HANDBOOK OF PRIMARY CARE PSYCHOLOGY

Handbook of Primary Care Psychology

EDITED BY

Leonard J. Haas

OXFORD
UNIVERSITY PRESS

2004

OXFORD
UNIVERSITY PRESS

Oxford   New York
Auckland   Bangkok   Buenos Aires   Cape Town   Chennai
Dar es Salaam   Delhi   Hong Kong   Istanbul   Karachi   Kolkata
Kuala Lumpur   Madrid   Melbourne   Mexico City   Mumbai   Nairobi
São Paulo   Shanghai   Taipei   Tokyo   Toronto

Copyright © 2004 by Oxford University Press, Inc.

Published by Oxford University Press, Inc.
198 Madison Avenue, New York, New York 10016

www.oup.com

Oxford is a registered trademark of Oxford University Press

Library of Congress Cataloging-in-Publication Data

Handbook of primary care psychology / edited by Leonard J. Haas.
p. cm.
ISBN 0-19-514939-4
1. Medicine and psychology—Handbooks, manuals, etc.   2. Primary
care
(Medicine)—Handbooks, manuals, etc.   I. Haas, Leonard J.
R726.5 .H345   2004
616′.001′9—dc22   2003021069

1 3 5 7 9 8 6 4 2
Printed in the United States of America
on acid-free paper

This volume is dedicated to Abby Gottsegen-Haas, Margot F. Haas, and Andrew G. Haas, who generously and graciously endured my preoccupation with this project for longer than I care to tabulate; to Rudolph Haas, MD, who seems to have imprinted his young son, me, with a primary care orientation by taking him along on house calls in rural Maine; and to Gerda Haas, who showed her son what it means to be a scholar and a writer.

Preface

To many psychologically distressed individuals, psychological services are either invisible or unattainable. Even the most conservative estimates reveal the staggering number of those with untreated psychological or psychiatric disturbances (e.g., Narrow et al., 2002). Additional huge numbers of patients with conditions such as hypertension, diabetes, functional gastrointestinal disorders, or low back pain could benefit from clinical health psychology interventions (Trask et al., 2002). Finally, untold numbers suffer from conditions such as cancer, dementia, infertility, or simple loneliness (Wedding, 2001). Although individuals in each of these categories may never seek psychological help on their own initiative, upward of 80% of them, at least in the United States, will visit their primary care physician in a given year (deGruy, 1996). The psychologist who intends to make a meaningful difference in the quality of health care for the population as a whole must be involved in the primary care setting (Coleman & Patrick, 1976).

This book is addressed to those psychologists. It is also is addressed to those who wish to practice primarily as primary care psychologists. It may also be interesting to a broader audience: mental health specialists of other disciplines, psychology trainees in medical settings, those with research interests in primary care mental health, primary care physicians, and other health and mental health practitioners. Its primary objective is to be worthy of its "handbook" appellation; it is also intended as a guidebook to the unfamiliar world of primary health care, a primer on a range of critical clinical issues, and a toolbox of quickly accessible clinical resources.

Primary care psychology is a complex arena in which to practice: It is both an emerging and a well-established area of professional psychology; it requires both a broad generalist approach to a wide variety of problems and the ability to focus in depth on complex issues. It requires negotiating a new role in a health care team that frequently does not consider psychology to be preeminent.

At the same time, primary care psychology is intensely rewarding: It allows psychologists to participate in a much broader range of issues and to provide help to a broader range of people for a broader range of problems. Involvement in the primary medical care system may reduce professional independence, but in return it offers the opportunity to influence a much larger system (Nolan, 1998).

This book has taken shape with several guiding principles: to be both practical and idealistic;

to provide specific tools to help in practice as well as a grounding in the philosophy of primary care; to be broad ranging and concise, so that the primary care psychologist will have in one volume ready access to a wide range of necessary information; to be written from an interdisciplinary perspective, in keeping with the philosophy of integrative primary care; to be written from a collaborative care perspective; and to be responsive to the constant evolution of best practices and best evidence by incorporating a companion Web site (www.primarycarepsych.com).

For well-trained psychologists, there is reassuring "old news" in this handbook as well. Specifically, considerable evidence in health psychology, behavioral medicine, psychoneuroimmunology, "patient-centered" medicine, and psychosocially informed primary care underscores the therapeutic power of empathy. The simple provision of a caring, understanding relationship is not only rare, but also increasingly more clearly related to important outcomes. Immersion in the primary care environment, in which such relationships can be dismissed as inefficient or soft-headed (Stein, 2003), should not lead psychologists to abandon their established skills in effective, empathic communication. A second bit of old news is that communication is crucial, particularly between physician and psychologist and between patient and psychologist. Poor communication leads to faulty assumptions and poor patient care. Throughout this book, the reader will find specific recommendations for primary care that will improve such communication.

OVERVIEW AND ORGANIZATION

The book is organized in four parts plus two Appendixes. In Part I, the emerging discipline of primary care psychology is delineated. The primary care medical system in the United States has been called the "de facto mental health system" (Narrow et al., 2002) because it is in this sector that the vast majority of mental health patients receive care. Yet that care is often suboptimum. Many cases of psychopathology go undetected by the pressured primary care physician, and many detected cases are inadequately treated. The primary care physician needs more help from psy-

chologists, and the initial chapters describe what kind of help we can offer, as well as what difficulties await the psychologist who pursues this line of service. Part I is based on two key concepts: first, that primary care psychology is as much an orientation to providing service as it is a specific set of services or specific physical location; and second, that the psychologist can both maintain his or her autonomy and participate in the larger medical system effectively as a team player.

Chapters in part I address the discipline of primary care psychology and its philosophical and historical framework (chapter 1); practical issues of functioning in a collaborative practice environment (chapter 2); a tool kit of psychological test instruments that may be useful to the practicing psychologist (chapter 3); and systems-level efforts to develop better integration and collaboration between mental health and primary care services (chapter 4).

Part II reviews the four medical specialties designated as primary care: family practice, internal medicine, pediatrics, and obstetrics-gynecology. These chapters offer an insider's view of each primary care specialty, with particular attention to how the primary care psychologist can collaborate effectively with these physicians. Each chapter also presents one or more cases that illustrate the types of psychologically related problems encountered in the specialty and how they are currently addressed. Practice-building strategies and mistakes to avoid are also included, as are useful perspectives on modern primary health care.

Paradoxically, to be efficient in primary care psychology demands a deep understanding of the persons who are patients and their life contexts. Part III provides such perspectives: The seven chapters in this section provide the generalist psychologist with perspectives that can help untangle the complex set of forces that act on the patients who seek our help.

In chapter 9, Jerome Kagan provides the practicing psychologist with a reminder of the developmental influences that have brought the patient to the point at which they seek help, and the chapter considers of a set of dimensions that form the boundaries of both human potential and human limitations.

Medicine is based on the biomedical model, but as Engel (1977) noted, there is a need for a more inclusive biopsychosocial model if we are to fully understand the person who is the patient. Psychology, too, to the extent it relies narrowly on the psychosocial model, is in need of a more comprehensive framework. Chapter 10, "Interpersonal and Family Systems Perspectives," reminds us that the individual exists in a social context. The chapter provides a concise review of systems concepts for the non-systems-oriented therapist, as well as useful examples of the interpersonal impact of symptoms and illnesses.

Because cultural competence is even more crucial in primary care psychology than in specialty psychology (U.S. Department of Health and Human Services, 2001), chapter 11 addresses cultural factors in patients' understanding of and response to mental health referrals and treatment; the chapter also includes useful tools to help the primary care psychologist achieve higher levels of cultural competence and describes the subcultures of primary care medicine, psychotherapy, and mental health.

Although psychologists may believe themselves to be expert in assessing and alleviating suffering, Eric Cassell's chapter 12 will deepen the understanding of suffering in the medically ill patient. Cassell argues that medicine, and perhaps psychology, can neglect the true meaning of suffering, and he reminds us that careful and attentive ears and eyes are necessary to discern the aspects of the person damaged by physical or mental illness. The chapter highlights the dimensions in which persons can experience injury and limitation, as well as the keys to alleviating suffering: transcendence, finding meaning in one's experience, community, and control.

To some extent, the healing arts have always involved providing renewed hope to the suffering. Chapter 13 offers an important analysis of this important element of effective health care as well as of its opposite, hopelessness, and suggests methods for implementing targeted hope-building and hopelessness-reducing treatment.

Psychologists and other behavioral and social scientists have developed countless models to address the often-imperfect link among intentions, clinician recommendations, and actual behavior change. With important roots in the transtheoret-ical model of behavior change (Prochaska et al., 1992), DiClemente and colleagues in chapter 14 provide an important overview of this crucial issue. The chapter provides insights and tools for psychologists to help patients follow through with both medical and psychological recommendations. The material may also allow the psychologist to provide helpful consultation and training to physicians, who are often frustrated when they encounter "noncompliant" patients.

The primary care psychologist practices in an environment that makes heavy use of diagnostic labels, mnemonics, algorithms, and treatment protocols, all designed to spare cognitive resources and promote time efficiency. For many psychologists, these aspects of the primary care setting will be useful antidotes to excessive contemplativeness. Yet, to work efficiently and at the same time maintain creativity and be consciously "present" for multiple and varying encounters, the primary care psychologist must overcome many of these pressures. Shelly Carson and Ellen Langer in chapter 15 remind us there are ways to nurture mindfulness and suggest ways we can use these techniques to help both our patients and ourselves respond creatively to pressure and stress. Their approach to mindfulness does not require meditation, but focuses on the aspect of mindfulness that involves transcending predetermined categories and transcending the priming influence of context.

Part IV addresses clinical conditions that are (a) common in the primary care environment (e.g., diabetes, low back pain, sleep disorders); (b) likely to be referred to the primary care psychologist (e.g., depression, anxiety, eating disorders, grief); and (c) treatable with well-established psychological interventions (e.g., smoking, obesity, heart disease). In keeping with the biopsychosocial approach, the clinical chapters are presented as a unified section (listed alphabetically, from alcoholism to work stress) with no attempt to separate them into mental, physical, or environmental categories. Because the primary care psychologist must often use tools other than psychotherapy, chapters include available evidence on the usefulness of extrapsychotherapeutic approaches (e.g., self-help groups, journal writing, reading, exercise) as well as suggestions for consultative approaches.

The primary care psychologist is frequently referred patients who have both psychological and medical problems (the psychological treatment may or may not be directly related to the medical problem) in which he or she does not specialize; thus, chapters on "medical" conditions are designed to provide a concise overview of what the mental health specialist should know to provide effective treatment.

The chapters on prototypically psychological disorders—alcoholism and other substance use disorders (chapter 16), anxiety (chapter 17), depression (chapter 22), eating disorders (chapter 25), personality disorders (chapter 33)—will be useful even to the psychologist familiar with these conditions because the presentation of these disorders is often different in primary care than in specialty care.

Seven chapters address issues that are so pervasive yet underdetected and undertreated in primary care patient populations that they should be reviewed when working with almost every referral: alcoholism, substance abuse, and prescription drug abuse (chapter 16); domestic violence (chapter 24); rape, sexual assault, and posttraumatic stress disorder (chapter 34); sleep disorders (chapter 37); smoking (chapter 38); stress (chapter 40); and work stress (chapter 41).

Abuse histories in particular are highly prevalent in primary care populations, especially among women. In addition to chapter 34 on rape, sexual assault, and posttraumatic stress disorder and chapter 24 on domestic violence, chapters addressing fibromyalgia and chronic fatigue syndrome (chapter 26) and sexual disorders affecting women (chapter 36) will be of particular help in working with abused women.

The common currency of medical settings is physical complaints, and it is not surprising that somatic symptoms and pain complaints form themes that constantly recur in work with primary care patients. In addition to chapter 39 on somatoform disorders and chapter 19 on back pain, important and helpful material on somatic expressions of distress can be found in chapter 26 on fibromyalgia and chronic fatigue syndrome and chapter 30 on irritable bowel syndrome and other functional gastrointestinal disorders.

Pain problems, as well as their psychological and pharmacological treatment, are addressed in chapters on suffering (chapter 12), back pain (chapter 19), cancer (chapter 20), and fibromyalgia and chronic fatigue syndrome (chapter 26).

Five chapters provide useful overviews of problems commonly encountered and treated by clinical health psychologists: back pain (chapter 19), diabetes (chapter 23), heart disease and essential hypertension (chapter 28), obesity (chapter 32), and smoking (chapter 38).

Although primary care physicians may be familiar with psychologists' ability to treat and help manage many common clinical conditions, as Kainz (2002) has noted, they may be less aware that psychologists can provide effective help for infertility (chapter 29), sexual disorders (chapters 35 and 36), sleep disorders (chapter 37), smoking (chapter 38), and end-of-life care (chapter 27). These chapters may help psychologists develop ways to expand primary care physicians' use of their services.

Regardless of psychologists' opinions on the role of medication in psychological treatment, involvement in primary care will mean involvement in a drug-saturated environment. Prescriptions are expected by most patients and are offered with regularity by most primary care physicians, and the effective primary care psychologist must have a working knowledge of common medications. Appendix A provides a concise summary of psychoactive medications common in primary care. Because patients do not always know whether they are taking a generic or branded medication or what class of medication they have been prescribed, Appendix A also provides an alphabetical list that translates generic into brand names and vice versa, as well as listing the class of medication. Appendix B is a review of current evidence regarding the effect of nonpsychoactive medications on mental and behavioral functioning. It also includes useful information on taking a drug history and reminds us that recent medication discontinuation and medication overdose are as much a concern as which medication the patient is presently taking.

GOING FURTHER

The array of materials for further study suggested by the various chapter authors was so extensive that a companion Web site was developed. Purchasers of this volume will be able to access the readers-only section of the Web site, which includes lists of books, audiovisual material, and Web sites available for further professional study. In keeping with the philosophy of primary care that patients should be active partners in managing their own health, the companion Web site also provides extensive listings of patient self-help resources. In addition, the Web site provides printable versions of the primary care tools included in this volume, including several history-taking guides and screening tools. We encourage readers to make use of this additional resource and to help the editor and authors make the handbook more useful. Access to the readers-only section of www.primarycarepsych.com is with the user name *reader* and the password *2004*.

ACKNOWLEDGMENTS AND FINAL WORDS

This is in many respects the book I wish I had when I began practicing primary care psychology over a dozen years ago. It has taken shape with the help and encouragement of many friends, family, and colleagues. I particularly want to acknowledge Danny Wedding, who provided encouragement and sage advice at crucial times; Leslie DiMella, who generously and discerningly reviewed material at key moments; Rick Steiner, who provided a much-needed sense of perspective; Kristen Christensen, who did yeo-woman service in readying the manuscript and helping to corral wayward authors; and Joan Bossert, who offered a steady and wise view of the "bigger picture" that bolstered editorial confidence when it flagged.

Primary care psychology is both old and new; it is both emerging and well established. It challenges and rewards. Above all, it demands multiple competencies and a breadth of knowledge and skill as well as an appreciation for the clinicians and patients who are one's partners in the healing endeavor. It is my hope that readers of this volume will find it a powerful and comprehensive tool in the development of their practices and the improvement of their ability to serve those who seek their help.

Regarding usage: In an attempt to slow down the steady industrialization of health care, the handbook refers to both psychologists and physicians as "clinicians" or "practitioners" rather than "providers." In an attempt to clearly identify recipients of services as individuals involved in relationships with clinicians, they are referred to as "patients" rather than "clients" (patients, and only patients, have doctors, whereas clients may have accountants, lawyers, or hairdressers; Hodgkiss, 2000).

References

Coleman, J. V., & Patrick, D. L. (1976). Integrating mental health services into primary medical care. *Medical Care, 14*(8), 654–661.

Engel, G. L. (1977). The need for a new medical model: A Challenge for biomedicine. *Science, 196*(4286), 129–135.

Hodgkiss, A. (2000). User, client or patient: What do we call people receiving treatment for mental health problems? *Psychiatric Bulletin, 24,* 441–443.

Kainz, K. (2002). Barriers and enhancements to physician–psychologist collaboration. *Professional Psychology: Research and Practice, 33,* 169–175.

Narrow, W. E., Rae, D. S., et al. (2002). Revised prevalence estimates of mental disorders in the United States: Using a clinical significance criterion to reconcile 2 surveys' estimates. *Archives of General Psychiatry, 59,* 115–123.

Nolan, T. W. (1998). Understanding medical systems. *Annals of Internal Medicine, 128,* 293–298.

Prochaska, J. O., DiClemente, C. C., et al. (1992). In search of how people change. *American Psychologist, 47,* 1102–1114.

Stein, H. (2003). Physician balint groups as an organizational laboratory of psychohistory. *Journal of Psychohistory, 30,* 226–253.

Trask, P. C., Schwartz, S. M., et al. (2002). Behavioral medicine: The challenge of integrating psychological and behavioral approaches into primary care. *Effective Clinical Practice, 5,* 75–83.

U.S. Department of Health and Human Services. (2001). *Mental health: Culture, race, and ethnicity. A supplement to mental health: A report of the surgeon general.* Rockville, MD: Author.

Wedding, D. (Ed.). (2001). *Behavior and medicine.* New York: Hogrefe and Huber.

Contents

Contributors

Graciela S. Alarcón, M.D., Professor of Medicine, University of Alabama, Birmingham

Kelly C. Allison, Ph.D., Instructor of Psychology in Psychiatry, Weight and Eating Disorders Program, University of Pennsylvania School of Medicine, Philadelphia

Mary G. Austrom, Ph.D., Clinical Associate Professor, Indiana Alzheimer's Disease Center, Department of Psychiatry, Indiana University School of Medicine, Indianapolis

Carla J. Berg, Clinical Psychology Training Program, University of Kansas, Lawrence

Robert I. Berkowitz, M.D., Associate Professor of Psychiatry, Weight and Eating Disorders Program, University of Pennsylvania School of Medicine, Philadelphia

Daniel Bluestein, M.D., M.S., Professor of Family and Community Medicine, Eastern Virginia Medical School, Norfolk

Beth C. Bock, Ph.D., Associate Professor, Department of Psychiatry and Human Behavior, Brown Medical School, Centers for Behavioral

and Preventive Medicine, Lifespan Academic Medical Center, Providence, Rhode Island

Laurence A. Bradley, Ph.D., Professor of Rheumatology and Immunology, University of Alabama, Birmingham

Brittany Briggs, M.A., Research Coordinator, Reproductive and Sexual Medicine Clinic, University of Washington Medical Center, Seattle

Charles K. Burnett, Ph.D., Dr.P.H., Clinical Assistant Professor of Medicine and Psychiatry, and Adjunct Assistant Professor of Psychology, University of North Carolina School of Medicine, Chapel Hill

Christopher M. Callahan, M.D., Associate Professor of Medicine, Cornelius and Yvonne Pettinga Scholar in Aging Research, Division of General Internal Medicine and Geriatrics, Indiana University Center for Aging Research, Regenstrief Institute Inc., Indianapolis

Robert M. Carney, Ph.D., Professor of Psychiatry, Washington University School of Medicine, St. Louis, Missouri

Bruce N. Carpenter, Ph.D., Associate Professor of Psychology and Director of Clinical Training, Department of Psychology, Brigham Young University, Provo, Utah

Shelley H. Carson, Ph.D., Lecturer in Psychology, Harvard University, Cambridge, Massachusetts

Kenneth R. Casey, M.D., Ph.D., Professor of Medicine, University of Utah, Salt Lake City

Eric Cassell, M.D., M.A.C.P., Clinical Professor of Public Health, Weil Medical College of Cornell University, New York, New York

A. Peter Catinella, M.D., M.P.A, Associate Professor and Vice Chair, Department of Family and Preventive Medicine, University of Utah, Salt Lake City

Alex Y. Chen, M.D., M.S.H.S., Assistant Professor of Pediatrics, Childrens Hospital Los Angeles, University of Southern California Keck School of Medicine

Kelly R. Chrestman, Ph.D., Clinical Psychologist, Center for the Treatment and Study of Anxiety, University of Pennsylvania, School of Medicine, Philadelphia

Leanne R. Cianfrini, M.A., Division of Rheumatology and Immunology, University of Alabama, Birmingham

Gretchen A. Clum, Ph.D., Research Associate, Department of Pediatrics, Johns Hopkins University, Baltimore, Maryland

Gerard J. Connors, Ph.D., Senior Research Scientist, Research Institute on Addictions, University at Buffalo, State University of New York

Barbara Cubic, Ph.D., Associate Professor of Psychiatry and Behavioral Sciences, Eastern Virginia Medical School, Norfolk

Laura A. Czajkowski, Ph.D., Associate Professor, Department of Psychiatry, University of Utah, Salt Lake City

Frank V. deGruy, M.D., Professor of Family and Preventive Medicine and Psychiatry, University of Colorado, Boulder

Carlo C. DiClemente, Ph.D., Professor of Psychology, and Chair, Psychology Department, University of Maryland, Baltimore County

Douglas A. Drossman, M.D., Professor of Medicine and Psychiatry, University of North Carolina School of Medicine, Chapel Hill

David Duncan, M.D., Assistant Professor, Department of Psychiatry, University of Utah, Salt Lake City

Jeanne L. Esler, Ph.D., Staff Psychologist, Department of Psychiatry, Rhode Island Hospital, Providence

Kevin Ferentz, M.D., Assistant Professor of Family Medicine, University of Maryland Medical School, Baltimore

Kenneth E. Freedland, Ph.D., Professor of Psychiatry, Washington University School of Medicine, St. Louis, Missouri

Jennifer Gafford, Ph.D., Faculty Psychologist, Family Medicine Residency Program at Forest Park Hospital, St. Louis, Missouri, and Clinical Assistant Professor of Community and Family Medicine, Saint Louis University School of Medicine

Geri-Ann Galanti, Ph.D., Associate Professor of Anthropology, California State University, Los Angeles

Russell E. Glasgow, Ph.D., Senior Scientist, Kaiser Permanente Colorado Clinical Research Unit, Denver

Kelly M. Glazer, M.S., Doctoral Candidate, Clinical Psychology Training Program, University of Utah, Salt Lake City

Karen Gunning, Pharm.D., B.C.P.S., Assistant Professor of Pharmacy Practice, Adjunct Assistant Professor of Family and Preventive Medicine, University of Utah, Salt Lake City

Leonard J. Haas, Ph.D., A.B.P.P., Professor of Family and Preventive Medicine, Director of Behavioral Science, Department of Family and Preventive Medicine, University of Utah, Salt Lake City

L. Kevin Hamberger, Ph.D., Professor of Family and Community Medicine, Medical College of Wisconsin, Racine Family Practice Center

Paul J. Hartung, Ph.D., Associate Professor of Behavioral Sciences, Northeastern Ohio Universities College of Medicine, Rootstown

Amy Heard-Davison, Ph.D., Clinical Instructor, Reproductive and Sexual Medicine Clinic, Department of Psychiatry and Behavioral Sciences, University of Washington Medical Center, Seattle

Julia R. Heiman, Ph.D., Professor of Psychiatry and Behavioral Sciences, and Director, Reproductive and Sexual Medicine Clinic, University of Washington School of Medicine, Seattle

Christopher R. Jones, M.D., Ph.D., Associate Professor of Neurology, University of Utah, Salt Lake City

Kirtly Parker Jones, M.D., Professor and Vice Chair for Educational Affairs, Department of Obstetrics-Gynecology, University of Utah, Salt Lake City

Jerome Kagan, Ph.D., Research Professor of Psychology, Harvard University, Cambridge, Massachusetts

Julia Kasl-Godley, Ph.D., Clinical Psychologist, Hospice Care Center, VA Palo Alto Health Care System, California

Randall E. Kolb, M.D., Professor of Family Medicine, University of Pittsburgh School of Medicine

Douglas G. Kondo, M.D., Chief Resident, Division of Child and Adolescent Psychiatry, Department of Psychiatry and Behavioral Sciences, Duke University Medical Center, Durham, North Carolina

Barbara M. Korsch, M.D, Professor of Pediatrics, Childrens Hospital Los Angeles, University of Southern California Keck School of Medicine

Ellen J. Langer, Ph.D., Professor of Psychology, Harvard University, Cambridge, Massachusetts

Jennifer Paul Leiser, M.D., Assistant Professor, Department of Family and Preventive Medicine, University of Utah, Salt Lake City

Sara M. Lewis, M.F.A., Research Associate, Childrens Hospital Los Angeles

John C. Linton, Ph.D., A.B.P.P., Associate Professor and Chief Psychologist, Departments of Behavioral Medicine and Family Medicine, West Virginia University School of Medicine, Charleston

Joseph LoPiccolo, Ph.D., Professor of Psychology, University of Missouri, Columbia

Steven Lovett, Ph.D., Director, Interprofessional Team Training and Development, VA Palo Alto Health Care System, California

Roger Luckmann, M.D., Professor of Medicine, Department of Family Medicine and Community Health, University of Massachusetts Medical School, Worcester

Michael K. Magill, M.D., Professor and Chair, Department of Family and Preventive Medicine, University of Utah, Salt Lake City

John S. March, M.D., M.P.H., Professor and Chief, Division of Child and Adolescent Psychiatry, Department of Psychiatry and Behavioral Sciences, Duke Child and Family Study Center, Duke University Medical Center, Durham, North Carolina

Nancy L. McKendree-Smith, Ph.D., Postdoctoral Fellow, Division of Rheumatology and Immunology, University of Alabama, Birmingham

Mark Mengel, M.D., Professor and Chair, Department of Community and Family Medicine, St. Louis University School of Medicine

Mimi Meyers, M.S.W., Teaching Faculty, Ackerman Institute for the Family, New York, New York

Scott T. Michael, Ph.D., Postdoctoral Fellow, Mental Illness Research, Education, and Clinical Center, VA Puget Sound Health Care System, Seattle, Washington

Paul A. Nutting, M.D., M.S.P.H., Director of Research, Center for Research Strategies, and Clinical Professor, Department of Family Medicine, University of Colorado Health Sciences Center, Boulder

Judith K. Ockene, Ph.D., Professor of Medicine, Division of Preventive and Behavioral Medicine, University of Massachusetts Medical School, Worcester

Akiko Okifuji, Ph.D., Associate Professor of Anesthesiology, Psychology, and Pharmacy Practice, Pain Research and Management Center, University of Utah, Salt Lake City

Trish Palmer, M.D., Assistant Professor, Department of Family and Preventive Medicine, University of Utah, Salt Lake City, and Educational Director, Pisacano Leadership Foundation, Lexington, Kentucky

Stacy C. Parenteau, Clinical Psychology Training Program, University of Kansas, Lawrence

Darshana Patel, M.D., Private Family Practice, Green Bay, Wisconsin

Lori Pbert, Ph.D., Associate Professor of Medicine, Division of Preventive and Behavioral Medicine, University of Massachusetts Medical School, Worcester

Mark A. Penn, M.D., M.B.A., Professor of Clinical Family Medicine, Northeastern Ohio Universities College of Medicine, Rootstown

Frederic W. Platt, M.D., Clinical Professor of Medicine, University of Colorado, Boulder

James W. Price, M.D., M.B.A., Program Director, Family Medicine Residency Program, and Chief of Family Medicine, Forest Park Hospital, St. Louis, Missouri, and Clinical Assistant Professor of Community and Family Medicine, Saint Louis University School of Medicine

Patricia A. Resick, Ph.D., Curators' Professor of Psychology, Director, Center for Trauma Recovery, University of Missouri, St. Louis

Nina Ross, M.D., Intern, Family Medicine, University of Virginia, Charlottesville

David B. Sarwer, Ph.D., Assistant Professor of Psychology in Psychiatry and Surgery, Weight and Eating Disorders Program, University of Pennsylvania School of Medicine, Philadelphia

Constance N. Scharf, M.S.W., Teaching Faculty, Ackerman Institute for the Family, New York, New York

Christopher N. Sciamanna, M.D., M.P.H., Assistant Professor, Department of Community Health, Brown Medical School, Centers for Behavioral and Preventive Medicine and The Miriam Hospital, Providence, Rhode Island

H. Russell Searight, Ph.D., M.P.H., Director of Behavioral Medicine, Forest Park Hospital Family Medicine Residency Program, St. Louis, Missouri, and Clinical Associate Professor of Community and Family Medicine, Saint Louis University School of Medicine

David Servan-Schreiber, M.D., Ph.D., Clinical Professor of Psychiatry, University of Pittsburgh School of Medicine

Judith A. Skala, R.N., Ph.D., Research Nurse Coordinator and Cognitive Behavior Therapist, Department of Psychiatry, Washington University School of Medicine, St. Louis, Missouri

Denise Small, R.Ph., Pharm.D., Clinical Pharmacy Specialist, University of Utah Hospital, and Adjunct Instructor, Department of Pharmacy Practice, University of Utah, Salt Lake City

Timothy W. Smith, Ph.D., Professor of Psychology, University of Utah, Salt Lake City

C. R. Snyder, Ph.D., M. Erik Wright Distinguished Professor of Clinical Psychology, Carnegie Foundation Distinguished Teaching Professor of Psychology, University of Kansas, Lawrence

Patrick R. Steffen, Ph.D., Assistant Professor of Psychology, Brigham Young University, Provo, Utah

Scott H. Stewart, M.D., Assistant Professor of Medicine, School of Medicine and Biomedical Sciences, University at Buffalo, State University of New York

Gary Tabas, M.D., F.A.C.P., Associate Professor of Medicine, University of Pittsburgh School of Medicine

Kathleen L. Tarr, M.D., Ph.D., Assistant Professor of Medicine, Saint Louis University School of Medicine

Tiffany L. Tibbs, Ph.D., Research Instructor, Department of Psychiatry, Washington University School of Medicine, St. Louis, Missouri

David Turok, M.D., Instructor, Department of Obstetrics-Gynecology, University of Utah, Salt Lake City

Frederick W. Unverzagt, Ph.D., Associate Professor, Indiana Alzheimer's Disease Center, and Department of Psychiatry, Indiana University School of Medicine, Indianapolis

Jennifer T. Van Horn, M.D., Instructor, Department of Obstetrics-Gynecology, University of Utah, Salt Lake City

Mary M. Velasquez, Ph.D., Assistant Professor of Family and Community Medicine, University of Texas Medical School at Houston

David Waters, Ph.D., Ruth Murdaugh Professor of Family Medicine, University of Virginia, Charlottesville

Danny Wedding, Ph.D., Professor of Psychiatry, University of Missouri–Columbia School of Medicine, and Director, Missouri Institute of Mental Health, Columbia

Margot Weinshel, M.S.W., R.N., Teaching Faculty, Ackerman Institute for the Family, New York, New York

Risa B. Weisberg, Ph.D., Assistant Research Professor of Psychiatry and Human Behavior, Brown University, Providence, Rhode Island

Kristin Kahle Wrobleski, Clinical Psychology Training Program, University of Kansas, Lawrence

Antonette M. Zeiss, Ph.D., Clinical Coordinator and Director of Training, Psychology Service, VA Palo Alto Health Care System, California

HANDBOOK OF PRIMARY CARE PSYCHOLOGY

I

THE DISCIPLINE OF
PRIMARY CARE PSYCHOLOGY

1

Primary Care, Psychology, and Primary Care Psychology

Leonard J. Haas
Frank V. deGruy

ILLUSTRATING THE PRIMARY CARE PSYCHOLOGY APPROACH

Sara James comes to the office of her primary care physician complaining of deep fatigue. Sara is a 36-year-old woman who works part time as a paralegal; she is married to a man who is a busy contractor, and she is the mother of three small children. She wonders if she has mononucleosis or perhaps a thyroid problem like her sister's. Her physician does a thorough physical examination and can find no evidence of poor thyroid functioning, infection, or any other biomedical explanation for her fatigue.

Scenarios like this occur many times every day in the offices of pediatricians, internists, family physicians, and gynecologists across the United States. What happens next depends on the training and attitudes of the primary care physician and the mental health professionals involved in the patient's care. This scenario could follow at least three different pathways:

The biomedical pathway: Suspicious that he hasn't exhausted all possibilities, the physician suggests

additional tests to Ms. James. Worried and eager to discover if she has something serious or not, Ms. James agrees and gets a full workup. When results are normal, her worries are not assuaged: She requests a referral to a specialist in "fatigue-related medicine." Her doctor reluctantly agrees and refers her to a rheumatologist. This specialist also cannot explain her condition with any known conventional diagnosis. Ultimately, she finds her way to an alternative medicine practitioner, who practices herbology; she receives a diagnosis of "multiple chemical sensitivities" and a prescription for aromatherapy and herbal remedies.

This scenario conforms to much existing data on the pathways patients commonly take in primary care when (as is the case in perhaps the majority of primary care visits) their symptoms have no medical explanation (e.g., Kroenke & Mangelsdorff, 1989). The physician who is unwilling to consider psychosocial or emotional causes of distress and dysfunction often begins to pursue increasingly rare conditions. Convinced that there is "something wrong," the patient (as 30% of Americans do) may turn to complementary and

5

alternative medicine, such as acupuncture, herbology, or aromatherapy. Or, the case could continue along a different path:

The psychiatric pathway: *Recognizing that women are more likely to experience depression and knowing from his care of Ms. James that her mother suffered from depression, the physician begins to suspect that the fatigue may be related to an underlying depression. He probes Ms. James about her mood and how her life has been going recently; she notes that things have been "a bit frustrating" at work, and she has found herself uncharacteristically out of sorts, even sad, since a coworker with whom she had a long and satisfying work relationship was transferred to another state. On further probing, she reveals that her sleep and appetite have both been disturbed, she has lost interest in sexual intimacy, and she becomes tearful every day. Believing that he has successfully diagnosed a case of major depressive disorder, the physician prescribes an antidepressant and suggests that Ms. James follow up with him in 1 month.*

This is probably the second most common scenario in primary care when the physician encounters a likely mental health problem. It has been known for many years that the majority of psychoactive medication prescriptions are written by primary care physicians and not by psychiatrists. However, it is also clear that prescribing antidepressants does not mean that the depression has been treated. In fact, the evidence suggests that as many as half of antidepressant prescriptions either are not filled or are taken improperly, and a considerable proportion of responses to them are placebo responses (Moncrieff, Wessely, & Hardy, 2001).

Psychiatric pathway continued: *One month later, Ms. James returns to her primary care physician, noting that she is still tired and admitting that she took the fluoxetine he prescribed for 1 week, found that it gave her diarrhea, and discontinued taking it. She briefly felt better and now again is tired and wonders what is going on. Telling her that she needs to have a thorough evaluation and empathizing with her difficulties taking the prescription, her physician suggests that Ms. James*

should restart the medication and also see a psychologist who specializes in depression. Although the psychologist's office is located several miles away in a different neighborhood and although the psychologist is on a different insurance panel, Ms. James agrees to make an appointment. Her physician suggests that she should return for a follow-up visit in 6 weeks.

This aspect of the case illustrates the traditional method of linking mental health and primary care arenas through referrals. However, this is an inefficient and often not helpful method because it puts additional barriers in the path of the patient who wishes to receive help. Assume for the sake of this illustration that Ms. James is able to overcome the obstacles that chiefly account for the dismal rate of successful referrals from primary care to specialty mental health care; she is able to schedule an appointment within a reasonable time, she is motivated enough to make her way across town to see the psychologist, and she is savvy enough about health care benefits to arrange to have the services reimbursed.

Psychiatric pathway continued: *At the initial appointment, the psychologist does a thorough history of Ms. James's symptoms and then begins to explore her self-esteem, her sense of loss, and her relationship with her husband. Ms. James rapidly becomes defensive and wonders why the psychologist needs to know all of these things. Can't the psychologist simply suggest a better medication or give her some techniques that will make her feel better? The psychologist reflects on whether she is resistant or has some deeper personality pathology that was misdiagnosed by the primary care physician. He returns to evaluating her symptoms and considers that perhaps she would be better diagnosed as having atypical somatoform disorder with depressive personality disorder features, rather than having major depressive disorder. He privately concludes she is "not a good candidate for therapy." He suggests that she try to think more optimistically and concludes the session, indicating that he can suggest a psychiatric referral or Ms. James could return for further work with him. She does not make a follow-up appointment.*

This scenario describes what we believe is a typical difficulty in traditional mental health practice as it relates to primary care. The primary care patient may or may not believe that she has a mental problem, and may or may not be ready to agree to psychological treatment. In addition, the presentation of common psychological problems in the primary care arena is often different from the presentation in specialty care, and the psychologist must be attuned to the ways in which psychological distress may be expressed. Consider the following as an alternative:

The primary care psychology pathway: *After exploring Ms. James's reluctance to restart fluoxetine and the fact that her improvement was probably not attributable to the medication, her physician suggests that she see a psychologist. Although privately worried that perhaps her doctor believes she is just a hypochondriac and is trying to get rid of her, Ms. James agrees so that she can at least say that she tried what he recommended. The psychologist, who practices in the physician's clinic 2 days each week, is able to see her that same afternoon for a brief initial visit. This session primarily involves the psychologist explaining psychological treatment to her and exploring her understanding of her condition. Ms. James expresses her puzzlement at the referral because she does not understand how "just talking" could help her and wonders if what she really needs is an energizing medication such as modafinil, which she has recently heard about on television.*

Agreeing that he will discuss this idea with the primary care physician at a later point, the primary care psychologist explains that it sometimes helps to talk over things that are on one's mind and briefly explores her symptomatology. She acknowledges that she experienced a significant loss when her colleague was transferred because she is quite isolated and lonely and agrees to come back in 3 days for a full psychotherapy session. After four additional sessions over the following 2 months and some "homework exercises" aimed at improving her social support, Ms. James indicates that she feels much better and feels no need for further counseling.

Although he recognizes that Ms. James is at risk for further depressive reactions, the psychologist agrees that she has made considerable prog-

ress and "leaves the door open" so that if she experiences similar symptoms in the future she will find it easier to come in for a short course of therapy. He then reviews with her the common symptoms of social isolation and depression and notes that, in her case, sadness and fatigue are warning signs that she is becoming isolated. He then dictates a brief note to her physician describing her progress and notes what the physician might see in the future that would suggest the need for further treatment.

Although this case is not meant to imply that all fatigue is masked minor depression, it does illustrate the need for the primary care psychologist to make services accessible and understandable to patients who may not initially understand the connection between the somatic symptoms they present to their primary care physicians and their emotional lives. Practicing psychology in primary care offers the opportunity to address mental health issues where they are most often presented; the opportunity to address the psychosocial aspects of medical complaints; and the prospect of helping the primary care system truly meet the needs of its patients without erecting more barriers to care. However, the practice of primary care psychology demands skills, attitudes, and a knowledge base broader than that typically obtained by the conventionally trained psychologist. This chapter addresses the nature of primary medical care, the need for psychologists' presence in primary medical care, and the elements that constitute effective primary care psychological practice.

WHAT IS PRIMARY CARE?

Elements of Primary Health Care

Primary health care as defined by the Institute of Medicine is "the provision of integrated, accessible health care services by clinicians who are accountable for addressing a large majority of personal health care needs, developing a sustained partnership with patients, and practicing in the context of family and community" (Donaldson, Yordy, Lohr, & Vanselov, 1996, p. 32). This definition contains most of the values espoused by the primary care disciplines, and encoded here are many of the behaviors expected from a primary care physician. Each of the descriptors is worthy of elaboration.

Integrated means that primary care physicians have a responsibility to coordinate care across settings (e.g., inpatient/outpatient), across specialists (e.g., primary care physician/rheumatologist or surgeon), across the physical/psychological dimension, and across domains of care (e.g., pharmacy, dentistry, nutrition). Fragmentation of care is one of the principal sources of medical errors and increased costs, and integration of medical and psychological care is one of the driving principles of this handbook.

Accessible means that the primary care physician or a partner who knows the patient should always be available to the patient. One important implication of this is that the primary care physician will be counting on the similar availability of any consultants, collaborators, or partners to share the care of the patient.

Accountable means that primary care physicians feel they have to answer for the care—all the care—their patient receives. At its best, this is a covenant between the primary care physician and the patient which implies that the primary care physician will stay with the patient through all health care experiences. This has important implications for the level of communication between primary care physicians and those sharing in the care of their patients.

The term *large majority of health care needs* emphasizes the breadth of care. Whatever concerns or symptoms patients present determine the content of primary care. Three years of postdoctoral training and conscientious continuing medical education prepares most primary care physicians to be competent to manage 80%–90% of all medical problems presented to them (Zvolensky, Eifert, Larkin, & Ludwig, 1999) and to find consultation or make a referral for the rest.

Sustained partnership implies continuity of care: "If you want me to, I'll stick with you forever."

The term *in the context of family and community* implies that any given "best" treatment might need to be modified according to family or community issues. Most experienced primary care physicians would agree that knowledge of these contexts profoundly affects the kind of care rendered and can dramatically improve its quality.

These concepts carry an additional implication, that the primary care physician is trained to take care of the *person* who has symptoms or problems rather than only taking care of the problems. Among other things, this integrative "whole person" approach ideally emphasizes the relationship between the psychological and the physical dimensions of health.

Who Practices Primary Care?

Primary medical care is "officially" provided by four federally designated medical specialties: general internal medicine, family practice, pediatrics, and obstetrics-gynecology. In addition, primary care is provided by nurse practitioners and physician assistants who practice in collaboration with physicians or practice under their licenses.

As of 2003, there were more than 283,000 primary care physicians in the United States, approximately one third of the total number of licensed physicians (Pasco & Smart, 2003).

Although all primary care specialties require some training and experience in psychiatry or behavioral science, family medicine and pediatrics generally offer the most extensive training in this area. It is common for primary care physicians to see patients who are depressed, anxious, "stressed," having psychosomatic symptoms, abusing alcohol or drugs; who are victims of domestic violence; and who manifest psychological reactions to medical illness. In younger primary care patients, conduct disorders, attention-deficit/hyperactivity disorder and developmental disabilities are common; in both pediatric and adult patient populations, family distress and family adjustment are critical issues (Pace, Chaney, et al., 1995).

WHY DOES PRIMARY CARE NEED PSYCHOLOGY?

Primary Care Patient Populations Have Significant Psychological Needs

Of all the generalist–specialist overlaps, the one between primary care and mental health care is the most extensive. It can be reasonably argued that every clinical problem is a behavioral prob-lem. The relationship between these dimensions of health is argued in more detail elsewhere (de-Gruy, 1996), and is only described briefly here. The psychological needs of primary care patients can be classified into three general categories, re-lated to (a) psychopathology or "true mental dis-orders," (b) stress-related symptoms and prob-lems related to chronic medical conditions or "behavioral health problems," and (c) member-ship in "vulnerable populations," including abuse victims, those who are socially isolated, and those who are economically disadvantaged.

Psychopathology

Despite the increased availability of mental health services and the proliferation of mental health professionals, epidemiological studies of Ameri-ca's mental health demonstrate that there is still a huge gap between the need and the available services. Very large numbers of the U.S. popula-tion have unmet mental health needs. Mental health problems are extremely disabling; it has been estimated that in the United States they rank second to cardiovascular disease in their im-pact on disability (Murray & Lopez, 1996). Al-though estimates of the prevalence of mental ill-ness in the United States have ranged as high as 25% (Kessler, Burns, et al., 1987), more conser-vative estimates that require clinical significance suggest an overall prevalence of 18.5% for adults (Narrow, Rae, et al., 2002). In addition, those with "subsyndromal" (or mild) mental health conditions also suffer significant disability or functional impairment (e.g., Olfson, Gilbert, et al., 1995; Wells, Stewart, et al., 1989).

Most individuals in need of mental health ser-vices will turn to the primary care physician as their first and sometimes only source of help (Cauce, Domenech-Rodriguez, et al., 2002; Ray, Raicti, et al., 1992); indeed, research suggests that half or more of common mental disorders are treated exclusively in the primary care sector (Bea & Tesar, 2002). In addition, nonpsychiatric physicians write most of the prescriptions for psy-choactive medications in the United States. For example, in 1988 approximately 80% of all U.S. prescriptions for psychotropic drugs were written by nonpsychiatrists, most of them primary care

physicians (Beardsley, Gardocki, et al., 1988). Primary care has been called the "de facto mental health system" in the United States (Schurman, Kramer, et al., 1985).

For a variety of reasons, psychologically dis-tressed patients experience increased physical symptomatology (Katon, Von Korff, et al., 1990; Kroenke, Spitzer, et al., 1994). Thus, whether or not they are seeking mental health care, patients with mental diagnoses show consistently higher utilization of medical resources than their unaf-fected counterparts, generally on the order of twice the baseline utilization rates (deGruy, 1996). In some cases, such as somatization disorder, the in-creased utilization is extraordinary—up to nine times the national norm (Smith, 1994).

Behavioral Health Problems

As health psychologists well know, behavioral, cognitive, interpersonal, and emotional factors are relevant to the management of most common and chronic illnesses. Trask and colleagues (2002) noted, for example, that cancer, chronic pain, cardiovascular disease, Crohn's disease, diabetes, and asthma all can be improved when treated with evidence-based health psychology techniques.

At a fundamental level, following through with help-seeking and medical recommendations for any condition is a behavioral issue (Codori & Nannis, 1990; Donovan & Blake, 1992; Lieber-man, 1996), as are "lifestyle prescriptions" such as exercise and diet (Meichenbaum & Turk, 1987) that can help prevent disease or keep it from worsening. What Glasgow and Nutting (see chapter 23) call *self-management problems* (also known as compliance, adherence, and follow-through problems) can be improved with psycho-logical treatment. Useful recent advances in psy-chological approaches to these issues have been made by Prochaska, DiClemente, and colleagues (1992) and Rollnick, Mason, and Butler (1999), among others.

Psychosocial Vulnerabilities

The primary care patient, especially the patient with mental health problems, is likely to be older, less educated, poorer, and a member of an ethnic minority group (U.S. Department of Health and

Human Services, 2001; Wells et al., 1989). For these patients, but not only for these patients, having a medical illness is not usually the reason for seeking primary medical care. The actual determinant of an individual's decision to seek medical care may have more to do with an emotional or interpersonal situation than with the severity of physical symptoms. Conversely, for many patients with psychological or psychosocial concerns, medical visits are generated by the physical symptoms of distress (Smith, Rost, et al., 1995). In addition, histories of abuse, trauma, and social isolation also affect physical health and the perception of symptoms (House, Landis, et al., 1988).

The Primary Care Physician Has Difficulty Meeting These Needs

The thrust of medical training and the situational demands on the primary care physician make it difficult to address the actual needs of the primary care patient for three reasons: the focus on biomedical conditions in traditional medical training, economic pressures that limit time with the patient, and competing demands that place psychological concerns at a lower priority.

Traditional Medical Training Focuses on Biomedical Conditions

Medical school and residency emphasize the biomedical, technical aspects of care, and psychosocial material is often considered secondary—even irrelevant and unscientific. There is no coherent medical psychology that is taught in every medical school (Kainz, 2002). Psychiatry for the most part focuses on evaluation and management of severe mental illness, leaving the primary care clinician "without support when he/she is trying to understand and deal with the ordinary mental distress, disorders and illness encountered in the daily practice of primary care" (deGruy, 1996, p. 299).

Economic Pressures Limit the Amount of Time the Physician Spends With the Patient

The average U.S. primary care visit lasts less than 13 minutes (Balkrishnan, Hall, et al., 2002), and patients often bring to this visit more problems (and sometimes more significant problems) than

their single "chief complaint." Although there are guidelines that help the primary care physician address patients' psychosocial concerns within the standard time constraints (Stewart, Brown, et al., 1995; Stewart & Lieberman, 1993), accumulating evidence suggests that addressing patients' concerns takes time (cf. Harman, Schulberg, et al., 2001), and the sense of time pressure is generally very high in normal primary care practices.

Competing Demands Place Psychological Concerns at a Lower Priority

Despite the fact that substantial amounts of mental care are presently being delivered by primary care physicians, a number of studies have shown that there is significant underdetection and undertreatment of mental illnesses by primary care physicians (Badger, deGruy, et al., 1994; Seltzer, 1989). In an average 15-minute visit, primary care physicians will be dealing with a patient's chief complaint, with two or three other active problems on the patient's problem list, with health promotion/disease prevention guidelines, and with a steady stream of specialist-recommended procedures and tests, such as glaucoma testing, prostate-specific antigen testing, digital rectal examinations, and so on. Small wonder primary care physicians do not consistently address mental distress or mental disorders, even if identified; they just do not always make it to the top of the list of most pressing concerns. Primary care physicians become understandably defensive when their rates of recognition and methods of management of mental health problems are criticized, arguing in part that, without adequate resources and with pressure to respond to other needs, they make rational decisions about the allocation of their time and effort (deGruy, 1996; Schwenk, 2002). Another important, regrettable dimension of primary care today is defensive medicine. As Hamberger, Ovide, and Weiner (1999) noted, "Doctors get sued for missing biomedical diagnoses, not psychosocial ones" (p. 102).

Access to the Specialty Mental Health Care System Is Limited by Stigma and Economics

Primary care patients typically do not view their emotional disorders as something apart from their general health, and a considerable number (up to one-half by some estimates) will refuse referral to a mental health professional (Olfson, 1991; Orleans, George, et al., 1985; Wickramasekera, 1989). Those who refuse tend to be high medical utilizers with unexplained physical symptoms, but refusals cut across all demographic and diagnostic groups of patients. Indeed, a certain portion of primary care patients recognizes their psychological disorders, but prefers to receive mental health care in medical settings, in part because this is not construed as "mental health care" (deGruy, 1996).

The stigma of mental illness and resistance to getting help in treating it is still a common cultural feature in the United States (Cole & Rajum, 1996). For example, Kessler and colleagues (2001) found that approximately 60% of adults with serious mental illness were not receiving regular treatment, the majority because they felt that they did not have an emotional problem. In addition, consistent with the stigma of seeking mental health care and the value of independence in this society, the most commonly reported reason for failing to seek treatment (72%) and treatment dropout (58%) was "wanting to solve the problem on their own."

Even those who wish to obtain specialty mental health services face significant barriers to access. Fisher and Ransom (1997) estimate that between one-third and one-half of primary care patients referred to mental health specialists do not achieve a first visit, often because of mental health clinicians' inaccessible offices, inconvenient office hours, lack of insurance, or restrictions on insurance coverage. Those who do finally successfully gain access to mental health care incur added costs because of the arbitrary separation of mental health and medical care systems (Coleman & Patrick, 1976; Strosahl, 2001).

DEFINING PRIMARY CARE PSYCHOLOGY

Having defined the need for a primary care psychology and begun to suggest what issues it should address, we now describe it in more detail, beginning with episodes from a "day in the life" of Dr. Emily Versatile, a psychologist in independent practice who spends 2 days each week in a primary care clinic.

Dr. Versatile's first patient of the day is Tanya Brown, a 53-year-old woman referred for smoking cessation. As they discuss what has made it difficult for Tanya to quit smoking, she describes an abusive 10-year marriage that ended recently. She has never discussed the abuse with anyone other than her children, who were quite unsupportive of her and did not believe that their father could have been abusive. This 45-minute discussion of her background proves enormously relieving to Tanya (she returns for three more sessions, in which smoking is still the main focus, but she notes that her mood and her self-esteem have increased dramatically).

Dr. Versatile's next patient is Saliri Mowese, a 32-year-old Somalian woman who is having difficulty parenting her adolescent son; on further exploration, it becomes clear that her emigration from Somalia followed some traumatic experiences in the civil war, and she is showing symptoms of posttraumatic stress disorder. The son, who is in the waiting room, is invited to join the session, and a productive discussion of the family's adjustment to life in the United States occurs. (Three more sessions over the following 6 weeks, focused on parenting, culture clash, and efforts to resolve posttraumatic stress disorder symptoms, result in much improved functioning; the patient gets a new job, and the son finds friends who are not delinquent.)

The third patient does not come in; Dr. Versatile takes the opportunity to sit in the break room and begins a conversation with Matt Hendricks, a primary care physician with whom she has collaborated for several years, about why he finds himself so tired and sad when working with a patient who has multiple unexplained physical ailments. They have a productive discussion of the relationship between this patient and the physician's hypochondriac complaining mother.

Dr. Versatile's next 5 hours are spent in a variety of ways: conventional psychotherapy sessions, brief "health and behavior interventions," parenting skills coaching, and evaluating new patients.

Her last patient of the day is Harry Dourman, a depressed 38-year-old man who seems unresponsive to the selective serotonin reuptake inhibi-

tor prescribed for him. Because a consultation was requested, Dr. Versatile asks that the medical assistant find his physician, who is able to join them for the visit. She finds that the most appropriate diagnosis appears to be bipolar-II disorder and suggests to the physician that a mood stabilizer might be more appropriate for such a condition than a selective serotonin reuptake inhibitor. She schedules the patient for a session the following week (to which she suggests he bring his wife) to begin to work on strategies to cope with his condition.

This range of activities and these rapid shifts in focus typify the challenges faced by psychologists who practice in the primary care setting. Primary care psychology is different from subspecialties of clinical health psychology, such as cardiac risk prevention, chronic pain management, cognitive rehabilitation, or psycho-oncology. Although it defies precise definition, primary care psychology draws heavily from clinical health psychology, behavioral medicine, developmental psychology, family psychology, systems theory, learning theory, and educational psychology as well as from the philosophy of primary care (Garcia-Shelton & Vogel, 2002; Strosahl, 2001).

Historical Perspective

Although modern primary care psychology is developing as a unique subdiscipline, the impulse that underlies its development is certainly not new. Efforts to improve medical–psychological collaboration have existed for years. Routh (1994), for example, noted that in 1911 the American Psychological Association established a committee on relations between psychology and medical education. The first account of a collaborative psychology–pediatric practice was published over 35 years ago (Smith, Rome, et al., 1967). Family therapists have been exploring collaboration with primary care clinicians, particularly family physicians, for almost that long (e.g., Doherty & Baird, 1983). Convincing arguments for more integrated care have been made from the beginning of this period of collaboration (e.g., Coleman & Patrick, 1976) to the present time (Samet, Friedmann, et al., 2001).

As Drotar (1995) described, developing effective collaboration is often time consuming and re-

quires sacrificing some of psychologists' hard-won independence. Yet, improved integration of psychological and primary care practice can be as simple for the psychologist as sending a copy of an intake report to a patient's family doctor. At the other extreme, efforts to integrate can be as far reaching as full integration into primary care systems, with no difference in patients seen, time allocated, or problems addressed (Strosahl, 2001). For independent practitioners of psychology, some intermediate level of collaboration will probably be most congenial.

A Way of Thinking Rather Than a Particular Service

Although many writers (e.g., Bray & Rogers, 1995; Coleman & Patrick, 1976; McDaniel, Haley, et al., 1998) emphasize "co-location" as an essential element, primary care psychology is as much a point of view as it is a set of procedures or physical proximity to primary care physicians. In addition to endorsing the philosophy of primary care, the primary care psychology approach includes a special regard for generalism; an integrative, biopsychosocial orientation; an awareness that resources are limited and must be managed effectively; a perspective on psychopathology that searches for and builds on existing competencies; attentiveness to opportunities for educational and preventive interventions; and a population-based perspective.

WHAT IS DIFFERENT ABOUT PRACTICING PRIMARY CARE PSYCHOLOGY?

The psychologist who wishes to practice effectively in the primary care environment must have an awareness of what is different about it. In this section, we consider several salient features, focusing on aspects of the patient, the physician, and the environment.

Primary Care Patients' Needs, Problems, and Expectations

We focus in this section on seven characteristics of primary care patients and their concerns.

1. *Many patients have both medical and psychological conditions.* The primary care psychologist must be familiar and comfortable with the reality of patients' medical conditions. Two thirds of primary care patients with a psychiatric diagnosis have a significant physical illness (Spitzer, Williams, et al., 1994), and chronic medical illnesses substantially increase the likelihood of depression. Also, the primary care psychologist must be conscious of two additional difficulties: Medical complications can masquerade as psychological symptoms (Morrison, 1997), and psychological symptoms are frequently expressed somatically by primary care patients (Kroenke et al., 1994).

2. *Patients' psychological problems are frequently "messy": multiaxial, comorbid with other conditions, and mixed with miscellaneous symptoms and subthreshold conditions.* Unlike specialty patient populations or patient populations selected for research on treatment effectiveness, problems may be less "cleanly" defined. For example, the initial research into the effectiveness of screening primary care patients for psychopathology (Spitzer et al., 1994) found that nearly one third of the respondents had three or more mental diagnoses. In the World Health Organization primary care study (Von Korff, Ormel, et al., 1992), patients with all but one of the specific diagnoses had comorbidity rates of about 50%.

The co-occurrence of depression and anxiety in the primary care patient is extensive (Parkerson, Broadhead, et al., 1996), as is the overlap of anxiety and panic disorder (Simon, Gureje, et al., 2001; Walker, Katon, et al., 2000); depression and panic disorder (Ronalds, Kapur, et al., 2002); and Axis I and Axis II problems (Sansone, Whitecar, et al., 2001). Relevant to this last point, significant prevalence of Axis II disorders, particularly borderline personality disorder, has been found in primary care populations, again much of it unrecognized and untreated (Gross, Olfson, et al., 2002). One implication drawn from these findings by several researchers is that effective integration of psychological services might allow intervention when problems are less entrenched (Coyne, Fechner-Bates, et al., 1994; Katon, 1987; Ransom, 1983).

3. *Patients frequently have abuse or trauma histories.* The prevalence of abuse and trauma histories is significant and is related to both overall levels of health as well as "somatic preoccupation" (Sansone et al., 2001) and depression (Walker et al., 2000).

4. *Patients may not consider themselves to have psychological problems.* A considerable number of patients follow through on psychology referrals because "the doctor told me to"; the primary care psychologist cannot take for granted that the patient understands or accepts the premises under which most psychological treatment is conducted. Thus, the effective primary care psychologist will be able to work from a health or competence perspective and not "over-pathologize" (Schroeder, 1997). The issue of stigma must be addressed early in treatment as well. Perhaps one of the subtlest changes required of the psychologist who practices in primary care is shifting away from the covert blaming of the victim that is embodied in much popular psychology and some psychosomatic theorizing about medical illnesses. Conversely, the behaviorally trained psychologist must recognize the biological realities of organic pathology and not insist that everything can be modified or cognitively restructured. A reasonable understanding of the realities of primary care medicine will be necessary to provide effective care to patients who have both medical and psychological problems or problems that manifest in both the medical and mental health areas (Wickramasekera, 1989).

5. *Patients may not expect or need psychotherapy.* The effective primary care psychologist must have an extensive awareness of community resources (Kates & Craven, 1998). In addition, primary care settings provide opportunities to develop programs in coordination with community agencies (Schroeder, 1997).

The primary care psychologist must also think beyond individual psychotherapy in considering how to deliver better care. Such "nontherapy" interventions as psychoeducational classes and support groups (Caudill, Schnable, et al., 1991; Kennell, Klaus, et al., 1991; Lorig, Mazonson, et al., 1993) and such self-help materials as books (Kemper, Lorig, et al., 1993) and videotapes (Robinson, Schwartz, et al., 1989) should be at the ready for the patients of the primary care psychologist. Meeting the informational needs of primary care patients may well be therapeutic and may prove to be a potent addition to the care provided by the primary care physician. For example, patients frequently need additional education about their antidepressants and other prescriptions.

6. *Patients may expect brief, practical, directive, and pharmaceutical-based treatment.* The effective primary care psychologist must be able to explain psychotherapy and counseling to patients unfamiliar with it and be able to raise patients' motivation without promising unrealistic outcomes. Ideally, the primary care psychologist should have the ability to focus on interventions that have immediate payoff (e.g., within a matter of days); this may involve helping the patient to appreciate the importance of small behavior changes.

In addition, the primary care psychologist should be an effective educator because he or she may need to explain the process of psychological change and help the patient to maintain motivation in the face of discouragement; still, it is important to note that a significant proportion of primary care patients will experience enormous relief simply from the caring, empathic attentive moments they experience in the primary care psychologist's office (Adler, 1997). In these cases, the psychologists' job is to help the patient develop some appreciation of the changes that may be necessary to maintain this relief.

7. *Care is often sought episodically.* It is quite common for primary care psychologists to see a patient for three sessions, resolve a focal problem, and then see the patient a year or more later for a new crisis. This is in keeping with the continuity-of-care model and practice in primary care, but it is quite different from the more thorough approach that "treats everything in one course of therapy" prominent in many mental health training programs. The primary care psychologist must become comfortable with episodic care and enable the patient to return for additional treatment if necessary.

"There's a Doctor in the House"

As noted, the fact that the patient has a relationship with a primary care physician has important implications for the primary care psychologist. Both formally and informally, the interdisciplinary team most often functions with the primary care physician as its leader; physicians are trained to have the final responsibility for their patients (Pace et al., 1995). Beyond this professional socialization lies an interpersonal reality; patients for the most part will have their longest-term relationships with the primary care physician and may see the primary care psychologist only intermittently. To build on this doctor–patient relationship and support it is a major shift for many psychologists. The primary care psychologist must avoid competing over who cares more for the patient or who "owns the patient" or triangulating the patient if the primary care physician and psychologist disagree on treatment plans. This raises three issues:

1. *The physician usually wants information about "his" or "her" patient.* The primary care environment will raise competing demands to reveal and withhold information; the primary care psychologist must be able to provide a safe and confidential environment for the patient (Strosahl, 1996) and at the same time be able to include the primary care physician and approach the patient's problems as much as possible as a team. Medical teams are used to sharing information fairly openly, and physicians may not understand why psychologists emphasize confidentiality so much. At the same time, psychologists' patients often expect confidentiality, and clarity about what information will be shared is critical (Haas & Malouf, 2002).

2. *The physician–patient relationship may be problematic.* Not uncommonly, the doctor–patient relationship itself will be a topic that the patient wants to address with the psychologist. Power issues are often present in medical care (for example, physicians may refuse to continue to treat patients who disagree with the treatment plan, or patients may fear that this will happen), and psychologists may hear complaints from patients about how their physicians dominate or intimidate them. Effectively balancing the competing demands of such a situation often requires family therapy skills.

The primary care psychologist may also have opportunities to help physicians accurately assess themselves and thereby improve the care they are able to provide (cf. Drotar, 1995). Accurate constructive feedback is a rare commodity in medical systems (Ende, 1983), and respectful colleagues who can help primary care physicians recognize their limits and perhaps expand them will be highly valued.

3. *Consultation and teamwork are essential.* Consultation should also be an important avenue of service delivery (Smith et al., 1995). Because the primary care physician will have an ongoing relationship with the patient, key elements of treatment may be achieved by helping the physician work differently with the patient. In addition, for patients who have not (yet) been referred, the primary care psychologist must be able to conduct an informal consultation. The ability to collaborate with professionals from other disciplines is not a prominent feature of current psychology training and must be cultivated (Schroeder, 1997). For example, a common way in which physicians consult with their colleagues and a way in which they commonly will check out the usefulness of mental health advice is the "curbside" or "corridor" consultation. It is important, if such a consultation is requested, for the psychologist to keep the advice hypothetical, brief, and practical. It is reasonable at this point to indicate one's availability for a referral. It is a common medical practice to give general answers to curbside consultation questions, but actually to request to see the patient before giving a detailed opinion, and this should be the standard of practice for psychologists as well.

The Primary Care Psychologist Practices in "the House of Medicine"

The practice of psychology in the primary medical care environment requires consideration of at least two issues:

1. *Psychology may be misunderstood, caricatured, or devalued.* The primary care psychologist will experience challenges to his or her professional status and must have a strong professional identity as well as a good sense of humor. Professional support is essential; for some psychologists who practice exclusively in the primary care setting, the pressure to prove themselves to their medical colleagues can pose the risk of neglecting self-care strategies (Cole-Kelly & Hepworth, 1991). As well, the psychologist must know very clearly the limits of his or her competence or capacity while remaining a generalist (Haas, 1993; Haas & Malouf, 2002). Ironically, the display of theoretical sophistication, a common way in which psychologists enhance their self-esteem among peers, will detract from their effectiveness with primary care physicians. The primary care physician is more likely to value practical, commonsense advice and even suggestions for phrasing interventions (Stewart & Lieberman, 1993).

2. *Medication is pervasive.* Patients expect to be diagnosed with a physical condition and given a prescription for it when they visit primary care physicians (Jackson & Kroenke, 2001). The psychologist who needs to increase patients' motivation to undertake psychological approaches to their problems will need to have effective patient education skills and the ability to point out everyday examples of "mind influencing body" (Wickramasekera, 1989). On the other hand, the psychologist who is skeptical of medication must be careful not to undermine patients' (sometimes shaky) motivation to follow through with medication prescriptions because it is clear that, for a number of psychological disorders, medication plus psychotherapy is superior to either alone (Nathan & Gorman, 2002). It is hard to be an effective primary care psychologist without being conversant with psychotropic medications and their effect on thinking, feeling, and behavior.

Because patients and physicians alike may request recommendations about medications or dosage, the primary care psychologist must be good at managing expectations and clarifying his or her role in regard to prescriptions. In many cases, the psychologist may indeed have more familiarity with effects of certain psychotropic medications than the primary care physician; in addition, the psychologist may recognize treatable psychopathology that the physician has overlooked and for which he or she could usefully prescribe. However, unless he or she practices in a state that has granted prescriptive authority to psychologists, this information must be phrased as general information rather than as specific recommendations for this patient (Haas & Malouf, 2002).

SUMMARY

Primary care psychology, although it defies easy definition, is a different approach than specialty mental health care, clinical health psychology, or behavioral medicine. The opportunity to provide psychological services in the primary care setting offers the possibility that the primary care psychologist can improve patients' health as well as the health care system itself. Primary care psychology requires preventive, educational, and consultative skills in addition to the full array of clinical skills possessed by the well-trained clinical psychologist. Primary care is integrated, continuous, generalist care, and this definition applies as much to psychologists as it does to physicians.

Primary care needs psychology to address the enormous amount of untreated psychopathology, the significant lifestyle and behavioral health problems, the psychological impact of chronic illness, and the combined psychological impact of being ill and being a member of a vulnerable population. Neither the pressured and overburdened primary medical care system nor the often-inaccessible specialty mental health system can easily meet these needs.

The practice of psychology in primary care settings must be adapted to the unique expectations and needs of the primary care patient, the existence of an ongoing relationship between the patient and the primary care physician, and the fact that psychological services are delivered in a medical environment.

The primary care psychologist must be a consummate generalist; have a competence-oriented, practical perspective; and be able to provide services that go well beyond conventional psychotherapy in working with the primary care patient and the primary health care team.

Effective work in primary care may result in some reduction of professional autonomy, but in return it offers the chance to affect a much larger system and to offer psychological service where it is desperately needed.

ADDITIONAL RESOURCES

Suggestions for further reading and Internet professional development resources are available at this book's companion Web site: www.primarycarepsych.com.

References

Adler, H. M. (1997). The history of the present illness as treatment: Who's listening, and why does it matter? *Journal of the American Board of Family Practice, 10*(1), 28–35.

Badger, L. W., deGruy, F. V., et al. (1994). Patient presentation, interview content, and the detection of depression by primary care physicians. *Psychosomatic Medicine, 56*, 128–135.

Balkrishnan, R., Hall, M. A., et al. (2002). Capitation payment, length of visit, and preventive services: Evidence from a national sample of outpatient physicians. *American Journal of Managed Care, 8*, 332–340.

Bea, S. M., & Tesar, G. E. (2002). A primer on referring patients for psychotherapy. *Cleveland Clinic Journal of Medicine, 69*, 113–114, 117–118, 120–122, 125–127.

Beardsley, R. S., Gardocki, G. J., et al. (1988). Prescribing of psychotropic medication by primary care physicians and psychiatrists. *Archives of General Psychiatry, 45*, 1117–1119.

Bray, J. H., & Rogers, J. C. (1995). Linking psychologists and family physicians for collaborative practice. *Professional Psychology: Research and Practice, 26*, 132–138.

Cauce, A. M., Domenech-Rodriguez, M., et al. (2002). Cultural and contextual influences in mental health help seeking: A focus on ethnic minority youth. *Journal of Consulting and Clinical Psychology, 70*, 44–55.

Caudill, M., Schnable, R., et al. (1991). Decreased clinic use by chronic pain patients: Response to behavioral medicine intervention. *Clinical Journal of Pain, 7*, 305–310.

Codori, A., & Nannis, E. (1990, August). *The logic of noncompliance: The patient's perspective.* Paper presented at the 98th meeting of the American Psychological Association, Boston.

Cole, S., & Rajum, A. (1996). Overcoming barriers to integration of primary care and behavioral health care: Focus on knowledge and skills. *Behavioral Health Care Tomorrow, 5*, 30–37.

Cole-Kelly, K., & Hepworth, J. (1991). Pressures for omnipotence, saner responses for family therapists in medicine. *Family Systems Medicine, 9*, 159–164.

Coleman, J. V., & Patrick, D.L. (1976). Integrating mental health services into primary medical care. *Medical Care, 14*, 654–661.

Coyne, J. C., Fechner-Bates, S., et al. (1994). Prevalence, nature, and comorbidity of depressive disorders in primary care. *General Hospital Psychiatry, 16*(4), 267–276.

deGruy, F. (1996). Mental health care in the primary care setting. In M. Donaldson, K. Yordy, K. Lohr, & N. Vanselov (Eds.), *Primary care:*

America's health in a new era (pp. 285–311). Washington, DC: Institute of Medicine, National Academy Press.

Doherty, W., & Baird, M. (1983). *Family therapy and family medicine: Toward the primary care of families.* New York: Guilford Press.

Donaldson, M., Yordy, K., Lohr, K., & Vanselov, N. (Eds.) (1996). *Primary care: America's health in a new era.* Washington, DC: National Academy Press.

Donovan, J. L., & Blake, D. R. (1992). Patient noncompliance: Deviance or reasoned decision-making. *Social Science and Medicine, 34,* 507–513.

Drotar, D. (1995). *Consulting with pediatricians: Psychological perspectives.* New York: Plenum.

Ende, J. (1983). Feedback in clinical medical education. *Journal of the American Medical Association, 250,* 777–781.

Fisher, L., & Ransom, D. C. (1997). Developing a strategy for managing behavioral health care within the context of primary care. *Archives of Family Medicine, 6,* 324–333.

Garcia-Shelton, L., & Vogel, M. (2002). Primary care health psychology training: A collaborative model with family practice. *Professional Psychology: Research and Practice, 33,* 546–556.

Gross, R., Olfson, M., et al. (2002). Borderline personality disorder in primary care. *Archives of Internal Medicine, 162,* 53–60.

Haas, L. J. (1993). Competence and quality issues in the performance of forensic psychologists. *Ethics and Behavior, 3,* 251–266.

Haas, L. J., & Malouf, J. L. (2002). *Keeping up the good work: A practitioners' guide to mental health ethics* (3rd ed.). Sarasota, FL: Professional Resource Press.

Hamberger, K., Ovide, C., & Weiner, E. L. (1999). *Making collaborative connections with medical providers.* New York: Springer.

Harman, J. S., Schulberg, H. C., et al. (2001). The effect of patient and visit characteristics on diagnosis of depression in primary care. *Journal of Family Practice, 50,* 1068.

House, J. S., Landis, K. R., et al. (1988). Social relationships and health. *Science, 241,* 540–545.

Jackson, J. L., & Kroenke, K. (2001). The effect of unmet expectations among adults presenting with physical symptoms. *Annals of Internal Medicine, 134*(9, Pt. 2), 889–897.

Kainz, K. (2002). Barriers and enhancements to physician–psychologist collaboration. *Professional Psychology: Research and Practice, 33,* 169–175.

Kates, N., & Craven, M. (1998). *Managing mental health problems: A practical guide for primary care.* Seattle, WA: Hogrefe & Huber.

Katon, W. (1987). The epidemiology of depression in medical care. *International Journal of Psychiatry and Medicine, 17,* 93–112.

Katon, W., Von Korff, M., et al. (1990). Distressed high utilizers of medical care. DSM-III-R diagnoses and treatment needs. *General Hospital Psychiatry, 12,* 355–362.

Kemper, D. W., Lorig, K., et al. (1993). The effectiveness of medical self-care interventions: A focus on self-initiated responses to symptoms. *Patient Education and Counseling, 21,* 29–39.

Kennell, J., Klaus, M., et al. (1991). Continuous emotional support during labor in a U.S. hospital. *Journal of the American Medical Association, 265,* 2197–2237.

Kessler, L. G., Burns, B. J., et al. (1987). Psychiatric diagnoses of medical service users: Evidence from the Epidemiologic Catchment Area Program. *American Journal of Public Health, 77,* 18–24.

Kessler, R. C., Berglund, P. A., et al. (2001). The prevalence and correlates of untreated serious mental illness. *Health Services Research, 36*(6, Pt. 1), 987–1007.

Kroenke, K., & Mangelsdorff, A. D. (1989). Common symptoms in ambulatory care: Incidence, evaluation, therapy, and outcome. *American Journal of Medicine, 86,* 262–266.

Kroenke, K., Spitzer, R. L., et al. (1994). Physical symptoms in primary care: Predictors of psychiatric disorders and functional impairment. *Archives of Family Medicine, 3,* 774–779.

Lieberman, J. A. R. (1996). Compliance issues in primary care. *Journal of Clinical Psychiatry, 7,* 76–82.

Lorig, K., Mazonson, P., et al. (1993). Evidence suggesting that health education for self-management in patients with chronic arthritis has sustained health benefits while reducing health care costs. *Arthritis and Rheumatology, 36,* 439–446.

McDaniel, S., Haley, W., et al. (1998). Psychological practice in primary care settings: Practical tips for clinicians. *Professional Psychology: Research and Practice, 29,* 237–244.

Meichenbaum, D., & Turk, D. C. (1987). *Facilitating treatment adherence: A practitioner's guidebook.* New York: Plenum Press.

Moncrieff, J., Wessely, S., & Hardy, R. (2001). Antidepressants using active placebos. *Cochrane Database of Systemitic Reviews, 1,* CD003012.

Morrison, J. (1997). *When psychological problems*

mask medical disorders: A guide for psychothera-pists. New York: Guilford Press.

Murray, C., & Lopez, A. (1996). *Global burden of disease*. Cambridge, MA: Harvard University Press.

Narrow, W. E., Rae, D. S., et al. (2002). Revised prevalence estimates of mental disorders in the United States: Using a clinical significance criterion to reconcile two surveys' estimates. *Archives of General Psychiatry, 59,* 115–123.

Nathan, P., & Gorman, J. (Eds.). (2002). *A guide to treatments that work* (2nd ed.). New York: Oxford University Press.

Olfson, M. (1991). Primary care patients who refuse specialized mental health services. *Archives of Internal Medicine, 151,* 129–132.

Olfson, M., Gilbert, T., et al. (1995). Recognition of emotional distress in physically healthy primary care patients who perceive poor physical health. *General Hospital Psychiatry, 17,* 173–180.

Orleans, C. T., George, L. K., et al. (1985). How primary care physicians treat psychiatric disorders: A national survey of family practitioners. *American Journal of Psychiatry, 142,* 52–57.

Pace, T. M., Chaney, J. M., et al. (1995). Psychological consultation with primary care physicians: Obstacles and opportunities in the medical setting. *Professional Psychology: Research and Practice, 26,* 123–131.

Parkerson, G. R., Broadhead, W. E., et al. (1996). Anxiety and depressive symptom identification using the Duke Health Profile. *Journal of Clinical Epidemiology, 49,* 85–93.

Pasco, T., & Smart, D. (2003). *Physician characteristics and distribution in the United States: 2003–4 Edition*. Chicago: AMA Press.

Prochaska, J. O., DiClemente, C. C., et al. (1992). In search of how people change. *American Psychologist, 47,* 1102–1114.

Ransom, D. (1983). Random notes; on building bridges between family practice and family therapy. *Family Systems Medicine, 1,* 91–96.

Ray, D. C., Raicti, M. A., et al. (1992). Effects of perceived responsibility on help seeking decisions among elderly person. *Journal of Gerontology: Psychological Services, 47,* 199–205.

Robinson, J. D., Schwartz, M. D., et al. (1989). The impact of fever health education on clinic utilization. *American Journal of Disabled Children, 143,* 698–704.

Rollnick, S., Mason, P., & Butler, C. (1999). *Health behavior change: A guide for practitioners*. Edinburgh, Scotland: Churchill Livingstone.

Ronalds, C., Kapur, N., et al. (2002). Determinants of consultation rate in patients with anxiety and depressive disorders in primary care. *Family Practice, 19,* 23–28.

Routh, D. (1994). *Clinical psychology since 1917: Science practice and organization*. New York: Plenum.

Samet, J. H., Friedmann, P., et al. (2001). Benefits of linking primary medical care and substance abuse services: Patient, provider, and societal perspectives. *Archives of Internal Medicine, 161,* 85–91.

Sansone, R. A., Whitecar, P., et al. (2001). The prevalence of borderline personality among primary care patients with chronic pain. *General Hospital Psychiatry, 23,* 193–197.

Schroeder, C. (1997). Conducting an integrated practice in a pediatric setting. In R. J. Illback, C. T. Cobb, & H. M. Joseph Jr. (Eds.), *Integrated services for children and families* (pp. 221–255). Washington, DC: American Psychological Association.

Schurman, R. A., Kramer, P. D., et al. (1985). The hidden mental health network. Treatment of mental illness by nonpsychiatrist physicians. *Archives of General Psychiatry, 42,* 89–94.

Schwenk, T. L. (2002). Diagnosis of late life depression: The view from primary care. *Biological Psychiatry, 52,* 157–163.

Seltzer, A. (1989). Prevalence, detection and referral of psychiatric morbidity in general medical patients. *Journal of the Royal Society of Medicine, 82,* 410–412.

Shapiro, S., Skinner, E. A., et al. (1984). Utilization of health and mental health services. Three Epidemiologic Catchment Area sites. *Archives of General Psychiatry, 41,* 971–978.

Simon, G. E., Gureje, O., et al. (2001). Course of hypochondriasis in an international primary care study. *General Hospital Psychiatry, 23(2),* 51–55.

Smith, E. E., Rome, L. P., et al. (1967). The clinical psychologist in the pediatric office. *Journal of Pediatrics, 71,* 48–51.

Smith, G. R., Jr. (1994). The course of somatization and its effects on utilization of health care resources. *Psychosomatics, 35,* 263–267.

Smith, G. R., Jr., Rost, K., et al. (1995). A trial of the effect of a standardized psychiatric consultation on health outcomes and costs in somatizing patients. *Archives of General Psychiatry, 52,* 238–243.

Spitzer, R. L., Williams, J. B., et al. (1994). Utility of a new procedure for diagnosing mental disorders in primary care. The PRIME-MD 1000 study. *Journal of the American Medical Association, 272,* 1749–1756.

Stewart, M., Brown, J., et al. (1995). *Patient-centered medicine: Transforming the clinical method.* Thousand Oaks, CA: Sage.

Stewart, M., & Lieberman, J. A. (1993). *The fifteen-minute hour: Applied psychotherapy for the primary care physician.* Westport, CT: Praeger.

Strosahl, K. (1996). Confessions of a behavioral therapist in primary care: The odyssey and the ecstasy. *Cognitive and Behavioral Practice, 3,* 1–28.

Strosahl, K. (2001). *Integrated behavioral healthcare: Prospects, issues and opportunities.* New York: Academic Press.

Trask, P. C., Schwartz, S. M., et al. (2002). Behavioral medicine: The challenge of integrating psychological and behavioral approaches into primary care. *Effective Clinical Practice, 5*(2), 75–83.

U.S. Department of Health and Human Services. (2001). *Mental health: Culture, race, and ethnicity. A supplement to mental health: A report of the surgeon general.* Rockville, MD: Author.

Von Korff, M., Ormel, J., et al. (1992). Disability and depression among high utilizers of health care. A longitudinal analysis. *Archives of General Psychiatry, 49,* 91–100.

Walker, E. A., Katon, W. J., et al. (2000). Predictors of outcome in a primary care depression trial. *Journal of General Internal Medicine, 15,* 859–867.

Wells, K. B., Stewart, A., et al. (1989). The functioning and well-being of depressed patients. Results from the Medical Outcomes Study. *Journal of the American Medical Association, 262,* 914–919.

Wickramasekera, I. (1989). Somatizers, the health care system and collapsing the psychological distance that the somatizer has to travel for help. *Professional Psychology: Research and Practice, 20,* 105–111.

Zvolensky, M. J., Eifert, G. H., Larkin, K. T., & Ludwig, H. A. (1999). Improving communication between clinical psychologists and primary care physicians: Implications for increasing the quality of rural mental health care. *Journal of Rural Community Psychology, 2,* 1–6.

2

Establishing and Maintaining a Psychological Practice in Primary Health Care

H. Russell Searight
James W. Price
Jennifer Gafford

Practice in primary care challenges a psychologist's decision making, efficiency, and clinical knowledge. Consider the following "slice of primary care psychology life," a composite of our experiences, but certainly within the realm of possibility for a primary care psychologist:

Dr. Mandelbrot practices in a family medicine clinic staffed by three family physicians and two nurse practitioners. Halfway through an evaluation of a patient with chronic low back pain, he is interrupted by a knock on the door. A physician colleague asks if he has a minute and describes a 71-year-old male currently in the office with reported memory loss as well as irritability and sleep disturbance. Mandelbrot excuses himself from his patient and spends 15 minutes administering a Geriatric Depression Scale as well as a brief mental status examination.

When finished, Dr. Mandelbrot finds the physician reading another patient's X-rays. Mandelbrot's colleague stops briefly and says, "What did you find? Should I start him on an antidepressant?" Mandelbrot responds, "He might very well respond because he does seem to be depressed,

but he may also have early stage dementia." The physician is handed a sheet of lab results; as he reviews them, he says, "What should I start him on, Prozac?" "That's certainly your call, but I've gotten the impression that sertraline [Zoloft] seems better for geriatric patients," Dr. Mandelbrot says. "Okay, I'll start him on 50 mg," says the colleague. Mandlebrot responds, "Do you think the fact that he is older than 65 would suggest he'd do better starting at a lower dose and gradually increasing? I can give you some feedback on how he's doing because I plan to see him again next week to further assess his memory and his ability to live independently." The physician begins to move toward the exam room where the next patient is ready; he calls over his shoulder, "Thanks a lot for your help; this patient confused me a bit."

As Dr. Mandelbrot walks through the clinic to rejoin his original patient, the nurse practitioner asks if he has a minute. She describes a 10-year-old boy with primary nocturnal enuresis: "He's been to the urologist; there's nothing medically wrong. I was going to start him on the nasal spray DDAVP. What do you think?" Dr. Mandelbrot spends about 30 seconds explaining that behavioral therapy with the bell and pad is more effective than medication if the parents and the patient are willing to accept about 2 weeks of sleep disruption. He tells her how to order the device and returns to the original patient, apologizing for the interruption.

The patient responds: "It doesn't bother me, I'm used to it. It's always this way when I come to the doctor." After obtaining a pain history, assessing psychiatric symptoms, and reviewing a recent orthopedic consultation, Mandelbrot describes how depression often amplifies pain: "If we treat your depression, it won't take your pain away, but because treatment will help your sleep, give you more energy, and improve your mood, you'll probably be able to tolerate the pain a bit better. Would you feel okay about my talking with your primary care doctor about your depression and medication options?" The patient agrees, and Mandelbrot also encourages him to increase his activity level gradually, structure his day with specific goals, and return in 2 weeks for relaxation training.

As this vignette illustrates, providing psychological services in primary care can be a substantial departure from traditional mental health training and practice models. Many psychiatric disorders are commonly diagnosed and treated in the primary care sector without mental health consultation (Miranda, Hohman, Attkisson, & Larson, 1994). A typical family physician or internist will diagnose and treat more patients with major depression, generalized anxiety, and panic disorder than many psychologists will see in a professional lifetime. However, "pure" psychiatric conditions are uncommon because mental health symptoms are typically intertwined with medical conditions and medication side effects.

For the psychologist, success in primary care requires openness, flexibility, self-direction, and a willingness to learn. This chapter proceeds from a very broad discussion of medical culture (Searight, 1994; Stein, 1990) to specific primary care knowledge and skills. The chapter begins by describing three key values: a generalist orientation, efficiency, and pragmatism. With these dimensions as a basis, psychologist–physician relationships, roles, and communication styles are exam-

ined. Because most psychiatric conditions in this setting are treated with psychotropic medications, we provide some guidelines concerning medication issues. Additional sections concern generating referrals, documentation, and the scope of primary mental health care.

FUNDAMENTAL PRIMARY CARE VALUES

The authors' collective experience teaching and practicing in primary care is the basis for most of this chapter. Our overarching philosophy is that effective primary care psychological practice requires respect for the dominant biomedical perspective (Searight, 1999). Psychologists entering medical settings will become quite frustrated if their goal is to convert their physician colleagues to the values or mores of mental health culture. The psychologist's in-depth description of patients' personality dynamics, conflicting etiological theories, and limitations of existing research will typically meet with a physician response of "Okay, that's interesting, but the patient I've asked you about is here now, and while we've been talking, two more patients have arrived." To be successful, psychologists need to adapt evaluation, treatment, and professional communication strategies to the primary care context.

Three core values dominate the primary care setting: a broad-based generalist perspective, efficiency, and pragmatism (Searight, 1994, 1999). Psychologists' training is often inconsistent with these values. As a result, the initial professional adjustment to primary care may be challenging. Each of these values is discussed in detail below.

Broad-Based Clinical Skills

Over the past 15 to 20 years, psychology graduate training has become increasingly specialized. Graduate psychology programs may focus on the psychosocial aspects of trauma and abuse, neuropsychological assessment, geriatrics, or pediatrics. By contrast, primary care is very broad based. In a typical family medicine clinic, a 2-year-old with tantrums may be followed by a geriatric patient in early stages of dementia. Training for primary care psychologists should, in many ways, parallel that of generalist physicians. Rather than having in-depth training in a specific area such as neuropsychology, pediatrics, adult psychotherapy, health psychology, trauma/abuse, or geriatrics, primary care practitioners should have broad-based knowledge in all of these areas. The emphasis is on information breadth rather than on a detailed, narrowly focused knowledge base. Note that this volume and other sources (e.g., McDaniel, Belar, Schroeder, Hargrove, & Freeman, 2002), although they include information on common psychiatric conditions (e.g., anxiety and mood disorders), also focus on common chronic medical conditions such as gastrointestinal disorders, diabetes, obesity, and upper respiratory infections. The path to other useful sources is given at the end of this chapter. Working knowledge of psychopharmacology, somatization, neuropsychological screening, pain management, consultation models, and organizational dynamics is also very helpful.

The fact that primary care involves an unselected patient population with tremendous diversity of problems means that pragmatism and efficiency become crucial. Clinically, a useful working standard is to be able to manage approximately 80% to 85% of presenting problems effectively with the remainder referred to mental health specialists, such as psychiatrists or tertiary care psychologists (Searight, 1999). The remaining 15% to 20% typically include specialized issues, such as autistic spectrum disorders or more severe psychiatric syndromes such as schizophrenia. This model parallels the way in which a primary care physician manages the more specialized medical needs of patients. As generalists, primary care psychologists should know when and how to refer patients for specialty mental health services for eating disorders, borderline personality disorder, or significant marital/family dysfunction.

The treatment course also varies. Primary care physicians typically see patients in several closely spaced visits to address acute focal problems and then may have regular maintenance appointments at longer intervals. Primary care psychologists often see patients in a similar format. Psychologists in this setting commonly see patients for one to three closely spaced visits, during which they focus on resolving acute symptoms. The patient may have no more contact until returning a year later with similar or different concerns. This

treatment model would likely be criticized as superficial by many psychotherapists providing long-term treatment. It is important to recognize, however, that primary care patients are more likely to view their interaction with psychologists similar to that with their physician.

Efficiency

Time consciousness is one of modern medicine's defining features. Speed, efficiency, and fiscal measures of time are core dimensions of primary care (Lee, 2000). Time has a different meaning in medical settings than in mental health settings (Searight, 1994, 1999). Primary care physicians in private practice may see 40 to 60 patients per day. Psychologists should recognize that the average primary medical care office visit is approximately 15 minutes long. Some primary care psychologists do maintain the typical 50-minute sessions. However, others (Strosahl, 2000; Stuart & Lieberman, 1993) have developed structured time-efficient models. Strosahl (2000) described consultation visits of 15 to 30 minutes. These encounters include several initial minutes of introduction and specific discussion of the physician's referral issue, and 5 to 10 minutes developing an overview of the problem, followed by 15 minutes of targeted behavioral treatment.

Pragmatism

As psychologists, our training makes us unique in our ability to complete comprehensive cognitive and personality evaluations, to compose detailed 10-page assessment reports and to respect the value of the traditional 50-minute psychotherapy session. Psychologists entering primary care may try to highlight these skills, demonstrating the depth of what we have to offer in understanding a single patient's personality dynamics and documenting this in a comprehensive, well-written, lengthy report. Indeed, psychologists take pride in their ability to explore, understand, and describe the human psyche, often in a language that only they can understand.

In contrast, primary care values emphasize practical information with immediately relevant consequences for patient care. Psychologists' education, however, often emphasizes theory and ideal rather than feasible diagnostic and treatment approaches. Traditionally trained psychologists typically require considerable reorientation for successful primary care practice.

Psychologists new to the primary care setting often find that much of their training does not appear to be valued and they may feel unappreciated by the pragmatic physician who expects a much simpler response to such a question as, "What can I do to minimize the disruption this patient causes the clinical staff every time she enters the office?" Similarly, the psychologist who delivers a 60-minute talk on posttraumatic stress disorder to a group of physicians that includes a thorough discussion of the disorder and the theoretical implications of alternative forms of treatment will be disappointed when the only question asked at the end is "Why not just give them Prozac? That's what the pharmaceutical rep suggested last week."

Psychologists entering primary care must critically examine elements of their practice that are comfortable and familiar and make pragmatic decisions about how to adapt these elements effectively to the primary care setting. Physicians typically seek very practical, concrete suggestions. For example, if a physician asks how to reduce the disruption of a particular patient, it would not be helpful for the psychologist to suggest scheduling the patient for a comprehensive personality evaluation 3 weeks later, only to have a detailed 5- to 10-page report completed for the physician in another 2 weeks. A more pragmatic approach might include scheduling a 1-hour session with the patient, relying primarily on the patient's history and clinical interview for diagnosis, and responding to the physician verbally and in a brief consultation note with a diagnosis and very specific management techniques. Similarly, in delivering a talk on posttraumatic stress disorder, physicians are more likely to appreciate a 30-minute lecture on how posttraumatic stress disorder presents in primary care and steps the physician can take in providing pharmacotherapy, facilitating access to appropriate services, and providing support to the patient.

Is the depth of psychological training even valued in this setting? Absolutely. Strong assessment and diagnostic skills can be very useful in the primary care setting, just in a more pragmatic form.

One of the core skills in our training is strong interviewing skills. Because psychiatric diagnosis is heavily dependent on self-report, psychologists are quite adept at eliciting relevant data from patients. This skill is particularly important in the primary care setting; it has been estimated that up to 80% of diagnostic information is derived from the patient's history (Lazare, Putnam, & Lipkin, 1995).

When testing is necessary, the primary care psychologist is likely to use a brief screening test and refer the patient for a more comprehensive evaluation if needed. The following case example illustrates how a psychologist can be helpful and informative to a primary care physician even without conducting an entire cognitive evaluation:

Joey is a 10-year-old boy in the fourth grade referred to Dr. Luminous by his primary care physician. The physician provides the following information in the child's medical record: misbehaves in school, yelled at teacher last week, spaces out, seems disinterested in school, missing assignments, fights with mom during homework, headaches every morning before school, teachers want medicine for child, no serious conduct problems.

Dr. Luminous conducts a clinical interview with the parents and child to learn that Joey feels "stupid" and hates school because it is "boring." His parents state that Joey is "very bright," but seems to have trouble reading and spelling, no matter how much they practice. In fact, he was retained in second grade because of these problems. Review of the family history reveals two cousins and an uncle with learning disabilities. Further history and teacher ratings on the Conners' Teacher Rating Scales do not suggest serious conduct problems or symptoms of attention-deficit/hyperactivity disorder. Although there are mild school-related anxiety and self-esteem issues that should be addressed, she is able to rule out major affective and anxiety disorders.

Dr. Luminous conducts cognitive screening with selected subtests of the Wechsler Intelligence Scale for Children–Third Edition (WISC-III) and Wide Range Achievement Test–Third Edition (WRAT-3), and the results of these measures strongly suggest the presence of verbal learning disabilities. She discusses these results with the parents and child and recommends a comprehen-

sive evaluation by the school district specialist. She provides them with a note to give the school counselor documenting the results of the screening and her general impressions. Finally, she follows up with the primary care physician verbally and in a consultation note, describing (1) her impressions that learning problems may be contributing to the child's disruptive behavior in the classroom, (2) steps taken to facilitate an appropriate evaluation, and (3) her plan for follow up with the patient.

With respect to intervention, psychologists often underestimate patients' willingness to receive and act on direct advice (Newfield, Kuehl, Joanning, & Quinn, 1987). Primary care patients often expect direct guidance (Strosahl, 2000) and may be frustrated with mental health clinicians' indirectness and quasi-socratic questioning style.

Psychologists are also well trained in research methodology. Although "research" may periodically conflict with real-world pragmatics, the heavy emphasis in psychology graduate programs on systematic empirical knowledge for guiding diagnosis and treatment as well as psychology's long research tradition are quite valuable in today's world of evidence-based medicine (Sackett, Straus, Richardson, Rosenberg, & Haynes, 2000). This empirical training allows psychologists to evaluate critically new research findings in clinical medicine and the efficacy of new treatments, such as psychotropic medications. Similarly, psychologists' recognition of the distinction between statistical and clinical significance as a standard is also very helpful in interpreting medical literature. POEM, an acronym for patient-oriented evidence that matters, is becoming a popular framework (e.g., "Does a high-fiber dietary supplement of wheat bran reduce the recurrence rate of colorectal adenomas?"; Vitanzu & Hong, 2000) for analyzing research findings among practicing primary care physicians. Psychology's scientist–practitioner philosophy is particularly suited for developing and critiquing POEMs.

Given the differences between traditional psychological training and the demands to be pragmatic in the primary care setting, traditionally trained psychologists will require considerable reorientation to be successful in this setting. One way to begin this process is to explore how the primary medical care literature addresses mental health issues. One of the core features of family medicine, for example, is an appreciation for behavioral medicine or the mental health aspects of patient care. Studying the ways in which mental health is addressed in family practice journals, such as *American Family Physician*, will offer the psychologist a window into the ways in which mental health issues are integrated by the physician into primary care. In turn, this perspective will provide direction to the psychologist in how to best answer referral questions, respond to "curbside" consultations, and tailor talks to this group of professionals.

Another important method of adapting effectively to the primary care setting is to ask for specific feedback from physicians with whom you have worked. How do your primary care colleagues evaluate, for example, your availability to them or their patients, the quality and format of your written and verbal consultations, your follow-up, and your ability to meet their patients' needs (Platt, chapter 6, this volume)?

THE PSYCHOLOGIST'S ROLES

Several factors can trigger a request for consultation from a primary care physician: uncertainty about the patient's condition ("Is this patient depressed?"); the possible contribution of psychological factors to a physical condition (e.g., pseudoseizures, tension headaches, noncardiac chest pain); difficulty managing or treating the patient's psychological issues within the time parameters of a primary care office visit; frustration with illness-related behavior (e.g., noncompliance with antihypertensive medication); or recognition that the patient's psychiatric problem exceeds the primary care provider's level of training. The boundary between "medical" and "psychological" problems is often fluid, with both dimensions interacting. Conditions such as irritable bowel syndrome, compliance with a diabetic regimen, or post-cerebrovascular accident rehabilitation are examples of this boundary diffusion.

At the time of referral, the psychologist should attempt to obtain concise written or verbal information from the physician about the consultation's purpose. If the psychologist is practicing in the same office and sharing a chart, referral information should be available in the medical record. Many consultation requests are vague ("Please evaluate patient" or "Full psychological evaluation"). Because an individual primary care physician may envision different roles of consultation or treatment by the psychologist with specific patients, it is important that the psychologist's role be clarified at the initiation of the referral. Often, the referring physician is aware of a patient's psychological distress or maladaptive behavior, but has not articulated a differential diagnosis or a targeted treatment concern. The psychologist can both assist the physician's case conceptualization and specify a referral issue by querying the physician: "What questions would you like me to try to answer?" "What decisions do you need to make about the patient?" "Do you plan on following the patient after I see him or her?" "Would you like me to follow the patient?"

The limited available research suggests that, once they refer a patient, primary care physicians want the psychologist to accept treatment responsibility for the patient's mental health concerns (Kushner, Diamond, Beasley, Mundt, Plane, & Robbins, 2000). Among primary care physicians, family physicians surveyed were evenly divided as to whether a mental health referral was for consultation only or for treatment. Pediatricians, on the other hand, preferred that the patient receive treatment when they made a referral (Kushner et al., 2000). All three groups surveyed—family physicians, pediatricians, and internists—expressed dissatisfaction with mental health professionals' communication with them about patients referred.

Psychologists who provide ongoing treatment for a referred patient should continue to communicate to the physician through succinct written or verbal summaries of the patient's course. For patients with psychiatric conditions, the psychologist's communication should include a description of the degree of specific symptom improvement. As an example, consider a patient treated for panic disorder with cognitive–behavioral therapy by a psychologist and with a selective serotonin reuptake inhibitor (SSRI) by an internist. The psychologist could provide feedback monthly to bimonthly about the number of panic attacks and their frequency, intensity, and duration as well as

the number of attacks that the patient was able to prevent from escalating. This information, in turn, will help the physician focus the next clinical encounter with the patient. Thus, the internist, on learning that the patient's panic symptoms are improved, might address other medical conditions or determine whether to increase or decrease SSRI dosages. Many physicians appreciate information about whether a referred patient made an initial appointment with the psychologist. Finally, even when patients are referred for more specialized, comprehensive psychological evaluations, physicians appreciate the psychologist's effort to translate lengthy, complicated assessment results into more understandable conclusions with practical implications. An illustrative example is provided in the section on documentation.

PSYCHOTROPIC MEDICATIONS

As noted in chapter 1, the majority of psychotropic medication prescriptions are written by primary care physicians. The majority of these prescriptions are for antidepressants, antianxiety agents, and stimulants. The role of psychologists in prescribing psychotropic medications is under debate in many state legislatures (Sammons, Gorny, Zinner, & Allen, 2000; VandenBos & Williams, 2000). Regardless of local regulations, however, primary care psychologists will often be asked for psychotropic medication recommendations.

Surveying psychologists practicing in a broad range of settings, VandenBos and Williams (2000) reported that over 90% of practicing psychologists had consulted with physicians about changing a patient's medication, over 85% participated in the initial decision to prescribe medication, 79% served as consultants for a health care team that included a member with prescriptive authority, and nearly 60% had recommended a physician prescribe a specific medication for a patient.

In primary care, the psychologist's role in pharmacology is best captured by the American Psychological Association's task force description of Level II training (American Psychological Association, 1992). Level I focuses on basic knowledge necessary for most independently practicing psychologists; Level II knowledge is required for psychologists collaborating with prescribing clinicians (Level III is the standard of direct prescribing authority). Level II education includes knowledge of basic pharmacokinetics, drug benefits and adverse effects, central nervous system effects of nonpsychotropic medications, analysis of pharmacology research, and professional collaboration skills (American Psychological Association, 1992; Phelps, Brown, & Power, 2002).

Typical graduate school clinical psychology curricula provide only partial Level II training. However, with the addition of 1 to 2 years of supervised clinical experience in medical settings, Level II skills are attainable. Level III training in independent prescribing is presently not readily accessible. In-depth course work in pharmacology, neuroanatomy, and pathophysiology complemented by approximately 2 years of intensive supervised experience (Phelps et al., 2002) are necessary to meet Level III standards.

Primary care physicians treat a broad spectrum of illness and disability. This breadth requires knowledge of an increasingly complicated array of pharmacotherapies. The psychologist can be extremely useful as a psychopharmacological consultant to the primary care physician by maintaining current knowledge about commonly used psychotropic medications. In addition, keeping up to date about new psychotropic medications is helpful so the psychologist can critically assess drug efficacy and side effects and summarize this information for the physician. Because of their background in research design, statistics, and measurement, psychologists are in a particularly good position to evaluate critically the evidence from clinical trials of psychotropic agents. Outcome measures typically include narrow-band instruments (e.g., Hamilton Depression Inventory) as primary indicators of drug efficacy. Appendix A presents a summary of current psychotropic medications, and the specific chapters on depression, anxiety, attention-deficit/hyperactivity disorder, and personality disorders present additional data.

Generally, written and oral communications, including recommendations about prescriptions, should be framed according to the relationship that the psychologist has with the physician (Hamberger, Ovide, & Weiner, 1999). If the psycholo-

gist does not have an ongoing professional relationship with the physician, it is recommended that medication issues be addressed very generally (e.g., "The patient does appear to have evidence of depression with pronounced vegetative symptoms; recommend evaluating for antidepressant medication"). When the physician and psychologist have an ongoing working relationship and the psychologist maintains current knowledge about psychotropic medications, including dosages, side effects, contraindications, and medication interactions, this knowledge can be used productively in making focused recommendations to the physician. ("This patient meets *DSM-IV* criteria for major depression. For patients of his age and sensitivity to medication side effects, starting on a low dose of an SSRI is recommended. Sertraline has been found to be particularly useful with patients in this age group. Dosage titration occurs gradually by 25-mg increments every 2 weeks.") Many psychologists may not be comfortable communicating this specifically and should only make specific recommendations if their training has been adequate.

Psychologists should appreciate that a patient's ongoing medical conditions or other pharmacotherapy often interact with psychotropic medications. For example, the SSRI fluoxetine (Prozac) appears to interact with warfarin (an anticoagulant) and increases coagulation time. It is hypothesized that this interaction occurs because the SSRIs may displace warfarin from protein-binding sites, thus leaving increased levels of biologically active (unbound) warfarin (Stoudemire & Moran, 1998). Psychologists should also be aware that many nonpsychotropic medications have an impact on cognition, emotion, and behavior; Appendix B summarizes current evidence. As an example, symptoms of dysphoric mood and decreased energy are occasional side effects of α-2 agonists, a class of antihypertensive drugs (Charney, Berman, & Miller, 1998).

DOCUMENTATION

The lengthy, detailed evaluation reports written by many psychologists are often perceived as unhelpful by primary care clinicians facing the significant time constraints inherent in today's medical practice. The physician is likely to become "lost" in the details when reports include multiple subtest scores, elaborate descriptions of underlying personality dynamics, and detailed family histories.

Adapting the consultation note to the primary care setting may be one of the most difficult tasks for the psychologist new to primary care. Psychologists are trained to provide enough detail from assessment data to support diagnostic conclusions several pages later. Whereas this information might be helpful to a therapist or educator, the primary care physician is most concerned with the final conclusions and recommendations. Keeping in mind the role as a consultant to the physician, rather than to the patient's school or therapist, may reduce dissonance in summarizing rather than detailing assessment findings. In addition to Table 2.1, which provides a suggested outline for a consultation note, chapter 21 also provides a suggested outline with additional detail regarding length and format.

A comparison of two approaches is illustrated by sections of psychological reports. Detailed personality descriptions, such as the following example from Exner (1993), are helpful to psychotherapists providing long-term, intensive treatment, but will be of minimal value to a primary care physician.

> In part, her overload state is created because she is more limited in accessible resources than is common for the adult. This seems to reflect a developmental lag that may have occurred because she sacrificed her own individuality in favor of her family's wants during earlier years, or it may simply be that she developed a strong commitment to a somewhat unrealistic Florence Nightingale–type role model prematurely. Whatever the cause, there are probably many unrecognized resources available to her that, if identified, could help to resolve the overload problem. A second factor contributing to the overload is considerable distress. Much of that distress seems to evolve from a sense of dissatisfaction with herself and an inability to express her feelings in ways that are not threatening to her. (p. 628)

In contrast, a concise summary, highlighting key behavioral concerns, their chronicity, and as-

Table 2.1 Suggested Headings for a Primary Care Psychological Consultation Note

Identifying Information
Reason for Referral
Current Medical Conditions
Medical History
Mental Health History
Current Medications
Social History
Substance Abuse History
Mental Status Examination
Test Results (if administered)
Summary
Diagnosis
Recommendations

sociated psychiatric conditions will be more helpful to the physician:

> The results of the current evaluation suggest that Susie is aware that the sexual abuse of her sister was wrong; however, she appears to be limited in terms of her capacity to process this issue verbally, intellectually, and emotionally. In addition, Susie's history does suggest the strong possibility of bipolar disorder, including episodes of disorganization in thinking and affective instability.

Where to Document

Primary care psychologists use several approaches to documentation. Those who practice in a medical clinic often write directly in medical records. Some psychologists in these settings maintain separate, secure files and restrict communication with referring physicians to verbal exchanges (Seaburn, Lorenz, Gunn, Gawinski, & Mauksch, 1996) or brief chart notes.

When documenting in an office-based medical record, it is helpful if the mental health notes are written on pages of different color or marked in some other way to indicate that these notes differ from the remainder of the medical record. Having a clear heading such as "Psychological Consultation" will orient the physician to the distinct nature of these communications. Although psychologists typically make some concessions to the medical format, such as brevity, frequent subheadings, specific diagnoses, and targeted recommendations, it is not usually necessary for the psychologist to adapt to a traditional medical charting format.

However, psychologists should be knowledgeable about common documentation systems, such as the SOAP (subjective, objective, assessment, plan) format (Springhouse, 1999). In this system, the note begins with the patient's subjective complaint ("Headache"), followed by objective observation ("Patient lying on exam table grimacing"), then proceeds to the clinician's assessment ("Tension headache") and plan ("Ibuprofen every 4–6 hours; stress management"). Each section may include additional supporting information. For example, the physical examination is typically documented under "Objective." However, if the psychologist clearly indicates that these are mental health visits that are documented, the physician will be prepared for a slightly different writing style and format.

Although only about 5% of physicians use electronic medical records (EMRs), it is likely that these computerized formats will become more common in the near future (Jue & Jerant, 2001). In terms of patient documentation, EMRs may be more efficient when the clinician has a structured format that can be stored as a template. Commonly repeated phrases and sentences can also be reproduced with specific terms inserted. EMRs are better suited to standardized medical encounters, such as school physicals or for reporting cognitive test results.

There are several advantages for patient care continuity when the psychologist writes progress notes in the primary care record. The psychologist may see the patient somewhat more frequently than the patient's primary care physician. By documenting these contacts, the psychologist will provide updated information for the patient's next physician visit. Psychologists practicing independently should send a letter or focused consultation note to the referring physician. This written communication includes a brief summary of relevant symptoms, complicating factors, diagnostic impression, and treatment recommenda-

tions. Treatment to be provided by the referring physician should be clearly delineated from interventions to be provided by the psychologist.

What to Document

Psychologists are often unsure about the degree of detail and content of information to be provided in a general medical record. For an initial patient assessment, a detailed consultation note is useful to the primary care physician. Table 2.1 summarizes common section headings for these evaluations. Typically, the amount of information under each major heading should be confined to three or four sentences. The psychologist should always remember that physicians tend to focus primarily on the summary, diagnosis, and recommendations sections. Those sections, although succinct, should provide a synopsis of relevant clinical material, a *DSM-IV* (*Diagnostic and Statistical Manual of Mental Disorders*, 4th ed.; American Psychiatric Association, 1994) diagnosis, and specific advice about treatment options.

In comparison with records in mental health settings, medical charts are more likely to be read by a third party, including insurance company representatives, attorneys, nursing staff, internal quality assurance representatives, Workers' Compensation personnel, Social Security reviewers, and often the patient. Psychological notes should always be written with an understanding that they will be read by a third party. As a result, particularly sensitive material (e.g., an extramarital affair, adults' childhood sexual abuse history, past illegal acts) is often deliberately omitted or stated more generally (i.e., "history of significant psychosocial childhood trauma" for childhood sexual abuse).

Sensitive information may be managed by verbal communication to the physician or by including two levels of mental health documentation in the record. A brief handwritten or dictated communication may be added to the progress note section of the medical record, with a more detailed, typed consultation report in a specific mental health part of the medical record. The progress note should include basic symptom description as well as diagnostic and treatment information without significant detail. Placing detailed mental health communications in a separate section will remind records personnel of their sensitive nature. Using a distinctive color of paper for psychological notes may also prevent inadvertent release along with general medical information. Ethically, psychologists should review records sent to non–health care professionals (e.g., schoolteachers, counselors, employers) in a face-to-face conversation with the patient to clarify any concerns.

What to Release

Many private organizations as well as state and federal facilities require a separate authorization to release mental health or substance abuse records. A general medical release may not suffice in these situations. Facilities receiving federal funding are likely to have more stringent standards. Conversely, psychologists should be aware that, when information is written in the patient's medical record, mental health data may be disclosed along with the remainder of the medical documents. New federal regulations, such as the Health Insurance Portability and Accountability Act (HIPAA), have increased attention to medical records privacy (Gostin, 2001).

For example, the common practice of faxing patient information can only occur with a high degree of security. The sending and receiving machines should be accessible only to those specifically authorized to have direct contact with medical records. For primary care practices that include psychologists, mandatory HIPAA patient privacy notices should include reference to psychotherapy notes. Psychologists may want to review guidelines and sample written policies from organizations such as the American Psychological Association Insurance Trust and adapt them to their own practice. Psychologists may need to broaden the HIPAA policy about disclosure of information in high-risk situations. In cases of threats to harm self or others, HIPAA regulations state that only the authorities should be notified. However, to protect public and patient welfare adequately, any pretreatment informed consent documents may need to be modified to include disclosures of risk status to family members and other health care professionals. When in doubt,

psychologists should discuss these issues with medical records specialists.

Patients often find mental health terminology confusing and frightening. Although it is common for patients to request and receive copies of their medical records, mental health records should not be directly released to patients or other non-professionals without reviewing the notes and clarifying content directly with the patient.

REFERRALS

Generating Referrals

A psychologist who genuinely understands and practices within the culture and values of primary care should be successful in maintaining a referral base. For psychologists interested in receiving new patients, some of the practice-building strategies employed by medical specialists will serve as additional guidelines. Practice announcements, typically printed as large engraved cards, should include name, degree, office phone number, and location, as well as a brief phrase describing any specialty interests. Additional relevant information may include the university from which graduate degrees were obtained as well as similar information for internships and postdoctoral fellowships (Hamberger et al., 1999). If the psychologist's practice is located near or in a medical office building, an open house may enhance visibility.

Providing brief talks for hospital or community-based organizations will also stimulate referrals. A 15- to 30-minute lunchtime talk, with lunch provided by the speaker, is consistent with pharmaceutical representatives' presentation format (Hamberger et al., 1999). Effective presentations to physicians differ from those to academic psychology audiences in several important ways. Pragmatism and clinical utility should be key principles for guiding any educational experience for primary care clinicians. Little attention should be devoted to theory and academic history of a clinical issue. Although psychologists are trained to emphasize citations and critically evaluate research designs, busy primary care physicians are unlikely to find these discussions useful (Hamberger et al., 1999; Searight, 1999).

Medical education often includes clinical protocols. Psychologists should consider adapting their information to this format. For example, a description of three key strategies for managing the "angry patient" and five tips for screening a child with behavioral problems are examples of familiar primary care formats. Case vignettes, particularly when based on primary care rather than psychiatric patients, can highlight the psychologist's contribution to diagnosis and treatment. Mental health topics addressed in *American Family Physician* provide examples of this format. Stylistically, physician conferences also tend to be structured with a lecture followed by a question-and-answer period versus the looser discussion format featured in many graduate psychology programs.

Psychologists are often unnecessarily fearful of "giving away" their knowledge to other health care clinicians. There is concern that these didactic conferences will simply result in providing the physician with "free" information that will be incorporated into medical practices so that the psychologist's services are not required. In our experience, this fear is unfounded. Most primary care physicians simply do not have the time or training necessary to supplant a psychologist. Thoughtful, practical, clinically relevant conferences typically stimulate referrals.

Psychologists should be aware that initial referrals from primary care physicians may be particularly challenging. Physicians who have not typically referred to psychologists in the past may initially refer patients with significant longstanding psychopathology. Physicians may feel overwhelmed or frustrated by these patients and may in part be seeking some relief. The psychologist should not overreact to these early challenging referrals. Instead, the response should include a professional consultation and verbal or written communication to the physician following the format described in the section on documentation. The physician may greatly appreciate the psychologist's confirmation that this patient is, indeed, difficult. In addition, physicians with limited experience in referring patients to psychologists may not be aware of the types of problems psychologists can realistically address. Brief, diplomatic education concerning these issues is often indicated. For example, more complicated, time consuming evaluations such as child custody evaluations, social security disability assessments, or psychological examinations for sensitive employment areas may not be the type of referrals the primary care psychologist most wants; in such cases, the referring physician can be helped to find appropriate resources.

Referral for Specialized Mental Health Care

The majority of patients with psychiatric conditions can be effectively managed collaboratively by the primary care physician and the psychologist. However, approximately 10% to 15% of patients will have more severe psychiatric conditions such as schizophrenia, complicated mood disorders that do not respond to typical pharmacotherapy, active drug or alcohol abuse, or a high level of self-injurious behavior. These patients typically require more intensive and specialized treatment than a primary care psychologist can provide. Therefore, the primary care psychologist should maintain a referral network of responsive secondary and tertiary care psychologists and other mental health specialists.

CONCLUSION

Psychologists beginning practice in a primary care setting may initially feel a strong urge to return to a traditional mental health setting. This feeling often stems from a frustrated disappointment that physicians do not appreciate the psychologist's wealth of theoretical and empirical knowledge. The emphasis on pragmatic action over detailed reflection may also be at odds with many psychologists' values.

A common pitfall leading to psychologists' disappointment is early attempts to convert internists, family physicians, obstetrician-gynecologists, and pediatricians to the mental health professional's worldview. The psychologist's mission of educating physicians to the value of detailed personality description, multigenerational genograms, or diverse theoretical perspectives is typically a frustrating failure. Successful primary care psychologists spend time understanding medical culture with its accompanying implicit and explicit norms (Stein, 1990). Physicians will value psychologists' contributions when this information is presented in the familiar medical context.

ADDITIONAL RESOURCES

Suggestions for further reading and Internet professional development resources are available at this book's companion Web site: www.primarycarepsych.com.

References

American Psychiatric Association. (1994). *Diagnostic and statistical manual of mental disorders* (4th ed.). Washington, DC: Author.

American Psychological Association. (1992). *Report of the APA Ad Hoc Task Force on Psychopharmacology*. Washington, DC: Author.

Charney, D. S., Berman, R. M., & Miller, H. L. (1998). Treatment of depression. In A. F. Schatzberg & C. B. Nemeroff (Eds.), *Textbook of psychopharmacology* (pp. 705–732). Washington, DC: American Psychiatric Press.

Exner, J. E. (1993). *The Rorschach: A comprehensive system* (Vol. 1, 3rd ed.). New York: Wiley.

Gostin, L. O. (2001). National health information privacy: Regulations under the health insurance portability and accountability act. *Journal of the American Medical Association, 285,* 3015–3021.

Hamberger, L. K., Ovide, C. R., & Weiner, E. L. (1999). *Making collaborative connections with medical providers: A guide for mental health professionals.* New York: Springer.

Jue, J., & Jerant, A. F. (2001). Electronic paper and pencil: Six steps to a low cost electronic medical record. *Family Practice Management, 5,* 33–40.

Kushner, K., Diamond, R., Beasley, J. W., Mundt, M., Plane, M. B., & Robbins, K. (2001). Primary care physicians' experience with mental health consultation. *Psychiatric Services, 52,* 838–840.

Lazare, A., Putnam, S. M., & Lipkin, M. (1995). Three functions of the medical interview. In M. Lipkin, S. M. Putnam, & A. Lazare (Eds.), *The medical interview: Clinical care, education, and research* (pp. 3–19). New York: Springer.

Lee, J. V. (2000). Doctoring to the music of time. *Annals of Internal Medicine, 132,* 11–17.

McDaniel, S. H., Belar, C. B., Schroeder, C., Hargrove, D. S., & Freeman, E. L. (2002). A training curriculum for professional psychologists in primary care. *Professional Psychology: Research and Practice, 33,* 65–72.

Miranda, J., Hohmann, A. A., Attkisson, C. C., & Larson, D. B. (Eds.). (1994). *Mental disorders in primary care.* San Francisco: Jossey-Bass.

Newfield, N. A., Kuehl, B. P., Joanning, H., & Quinn, W. H. (1987, October). *A mini ethnography of the family therapy of adolescent drug abuse: The ambiguous experience.* Paper presented at the 45th annual meeting of the American Association for Marriage and Family Therapy, Chicago.

Sackett, D. L., Straus, S. E., Richardson, W. S., Rosenberg, W., & Haynes, R. B. (2000). *Evidence based medicine: How to practice and teach EBM* (2nd ed.). Edinburgh, Scotland: Churchill Livingston.

Sammons, M. T., Gorny, S. W., Zinner, E. F., & Allen, R. P. (2000). Prescriptive authority for psychologists: A consensus of support. *Professional Psychology: Research and Practice, 31,* 604–609.

Seaburn, D. B., Lorenz, A. B., Gunn, W. B., Gawinski, B. A., & Mauksch, L. B. (1996). *Models of collaboration: A guide for mental health professionals working with healthcare practitioners.* New York: Basic Books.

Searight, H. R. (1994). Psychosocial knowledge and allopathic medicine: Points of convergence and departure. *The Journal of Medical Humanities, 15,* 221–232.

Searight, H. R. (1999). *Behavioral medicine: A primary care approach.* Philadelphia: Taylor & Francis.

Springhouse. (1999). *Mastering documentation* (2nd ed.). Springhouse, PA: Author.

Starr, P. (1982). *The social transformation of American medicine.* New York: Basic Books.

Stein, H. (1990). *American medicine as culture.* Boulder, CO: Westview Press.

Stoudemire, A., & Moran, M. G. (1998). Psychopharmacology in the medically ill patient. In A. F. Schatzberg & C. B. Nemeroff (Eds.), *Textbook of Psychopharmacology* (2nd ed., pp. 931–959). Washington, DC: American Psychiatric Press.

Strosahl, K. (2000). The psychologist in primary health care. In A. J. Kent & M. Hersen (Eds.), *A psychologist's proactive guide to managed mental health care* (pp. 87–112). Mahwah, NJ: Lawrence Erlbaum.

Stuart, M. R., & Lieberman, J. A. (1993). *The 15 minute hour: Applied psychotherapy for the primary care physician* (2nd ed.). Westport, CT: Praeger.

Vanden Bos, G. R., & Williams, S. (2000) Is psychologists' involvement in the prescribing of psychotropic medication really a new activity?

Professional Psychology: Research and Practice, 31, 615–618.

Vitanzo, P. C., & Hong, E. W. (2000). Does a high-fiber dietary supplement of wheat bran reduce the recurrence rate of colorectal adenomas? *Journal of Family Practice, 49,* 656.

3

Psychological Assessment in Primary Care

John C. Linton

The roles that psychologists assume with primary care clinicians vary from setting to setting (Bendell-Estroff & Bernal, 2001). Psychologists can be integral members of the primary care practice with a full-time office on site, they can consult with primary care clinicians on a regular basis from an off-site office, or they can take referrals from primary care settings for treatment in clinics or private offices. They bring a wide variety of professional skills to the primary care setting in each of these roles, and one unique and important skill is psychological assessment (Rozensky, Sweet, & Tovian, 1997).

Diagnostic assessment has formed the core of medical practice since ancient times. Psychological assessment also has a long and distinguished history. Assessment defined the beginnings of clinical psychology and continues to be a foundation skill in professional psychology training programs. The popularity of psychological assessment has waxed and waned over time, but continues to help define what other professionals expect from experts in the psychological sciences and practice. This chapter focuses on potential assessment-related roles for psychologists in primary care,

presents practical suggestions for conducting psychological assessments in primary care, and presents a selection of useful evaluation tools.

Primary care presents unique challenges to the practice of effective psychological assessment. A prominent challenge is time: medical environments, and the primary care environment in particular, operate on a timescale that is largely unfamiliar to psychologists. Turnaround for scheduling patients and providing assessment reports is sometimes expected within hours rather than days or weeks. Primary care physicians vary considerably in their receptiveness (and even their awareness) of psychological assessment and its value. Primary care physicians may not provide the same clarity in their referral questions as other mental health specialists would; indeed, they may simply ask for a specific test without clearly stating the reason they are requesting it.

Diagnostic instruments standardized on psychiatric populations must be used cautiously in primary care, especially because somatic presentations or symptomatologies that do not reach the threshold for formal diagnosis according to the *DSM-IV* (*Diagnostic and Statistical Manual of Men-*

tal Disorders, 4th ed.; American Psychiatric Association, 1994) are common in primary care and make diagnosis more complex (Derogatis & Lynn, 2000). Last, patients often have coexisting medical problems that mimic or contribute to the psychological or behavioral symptom picture.

As Searight, Price, and Gafford (chapter 2) emphasize, the primary care environment is highly pragmatic. This can pose a challenge to the primary care psychologist accustomed to focusing the psychological assessment process on arriving at a definitive (usually *DSM-IV* related) diagnosis. In primary care, such an end point is less necessary or desirable; rather, the focus is on assessment that results in practical implications for patient management and improvement of functioning (Bendell-Estroff & Bernal, 2001; Peek & Heinrich, 2000).

APPROACHES TO INCORPORATING PSYCHOLOGICAL ASSESSMENT INTO A PRIMARY CARE PRACTICE

Primary care psychologists can use their expertise in assessment in at least two ways in addition to the customary use of assessment as an aid to psychological treatment planning and monitoring: They can help primary care physicians use appropriate screening or case-finding tools, and they can provide diagnostic information to primary care physicians in a consultative capacity.

Helping Primary Care Physicians Use Appropriate Screening or Case-Finding Tools

Identifying psychological disorders earlier in the course of the illness may allow treatment that prevents the condition from worsening. In addition, patients with undetected psychiatric disorders overuse medical resources; for both of these reasons, screening should provide cost savings as well as improved health outcomes (Derogotis & Lynn, 2000; Sperry, Brill, Howard, & Grissom, 1996). Diagnostic tests, particularly in the form of screens, are available to primary care clinicians from a variety of sources, including pharmaceutical companies, professional publications, and the Internet. The sheer number and complexity of

these instruments can be daunting for a busy primary care clinician.

Psychologists can provide consultation to their medical colleagues by evaluating tests in several domains and recommending those best suited for the specific primary care office. A psychologist must first study and understand the culture of primary care in general and the specific primary care setting in question before deciding which tests to recommend, but some general guidelines are available.

The ideal screening tool is both highly sensitive (few false negatives) and highly specific (few false positives). Understanding sensitivity and specificity is helpful in ruling in or ruling out a particular diagnosis; the clinician must pay careful attention to both, as well as to "prior probability" (e.g., base rates), because these change the usefulness of positive screening results (Sackett, Straus, Richardson, Rosenberg, & Haynes, 2000). Because screening does pose some risk to patients (most notably false labeling with a "mental illness"), it should be implemented only for problems that represent significant morbidity and for which effective treatments exist (Derogotis & Lynn, 2000; Linton & Cody, 2001). Finally, and crucially, screening in primary care is useful only when resources are available to treat the problems uncovered (Coyne, Thompson, Palmer, & Kagee, 2000) and when screening results are relevant to decisions like medication management, referral to a behavioral health specialist, or hospitalization (Kush, 2001).

It is also important to recognize the practical implications of screening used in the primary care medical office. Maruish (2000) notes that one should consider how easily and rapidly the test can be administered and scored and how quickly staff can be trained to integrate the screening procedure into the daily flow of work.

Providing Diagnostic Information to Primary Care Physicians in a Consultative Capacity

Primary care clinicians frequently are aware that psychological factors are causing or complicating their patients' problems, and an important role for the primary care psychologist is as a consultant on diagnostic and treatment issues. Psychological assessment may help identify personality styles that are complicating the patient's response to medical treatment, aspects of the medical condition that may be particularly stressful given the patient's psychology, and psychological conflicts that are expressed somatically.

An interesting aspect of psychological test instruments is that some patients find completing them less threatening than discussing their problems and psychological symptoms face-to-face. Patients may experience taking these tests as more akin to laboratory tests used for annual physicals and be more candid in their responses.

PRINCIPLES OF PRIMARY CARE PSYCHOLOGICAL ASSESSMENT

When the primary care psychologist is called on to provide diagnostic information, the following six rules of thumb may prove useful.

1. *Pay attention to the patient who is not in your office.* If referred patients fail to show up, the referring office should be notified, and a brief letter should be sent to the referring clinician for the patient's file. In a busy primary care practice, it is easy to refer a patient and, if no report is forthcoming, to assume that the patient followed through, but that the psychologist did not. If asked, the ambivalent patient may claim confusion about the referral, claim that no one ever called, or otherwise blame the psychologist. A chart note or brief communication informing the referring physician of the situation can prevent this sort of misunderstanding.

2. *Use practical measures.* Multidimensional measures such as the Minnesota Multiphasic Personality Inventory-2 (MMPI-2) and the Millon scales are comprehensive but lengthy, both to administer and interpret (Linton & Cody, 2001). Frequently, they offer more data than a busy primary care physician needs and increase the cost. However, for complex cases on which the psychologist is asked to consult because of a diagnostic dilemma for the primary care clinician, a complete personality battery may be in order. Most often, a more narrowly focused tool may suit the purpose better (suggestions are given in a separate section).

3. *Write useful reports.* A common mistake

psychologists make in providing feedback to referring primary care clinicians is to write a report that is too intricate and long and not directly tied to the referral question. After a thorough diagnostic interview and testing, it is tempting to write an extensive report with a great deal of detail. In fact, the referring clinician is likely to read only the summary and conclusions. So thought should be given to how clearly these sections communicate a final estimate of the patient and what course of action is recommended, either for the referring clinician or a behavioral health expert. Another error is to lose sight of the referral question. Frequently, primary care clinicians refer to consultants for the answer to a specific question. When they receive a report back, they expect the question to be answered and to have the consultant point out inconsistencies in findings that are difficult to explain.

4. *Write reports that are appropriate for the primary care environment.* In primary care, it is not unusual for a clinician to provide a copy of consultant reports to the patient on request. Omit highly sensitive information that could prove embarrassing for the patient unless it is vital to the findings and necessary for the referral source to know. Omit jargon if possible; in addition to the primary care physician (who may not be familiar with psychological terminology), the report could be read by teachers, attorneys, or family members. It may be valuable to write a summary that can be given to the patient or other nonclinicians.

5. *Recognize when preliminary rapid communication of findings is necessary.* As noted, primary care physicians often have tighter timetables for making treatment decisions than do mental health specialists. The psychologist must strike a balance between responding in a timely fashion and doing so prematurely, before all the data are available and a coherent formulation developed. At times, a brief preliminary note or phone call summarizing findings may be necessary. If brief notes are written about a patient before the report is completed, be sure to indicate that further information will follow so the referring clinician does not think this is the final report.

6. *Do not compromise your standards.* Regardless of the setting in which it is provided, the psychological report must still meet professional standards. Sweet (1991), Olin and Keatinge (1998),

and others have noted: consent and confidentiality issues must be documented. The findings must be based on data, not intuition. Raw data should not be included in the report unless it is provided to a professional who can interpret it. Reports should address patient strengths as well as negative findings. The report should not contain errors. If testing involves compensation or civil or criminal proceedings, the possibility of dissimulation must be considered. As capable psychologists well know, psychological assessment refers to more than testing; a comprehensive diagnostic interview (at the minimum) should accompany formal testing.

INTEGRATING A PSYCHOLOGICAL ASSESSMENT PRACTICE INTO PRIMARY CARE

At least initially, integration is a "high-maintenance" project. It takes considerable effort and planning to understand various primary care practices and how they operate, appreciate each of their unique needs, involve yourself in the practice by regular contact, and become a professional held in high regard as having a skill of value to the setting. The primary care psychologist may have to "sell" the benefits of assessment to both physicians and patients. In contrast to specialty mental health settings, in primary care neither the clinician nor the patient wants the symptoms of record to be psychological. The preference is to have something to treat, to medicate, to "fix" in the short visits necessary in that environment. Primary care physicians therefore tread lightly when broaching the suggestion for psychological assessment, and patients seldom embrace it warmly.

Physicians tend to be very case oriented, and if a consultant does a good job on the first few cases, more referrals can be expected in short order. As the pace picks up, it is important to develop a method of triage; that is, communication with the primary care clinician to determine which referrals are to be done immediately and which can wait.

Although paper-and-pencil tests remain popular, scannable test forms or computer-assisted administration and scoring programs are very useful when rapid response is necessary. The cost of these methods must be balanced against the benefits of immediacy. Olin and Keatinge (1998, pp. 265–268) described those available with computer software. Additional information on testing, including standards and online availability, is available from the American Psychological Association Science Directorate Web site (www.apa.org/science/testing.html). A listing of test publishers and suppliers can be found in Olin and Keatinge's work (1998, pp. 268–269).

The primary care psychologist may also wish to offer assessment services that go beyond traditional psychological testing. Primary care clinicians often need careful evaluation of their patients' nutritional patterns, exercise habits, sleep patterns, occupational stress, and interpersonal functioning. Some general health measures are described below, and other chapters in this volume address assessment tools in these additional areas.

ITEMS THAT SHOULD BE INCLUDED IN THE PRIMARY CARE PSYCHOLOGIST'S ASSESSMENT TOOL KIT

A wide variety of issues may need assessment in primary care, and psychologists may have their own favorite assessment tools. A full review of all available tools is beyond the scope of this chapter. However, nine categories of tools and selected instruments that are worthy of consideration are listed below. The primary care psychologist should be comfortable with at least one tool in each category.

A Quick, Reliable Screen for the "Big Five" Psychological Disorders

The standout tool in this category is the Patient Health Questionnaire (PHQ) (Spitzer, Kroenke, Williams, & the PHQ Primary Care Case Study Group, 1999). The PHQ is a self-administered form of the PRIMary Care Evaluation of Mental Disorders (PRIME-MD) and was designed for ease of use in primary care settings. Patient responses can be rapidly totaled to determine if they meet criteria for one or more of the "big five" psychological disorders—mood disorder, anxiety disorder, substance abuse, eating disorder, or somatoform disorder—by applying diagnostic algorithms abbreviated at the bottom of each page. An even briefer version, the PHQ-9, focuses only on anxiety and depression (Hahn, Kroenke, Williams, & Spitzer, 2000).

A Good Global Psychiatric Symptom Index

The Symptom Checklist 90–Revised (SCL-90R) (Derogatis, 1977) is a 90-item, multidimensional self-report symptom inventory that is quite widely used. It measures symptomatic distress in nine primary dimensions, such as somatization, depression, anxiety, and hostility and yields three global indices of distress.

Two additional candidates are (a) the Brief Screening Inventory (Derogatis & Spencer, 1982), a shortened form of the SCL-90 that measures the same nine symptom dimensions and three global indices of distress, but does so using only 53 items; and (b) the General Health Questionnaire (Goldberg, 1972), a 60-item self-report inventory with four subscales (somatic symptoms, anxiety and insomnia, social dysfunction, and severe depression). It is widely used in general medical populations, and abbreviated forms are also available.

A Good Multidimensional Psychological Inventory

The most commonly used tests include the MMPI-2 and the Millon scales (Linton & Cody, 2001). The Personality Assessment Inventory (Morey, 1991) is an increasingly popular alternative to the MMPI-2.

Tools for Depression, Anxiety, and Substance Abuse

The conditions of depression, anxiety, and substance abuse are so prevalent in primary care that the psychologist should have a focused tool for assessing each condition; these tools can be used for monitoring patients' response to treatment as well.

Depressive Disorders

The Beck Depression Inventory (BDI; Beck & Steer, 1993b) is a 21-item, unidimensional self-report inventory with many revisions and abbreviated versions, such as the BDI-II (Beck, Steer, & Brown, 1996). It can be used as a first-tier screening test or a second-tier tool to assess the level of distress in patients who have been previously identified as depressed. The BDI-II may also differentiate reactive and transitory sadness from an independent mood disorder (Kush, 2001). It can be used for patients aged 13 years to adult and meets the 2-week requirement for depression in the *DSM-IV*. It can be completed in 5 to 10 minutes and can be scored rapidly. The BDI Primary Care (BDI-PC; Beck, Steer, Ball, Ciervo, & Kabat, 1997) is a version using only seven items, but presents a risk for false negatives because of missing symptoms that are not covered in this shortened version. In addition to these measures for depression, the Beck Hopelessness Scale (Beck, Kovacs, & Weissman, 1975) is a brief self-report scale that is particularly sensitive to suicidal ideation or intent.

The Center for Epidemiological Studies Depression Scale (CES-D; Radloff, 1977) is is a 20-item, self-report depression scale that assesses the patient's level of functioning and perceived mood over the previous 7 days. It reflects four dimensions: depressed affect, positive affect, somatic problems, and interpersonal problems.

The Hamilton Rating Scale for Depression (HAM-D; Hamilton, 1967) is a clinician-administered tool of 21 items, each measuring a depressive symptom. The HAM-D is less practical to use in primary care settings than a self-report test like the BDI and tends to be utilized more often in research, such as in clinical trials for antidepressant medication.

The Geriatric Depression Scale (GDS; Yesavage et al., 1983) was developed to measure depressive symptoms in geriatric patients and to address the limitations of self-report measures of depression used with older adults (for example, somatic items such as disorders of sleep and sexual functioning are not reliable markers for depression in older patients). The GDS is a yes/no format in response to 30 items, although a short form of 15 items has also been standardized to increase the ease of administration (Scogin, Rohen, & Bailey, 2000).

Anxiety Disorders

Anxiety is more complex to measure than depression because there are so many subsyndromes, such as generalized anxiety, obsessions and compulsions, and symptoms of panic. The primary care clinician is seldom interested in the measurement of these syndromes, instead needing a general picture of the anxiety, with referral for more specific evaluation if needed.

The Beck Anxiety Inventory (BAI; Beck & Steer, 1993a) is the most practical tool for the assessment of anxiety in primary care settings (Kush, 2001). The BAI is a 21-item scale that is used with adolescents and adults. It includes items reflecting both psychological and biological anxiety, which allows the assessment of panic symptoms and generalized anxiety disorder (GAD), which are often seen in primary care settings because of the somatic presentation of anxiety that the patient might think is caused by a cardiac condition. The BAI can also call attention to anxiety levels that do not reach the threshold for anxiety disorders, but still cause distress to the patient (Kush, 2001).

The Hamilton Anxiety Scale (HAS; Hamilton, 1959) is a 14-item, clinician-administered rating scale. Each of the items represents a specific manifestation of anxiety and is rated by the clinician on a 5-point scale. The items reflect both somatic and cognitive symptoms. Like the HAM-D, the HAS is impractical for regular use in the primary care setting and tends to be utilized more to measure outcome in clinical anxiolytic drug trials. The HAS allows a more thorough evaluation of anxiety and may be used more as a second-tier assessment with patients who have already reported symptoms of anxiety.

Substance Abuse Disorders

The CAGE Questionnaire is probably the simplest and best-known screening device for assessing patients in primary care who experience social problems or clinical symptoms because of the use of alcohol or recreational drugs, but do not admit to these problems during routine medical visits. The CAGE asks if patients have ever felt the need to cut down on their drinking, felt annoyed by someone criticizing their drinking, felt guilty about drinking, or ever had the need for a drink first thing in the morning, an "eye opener." Israel et al. (1996) reported that, although most primary care clinicians have heard of the CAGE, they do not know the questions and in general feel unprepared to assess and treat chemical dependency, so it might fall to the psychologist to screen using the CAGE.

The Drug Abuse Screening Test (DAST-20; Skinner, 1982) was developed to screen for the abuse of illegal, over-the-counter, and prescribed drugs. It is not used for the assessment of alcohol abuse. It is self-administered and takes about 5 minutes to complete. It asks 20 questions that measure symptoms over the previous 12 months. The symptoms are summarized, and the patient's drug abuse is categorized along a continuum from "low abuse" to "severe abuse."

The Alcohol Use Disorders Identification Test (AUDIT; Allen, Reinert, & Volk, 2001) is a 10-item, self-report measure used for alcohol abuse screening in primary care. The AUDIT was developed in a six-country collaborative effort through the World Health Organization. Test items address alcohol intake, alcohol dependence, and adverse consequences of drinking. It is available through the World Health Organization and can be administered in about 2 minutes orally, in writing, or via computer.

A Useful Intellectual Assessment Tool

Although primary care psychologists receive few requests for intellectual assessment, more commonly they may want to include a brief intellectual assessment as part of overall evaluation or treatment planning or consultation. The Kaufman Brief Intelligence Test (Kaufmann & Kaufman, 1990) yields scores highly correlated with verbal and performance IQs measured by more comprehensive testing. It takes 15 to 30 minutes to administer, is easy to learn, and is a good choice when more than an estimate from a limited set of intelligence subtests is needed but there is no time for a complete intellectual evaluation.

A Cognitive Impairment Tool

Memory and cognitive changes are most thoroughly assessed by specialists, and it is unlikely that the generalist primary care psychologist would be in a good position to give a full neuropsychological battery. There are, however, a number of cognitive screening tests that may help determine whether a more comprehensive evaluation is necessary. Screening can help detect the early stages of dementia and, importantly, help to distinguish it from pseudodementia caused by depression (Strain et al., 1988).

The Mini-Mental State Examination (MMSE; Folstein, Folstein, & McHugh, 1975) is an 11-item, clinician-administered exam that assesses six aspects of cognitive functioning, such as orientation, recall, and praxis. It is most sensitive to moderate-to-severe impairment. The MMSE is familiar to many primary care clinicians, but can also be used routinely by psychologists. It is brief and relatively easy to administer and score.

The Dementia Rating Scale (DRS; Mattis, 1988) provides a short-form measure of cognitive functioning in patients with known cortical impairment, especially those with the degenerative type. The DRS presents 36 tasks and five subscales involving attention, initiation/perseveration, construction, conceptualization, and memory. It provides more clinical information than the MMSE, but takes longer to administer.

The Wechsler Memory Scale (WMS; Wechsler, 1997) is a widely used test that can be given to patients from the ages of 16 to 89 years. It is well researched and is sound psychometrically. The WMS takes longer to administer than the DRS or MMSE, but yields much more information. An additional advantage is that the WMS-III was standardized with the WAIS-III, and therefore allows comparison between a patient's intelligence and specific memory abilities (Olin & Keatinge, 1998).

The Cognistat (Northern California Neurobehavioral Group, 1995) is a test of global cognitive functioning that takes about a half hour to administer and score. It is easy to use and is most sensitive to serious cognitive dysfunction. If the patient performs within the normal range it may indicate there is no dysfunction or that mild problems have been missed.

The Cognitive Capacity Screening Examination (Jacobs, Berhard, Delgado, & Strain, 1977) is a 30-item test to detect diffuse cognitive disorders in medical populations; it is more sensitive than is the MMSE to mild cognitive symptoms.

The Cognitive Test for Delirium (Hart et al., 1995) is a nonverbal, examiner-administered test that evaluates orientation, attention span, memory, comprehension, and vigilance. It can be administered and scored in 15 minutes and has high levels of sensitivity and specificity for delirium.

The Neuropsychological Impairment Scale (NIS; O'Donnell, DeSoto, DeSoto, & Reynolds, 1994) is one of the few self-report measures of cognitive functioning; most other tools use performance measures (Kush, 2001). It comprises 95 items written on a fifth-grade level and can be completed in 15 to 20 minutes. It is designed primarily to identify potential cognitive impairment and may be best used as a first-tier screen.

General Health Assessment Tool

In addition to expanding the range of assessment services, general health screening may allow the psychologist to focus on early intervention as a form of prevention and address the impact of medical problems on the patient's quality of life. The "impairment" question from the PHQ can be used for this purpose as well (Spitzer, Williams, Kroenke, Hornyak, & McMurray, 2000).

The 36-item Short Form Health Survey (SF-36; Ware, Snow, Kosinski, & Nagle, 1993) is a well-regarded, widely used, self-administered general health profile that yields scores on eight scales measuring function and well-being: physical function, physical role, bodily pain, general health, vitality, social function, emotional role, and mental health. It has been used in over 1,200 studies examining a wide variety of medical, surgical, and behavioral conditions (Wetzler, Lum, & Bush, 2000). It can be used to monitor perception of overall health, estimate the burden of different health conditions, measure treatment effects in clinical trials, screen patients for referral, and monitor outcomes in a wide variety of medical and rehabilitation patients. It has also been widely used in program evaluation to mark intervention effectiveness. It can be completed in 10 minutes and is popular with patients, who feel their viewpoint is being considered when they are asked to take it. It is particularly helpful with those who have multiple, ill-defined complaints because it allows busy primary care clinicians to focus their listening on those concerns the patient deems most important.

Ware, Kosinski, and Keller (1994) developed an even shorter version of the SF-36, the SF-12. A subset of 12 items from the SF-36 comprises this survey, which can be printed on one or two pages and self-administered in about 2 minutes. The SF-12 has been found to reproduce more than 90% of the variance in the SF-36 physical and mental component summary scales. As such, it is seen as a valid and practical method for obtaining most of the information from the SF-36 and is a plausible alternative to the SF-36 for measuring health status. The SF-12 is particularly useful in clinical and research situations in which a shorter survey is required. However, because a single item is scored on more than one scale (contextual, weighted scoring), a computerized scoring program is necessary to interpret results.

The Duke Health Profile (DUKE-17; Parkerson, Broadhead, & Tse, 1990) is a 17-item, self-report instrument that is composed of six measures (physical, mental, social, general, perceived health, and self-esteem) and four dysfunction measures (anxiety, depression, pain, and disability). It is a brief tool for measuring health as an outcome of medical intervention and health promotion and represents a shortened version of research scales used at Duke University Medical Center. It correlates well with other health measurement instruments and is responsive to clinical change.

The Health-Related Quality of Life (HRQOL; Hays, Cunningham, Beck, Shapiro, & Ettl, 1995) is used in general health care settings to measure concepts such as health perception, social functioning, level of energy, freedom from pain, leisure and social activities, sexual functioning, family life, and friendships. Although the tool was standardized on patients with HIV, it has been used with patients who have other chronic diseases and to measure overall life satisfaction in patients who are not experiencing significant illness.

Relationship Assessment Instruments

Although it can be challenging to specify who constitutes a patient's family (Rozensky et al., 1997), interpersonal assessment can often provide important insights into causes of the patient's problems and routes to solutions. Family assessment can include family structure and patterns, communication style, strengths and resources, family life cycle, and specific illness-related concerns of family members (Rozensky et al., 1997). Because primary care physicians rarely refer for family assessment, the psychologist must often take the initiative in this regard. A basic genogram can be a useful tool to establish information about relationships with significant others in the patient's life. A list of potential assessment instruments, mostly rating scales and inventories, suggested for use with families in medical settings can be found in the work of Rozensky et al. (1997).

Useful Pediatric Tools

Although this volume focuses on the adult primary care patient, the primary care psychologist will commonly encounter questions about children. Although pediatricians are the most common source of child assessment referrals, family physicians commonly treat both adult and child patients. In addition, although the other primary care specialties do not see children, their adult patients may have questions about their children, and the primary care physician may well refer to a psychologist who they know well, despite the fact that he or she is not a child psychologist. Thus, it is helpful for the generalist primary care psychologist to have available some useful pediatric and parenting instruments.

The Eyberg Child Behavior Inventory is is a well-validated, 36-item questionnaire that parents can complete in several minutes, and the pediatric clinician can review it quickly. It includes questions about behavior at bedtime and mealtime and is particularly suited to identify children at risk for disruptive behavior problems (Eyberg & Ross, 1978; Robinson, Eyberg, & Ross, 1980). Problems are categorized by frequency and intensity.

The Pediatric Symptom Checklist (Jellinek & Murphy, 1990) is a 35-item tool that measures the presence of emotional or behavioral symptoms. Scoring is rapid, and a single score is generated. Cutoff scores reflect the severity of problems that have been empirically determined for children aged 4 to 12 years.

Rating scales are commonly used to measure and quantify behavior in children, adolescents, and parents. The Connors Rating Scales (Conners, 1997) are probably the most widely known; they can be rapidly administered and scored and can be used with children from 3 to 17 years old. The Connors scales can be given to both parents and teachers.

The Achenbach Rating Forms (cf. Achenbach, 1991), also known as the Child Behavior Checklist (CBCL), are also used frequently for rating behavioral and emotional problems in children. The CBCL is more time consuming to administer and score than the Connors scales, but the CBCL gives an extensive picture of the child and includes positive characteristics in addition to symptoms and problem behaviors.

The Parenting Stress Index (PSI; Abidin, 1995) screens for stress in the parent–child relationship. The PSI identifies dysfunctional parenting and predicts the potential for adjustment problems in children and behavioral problems in parents. It is designed to be used primarily with parents who have children younger than 6 years old, but can used by parents with children as old as 12 years. It consists of 101 items written at the fifth-grade reading level and can be self-administered in about 25 minutes, either in a paper-and-pencil format or online using the PSI Software Portfolio, which automatically scores item responses and generates a report.

SUMMARY

Assessment has waxed and waned in popularity, but is still a mainstay in professional psychology, with unique applications in primary care. In addition to using psychological test instruments in the diagnosis and treatment of their own patients, primary care psychologists can assist primary care clinicians in screening patients for behavioral health problems and can provide psychological assessment findings in consultative capacity. To provide psychological assessment services most effectively, care must be taken to understand the unique nature of the primary care patient and the unique constraints of the primary care environment. The primary care psychologist must maintain appropriate professional testing standards and at the same time recognize the need for speed and the need to focus on functional abilities more than on diagnostic purity. Integrating an assessment practice into the primary care environment poses challenges in selecting appropriate tools, developing appropriate procedures, and communicating results appropriately. The primary care psychologist is in a good position to expand the range of assessment services to include such issues as general health, parenting stress, sleep habits, and health-promoting behaviors.

References

Abidin, R. R. (1995). *Parenting stress index* (3rd ed.). Lutz, FL: Psychological Assessment Resources.

Achenbach, T. M. (1991). *Manual for the child behavior checklist/4–18 and 1991 profile*. Burlington: University of Vermont, Department of Psychiatry.

Allen, J. P., Reinert, D. F., & Volk, R. J. (2001). The alcohol use disorders identification test: An aid to recognition of alcohol problems in primary care patients. *Preventive Medicine, 33,* 428–433.

American Psychiatric Association. (1994). *Diagnostic and statistical manual of mental disorders* (4th ed.). Washington, DC: Author.

Beck, A. T., Kovacs, M., & Weissman, A. (1975). Hopelessness and suicidal behavior: An overview. *Journal of the American Medical Association, 234,* 1146–1149.

Beck, A. T., & Steer, R. A. (1993a). *BAI, Beck anxiety inventory manual*. San Antonio, TX: Psychological Corporation.

Beck, A. T., & Steer, R. A. (1993b). *Manual for the Beck depression inventory*. San Antonio, TX: Psychological Corporation.

Beck, A. T., Steer, R. A., Ball, R., Ciervo, C. A., & Kabat, M. (1997). Use of the Beck Anxiety and Depression Inventories for primary care with medical outpatients. *Psychological Assessment, 4,* 211–219.

Beck, A. T., Steer, R. A., & Brown, G. K. (1996). *Manual for the Beck depression inventory–II.* San Antonio, TX: Psychological Corporation.

Bendell-Estroff, D., & Bernal, P. (2001). Recognizing and treating psychopathology in primary care medicine. In D. Wedding (Ed.), *Behavior and medicine* (pp. 407–415). New York: Hlogrefe and Huber.

Conners, C. K. (1997). *CRS-R manual.* North Tonawanda, NY: MHS.

Coyne, J. C., Thompson, R., Palmer, S. C., & Kagee, A. (2000). Should we screen for depression? Caveats and potential pitfalls. *Applied and Preventive Psychology, 9,* 101–121.

Derogatis, L. R. (1977). *SCL-90-R: Administration, scoring and procedures manual–I.* Baltimore, MD: Clinical Psychometric Research.

Derogatis, L. R., & Lynn, L. L. (2000). Screening and monitoring psychiatric disorder in primary care populations. In M. Maruish (Ed.), *Handbook of psychological assessment in primary care settings* (pp. 115–152). Mahwah, NJ: Erlbaum.

Derogatis, L. R., & Spencer, P. M. (1982). *BSI administration and procedures manual I.* Baltimore, MD: Clinical Psychometric Research.

Eyberg, S. M., & Ross, A. W. (1978). Assessment of child behavior problems: The validation of a new inventory. *Journal of Clinical Child Psychology, 7,* 113–116.

Folstein, M., Folstein, S., & McHugh, P. (1975). Mini-Mental State. *Journal of Psychiatric Research, 12,* 189–198.

Goldberg, D. (1972). *The detection of psychiatric illness by questionnaire.* Oxford, U.K.: Oxford University Press.

Hahn, S. R., Kroenke, K., Williams, J. B. W., & Spitzer, R. L. (2000). Evaluation of mental disorders with the PRIME-MD. In M. Maruish (Ed.), *Handbook of psychological assessment in primary care settings* (pp. 191–255). Mahwah, NJ: Erlbaum.

Hamilton, M. (1959). The assessment of anxiety states by rating. *British Journal of Medical Psychology, 32,* 50–55.

Hamilton, M. (1967). Development of a rating scale for primary depressive illness. *British Journal of Social and Clinical Psychology, 6,* 278–296.

Hart, R. P., Levenson, J. L., Sessler, C. N., Best, A. M., Schwartz, S. M., & Rutherford, L. E. (1995). Validation of a cognitive test for delirium in medical ICU patients. *Psychosomatics, 37,* 533–546.

Hays, R. D., Cunningham, W. E., Beck, C. K., Shapiro, M. F., & Ettl, M. K. (1995). Health-related quality of life in HIV disease. *Assessment, 2,* 363–380.

Israel, Y., Hollander, O., Sanchez-Graig, M., Booker, S., Miller, V., Gingrich, R., & Rankin, J. G. (1996). Screening for problem drinking by the primary care physician-nurse team. *Alcoholism: Clinical and Experimental Research, 20,* 1443–1450.

Jacobs, J., Berhard, M., Delgado, A., & Strain, J. (1977). Screening for organic mental syndromes in the medically ill. *Annals of Internal Medicine, 86,* 40–46.

Jellinek, M. S., & Murphy, J. M. (1990). The recognition of psychosocial disorders in pediatric practice: The current status of the Pediatric Symptom Checklist. *Journal of Developmental and Behavioral Pediatrics, 11,* 273–278.

Kaufmann, A. S., & Kaufman, N. L. (1990). *Manual for the Kaufman brief intelligence test.* Circle Pines, MN: American Guidance Service.

Kush, F. R. (2001). Primary care and clinical psychology: Assessment strategies in medical settings. *Journal of Clinical Psychology in Medical Settings, 8,* 219–228.

Linton, J. C., & Cody, S. (2001). Assessment of patients. In D. Wedding (Ed.), *Behavior and medicine* (pp. 279–297). New York: Hlogefe and Huber.

Northern California Neurobehavioral Group. (1995). *Manual for the Cognistat.* Fairfax, CA: Author.

Maruish, M. E. (2000). General consideration introduction. In M. Maruish (Ed.), *Handbook of psychological assessment in primary care settings* (pp. 3–43). Mahwah, NJ: Erlbaum.

Mattis, S. (1988). *Dementia rating scale—professional manual.* Odessa, FL: Psychological Assessment Resources.

Morey, L. C. (1991). *Personality assessment inventory (PAI).* Lutz, FL: Psychological Assessment Resources.

O'Donnell, W. E., DeSoto, C. B., DeSoto, J. L., & Reynolds, D. M. (1994). *The neuropsychological impairment scale (NIS) manual.* Los Angeles: Western Psychological Services.

Olin, J. T., & Keatinge, C. (1998). *Rapid psychological assessment.* New York: Wiley.

Parkerson, G. R., Broadhead, W. E., & Tse, C. J. (1990). The Duke Health Profile. *Medical Care, 28,* 1056–1072.

Peek, C. J., & Heinrich, R. (2000). Integrating behavioral health and primary care. In M. Maruish (Ed.), *Handbook of psychological assessment in primary care settings* (pp. 43–93). Mahwah, NJ: Erlbaum.

Radloff, L. S. (1977). The CES-D scale: A self-report depression scale for research in the general population. *Applied Psychological Management, 1*, 385–401.

Robinson, E. A., Eyberg, S. M., & Ross, A. W. (1980). The standardization of an inventory of child conduct problem behaviors. *Journal of Clinical Child Psychology, 9*, 22–29.

Rozensky, R. H., Sweet, J. J., & Tovian, S. M. (1997). *Psychological assessments in medical settings*. New York: Plenum, pp. 6–7.

Sackett, D. L., Straus, S. E., Richardson, W. S., Rosenberg, W., & Haynes, R. B. (2000). *Evidence-based medicine: How to practice and teach EBM*. London: Churchill Livingstone.

Scogin, F., Rohen, N., & Bailey, E. (2000). Geriatric depression scale. In M. Maruish (Ed.), *Handbook of psychological assessment in primary care settings* (pp. 491–508). Mahwah, NJ: Erlbaum.

Skinner, H. A. (1982). *The drug abuse screening test (DAST): Guidelines for administration and scoring*. Toronto, Canada: Addiction Research Foundation.

Sperry, L., Brill, P. L., Howard, K. I., & Grissom, G. R. (1996). *Treatment outcomes in psychotherapy and psychiatric interventions*. New York: Brunner/Mazel.

Spitzer, R. L., Kroenke, K., Williams, J. B., & the PHQ Primary Care Case Study Group. (1999). Validation and utility of a self-report version of the PRIME-MD. *Journal of the American Medical Association, 282*, 1737–1744.

Spitzer, R. L., Williams, J. B., Kroenke, K., Hornyak, R., & McMurray, J. (2000). Validity and utility of the PRIME-MD patient health questionnaire in assessment of 3000 obstetric-gynecologic patients: the PRIME-MD Patient Health Questionnaire Obstetrics-Gynecology Study. *American Journal of Obstetrics and Gynecology, 183*, 759–769.

Strain, J. J., Fulop, G., Lebovits, A., Ginsberg, B., Robinson, M., Stern, A., Charap, P., & Gany, F. (1988). Screening devices for diminished cognitive capacity. *General Hospital Psychiatry, 10*, 16–23.

Sweet, J. J. (1991). Psychological evaluation and testing services in medical settings. In J. Sweet, R. Rozensky, & S. Tovian (Eds.), *Handbook of clinical psychology in medical settings* (pp. 291–315). New York: Plenum Press.

Ware, J. E., Kosinski, M., & Keller, S. D. (1994). A 12-item short-form health survey. *Medical Care, 34*, 220–233.

Ware, J. E., Snow, K. K., Kosinski, M., & Nagle, G. (1993). *SF-36 Health Survey: Manual and interpretation guide*. Boston: New England Medical Center, The Health Institute.

Wechsler, D. (1997). *WMS-III administration and scoring manual*. San Antonio, TX: Psychological Corporation.

Wetzler, H. P., Lum, D. L., & Bush, D. M. (2000). Using the SF-36 Health Survey in primary care. In M. Maruish (Ed.), *Handbook of psychological assessment in primary care settings* (pp. 583–622). Mahwah, NJ: Erlbaum.

Yesavage, J. A., Brink, T. L., Rose, T. L., Lum, O., Huang, V., Adey, M., & Leirer, V. O. (1983). Development and validation of a geriatric depression screening scale: A preliminary report. *Journal of Psychiatric Research, 17*, 37–49.

4

Models of Integrated Care in Primary Care Settings

Danny Wedding
Mark Mengel

WHY DO WE NEED INTEGRATED PRACTICE?

Integrated practice can occur in a variety of contexts and involves a large number of different health professionals. This chapter examines the specific collaboration of primary care physicians (most often family practitioners or internists) and mental health specialists (most often psychologists and social workers). Although there are salient difficulties associated with intraprofessional collaboration (e.g., psychiatrists working with their primary care physician colleagues), there are particular challenges and opportunities associated with interprofessional collaboration, and these are our current concern. We hope an examination of current models of integrated practice will help identify creative approaches to collaboration in practice. Breaking out of the "silos" that result from our traditions of training and professional enculturation offers practitioners an opportunity to grow both personally and professionally and should result in more effective and efficient diagnosis and treatment of patients.

The delivery of mental health services in the United States consists of a pastiche of public and private mental health services, often referred to as the de facto mental health system. This system involves four primary sectors: (a) specialty mental health care, with services provided by mental health professionals with specialized training (psychologists, psychiatrists, psychiatric nurses, and social workers); (b) primary medical, with services provided by professionals with generic health and medical training (family physicians, internists, nurse practitioners, pediatricians, etc.); (c) human services, with care provided by professionals and paraprofessionals with other than health training (e.g., probation officers, religious groups, teachers, and similar helping professions); and (d) voluntary support networks, which include groups like Alcoholics Anonymous that focus on education and support.

It is obvious that collaborative care can occur in any of these settings, but we are most interested in mental health care provided in the primary medical sector, and we believe collaboration at this level holds the most promise for delivering high-quality behavioral health services to the largest number of people in a way that enhances the clinician–patient relationship and still controls costs.

It is helpful to think of collaborative care as existing on a continuum that ranges from respectful, collegial, and generally harmonious ad hoc coordination of patient care activities (the extant model in most primary care practice settings) to integrated care, a model in which clinicians from multiple disciplines work closely in daily contact to ensure that all of the biopsychosocial needs of each patient are addressed. In settings of this type, many of the traditional trappings associated with occupational status and prestige are sacrificed in the interest of team harmony, continuing education for all members of the team, and the best interests of the patient. (For example, we frequently work on a team with the mother of a child with fetal alcohol syndrome; although this individual has appropriate, but relatively modest, academic credentials, we listen carefully to her suggestions because of the vast expertise she has developed from reading, lecturing, and researching the disease that afflicts her son.)

The importance of collaborative care in the primary medical sector is underscored by the frequency with which psychological problems present in primary care settings. Over 40 years ago, Cummings and colleagues initiated a seminal series of studies that documented that 60% of physician visits were by patients who had no physical illness or whose psychological problems were exacerbating their physical illness (Cummings & Follette, 1968; Cummings, Kahn, & Sparkman, 1962; Follette & Cummings, 1967).

These findings of Cummings and colleagues have been replicated and extended in a series of influential studies (Badger, 1994; Ballenger, 1987; Barrett, Barrett, Oxman, & Gerber, 1988; Bridges & Goldberg, 1985; Kessler, Burns & Shapiro, 1987; Lebowitz et al., 1997; Regier, Goldberg, & Taube, 1978; Regier et al., 1993; von Korff, Ormel, Katon, & Lin, 1992; West, 1979). Kroenke and Mangelsdorff (1989), for example, found that 40% of outpatient visits could be attributed to 1 of 10 core symptoms (chest pain, fatigue, dizziness, headache, swelling, back pain, shortness of breath, insomnia, abdominal pain, and

numbness); however, a biological cause could be identified for the symptoms in only 26% of primary care visits.

Brown and Schulberg (1995) reported that depression and anxiety were the most common psychiatric disorders among ambulatory medical patients, and that these disorders were associated with significant levels of functional disability. A recent review of emotional disorders by Coyne and colleagues (Coyne, Thompson, Klinkman, & Nease, 2002) has argued that, although these disorders are more likely to present in primary care settings than in mental health settings, they are often undetected or inadequately treated .

Depression offers a specific example of the potential importance of collaborative practice. Only one of three depressed patients will seek direct care for depressive symptoms (Goodnick, Henry, & Buki, 1995); of these, 70%–90% will seek treatment from a primary care physician (Blacker & Clare, 1987). However, although depression is a common and disabling disease, the correct diagnosis will be missed for half of the patients presenting with depression in traditional primary care settings (Coyne, Schwenk, & Fechner-Bates, 1995). Even when the correct diagnosis is made, many of these patients will receive less-than-optimal doses of antidepressant medications (Wells, Katon, Rogers, and Camp, 1994), and few will be referred for psychological treatment.

Despite the ubiquity of behavioral health problems in primary care settings, up to two thirds of patients meeting diagnostic criteria for mental illness have these problems go undetected by primary care clinicians (deGruy, 1996; Spitzer et al., 1994), underscoring the importance of a collaborative approach to the delivery of health care services for this population. According to Stoeckle (1995), "Patients bring [to the medical visit] not only the bodily complaints, but also the circumstances of their every day lives—who they are and who they hope to be" (p. 147). We believe most mental health and behavioral health problems can—and should—be treated in a primary care setting; however, if adequate treatment is to occur, it will require genuine integration of services and close collaboration between primary care physicians and clinicians with specific training in the identification of behavioral health problems and the delivery of meaningful, evidence-based treatments.

Patients with substance abuse problems are also commonplace in primary care settings (Sullivan & Fleming, 1997), and individuals with co-occurring health and substance abuse problems offer rich opportunities for the collaboration of primary care physicians and mental health providers (Brach et al., 1995). The National Household Survey on Drug Abuse estimated that 12.8 million Americans (about 6% of the population aged 12 years and older) currently use illicit drugs; about 32 million Americans (15.8% of the population) had engaged in binge or heavy drinking (five or more drinks on the same occasion at least once in the previous month) (Sullivan & Fleming, 1997). Fleming and Barry (1992) reported that alcohol-related disorders occur in up to 26% of general medical clinic patients. Despite the prevalence of substance use disorders, it has been well documented that physicians often fail to identify alcoholics when these patients are admitted to the hospital (Buchsbaum, Buchanan, Poses, Schnoll, & Lawton, 1992; Cleary, Miller, Bush, Warburg, Delbanco, & Aronson, 1988; Moore, Bone, Geller, Mamon, Stokes, & Levine, 1989).

Brief interventions, appropriate for a primary care setting, can substantially reduce hazardous drinking, a behavior that has enormous negative effects on public health (Fleming, Mundt, French, Manwell, Stauffacher, & Barry, 2002; Kahan, Wilson, & Becker, 1995). It is critical for all primary care physicians to develop skills in identifying, treating, and (when necessary) referring patients who are chemically dependent.

As the prevalence of chronic illness increases in our society (Anderson & Knickman, 2001), a collaborative approach between physicians and mental health professionals holds the greatest promise for meeting the needs of these patients (Von Korff, Gruman, Schaefer, Curry, & Wagner, 1997; Wagner et al., 2001). To implement evidence-based interventions with a well-defined population of chronically ill patients, a collaborative, team-based approach holds the potential for improving self-management skills among such patients (Von Korff et al., 1997) and would help encourage the behavioral change efforts necessary to improve a patient's risk status, such as smoking cessation, implementation of a healthy diet, or exercise program initiation. Recent research has shown that primary care physicians have very little time to engage in such vital work (Dovey, Green, & Fryer, 2000).

The aging of the U.S. population is yet another reason why it is imperative for behavioral health services to be available in primary care settings. The 1999 Surgeon General's Report on Mental Health noted that 19.8% of the older adult population has a diagnosable mental disorder during a 1-year period; these figures do not include individuals with severe cognitive impairments such as Alzheimer's disease (*Mental Health: A Report of the Surgeon General*, 1999). However, the stigma of mental illness is especially acute in elderly populations, and older adults with psychiatric disorders frequently seek health care services in primary care settings, in which the detection and management of behavioral health problems can be maximized by collaborative care between primary care physicians and mental health providers.

Over half of older persons who receive mental health care are treated by their primary care physician (Lebowitz et al., 1997). There are multiple reasons for this: Seeing a primary care physician does not have the stigma associated with consultation with a psychiatrist or psychologist; insurance policies often encourage use of primary care, which tends to be less expensive than specialty mental health care; and primary care is more convenient and accessible (U.S. Department of Health and Human Services, 2001). A report in the *Archives of General Psychiatry* documented the "upcoming crisis in geriatric mental health care" that is likely to result as a consequence of the aging of the U.S. population (Jeste et al., 1999).

The American Geriatrics Society (1993), noting that 1% or fewer elderly persons in the community receive psychiatric care, has recommended that the National Institute of Mental Health fund "training programs in interdisciplinary mental health care for the elderly that includes the disciplines of medicine, psychiatry, psychology, psychiatric nursing, and clinical social work. Training programs need to recognize that most mental health care takes place in the primary care setting."

The importance of collaborative care is highlighted by Healthy People 2010, which set an explicit goal of increasing "the number of persons seen in primary health care who receive mental health screening and assessment" (U.S. Department of Health and Human Services, 2000). Although these objectives can be met by integrating behavioral health services into primary care settings (Blount, 1998b), few clinical psychology programs adequately prepare students for collaborative care (American Psychological Association, 1998), and the recent introduction of Health Insurance Portability and Accountability Act regulations makes collaborative care relationships more difficult. However, despite the absence of formal training in collaborative care, many psychologists have independently established meaningful and mutually satisfying collaborative practices with their primary care colleagues (Rabasca, 1999). Our personal belief is that the most exciting work in collaborative primary care is found in U.S. and Canadian community and family medicine departments, and this chapter highlights the best of these programs.

The importance of collaborative practice has been underscored by policy decisions of the Accreditation Council for Graduate Medical Education (ACGME). Effective July 1, 2001, ACGME began requiring that residency programs develop pilot programs to meet core competency requirements to promote an integrated collaborative approach to care. Under the new ACGME guidelines, residency programs seeking accreditation bear the burden for demonstrating and documenting that they are teaching residents to work collaboratively with other professionals. The significance of social–behavioral sciences for the practice of medicine is specifically acknowledged in the ACGME guidelines for accreditation.

Family practice residency training programs in the United States and Canada have been leaders in teaching residents about the importance of multidisciplinary approaches and the merits of an integrated approach to health care delivery. The majority of these programs have a behavioral scientist on the faculty who not only teaches about the value of an integrated approach to primary care, but also models such an approach clinically. These programs can serve as exemplars for other residency programs working to meet the new ACGME accreditation guidelines.

PRIOR RESEARCH ON COLLABORATIVE PRACTICE

The Importance of Engel's Biopsychosocial Model

During the quarter century that has elapsed since George Engel first proposed a biopsychosocial model of health care delivery (Engel, 1977), there has been a spate of research documenting the connections among the biological, psychological, and social parameters of health (see Wedding, 2001, for an overview). In addition, a growing body of literature addresses psychosocial factors that influence and predict health outcomes across different diseases; these factors have been referred to as "shared psychosocial determinants" (Sobel, 1995). Writing about the impact of these psychosocial determinants, Sobel (1995) stated:

> Thoughts, feelings, and moods can have a significant effect on the onset of some diseases, the course of many, and the management of nearly all. Many visits to the doctor are occasioned by psychosocial distress. Even in those patients with organic medical disorders, functional health status is strongly influenced by mood, coping skills, and social support, yet the predominant approach in medicine is to treat people with physical and chemical treatments that neglect the mental, emotional, and behavioral dimensions of illness. This critical mismatch between the psychosocial health needs of people and the usual medical response leads to frustration, ineffectiveness, and wasted health care resources. . . . Rather than targeting specific diseases or behavioral risk factors, these psychosocial interventions may operate by influencing underlying, shared determinants of health such as attitudes, beliefs, and moods. (p. 234)

Referrals to Behavioral Health Specialists

Although referral by primary care physicians to behavioral health providers appears to pay homage to the biopsychosocial model and addresses the issue of shared psychosocial determinants, the referral system itself is intrinsically flawed and ineffectual. Put simply, patients typically ignore their physicians' recommendations to seek counseling or therapy. Glenn (1987) reported his initial interest in collaborative practice resulted from the realization that the majority of the patients he referred never kept their appointments. Bloch (1993) noted, "While [referral] conforms to the biopsychosocial model, it is often flawed and expensive. Patients and biomedical providers alike interpret referral as a sign of failure, rejection, and, often, pejorative labeling. Schematically, it signifies dysfunction at the provider/patient interface" (p. 4, cited in Blount, 1998).

Integrated Health Care

Co-location, joint training, and shared continuing education of primary care providers and mental health specialists define integrated behavioral health care. The idea is surprisingly simple, but it has proved difficult to implement fully for a variety of reasons, including the sociology of professions, our history of training health care providers in disparate settings, and fears of loss of power and autonomy by high-status providers, most often physicians. However, when the model has been implemented and tested, it has been found effective and satisfying for both patients and those providers working in the integrated system (Cummings, 1997).

Although referrals are obviously made in an integrated care context, they occur within the practice rather than outside it, putting patients at ease because their care is both continuous and coordinated. The transfer of the patient from primary care provider to consultant is facilitated by introductions that are often made in person, typically requiring no more than a short walk down a hallway to the office of a behavioral care colleague. The confidence of the primary care physician in the consultant is reinforced by the patient's realization that these individuals share office space and staff, and that they have developed a long-term, linked, and coordinated practice. The proximity of provider offices diminishes any concerns patients may have about being perceived as "neurotic" and foisted onto someone else; this is particularly important in patients with psychological concerns who may deeply resent any suggestion that their problems are "all in their heads."

The History of Integrated Care

Cummings developed the first truly integrated collaborative care model in 1962 at the Kaiser Permanente Medical Center in San Francisco, California (Cummings, 1997). Behavioral care providers (mostly psychologists and social workers) were co-located with physicians. Don Lipsett, M.D., instituted a subsequent and similar experiment in integrative care at Boston's Beth Israel Hospital in 1974 (Cummings, 1997).

Cummings' pioneering model became the blueprint for a systemwide integrated network in the Kaiser northern California region. This huge experiment involved 2.4 million "covered lives." This total pool of northern California Kaiser enrollees was divided into cohorts of 20,000 individuals assigned to truly multidisciplinary teams. In effect, each cohort of 20,000 comprised a small group practice. The ratio of primary care physicians to psychologists was maintained at a 6:1 level in the Kaiser model. Each group practice had its own budget and hired its own support staff. The beauty of this model is that the practices of each cohort team could be compared in terms of their efficacy and effectiveness, and each team could learn from the experiences of the others (N. Cummings, personal communication, September 17, 2002; Kent & Gordon, 2001).

We believe that integrated behavioral health care—as defined above by the co-location and joint training and continuing education of primary care providers and mental health specialists—holds the greatest promise for addressing the shared psychosocial determinants found so frequently in primary care settings. This model fosters mutual respect and camaraderie among providers, trust and confidence among patients, and a healthy sense that "we're all in this together."

Research Support

A growing body of evidence supports the benefits associated with an integrated care model. For example, Katon et al. (1999) examined a group of 228 patients recognized as depressed by their primary care physicians and treated with antidepressants. Patients were randomly assigned to a collaborative care intervention ($n = 114$) or usual care ($n = 114$) by the primary care physician. Patients in the intervention group received enhanced education and increased frequency of visits by a mental health specialist. Those in the intervention group showed greater adherence to medication regimens, and they were more likely to rate quality of care as good to excellent. Intervention patients showed a significantly greater decrease in severity of depressive symptoms over time and were more likely to have recovered fully at 3 and 6 months. The authors concluded that the collaborative care program resulted in significant improvements in (a) adherence to antidepressants, (b) satisfaction with care, and (c) treatment outcomes.

Other Advantages

There are other advantages to integrated care in addition to improved patient care. For example, collaborative care is cost-effective and can often help prevent expensive emergency room visits, specialty consultation, and hospitalization (Blount, 1998; Budman, Demby, & Feldstein, 1984; Cummings, Dorken, Pallack, & Henke, 1990; deGruy,

1996; Jones & Vischi, 1979; Katon, 1995; Mumford, Schlesinger, & Glass, 1981; Mumford, Schlesinger, Glass, Patrick, & Cuerdon, 1984). In addition, collaborative care environments are congenial work settings in which physicians and nonphysician providers work side by side, each appreciating the training, background, skills, and special expertise the other brings to the treatment and consulting experience. Blount (1998) documented that primary care physicians are happier working in integrated settings. This fact may be important in respect to the overall costs of health care insofar as staff turnover can add considerably to the overall costs of operation in a health care setting. A summary of these and other compelling reasons for collaborative care is provided in Table 4.1.

INTEGRATED CARE FOR PATIENTS WITH CHRONIC DISEASES

Von Korff and colleagues (1997) built a strong case for collaborative care for all patients with chronic illnesses, arguing that good collaborative care has four essential components:

(1) Collaborative definition of problems, in which patient-defined problems are identified along with medical problems diagnosed by phy-

Table 4.1 Key Reasons for Integrating Primary Care

1. Patients come with undifferentiated problems.

2. For problems that are clearly psychological or psychiatric in nature, such as depression and anxiety, primary care medical settings are the predominant locus of treatment.

3. When the primary care service is a better fit for the way patients present, there is better adherence to treatment regimes, which leads to better outcomes.

4. Even when trained in psychiatry and counseling, physicians cannot be expected to address the entire array of psychological/psychiatric problems that present in primary care, and referral out is often a poor alternative.

5. Collaborative care is the best way of potentiating the skills of primary care physicians in dealing with the psychosocial aspects of primary care.

6. Primary care clinicians are happier with their work in integrated settings.

7. Patients are more satisfied with their care in integrated settings.

8. Integrated, collaborative care appears to be a break-even or cost-saving move in the long run.

9. Integrated primary care settings are the best laboratories for the further development and refinement of primary medical services.

Adapted from Blount (1998a).

sicians; (2) Targeting, goal setting, and planning, in which patients and clinicians focus on a specific problem, set realistic objectives, and develop an action plan for attaining those objectives in the context of patient preferences and readiness; (3) Creation of a continuum of self-management training and support services, in which patients have access to services that teach skills needed to carry out medical regimens, guide health behavior changes, and provide emotional support; and (4) Active and sustained follow-up, in which patients are contacted at specified intervals to monitor health status, identify potential complications, and check and reinforce progress in implementing the care plan. These elements make up a common core of services for chronic illness care that need not be reinvented for each disease. (p. 1097)

Consider the following case example:

A 16-year-old patient with Type I diabetes had a history of good control of his blood glucose levels for many years; however, two successive elevated hemoglobin A1c (HgA1c) (a common laboratory measure of glycemic control) readings left his family physician concerned about compliance issues. The team social worker discussed the boy's situation with his parents, who reported that he has started to drink beer and disregard his diet after recently breaking up with his girlfriend.

The team psychologist noted that money for gas is an important reinforcer for this young man and recommended a behavior modification program in which "cash for gas" is made contingent on HgA1c levels of 8% or less. He also volunteered to see the patient periodically to assess his depression. The team nurse noted that the boy has never had any other girlfriend and lacks social skills; she has special training in this area and volunteered to provide assertion training.

The physician discussed these recommendations with the patient on his next visit and, after obtaining the patient's consent, introduced him to both the nurse and the psychologist. Each saw him for three sessions in addition to his regular office visits; his physician, between patients, dropped by for one of the social skills training sessions and offered encouragement. The teenager reported on his next visit that he had a new girlfriend, and he is quite happy in this relationship.

His HgA1c level on this visit was 7.2, well within acceptable limits.

Wagner (2000) has reinforced the above points in his review of the literature on the primary care (collaborative) team, adding that success is enhanced if team member roles are clearly defined, they are trained for their roles, physicians are willing to share care, and the organization possesses sufficient resources and supportive management to enable the team to function. A system in which an intransigent physician insists on having final authority for all patient decisions is not likely to be successful; likewise, any system that is too short-staffed to allow time for consultation and conversation between team members is doomed to fail.

The Importance of Triage

Strosahl (1998) has argued that primary care health professionals must be able to provide evidence-based treatment across a variety of disorders and implement triage when specialty mental health care is required. In a different article, Strosahl et al. (1994) provided examples of the successful integration of behavioral health services and primary care in health maintenance organization (HMO) settings. Lazarus (1995) has described the problems that occur in collaborative practice and offered general guidelines to assist in the treatment of behavioral disorders in managed care settings. Lazarus's recommendations included giving primary care physicians clear instructions how to triage psychiatric patients, having these physicians encourage their patients to contact their mental health therapist directly, scheduling meetings between the primary care physician and the mental health specialist, and coordinating medication management.

A Tripartite Continuum

Strosahl (1998) has proposed a tripartite continuum of care in primary behavioral health care. The three levels of care in this model are, from lowest to highest, behavioral health consultation (judged to be appropriate for 60% of the primary care population), specialty consultation (appropriate for 30% of primary care patients), and integrated care programs (necessary for 10% of the primary care population). All three levels can be applied in primary care settings.

For example, at the first level, a family physician might feel entirely comfortable treating a patient's depression and would require little assistance, but would take comfort in knowing that a clinical psychologist with considerable experience in the treatment of mood disorders was just down the hall. The physician and psychologist might discuss the issues involved in the patient's care over coffee (with appropriate safeguards for patient confidentiality under the Health Insurance Portability and Accountability Act of 1996 standards), but consultation per se would not be necessary.

However, if the patient became acutely suicidal and appeared to be getting worse in spite of treatment, specialty consultation might be appropriate, and the physician could personally escort and introduce the patient to the psychologist, who would assess the magnitude of depression, make an informed assessment of the patient's prognosis, and make recommendations for potential alterations in the treatment plan. These changes might include adjustments in the choice and level of medication prescribed.

At the third level, integrated care, the physician and psychologist would both meet routinely (and sometimes jointly) with the patient. The physician might focus primarily on medication and physical concerns, and the psychologist might focus primarily on teaching the patient cognitive–behavioral techniques to use to cope with an entrenched set of self-defeating beliefs; however, each clinician would remain invested and informed of the activities and plans of the other, and each would be involved and invested in the treatment prescribed. Care would be integrated, coordinated, and orchestrated, and the patient would be able to avoid the cacophony that sometimes results from multiple clinicians making recommendations that are discordant at best and conflicting at worst.

TRAINING FOR COLLABORATIVE PRACTICE

Strosahl (1998) has emphasized that providing genuine collaborative care involves much more than simply providing therapy services in a primary care setting; in fact, the word *therapy* is unlikely to be heard, and patient contacts are far more likely to involve discussions of stress, coping, and adaptation. In the case example, these recommendations could come from either the psychologist or the primary care physician.

HMOs have had an early leadership role in supporting collaborative care in primary care settings, and the Kaiser Permanente programs have been particularly noteworthy. At the Kaiser Permanente Medical Center in San Jose, California, for example, health psychologists work in proximity to primary care clinics; make appointments through the same mechanisms as primary care physicians; conduct frequent "curbside" consults and direct, same-day, "warm handoffs" of patients from the primary care physicians; and participate in all team activities, including meetings, educational sessions, and clinical case discussions. Challenges associated with this close collaboration according to Gordon and Kent (2002) include

> working on an abbreviated appointment schedule (30-minute appointments for new patient evaluations and 15- to 30-minute appointments for return visits); focusing almost exclusively on brief psychotherapeutic interventions; communicating with the primary care physicians concisely; emphasizing diagnosis and management in a practical manner and avoiding in-depth psychological analysis and jargon; abbreviating charting with careful attention to ethical issues and confidentiality; and having strong group skills. All of these changes reflect the fast-paced culture and mindset of primary care. (p. 2)

Examples of Model Programs

A number of programs have begun to integrate the training of mental health professionals and primary care residents, especially family medicine programs. Since the birth of family practice in 1969, its residency training programs have had to include a longitudinal curriculum in the behavioral sciences to meet accreditation requirements. Remarkably, this requirement has resulted in a behavioral science faculty (psychologists, marriage and family therapists, social workers, and other mental health professionals) that comprises about 30% of the total faculty in family medicine departments (Holloway et al., 1995). With such a behavioral science presence in family medicine training programs, it is not surprising that these training programs have spawned some of the most innovative collaborative models of care.

An excellent example of how inclusion of a behavioral science requirement into the training of family practice residents can result in collaborative care models and joint training of mental health professionals is the University of Washington's (Seattle, WA) family practice residency program. Under the direction of Larry Mauksch, the behavioral science faculty trains family practice residents, offers internships to mental health professionals, and trains a fourth-year psychiatric resident. The teaching and clinical role of mental health professionals in the program allow two common barriers to collaborative practice to be surmounted: (a) physician discomfort and lack of skill in managing patients with emotional distress and (b) lack of appropriate referral resources available that patients are comfortable using. Because mental health professionals are on site and immediately available, they can consult with residents immediately when a patient presents with a mental health or behavioral issue, modeling core skills. Mental health professionals can be brought into the exam room quickly to meet patients before they leave the family practice center, and this introduction greatly facilitates the patients' ability to keep their first appointment with the mental health professional. "Hallway consultations" between physicians and mental health professionals also occur frequently within the family practice center, and occasionally, as their schedules allow, joint conferences for planning, teaching purposes, or provider transitions are held between physicians and mental health professionals.

Although mental health professionals at times find it difficult to communicate with physicians in this program, particularly with those residents who are on off-site rotations, the fact that the program is a teaching program as well as a clinical practice affords financial resources that would not have been present in a purely clinical program. The last essential ingredient in the development of the University of Washington's collaborative practice model was the support of leadership within the department (L. Mauksch, personal communication, June 19, 2002). For a more thorough review of the role of behavioral sciences in family medicine, see the work of Fischetti and McCutchan (2002).

Another excellent shift at some universities is to locate their clinical psychology training programs within the health sciences centers rather than in more traditional colleges of arts and sciences, providing psychology students greater opportunities to interact with, learn from, and teach other health care professionals; the University of Florida at Gainesville's program is an excellent example of this practice. Even in those universities where clinical training is conducted in traditional departments, an increasing number of academic health centers are housing clinical psychologists in independent departments of health psychology (e.g., the University of Missouri–Columbia).

One example of a successful collaborative behavioral health care training program is the Health Psychology Postdoctoral Fellowship in Primary Care program at the University of Mississippi Medical Center, Jackson. This 2-year program involves supervised clinical, teaching, and research experience. Training is based on a cognitive–behavioral orientation and strongly emphasizes a scientist–practitioner model. The program goal is to prepare psychologists to work in interdisciplinary teams in primary care settings. Fellows receive weekly supervision in the assessment and treatment of primary care patients. Physician faculty and residents refer patients for a wide variety of psychological difficulties. Fellows provide outpatient clinical services in the department's two outpatient primary care clinics and have the option of attending inpatient rounds and receiving inpatient hospital experience with the family medicine team. Fellows also contribute to the didactic training of family practice residents, pharmacy residents, dental students, and medical students by preparing and presenting lectures and seminars on a variety of behavioral and health issues. Fellows also contribute to the supervision of predoctoral psychology students pursuing externship experiences with the Department of Family Medicine.

At the postdoctoral level, the Department of Family Medicine and Community Health at the University of Massachusetts, Worcester, has established a postdoctoral fellowship in primary care psychology; this fellowship is actually embedded within the family medicine residencies. This is a 2-year, full-time, training and service experience designed to prepare clinical and counseling psychologists to work in the clinical service, research, and training settings associated with primary medical care. Fellows in this program receive significant opportunities to teach behavioral science to family practice residents, to teach family practice residents to work collaboratively with behavioral health specialists in providing primary care services, and to conduct research on primary care questions. The program's Web site notes:

> Every effort is made to identify fellows as part of a resident class. Having behavioral health providers as peers in their training helps residents develop the personal relationships on which collaboration is based. Having family practice residents as peers in their training helps the fellows develop familiarity with the primary care setting in an environment of support where help with the vagaries of "medical culture" is easily available.

Other postdoctoral fellowship programs in primary care health psychology have been developed by the Consortium for Advanced Psychology Training in Flint, Michigan, affiliated with Michigan State University Flint Area Medical Education. The programs are designed to foster collaboration between psychology and medicine within a variety of health care settings.

The Program in Human Sexuality, in the Department of Family Practice and Community Health at the University of Minnesota Minneapolis, offers postdoctoral fellowships for psychologists in behavioral medicine and human sexuality. The behavioral medicine fellowship has four primary goals: (a) providing training in the integration of behavioral medicine into the primary care setting; (b) assisting in the development of skills as an educator of resident physicians in behavioral medicine; (c) facilitating greater skill in psychotherapy; and (d) promoting growth and skill in research design, analysis, and report writing. Fellows in this program work with psychology faculty to train family medicine residents in communication skills and the physician–patient relationship, and they teach psychosocial factors in the context of health, illness, and disease; management of psychological disorders in the primary care setting; basic counseling skills; and physician health maintenance and self-care.

Military training programs have been leaders in their integration of meaningful learning experiences for psychologists in the context of primary care. For example, a 2-year fellowship in clinical health psychology at Brooke Army Medical Center in San Antonio, Texas, is designed to provide the skills needed to provide psychological services for primary care medical clinics. The Air Force is also developing a servicewide program for integrating psychological consultation into primary medical care facilities, and the psychology internship at Wilford Hall Air Force Base (San Antonio, TX) is one of the agencies at the forefront of this effort.

The historical separation of medical students and residents (typically trained in tertiary hospital settings) and psychology students (typically trained in arts and sciences programs located on a university's main campus) presents significant barriers to effective communication and collaboration. Other barriers include differences in student backgrounds and professional cultures, differing time constraints (more dramatic in medicine), and different professional expectations.

Zvolensky, Eifert, Larkin, and Ludwig (1999) have proposed a variety of methods to improve communications between clinical psychologists and primary care physicians (e.g., having psychologists give grand rounds, publish articles in primary care journals, and become more involved in residency training in primary care settings). Garcia-Shelton and Vogel (2002) described a model for the postdoctoral training of health psychologists in primary care settings; this model requires a 2-year commitment and involves close and collaborative interaction with family practice residents and staff.

Some programs require explicit and formal training in the behavioral sciences to help physicians develop therapeutic skills as well as skills in recognition and assessment. Perhaps the best-known and most successful fellowship in this area is the Family Systems Medicine Fellowship developed by Thomas Campbell and Susan McDaniel in New York at the University of Rochester's Department of Family Medicine. Primary care physicians can join this program after their residency training is completed. Primary care physicians in this program are enrolled in a 2-year fellowship in which the supervision model offers live supervision and is much more akin to training in psychotherapy than the passive preceptor model of training traditionally used in medical care. Joint training with mental health professionals is an integral part of the program. The University of Rochester has expanded its fellowship offerings to include a fellowship on behavioral change and prevention and a fellowship for mental health professionals called the Medical Family Therapy Fellowship, which provides mental health professionals training in a medical environment.

Although not initially organized as a training model, Programs of All-Inclusive Care for the Elderly (PACE) are seen as a viable model for training multiple disciplines, not just clinicians or mental health professionals, in true interdisciplinary collaborative care. The PACE model was started in San Francisco at On Lok (Eng, Pedulla, Eleazer, McCann, & Fox, 1997). Because of a demonstration project funding from the Robert Wood Johnson Foundation, additional funding from the John A. Hartford Foundation, and interest from the U.S. government, the PACE model has rapidly spread across the country and was fully operational in 25 sites by 2001.

Under a waiver program, PACE programs receive capitated payments from Medicaid and Medicare to keep seniors eligible for a nursing home active in the community. Using a multidisciplinary team-based model (including physicians, nurses, physical therapists, occupational therapists, social workers, recreational therapists, mental health professionals, and administrators), PACE is responsible for all the health care needs of their clientele, often referred to as a "social HMO," because PACE funds can be used for nontraditional interventions to keep their clientele healthy (e.g., buying an air conditioner for a patient's home during a heat wave). Team meetings with all professionals occur first thing in the morning daily, with patients reassessed every 3 to 6 months.

The initial evaluation of patients requires a 2-day assessment by all health professionals. Using such an intense approach to care, many PACE programs have been able to document substantial improvements in health outcomes from what would have been expected if these patients remained in the usual care system or were placed in a nursing home (Williamson, 2000; Eng et al., 1997; www.natlpaceassn.org). We believe PACE sites are ideal training grounds for health professionals who want to learn about interprofessional collaborative care directed at frail elders.

SUMMARY

Substantial research evidence as well as clinical experience suggests that mental health services can be integrated successfully with primary care medical services. This integration benefits both patients and clinicians, and occurs along a continuum that moves from less integrated to more integrated care: behavioral health consultation; specialty consultation; integrated care. While we believe almost all patients respond to and benefit from integrated care, the elderly and those patients with addictions, chronic illnesses, and specific mental health problems such as depression are the most likely to be helped by active efforts to coordinate and concatenate mental health and primary health services. The importance of integrated care has been emphasized by numerous political entities, professional groups, accreditation bodies, and practice organizations. The most dynamic and successful models of integrated care are found in community and family medicine training programs in the United States and Canada, and a number of these programs are described. We believe integrated care increasingly will be recognized as the sine qua non for comprehensive health care in the twenty-first century.

ADDITIONAL RESOURCES

Suggestions for further reading and professional development resources are available at this book's companion Web site: www.primarycarepsych.com.

References

American Geriatrics Society. (1993). *Policy statement*. Developed by the AGS Public Policy Committee and approved May 1987 by the

AGS Board of Directors. Reviewed November 1990, April 1993. Retrieved August 11, 2002, from http://www.americangeriatrics.org/products/positionpapers/mentalhl.shtml

American Psychological Association. (1998). *Interprofessional health care services in primary care settings: Implications for the education and training of psychologists* (SAMHSA/HRSA Work Order No. 97M220464). Washington, DC: Author.

Anderson, G., & Knickman, J. (2001). Changing the chronic care system to meet people's needs. *Health Affairs, 20*(6), 146–160.

Badger, L. W. (1994). Patient presentation, interview content, and the detection of depression by primary care physicians. *Psychosomatic Medicine, 56,* 128–135.

Ballenger, J. (1987). Unrecognized prevalence of panic disorder in primary care, internal medicine and cardiology. *American Journal of Cardiology, 60,* 39J–47J.

Barrett, J., Barrett, J., Oxman, T., & Gerber, P. (1988). The prevalence of psychiatric disorders in a primary care practice. *Archives of General Psychiatry, 45,* 1100–1106.

Blacker, C., & Clare, A. (1987). Depressive disorder in primary care. *British Journal of Psychiatry, 150,* 737–751.

Bloch, D. A. (1993). The full service model: An immodest proposal. *Family Systems Medicine, 11,* 1–7.

Blount, A. (1998a). *Integrated primary care: The future of medical and mental health collaboration.* New York: Norton.

Blount, A. (1998b). Introduction to integrated primary care. In A. Blount (Ed.), *Integrated primary care: The future of medical and mental health collaboration* (pp. 1–43). New York: Norton.

Brach, C., Falik, M., Law, C., Robinson, G., Trent-Adams, S., Ulmer, C., & Wright, A. (1995). Mental health services: Critical component of integrated primary care and substance abuse treatment. *Journal of Health Care for the Poor and Underserved, 6,* 322–341.

Bridges, K. W., & Goldberg, D. P. (1985). Somatic presentation of *DSM-III* psychiatric disorders in primary care. *Journal of Psychosomatic Research, 29,* 563–569.

Brown, C., & Schulberg, H. (1995). The efficacy of psychosocial treatments in primary care: A review of randomized clinical trials. *General Hospital Psychiatry, 17,* 414–424.

Buchsbaum, D. G., Buchanan, R. G., Poses, R. M.,

Schnoll, S. H., & Lawton, M. J. (1992). Physician detection of drinking problems in patients attending a general medicine practice. *Journal of General Internal Medicine, 7,* 517–521.

Budman, S. H., Demby, A. B., & Feldstein, M. L. (1984). A controlled study of the impact of mental health treatment on medical care utilization. *Medical Care, 22,* 216–222.

Cleary, P. D., Miller, M., Bush, B. T., Warburg, M. M., Delanco, T. L., & Aronson, M. D. (1988). Prevalence and recognition of alcohol abuse in a p rimary care population. *American Journal of Medicine, 85,* 466–471.

Coyne, J., Thompson, R., Klinkman, M. S., & Nease, D. E., Jr. (2002). Emotional disorders in primary care. *Journal of Consulting and Clinical Psychology, 70,* 798–809.

Coyne, J. C., Schwenk, T. L., & Fechner-Bates, S. (1995). Nondetection of depression by primary care physicians reconsidered. *General Hospital Psychiatry, 17,* 3–12.

Cummings, N. A. (1997). Pioneering integrated systems. In N. A. Cummings, J. L. Cummings, & J. N. Johnson (Eds.), *Behavioral health in primary care: A guide for clinical integration* (pp. 23–35). Madison, WI: Psychosocial Press (International Universities Press).

Cummings, N. A., Dorken, H., Pallak, M. S., & Henke, C. (1990). *The impact of psychological intervention on healthcare utilization and costs.* South San Francisco, CA: Biodyne Institute.

Cummings, N. A., & Follette, W. T. (1968). Psychiatric services and medical utilization in a prepaid health plan setting, Part 2. *Medical Care, 6,* 31–41.

Cummings, N. A., Kahn, B. I., & Sparkman, B. (1962). *Psychotherapy and medical utilization: A pilot study.* Oakland, CA: Annual Reports of Kaiser Permanente Research Projects.

deGruy, F. (1996). Mental health care in the primary care setting. In M. S. Donaldson, K. D. Yordy, K. N. Lohr, & N. A. Vanselow (Eds.), *Primary care: America's health in a new era* (pp. 285–311). Washington, DC: National Academy Press.

Dovey, S., Green, L., & Fryer, G. E. (2000). Educating doctors to provide counseling and preventive care: Turning 20th century professional values head over heels. *Education for Health, 13,* 307–316.

Eng, C., Pedulla, J., Eleazer, G. P., McCann, R., & Fox, N. (1997) Program of all inclusive care for the elderly (PACE): An innovative model of integrated geriatric care and financing. *Jour-*

nal of the American Geriatric Society, 45, 223–232.

Engel, G. L. (1977). The need for a new medical model: A challenge for biomedicine. *Science, 196,* 129–136.

Fischetti, L. R., & McCutchan, F. C. (2002). A contextual history of the behavioral sciences in family medicine revisited. *Family Systems and Health, 20,* 113–129.

Fleming, M. F., & Barry, K. L. (1992). Clinical overview of alcohol and drug disorders. In M. F. Fleming & K. L. Barry (Eds.), *Addictive disorders* (pp. 3–21). St. Louis, MO: Mosby.

Fleming, M. F., Mundt, M. P., French, M. T., Manwell, L. B., Stauffacher, E. A., & Barry, K. L. (2002). Brief physician advice for problem drinkers: Long-term efficacy and benefit-cost analysis. *Alcoholism: Clinical and Experimental Research, 26,* 36–43.

Follette, W. T., & Cummings, N. A. (1967). Psychiatric services and medical utilization in a prepaid health plan setting. *Medical Care, 5,* 25–35.

Garcia-Shelton, L., & Vogel, M. E. (2002). Primary care health psychology training: A collaborative model with family practice. *Professional Psychology: Research and Practice, 33,* 546–556.

Glenn, M. L. (1987). *Collaborative health care: A family oriented approach.* New York: Praeger.

Goodnick, P., Henry, J., & Buki, V. (1995). Treatment of depression in patients with diabetes mellitus. *Journal of Clinical Psychiatry, 56,* 128–136.

Gordon, M., & Kent, J. (2002). *Integrating health psychology, primary care.* Retrieved August 13, 2002, from http://www.medinfosource.com/mb/mb991201b.html

Holloway, R. L., Marbella, A. M., Townsend, J. M., Tudor, J. M., Tollison, J. W., Saultz, J. W., et al. (1995). Defining the need for faculty in family medicine: Results of a national survey. *Family Medicine, 27,* 98–102.

Jeste, D. V., Alexopoulous, G. S., Bartels, S. J., Cummings, J. L., Gallo, J. J., Gottlieb, G. L., Halpain, M. C., Palmer, B. W., Patterson, T. L. Reynolds, C. F., and Lebowitz, B. D. (1999). Consensus statement on the upcoming crisis in geriatric mental health care. *Archives of General Psychiatry, 56,* 848–852.

Jones, K. R., & Vischi, T. R. (1979). Impact of alcohol, drug abuse and mental health treatment on medical care utilization: A review of the literature. *Medical Care, 17,* 1–82.

Kahan, M., Wilson, L., & Becker, L. (1995). Effectiveness of physician-based interventions with problem drinkers: A review. *Canadian Medical Association Journal, 152,* 851–859.

Katon W. (1995). "Will improving detection of depression in primary care lead to improved depressive outcomes? [editorial; comment]." *General Hospital Psychiatry, 17*(1), 1–2.

Katon, W., Von Korff, M., Lin, E., Simon, G., Walker, E., Unutzer, J., et al. (1999). Stepped collaborative care for primary care patients with persistent symptoms of depression: A randomized trial. *Archives of General Psychiatry, 56,* 1109–1115.

Kent, J., & Gordon, M. (2001). Programmatic approaches to care and outcomes: The medical co-management group appointment. In N. A. Cummings, W. O'Donohue, S. C. Hayes, & V. Follette (Eds.), *Integrated behavioral healthcare: Positioning mental health practice with medical/surgical practice* (pp. 77–90). San Diego, CA: Academic Press.

Kessler, L., Burns, B., & Shapiro, S. (1987). Psychiatric diagnoses of medical service users: Evidence from the Epidemiologic Catchment Area program. *American Journal of Public Health, 77,* 18–24.

Kroenke, K., & Mangelsdorff, A. D. (1989). Common symptoms in ambulatory care: Incidence, evaluation, therapy and outcome. *American Journal of Medicine, 86,* 262–266.

Lazarus, A. (1995). The role of primary care physicians in managed mental health care. *Psychiatric Services, 46,* 343–345.

Lebowitz, B., Pearson, J., Schneider, L., Reynolds, C., Alexopoulos, G., Bruce, M., Conwell, Y., Katz, I., Meyers, B., Morrison, M., Mossey, J., Niederehe, G., & Parmelee, P. (1997). Diagnosis and treatment of depression in late life: Consensus statement update. *Journal of the American Medical Association, 278,* 1186–1190.

Mental health: A report of the surgeon general. (1999). Washington, DC: U.S. Government Printing Office.

Moore, R. D., Bone, L. R., Geller, G., Mamon, J. A., Stokes, E. J., & Levine, D. M. (1989). Prevalence, detection, and treatment of alcoholism in hospitalized patients. *Journal of the American Medical Association, 261,* 403–407.

Mumford, E., Schlesinger, H. J., & Glass, G. V. (1981). Reducing medical costs through mental health treatment. In A. Broskowski, E. Marks, & S. H. Budman (Eds.), *Linking health and mental health* (pp. 257–273). Beverly Hills, CA: Sage.

Mumford, E., Schlesinger, H. J., Glass, G. V., Patrick, C., & Cuerdon, T. (1984). A new look at evidence about reduced cost of medical utilization following mental health treatment. *American Journal of Psychiatry, 14,* 1145–1158.

Rabasca, L. (1999). More psychologists are building up their practices by partnering with primary-care physicians. *American Psychological Association Monitor Online, 30*(4). Retrieved August 10, 2002, from http://www.apa.org/monitor/apr99/doc.html

Regier, D., Goldberg, I., & Taube, C. (1978). The de facto mental health services system. *Archives of General Psychiatry, 35,* 685–693.

Regier, D., Narrow, W., Rae, D., Manderscheid, R., Locke, B., & Goodwin, F. (1993). The de facto mental health and addictive disorders service system. *Archives of General Psychiatry, 50,* 85–94.

Sobel, D. S. (1995). Rethinking medicine: Improving health outcomes with cost-effective psychosocial interventions. *Psychosomatic Medicine, 57,* 234–244.

Spitzer, R., Williams, J., Kroenke, K., Linzer, M., deGruy, F., Hahn, S., Brody, D., & Johnson, J. (1994). Utility of a new procedure for diagnosing mental disorders in primary care: The PRIME-MD 1000 Study. *Journal of the American Medical Association, 272,* 1749–1756.

Stoeckle, J. D. (1995). Patients and their lives: Psychosocial and behavioral aspects. In M. Lipkin, S. M. Putnam, & A. Lazare (Eds.), *The medical interview: Clinical care, education, and research frontiers of primary care* (p. 147–152). New York: Springer-Verlag.

Strosahl, K. (1998). Integrating behavioral health and primary care services: The primary mental health care model. In A. Blount (Ed.), *Integrated primary care: The future of medical and mental health collaboration* (pp. 139–166). New York: Norton.

Strosahl, K., Robinson, P., Heinrich, R. L., Dea, R. A., Del Toro, I., Kisch, J., et al. (1994). New dimensions in behavioral health/primary care integration. *HMO Practice, 8,* 176–179.

Sullivan, E., & Fleming, M. (Consensus Panel Co-Chairs). (1997). *A guide to substance abuse services for primary care clinicians: Treatment Improvement Protocol (TIP) Series 24* (DHHS Publication No. SMA 97–3139). Rockville, MD: Center for Substance Abuse Treatment.

U.S. Department of Health and Human Services. (2000). *Healthy people 2010.* Washington, DC: U.S. Government Printing Office.

U.S. Department of Health and Human Services. (2001). *Administration of aging report: Older adults and mental health: Issues and opportunities.* Washington, DC: U.S. Government Printing Office.

Von Korff, M., Gruman, J., Schaefer, J., Curry, S. J., & Wagner, E. H. (1997). Collaborative management of chronic illness. *Annals of Internal Medicine, 127,* 1097–102.

Von Korff, M., Ormel, J., Katon, W., & Lin, E. (1992). Disability and depression among high utilizers of health care. A longitudinal analysis. *Archives of General Psychiatry, 49,* 91–100.

Wagner, E. H. (2000). The role of patient care teams in chronic disease management. *British Medical Journal, 320,* 569–572.

Wagner, E. H., Glasgow, R. E., Davis, C., Bonomi, A. E., Provost, L., McCulloch, D. M., Carver, P., & Sixta, C. (2001). Quality improvement in chronic illness care: A collaborative approach. *Journal of Joint Commission on Health Care Quality, 27,* 63–80.

Wedding, D. (2001). *Behavior and medicine.* Göttingen, Germany: Hogrefe & Huber.

Wells, K. B., Katon, W., Rogers, B., & Camp, P. (1994). Use of minor tranquilizers and antidepressant medications by depressed outpatients: Results from the Medical Outcomes Study. *American Journal of Psychiatry, 151,* 694–700.

West, N. D. (1979). *Psychiatry in primary care medicine.* Chicago: Year Book Medical.

Williamson, J. D. (2000). Improving care management and health outcomes for frail older people: Implications of the PACE model. Program for All-Inclusive Care of the Elderly. *Journal of the American Geriatric Society, 48,* 1373–1380.

Zvolensky, M. J., Eifert, G. H., Larkin, K. T., & Ludwig, H. A. (1999). Improving communication between clinical psychologists and primary care physicians: Implications for increasing the quality of rural mental health care. *Journal of Rural Community Psychology, 2,* 1–6.

II

THE PRIMARY CARE
MEDICAL SPECIALTIES

5

Family Medicine

A. Peter Catinella
Jennifer Paul Leiser

Meet Dr. Helen, a family practice physician in a busy private practice. Dr. Helen is a graduate of a 3-year family medicine residency. She is board certified in family practice. She encounters patients with mental health problems on a daily basis. Dr. Helen feels she is one of a unique group of doctors that has the privilege of caring for individuals and families at all stages of the life cycle.

Family practice is an official medical specialty under the jurisdiction of the American Board of Family Practice. To qualify as a specialty, a field carries a unique focus of care and special training to justify that designation. Specialties define their unique focus of care using several criteria. Some specialties, such as pediatrics or internal medicine, focus on patients of a certain age. Some, like obstetrics and gynecology, care for patients of one gender. Some care for patients experiencing certain kinds of disease or disease of certain organs, such as oncology or cardiology. Some focus on a certain set of therapeutic skills, such as general surgery. Family physicians describe themselves as another kind of specialist.

Family physicians are specialists in primary care: the care of individuals throughout the life cycle, focusing on the whole person in the context of their family and social relationships and the common medical conditions they may experience. Several other specialties claim status as primary care physicians; these include obstetrics and gynecology, pediatrics, and internal medicine. However, no other specialty promises to care for individuals from conception until death regardless of age, gender, or medical condition.

Prior to family practice becoming the 20th medical specialty in 1969, primary care had not yet been formally developed. In the middle of the 20th century, most medical care was provided by generalists, also known as general practitioners. These doctors attended a 4-year medical school and then completed a 1-year internship before going into practice on their own. They provided longitudinal care for a community of patients and used consultants for complex cases.

As basic medical science and technology advanced, greater emphasis was placed on specialty knowledge. Physician training occurred almost exclusively in academic hospitals, in which students were exposed mainly to rare and complex problems. There was less exposure to health conditions found commonly in the larger community (White, Williams, & Greenberg, 1961). A large majority of physicians chose disease- or organ-defined specialties for their career.

Several physicians wrote that such specialization was to herald a new era of technical medicine, and that general medical care would soon be an artifact of the past (Code, 1970; Moser, 1974). Others were alarmed at the loss of the generalists' personal knowledge of the patient over the life cycle and the loss of emphasis on the patient as a whole person rather than a collection of organ systems. They wrote that the growth of technology and medical advancements demanded a new type of generalist, one who would be knowledgeable in the latest medical advances and preserve the humanistic traditions of medicine (Butler, 1966; Menke, 1970).

Dr. Helen has been in private practice for three years. Her practice is in an urban area where consultation with other professionals is relatively easy. The opportunity to participate in the care of all members of a family is what attracted Dr. Helen to family medicine. She explains it as follows:

Dr. Helen: I entered family practice because I wanted to play a role in the lives of people of all ages. I am proud to be part of a specialty that cares for the whole person and turns no one away. There is no one whom I cannot see because they are the wrong age, the wrong gender, or have the wrong organ system malfunctioning. My training taught me to understand a person in the context of social relationships. Having the mother, husband, child, and grandparents seeking care and guidance from me allows me to understand the dynamics of their relationships and how these dynamics affect their health and well-being. I see my patients as whole persons, and I try to provide care that will enhance their overall well-being and quality of life. I emphasize preventive care, health promotion, and improving the health of the community in which my patients live.

Dr. Helen may bristle a bit if you refer to her as a "general practitioner." The law in most states still allows physicians to be licensed and to go into practice after a 1-year internship. These physicians may be called general practitioners; however, they are not board certified. When family practice was founded as a specialty, training increased from a 1-year internship to a 3-year residency, followed by board certification by the American Board of Family Practice. Dr. Helen takes pride in the depth and breadth of her residency training. Dr. Helen's hospital-based training included adult and pediatric medicine; obstetrics and gynecology; general surgery; surgical specialties such as orthopedics, urology, otolaryngology, ophthalmology, and psychiatry. Her training focused on ensuring competency in diagnosis and management of the late manifestations and complications of the large majority of common diseases.

More than any other specialty, family practice training emphasizes the clinic setting. Dr. Helen's training in ambulatory medicine had several goals. It taught her how to identify and manage disease early in its course. She learned to promote health and prevent the development of disease. She learned to manage common chronic illnesses such as diabetes and high blood pressure. She was trained in understanding family life cycles and family dynamics, a model known as the biopsychosocial model of care. She values communication skills as the cornerstone of the doctor–patient relationship.

She often develops long-term plans for her patients, anticipating a longitudinal relationship that allows time to build trust and mutual understanding. She acknowledges psychological health as part of her patients' overall health. In fact, her residency program was required to have a behavioral specialist as a member of the faculty for accreditation of the program. This may seem unremarkable today, but it was a substantial deviation from standard medical training at its conception (Stephens, 1987). Although the content of family physicians' behavioral science training has evolved with changes in medical practice, it is still a basic element of family practice training.

Of course other specialties include training in behavioral sciences, but no specialty emphasizes it as much as family practice. Gaufberg and colleagues (2001) reported that, on average, family practice trainees received 352 hours of psychosocial training compared to 118 hours for internal medicine trainees. This training includes performing a mental status examination, interviewing techniques, treatment of substance abuse and addictive disorders, psychiatric differential diagnosis, social and ethical issues, psychopharmacology, psychotherapy, counseling, and behavioral interventions. As a result, family physicians identify, manage, and refer a wide range of mental health disorders.

Has this experiment in creating a new primary care specialty been successful (Green & Fryer, 2002)? Data from various sources suggest it has been. Of patients claiming a single physician as their usual medical provider, 62% cite a family physician as their provider, with internal medicine next in frequency at 16% (Graham et al., 2002). The National Ambulatory Medical Care Survey collects annual data on physician office visits and characteristics of physician practices and patients. Of 823.5 million office visits in 2000, there were 24.1% to general and family physicians, compared to 15.2% to internists and 12.6% to pediatricians. Yet, general and family physicians make up only 17.1% of office-based physicians (U.S. Department of Health and Human Services, 2002).

The most common reasons for visits to family physicians include annual or employment examinations, upper respiratory symptoms, hypertension, back and other musculoskeletal problems, skin rash, diabetes mellitus, allergy problems, well-baby examinations, and depression. For patients who suffer from common chronic mental health issues such as depression, they report family physicians serve as their usual source of care in 62% of cases, compared to 22.9% who report using internists (Green & Fryer, 2002). On average, a family physician cares for about 2,000 patients and works 47 weeks a year. The mean time spent with a patient is 17.0 minutes per visit, compared to 19.7 minutes for an internist and 15.4 minutes for a pediatrician (Cherry & Woodwell, 2002).

Family practitioners are the backbone of care for Americans in rural areas. Family physicians make up one in four physicians practicing in nonmetropolitan statistical areas, although specialists in internal medicine and pediatrics each constitute about 10% of the providers in these areas (U.S. Department of Health and Human Services, 2002). Of family physicians, 13% practice in communities of fewer than 20,000 people (American Academy of Family Physicians, 2002). In fact, the presence of family physicians in rural areas keeps 58% of existing U.S. counties from becoming areas with a primary care health personnel shortage, a designation indicating a physician-to-population ratio of less than 1:3,500 (Fryer, Green, & Dovey, 2001).

Family practice lives up to its name by caring for multiple family members. In a cross-sectional study of 138 family physicians, 4,454 direct observations were made on outpatient visits. The patient's family members were present at almost one third of visits, and issues involving an absent family member occurred in 18% of visits. There were 75% who reported that their family members saw the same family physician (Medalie, Zyzanski, Langa, & Stange, 1998).

On a typical Monday morning, Dr. Helen enters her office and finds her medical assistant Tom waiting for her. Together, they review the morning's schedule. Ten patients are scheduled, and several more have called for appointments for acute problems. Dr. Helen and Tom plan the morning:

Dr. Helen: Mr. Jenkins's daughter will be accompanying him. She's worried about his balance and wonders if he should consider assisted living. Mrs. Palmero will be in with her newborn; call the hospital and find out what he weighed at discharge. Fred Kooper called me last week to tell me that his blood pressure readings are worse. Would you make sure you take two blood pressure readings 5 minutes apart? Pam Gaston thinks she has a bladder infection, so go ahead and get a urine sample.

Tom: Margaret Dupre called for an appointment. She says it's urgent but wouldn't tell me anything else. I booked her for a 10-minute slot; that's all we have open.

Dr. Helen: Okay, we'll see what she wants. I started her on antidepressants last month. I hope she isn't getting worse. Oh, on Paul Philips, get a film on his right wrist. I was the

*team physician at his last track meet and I
want to make sure he didn't break his navicu-
lar bone last week. It looks like Dave O'Neill
is applying for disability. I'll need a little extra
time with him. Make sure his old records are
on the chart.*

A look at Dr. Helen's schedule provides insight
into a key frustration of family physicians: lack of
time (Yarnall, Pollak, Ostbye, Krause, & Michener, 2003). Financial pressures in many practices
force more patients into every workday. Patients
with acute illnesses need to be seen promptly.
Those with mental health problems may be unwilling to reveal the real reason for their visit to
the person scheduling the appointment, making
it difficult to plan an appropriate visit length.

Dr. Helen has several methods for addressing
her patients' mental health needs in this context.
First, her knowledge of the patient's medical history and family support helps her put problems
into context quickly. She will be attuned to cues
from her patients that depression is developing.
If a patient whom she knows has an anxiety disorder presents confusing physical symptoms, she
can more confidently assess the true problem.
Second, Dr. Helen is skillful at collaborating with
mental health professionals. She can make an initial assessment, initiate medication, and rule out
other medical problems as contributors. She can
provide brief supportive care in the context of
the ongoing relationship with the patient. When
the patient needs more in-depth or ongoing psychotherapy, Dr. Helen will refer to a mental
health professional.

If Dr. Helen were asked about the typical
mental health needs of her patients, her response
might sound like this:

Dr. Helen: It depends on the patient's age. In chil-
    dren and adolescents, I have diagnosed anxiety,
    attention-deficit disorder, substance abuse, de-
    pression, and eating disorders. In adults, de-
    pression and anxiety seem most prevalent,
    although a fair number of substance abuse dis-
    orders are identified. I often must diagnose
    personality disorders so I can appropriately
    modify my approaches to compliance issues or
    other aspects of care. Finally, in the elderly,
    dementia and depression are my most com-
    mon mental health diagnoses. Understanding

people's lives, their perspectives and how they
process information, the assumptions they
work under, and the dynamics they create are
all essential pieces of information and data for
me. I can use my knowledge of family systems
theory, models of change, and brief counseling
techniques on many aspects of a patient's care.
I rely a lot on my referral sources, though,
when I observe longer or more intense care
will be required or if I believe the case exceeds
my limits of competency.

Dr. Helen is experienced in diagnosing and
treating a number of psychiatric conditions. Her
practice includes a large number of patients with
depression, anxiety disorders, and substance abuse.
Some patients feel stigmatized when seeing a psychiatrist, so she may be the only physician they
are willing to see. Dr. Helen is likely to request a
consultation from a psychiatrist in cases of poor
response to treatment, multiple psychiatric diagnoses, psychotic disorders, and bipolar disorder.
After stabilization by the psychiatrist and establishment of an optimal medication regimen, Dr.
Helen may accept responsibility for ongoing medical management. Even for patients under a psychiatrist's care, Dr. Helen expects to see the patient for any other medical issues that may arise.
Dr. Helen will also refer to a psychiatrist if she
believes there is a significant suicide risk.

Dr. Helen is likely to refer to a clinical psychologist or social worker if her patients have significant psychosocial issues that have an impact
on their mental health. She may also request a
consultation if there is a question of the precise
psychiatric diagnosis. This is very helpful to her
in tailoring the patient's medications. She recognizes that clinical psychologists often have a good
working knowledge of medication options for
various conditions, and she is open to suggestion
on these choices. Her knowledge of the patient's
other medical conditions also helps her choose
appropriate medications. She may request the assistance of a psychologist if a patient's mental
health issues are complicating care for other medical conditions.

Monday morning is always busy in Dr. Helen's
office. Patients with acute illnesses that have not
resolved over the weekend call for appointments.
Tom has double-booked the schedule to accommodate several such patients. By the time Marga-

ret Dupre arrives, Dr. Helen is already about 25 minutes behind schedule.

Margaret is 39 years old. She works part time as a teacher's aide. He husband is a manager at a convenience store and works 50 or more hours per week. The Dupres have two children, aged 4 and 5 years. The husband's company provides health insurance, but benefits for mental health are limited, and copayments are higher. Money is tight at their household. Last month, Margaret visited Dr. Helen with complaints of fatigue and insomnia. A brief medical examination showed no obvious abnormalities. Laboratory work ruled out thyroid disorders or anemia as the cause. Dr. Helen delivered the two children, and she recalled Margaret's bout of postpartum depression after the younger child's birth. She diagnosed Margaret with depression and started her on medication.

Today, the situation appears to have worsened. On entering the exam room, Dr. Helen immediately notes Margaret's haggard appearance. Under gentle questioning by Dr. Helen, Margaret begins to sob. The insomnia is worsening, rather than improving, with medication. Her sense of hopelessness has deepened, and she questions whether she is really of any use to her family. She missed work 3 days last week and spent most of the weekend in bed. Her husband was unable to find a substitute at work, so he dropped Margaret off today. Her mother came over to get the children to school and day care. With downcast eyes, she admits to a suicide plan. She is evasive about her possible method and does not answer when Dr. Helen asks her to contract for safety. Dr. Helen recognizes that her patient is at a moderate risk of suicide, and that urgent intervention is needed. She excuses herself from the exam room to arrange a consultation.

In the hallway, Tom notes that he has filled the other exam rooms with patients who are waiting to be seen. Dr. Helen has spent 20 minutes with Margaret, so she is now 35 minutes behind schedule. Dr. Helen calls her insurance clerk to see which psychiatrist in the area might be covered on Margaret's health plan. It is a plan that is not familiar to the clerk, so she tells Dr. Helen she will call the insurance company to find out. Dr. Helen instructs Tom to try to reach Margaret's husband at work. The insurance clerk calls on the intercom to say that she reached an answering machine at the insurance company and left a message, but she will keep trying.

Family physicians experience unique challenges interacting with the mental health system. Insurance companies frequently have a limited panel of mental health clinicians who are eligible for coverage. Because of constantly changing provider panels, Dr. Helen has difficulty developing and maintaining collegial relationships with these professionals. She experiences frustration at the difficulty of obtaining mental health consultation for her patients in need.

Dr. Helen: If my patient is suffering from a life-threatening heart condition, I can have a cardiologist at her side in a matter of minutes. However, for a life-threatening psychiatric condition, I have to make multiple calls, and I never know who may be going to see her. Insurance companies don't seem to realize how serious these situations can become.

Many insurance plans limit reimbursement for mental health care. Although Dr. Helen is well trained in this field and provides cost-effective care, she may receive reduced insurance reimbursement compared with a similar level of service for a medical problem. Some of her colleagues in family medicine submit insurance claims listing the patient's symptoms of insomnia or fatigue, rather than the true diagnosis of depression, in the belief that this will result in better reimbursement. Dr. Helen has been successful in obtaining payment using specific CPT-4 (current procedural terminology) procedure codes (American Medical Association, 2003) for medical management of mental health conditions, but insurance payment policies are always changing. The lack of reimbursement is also a barrier to many of her patients in obtaining psychotherapy. Dr. Helen keeps a list of providers who accept reduced or sliding scale payments for her patients who cannot otherwise access mental health care.

Dr. Helen places a call to a local psychiatrist who has consulted for her in the past. He is making rounds at the hospital and cannot be reached. She leaves a message with his answering service. She also calls a clinical psychologist she knows. The psychologist is in session and does not take calls during sessions. Dr. Helen leaves a message on the answering machine. Her receptionist calls on the intercom to say that Mr. Dank, her 11:00 a.m. patient, needs to get back to work and is wondering how much longer he will have to wait. Dr. Helen estimates it will be at least another half hour, and the patient leaves without being seen. He is unhappy and plans to file a complaint with the office manager. Tom reports he has been unsuccessful in reaching the husband at work. He does speak to Margaret's mother at home, and she promises to try to reach Mr. Dupre. Dr. Helen checks on Margaret, who is still waiting in the exam room. Margaret is red-eyed and seems a bit more agitated. Dr. Helen apologizes for the wait and goes into the next exam room, where a man with chronic back pain is waiting for a disability examination.

Family physicians may also interact with other mental health clinicians. Those lucky enough to practice in areas with good institutional support may be able to access the services of social workers or case managers. These professionals may assist the family physician in providing patient or family counseling or accessing other community resources. Family physicians realize a team-based approach can help them cope with some of the most challenging aspects of patient care.

Tom interrupts Dr. Helen in the middle of her next exam. The insurance company has confirmed that the psychiatrist Dr. Helen wishes to consult is an eligible provider. The psychiatrist returns Dr. Helen's call and promises to meet Margaret at the emergency room for a consultation. Margaret's husband also calls, and Dr. Helen shares her concerns with him. He is concerned and says he will come to the office to drive Margaret to the emergency room. Dr. Helen then returns to complete the disability exam and finish her morning. Her sack lunch will need to be eaten in about 5 minutes so she can start the afternoon session on time. She is relieved that she has helped Margaret access appropriate care.

Dr. Helen desires an effective collegial relationship with mental health specialists. From her perspective, this includes several elements. First, she most wishes for colleagues who understand that her relationship with the patient is a long-term one, typically much longer than any psychotherapist will have with the patient. Regular communication with the mental health specialist ensures that each member of the team understands the care plan. Communication can be in the form of a phone call, a letter, or a copy of a progress note, depending on urgency.

Dr. Helen recognizes the importance of confidentiality for her patients. However, the unique confidentiality practices of the mental health field sometimes frustrate her. When Dr. Helen refers a patient to another medical specialist, she expects to communicate with that specialist by phone or letter to let him or her know the reason for the referral. She also receives communication back, outlining the specialist's assessment of the patient and the planned treatment. A referral to a mental health professional often results in no communication at all. If she attempts to communicate directly, she may be told the patient has not specifically authorized the communication, so no information can be provided. Dr. Helen believes this contributes to fragmented care. She would ideally like to know the patient's diagnosis, recommendations for medication management, and the ongoing plan of therapy. She would like to be informed of major changes in the patient's condition, such as suicide gestures or hospitalizations, and of important life events that may have an impact on other aspects of the patient's health.

Dr. Helen recalls the case of a severely depressed patient who attempted suicide: "I saw her in my office, and I recognized the severity of her depression. I started her on antidepressants and referred her for an urgent psychiatric appointment. That psychiatrist saw her and made adjustments to her medications. The patient became more suicidal and attempted an overdose. When she was admitted to the intensive care unit, a second psychiatrist saw her and managed her care in the hospital. After discharge, a third psychiatrist saw her for aftercare. She then returned to my care. None of the psychiatrists communicated with me about her management."

Dr. Helen believes that insurance company limitations and practice organization by mental health professionals contribute to more fragmented care. She interrupts patient visits regularly to take calls from other clinicians, and she hopes this professional courtesy can be returned.

Dr. Helen is willing to assist mental health specialists as a resource. She can provide medical management of clients the psychologist identifies as needing medication. She is happy to accept the referral of patients who do not have a primary care physician.

If you ask Dr. Helen how she would like to get acquainted with a psychologist who is new to her community, she might answer as follows:

"I am always looking for qualified mental health professionals to whom I can refer patients. Of course, a personal recommendation from a psychologist or physician that I already know is the strongest introduction. It is so difficult for me to communicate with psychologists that it always makes a great impression if someone takes the time to call me about my patient. I attend continuing medical education sessions at the local hospital, and a well-prepared presentation by a psychologist would help me with my education as well as introduce me to a local referral resource. It helps me to know which insurance plans cover the psychologist because low insurance reimbursement is a barrier to many of my patients. Referring a patient blindly to a psychologist listed in their insurance book is not very satisfying. However, if that psychologist made an effort to communicate with me after seeing my patient, it would make me more inclined to refer future patients, especially if I get positive reports from the patient about the therapy experience."

Mental health specialists and family physicians can collaborate in ways beyond direct patient care. Behavioral scientists serve as faculty in family practice residencies. Mental health specialists are often welcomed if they can offer lectures and seminars on timely issues in primary care mental health. Family practitioners also recognize the skill of mental health professionals in areas such as interviewing and communication skills, ethics, the patient-physician relationship, and family systems theory. Community medicine experience is required for family practice training. This experience includes community health needs assessment, service-learning experiences, the study of social science applications to clinical medicine, and the integration of public health with medical practice. Community experiences provide family physicians with a knowledge of local resources and, more often than not, foster a sense of social consciousness and patient advocacy once they realize how limited such resources are.

Family practice is rooted in values such as compassion, empathy, trust, listening, and respect (Rakel, 2000). The specialty developed in response to a medical climate that began to place technology over touch, curing over caring, and physician paternalism over patient-centered care. The rapid growth of family practice over the last three decades provides testimony to its success and its more holistic approach. People bring illness, not disease, to the attention of the physician. They seek hope and comfort, not merely drugs and procedures. Family physicians are and will remain natural collaborators with mental health professionals.

References

American Academy of Family Physicians. (2002). *Population of community in which primary offices of family physicians are located.* Retrieved April 25, 2003, from http://www.aafp.org/x779.xml

American Medical Association. 2003. *Current procedural terminology,* 4th ed. Chicago: Author.

Butler, A. M. (1966). Medicine and changing times. *New England Journal of Medicine, 274,* 1119–1120.

Cherry, D., & Woodwell, D. (2002). *National Ambulatory Medical Care Survey: 2000 summary. Advance data from vital and health statistics; No. 328.* Hyattsville, MD: National Center for Health Statistics.

Code, C. F. (1970). Determinants of medical care—A plan for the future. *New England Journal of Medicine, 283,* 679–685.

Department of Health and Human Services, Centers for Disease Control and Prevention, National Center for Health Statistics. (2002). *2000 National Ambulatory Medical Care Survey* (Version CD-ROM Series 13, No. 32; Sets 2.0, Rev. 805).

Fryer, G., Green, L., & Dovey, S. (2001). The United States relies on family physicians unlike any other specialty. *American Family Physician, 63,* 1669.

Gaufberg, E. H., Joseph, R. C., Pels, R. J., Wyshak, G., Wieman, D., & Nadelson, C. C. (2001). Psychosocial training in U.S. internal medicine and family practice residency programs. *Academic Medicine, 76,* 738–742.

Graham, R., Roberts, R., Ostergaard, D., Kahn, N., Pugno, P., & Green, L. (2002). Family practice in the United States: A status report. *Journal of the American Medical Association, 288,* 1097–1101.

Green, L. A., & Fryer, G. E., Jr. (2002). Family practice in the United States: Position and prospects. *Academic Medicine, 77,* 781–789.

Medalie, J. H., Zyzanski, S. J., Langa, D., & Stange, K. C. (1998). The family in family practice: Is it a reality? *Journal of Family Practice, 46,* 390–396.

Menke, W. G. (1970). Divided labor: the doctor as specialist. *Annuals of Internal Medicine, 72,* 943–950.

Moser, R. H. (1974). Editorial: An anti-intellectual movement in medicine? *Journal of the American Medical Association, 227,* 432–434.

Rakel, R. E. (2000). Compassion and the art of family medicine: From Osler to Oprah. *Journal of American Board Family Practice, 13,* 440–448.

Stephens, G. G. (1987). Developmental assessment of family practice: An insider's view. In W. J. Doherty, C. E. Christianson, & M. B. Sussman (Eds.), *Family medicine: The maturing of a discipline* (pp. 1–21). New York: Haworth Press.

White, K., Williams, T., & Greenberg, B. (1961). The ecology of medical care. *New England Journal of Medicine, 265,* 885–892.

Yarnall, K. S., Pollak, K. I., Ostbye, T., Krause, K. M., & Michener, J. L. (2003). Primary care: Is there enough time for prevention? *American Journal of Public Health, 93,* 635–641.

6

Internal Medicine

Frederic W. Platt

Mr. Arnold is a 60-year-old architect who lives with his wife, one dog, and one cat. He considers himself generally well, but has diabetes, hypertension, and recurrent backache. Today, he comes to see his physician, Dr. Xavier, because of a 3-day illness that consists of fever, productive cough with yellow sputum, and pain in the right side of his chest when he coughs or breathes deeply. He has been working with this same physician for 12 years and believes that the doctor knows him well and has his best interests at heart. His wife has also consulted Dr. Xavier in the past. She is quite healthy and usually appears at the office once a year for a "well-woman exam."

Mr. Arnold knows that this doctor will either solve his problems or find someone else to do so. In the past, when Mr. Arnold developed urinary obstruction, Dr. Xavier referred him to a urologist. Other than that one referral, Dr. Xavier has been able to care for all Mr. Arnold's medical problems during the last 12 years. On this day, they meet in Dr. Xavier's office, a small suite in a medical office building attached to the hospital. Mr. Arnold does not enter the hospital proper; his current care is accomplished by repeated visits to the of-fice and a chest X-ray obtained in a radiology suite in the same building.

Dr. Xavier spends about 40 minutes with Mr. Arnold on this visit and sees him again three times over the next 2 weeks for shorter visits. He diagnoses a right middle lobe pneumonia, obtains the confirming chest X-ray, has some blood tests drawn, and prescribes an oral antibiotic on the first visit. He reviews the status of the patient's diabetes, obtains a finger-stick blood sugar, and makes an alteration in the patient's medication for that problem. He scans the vital signs obtained by his nurse, repeats the blood pressure himself, and discusses medication with Mr. Arnold. The interview takes about 20 minutes, the physical examination about 10 minutes, and the discussion of diagnosis and treatment about 10 minutes on this first visit.

A PEDIATRICIAN FOR ADULTS

Dr. Xavier is an internist, a specialist in internal medicine, who practices primary care medicine rather than consultative secondary care. Most of his work actually takes place in his office. On a typical day, he sees 20 patients in the office and 2 in the hospital. Other internists in the same community work entirely in the hospital, calling themselves "hospitalists," or subspecialize in compartments of internal medicine such as cardiology, gastroenterology, or endocrinology. All describe their work as "limited to diseases of adults" and say that they do not do major surgery or deliver babies.

When pressed for a definition of his work, Dr. Xavier says that he is "a pediatrician for adults." He says that nobody seems to know what an internist is, but everyone knows what a pediatrician is. Because his patients are likely to come to him first rather than be referred from another doctor, he considers his work to be "primary care."

Dr. Xavier is proud to be an internist. He traces his lineage back to Hippocrates, who, Dr. Xavier says, "must have been an internist" because, in his famous oath, he urged other doctors "not to cut." In the long history of doctoring, physicians have been a different breed from surgeons. In England, for example, surgeons were for many years a lower social order, less well educated, often originated as barbers, and were called "Mister"; physicians were better educated and referred to as "Doctor." When Dr. Xavier entered his practice over 20 years ago, there were still internists who listed their field as "internist and diagnostician."

That is how Dr. Xavier pictures himself—a thoughtful person who knows much about the diseases and ailments of adults and who can and will sort them out for his patients. He also thinks he has a central role in the constellation of physicians. Dr. Xavier is proud of the fact that, when writing chart notes for a hospitalized patient, he heads his note "Medicine." Other specialists head their notes "Urology" or "Dermatology," but internists place their claim to the center of their universe with their designation, "Medicine." He says that internal medicine much like the oboe—it sits in the middle of the medical orchestra.

Of course, Dr. Xavier understands that doing his work well requires him to understand more than the pathophysiology, diagnosis, and treatment of disease; he also has to understand the person wrapped around the disease, but he has had little formal training in that task. How could

that be? It has something to do with the centrality of the disease theory in contemporary medical education.

THE DISEASE THEORY AND MEDICAL PROGRESS

Asked what they think was the most important medical invention in the history of medicine, students name antibiotics, the stethoscope, the X-ray, and other developments. But surely our most important invention was disease theory. Beginning about 200 years ago with French, German, and English practitioners, we have become more and more enthralled with this theory. It goes something like this: 300 years ago, if you were ill, your doctor considered the sort of person you were and tried to sort out how your personality, your gender, your religious focus, your "humors," and your character might be out of order. If you had a cough and chest pain, your problem was quite different from the problem of a person half your size, of different religion, and of different temperament and character who also happened to have cough and chest pain.

Gradually, we came to focus on the illness itself and created a concept of disease. If you have a community-acquired pneumonia and so does that other person, all those previous considerations have little import. The doctor simply has to know what organisms cause community-acquired pneumonias, what antibiotics might cure them, and what conflicting effects of your many medications are worrisome. Your personality has little to do with the matter. The disease is the focus and the issue.

Progress in medicine in the last two centuries has come about through this disease theory. We teach our medical students disease theory throughout their medical curriculum—and we teach little else. Our graduating doctors are experts in diseases: their causes, presentations, diagnosis, and treatment. We further train our doctors to focus on diseases of one organ or organ system; they become gastroenterologists or cardiologists. We have specialists in the diseases of eyes (ophthalmologists), and even in diseases of the back of the eye (retinologists).

So it is not surprising that Dr. Xavier's medical training prepared him well for the care of diseases, but not so well for the care of the person of the patient. He experiences this in daily frustrations with patient behavior—patients who fail to follow his recommendations, patients who are angry, patients who want telephone diagnosis and treatment, and countless other communication and interaction syndromes. Dr. Xavier says that 50% of his difficulties come from the patients themselves and recognizes that he has been ill prepared for that struggle. He has been known to say that "medicine would be fun if it weren't for the patients." He says that sometimes it seems as if there is a war going on between himself and his patients to see who will get control of the conversation. Unfortunately, he has not read Mishler's (1984) description of that battle.

There are several excellent textbooks of medical interviewing that might help Dr. Xavier (e.g., Coulehan & Block, 2001; Feldman & Christensen, 1997; Kleinman, 1988; Lipp, 1986; Platt & Gordon, 1999; Weisberg, 1994) and many training programs organized by groups such as the Society for Teachers of Family Medicine, the American Academy on Patient and Physician, and the Bayer Institute for Health Care Communication. He might try some of them for starters. Then he would be able to balance his knowledge of diseases with knowledge of the central science needed to work with patients: communication.

AN INTERNAL MEDICINE EDUCATION

Dr. Xavier received his bachelor's degree in biological sciences and his medical degree 4 years later. He then spent 3 years in postgraduate residency training at a "teaching hospital" affiliated with the local medical school. He then took and passed the certifying examination of the American Board of Internal Medicine. He is a member of an educational organization of internists, the American College of Physicians, and goes to their annual meetings to further his education. He attends educational meetings once or twice a week at his hospital, but says that his most important educational activity now is frequent conversations with colleagues at lunch at the hospital or by phone when they share patients. He reads an article or two each day from the stack of subscribed and unsolicited journals that pile up in his office. More helpful to him are the hospital library and the librarian, who finds pertinent articles when he has a puzzling patient disease problem.

European physicians call this sort of medical practice *general practice* even though it omits obstetrics and pediatrics. They use that term as we would use *primary care*. In the United States, *general practice* (GP) is used to denote the practice of an all-purpose doctor with very little training after medical school, usually 1 year of postgraduate training called internship. (Paradoxically, the doctors with the least training were expected to have the greatest breadth of knowledge and capabilities.) In the United States, the term GP has vanished, to be replaced by family practice, describing the work of doctors with training similar to that of Dr. Xavier, but in slightly greater breadth and slightly less depth. A current family practice doctor might see younger and healthier patients, might include children and infants, might even do some surgery and deliveries, especially in areas less well served by numbers of subspecialists.

Internists practicing in areas with many subspecialists tend to work mostly as primary care physicians. Those practicing in areas less well covered tend to act more as consultants to other primary care doctors, mostly family practitioners. But there is no constant model of practice in internal medicine, and the more than 100,000 doctors in the United States who claim that specialty practice in highly varied and variable situations.

Is Dr. Xavier typical of internists? Perhaps, but internists vary considerably. Dr. Xavier is midway in his career and admits that he may no longer be quite current with all the newer drugs and tests, but he believes that he is now better than average at communicating with his patients—a bit more skilled at resolving strange interactions and at working with the patients who come wrapped around their diseases.

Dr. Xavier says that, although his patients' ages distribute as they do in the population, his time is spent predominantly with his older patients because they are sicker. Contrasting himself with "geriatricians," he says that they do much the same work with much the same patients except that he does little care of demented Alzheimer's patients in nursing homes, and his friends the geriatricians do a lot of that sort of work.

MENTAL HEALTH
AND INTERNAL MEDICINE

Dr. Xavier cares for about 2,000 persons, aged 15 to 105 years, all of whom suffer from the usual emotional issues and illnesses. He treats anxiety and panic disorders, grief and loss, and major depressions and works with patients with every possible character trait and pattern. He uses a lot of benzodiazepine tranquilizers, a lot of serotonin reuptake inhibitor antidepressants, and a lot of tricyclic antidepressants. He works with patients on behavior change issues regarding alcoholism, the use of cigarettes, and obesity. He works with psychologists, psychiatric social workers, and other mental health specialists, mostly by phone conversations about their shared patients.

Some internists are less capable of or interested in focusing on their patients' mental and psychic problems (substance abuse, depression, anxiety), and some are more so. A mental health worker might well be puzzled about this varying threshold of awareness about psychological issues on the part of internists. Such issues play little part in the training of internists, but a large part in their patients' problems. Most practicing internists come to realize that mental and psychological problems are ubiquitous. They often learn on the job. But they do not always reach the same understanding as clinicians trained in psychology or psychiatry.

For example, Dr. Xavier says that he has a theory about psychosomatic disease. He says he is not sure that emotional issues translate to physical symptoms, but he thinks that patients suffer quietly with their physical symptoms until emotional issues appear (trouble at home or work) and then come to the doctor with those same physical symptoms. He says, "It isn't something about the disease that brings the patient to the doctor, but rather it is something about the patient."

He has grudgingly admitted that he has to know his patient's social, home, and work stories "a little bit" to help them with their diseases. On occasion, at medical meetings, he has attended sessions in "motivational interviewing" and "behavior change strategies." He has heard about staging behavior change and understands that empathy works better than leaning on a patient. Still, he says he would "rather just tell the patient what to do and have him do it." He says he himself is "probably in the contemplative stage" about becoming a change artist for his patients.

Dr. Xavier says that he would really vastly prefer to have his patients' mental illnesses, psychological foibles, behavior disorders, and tendency not to comply with his directions all treated by a mental health expert. Unfortunately, he has no such expert in his office and finds it difficult to get his patients to such a person because of their own "resistance" and the obstructions created by their insurance and health maintenance organization (HMO) programs. He has a favorite psychiatrist and two favorite psychologists to whom he is occasionally able to refer patients. However, he says that the vast majority of his patients are tied into a limited group of psychotherapists he does not know personally or professionally. He says dealing with them is a problem because they are hard to reach by phone and seldom are available when he calls them. He cites this situation as a not-rare frustration:

Dr. Xavier: I cared for Mrs. B. for 15 years, and recently she has been more and more depressed. Despite my medications and our discussions, she seemed to be getting worse, so I sent her to the emergency room for an evaluation by the mental health person there. After a few hours, I got a call from the admitting mental health person saying that he agreed with my appraisal and that he would admit Mrs. B. to another hospital where her HMO had a contract. He would arrange for the psychiatrist at that hospital to call me the next day. Four days later, I hadn't heard word one, so I called that hospital; after being put on hold several times and having to listen to that excruciating hold music, finally some nameless person came on the line to tell me that they could not tell me anything at all because the patient was on a psychiatry unit, and all information was "privileged." I was livid!

At the heart of this example of bad communication lies the issue of "Just whose patient is this?" A sense of ownership may lead to exaggerated concern for privacy issues. Dr. Xavier thinks that any patient "belongs to" that person himself or herself, not to any clinician. He bristles at the competitiveness that doctors display in their use of phrases such as "my patient." He thinks real teamwork in the medical profession should include an enormous amount of communication. He says that mental health people are bad at this, but so are other subspecialists, who all act as if their own bit of the patient was the whole thing. Dr. Xavier believes that the only difference with mental health workers is their claim to a special need for confidentiality, usually without ever discussing that need with the patient or asking about the possibility of sharing information with a primary care doctor. Dr. Xavier says that he doubts that the caretaker on the psychiatry unit ever asked Mrs. B. if they could or should talk with him, but he is sure that the patient will be returned to him and that he will be ignorant of all that occurred and will have missed any help from the mental health expert.

The Need to Improve Communication

Barring a major structural change in American medicine, perhaps a return to the freer referral styles of the past, Dr. Xavier says that what would help him most with his patients would be for mental health people to recognize his central role with his patients and communicate better, preferably by phone. He says that he would like each mental health person to always ask every patient for the name and phone number of their primary physician, then always ask if they can have permission to communicate with that doctor, and then always call that doctor. Dr. Xavier notes that he may care for a patient for 15 years; then, he will refer the patient to the mental health expert, who will see the patient eight times; and then the patient will return to Dr. Xavier for the next 5 years, with Dr. Xavier none the wiser for this mental health "consultation" and no more capable of working well with his patient. He believes that he has much to learn from mental health people, but that they are terrible at sharing their understandings and insights with him.

Making New Connections

If a psychologist wanted to connect with Dr. Xavier or other internists and become one of those valued mental health people on the referral list, he or she might try the following suggestions:

1. Take an internist to lunch (or breakfast). Nothing beats a face-to-face conversation. Ask the physician to tell you what internists do and what they want from mental health experts. Tell the doctor that you have just read a chapter about internists and are curious to learn if they are in need of psychologists for referral, the issues with which they are struggling, or whether they might like a noon talk or other educational activity.
2. Explore these issues with your own primary care physician if this is an internist.
3. Contact the local branch of the American College of Physicians (which can be found at www.acponline.org/chapters) to find out about local or regional meetings and to learn about local issues of concern to internists.
4. For a local or regional psychology meeting, develop a presentation that concerns complaints of internists as they try to learn about good psychologists to whom they can refer.
5. Refer a patient. If you are treating a patient who does not have a primary care physician, inquire if particular internists are taking new patients.
6. Finally, psychologists can network through the primary care physicians of their patients. "Do you have a regular doctor? Could I make contact with that doctor?"

In doing these things, however, the psychologist should keep in mind that there are particular qualities that Dr. Xavier values. First, Dr. Xavier will want to know if the psychologist is good for his patients: attentive, a good listener, perceptive about the patient as a person, focused on the real issues, a caring and concerned clinician. Dr. Xavier will not much care what the psychologist's theoretical school of therapy is, but will want the psychologist to display the sort of behavior to patients that Carl Rogers would have recommended. Second, Dr. Xavier definitely wants to be kept in the picture (especially if he referred the patient). Dr. Xavier may have a relationship with the patient that spans decades and may have learned quite a lot, gathered in small bits over a long relationship, about the patient's issues. Any psychologist who works with Dr. Xavier should definitely assume that he cares about how those issues are resolved.

WHERE WE ARE GOING

Thirty years ago, the typical primary care internist had 12 patients in the hospital and 12 in the office every day. The doctor had the opportunity to converse with colleagues, nurses, and other doctors while making rounds in the hospital. Those conversations served many functions—personal and professional. They allowed informal consultations and coherent team care of patients, diminished the anguish of ubiquitous medical uncertainty, and gave the physician a great deal of security and comfort.

Today, the ratio of hospital to clinic patients has changed dramatically. Outpatient procedures have improved; drug therapy is better; and insurance pressures push patients out of the hospital earlier. As a result, each doctor is in the hospital much less, and contact with peers and colleagues has vastly diminished. Doctors are more isolated and lonelier. Their work loses some of its joy, and their anxiety increases.

The structure of American medicine is highly in flux. Capitated HMOs seem to be on the way out, but managed care will probably be here forever. Payment schemes seem to be designed to destroy primary care medicine, paying much more for procedure time than they do for cognitive, being-with-the-patient time. Despite efforts such as the resource-based relative-value system, this massive payment inequity continues and, in fact, worsens. Many primary care doctors throughout the nation are retiring early, partly because they can (having acquired enough wealth in "better times") and partly because they are distraught about HMO interference, Medicare payment cuts, paperwork, increasingly litigious patients, and the loneliness of medical practice.

Medical (i.e., disease-focused) progress has been immense and will probably continue. We are at the edge of usable genetic knowledge and techniques. Minimally invasive surgery is becoming more common. The understanding of disease and our ability to treat it is growing rapidly. All are to the good, and all are a source of professional joy. But the cost of this care continues to mount, and doctors increasingly find themselves in the middle of economic arguments and issues.

Then there are all the behavior issues that produce the very diseases Dr. Xavier is so avid to diagnose and treat. He says he would be better off if he could help his patients smoke less rather than diagnose the lung cancer that appears 20 years later. Dr. Xavier and his internist colleagues might benefit from reading or training in some of the newer skills of behavior modification, perhaps starting with Miller and Rollnick's (1991) wonderful book, *Motivational Interviewing*. Other such resources include the works of Levinson, Cohen, Brady, and Duffy (2001); Keller and White (1997); Prochaska, Norcross, and Diclemente (1994); and Rollnick, Mason, and Butler (2000).

Because many of their patients come to them with problems related to cigarette smoking, overeating, alcohol use, lack of exercise, and failure to adhere to medical recommendations, Dr. Xavier and his colleagues might feel much better about their work if they have improved skills in this area of medical practice. Perhaps their mental health colleagues can help them to learn such skills. Meanwhile, mental health folk might read about teamwork and, of course, if not versed in motivational interviewing, might read some of the same references (Stoeckle, Ronan, Emanuel, Ehrlich, & Hughes, 2002; Suchman, Botelho, & Hinton-Walker, 1998).

In short, we are in a time of much change, a challenge to us all. Asked what internists and mental health workers could do to improve matters, Dr. Xavier says, "just talk with one another."

References

Coulehan, J. L., & Block, M. R. (2001). *The medical interview: Mastering skills for clinical practice* (4th ed.). Philadelphia: Davis.

Feldman, M. D., & Christensen, J. F. (Eds.). (1997). *Behavioral medicine in primary care: A practical guide.* Stamford, CT: Appleton and Lange.

Keller, V. F., & White, M. K. (1997). Choices and changes: A new model for influencing patient health behavior. *Journal of Clinical Outcomes Management, 4*(6), 33–36.

Kleinman, A. (1988). *The illness narratives: Suffering, healing and the human condition.* New York: Basic Books.

Levinson, W., Cohen, M. S., Brady, D., & Duffy, F. D. (2001). To change or not to change: sounds like you have a dilemma. *Annuals of Internal Medicine, 135,* 386–391.

Lipp, M. R. (1986). *Respectful treatment: A practical handbook of patient care* (2nd ed.). New York: Elsevier.

Miller, W. R., & Rollnick, S. (1991). *Motivational interviewing: Preparing people to change addictive behavior.* New York: Guilford.

Mishler, E. G. (1984). *The discourse of medicine: Dialectics of medical interviews.* Norwood, NJ: Ablex.

Platt, F. W., & Gordon, G. H. (1999). *Field guide to the difficult patient interview.* Philadelphia: Lippincott.

Prochaska, J. O., Norcross, J. C., & Diclemente, C. C. (1994). *Changing for good.* New York: Avon.

Rollnick, S., Mason, P., & Butler, C. (2000). *Health behavior change: A guide for practitioners.* Edinburgh, Scotland: Churchill Livingstone.

Stoeckle, J. D., Ronan, L. J., Emanuel, L., Ehrlich, C., & Hughes, C. C. (2002). *Doctoring together: A physician's guide to manners, duties and communication in the shared care of patients.* Boston: Massachusetts General Hospital Press.

Suchman, A. L., Botelho, R. J., & Hinton-Walker, P. (1998). *Partnerships in healthcare: Transforming relational process.* Rochester, NY: University of Rochester Press.

Weisberg, J. (1994). *Does anybody listen? Does anybody care?* Englewood, CO: MGMA.

7

Pediatrics

Barbara M. Korsch
Alex Y. Chen
Sara M. Lewis

WHAT IS PEDIATRICS?

Pediatrics is the specialty devoted to the care of children. Pediatrics requires expert knowledge about children, not only regarding childhood diseases. Pediatricians care for patients between birth and 18 years of age. In 1996, there were approximately 34,100 pediatricians in the United States (Chang & Halfon, 1997; Randolph & Pathman, 2001). Pediatricians are distributed somewhat unevenly in the United States; there are relatively more pediatricians available in urban areas as compared to rural areas. On average, there is 1 pediatrician per 7,150 children in urban areas and 1 pediatrician per 24,400 children in rural America (Randolph & Pathman, 2001).

Why Pediatrics Is Considered a Primary Care Specialty

Pediatricians provide comprehensive long-term care to children. Most general pediatricians are community practitioners. There are also subspecialties in pediatrics, including intensive care, emergency care, cardiology, and others.

Distinguishing Pediatrics From Related Specialties

Pediatrics as a specialty defines itself by an age range of patients. Pediatricians are both primary care physicians and specialists because of their unique in-depth knowledge of childhood growth and development and the diseases of childhood.

History of Pediatrics as a Specialty

Authorities in India and China at least 2,000 years ago recognized that children are a different group of patients from adults (Colon & Colon, 1999). Pediatrics as a specialty is believed to have existed since 1889, when the first scientific session of the American Pediatric Society was held in Washington, DC. At that time, Sir William Osler noted that pediatrics was the last specialty to separate from general medicine. The founding of the *Journal of Pediatrics* in 1948 is another milestone. Since that time, numerous other pediatric journals have appeared. In 1960, as the emphasis in pediatric medicine shifted from inpatient care to ambulatory services, the Ambulatory

Pediatric Association was founded. Several other pediatric scientific clinical associations grew and flourished throughout the last century.

Initially, pediatrics focused heavily on infant nutrition because malnutrition was one of the leading causes of death in infancy and childhood (Brosco, 2001). Infectious disease and preventive immunizations were also emphasized early on because these were among the most acute concerns of society at the time. Psychosocial aspects of medicine were not the explicit focus of pediatric practice and training, although good clinicians were always aware of them.

Credentialing in Pediatrics

Following medical school, physicians must undergo a 3-year residency program and pass a board certification examination to qualify as pediatricians. Additional training is often available through fellowships that allow the pediatrician to specialize in subareas of the field, such as pediatric cardiology. Board certification typically involves a written examination. Once the pediatrician is board certified, he or she must recertify every 7 years. Board certification is offered by the American Board of Pediatrics.

Future Challenges for Pediatric Practice

The past 20 years have witnessed an increasing number of children living in poverty. Poor children not only have greater physical health needs in terms of health maintenance and prevention, but also have greater mental health needs. Low socioeconomic status heightens the risk for social, emotional, and behavioral problems (Briggs-Gowan, Carter, Skuban, & Horwitz, 2001). Rates of these problems are up to two times higher in children of low socioeconomic status than among children with higher socioeconomic status (Jellinek et al., 1999). The pediatric population in the United States has also increased in diversity ethnically and culturally. Pediatricians and mental health professionals will have to become more culturally sensitive and culturally competent in the provision of care. American families are also more and more frequently single-parent families or families with two wage earners (Task Force, 2000). Children's developmental, social, and emo-

tional needs may now need to be approached in light of the reality of new family structures.

Children in the United States may also have increasing mental health needs. Based on findings from the National Health Interview Survey on Disability (National Health Interview Survey 1994–1995), Newacheck, Strickland, and Shonkoff (1998) identified 15% to 18% of children in the United States as having chronic health conditions (developmental, physical, and mental). Approximately half of those children have developmental disabilities, mental impairments, or psychological conditions (ranging from attention-deficit/hyperactivity disorder [ADHD] to psychosis). Among the five most common pediatric chronic conditions, three are mental health and developmentally related: adolescent depression, ADHD, and mental retardation/cerebral palsy (Task Force, 2000). Recent estimates of the economic burden of pediatric mental health disorders approached $12 billion per year (Ringel & Sturm, 2001). Close collaboration between pediatricians and mental health professionals is going to be required to address these needs.

In individual practice, the majority of pediatricians in the United States practice in groups of 2 to 10 pediatricians; often there are "midlevel providers" such as pediatric nurse practitioners or physician assistants in the practices. Managed health care has shaped other models of pediatric care, such as multispecialty care. Restructuring of current practices may be necessary to meet future needs, especially in relation to mental health issues.

Modern pediatric practices emphasize wellness care, health supervision, and preventive medicine in addition to diagnosis and treatment of disease.

TYPICAL PATIENT PROBLEMS IN PEDIATRICS

In a busy Los Angeles, California, managed care pediatric clinic where a new patient visit is only allotted 15 minutes, a 2-year-old boy, Garcia, comes to the office for the first time with his mother to see the general pediatrician. The mother states that they had recently moved from Mexico, and that she is concerned about the fact that her child has only spoken a word that resembles "mama."

Dr. Little, the pediatrician, sought to elicit a more thorough history with her limited medical Spanish. She learned that the child does not play much but appears to have good motor skills. The mother's brother died young from some disease. Dr. Little asks one of the nurses to come in and translate for her; while she waits, she notices young Garcia will not make eye contact with her. Finally, the nurse is able to free herself to come in, and she obtains the information that the mother's brother died from some kind of kidney problem.

After examining the child, Dr. Little is now behind schedule. She orders a hearing evaluation to see if the child can hear. She considers whether Garcia is just a slow starter because of the family's social problems (moving from Mexico, lack of time to read to him, divorce). The possibility of autism is considered.

Dr. Little orders the hearing evaluation and spends another 15 minutes explaining everything to the mother through an interpreter even though she is already behind schedule. At the end of the day, she realizes that young Garcia has no insurance, only basic Medicaid, and that her group will only be reimbursed $20 for the visit. Over the next few weeks, she will follow up on the result of the hearing evaluation and refer young Garcia for evaluation of developmental delay and possible autism.

Pediatricians are often the first professionals to identify psychosocial issues in their patients. An increasing number of patients visit pediatric offices to consult about behavioral and psychosocial problems as their primary concern: hyperactivity, toileting issues, sleep problems, and feeding difficulties. Family dysfunction, divorce, adoption, foster care, and many social problems are presented to the pediatrician because they have an impact on a child's adaptation. Pediatricians are also called on to settle educational dilemmas.

There are a great many new concerns for the pediatrician in relation to the mental health aspects of chronic illness. Patients are surviving longer and are undergoing technically complex and possibly traumatic treatments. Traditionally, for many medical conditions, removal of symptoms was the central goal, but in modern pediatric practice, the impact of treatment on other aspects of the child's development must be considered. For example, if the treatment for a child's seizures makes the child so sleepy that the child cannot participate in normal activities, this may be considered inappropriate treatment.

TYPICAL MENTAL HEALTH NEEDS OF PEDIATRICS PATIENTS

The problems that pediatricians face most frequently include feeding and sleep problems, maladaptive behavior in school or at home, temper tantrums, functional abdominal pain and other psychosomatic symptoms, and depression.

Many consultations are related to hyperactivity and attention-deficit disorder. These consultations are often recommended by teachers. In these cases, the expectation is that the doctor will prescribe medication on the basis of the observations of others. Parents are scheduling appointments with their child's pediatrician specifically for medications. These visits can be difficult for the pediatrician because the parents are responding to pressure from the teacher and are often frustrated. If the pediatrician does not feel that medication is appropriate, the conflict may be difficult to resolve, and the parents may reject a referral to a mental health specialist.

The pediatrician is often the first one to be confronted with family dysfunction, maternal depression, domestic violence, or child neglect or abuse. In all these situations, consultations or at least cooperation with mental health professionals are indicated and are not always readily available. Families often look for quick solutions or nonexistent medicinal remedies. Often they are not ready to accept a mental health referral and do not follow through with recommendations to seek counseling (Phillips, Clawson, & Osinski, 1998; U.S. Surgeon General, 1999).

TYPICAL PEDIATRICIAN INTEREST IN TREATING PSYCHIATRIC OR BEHAVIORAL PROBLEMS

Because more than half of the families presenting to the pediatrician's practice have complaints in the behavior and psychosocial sphere, pediatricians have consistent need for consultation and cooperation with mental health professionals. However, the bulk of mental health issues continue to be addressed and treated in the pediatrician's office rather than in an outside mental health agency. If given a choice, the mental health aspects of pediatric practice might not be the pediatrician's preference. As the profession and pediatric training evolve to meet the demands of managed care, more and more pediatricians may prefer organized well-child visits and visits focused on a single medical problem. Many prefer patient care in hospital settings, or intensive care or emergency room pediatrics, but for most practitioners, mental health problems are a major focus for their daily practices.

The Pediatrician's Typical Level of Training in Psychiatry/Behavioral Science and Range of Expertise

There is increasing emphasis in undergraduate and graduate pediatric training on psychiatry and behavioral science as the need for these services becomes more apparent. The need for increased residency training in behavioral and developmental pediatrics continues to be emphasized in the literature (Burklow, Vaughn, Valerius, & Schultz, 2001; Committee on Psychosocial Aspects, 2001). Some of the most acute problems in communities relate to psychosocial issues (e.g., violence, drug use, etc.).

Curricula in undergraduate medical schools have changed, and graduate training emphasizes progressively more the behavioral aspects of pediatric practice. In fact, a rotation in behavioral pediatrics is now mandatory. In addition, competence in communicating with patients is one of the goals of all pediatric residency programs, and programs must document how this is accomplished.

Many academic centers offer pediatric behavioral fellowships, 1 to 3 years long, that provide advanced training in developmental pediatrics and specific conditions, such as ADHD, autism, and learning disabilities. Pediatricians can now also obtain board certification in developmental/behavioral pediatrics (for more information, see the American Board of Pediatrics Web site, www.

abp.org). The Society of Behavioral Pediatrics and the *Journal of Developmental and Behavioral Pediatrics* are other focal points for pediatricians with behavioral interests. Behavioral fellowships are often interesting to experienced pediatricians who realize that mental health issues are essential parts of their practices.

Key Frustrations of Pediatricians, Especially in Relation to Mental Health Issues

Like most other primary care practitioners, conscientious pediatricians are increasingly frustrated with systems problems such as limited time and inadequate reimbursement. These issues are most acutely perceived when it comes to the mental health aspects of patient problems. There are no remunerative laboratory tests and few quick, gratifying remedies.

When pediatricians are asked which patients are most frustrating, patients with multiple problems are often listed first, and those with psychosomatic complaints come shortly thereafter. These patients have obvious mental health concerns that need to be addressed, an activity that is often lengthy and frustrating for both patient and physician. Traditional medical education does not include adequate teaching of behavioral issues; assessment and management skills likewise may not be adequately taught.

At a more basic level, medical education not only fails to nurture the humanism of the young idealistic student, but also actually teaches the student not to be open to feelings that may be disturbing.

Pediatricians' expectations for their future careers may be inappropriate. The old paradigm of "find it and fix it" has not been replaced. They expect to be "doing" more than listening. Making a quick diagnosis and prescribing the appropriate medication (or better yet, "cure") are what they like and all too rarely do.

Another source of frustration lies in the limited resources for referral and treatment for those patients who need mental health attention. Pediatricians are rarely taught effective ways of making a mental health referral. There is too often poor communication with mental health personnel, which leaves pediatricians with a complex, dissatisfied patient. In addition, it must be mentioned that pediatricians are historically reimbursed at a lower rate on average than most other general and specialty practitioners, even though their training and responsibilities seem to justify reimbursement at a higher rate.

How Mental Health Specialists Can Collaborate Effectively With Pediatricians

In the 1950s, Haggarty coined the term *new pediatrics* (Ambulatory Pediatric Association, 1990). He urged and supported changes in pediatric education that would lead to greater competence of the pediatrician to deal with these issues in comprehensive care and to a clearer recognition of the potential of working in collaboration with experts and practitioners from the mental health profession.

Over the last few decades, there have been various patterns for collaborating with clinicians from the fields of social work, public health nursing, education, and so on. A number of teams were devised to include psychiatrists or psychologists either to work directly with the patient and family or to help and supervise pediatricians in their work with the patient. Social workers have traditionally worked in the pediatric setting, although their role also has changed over time. Although they used to be sought out for community resources and practical issues, they are now increasingly called on to help in clinical evaluation and therapy with the child or family.

From the beginning, the discipline of clinical psychology seemed to offer a very promising combination of relevant basic science combined with clinical skill and experience. This particular kind of cooperation is presently the most common team effort for taking care of the increasing number of behavioral and emotional problems facing the pediatric practitioner. One reason for the productive collaboration of pediatrics and psychology lies in the facts that one of the basic sciences for pediatrics is child development and that clinical psychologists usually have in-depth training in this field.

Particularly in the pediatric office setting, psychologists can provide valuable consultation for physicians. Psychologists are able to evaluate the severity of a psychosocial problem by meeting with the child or parent. They can then determine the most appropriate disposition for the child, ranging from outpatient family counseling to inpatient psychiatric hospitalization in the most severe cases. They can also collaborate with pediatricians by providing assessments of children for disorders such as ADHD or learning disabilities. Their assessments can help guide the physician regarding the potential efficacy of prescribing medications. They can assist the parents in requesting an individual education plan (special education) for their child at school.

Common Mistakes of Mental Health Specialists in Relating to Pediatricians and How They Can Be Avoided

One of the most common mistakes psychologists make in working with pediatricians is that they refuse to share any data about the patient after the referral has been made. This often leaves pediatricians feeling that they have been excluded from the care of the patient. If the pediatrician the family knows and trusts initiates and supports the referral, the family is often more receptive to treatment.

Experienced pediatric practitioners know that it is rarely wise to refer a family to a mental health specialist on a first visit. Unless the family specifically requests such a referral, it often makes them feel judged, rejected, and poorly understood. If the referral is proposed in a collaborative spirit, with the pediatrician as part of the treatment team, the results will usually be better.

Recommendations for Collaborative Practice

The psychologist who wishes to establish effective working relationships with pediatricians might consider the following strategies. First, give a talk to pediatricians regarding mental health referrals. Second, contact local pediatricians and explore their interest and available resources for having a psychologist as part of their staff to provide immediate on-site consultations and other services. Often, a simple phone call to discuss issues related to an existing patient or an introductory phone call to introduce the mental health practice to pediatricians in the area may lead to further discussions on collaborations and referral patterns. In the past, lunch meetings were thought of as a good way to form connections; however, in busy managed care practices, physicians rarely have the luxury of a long lunch hour. Good communication and feedback from the psychologist to the pediatrician is the key to long-lasting professional relationships. Pediatric residency or fellowship trainings that incorporate interdisciplinary team management concepts can be very useful in alerting pediatricians to the potential of collaboration with other professionals.

When a mental health professional is part of the health care team, a number of effective patterns of collaboration can be developed. This is true in private practice as well as in other clinic settings. For example, when a pediatrician encounters a problem related to mental health, the on-site consultant is engaged, and a joint plan is developed for further assessment or appropriate intervention. Empowering the parents to request an individual education plan, jointly exploring family dynamics concerning discipline problems, and pointing out reinforcement of undesirable attention-getting behaviors are all common examples of situations that can be helped on the spot with this approach, as illustrated by the following case example:

A little girl who had choked on chow mein noodles developed a phobia of eating and lost 8 kilograms in 3 weeks. When the child was brought to her pediatrician, the pediatrician asked the mother and child to meet with him and the clinic's child psychologist. The child psychologist provided diagnostic clarification (e.g., anxiety/ phobia vs. eating disorder) and talked extensively with the mother about setting up a reward/contingency program to reinforce appropriate caloric intake. With the pediatrician, the psychologist then followed the child's progress.

It has also been shown that mental health referral is more likely to be successful with this team approach, reducing noncompliance with mental health referrals from approximately 60% when the mental health professional was off site to about 30% when the mental health expert was part of the team (D. Meichenbaum, personal communication, April 23, 2002).

FUTURE DIRECTIONS OF PEDIATRICS

The future of pediatrics is very difficult to predict at this time of rapid change in our society, in health economics, and in patterns of care. Some believe pediatricians might develop into specialists rather than primary care practitioners, which of course would require a drastic change in both preparation and practice. Others feel that, by including behavioral and psychosocial training, primary care pediatricians would more adequately meet patient needs and provide more service to the community.

As our community is becoming more complex, we are recognizing more patients and families with primary concerns that relate to psychosocial, emotional, and behavioral problems. Traditional medical education did not prepare pediatricians adequately for this part of their practice nor emphasize the need for cooperation with other health professionals in responding to these issues. Last but not least, pediatricians increasingly face the complex and severe problems encountered by the long-term survivors of dramatic new treatment modalities for previously terminal diseases.

ACKNOWLEDGMENT   We gratefully acknowledge Stephanie Marcy, our on-site psychologist, for her insights and help with this chapter.

References

Ambulatory Pediatric Association. (1990). *30th anniversary—The Ambulatory Pediatric Association: Its history and the collection of the George Armstrong Lectureships (1960–1990)*. McLean, VA: Author.

Briggs-Gowan, M. J., Carter, A. S., Skuban, E. M., & Horwitz, S. M. (2001). Prevalence of social-emotional and behavioral problems in a community sample of 1- and 2-year-old children. *Journal of the American Academy of Child and Adolescent Psychiatry, 40,* 811–819.

Brosco, J. P. (2001). Weight charts and well-child care: How the pediatrician became the expert in child health. *Archives of Pediatrics and Adolescent Medicine, 155,* 1385–1389.

Burklow, K. A., Vaughn, L. M., Valerius, K. S., & Schultz, J. R. (2001). Parental expectations regarding discussions on psychosocial topics during pediatric office visits. *Clinical Pediatrics, 40,* 555–562.

Chang, R. K., & Halfon, N. (1997). Geographic distribution of pediatricians in the United States: An analysis of the fifty states and Washington, DC. *Pediatrics, 100,* 172–179.

Colon, A. R., & Colon, P. A. (1999). *Nurturing children: A history of pediatrics.* Westport, CT: Greenwood Press.

Committee on Psychosocial Aspects of Child and Family Health, American Academy of Pediatrics. (2001). The new morbidity revisited: A renewed commitment to the psychosocial aspects of pediatric care. *Pediatrics, 108,* 1227–1230.

Jellinek, M. S., Murphy, J. M., Little, M., Pagano, M. E., Comer, D. M., & Kelleher, K. J. (1999). Use of the Pediatric Symptom Checklist to screen for psychosocial problems in pediatric primary care: A national feasibility study. *Archives of Pediatrics and Adolescent Medicine, 153,* 254–260.

Newacheck, P. W., Strickland, B., & Shonkoff, J. P. (1998). An epidemiologic profile of children with special health care needs. *Pediatrics, 102,* 117–123.

Phillips, S., Clawson, L., & Osinski, A. (1998). Pediatricians' pet peeves about mental health referrals. *Adolescent Medicine, 9,* 243–258.

Randolph, G. D., & Pathman, D. E. (2001). Trends in the rural–urban distribution of general pediatricians. *Pediatrics, 107,* E18.

Ringel, J. S., & Sturm, R. (2001). Financial burden and out-of-pocket expenditures for mental health across different socioeconomic groups: Results from HealthCare for Communities. *Journal of Mental Health Policy and Economics, 4*(3), 141–150.

Task Force on the Future of Pediatric Education. (2000). The future of pediatric education II. Organizing pediatric education to meet the needs of infants, children, adolescents, and young adults in the 21st century. *Pediatrics, 105,* 157–212.

U.S. Surgeon General's Report on Mental Health. (1999). Retrieved August 11, 2002, from http://www.surgeongeneral.gov/library/mentalhealth/home.html

8

Obstetrics-Gynecology

David Turok
Jennifer T. Van Horn

Vignettes from a composite "day in the life" for Dr. Marjorie Fecund, a primary care obstetrician-gynecologist, might look something like the following:

When Dr. Fecund arrives at her office this particular morning, the first of her 15 prenatal patients is already waiting. Reviewing her day's schedule and hoping she is not double-booked too much, Dr. Fecund estimates that if she spends about 5 to 10 minutes on average directly with each patient, she will not be too much behind schedule by the end of the day (i.e., she will probably leave the office about 6:00 p.m.).

Her third patient, Shirley Waverly, is in the first trimester of pregnancy; she seems tense and upset. Dr. Fecund recalls that Shirley's first pregnancy ended in a miscarriage, and this precipitated considerable stress. In fact, Dr. Fecund put her on selective serotonin reuptake inhibitors for 6 months following the miscarriage.

Today, she asks Shirley what is wrong. Shirley reveals that her husband threatened that unless she ends this pregnancy (which she wants), he

will leave her. Dr. Fecund acknowledges that this is a very difficult situation that requires more than the 10 minutes she has available in today's appointment and offers Shirley a longer appointment later in the week. Shirley bursts into tears at this, and Dr. Fecund recommends she contact a therapist. Not knowing who is a provider on Shirley's plan (and in fact not really having a clear recommendation), Dr. Fecund suggests that Shirley ask the office manager to find her a therapist who is on her panel.

In the midst of seeing her next few patients, Dr. Fecund is paged to the hospital to do an emergency cesarean section for a patient in labor. The remainder of the patients this morning are asked if they would like to reschedule, and about half of them do so. Two hours later, Dr. Fecund returns to see her office patients.

By midafternoon, she has seen a combination of patients with obstetric and gynecologic issues: Joan Jasper is healthy and very excited as she is now 2 weeks from her due date with her first pregnancy. Colleen O'Malley is the 80-year-old mother of a perimenopausal patient of Dr. Fe-

cund's who came in for routine gynecologic care. Ms. O'Malley is a widow who lives independently, although her daughter is concerned about her increasing forgetfulness. Dr. Fecund performs a physical exam and is relieved to learn that the patient's very thorough internist is managing all of her medical issues and has initiated a conversation regarding future assisted-living options. Sara W. is a 17-year-old who recently became sexually active. She has not yet used a method of contraception, but has come in today because she does not want to become pregnant. She is ecstatic at the news of a negative pregnancy test and wants to begin the contraceptive patch. She is also a smoker who is not interested in quitting at this time and notes that "all of my friends smoke."

Dr. Fecund's last patient of the day is Tracy Behr. She was diagnosed with postpartum depression in the month after the birth of her now 2-year-old daughter. Dr. Fecund was present at the delivery and remembers referring Tracy to a psychiatrist when her symptoms worsened after several weeks of treatment. Dr. Fecund never received information regarding Tracy's mental health care and has not seen her since then. Now she has returned because she feels comfortable with Dr. Fecund.

It turns out that Tracy has tried two different antidepression medications and neither worked. Her symptoms of poor sleep, weight gain, and feelings of worthlessness have persisted. Throughout the visit, Tracy's daughter Emily is crying, throwing patient handouts around the room, and trying to climb onto the exam table. Tracy expresses her tremendous disappointment in her parenting skills. While Emily is pulling on Tracy's sleeve, an area of bruising on Tracy's arm is exposed.

This prompts Dr. Fecund to ask of any other areas of injury and the possibility of domestic violence. At this point, Tracy begins crying as she relates to Dr. Fecund her husband's increasingly abusive behavior. Dr. Fecund turns the conversation to offering support for Tracy and then suggests documenting the presence of her injuries and finally referring her to a counseling center for women exposed to domestic violence.

These few of the roughly 30 patient encounters that Dr. Fecund will have on a typical day illus-

trate some of the psychosocial aspects of primary care obstetrics-gynecology.

Obstetrician-gynecologists specialize in the medical care of women, including care related to pregnancy and the reproductive tract. Obstetrics and gynecology is a complex specialty. It includes both medical and surgical aspects of care and both inpatient and outpatient medicine. The Association of American Medical Colleges defines an obstetrician-gynecologist as a physician who "possesses special knowledge, skills and professional capability in the medical and surgical care of the female reproductive system and associated disorders. This physician serves as a consultant to other physicians, and as a primary care physician for women" (American Association of Medical Colleges, 2002). The American College of Obstetrics and Gynecology (ACOG) puts it more simply in the logo on their web site: "Women's health care physicians" (http://www.acog.org; retrieved May 30, 2003). Approximately 41,000 obstetrician-gynecologists are practicing in the United States (Pasco & Smart, 2003), and the majority practice some form of primary care.

TRAINING

The obstetrician-gynecologist completes 4 years of residency training. The obstetrical portion of training includes emphases on preconception health, pregnancy, labor and childbirth, postpartum care, genetics, genetic counseling, and prenatal diagnosis. The gynecologic portion of residency training covers women's general health, including care of reproductive organs, breasts, and sexual function. Gynecologists also screen for cancer at multiple sites, manage hormonal disorders, treat infections, and are trained in surgery to correct or treat pelvic organ and urinary tract problems, including cancer of the reproductive organs. Three years of fellowship training is required to practice in one of the subspecialty areas (e.g., gynecologic oncology, maternal-fetal medicine [high-risk pregnancies], reproductive endocrinology [problems of hormone and reproductive function], and urogynecology [urogenital prolapse and incontinence]). There is little exposure to psychiatry or psychology in most training programs.

OBSTETRICS-GYNECOLOGY AS A PRIMARY CARE SPECIALTY

Although obstetrics-gynecology is frequently considered a secondary or tertiary care medical specialty, obstetrician-gynecologists often serve as primary care physicians for their patients. Indeed, the majority of women aged 20 to 40 years get their primary medical care from their obstetrician-gynecologist (Ling, Laube, Nolan, Smith, & Stovall, 1996). Seltzer (1998) noted "most of us serve as the principal or only physician for at least a subset of our patients" (p. 3). In a 1992 survey of obstetrician-gynecologists, more than half indicated that they spend more than half of their time providing primary and preventive care (Seltzer, 2002). Nonetheless, it is also true that a number of women patients also have another primary care physician.

Federal legislation has now designated obstetrician-gynecologists as primary care physicians. In addition, recently enacted Medicare statutes allow women to choose an obstetrician-gynecologist as their primary care physician (Fink et al., 2001). In 1993, ACOG formed a task force on primary and preventive health care that identified three levels of care that could be provided by obstetrician-gynecologists: traditional specialty care, primary and preventive care, and extended primary care. The ACOG definition of extended primary care fits most closely with that of the Institute of Medicine (Donaldson, Yordy, Lohr, & Vanselov, 1996): "first-contact, comprehensive and ongoing care." Still, a majority of obstetrician-gynecologists provide gynecologic care as well as some nongynecologic care. In 1996, a primary care requirement was implemented in residency training.

PRACTICE IN OBSTETRICS-GYNECOLOGY

Obstetrician-gynecologists practice in a range of settings, from solo independent practices to large group and public practices. A typical obstetrician-gynecologist sees roughly 30 outpatients per day in visits approximately 15 minutes long for obstetrical patients and 15 to 30 minutes long for gynecology patients. It is common for the obstetrician-gynecologist to spend 2 to 3 days per week in the office and 1 day operating in the hospital. In addition, unpredictable hospital visits are required to deliver babies. As noted, most women seek care from obstetrician-gynecologists during the childbearing years, but often they develop close relationships with their physicians and continue to visit them as their primary care physician. Depending on their location, an increasing number of obstetrician-gynecologists may have midlevel practitioners, such as nurse practitioners or certified nurse midwives, in their practices. These practitioners may have longer visits with patients and focus more on general health, prevention, other primary care issues, or mental health issues.

Typical Patient Problems

The most common disorders treated by primary care obstetrician-gynecologists besides prenatal and postpartum care are menstrual disorders, pelvic pain, pelvic infections, infertility, incontinence, abnormal pelvic masses, contraception management, menopause management, and abnormal Pap smears.

Mental/Behavioral Health Aspects of Obstetrics-Gynecology

Many of the common complaints and problems brought to obstetrician-gynecologists by their patients have a strong mental/behavioral health component. Pregnancy is the most common "problem" brought to the obstetrician-gynecologist. Although for most obstetrical patients the prospect of giving birth is satisfying, it is important to realize that pregnancy carries with it enormous physiological and psychological changes. Even "uncomplicated" pregnancy involves a weight gain of 25 to 35 pounds, an increase in blood volume of roughly 50%, and the growth and emergence of a 7-pound newborn human who permanently alters the family structure, all within a 40-week period. Thus, although pregnancy will ideally be uncomplicated, it is never uneventful.

In cases of complicated pregnancy, there may be health risks for the mother and survival risk or potentially lifelong developmental problems for the newborn. In addition, the prevalence rates of psychiatric problems in the population at large suggest that 15% to 25% of pregnant women will have preexisting mental health problems that may be worsened by the pregnancy. For women who are not in this risk group but who experience a complicated pregnancy, there is a greater likelihood of associated mental illness; in fact, Kendell, Chalmers, and Platz (1987) found a threefold increase in the rate of psychiatric admissions in the month following delivery compared to the previous 2 years. Although postpartum depression is not as prevalent as once believed, it is still an issue for approximately 8% to 15% of mothers (Cox, Murray, & Chapman, 1993; Pop, Essed, de Geus, van Son, & Komproe, 1993), and the consequences of untreated postpartum depression can be significant.

Domestic violence is another issue of concern, with reported prevalence rates of 1% to 20% during pregnancy (Gazmararian et al., 1997).

The association of pelvic pain with abuse history is recognized by most primary care obstetrician-gynecologists; however, it is difficult to establish a causal relationship between the two. In addition, chronic pelvic pain and depression often coexist, and pelvic pain can be a prominent symptom of somatoform disorder as well.

Obstetrician-gynecologists also have begun to focus more on smoking cessation for their pregnancy patients because accumulating evidence suggests both that smoking during pregnancy poses risks to the developing fetus and that the time of pregnancy is one when smoking cessation efforts may be more likely to succeed.

Other issues of particular concern to women that might be commonly brought to their gynecologist would include sexual assault, rape, premenstrual syndrome, and menopausal mood changes.

Frustrations of Obstetrician-Gynecologists in Relation to Mental Health Issues

The interest of obstetrician-gynecologists in treating their patients' psychological conditions varies considerably. At one extreme, some obstetrician-gynecologists have obtained training in psychiatry; at the other end of the continuum, other obstetrician-gynecologists find frustrating the subtle (they might call it vague) and lengthy process of

psychological assessment and improvement. Surgical techniques, in contrast, are precise and fairly rapid in their effects.

Diagnostic uncertainty also frustrates some obstetrician-gynecologists. Most physicians are accustomed to ordering and obtaining laboratory and radiological tests of physiological measures that are precise in their results. In addition, most complaints can be assessed with a physical examination that provides direct sensory data to the physician. In contrast, the somewhat murky process of assessing many psychological complaints, especially psychosomatic ones, is a barrier to their enthusiastic treatment of such issues.

Even those obstetrician-gynecologists who are eager to help with their patients' psychological well-being face a number of barriers to doing so. The primary barrier is time. As noted in the vignette, the typical obstetrical visit is 5 to 10 minutes long, and there are many medical issues that may need to be addressed. Second, even if time is spent in psychiatric assessment and office counseling, reimbursement for these activities is often difficult to obtain. Limited resources for referral and treatment are further barriers. Although it may be easy for obstetrician-gynecologists to find a pediatrician to refer their patients for postnatal care, they are often unclear who in the mental health community would be good referral resources for their patients.

Suggestions for Effective Collaboration Between Mental Health Practitioners and Obstetrician-Gynecologists

The psychologist who is interested in further collaboration with obstetrician-gynecologists could consider any of the following strategies:

1. The women the psychologist is currently treating may well have an obstetrician-gynecologist as their primary care physician. The psychologist could request permission to collaborate with the obstetrician-gynecologist. Most obstetrician-gynecologists would appreciate this information and would be more likely to refer patients in the future.
2. For patients who do not have an obstetrician-gynecologist or a primary care physician, the psychologist could provide a referral to an obstetrician-gynecologist after

determining that the obstetrician-gynecologist of choice is taking new patients.

3. Once contact has been made with an obstetrician-gynecologist, it is reasonable to inquire if they have particular needs with which the primary care psychologist could help. Particularly if the psychologist offers treatment for smoking, obesity, depression, relationship problems, infertility, and domestic violence, these would be of interest to the obstetrician-gynecologist.

4. The psychologist could call the local ACOG chapter or obstetrics-gynecology department of a local medical school or hospital and offer to give a talk on a relevant topic. There are often annual meetings of local obstetrics-gynecology societies, and large clinics even have their own conference times at which a presentation might be welcome. Such a talk might range from "what services I provide and how to refer to me" to a specific presentation on a psychological topic of relevance to women's health.

Qualities obstetrician-gynecologists seek in any specialist to whom they would refer include having respect for their ongoing relationships with their primary care patients, keeping them informed of relevant aspects of treatment, and being supportive of their work with their patients. All of these principles would apply to psychologists who wish to collaborate with an obstetrician-gynecologist. Of course, fundamentally, the obstetrician-gynecologist wants to collaborate with psychologists who treat their patients well and do good work.

Avoiding Common Mistakes of Mental Health Specialists in Relating to Obstetrician-Gynecologists

It is important that psychologists recognize the pace of obstetrical care. Not uncommonly in obstetrics, decisions about care take place in a matter of minutes; prompt responsiveness to the obstetrician-gynecologist's requests will be highly appreciated, and lengthy delays in response will not. The primary care psychologist should keep in mind that an average "page return time" for the obstetrician-gynecologist is 2 to 5 minutes, and the obstetrician-gynecologist may have little pa-tience with a call return time that is measured in hours or days.

FUTURE DIRECTIONS OF OBSTETRICS-GYNECOLOGY OF INTEREST TO PSYCHOLOGISTS

As in almost all areas of medicine, the field of obstetrics and gynecology is evolving into more specialized care and is likely to be affected strongly by the "genomic revolution." For example, the increased availability of prenatal genetic tests, and even genetic testing of preimplantation in-vitro embryos, will have significant impact. Couples may be required to make agonizing choices about pregnancy outcome, and psychologists could provide help to patients making these difficult decisions. Psychologists could also help gynecologic patients decide whether to undergo screening for genetic cancer syndromes (the psychological implications in these situations include the uncertainty of diagnosis and implications for offspring).

References

American Association of Medical Colleges. (2002). Careers in medicine: obstetrics-gynecology. Retrieved May 29, 2003, from http://www.aamc.org/students/cim/pub_obgyn.htm

American College of Obstetrics and Gynecology Task Force of Primary and Preventive Health Care. (1993). *The obstetrician-gynecologist and primary-preventive healthcare.* Washington, DC: Author.

Cox, J. L., Murray, D. L., & Chapman, G. (1993). A controlled study of the onset duration and prevalence of postnatal depression. *British Journal of Psychiatry, 163,* 27–31.

Donaldson, M., Yordy, K., Lohr, K., & Vanselov, N. (Eds.). (1996). *Primary care: America's health in a new era.* Washington, DC: National Academy Press.

Fink, K. S., Baldwin, L. M., Lawson, H. W., Chan, L., Rosenblatt, R. A., & Hart, L. G. (2001). The role of gynecologists in providing primary care to elderly women. *Journal of Family Practice, 50,* 153–158.

Gazmararian, J. A., Lazorick, S., Spitz, A. M., Ballard, T. J., Saltzman, L. E., & Marks, J. S. (1997). Prevalence of violence against pregnant women. *Journal of the American Medical Association, 277*(14), 1125.

Kendell, R. E., Chalmers, J. C., & Platz, C. (1987). Epidemiology of puerperal psychoses. *British Journal of Psychiatry, 150,* 662.

Kessler, R. C., Barker, P. R., Colpe, L. J., Epstein, J. F., Gfroerer, J. C., Hiripi, E., et al. (2003). Screening for serious mental illness in the general population. *Archives of General Psychiatry, 60,* 184–189.

Ling, F. W., Laube, D. W., Nolan, T. E., Smith, R. P., & Stovall, T. G. (1996). *Primary care in gynecology.* Baltimore, MD: Williams and Wilkins.

Pasco, T., & Smart, D. (2003). *Physician characteristics and distribution in the United States: 2003–4 Edition.* Chicago: AMA Press.

Pop, V. J. M., Essed, G. G. M., de Geus, C. A., van Son, M. M., & Komproe, I. H. (1993). Prevalence of post partum depression? *Acta Obstetricia et Gynecologica Scandinavica, 72,* 354.

Seltzer, V. L. (1998). Obstetrician gynecologists: Women's health care physicians. *Obstetrics and Gynecology, 91,* 1–5.

III

PERSPECTIVES AND ISSUES

9

Developmental Perspectives

Jerome Kagan

A deep understanding of adolescents or adults who have developed beliefs, habits, or moods that interfere with adaptation to their society is difficult because a large number of conditions make separate contributions to each particular individual profile. Some conditions are biological; others are derivative of family experiences during the opening decade; still others are traceable to the social class of the child's family, birth order, school performance, and the historical era during which the adolescent years are spent. And some events are unpredictable. If Justice Fortas had not been a member of the Supreme Court when Harry Truman was president, Lyndon Johnson would not have been elected to Congress; as a result, he probably would not have become president of the United States. If Charles Darwin's uncle had not agreed to travel half a day to persuade Charles's father to let his son go on the *Beagle* voyage, Alfred Wallace might have been celebrated as the theorist of evolution.

This chapter describes some of the major factors that affect the varied personality profiles of adolescents and adults, presented in the order in which each exerts its most important influence.

The factors are temperament, parental behaviors toward and with the child, parental values, identifications, social class, birth order, school failure or success, and historical era. However, the method used to generate data must be addressed first because the validity of every scientific conclusion depends on the nature of the evidence. Unfortunately, the quality of evidence documenting the influence of each of the factors is uneven. It is strongest for the effects of temperament, social class, and historical era and weaker for the others. Because questionnaires and interviews are the most common source of information in this domain, it is useful to consider the validity of this form of information.

THE PROBLEMS WITH SELF-REPORT

The notion of self was central to the conceptualization of personality by American psychologists in the 19th and the first half of the 20th century because the referent for personality was the whole person rather than any particular trait. However, history has eroded this position. Freudian ideas became less attractive after World War II, and psychologists returning to the university, who wanted to make their discipline more scientific, insisted that all concepts should rest on objective data rather than on intuition or abstract philosophical concepts. As a result, a cadre of technically trained psychologists exploited the niche that psychoanalysts had occupied and argued that factor analysis of the answers provided by young adults, usually middle-class, white college students filling out questionnaires, could reveal the fundamental dimensions of personality. The most popular personality dimensions, called the Big Five, are based entirely on answers to questionnaires. The problem with these concepts is that questionnaires represent a very particular form of evidence.

Physicians would not rely only on patients' verbal reports to decide on the basic human diseases; economists would not rely only on interviews with consumers to discover fundamental concepts in economics; and few cognitive psychologists would analyze adults' descriptions of their perceptions, memories, and problem solutions to infer the basic cognitive competencies. A personality type is a stable profile of behaviors, beliefs, motives, and moods that differentiates one group of individuals from others, and questionnaires are an inadequate basis for inferring the number of personality types within a culture. Explanations of personality based on other sources of data—observed behavior with or without biological measurements—would reveal that each personality type combines inherited temperamental biases with a cascade of experiences (Kagan, 2002). I consider first the temperamental biases that influence personality development.

THE ROLE OF TEMPERAMENT

A temperamental quality is a relatively stable psychobiological profile, under some genetic control, that combines behavior, emotion, and physiology. At present, the physiological features that are the presumed foundation for each of the large number of temperaments have not been discovered. As a result, scientists rely either on responses to questionnaires or, less often, on behavior to classify a child as a member of a particular temperamental group. It is likely that many, but not all, temperaments will be the result of variations in neurochemistry. The brain contains a very large number of different molecules, along with their receptors, and variation in the concentration of the molecules and the density and location of the receptors affects the excitability of neuronal ensembles and the circuits to which they belong. If children inherit different concentrations of these molecules or different densities of the relevant receptors, there will be a very large number of temperament types.

For example, an enzyme called dopamine-beta-hydroxylase, which is under some genetic control, is necessary for the final step in the synthesis of norepinephrine. Children with very low levels of this enzyme will have low levels of norepinephrine. Because norepinephrine in the brain increases the probability of a fear state, children with low levels of this enzyme should be less fearful. Evidence indicates that boys with conduct disorder, who seem to be minimally fearful of punishment, have very low levels of this enzyme (Rogeness et al., 1988).

Although variation among young children in irritability, activity level, laughter, and attentional style might be temperamental, a great deal of research on temperament has been related to the Thomas and Chess types, called easy versus slow to warm up (Thomas & Chess, 1963). The latter child is shy and timid in unfamiliar social situations; the former is sociable and affectively spontaneous. These two qualities are among the most stable and heritable in human personality, with heritability coefficients ranging between 0.3 and 0.6 (Kagan, 1994). The shy, timid child has also been called the inhibited child; the social, fearless child has been called the uninhibited child.

Children who are inhibited in the second and third years are different from those who are uninhibited as early as 4 months of life. One group of 4-month-old infants, called high-reactive infants, displays a pattern of high motor activity and crying when presented with unfamiliar visual, auditory, and olfactory stimuli. These children are biased to become inhibited children. By contrast, infants who show low levels of motor activity and minimal crying to the same stimulus events, called low-reactive infants, are likely to become un-inhibited in the second and the third years. The behavioral differences between high- and low-reactive infants can be understood if it is assumed that the two groups differ in excitability of the amygdala and its projections to the cortex, brain stem, and autonomic nervous system.

HIGH- AND LOW-REACTIVE INFANTS

I have been following a large group of middle-class, Caucasian children, initially classified at 4 months as high or low reactive, through age 11 years; at that time, their behavior and physiological profiles were evaluated. Four biological signs that imply an excitable amygdala are (a) greater activation of the right rather than the left hemisphere, (b) a large brain stem–evoked potential from the inferior colliculus, (c) a reactive sympathetic nervous system, and (d) a large event-related potential at 400 ms to discrepant visual scenes. About one of every five high reactives and one of every three low reactives preserved both the expected behavioral and their biological patterns at age 11 years. However, fewer than 5% of the children from these two groups developed behavioral and biological profiles characteristic of the complementary temperamental category.

This means that the infant's temperament constrains the likelihood of developing a particular outcome. That is, it can be predicted with great confidence that a high-reactive infant will not be an extremely ebullient, fearless, sociable child who has low cortical and autonomic arousal. Analogously, it is certain that a low-reactive infant will not be an extremely timid, fearful adolescent with high levels of biological and cortical arousal. But prediction of the specific traits each type will possess during adolescence is far less certain.

The suggestion that each temperament constrains more outcomes than it determines applies to environmental conditions as well. If all that is known about a sample of children is that they were born to economically secure, well-educated, nurturant parents and their adult profile must be predicted, the most accurate guesses will refer to characteristics that will not be actualized—criminality, school failure, psychosis, homelessness, and drug addiction. However, predictions of the specific characteristics that will be part of the adult's personality are less likely to be correct. When the promises of the genome project are met and parents will be able to request a complete genomic analysis of their newborn, an expert will be able to tell the parents what the infant will *not* become (schizophrenic, a creative composer), but will be unable to inform them about the characteristics that infant will possess two decades later.

Temperament and Feeling Tone

The quality of a person's perceived body tone, which is influenced by their temperament, has a profound influence on personality development. Spontaneous activity within the body—by the heart, blood vessels, muscles, and gut—is transmitted first to the amygdala and from there to the orbitofrontal prefrontal cortex. If this information pierces consciousness, it motivates the person to interpret the unexpected change in feeling.

Individuals who possess a feeling tone characterized by tension or uneasiness will be motivated to understand why they feel this way. A frequent first guess, especially in Western society, is that they probably violated one of their ethical standards. For example, the person may wonder if he or she had been rude to a friend, harbored a prejudice, or had not made enough of his or her life. The list of possible moral lapses is so long that few will have trouble finding some ethical flaw to explain the unwelcome feeling and, as a consequence, will experience a moment of guilt. This tendency is stronger among inhibited than among uninhibited children because the former possess high sympathetic tone and often become upset when criticized by parents for minor misbehaviors.

Temperament Interacts With Culture

Although temperament makes an important contribution to personality, the individual's past history and current life context are equally significant. A low-reactive infant living in an urban setting in America who experiences a history of inconsistent socialization for asocial or aggressive behavior is at a slightly higher than normal risk for a delinquent career, especially if the child lives in an urban neighborhood provocative of anger, frustration, and temptations to asocial behavior. Some boys diagnosed with conduct disorder display very low heart rates and blood pressures, implying that they might have a higher threshold for becoming fearful of harm or punishment (Raine, Venables, & Williams, 1990). This same child is at far less risk if raised by parents who socialize asocial behavior in an isolated village in Manitoba, Canada.

Although the absolute risk is low, high-reactive infants are a bit more likely than others to develop symptoms of social anxiety during adolescence and adulthood, especially if raised in large cities by parents who fail to help the child deal with unfamiliar events. About 20% of 7-year-old children who had been high-reactive infants showed symptoms of anxiety, compared with less than 5% of all other children. The defining features of social anxiety are feelings of tension, shame, or anxiety linked to meeting new people and worrying about their evaluations. A classic symptom is reluctance to eat in a restaurant because of uncertainty over the proper rituals to implement in a public place. By contrast, phobic patients are afraid of such objects as spiders, snakes, heights, or large animals. None of these objects is unfamiliar, and none evaluates the patient.

The source of the apprehension of the phobic is the possibility of harm or contamination. Panic disorder is characterized by unpredictable surges in autonomic activity that produce a rapid heartbeat, dry mouth, sudden sweating, irregular breathing, or a feeling of suffocation. These unexpected bodily changes can be frightening, especially if the person interprets them as signs of an imminent heart attack or, perhaps, of going crazy. The patients who develop a strong conditioned fear of the next autonomic surge may decide to remain at home; they are called *agoraphobic*. Thus, social anxiety, phobia, and panic disorder are symptom clusters with special biologies and distinctive thoughts about the target of their fear. It appears that high-reactive infants are especially vulnera-

ble to social anxiety but not to the other two symptom categories.

Temperament, history, and current context are not additive, and each has its most important influence at different periods in development. Although the temperamental contribution exerts its force first, the social environment begins to shape infants of varied temperaments into different profiles within the first year.

Advantages and Disadvantages of Each Type

Although many American parents assume that low-reactive children have all the advantages, each of the two temperament types has both advantages and disadvantages in contemporary American society. A technological economy requires a college education, and the better the college, the higher the probability of attaining a challenging and economically productive career. The high-reactive individual is more concerned over failure to obtain good grades and, therefore, is more likely to have an academic record that will gain admission to a better college.

In addition, our society needs adults who prefer to work in settings in which they can titrate their uncertainty. These adults often choose intellectual vocations because this work allows some control over each day's events in settings in which unanticipated interactions with strangers can be held to a minimum. American society requires these vocational roles and rewards such individuals with respect and financial security. Further, contemporary adolescents are confronted with many temptations that promise pleasure, peer acceptance, and self-enhancement if they are willing to take some risks. Driving at high speeds, experimenting with drugs, enjoying unprotected sex, and cheating on examinations are four temptations with potentially undesirable consequences.

There are advantages to being a low-reactive infant who becomes an uninhibited child. Sociability and a willingness to take career and economic risks are adaptive traits in contemporary America. The young adult who was willing to leave home to attend a better college or accept a better job is likely to gain a more challenging position than one who stays close to home because of a reluctance to confront the uncertainties of a distant place. Thus, the account is balanced. Each temperament type has a set of burdens and a set of opportunities.

FAMILY EXPERIENCE

Variation in parental behavior toward children assumes its greatest importance during the first decade of a child's life (Maccoby, 1980). Parents provide several classes of experience that can have a profound influence on children. One of the most robust scientific facts is that a child's mental and cognitive development is facilitated if parents provide a great deal of stimulus variety and promote language development in their children (Kagan, 1984). Hence, parents who play with and talk to their children and present them with a degree of variety that can be understood will promote cognitive development. Therefore, academic success, which influences adult personality in our culture, is partially dependent on parental behavior with young children.

Parents also influence children through praise and punishment of particular actions and values. The ethical standards a child learns are due, in part, to the behaviors and intentions that are rewarded or punished. If parents are consistent in disciplining the child for disobedience, they are likely to create a 5-year-old who does not seriously violate family and community norms. If a parent praises school success, the child is likely to be concerned with school performance, at least during the elementary years.

A third source of influence involves parental communications indicating that they value their child. This experience has become more important in our society during the last two centuries than it was in the past. Humans have a pervasive tendency to evaluate themselves as good or bad (Kagan, 1984). Children who grow up in third world villages and who have to gather wood, help prepare supper, take care of infants, and wash clothes realize that they are of value to the family and, therefore, know they are good. As a result, no parent has to tell his or her children that they are loved. Children know they are of value.

Unfortunately, most middle-class children in contemporary American society make no contribution to their family and therefore must be reassured of their goodness. That is one reason for the importance of parental behaviors and communications that inform the child that he or she is valued. However, parents can love the child and not display a great deal of physical affection. For example, John Stuart Mill recalled that his father was a wonderful person, but not an emotionally close one (Mill, 1871). Because our culture equates parental love with kissing and embracing, some modern Americans have a hard time understanding that a child can feel loved, and can love a parent, even though there is not a great deal of physical affection between them.

All parents affect their children, indirectly, through a process called *identification*, which can be extremely important. Children assume that they possess some of the psychological qualities of their parents and often experience vicarious affect when the parent experiences an emotional event. These two phenomena define identification. The child with a parent who is popular and talented will assume that she, too, has some of those characteristics and will experience pride in that fact. However, many parents find it difficult to hide their less admirable traits, and if the parent is perceived as incompetent, unpopular, or unjust, the child may be ashamed or anxious.

THE INFLUENCE OF SOCIAL CLASS

Children identify not only with their parents and close relatives, but also with their ethnic and social class groups. The signs young children use to construct the category of class include residence, neighborhood, and material possessions. Most 7-year-olds have no trouble distinguishing drawings of homes that represent poor and wealthy families. But because parents do not usually remind their children of their social class category and no special rituals or holidays define class membership, discovery of one's social class is conceptually difficult and less uniform and does not form before 6 or 7 years of age.

Class has a greater potential for shame in the United States than it does in many other countries because many Americans believe that hard work and intelligence are all that are needed to gain the wealth that has become, in this century, a primary feature of personal worth. Ten-year-olds who identify with the status of their economically disadvantaged families are vulnerable to feelings of shame or impotence if they wonder whether their parents are lazy or incompetent.

However, identification with a less advantaged social class can provide some protection against shame or guilt if the young adolescent generates reasons for the family's class position that remove some of the responsibility for their status. These protective beliefs include the notions that the rich are corrupt and morally flawed; secure jobs in a capitalist society are scarce; and employers are prejudiced against the poor. Each of these interpretations permits the adolescent who identifies with a disadvantaged family to mute some dysphoria. These protections are becoming more difficult to exploit as American society tries to eliminate prejudice and provide more opportunities for the poor. As the psychological protection is torn away, adolescents from poor families confront their status without a healing rationalization.

Of course, the number of poor families in the city or town affects the strength of the identification with the family's social class. A belief in a family's economic disadvantage is most distinctive in societies in which many are affluent, as is true for modern Western nations. Although over 90% of residents in many isolated villages in underdeveloped countries are poor in an absolute sense, they often feel less hopelessness because the individuals are less conscious of the difference between their economic status and that of those who live in large cities hundreds or thousands of miles away.

Conversely, identification with a privileged family can help protect the child against anxiety. George Homans (1984), an influential Harvard sociologist, noted in a memoir written shortly before his death that he coped with his intense childhood anxiety over his poor school grades and unpopularity with peers by reminding himself that he could trace his pedigree back to John Adams. Every child is emotionally moved by stories of heroic family members who possessed qualities symbolic of strength, bravery, compassion, or unusual intelligence. Pulitzer Prize–winning author Frank McCourt's chronically unemployed and occasionally drunk father reminded him that, as a son of Ireland, he possessed the courage of those who came before him. These family myths help children cope with anxiety, shame, and guilt.

BIRTH ORDER

The child's birth order, whether first, second, third, or last-born, also contributes to personality. If scientists compare 1,000 firstborns with 1,000 later-borns from the same social class, the former are generally more responsible, obtain higher grades, attend better colleges, and commit fewer crimes (Sulloway, 1996). Further, when a stress or challenge occurs, firstborns are less likely than later-borns to develop psychological symptoms. By contrast, later-borns are more pragmatic, less idealistic, a little more rebellious, and more likely to develop psychological problems (Sulloway, 1996).

One interpretation of this fact requires the assumption that a firstborn growing up in a traditional American home perceives the world as relatively orderly because parents are predictably nurturant and consistently discipline high standards for accomplishment. The firstborn child identifies with the parents and perceives the world as a just place where, if one does what one is told, all will be well. As firstborn 6-year-olds leave home to enter school, they ask implicitly, "What is it that you want me to do?"

The world looks different to later-borns. Imagine a later-born 2-year-old who suddenly confronts a firstborn intruding into his or her sphere of activity. Firstborns seize toys from their younger siblings, are permitted to stay up later at night, and receive more expensive presents on birthdays and at Christmas. One reasonable outcome of these differences is that later-borns see the world as a little unjust; firstborns see it as fair. As a result, firstborns are more concerned with the approval of authority, want to keep harmonious relations with parents and teachers, and have greater trust of, but less hostility toward, authority than later-borns.

Firstborns who select science as a vocation are more likely to reject a new theory if it is opposed by older, respected scientists. More defiant later-borns are likely to favor the new theory. Frank Sulloway (1996) studied a large number of revolutions in science where the creative discovery was of concern to the larger society. Some of these revolutions included the ideas of Copernicus, Bacon, Freud, and Darwin. Sulloway determined what eminent scientists of the same era said about each revolutionary idea in the 10-year period following its original dissemination and whether the scientist was for or against the new idea and whether the scientist was a firstborn or later-born. Scientists who agreed with the new idea were likely to be later-borns; those who opposed it were likely to be firstborns. Thus, a scholar's attitude toward a new scientific idea is influenced by birth order.

SCHOOL SUCCESS

The child's history of success or failure in school is an important developmental factor in personality development in modern societies because personal achievement is valued, and a technical vocation, which permits achievement, usually requires college or postgraduate training. Success in school always depends on the child's intellectual abilities, but it also depends on the size of the community. If the child's talent is held constant, the probability of success is greater if the child attends a small school in a smaller town or city rather than a large school in an urban area.

Consider two 9-year-old girls with IQs of 120 who are popular and have nurturing parents. One girl lives in a small town in Missouri; the other lives in Chicago. The former will confront very few girls as successful as she is, and if she stays in this town through high school, will graduate with a perception of herself as extremely talented because she compares herself with the other girls in the town and recognizes she is in the top 5% of her peer group. The girl growing up in Chicago will know over 100 girls who are more talented than she is and, as a result, will learn humility. A majority of the first group of astronaut candidates grew up in small towns that did not have museums, aquariums, or large libraries. If a person is going to succeed in life in an extraordinary way, it is necessary to have an illusion about self. The adolescent must believe that he or she is more talented or courageous than others. This illusion is harder to establish if there are several hundred children of the same age who are more able, attractive, or courageous.

HISTORICAL ERA

The historical era during which the adolescent years are spent can influence adult personality. Although the years of age from 4 to 8 are important for the establishment of identifications, 8-year-olds are too young to understand the deep premises of their society. For example, religious piety permeated life in 17th century New England, and children growing up during this era could not have known that the devil was a premise and not a fact.

The important intellectual advances that emerge at 13 to 16 years of age motivate youths to brood about their beliefs because their experiences are often inconsistent with their childhood ideas. However, at unpredictable times, historical events, like a war or an economic depression, provoke changes in ideology as the adolescent contrasts the beliefs held prior to the historical event with those generated by the new social conditions. Adolescents who are beginning to synthesize the assumptions they will rely on for the rest of their lives are especially receptive to historical events that challenge their existing beliefs. Contemporary youths in Bosnia and Afghanistan have witnessed cruelties that will make deep skeptics of their generation. It will make little difference to many 18-year-olds in these countries whether they had caring or indifferent mothers if they lived through rape, artillery shells, and the senseless death of friends and family.

The economic depression in America from 1930 to 1940 left about one third of American families chronically anxious over their economic security. Children were reminded daily that they should be careful with their clothes, mothers skimped on meals, and fathers drove rusty cars. A large proportion of Americans who were adolescents during those years, now in their seventh or eighth decade, saved more money than the generation before or after them and conducted their lives with a continuous concern over financial loss.

As a young man, Samuel Beckett witnessed the anarchy that tore through Ireland in the early decades of the last century. He probably exploited his childhood memory of the senseless violence of the Easter uprising when he had one of the tramps in *Waiting for Godot* say, "This has become merely insignificant," and let the other reply, "Not enough." Protest against the Vietnam War at the end of the 1960s turned large numbers of privileged American adolescents against the values of their parents and established authority. High school youths defiantly left their classrooms to march in protest against the war and got away with it. It is heady for a 16-year-old to defy the rules of authority and avoid punishment. These experiences erode a tendency to worry over coming to work at 9 a.m. and leaving at 4 p.m. Many of these middle-class youths thumbed their nose at authority because they happened to be born during a thin slice of time when segments of American society were uncertain which behaviors were legitimate. When history tears a hole in the fabric of consensual assumptions, the mind flies through it into a space free of hoary myth to invent a new conception of self, ethics, and society.

The historical era in which one lives also influences a person's interpretation of symptoms. The diary of John Cheever, who was born in 1912 and died in the second half of the 20th century, and the diary and letters of Alice James, William and Henry James's sister, who died about 100 years earlier than Cheever, suggest that both writers inherited a similar diathesis for a melancholic mood. But Cheever, whose premises about human nature were formed when Freudian theory was popular, assumed that his depression was because of childhood experiences, and he relied on psychotherapy to overcome the conflicts he imagined his family had created. By contrast, Alice James, born in the summer of 1848, believed, with the majority of her contemporaries, that she inherited her dour mood, and her childhood experiences were irrelevant. Public and medical opinion assumed that women, especially those who were well educated, were susceptible to depression because they inherited an insufficient supply of psychic energy. Thus, when Alice James had a serious depression at 19 years of age, she assumed it was because of her heredity and decided, after a decade of suffering, that she wished to die. The different cultural contexts in which

these two writers lived exerted profound influences on their understanding of their moods and the coping strategies they selected.

SUMMARY

The development of a life, like the development of a freak storm, requires the conjunction of a large number of independent factors coming together over the first two decades. I suggest that the child's belief (or lack of belief) in personal virtue, which is influenced by many factors, is a seminal determinant of personality and pathology.

Humans are motivated for two different goals each time they select one action over an alternative. One goal is the attainment of a feeling of pleasure that originates in one or more of the sensory modalities. The second, qualitatively different, goal has its origin in thought rather than sensation. The desired psychological state is a conceptual consonance between a moral standard and an action or belief. When the experience of consonance occurs, the individual momentarily experiences a special feeling because his or her behavior, or acquired property, is in accord with a representation personally categorized as "good." No word in English names this feeling with precision, but *virtue* comes close. People eat cake for the sensory delight of its taste, but on occasion, will refuse cake to remain loyal to a standard that urges avoidance of too many calories.

Children and adults spend a great deal of every day testing their competence against a standard. Six-year-olds build sand castles and adults climb rugged mountains because implementing actions that are guided by an idea of perfection is as much a biologically prepared disposition as the pursuit of sweet tastes and the avoidance of pain. After each person protects the self from harm or privation, the affirmation of self's virtue takes precedence over the search for sensory pleasure for most hours of each day.

The pursuit, and eventual capture, of more power, status, wealth, romance, and good brandy, which contemporary Western society treats as sensory pleasures, can be strategies to affirm one's virtue. In societies in which frugality is prized, as in Puritan New England, individuals hide their wealth. In contemporary America, where wealth has become an unconflicted sign of virtue, one feels obligated to display it. A winter holiday in the Caribbean often serves as a motive to do what one ought to do as frequently as it serves the wish to avoid blizzards. "I am doing what I should be doing" is often the silent voice behind a louder declaration, "I am doing what I enjoy."

The human moral sense, like a spider's web, is a unique product of evolution that has been maintained because it ensures our survival. The variation among children, adolescents, and adults in the belief that they do or do not possess virtue is central to their personality and the symptoms they might develop.

Despite the extraordinary variety in human skills, prevalent moods, and beliefs, which are a product of temperament and experience, every person seeks the same set of fundamental goals. Humans wish to be free of hunger, privation, harm, criticism, rejection by those whom they adopt as reference groups, and doubt over personal virtue. Doubt can be the product of a perception of lower status, childhood identifications with role models they regard as lacking virtue, failure at the tasks society requires, and a dysthymic feeling tone that the individual interprets as guilt.

Although it takes almost 20 years to create a coherent judgment of the self's virtue, once that judgment is made, it is difficult, but not impossible, to change. This dynamic can be phrased in a different way, although the deep meaning is similar.

Each life history creates nodes of uncertainty over one's level of talent, acceptability to others, wealth, status, and moral character. A particular source of uncertainty that is chronic, or felt with intensity, during the childhood and adolescent years can produce a persistent doubt over the self's virtue. The clinician's task is first to diagnose the patient's profile of uncertainties and then help the patient understand that the anxiety, depression, or maladaptive symptoms that accompany their beliefs are constructions that can be altered through intellectual analysis of their source and conscious attempts to gain goals that will refute the distorted judgment. The patient with social anxiety can be persuaded that

the anticipation of a stranger's criticism is exaggerated by having the patient confront the source of the fear. The depressed patient can be helped to appreciate that his or her apathy and lack of vitality are the product of a fatalism that feeds on an exaggerated shame or guilt and reluctance to engage challenges that have the risk of failure.

The course of each life can be likened to that of a traveler whose knapsack is slowly filled with doubts, dogma, and desires during the first dozen or so years. Each person spends the adult years trying to empty the heavy load in the knapsack until he or she can confront the opportunities present in each fresh day. Some adults approach this state; most carry their collection of uncertainties, prejudices, and frustrated wishes into middle and old age, trying to prove what must remain uncertain and raging wildly at ghosts.

References

Homans, G. C. (1984). *Coming to my senses: The autobiography of a sociologist.* Somerset, NJ: Transaction Publishers.

Kagan, J. (1984). *The nature of the child.* New York: Basic Books.

Kagan, J. (1994). *Galen's prophecy.* New York: Basic Books.

Kagan, J. (2002). *Surprise, uncertainty, and mental structures.* Cambridge, MA: Harvard University Press.

Maccoby, E. E. (1980). *Social development.* New York: Harcourt.

Mill, J. S. (1871). *Autobiography.* New York: Henry Holt.

Raine, A., Venables, P. H., & Williams, M. (1990). Autonomic orienting responses in 15 year old male subjects and criminal behavior at age 24. *American Journal of Psychiatry, 147,* 933–937.

Rogeness, G. A., Maas, J. W., Javors, M. A., Masedo, C. A., Harris, W. R., & Hoppe, S. K. (1988). Diagnoses, catecholamines, and plasma dopamine-hydroxylase. *Journal of the American Academy of Child and Adolescent Psychiatry, 27,* 121–125.

Sulloway, F. (1996). *Born to rebel.* New York: Pantheon.

Thomas, A., & Chess, S. (1963). *Behavioral individuality in early childhood.* New York: New York University Press.

10

Interpersonal and Family Systems Perspectives

David Waters

Nina Ross

In this chapter, we address the importance to primary care psychologists of an interpersonal-systemic view of persons and their medical and psychological problems. Although the interpersonal aspects of health care have been particularly important in family medicine, a field whose name bespeaks commitment to each patient's context, it is important in all aspects of primary care. Awareness of context facilitates sensitivity to the interpersonal aspects of the practice of medicine. Furthermore, delivery of the highest quality health care requires attention to each patient's unique social context. Psychologists can help physicians look beyond each disease episode to the web of relationships in which the patient is integrated, thereby facilitating broader systemic thinking that may ultimately bring greater healing to patients and their families.

We intend this chapter to be a summary of basic principles, a reminder of their roots for those psychologists well trained in family systems approaches to treatment, and a concise introduction to family systems concepts for those less familiar with these approaches. We also consider

primary care psychologists as valuable consultants to physicians in "systems thinking"; thus, a primary care psychologist with an interpersonal-systems perspective can informally teach his or her primary care physician counterpart about the interpersonal and systemic aspects of patient problems. However, to best help physicians think about illness with psychological sophistication, psychologists need to speak in the medical idiom, using examples and stories to which physicians can relate.

With this in mind, the concepts in this chapter are illustrated with medical case histories that can be used to engage and inform primary care physicians. The psychologist's ability to look at behavior in context brings much-needed perspective to medical care. This perspective can be especially useful when "treatment as usual" is not helping. Physicians remain focused on the individual patient, invoking concepts such as noncompliance. The psychologist trained in systemic thinking may be able to step back and find contextual explanations for the apparent treatment failure. Consider the following case history:

John Martin is a 62-year-old man with end-stage chronic obstructive pulmonary disease, a lung disease caused by years and years of heavy smoking. His lung function is so poor that he must use constant supplemental oxygen. John has been in a nursing home for several months but was asked to leave after a nurse found him smoking yet again. His smoking while on oxygen is extremely dangerous, yet he adamantly refuses to quit.

John's wife, Margaret, took him back home and began the arduous task of caring for him without any help. John was largely confined to bed, incapable of preparing his own meals, and frequently incontinent. He also had spells when his breathing worsened, causing him to become somnolent and confused as the levels of carbon dioxide in his blood increased.

John was brought to the hospital by a rescue squad one morning after such a spell; his wife found him wheezing in bed and was unable to arouse him. On admission, his chest X-ray showed no obvious cause for his worsened breathing. He was treated with steroids and inhaled medications, and his condition improved. Despite his improved breathing, however, John remained listless and depressed, refusing to discuss his continued smoking or plans for discharge from the hospital. Notably, Margaret had not yet come to the hospital after 2 full days. Members of the inpatient team tried to call her at home without success. Frustrated and confused, the team asked the help of the psychologist on the service.

When the team met with Margaret, she emphasized that she was not able to take her husband home at this time; John was belligerent and demanding, and she was so tired. Furthermore, she resented the fact that her husband continued to smoke; it seemed to her that he was bringing trouble onto himself. And she was scared each time she went into his room and was unable to wake him. She lived in fear that she would someday find him dead.

The physician and the psychologist met with Margaret and John together. They helped Margaret to articulate her fears about taking her husband home. John replied that he knew Margaret was afraid, and he did not want to go home to be a burden on her. He explained that he was not trying to get better because there was nothing to get better for; he did not care if he died because there was nothing to live for.

With help from the team, husband and wife discussed how they could both take better care of each other. Margaret learned some management strategies to cope better with John's lung disease, and John brainstormed about ways to share the household chores despite his physical limitations. They talked about their mutual anger and the stalemate that had kept them distant from each other for the last few months. Finally, they agreed that John should return home if adjustments in their home life could be made, and they planned the first round of those adjustments. John was discharged the next day, and the couple was seen regularly in follow-up.

Consider the culture of modern medicine that John and Margaret encountered in the hospital. Our health care system encourages reductionistic thinking at the expense of systemic considerations. The doctor–patient relationship is revered as a privileged exchange between two individuals. Although this view may serve the important concepts of confidentiality and trust, its narrow focus may also exclude crucial players from the therapeutic alliance. Similarly, diagnostic systems, both medical and psychiatric, make no mention of interpersonal effects. We diagnose clinical depression with no simple way to indicate that the depression may be a rational response to being beaten or betrayed. We diagnose tension headaches without any direct way to link the headaches to an overwhelming personal reality that logically leads to muscle tension. Our reimbursement system reinforces this notion that illness is confined to the individual. No billing codes exist for "poorly controlled diabetes secondary to destructive family influences" or "depression due to chaotic family functioning."

Unfortunately, this medical reductionism fails to capture the complexity of human illness. Disease (the physical experience) is a highly individual affair; illness (the lived experience of having a disease) is a social phenomenon. Medical interventions begin with the patient, but quickly radiate to the patient's interpersonal world. Similarly, illness brings consequences and meaning that reach far beyond the individual patient. Accordingly, it is naive and sometimes even dangerous to ignore the systemic aspects of illness. It does not help to persuade the overweight husband to eat differently if his wife, who does all the cooking, perceives the changes as a criticism of her cooking or merely another demand from a demanding man. Well-designed treatment plans will fail if the caregiver becomes depressed and overwhelmed under the regimen. The effective physician must possess a working awareness of the power of the intimate group in creating, maintaining, improving, or exacerbating illness. As experts in human behavior, psychologists have an ideal opportunity to keep the power of intra- and interpersonal events in focus as medical colleagues try to effect changes in individual patients' health.

A PRIMER ON SYSTEMIC THINKING

As we move toward a broader understanding of patients and their interpersonal contexts, we look to systems theory for general concepts and principles. How do systems work? How can systems thinking improve medical care? It is useful to review the essential qualities of systems and how they affect—or even control—human behavior. We underline five of the basic principles of systemic thinking here.

First, the concept of a system, as expressed in general systems theory (von Bertalanffy, 1968) posits that everything constitutes a system, from the tiny system of an individual atom to the vast system of the entire universe. A system is merely a complex of interrelated parts, functioning together in mutually affecting ways. Certainly, the body is a system; the functioning of the whole depends on the functioning of many interrelated parts. Kidney failure leads to an increase in circulating urea, and high levels of urea then decrease cognitive functioning. Gastric ulcers can bleed, lowering red blood cell counts and precipitating heart attacks. Physicians are well versed in this kind of physiological systems theory; they are not accustomed to applying those same principles to the interrelated parts of a family or community. The notion that systemic relationships do not end

at the skin, but go on interpersonally as well, should be a short conceptual leap.

Second, these complexes of interrelated parts are not merely connected, but are connected such that all parts have an impact on other parts and on the whole. As a rule, it is not possible to change a single part of a system in isolation; change begets additional change. Again, this principle is not lost on physicians at the physiological level, but they can be slow to consider it on an interpersonal level. When treating a smoker, it should be (but is not) routine to inquire about the spouse's smoking status, for example. When counseling on diet and exercise, it should be (but is not) routine to enlist the help of a patient's family and friends. Medicine overemphasizes the ability of the individual to make autonomous changes as though he or she were not part of a larger whole.

Third, systems are inherently conservative in that they attempt to maintain dependable patterns of functioning, as if stability might increase efficiency and change might increase risk. This *homeostatic impulse* means that systems find ways to incorporate changes so that the system can continue to function in as stable a manner as possible. For example, a woman whose husband's illness deprives her of companionship, sexual pleasure, and a hoped-for future will more often adapt than break off her marriage. She may reach out to new friends or a new job, learn to find fulfillment in caring for her husband, or develop a rich fantasy life to endure her isolation. All of these shifts maintain homeostasis by enabling married life, with its many stable satisfying elements, to continue in the face of major illness, a life-changing event. Homeostatic impulses can be both adaptive and maladaptive. They are adaptive to the extent that they allow systems to incorporate difficulties without breaking down. They become maladaptive when they stifle growth by encouraging individuals to accommodate systemic changes in unhealthy ways.

The Greenes' fourth child, Davy, was born with spina bifida, a serious birth defect in which the spinal cord fails to develop properly. Over time, their devastation gave way to quiet determination, and the family instituted all of the special care that Davy's condition required. Life became centered on feedings, physical therapy, and doctors' appointments. Davy flourished under the family's devoted care, but with time, this focus became disruptive to family life. Davy's parents began to pull away from each other. They justified the neglect of their marriage to themselves, saying, "We just have too much else on our minds." The couple stayed at home, losing touch with friends and neglecting the various interests that had previously filled their leisure time.

The other children were taught to remain quiet about their own needs so that Davy's many needs could be met; whenever they asked for attention or affection, they were subtly shamed. Robert, the second oldest child in the family, had been an easy-tempered boy; when he began to have angry outbursts at school and at home, his parents immediately began to talk about sending him to live with cousins. The family had adapted well to Davy's birth in terms of disease management, but the patterns of functioning now in place were rigid and unresponsive to the needs of the rest of the family.

Fourth, systems seek and maintain homeostasis using whatever means necessary; fifth, with homeostasis established, they resist change. As a general rule, change is threatening to organisms of all kinds. All species have (and like) their patterns and regularities, and attempts to change an individual or a system are usually met with considerable resistance.

Robert was suspended from school, and the family pediatrician sensed that the Greenes were doing poorly. The pediatrician referred the family to a therapist, who immediately observed that all of the family members were struggling with the changes that the family structure had been forced to absorb. The therapist tried to discuss these changes and was told by Mrs. Greene, "I have a child to keep alive here! Everybody just needs to accept my priorities." As the others indicated that the current family balance was not working, the mother became angrier and more insistent. "I'd love to meet everyone's needs," she said, "but first things come first." She was unable to consider alternative ways to organize the family. When Mr. Greene was asked for his opinion, he

could only say, "Listen to my wife. There's no point in disagreeing with her—she's always right anyway." Both parents rejected the possibility of change; the mother feared that change would kill Davy, and the father felt helpless to oppose his wife.

Even when there are obviously dysfunctional patterns, it can be surprisingly difficult to get members of a system to review its functioning and institute change.

Thus, we have reviewed some basic principles of systems functioning: Systems are actively interconnected at multiple levels; they seek and try to maintain homeostatic functioning; and they resist change. What are the practical implications of these principles for medical care? It must be remembered that illness takes place in the context of emotional and social systems; these systems include family, friends, and community in addition to the actual patient. A seemingly simple medical intervention—"I want you to lose some weight"— may appear to be an isolated new variable, but it is introduced into a complicated array of mutually dependent elements. Change is not easily absorbed by such systems, and the admonition to lose weight no longer seems so simple.

The remainder of this chapter applies systemic principles and concepts of family intervention to clinical medicine. We first consider the family life cycle; next, we consider the effect of an individual's illness on the life of a family. We then reverse the perspective to explore the ways in which family life and social context (or lack thereof) can shape illness. Finally, we discuss the reality of the cycle in which illness and family interact; with illness affecting family and family affecting illness. This cycle continues, often with no obvious starting point and no end. Medicine in context, the hallmark of family medicine, requires physicians and psychologists alike to understand and anticipate this cycle.

The Greenes' family therapist established rapport with the family and began to explore the rigid structure in place. As Mrs. Greene relaxed, she was able to talk about her own childhood experience of feeling neglected in spite of her serious asthma. Her parents had "left her to her own devices," and she was not about to repeat that ne-

glect with Davy. With the therapist's help, the other children were able to say, "That's how we feel—like you are forcing us to take care of ourselves without any help."

Mrs. Greene realized that parental attention and care are crucial for healthy children as well as sick ones, and she speculated that perhaps she had overcorrected for her parents' style. Mr. Greene was then helped to take a more active role in the family, both assisting his wife with daily responsibilities and confronting her gently when she lost perspective. Communication within the family improved, and Davy's disease became part of family life instead of the center of it.

THE FAMILY LIFE CYCLE

Like all living systems and organisms, families have a relatively predictable and important life cycle. It is important to be mindful of this developmental cycle; as with most developmental paradigms, if challenges are not met when they should be, they tend to have long-term effects and to create cumulative trouble. Thus it is important to review the normal cycle of families, with attention to the tasks and dangers of each stage along with opportunities for therapeutic impact. Although a variety of life cycle stages has been identified by various theorists (e.g., Goldenberg & Goldenberg, 1998; Walsh, 2003), we briefly touch on five stages characteristic of the nuclear family: the establishment of the family, the birth of the first child, the children starting school, the children leaving home, and the children becoming their parents' parent. It is also important to note that all of these stages are really processes that happen over time rather than discrete events (Medalie, 1979).

Establishment of the Family

The first task of any new family unit is to establish itself as an independent entity with its own boundaries and rules. In the normal family life cycle, this means that there is a primary transfer of loyalty from the family of origin of each partner to the new family. Pragmatically, what this means is that the new family becomes its own rule maker and is not dominated by the old family

rules. The failure to do this is potentially very problematic; it is the source of mother-in-law jokes because they refer to the loyalty battle between old family and new family.

Thus if the couple does not accomplish this task, they remain subject to the rules they grew up with and lack the requisite autonomy to establish their own values. A couple is courting trouble in terms of their own development if, when Mother comes to visit, "I just can't say no when she moves all our furniture around, even though I resent it," or, "If they invite us on a vacation, we have to go, or it will break their hearts." These patterns tend not to go away in time (unless the parents die) but to get stronger, and they can become a source of major resentment and distance. Such difficulty also often reflects the difficulty of the couple in growing up and taking an adult position in other ways as well.

The Birth of the First Child

The challenge of the birth of the first child is to maintain the couple's connection as they add the new baby to the family. For many couples, the addition of children effectively means the end of a couple's life together as everything becomes organized around the kids. Couples stop going out together ("I couldn't stand to leave the baby!") and stop making choices based on their needs. Often, the sexual relationship never fully recovers—in some cases, never really recovers at all—from the hiatus around the birth and the new demands. Couples can become quite estranged and distant but not even notice it because the new addition provides a strong centerpiece to family life.

The task for new parents is to add the parental role to the lovers' role, not replace it; the establishment of new rituals for getting together is vital. Couples who used to have fun by taking off for the weekend with friends or treating themselves to a weekend at a fancy hotel need to find replacements for those activities rather than eliminating them. Husbands sometimes give in resentfully to the pressure to organize everything around the kids and harbor a sense of displacement that is not good.

A primary care physician can ask the couple at 6 months if an evening out without the baby now is something that would be enjoyable. If the couple had been accustomed to "couple time" and no longer arranges for any, they may be courting trouble, and it can be helpful to interrupt the emerging pattern.

The Children Go Off to School

The significance of this milestone is that, when it is time for children to go to school, parents have to relinquish a major degree of control for the first time. Preschool and other early arrangements tend to be private and contractual, and parents can have a major influence and move the child if they are not satisfied. When the child enters public school (or private school for that matter), the parents need to start to give the message, "You need to work within the rules," so the child learns to adapt and cooperate effectively. If parents send the child the message, "You are special, and you shouldn't have to put up with anything difficult," they are failing their child. Children learn how to take responsibility for their behavior in a major way in the crucible of public schooling, and parents who undermine that process are not succeeding at an important developmental task.

The other issue at this stage is the question of "letting go" generally. Part of sending a child off to school is realizing that he or she is going to become more autonomous, that friends will begin to compete actively with family for interest and time, and that outside influences—"Everybody else gets to do it!"—start to have a major impact on the child. Families who can only fight that, and hold on tighter, are in for a tough ride. Likewise, parents who make a loyalty test of a child's natural interest in the larger world—"You'd rather go to Bobby's than be with Mommy??!!"—are teaching a child that growing up is dangerous and hurtful.

The Children Leave Home

The stage of the children leaving home is the logical extension of the preceding stage. Parents who have handled the autonomy issue well will have less trouble at this stage (another example of the cumulative nature of these stages and how early failures will have later ramifications). The task in this stage is to let go effectively as kids start to move out toward college, work, or marriage. This is not an event, but a long-term process that begins with parents letting go bit by bit as children get older.

Parents who maintain strict, top-down rule systems until a child's 18th birthday, for example, are setting up a crisis for a child with a lot of pent-up energy and no practice in self-management. Parents need to involve children more and more in their own choices as they get older and to face their declining control of the child with grace and sensitivity. Parents who arrive at the child's leaving with the illusion that they are still in control will have a difficult time setting the child on a healthy path.

A different, but equally difficult, path is set for the child who gets the message, "You are our whole life." Even if that message is given alongside apparent freedom and autonomy, children in that position do not have much freedom because so much is riding on their every move. "If I get a C in this course it will kill my parents" or "If I don't go into the family business, my father will die" are heavy and unnatural burdens for children who need to find their own paths.

The Children Begin to Become Their Parents' Parent

The last family developmental stage is built around the natural changes of aging and loss of function in older parents. It is natural and expected that children will begin to have a quasi-parental role with their own parents. What is required to accomplish this is that all parties gracefully acknowledge this change and allow it to happen. The father who insults the son who tries to help him with the finances he can no longer manage is making an unnecessary crisis out of a natural transition. Similarly, the child who enacts this stage with harshness or revenge in mind is making the worst of an important developmental task.

All of these family developmental tasks are important elements of systemic awareness; it is this consciousness of context that allows primary care psychologists and primary care physicians to recognize when a particular aspect of the patient's family or its development needs attention. Awareness of the family life cycle can also help the clinician to normalize the challenges of remaining healthy within a healthy family system.

AN INDIVIDUAL'S ILLNESS HAS INTERPERSONAL IMPACT

Family process and medical realities interact in sometimes subtle but pervasive ways. Disease afflicts individual patients, but consequences of disease ripple outward. Even transient illnesses can have powerful interpersonal impacts; for example, a mother misses work when her son catches a cold and becomes anxious about her job tenure. Or, in a more complex example, consider the marital strains that result when disability necessitates drastic changes in roles and household responsibilities.

These effects are not just abstract systems concepts. Consider excerpts from qualitative studies of the familial impact of disease. Maughan, Heyman, and Matthews (2002) interviewed women and their husbands following diagnosis and treatment of gynecological cancer. The patients had diagnoses of cervical, vaginal, or vulvar cancer, and most of them had undergone extensive surgery as part of their treatment; the men were asked to describe their experiences of their wives' illnesses.

Husband A: No, I wouldn't have said I was ready [for her to come home]. I would have much preferred she'd been in the hospital longer, but she didn't want to be there. She'd just had enough, you know, she wanted to be home. . . . When you've never done that type of thing [catheter care] before, it's quite frightening to see it all.

Husband B: I wouldn't say that it has been easy [resuming intercourse]; it kind of puts you off, doesn't it. You know. I don't want to hurt her, for one thing, and then to be honest, I just kind of lost interest as well, which is strange.

Husband C: She came back from the hospital a different person. Her temperament had changed. Like I say, she was nice, easygoing, and would always have a smile on her face. Now, I can't get near her or anything. She is not the same person. . . . She snaps and swears at the kids, and she won't let me near her.

One person's illness can cause tremendous disruption of marital and familial life, as demonstrated in these first three quotations. Alienation, divorce, and child psychopathology are possible outcomes of serious disease such as gynecological cancer if there is no help from the professional side.

The second study illustrated the interpersonal impact of Parkinson's disease (Habermann, 2000, pp. 1412–1413). Spouses of individuals with Parkinson's disease had these things to say about the challenges they faced:

Husband A: The hardest thing is seeing her like this, seeing her and sensing her frustration, unhappiness, with the situation. The frustration of not being able to deal with it, not being able to make it better. Trying to change medications, do exercises, and it just never gets better.

Wife A: Probably socially, you're not invited to as many things as you used to be because it's harder for him to converse or them to feel comfortable and converse with him. We were used to being invited to a lot of dinner groups and things, . . . but I've noticed a decline socially, a smaller circle.

Wife B: I think the closeness we had has changed. It's hard to put it into words. It's a feeling, the physical part is different. Sometimes it's hard when he is having a lot of symptoms. But . . . we still have a good relationship at times as far as the intimacy goes.

Wife C: There were a whole lot of things we couldn't talk about because they were affected by his condition, and he refused to talk about it. I was seriously thinking about leaving because I couldn't stand around and watch. He was not eating, he looked horrible, like he was going to fall over and die, and I couldn't, just couldn't do it. I couldn't stand around and watch that happen, and I couldn't seem to find anything to do to change that.

These speakers reflected on one of the most difficult aspects of prolonged illness: Family members must watch their loved one change and suffer. Feelings of powerlessness and helplessness can be overwhelming for the family as well as the patient, leading to confusion, depression, and despair. In keeping with systems principles, it can be anticipated that every one of these challenges will have larger effects as they force other changes.

Partners of dialysis patients were interviewed by White and Grenier (1999, pp. 1316–1317):

Husband A: It [dialysis] affects me to the point of frustration. It doesn't matter how much I do for my wife, we know there is no light at the end of the tunnel.

Husband B: We cope as long as I stay healthy. Otherwise, heaven knows what would happen if I were sick.

Wife A: It's affected our sex life. We had a very good sex life, and now we're too tired half the time. I hope that comes back. He feels the same as I do.

These studies and others illustrate several common themes:

1. Changes in family roles are keenly felt when a family member becomes ill. All aspects of familial functioning, from child care to sick care to extended family relations, may need to be renegotiated.

2. Both patient and caregiver can experience significant isolation—from each other, from family and friends, and from cherished activities. Hobbies may no longer seem as important, and those people not intimately involved with the illness may be pushed aside.

3. The loss of sexual intimacy can be a significant and painful change in a couple's life. Sexual intimacy may fall victim to fatigue, disgust, disability, or just radically changed circumstances; in any case, its loss can lead to further stress on an already strained relationship.

4. Finally, the burden of caregiving must not be underestimated. Most people are unprepared for the caregiving role, yet few people can refuse. Caregiving can be a lonely and exhausting job, and it is usually superimposed on existing responsibilities. Compassion and support for caregivers can go a long way toward helping families cope with chronic illness.

Despite the foregoing problems, the interpersonal impacts of illness are not always negative. Serious illness also has the potential to draw families together and to refocus their priorities.

Adjustments in roles and responsibilities can be healthy, forcing families to reconsider homeostatic strategies that have become outdated or maladaptive, engendering new conversations and awareness. Illness can even foster renewed appreciation for the love and support that families provide. The process of providing needed guidance, support, and appreciation for adaptive solutions can help families grow immeasurably in the face of hard times.

HOW THE PRIMARY CARE PSYCHOLOGIST CAN HELP

Having discussed the many ways in which illness disrupts family life, let us now consider the role of the systems-oriented psychologist working in a primary care medical setting. How can the psychologist (or physician, with support and guidance) help patients and families minimize the impact of major illness? Here are some major ways to lessen the burden of disease:

1. *Offer anticipatory guidance.* Help everyone—patients, caregivers, immediate and extended family—to anticipate what some of the challenges may be so they can recognize and talk about challenges as they happen. Guidance indirectly labels difficulties as normal and expectable, taking away much of the shame and confusion.

2. *Ask the right questions.* Patients or caregivers might not raise these issues spontaneously, but may well be ready to talk if asked. So, one might say, "These illnesses are hard on husbands, too. How are you holding up?"

3. *Ask about people not present.* "How are the kids reacting?" "How is her mom taking all this?"

4. *Listen to the answers.* Pro forma questions are not enough; model a good dialogue and an empathic ear. The point of anticipatory guidance is as much to engender a useful conversation as to head off a particular problem. So, if the husband referenced in item 2 answers with how his wife is doing, the psychologist might say, "I'm glad to hear she's doing better; I was wondering about *you.*"

5. *Refer to services.* Many people do not know about available services or are reluctant to use them. Help people overcome shyness, shame, and other barriers to the many services available, especially support groups, which can help with depression and isolation. (This implies that you know about the available services.) Follow up regularly on whether the resources are actually used.

6. *Do not overlook technology.* Most organizations that support patients and families with particular diseases have well-run Web sites. Encourage computer-literate patients to look online for information and support and try to help people without computers to find a way to make the same connections (for example, using public terminals at their local libraries).

7. *Give advice that supports family life and family rituals.* The physician or psychologist can strongly encourage maintenance of the positive aspects of family life. Burdened, exhausted, or discouraged families often forgo important rituals such as birthdays, holidays, or church-going; family meals are often the first to go. The more discouraged a family becomes, the more important these rituals are in maintaining a sense of hope and viability in the family. In some cases, new rituals must be devised to fit the circumstances. (For example, if the father is bedridden and requires constant supervision, ask the minister to hold a service in the family home.)

8. *Help people talk to one another.* Communication often breaks down quickly in hard times; people do not know what they are allowed to say. Teach people that they need to talk more, not less, as times get worse. Sharing each other's anxieties and fears can restore and revitalize relationships. Secrets are almost always a bad idea; they seldom stay secret, and they block other direct communication. Meeting with family members in addition to the patient may be needed to unblock communication.

9. *Encourage self-care for all family members.* Supporting recreation is very important. In hard times, many families constrict emotionally and avoid relaxation, fun, and play. Even if a family member is suffering, it may not be disrespectful for other family members to find some aspects of life enjoyable. Likewise, we must encourage or even insist that caregivers get out and take care of themselves. A dedicated caregiver may need professional support for improving self-care, but this may be crucial to the caregiver's survival.

Disease may begin with an individual patient, but illness quickly affects each member of the patient's family. The professional voice can be used in many positive and constructive ways to help families minimize the disruption of serious illness. Physicians may need help from their primary care psychologist colleagues in working with families in these ways as challenging situations develop. A perceived lack of medical solutions should not prevent the physician (or the psychologist) from bringing healing suggestions to a family.

FAMILIES AND PSYCHOSOCIAL PROCESSES SHAPE ILLNESS

Family processes also shape illnesses, largely through individual and collective coping styles. Although some families rally in the face of a difficult diagnosis or treatment course, there are other families in which serious illness magnifies conflicts, complicates treatment, and even undermines recovery.

Psychologists and physicians alike accept the notion that the entire family must be considered when treating a sick child. Children rely on adults for their medical care. More subtly, children are extremely sensitive to the overall emotional climate of the family. Thus, familial effects go beyond simple variables such as whether parents give children their prescribed medications (although that is an important variable not only for the outcome of a particular disease, but also because it may well teach lasting lessons about how to respond to medical instructions).

Family influences may be especially important in the chronic diseases of childhood. As an example, Jacobsen et al. (1994) followed 61 children and adolescents with new-onset insulin-dependent diabetes. Diabetic control was assessed over a 4-year period using periodic blood tests. Several family characteristics were significantly associated with better blood sugar control, including increased expressivity, high levels of cohesiveness, and low levels of conflict. Although these findings do not demonstrate causality, they do illustrate the link between communication and disease outcomes in children with diabetes.

A similar study examined the influence of family dynamics on disease outcomes in children with cystic fibrosis (Patterson, Budd, Goetz, & Warwick, 1993). Cystic fibrosis (CF) is a chronic disease that requires arduous therapy at home, including antibiotics, chest physical therapy, aerosols, pancreatic enzyme replacement, and vitamins. Optimal treatment for children with CF requires a huge investment of time and family resources. This study found improved lung function in CF patients when both parents' coping styles emphasized family integration, support for self, and medical consultation. Armed with these data, physicians should assess family dynamics when faced with concerns about treatment compliance in this difficult disease. A confrontational approach by the physician—"You've *got* to do these therapies"—may create shame or drive parents away instead of delivering the intended sense of urgency. Physicians will have more success if they tailor their approaches to the unique dynamics of each family; psychologists can help physicians to understand this principle as well as to learn ways of enacting it. Above all, an open, supportive relationship with families (even if they are currently doing a poor job) is the best single way to help them focus on the vital aspects of parenting an ill child well.

Fewer studies have examined the influence of family dynamics on diseases of adulthood. Certainly, adults are also susceptible to family influences, so it can be assumed that similar results would be found. Consider the adult patient with end-stage renal disease who must adhere to strict dietary and fluid restrictions. Every ounce of liquid consumed must be measured and recorded, and every bite of food must be analyzed for its content of various salts. Familial support and cohesiveness would clearly make it easier for this patient to make the major lifestyle changes necessary for compliance with the restrictions.

Family interactions can shape a patient's reaction to illness as well as the patient's subsequent illness behavior. Is it possible that families and illness could also be related in a causal manner? Can psychosocial stressors such as familial conflict precipitate illness? This causal relationship between family and illness has been difficult to demonstrate. Nonetheless, there is a substantial body of literature on the link between social stressors and illness (e.g., Holmes & Rahe, 1967; Musante et al., 2000) based on research demonstrating that the accumulation of stress, measured by a point system, leads to a great increase in the likelihood of sickness (Miller & Rahe, 1997).

More recent work in psychoneuroimmunology suggests the biological mediating mechanisms that explain these findings (cf. Kiecolt-Glaser, McGuire, Robles, & Glaser, 2002).

HOW THE PSYCHOLOGIST CAN HELP BROADEN THE FOCUS OF MEDICINE TO INCLUDE BIOPSYCHOSOCIAL ISSUES

We suggest in this section five ways of operating that may help make primary care more biopsychosocial: integration of mind and body aspects from the beginning; enlistment of family members as allies; recognition that symptoms often have a function in the family; inclusion of the family in your thinking even when working with only one member; and remembering that the family, the patient, and the physician form a triangle.

Integrate Mind and Body Aspects From the Beginning

Never attribute disease to psychological or familial factors by exclusion. Every psychologist dreads the referral that was begun with, "Well, your body checks out fine, so I think it's time to call in the psychologist." If the physician starts the diagnostic process with inclusive ideas such as "This kind of stomach problem is usually a function of both physical and emotional processes, and we need to pay attention to both," the patient will be more receptive to considerations of systemic and psychological variables later. Avoid either-or thinking; it is always about the balance of mind and body, not which one is "really the issue."

Enlist Family Members as Allies

The family is a great potential ally in working with any number of illnesses and should be treated as such. The majority of families are eager to help their family member, and they want to contribute to treatment. In the rare case when the family is interfering with progress, it is even more important to understand how the family works. Accordingly, have a low threshold for bringing family members into the office as a case becomes confusing or blocked. Obtain information about family context and use it.

Recognize That Symptoms Often Have a Function in the Family

Recognizing the interpersonal or transactional functions of symptoms is very important in primary care. People are not blamed for their physical problems in the same way as they are blamed for their emotional or behavioral ones, and this attaches value to medical symptoms. Every child who has escaped school with a "stomachache" knows this. "Not tonight dear, I have a headache" is a cliché, but it works because it is harder to argue with a headache than with simple disinterest. However, it is important to remember that even though symptoms have interpersonal effects, this does not prove that they were deliberately used to achieve those effects.

Include the Family in Your Thinking, Even When Working With Only One Member

Family genograms (McGoldrick & Gerson, 1985) or other pictorial maps of all the people who make up a family can provide a quick overview of the multiple roles assumed by each member of the family. Psychologists can also use such visual aids to enrich their thinking about difficult cases. Families can be "brought into" treatment in other ways as well. Patients can be encouraged to write a letter to particular family members, conference

calls can be arranged, and "interpersonal homework" can be assigned.

Remember That the Family, the Patient, and the Physician Form a Triangle

Only in the simplest, most straightforward encounters is medicine a dyadic process. More often, the patient's family is apt to be a third element in the relationship. The family's belief in the physician, the patient's susceptibility to family influences, the doctor's openness to family ideas, and other forces guarantee that the family is what Doherty and Baird (1983) have called "the ghost in the room" (p. 12).

Dorothy, aged 61 years, was repeatedly found to have blood sugar readings in the 400s at visits to her family physician. Her physician pushed harder and harder for her to take her insulin, check her blood sugar regularly, and alter her diet. Dorothy always said she would, but then nothing ever changed.

Dorothy's oldest daughter accompanied her to the clinic one day, and the physician invited her into the examining room. The physician said to her, "I'm really worried about your mom. She's not taking good care of herself." The daughter was amazed: "That's not what Mom says! She says she's doing fine, and you agree!" The physician looked at the mother, who sheepishly said, "I don't want everyone worrying about me! You all have more important things to worry about," and then named her greater concerns: finances, health of children and grandchildren, and so on.

As the three of them talked, it emerged that the mother was not filling her prescriptions for financial reasons. She was also reluctant to share her health concerns with her children so as not to "distract" the rest of the family. The daughter, near tears, impressed on her mother how important she was to the whole family, and she vowed to call a family meeting to educate everyone about Dorothy's diabetes. The physician offered to take part in that meeting, but they decided to start with just the family.

Within 1 month, Dorothy's blood sugar readings were down dramatically as the family rallied around her needs and made it their business to "make sure Momma stays well." The physician routinely stayed in touch with the daughter after that, with the mother's consent, and Dorothy continued to manage her disease more effectively.

LACK OF FAMILY AS A RISK FACTOR FOR ILLNESS

In our discussion of families and illness, we must briefly mention the patient who does not have a family or other source of intimate social support. Systemic thinking leads to notice of an absence of social connectedness as clearly as various patterns of familial interactions are noticed. Social isolation itself may be a risk factor for physical disease (House, Landis, & Umberson, 1988).

In an early classic study of this issue, Berkman and Syme (1979) followed 6,928 adults in Alameda County, California, over a 10-year period. Information was gathered regarding marriage, contact with close friends and relatives, church membership, and group associations. In each of these categories, people with social ties and relationships had significantly lower mortality rates than people without such ties. Moreover, the intimate ties of marriage and family were stronger predictors of decreased mortality than more casual social contacts.

A similar study interviewed over 3,000 male survivors of heart attack (Ruberman, Weinblatt, Goldberg, & Chaudhary, 1984). Social isolation was found to increase mortality significantly following myocardial infarction. Social isolation has been posited to be a stronger predictor of heart attacks than high cholesterol (Musante et al., 2000). The implication of these findings is that reducing social isolation may improve disease outcomes.

For example, Spiegel, Bloom, Kraemer, and Gottheil (1989), in a study of 86 women with metastatic breast cancer, found that patients enrolled in a support group lived an average of 18 months longer than patients receiving medical treatment alone. The authors speculated that groups serve to counter the social alienation that often divides cancer patients from their family and friends. Support groups provide a safe forum for discussion and a peer group with similar experiences.

Social isolation is a valid target for therapeutic interventions. Helping people try to get back in touch with lost family or friends, or supporting such activities as going to church, joining a club or group, or resolving an old enmity can make a significant difference in people's outlook and health (Larson, Larson, & Johnson, 2001).

BRINGING FAMILY THERAPY INTO PRIMARY CARE PRACTICE

Although the time-pressured primary care physician may attempt to refer the patient and family to a psychologist, there are times when the physician, who knows the family best, should work with the family. Doherty and Baird (1983) suggested conditions under which it is appropriate for the physician to work directly with families:

1. *Family transition problems*: addition or subtraction of family members, by loss or developmental change, or similar changes that significantly alter a family's structure. This is a large category, and it is one every family will experience sooner or later, usually multiple times. Comfort with helping families adapt to transitions is a prime skill for primary care physicians to develop.
2. *Problems of recent origin*: a new depression, a new outbreak of bad behavior from a normally tractable child, and so on. The family physician may be ideally poised to point out problems that the family has not yet recognized or to react quickly when they bring something new and worrisome to his or her attention. All problems are easier to solve, or at least affect, early on than after they are entrenched.
3. *Illness-related problems.* These problems naturally involve the physician, and the physician can moderate the disruptive or problematic aspects of illness by anticipating them and by convening the family to explain their part in adapting to new circumstances.

Of course, physicians differ in their interest in and aptitude for family intervention; a good collaborative arrangement with a primary care psychologist can help the patients and families of primary care physicians who are less willing or able to focus on these issues, while maintaining the patient's and family's relationship with the primary care physician.

Whether a physician or a psychologist works with a given family, it is helpful to remember some basic principles of family therapy that can easily carry over into the medical setting. This is especially important for people without formal training in family therapy. To provide some guidance, we offer the following principles:

1. Think of the patient as part of the system, not the primary source of the problem. Family therapists always speak of the "identified patient" rather than the "patient" to signify that the person presenting with a problem may not be the source of the trouble. No one has a problem in isolation.

2. If things are not adding up and making sense, you probably need more data and another point of view. An old family therapy adage says, "When you're confused, or the picture isn't clear, add family members."

3. Get the family together early and often. Model a systemic outlook by having a low threshold for family input. Teach people that both physical illness and psychological distress are family affairs by including family members.

4. Remember that all families have covert rule systems. Examples might include, "Mom is never wrong, so don't argue with her," "Be happy, there's never any reason to be down," or "Anger is not allowed." It is important for the professional with access to the family structure to identify and (it is hoped) affect these rule systems. One of the basic tasks of the person working with a family is to "make the invisible visible," that is, notice and bring out the invisible rule system for discussion and review. In the same vein, the family therapist tries to "say the unsayable," that is, name the processes that are endemic to family functioning but not spoken. Thus, a person meeting with the family that has lost a matriarch might say, "No one ever talks about having gotten mad at Grandma, even though she did some pretty upsetting things. Is getting mad at her allowed?"

5. Respect family processes. Do not think in terms of families being "sick" or "dysfunctional" or not; instead, try to understand instead how they work, why they work that way, and which parts of their functioning are or are not effective. Although the professional tendency is to put things into categories—pathological categories being a perennial favorite—it is more useful to think in terms of adaptation. Why did this family evolve that particular pattern? What made them accept and incorporate this way of working? All families are dysfunctional in some ways and not others; learn what works for them and why. If the behavior or adaptation attempt is truly dysfunctional, you can help them see that it cannot work and to find something that works better.

CONVENING THE FAMILY

Both primary care psychologists and primary care physicians may be somewhat challenged, or even overwhelmed, by the prospect of working with more than one person at a time, even if they are capable of thinking systemically. There is a substantial body of clinical literature on the art and science of convening families, conducting family meetings, undertaking basic (and advanced) family therapy; a full consideration is beyond the scope of this chapter. Such works as those of Doherty and Baird (1983), and McDaniel, Hepworth, and Doherty (1992) treat these issues in greater depth.

CONCLUSION

Learning to think systemically and interpersonally in the highly focused, individualistic world of clinical medicine is a skill that can have tremendous potential impact. Primary care physicians have an enormous opportunity to help patients understand their illness as part of a larger whole and to help families make sense of the impact a loved one's illness has on them. The challenge for the psychologist who works with physicians who are willing to struggle with this is to help them feel comfortable with the great complexity of interpersonal and family processes. Families are our basic societal unit for caring for and protecting the individuals we love. Knowing how to meet them "where they are," include them in important moments, and help them adapt to and support difficult transitions and crises is a tremendous contribution.

Physicians and primary care psychologists can take better care of their patients if they are aware of the family issues that are impinging on the patient and can have an impact far beyond the medical one. Psychologists have the opportunity to help physicians broaden the narrow view of their training and take a larger, more systemic perspective that will offer a new perspective on illness and care. Representing that viewpoint and helping physicians learn to think more broadly is a valuable contribution.

References

Berkman, L. F., & Syme, S. L. (1979). Social networks, host resistance, and mortality: A 9-year follow-up study of Alameda County residents. *American Journal of Epidemiology, 109,* 196–204.

Doherty, W. J., & Baird, M. A. (1983). *Family therapy and family medicine: Toward the primary care of families.* New York: Guilford Press.

Goldenberg, H., & Goldenberg, I. (1998). *Counseling today's families* (3rd ed.). Pacific Grove, CA: Brooks/Cole.

Habermann, B. (2000). Spousal perspective of Parkinson's disease. *Journal of Advanced Nursing, 31,* 1409–1415.

Holmes, T. H., & Rahe, R. H. (1967). The social readjustment rating scale. *Journal of Psychosomatic Research, 11,* 213–218.

House, J. S., Landis, K. S., & Umberson, D. (1988). Social relationships and health. *Science, 241,* 540–545.

Jacobsen, A. M., Hauser, S. T., Lavori, P., Willett, J. B., Cole, C. F., Wolfsdorf, J. I., Dumont, R. H., & Wertlieb, D. (1994). Family environment and glycemic control: A four-year prospective study of children and adolescents with insulin-dependent diabetes mellitus. *Psychosomatic Medicine, 56,* 401–409.

Kiecolt-Glaser, J. K., McGuire, L., Robles, T. F., & Glaser, R. (2002). Psychoneuroimmunology: Psychological influences on immune function

and health. *Journal of Consulting and Clinical Psychology, 70,* 537–547.

Larson, D. B., Larson, S. S., & Johnson, B. R. (2001). Families, relationships, and health. In D. Wedding (Ed.), *Behavior and medicine* (pp. 11–30). Seattle, WA: Hogrefe & Huber.

Maughan, K., Heyman, B., & Matthews, M. (2002). In the shadow of risk: How men cope with a partner's gynecological cancer. *International Journal of Nursing Studies, 39,* 27–34.

McDaniel, S. H., Hepworth, J., & Doherty, W. J. (1992). *Medical family therapy: A biopsychosocial approach to families with health problems.* New York: Basic Books.

McGoldrick, M., & Gerson, R. (1985). *Genograms in family assessment.* New York: Norton.

Medalie, J. (1979). The family life cycle and its implications for family practice. *Journal of Family Practice, 9,* 47–56.

Miller, M. A., & Rahe, R. H. (1997). Life changes scaling for the 1990s. *Journal of Psychosomatic Research, 43,* 279–92.

Musante, L., Treiber, F. A., Kapuku, G., Moore, D., Davis, H., & Strong, W. B. (2000). The effects of life events on cardiovascular reactivity to behavioral stressors as a function of socioeconomic status, ethnicity, and sex. *Psychosomatic Medicine, 62,* 760–767.

Patterson, J. M., Budd, J., Goetz, D., & Warwick, W. J. (1993). Family correlates of a 10-year pulmonary trend in cystic fibrosis. *Pediatrics, 91,* 383–389.

Ruberman, W., Weinblatt, E., Goldberg, J. D., & Chaudhary, B. S. (1984). Psychosocial influences on mortality after myocardial infarction. *New England Journal of Medicine, 311,* 552–559.

Spiegel, D., Bloom, J. R., Kraemer, H. C., & Gottheil, E. (1989). Effect of psychosocial treatment on survival of patients with metastatic breast cancer. *Lancet, 14,* 888–891.

von Bertalanffy, L. (1968). *General systems theory.* New York: Braziller.

Walsh, F. (Ed.). (2003). Normal family processes: Growing diversity and complexity. New York: Guilford Press.

White, Y., & Grenyer, B. (1999). The biopsychosocial impact of end-stage renal disease: The experience of dialysis patients and their partners. *Journal of Advanced Nursing, 30,* 1312–1320.

11

Cultural Perspectives

Leonard J. Haas
Geri-Ann Galanti

It is not overstating the situation to call any encounter between a primary care psychologist and a patient cross-cultural, even if both parties are native to the same U.S. region and belong to the same social class; regardless of their cultural background, substantial percentages of primary care patients will not necessarily understand or agree with the "culture" of mental health care. The situation becomes even more complex if the patient is a member of a U.S. minority group or identifies with a non-U.S. culture.

Beyond the issue of overcoming the "culture clash" between medical and psychological care, cultural issues are prominent for primary care psychologists because U.S. society has become more culturally diverse (Judy & D'Amico, 1997; U.S. Census Bureau, 2001) and because primary care draws from this broader range of cultures. Furthermore, there are culture-specific responses to both mental and physical illnesses that must be considered to provide effective care. Despite these facts, culture is easy to overlook in the time-pressured primary care environment, and as Synder and Kunstadter (2001) pointed out, "If you don't think of it, you won't see it" (p. 55).

It is important for the primary care psychologist to understand basic concepts of cultural analysis. It is also important to be able to apply these tools not only to other cultures, but also to one's own. For the primary care psychologist, this means an understanding of common themes in current U.S. culture and how they may or may not dovetail with the values of the mental health disciplines or the values of medicine. A full understanding of patients' illnesses, their response to health care advice, and their adherence to treatment regimens depends on understanding social and cultural influences on human behavior in health and illness. Although a full consideration of spirituality and religion in relation to culture is beyond the scope of this chapter, it is also important to recognize that, in many cultures, including those in the Middle East, religion and culture are deeply intertwined.

A useful "spiritual assessment tool," FICA, was proposed by Pulchalski and Romer (2000). These authors suggested that the clinician inquire about the patient's faith, the influence of spiritual beliefs on his or her behavior, the patient's connection to a community of fellow believers, and how the patient would like the clinician to address spirituality.

CULTURE AND CULTURAL CONCEPTS DEFINED

Although there are numerous definitions of culture, a useful formal definition (Merriam-Webster's Collegiate Dictionary, 2003) is as follows: "Culture (n.): customary beliefs, social forms, and material traits of a racial, religious, or social group." More broadly, culture is "the beliefs, values, social structures, situational behavioral expectations, language and technology shared by a group of people" (Synder & Kunstadter, 2001, p. 49).

Ethnicity is closely related to the concept of culture, and the two are often used interchangeably. Technically, however, ethnicity is a social category based on perceptions of shared culture or ancestry; culture refers to shared beliefs and behaviors.

Culture is considered an attribute of ethnic, religious, national, and other social groups, including professional groups such as physicians and psychologists. These attributes endure over time and are passed formally and informally to new members of the group. Cultural concepts are guidelines, both implicit and explicit, that give individuals ways to view the world, respond to it emotionally, and behave in it. Culture can be described as an inherited "lens" of shared concepts through which individuals perceive and understand the world in which they live (Helman, 1991, p. 376).

Culture is largely "invisible" to its members. A student from a particular ethnic group, hearing an anthropologist describe the customs of the group, may well exclaim, "Oh! I didn't realize that was cultural. I thought that was just the way my family did things." Often, it takes an outsider to "see" culture.

Culture must be maintained. Members of a culture who are geographically dispersed can connect through ritual events or through regular gatherings or communication.

Growing up within any society is a form of enculturation, as opposed to *acculturation*, the process of taking on a new culture. Both of these processes occur through learning and using the shared language, symbols, myths, and rituals. Enculturation also involves joining and learning the patterns of particular subcultures (Helman, 1991). Enculturation also means learning how to define who is "one of us," who is to be respected, who can be dominated, who is responsible for which activities or types of labor, how conflict should be resolved, what causes and what cures illness, and what are the proper means to express distress, among other issues (Helman, 1991). Although enculturation is rarely stressful, acculturation often is. We discuss acculturation stress in a separate section.

Culture is not uniform. Every culture includes subcultures, smaller groups of people within a larger culture who share certain characteristics not shared by the culture at large. At the minimum, age or gender groupings can constitute subcultures. In addition, members of the culture or subculture may disagree about the interpretation of the cultural rules.

Despite internal subcultural differences, cultures can be differentiated on several broad dimensions. As an important example, cultures can be considered more egocentric or individual based or more sociocentric or group based. U.S. culture is highly individualistic. In fact, the U.S. health care system makes this individualistic independence a legal fact: Husbands cannot decide about medical procedures for their wives, for example. Similarly, in U.S. mental health culture, evidence of overconcern for others can be considered pathological (e.g., "codependent," "merged," "poor boundaries," etc.). Other cultures are much more communal. It would be expected, for example, that a traditional Mexican woman would consult her husband before agreeing to surgery or to a referral for psychotherapy.

Another broad dimension on which cultures may differ is modal family structure. U.S. society considers normative the egalitarian nuclear family household, with husbands and wives sharing equal authority. In contrast, the extended family household is the norm in many parts of the world, with several generations living under one roof. Often, these family units are hierarchical, and individuals within the family are not equal. Men are dominant over women, parents over children, and older siblings over younger siblings.

Cultures establish norms about the proper roles

of men and women, "men's work" and "women's work." In U.S. culture, gender equality is considered the norm (although there are clearly U.S. subcultures that define the roles very distinctly), and medical culture is aligned with this value. It is considered appropriate for women physicians to treat male patients, for example, and vice versa. Psychological culture also values gender equality. In fact, depending on the presenting problem, evidence of overvaluing certain aspects of women's or men's functioning or denying that each gender could potentially function as well as the other might be considered pathological.

Cultural rules constrain what can be communicated, to whom, and in what manner. In U.S. medical culture, full disclosure of private information, including intimate details of physical and mental functioning, is expected from patients. In U.S. psychological culture as well, full disclosure is expected, and unusual secretiveness can be considered pathological (labeled, for example, as "paranoid" or "resistant"). However, in Norwegian culture, it is considered rude and disrespectful to say anything negative about one's family members; thus, a Norwegian patient may withhold such information out of politeness rather than feelings of guilt about "unacceptable" feelings (McGoldrick & Giordano, 1996). Many Arabs value the privacy of the family and until their trust is gained, responses to questions will be aimed at pleasing the interviewer, saving face, and absolving the family from responsibility (Lipson & Meleis, 1983).

As spoken language differs from culture to culture, so does nonverbal communication. Lack of eye contact in U.S. culture is generally thought to indicate discomfort with the topic, evasiveness, or lying. However, in Asian culture, it may signify respect for a superior, whereas to look someone directly in the eye implies a claim of equality. In many Middle Eastern cultures, men and women may avoid direct eye contact to maintain sexual propriety. In many Native American cultures, direct eye contact has the potential to result in soul loss or soul theft and may be avoided for that reason.

Personal space varies from culture to culture. The typical distance two Anglo Americans will stand from each other is 3 feet. If someone stands closer, they invade "personal space" and are often perceived as "pushy" or "aggressive." Those who stand too far away, on the other hand, are often seen as "cold" or "distant." Yet normal personal distance for Middle Easterners is about 2 feet, and for Japanese, it is 4 feet. These cultural differences can lead to assumptions about "pushy Arabs" and "standoffish Japanese" that are unwarranted.

Cultural rules concerning the use of silence differ. In U.S. culture, silence as response to a question would be unexpected; it is normative for questions to be answered rapidly, even if the answer is no more than "I don't know" or "I need to think about that." In contrast, it is customary in many Native American tribes to give thought to questions, and a Native American might sit silently for minutes pondering a question. This behavior could be judged inappropriately as ignoring the question, as discomfort with the question, or as reflecting a hearing problem.

Cultures also incorporate aspects of spirituality. As Helman (1991, p. 378) put it, cultural rules influence "what is more appropriate for the condition—penitence or penicillin."

CULTURE AND ILLNESS

Is illness a cultural concept? In many respects, yes. Formally, *illness* is defined as an involuntary state that prevents an individual from performing customary tasks or fulfilling social role obligations. The person who is sick is "excused" from these obligations. In contrast, voluntary decisions not to perform work or meet obligations may be considered inconsiderate, deviant, sinful, or even criminal. From a sociological perspective, *disease* is the biological condition, *illness* reflects the way the individual perceives the disease, and *sickness* refers to how society perceives the individual. Thus, for example, someone with hypertension may have a disease, but not an illness if they perceive themselves as well; someone who is HIV positive may feel well, but be perceived as sick and therefore avoided.

The sick individual does, however, have responsibilities; in most cultures, the afflicted are usually expected to make efforts to get better, seek care, and comply with approved healers' treatment recommendations.

Cultural differences affect whether an experience is labeled as an illness, the type of illness it is considered to be, and which (if any) treatment is appropriate. In U.S. culture, mind and body have long been seen as separate entities to be treated by different types of practitioners. Since the advent of holistic medicine in the 1970s, this is changing, but there is still a division of labor between physicians who treat the body and psychotherapists who treat the mind. This is not the case in other cultures. For example, in most traditional African cultures, mind and body are seen as an integrated unit, and the same practitioner may treat mental, emotional, and physical illnesses. As another example, the Mexican *curandera* may use herbs or rituals to treat any ailment that leaves the patient not feeling "well."

Cultures generally espouse one of the following three major systems of disease explanation (Mutha, Allen, & Welch, 2002). *Biomedical systems*, dominant and developed in the Western world, conceptualize disease as a result of abnormalities in the structure and function of body organs and systems. Basic cause-and-effect mechanisms, as seen in physics and chemistry, are invoked. Pathogens (bacteria and viruses), toxins, biochemical alterations, stress, injury, or aging may be causes of disease. *Naturalistic systems*, prevalent in Asian countries and to some extent in Latin cultures, consider disease to be a result of imbalance in certain natural elements, especially heat and cold. *Personalistic systems*, most common in Africa, the Caribbean, West Indies, and Native American cultures, consider disease to be a result of the actions of sensate agents that are supernatural, nonhuman, or human (e.g., ghosts, evil spirits).

People in non-Western and preliterate societies may believe in illnesses not recognized by Western biomedicine. These include exotic diseases such as *windigo*, found among Ojibwa Indians, in which the patient starts running around crazily and tries to eat people; *koro*, found in Malaysia, in which a man believes his penis is disappearing; as well as more "ordinary" ailments such as evil eye and *susto*. The latter, found among Latin Americans, is thought to result from fright, which causes the soul to leave the body. It may often appear as depression. Such illnesses generally require the treatment of a traditional prac-

titioner. The converse applies as well, of course: Diseases such as bulimia, anorexia, attention-deficit disorder, premenstrual syndrome, and Epstein-Barr virus could be seen as folk illnesses by a clinician from another culture because they are recognized only in Western societies.

Note that U.S. culture is not entirely consistent in its biomedical orientation. For example, certain diseases such as obesity, alcoholism, depression, venereal disease, and HIV/AIDS are often considered shameful examples of personal failure (Lazare, 1987). Cancer is also considered by some "new age" theorists as evidence of personal failure.

CULTURE AND PATIENTHOOD (HELP-SEEKING)

Becoming ill, at least in the United States, means encountering the U.S. health care system, a culture unto itself. What is the culture of medicine in North America? Modern medical practice includes the core values of autonomy, value of human life, honesty, and confidentiality. These values can conflict, and cultural differences in values make the conflicts worse. The culture of U.S. medicine also has many values in common with the culture of science, for example, the belief in the discoverability of physical causes of symptoms, the distrust of data that cannot be measured, the valuing of objective over subjective data, the dualistic approach, the belief in progress (which implies that more recently developed techniques are better), and physical health as separate from mental or spiritual health.

In U.S. health care, prescription medications are frequently prescribed or given. The patient is expected to be able to provide informed consent. There is a biological explanation for symptoms, or else they are "nothing." It is appropriate that the patient be informed about all aspects of care, including the diagnosis. It is not appropriate to use herbal or complementary medicine. Standardization of treatment is important. Patient "activism" is expected. Future orientation is heavily emphasized.

The medical subculture of primary care has its own values (Synder & Kunstadter, 2001), which emphasize first contact, and comprehensive and longitudinal care. One assumption that stems from these values is that the patient should see one clinician as his or her primary care provider. In other cultures, this may be less clear.

Other aspects of U.S. health care culture that may be different in other cultures are the relatively low threshold for seeking professional care and the relatively high emphasis on prevention and "health promotion." However, because Western culture values stoicism in men, there are gender variations, with U.S. men being much more reluctant to seek care. In more traditional cultures, the main site of primary care health care is not in the physician's office, but within the family, in which illness is first recognized, named, and then dealt with, usually by mothers or grandmothers (Helman, 1991).

Social obligations affect medical help-seeking decisions as well. In the United States, decisions about seeking care or accepting care are generally made by the individual or by the parent if the individual is a child. It is not necessary to consult with the head of the family or other authority figure. Some patients, not necessarily always from non-U.S. cultures, might refuse treatment that would improve their condition if the treatment would burden their family.

CULTURE AND PSYCHOPATHOLOGY

Judgments of mental or behavioral abnormality are highly influenced by cultural factors. Cultural factors can contribute to underrecognition of psychopathology because of cultural "filtering" of symptoms. Conversely, overdiagnosis of psychopathology can result from misunderstanding behavior that would be appropriate in the individual's native culture. In addition, cultural or immigrant status may itself be a risk factor for psychological disorder.

Cultural Variables Can Filter the Expression of Symptoms

There are cultural differences in whether "mood" symptoms are expressed with the emotion of sadness or by somatic complaints instead of sadness or guilt (American Psychiatric Association, 1994).

Complaints of nerves and headaches in Latino and Mediterranean cultures; of weakness, tiredness, or "imbalance" in Chinese and other Asian cultures; of "problems of the heart" in Middle Eastern cultures; or of being heartbroken among the Hopi may all be ways to express the depressive experience.

In some cultures, different aspects of a disease may be considered differentially serious. For example, in the case of manic depression, the British, who tend to value emotional control, are often more concerned about the manic phase; the more emotionally expressive Americans are more disturbed by the depressive phase. Anxiety disorders are also affected strongly by cultural norms. For example, in Asian cultures, in which mental illness is highly stigmatized, individuals will often somaticize their anxiety and seek medical care for the associated symptoms (McGoldrick & Giordano, 1996). In cultures in which emotional problems are more acceptable, anxiety may be expressed cognitively. Although DSM-IV (Diagnostic and Statistical Manual of Mental Disorders, fourth edition; American Psychiatric Association, 1994) characteristics of panic disorders have been found in epidemiological studies worldwide, in some cultures (e.g., certain African and Native American cultures) panic disorder symptoms may take the form of intense fear of witchcraft or magic. Social phobia may present as persistent or excessive fears of giving offense to others in social situations instead of being embarrassed. Among certain Asian cultures, particularly Japanese and Korean, social phobia symptoms may take the form of extreme anxiety that eye contact, blushing, or body odor will offend others (American Psychiatric Association, 1994).

Misunderstanding of Culturally Normative Expressions as Psychopathology

It is not uncommon for Portuguese individuals, for example, to experience visual and auditory hallucinations following the death of a loved one. A Portuguese patient or one from a culture with similar means of expression could easily be evaluated by a U.S. mental health specialist as suffering from a delusional disorder.

As a second example, consider the diagnosis of agoraphobia: Because some cultural or ethnic groups, including many from the Moslem Middle East and Africa, restrict the participation of women in public life, this must be distinguished from agoraphobia. Similarly, obsessive-compulsive disorder may be diagnosed mistakenly in patients from cultures that have prescribed ritual behavior, or life transitions and mourning may intensify ritualistic behavior that could look obsessive to an outsider unfamiliar with the culture. Appropriate diagnosis is aided by considering whether mental and behavioral symptoms typically exceed cultural norms, occur at times and in places judged inappropriate even by others of the same culture, and interfere with social role function.

> Esperlita Vega, a Filipino American nurse, has been seeing visions of her aunt and uncle, who were recently killed in a car accident during a visit to the United States. The hallucinations began a week after their funeral. She has had trouble sleeping and has lost her appetite. When Esperlita shared her experience with an Anglo American nurse, she was advised to get psychiatric help. Her colleague feared that Esperlita was having a nervous breakdown. However, when Esperlita shared her story with a Filipino coworker, her Filipino colleague suggested that Esperlita's dead relatives were having trouble making the journey to the next world because they had died in a foreign country and lacked the proper burial ritual. She considered Esperlita's visions normal rather than a sign of impending psychosis.
>
> Convinced of her colleague's interpretation, Esperlita and her family offer masses for her departed aunt and uncle and light candles on their graves each night. At the end of 2 weeks, the visions disappear, Esperlita is able to sleep undisturbed, and her appetite returns (Galanti, 1997, pp. 114–115).

Misdiagnosis of Acculturation Problems as Psychopathology

Acculturation problems may be misdiagnosed as psychopathology. For example, personality disorders may be confused with problems associated with acculturation following immigration. Immigrants who are "frozen" emotionally by the overstimulation of American life can be mistakenly perceived as cold, hostile, and indifferent and diagnosed with schizoid personality traits. In addition, certain personality traits are more valued in certain cultures than others. For example, many Asian women are socialized to be passive, a trait often seen as needing "fixing" in a culture such as that in the United States, which values assertiveness.

Similarly, it will be rather easy to diagnose paranoid personality disorder in members of minority groups, immigrants, refugees, or others who are guarded and defensive because they are unfamiliar with the mental health treatment setting or have experienced discrimination in the larger society. It is important that psychologists seek to help patients determine to what extent their problems may stem from racism or bias. For example, ethnic minorities may develop defensive behaviors in what is termed a "healthy paranoia" in response to discrimination (American Psychological Association, 1998). Nonetheless, acculturative stress may itself be a risk factor for psychopathology (Williams & Berry, 1991).

Cultural Risk Factors

The threshold for alcohol abuse, for example, is strongly affected by cultural traditions surrounding the use of alcohol for social, religious, and family activities. In the United States, Latino males have somewhat higher rates of alcohol consumption; Latino females have lower rates than females from white and African groups (American Psychiatric Association, 1994).

An additional example is somatization. Although this condition is diagnosed only rarely in men, there may be a higher incidence of somatization among Greek and Puerto Rican men (American Psychiatric Association, 1994). A further example is that of the norms in Chinese society, in which one can legitimately seek rest and care for somatic complaints, but not psychological distress. Not surprisingly, somatization disorders are more prevalent in such societies (Tseng & Shu, 1980). Although posttraumatic stress disorder is not strictly a cultural risk factor, it should be considered more likely in individuals who have recently emigrated from areas of considerable social unrest or civil conflict. These patients, however, may not be eager to reveal experiences of torture and trauma, especially if their immigrant status is somewhat vulnerable.

CULTURE AND PSYCHOLOGICAL PATIENTHOOD

Rosa Jimenez, a middle-aged Hispanic woman, visits her physician complaining of chest pains. Tests indicate no underlying physical cause. She responds to the physician's attempt at obtaining a medical history with only brief answers. She cries throughout the interview, even after her chest pain ceases, and says nothing when the physician asks her why she is depressed. When her adult daughter arrives, she explains that Rosa has been distraught since her husband left home 2 weeks earlier. At this, Rosa cries out, "No, no! You must not say anything. It's private." Her daughter quietly replies that she cannot stand to see her mother suffer and is concerned about her chest pains. At this point, the physician suggests that Rosa might want to talk to one of the staff psychiatrists. Her response is adamant: "No! No other people should know about this!" (Galanti, 1997).

U.S. culture is highly individualistic, especially concerning psychosocial problems. In reality, however, the individual's symptoms can only be fully understood in relation to the context—social, cultural, and emotional—in which he or she is embedded (Helman, 1991).

Seeking help for psychological difficulties (or accepting a referral to a primary care psychologist) poses a problem for many patients, not all of whom are from non-U.S. cultures. Culture-related barriers to mental health care include the perception of stigma, the belief that depression is caused by life experiences, that problems should not be discussed outside the family, that health care professionals cannot be trusted, and that psychotropic medication may be addictive.

The stigma of mental illness is great in many cultures, including Anglo American culture. The issue of stigma is particularly of concern in Asian cultures. In these cultures, mental illness is generally thought to be inherited; thus, if one family member is mentally ill, not only will it bring great

shame to the entire family, it will also reduce the marital opportunities for the other members of the family. Chinese natives studying in the United States, for example, are often astounded to learn that many Americans seek psychotherapy for minor problems. In China, the category "neurotic" does not exist; there is only sanity or severe mental illness. A Chinese psychiatrist of G. G.'s acquaintance noted that his parents told their friends only that he was a "doctor" because they were ashamed of his association with the mentally ill.

An additional barrier to mental health help-seeking is that certain minority ethnic groups may believe that the proper source of help for emotional or behavioral problems is the church (African Americans) or the family (Hispanics or Middle Easterners, for example) because personal issues should not be discussed with "outsiders."

Another barrier to effective use of U.S. mental health care involves cultural attitudes toward "nondirectiveness." U.S. mental health culture values personal choice and autonomy, and many clinicians strenuously avoid giving advice. Patients from patriarchal, hierarchical cultures often expect the therapist to tell them what to do and have difficulty remaining in treatment without "answers." In addition, in such cultures, the clinician who must ask a lot of questions before making a diagnosis is seen as inferior to the one who knows without asking and then proceeds to tell the patient what to do (Galanti, 1997).

The mental health value of full self-disclosure by the patient with relatively little reciprocal self-disclosure by the therapist can also pose problems. Patients from some cultures would strongly wish for self-disclosure to be reciprocal; many Arab Americans, for example, might expect the therapist to reveal personal information in exchange for the personal information that they shared and would mistrust a therapist who did not do so. Reciprocity is important in many Asian cultures as well, although it often takes material form. For example, when someone does something for another, something is owed in exchange. If the exchange is not completed, the person receiving the kindness is in the other's debt. Because this is an uncomfortable position, it is extremely important not to let such indebtedness occur. A gift to the therapist satisfies the reciprocal obligation, but such an action might make a U.S. clinician uncomfortable or lead to overinterpretation of psychopathology.

The issue of diagnosis also has cultural implications. In U.S. mental health culture, as in U.S. medical culture, diagnosis is considered necessary for proper treatment, and the diagnosis must be communicated to the patient. In other cultures (e.g., certain rural Southeast Asian societies), naming a potential condition may be considered wrong. In these cultures, for example, a consent form that indicated possible outcomes would be felt to increase the chance of their occurrence.

The hierarchical nature of the Asian family presents a special challenge for therapists because, in many forms of American psychotherapy, issues of conflict with parents are investigated as a source of emotional issues. Asian patients may consider it disrespectful to say anything negative about their parents because they gave life, sacrificed for their children, and so on. Therefore, they are owed everything, especially respect. Helping these individuals meet the obligation of filial piety and at the same time take care of their own needs is a special psychotherapeutic challenge.

An additional issue can arise regarding cultural rules for child rearing. Many hierarchical cultures are discipline oriented. Corporal punishment of children may be normative. Finding the appropriate balance between respecting cultural values and meeting the ethical and legal obligation to protect children from abuse may also become a therapeutic challenge.

Finally, cultural aspects of domestic violence may pose difficult therapeutic choices. Domestic violence is difficult for women to discuss even when they are native to the United States; for women from cultures that foster male dominance, there may be additional barriers. Not only might the woman consider spousal abuse "normal," she may be financially dependent on her husband, and greater stigma may be attached to divorce.

ACHIEVING CULTURAL COMPETENCE

The culturally competent primary care psychologist will acquire knowledge, attitudes, and skills that allow effective care of patients from a variety of backgrounds. Many psychologists may already be familiar with the American Psychological Association's (1998) *Guidelines for Providers of Psychological Services to Ethnic, Linguistic, and Culturally Diverse Populations*; in this section, we present a number of suggestions for culturally competent work in the multicultural primary care environment.

1. Use cultural understanding to generate hypotheses rather than to stereotype. Consider the following example:

   A hospital nurse was caring for a very ill Native American patient who had been refusing all food and medication. He appeared to be slowly dying. The nurse, knowing that some Native Americans use traditional healers, asked him if he would like to see a medicine man. His face lit up at her question, and he nodded affirmatively. It took considerable effort, but she was able to arrange for a medicine man to perform a traditional ritual involving burning incense and chanting and for the patient to go through a purification ritual in a sweat lodge. Although the other nurses thought she was "crazy" for arranging all of this, the patient suddenly began to eat and take his medication. His health started to improve, and he eventually recovered (Galanti, 2004).

   Had this nurse invited a medicine man without asking the patient if he wanted one, she would have been stereotyping him. But knowing that medicine men are part of his traditional culture and asking him if he would like to see one, she used a generalization that likely helped to save his life. It is important that the clinician have some knowledge of the patient's cultural background because it is unlikely that the patient will volunteer such information. The patient in this example never asked to see a medicine man; it was the culturally competent nurse who first raised the issue.

2. Understand your own culture. A set of useful questions is given in Table 11.1.

3. Understand how the culture of medicine and psychology might pose problems for the individual. Recognize that specific be-

Table 11.1 Defining Your Cultural Identity

1. How would you describe your cultural identity?

2. What do you appreciate most about your group or culture?

3. What would you change about your group or culture?

4. What are common misconceptions about your group or culture?

5. Describe your first experience with a culture other than your own.

6. Identify one group or culture with which you feel most comfortable and why.

7. Identify one group with which you feel the least comfortable and why.

Adapted from Najm and Lenahan (1998).

havioral patterns, such as adherence to time schedules, willingness to talk about family matters, deference to authority, competitive versus cooperative attitudes, and religious and spiritual beliefs about causes and cures for disorders may affect the individual's willingness to accept mental health care. It is also important to recognize that there may be cultural biases in the assessment tools used.

4. Value the ability to communicate well with patients of diverse backgrounds as a clinical skill. Not only should primary care psychologists consider cultural competence a necessary skill, but also, the effective clinician should be able to recognize when lack of knowledge of a patient's culture is compromising the ability to provide good care.

5. Include cultural factors in a complete assessment of the patient. In addition to including culture as an explanatory factor when assessing a patient's difficulties, it is helpful to understand the broader context in which the patient functions (e.g., What is happening to people of that group and how does that affect them?). Be curious. Recognize that cultural aspects of identity and self-esteem are important to patients and avoid demeaning these.

6. Inquire about culturally appropriate ways of handling the situation; find out what the patient wants you to know about his or her culture; explore common ways in which people of that background obtain treatment for conditions like this.

7. Be capable of assessing acculturation stress (see Table 11.2).

8. If possible, conduct assessment and treatment in the preferred language of the patient. This suggestion implies that the primary care psychologist not fluent in the patient's preferred language must be capable of using an interpreter. Especially for psychotherapy, be cautious about use of family members as translators because they may introduce their own biases and may "already know" what is wrong with their family member. This is most difficult with children acting as translators for their parents. Ideally, professional translators are used and the consultation room is arranged in such a way that the clinician can look directly at the patient and address the patient, not the translator.

9. Keep cultural issues in perspective. Be cautious about "overculturalizing." Although it is important to be sensitive to culture differences, it is possible to place too much emphasis on ethnicity and culture. In a similar fashion, stereotypic cultural explanations for pathology may serve to minimize it. For example, dismissing a patient's alcoholism because "he is a hard-

Table 11.2 Assessing Acculturation and Acculturative Stress

1. What language do you usually use with your parents, children, spouse, or friends?[a]

2. In what language do you think, dream, or have emotional experiences?[a]

3. In what language do you listen to the radio, watch TV, or read?[a]

4. What has the process of adapting to a new language, new diet, new culture, new rules, or new expectations been like for you?

5. What do you think are the benefits and the drawbacks of integrating into this culture?

6. How do you think of yourself in relation to the majority culture?

Adapted from Gonzales (1998).
[a]In general, those from non-English-speaking groups who report using their native language in all or most of these settings are less likely to be assimilated or integrated into the majority culture.

drinking Irishman" would be both over-emphasizing cultural factors and overlooking a treatable condition. When working with the culturally different, consider whether it is appropriate to view the individual or family any differently from those in your own ethnic or cultural group (American Psychological Association, 1998).

10. Regardless of the patient's cultural context, consider the patient's actual goals in seeking treatment (La Roche & Maxie, 2003). Cultural factors are often confounded with other variables, particularly education and socioeconomic status. Often, the realistic problems of poverty, unemployment, child care, and the like are more prominent for a minority patient (Sundberg & Gonzales, 1981). In general, it is important to understand the following considerations (adapted from Kleinman, Eisenberg, & Good, 1978):

- Why the patient is seeking care at this time
- What the patient thinks is the nature of the problem
- What the patient thinks is the cause of the problem
- What the patient expects of the clinician
- How specifically the patient wants the clinician to help
- How the patient feels about receiving psychological care

SUMMARY

Because of the increasing diversity of the U.S. population, and the increasing diversity of the primary care patient population, the primary care psychologist must be capable of assessing and managing cultural obstacles to effective care. In addition, because primary care medicine and mental health care are subcultures themselves, it is useful to approach any encounter with a primary care patient or physician with a cross-cultural perspective. Cultural and subcultural perspectives on health and illness, on power and shared decision making, on privacy and community, among other issue, are important to understand. Psychologists' awareness of their personal and professional cultural "filters" is also important in providing culturally competent care in the primary care enviroment.

ADDITIONAL RESOURCES

Suggestions for further reading and professional development resources are available at this book's companion Web site: www.primarycarepsych.com.

ACKNOWLEDGMENT   G. G. would like to thank the following individuals for generously sharing their insights and knowledge: Sylvia Bercovici, Len Epstein, Karen Michaels, Victoria Mihich, and Joanna Poppink.

References

American Psychiatric Association. (1994). *Diagnostic and statistical manual of mental disorders* (4th ed.). Washington, DC: Author.

American Psychological Association. (1998). *Guidelines for providers of psychological services to ethnic, linguistic, and culturally diverse populations*. Washington, DC: Author.

Galanti, G. (1997). *Caring for patients from different cultures*. Philadelphia: University of Pennsylvania Press.

Galanti, G. (2004). *Caring for patients from different cultures* (3rd ed.). Philadelphia: University of Pennsylvania Press.

Gonzales, J. C. (1998). Measures of acculturation. In G. P. Koocher, J. C. Norcross, & S. S. Hill (Eds.), *Psychologist's desk reference* (pp. 70–73). New York: Oxford University Press.

Helman, C. G. (1991). The family culture: A useful concept for family practice. *Family Medicine, 23*, 376–381.

Judy, R., & D'Amico, C. (1997). *Workforce 2020*. Indianapolis, IN: Hudson Institute.

Kleinman, A., Eisenberg, L., & Good, B. (1978). Culture, illness, and care: Clinical lessons from anthropologic and cross-cultural research. *Annals of Internal Medicine, 88*, 251–258.

La Roche, M. J., & Maxie, A. (2003). Ten considerations in addressing cultural differences in psychotherapy. *Professional Psychology: Research and Practice, 34*, 180–186

Lazare, A. (1987). Shame and humiliation in the medical encounter. *Archives of Internal Medicine, 147*, 1653–1658.

Lipson, J. G., & Meleis, A. I. (1983). Issues in health care of Middle Eastern patients. *Western Journal of Medicine, 139,* 854–861.

McGoldrick, M., & Giordano, J. (1996). Overview: Ethnicity and family therapy. In M. McGoldrick, J. Giordano, & J. K. Pearce (Eds.), *Ethnicity and Family Therapy* (pp. 1–27). New York: Guilford Press.

Merriam Webster's Collegiate Dictionary (11th Ed.). (2003). Springfield, MA: Merriam-Webster.

Mutha, S., Allen, C., & Welch, M. (2002). *Toward culturally competent care: A tool box for teaching communication strategies.* San Francisco: University of California–San Francisco Press.

Najm, W., & Lenahan, P. M. (1998, May). *Teaching medical students cross cultural health care.* Paper presented at the annual convention, Society of Teachers of Family Medicine, San Francisco, CA.

Pulchalski, C., & Romer, A. (2000). Taking a spiritual history allows clinicians to understand patients more fully. *Journal of Palliative Medicine, 3,* 129–137.

Sundberg, N., & Gonzales, L. (1981). *Cross cultural and cross ethnic assessment: Overview and issues.* San Francisco: Jossey Bass.

Synder, D., & Kunstadter, P. (2001). *Providing health care in a multicultural community.* In D. Wedding (Ed.), *Behavior and medicine* (3rd ed., pp. 49–59). Seattle, WA: Hogrefe and Huber.

Tseng, W. S., & Shu, J. (1980). Minor psychological disturbances of everyday life. In H. C. Triandis & J. G. Draguns (Eds.), *Handbook of cross cultural psychology: Vol. 6, Psychopathology* (pp. 61–97). Boston: Allyn and Bacon.

U.S. Census Bureau. (2001). *U.S. Census 2000, Summary Files 1 and 2.* Retrieved July 3, 2003, from http://www.census.gov

Williams, C. L., & Berry, J. W. (1991). Primary prevention of acculturative stress among refugees: Application of a psychological theory and practice. *American Psychologist, 46,* 632–641.

12

The Nature and Psychology of Suffering

Eric Cassell

Despite the age-old obligation of physicians to relieve human suffering, little attention is explicitly given to the problem of suffering in medical education, research, or practice. I begin by focusing on a modern paradox: Even in the best settings and with the best physicians, it is not uncommon for suffering to occur not only during the course of a disease, but also as a result of its treatment. The understanding of this paradox and its solution requires an understanding of what suffering is and how it relates to medical care.

A 35-year-old sculptor with cancer of the breast that had spread widely was treated by competent physicians employing advanced knowledge and technology and acting out of kindness and true concern. At every stage, the treatment as well as the disease were a source of suffering to her.

She was frightened and uncertain about her future, but could get little information from her physicians, and what she was told was not always the truth. She was unaware, for example, that the radiation therapy to the breast (in lieu of a mastectomy) would be so disfiguring. After her ova-

ries were removed and she received a regimen of medications that were masculinizing, she became obese, she grew facial and body hair of a male type, and her libido disappeared. When the tumor invaded the nerves near her shoulder, she lost strength in the hand she used to sculpt and became profoundly depressed.

At one time, she had watery diarrhea that would occur unexpectedly and often cause incontinence, sometimes when visitors were present. She could not get her physicians to give her medication to stop the diarrhea because they were afraid of possible disease-related side effects (although she was not told the reason).

She had a pathological fracture of her thigh resulting from an area of cancer in the bone. Treatment was delayed while her physicians openly disagreed about pinning her hip. The view that it was wrong to operate on someone with such a poor prognosis prevailed. She remained in traction, but her severe pain could not be relieved. She changed hospitals and physicians, and the fracture was repaired. Because of the extent of metastatic disease in the unrepaired leg, she was advised not to bear weight on it for fear that it might also break—a possibility that haunted her.

She had come to believe that it was her desire to live that would end each remission because every time that her cancer would respond to treatment and her hopes would rekindle, a new manifestation would appear. Thus, when a new course of chemotherapy was started, she was torn between her desire to live and her fear that allowing hope to emerge again would merely expose her to misery if the treatment failed. The nausea and vomiting of the chemotherapy were distressing, but no more so than the anticipation of hair loss (but the hair loss itself was not as distressing as she had thought, and she never wore the wig that had been made in advance).

In common with most patients with similar illnesses, she was constantly tortured by fears of what tomorrow would bring. Each tomorrow was seen as worse than today, as heralding increased sickness, pain, or disability—never as the beginning of better times. Despite the distress caused by such thoughts, she could not think otherwise. She felt isolated because she was not like other people and could not do what other people did. She feared that her friends would stop visiting her. She was sure she would die.

This young woman had severe pain and other physical symptoms that caused her suffering. But, she also suffered from threats that were social and others that were personal and private. She suffered from the effects of the disease and its treatment on her appearance and her abilities. She also suffered unremittingly from her perception of the future.

What can this case tell us about the relief of suffering? Three facts stand out. The first is that this woman's suffering was not confined to physical symptoms. The second is that she suffered not only from her disease but also from its treatment. The third fact is that one could not anticipate what she would describe as a source of suffering; like other patients, she had to be asked. Some features of her condition she would call painful, upsetting, uncomfortable, distressing, but not a source of suffering. In these characteristics, her case is ordinary.

When I ask sick patients whether they are suffering, they often have a quizzical expression—they are not sure what I mean. One patient, who said he was not suffering, had metastatic cancer of the stomach from which he knew he would shortly die. On the other hand, a woman who felt her suffering bitterly was waiting in the hospital for her blood count to return to normal after it had been long depressed by chemotherapy. Aside from some weakness, she was otherwise well and would remain so. Another patient, someone who had an operation for a minor problem and was in little pain and not seemingly distressed, said that even coming into the hospital had been a source of suffering.

When I discuss the problem of suffering with laypersons, they are shocked to discover that it is not directly addressed in medical education. My physician colleagues of a contemplative nature were surprised at how little they knew about the problem and how little thought they had given it, whereas medical students were not sure of the relevance of the issue of suffering to their work.

The relief of suffering, it would appear, is considered one of the primary ends of medicine by patients and the general public, but not by the medical profession, judging by medical education and the responses of students and colleagues. Currently, even though suffering is more widely discussed and has been the subject of conferences and some publications, it is infrequently recognized as such and inadequately treated. As in the care of the dying, patients and their friends and families do not divide up suffering into its physical and nonphysical sources the way doctors do (Cassell, 1972). A search of the medical and social science literature (Psychological Abstracts, Citation Index, and Index Medicus) does not help in understanding what suffering is; the word *suffering* is most often coupled with the word *pain*, as in "pain and suffering."

Although pain and suffering are not synonymous, physical pain remains a major cause of human suffering and is the primary image formed by people when they think about suffering. However, no one disputes that pain is only one among many sources of human suffering. With the notable exception of the work of Bakan (1968), the medical literature did not bring me closer to understanding medicine's relationship to suffering because the topic is rarely discussed. Yet in their fight against scourges such as cancer and heart disease (and in former times, the infectious plagues), doctors and their patients share a common goal and dedication to eliminating the causes of suffering.

In view of the long history of medicine's concern with the relief of sources of suffering, it is paradoxical that patients often suffer from their treatment as well as their disease. The answer seems to lie in a historically constrained and presently inadequate view of the ends of medicine. Medicine's traditional concern primarily for the body and for physical disease is well known. In addition, the widespread effects of the mind-body dichotomy on medical theory and practice are also known. Indeed, I hope to show that the dichotomy itself is one of the sources of the paradox of doctors causing suffering in their attempts to relieve it.

Today, as ideas about the separation of mind and body are changing, physicians are concerned with new aspects of the human condition. One critic, Illich (1976), complained of an overbearing medicalization of humanity. For him, any concern of the medical profession that does not have to do with the body enters the domain of the spiritual. Although many may share his concern, the fact remains that the profession of medicine is being pushed and pulled into new areas (sometimes contradictorily) both by its technology and by the demands of its patients. Attempting to understand what suffering is and how physicians might truly be devoted to its relief offers the primary care psychologist an opportunity to help physicians transcend the dichotomies between mind and body, subjective and objective, person and object.

The remainder of this chapter is devoted to three points. The first is that suffering is experienced by persons. In the separation between mind and body, the concept of person, or personhood, has been associated with mind, spirit, and the subjective. However, as I show, person is not merely mind, merely spiritual, nor only subjectively knowable. Person has many facets, and it is ignorance of them that actively contributes to patients' suffering. The understanding of the place

of person in human illness requires a rejection of the historical dualism of mind and body.

The second point derives from my interpretation of clinical observations: Suffering occurs when an impending destruction of the person is perceived; it continues until the threat of disintegration has passed or until the integrity of the person can be restored in some other manner. It follows, then, that although it often occurs in the presence of acute pain, shortness of breath, or other bodily symptoms, suffering extends beyond the physical. Most generally, suffering can be defined as the state of severe distress associated with events that threaten the integrity of the person.

The third point is that suffering can occur in relation to any aspect of the person, and these aspects extend much beyond the boundary of the skin. What follows is a somewhat simplified topography of persons that illustrates the extent of personhood and its relationship to suffering.

"PERSON" IS NOT "MIND"

The concept of person is not the same as the concept of mind. The idea of person is not static; it has gradually changed over history. The split between mind and body that has so deeply influenced our intellectual history and our approach to medical care was proposed by René Descartes to resolve certain philosophical issues. There is some reason to believe that Descartes's proposal, whatever other origins it may have had, was a successful political solution that allowed science to escape the smothering control of the church.[1] However, Descartes lived in a religious era in which it might have been justly claimed that what is nonbody is within the spiritual domain. In such eras, which include every social period until the recent past, spiritually derived rules governed virtually every aspect of life. But the general concept of the person has broadened over time, and the spiritual realm (equated with religion) has diminished.

The decline of the spiritual includes two simultaneous changes: an enlarged belief in a self as a legitimate entity apart from God and a decline in the power of belief. Changes in the meaning of concepts like *person* occur with changes in society, but the words for the concepts remain the same. This fact tends to obscure the depth of the transformations that have occurred in the meaning of *person*. People simply are persons in this time, as in past times, and have difficulty imagining what it might be like to be a person in an earlier period when the concept was more restrictive.

For example, the uniquely individual nature of persons is something taken for granted (the words *individual* and *person* are often used interchangeably); yet, the idea of individuality (in our sense) did not appear in Western tradition until around the 12th century (Morris, 1973). Political individualism is fundamental to our national heritage, yet its origins are in the 17th century; only in the last century has it come to stand for the unprecedented degree of personal freedom we enjoy. The recent stress on individual differences rather than on political equality is a predictable new direction of self-image. The key word is *self*.

What the last few decades have witnessed is an enlargement of that aspect of the person called the self. The contemporary identification of self (or self-awareness) and person is a case of mistaken identity, like the confusion of mind for person. In its contemporary usage, my self is one aspect of my person that may be known to me and may even be a condition of personhood. But there are parts of my person that can only be known to others, just as there are parts of my self that can only be known to me. Self is that aspect of person concerned primarily with relations with oneself. Other parts of a person involve relations with others and with the surrounding world. Self is only one part of person, included in but not synonymous with personhood (Zaner, 1981). Similarly, one cannot divorce the concept of person from the notion of mind, but the two are not interchangeable.

The mind-body dichotomy of the past and the contemporary perspective of science effectively separate human beings from nature (including their bodies). In this view, the body belongs to medical science, but there is no place for person. The only remaining place for the idea of person is in the category of mind. When the mind is problematic (not identifiable in objective terms), its very reality diminishes for science and so does

that of person. The concept of person then becomes identified with mind, the spiritual, and the subjective for lack of an alternative place in medicine's objective categories. Therefore, as long as the mind-body and similar dichotomies are accepted, suffering is either subjective and thus not truly "real"—not within medicine's domain—or identified exclusively with bodily pain. Not only is the identification of suffering with bodily pain misleading and distorting because it depersonalizes the sick patient, but also it is itself a source of suffering.

Finally, how suffering can be brought on by something in the body (like pain) cannot be understood until it is realized that nothing happens solely to the body. We are of a piece—whatever happens to one part happens to the all, and what happens to the whole of us happens to every part. As a consequence, it is not possible to treat sickness as something that happens solely to the body without risking damage to the person. An anachronistic division of the human condition into what is medical (having to do with the body) and what is nonmedical (the remainder) has given medicine too narrow a notion of its calling. Because of this division, physicians may, in concentrating on the cure of bodily disease, do things that cause the patient as a person to suffer. Psychologists may have the opportunity to intervene directly with patients in these too common situations or to help physicians broaden their focus to include the person rather than just the disease.

AN IMPENDING DESTRUCTION OF PERSON

Suffering is ultimately a personal matter, something with a presence and extent that can only be known to the sufferer. Patients sometimes report suffering when it is not expected or do not report suffering when it can be expected. Further, people often say that they know another is suffering greatly and then ask and find that the other person does not consider himself or herself to be suffering. Finally, a person can suffer enormously at the distress of another, especially if the other is a loved one. But, as is clarified in this chapter, suffering exists, and often can only be understood, in the context of others.

Suffering itself must be distinguished from its uses. In some theologies, especially the Christian, suffering has been seen as presenting the opportunity of bringing the sufferer closer to God. This "function" of suffering is at once its glorification and relief. If, through great pain or deprivation, someone is brought closer to a cherished goal, that person may have no sense of having suffered, but instead may feel enormous triumph. To an observer, the only apparent thing may be the deprivation. This cautionary note is especially important because people are often said to have suffered greatly, in a religious context, when it is known only that they were injured, tortured, or in pain, not whether they suffered.

Although pain and suffering are closely identified in the minds of most people and in the medical literature, they are phenomenologically distinct. The difficulty of understanding pain and the problems of physicians in providing adequate relief are well known (Goodwin, Goodwin, & Vogel, 1979; Kammer & Foley, 1981; Marks & Sacher, 1973). The greater the pain, the more it is believed to cause suffering. However, some pains, like those of childbirth, can be extremely severe and yet considered uplifting. The perceived meaning of pain influences the amount of medication required to control it. For example, a patient reported that she had initially believed that the pain in her leg was sciatica, and that she could control it with small doses of codeine, but when she discovered that it was caused by the spread of malignant disease, much greater amounts of medication were required for relief. Patients can writhe in pain from kidney stones and not be suffering (by their own statement) because they "know what it is." In contrast, people may report considerable suffering from apparently little pain when they do not know its source.

There are three other times when suffering in close relation to pain is commonly reported. The first is when the pain is so severe that it is virtually overwhelming—the pain of a dissecting aortic aneurysm is of that type. The second is when the patient does not believe that the pain can be controlled. The suffering of patients with terminal cancer can often be relieved by demonstrating

that their pain truly can be controlled. These patients will then often tolerate the same pain without any medication, preferring the pain to the side effects of their analgesics. The third is pain that is not overwhelming, but that continues for a very long time, so it seems that the pain is endless. Physicians commonly tell patients that they will "get used to the pain," but that rarely happens. What patients learn is both how little tolerance other people have for their continued report of pain and how pain becomes less bearable the longer it continues. Patients with recurrent pain even suffer in the absence of their pain by merely anticipating its return, as do people with severe frequent migraine headaches, who constantly worry whether a migraine will appear to ruin yet another important occasion.

In sum, people in pain frequently report suffering from pain when they feel out of control, when the pain is overwhelming, when the source of the pain is unknown, when the meaning of the pain is dire, or when the pain is apparently without end. In these situations, persons perceive pain as a threat to their continued existence—not merely to their lives, but to their integrity as persons. That this is the relation of pain to suffering is strongly suggested by the fact that suffering can often be relieved in the presence of continued pain by making the source of the pain known, changing its meaning, and demonstrating that it can be controlled and that an end is in sight. These same facts apply to other physical sources of suffering, such as shortness of breath.

It follows, then, that suffering has a temporal element. For a situation to be a source of suffering, it must influence the person's perception of future events. "If the pain continues like this, I will be overwhelmed"; "If the pain comes from cancer, I will die"; "If the pain cannot be controlled, I will not be able to take it." Note that, at the moment the individual is saying, "If the pain continues like this, I will be overwhelmed," he or she is not overwhelmed. At that moment, the person is intact. Fear itself always involves the future. In the case example that began this chapter, the patient cannot give up her fears; she cannot relinquish her sense of future despite the agony the fears cause her. Because of its temporal nature, suffering can frequently be relieved in the face of continued distress by causing the sufferers to root themselves in the absolute present: "This moment and only this moment."

Unfortunately, that is difficult to accomplish. It is noteworthy, however, that some Eastern theologies suggest that desire is the source of human suffering. To end suffering, one must give up desire. To give up desire, one must surrender the enchantment of the future. As suffering is discussed in the other dimensions of person, note how suffering would not exist in the absence of the future.

To move from the body as a source of suffering to suffering that arises from the other dimensions of person, two other aspects of pain that cause suffering should be mentioned. The first is when physicians do not validate the patient's pain. If no disease is found, physicians may suggest that the patient is "imagining" the pain, that it is "psychological" (in the sense that it is not real), or that he or she is "faking." Somewhat similar is that aspect of the suffering of patients with chronic pain who discover that they can no longer talk to others about their distress. In the former case, the person comes to distrust his or her perceptions of self, and in both instances, the social isolation adds to the person's suffering.

Another aspect essential to understanding suffering is the relation of meaning to the way in which illness is experienced. The word *meaning* has a number of different commonly employed senses that make for difficulties when we are not clear about which kind of meaning we mean. For example, when we say that the search for meaning is important or that people search to find meaning in life, or in the world, or in what has happened, we are referring to a special sense of the word *meaning*. Here, what something means is its meaning to a particular individual. Not individual in the sense that everybody sees things a little differently, but individual in reference to the fundamental things that characterize that person.

In other words, when I look to the world to find meaning, I find that there are things in the world—circumstances, opportunities, events, people, ideas, or perhaps groups with ideas or goals—that fit right in with my values, give me a chance to fit in or do things, or give me purpose in relationship to these things; finally, in the way that I can admire and find myself in these things, they give me self-worth. It can be seen that finding meaning, in this sense of meaning, might have an important therapeutic impact on persons as they discover how much more there is for them and how much more worth they have in view of what they find (or are helped to find) in the world.

Another characteristic of meaning when it is used in this fashion is that it is quite stable. That is because your values and your purposes, what is fundamentally important to you, and how you see yourself in relationship to the world, if they change at all, change slowly. People may suffer when their world ceases to have meaning in that sense, and sometimes finding meaning (of that kind) may be a help to the suffering person.

There is another kind of meaning that is crucial to understanding suffering. The type of meaning that may precipitate suffering is more often changeable, shifting from moment to moment as events, circumstances, and relationships swirl around and demand the assignment of meaning. Although the assignment of the meaning is, as always, within the person, the source of the meaning is in the changing world. The perception of what is happening may suddenly shift, demanding a shift in meaning, for example, when the actions of a physician or nurse, previously seen as benevolent, are suddenly perceived as terribly threatening. Or utterances take on a new meaning as circumstances change.

With the change in meaning secondary to the new perception come shifts in the cognitive, emotional, physical, and spiritual impact of what is happening. For the same word, event, object, or relationship, a person may simultaneously have a cognitive meaning, an affective or emotional meaning, a bodily meaning, and a transcendent or spiritual meaning (Cassell, 2003). This may result in contradictions in the different levels of meaning. For example, for a patient receiving chemotherapy, the word *chemotherapy* could be shown to elicit simultaneously a cognitive meaning that included his beliefs about the cellular mechanism of drug action, the emotion of fear, the bodily sensation of nausea, and the transcendent feeling that God would protect him. Normally, all those levels of meaning are jumbled, but together they constituted the meaning for that patient of the word *chemotherapy* (Cassell, 2003, p. 179).

Meanings are dynamic, not fixed or static. They include where things come from and what they become. Apples come from trees and become applesauce. Fall on your wrist on the ice and not only does the thought of the fracture come to awareness, but also the thought of the impairment that will follow. Thus, meanings contain predictions, and predictions lead to the foretaste of experience. Think of how your foot feels when the next step going down is not in its expected place (walking down a stationary escalator, for example). The failed expectation of sensation produces its own sensation.

Meanings and their resultant predictions not only are a result of experience but also modify the ongoing experience and even its physical sensations (from moments to months), so that they are reinforced, amplified, or diminished. As a consequence, the meanings assigned by the person to the suffering may change how the patient (and others) behaves or even what happens in the body. The whole process of the assignment of meanings may occur below awareness, out of consciousness, or may be unconscious in the psychodynamic sense. Despite their complexities, the meanings the patient assigns to the illness experience and suffering offer opportunities for intervention. When meanings are changed, the body and the suffering may also be altered.

A SIMPLIFIED DESCRIPTION
OF THE PERSON

Unlike objects of science, persons cannot be reduced to their parts to understand them better. But a simple topography of person may be useful in understanding the relation between suffering and the goals of medicine.

Persons have personality and character. All parents know that personality traits appear within the first few weeks to months of life and are remarkably durable over time. Some personalities handle some illnesses better than others. What may be destructive for one person is easily tolerated by another, but some stresses that may accompany illness, such as loss of control, are universally difficult to bear. Individuals vary in character as well as personality. Some people do, in fact, have "stronger" character than others and

bear adversity better. Some are good, kind, and tolerant under the stress of terminal illness; others become mean and strike out when even mildly ill.

A person has a past—things done and places visited, accomplishments and failures. The lived past is a story that has taken place over time and in many places, and has involved countless others. The experiences gathered during one's life are a part of today as well as yesterday. Events of the present can be checked against the past, and events of the past contribute to the meanings assigned to present happenings.

It would be an error to think that the past is simply memories stored in some old mental filing cabinet. Rather, the constant flow of happenings reinforces some past experiences and dilutes others. Memory exists in the nostrils and the hands as well as in other body parts. A fragrance drifts by, and an old memory is evoked. My feet have not forgotten how to roller skate, and my hands remember skills I was hardly aware I had learned. When these memories and past experiences involve sickness and medical care, they can influence present illness and medical care. They can stimulate fear or confidence, bodily symptoms, and even anguish. It damages people to rob them of their past, deny the truth of their memories, or mock their fears and worries. A person without a past is incomplete.

Life experiences, previous illness, and experiences with doctors, hospitals, medications, deformities and disabilities, pleasures and successes, or miseries and failures form the net of meanings that is the background for illness. The personal meaning of the disease and its treatment arise from the past as well as the present. If cancer occurs in a patient with self-confidence resulting from many past achievements, it may give rise to optimism and a resurgence of strength. Even if fatal, the disease may not produce the destruction of the person, but rather reaffirm his or her indomitability. The outcome would be different in a person for whom life had been a succession of failures.

Like an old wound that aches when it rains, one can suffer again the injuries of yesterday. The lived past provides other occasions for suffering. It may simply be lost, as in the case of amnesia, leaving the person less whole. Or its truth may be denied by the events of today, as in "All my life I believed in . . . , and now, when it is too late to change, it turns out not to be true."

A person has a family. The intensity of family ties cannot be overemphasized; people frequently behave as if they were physical extensions of their parents. Things that might cause suffering in others may be borne without complaint by someone who believes that the disease is part of the family identity and thus inevitable. I remember a man with polycystic kidney disease who was quite proud of his ultimately fatal disease because he was finally "one of them," like his mother and sister. Many diseases for which no heritable basis is known are also acceptable to an individual because others in the family have been similarly afflicted. What seems to count is the connection of the individual to the family. One of my patients, dying of cancer of the lung, literally shrugged his shoulders over his impending death from the disease that killed his father and two brothers. His children suffered at his bedside. He was fulfilling his destiny while they were losing a father. Just as a person's past experiences give meaning to the present, so do the past experiences of the person's family. They are part of the person.

A person has a cultural background. It is well known that socially determined factors such as diet, environment, and social behaviors contribute to disease patterns. Because culture also contributes to beliefs and values, cultural factors play a part in the effects of disease on a person. Culture defines what is meant by masculine or feminine, what clothes are worn, attitudes toward the dying and the sick, mating behavior, the height of chairs and steps, attitudes toward odors and excreta, where computers are placed and who uses them, bus stops and bedclothes, and how the aged and the disabled are treated. These things, mostly invisible to the well, have an enormous impact on the sick and can be a source of untold suffering. They influence the behavior of others toward the sick person and that of the sick toward themselves. Cultural norms and social rules regulate whether someone can be among others or will be isolated, whether the sick will be considered foul or acceptable, and whether they are to be pitied or censured.

With this in mind, it can be seen how someone devoid of physical pain, perhaps even devoid of "symptoms," can suffer. People can suffer from what they have lost of themselves in relation to the world of objects, events, and relationships. Such suffering occurs because our intactness as persons, our coherence and integrity, comes not only from intactness of the body but also from the wholeness of the web of relationships with self and others. We realize also that, although medical care can reduce the impact of sickness, inattentive care can increase its disruption.

A person has roles. I am a father, a physician, a teacher, a husband, a brother, an orphaned son, an uncle, and a friend. People are their roles (whatever else they may be), and each role has rules. Together the rules that guide the performance of roles make up a complex set of entitlements and limitations of responsibility and privilege. By middle age, the roles may be so firmly set that disease can lead to the virtual destruction of a person by making the performance of his or her roles impossible. Whether it is a doctor who cannot doctor or a parent who cannot parent, the individual is unquestionably diminished by the loss of function. I am aware that the "sick role" allows patients to be excused from their usual role requirements but, in practice, the concept of the sick role has not been very useful (although it offers some insight into illness behavior). Here, as in each facet of person, the degree of suffering caused by the loss varies from person to person.

There is no self without others; there is no consciousness without a consciousness of others, no speaker without a hearer, no dreamer who does not dream in relation to others, no act or object or thought that does not somehow encompass others. There is no behavior that is not, was not, or will not be involved with others, even if only in memory or reverie. The degree to which human interactions are literally physically synchronized is amazing. Take away others, remove sight or hearing, let the ability to synchronize activities be injured, and the person begins to be diminished. Everyone dreads becoming blind or deaf, but these are only the most obvious injuries to human interaction. There is almost no limit to the ways in which humans can be cut off from others and then suffer the loss. It is in relationships with others that sexuality, giving and receiving love, and happiness, gratitude, anger, and the full range of human emotionality find expression. Therefore, in this dimension of the person, illness may injure the ability to express emotion.

Furthermore, the extent and nature of a sick person's relationships strongly influence the degree of suffering that a disease may produce. There is a vast difference between going home to an empty apartment or returning to a network of friends and family after hospitalization. Illness may occur in one partner of a long and strongly bound marriage, or it may be the last straw in a union that was falling apart. Suffering caused by the loss of sexual function associated with some diseases depends not only on the importance of sexual performance to the sick person but also on its importance in his or her relationships. The impact of the kind of relationships a patient has was brought home to me as I sat at the bedside of a dying man who wanted to stop the futile treatments given for his malignancy. His wife sat stunned after hearing him speak and then screamed, "Damn you, you're just trying to get out and leave me like you always have."

A person has a relationship with himself or herself. Self-esteem, self-approval, and self-love (and their opposites) are emotional expressions of the relationship of a self to itself. To behave well in the face of pain or sickness brings gratification just as to behave poorly in these situations may leave lifelong disappointment in its wake. The old-fashioned words *honor* and *cowardice* stand for states that are much more with us than their lack of currency would suggest. In our times, we have been more concerned with relationships with others than with ourselves (Storr, 1988). Nonetheless, suffering may follow on failing oneself if the failure is profound enough.

A person is a political being. A person is, in the larger sense of political, equal to other individuals, with rights, obligations, and the ability to redress injury by others and by the state. Sickness can interfere here, producing the feeling of political powerlessness and lack of representation. The recent successes in the drive to restore the disabled to parity are notable in this regard. All relationships between people, in addition to whatever else they may be, are relationships of power: of subordinance, dominance, or equipotence. The powerlessness of the sick person's body and the ability of others to control the person by controlling the body are part of the political dimension of illness. The change in the relationship of doctor and patient described here represents a change in their relative power. However, the fundamental political loss and source of suffering in this dimension of person derives less from the actions of others as from disease itself.

Persons do things. They act, create, make, take apart, put together, wind, unwind, cause to be, and cause to vanish. They know themselves and are known by these acts. More than the requirements of a role, more than is necessary in a relationship, more than they know themselves, and some more (or less) than others, things come out of their mouths or are done by their hands, feet, or entire bodies that express themselves. When illness makes it impossible for people to do these things, they are not themselves.

As psychologists know better than most, persons are often, to one degree or another, unaware of much that happens to them and why. Thus some things in thought cannot be brought to awareness by ordinary reflection, memory, or introspection. The structure of the unconscious is pictured quite differently by different scholars, but most students of human behavior accept that such an interior world exists. People can behave in ways that seem inexplicable and strange even to themselves, and the sense of powerlessness the person may feel in the face of such behavior can be a source of great distress.

Persons have regular behaviors. In health, the details of day-to-day behavior are taken for granted. From the moment of awakening in the morning to the manner of sleep at night, a person's behavior follows a customary pattern. Persons know themselves to be well as much by whether they behave as usual as by any other set of facts. If they cannot do the things they identify with the fact of their being, they are not whole.

Every person has a body. The relation with one's body may vary from identification with it to admiration, loathing, or constant fear. There are some who act as though their body's only purpose was to carry their heads about. The body may even be a representation of one parent, so that when something happens to that person's body, it is as though an injury was done to a parent. Into this relationship with the body every illness must fit. Disease can so alter the relationship that the body is no longer seen as a friend but as an untrustworthy enemy. This is intensified if the illness occurs without warning so that the person comes to distrust his or her perceptions of the body. As illness deepens, the person may feel increasingly vulnerable or damaged. Much was made a few years back of the concept of body image and the suffering caused by disease-induced alterations of that image. The body does not actually have to be altered to cause damage to the wholeness of the person; damage to the person's relationship with the body is sufficient.

Everyone has a secret life. Sometimes it takes the form of fantasies and dreams of glory, and sometimes it has a real existence known to only a few. Within that secret life are fears and desires, love affairs of the past and present, hopes or fantasies, and ways of solving the problems of everyday life known only to the person. It is proper that they remain secret because they arise from a discrete part of human existence—a separate, private life that cannot be predicted from what is known of the public person. Modesty is not merely a behavior that hides one from public view; it hides the parts of a person that are none of the public's business. Disease may destroy not only the public person but also the secret person. A secret beloved friend may be lost to a sick person because he or she has no legitimate place by the sickbed. When that happens, the sick person may have lost that part of life that made tolerable an otherwise embittered existence. The loss may be of only the dream, the wish, or the fantasy (however improbable) that one day might have come true. Such loss can be a source of great distress and intensely private pain.

Every person has a perceived future. Events that one expects to come to pass vary from expectations for one's children to a belief in one's creative ability. Intense unhappiness results from a loss of that future—the future of the individual person, of children, and of other loved ones. It is in this dimension of existence that hope dwells. Hope is one of the necessary traits of a successful life. No one has ever questioned the suffering that attends the loss of hope.

Everyone has a transcendent dimension—a life of the spirit, however expressed or known. Considering the amount of thought devoted to it through the ages, the common wisdom contains very little about transcendence, which is all the more remarkable given its central place in the relief of suffering. It is most directly dealt with in mysticism and in the mystic traditions both within and outside formal religions. Spirituality seems to me, however, to be part of everyday life, much as is emotion. It also seems evident that the frequency with which people have intense feelings of bonding with groups, with ideals, or with anything larger and more enduring than the person—of which patriotism is one example—is evidence of the universality of human transcendence. The quality of being greater and more lasting than an individual life gives this aspect of persons its timeless dimension. However, the profession of medicine appears to ignore the human spirit. When I see patients in nursing homes who seem to go on forever, existing only for their bodily needs, I wonder whether it is not their transcendent dimension that they have lost.

THE NATURE OF SUFFERING

For purposes of explanation, I have outlined various parts that make up a person. However, persons cannot be reduced to their parts so that they can be better understood. Reductionist scientific methods, so successful in other areas of human biology, are not as useful for the comprehension of whole persons. My intent is to suggest the complexity of persons and the potential for injury and suffering that exists in each of us. All the aspects of personhood—the lived past, the family's lived past, culture and society, roles, the instrumental dimension, associations and relationships, the body, the unconscious mind, the political being, the secret life, the perceived future, and the transcendent-being dimension—are susceptible to damage and loss.

Injuries (e.g., the sense of having been assaulted or destabilized by sickness or its treatment; Daneault et al., 2003) may be expressed by sadness, anger, loneliness, depression, grief, unhappiness, melancholy, rage, withdrawal, or yearning. We acknowledge the individual's right to have and give voice to such feelings, but we often forget that the affect is merely the outward expression of the injury, much as speech is of thought, and is not the injury itself. We know much less about the nature of the injuries themselves, and what we know has been learned largely from literature and the other arts, not from medicine.

If the injury is sufficient, the person suffers. The only way to learn whether suffering is present is to ask the sufferer. We all recognize certain injuries that almost invariably cause suffering: the death or suffering of loved ones, powerlessness, helplessness, hopelessness, torture, the loss of a life's work, deep betrayal, physical agony, isolation, homelessness, memory failure, and unremitting fear. Each is both universal and individual. Each touches features common to us all, yet each contains features that must be defined in terms of a specific person at a specific time.

THE MELIORATION OF SUFFERING

One might ask why everybody is not suffering all the time. In a busy life, almost no day goes by that a little chip is not knocked off one or another of the parts of a person. Obviously, one does not suffer merely at the loss of a piece of oneself but instead when intactness cannot be maintained or restored. Yet I suspect more suffering exists than is known. Just as people with chronic pain learn to keep it to themselves because others lose interest, so may those with chronic suffering.

There is another reason why each injury— even large assaults—may not cause suffering. Persons are able to enlarge themselves in response to damage, so that rather than being reduced by injury, they may indeed grow. This response to suffering has led to the belief that suffering is good for people. To some degree, and in some individuals, this may be so. We would not have such a belief, however, were it not equally common knowledge that persons can also be destroyed by suffering. If the leg is injured so the athlete can never run again, the athlete may compensate by learning another sport, skill, or mode of expression. And so it is with the loss of relationships, loves, roles, physical strength, dreams, and power. The human body may not have the capacity to grow another part when one is lost, but the person has.

The ability to recover from loss without succumbing to suffering is sometimes called resil-

iency, as though merely elastic rebound is involved. But it seems more as if an inner force is withdrawn from one manifestation of person and redirected to another. If a child dies and the parent makes a successful recovery, the person is said to have "rebuilt" his or her life. The verb suggests, correctly I think, that the parts of the person are assembled in a new manner, allowing renewed expression in different dimensions. If a previously active person is confined to a wheelchair, intellectual or artistic pursuits may occupy more time and energy. Total involvement in some political or social goal may use the energy previously given to physical activity. We see an aged scholar, for whom all activity is restricted by disease and infirmity, continue to pursue the goals of a lifetime of study, and we marvel at the strength of "the life of the mind."

Recovery from suffering often involves borrowing the strength of others as though persons who have lost parts of themselves can be sustained by the personhood of others until their own recovers. This is one of the latent functions of physicians: lending strength. A group also may lend strength: Consider the success of groups of the similarly afflicted in easing the burden of illness (e.g., women who have had a mastectomy, people with ostomies, fellow sufferers from a rare sickness, or even the parents or family members of the diseased).

Meaning and transcendence offer two additional ways by which the destruction of a part of personhood or threat to its integrity are meliorated. The search for the meaning of human suffering has occupied humanity on individual and cultural levels throughout history. Assigning meaning—enlarging significance and positive importance—to the injurious condition often reduces or even resolves the suffering associated with it. Most often, a cause for the injury is sought within past behaviors or beliefs. Thus, the pain or threat that causes suffering is seen as not destroying a part of the person because it is part of the person by virtue of its origin within the self. The concept of Karma in Eastern theologies is a complex form of that defense against suffering because suffering is seen to result from behaviors of the individual in previous incarnations.

In our culture, taking the blame for harm that comes to oneself because of the unconscious mind reduces suffering by locating it within a coherent set of meanings. Physicians are familiar with the question: "Did I do something to make this happen?" A striking example of this mechanism is when a woman takes the blame for rape as if she had done something to invite it. It is more tolerable for a terrible thing to happen because of something one has done—and even suffer the guilt—than that it be simply a stroke of fate, a random, chance event. Like Job's friends warding off the possibility that God is not just, others around the victim often encourage self-blame.

Transcendence is probably the most powerful way in which one is restored to wholeness after an injury to personhood. When experienced, transcendence locates the person in a far larger landscape. The sufferer is not isolated by pain but is brought closer to a transpersonal source of meaning and to the human community that shares that meaning. Such an experience need not involve religion in any formal sense; however, in its transpersonal dimension, it is deeply spiritual. Patriotism provides another example of transcendence as a means for relieving personal agony, as in Nathan Hale's last words, "I only regret that I have but one life to lose for my country."

WHEN SUFFERING CONTINUES

What happens when suffering is not relieved? If suffering occurs when there is a threat to the integrity of the person or a loss of a part of the person, then suffering will continue if the person cannot be made whole again. Little is known about this aspect of suffering. Is much of what is called depression actually unrelieved suffering? Considering that depression commonly follows the loss of loved ones, business reversals, prolonged illness, profound injuries to self-esteem, and other damages to person, the possibility is real. In many chronic or serious diseases, persons who "recover" or who are seemingly successfully treated do not return to normal function. Despite a physical cure, they may never again be employed, recover sexual function, pursue career goals, reestablish family relationships, or reenter the social world. Such patients may not have recovered from the nonphysical changes that occur with life-threatening illness. Consider the dimensions of person described in this chapter, and it is difficult to think of one that is not threatened or damaged in profound illness. It should come as no surprise to discover that chronic suffering frequently follows in the wake of disease. It should also be no surprise that antidepressant medications often fail to relieve suffering because none are FDA-approved for restoring meaning or personhood.

The paradox with which this chapter began—that suffering is often caused by the treatment of the sick—no longer seems puzzling. How could it be otherwise, when medicine has concerned itself so little with the nature and causes of suffering? This lack is not a failure of good intentions. No one is more concerned about the relief of pain or the restoration of lost function than the physician. Instead, it is a failure of knowledge and understanding. We lack knowledge because, in working within the constraints of a dichotomy contrived in a historical context far removed from our own, we have artificially circumscribed our task in caring for the sick.

Problems of staggering complexity arise when we attempt to understand all the known dimensions of person and their relationship to illness and suffering, yet these problems are no greater than those initially posed in trying to find out how the body worked. The difficulty is not how to finish solving the problems—it is how to start. But if medicine and the healing arts are again to be directed toward the relief of human suffering, the need is clear.

Note

1. Richard Zaner (1988, p. 106 ff.) argued convincingly that, regarding the mind-body dichotomy, Descartes has been treated unfairly by history; he knew full well that no such separation is possible.

References

Bakan, D. (1968). *Disease, pain, and sacrifice*. Boston: Beacon Press.

Cassell, E. J. (1972). Being and becoming dead. *Social Research, 39*, 528–542.

Cassell, E. J. (2003). *The nature of suffering* (2nd ed.). New York: Oxford University Press.

Goodwin, J. S., Goodwin, J. M., & Vogel, A. V.

(1979). Knowledge and use of placebos by house officers and nurses. *Annals of Internal Medicine, 91,* 106–110.

Illich, I. (1976). *Medical nemesis: The expropriation of health.* New York: Bantam Books.

Kammer, R. M., & Foley, K. M. (1981). Patterns of narcotic drug use in Canada. *Annals of the New York Academy of Science, 362,* 161–172.

Marks, R., & Sacher, E. (1973). Undertreatment of medical patients. *Annals of Internal Medicine, 78,* 173–181.

Morris, C. (1973). *The discovery of the individual.* New York: Harper Torchbooks.

Storr, A. (1988). *A return to the self.* New York: Ballantine Books.

Zaner, R. (1981). *The context of self.* Athens, OH: Ohio University Press.

Zaner, R. (1988). *Ethics and the clinical encounter.* Englewood Cliffs, NJ: Prentice-Hall.

13

Hope and Hopelessness

C. R. Snyder
Kristin Kahle Wrobleski
Stacy C. Parenteau
Carla J. Berg

The primary care psychologist will encounter many patients without hope. The patient who is referred to the primary care psychologist often has difficulty finding the motivation to follow the treatment regimen or cannot find a way to overcome the many obstacles that result from several comorbid conditions. Although hope has not been a clear focus of cognitive–behavioral therapists or clinical psychologists in general, the treatment approach can be enhanced by including it.

> Mr. L. is a 56-year-old man with long-standing hypertension and high cholesterol who has recently been diagnosed with congestive heart failure. His physician refers him to the psychologist because he has begun missing follow-up appointments and has been failing to take his medication because "it's no use." His physician believes Mr. L. is depressed. Mr. L. agrees to see the psychologist for one visit to placate his doctor, but expresses deep pessimism about the point of talking about his problems or his future because "it's hopeless."

Although it would be typical to describe Mr. L. as depressed, we believe that a focus on hope-

lessness offers an important avenue of treatment. In this chapter, we address this process of working with the hopeless patient. Our suggested hope-based approach reaches beyond building the patient's self-efficacy in a specific area or helping the patient with goal-setting strategies. This approach includes a more comprehensive conceptualization and approach to working with situations in which the patient feels hopeless, and it teaches patients to reengage in goal-setting strategies, building skills to help reach goals and staying motivated enough to complete a goal.

When faced with terminal or chronic diagnoses, patients commonly are unable to think of how to move forward in their lives. Lacking positive future orientations, hopeless patients become vulnerable not only to ordinary stressors, but also to magnified symptoms when physically ill. We hasten to note, however, that hopelessness does not have to accompany chronic or terminal illnesses, and the primary care psychologist plays a pivotal role in helping the patient to become hopeful.

In this chapter, we give clinicians a framework for understanding hope, as well as suggestions for incorporating "hope enhancement" into psychotherapy. To that end, we answer the following questions: What is hope? How are hope and physical health related? How can we recognize hopelessness? How can the psychologist help the patient to rebuild hope? Last, we provide a case study to illustrate how hope theory can be used in psychotherapy for a patient with a medical illness.

WHAT IS HOPE?

Hope is defined as "desire accompanied by expectation of or belief in fulfillment; and as the expectation of fulfillment or success, as well as someone or something on which hopes are centered, e.g., something hoped for" (*Merriam-Webster Online Dictionary*). Snyder (1994) expanded on the lay understanding of hope to develop the "hope theory," which has received considerable attention from social scientists. In Snyder's formulation, hope centers on the goal pursuit process and encompasses a person's perceived capacities to find the ways of achieving goals while staying interested in reaching the goal.

In the context of hope theory, goals are presented as the object of future-oriented thinking. Based on the centrality of goal thinking, hope theory is a cognitive model that involves the perceived ability to find the (a) pathways to reach desired goals and (b) motivation, or agency, to move toward those goals along selected routes. So conceptualized, hope is a traitlike thinking process that develops in early childhood and is maintained throughout the life span. In contrast, hopelessness is a lack of hopeful thinking, or a lack of goals, pathways, or motivation. Furthermore, the hopeless person frequently attaches a negative emotional response to this cognitive set, such as a feeling of despair.

COMPONENTS OF HOPE

Within the hope theory mental trilogy of goals, pathways, and agency, goals are the object of the thinking process (Snyder, 1994). These goals generally are categorized as either approach or avoidance in content. Approach goals involve the continuation of an ongoing goal pursuit or the ac-

complishment of a new feat that is built on a previous goal. For instance, a high-hope cardiac rehabilitation patient who has lost 10 pounds (on doctor's orders) since his last checkup will set an approach goal of losing another 15 pounds by his next checkup. An asthma patient may set an avoidance goal of not presenting to the emergency room because of an asthma attack for an entire month.

The absolute certainty of accomplishing a goal is not necessary. On the contrary, hopeful persons appear to set goals that stretch their limits and abilities. These "stretch" goals are challenges, and hopeful persons may not be completely certain of achieving their stretch goal (Snyder, 2002). For example, a stroke patient who uses a walker may set a goal of using only a cane to walk within 4 weeks, even though the patient's physical therapist might believe that it would be 5 weeks before the patient is ready. The patient's goal is not completely unrealistic; it just sets up a greater challenge.

The second part of the mental trilogy involves pathways thinking or the perceived capacity to produce appropriate steps to achieve one's goals. For instance, a patient suffering from bipolar depression may identify several pathways that serve a goal of managing her illness, including taking her medication as prescribed, attending a bipolar disorder support group, and continuing in individual psychotherapy. A patient with early-stage cancer might set a goal of being cancer free. Consequently, she identifies a variety of pathways to "beat" the cancer, including attending all her radiation therapy appointments, clearly communicating any new symptoms to her oncologist, attending a cancer support group, and reading articles on cancer prevention and treatment. Again, the pathways are any steps that a person is taking to achieve a given goal.

Third, agency is the motivational component of the hope mental trilogy that allows a person to move along the pathways toward a goal. Agency thinking is linked to energy-building behaviors, such as eating well-balanced meals and getting enough sleep. A high-hope patient suffering from multiple sclerosis may decide to take a nap during his lunch break to have enough energy to stay focused during the rest of the day at work. In addition, agency thought often involves motivational self-talk, such as, "I can do this," "I will beat this disease," and the like (Snyder, LaPointe, Crowson, & Early, 1998). In another example, a transplant patient might use statements such as "I will stay as healthy as possible" and "I will make it through this."

Although hope theory primarily conceptualizes hope in cognitive terms, Snyder, Ilardi, et al. (2000) also identified certain emotional states that correspond with high or low hope. In this regard, the high-hope person (as measured by the Hope Scale, described in the next section) works within a positive emotional frame and reports more positive feelings, such as contentment and happiness. Accordingly, inadequate or ineffective pathways are easily identified because the accompanying frustration is antithetical to the high-hope person's typical positive emotional frame of reference. High-hope people are able to identify ineffective pathways quickly, and they have the necessary agency to undertake a search for alternative pathways.

Thus, by identifying the ineffective pathways that contribute to a sense of goal blockage, high-hope persons can try other, more successful pathways. In this process of jettisoning unproductive routes and finding more productive avenues to their goals, high-hope people are able to maintain a positive emotional equilibrium.

Conversely, patients who are not engaging in hopeful thinking are likely to report *feeling* hopeless rather than *thinking* hopelessly. Low-hope people cannot readily overcome ineffective pathways, and even minor setbacks quickly lead to counterproductive cognitions about their inabilities to reach their goals. This results in a cycle of increased attention to that which is not going right rather than the consideration of positive new directions. For such low-hope persons, therefore, the thoughts continue to fuel negative emotions, and this catastrophic cycle continues. The clinician should be mindful that the patient is likely to identify hopelessness as a deeply felt emotion rather than a lack of pathways or agency.

MEASURING HOPE

People see themselves as having differing capacities for summoning pathways and agency thoughts.

These different self-referential, goal-directed thoughts are reflected in their scores on the Hope Scale. Using this definition of hope, Snyder and colleagues (1991) developed and validated the Trait Hope Scale (see Table 13.1) as a self-report index of enduring, cross-situational hopeful thinking. This Hope Scale offers a total hope score and subscores for pathways and agency. In addition, the Adult State Hope Scale (Snyder et al., 1996) and the Children's Trait Hope Scale (Snyder et al., 1997) can be used to assess hope.[1] We recommend using the multi-item Hope Scale because

Table 13.1 The Trait Hope Scale

Directions: Read each item carefully. Using the scale shown below, please select the number that best describes YOU and put that number in the blank provided.

1 = Definitely False
2 = Mostly False
3 = Somewhat False
4 = Slightly False
5 = Slightly True
6 = Somewhat True
7 = Mostly True
8 = Definitely True

__ 1. I can think of many ways to get out of a jam.

__ 2. I energetically pursue my goals.

__ 3. I feel tired most of the time.

__ 4. There are lots of ways around any problem.

__ 5. I am easily downed in an argument.

__ 6. I can think of many ways to get the things in life that are most important to me.

__ 7. I worry about my health.

__ 8. Even when others get discouraged, I know I can find a way to solve the problem.

__ 9. My past experiences have prepared me well for my future.

__10. I've been pretty successful in life.

__11. I usually find myself worrying about something.

__12. I meet the goals that I set for myself.

Notes: When administering the Trait Hope Scale, it is called the Future Scale or Goal Scale. The Agency subscale is derived by summing Items 2, 9, 10, and 12; the Pathways subscale score is derived by adding Items 1, 4, 6, and 8. The remaining items are distracters. The total Hope Scale score is derived by summing the four agency and four pathways items. The scale is reprinted with the permission of C. R. Snyder and the American Psychological Association, © 1991, *Journal of Personality and Social Psychology*.

simply asking the patient how much hope she or he has can be unreliable.

In this regard, a maxim of assessment is that several items (or questions) produce a more consistent and thorough sampling of a given concept than does one item. Likewise, merely asking one question about hope level is too dependent on the patient's conceptualization of hope, which may or may not include the pathways and agency components. The Hope Scale allows the clinician to compare pre- and posttreatment scores regardless of the patient's subjective and evolving understanding of "hope." Also, the Hope Scale is useful in identifying whether the patient struggles more with summoning motivation or identifying pathways, which then informs the focus of the intervention.

In summary, hope theory reflects a cognitive process that involves pathways and agency thinking about one's capacity to pursue goals. Such hopeful thoughts also have causal influences on persons' emotional states. That is, successful goal pursuits beget positive emotions, whereas perceived lack of success in goal pursuits yields negative emotions (for empirical support, see Snyder et al., 1996).

On this point, consider a high-hope patient with Parkinson's disease who has met her goal of learning as much as possible about her disease by attending seminars, talking to her doctor, and reading books on coping with the illness. This patient is likely to feel more in control and positive than another Parkinson's patient who is low in hope and cannot come up with a goal now that her primary goal of curing Parkinson's is not possible. Indeed, the latter patient is likely to report feeling a sense of hopelessness.

The Trait Hope Scale provides a reliable and valid measure of an adult's perceived ability to identify pathways and to summon the necessary motivation to use those pathways. Furthermore, high-hope people readily adapt their pathways to particular circumstances and are able to produce the requisite agency thought and channel it to the best pathways for particular goal pursuits. Low-hope persons, on the other hand, struggle to adapt their pathways to the situation and wrestle with finding enough motivation to use any pathways that are found. A high-hope person with Type 1 diabetes keeps herself motivated by using positive self-talk statements such as "I want to have children," which reminds her that keeping her blood sugar level as steady as possible is important during pregnancy. She also relies on her friends for moral support and works on her assertiveness skills to feel comfortable communicating her eating schedule to friends and coworkers. On the other hand, a low-hope person with Type 1 diabetes does not test her blood sugar regularly because she sees it as a futile effort to control an incurable illness. Consistent with this attitude, she has not taken steps to maintain a more regular eating and sleeping schedule and is uncomfortable asking for any special accommodations.

RELATIONSHIP OF HOPE WITH PHYSICAL HEALTH

As a construct of individual differences, hope should differentially predict how individuals cope with impediments to their goals. For purposes of this chapter, we focus on the relationship between levels of hope and health-related impediments and markers. Numerous empirical investigations have shown that hope acts as a buffer against distress and despair in individuals with medical illnesses (for review, see Snyder, 2002). This occurs through a variety of mechanisms. For instance, hope has been linked to other adaptive psychological processes, such as benefit finding (identifying the positive, but unexpected, consequences of a difficult situation), that lead to increased emotional well-being in patients with various medical conditions (Abbey & Halman, 1995). In hope theory terms, the positive appraisals and benefit-finding promote a sense of agency in people who are struggling with illnesses. For instance, Ms. J., a breast-cancer survivor, noted that, although she had to go through surgery and chemotherapy, the long car drive to the hospital allowed her a lot of time to talk to and reconnect with her once-estranged mother.

Hope also is predictive of other positive coping strategies, such as emotional expression. In this regard, Stanton et al. (2000) found that high-hope breast cancer patients who engaged in emotionally expressive coping had fewer medical appointments and reported less overall distress than did their low-hope counterparts. For high-hope cancer patients, therefore, emotional expression may help clarify goals that facilitate continued goal pursuit (Stanton et al., 2000).

In another study by Irving, Snyder, and Crowson (1998), the relationship of dispositional hope to various self-reported cancer-related coping activities was examined in 115 college women. Results showed that high-hope compared to low-hope women were significantly more knowledgeable about cancer, even when controlling statistically for academic achievement, experience with cancer among family and friends, and positive and negative affectivity. Participants also were asked to list coping strategies in the imagined phases of cancer. High-hope women listed significantly more hope-related coping responses during the different phases of the cancer diagnosis and treatment process, and they did so even when the variances related to the previously mentioned variables were controlled statistically. This last finding may reflect both pathways thinking and the agency thinking that may be synonymous with a person's "fighting spirit" when faced with adversity.

HOPELESSNESS AND THE DEVELOPMENT OF MEDICAL ILLNESSES

Hopelessness may also play a role in the development of medical illnesses. Anda et al. (1993) found a positive correlation between hopelessness and both fatal and nonfatal ischemic heart disease in adults aged 45 to 77 years. In this regard, Snyder, Feldman, Taylor, Schroeder, and Adams (2000) theorized that higher hope people are more likely to engage in primary prevention strategies. Furthermore, when a disease process cannot be prevented, the higher hope patients are able to conceptualize strategies for continuing on plausible pathways toward reachable goal pursuits. For instance, higher hope individuals with total visual impairments reported having a more sociable and confident coping style than their lower hope counterparts (Jackson, Taylor, Palmatier, Elliott, & Elliott, 1998).

In the primary care setting, a variety of factors is likely to influence a patient's subjective level of hopelessness. The severity and prognosis of an illness are two key factors that exacerbate hopelessness. More severe illnesses will restrict the patient's available pathways. For instance, a patient with mild chronic bronchitis may have to restrict certain social activities during an acute flare-up of bronchitis. A patient with emphysema, on the other hand, may eventually be unable to leave the house because he or she cannot walk more than 10 steps at a time before needing to rest. The type of disability also can influence the onset and continuation of hopelessness. A patient with decreased mobility after a hip replacement only may need to make minor adjustments to daily activities, such as using a walker. A person with macular degeneration, however, would eventually have to stop driving and would require assistance with most basic activities, such as grocery shopping and paying bills.

RECOGNITION OF HOPELESSNESS

The previously described studies illustrate the importance of hope for coping successfully with physical illnesses. Persons with high levels of hope find effective physical and psychological pathways to navigate their illnesses. For those with high hope rather low hope, the health-related impediments are overcome, and the future-oriented, goal-directed thought processes are maintained. The high-hope thought processes are largely self-correcting in that goal or pathways blockages are quickly identified and adapted, and the requisite agency thoughts are readily available. Unfortunately, not everyone has elevated hope. For people with lower levels of hope, life's challenges are not so easily overcome. As stated, hopelessness in the context of Snyder's hope theory is the absence of agency and pathways goal-directed thinking. Furthermore, we would point out that hopelessness can reflect deficiencies in any of the goals, pathways, or agency components of hope theory. In this regard, we return to the cases of Mr. L. and Ms. C. for a glimpse of a hopeless patient in therapy.

Low-hope compared to high-hope people are less likely to "let go" of goals that are no longer feasible (Snyder, 1998). For example, those with low hope may continue to pursue unattainable goals (thereby leading to further demoralization), or they may be unable to identify plausible alternative goals, a process we call *regoaling*.

> Mr. L., for instance, struggled to conceptualize any goal other than a full recovery. Given the chronic nature of congestive heart failure, however, he realistically could no longer look forward to a full recovery. Faced with the evidence that his goal was no longer attainable, he was stymied in identifying an alternative goal. He was bewildered when asked about his other life goals.

> Ms. C. had always counted on having children with her husband. After establishing herself in her career, Ms. C. and her husband began trying to conceive a child when she was 35 years old. After 2 years without a pregnancy, they consulted a fertility expert, who suggested in vitro fertilization as their best option. After several failed in vitro fertilization trials, Ms. C. still maintained her goal of having her own children.

An inability to construe new pathways also can contribute to low hope. When a given pathway no longer leads to a goal, high-hope persons quickly will identify alternative paths so as to continue their goal pursuits. Low-hope persons, however, cannot find new routes. This inability to shift from one pathway to another also exemplifies a sense of hopelessness. The inability to identify these new pathways likely is a combination of several factors, including an unyielding commitment to an established pathway and difficulty with thinking creatively in the stressful context of failing to move closer to a goal.

> Mr. L. reported that he had good social support from family and friends. Continuing these relationships, however, was a struggle. His physician's recommendations included many strict dietary restrictions, but Mr. L. had the habit of going out for steak and beer once a week with his pals. This social ritual included drinking Scotch and having a cigar. He had begun avoiding these gatherings because he could not figure out how to work his new diet into these old habits.

> Ms. C. maintained her goal of wanting to become a parent. She was very close to her two sisters, who had successfully given birth to their own children. Ms. C.'s involvement in her sisters' pregnancies had so intensified her commitment to having children the "natural way" that she struggled to accept surrogacy or adoption as plausible alternatives because, with those options, she would not have the full experience of motherhood. She fixated on in vitro fertilization as her only choice.

A third factor that contributes to hopelessness is a lack of agency. As mentioned, the successful completion and adaptation of pathways fosters agency, which in turn provides the impetus to continue the goal pursuit process. Low-hope persons, however, lack the drive to implement pathways and pursue their goals. Therapists may see this when patients complain of being without motivation or follow suggestions with a "Yes, but . . ." and a long list of reasons why the stated goals or pathways are impossible to implement.

> Mr. L.'s initial reaction to the congestive heart failure diagnosis was, "Why bother?" Because of the chronic and terminal nature of this illness, he had trouble following any diet or exercise plan. This further robbed him of mental energy. Introverted by nature, he also had trouble reaching out to his spouse and family members for much-needed emotional support.

> Ms. C.'s struggles with infertility were made worse by her discomfort sharing her emotions with her husband and sisters. She became very discouraged after her last failed in vitro fertilization attempt. Because she had decided not to tell her sisters, she cut off the possibility of them giving moral support. Feeling isolated from her sisters furthered her feelings of hopelessness.

HOW THE PSYCHOLOGIST CAN HELP THE PATIENT REBUILD HOPE

Just as hope can help people successfully manage and overcome medical conditions via primary and secondary prevention strategies, illness-related hopelessness stops goal pursuit processes (Snyder, Feldman, et al., 2000). As such, the tenets of hope theory offer succinct methods by which psychologists can address illness-related impediments to patient life goals. These hope principles may extend from managing a chronic illness to helping a patient die with dignity (Gum & Snyder, 2002). Although we have presented hope as a traitlike construct in this chapter, many hopeful "skills" can be learned, thereby raising patient levels of hope. These hope skills center on goal formulation, pathways identification, and agency initiation.

The following guidelines should be useful in formulating a hope-based approach to treatment:

- Establish a thorough understanding of the patient's diagnosis, treatment regimen, and prognosis. These will help determine the nature of goals and limits on pathways and agency. For instance, a terminal illness may require the psychologist to conceptualize hope in terms of goals that focus on bringing closure to relationships and seeking palliative care rather than a cure.
- Talk to the patient's primary care physician to provide for continuity of care and to obtain a sense of the working relationship between the patient and doctor. Patients may need to build communication and coping skills if they have difficulty dealing with their physicians.
- Assess the patient's understanding of his or her illness. Determine if the patient can identify how the illness is having an impact on his or her goals.
- Evaluate the patient's relationships with family and friends. Assess the degree to which the family or friends understand the particular illness, along with their involvement in the patient's treatment. Families are an excellent resource for providing agency to patients in the pursuit of their goals.
- Administer the Trait Hope Scale (Table 13.1) to (a) establish a baseline measure for later comparison and tracking improvements and (b) identify particular deficits (e.g., a patient may be low in pathways and high in agency or high in pathways and low in agency).
- As a clinician, be mindful of maintaining your own level of hope. Treatment goals will need to be reevaluated on a constant basis, and the pathways for helping patients will vary. Make sure to consult with other clinicians for ideas on how to help patients reach goals. Finally, maintain a healthy life outside work to maintain your own sense of agency.

APPLYING THE PRINCIPLES OF HOPE THEORY

After assessing the patient's hope level and determining the course and symptoms for the particular disease process, the psychologist then can address the goal, pathways, and agency components of the intervention. At this stage, the patient should be educated as to the components of hope along with the rationale for including this type of intervention. The rationale might include examples of hopeful thinking and how this process will allow patients to live full lives despite their physical illnesses. It is important for the clinician to teach the concepts of hope early in treatment and to explain how various coping strategies might act as pathways toward a given goal. Teaching hope theory to patients gives them a framework on which to build other coping, goal-setting, and skill-building techniques.

The generalizability of hopeful skills should be emphasized as patients move beyond the constraints of their illnesses to expand their goals. We encourage therapists from all theoretical orientations to consider how incorporating hope into their approach might enhance the patient's therapeutic experience. Hope theory in the context of psychotherapy is meant to provide the therapist and patient with a fresh perspective that promotes a future orientation even if the future includes difficulties stemming from physical illness or challenges because of a mental illness. We remind clinicians that, in the earliest sessions, patients' feelings of hopelessness will need to be validated even as the active hope-building process begins. Also, it is common for patients to feel sad about letting go of goals that were once very important to them. We encourage clinicians to give their patients time in sessions to grieve the loss of earlier goals.

The following steps outline the application of the hope-building process to the therapeutic endeavor:

- Help patients articulate their primary goals and discuss adjusting these goals according to the limitations produced by their illnesses. If a goal is no longer feasible given the patient's current circumstances, help the patient regoal or develop an adapted or alternative goal.

Prior to her diagnosis of rheumatoid arthritis, Ms. D. had a goal of traveling to every continent in the world. Her increasing medical bills and lower energy levels made her goal of traveling the world an impossibility. She readjusted this goal to her present circumstances and established a new goal of visiting all the neighboring states.

- Work with patients to generate pathways toward their goals. Again, these pathways must be appropriate to the restrictions related to the particular diseases. Patients may use activities such as listing as many pathways as possible, consulting with friends and family, doing Internet searches, and the like to find creative solutions. Some patients may have extreme difficulty in generating alternative pathways. Clinicians should help these patients identify a default pathway, such as talking to a particular friend who is great at problem solving, or setting a follow-up appointment with the psychologist when a particularly difficult situation arises.

Mr. J. suffered from severe age-related hearing loss. He was referred to the psychologist because of the primary physician's concerns about Mr. J.'s increasing social isolation. The barriers to Mr. J.'s usual pathways for maintaining his friendships and associations were assessed. His most obvious pathway toward becoming more social was to get fitted for hearing aids. He and the psychologist also worked on a variety of communication strategies, such as facing people directly when talking and going to quieter restaurants to minimize noise interference.

- Introduce the agency component of hope. It is important to explore what has helped patients to reach their goals in the past, along with the present motivators that might be available to them. Encourage lifestyle choices that promote energy levels, such as proper nutrition, exercise, and healthy sleep habits.

Although Mr. R., who suffered from rheumatoid arthritis, was very good at adapting his pathways to his condition, he struggled to find the motivation to work on his goal of going back to school for an associate's degree. He and his psychologist identified the time of day

when he had the most energy (morning) and set this time aside for making phone calls to the local college and setting up necessary appointments. Mr. R. also wrote down his goal on a piece of paper and taped it to his refrigerator door as a reminder of what he was working toward. He also found it helpful to jot down positive thoughts whenever he had difficulty getting moving on a project.

To address the various appropriate issues in imparting hopeful thinking, we prepared a flowchart for psychological practitioners. Figure 13.1 addresses the factors necessary for hopeful thinking. We encourage practitioners to consider this form for their own use or perhaps for patient homework assignments.

To illustrate further the principles of hope theory within a therapeutic context, we present a case study of Mr. V., a patient seen on an outpatient basis (by K. K. W.) for whom hope-building skills were incorporated into the broader treatment.

Mr. V. is a 64-year-old Hispanic male with Type 1 diabetes and hypertension. His psychiatrist referred him to the outpatient mental health clinic because of concerns regarding medication compliance and his handling of life stressors.

What are the patient's main goals in life? Mr. V. said that his main goals are to stay healthy and to spend quality time with his family.

Are those goals still reasonable given his particular disease processes? Neither the diabetes nor hypertension precluded his staying healthy or spending time with his family. It was imperative, however, that Mr. V. be very specific about what he understood "staying healthy" to mean. In this instance, he rephrased his goal in more specific terms as "not allowing my health to deteriorate."

If the goals are reasonable, what pathways will help the patient to reach them? Mr. V. was somewhat aware of what he needed to do to keep both of his medical conditions under control, but he formulated a better plan after engaging in some educational activities on symptoms and symptom management. For ex-

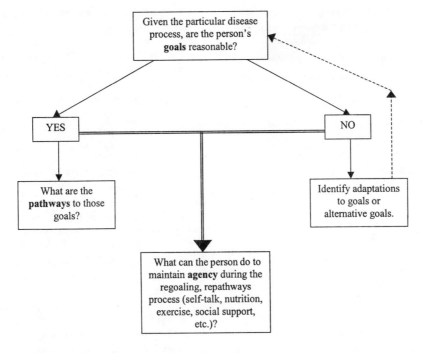

Figure 13.1 Putting hope theory into practice.

ample, we identified several pathways to manage the diabetes and hypertension.

First, there was moderate exercise. Mr. V. said that he liked going for walks. As such, he picked a half-hour time block 4 days a week to go walking at a park near his house. An anticipated pathway blockage was that he did not want to go walking alone. Therefore, whenever possible, Mr. V. included his children and grandchildren in these walks.

Second, he needed to eat better. Fortunately, Mr. V.'s wife did most of the cooking, and she carefully provided a balanced diet. This patient's particular struggle involved snacking on cookies or candy bars. He agreed, however, to purchase sugar-free cookies and healthy snacks and to limit snacks to one between meals.

Third, Mr. V. had to do a better job of adhering to his medication regimen. This pathway was broken down into several smaller pathways that involved (a) keeping all medications together and putting them into a pill organizer; (b) placing reminder notes on the bathroom mirror and refrigerator; and (c) marking each pill bottle with a "refill date" for replenishing his supplies of each pre-

scription (the second to the last bottle of insulin also was marked with a refill reminder).

What can the patient do to maintain agency during the hope-building process?

A substantial part of Mr. V.'s motivation came from his family. He felt remoralized and more confident because they were involved in his exercise plan. When he did walk by himself, he struggled to muster the necessary motivation. He found that positive self-talk was extremely helpful. For him, the reminders of the health benefits included statements such as "Walking brings down my blood pressure," "Exercise increases circulation," and "I feel less stressed when I'm walking." Mr. V. also discovered that looking at pictures of his grandchildren was a good motivator for maintaining healthy habits. This was especially helpful for his diet, for which he came up with the clever idea of placing pictures of his family on the refrigerator door.

When working with a hopeless patient such as Mr. V., the primary care psychologist initially may need to be directive about applying hope-building skills when the patient's illness presents an obsta-

cle to the goal pursuit process. Mr. V. provides an example, however, of how patients can begin to incorporate hopeful thinking into their daily lives. As sessions progressed, he began to articulate other life goals, including building a more active social life. With little help from his therapist he identified several pathways that he already was trying to attain this goal. Furthermore, he reported how he arranged his social engagements so that they would not interfere with his medication or meal schedules.

CONCLUSION: THERE IS HOPE

Helping patients to cope with serious, chronic illnesses is a complex and challenging task. We believe that hope theory offers a clinically useful perspective on what the patient is experiencing, and that this model can help practitioners conceptualize how a medical illness can impair the patient's ability to pursue goals actively. Pragmatically, the concepts of hope theory are easily adapted to a variety of therapeutic orientations, including cognitive–behavioral therapy (Snyder, Ilardi, et al., 2000). Patients who are able to maintain hope in the face of illness are proof that hope is not dependent on physical health. Even when an illness does lower hope, however, the good news is that hope can be rekindled.

Note

1. The State Hope Scale (Snyder et al., 1996) has three pathways and three agency items that measure an adult's level of hope "right now." The Children's Trait Hope Scale (Snyder et al., 1997) contains three pathways and three agency items, and it is appropriate for measuring the enduring hope levels of children between the ages of 8 and 15 years.

References

Abbey, A., & Halman, L. (1995). The role of perceived control, attributions, and meaning in members of infertile couples' well-being. *Journal of Social and Clinical Psychology, 14,* 271–296.

Anda, R., Williamson, D., Jones, D., Macera, C., Eaker, E., Glassman, A., & Marks, J. (1993). Depressed affect, hopelessness, and risk of ischemic heart disease in a cohort of U.S. adults. *Epidemiology, 4,* 285–294.

Gum, A., & Snyder, C. R. (2002). Hope and coping with terminal illness. *Journal of Palliative Medicine, 5,* 883–894.

Irving, L. M., Snyder, C. R., & Crowson, J. J., Jr. (1998). Hope and coping with cancer by college women. *Journal of Personality, 66,* 195–214.

Merriam-Webster Online Dictionary. (2003). Retrieved April 24, 2003, from http://www.m-w.com/netdict.htm

Jackson, W. T., Taylor, R. E., Palmatier, A. D., Elliott, T. R., & Elliott, J. L. (1998). Negotiating the reality of visual impairment: Hope, coping, and functional ability. *Journal of Clinical Psychology in Medical Settings, 5,* 173–185.

Snyder, C. R. (1994). *The psychology of hope: You can get there from here.* New York: Free Press.

Snyder, C. R. (1998). A case for hope in pain, loss, and suffering. In J. H. Harvey, J. Omarzu, & E. Miller (Eds.), *Perspectives on loss: A sourcebook* (pp. 63–79). Washington, DC: Taylor and Francis.

Snyder, C. R. (2002). Hope theory: Rainbows of the mind. *Psychological Inquiry, 13,* 249–275.

Snyder, C. R., Feldman, D. B., Taylor, J. D., Schroeder, L. L., & Adams, V. H. (2000). The roles of hopeful thinking in preventing problems and enhancing strengths. *Applied and Preventive Psychology, 9,* 249–270.

Snyder, C. R., Harris, C., Anderson, J. R., Holleran, S. A., Irving, L. M., Sigmon, S. T., Yoshinobu, L., Gibb, J., Langelle, C., & Harney, P. (1991). The will and the ways: Development and validation of an individual-differences measure of hope. *Journal of Personality and Social Psychology, 60,* 570–585.

Snyder, C. R., Hoza, B., Pelham, W. E., Rapoff, M., Ware, L., Danovsky, M., Highberger, L., Rubinstein, H., & Stahl, K. J. (1997). The development and validation of the Children's Hope Scale. *Journal of Pediatric Psychology, 22,* 399–421.

Snyder, C. R., Ilardi, S. S., Cheavens, J., Michael, S. T., Yamhure, L., & Sympson, S. (2000). The role of hope in cognitive-behavior therapies. *Cognitive Therapy and Research, 24,* 747–762.

Snyder, C. R., LaPointe, A. B., Crowson, J. J., & Early, S. (1998). Preferences of high- and low-hope people for self-referential feedback. *Cognition and Emotion, 11,* 807–823.

Snyder, C. R., Sympson, S. C., Ybasco, F. C., Borders, T. F., Babyak, M. A., & Higgins, R. L. (1996). Development and validation of the State Hope Scale. *Journal of Personality and Social Psychology, 70,* 321–335.

Stanton, A. L., Danoff-Burg, S., Cameron, C., Bishop, M., Collins, C. A., Kirk, S. B., Sworowski, L. A., & Twillman, R. (2000). Emotionally expressive coping predicts psychological and physical adjustment to breast cancer. *Journal of Consulting and Clinical Psychology, 68,* 875–882.

14

Health Behavior Change and the Problem of "Noncompliance"

Carlo C. DiClemente
Kevin Ferentz
Mary M. Velasquez

Compliance is the term used to indicate how well the patient executes medical and health care clinicians' directives intended to foster symptomatic relief, disease management, and prevention of future illness. Chronic illness and preventable conditions are leading causes of death and disability in the United States; patient cooperation and compliance are critical to management and prevention of such chronic conditions as diabetes, cardiovascular disease, cancer, obesity, chronic lung disease, HIV, and other conditions (Meichenbaum & Turk, 1987; Stuart, 1982). The costs of noncompliance are significant for the doctor, the patient, and the health care system. Loss of staff time, inadequate dosage of medications, expensive procedures, overreliance on intensive treatment settings, medical complications, disability, and premature death are all consequences of poor compliance with required or recommended treatment procedures and behavior changes.

Compliance is an issue for all psychological assessment and therapy procedures. It is particularly salient for medical interventions that involve taking prescribed medications, keeping appointments for visits or medical testing, following specific regimens like glucose monitoring, or making lifestyle changes in such areas as diet, exercise, alcohol, tobacco, and illicit drug use (Baekelund & Lundwall, 1975; Brownell & Cohen, 1995; Burke, Dunbar-Jacob, & Hill, 1997; DiClemente & Scott, 1997; Paykel, 1995). Physicians are often taught that the professional's role is to make recommendations and the patient's role is to follow them, that is, "be compliant."

In fact, compliance is difficult to predict, and clinicians significantly overestimate the percentage of their patients that follow recommendations. Research has demonstrated that sociodemographic factors—age, race, gender, level of education, occupation—or how long the patient has had the illness are not reliable factors in predicting compliance. Moreover, patients who are "noncompliant" are often avoided by their clinicians and are viewed as undesirable and difficult, resistant, and stubborn (Friedman & DiMatteo, 1990). From this perspective, compliance appears to be almost entirely the patient's problem.

However, professionals who prescribe complex tasks and assume compliance are underestimating the task, the patient, and the problem

(Christiansen, 2000; Eraker, Kirscht, & Becker, 1984). Patients are not passive participants in health care interaction; they have lifestyles, ideas, values, and constellations of behaviors that may conflict with the clinician's recommendations. It is simplistic to assume that patients will comply with recommendations simply at the request of the clinician. Even for the acquiescent and conscientious patient, follow-through or compliance is often problematic.

Compliance with treatment recommendations and medical regimens often requires complicated behavior changes and a shifting of patterns of behavior and priorities in the life of the patient. Health care clinicians, who themselves often fail to comply with recommended healthy behaviors and screening activities, frequently underestimate task demands. Even prescriptions that "simply" require a patient to take a single dose of medication three times a day require significant changes in daily routine. In fact, simply switching a dosing from twice a day to three times a day increases the complexity of the task dramatically for anyone who is active outside the home and would need to manage a midday dose. The complicated regimens of medication and behavior changes offered to HIV-positive patients and those with diabetes and cardiovascular disease are much more challenging (Fogarty et al., 2002; Kiortsis, Giral, Bruckert, & Turpin, 2000). Understanding task demands and appreciating the complexity of prescribed treatment recommendations are essential first steps in promoting patient cooperation and adherence to recommendations.

Compliance or adherence issues are central to the role of the psychologist in primary care settings. However, although psychologists are well trained in therapeutic techniques, many psychology training programs do not adequately address the problem of adherence and the process of behavior change involved when patients are inconsistent in their attendance or participate only halfheartedly in therapeutic and behavior change activities. For example, dropout rates among psychiatric patients are between 31% and 56% prior to the fourth session, and only 58% of scheduled psychotherapy appointments are kept (DiClemente & Scott, 1997; Mattson et al., 1998). For all types of health behaviors, adherence rates range from 20% to 80% (Burke et al., 1997).

Clearly, the problem of compliance is a critical one to understand and address in the training and practice of primary care psychology.

We believe that collaborative prescribing and problem solving is the secret to maximizing patient participation in the process of health behavior change. We use the terms *adherence*[1] and *compliance* interchangeably in this chapter with the understanding that, for medical treatment plans to be implemented effectively, patients must be active participants convinced of the value and efficacy of the prescription and in possession of a personal plan of action. They must also be committed to implementing that plan and to accomplishing effectively the various tasks required to meet the recommendations of the health care clinician. We describe some of the existing models for understanding adherence to medical regimens and lifestyle changes, then suggest a framework for practitioners working with adherence issues, and, finally, we offer some practical strategies for enhancing adherence.

MODELS FOR ENHANCING ADHERENCE

Models that address the problem of adherence can be categorized as (a) cognitive–behavioral and social learning models; (b) models focused on patient perceptions; (c) motivation-minimizing technological modifications; and (d) behavior change models.

Cognitive–Behavioral and Social Learning Approaches

Meichenbaum and Turk, in their 1987 text on facilitating treatment adherence, identified three broad categories of nonadherence and identified specific behaviors relevant to each. They highlighted the fact that adherence is a complex, dynamic phenomenon that changes over time. Research confirmed the fact that adherence rates decrease over time, and that adherence to one part of a proposed treatment plan does not necessarily indicate cooperation with other aspects of the plan (Evangelista & Dracup, 2000; Kravitz et al., 1993). The three broad categories Meichenbaum and Turk identified are (a) prescription and drug taking, (b) treatment attendance and participation, and (c) health behavior changes (see Table 14.1). They argued that each type of adherence problem is different and requires the use of slightly different strategies.

The strategies that they suggest include (a) enhancing the relationship between the patient and clinician, which includes focusing on patient concerns and expectancies and improving the communication process; (b) improving patient education, giving the patient all the relevant information about the treatment and ways to simplify it; (c) using behavior modification approaches of self-monitoring, goal setting, behavioral contracting, and reinforcement procedures; and (d) teaching self-regulatory skills of problem solving, coping, attribution retraining, and interpersonal skills development. They described a comprehensive array of strategies and discussed enlisting family and community supports.

Bandura's work supported and added to this array with his social cognitive theory, particularly his focus on self-efficacy as a critical mediator of behavior change (Bandura, 1977, 1986, 1997). This theory has been applied extensively in health behavior settings, and efficacy-enhancing interventions for health behaviors have been studied (Strecher, DeVellis, Becker, & Rosenstock, 1986). A unique contribution of self-efficacy theory is its inclusion of individuals' assessment of their confidence or efficacy to perform the behavior in the analysis of task dimensions.

For example, a complete evaluation of an individual's efficacy to take a prescription would describe in detail the behavior and ask about various types of situations that could hinder adherence (Bandura, 1977; DiClemente, Fairhurst, & Piotrowoski, 1995). Specifically, patients might be asked to rate their confidence (on a scale of 1 to 10) in their ability to take the prescribed medication three times a day, on a weekday, on a weekend, when on vacation, when very busy, and when stressed. This evaluation could help pinpoint situations when a patient would have difficulty and suggest specific areas for intervention and problem solving.

Table 14.1 Types of Adherence Problems

Prescription and drug-taking errors

1. Failing to fill the prescription
2. Failing to take the medication as prescribed (partial adherence)
3. Taking other medication or combining medications not prescribed

Treatment attendance and participation problem

1. Delay in seeking care for a medical problem
2. Failing to enter or participate in a prescribed treatment program or regimen
3. Failing to keep scheduled appointments for testing or follow-up
4. Terminating treatments prematurely

Health behavior change difficulties

1. Failing to implement behavior change instructions
2. Failing to follow prescribed health behavior programs
3. Creating idiosyncratic and ineffective treatment regimens
4. Substituting one's own program for the recommended treatment regimens

Adapted from Meichenbaum and Turk (1987).

Patient Perception and Health Promotion Models

Several health behavior models focus on patients' beliefs and intentions; we highlight two—reasoned action and health beliefs—in this section. The health belief model focuses on the patient's perceptions of vulnerability and his or her view of the effectiveness of the treatment as the key elements of seeking treatment and following prescribed regimens. Rosenstock, Strecher, and Becker (1988) identified four critical dimensions that lead patients to take effective action: (a) perceived susceptibility to the illness or problem, (b) perceived seriousness of the threat or problem, (c) the conviction that the action will be effective in dealing with the problem and not be so costly as to negate its usefulness, and (d) prompts or cues to make the change or follow the prescribed course of action. This focus on patient cognitions and motivation was innovative and has been included in more recent health communication models that focus not only on the individual clinician's communication, but also on social communication and media messages (Ockene, Hayman, Pasternak, Schron, & Dunbar-Jacob, 2002).

In their theory of reasoned action, Ajzen and Fishbein (1980) highlighted expectancies about potential outcomes and beliefs about norms (e.g., how significant others would act in similar situations), as well as intentions to implement the action. The revised theory of planned behavior highlights an added third determinant, perceived behavioral control. This concept assumes that a person's evaluation of the pros and cons of the behavior as well as the perception of his or her self-efficacy to perform the behavior affect motivation (Azjen, 1985, 2002). Thus, this theory emphasizes both outcome expectations (cognitions focused on the expected *outcome* of the behavior) and efficacy expectations, or the *perceived ability and confidence* to perform the behavior across situations.

Motivation-Minimizing Technological Approaches

"Engineering" alternatives that lessen the burden on the patient of the prescribed health behavior have become a very active arena for what can be labeled "motivation-minimizing" adherence enhancement initiatives. These approaches have been most extensively employed in medication approaches. For example, medroxyprogesterone (Depo Provera) is an injectable birth control medication that requires only one dose every 3 months. For smokers, the nicotine patch is replaced only periodically and does not require chewing gum on a regular basis. Other efforts to minimize motivation include aids such as programmed telephone reminder calls, E-mail prompts, and day-labeled pill dispensers (Guthrie, 2001; Ockene et al., 2002).

Behavior Change Models

Although all of the models and theories that have been described focus on various aspects of behavior change as components of their perspectives, some recent models attempt to understand the broader process of behavior change. We highlight the stages of health behavior change in this section.

The most widely known and used model in this area is the transtheoretical model of intentional behavior change (DiClemente, 2003; Pro-

chaska & DiClemente, 1984; Prochaska, DiClemente, & Norcross, 1992; Prochaska, Norcross, & DiClemente, 1994). In this model, change is viewed as a progression from an initial precontemplation stage, in which the person is not currently considering change, to contemplation, in which the individual considers advantages and disadvantages of change, and then to preparation, during which planning and commitment are secured. Successful accomplishment of these initial stage tasks leads to taking action to make the specific behavioral change that, if successful, leads to the final and fifth stage of change, maintenance, in which the person works to maintain and sustain long-term change (DiClemente & Prochaska, 1998; Prochaska et al., 1992).

The stage-of-change model appears to be applicable to the process of intentional change of health behaviors whether that change occurs with or without the assistance of a clinician, an intervention, or a treatment program (DiClemente & Prochaska, 1998; Norcross, Ratzin, & Payne, 1989). The tasks of the different stages offer a template for understanding what aspects need attention to create successfully maintained change. Because medical prescriptions and treatment regimens require personal behavior change continued over some period of time, this process-of-change model is relevant for health behavior change (see Table 14.2). These stages have been used to assess the patient's position in this process of change and assist the patient in moving successfully through the stages for a wide range of health behaviors, including exercise and physical activity, diet, condom use, diabetes management, asthma, and substance abuse (Brown-Peterside, Redding, Ren, & Koblin, 2000; Glanz et al., 1994; Grimley, Prochaska, Veclicer, & Prochaska, 1995; Marcus, Rossi, Selby, Niaura, & Abrams, 1992; Ruggiero, 2000; Schmaling, Afari, & Blume, 2000; Timpson et al., 2001; Velasquez, Gaddy-Maurer, Crouch, & DiClemente, 2001).

All these models hold important implications for intervention. Persuasive communication, signed agreements and contingency contracting, and self-monitoring and self-efficacy enhancement procedures have been successful in improving compliance to cardiovascular and other disease prevention (Burke et al., 1997; Neale, 1991; Sorenson et al., 1998) and have been included in ad-

Table 14.2 Stages of Change and Adherence Tasks and Strategies

Precontemplation stage

  Adherence tasks:

    Become aware of risk posed by condition

    Recognize need to take action to manage the condition or health risk

  Clinician strategies:

    Personalize feedback

    Educate

    Enhance motivation

    Identify relevant role models

    Increase patient's sense of vulnerability

    Increase positive expectancies

Contemplation stage

  Adherence tasks:

    Resolve decisional ambivalence

    Make the decision to act

    Change problematic beliefs

    Eliminate/reduce barriers to action

    Develop positive outcome and efficacy expectancies

  Clinician strategies:

    Increase positive outcome expectations for adherence

    Increase positive expectancies

    Challenge dysfunctional beliefs

    Help eliminate/reduce barriers

    Address cultural issues

Preparation stage

  Adherence tasks:

    Understand task demands

    Develop acceptable, effective, detailed adherence plan

    Increase commitment to take action

  Clinician strategies:

    Develop task and option priorities

    Increase self-efficacy

    Support planning and commitment

    Evaluate task demands and needed skills

Action stage

  Adherence tasks:

    Follow agreed on prescribed regimen

    Revise/refine plans

    Overcome barriers to adherence

    Continue commitment

  Clinician strategies:

    Reinforce self-efficacy

    Train in relevant skills

    Refine plans

    Offer aids

    Engage social support

    Develop behavioral contracts

    Implement reinforcement procedures

Maintenance stage

  Adherence tasks:

    Sustain behavior changes

    Integrate changes into lifestyle

    Avoid relapse

    Create supportive environments and engage social supports

  Clinician strategies:

    Address barriers

    Design relapse prevention strategies

    Promote social support seeking

    Provide reinforcement

    Highlight benefits of risk reduction and problem management

herence task force recommendations (Ockene et al., 2002).

Strategies to increase the patient's perceived susceptibility to the health problem and participation in the change process include assessing irrational beliefs, asking patients to complete personal risk assessments and providing feedback, or presenting results of medical tests compared with population norms (Christiansen, Moran, & Wiebe, 1999; Clifford, Tan, & Gorsuch, 1991; DiClemente, Marinilli, Singh, & Bellino, 2001). In addition, completing a decisional balance exercise can assist the patient identify benefits and barriers (Rollnick, Mason, & Butler, 1999). To do this, clinicians can simply write "costs" and "benefits" (or "pros" and "cons") at the top of a blank form and ask the patient to list his or her thoughts about each category.

Another approach is to use "scaling rulers" in which the clinician asks the patient to rate, on a scale of 0 to 10, how serious it would be if they were to develop a particular health problem, how susceptible they feel to a particular disorder, how important a particular behavior change or recommended course of action is to them, and how confident they would be that they could do it if they wanted (Rollnick et al., 1999). This type of dialogue fosters communication between the clinician and patient, makes the patient feel "listened to," helps the clinician gauge the patient's feelings of vulnerability, and corrects any existing misconceptions about the health problem or the prescription for change. Motivation-enhancing types of communication have been promoted and supported as more effective ways to engage change (Miller & Rollnick, 1991, 2002.)

A COMPREHENSIVE APPROACH TO IMPROVING ADHERENCE

Adherence to health behavior regimens and recommendations involves three key elements: patient, clinician, and task. All three must be considered to develop a comprehensive approach for improving adherence to health behavior recommendations that ultimately will lead to improved health and quality of life. Patient-focused efforts include approaches that focus on patients' intentions, expectancies, motivations, and change process. Task-focused approaches have concentrated on requirements of the recommendations or to modifications of the task or task demand on the patient. Finally, clinician-focused (and health care systems–focused) efforts include changes in communication style, mode of message delivery, and the like. We suggest that all three aspects are needed to create an effective and comprehensive strategy to improve compliance rates among patients across the broad spectrum of health behaviors. We describe the role of each of the three critical components needed for effective compliance in detail and how they contribute to a collaborative approach to increasing adherence.

Patient Role

The patient must understand what is asked and understand how this action is connected with the problem being addressed. Although there are some patients who would simply follow the recommendations given by someone in authority regardless of whether it made sense to them (Blass, 1992; Milgram, 1963), these patients represent a diminishing minority of the patient population. Most will need information and understanding to keep the appointment or implement the prescription (Hardy, O'Brien, & Furling, 2001). However, this presupposes some agreement between patient and clinician that there is actually a health problem or risk that needs to be treated.

Precontemplators, who are not considering making prescribed changes, represent individuals with a range of reasons for not following the prescription. There are those who are unconvinced that there is a problem of sufficient magnitude to require action and do not acknowledge personal susceptibility or vulnerability as described in the health belief model. For example, the male patient who believes that he is in good shape and that there is no danger of a heart problem does not see his cholesterol level as relevant. In addition, there are those precontemplators who believe that they cannot make the required changes (insufficient self-efficacy; Bandura, 1977, 1997) or who simply resist being told what to do (DiClemente & Velasquez, 2002). These patients either cannot or will not follow a demanding diet, for example.

Finally, there are those patients who do not believe that the behavior change recommended is reasonable or will produce the desired health benefits. As described in the social learning model, their outcome expectancies for the prescribed behavior are insufficient to promote a serious consideration of this recommended procedure. For example, patients tell us that using condoms at every sexual encounter with a steady partner you can trust appears to be excessive or taking all their prescribed antiretroviral medication seems useless because it will not make anyone HIV negative. Learned helplessness, psychological reactance, and other models of self-regulation address these issues as well (Abramson, Seligman, & Teasdale, 1978; Brehm, 1966; Carver & Scheier, 1998).

Thus, to adhere conscientiously to health behaviors, patients have to believe that the health problem is of sufficient importance to them to consider taking action. They then need to become convinced of the reasonableness and effectiveness of the prescription and reassure themselves of their self-efficacy to perform the behavior to begin the "buy in" and collaborate in the change process (Rollnick et al., 1999; Stewart et al., 1995; Velasquez, Wright, & Ingersoll, in press).

Decision making occurs during the contemplation stage in the transtheoretical model and largely consists of costs-benefits analysis. For example, considerations like "monitoring my glucose will ensure that I can spend more quality time with my family and reduce the risks of complications of my diabetes" would support adherence. A decisional balance tipped in favor of the behavior supports a solid decision to take action and, according to the theory of planned behavior, creates an intention to follow the prescription.

Once convinced of the need for change and the value of the prescribed behavior, patients often still need assistance in overcoming any remaining ambivalence. For example, even though a patient knows that his or her current behavior is health threatening and sees the value in changing, it is common to still hold mixed feelings about the behavior. Many patients in medical settings report that they feel a conflict between their goal to live a long life, which might be achieved by following a recommended regimen, and their quality of life, which often includes engaging in

an array of unhealthy but enjoyable behaviors. Therefore, it is important to analyze the patient's personal concerns about the change required by the prescription or regimen and how that change will affect his or her life. It is also important in this stage to address any cultural and religious considerations that may be helpful in promoting decision making and resolving ambivalence (DiClemente, 2003).

The next step (preparation stage) in the process of improving adherence is for the patient to generate the commitment and develop a plan or strategy that will make implementation of the prescription feasible. For patients preparing to make a change, the prescribed behavior must become a priority in their lives. That is, the prescribed medication regimen, regular physical activity, monitoring glucose levels, dietary change, or elimination of risky behaviors like smoking has to fit into the current "life space" of the individual.

For example, individuals going through a divorce, stressful work times, or personal losses find smoking cessation particularly problematic because of the stress management role of cigarettes in their lives. As another example, beginning a diet the week before going on a vacation cruise can offer additional barriers to adherence. The importance of the health behavior change in the context of the individual's life is an important consideration that must be explored. Often, other activities have to be curtailed, other responsibilities managed, and some desirable behaviors modified. This requires a strong commitment to continue to adhere and a plan of action to guide patient adherence. An adequate understanding of the task and the skills needed to implement the tasks is critical in planning change.

For patients in the action stage, a focus on commitment and skill acquisition is central. To be able to self-administer glucose injections, for example, the patient has to be able to use a syringe properly and overcome any anxiety related to needles. To quit smoking, the patient has to learn how to manage emotions and other cues to light up, tolerate withdrawal, find alternative stress reducers, and so on.

Change plans may have to be modified as the individual begins to take action because it is difficult to anticipate how the plan will play out in the day-to-day life of the individual. Once the patient has found a comfortable, or at least tolerable, way to accomplish the recommended health behavior, it may take months to firmly establish the new pattern of behavior. Many compliance studies have demonstrated that initial adherence erodes over time, a phenomenon known as relapse (Dew, Roth, Thompson, Kormos, & Griffith, 1996).

Maintaining change over time is the final step in the process of change. The new behavior has to be sustained over time despite the many changes in the patient's life. For example, physical activity and dietary regimens have to endure across changes in seasons, jobs, marital status, shifts in friendships, residences, and health status. Challenges to the new pattern of behavior have to be met with continued adherence and avoidance of relapse. Once the health behavior becomes well integrated into the patient's life, the effort and energy needed to sustain this pattern can be reduced. Monitoring glucose levels, doing breast self-exams, not smoking, taking daily doses of cholesterol-lowering medication, eating adequate servings of fruits and vegetables, or keeping physically active eventually become permanent activities that are a normal part of the patient's life.

Clearly, the challenges for maintenance of behavior change are different for behaviors that are prescribed for only a set period of time or until the desired health effects are obtained, as is the case with some physical rehabilitation programs and medication regimens. Moreover, health regimens that require continually changing recommendations over time (shifting medications, changing multiple behaviors) pose additional challenges because patients are asked to change patterns of behavior continually.

Task Demands

To understand and promote adherence, health care clinicians and health promotion professionals should perform task analyses for all the prescribed regimens that they offer. This requires analyzing exactly what is asked of the patient in terms of various dimensions of the regimen, like the frequency of the behavior, the required activities, or the level of skill needed to perform the task. The rule of thumb should be to prescribe

the least burdensome regimen to achieve the most health benefit.

The nature and extent of the task should also be part of the collaboration and negotiation that occurs between clinician and patient. Although maximum benefit could be achieved with a complicated, multibehavior, extensive, and intensive set of prescriptions, simply giving these to the patient and demanding performance is a recipe for noncompliance. The clinician indicates which tasks are most important to avoid overwhelming the patient and creating a sense of helplessness.

There are really two dimensions to this priority setting. The first consists of determining which of the recommended behaviors has the greatest possibility of yielding the most health benefit. The second dimension requires determination of which of the recommended behaviors has the greatest probability of adoption by the patient. Negotiations can be based on the benefits of compliance or the costs of noncompliance.

Rollnick et al. (1999) described an "agenda-setting" technique in which the clinician presents the patient with a paper that has several circles depicting multiple behaviors involved in addressing a particular health problem. For example, a diabetic patient is presented with pictures representing a bottle of medication, a piece of pie, a pack of cigarettes, and a person exercising. Using this technique, the clinician asks the patient which of these behaviors is most important and relevant for them to address, which they would like to discuss that day, or which they are most ready to change. This type of approach can be very helpful both in establishing the stage of change of the patient for each health behavior and in establishing a respectful collaboration between patient and clinician. This patient-centered approach is also very different from the directive, clinician-centered types of consultations and recommendations often found in medical settings (Friedman & DiMatteo, 1990; Rollnick et al., 1999; Stewart et al., 1995).

Clinician Role

As is obvious in the discussion here, understanding, designing, and negotiating acceptable task demands begins to define the clinician's role in promoting adherence. The clinician has the responsibility of creating accessible and effective regimens and prescriptions, providing the understanding and expectations that would facilitate adherence to that prescribed plan of action, enhancing motivation and promoting the process of change, providing training for the skills needed to comply with the tasks, and offering support and assistance in both the action and maintenance phases of the change process (Table 14.2).

Prescribing and Prioritizing

If the clinician simply lists a large number of changes that the patient "must" make, the patient can become overwhelmed and immobilized (Meichenbaum & Turk, 1987). Necessary activities should be distinguished from recommended or optimal ones. Clinicians should be aware of the different challenges and respond by segmenting recommendations in order of importance and impact as described above.

Increasing Understanding and Expectations

Patients have varying levels of knowledge and sophistication about medical conditions and health care. They also differ in their "need to know." For some patients, a simple explanation of how this particular activity will have a direct impact on their condition (e.g., physical activity increases blood flow and strengthens the heart) will suffice. For others, a more complicated explanation that goes into the more technical aspects may be needed, illustrating how physical activity or exercise increases metabolic activity, has an impact on the immune system, and increases blood flow to the brain and peripheral areas of the body.

The same is true for helping patients become convinced of the seriousness of their condition and the need for change. Providing precontemplators with personalized, relevant, and compelling information about their condition and addressing their reservations about the existence of the problem or the need to change are essential. Responding honestly and objectively to the concerns of the patient increases understanding and helps create the cognitive map that will support active adherence.

Whenever the clinician can offer information about how specific symptoms observed in the pa-

tient would be relieved by compliance or exacerbated by noncompliance, it can increase the subjective expected utility of the prescribed behavior change. Tailoring the regimen to the patient's personal risk, personal history, personal goals, and desired lifestyle improves compliance; likewise, providing information that is specific to this patient or class of patients rather than generic may increase motivation for change. All of us believe that we are unique, and that what is true of others is not necessarily true of ourselves. This belief can help or hinder making the connections between the prescription and the problem. This personal perspective also includes cultural, ethnic, and religious considerations relevant to the patient.

Another important element of the clinician's role in promoting adherence is providing the proper expectations about the prescribed regimen. Appropriate expectation about benefits seems to be an essential element that contributes to the decision to comply with the recommended behavior changes. Moreover, just as physicians are required to give the patient some warning about the most important potential side effects of a prescribed medication, clinicians should acknowledge the potential negative aspects of any recommendation. Credibility is enhanced when the patient believes that the clinician is "leveling" with him or her.

For example, it is important to acknowledge that a particular regimen is difficult. It may be appropriate to disclose that the clinician struggles to eat a diet low in fat as well. It can be helpful to discuss general compliance rates to indicate that others have found it difficult. However, this is also the time and place for examples to provide relevant models of patients who have been able to make the change and clearly received many benefits from complying.

Asking patients about their expectations or any relevant role models that they have known is also an excellent strategy. Often, patients know someone who had a similar condition. They will compare recommendations and use knowledge from that person to guide their decision about whether to comply with a prescribed behavior.

In any case, it is the responsibility of the clinician to offer a compelling rationale and solid reasons to support the effectiveness of the prescribed behavior and to assist the patient in creating expectancies that link the behavior to desired outcomes. The trust that the clinician is giving adequate and accurate information is, of course, the result of having established an atmosphere of honesty and respect between the patient and the clinician. It is well documented that the nature and quality of the relationship between the clinician and the patient influences adherence to treatment recommendations (Meichenbaum & Turk, 1987; Stewart et al., 1995).

Enhancing Motivation and Promoting the Process of Change

One of the most important aspects of the clinician's role in enhancing adherence is strengthening the patient's motivation to make the changes required. Although the term motivation is often used in the literature on behavior change, it can be an elusive concept. For our purposes, motivation is best defined as readiness to accomplish the various tasks identified in the stages of change in order to establish and maintain the new behavior (DiClemente, 2003). Education is a necessary, but not sufficient, strategy to assist patients through the change process. Motivational enhancement has often been the missing link in improving adherence and compliance (DiClemente, 1999; DiClemente et al., 2001; Miller & Rollnick, 1991, 2002; Rollnick et al., 1999). Motivational interviewing has concentrated on basic principles of brief interventions. These include the primary assumption that the patient is in charge of the change. Principles include listening with empathy and sophisticated summarizing as powerful strategies to promote consideration and planning for change. They also include "rolling with resistance" as an effective way to manage patients' reluctance, rebellion, or rationalization. This term means that clinicians should allow, and even encourage, the patient to express negative feelings about the prospect of behavior change without feeling threatened or trying to convince the patient to feel differently (see Rollnick et al., 1999, for a variety of strategies to roll with patient resistance in medical settings). A final principle in motivational interviewing is support of the patients' confidence, or efficacy, in their ability to

accomplish the task as a way to assist them in successfully negotiating the stages of change.

These principles offer clinicians a set of basic strategies to use in interacting with patients. Rollnick and colleagues (1999) have demonstrated that this approach can be used in a consultation setting to structure conversations around the importance of the change, the confidence that the patient can implement the change, and finally the readiness to make the change. This negotiation allows the patient to identify along with the clinician the goal of change and to set priorities among the changes that need to be made.

The motivational enhancement approach fits nicely with the emphasis on shifting the decisional considerations toward change, increasing commitment and developing a viable change plan, enacting and revising the plan, using the behavioral coping mechanisms necessary to achieve success, and finally integrating the new behavior solidly into the behavioral repertoire and lifestyle of the individual (DiClemente & Velasquez, 2002). The stages of change outline the tasks that need to be accomplished. The motivational enhancement approach provides some skills and principles that help in assisting the patient to accomplish these tasks.

Skills Training for Compliance

Many of the regimens and tasks recommended to protect and promote health require a rather complicated set of behaviors. For example, the "medication cocktail" prescribed for HIV patients often requires multiple doses of different types of medication taken at specific times with other specifications about whether they are to be taken with food. Diets require extensive preparation in selecting and preparing the proper foods. Self-administration of insulin requires glucose monitoring and use of a syringe. The discussion of task demands above outlined the scope of tasks that patients are often asked to perform. Clearly, some of these tasks, if not all, require skills as well as knowledge.

The more complicated and time-consuming role for a clinician would be to provide the information or counseling needed about the procedure and assist in training patients in the necessary skills. Primary care clinicians often feel that they do not have the time to devote to this type of negotiation and collaboration. If patients need extensive or detailed information or any skill training is needed to enhance adherence, this task often is delegated to the nurse, dietician, or health educator.

However, the links between the prescription and the ancillary information or training are often incomplete or weak. Skill development and training can get lost in the referral system. The link between the primary care clinician and the ancillary health professionals needs to be established clearly and facilitated for it to be effective in supporting adherence. In addition, there appears to be a clear and compelling role for a behavior change specialist with a background in psychology to help increase adherence across a wide range of health behaviors.

Ongoing Support

The final, but important, aspect of the clinician's role in promoting adherence is to provide support to the patient during the entire process of change. From the patient's perspective, the prescription could not have been that important if the clinician does not follow up with the patient or even mention the recommendation at the next visit. Reminder phone calls have been found to increase compliance; arranging for follow-up and a check-up and sending feedback and reminders in the mail have all been helpful in increasing adherence (Burke et al., 1997; Kirkman et al., 1994; Ockene et al., 2002). Continued contact does seem to have a significant impact. Providing support and engaging support systems can be valuable aids to creating compliance and promoting behavior change.

TRAINING FOR ADHERENCE ENHANCEMENT

We have proposed some principles and strategies for improving compliance. Next, we provide some basic training tips for helping physicians, health psychologists, and other health care clinicians to learn how to work collaboratively with patients. Some are rather simple techniques for enhancing communication between patient and clinicians to increase the likelihood that patients will comply with a clinician's advice. Patients will be more likely to follow recommendations if they understand clearly what those recommendations are and why they are being made. In addition, patients are more likely to follow recommendations when they believe their clinician has been truly listening to their complaints. More curricular time should be devoted in professional and medical schools to teaching techniques that enhance adherence and compliance.

Although the initial history and physical may not appear to be an opportunity for increasing patient motivation, we have found that is actually an optimal time for setting the wheels of change in motion. For example, rather than asking a cigarette smoker the number of cigarettes he or she smokes in a day, the practitioner can elicit much more information about the patient by asking an open-ended question such as, "Tell me about your smoking on a typical day." The practitioner may even choose to break the day into segments and ask patients to describe their smoking from the time they get up in the morning through noon. This technique takes only a few minutes longer, but the practitioner learns about the patient's lifestyle, including cues to smoke, and typically obtains a much more accurate estimate of the number of cigarettes smoked in a day.

This technique can be used with a variety of problem behaviors, including diet, exercise, and medication adherence. Many patients report that this strategy alone increases their motivation to change because it allows them to examine and discuss their problem behaviors in a nonthreatening way. It also increases self-monitoring following the interview. This can also begin the communication pattern that can be used in subsequent visits to enhance collaboration between patient and clinician.

Another important skill to learn is how to give and receive feedback in interactions with the patient. Summarizing and offering feedback also gives patient and clinician an opportunity to clarify misunderstandings and helps evaluate how much the patient has benefited from educational efforts.

It is critical that patients be given specific, concrete, and detailed information and instructions. Telling a patient to "lose weight" or "cut down on salt because it is not good for you" are examples of recommendations that are too vague. Patients are more likely to respond to the specific recommendation "to reduce your high blood pressure, remove salt from the table and do not add salt to food during cooking." A patient might be told to decrease intake by 200 calories each day and to try to lose 5 pounds before the next office visit. Such advice is concrete and easier to follow than the general advice, "You need to go on a diet."

The patient's perception of his or her relationship with the clinician can have a significant impact on whether the patient will follow the advice. Patients are more likely to follow recommendations if they perceive the clinician as friendly, interested, respectful, and supportive.

Patients' lack of adherence can lead to frustration and a sense of hopelessness on the part of the clinician. It is important for clinicians to pay attention to their own reactions to patients who do not comply with recommended health behavior change. It is helpful to keep in mind that non-adherence is not invariably maladaptive and may represent the patient's attempt to exert some degree of control over his or her illness and treatment. Or the decision not to adhere may be based on a logical analysis that the costs of adhering to the prescribed medical regimen outweigh the potential gains. It is critical to keep in mind that patients almost always enter treatment not as "blank slates," but with certain expectations about their illness and what should take place. They typically have their own ideas and beliefs about their disorder and its etiology, course, prognosis, and treatment.

Patients cannot be expected to follow recommendations if they do not remember them. There are various techniques that can be used to enhance the recall of information. For example, clinicians should remember to give the most important information first because we tend to remember better the first things we are told. Clinicians should also give manageable amounts of information at a time and should stress the importance of the instructions. It is helpful to summarize the instructions at the end of the visit, and writing down the instructions helps patients remember them, especially if they are written down on a prescription pad. Phone calls by staff and other follow-up strategies can also be used to answer questions about the protocol and prompt adherence to recommendations.

There are also techniques to detect noncompliance in patients. The simplest thing to do is to question the patient in a matter-of-fact, nonjudgmental, and nonthreatening manner if the treatment response is slow or insufficient. Half of patients will admit noncompliance. Patients who admit to having difficulty in following recommendations are most responsive to interventions. Using the ubiquity approach is helpful, that is, "Many patients have trouble taking their medications every day. Are you missing any doses of medication? How often?" This allows the patient to save face (Bond & Hussar, 1991). Clinicians should be aware of patients whose appointment keeping is erratic because they are much less likely to be following recommendations in general. For example, half of patients with hypertension drop out of treatment in the first year after diagnosis, and an additional 25% drop out over the next 5 years. The dropout rate can be decreased by using techniques such as appointment reminders, making advance appointments, phoning patients to make appointments, and using postcard reminders (Gariti et al., 1995; Koren, Bartel, & Corliss, 1994) as well as by explaining that follow-up visits are important even if, or especially if, there has been difficulty adhering to the regimen.

Established techniques, approaches, and strategies can clearly improve adherence and health outcomes (Ockene et al., 2002; Roter et al., 1998). The challenge remains how to give clinicians the training needed and offer the support systems that could implement these interventions. Some basic adherence enhancement skills outlined above include empathy, respectful and clear collaborative communication skills, understanding task demands, working with patients to prioritize health behavior changes, and good, understandable information and instructions.

However, it is clear that some specialized skills are needed in promoting behavior change, particularly for difficult patients, those unwilling to comply, and those with multiple and complex prescribed medical regimens. These specialized skills include more advanced counseling and motivational enhancement skills, training in cognitive–behavioral interventions, including family and significant others in the consultation, and managing problems in other nonmedical areas of patient functioning.

SUMMARY

Although adherence is ultimately the responsibility of the patient, there are various techniques that physicians, primary care psychologists, and other health care professionals can employ to help the patient follow through. The attitude must be one of partnership, creating a solid working relationship between patient and clinician. Adherence and motivation to follow prescribed health regimens are enhanced by improving communication between clinician and patient, heightening the patients' perceptions of the importance of the prescription to achieve valued outcomes, improving patient recall, enhancing coping skills and strategies, assessing successes and difficulties in achieving compliance, and making changes in appointment and follow-up procedures. A careful analysis of the various tasks of the patient and the important interactions among clinician characteristics, task demands, and patient characteristics can significantly increase adherence.

ACKNOWLEDGMENTS   We would like to thank Angela Marinilli, Manu Singh, and Lisa Kan for their assistance in preparing this chapter. We would also like to acknowledge support of the National Cancer Institute, National Institute of Alcoholism and Alcohol Abuse, National Heart Lung and Blood Institute, and the National Institute on Drug Abuse for funding projects that contributed to the information and research presented in this chapter.

Note

1. Adherence is the preferred term because it connotes a more collaborative and less hierarchical relationship between clinician and patient and can more readily reflect degrees of completion in enacting the recommended behavior.

References

Abramson, L. Y., Seligman, M. E. P., & Teasdale, J. D. (1978). Learned helplessness in humans: Critique and reformulation. *Journal of Abnormal Psychology, 87,* 49–74.

Ajzen, I. (1985). From intentions to actions: A theory of planned behavior. In J. Kuhl & J. Blackman (Eds.), *Action control: From cognition to behavior* (pp. 11–39). Berlin: Springer-Verlag.

Ajzen, I. (2002). Perceived behavioral control, self-efficacy, locus of control, and the theory of planned behavior. *Journal of Applied Social Psychology, 32,* 1–20.

Ajzen, I., & Fishbein, M. (1980). *Understanding attitudes and predicting social behavior.* Englewood Cliffs, NJ: Prentice-Hall.

Baekeland, F., & Lundwall, L. (1975) Dropping out of treatment: A critical review. *Psychological Bulletin, 82,* 738–783.

Bandura, A. (1977). Self-efficacy: Toward a unifying theory of behavioral change. *Psychological Review, 84,* 191–215.

Bandura, A. (1986). *Social foundations of thought and action: A social cognitive theory.* Englewood Cliffs, NJ: Prentice-Hall.

Bandura, A. (1997). *Self-efficacy: The exercise of control.* New York: Freeman.

Blass, T. (1992). The social psychology of Stanley Milgram. In M. P. Zanna (Ed.), *Advances in experimental social psychology* (Vol. 25, pp. 277–328). San Diego, CA: Academic Press.

Bond, W. S., & Hussar, D. A. (1991). Detection methods and strategies for improving medication compliance. *American Journal of Hospital Pharmacy, 48,* 1978–1988.

Brehm, J. W. (1966). *A theory of psychological reactance.* New York: Academic Press.

Brownell, K. D., & Cohen, L. R. (1995). Adherence to dietary regimens, 2: Components of effective interventions. *Behavioral Medicine, 20,* 155–164.

Brown-Peterside, P., Redding, C. A., Ren, L., & Koblin, B. A. (2000). Acceptability of a stage-matched expert system intervention to increase condom use among women at high risk of HIV infection in New York City. *AIDS Education and Prevention, 12,* 171–181.

Burke, L. E., Dunbar-Jacob, J. M., & Hill, M. N.

(1997). Compliance with cardiovascular disease prevention strategies: A review of the research. *Annals of Behavioral Medicine, 19,* 239–263.

Carver, C. S., & Scheier, M. F. (1998) *On the self-regulation of behavior.* New York: Cambridge University Press.

Center for the Advancement of Health. (1999). *Patients as effective collaborators in managing chronic conditions.* New York: Millbank Memorial Fund.

Christensen, A. J. (2000). Patient-by-treatment context interaction in chronic disease: A conceptual framework for the study of patient adherence. *Psychosomatic Medicine, 62,* 435–443.

Christensen, A. J., Moran, P. J., & Wiebe, J. S. (1999). Assessment of irrational health beliefs: Relation to health practices and medical regimen adherence. *Health Psychology, 18,* 169–176.

Clifford, P. A., Tan, S. Y., & Gorsuch, R. L. (1991). Efficacy of a self-directed behavioral health change program: Weight, body composition, cardiovascular fitness, blood pressure, health risk, and psychosocial mediating variables. *Journal of Behavioral Medicine, 14,* 303–323.

Dew, M. A., Roth, L. H., Thompson, M. E., Kormos, R. L., & Griffith, B. P. (1996). Medical compliance and its predictors in the first year after heart transplantation. *Journal of Heart and Lung Transplant, 16,* 631–645.

DiClemente, C. C. (1999). Motivation for change: Implications for substance abuse. *Psychological Science, 10,* 209–213.

DiClemente, C. C. (2003). *Addiction and change: How addictions develop and how addicted people change.* New York: Guilford Press.

DiClemente, C. C., Fairhurst, S. K., & Piotrowski, N. A. (1995). Self-efficacy and addictive behaviors. In J. Maddux (Ed.), *Self-efficacy, adaptation and adjustment: Theory, research and application* (pp. 109–141). New York: Plenum Press.

DiClemente, C. C., Marinilli, A. S., Singh, M., & Bellino, L. E. (2001). The role of feedback in the process of health behavior change. *American Journal of Health Behavior, 25,* 217–227.

DiClemente, C. C., & Prochaska, J. O. (1998). Toward a comprehensive, transtheoretical model of change: Stages of change and addictive behaviors. In W. R. Miller & N. Heather (Eds.), *Treating addictive behaviors* (4th ed., pp. 3–24). New York: Plenum Press.

DiClemente, C. C., & Scott, C. W. (1997). Stages of change: Interaction with treatment compliance and involvement. In L. S. Onken, J. D. Blaine, & J. J. Boren (Eds.), *Beyond the therapeutic alliance: Keeping the drug-dependent individual in treatment* (pp. 131–156). Rockville, MD: National Institute on Drug Abuse.

DiClemente, C. C., & Velasquez, M. (2002). Motivational interviewing and the stages of change. In W. R. Miller & S. Rollnick (Eds.), *Motivational interviewing* (2nd ed., pp. 201–216). New York: Guilford.

Eraker, S. A., Kirscht, J. P., & Becker, M. H. (1984). Understanding and improving patient compliance. *Annals of Internal Medicine, 100,* 258–268.

Evangelista, L. S., & Dracup, K. (2000). A closer look at compliance research in heart failure patients in the last decade. *Progress in Cardiovascular Nursing, 15,* 97–103.

Fogarty, L., Roter, D., Larson, S., Burke, J., Gillespie, J., & Levy, R. (2002). Patient adherence to HIV medication regimens: A review of published and abstract reports. *Patient Education and Counseling, 46,* 93–108.

Friedman, H. S., & DiMatteo, M. R. (1990) Patient-physician interactions. In S. A. Shumaker, E. B. Schron, & J. K. Ockene (Eds.), *The handbook of health behavior change* (pp. 84–101). New York: Springer.

Gariti, P., Alterman, A. I., Holub-Beyer, E., Volpicelli, J. R., Prentice, N., & O'Brien, C. P. (1995). Effects of an appointment reminder call on patient show rates. *Journal of Substance Abuse Treatment, 12,* 207–212.

Glanz, K., Patterson, R. E., Kristal, A. R., DiClemente, C. C., Heimendinger, J., Linnan, L., et al. (1994). Stages of change in adopting healthy diets: Fat, fiber and correlates of nutrient intake. *Health Education Quarterly, 21,* 499–519.

Grimley, D. M., Prochaska, J. O., Velicer, W. F., & Prochaska, G. E. (1995). Contraceptive and condom use adoption and maintenance: A stage paradigm approach. *Health Education Quarterly, 22,* 20–35.

Guthrie, R. M. (2001). The effects of postal and telephone reminders on compliance with pravastatin therapy in a national registry: Results of the first myocardial infarction risk reduction program. *Clinical Therapeutics, 23,* 970–980.

Hardy, K. J., O'Brien, S. V., & Furlong, N. J. (2001). Information given to patients before appointment and its effect on non-adherence rate. *British Medical Journal, 323,* 1298–1300.

Kiortsis, D. N., Giral, P., Bruckert, E., & Turpin, G. (2000). Factors associated with low compliance with lipid-lowering drugs in hyperlipidemic patients. *Journal of Clinical Pharmacy and Therapeutics, 25*, 445–451.

Kirkman, M. S., Weinberger, M., Landsman, P. B., Samsa, G. P., Shortliffe, E. A., Simel, D. J., et al. (1994). A telephone-delivered intervention for patients with NIDDM: Effect on coronary risk factors. *Diabetes Care, 17*, 840–846.

Koren, M. E., Bartel, J. C., & Corliss, J. (1994). Interventions to improve patient appointments in an ambulatory care facility. *Journal of Ambulatory Care Management, 17*, 76–80.

Kravitz, R. L., Hays, R. D., Sherbourne, C. D., DiMatteo, M. R., Rogers, W. H., Ordway, L., et al. (1993). Recall of recommendations and adherence to advice among patients with chronic medical conditions. *Archives of Internal Medicine, 153*, 1869–1878.

Marcus, B. H., Rossi, J. S., Selby, V. C., Niaura, R. S., & Abrams, D. B. (1992). The stages and processes of exercise adoption and maintenance in worksite sample. *Health Psychology, 11*, 386–395.

Mattson, M. E., Del Boca, F. K., Carroll, K. M., Cooney, N. L., DiClemente, C. C., Donovan, D., Kadden, R. M., McRee, B., Rice, C., Rycharik, R. G., & Zweben, A. (1998). Project MATCH Research Group. Compliance with treatment and follow-up protocols in Project MATCH: Predictors and relationship to outcome. *Alcoholism: Clinical and Experimental Research, 22*, 1328–1339.

Meichenbaum, D., & Turk, S. (1987). *Facilitating treatment adherence: A practitioner's guidebook.* New York: Plenum Press.

Milgram, S. (1963). Behavioral study of obedience. *Journal of Abnormal and Social Psychology, 67*, 371–378.

Miller, W. R., & Rollnick, S. (1991). *Motivational interviewing: Preparing people to change addictive behavior.* New York: Guilford Press.

Miller, W. R., & Rollnick, S. (2002). *Motivational interviewing: Preparing people for change* (2nd ed.). New York: Guilford Press.

Neale, A. V. (1991). Behavioural contracting as a tool to help patients achieve better health. *Family Practice, 8*, 336–342.

Norcross, J. C., Ratzin, A. C., & Payne, D. (1989). Ringing in the new year: The change processes and reported outcomes of resolutions. *Addictive Behaviors, 14*, 205–212.

Ockene, I. S., Hayman, L. L., Pasternak, R. C.,

Schron, E., & Dunbar-Jacob, J. (2002). Task Force #4—adherence issues and behavior changes: Achieving a long-term solution. *Journal of the American College of Cardiology, 40*, 630–640.

Paykel, E. S. (1995). Psychotherapy, medication combinations, and compliance. *Journal of Clinical Psychiatry, 56*(Suppl.), 24–30.

Prochaska, J. O., & DiClemente, C. C. (1984). *The transtheoretical approach: Crossing traditional boundaries of therapy.* Malabar, FL: Krieger.

Prochaska, J. O., DiClemente, C. C., & Norcross, J. (1992). In search of how people change. *American Psychologist, 47*, 1101–1114.

Prochaska, J. O., Norcross, J. C., & DiClemente, C. C. (1994). *Changing for good.* New York: Avon.

Rollnick, S., Mason, P., & Butler, C. (1999). *Health behavior change: A guide for practitioners.* London: Churchill Livingstone.

Rosenstock, I. M., Strecher, V. J., & Becker, M. H. (1988). Social learning theory and the health belief model. *Health Education Quarterly, 15*, 175–183.

Roter, D. L., Hall, J. A., Merisca, R., Nordstrom, B., Cretin, D., & Svarstad, B. (1998). Effectiveness of interventions to improve patient compliance: A meta-analysis. *Medical Care, 36*, 1138–1161.

Ruggiero, L. (2000). Helping people with diabetes change behavior: From theory to practice. *Diabetes Spectrum, 13*, 125.

Schmaling, K. B., Afari, N., & Blume, A. W. (2000). Assessment of psychological factors associated with adherence to medication regimens among adult patients with asthma. *Journal of Asthma, 37*, 335–343.

Sorenson, J. L., Mascovich, A., Wall, T. L., DePhillipis, D., Batki, S. L., & Chesney, M. (1998). Medication adherence strategies for drug users with HIV/AIDS. *AIDS Care, 10*, 297–312.

Stewart, M., Belle-Brown, J., Wayne-Weston, W., McWhinney, I. R., McWilliam, C. L., & Freeman, T. R. (1995). *Patient-centered medicine: Transforming the clinical method.* Thousand Oaks, CA: Sage.

Strecher, V. J., DeVellis, B. M., Becker, M. H., & Rosenstock, I. M. (1986). The role of self-efficacy in achieving behavior change. *Health Education Quarterly, 13*, 73–92.

Stuart, R. B. (Ed.). (1982). *Adherence, compliance and generalization in behavioral medicine.* New York: Brunner/Mazel.

Timpson, S. C., Pollak, K. I., Bowen, A. M., Williams, M. L., Ross, M. W., McCoy, C. B., et al. (2001). Gender differences in the processes of change for condom use: Patterns across stages of change in crack cocaine users. *Health Education Research, 16,* 541–553.

Velasquez, M. M., Gaddy-Maurer, G., Crouch, C., & DiClemente, C. C. (2001). *Group treatment for substance abuse: A stage of change treatment manual.* New York: Guilford Press.

Velasquez, M. M., Wright, K., & Ingersoll, K. S. (in press). Treatment adherence and cardiovascular disease. In G. Fowler (Ed.), *Twenty common problems in cardiology.* New York: McGraw-Hill.

15

Mindful Practice for Clinicians and Patients

Shelley H. Carson
Ellen J. Langer

The clinician in a primary care environment works in an atmosphere that rewards efficiency, speed, and productivity. Within this fast-paced environment with its multiple distractions and interruptions, it seems convenient and efficient for the therapist to rely on automatic or over-learned responses to oft-seen clinical symptoms. Overlearned responses, however, may be *mindless* in that they actually reduce efficiency by limiting the nature of the therapeutic intervention to mind-sets that may be stereotyped, repetitive, and contextually ineffective. In a similar vein, the patient may be responding mindlessly by interpreting his or her current situation from a rigid and precategorized point of view that interferes with effective treatment. Increasing mindfulness rather than mindlessness can help patients recast their experiences in a different light as well as help clinicians approach patients' problems from a different perspective.

In this chapter we review the theory of mindfulness/mindlessness and discuss how a mindful perspective can promote better mental health in patients as well as clinicians. We also discuss spe-cific areas of concern in the primary care setting and ways that a mindful perspective can have a useful impact on the decisions of the mental health professional regarding diagnostic issues and coordination with the primary care physician and staff.

MINDFULNESS/MINDLESSNESS THEORY

The theory of mindfulness/mindlessness is distinct from the Buddhist tradition of mindfulness meditation that has been incorporated into thera-pies such as dialectical behavior therapy (Line-han, 1993). Although various forms of medita-tion indeed may bring about a postmeditation state of mindfulness, the concern here is with mindfulness without meditation (Langer, 1989, 1992, 1997; Langer & Moldoveanu, 2000).

Mindfulness is a flexible state of mind that re-sults from drawing novel distinctions about the situation and the environment. When we are mindful, we are actively engaged in the present and sensitive to both context and perspective. The mindful condition is the result of, and also the continuing cause of, actively noticing new things. When we are mindful, we may notice new aspects of our experience on many levels simultaneously, from molecular perceptions to higher level metaphorical insights. Mindful thinking typically is guided by rules and routines, but it is not governed by them.

As an exercise in mindfulness, consider reading this chapter from the perspective of the clinician, the perspective of the patient, the perspective of the patient's spouse, or the perspective of a researcher. Different aspects of the chapter will become important depending on the perspective. By reading from several perspectives, we derive fuller understanding of the material. The ability to perceive experiences in many lights and to choose the light appropriate for the current moment is characteristic of the mindful approach.

In contrast, *mindlessness* is a state of rigidity in which we adhere to a single perspective and act like automatons. When we are mindless, we are trapped in rigid mind-sets and are oblivious to context or perspective. We pigeonhole our experience of the world into rigid categories. Mindless thought processing and behavior are governed by rules, routines, and categories that have been established for us, or by us, in the past. Much of what we learn is information that has been imparted to us by an authority or has been presented to us in absolute language.

We often accept this information mindlessly and become trapped within a single perspective, oblivious to how things could be construed otherwise. In fact, we often view and accept our own personal experience mindlessly, unaware that we could have processed the experience from an alternate perspective or even from multiple alternate perspectives. We come to accept our original categorization of material, whether it stems from an attitude we were taught by an authority or from our own early experience as immutable truth; that is, we become cognitively committed to one way of seeing it. When information and experience are processed mindlessly, the potential for reconsideration is abandoned.

Our learned emotional responses to people, things, ideas, and even ourselves control our well-being. All too often, these emotional responses have been learned mindlessly. Although mindless responses can impart a (false) sense of stability and certainty, many studies have found that increasing mindful responses results in greater competence, health, positive affect, creativity, and reduced burnout (see Langer, 1989, 1997, for review of research).

The essence of mindfulness theory, then, is that a flexible mind-set in which we remain actively engaged in the process of drawing novel distinctions about our environment is more beneficial than a mind-set in which we are judgmental and rigid, sacrificing flexibility for a sense of certainty.

Arguments against mindfulness theory insist that cognitive work, such as actively drawing novel distinctions, is effortful. According to this argument, reliance on cognitive commitments (preformed rigid judgments about objects, persons, situations) and schemas (models that describe "how the world is") is more efficient because this saves mental energy that can be directed elsewhere. The alternative, a mindful engagement with the situation, is (erroneously) believed to lead to "analysis paralysis," which stifles decisive, purposeful action.

The point of mindful thinking, however, is not to fail to establish schemas or categories, but rather to make use of flexible categories and schemas that describe "how things may be" rather than single-mindedly presuming "how they are." The environment, after all, is filled with changing and even conflicting data. To make the best decisions, schemas need to be updated regularly.

This differs from mindless processing, in which there is a tendency to fortify schemas and cognitive commitments with confirming data and to ignore or refute disconfirming data. Therefore, schemas may still be mindfully employed, but the mindful aspect is relating the schema to the context and perspective and making an active judgment as to whether the schema applies. Just as the hallmark of a great quarterback is improvisation if the play starts to fall apart, the mindful individual is actively observing the environment and will be able to improvise when a life situation does not conform to a prescribed schema.

For this to happen, the mindful individual needs to be able to recategorize and revalue events as they unfold. The way to accomplish this is to be aware not to confuse the stability of the mind-set with the stability of the underlying phenomenon. Things in the world are changing all the time whether or not our beliefs are rigidly attempting to hold them still.

THE IMPORTANCE OF MINDFULNESS/MINDLESSNESS THEORY FOR MENTAL HEALTH CLINICIANS

The mindfulness/mindlessness distinction is particularly useful to clinicians in the field of mental health. One of the underlying principles of mental illness is that behavior that is currently maladaptive may have been adaptive, or at least appeared adaptive to the patient, at its inception. Thus, the alcoholic who was heartbroken over a breakup with a girlfriend found relief from pain when he had a couple of drinks. Similarly, the agoraphobic found relief from anxiety and panic symptoms when restricting herself to smaller and smaller areas around the home. The problem, of course, occurs when the once-adaptive behavior crystallizes into a rigid pattern of maladaptive behavior with no other options available from the perspective of the sufferer.

This original grain of adaptiveness may be found in much behavior that has grown to be problematic. Disordered behavior is generally rigid and automatic. Most disordered behavior, therefore, may be seen as a subset of mindless behavior, characterized by rigidity and a single-perspective point of view. The problem, then, is not the original behavior, but rather continuing the behavior once the context has changed.

If mental disorders are often characterized by mindlessness, then perhaps teaching mindfulness to patients will improve their mental health. Increasing mindfulness does not rest on alleviating symptoms per se, but on teaching that a response to every situation, every person, and every event may be (a) viewed from multiple perspectives; (b) categorized as positive, negative, or neutral (and recategorized as the situation changes); and (c) controlled by the individual. That is, once the individual has learned that there are options for conceptualizing experience, he or she may then realize that there are also options for responding to the experience both emotionally and behaviorally. Having a wider selection of response options should lead to a greater sense of personal control over responses to situations and events.

N. E. was a 16-year-old female high school student diagnosed with Grave's disease. Pharmaceutical treatment led to a substantial and rather rapid weight gain. She was referred to the psychologist by her primary care physician for school refusal and for refusal to take her medications, thus risking medical complications, including heart damage. When interviewed by the psychologist, N. E. stated that she hated her body, and she hated her mother (whom she blamed for giving her "bad thyroid genes"). She had kept her illness a secret from her friends and insisted that she would not go back to school to face them while she looked like a "beached whale." N. E. saw herself as a victim of her bloated body.

Although school attendance and drug compliance were the primary behavioral goals of therapy, her therapist realized that N. E. had mindlessly categorized her illness, her medications, her weight gain, her own body, and even her mother as "bad." She had also mindlessly categorized her friends and classmates as people who would ridicule her for her weight gain.

In therapy, the clinician helped N. E. explore a number of alternate perspectives from which she could view her relationship to her illness. Eventually, N. E. chose to view her current situation as a quest—a quest seeking wellness—and an opportunity to prove herself. She began to view the excess body weight not as a failure of self-discipline, but as a temporary tribulation her body must pass through on the way to her final prize of good health. The idea that she was successfully shouldering excess weight in the service of a nobler cause actually made her feel more self-confident than she had felt before she was diagnosed. She now viewed her medications and her mother as allies in the quest. When N. E. returned to school, she found that most of her classmates were extremely supportive and admired her for her positive attitude. Realizing that she could change her perspective and did not need to be trapped in the "victim" mind-set led directly to the behavioral changes stipulated as N. E.'s therapy goals.

Note that after mindfully exploring a number of perspectives, the patient—not the therapist—chose the perspective from which she would view her illness.

Of course, the idea of viewing a problem from a different perspective is not new to the field of psychopathology. Selecting a new theory or perspective and then testing it in the real world is the heart of Beck's cognitive therapy (Beck, Rush, Shaw, & Emery, 1987). However, one difference between cognitive therapy and mindfulness theory is that mindful thinking requires us to think of multiple alternate perspectives rather than a single alternative, so that one rigid way of viewing a situation or event is not replaced with another that may itself become maladaptive if the context changes.

In many therapeutic situations, the therapist helps the patient by putting the patient's problem in another context from a different perspective. Unwittingly, however, if this perspective is taken as reasonable, the patient is likely to see it as the only correct interpretation. As a result, accepting this new therapist-offered interpretation is likely to lead to increased dependence on the therapist and decreased trust of the patient in his or her own ability to see clearly. Alternatively, the deceptively simple change to multiple (more than two) perspectives should result in a decrease in the patient's willingness to accept any single interpretation as necessarily true; a decrease in dependence on the therapist; a decrease in the likelihood that the therapist will get locked into any particular view; and an increase in mindfulness for both the therapist and the patient.

Mindfulness theory seeks to unlock the rigid perspective that underlies maladaptive thinking by increasing uncertainty. Again, when we are "certain," we are confusing the stability of our own mind-set with the stability of the underlying phenomenon. The more reasonable alternatives one can envision to explain a negative experience or situation, the less likely it becomes that any single explanation is correct. Thus, exercises in alternative explanations may increase a patient's uncertainty in the "locked" point of view. In this manner, the patient may come to terms with the negative experience by coming to understand that his or her interpretation of the experience can fluctuate and can be controlled.

In summary, mindless mental processing may be a common feature of mental disorder. Adopting a mindful perspective may help patients process and interpret information in a less rigid and precategorized manner. This flexibility, in turn, may open the possibility of reinterpretation of information in a more adaptive manner and may aid in the treatment of the disorders most often seen in the primary care setting. At the end of this chapter, we include several techniques explored in our laboratory for increasing mindfulness.

SOME ISSUES OF MINDFULNESS/ MINDLESSNESS IN THE PRIMARY CARE SETTING

The primary care environment presents the potential for mindless processing in several ways. First, the purpose of the setting is to diagnose (categorize) and treat both physical and emotional problems efficiently. The need to categorize problems exerts pressure to pigeonhole the presenting concerns of patients. Second, to be efficient financially, the system has a hierarchical arrangement of staff and encourages rapid processing of patients. This means that there may be both time pressure and the pressure of playing a role in the hierarchy on clinicians and other staff members. Both types of pressure may affect the mindful quality of service. These and other issues relevant to the primary care setting may be viewed through the lens of mindfulness theory, and we present them as food for thought rather than absolute problems to be addressed.

Mindful Classification of Symptoms and Disorders

The very act of classifying an individual as a patient tends to color our view of his or her behavior. Certain behaviors or thinking patterns are seen as problematic when viewed within the confines of the therapeutic setting. If these same behaviors are viewed outside the therapeutic setting, they might be seen as variants of "normal" behavior.

This observation was confirmed in a study we performed at Yale (Langer & Abelson, 1974). In this study, two groups of clinicians were shown a videotape of a rather ordinary looking man being interviewed. One group of clinicians had been trained to avoid the use of labels; the other group had not received this training. Half of the clinicians in each group were told the man was a job applicant, and half were told he was a patient. The clinicians who were told the man was a job applicant, as well as members of the patient group who had received the special training, rated the man's behavior as well adjusted. Many of the clinicians who viewed the man as a patient, however, rated him as having serious psychological problems. The results of this study suggested that categorization of an individual may automatically and mindlessly activate a lens through which all of that individual's behaviors are viewed. (For another demonstration of the mindless classification of patients, see Rosenhan's classic 1973 study, "On Being Sane in Insane Places.") Awareness that the category of patient may be accompanied by an automatic tendency to view even normal activity as problematic will allow us to be more mindful of our own interpretations of patient behavior.

As mentioned above, we transform experiences into models or templates for behavior called schemas. We also organize the world by creating categories and attempting to place all objects and experiences within our personal categorical system. Developmental researchers tell us that one of the earliest categorizations we make is between "me" and "not me." Researchers on the biological basis of emotions suggest that we instinctively categorize things as "safe" or "not safe" and as "friend" or "foe" on the basis of very little information indeed.

For our ancestors, who needed to make immediate life-and-death distinctions between a bison (potential food source) and a saber-toothed tiger, the habit of quick classification into preexisting categories was adaptive. However, in the modern world of rapidly changing information and experience, premature cognitive commitment to a category may limit the ability to respond to situations adaptively. Once categorized, objects or events may become locked in. We believe we have "pegged" that experience or object, and we cease making new distinctions about it. To create new and fluid categories is a mindful activity. To

rely on rigid categorizations or on the categorization of things made years in the past is mindless.

As mental health clinicians, however, our work is based on rapid and efficient categorization. We efficiently classify the problems of our patients into categories of symptoms; then, if appropriate, we categorize the symptoms into previously established diagnostic categories of mental disorder. How can we best retain a mindful perspective when pigeonholing problems is our profession?

Mindful Categorization of Symptoms

Most of us learned early in our psychological training to categorize certain behaviors or thought patterns as symptoms. Further, we learned to categorize anything called a symptom as bad, something to get rid of, undesirable. Often, we think about such symptoms mindlessly instead of considering the context of the symptom.

Many symptoms, however, can be considered adaptive in certain contexts. For instance, overeating may be a symptom of an eating disorder, but it is also associated with holidays and celebrations; elevated or expansive mood is a symptom of mania, but it can also occur in reaction to a personal accomplishment and pride. Insomnia can provide time to write a term paper, read a book, or watch a movie.

It is, regrettably, not uncommon to psychopathologize even normal behavior. For instance, we often say someone is obsessed with an idea. If we are mindful, however, we might say instead that he or she is passionate about the idea. Thomas Edison was obsessed with the idea of inventing an electric light bulb, and Isaac Newton was obsessed with delineating the universal laws of gravity. Both lost sleep and forgot to eat meals during extended periods of work. Were they obsessed or passionate? In our laboratory, we have examined another symptom: the inability to concentrate. Research with children and adults with attention-deficit/hyperactivity disorder indicated that, when novel stimuli in the environment are reduced, the inability to concentrate disappears. This research suggested that the concept of "distraction" may be reformulated as "otherwise attracted" (see Langer, 1997). The point is that so-called symptoms may be interpreted from many perspectives, and that the valence of a symptom may change contextually (cf. Carson, Shih, & Langer, 2001).

Even if a symptom is causing distress to a patient in the present situation or context, the clinician and patient may be able to envision contexts in which the symptom might be beneficial. The very act of visualizing such contexts may lessen the rigidity with which a symptom distresses a patient. For instance, consider a patient who has difficulty falling asleep at night because he or she is "obsessing" about a problem. If we subscribe to the mindless assumption that we should fall asleep almost immediately upon hitting the pillow, then of course any failure to do so will be viewed as a pathological symptom. However, if we view the period before sleep as a proper time to address the day's concerns mentally, then the obsessing looks more like problem solving. It is often the failure to find the solution to a "problem" that leads us to feel we are obsessing about it; if we "figured it out" during our late-night rumination, the next day we probably would be unlikely to think of ourselves as obsessed. Literature in the field of creativity research repeatedly indicates that mulling over a problem before sleep activates unconscious or implicit mental processing that may lead to insightful solutions. When viewed in this light, the patient may see that obsessing about a problem at night may be part of a problem-solving process that may prove beneficial in the long run.

> C. B. was a 48-year-old male airline pilot on medical leave for vision difficulties caused by a detached retina. Although the retina was successfully repaired, C. B.'s primary care physician informed him that he could no longer run 3 miles a day without permanently injuring his eyesight. The patient nevertheless continued to run. His physician then referred him to a psychologist with a request to treat his "compulsive running."
>
> After determining that C. B. was not attempting to use his vision difficulties to avoid returning to flight status, the therapist began response prevention treatment for the "running problem." After several sessions, however, C. B. announced he was terminating therapy, claiming that running was very important to him. At this point, the therapist reviewed treatment objectives from a mind-
> ful perspective. Was the patient's regular running routine actually a symptom to be eradicated, or could it be viewed as a positive element of the patient's life? Choosing the latter perspective, the clinician worked jointly with C. B. to develop running paradigms, such as running in waist-high water or running on a treadmill while resting the upper body on a support scaffold, which would not unnecessarily jar the retina. The patient was able in this way to continue a running program on a limited basis without endangering his vision.

Note that when running was viewed as a compulsive symptom, treatment was ineffective. However, when the patient's desire to run was viewed in a benign light, an acceptable behavior modification program succeeded.

In summary, symptoms may be neutral or even beneficial to patients in some contexts and under some conditions. Rather than automatically categorizing these symptoms as negative, mindfully consider each symptom or behavior and not only its current value, but also its potential value to the patient before relegating it to the criteria-for-diagnosis category.

Mindful Categorization of Disorders

A second potential area for mindless categorization is the classification of mental disorder. The benefits of the current classification system are irrefutable: It provides a basis for formulating treatment, justification for reimbursement from third parties such as insurance companies, a basis for continuing research, and a shorthand for scientific communication of large amounts of information about individual behavior. Rigid adherence to the classification system as it stands today, however, would constitute mindless behavior. The accepted classification system as represented in the *Diagnostic and Statistical Manual of Mental Disorders*, fourth edition (*DSM-IV*; American Psychiatric Association, 1994) is itself fluid and changing.

For example, patients diagnosed as schizophrenic prior to 1980 in the United States might well be diagnosed with bipolar disorder under today's criteria. Yet many patients diagnosed prior to 1980 still carry the diagnosis of schizophrenia without benefit of review. It is very difficult not to be affected by the prior diagnoses that a patient has received. It is more mindful to think of a diagnosis as a fluid, changing condition rather than as a rigid, fixed category into which a patient can be pegged.

Another consideration about the *DSM* classification system is that it may, to some extent, reflect the political views of society and not necessarily the afflictions of the patient. Until 1980, for instance, homosexuality was considered a disorder. Other disorders affected by politics include posttraumatic stress disorder, passive–aggressive personality disorder, premenstrual dysphoric disorder, and masochistic personality disorder (American Psychiatric Association, 1994). To the extent that *DSM* reflects political viewpoints, a dose of mindful reflection may be more beneficial to the patient than rigid adherence to the criteria of disorders.

Mindfulness and Mind-Body Dualism

Woody Allen asked in *Getting Even*, "Is there a split between mind and body, and if so, which is it better to have?" Traditional Western training in both medicine and psychiatry has emphasized a mind-body dualism that suggests disorder has either a physical (body) or a mental/emotional (mind) etiology. The mindless categorization of disorder into physical and mental, however, may have serious consequences. There is now ample evidence that negative emotions (anger, fear, and stress) may have direct and indirect links to cardiovascular disease and to dysregulation of the immune system, potentially leading to infectious diseases, asthma, and even cancer (see Leventhal & Patrick-Miller, 2000, for a review). In contrast, positive emotional states may lead to improved physical health and improved functioning of the immune system (see Salovey, Rothman, Detweiler, & Steward, 2000, for a review). Physical ailments, in turn, can lead to emotional dysregulation in the form of depression, fear/anxiety, and anger/irritability.

E. E. was a 32-year-old housewife referred to the psychologist by her primary care physician after extensive tests on her severe back and neck pain revealed no physical cause. The doctor suspected that her symptoms, which were so severe that she could barely walk, were caused by stress.

When interviewed by the primary care psychologist, E. E. described a home life that was dominated by an abusive and demanding mother-in-law. The situation had recently worsened when E. E.'s husband insisted that his brother, who was recovering from a leg amputation resulting from his failure to comply with treatment for diabetes, move in with them. E. E. spent most of her day waiting on the in-laws, who were never satisfied with her efforts. E. E. felt she must work even harder to avoid her husband's harsh rebukes. She was worried that if she did not please her in-laws, her husband would leave her.

The psychologist began working with E. E. to help her view her situation from a variety of perspectives. How does her life with the demanding in-laws appear to the neighbors, the postman, or the living room sofa? Is it necessary to be a servant to one's in-laws in order to be a "good wife"? Can she see herself in other roles, such as an independent elementary school teacher (her former position) with her own apartment? Can she see herself returning to school to study her passion of interior design?

E. E. is still living with the demanding in-laws; she states that this is a choice she is making for the present. She may choose another option in the future. In the meantime, she claims that viewing her life from a variety of perspectives and knowing she can choose which perspective is appropriate for her at this time has changed her life. Her back pains only flare up occasionally, and E. E. claims to use them as an indicator that she has slipped into her old, rigid mind-set of playing the servant. She then puts her feet up and reviews her current options. Mindful examination of her life appears to be improving her physical as well as her emotional health.

In summary, given the preponderance of current research evidence that indicates the inseparability of mind and body, the perspective of mindfulness suggests that we look at how each physical symptom may affect the patient's emotional state and, conversely, how emotional symptoms—and the interpretation of situations and events—may directly or indirectly affect the physical health of the patient. The importance of helping patients reframe or reinterpret stressful situations in a mindful fashion gains importance when the ramifications of stress for one's health are considered.

Mindfulness and Role-Playing in the Primary Care Setting

Role-Playing and Staff Members

The primary care setting is by necessity organized hierarchically; unfortunately, this can result in a situation in which medical personnel, from doctors to nurse's assistants to patients, are organized in a descending order of status. Individuals may unwittingly act and communicate mindlessly according to their roles in the hierarchy rather than in accordance with their knowledge of a given situation.

Psychologist Robert Cialdini (1993) cited an incident that is truly an example of mindless action in the medical hierarchy. After treating a patient's earache, a physician wrote a prescription for medication to be administered in the "R ear." The nurse, without considering that medication for an earache might be prescribed for the "Right ear" mindlessly proceeded to inject the medication into the patient's rear. Numerous malpractice cases describe incidents in which a nurse silently questioned the dosage of a medication, but administered it anyway because "the doctor prescribed it."

Psychologists and other mental health clinicians may find themselves sandwiched into such a hierarchy, replete with certain role expectations. We believe that, through mindful observation and awareness of role expectations in the setting, clinicians can make overtures toward other staff members that allow them to communicate in confidence outside their prescribed role in the hierarchy. It may be possible for primary care psychologists, through awareness of the pitfalls of role-based communication, to take an active and mindful lead in ensuring that all members of the staff feel comfortable in expressing doubts and suggestions about patient diagnosis and treatment.

Role-Playing and the Patient

Besides the hierarchical roles unwittingly played by staff members, patients may also play implicit roles. Patients may unwittingly, for example, perceive themselves as victims—of disease, of "the

system," or of their own temperaments and emotions. Unfortunately, this role is sometimes encouraged by outside agents, such as personal injury attorneys and patient advocacy groups, who may have a stake in portraying the ill or injured patient as a victim. The downside for patients is, of course, that victimization removes their perception of control over their situation. They learn to feel helpless about their circumstances.

This learned helplessness and its relationship to depression and disease was described by Martin Seligman (1975) in his famous animal experiments of the 1970s. When animals, as well as humans, perceive that they have no control over their situation or environment, they eventually "give up" and make no effort to help themselves.

Patients, however, are not victims unless they decide to be. A mindful examination of patients' experience from multiple perspectives can help them discover that there are multiple possibilities for control over their behavior and circumstances. They need not be victims of disease, poor parenting, a hostile society, or even their own genes. Once people self-label, experiences that might be in opposition to the label go unnoticed, and the problems associated with the label seem much more pronounced (cf. Langer, Janis, & Wolfer, 1975).

In summary, in the primary care setting, every individual may be cast in a definitive role that he or she plays mindlessly. A mindful handling of the situation suggests that the clinician first be aware of times when an individual may be communicating through his or her implicit role in the medical hierarchy; second, the clinician must be willing to help each individual see possibilities outside that role and to feel comfortable outside the role. Patients, who may feel like victims of their own physical or mental ailments, can be mindfully presented with a variety of options for reframing their experience. By learning to view their situation from a mindful perspective, they can increase their tolerance of unpleasantness and uncertainty and examine the more positive aspects of their circumstances, even as they work to change them.

Mindfulness and the Time-Pressured Setting

We mentioned that opponents of mindfulness theory believe that mindful consideration of alternate perspectives is time and energy consuming. Cognitive commitments, categorizing experience based on a one-time exposure, and examining experience from a single perspective seem more efficient. We have heard clinicians, after all, brag about the speed with which they reliably render a diagnosis. In a primary care setting in which time with each patient is limited, the mindless pigeonhole method may seem more expeditious, but is it?

The true "expert" in this (or any) field is always a student as well as a skillful practitioner, growing in expertise through openness to new learning and new perspectives. Remaining mindful does not mean that we cannot bring all our training and years of experience to bear on the diagnosis and treatment of a patient. However, remaining mindful does mean that, even as a diagnosis and treatment plan are formulated, we remain open to new observations and information, and we remain willing to change our preconceived notions in accordance with changes in context.

A second pitfall of the time pressure exerted by the primary care setting is that clinicians may actually be focusing attention on the flow of patients rather than on the needs of the current patient. Clinicians report being mentally preoccupied with the next patient or with one seen earlier in the day. When the therapist engages mindfully, however, with the individual currently being seen, mental carryover from previous cases or thoughts of future cases will be eliminated. In other words, mindfulness works in opposition to boredom to refocus the clinician's attention on the possibilities of the present. This attentional shift should result in greater psychological well-being for the clinician as well as for the patient.

METHODS OF INCREASING MINDFULNESS

The following suggestions for increasing mindfulness are adaptations of experimental manipulations and of observations we have made in our investigations of the effects of mindfulness and mindlessness on health, learning, and communication processes. They represent only a few of the potential methods for teaching others to mind-fully envision alternative models for "how things are."

1. *Actively observe novel distinctions.* Observing new distinctions increases positive affect and also increases interest in the event, object, behavior, or situation (Langer & Pietrasz, 1995). When patients are instructed to actively notice a specific number of new things about a maladaptive behavior (and to consider how each aspect may be advantageous), they may begin to see the behavior in a less rigid light. When the rigidity of the behavior is reduced, patients may feel they have more behavioral options. This in turn may allow them to regain a feeling of control over their behavior. For example, when binge eaters are prompted to keep a food journal (prompting them to notice novel aspects of their present eating behavior, such as emotional state, time of day, what they are thinking, what they are eating), they report feeling more in control of their eating behavior.

2. *Introduce information in a conditional way, replacing "certainty" words with "possibility" words.* When authority figures replaced the words "is" and "are" with "may be" and "could be" in our research, participants responded with increased production and creativity (see Langer & Moldoveanu, 2000, for a review). Clinicians can replace the words "is" and "are" with "may be" and "could be" in their discussions with patients. In addition, patients can be instructed to use possibility words in their narratives. The very act of replacing the certainty of their convictions with the possibility that things may be true will also open up the possibility that things may not be as the patient currently interprets them. This, in turn, creates a mind-set open to new interpretations.

3. *Contemplate puzzles and paradoxes.* Human lives are full of paradoxes. For example, we may both love and hate our parents or our bodies. We may at once feel victimized by and responsible for an illness or a seemingly intolerable situation. Actively thinking about paradoxes increases the ability to tolerate ambiguity (and decreases the anxiety associated with uncertainty). Increased tolerance of uncertainty is a hallmark of mindfulness. Suggest that patients contemplate a paradox or a puzzle several times a week, from the sublime (How can light be both a particle and a wave?) to the comical (When does $1 + 1 = 1$?

One answer: when adding one wad of gum to one wad of gum). Here, for example, is a paradoxical puzzle on the nature of relativity: What stays fixed in the same corner, yet travels the world? One answer: a stamp.

4. *Add humor to the situation.* Have patients purposefully find something humorous about their situation. Humor itself relies on mindfulness by forcing us to see a new and unexpected side to a given situation. (This is why a joke already heard and remembered, without being newly considered, is rarely funny.)

5. *View the situation from multiple perspectives.* Ask the patient to relate his or her problem as seen from the perspective of different people. This may include the perspective of others involved in the situation (and, if appropriate, the humorous perspective of fictional observers, such as a dentist or a hairdresser).

6. *Consider alternative understandings of the problem.* How many ways can the problem be viewed as useful? In what contexts could the problem be considered useful? For example, Alloy and Abramson's (1979) classic research into depressive realism suggested that depressed states of mind may lead to more accuracy and realism in evaluating certain situations. In a like manner, all problems can be seen as useful in some contexts. Viewing problems as having a potential silver lining, no matter how remote the possibility of that silver lining, may serve to decrease a patient's fear of or resentment of the clinical problem. For example, when N. E., the 16-year-old patient described above, viewed her experience with Grave's disease as a quest for health, she found that working through the treatment had positive benefits. The difference between an ordeal and an adventure may be in how one looks at it.

7. *Examine positive experiences that fall outside the diagnosis* (e.g., moments of joy). The purpose of examining positive experiences alongside symptomatic concerns is not to whitewash difficulties. Rather, a journey outside diagnostic concerns serves two purposes: First, it keeps the current difficulties from usurping the entire mental landscape and puts current concerns into some perspective. Second, a growing body of research indicates that an increase in positive mental state, even a mild increase such as that experienced from remembering positive events, markedly influences mental flexibility and creative problem solving (Langer et al., 1975; also see Isen, 2000, for a review). Thus, the chances of finding a mindful solution to a problem are increased by the remembrance of positive events.

8. *Start a mindfulness journal.* Make a point to begin or end each day by writing down the significant events of the day. Look back on the events with the purpose of observing new things and new perspectives about them. Practice at mindfully viewing events and situations in retrospect will enhance the ability to mindfully experience events and situations at the time they occur.

SUMMARY

In this chapter, we introduced the concepts of mindfulness and mindlessness. Mindfulness is a state of actively seeking novel distinctions in one's present situation. It is a state of remaining actively open to new ways of experiencing the environment. Mindlessness, in contrast, is running on automatic pilot, assigning new experience to old categories previously developed. It is looking at all experience from a single perspective and never questioning that perspective.

We also discussed ways that the mindfulness/mindlessness distinction may have an impact on the clinician in the primary care setting. We looked at the general ways in which clinicians may help patients mindfully reinterpret their experience and improve their mental health. As patients increase in mindfulness, they will tend to respond less frequently with precommitted maladaptive patterns.

We also looked at the specific ways mindlessness may be introduced into the primary care system and how clinicians may avoid these pitfalls. These include the following:

- Evaluating symptoms mindfully (for both their negative and potentially positive impact on patients) before considering them criteria for diagnosing a disorder.
- Thinking mindfully about diagnostic labels and viewing diagnostic categories as fluid and contextually dependent.
- Keeping in mind the role that other staff

members may be enacting and communicating with staff members in a way that encourages them to think outside their roles.

- Helping patients to see themselves not only within their role as a patient, but also as individuals full of possibilities and not limited by either the medical or mental diagnostic label.

There are no actual rules for increasing mindfulness, only a willingness to actively seek out what is new and what is possible. There are also no rules for decreasing mindlessness, only a willingness to suspend cognitive commitments long enough to envision alternative perspectives.

The more alternatives one can envision, the more possibilities one sees for enriching and improving the experience of life. The main point of this chapter is to suggest that one of the greatest gifts we can provide patients is the ability to conceptualize their present experience in terms of many possible interpretations. We can actively change our interpretations, and the behaviors they encourage, whenever it is to our benefit to do so. This is *mindfulness*. This knowledge can make a true difference in our lives and in the lives of our patients.

References

Alloy, L. B., & Abramson, L. Y. (1979). Judgment of contingency in depressed and nondepressed students: Sadder but wiser? *Journal of Experimental Psychology: General, 108*, 441–485.

American Psychiatric Association. (1994). *Diagnostic and statistical manual of mental disorders* (4th ed.). Washington, DC: Author.

Beck, A. T., Rush, A. J., Shaw, B. F., & Emery, G. (1987). *Cognitive therapy of depression.* New York: Guilford Press.

Carson, S., Shih, M., & Langer, E. (2001). Sit still and pay attention? *Journal of Adult Development, 8*, 183–188.

Cialdini, R. B. (1993). *Influence: The psychology of persuasion.* New York: Quill/W. Morrow.

Isen, A. M. (2000). Positive affect and decision making. In M. Lewis & J. M. Haviland-Jones (Eds.), *Handbook of emotions* (2nd ed., pp. 417–435). New York: Guilford Press.

Langer, E. J. (1989). *Mindfulness.* Reading, MA: Addison-Wesley.

Langer, E. (1992). Matters of mind: Mindfulness/mindlessness in perspective. *Consciousness and Cognition, 1*, 289–305.

Langer, E. J. (1997). *The power of mindful learning.* Reading, MA: Addison-Wesley.

Langer, E. J., & Abelson, R. (1974). A patient by any other name . . . : Clinician group differences in labelling bias. *Journal of Consulting and Clinical Psychology, 42*, 4–9.

Langer, E. J., Janis, I., & Wolfer, J. (1975). Reduction of psychological stress in surgical patients. *Journal of Experimental Social Psychology, 11*, 155–165.

Langer, E. J., & Moldoveanu, M. (2000). The construct of mindfulness. *Journal of Social Issues, 56*, 1–9.

Langer, E., & Pietrasz, L. (1995). *From reference to preference.* Unpublished manuscript, Harvard University, Cambridge, MA.

Leventhal, H., & Patrick-Miller, L. (2000). Emotions and physical illness: Causes and indicators of vulnerability. In M. Lewis & J. M. Haviland-Jones (Eds.), *Handbook of emotions* (2nd ed., pp. 523–537). New York: Guilford Press.

Linehan, M. M. (1993). *Skills training manual for treating borderline personality disorder.* New York: Guilford Press.

Rosenhan, D. L. (1973). On being sane in insane places. *Science, 179*, 250–258.

Salovey, P., Rothman, A. J., Detweiler, J. B., & Steward, W. T. (2000). Emotional states and physical health. *American Psychologist, 55*, 110–121.

Seligman, M. E. P. (1975). *Helplessness: On depression, development and death.* San Francisco: W. H. Freeman.

IV

CLINICAL CONDITIONS

IV

CLINICAL CONDITIONS

16

Alcohol and Other Substance Use Disorders

Gerard J. Connors
Scott H. Stewart

Alcohol and other substance use disorders are among the most imposing problems facing health care systems today. This is particularly true in primary care settings because alcohol and other substance misuse is associated with a wide range of medical problems, including hypertension, diabetes, gastrointestinal disorders, sexually transmitted diseases, family violence, trauma, depression, anxiety, and thought disorders (Fleming & Manwell, 2000). Unfortunately, physicians and mental health professionals alike often fail to assess systematically for alcohol and other substance use disorders. Despite the lack of attention paid to addictive disorders in many clinical training programs, psychologists are particularly well qualified to treat these problems (Miller & Brown, 1997); in particular, the primary care psychologist can offer "low-threshold entry points" (Washburn, 2003) for patients who need alcohol or drug abuse treatment.

In this chapter, we begin with an overview of alcohol and other substance use disorders, including the diagnostic criteria for abuse and dependence, epidemiological data, a description of the natural history of these disorders, and an over-view of alcohol- and substance-related medical disorders. Strategies for identifying alcohol and other substance use disorders are then described. The following section addresses treatment issues, including barriers to treatment, treatment setting options, effective psychological and psychopharmacological treatments, family involvement in the treatment endeavor, self-help group involvement, and the problem of relapse. Remaining sections of the chapter address innovative collaborative care arrangements and secondary prevention interventions potentially available for use in medical environments.

DIAGNOSTIC CRITERIA

The diagnostic system used most widely in the United States for the assessment of alcohol and other substance use disorders is the fourth edition of the *Diagnostic and Statistical Manual of Mental Disorders* (*DSM-IV*; American Psychiatric Association, 1994). (A parallel system, the *International Statistical Classification of Diseases, 10th Revision* [*ICD-10*; World Health Organization, 1992] is widely used outside the United States.) The *DSM-IV* criteria for alcohol dependence are outlined in Table 16.1.

Because alcohol use disorders are so highly prevalent among patients in medical environments, the diagnostic criteria presented in the table have been modified from their proposed use in the diagnosis of substance use disorders to reflect only alcohol use and its consequences. Of course, the criteria are applicable to other substance use disorders as well. As can be seen in Table 16.1,

a diagnosis of alcohol dependence is warranted when three or more indicators of impairment are identifiable over the course of a 12-month period.

An alcohol or other substance use disorder that does not meet the criteria for dependence is labeled "[alcohol] abuse," and the *DSM* criteria are provided as well in Table 16.1. Review of these criteria reveals that the category of "alcohol abuse" focuses on health damage (psychological or physical) and on social, legal, or vocational consequences.

Table 16.1 *DSM-IV* **Diagnostic Criteria for Alcohol Dependence and Alchol Abuse**

Alcohol dependence	Clustering of symptoms—A maladaptive pattern of alcohol use, leading to clinically significant impairment or distress as manifested by three or more of the following occurring at any time during the same 12-month period:
Tolerance	Need for markedly increased amounts of alcohol to achieve intoxication or desired effect or reduced effect with continued use of the same amount of alcohol
Withdrawal	The characteristic withdrawal syndrome for alcohol, or alcohol or a closely related substance is taken to relieve or avoid withdrawal symptoms
Impaired control	Persistent desire, or one or more unsuccessful efforts to cut down or control drinking
Drinking in larger amounts or over a longer period than the person intended	
Neglect of activities	Important social, occupational, or recreational activities given up or reduced because of drinking
Time spent drinking	A great deal of time spent in activities necessary to obtain alcohol, to drink, or to recover from its effects
Drinking despite problems	Continued drinking despite knowledge of having a persistent or recurrent physical or psychological problem that is likely to be caused or exacerbated by alcohol use
Duration criteria	No duration criterion specified; however, dependence criteria must be met within the same year and must occur repeatedly as specified by duration qualifiers associated with criteria (such as "often," "persistent," and "continued")

Criterion for subtyping:

  With physiological dependence: Evidence of tolerance or withdrawal

  Without physiological dependence: No evidence of tolerance or withdrawal

Alcohol abuse

A. A maladaptive pattern of alcohol use leading to clinically significant impairment or distress, as manifested by one or more of the following, occurring within a 12-month period:

  1. Recurrent drinking resulting in a failure to fulfull major role obligations at work, shcool, or home

  2. Recurrent drinking when it is physically hazardous

  3. Recurrent alcohol-related legal problems

  4. Continued alcohol use despite having persistent or recurrent social or interpersonal problems caused or exacerbated by the effects of alcohol

B. The symptoms have never met the criteria for alcohol dependence

Adapted from National Institute on Alcohol Abuse and Alcoholism (1995a).

EPIDEMIOLOGY

Survey data indicated that approximately 4.5% to 6% of the U.S. population meet *DSM-IV* criteria for current alcohol abuse or dependence (Grant, 1997). These disorders are about twice as common among men, with inverse associations between the probability of dependence and age, education, and income. It is often assumed that problem drinkers are overrepresented in general medical settings, but this may be a result of prevalence studies completed in clinics serving high-risk populations. Studies of the use of alcohol and medical services by the general population suggested that problem drinkers have a similar prevalence in medical settings as they do in the general population. Nevertheless, alcoholism is common in medical settings and probably is underdiagnosed.

The prevalence of other drug abuse has been less studied in medical settings. Results of the 2001 U.S. National Household Drug Survey (Substance Abuse and Mental Health Services Administration, 2001) provided estimates on the prevalence of illicit drug abuse and dependence in the general population. Illicit drugs include marijuana, cocaine, heroin, hallucinogens, inhalants, and nonmedical use of prescription medications. Approximately 7% of the population aged 12 years and older were estimated to have used an illicit drug within the previous month. Of these, about 56% used marijuana only, and 44% used another illicit drug with or without concurrent marijuana use. Approximately half of these current illicit drug users were estimated to have experienced consequences that were consistent with abuse or dependence. Illicit drug abuse, often accompanied by alcohol abuse, peaks at ages 18 to 20 years, with a rapid decline thereafter.

Men are more likely to use illicit drugs than women, except for the use of prescription drugs for nonmedical purposes, which is similar for both sexes. Risk factors for illicit drug use include low education, unemployment, urban residence, and criminal history. Certainly, those who misuse prescription drugs are overrepresented in medical settings, but it is not known if this is true for other illicit drug users. Nevertheless, the medical complications of such drug use are frequently encountered, particularly in clinics serving high-risk populations.

NATURAL HISTORY

In the general population, the incidence of initial alcohol use begins to rise steeply at about 14 years of age. Beyond the mid-20s, the incidence of initiation is lower, with only a slow increase in the probability of using alcohol throughout the remainder of the life span. Problem drinking initially occurs most often in adolescence through the early 30s, and those who reach the age of 35 years with few adverse sequelae of drinking are unlikely to develop alcohol dependence (Grant, 1997). These patterns are likely mirrored in populations utilizing primary care services.

Alcohol dependence is often characterized by remissions and relapses rather than constant daily drinking, complicating studies of the natural history of dependence. A significant proportion of patients with alcohol dependence (20% or more) will have long-term or permanent remissions without benefit of treatment. Others will seek treatment in specialty settings or attend self-help groups, with a 40% to 60% probability of long-term remission (American Psychiatric Association, 1994; Schuckit et al., 2001). However, a substantial percentage of individuals will suffer from persistent dependence with a high risk for medical sequelae. This subgroup receives a disproportionate share of treatment by medical personnel.

Understanding the natural history of dependence on illicit drugs is also complicated by the relapsing-remitting pattern of the disorders and the difficulty of obtaining accurate reports about illegal behaviors. Studies performed in specialty settings may primarily include those experiencing the most adverse consequences of drug use, who present with relatively low rates of remission and high mortality rates (Hser, Anglin, & Powers, 1993). In the general population, the relatively high prevalence of drug use among adults aged 18 to 25 years compared to the lower prevalence among those older than 25 years suggests that most illicit drug users will stop using drugs (Substance Abuse and Mental Health Services Administration, 2001). Within the currently using population, there clearly exists a subset with severe addiction and a poorer prognosis.

TYPICAL PRESENTATION

Although no comprehensive surveys of presenting complaints in alcoholic patients have been conducted, it is safe to assert that patients generally do not visit primary care physicians because of concerns about their drinking. Rather, they are likely to present with symptoms that are secondary to excessive alcohol or other drug use. In clinical practice, the more common signs and symptoms attributable to alcohol abuse are caused by diseases of the gastrointestinal tract, cardiovascular system, and nervous system. Heavy use may also directly impair diabetes control.

Gastrointestinal disorders include gastritis, peptic ulcer disease, pancreatitis, and liver disease and range from clinically mild to life threatening. Common cardiovascular sequelae of heavy drinking include hypertension, cardiac arrythmia, and congestive heart failure. Hypertension is very common in primary care settings, and alcohol abuse should be considered in patients with newly diagnosed hypertension as well as those whose blood pressure proves difficult to control.

There are many neurological effects of chronic, heavy alcohol consumption, including degeneration of the central and peripheral nervous systems. Acutely, alcohol withdrawal is a common cause of delirium and seizure. Poor diet may lead to vitamin deficiencies, occasionally resulting in acute encephalopathy and, if not urgently treated, chronic neurological sequelae.

Other disorders associated with alcohol abuse are typically less dramatic and may not be recognized as secondary to alcohol. These include various skin disorders, amenorrhea, gouty arthritis, parotid gland enlargement, insomnia, and symptoms of depression. For a full review of medical conditions caused or influenced by alcoholism or other drug abuse, see Stein (1999).

Abuse of other drugs leads to other clinical presentations (Cherubin & Sapira, 1993). Patients who abuse prescription drugs (commonly narcotic analgesics, sedatives, and stimulants) may present with symptoms of pain, anxiety, or sleep disorders. Such symptoms may be feigned to obtain the specific drug of abuse. These patients often "doctor shop" until the desired prescription is provided. In practice, it is often difficult to differentiate legitimate indications for potentially addictive drugs from drug-seeking behavior. Cocaine users may present with cardiovascular or neurological symptoms from vascular effects of this drug or pulmonary symptoms if the drug is inhaled. Intravenous drug abuse is characterized by many infectious complications, such as HIV, infections at injection sites, endocarditis, or abscess formation from blood-borne dissemination of injected organisms.

Drug abuse in general promotes high-risk sexual behavior, with an increase in HIV infection and other sexually transmitted diseases. Compulsive drug seeking, the adverse consequences of drug abuse, and social factors associated with drug abuse may also interfere with care plans for any chronic medical condition.

SCREENING

Screening refers to the application of assessment procedures to identify persons with alcohol and other substance use problems and consequences or who are at risk for such difficulties. Screening can also set the stage for subsequent assessment and intervention (Connors & Volk, in press).

Screening Measures

A variety of psychometrically sound screening measures have been developed for use in a range of settings (for a review, see Connors & Volk, in press). Many of these measures are brief, inexpensive or free, and easy to administer.

Among the most frequently used screening measures are the CAGE (Mayfield, McLeod, & Hall, 1974) and the Alcohol Use Disorders Identification Test (AUDIT; Saunders, Aasland, Babor, DeLaFuente, & Grant, 1993). The CAGE (see Table 16.2) is a 4-item measure that can be administered verbally or in written form. A cutoff score of 2 items answered "yes" appears to work most productively for sensitive and accurate identification (Ewing, 1984; Jacobson, 1989). The AUDIT is a 10-item screening measure designed specifically for use in primary care settings, al-

Table 16.2 The CAGE Questionnaire

Have you ever felt you should cut down on your
  drinking?

Have people annoyed you by criticizing your
  drinking?

Have you ever felt guilty about your drinking?

Have you ever had a drink first thing in the morning
  (eye opener)?

Note: The test name is an acronym of letters of words from
the four items (cut down, annoyed, felt guilty, eye opener).
A cutoff score of two "yes" responses is generally used. From
Mayfield, McLeod, and Hall (1974).

though research has shown that it is suited for use
in a wide range of other settings (Saunders et al.,
1993). The AUDIT is shown in Table 16.3. An
individual's responses to each of the items is
given a score, and the total score is calculated by
adding the scores for each of the items. The minimum, or cutoff, score for possible identification of
an alcohol problem is 8. An advantage of the
AUDIT over the CAGE is that the former gathers
information on quantity and frequency of alcohol
consumption. The AUDIT also has greater potential for eliciting indications of a broader range of
alcohol use dysfunction and associated risk.

Fewer options are available for screening for
other drug abuse. One that is widely used, the
Drug Abuse Screening Test (DAST; Skinner, 1982)
includes 20 items on drug use consequences (yes/
no response format), with a score of 6 or higher
indicative of drug problems. A more recently developed tool is the Alcohol, Smoking, and Substance Involvement Screening Test (ASSIST;
World Health Organization ASSIST Working
Group, 2002). The ASSIST was developed to
identify substance use and related problems among
primary care patients. It is composed of 8 items
and takes less than 5 minutes to complete.

Even briefer strategies have emerged in recent
years. As examples, Cyr and Wartman (1988)
proposed use of two screening questions, and
Williams and Vinson (2001) described use of a
single question. Brown, Leonard, Saunders, and
Papasouliotis (2001), in an effort to assess both
alcohol and other substance abuse, developed a
Two-Item Conjoint Screen (called the TICS).
The items associated with these three screening
strategies are shown in Table 16.4.

Once alcohol or other substance misuse is

identified through screening, the clinician must
gather more detailed information on the patient's
alcohol/substance use. The initial focus is on the
nature and extent of use, consequences (e.g., so-
cial/vocational, psychological, physical), and extent to which the patient's behavior meets the
diagnostic criteria. Such an endeavor is ideally
collaborative; the clinician should attempt to be
nonjudgmental, use open-ended questions, and
use reflective listening (e.g., Miller & Rollnick,
2002). A measure available for guiding the assessment of alcohol and other substance use and consequences is the Addiction Severity Index (ASI;
McLellan et al., 1992). In addition, structured
clinical interviews (such as the Diagnostic Interview Schedule for *DSM-IV*) are available for
making diagnostic determinations (see review by
Maisto, McKay, & Tiffany, in press).

Biological Indicators

Screening for alcohol and other substance use
disorders can also be conducted with biological
assessments. These biomarkers have received particular attention in screening for alcohol consumption (e.g., Allen, Sillanaukee, Strid, & Litten, in press). Blood tests, as an example, provide
useful information on recent (past few weeks)
and longer term (years) heavy alcohol use. Typically, this involves examination of elevations in
certain liver enzymes. Most frequently studied
are aspartate aminotransferase (AST), alanine
aminotransferase (ALT), and gamma-glutamyl-
transferase (GGT) (e.g., Allen et al., in press).
Mean cell volume (MCV), a test for alteration in
blood cells, also can be used to test for recent
heavy drinking. Although past heavy drinking can
significantly elevate readings on each of these
tests, GGT is the most sensitive to changes.

Biological screening for drug problems is primarily accomplished with urinalysis. Urinalysis
provides an index of use over the past 2 to 3 days
for most drugs of abuse and over a week or longer
in the case of heavy marijuana or phencyclidine
use (Schwartz, 1988). Primary care physicians
and mental health professionals are in an excellent position to collaborate on the interpretation
of such test results, alone and in concert with
other screening and assessment findings, and in
presenting the findings to the patient.

Table 16.3 The Alcohol Use Disorders Identification Test (AUDIT)

1. How often do you have a drink containing alcohol?

   | Never | Monthly or less | Two or four times a month | Two to three times a week | Four or more times a week |

2. How many drinks containing alcohol do you have on a typical day when you are drinking?

   | 1 or 2 | 3 or 4 | 5 or 6 | 7 or 9 | 10 or more |

3. How often do you have six or more drinks on one occasion?

   | Never | Less than monthly | Monthly | Weekly | Daily or almost daily |

4. How often during the last year have you found that you were not able to stop drinking once you had started?

   | Never | Less than monthly | Monthly | Weekly | Daily or almost daily |

5. How often during the last year have you failed to do what was normally expected from you because of drinking?

   | Never | Less than monthly | Monthly | Weekly | Daily or almost daily |

6. How often during the last year have you needed a first drink in the morning to get yourself going after a heavy drinking session?

   | Never | Less than monthly | Monthly | Weekly | Daily or almost daily |

7. How often during the last year have you had a feeling of guilt or remorse after drinking?

   | Never | Less than monthly | Monthly | Weekly | Daily or almost daily |

8. How often during the last year have you been unable to remember what happened the night before because you had been drinking?

   | Never | Less than monthly | Monthly | Weekly | Daily or almost daily |

9. Have you or someone else been injured as a result of your drinking?

   | No | Yes, but not in the last year | Yes, during the last year |

10. Has a relative or friend or a doctor or other health worker been concerned about your drinking or suggested you cut down?

   | No | Yes, but not in the last year | Yes, during the last year |

Note: Questions 1–8 are scored 0, 1, 2, 3, or 4 (with higher scores accorded to responses reflecting greater drinking or more frequent consequences). Questions 9 and 10 are scored 0, 2, or 4 only. The minimum score is 0 (for nondrinkers) and the maximum possible score is 40. A score of 8 or more indicates a strong likelihood of hazardous or harmful alcohol consumption. From Saunders et al. (1993).

TREATMENT ISSUES

Symptoms of drug abuse often lead to detection of substance abuse by physicians. However, therapists are often the first to diagnose and treat these disorders. In this sensitive situation, the autonomy of the patient must be recognized; nonetheless, the therapist should candidly discuss his or her concerns with the patient and obtain the patient's consent to share these with the primary care physician. Although the therapist may deliver the major share of treatment for a substance use disorder, collaborative care is optimal. Physician interest in the patient's progress can facilitate treatment, medical complications of drug use may be detected early, and routine preventive care (often underutilized by those with substance use disorders) may be provided. If the physician is comfortable with pharmacotherapy for substance abuse, this may also be incorporated into a comprehensive treatment plan.

Barriers to Acceptance of Diagnosis or Treatment

A variety of impediments to the acceptance of a diagnosis or a recommendation for treatment can emerge in any given case (Donovan & Rosengren, 1999). Some of these barriers reflect logistical impediments, such as treatment costs, availability or

Table 16.4 Recent Brief Screening Approaches

Cyr and Wartman (1988):
  Have you ever had a drinking problem?
  When was your last drink?

Williams and Vinson (2001):
  When was the last time you had more than x
  drinks in 1 day? (where $x = 4$ for women and 5
  for men)

Brown et al. (2001):
  In the past year, have you ever drunk or used
  drugs more than you meant to?
  Have you felt you wanted or needed to cut down
  on your drinking or drug use in the last year?

Note: For the Cyr and Wartman items, a positive response to the first item or a response of within the past 24 hours to the second would be considered a positive indication. For the Williams and Vinson item, a response of within the last 3 months would be considered positive. For the Brown et al. items, a positive response to either would be considered positive.

cost of transportation, lost time from work, and child care or family responsibilities. The extent to which these impediments will play a role in the case of a given patient can vary considerably (Cunningham, Sobell, Sobell, & Gaskin, 1994). Typically, however, the patient does not accept the suggestion or judgment that a problem exists. Often, this lack of acceptance has been referred to as denial or resistance, although such concepts have not been found particularly useful in the treatment of alcohol and other substance use disorders (e.g., Miller, 1985). Instead, it may be more useful to focus on motivation, which can be viewed as the "flip side" of denial and resistance. Such a focus allows the clinician to focus on increasing the patient's motivational readiness to change. Motivational interventions aim to "increase the probability of entering, continuing, and complying with an active change strategy" (Miller, 1985, p. 88). Representative clinician actions, according to Miller and Rollnick (2002), include providing nonjudgmental feedback, giving advice regarding making change, decreasing the desirability of the substance being misused, expressing empathy, working to remove barriers to change, and providing choices. Hartnoll (1992) notes that the decision to seek help

is mediated by perceptions and interpretations on the part of the drug user and important others regarding the significance of a person's drug use and its consequences, regarding the nature and availability of different options for the future, and regarding the perceived need for, and value (and costs) of seeking help. (p. 431)

Treatment Settings

Clinical services for alcohol and other substance use disorders are available in a range of settings. The most common groupings are residential programs, partial hospitalization/intensive outpatient programs, and outpatient programs. Decisions on which setting might best meet the needs of a given patient are typically made on the basis of severity of dependence, previous treatment history (if any), cognitive and physical functioning (including potential for withdrawal), family and social supports, and the variety of logistical variables described in the context of potential barriers to treatment.

Treatment intensity or "level-of-care" issues have been receiving considerable attention (Gastfriend, 1999). Best known of the efforts to operationalize level-of-care decisions is the American Society of Addiction Medicine (ASAM, 1996) *Patient Placement Criteria for the Treatment of Substance-Related Disorders*. The ASAM materials identify a range of levels of care, including early intervention, detoxification, outpatient, intensive outpatient, medically monitored intensive inpatient, and medically managed intensive inpatient.

Effective Treatments

Psychological Interventions

Summaries of treatment outcome research for alcohol and other substance abusers have indicated that it is effective (e.g., Carroll, 1998b; Institute of Medicine, 1990). However, there is no single treatment intervention that works for all persons with alcohol and other substance use disorders. Accordingly, it is important that health care professionals as well as addictions specialists be diligent in determining the unique needs of the patients they assess and the settings and interventions best suited to address those needs.

Comprehensive reviews of specialty treatments for persons with alcohol and other substance use disorders are available elsewhere (e.g., Carroll, 1998b; McLellan et al., 1996; Miller, Andrews, Wilbourne, & Bennett, 1998). Although many specialty alcohol and substance abuse treatment approaches may be generalizable to the primary care setting, we highlight in this chapter two approaches that may be particularly feasible in primary care settings: motivational enhancement and cognitive–behavioral interventions.

Motivational enhancement approaches have been found to be an effective means of promoting positive changes in health behavior (Burke, Arkowitz, & Dunn, 2002). The approach is both patient centered and directive, with the patient enlisted as an active participant in decision making. The variation of this approach most often used in working with alcohol and other substance abusers is motivational interviewing (Miller & Rollnick, 2002). The key objectives for the clinician are to help the patient become aware of the need to change, increase the patient's motivation to make change, and discuss plans for change. Addressing patient ambivalence about change is very important, as is establishing rapport with the patient, working with the patient to set an agenda for interactions, assessing the patient's initial views on the importance of making change (and associated readiness to change), and developing a change plan. More detailed descriptions of these clinical strategies can be found in the work of Miller and Rollnick (2002) and Rollnick, Mason, and Butler (1999).

Cognitive–behavioral interventions include a wide range of clinical procedures based on principles of learning and behavior change. For many patients, a particular focus is placed on the assessment and training of interpersonal and self-management skills. With alcoholic patients and other substance abusers, the primary goal typically is the development of skills to achieve and maintain abstinence. A thorough functional analysis of the patient's drinking or drug behavior, with particular attention to the antecedents of such behavior, helps identify specific skills the patient needs to develop.

Comprehensive manuals describing cognitive–behavioral interventions are available (e.g., Carroll, 1998a; Kadden et al., 1992). Among the modules most often applied are those addressing problem solving, assertiveness, drink refusal, stress management, coping with craving, interpersonal skills, managing negative moods and depression, and coping with any relapses that might occur. Research on the use of such interventions has supported their effectiveness in reducing and eliminating alcohol and other substance use (Carroll, 1998b; Miller et al., 1998).

As interventions are implemented, it is crucial to perform ongoing assessments of response to treatment. These ongoing assessments would focus on reductions in alcohol and other substance use and misuse, reductions in consequences, increases in abstinent days, and improved life functioning more generally (e.g., improvements in family, vocational, and health functioning). If use is not moderated or eliminated or if adverse consequences of use persist, the primary care psychologist should consider referral to a specialty program.

Pharmacotherapy for Alcohol Abuse

The two main goals in the pharmacotherapy of drug addictions are detoxification and maintenance of remission. Alcohol withdrawal is often mild and does not require treatment. More severe withdrawal is manifested by vital sign instability (tachycardia, hypertension, fever), anxiety, and occasionally delirium. The mainstays of pharmacotherapy for withdrawal, when required, are benzodiazepines (Mayo-Smith, 1997). For milder symptoms, these may be administered as needed, but a regular dosing schedule is necessary for more advanced withdrawal.

Primary care physicians may perform alcohol detoxification on an outpatient basis for patients who are not experiencing active withdrawal symptoms or have milder symptoms and wish to stop drinking. Algorithms are available to guide such therapy, including appropriate patient selection and dosing guidelines (Prater, Miller, & Zylstra, 1999). More severe withdrawal often requires hospital admission. Other drugs have been studied in the treatment of alcohol withdrawal, including clonidine, beta-blockers, and anticonvulsants, but their efficacy has not been well established. For patients who are intolerant of benzodiazepines, barbiturates are an acceptable alternative in inpatient settings. Detoxification and maintenance therapy for narcotic addiction overlap, with opioid agonists used for both treatment goals.

For maintenance therapy, several drugs have been used for treating alcohol dependence, including disulfiram (Antabuse), naltrexone (ReVia), acamprosate (Campral), and ondansetron (Zofran) (Anton, 2001). Disulfiram is an inhibitor of aldehyde dehydrogenase, which catalyzes the breakdown of acetaldehyde to carbon dioxide and water. Acetaldehyde is the major product of the oxidation of ethanol and is toxic if not rapidly metabolized. Accumulation of acetaldehyde results in the disulfiram-alcohol reaction (uncomfortable flushing, dyspnea, nausea, and vomiting). Avoidance of these unpleasant symptoms is the basis for the efficacy of this agent. On rare occasions, a severe disulfiram-alcohol reaction may lead to hypotension and shock, chest pain, or heart attack. Therefore, patients with a history of heart disease should not receive disulfiram. Patients should be advised to avoid any alcohol (including alcohol in over-the-counter medications), and the antibiotic metronidazole should not be prescribed concurrently. Both lack of compliance and the potential for severe reactions have limited the usefulness of this agent.

Naltrexone is an opioid receptor antagonist, and was approved by the Food and Drug Administration for the treatment of alcohol dependence in 1994. This agent acts by decreasing craving for alcohol. Controlled clinical trials have shown mixed results. The drug appears to have efficacy in maintaining abstinence and perhaps in decreasing the amount of alcohol consumed per drinking day among compliant patients. There may be an interaction of naltrexone treatment with counseling; some evidence suggests that the drug is effective only as an adjunct to cognitive–behavioral therapy. Additional trials are ongoing. The drug is usually well tolerated, although mild nausea is common. Patients using narcotic medications or illicitly using narcotics and patients with liver disease should not receive naltrexone.

Acamprosate has been used extensively in Europe and is currently undergoing clinical trials in the United States, both alone and with concurrent naltrexone. The drug is a synthetic amino acid derivative and is well tolerated. Several clinical trials have shown a decrease in the quantity and frequency of alcohol use and an increase in abstinence among patients who remain compliant with this drug. Similar to naltrexone, however, results in clinical settings have been mixed.

Ondansetron is an antagonist of a subset of serotonin receptors. Clinical trials have suggested that, in concert with cognitive–behavioral therapy, this drug has some efficacy in the treatment of early-onset alcoholism, decreasing the amount of alcohol consumed, and perhaps increasing the percentage of days abstinent. No conclusive evidence exists on the efficacy of other serotonergic agents, such as the selective serotonin reuptake inhibitors, but these drugs continue to be studied and may prove useful in a subset of patients with alcohol dependence.

None of these drugs is curative, and their use should be accompanied by appropriate counseling and social support. For this reason, primary care clinicians rarely prescribe these agents, and most patients receiving them will be receiving treatment for their alcohol dependence in specialty settings. Noncompliance is an important reason for treatment failure regardless of which agent is prescribed.

Pharmacotherapy for Drug Abuse

Methadone (Dolophine, Methadose), a long-acting opioid, is the main drug used in the treatment of narcotic addiction. Controlled use and weaning of this drug are intended to minimize the adverse consequences of drug-seeking behavior while limiting withdrawal symptoms. The drug is generally prescribed and administered daily in federally licensed specialty clinics. Levomethadyl (ORLAAM) is available as a second-line agent, but is not commonly used because an association has been found with potentially fatal cardiac arrythmia. Buprenorphine (Buprenex, Subutex), a partial opioid agonist, may be safer than methadone because of a lower risk for overdose and withdrawal symptoms. This drug may also be administered three times weekly as opposed to daily. Buprenorphine and the combination of buprenorphine with naloxone have recently received Food and Drug Administration approval for the treatment of narcotic addiction. Because buprenorphine has less abuse potential than methadone, federal restrictions on its use are reduced. Providers must have prior training and certification in the use of buprenorphine for narcotic abuse, as well as an additional Drug Enforcement Agency (DEA) registration number. Some primary care clinicians will obtain credentials to prescribe this drug if they have a special interest in substance use disorders. Naltrexone has met with limited success for narcotic addiction because of very poor compliance, although when closely monitored (such as in treating impaired physicians), this agent can be effective. There are no proven pharmacotherapeutic options for the treatment of dependence on other commonly abused drugs.

Family Involvement

The family, and other persons with significant ties to the patient, can play a pivotal role in the treatment of alcohol and other drug use (McCrady & Epstein, 1996; O'Farrell & Fals-Stewart, 1999). Involving the patient's spouse/partner or other family members allows for assessment of and intervention on reciprocal relationships within the family that may be contributing to the alcohol or substance use problem. Family sessions typically address such matters as identification of interpersonal dysfunction, improving communication of thoughts and feelings, and addressing "enabling" (McKay, 1996). More detailed descriptions of family interventions are available (e.g., Connors, Donovan, & DiClemente, 2001; O'Farrell, 1993).

Self-Help Groups

Alcoholics Anonymous (AA) is the prototype mutual-help organization and a commonly sought source of help for alcohol and other substance-related problems. Examples of other such groups include Rational Recovery, Secular Organizations for Sobriety, Women for Sobriety, and Self-Management and Recovery Training (SMART) for alcohol-related problems and Narcotics Anonymous and Cocaine Anonymous for other drug problems (although many drug abusers predominantly attend AA meetings). AA is the largest of these organizations, with an estimated 1 in 10 Americans attending an AA meeting in their lifetime (McCrady & Miller, 1993).

Such programs have been beneficial to many individuals in the contexts of initiating abstinence and especially maintaining abstinence, and some

empirical support for this estimation is available (e.g., Emrick, Tonigan, Montgomery, & Little, 1993). Although many have benefited from their involvement in mutual-help groups, not all affiliate with them. One clinical approach to use with patients is to recommend attending some initial minimum number of meetings and then assessing the "fit" between the patient and the mutual-help group.

The Problem of Relapse

Relapse is common. Litman (1980) has characterized alcoholism as a "relapsing condition." Fortunately, considerable attention has been devoted to the issue over the past two decades (see Marlatt & Gordon, 1985). This has resulted in the identification of the types of situations associated with the return of alcohol and substance use. In this regard, Marlatt and Gordon (1985) have found that most patients attribute their relapses to intrapersonal determinants, particularly in situations that involve negative emotional states. This has resulted in clinical efforts to help patients identify situations that are "high risk" for triggering renewed alcohol or other drug use, along with the development of coping skills to help the patient address such situations without using substances.

Innovative Collaborative Care Arrangements

Health care in the United States is generally characterized by separate systems providing medical care and addiction treatment. However, several small studies have evaluated collaborative arrangements, generally providing medical care and treatment for substance abuse in the same facility (Chick, Lloyd, & Crombie, 1985; O'Toole, Strain, Wand, McCaul, & Barnhart, 2002; Umbrict-Schneiter, Ginn, Pabst, & Bigelow, 1994) or encouraging specialty addiction treatment among medical or surgical inpatients (Dunn & Ries, 1997). Such programs provide specific links between medical and substance abuse care and have shown some benefit in terms of increasing utilization of both addiction treatment and general medical care. As a whole, the literature suggests that establishment of collaborative referral patterns between primary care practices and substance abuse treatment will benefit patients referred from general medical to specialty settings and vice versa.

SECONDARY PREVENTION OF ALCOHOL PROBLEMS

Recent years have witnessed a greater appreciation of the heterogeneity of alcohol-related problems. The influential Institute of Medicine report *Broadening the Base of Treatment for Alcohol Problems* (1990) argued that alcohol consumption and drinking problems are best viewed as falling on a continuum ranging from low/few to heavy/severe. Such a conceptualization acknowledges that cases other than severe cases (i.e., alcoholism, severe dependence) can and do exist, and that other types of interventions and treatment goals can be pursued to address them. Secondary prevention interventions are an effective response to alcohol-related dysfunction among lower severity problem drinkers (Connors, 1993; Rosenberg, 1993).

These interventions typically entail use of packages of cognitive–behavioral strategies designed to reduce drinking and minimize risks associated with any drinking that does occur. As such, the treatment goal is moderated drinking as opposed to abstinence. Treatment components typically include self-monitoring, functional analysis of drinking, goal setting, and drinking moderation strategies. Self-help manuals focused on reducing alcohol consumption are available for use (e.g., Miller & Munoz, 1982; Robertson & Heather, 1985; Sanchez-Craig, 1984; Vogler & Bartz, 1982).

Primary care–based screening and brief intervention have been extensively studied for heavy drinkers meeting *ICD-10* criteria for hazardous or harmful consumption. Such an approach may decrease progression to abuse or dependence and has been shown to reduce the quantity as well as frequency of alcohol consumption and to reduce some adverse consequences of heavy consumption (Fleming et al., 2002; Wilk, Jensen, & Havighurst, 1997). The screening component generally utilizes a validated instrument such as the CAGE or AUDIT. This is followed by a brief motivational counseling intervention. Counseling includes feedback about current drinking habits, an emphasis on the patient's responsibility to change, specific advice on moderating alcohol consumption, an empathic clinician approach, and efforts to enhance the patient's self-efficacy (National Institute on Alcohol Abuse and Alcoholism, 1995b).

SUMMARY

Given their widespread prevalence in primary care settings, it is critical that alcohol and other substance use and abuse be identified and addressed. The primary care psychologist can provide flexible, tailored, accessible treatment that may be more acceptable to the less severely impaired primary care patient.

A number of brief, reliable, and valid measures are available for alcohol and other substance use problems. Biological assessments, such as blood and urine tests, also can be used for purposes of screening in high-risk settings. Motivational interventions are often useful to increase the likelihood that patients will commit to making changes in their alcohol and substance misuse. A variety of treatment settings are available for the provision of addiction-specific services. These include residential programs, intensive outpatient programs, and outpatient programs.

Effective treatments are available for persons with alcohol and other substance use problems. These include psychological treatments, such as cognitive–behavioral interventions, and pharmacological agents. Mutual-help organizations, such as AA, have been beneficial for many individuals seeking to initiate and maintain abstinence. The establishment of referral arrangements between primary care practitioners and addiction-specific treatment programs holds considerable potential benefit for patients with alcohol and other substance use problems. Secondary prevention interventions that focus on drinking moderation have been useful in working with patients without histories of severe dependence on alcohol.

ADDITIONAL RESOURCES

Suggestions for further reading and professional development resources are available at this book's companion Web site: www.primarycarepsych.com.

References

Allen, J. P., Sillanaukee, P., Strid, N., & Litten, R. Z. (in press). Biomarkers of heavy drinking. In J. P. Allen & V. Wilson (Eds.), *Assessing alcohol problems: A guide for clinicians and researchers* (rev. ed.). Bethesda, MD: National Institute on Alcohol Abuse and Alcoholism.

American Psychiatric Association. (1994). *Diagnostic and statistical manual of mental disorders* (4th ed.). Washington, DC: Author.

American Society of Addiction Medicine. (1996). *Patient placement criteria for the treatment of substance-related disorders.* Chevy Chase, MD: Author.

Anton, R. F. (2001). Pharmacologic approaches to the management of alcoholism. *Journal of Clinical Psychiatry, 62*(Suppl. 20), 11–17.

Brown, R. L., Leonard, T., Saunders, L. A., & Papasouliotis, O. (2001). A two-item conjoint screen for alcohol and other drug problems. *Journal of the American Board of Family Practice, 14,* 95–106.

Burke, B. L., Arkowitz, H., & Dunn, C. (2002). The efficacy of motivational interviewing and its adaptations: What we know so far. In W. R. Miller & S. Rollnick (Eds.), *Motivational interviewing: Preparing people for change* (pp. 217–250). New York: Guilford Press.

Carroll, K. M. (Ed.). (1998a). *Therapy manuals for drug addiction: Manual 1, A cognitive-behavioral approach: Treating cocaine addiction.* Bethesda, MD: National Institute on Drug Abuse.

Carroll, K. M. (1998b). Treating drug dependence: Recent advances and old truths. In W. R. Miller & N. Heather (Eds.), *Treating addictive behaviors* (2nd ed., pp. 217–229). New York: Plenum Press.

Cherubin, C. E., & Sapira, J. D. (1993). The medical complications of drug addiction and the medical assessment of the intravenous drug user: 25 years later. *Annals of Internal Medicine, 119,* 1017–1028.

Chick, J., Lloyd, G., & Crombie, E. (1985). Counseling problem drinkers in medical wards: A controlled study. *British Medical Journal, 290,* 965–967.

Connors, G. J. (1993). Drinking moderation training as a contemporary therapeutic approach. *Drugs and Society, 8,* 117–134.

Connors, G. J., Donovan, D. M., & DiClemente, C. C. (2001). *Substance abuse treatment and the stages of change: Selecting and planning interventions.* New York: Guilford Press.

Connors, G. J., & Volk, R. J. (in press). Screening for alcohol problems among adults. In J. A. Allen (Ed.), *Assessing alcohol problems: A guide for clinicians and researchers* (2nd ed.). Bethesda, MD: National Institute on Alcohol Abuse and Alcoholism.

Cunningham, J. A., Sobell, L. C., Sobell, M. B., & Gaskin, J. (1994). Alcohol and drug abusers' reasons for seeking treatment. *Addictive Behaviors, 19,* 691–696.

Cyr, M., & Wartman, S. (1988). The effectiveness of routine screening questions in the detection of alcoholism. *Journal of the American Medical Association, 259,* 51–54.

Donovan, D. M., & Rosengren, D. B. (1999). Motivation for behavior change and treatment among substance abusers. In J. A. Tucker, D. M. Donovan, & G. A. Marlatt (Eds.), *Changing addictive behavior* (pp. 127–159). New York: Guilford Press.

Dunn, C. W., & Ries, R. (1997). Linking substance abuse service with general medical care: Integrated, brief interventions with hospitalized patients. *American Journal of Drug and Alcohol Abuse, 23,* 1–13.

Emrick, C. D., Tonigan, J. S., Montgomery, H., & Little, L. (1993). Alcoholics Anonymous. What is currently known? In B. S. McCrady & W. R. Miller (Eds.), *Research on Alcoholics Anonymous: Opportunities and alternatives* (pp. 41–76). New Brunswick, NJ: Rutgers Center of Alcohol Studies.

Ewing, J. A. (1984). Detecting alcoholism. The CAGE questionnaire. *Journal of the American Medical Association, 252,* 1905–1907.

Fleming, M., & Manwell, L. B. (2000). Epidemiology. In G. Zernig, A. Saria, M. Kurz, & S. S. O'Malley (Eds.), *Handbook of alcoholism* (pp. 271–286). Boca Raton, FL: CRC Press.

Fleming, M. F., Mundt, M. P., French, M. T., Manwell, L. B., Stauffacher, E. A., & Barry, K. L. (2002). Brief physician advice for problem drinkers: Long-term efficacy and benefit-cost analysis. *Alcoholism: Clinical and Experimental Research, 26,* 36–43.

Gastfriend, D. R. (1999). Patient placement criteria. In M. Galanter & H. D. Kleber (Eds.), *Textbook of substance abuse treatment* (2nd ed., pp. 121–127). Washington, DC: American Psychiatric Press.

Grant, B. F. (1997). Prevalence and correlates of alcohol use and *DSM-IV* alcohol dependence in the United States: Results of the National

Longitudinal Alcohol Epidemiologic Survey. *Journal of Studies on Alcohol, 58,* 464–473.

Hartnoll, R. (1992). Research and the help-seeking process. *British Journal of Addiction, 87,* 429–437.

Hser, Y., Anglin, M. D., & Powers, K. (1993). A 24-year follow-up of California narcotics addicts. *Archives of General Psychiatry, 50,* 577–584.

Institute of Medicine. (1990). *Broadening the base of treatment for alcohol problems.* Washington, DC: National Academy Press.

Jacobson, G. R. (1989). A comprehensive approach to pretreatment evaluation: I. Detection, assessment, and diagnosis of alcoholism. In R. K. Hester & W. R. Miller (Eds.), *Handbook of alcoholism treatment approaches: Effective alternatives* (pp. 17–53). New York: Pergamon Press.

Kadden, R., Carroll, K., Donovan, D., Cooney, N., Monti, P., Abrams, D., Litt, M., & Hester, R. (Eds.). (1992). *Cognitive-behavioral coping skills therapy manual: A clinical research guide for therapists treating individuals with alcohol abuse and dependence.* Bethesda, MD: National Institute on Alcohol Abuse and Alcoholism.

Litman, G. K. (1980). Relapse in alcoholism: Traditional and current approaches. In G. Edwards & M. Grant (Eds.), *Alcoholism treatment in transition.* Baltimore, MD: University Park Press.

Maisto, S. A., McKay, J. R., & Tiffany, S. T. (in press). Diagnosis. In J. Allen (Ed.), *Assessing alcohol problems: A guide for clinicians and researchers* (rev. ed.). Bethesda, MD: National Institute on Alcohol Abuse and Alcoholism.

Marlatt, G. A., & Gordon, J. R. (1985). *Relapse prevention.* New York: Guilford Press.

Mayfield, D., McLeod, G., & Hall, P. (1974). The CAGE questionnaire: Validation of a new alcoholism screening instrument. *American Journal of Psychiatry, 131,* 1121–1123.

Mayo-Smith, M. F. (1997). Pharmacological management of alcohol withdrawal. A meta-analysis and evidence-based practice guidelines. *Journal of the American Medical Association, 278,* 144–151.

McCrady, B. S., & Epstein, E. E. (1996). Theoretical bases of family approaches to substance abuse treatment. In F. Rotgers, D. Keller, & J. Morgenstern (Eds.), *Treating substance abuse: Theory and technique* (pp. 117–142). New York: Guilford Press.

McCrady, B. S., & Miller, W. R. (1993). The importance of research on Alcoholics Anonymous. In B. S. McCrady & W. R. Miller (Eds.), *Research on Alcoholics Anonymous: Opportunities and alternatives* (pp. 3–12). New Brunswick, NJ: Rutgers Center of Alcohol Studies.

McKay, J. R. (1996). Family therapy techniques. In F. Rotgers, D. Keller, & J. Morgenstern (Eds.), *Treating substance abuse: Theory and technique* (pp. 143–173). New York: Guilford Press.

McLellan, A. T., Kushner, H., Metzger, D., Peters, R., Smith, I., Grissom, G., Pettinati, H., & Argeriou, M. (1992). The fifth edition of the Addiction Severity Index. *Journal of Substance Abuse Treatment, 9,* 199–213.

McLellan, A. T., Woody, G. E., Metzger, D., McKay, J., Durrell, J., Alterman, A. I., & O'Brien, C. P. (1996). Evaluating the effectiveness of addiction treatments: Reasonable expectations, appropriate comparisons. *Milbank Quarterly, 74,* 51–85.

Miller, W. R. (1985). Motivation for treatment: A review with special emphasis on alcoholism. *Psychological Bulletin, 98,* 84–107.

Miller, W. R., Andrews, N. R., Wilbourne, P., & Bennett, M. E. (1998). A wealth of alternatives: Effective treatments for alcohol problems. In W. R. Miller & N. Heather (Eds.), *Treating addictive behaviors* (2nd ed., pp. 203–216). New York: Plenum Press.

Miller, W. R., & Brown, S. A. (1997). Why psychologists should treat alcohol and drug problems. *American Psychologist, 52,* 1267–1279.

Miller, W. R., & Munoz, R. F. (1982). *How to control your drinking* (2nd ed.). Albuquerque: University of New Mexico Press.

Miller, W. R., & Rollnick, S. (2002). *Motivational interviewing: Preparing people to change addictive behavior* (2nd ed.). New York: Guilford Press.

National Institute on Alcohol Abuse and Alcoholism. (1995a). *Alcohol alert* (No. 30, PH 359). Rockville, MD: Author, Scientific Communications Branch, Office of Scientific Affairs.

National Institute on Alcohol Abuse and Alcoholism. (1995b). *Physicians guide to helping patients with alcohol problems.* Bethesda, MD: Author.

O'Farrell, T. J. (Ed.). (1993). *Treating alcohol problems: Marital and family interventions.* New York: Guilford Press.

O'Farrell, T. J., & Fals-Stewart, W. (1999). Treatment models and methods: Family models. In B. S. McCrady & E. E. Epstein (Eds.), *Addictions: A comprehensive guidebook.* (pp. 287–305). New York: Oxford University Press.

O'Toole, T. P., Strain, E. C., Wand, G., McCaul, M. E., & Barnhart, M. (2002). Outpatient treatment entry and health care utilization after a combined medical/substance abuse intervention for hospitalized medical patients. *Journal of General Internal Medicine, 17,* 334–340.

Prater, C. D., Miller, K. E., & Zylstra, R. G. (1999). Outpatient detoxification of the addicted or alcoholic patient. *American Family Physician, 60,* 1175–1183.

Robertson, I., & Heather, N. (1985). *So you want to cut down your drinking? A self-help manual for controlled drinking.* Edinburgh: Scottish Health Education Group.

Rollnick, S., Mason, P., & Butler, C. (1999). *Health behavior change: A guide for practitioners.* London: Harcourt Brace.

Rosenberg, H. (1993). Prediction of controlled drinking by alcoholics and problem drinkers. *Psychological Bulletin, 113,* 129–139.

Sanchez-Craig, M. (1984). *A therapist's manual for secondary prevention of alcohol problems: Procedures for teaching moderate drinking and abstinence.* Toronto: Addiction Research Foundation.

Saunders, J. B., Aasland, O. G., Babor, T. F., DeLaFuente, J. R., & Grant, M. (1993). Development of the Alcohol Use Disorders Identification Test (AUDIT): WHO collaborative project on early detection of persons with harmful alcohol consumption. *Addiction, 88,* 791–804.

Schuckit, M. A., Smith, T. L., Danko, G. P., Bucholz, K. K., Reich, T., & Bierut, L. (2001). Five-year clinical course associated with *DSM-IV* alcohol abuse or dependence in a large group of men and women. *American Journal of Psychiatry, 158,* 1084–1090.

Schwartz, R. H. (1988). Screening for drug use in adolescents: The other side of the coin. *Journal of Pediatrics, 112,* 328.

Skinner, H. A. (1982). The drug abuse screening test. *Addictive Behaviors, 7,* 363–371.

Stein, M. D. (1999). Medical consequences of substance abuse. *Psychiatric Clinics of North America, 22,* 351–370.

Substance Abuse and Mental Health Services Administration. (2001). *Results from the 2001 National Survey on Drug Abuse.* Rockville, MD: Author.

Umbrict-Schneiter, A., Ginn, D. H., Pabst, K. M., & Bigelow, G. E. (1994). Providing medical care in methadone clinic patients: Referral vs. on-site care. *American Journal of Public Health, 84,* 207–210.

Vogler, R. E., & Bartz, W. R. (1982). *The better way to drink.* New York: Simon and Schuster.

Washburn, A. (2003). *Why psychologists should know how to treat substance use disorders.* Psychnet. Retrieved June 15, 2003, from www.apa.org

Wilk, A. I., Jensen, N. M., & Havighurst, T. C. (1997). Meta-analysis of randomized controlled trials addressing brief interventions in heavy alcohol drinkers. *Journal of General Internal Medicine, 12,* 274–283.

Williams, R., & Vinson, D. C. (2001). Validation of a single screening question for problem drinking. *Journal of Family Practice, 50,* 307–312.

World Health Organization. (1992). *International classification of diseases and related health problems* (10th revision). Geneva: Author.

World Health Organization ASSIST Working Group (2002). The Alcohol, Smoking and Substance Involvement Screening Test (ASSIST): Development, reliability and feasibility. *Addiction, 97,* 1183–1194.

17

Anxiety Disorders

Jeanne L. Esler
Risa B. Weisberg
Christopher N. Sciamanna
Beth C. Bock

The majority of patients suffering from anxiety and other psychological disorders in primary care settings are not recognized, and even fewer are treated effectively. There are significant numbers of such patients, and their anxiety disorders often have a chronic and persistent course, especially panic disorder with agoraphobia, posttraumatic stress disorder (PTSD), and social anxiety disorder (Weisberg, Culpepper, & Keller, 2002). Because anxiety disorders are chronic in nature, typically displaying patterns of exacerbation and remission often associated with life stress, these patients form a substantial core of the practices of primary care physicians (PCPs) (Barlow, 2001; Brown & Barlow, 1995).

When primary care psychologists are able to identify and treat anxiety disorders adequately, this will likely reduce unnecessary and often ineffective medical utilization by these patients. The psychologist has a crucial role to play in the improved identification and treatment of anxiety disorders in primary care settings. Primary care psychologists can help PCPs detect and refer patients with anxiety; ideally, they can also provide treatment in the familiar and accessible primary

care setting. Not only is this more convenient for the patient, but also it may decrease the stigma associated with seeking psychological services.

In this chapter, we review the prevalence of anxiety disorders in primary care, the role of the primary care psychologist, nonpsychological causes of anxiety, conditions that often occur concurrently with anxiety, the presentation of anxious patients in primary care settings (including case examples of the five most common anxiety disorders), and "subthreshold" presentations and their treatment. We also include recommendations for prevention, assessment, and treatment of anxiety disorders in primary care settings, as well as suggestions for successful collaboration between PCPs and psychologists.

PREVALENCE OF ANXIETY DISORDERS

Community surveys have indicated that anxiety disorders are the single most prevalent class of mental disorders in the population at large, with 1-year estimates ranging from 13% to 17% (Kessler et al., 1994; Regier et al., 1984). Thus, the prevalence of anxiety disorders is greater than any other major class of disorder, including mood and addictive disorders. Anxiety disorders are among the most common mental health problems seen in the primary care setting (e.g., Nisenson, Pepper, Schwenk, & Coyne, 1998; Ormel et al., 1994; Weiller, Bisserbe, Maier, & Lecrubier, 1998). This is significant given that more than half of patients with an anxiety disorder receive their treatment from a primary care provider without consultation from a mental health specialist (Harman, Rollman, Hanusa, Lenze, & Shear, 2002; Price, Beck, Nimmer, & Bensen, 2000; Shear & Shulberg, 1995). Because the majority of patients with psychiatric disorders initially present to PCPs, physicians working in primary care and family medicine represent the front line of care and frequently act as gatekeepers to mental health specialty services through referral (Beardsley, Gardocki, Larson, & Hidalgo, 1988; Weiller et al., 1998).

ROLE OF THE PRIMARY CARE PSYCHOLOGIST

Although only one third of patients with anxiety disorders seek psychological treatment (Fifer et al., 1994; Ohayon, Shapiro, & Kennedy, 2000; Regier et al., 1993), the number of individuals this represents is staggering. In the United States, the number of physician office visits in which a diagnosis of anxiety was recorded increased from 9.5 million per year in 1985 (1.9% of all office visits) to 11.2 million per year in 1993–1994 (1.6%) and to 12.3 million per year in 1997–1998 (1.5%; Harman et al., 2002). This presents a tremendous opportunity for the primary care psychologist who works closely with a PCP. Not only are PCPs the first health care professionals many patients with anxiety disorders see, PCPs are often the only providers from which patients with anxiety disorders seek and receive treatment.

Because at least 50% of patients with psychological disorders receive all or part of their care from PCPs, underdiagnosis and inadequate treatment are major concerns (Ford, 1994). It is imperative that primary care psychologists assist PCPs in identifying patients with anxiety disorders. Failure of physicians to diagnose the presence of anxiety disorders may be attributed to a variety of causes.

First, physicians may not make referrals to mental health specialists because they do not identify the need for mental health referrals, especially when anxious patients focus on the physical symptoms of anxiety and not the cognitive symptoms of distress. Next, if the anxiety disorder is identified, PCPs may prefer to initiate treatment themselves, most typically with a selective serotonergic reuptake inhibitor (SSRI). This may be done more frequently in settings without a primary care psychologist because making a referral to a mental health specialist is inconvenient or time consuming for the physician or the patient. Next, patients may also diagnose themselves as having an anxiety disorder and request medication from their PCPs instead of initiating treatment with an unknown mental health clinician. This has become increasingly common with the recent increase in direct-to-consumer advertising by pharmaceutical companies, especially for SSRIs. Finally, patients may not follow through with mental health referrals made by PCPs because of stigma, the time commitment required for psychotherapy, apprehension about seeking treatment in a new setting, or cost or lack of insurance coverage for this specialized service. These reasons convincingly demonstrate the need for primary care psychologists.

PREVENTION

If psychologists treat only those patients referred to them by PCPs, they will miss many who could benefit from their help. The psychologist working in primary care should assume that referred cases are just the tip of the iceberg so to speak. Psychologists may wish to publicize their services within the primary care settings, letting both PCPs and patients know that they are available. PCPs may need help in identifying patients; patients may benefit from direct-to-consumer education about the benefit of seeking psychological services. Early intervention with basic stress management techniques, including cognitive techniques and relaxation exercises, may be beneficial. This could be conducted in a patient-initiated group format. In addition, self-help materials could be distributed to patients. Last, primary care psychologists may consider implementing routine screening of primary care patients for anxiety disorders.

SCREENING AND FURTHER ASSESSMENT

When a primary care psychologist receives a referral from a physician for a patient with anxiety disorder, it is imperative that a careful psychological diagnostic workup be completed. This is because PCPs often do not differentiate between the different types of anxiety disorders. For example, in a large study of office-based physician practices in the United States, 70% of anxiety disorder visits to PCPs were coded as "anxiety state, unspecified" (Harman et al., 2002). This is most likely because of short PCP visit times (typically a 15-minute office visit), as well as lack of specific expertise in psychological assessment. Moreover, from the perspective of the PCP, differentiating between anxiety disorders (e.g., panic disorder vs. social phobia) may not always be deemed necessary given that the initial treatment by PCPs may be similar, regardless of the disorder. For example, PCPs commonly initiate treatment with a course of SSRI medication.

However, differential diagnosis between the anxiety disorders and other psychological disorders is crucial for providing appropriate treatment and must be done by the primary care psychologist. For example, if a patient was incorrectly diagnosed with panic disorder when in fact the patient had social phobia, exposure-based treatments might be ineffective if they were focused on panic disorder (e.g., fear of physical symptoms) and not on social situations (e.g., fear of embarrassment or humiliation). Therefore, accurate psychological assessment and diagnosis are essential for effective treatment.

Psychiatric comorbidity rates are high among primary care patients, making it even more difficult to diagnose primary care patients with anxiety disorders accurately. For example, over 40% of participants in the Primary Care Anxiety Project (PCAP), a naturalistic, longitudinal study of anxiety disorders in primary care patients, were diagnosed with more than one anxiety disorder; over 70% were diagnosed with more than one Axis I disorder (Rodriguez, Weisberg, Machan, Culpepper, & Keller, 2002). Therefore, it is the role of the primary care psychologist to conduct a thorough psychological assessment.

Semistructured interviews are valuable for contributing to reliable differential diagnosis and the systematic assessment of issues related to a functional analysis of behavior (White & Barlow, 2001). A commonly used and empirically supported semistructured interview for anxiety disorders is the Anxiety Disorders Interview Schedule for *DSM-IV* (ADIS-IV; DiNardo, Brown, & Barlow, 1994). We strongly recommend that mental health clinicians inform PCPs of all psychological assessments, resulting diagnoses, and treatment plans.

NONPSYCHOLOGICAL CAUSES OF ANXIETY

Primary care psychologists should be aware that several medical conditions may imitate anxiety disorders (e.g., White & Barlow, 2001). These include endocrine disorders (e.g., hyperthyroidism, hypoglycemia, pheochromocytoma, Cushing's syndrome, menopause); cardiovascular disorders (e.g., myocardial infarction, mitral valve prolapse, arrhythmias, congestive heart failure, hypertension); and neurological disorders (e.g., epilepsy, Huntington's disease, multiple sclerosis, vestibular disorders). In some cases, the primary care psychologist may be the one to recommend that the physician rule out these medical conditions before beginning psychological treatment.

An additional important cause of anxiety may be pharmaceutical. Primary care psychologists must obtain an adequate history of the patient's use of all drugs and substances, including prescription and over-the-counter medication, "recreational" drugs, herbal remedies, and diet drugs. The psychologist should be aware that the following drugs and substances or reactions to them may exacerbate (or produce) anxiety: anticholinergic drugs; marijuana and other drugs that alter perception; stimulant drugs of abuse; sympathomimetic drugs (decongestants, B-2 bronchodialators, weight-reduction agents); thyroid hormone, xanthine-containing drugs (bronchodialators with theophylline, many over-the-counter cold and arthritis remedies, caffeine); and withdrawal symptoms of sedatives/hypnotics, alcohol, caffeine, and tobacco (Roca, 1991). Appendix B contains additional information on the psychiatric effects of commonly prescribed medications.

The primary care psychologist must be cognizant that an anxiety disorder diagnosis may also be a significant risk factor for suicidal ideation and suicide attempts and screen accordingly. This is especially true for panic disorder (Fleet, Dupuis, Kaczorowski, Marchand, & Beitman, 1997), PTSD (Briere & Zaidi, 1989), and social anxiety disorder (Lang & Stein, 2001). Suicidal ideation among primary care patients is highly associated with panic disorder and comorbid major depression (odds ratio [OR] 15.4) or panic attacks and comorbid major depression (OR 7.9; Goodwin et al., 2001). Because the offices of PCPs are frequently the first and only place where treatment is sought and received for many patients with anxiety disorders, primary care psychologists should educate PCPs about this matter and help establish a routine screen for suicidal ideation, plan, and intent.

COMORBIDITIES

Because an anxiety disorder diagnosis does not rule out the existence of physical disorders (and vice versa), primary care psychologists are encouraged to be aware of all physical and psychiatric disorders and their interactions. From the perspective of the biopsychosocial model, it is important to recognize that many chronic physical conditions are exacerbated or maintained by high levels of anxiety. For example, gastric ulcers, hypertension, migraines, coronary artery disease, asthma, and many pain conditions often co-occur with anxiety disorders (e.g., White & Barlow, 2001). Frequently, the identification and treatment of these anxiety disorders will also improve the status of the ongoing physical condition.

Some anxiety disorders may frequently co-occur with medical conditions. For example, primary care patients with PTSD were more likely to have other medical problems, including ane-

mia, arthritis, asthma, back pain, diabetes, eczema, kidney disease, lung disease, and ulcer (Weisberg, Bruce, et al., 2002). Complications introduced by comorbid medical conditions, especially chronic illnesses such as diabetes, hypertension, arthritis, asthma, and cardiovascular disease, may complicate psychological treatments.

PRESENTATION OF ANXIOUS PATIENTS IN PRIMARY CARE SETTINGS

Recognizing anxiety and mood disorders in the context of correctly identifying a variety of physical disorders is a very difficult task for PCPs. Broadhead (1994) noted that the presentation of psychological symptoms may be somewhat different in primary care settings compared with more traditional mental health settings, and that cultural variations in the expression of anxiety symptoms often confuse the picture further for the PCP. Indeed, expressions of anxiety are often tightly integrated with specific cultural idioms, which may vary greatly from one culture to another, requiring some knowledge of these cultural expressions (Barlow, 2001).

Commonalities among most patients with anxiety disorders in primary care settings include the fact that patients will generally be more focused on physical and somatic symptoms and less focused on psychological and cognitive symptoms. This is somewhat self-evident from the setting in which patients seek care. Primary care patients may initially resist the idea that their symptoms are psychological rather than physical in origin and may continue to seek physical explanations for their symptoms. A 2001 survey examined reasons primary care patients with anxiety disorders did not receive psychotherapy (Weisberg, Culpepper, & Keller, 2001); the most common reasons were (a) not believing the problem was treatable, (b) not believing in the value of psychological therapy, and (c) no physician recommendation for therapy.

Patients presenting to primary care settings who are ultimately diagnosed with anxiety commonly report cardiac, gastrointestinal, and neurological symptoms (Katon, 1984). Most often, the pattern of symptoms is not well explained by identifiable physical illnesses (Van Hemert, Hengeveld, Boek, Rooijmans, & Vandenbroucke, 1993). Chest pain in the absence of clinical evidence of cardiac disease is a common presentation of anxiety in primary care settings; frequently, patients with these complaints meet criteria for panic disorder (Yingling, Wulsin, Arnold, & Rouan, 1993). In primary care settings, individuals with panic disorder had an average of 14.1 somatic symptoms, as compared with 7.3 symptoms in a control group (Katon, Vitaliano, Russon, Jones, & Anderson, 1987). The authors noted that the somatic focus of many individuals with panic disorder often leads to misdiagnosis of physical problems.

Panic Disorder and Panic Disorder With Agoraphobia

Mr. D., a 38-year-old married male business executive, seeks treatment from his PCP after going to the emergency department on several occasions in the past month with episodes of intense chest pain, shortness of breath, palpitations, dizziness, and feeling like he was dying. These episodes occurred while he was at home in the evening, typically while he was watching television. Medical evaluation reveals a normal electrocardiogram and a normal exercise stress test. Mr. D. has no psychiatric history and does not use alcohol or drugs, but is obese and has high cholesterol. In addition, his father recently experienced a nonfatal heart attack. Since these episodes occurred, Mr. D. has avoided physical activities that make his heart beat quickly, including exercise, watching exciting sporting events, climbing stairs and any interpersonal interaction involving confrontation for fear that he may trigger another episode of chest pain and associated symptoms. This avoidance of confrontation has greatly affected his work productivity.

Panic disorder is characterized by recurrent, unexpected periods of intense fear or discomfort in which four (or more) symptoms develop abruptly and reach a peak within 10 minutes (panic attacks). The panic attacks must be followed by persistent concern about having additional attacks, worry about the implications of the attack or its consequences, or a significant

change in behavior (American Psychiatric Association [APA], 1994).

Epidemiological studies worldwide indicated the lifetime prevalence of panic disorder is between 1.5% and 3.5%, with a 1-year prevalence rate between 1% and 2% (APA, 1994). In addition, about 33% to 50% of individuals with panic disorder also have agoraphobia (anxiety about, or avoidance of, places or situations from which escape might be difficult; APA, 1994). Compared to men, women report more than two times greater incidence (Katerndahl & Realini, 1993).

Patients with panic disorder present differently in primary care settings (as compared to mental health settings) in that they are more focused on physical symptoms (e.g., chest pain, shortness of breath, and dizziness) and less focused on the cognitive symptoms of panic (e.g., fear of going crazy). Moreover, medical settings are used far more frequently than mental health settings to care for panic attacks; specifically, 49% of patients with panic attacks in the community sought treatment in medical settings, as compared with 26% who sought help from mental health practitioners (Katerndahl & Realini, 1995). This is somewhat problematic given that panic disorder is not generally recognized in medical settings. Of patients with panic disorder, 70% see an average of 10 physicians before receiving a correct diagnosis (Sheehan, 1982). Of patients with panic disorder, 61% are not recognized in the primary care setting as having an anxiety disorder (Spitzer et al., 1994), and 98% are not correctly identified in emergency departments (Fleet et al., 1996). Not surprisingly, patients with panic disorder have more medical utilization than individuals without panic disorder (Roy-Byrne et al., 1990).

Social Anxiety Disorder (Social Phobia)

Ms. E., a 31-year-old, single human resources consultant, seeks evaluation from her PCP for "episodes of excessive sweating" and tells her physician she is certain she must have a glandular disorder. On further clarification, Ms. E. states that she was recently promoted, and her job now requires her to lead training workshops regularly. She reports that while she leads these seminars, she sweats profusely and feels very warm, dizzy, and lightheaded; these symptoms often will persist all day. She wants to quit her job because of the "excessive sweating" and feels embarrassed and humiliated that she cannot control the sweating. She reports no significant medical or psychiatric history, but a history of heavy alcohol use at social events while in high school and college. She reports that she currently only drinks on weekends, but feels very uncomfortable in social situations unless she has several gin-and-tonics.

Social anxiety disorder is characterized by a marked and persistent fear of one or more social or performance situations in which the individual fears that he or she will act in a way (or exhibit anxiety symptoms) that will be humiliating or embarrassing (APA, 1994). The person recognizes that the fear is excessive or unreasonable, that exposure to the feared social situation invariably provokes anxiety, and the person avoids the situation or endures it with intense anxiety or distress.

Community-based and epidemiological studies have reported a lifetime prevalence of social anxiety disorder ranging from 3% to 13% (APA, 1994). Social anxiety disorder typically has an onset between 15 and 18 years of age (Lang & Stein, 2001), but may also appear abruptly following a stressful or humiliating experience (APA, 1994). The course is often continuous, and duration is frequently lifelong. Social anxiety disorder is frequently comorbid with other anxiety disorders (56.9%), affective disorders (41.4%), and substance abuse disorders (39.6%; Magee, Eaton, Wittchen, McGonagle, & Kessler, 1996). Social anxiety disorder is one of the most commonly undiagnosed and untreated psychological disorders in primary care and community and mental health settings (Katzelnick & Greist, 2001).

For primary care patients with social anxiety disorder, the typical presentation may be different in that they may initially focus on the physical symptoms of disorder without making the connection that symptoms occur exclusively in social or performance situations (e.g., while speaking in front of others). For example, social phobia has been associated with several physical comorbidities, including peptic ulcer disease (Davidson,

Hughes, George, & Blazer, 1993) and increased outpatient medical utilization (e.g., Lang & Stein, 2001). Other factors that may be different in primary care patients include motivation for treatment and willingness to follow through with treatment. If patients are concerned about the physical symptoms of social anxiety, they may seek medication from a primary care provider; if they want exposure-based therapy, they would likely present to a mental health setting.

Generalized Anxiety Disorder

Mr. H. is a 55-year-old biologist who recently separated from his wife. He reports a lifelong history of being prone to worry and "bad nerves." He is currently experiencing great difficulty sleeping, feels tired all the time, and has continuous tightness in his chest and upper back pain, which he especially notices at the end of the day. Apart from chronic back pain and irritable bowel syndrome, he has no other medical history. Physical examination, electrocardiogram, and stress tests were normal. Mr. H. also states that "little things make me jump," and he has trouble controlling his thoughts about all the things that he has to get accomplished for the next day.

Generalized anxiety disorder (GAD) is characterized by excessive anxiety and worry occurring more days than not for at least 6 months. In addition, there are often multiple foci of worries, and they are difficult to control (APA, 1994). Moreover, the anxiety and worry are associated with at least three of the following six symptoms: restlessness or feeling keyed up or on edge, being easily fatigued, difficulty concentrating or mind going blank, irritability, muscle tension, and sleep disturbance (APA, 1994).

The lifetime prevalence rate of GAD is reported to be 5%, and the 1-year prevalence rate is about 3% (APA, 1994). The typical onset of GAD is during childhood or adolescence, but may occur after age 20. The typical course is chronic but fluctuating and often is exacerbated during times of stress (Keller, 2002). In a recent study of GAD in primary care, 3.5% of 20,000 patients met criteria for pure GAD and 1.6% for comorbid GAD/major depression (Wittchen et al., 2002).

GAD is rarely diagnosed in primary care settings (Culpepper, 2002). When a GAD patient does seek care, the typical presentation may focus on somatic symptoms such as chronic chest tightness, difficulty sleeping, or muscle tightness. Many patients seeking treatment from PCPs will be seeking medications such as sleep aids or treatment for muscle and backaches.

Posttraumatic Stress Disorder

> Ms. C. is a 20-year-old college student seeking treatment from her PCP because of chronic back pain that she has been experiencing ever since she was in a serious rollover car accident 10 months ago, after which her passenger was hospitalized for 3 months. In addition, Ms. C. has difficulty sleeping, reports having trouble concentrating on her schoolwork, and is in danger of failing several classes. On further assessment, Ms. C. reports recurrent distressing dreams of the car accident and extreme anxiety while driving. As a result, she states that she has stopped driving entirely. Moreover, she feels irritable and distant from others, has dropped out of her sorority, and does not expect to have a career or normal life span.

For PTSD, the person experienced, witnessed, or was confronted with an event that involved actual or threatened death or serious injury, and the response involved intense fear, helplessness, or horror. In addition, the traumatic event is persistently reexperienced, the person persistently avoids stimuli associated with the trauma and also experiences persistent symptoms of increased arousal (APA, 1994).

Prevalence rates in community-based studies revealed a lifetime prevalence for PTSD ranging from 1% to 12.3% (cf. Bruce et al., 2001). Between 70% and 75% of the general population in the United States have been exposed to a traumatic event that meets the stressor criteria for PTSD (Green, 1994; Resnick, Kilpatrick, Dansky, Saunders, & Best, 1993). PTSD can occur at any age, and symptoms usually begin within 3 months

after the trauma. Duration of the symptoms varies, with half of individuals experiencing remission within 3 months, but many others have persisting symptoms after 12 months (APA, 1994).

Individuals exposed to traumatic events are high utilizers of health care, increasing the likelihood that these patients will be encountered in primary care settings (Samson, Bensen, Beck, Price, & Nimmer, 1999). However, the diagnosis of PTSD and not the experience of traumatic events alone seems to be the predictor of increased general medical complaints (Weisberg, Bruce, et al., 2002).

The typical presentation of PTSD in primary care patients often differs from the presentation of PTSD in a mental health setting. For example, if patients are injured as a result of the trauma, the focus of the initial treatment in a primary care setting may be on the physical injury. Among primary care patients with PTSD, five of the six types of trauma most frequently reported in the PCAP sample were traumas that may be associated with physical injury (serious accident involving a car or work, rape, attack with intent to kill, attack with weapon, and serious injury; Weisberg, Culpepper, & Keller, 2002). In a primary care setting, patients may focus on somatic symptoms such as sleep problems or feeling on edge or on anger management problems. The presence of PTSD may also make some patients noncompliant with PCP treatment recommendations; for example, a female sexual abuse survivor may avoid gynecological exams.

It is also important to recognize that not all trauma survivors meet criteria for PTSD. For example, in a large study of 502 primary care patients who met criteria for at least one anxiety disorder, 17% reported no history of trauma; 46% had experienced a traumatic event, but did not have PTSD; and 37% met criteria for PTSD (Weisberg, Bruce, et al., 2002). Moreover, because of the frequent emotional pain associated with the trauma, many primary care patients who have PTSD may also not be motivated to seek treatment and may not be willing to discuss their traumatic experiences with a mental health professional. Finally, many patients may not have been diagnosed with PTSD or may not understand the connection between past trauma and current physiological reactivity or other psychological symptoms (Samson et al., 1999).

Obsessive-Compulsive Disorder

Mrs. W. is a 29-year-old homemaker and mother of a 3-year-old child. During a routine physical exam with her PCP, Mrs. W. complains of "excessively dry" hands and requests a prescription medication. Further inspection of her hands reveals significant dryness, cracking, and bleeding of the skin. On further clarification, Mrs. W. states that she washes her hands "constantly," between 50 and 60 times per day, taking about 2 hours total per day. She states that this behavior began after the birth of her first child because she was fearful she would transmit a "deadly disease" to her infant. She states that these thoughts and this behavior significantly interfere with her daily routine.

Obsessive-compulsive disorder (OCD) is characterized by obsessions, which are recurrent, persistent thoughts that cause marked anxiety and distress, or compulsions, which are repetitive behaviors or mental acts that the person feels driven to perform to reduce distress (APA, 1994). These obsessions or compulsions cause marked distress, are time consuming (lasting more than 1 hour per day), or interfere significantly with functioning. The person recognizes that the obsessions or compulsions are excessive or unreasonable.

Epidemiological studies of community samples suggested that the lifetime prevalence of OCD is 2.5%, and the 1-year prevalence is 1.5% to 2.1%. Some estimates of OCD spectrum disorders in primary care settings are as high as 10% (Higgins, 1996). OCD typically begins in adolescence, and males have an earlier age of onset than females.

SUBTHRESHOLD PRESENTATIONS AND THEIR TREATMENT

There is mounting evidence that subthreshold or subclinical presentations of anxiety disorders are also significantly impairing for some patients (Barlow & Campbell, 2000). In addition to patients with Axis I disorders, another 5% of patients in primary care may experience subsyndromal anxiety and depressive symptoms that may warrant treatment (Roy-Byrne et al., 1994).

Treatments for full-criteria syndromes are likely effective for subthreshold patients, although specific studies addressing differences in treatment for patients with full diagnostic criteria versus subthreshold patients are lacking. However, it would be expected that medications (such as SSRIs, etc.) would provide benefit even if an individual does not meet full criteria for an anxiety disorder. Similarly, with psychotherapeutic approaches such as cognitive–behavioral therapy, because the focus would be on existing anxious cognitions and avoidance behavior, treatment should also be effective. Clearly, more research is needed in this area.

The question of whether there is any preventive benefit to treating subthreshold conditions has similarly not been adequately addressed. Longitudinal research following subthreshold cases of anxiety over time is necessary to see if they would exacerbate over time without treatment. Although subthreshold cases of anxiety have not been systematically examined, some research has been done on mixed anxiety-depressive disorder. In the PCAP, most cases of mixed anxiety-depressive disorder remitted on their own, without treatment, within a year (Weisberg, Culpepper, & Keller, 2002). However, these results were based on a small sample ($N = 10$), so they are far from conclusive. Clearly, more research is warranted in this area as well.

There are many other disorders in the spectrum of anxiety disorders that are beyond the scope of this chapter, including specific phobia, adjustment disorder with anxious mood, acute stress disorder, agoraphobia without panic, anxiety due to a general medical condition, substance-induced anxiety disorder, mixed anxiety-depressive disorder, and anxiety disorder not otherwise specified. A resource for further study in such areas includes Barlow's (2001) *Anxiety and Its Disorders*.

CHOICE OF TREATMENT IN PRIMARY CARE

We provide a broad overview of the current status of treatment choices for individuals with anxiety disorders. Although effective psychological and psychopharmacological treatments have been established for all the anxiety disorders, these treatments are often underutilized. Studies have suggested that patients with anxiety disorders are seldom treated and, when they are treated, often receive ineffective treatments. Findings from the Epidemiologic Catchment Area study (Regier et al., 1993), for example, suggested that only approximately 1 in 3 patients with a diagnosed anxiety disorder was receiving any treatment, let alone an effective treatment. More recent studies have suggested that little has changed. For example, a phone survey of 1,832 adults to assess anxiety and mood disorders concluded that only one third of the individuals diagnosed in the study were receiving treatment from their physicians for their anxiety or mood disorder (Ohayon et al., 2000).

In a large, naturalistic, multicenter, longitudinal study of primary care anxiety patients (PCAP), 504 patients meeting *DSM-IV* (*Diagnostic and Statistical Manual of Mental Disorders*, fourth edition; APA, 1994) criteria for one or more anxiety disorders were asked if they were receiving mental health treatment (Weisberg, Haisley, Machan, Culpepper, & Keller, 2001). Only half of primary care patients with anxiety disorders were receiving any treatment: 21% received medication only, 6% received psychotherapy only, 24% received both medication and psychotherapy, and 49% were untreated (Weisberg, Culpepper, et al., 2001). Detailed evaluation of the efficacy of psychosocial and pharmacological treatments for each anxiety disorder is beyond the scope of this chapter (for a review, see Nathan & Gorman, 2001).

Whether treatment is psychological or pharmacological, when the presentation of an anxiety disorder is somatic, treatment should be initiated in a sensitive manner. Specifically, we recommend using the biopsychosocial approach to minimize the issue of whether the somatic complaint is "all in the patient's head" (McDaniel, 1995). The biopsychosocial model does not force an "either/or" view of the patient's condition as medical (biological) or psychological. The biopsychosocial model is based on the following principles:

1. Most illness, whether physical or psychological, is influenced and determined by biological, psychological, and social phenomena.
2. Biological, psychological, and social variables influence the predisposition, onset, course, and outcome of most illnesses.
3. Better patient outcomes are achieved when therapeutic interventions are based on evaluation of the relationship among biological, psychological, and social variables (Cohen-Cole & Levinson, 1994).

By conceptualizing somatic complaints in this way, patients do not need to make the attribution that their physical symptoms are caused by psychological factors exclusively.

Psychological Treatments

Psychological treatments for anxiety disorders that have received empirical support include cognitive, behavioral, and exposure-based techniques as well as various self-regulation techniques, including progressive muscle relaxation, biofeedback, self-hypnosis, and meditation. In general, cognitive–behavioral approaches have received the most support (Barlow & Lehman, 1996). As stated, referrals to primary care psychologists likely just represent a small portion of all patients with anxiety disorders in primary care settings; proper identification and referral could easily overwhelm the resources available. Therefore, alternatives to the traditional one-to-one psychotherapy office visit may be necessary.

Many of the empirically supported treatments are available in manual or workbook form, so that they can be handed directly to the patient working under the supervision of a psychologist or other mental health specialist (e.g., Barlow & Craske, 1994). This approach would be a good option for the busy primary care psychologist. Thus, these treatments can be prescribed much like a medication, in the context of good general psychological care and attention to idiosyncratic problems that arise during the course of this treatment (Craske & Barlow, 1989). Evidence is accumulating that supports the viability of this type of approach to treat each specific psychological disorder, even with minimal therapist contact (e.g., Cote, Gauthier, Laberge, Cormier, & Plamondon, 1994).

Other studies have indicated that structured psychological interventions can be delivered in briefer format than has been customary, with beneficial results for a number of patients (e.g., Craske, Maidenberg, & Bystritsky, 1995; Roy-Byrne, Katon, Cowley, & Russo, 2001). Finally, self-help treatments, such as reading books or information on the Internet, are also helpful, but generally less so than therapist-based treatments.

In view of the enormous numbers of patients presenting with psychological disorders in primary care settings, one of the major problems facing psychologists and other mental health practitioners today is the dissemination of effective psychological treatments to those who need them (Barlow, Lerner, & Esler, 1996). There is also wide agreement that primary care settings will become an increasingly important arena for the delivery of behavioral health care, and that psychologists and other mental health professionals need to embrace changes and practice patterns that allow effective participation in primary care settings (DiBartolo, Hofmann, & Barlow, 1995; Liebowitz & Barlow, 1995).

Pharmacological Treatments

Pharmacological treatments for anxiety disorders that have been empirically supported include the use of SSRIs, benzodiazepines, tricyclic antidepressants, buspirone (Buspar), beta-blockers, and antihistamines (Liebowitz & Barlow, 1995; White & Barlow, 2001). Although benzodiazepines and tricyclic antidepressants historically have been the pharmacological mainstay of anxiety disorder treatment, SSRIs, selective serotonin and norepinephrine reuptake inhibitors (e.g., venlafaxine), and buspirone are also proven to be effective. Given their favorable side-effect profile and lower risk of tolerance, rebound anxiety, and withdrawal symptoms, SSRIs, selective serotonin and norepinephrine reuptake inhibitors, and buspirone should be considered first-line agents for most patients who require pharmacotherapy for anxiety disorder.

Further information on antianxiety medications can be found in Appendix A. Primary care psychologists are encouraged to keep informed of psychopharmacology developments as they are frequently in the position to offer suggestions to the PCPs, who are often the only prescribing physicians involved with the treatment of the primary care patient.

In the PCAP study, patients with anxiety disorders who were taking psychotropic medications were as likely to be receiving the prescription from their PCPs as from a psychiatrist. SSRIs were the psychotropic medication prescribed most frequently (63%), followed by benzodiazepines (38%), other antidepressants (28%), tricyclics (12%), and other anxiolytics (4%; Weisberg, Culpepper, et al., 2001). Although effective medications exist, a number of studies have suggested that medication is often prescribed inappropriately or at an incorrect dosage (Shear & Schulberg, 1995). Although both PCPs and psychiatrists most commonly prescribed SSRIs, PCPs on average prescribed a lower dose of the SSRIs than did psychiatrists.

COLLABORATION BETWEEN PHYSICIANS AND PRIMARY CARE PSYCHOLOGISTS

The main benefits that the primary care psychologist can give to the PCP are in (a) identifying patients with anxiety disorders; (b) providing psychological treatments for psychological disorders, such as cognitive–behavioral therapy; and (c) having familiarity with new developments in psychopharmacology. Physicians receive very little training on the psychological treatments of psychological disorders and can benefit from, over time, informal training by the primary care psychologist on the proper use, timing, and concomitant use of medications with these psychotherapy modalities. It is important for the primary care psychologist to be aware of ways in which the patient's psychological treatments can interact with their other, often multiple, medical problems. In addition, it is critical for the primary care psychologist to confirm any and all psychological diagnoses made by PCPs as PCPs receive little training in the proper diagnoses of psychological disorders.

Psychologists in primary care settings must be aware of possible patient barriers to acceptance of a psychological diagnosis or of treatment. In addition, many physicians endorse the widespread belief that patients who are not seeking care in a mental health setting will be resistant to psychiatric labeling, accepting a psychological referral, or "talking" about their problems. However, a study suggested patients with panic disorder seen in primary care are willing to see psychotherapists (95%–100%), see psychiatrists (86%–96%), and take psychotropic medications (87%–100%; Johnson et al., 2000).

Primary care psychologists may choose to include family members in treatment to increase patient acceptance. In addition, primary care psychologists may choose to offer patients nonpsychotherapy behavioral approaches to treatment, such as self-help groups, self-help treatments, or relaxation exercises.

Psychologists or other mental health practitioners in primary care settings should be aware of the consultation needs of PCPs. Primary care psychologists should avoid the mistakes of writing consultation notes that use excessive psychological terminology or are unfocused and lengthy. Moreover, consultation notes must be timely. For a suggested outline of a consultation note, see chapters 2 and 21. Physicians may be reluctant to make referrals to mental health clinicians because they may be time consuming for the physician to arrange or because physicians believe that patients will not follow through with such referrals. This underscores the need for on-site primary care psychologists. Whenever possible, psychologists should consider innovative collaborative care arrangements, such as being on site as consultants to decrease stigma, integrate treatment into regular care, and to provide short-term treatments (Pace, Chaney, Mullins, & Olson, 1995).

SUMMARY

The prevalence of anxiety disorders is greater than that of any other major class of disorder, including mood and addictive disorders. Individuals with anxiety disorders are more likely to seek treatment from a PCP than from a mental health professional. The majority of patients with anxiety disorders in primary care are not recognized, and even fewer are treated effectively. Behavioral health care specialists, particularly psychologists, are more clinically effective and more cost-effec-

tive in providing treatment than overburdened PCPs. Because the large number of these patients precludes individual assessment and intervention, more efficient models for the delivery of behavioral health care in primary care must be developed. Alternatives to the traditional one-to-one psychotherapy office visit should all be considered, including group treatments, self-directed treatments, and brief (even one-session) interventions. When possible, we recommend that psychologists consider innovative collaborative care arrangements, such as being on site in primary care offices to decrease stigma, integrate treatment into regular care, and provide short-term treatments.

ADDITIONAL RESOURCES

Suggestions for further reading and professional development resources are available at this book's companion Web site: www.primarycarepsych.com.

References

American Psychiatric Association. (1994). *Diagnostic and statistical manual of mental disorders* (4th ed.). Washington, DC: Author.

Barlow, D. H. (2001). *Anxiety and its disorders: The nature and treatment of anxiety and panic* (2nd ed.). New York: Guilford Press.

Barlow, D. H., & Campbell, L. A. (2000). Mixed anxiety-depression and its implications for models of mood and anxiety disorders. *Comprehensive Psychiatry, 41*(Suppl. 1), 55–60.

Barlow, D. H., & Craske, M. G. (1994). *Mastery of your anxiety and panic: II.* Albany, NY: Graywind.

Barlow, D. H., & Lehman, C. L. (1996). Advances in the psychosocial treatment of anxiety disorders: Implications for national health care. *Archives of General Psychiatry, 53,* 727–735.

Barlow, D. H., Lerner, J. A., & Esler, J. L. (1996). Behavioral health care in primary care settings: Recognition and treatment of anxiety and its disorders. In R. J. Resnick & R. H. Rozensky (Eds.), *Health psychology through the life span: Practice and research opportunities.* (pp. 133–148). Washington, DC: American Psychological Association.

Beardsley, R. S., Gardocki, G. J., Larson, D. B., & Hidalgo, J. (1988). Prescribing of psychotropic medication by primary care physicians and psychiatrists. *Archives of General Psychiatry,* 45, 1117–1119.

Briere, J., & Zaidi, Y. (1989). Sexual abuse histories and suicide in female psychiatric room patients. *American Journal of Psychiatry, 146,* 1602–1606.

Broadhead, W. F. (1994). Presentation of psychiatric symptomatology in primary care. In J. Miranda, A. A. Hohmann, C. C. Attkisson, & D. B. Larson (Eds.), *Mental disorders in primary care* (pp. 139–162). San Francisco: Jossey-Bass.

Brown, T. A., & Barlow, D. H. (1995). Long-term outcome in cognitive-behavioral treatment of panic disorder: Clinical predictors and alternative strategies for assessment. *Journal of Consulting and Clinical Psychology, 63,* 754–765.

Bruce, S. E., Weisberg, R. B., Dolan, R. T., Machan, J. T., Kessler, R. C., Culpepper, L., & Keller, M. B. (2001). Trauma and posttraumatic stress disorder in primary care patients. *Primary Care Companion of the Journal of Clinical Psychiatry, 3,* 211–217.

Cohen-Cole, S. A., & Levinson, R. M. (1994). The biopsychosocial model in medical practice. In A. Stoudemire (Ed.), *Human behavior: An introduction for medical students* (pp. 22–63). Philadelphia: Lippincott.

Cote, G., Gauthier, J. G., Laberge, B., Cormier, H. J., & Plamondon, J. (1994). Reduced therapist contact in the cognitive-behavioral treatment of panic disorder. *Behavior Therapy, 25,* 123–145.

Craske, M. G., & Barlow, D. H. (1989). *Mastery of your anxiety and panic.* Albany, NY: Graywind.

Craske, M. G., Maidenberg, E., & Bystritsky, A. (1995). Brief cognitive-behavioral vs. nondirective therapy for panic disorder. *Journal of Behavior Therapy and Experimental Psychiatry, 26,* 113–120.

Culpepper, L. (2002). Generalized anxiety disorder in primary care: Emerging issues in management and treatment. *Journal of Clinical Psychiatry, 63*(Suppl. 8), 35–42.

Davidson, J. R. T., Hughes, D. L., George, L. K., & Blazer, D. G. (1993). The epidemiology of social phobia: Findings from the Duke Epidemiological Catchment Area Study. *Psychological Medicine, 23,* 709–718.

DiBartolo, P. M., Hofmann, S. G., & Barlow, D. H. (1995). Psychosocial approaches to panic disorder and agoraphobia: Assessment and treatment issues for the primary care physician. *Mind/Body and Medicine, 1,* 1–12.

DiNardo, P., Brown, T. A., & Barlow, D. H. (1994). *Anxiety disorders interview schedule for DSM-IV.* San Antonio, TX: Graywind/ Psychological Corporation.

Fifer, S. K., Mathias, S. D., Patrick, D. L., Majonson, P. D., Lubeck, D. P., & Buesching, D. P. (1994). Untreated anxiety among adult primary care patients in a health maintenance organization. *Archives of General Psychiatry, 51,* 740–750.

Fleet, R. P., Dupuis, G., Kaczorowski, J., Marchand, A., & Beitman, B. D. (1997). Suicidal ideation in emergency department chest pain patients: Panic disorder a risk factor. *American Journal of Emergency Medicine, 15,* 345–349.

Fleet, R. P., Dupuis, G., Marchand, A., Burelle, D., Arsenault, A., & Beitman, B. D. (1996). Panic disorder in emergency department chest pain patients: Prevalence, comorbidity, suicidal ideation, and physician recognition. *American Journal of Medicine, 101,* 371–378.

Ford, D. E. (1994). Recognition and under-recognition of mental disorders in adult primary care. In J. Miranda, A. A. Hohmann, C. C. Attkisson, & D. B. Larson (Eds.), *Mental disorders in primary care* (pp. 186–205). San Francisco: Jossey-Bass.

Goodwin, R., Olfson, M., Feder, A., Fuentes, M., Pilowsky, D. J., & Weissmann, M. M. (2001). Panic and suicidal ideation in primary care. *Depression and Anxiety, 14,* 244–246.

Green, B. L. (1994). Psychosocial research in traumatic stress: An update. *Journal of Traumatic Stress, 7,* 341–362.

Harman, J. S., Rollman, B. L., Hanusa, B. H., Lenze, E. J., & Shear, M. K. (2002). Physician office visits of adults for anxiety disorders in the United States, 1985–1998. *Journal of General Internal Medicine, 17,* 165–172.

Higgins, E. S. (1996). Obsessive-compulsive spectrum disorders in primary care: The possibilities and the pitfalls. *Journal of Clinical Psychiatry, 57,* 7–9.

Johnson, M. R., Gold, P. B., Siemion, L., Magruder, K. M., Frueh, B. C., & Santos, A. B. (2000). Panic disorder in primary care: Patients' attributions of illness causes and willingness to accept psychiatric treatment. *International Journal of Psychiatry in Medicine, 30,* 367–384.

Katerndahl, D. A., & Realini, J. P. (1993). Lifetime prevalence of panic states. *American Journal of Psychiatry, 150,* 246–249.

Katerndahl, D. A., & Realini, J. P. (1995). Where do panic attack sufferers seek care? *Journal of Family Practice, 40*, 237–243.

Katon, W. (1984). Panic disorder and somatization: Review of 55 cases. *American Journal of Medicine, 77*, 101–106.

Katon, W., Vitaliano, P. P., Russon, J., Jones, M., & Anderson, K. (1987). Panic disorder: Spectrum of severity and somatization. *Journal of Nervous and Mental Disease, 175*, 12–19.

Katzelnick, D. J., & Greist, J. H. (2001). Social anxiety disorder: An unrecognized problem in primary care. *Journal of Clinical Psychology, 62*(Suppl. 1), 11–15.

Keller, M. B. (2002). The long-term clinical course of generalized anxiety disorder. *Journal of Clinical Psychiatry, 63*(Suppl. 8), 11–16.

Kessler, R. C., McGonagle, K. A., Shanyang, Z., Nelson, C. B., Hughes, M., Eshleman, S., Wittchen, H.-U., & Kendler, K. (1994). Lifetime and 12-month prevalence of *DSM-III-R* psychiatric disorders in the United States: Results from the National Comorbidity Survey. *Archives of General Psychiatry, 51*, 8–19.

Lang, A. J., & Stein, M. B. (2001). Social phobia: Prevalence and diagnostic threshold. *Journal of Clinical Psychiatry, 62*(Suppl. 1), 5–10.

Liebowitz, M., & Barlow, D. H. (1995). Panic disorder: The latest on diagnosis and treatment. *Journal of Practical Psychiatry and Behavioral Health, 1*, 10–19.

Magee, W. J., Eaton, W. W., Wittchen, H. U., McGonagle, K. A., & Kessler, R. C. (1996). Agoraphobia, simple phobia, and social phobia in the National Comorbidity Survey. *Archives of General Psychiatry, 53*, 159–168.

McDaniel, S. H. (1995). Collaboration between psychologists and family physicians: Implementing the biopsychosocial model. *Professional Psychology: Research and Practice, 26*, 112–117.

Nathan, P. E., & Gorman, J. M. (1998). *A guide to treatments that work.* New York: Oxford University Press.

Nisenson, L. G., Pepper, C. M., Schwenk, T. L., & Coyne, J. C. (1998). The nature and prevalence of anxiety disorders in primary care. *General Hospital Psychiatry, 20*, 21–28.

Ohayon, M. M., Shapiro, C. M., & Kennedy, S. H. (2000). Differentiating *DSM-IV* anxiety and depressive disorders in the general population: Comorbidity and treatment consequences. *Canadian Journal of Psychiatry, 45*, 166–172.

Ormel, J., Von Korff, M., Ustun, B., Pini, S., Kor-

ten, A., & Oldehonkel, T. (1994). Common mental disorders and disability across cultures: Results from the WHO collaborative study on psychological problems in general health care. *Journal of the American Medical Association, 272*, 1741–1748.

Pace, T. M., Chaney, J. M., Mullins, L. L., & Olson, R. A. (1995). Psychological consultation with primary care physicians: Obstacles and opportunities in medical settings. *Professional Psychology: Research and Practice, 26*, 123–131.

Price, D., Beck, A., Nimmer, C., & Bensen, S. (2000). The treatment of anxiety disorders in a primary care setting. *Psychiatric Quarterly, 7*, 31–45.

Regier, D. A., Myers, J. K., Kramer, M., Robins, L. N., Blazer, D. G., Hough, R. L., Eaton, W. W., & Locke, B. Z. (1984). The NIMH epidemiologic catchment area: Historical context, major objectives, and study population characteristics. *Archives of General Psychiatry, 41*, 934–941.

Regier, D. A., Narrow, W. E., Rae, D. S., Manderscheid, R. W., Locke, B. Z., & Goodwin, F. K. (1993). The de facto U.S. mental and addictive disorders service system: Epidemiologic catchment area prospective 1-year prevalence rates of disorders and services. *Archives of General Psychiatry, 50*, 85–94.

Resnick, H., Kilpatrick, D. G., Dansky, B. S., Saunders, B. E., & Best, C. L. (1993). Prevalence of civilian trauma and posttraumatic stress disorder in a representative national sample of women. *Journal of Consulting and Clinical Psychology, 61*, 984–991.

Roca, R. P. (1991). Anxiety. In L. R. Barker, J. R. Burton, & P. D. Zieve (Eds.), *Principles of ambulatory medicine* (3rd ed., pp. 128–142). Baltimore, MD: Williams and Wilkins.

Rodriguez, B. F., Weisberg, R. B., Machan, J. T., Culpepper, L., & Keller, M. B. (2002, March). *Comorbidity in anxiety disorder patients seen in general medical practices.* Poster presented at the annual meeting of the Anxiety Disorders Association of America, Austin, TX.

Roy-Byrne, P., Katon, W., Broadhead, W. E., Lepine, J. P., Richards, J., Brantley, P. J., Russo, J., Zinbarg, R., Barlow, D., & Liebowitz (1994). Subsyndromal (mixed) anxiety-depression in primary care. *Journal of General Internal Medicine, 9*, 507–512.

Roy-Byrne, P. P., Katon, W., Cowley, D. S., & Russo, J. (2001). A randomized effectiveness trial of collaborative care for patients with panic disorder in primary care. *Archives of General Psychiatry, 58,* 869–876.

Roy-Byrne, P. P., Stein, M. B., Russo, J., Mercier, E., Thomas, R., McQuaid, J., Katon, W. J., Craske, M. G., Bystritsky, A., & Sherbourne, C. D. (1990). Panic disorder in the primary care setting: Comorbidity, disability, service utilization, and treatment. *Journal of Clinical Psychiatry, 60,* 492–499.

Samson, A. Y., Bensen, S., Beck, A., Price, D., & Nimmer, C. (1999). Posttraumatic disorder in primary care. *Journal of Family Practice, 48,* 222–227.

Shear, M. K., & Schulberg, H. C. (1995). Anxiety disorders in primary care. *Bulletin of the Menninger Clinic, 59,* A73–A85.

Sheehan, D. (1982). Current concepts in psychiatry: Panic attacks and phobias. *New England Journal of Medicine, 307,* 156–158.

Spitzer, R. L., Williams, J. B. W., Kroenke, K., Linzer, M., deGruy, F. V., Hahn, S. R., Brody, D., & Johnson, J. G. (1994). Utility of a new procedure for diagnosing mental disorders in primary care: The PRIME-MD 1000 study. *Journal of the American Medical Association, 272,* 1749–1756.

Van Hemert, A. M., Hengeveld, M. W., Boek, J. H., Rooijmans, H. G. M., & Vandenbroucke, J. P. (1993). Psychiatric disorders in relation to medical illness among patients of a general medical out-patient clinic. *Psychological Medicine, 23,* 167–173.

Weiller, E., Bisserbe, J. C., Maier, W., & Lecrubier, Y. (1998). Prevalence and recognition of anxiety syndromes in five European primary care settings. *British Journal of Psychiatry, 173* (Suppl. 34), 18–23.

Weisberg, R. B., Bruce, S. E., Machan, J., Dolan, R. T., Culpepper, L., & Keller, M. B. (2002). Non-psychiatric medical illness in primary care patients with trauma histories and post-traumatic stress disorder. *Psychiatric Services, 53,* 848–854.

Weisberg, R. B., Culpepper, L., & Keller, M. B. (2001, November). *The underutilization of cognitive-behavioral therapy techniques in a sample of primary care patients with anxiety disorders.* In R. B. Weisberg (Chair), Dissemination of Cognitive-Behavioral Therapy for Anxiety Disorders to Medical Settings. Paper presented at the meeting of the Association for Advancement of Behavior Therapy, Philadelphia, PA.

Weisberg, R. B., Culpepper, L., & Keller, M. B. (2002, May). *The occurrence and course of mixed anxiety-depressive disorder in a sample of primary care patients.* Paper presented at the meeting of the American Psychiatric Association, Philadelphia, PA.

Weisberg, R. B., Haisley, E., Machan, J., Culpepper, L., & Keller, M. B. (2001, October). *Psychiatric treatment in primary care patients with anxiety disorders.* Poster presented at the meeting of the North American Primary Care Research Group, Halifax, Nova Scotia, Canada.

White, K. S., & Barlow, D. H. (2001). Panic disorder and agoraphobia. In D. H. Barlow (Ed.), *Anxiety and its disorders: The nature and treatment of anxiety and panic* (2nd ed., pp. 328–379). New York: Guilford Press.

Wittchen, H.-U., Kessler, R. C., Beesdo, K., Krause, P., Hofler, M., & Hoyer, J. (2002). Generalized anxiety and depression in primary care: Prevalence, recognition, and management. *Journal of Clinical Psychiatry, 63*(Suppl. 8), 24–34.

Yingling, K. W., Wulsin, L. R., Arnold, L. M., & Rouan, G. W. (1993). Estimated prevalences of panic disorder and depression among consecutive patients seen in an emergency department with acute chest pain. *Journal of General Internal Medicine, 8,* 231–235.

18

Attention-Deficit/Hyperactivity Disorder in Children and Adults

Douglas G. Kondo
John S. March

Attention-deficit/hyperactivity disorder (ADHD) is a heterogeneous neuropsychiatric behavioral disorder characterized by inattention, hyperactivity, and impulsivity of varying severity (March, Wells, & Conners, 1995). ADHD by definition begins in childhood and frequently leads to profound academic and social impairments across multiple settings (Barkley, 1998). In fact, the disorder is the most common cause for referral of children to mental health and primary care providers alike (Bird, Gould, & Staghezza, 1993) and is among the most prevalent chronic health conditions affecting school-aged children.

Like many chronic medical disorders, ADHD affects not only patients, but also their families, often in a deleterious way. The families of children with ADHD experience more stress, feelings of parental incompetence, marital discord, marital disruption, and social isolation than do controls (Edwards, Schulz, & Long, 1995); researchers have also documented an association with higher levels of parental alcohol consumption (Pelham & Lang, 1993) and parental psycho-

logical distress and depression (Barkley, Fisher, Edelbrock, & Smallish, 1991).

Rates of physician office diagnosis of ADHD have increased in recent years, reflecting an increase in educationally based referrals after the disorder became eligible as "other health impaired" under section 504 of the federal law known as the Rehabilitation Act, which applies to all education agencies that receive funding from a U.S. government source.

Although ADHD was once conceptualized as a disorder of childhood, evidence is accumulating that the condition persists across the life cycle. One third of children with ADHD will exhibit the full set of symptoms as adults—albeit in altered form—and as many as 60% of adults continue to have at least one functionally impairing symptom (Shaffer, 1994).

Primary care practitioners are frequently asked to evaluate patients for ADHD, and the opportunity to reinstate appropriate educational and psychosocial development, together with the high psychiatric comorbidity rates in untreated ADHD, makes early recognition and management of the disorder essential. When the disorder has gone undiagnosed in an adult, diagnosis and treatment can still have a significant impact on a patient's occupational and psychosocial functioning.

EPIDEMIOLOGY

Epidemiological studies of ADHD have yielded a prevalence of 1.7% to 16%, depending on the population studied (Goldman, Genel, Bezman, & Slanetz, 1998), and it was reported from a community sample that 10% of school-aged children had received the diagnosis of ADHD, and that 7% were undergoing pharmacological treatment (Rowland et al., 2002). In elementary school-aged children, boys are more affected than girls, with male:female ratios that range from 2:1 to 9:1, depending on the diagnostic subtype and the setting; clinically referred children are much more likely to be male (American Psychiatric Association [APA], 2000a). This gender referral bias may reflect a predominance of inattentive, cognitive, and executive functioning symptoms in girls, as compared with the concomitant disruptive, aggressive, and impulsive behaviors frequently seen in boys. With publication of the APA's *Diagnostic and Statistical Manual of Mental Disorders*, fourth edition (*DSM-IV*), more females have been diagnosed with the predominantly inattentive subtype of ADHD (Wolraich, Hannah, Baumgaertel, & Feurer, 1998). One study observed that, among children rated by teachers as meeting criteria for ADHD of any subtype, fewer girls than boys are diagnosed or treated with stimulants (Wolraich, Hannah, Pinnock, Baumgaertel, & Brown, 1996).

The scientific literature concerning ADHD in adults, although a small body of work compared with that for children with ADHD, definitively supports the validity of the diagnosis of ADHD in adults (Faraone et al., 2001). As public awareness and media coverage of the disorder increase, primary care clinicians will increasingly be called on to diagnose and treat ADHD in both young adults and the middle-aged population.

SYMPTOM PICTURE AND PRESENTATION

Beginning with Still's (1902) description of children suffering from deficient "volitional inhibition" and "moral control," the behavioral picture of ADHD has been known by a variety of names to generations of clinicians, parents, and teachers. By the mid-20th century, ADHD was thought to result from neurological injury, and the disorder was given the appellation minimal brain dysfunction (Clements & Peters, 1962). Later, the emphasis in diagnosis shifted to motoric hyperactivity, and the term hyperkinetic reaction of childhood was applied. Recent acronyms, in particular attention-deficit disorder (ADD) and its doppelganger ADHD, reflect the current emphasis on the concept of inattention and hyperactive/impulsive behavior that define the core symptoms of the disorder. One problem with this concept has been that all the symptoms are developmentally normal and appropriate at certain ages, which often prompts laypersons and professionals either to dismiss the diagnosis as fictional or to assume that it is real and that their child (or their patient) must have it.

Not surprisingly, the presentation of ADHD varies considerably with age. For example, very young children cannot be expected to attend as well as older adolescents; conversely, adolescents are generally less hyperactive and impulsive than preschool youngsters. Table 18.1 summarizes important developmental differences in the ADHD symptom picture as the disorder presents in preschool, middle childhood, adolescence, and adulthood. A quick scan indicates that the core symptoms of distractibility, poor sustained attention, and hyperactive and impulsive behavior are present in each age grouping. However, the relative importance of each of these dimensions varies with age, and the contexts in which the symptoms manifest also differ remarkably as children develop into young adults.

Notwithstanding these developmental differences, ADHD symptoms most often show up in situations that demand sustained attention and are boring and hard. For example, the work of most children is school, so it is expectable that school-based symptoms form a large part of the

Table 18.1 Developmental Differences in Presentation of Attention-Deficit/Hyperactivity Symptoms

Preschool	Middle Childhood	Adolescence	Adult
Inattentive	Distractible	Daydreams	Disorganized
Excitable	Hyperactive	Poorly organized	Has poor concentration
Hyperactive	Poorly organized	Restless	Does not finish things
Fidgety	Fails to complete	Poor follow-through	Procrastinates
Noisy	Disruptive in class	Requires direction	Impulsive
Aggressive	Bored all the time	Risky behaviors	Has affective dyscontrol
Stubborn	Interrupts		Anxious
Has temper tantrums	Cannot wait turn		Substance abuse
Has accidents			Antisocial

symptom presentation. Thus, when stimulus salience is low, as in doing math homework, ADHD symptoms are more likely than when stimulus salience and interactivity is high, as in playing video games.

This perhaps accounts for the finding that the modal age at diagnosis is 9 years, corresponding to the third grade, and that most referrals for clinical treatment originate with teachers and school administrators raising concerns about a child's disruptive behavior, academic underachievement, hyperactivity, lack of cooperation, or aggression. Similarly, symptoms are predictably less of a problem—or may even temporarily disappear—in highly structured or novel settings, when the child is engaged one-to-one with a sympathetic adult, when the child is intimidated and afraid, or when the child is physically ill. Such context-specific variability in symptom expression is typical of the disorder and should not be misconstrued as malingering by the affected child. The following cases illustrate ADHD in various scenarios.

Sierra was a 15-year-old female who presented after being retained at the end of ninth grade. A review of the text revision of DSM-IV (DSM-IV-TR) ADHD (APA, 2000a) criteria with the patient and her mother was equivocal. Psychological testing revealed a full-scale IQ of 112, which seemed discordant with her cumulative grade point average of 1.7. No learning disorders (LDs) were identified, but Sierra scored more than 1 standard deviation below normal on the Freedom From Distractibility Index. Teacher reports noted good behavior, but contained impressions of Sierra as "unmotivated" and "not a hard worker." The clinical interview revealed a long history of struggles with mathematics and any academic task involving reading comprehension. The patient endorsed a sense of frustration and disorganization in school, a tendency to be distracted by other students' sounds and movements in class, and frequent daydreaming during lectures. Continuous Performance Test (CPT) results were reported as "markedly atypical" across more than half the indices.

Ten weeks after a titration trial of a long-acting stimulant, the patient reported that she was placed on her school's honor roll for the first time and was making plans to attend community college to become a nurse or computer programmer.

Dominick was a 44-year-old male who presented for evaluation of possible depression. Several months earlier, he had received a promotion to management at the factory where he worked, and the increased demands for organization and multitasking were overwhelming to him. After years of good performance reviews, he received a poor one and felt demoralized. Family history revealed that his daughter, who lived out of state with her mother, was undergoing stimulant treatment for ADHD. Social history revealed that he was a "terrible student" who "barely made it out of high school."

Administration of the Conners Adult Diagnostic Interview for DSM-IV revealed that Dominick met criteria for the combined type of ADHD in childhood and for the inattentive type as an adult. A clinical interview, Beck Depression Inventory, and Hamilton Rating Scale for Depression were not suggestive of major depression.

Within 2 weeks of beginning a low-dose trial of a long-acting stimulant, he reported that his desk was cleared of memos and reports "for the first time in months," and that several coworkers had commented on his increased productivity. His mood symptoms cleared, and to his surprise, he started reading science fiction novels during his lunch hour, a pastime he had given up in middle school.

Charles was a third grader who was seen at a school-based health and wellness clinic. He was referred by his teacher for lack of focus, hyperactivity, and a tendency to complete worksheets immediately by "scribbling just anything" into the blank spaces. He rarely turned in homework assignments and frequently disrupted class by talking and provoking the other students. The patient was unable to remain quiet, despite frequent redirection. He would continuously make musical sounds with his mouth and simultaneously tap out rhythms on his desk with his wrist and knuckles. Conners teacher scales clearly pointed to the presence of ADHD. Charles himself was aware of his hyperactivity, but stated, "Cookies and chocolate make me hyper. I don't eat them." After some hesitation, he vigorously denied any frustration with academics, calling his schoolwork "easy."

Charles's mother did not attend the first two appointments that were made for her at the clinic. She presented for the third, and although she endorsed all but one of the DSM-IV-TR criteria for the combined subtype of ADHD, she insisted that Charles's activity level was a sign that he was "strong and healthy." She was able to admit that he frequently disrupted church services and had few close friends, but she vehemently refused to consider a medication trial. As the consultation continued, she blamed Charles's teacher and the school for his lack of academic progress. She compared his school problems with her own, noting that she had a tenth-grade education.

Charles was retained at the end of third grade, and he was transferred to a self-contained classroom for "behaviorally and emotionally handicapped" children.

Jules was a 29-year-old female living with her parents who presented for evaluation at an ADHD specialty clinic. She and her parents wondered if ADHD was the reason for her lack of occupational advancement because a cousin had "turned it around completely" since being placed on medication. The parents were high-functioning professionals and had sent Jules, their youngest child, to a private high school. She attended three private colleges over 7 years and had eventually obtained a degree at the local state college. Jules's older siblings had each obtained an advanced degree; one was a surgeon and the other an investment banker.

Review of Jules's elementary and middle school records revealed no academic struggles or behavioral concerns. The initial interview revealed no history of trauma or abuse, but did indicate a significant anxiety component. As a youth, Jules had displayed symptoms of separation anxiety, social anxiety, and generalized anxiety. On structured clinical interview, Jules met criteria for current generalized anxiety disorder and dysthymic disorder. Substance abuse history revealed daily alcohol use and binge drinking on weekends with friends from college. When a urine drug screen came back positive for THC (marijuana), Jules admitted to daily use dating back several years.

Jules began outpatient substance abuse treatment, but soon dropped out because she felt she was "not like those people." Her anxiety and depressive symptoms were treated with venlafaxine-XR and a 12-week course of cognitive–behavioral therapy. Her mood and anxiety symptoms cleared. Although she continued to drink and smoke cannabis socially, her level of usage declined, and she was able to find and keep a job in an art gallery.

Larry was a 5-year-old male living in foster care. He presented with his social worker and foster parent after being expelled from four different preschools for noncompliant behavior and fighting. Larry's social worker reported that his mother smoked crack cocaine and cigarettes while she was pregnant with him, and that Larry was born prematurely. Larry was a handsome, friendly child who was unable to remain seated in the office; more often than not, he was on the floor or under the couch. Without seeking permission, he opened several sets of toys and soon had them strewn around the office; he ignored his foster parent's instructions to put one toy away before opening another. He frequently interrupted the interview, and at one point sprinted suddenly out of the office, shouting "I need a drink of water!" Shortly after returning, he announced, "I'm bored!"

Preferring a psychosocial approach, Larry's foster mother enrolled in parent training classes, and his preschool agreed to create a daily report card (DRC) for him. A home behavior program that offered special snacks and video game time for positive DRCs was put into place. All instances of school aggression were reported on the DRC, and on Saturdays, Larry was allowed to go for ice cream or a fast-food lunch if his DRCs were aggression free on four of the five previous school days. Without medication, Larry was able to remain in good standing at his fifth preschool and won several ribbons for his lively performance at the end-of-the-year talent show.

Viola was a 9-year-old female living with her grandmother because of her mother's intractable substance abuse and related incarceration. The patient's grandmother became concerned when she noticed the protracted amount of time she was spending on her fourth-grade homework each night. The clinical interview and Conners scales were strongly suggestive of ADHD. The patient expressed concern that if her reading skills did not improve, she would not graduate from high school and would therefore be "unemployed and homeless like my mom."

The school agreed to perform IQ and achievement testing; reading disorder and disorder of written expression were identified. An individualized education program (IEP) was created for Viola, providing resource teaching and one-on-one language arts tutoring. Trials of three stimulants each resulted in moodiness, insomnia, and distressing motor tics. Her appetite also decreased markedly, and over a period of 4 months, she lost 11 pounds. Atomoxetine was well tolerated and, in the grandmother's estimation, the time Viola spent on homework was halved. Viola was referred to a mentoring program and paired with a college student, who encouraged and reinforced her interest in furthering her education.

DIAGNOSING ADHD IN CHILDREN

The diagnosis of ADHD is a clinical one based on a comprehensive medical and psychosocial history in addition to current observations of the patient's behavior across multiple settings. School, home, and social interactions are typically the main areas of concern. Symptoms and functional impairment must begin early in life, persist over time, and be present in more than one domain of the patient's life; that is, ADHD cannot be diagnosed if the patient's problems are limited to the home environment, while functioning and development in academic and social situations are normal. No laboratory blood test, neuropsychological test, or imaging study alone can definitively make or rule out the diagnosis. Table 18.2 lists the diagnostic criteria for ADHD. Note that there are four subtypes of ADHD based on the symptom cluster in which the patient exhibits at least six of nine symptoms: combined type (inattentive and hyperactive-impulsive), predominantly inattentive type, predominantly hyperactive-impulsive type, and ADHD not otherwise specified.

When considering the diagnosis of ADHD, it is critical to remember that no single source of data is adequate for an accurate diagnosis. We emphasize that there must usually be at least three major data sources: (a) developmental history and risk assessment, (b) parent and teacher rating scales, and (c) neuropsychological evaluation.

Developmental History and Risk Assessment

A comprehensive developmental history is essential to document early risk factors and to establish that the disorder did indeed demonstrate onset during early childhood. Routine inquiry regarding the genetic, medical, temperament, and environmental risks for ADHD is beneficial in at least three ways.

Table 18.2 Diagnostic Criteria for Attention-Deficit/Hyperactivity Disorder

A. Either 1 or 2
   1) Six (or more) of the following symptoms of **inattention** have persisted for at least 6 months to a degree that is maladaptive and inconsistent with developmental level:

Inattention
    a) Often fails to give close attention to details or makes careless mistakes in schoolwork, work, or other activities
    b) Often has difficulty sustaining attention in tasks or play activities
    c) Often does not seem to listen when spoken to directly
    d) Often does not follow through on instructions and fails to finish schoolwork, chores, or duties in the workplace (not due to oppositional behavior or failure to understand instructions)
    e) Often has difficulty organizing tasks and activities
    f) Often avoids, dislikes, or is reluctant to engage in tasks that require sustained mental effort (such as schoolwork or homework)
    g) Often loses things necessary for tasks or activities (e.g., toys, school assignments, pencils, books, or tools)
    h) Is often easily distracted by extraneous stimuli
    i) Is often forgetful in daily activities

   2) Six (or more) of the following symptoms of **hyperactivity-impulsivity** have persisted for at least 6 months to a degree that is maladaptive and inconsistent with developmental level:

Hyperactivity
    a) Often fidgets with hands or feet or squirms in seat
    b) Often leaves seat in classroom or in other situations in which remaining seated is expected
    c) Often runs about or climbs excessively in situations in which it is inappropriate (in adolescents or adults, may be limited to subjective feelings of restlessness)
    d) Often has difficulty playing or engaging in leisure activities quietly
    e) Is often "on the go" or often acts as if "driven by a motor"
    f) Often talks excessively

Impulsivity
    g) Often blurts out answers before questions have been completed
    h) Often has difficulty awaiting turn
    i) Often interrupts or intrudes on others (e.g., butts into conversations or games)

B. Some hyperactive/impulsive or inattentive symptoms that caused impairment were present before 7 years of age.

C. Some impairment from the symptoms is present in 2 or more settings (e.g., at school [or work] or at home).

D. There must be clear evidence of clinically significant impairment in social, academic, or occupational functioning.

E. The symptoms do not occur exclusively during the course of a pervasive developmental disorder, schizophrenia, or other psychotic disorder and are not better accounted for by another mental disorder (mood disorder, anxiety disorder, dissociative disorder, or personality disorder).

Code based on type:

314.01 Attention-Deficit/Hyperactivity Disorder, Combined Type: if both criteria A1 and A2 are met for the past 6 months

314.00 Attention-Deficit/Hyperactivity Disorder, Predominantly Inattentive Type: if criterion A1 is met but criterion A2 is not met for the past 6 months

314.01 Attention-Deficit/Hyperactivity Disorder, Predominantly Hyperactive, Impulsive Type: if criterion A2 is met but criterion A1 is not met for the past 6 months

314.9 Attention-Deficit/Hyperactivity Disorder Not Otherwise Specified

Reprinted with permission from the *Diagnostic and Statistical Manual of Mental Disorders*, 4th ed. (DSM-IV). Copyright 1994, American Psychiatric Association.

First, a careful inquiry, couched in a developmental framework, often stimulates recall and associations regarding other important information. The entire context of the present clinical problem, including family psychiatric history, early development, school history, family environment, previous response to treatment, and current functioning are generally required. Much of this can be obtained efficiently by mailing to the parent or guardian appropriate forms prior to the clinical interview.

Second, the inquiry serves to convince the parents that the clinician is serious in believing that ADHD has important biological roots. At the same time, it affirms the importance of environmental factors that may contribute to the exacerbation of symptoms and can be altered by behavioral intervention. Often, this approach counteracts the parent-blaming that the patient's parents have experienced from family, school, or professional contacts. In fact, forming such an alliance with the parents permits and encourages them to admit voluntarily some of the actual shortcomings in their parenting practices. Parents are much more willing to admit that they have handled a problem poorly if the clinician has made it clear that they did not "cause" the problem in the first place.

Third, it is essential to identify the various risks and protective factors to make a valid diagnosis. A family history of diagnosed—or symptomatology suggestive of—ADHD, oppositional defiant disorder (ODD), and antisocial behavior is helpful in the overall assessment of risk factors. Similarly, stress during and after pregnancy as well as fetal exposure to toxins such as cocaine or nicotine are additional risk factors that may have important implications for both biological and psychosocial effects on development.

Parent and Teacher Rating Scales

It is especially important to attend to the relationship between the child and his or her parents and teachers. Children with ADHD are consistently more negative, off task, and less compliant than normal children; as a result, parents of children with ADHD frequently are more harsh, negative, and avoiding of their children, beginning in preschool and worsening in adolescence with the development of conduct problems (Anastopoulos, Guevremont, Shelton, & DuPaul, 1992). In fact, patients often present for mental health services when these problems begin to generalize outside the family to school and peer settings. Thus, it is essential to obtain systematic information from parents or main adult caregivers and from the child's schoolteachers.

Norm-based rating scales offer the most efficient way to collect information about both internalizing and externalizing behavioral disturbances at home and school (APA, 2000b). These instruments generally demonstrate high reliability and validity and effectively discriminate between well-diagnosed ADHD and other disorders. In contrast to disruptive behavior symptoms, parents and teachers often do not recognize internalizing symptoms of anxiety and depression. Because identification of these commonly comorbid disorders is important for both diagnosis and successful treatment planning, it is important to assess for them when evaluating a child for ADHD. A compendium of commonly utilized instruments is presented in Table 18.3.

Neuropsychological Evaluation

Despite abundant data linking abnormalities in brain function to psychopathology, standard criteria for identifying mental disorders in children and adolescents have largely relied on behavioral symptoms. Unfortunately, the diagnostic criteria for ADHD do not operationalize certain critical neuropsychological constructs (distractibility, sustained attention, impulse inhibition, visual and phonological decoding skills, and visuospatial-organizational skills) that ADHD and its comorbid conditions often have in common.

Although there is no pathognomonic test finding that leads unequivocally to a diagnosis of ADHD, a brief neuropsychological evaluation is often helpful in gaining insight into some of the possible variations in ADHD that present in clinical practice as well as in understanding the comorbid cognitive and academic problems that often accompany the disorder. One such measure, the CPT, is now in widespread clinical use for evaluating sustained attention in children with ADHD and other neuropsychiatric disorders.

Table 18.3 Rating Scales Used in ADHD Evaluations of Adults and Children

For adults
- Conners Adult ADHD Rating Scales (CAARS) (Multi-Health Systems Inc., 1998)
- Conners Adult ADHD Diagnostic Interview for DSM-IV™ (CAADID) (Multi-Health Systems Inc., 2001)
- Wender Utah Rating Scale (WURS) (University of Utah, 1993)

For children and adolescents
- Conners-March Developmental Questionnaire (CMDQ) (Multi-Health Systems Inc., 1999)
- Conners Parent Rating Scale (CPRS), revised version: Long Form, ADHD Index Scale (Multi-Health Systems Inc., 1997)
- Conners Teacher Rating Scale (CTRS), revised version: Long Form, ADHD Index Scale (Multi-Health Systems Inc., 1997)
- Swanson, Nolan, and Pelham Rating Scale (SNAP-IV) (University of California, 1995)
- Multidimensional Anxiety Scale for Children (MASC) (Multi-Health Systems Inc., 1997)
- Children's Depression Inventory (CDI) (Multi-Health Systems Inc., 1992)

The CPT, which comes in a variety of commercial formats administered on a personal desktop computer, is a brief (15-minute) and objective method of assessing a variety of functions of arousal, vigilance, and impulse control. Because of the subjectivity of most history, interview, and rating methods, the CPT may help validate and confirm neuropsychological deficits that might otherwise be considered by parents and teachers as motivational. Conversely, the absence of demonstrated performance deficits may point to attention deficits that are secondary to poor motivation rather than dysfunction in neurocognitive processing. It is important, however, that the CPT not be presented to parents as "the test for ADHD." Because of its formality and the fact that it is administered and scored via computer, laypersons often have misconceptions regarding its diagnostic value. With odds ratios less than 1.2 (equivalent to sensitivity and specificity less than 70%), commercially available CPTs are an adjunctive measure in the assessment of ADHD and cannot substitute for a thorough history, interview, and review of patient records.

Most important, levels of intelligence (IQ) and educational achievement must be ascertained to determine whether a comorbid LD is present. Children with a significantly lower verbal than performance IQ may suffer from reading or language processing disorders that require specific remediation, and such a discrepancy usually indicates the need for further testing to determine whether the phonological or visual subtype of reading disorder is present. Children with a markedly lower performance than verbal IQ also are quite common.

These children may represent a distinct subtype of ADHD characterized more by inattention, disorganization, and daydreaming (distraction by interoceptive cues) than by hyperactive-impulsive behavior (Pennington, 1991). On neuropsychological testing, impaired visuospatial-organizational functioning is commonly present, and LDs typically involve mathematics, reading comprehension, and expressive written language. Often, the clinician can identify this particular pattern of cognitive deficits simply by inquiring about these problems while taking the medical history and reviewing previous psychoeducational evaluations.

Once a child is identified as having ADHD, a comprehensive psychoeducational evaluation is necessary owing to the elevated rate of comorbid LDs in ADHD. Current recommendations call for the administration of the Wechsler Intelligence Scale for Children–Third Edition (WISC-III) and the Woodcock-Johnson Psychoeducational Battery.

DIAGNOSING ADHD IN ADULTS

The issue of ADHD in adults has received considerable media attention in recent years, leading to concerns about overdiagnosis. It is important for clinicians to keep an open mind, recalling the scientific data regarding the persistence of symptoms and impairment into adulthood. Parents often seek personal evaluation after their children are diagnosed with ADHD, giving them insight into their childhood experiences. In many cases, the diagnosis of ADHD was obscured by comorbid psychiatric disorders, or the patient was simply deemed a poor student by parents and teachers. In others, ADHD escaped detection because of the patient's superior IQ, learned coping strategies, compliant behavior, or structured and tolerant home and school environments (Ratey, Greenberg, Bemporad, & Lindem, 1992). Adults with ADHD may exhibit a particular profile of impaired performance in tasks that demand sustained attention, set shifting, and use of working memory (Gallagher & Blader, 2001).

Although a similar method of assessment involving history, rating scales, and neuropsychological testing is appropriate for adults, the diagnosis is intrinsically more difficult because of problems related to the patient's retrospective recall, the absence of contemporary school data, and the increased prevalence of comorbidity, particularly substance abuse (Shaffer, 1994). A four-pronged approach is recommended for establishing a diagnosis of adult ADHD in clinical practice:

1. Use a standardized form of retrospective self-report of childhood symptoms (see Table 18.3).
2. Confirm by interview that the developmental course fits the general picture of ADHD in childhood (symptoms that appeared early; both academic and behavioral problems in school; significant impairment in social and parental relationships; early hyperactive-impulsive behavior that may decrease with age; and inattentive symptoms becoming central in adulthood).
3. Use third-party informants, preferably parents (who can fill out a childhood rating scale as they recall their child prior to age 7 years), or a spouse or sibling who can report on current behavior. If possible, obtain childhood school academic records and psychoeducational testing to confirm parent and patient reports.
4. Establish neuropsychological deficits by testing with CPT, the Verbal scale of the

Wechsler Adult Intelligence Scale (WAIS), the Block Design subtest of the WAIS, and a standardized reading and mathematics assessment.

Although imperfect, these four methods taken together provide both objective and historical information to substantiate the adult residual of ADHD and in turn provide a sound basis for developing a treatment plan. It is vital to cover the full diagnostic spectrum when evaluating adults with this disorder. Depression, anxiety, substance abuse, and the effects of years of aversive life experiences and personal and professional underachievement often require that treatment take into consideration complex existential issues, as well as problem-focused psychological interventions targeting specific psychiatric symptoms. Pharmacological treatment alone will not restore self-esteem, balance a checkbook, stabilize a marriage, or permit a patient to realize career goals; confronting simplistic expectations about the benefits of medication is better achieved when the range of psychological issues confronting the adult patient with ADHD has been carefully defined.

DIFFERENTIAL DIAGNOSIS AND COMORBIDITY

The differential diagnosis in ADHD is a broad one, encompassing a range of both psychological and medical conditions. A practical, but by no means exhaustive, list of diagnostic considerations is shown in Table 18.4. In a primary care setting, the relative number of patients who have a medical condition that accounts for their ADHD-like symptoms is small, but as a rule, a survey of the patient's general health should be undertaken. When working with children, a review of systems together with an assessment of nutritional status and progression along standardized height and weight curves forms a reasonable baseline. The decision to order laboratory tests to check for anemia, thyroid dysfunction, lead poisoning, and substance abuse should be based on the history and physical exam. Obstructive sleep apnea is one disorder that can easily be missed if the interviewer does not probe for the symptoms

Table 18.4 Differential Diagnosis of ADHD in Children and Adults

Age-appropriate behaviors in an active child

Patient who does not manifest clinically significant impairment

Ongoing neglect, trauma, or abuse

Psychiatric
  Posttraumatic stress disorder
  Adjustment disorders
  Depressive disorders
  Anxiety disorders
  Mental retardation
  Autism spectrum disorders
  Borderline intellectual functioning
  Bipolar spectrum disorders
  Oppositional defiant disorder
  Conduct disorder
  Substance abuse disorders
  Personality disorders
  Dissociative disorders

Medical
  Obstructive sleep apnea
  Hyperthyroidism
  Thyroid hormone resistance
  Anemia
  Vision and/or hearing impairment
  Side effects of medication
  Seizure disorder
  Traumatic brain injury
  Brain tumors (frontal, parietal, temporal)
  Central nervous system infection
  Environmental exposure (e.g., lead)
  In utero exposure (e.g., cocaine, nicotine, alcohol)
  Sydenham's chorea
  Chronic obstructive pulmonary disease
  Renal or hepatic insufficiency
  Multiple sclerosis
  Anoxic encephalopathy
  Dementia
  Delirium

of loud snoring, labored breathing, and periodic apnea during sleep. In children, the diurnal effects of obstructive sleep apnea can mimic the presentation of ADHD, producing inattention, oppositionality, decreased academic performance, and motor restlessness (Hansen & Vandenber, 1997). Insufficient sleep because of environmental factors should also be considered.

Perhaps the most important considerations are the first three items listed in Table 18.4. First, the child may be exhibiting a normal variant of age-

and developmentally appropriate behaviors. It is important to keep in mind that parental distress, although essential for the evaluation of the overall clinical picture, is not a criterion for the diagnosis of ADHD. When parents are struggling with inappropriate expectations for their child's behavior, reassurance, psychoeducation around developmental norms, and simple parenting tips may be all that is needed. Second, it must be remembered that, even if a child exhibits a full complement of ADHD symptoms, the diagnostic criteria are not met if the child does not show evidence of impairment in two or more settings, along with clinically significant impairment in school, at work, or in social relationships (APA, 2000a). Third, as in all clinical encounters with children, it is of utmost importance to explore the possibility that the presenting symptoms are best accounted for by neglect, trauma, or abuse.

In terms of the psychiatric differential diagnosis of ADHD, disorders from every sphere of the *DSM-IV-TR* are relevant. One of the most common confounding conditions is posttraumatic distress disorder, which can effectively mimic ADHD in terms of distractibility, inattentiveness, and impairment in academic and social functioning. Similarly, children with mood or anxiety disorders are often thought by parents or teachers to be exhibiting signs of ADHD. A small percentage of children will have academic difficulty secondary to subaverage intelligence, LD, or both, but not to ADHD.

Disorders of adjustment are common in the wake of major changes in a child's life, such as parental divorce, a family move, or a change in schools; the resulting disruption in functioning should not be attributed to ADHD, particularly if the child did not display symptoms prior to age 7 years. The developmental disorders, including autistic disorder and its accompanying spectrum disorders, and mental retardation should be the focus of clinical concern in cases when they are present. Finally, severe and persistent mental illnesses such as bipolar disorder and schizophrenia can present in childhood, and it is good practice to consider the mood and psychotic disorders whenever a mental health consultation is performed.

A range of psychiatric conditions can co-occur with ADHD, and comorbidity is present in as many as two thirds of clinically referred children. Grouped with ADHD in the "disruptive behavior disorders" are ODD and conduct disorder (CD). ODD and CD are comorbid with ADHD in 25% to 35% of children (Green & Atkins, 1999). ODD includes persistent symptoms of "negativistic, defiant, disobedient, and hostile behaviors toward authority figures," and patients with CD exhibit "a pattern of behavior in which the basic rights of others or major age-appropriate social norms or rules are violated" (APA, 2000a, p. 85). The coexisting association between ADHD and anxiety disorders has been estimated at 25% (Green & Atkins, 1999), and the coexistence of mood disorders with ADHD is approximately 18% (American Academy of Pediatrics, 1996). Approximately 20% to 25% of children with ADHD also have one or more LDs, although LD appears to be independent of ADHD (Pliszka, 2000). Because patient functioning and response to treatment are affected by the presence of comorbidities, a thorough evaluation for ADHD always includes assessment for coexisting conditions.

TREATMENT: PSYCHOSOCIAL AND PHARMACOLOGICAL APPROACHES

Overview

Although pharmacological treatment with stimulant medication is the most common form of treatment for patients with ADHD, psychosocial interventions are an essential component of treatment for the majority of children with the disorder (March, Wells, & Conners, 1996). For example, psychosocial treatments may be the only treatment available for ADHD children who do not respond to treatment with stimulants, for children who experience intolerable side effects, or for children whose parents refuse informed consent for the use of medication.

For other children with ADHD who display comorbid LD and disruptive behavior disorders, there are many reasons to recommend that psychosocial treatment be combined with pharmacotherapy. First, exclusive treatment with stimulant medication is not maximally effective because many have a clinically significant level of residual symptoms, even at very high doses. Second, stimulant medication may not affect the full range of symptoms in a child with ADHD and other comorbid conditions. Although improvements may be seen in the core ADHD symptoms (i.e., attention, hyperactivity, impulsivity), patients may continue to exhibit oppositional and aggressive behavior, academic underachievement, and poor peer and family relationships. These domains are potentially amenable to psychosocial treatment. A final limitation of stimulant monotherapy has to do with its applicability to in-home behavior problems. Many parents or physicians limit the use of stimulants to school hours during the 9 months of the academic year in an effort to avoid growth suppression, sleep disruption, and other medication side effects. This leaves parents to their own devices in managing impulsive, oppositional, and disruptive behavior in the late afternoons, evenings, weekends, and summers. For all of the above reasons, psychosocial treatment continues to be utilized and studied, especially in combination with stimulant medication.

Psychosocial Treatment With Children

Psychosocial treatment for pediatric ADHD patients optimally involves a clinical behavior therapy approach that focuses on the child, the parents, and the school (Pelham & Fabiano, 2000). Intervention with parents typically takes the form of parent training (PT), also known as parent management training, which is designed to teach parents skills and techniques for managing disruptive, impulsive, and oppositional behaviors in the home and in the community (Wells et al., 2000). Intervention in the school takes the form of consultation with teachers regarding the establishment of behavior management systems in the classroom. In addition, systems that tie the school and home together in a direct, cooperative effort are increasingly utilized for improving school behavior and academic performance. Multimodal treatment has become the standard of care for ADHD.

Parent Training

In PT for ADHD, parents are taught a specific set of behavior management skills geared toward the behavioral excesses and deficits displayed by their children (Mabe, Turner, & Josephson, 2001). Common targets in PT programs for ADHD include improving the general family emotional climate, parent skills for noting and positively reinforcing children's prosocial behavior, and parent skills for confronting disruptive behavior with effective antecedents and consequences. For example, parents are taught skills such as (a) spending structured, positive time with their children; (b) consistently attending to compliance, also known as "catch your child being good," and applying immediate reinforcers and verbal compliments on these occasions; (c) teaching their children to engage in independent, on-task behavior; (d) giving effective instructions and establishing developmentally appropriate rules and expectations with their children; and (e) applying very specific, predetermined consequences to negative child behaviors.

Common child behavior targets for children with ADHD are (a) noncompliance to parental instructions and other oppositional behavior; (b) aggression in the home with family members, relatives, and guests; (c) impulsive, disruptive behaviors within the family; and (d) inability to engage in independent behavior while the parent is busy. Because youngsters with ADHD frequently present management problems outside the home, parents are also taught to design and implement behavior management programs for use on outings such as shopping, dining out, church, or visiting friends and relatives. Consistent application of rewards and consequences gradually shapes the patient's behavior. Innovative PT programs for ADHD have included stress management for parents as well as training parents to become advocates for their child in the school system.

Despite the fact that PT has become almost a sine qua non of the psychosocial treatment of ADHD (Cantwell, 1996), there is a lack of evidence that combining PT with medication results in better outcomes than those achieved with medication alone (MTA Cooperative Group, 1999). Despite a burgeoning literature, fundamental scientific questions remain regarding effect size, scope, and durability of treatment with PT (Kazdin, 1997). Another limitation is that PT is not an option for all ADHD families for a variety of reasons. Among these are third-party payers' reluctance to cover the procedure, a lack of

dissemination, and the inability of some parents to commit to this treatment. Nonetheless, because PT is effective as monotherapy for ADHD, it remains the treatment of choice for children who do not respond to pharmacotherapy, whose parents refuse informed consent for medication, or who are forced to discontinue pharmacological treatment because of adverse events. One manualized, short-term, empirically validated PT system is parent-child interaction therapy (Hembree-Kigin & McNeil, 1995). A systematic review of the evidence for PT is available through the Cochrane Library (Zwi, Pindoria, & Joughlin, 2003).

School Interventions

A major aspect of the psychosocial treatment of ADHD is the use of behavior management strategies in the classroom. Many school personnel are familiar with the principles that are involved owing to the large number of children diagnosed with ADHD and the legal requirement that they create a 504 plan or IEP for each child who needs one.

A variety of different behavioral techniques have been developed for use in schools (Altmeier & Horwitz, 1997). A cueing system can prompt a teacher to monitor a child's behavior regularly and to deliver positive attention at frequent intervals (e.g., every 15 to 30 minutes) and to ignore negative behaviors whenever possible. A token economy may be established in which academic performance and behavioral targets are rewarded, and there is a "response cost" for inappropriate behavior. Consequences for negative behavior can be individual or group based. Group rewards can be effective when peer attention for disruptive behavior is competing with teacher-dispensed rewards for prosocial behavior.

A key facet of school-based interventions for ADHD is the continuity between the classroom and the home. The child is taught that compliant school behaviors will benefit him or her at home. A DRC system ties the family and school together in a cooperative effort. Teachers write a brief report or award a sticker at the end of the day (e.g., smiling face vs. frowning face; green light vs. red light). The first criterion the child must fulfill to receive a daily reward (e.g., video game, television, or computer time) is successful home delivery of the DRC. Parents then deliver backup rewards and consequences at home. Importantly, a bad day or failure to bring home the DRC on one day has no effect on the child's opportunity to earn privileges on the next. If the child has received positive DRCs on a prespecified number of days, a larger backup reward may be earned on the weekend. Eventually, the system is gradually rescinded when compliant behavior has become habitual. The key is constructing the system so that the locus of control lies within the child; inevitably, the child will act in his or her best interests.

Intervention With the Child

Individual psychotherapy with ADHD children is often of limited utility, but may be required if comorbid mood, anxiety, or substance abuse disorders are present. For some children, individual work focusing on themes of self-esteem, demoralization, and a lack of competence and mastery can be helpful in engaging the child in a therapeutic alliance and improving compliance with treatment. Anger management, impulse control, and improvement in social skills are other areas that may be addressed in individual psychotherapy. Children with ADHD who are in foster care or whose parents have divorced may benefit from a mentoring program that pairs them with a young adult. An organizational intervention that many students employ is a homework planner in which assignments are recorded as they are given throughout the day.

Pelham and Hoza (1996) developed an 8-week intensive summer treatment program that is now employed by several university-based clinics around the country. Treatment consists of 3 hours of daily classroom work and several recreation-based group activities during which social skills are taught and reinforced. In addition, sports skills training sessions are included because children with ADHD often suffer from poor motor skills and inattentiveness. A "buddy system" is utilized to facilitate the formation of dyadic friendships. Summer school staffers utilize behavioral management techniques in working with the children throughout the 9-hour day. Children also receive stimulant medication during the

camp day to maximize the combined treatment effects of medication and this intensive psychosocial treatment. The cost of the intensive, 8-week summer treatment program is less than a 1-year course of weekly individual psychotherapy, and it appears to have superior effectiveness in addressing the deficits of these children.

Treatment of the Adult With ADHD

Adults seen for treatment of ADHD display a wide range of clinical presentations. One group displays a high rate of chemical dependency and antisocial behavior, with the rate of antisocial personality disorder in some follow-up samples as high as 25%. Another group with perhaps greater cognitive endowment and protective psychosocial factors presents with a chronic sense of occupational and social underachievement and resulting demoralization. Taken as a whole, adults with ADHD display a high rate of comorbidity (Biederman et al., 1993), with one clinic reporting that just 12% of adults with ADHD had no comorbid psychiatric diagnosis (Shekim, Asarnow, Hess, Zaucha, & Wheeler, 1990).

Therefore, a primary task in working with adults with ADHD is the identification and treatment of comorbid disorders. Education for patients and their families about ADHD comprises another important aspect of treatment, and supportive cognitive–behavioral individual psychotherapy is often helpful in dealing with the losses attributable to the disorder, as well as the incorporation of a new set of cognitive abilities that are suddenly acquired in adult life with successful medical treatment.

With the growing societal awareness of adult ADHD, a number of approaches have been devised to meet the needs of individuals who are eager to improve on what many perceive as a lifetime of heretofore unexplained disorganization and underachievement. A burgeoning self-help literature, represented by Hallowell and Ratey's (1994) *Driven to Distraction: Recognizing and Coping With Attention Deficit Disorder From Childhood Through Adulthood*, brought notice to the disorder and offered coping strategies designed to improve functioning, productivity, relationships, and overall life satisfaction. The National Institutes of Health has begun sponsoring clinical trials of cognitive–behavioral therapy for adults with ADHD, and the results will help guide future best practices treatment strategies. A new intervention, ADHD life coaching, has sprung up around the country, offering assistance to adults with ADHD; clinicians should inform patients that this approach has not been scientifically investigated or empirically validated.

Pharmacological Treatment of Children

From an evidence-based medicine (EBM) perspective, the stimulants methylphenidate, dextroamphetamine, amphetamine-dextroamphetamine, dexmethylphenidate, and pemoline are first-line agents and the standard of care in the medical treatment of ADHD. This is based on randomized, controlled clinical trials that have repeatedly demonstrated the efficacy of these compounds.

More is known about the use of stimulants in children than about any other pediatric medication. The scientific literature on the use of stimulants in school-aged children includes over 100 trials involving more than 4,500 children; the body of literature on preschool children, adolescents, and adults is smaller, but is rapidly expanding. In addition to short-term efficacy studies, the demonstrated benefits of stimulant treatment have been extended to 14 months with the publication of the landmark MTA study (MTA Cooperative Group, 1999).

Notwithstanding the controversy that often surrounds the administration of controlled substances to children, stimulants are generally effective, well tolerated, and—most important—carry the potential for dramatic improvements in the functioning of the child at home, in school, and in the community. Much of the scientific literature has been based on the study of immediate-release preparations of stimulants such as Ritalin and Dextrostat. Although clinically efficacious, these compounds have the disadvantage of short serum half-life; this gives rise to clinical issues such as maintaining adherence to a regimen that calls for dosing three or four times daily, frequent peaks and valleys of stimulant effect, and the stigma some children and their guardians feel when the child is sent to the school nurse for repeated administration of medication. A variety of sustained release stimulant preparations has become available, such as Adderall-XR, Concerta, Metadate-CD, and Ritalin-LA. The long-acting stimulants have several advantages: medication effects that last through the school day, fewer serum level peaks and valleys, and (in theory) less diversion potential because of a lack of a euphoric effect sometimes observed with immediate-release preparations.

Approximately 85% to 90% of children with ADHD will respond if prescribed sequential adequate trials of three stimulants (Elia, 1993). However, some children will be stimulant nonresponders, others will discontinue stimulants because of adverse events, and some guardians will wish to explore pharmacotherapy but refuse informed consent for a stimulant because of personal preference. For these families and their physicians, remaining options include the heterocyclic antidepressant bupropion, the tricyclic antidepressants (TCAs), and the alpha-adrenergic agonists clonidine and guanfacine. In addition, a nonstimulant compound, atomoxetine, was introduced in the U.S. market in 2002. Atomoxetine is not a controlled substance and will therefore likely find a niche with primary care clinicians who treat patients with ADHD, if efficacy reports are replicated in clinical practice and adverse drug reactions are infrequent.

Bupropion demonstrated positive effects on hyperactivity, conduct, and cognition in one clinical trial (Conners et al., 1996), and in another study, bupropion appeared not statistically significantly different from methylphenidate (Barrickman et al., 1995). In clinical practice, it can be combined with a stimulant when a comorbid depressive disorder is present or used as an augmentation strategy for patients who are partial responders to stimulant monotherapy.

The TCAs imipramine, desipramine, and nortriptyline have all shown benefit in controlled trials in ADHD (March et al., 1996). Because of the narrow margin of safety, the potential for cardiovascular complications, and their lethality in overdose, TCAs are used with caution in patients with ADHD and are generally reserved for cases in which other treatment strategies have failed. Baseline cardiac assessment and periodic electrocardiogram monitoring is mandatory.

The alpha-adrenergic agonists clonidine and guanfacine have limited support in the literature as monotherapies in ADHD, particularly with respect to cognitive processing and academic performance. Clinical experience suggests that they may be useful in curbing activity level, improving frustration tolerance, and decreasing aggression and defiance in a subgroup of children with ADHD. Although widely used successfully in conjunction with stimulants, this practice is controversial because of a series of case reports regarding the deaths of four children while taking a combination of methylphenidate and clonidine (Popper, 1995).

A variety of other agents, including neuroleptics, selective serotonin reuptake inhibitors, anticonvulsants, and lithium, have been tried as treatments for ADHD in children (Green, 1995). However, unless there is a comorbid indication, their use in treating ADHD symptoms is not recommended. This is especially true for the low-potency neuroleptic thioridazine. Once a popular treatment for "minimal brain dysfunction" and "hyperkinesis," its use as a behavioral control agent in the child with ADHD is contraindicated because of the potential for neuroleptic-related side effects, including extrapyramidal symptoms, cognitive blunting, and especially tardive dyskinesia.

A user-friendly, straightforward algorithm for the medical management of childhood ADHD was published by the Texas Children's Medication Algorithm Project (the Texas algorithm; Pliszka et al., 2000). It provides the busy clinician with a concise six-stage treatment decision tree that includes dosing guidelines and that is based on an expert consensus emerging from an EBM review of the scientific literature.

Pharmacological Treatment of Adults

Pharmacotherapy of adults with ADHD is guided by the same principles as for children. Baseline and ongoing assessment of target symptoms is undertaken. As in children, stimulants are first-line therapy for adults with ADHD. The dose-response relationship appears to be more variable in adults, and adults may be more sensitive to both the therapeutic and side effects of the stimulants. The body of scientific literature addressing the treatment of ADHD in adults is small, albeit growing; for now, the clinician is faced with an upward extrapolation from the pooled experience with children, in much the same way that a downward extrapolation has been the rule in treating psychiatric disorders in children for which we only have replicated data in the adult population.

TREATMENT COURSE AND REFERRAL

As noted, a significant proportion of children with ADHD will continue to have symptoms and impairment into adulthood. Notwithstanding this fact, many parents will ask their clinician, "How long does she have to be on medication?" or "When will she grow out of this?" At such times, it is useful to make comparisons with other chronic medical conditions and simply to state that treatment makes sense only in the event that the family feels the observed benefits outweigh the risks, including the risks of *not* treating the ADHD. Reassurance is offered in the form of a reminder that the "consent" in informed consent rests at all times *entirely* with the patient and the patient's family.

Psychoeducation continues with a discussion of the natural history of the disorder. Cantwell (1985) described three broad categories of outcomes in untreated ADHD. The first is described as the developmental delay outcome, which occurs in up to 30% of patients. These children cease manifesting impairing symptoms sometime during adolescence or early adulthood. The second category is the continual display outcome, occurring in about 40% of subjects. These patients display continuous impairment, along with a host of comorbid (and possibly secondary) psychiatric and social difficulties. The third developmental trajectory Cantwell labeled developmental decay, which is seen in up to 30% of subjects with ADHD. These children not only continue to display ADHD symptoms, but also develop serious psychopathology, such as alcoholism, drug abuse, and antisocial personality disorder.

The decision regarding when to refer to a subspecialist in child and adolescent psychiatry is a complex one. Most primary care physicians are comfortable prescribing stimulants and can utilize the Texas algorithm to excellent advantage.

Psychologists working in primary care practices can provide an array of services to children with ADHD, including individual psychotherapy, psychological and achievement testing, parent training, and coordination of school-based services. In the event of referral, ongoing collaboration with the primary care physician and the child and adolescent psychiatrist is essential.

Pediatricians and family physicians often choose to refer children who do not respond to several stimulant trials and who appear to be candidates for polypharmacy. In cases that appear treatment resistant, consultation may be sought to confirm or clarify the diagnosis. Another common reason for referral is the development of impairing psychiatric comorbidities such as a mood, anxiety, or substance abuse disorder. Many children with prominent aggression, hostility, and a history of violence are referred for evaluation at mental health clinics. Finally, there are a number of indications for which psychiatric referral is strongly recommended, including (a) psychiatric hospitalization; (b) suicidal statements or gestures; (c) signs and symptoms suggestive of severe and persistent mental illness; (d) persistent dangerousness to self or others; (e) persistent nontrivial property destruction; and (f) retention at the end of a school year on academic or behavioral grounds.

SUMMARY

ADHD is a common neuropsychiatric disorder that adversely affects the lives and development of children, adolescents, and adults worldwide. Although the research literature is inconclusive regarding the genetics and neurobiology of ADHD, emerging evidence suggests that the disorder is characterized by variations in specific information processing functions within the central nervous system. Among these are short-term orientation, executive functioning, working memory, sustained attention, impulse suppression, and the regulation of motor behavior—all of which in turn depend on central nervous system regulation of arousal, reward, and coordination mechanisms.

Both genetic and environmental factors appear to play a role in the pathogenesis of ADHD, with the latter clearly critical in the adaptive or maladaptive elaboration of the ADHD symptom picture. Many patients with ADHD have problems beyond those confined to the disorder's core symptoms of inattention, hyperactivity, and impulsivity. Some, such as academic underachievement, poor peer relations, and family conflicts, are often secondary to ADHD; others, such as comorbid psychiatric disorders and LDs, may represent independent neurodevelopmental constraints to normal development. Because the presence of ADHD in a patient can affect the functioning of the patient's entire family, primary care clinicians would do well to screen for signs of increased stress, substance abuse, and depression in family members.

Each child, adolescent, or adult presenting for evaluation of possible ADHD deserves a comprehensive psychological and medical assessment culminating in a problem-focused treatment plan that squares with the treatment preferences of the patient or the patient's guardian. Such plans often call for multimodal treatment utilizing a combination of psychosocial and pharmacological interventions administered by a multidisciplinary treatment team. With these guiding principles, the great majority of persons with ADHD can be restored to an improved developmental trajectory. For this reason, ADHD is one of the most satisfying disorders to treat in the field of mental health.

Limitations are apparent in the scientific literature with regard to several aspects of the treatment of ADHD: (a) long-term outcomes; (b) how best to combine treatments; (c) the quantified impact of medication or psychosocial interventions across divergent outcome measures, sexes, ages, and ADHD diagnostic subtypes; (d) objective assessment procedures; and (e) which patient traits under which circumstances predict treatment response. What we can confidently conclude for now is that the experimental literature is definitive regarding the positive benefits of short-term stimulant treatment for ADHD in children and adolescents. Psychosocial treatments and educational interventions also have demonstrable short-term benefits and may prove to improve long-term outcome substantially, alone or in combination with pharmacotherapy. Thus, it appears that multimodal treatment, thoughtfully applied over time, is most likely to facilitate developmentally appropriate functioning in children, adolescents, and adults with ADHD.

ADDITIONAL RESOURCES

Suggestions for further reading and professional development resources are available at this book's companion Web site: www.primarycarepsych.com.

ACKNOWLEDGMENT   This work was supported in part by an NIMH Scientist Development Award for Clinicians (1-K20-MH00981-01) to Dr. March.

References

Altmeier, W. A., 3rd, & Horwitz, E. (1997). The role of the school in the management of attention deficit hyperactivity disorder. *Pediatric Annals, 26,* 737–744.

American Academy of Pediatrics. (1996). *The classification of child and adolescent mental diagnoses in primary care: Diagnostic and statistical manual for primary care (DSM-PC), child and adolescent version.* Elk Grove Village, IL: Author.

American Psychiatric Association. (1994). *Diagnostic and statistical manual of mental disorders.* 4th ed. Washington, DC: Author.

American Psychiatric Association. (2000a). *Diagnostic and statistical manual of mental disorders text revision: DSM-IV-TR* (4th ed., rev.). Washington, DC: Author.

American Psychiatric Association. (2000b). *Handbook of psychiatric measures.* Washington, DC: Author.

Anastopoulos, A. D., Guevremont, D. C., Shelton, T. L., & DuPaul, G. J. (1992). Parenting stress among families of children with attention deficit hyperactivity disorder. *Journal of Abnormal Child Psychology, 20,* 503–520.

Barkley, R. A. (1998) *Attention-deficit hyperactivity disorder: A handbook for diagnosis and treatment* (2nd ed.). New York: Guilford Press.

Barkley, R. A., Fisher, M., Edelbrock, C. S., & Smallish, L. (1991). The adolescent outcome of hyperactive children diagnosed by research criteria. III: Mother–child interactions, family

conflicts, and maternal psychopathology. *Journal of Child Psychology and Psychiatry, 32,* 233–256.

Barrickman, L. L., Perry, P. J., Allen, A. J., Kuperman, S., Arndt, S. V., Herrmann, K. J., & Schumacher, E. (1995). Bupropion versus methylphenidate in the treatment of attention deficit hyperactivity disorder. *Journal of the American Academy of Child and Adolescent Psychiatry, 35,* 649–657.

Biederman, J., Faraone, S. V., Spencer, T., Wilens, T., Norman, D., Lapey, K. A., Mick, E., Lehman, B. K., & Doyle, A. (1993). Patterns of psychiatric comorbidity, cognition, and psychosocial functioning in adults with attention deficit hyperactivity disorder. *American Journal of Psychiatry, 150,* 1792–1798.

Bird, H. R., Gould, M. S., & Staghezza, B. M. (1993). Patterns of diagnostic comorbidity in a community sample of children aged 9 through 16 years. *Journal of the American Academy of Child and Adolescent Psychiatry, 32,* 361–368.

Cantwell, D. P. (1985). Hyperactive children grown up. What have we learned about what happens to them? *Archives of General Psychiatry, 42,* 1026–1028.

Cantwell, D. P. (1996). Attention deficit disorder: A review of the past 10 years. *Journal of the American Academy of Child and Adolescent Psychiatry, 35,* 978–987.

Clements, S. D., & Peters, J. E. (1962). Minimal brain dysfunction in the school-aged child. *Archives of General Psychiatry, 6,* 185–197.

Conners, C. K., Casat, C. D., Gualtieri, C. T., Weller, E., Reader, M., Reiss, A., Weller, R. A., Khayrallah, M., & Ascher, J. (1996). Bupropion hydrochloride in attention deficit disorder with hyperactivity. *Journal of the American Academy of Child and Adolescent Psychiatry, 35,* 1314–1321.

Edwards, M. C., Schulz, E. G., & Long, N. (1995). The role of the family in the assessment of attention deficit hyperactivity disorder. *Clinical Psychology Review, 15,* 375–394.

Elia, J. (1993). Drug treatment for hyperactive children. *Drugs, 46,* 863–871.

Faraone, S. V., Biederman, J., Spencer, T. J., Wilens, T., Seidman, L. J., Mick, E., & Doyle, A. (2000). Attention-deficit/hyperactivity in adults: An overview. *Biological Psychiatry, 48,* 9–20.

Gallagher, R., & Blader, J. (2001). The diagnosis and neuropsychological assessment of adult attention deficit/hyperactivity disorder: Scientific study and practical guidelines. *Annals of the New York Academy of Science, 931,* 148–171.

Goldman, L. S., Genel, M., Bezman, R. J., & Slanetz, P. J. (1998). Diagnosis and treatment of attention-deficit/hyperactivity disorder in children and adolescents. *Journal of the American Medical Association, 279,* 1100–1107.

Green, M., Wong, M., & Atkins, D. (1999) *Diagnosis of attention deficit/hyperactivity disorder: Technical review 3.* Rockville, MD: U.S. Department of Health and Human Services.

Green, W. H. (1995). The treatment of attention-deficit hyperactivity disorder with nonstimulant medications. *Child and Adolescent Psychiatric Clinics of North America, 4,* 169–195.

Hallowell, E. M., & Ratey, J. J. (1994). *Driven to distraction: Recognizing and coping with attention deficit disorder from childhood through adulthood.* New York: Simon and Schuster.

Hansen, D. E., & Vandenber, B. (1997). Neuropsychological features and differential diagnosis of sleep apnea syndrome in children. *Journal of Clinical Child Psychology, 26,* 304–310.

Hembree-Kigin, T. L., & McNeil, C. B. (1995). *Parent–child interaction therapy: A step-by-step guide for clinicians.* New York: Plenum.

Kazdin, A. E. (1997). Parent management training: Evidence, outcomes, and issues. *Journal of the American Academy of Child and Adolescent Psychiatry, 36,* 1349–1356.

Mabe, P. A., Turner, M. K., & Josephson, A. M. (2001). Parent management training. *Child and Adolescent Psychiatric Clinics of North America, 10,* 451–464.

March, J. S., Conners, C. K., Erhardt, D., & Johnston, H. F. (1995). Pharmacotherapy of attention-deficit hyperactivity disorder. In J. W. Jefferson & J. H. Greist (Eds.), *Psychiatric clinics of North America: Annual of drug therapy* (Vol. 2, pp. 187–213). Philadelphia: Saunders.

March, J. S., Wells, K., & Conners, C. K. (1995). Attention-deficit/hyperactivity disorder part I: Assessment and diagnosis. *Journal of Practical Psychiatry and Behavioral Health, 1,* 219–228.

March, J. S., Wells, K, & Conners, C. K. (1996). Attention-deficit/hyperactivity disorder part II: Treatment strategies. *Journal of Practical Psychiatry and Behavioral Health, 2,* 23–32.

MTA Cooperative Group. (1999). A 14-month randomized clinical trial of treatment strategies for attention-deficit/hyperactivity disor-

der. The MTA cooperative group. Multimodal treatment study of children with ADHD. *Archives of General Psychiatry, 56,* 1073–1086.

Pelham, W. E., Jr., & Fabiano, G. A. (2000). Behavior modification. *Child and Adolescent Psychiatric Clinics of North America, 9,* 671–688.

Pelham, W. E., Jr., & Hoza, B. (1996). Intensive treatment: Summer treatment program for children with ADHD. In B. Hoza & P. S. Jensen (Eds.), *Psychosocial treatments for child and adolescent disorders: Empirically based strategies for clinical practice* (pp. 311–341). Washington, DC: American Psychiatric Association.

Pelham, W. E., Jr., & Lang, A. R. (1993). Parental alcohol consumption and deviant child behavior: Laboratory studies of reciprocal effects. *Clinical Psychology Review, 13,* 763–784.

Pennington, B. F. (1991). *Diagnosing learning disorders: A neuropsychological framework.* New York: Guilford Press.

Pliszka, S. R. (2000). Patterns of psychiatric comorbidity with attention-deficit/hyperactivity disorder. *Child and Adolescent Psychiatric Clinics of North America, 9,* 525–540.

Pliszka, S. R., Greenhill, L. R., Crismon, M. L., Sedillo, A., Carlson, C., Conners, C. K., et al. (2000). The Texas children's medication algorithm project: Report of the Texas Consensus Panel on Medication Treatment of Childhood Attention-Deficit/Hyperactivity Disorder. Part I. *Journal of the American Academy of Child and Adolescent Psychiatry, 39,* 908–919.

Popper, C. W. (1995). Combining methylphenidate and clonidine: Pharmacologic questions and news reports about sudden death. *Journal of Child and Adolescent Psychopharmacology, 5,* 157–166.

Ratey, J. J., Greenberg, M. S., Bemporad, J. R., & Lindem, K. J. (1992) Unrecognized attention-deficit hyperactivity disorder in adults presenting for outpatient psychotherapy. *Journal of Child and Adolescent Psychopharmacology, 2,* 267–275.

Rowland, A. S., Umbach, D. M., Stallone, L., Naftel, A. J., Bohlig, E. M., & Sandler, D. P. (2002). Prevalence of medication treatment for attention deficit-hyperactivity disorder among school children in Johnston County, North Carolina. *American Journal of Public Health, 92,* 231–234.

Shaffer, D. (1994). Attention deficit hyperactivity disorder in adults. *American Journal of Psychiatry, 151,* 633–638.

Shekim, W. O., Asarnow, R. F., Hess, E., Zaucha,

K., & Wheeler, N. (1990). A clinical and demographic profile of a sample of adults with attention deficit hyperactivity disorder, residual type. *Comprehensive Psychiatry*, *31*, 416–425.

Still, G. F. (1902). Some abnormal psychical conditions in children. *Lancet*, *1*, 1008–1012, 1077–1082, 1163–1168.

Wells, K. C., Pelham, W. E., Kotkin, R. A., Hoza, B., Abikoff, H. B., Abramowitz, A., et al. (2000). Psychosocial treatment strategies in the MTA study: Rationale, methods, and critical issues in design and implementation. *Journal of Abnormal Child Psychology*, *28*, 483–505.

Wolraich, M. L., Hannah, J. N., Baumgaertel, A., & Feurer, I. (1998). Examination of *DSM-IV* criteria for attention deficit/hyperactivity disorder in a county-wide sample. *Journal of Developmental and Behavioral Pediatrics*, *19*, 162–168.

Wolraich, M. L., Hannah, J. N., Pinnock, T. Y., Baumgaertel, A., & Brown, J. (1996). Comparison of diagnostic criteria for attention-deficit hyperactivity disorder in a county-wide sample. *Journal of the American Academy of Child and Adolescent Psychiatry*, *35*, 319–324.

Zwi, M., Pindoria, S., & Joughlin, C. (2003). Parent training interventions in attention-deficit/hyperactivity disorder [Protocol]. *Cochrane Database of Systematic Reviews*, Volume 3 Retrieved February 3, 2004 via OVID database.

19

Back Pain

Akiko Okifuji
Trish Palmer

Pain related to back problems is a prevalent medical condition and one of the most cited reasons for primary care visits (Bigos, Bowyer, Braen, Brown, Deyo, Haldeman, et al., 1994). A large-scale population study estimated a point prevalence rate of 28.4% and a lifetime incidence rate of 84.1% for low back pain in adults (Cassidy, Carroll, & Cote, 1998). Back pain is quite costly, accounting for over 156 million lost workdays for employed individuals (Bigos et al., 1994). Of those in the United States with back pain, only 15% to 20% seek medical care. For the majority of these individuals, it is a relatively transient problem and remits spontaneously.

A significant number of people with back pain undergo surgery in an attempt to correct a spinal abnormality. Approximately 280,000 back surgeries are performed in the United States each year (Taylor, Deyo, Cherkin, & Kreuter, 1994). Of these surgeries, 85% are laminectomies and discectomies; most of the remainder are spinal fusions. A cost-effectiveness analysis of back surgeries (Malter, Larson, Urban, & Deyo, 1996) indicated that, on average, such surgery extends a healthy quality of life by 5 months. However,

there is a substantial number of patients whose back pain becomes chronic even after "successful" surgery (i.e., the physical pathology is corrected). It is estimated that between 10% and 40% of patients undergoing back surgery become chronic pain patients with "failed back surgery syndrome" (Hoffman, Wheeler, & Deyo, 1993; Turner, Ersek, Herron, & Deyo, 1992).

In the United States, it is estimated that 5.2 million people are disabled by persistent back pain, with half becoming permanently disabled. The costs of chronic back pain to the economy are staggering, with an annual estimated health care expenditure of $20 billion. In addition, the expense associated with indemnity costs, lost tax revenue, and lost productivity is at least three times that of the direct health care costs.

It is important to realize, however, that back pain is not an illness. Rather, it is a descriptive category indicating the presence of pain in the paraspinal region. The onset may be insidious or may follow an injury. The pathophysiology of back pain varies from case to case. It is difficult to describe a "typical back pain patient." A meta-analysis evaluating comprehensive pain treatment programs (Flor, Fydrich, & Turk, 1992) suggested that chronic pain patients (the largest segment of which encompasses those with low back pain) are referred to such programs at an average age of 45 years and after a mean duration of pain of 7 years.

Although most pain syndromes are more prevalent in women than in men, chronic back pain seems to be more equal in sex distribution, probably because of the higher risk among men, who perform physically demanding work and have work-related injuries to the back.

MULTIDIMENSIONAL CONCEPTUALIZATIONS OF PAIN

In general, pain is considered a sign indicating a disease or injury; thus, many people consider it a "physical phenomenon" with an isomorphic relationship between the extent of organic pathology and pain severity. Scholars and clinicians have conventionally accepted this assumption of pain etiology for centuries. On the other hand, when pain could not be explained by physical findings, as in many cases of chronic back pain, pain was considered "mental." This Cartesian mind-body dualism has for centuries been the dominant way of understanding pain.

A major breakthrough in our understanding of pain was the gate-control model of pain (Melzack & Wall, 1965), in which three systems are postulated to be related to the processing of nociceptive (painful) stimulation: sensory-discriminative, motivational-affective, and cognitive-evaluative. All three systems are thought to contribute to the subjective experience of pain. Thus, the gate-control theory specifically includes psychological factors as an integral aspect of the pain experience. It emphasizes the central nervous system mechanisms and provides a physiological basis for the role of psychological factors in chronic pain.

The gate-control model describes the integration of peripheral stimuli with cortical variables, such as mood and anxiety, in the perception of pain. The physiological details of the gate-control model have been challenged, and it has been reformulated more than once. Nevertheless, this theory has had enormous heuristic value in stimulating further research in the basic science of pain mechanisms as well as in spurring new clinical treatments.

As an outgrowth of this earlier theorizing, the biopsychosocial model has been instrumental in the development of cognitive–behavioral treatment approaches for various clinical pain disorders. It provides an integrated model for chronic pain that incorporates purely mechanical and physiological processes as well as psychological and social contextual variables that may cause and perpetuate pain. The biopsychosocial model views illness as a dynamic and reciprocal interaction among biological, psychological, and sociocultural variables that shape the person's response to pain (Turk, 1996).

The biopsychosocial model of pain presumes the presence of physical changes in the muscles, joints, or nerves that generate nociceptive input to the brain. At the periphery of the nervous system, nociceptive fibers transmit sensations that may or may not be interpreted as pain. Such a sensation is not experienced as pain until subjected to higher order psychological and mental processing that involves perception, appraisal, and behavior. Perception involves the interpretation of nociceptive input and identifies the type of pain (e.g., sharp, burning, aching). Appraisal involves the meaning that is attributed to the pain and that influences subsequent behaviors. The individual may choose to ignore the pain and continue working, walking, socializing, and engaging in previous levels of activity; alternatively, he or she may leave work, refrain from all activity, and assume the "sick role." In turn, this interpersonal role is shaped by responses from significant others that may promote the healthy and active response or the sick role.

LEARNED RESPONSES TO PAIN

No learning is required to activate nociceptive receptors; pain is an intrinsic human response. Pain is inherently aversive, prompting us to escape from it and subsequently to avoid, modify, or cope with cues associated with a potentially painful experience. Acutely, avoidance of activity may be a protective device and an essential step toward healing (for example, favoring a leg with a sprained ankle). However, at some point, rehabilitation requires that we resume our normal life activities. Unfortunately, some people develop a conditioned fear of physical activities because such activities may temporarily aggravate pain. Avoidance of pain is a powerful rationale for reduction of activity in patients with back pain (Vlaeyen, Kole-Snijders, Boeren, & van Eek, 1995). Many patients with back pain express fear of aggravating their pain, and muscle soreness associated with exercise functions as a justification for further avoidance. Although it may be useful to reduce movement in the acute stage, over time, anticipatory fear of pain and avoidance of activities may become generalized to a wide range of life functioning, including work, leisure, and sexual activities.

Waddell, Newton, Henderson, Somerville, and Main (1993) reported that fear avoidance beliefs about physical activities and work are more strongly related to disability and work loss than are biomedical variables and actual pain. They concluded that "fear of pain and what we do about it is more disabling than the pain itself" (p. 164).

Additional support for the importance of fear avoidance and fear of injury (reinjury) beliefs has been reported by a number of investigators (Crombez, Vlaeyen, Heuts, & Lysens, 1999; Vlaeyen et al., 1995). For example, Klenerman et al. (1995) studied patients in primary care with acute back pain. They found that a set of psychological variables (including fear avoidance) were the most powerful predictors of chronic disability. Vlaeyen et al. (1995) observed that fear of movement, injury, or reinjury was a better predictor of self-reported disability than biomedical signs and symptoms or reported pain severity.

When a person experiences pain, the immediate behavior is withdrawal in an attempt to escape from it. Such pain behaviors are adaptive and appropriate. According to Fordyce (1976), however, these behaviors can be maladaptively maintained via reinforcement. For example, if limping and groaning are always followed by sympathetic attention and solicitous help from family, then positive feedback from the pain behavior reinforces the behavior; thus, the likelihood of that behavior recurring increases. Although such behavior is appropriate and adaptive during the active healing of the tissue damage, once the

learned behavioral pattern is established, the behavior is likely to be controlled by external contingencies of reinforcement, not by the initial purpose of protecting the injured area.

Social learning has received some attention in relation to acute pain and in the development and maintenance of chronic pain states. For example, children acquire attitudes about health and styles of symptom perception from their parents and social environment; culturally acquired perceptions and interpretations of symptoms may determine how people deal with illness; and the observation of others in pain provides models to imitate.

Pain and Malingering

It should be noted that the patient with pain does not exhibit pain behavior to obtain reinforcers because pain behavior is more likely to be the result of a gradual process of shaping. In this regard, it is important not to make the mistake of viewing pain behavior as malingering. Malingering involves the patient *consciously and purposely* falsifying a symptom such as pain for secondary gain. Contrary to the beliefs of many third-party payers, there is little support for the contention that outright malingering is prevalent (Craig & Hill, 1999).

PAIN-RELATED COGNITIVE PROCESSES

Various cognitive factors have been demonstrated to influence the perception of pain as well as adaptation to pain. Attentional factors are important in the pain experience because pain is a conscious experience. Our attentional resource is limited, and when greater attention is allocated to sensory processing, greater pain perception can be expected. For example, subjects show attenuated neural activities in the somatosensory region, periaqueductal gray matter, and the anterior cingulate cortex while engaging in a cognitively distracting task (Bantick et al., 2002; Longe et al., 2001). This is the basis for anecdotes of remarkable pain control, such as athletes continuing to play despite serious injury or soldiers' injuries becoming unbearable only after they have retreated to a safe place.

In addition, variable responses to experimentally induced pain are commonly observed when subjects' expectations are manipulated. Beliefs about pain interact with attention to, and appraisal of, sensory events. Thus, individuals expecting a noxious experience may allocate greater attention and interpret the sensory experience as more aversive than those who do not. A 2002 imaging study using functional magnetic resonance imaging (fMRI) also supported the possibility that expectations about pain likely contribute to the modulation of pain; increased activities in the primary somatosensory cortex can be evoked by the mere anticipation of pain without the actual pain experience (Porro et al., 2002).

Considerable experimental evidence exists on the effects of pain-specific thoughts on physiological reactions. Jamner and Tursky (1987), for example, showed that migraine headache patients exhibit significant elevation in their skin conductance in response simply to seeing words related to migraine headaches. Similarly, Flor, Birbaumer, Schugens, and Lutzenberger (1992) showed that patients with back pain tend to show a significant increase of muscle tension in their paraspinal regions when discussing their pain, whereas such elevation is not observed when discussing other matters. In addition, when these patients were resting and not discussing their pain or stress, their back muscle tension level was no higher than that of non–back pain patients or healthy individuals. Neither non–back pain patients nor healthy individuals showed elevations in muscle tension when discussing severe stresses. Clearly, pain-related thought processes, even in the absence of actual pain experience, can trigger the physiological responses that may contribute to the overall pain experience in patients with back pain.

Cognitive Errors

Maladaptive cognition, or cognitive error, contributes to distress and disability associated with pain. Several lines of research have indicated that catastrophizing (extremely negative thoughts about one's plight no matter how unlikely such negative outcomes may be) and adaptive coping strategies (discussed below) are important in determining a person's reaction to pain. Individuals who spontaneously catastrophize report greater pain than those who do not (Severeijns, Vlaeyen, van den Hout, & Weber, 2001), and catastrophizing appears to be a particularly potent influence on pain and disability (Jensen, Turner, Romano, & Karoly, 1991).

Moreover, if individuals believe that their pain is uncontrollable, pessimism and depreciation of their coping skills persist. On the other hand, if individuals believe that they are able to use coping skills effectively (self-efficacy beliefs), their tolerance to aversive situations increases. These cognitions seem to influence physiological and behavioral aspects of pain reciprocally. For example, Bandura, O'Leary, Taylor, Gauthier, and Gossard (1987) showed the positive effect of self-efficacy beliefs on the pain experience, which could be reversed by the administration of naloxone (an opioid antagonist), suggesting the direct effects of thoughts on endogenous opioids (endorphins).

EMOTION AND PAIN

As the International Association for the Study of Pain (1986, p. S217) noted, "Pain is unquestionably a sensation in a part or parts of the body but it is also always unpleasant and therefore also an emotional experience." The affective factors associated with pain include many different emotions, but they are primarily negative in quality. Specifically, affects of depression and anger are prominent, as we discuss in this section. In addition, fear and anxiety occur as natural consequences of the pain experience, as discussed above. The negative emotion and pain seem to have a dynamic relationship. For example, it is noteworthy that anxiety has been shown to potentiate pain severity during medical or dental procedures (Karadottir et al., 2002; Manyande et al., 1995) as well as after surgery (Feinmann, Ong, Harvey, & Harris, 1987).

Depression and Pain

The most studied negative affect in pain is depression. Depression as a clinical syndrome, as well as depressed mood, is quite prevalent in people suffering from pain. Approximately 50% of people suffering from chronic pain, for example, are depressed (Romano & Turner, 1985). Conversely, people suffering from major depressive disorder exhibit a diminished pain threshold (Adler & Gattaz, 1993). The causal relationship between depression and pain has been debated for years. Mood disorder may be a long-standing issue, related to the functional loss associated with chronic pain, or both.

However, research (e.g., Rudy, Kerns, & Turk, 1988; Turk, Okifuji, & Scharff, 1995) has suggested that the relationship is not likely to be a direct one; rather, it is mediated by perceived functional interference and control over pain. Suppose, for example, two people are suffering from a similar level of back pain. One person feels that, despite the pain, she could still enjoy her life by engaging in a modified level of recreational activities and by seeking out new hobbies that will not aggravate her pain. On the other hand, the second individual feels that there is nothing he can enjoy in his life because of his pain. Even though these two people have an equivalent level of pain, it is their mood that modifies their perception of their pain and ability to participate in activities.

Anger and Pain

Another affective component particularly pertinent to chronic pain is anger. Anger has been widely observed in individuals with chronic pain. Pilowsky and Spence (1976) reported an incidence of "bottled-up anger" in 53% of patients with chronic pain. Kerns, Rosenberg, and Jacob (1994) noted that the internalization of angry feelings was strongly related to measures of pain intensity, perceived interference, and reported frequency of pain behaviors. Other research (Bruehl, Burns, Chung, Ward, & Johnson, 2002) has suggested that it is not just the experience of anger but how people manage their anger (i.e., expression of anger) that may influence the pain perception via the endogenous opioid system.

Frustrations related to persistence of symptoms, limited information on etiology, and repeated treatment failures along with anger toward employers, insurance carriers, the health care system, family members, and themselves all contribute to the general dysphoric mood of these patients. It would be reasonable to expect that the presence of anger may serve as an aggravating factor because anger is associated with increased autonomic arousal, decreased motivation, and rejection of rehabilitation and disability management (rather than curative treatment) approaches. This issue is worthy of further study.

Emotional Reactions to Chronicity of Back Pain

The majority of people who experience back pain expect it to remit within a few weeks. When pain persists beyond the expected healing period, they are likely to pursue medical consultation that may lead to various diagnostic tests, such as an electromyelographic study, magnetic resonance imagery (MRI), computerized tomography (CT) scan, or diagnostic nerve blocks. Most patients, as well as clinicians, expect to find some pathological abnormality in the spinal area to explain the presence and extent of the back pain. However, in a large number of patients with severe pain syndrome, exact pathology cannot be objectively identified. Conversely, imaging studies using CT scans and MRI often reveal the presence of significant pathology in up to 35% of asymptomatic individuals (Jensen et al., 1994; Wiesel, Tsourmas, Feffer, Citrin, & Patronas, 1984).

The psychosocial consequences of uncertain diagnosis and pathology underlying the disabling pain can be staggering. The lack of "credibility" for their pain makes it difficult for patients to communicate effectively about their pain with others, and subsequently they may become socially withdrawn. Efforts to convince others of the authenticity of the pain may contribute to the somatic preoccupation and emotional distress associated with chronic pain.

Some patients feel that clinicians think that they are "nutcases," and that their pain is "imagined" or "all in their head" and may actually amplify their pain complaints to convince clinicians that indeed their pain is real. Unfortunately, this often results in inconsistent examination findings and reinforces the stereotype of chronic pain patients as somaticizers, "doctor shoppers," and even malingerers. These dynamics may also drive patients to seek additional diagnostic and invasive treatment procedures.

COPING

Successful self-regulation of pain depends on each individual's coping strategies—their specific ways of dealing with pain, adjusting to pain, and reducing or minimizing pain and distress caused by pain. Coping action is a spontaneously employed action that has specific purpose and intention, and it can be assessed in terms of overt and covert behaviors (Jensen et al., 1991). Overt behavioral coping strategies include rest, medication, and use of relaxation techniques. Covert coping strategies include various means of distracting oneself from pain, reassuring oneself that the pain will diminish, seeking information, and problem solving. Coping strategies are thought to alter both the perceived pain intensity and the ability to manage or tolerate pain so as to continue everyday activities.

It is important to note that coping can be beneficial or detrimental in the management of pain. Studies have found the active coping strategies (e.g., efforts to function in spite of pain or to distract oneself from pain, such as activity or ignoring pain) to be associated with adaptive functioning. Passive coping strategies (e.g., depending on others for help in pain control and restricted activities) are related to greater pain and depression (Keefe, Brown, Wallston, & Caldwell, 1989). In a number of studies, it has been demonstrated that, if instructed in the use of adaptive coping strategies, pain intensity decreases and tolerance of pain increases (DeGood & Sjutty, 1992).

TREATMENT IMPLICATIONS

Psychological Targets for Pain Patients Seen by the Primary Care Psychologist

Whether the primary care psychologist focuses on psychoeducation, psychotherapy, or behavior modification, it is important to focus on the following key psychological elements that contribute to the patient's pain: pain beliefs, mood, and stress management.

Pain Beliefs

It is important for clinicians to understand how patients with back pain conceptualize their plight and to help them understand the multifactorial nature of chronic pain. Many patients with back pain subscribe to the dualistic biological model of pain; they maintain the belief that their pain is caused by significant spinal or nerve damage that diagnostic testing has failed to detect. These patients tend to remain passive in their approach to treatment and depend on medications or procedures done to them, rather than active participation in rehabilitation.

These patients need to learn that, regardless of the presence or extent of pathology, a sedentary lifestyle worsens their condition. The importance of maintaining life activities to preserve the quality of life and minimize suffering associated with chronic pain cannot be overstated. A better understanding of the concepts of pain, disability, and rehabilitation is a critical first step in recovery for many patients with chronic low back pain.

Mood

As noted, psychological distress is commonly experienced by patients with chronic low back pain. Mood closely interacts with pain, leading to further reduction in pain tolerance, lethargic lifestyle, and limitation in available coping resources. In turn, a sedentary and lethargic lifestyle often increases social isolation as well as physical deconditioning. As discussed in the previous section, personal interpretation of one's plight mediates the relationship between pain and depression. It is thus critical for a psychologist to evaluate not only mood, but also its relation to how patients perceive their pain and disability. It is not uncommon to find patients holding overly pessimistic perspectives of their life conditions because of pain. Such beliefs may become an important treatment target in improving patients' emotional well-being.

Stress Management

Living with pain is stressful. Indeed, many patients report that stress is one of the major factors that exacerbates their pain. Mechanisms through which stress affects pain are most likely multifactorial. One of the common features in back pain, however, is increased muscle tension in the paraspinal region in response to stressors. Psychosocial education regarding pain, disability, and stress, as well as behavioral skill training to countercondition tension (e.g., progressive muscle relaxation), is often beneficial.

Specialty Care

The most promising approach for chronic, intractable low back pain is treatment at a multidisciplinary pain clinic (Table 19.1), in which clinicians from several disciplines work together as a team. Table 19.2 lists the general role of core team members of a multidisciplinary pain care team. The philosophy underlying the approach is rehabilitative rather than curative. The general goal is to decrease functional disability and improve quality of life via physical activation, psychoeducation, self-management skill training, and appropriate medical regimens. Patients are active participants in the treatment team rather than passive recipients of clinical care. As of 2001, there were 443 accredited pain management programs, clinics, and pain centers in the United States (Marketdata-Enterprises, 2001). The International Association for the Study of Pain (Loeser,

1992) classified them as multidisciplinary pain centers, multidisciplinary pain clinics, pain clinics, or modality-oriented clinics.

Patients with back pain make up the largest segment (55%) of the pain center population (Marketdata-Enterprises, 2001). Patients are generally referred by their primary care physicians, physiatrists, neurologists, or orthopedic surgeons. Actual implementation of the treatment program varies depending on the resources available. There are inpatient programs, day treatment programs, and outpatient programs. Inpatient programs, because of their cost and labor-intensive nature, are quite rare, and most have been transformed into day treatment programs.

Day treatment programs are generally 3 to 4 weeks long and usually involve patients in 4 hours of actual performance-based treatment (physical therapy, occupational therapy, relaxation) plus 4 hours in classroom-based group and individual therapies (psychoeducational classes, body mechanics, cognitive–behavioral groups, individual psychotherapy). Intensive multidisciplinary pain treatment programs based on the biopsychosocial model for chronic and subacute low back pain have repeatedly demonstrated efficacy in pain reduction and functional improvement (Guzman et al., 2002; Karjalainen et al., 2001). Not all patients require intensive systematic programs, however. Many patients may benefit from multi-

Table 19.1 Classification of Pain Centers

Modality-oriented clinic: Offers a specific type of treatment, but does not provide comprehensive assessment or management. It has no emphasis on an integrated, comprehensive team approach. The clinic may not be pain specific, but rather is defined by a single modality in which the clinic specializes (e.g., massage therapy, acupuncture).

Pain clinic: Focuses on diagnosis and management of patients with chronic pain and may specialize in the assessment and treatment of specific pain diagnoses (e.g., back pain, headaches).

Multidisciplinary pain clinic: Staffed by a team of clinicians, including physicians of different specialties and other health care providers who specialize in the diagnosis and management of chronic pain. It does not include research and teaching activities in its regular program.

Multidisciplinary pain center: Includes a range of health care professionals specializing in pain diagnosis and management, such as physicians, psychologists, nurses, physical therapists, occupational therapists, and other specialty care providers. The primary clinical approach is an integrated, multimodal approach. It is generally affiliated with a major health science institution and has research and teaching activities as a part of its regular operations.

Modified from Loeser (1992).

Table 19.2 Roles of Clinicians in a Multidisciplinary Pain Care Team

Physician
  Diagnosis of pain and medical conditions
  Evaluation of associated pathological conditions
  Medication management
  Provision of medical procedures (nerve blocks)
  Patient education (medication issues, importance of self-management)

Nurse/medical assistant
  Taking patient histories
  Assistance to physicians in dispensing and adjusting medications
  Patient education (healthy lifestyle, sleep, hygiene)

Physical therapist
  Review of musculoskeletal conditions
  Development of exercise regimen
  Instruction, supervision of exercise regimen for physical fitness, strength, flexibility
  Patient education (body mechanics, musculoskeletal aspects of chronic paint)

Occupational therapist
  Evaluation of body mechanics and energy conservation
  Instruction and supervision of work-related physical activities
  Consultation for modifying work specification

Psychologist
  Evaluation of past and current psychosocial issues relevant to patient's pain
  Diagnosis of psychiatric disorders
  Provision of stress and pain management skill training
  Modification of pain behaviors and maladaptive cognition
  Provision of psychological treatment
  Patient education (perception, social contingency)

disciplinary pain care on an outpatient basis. Such care generally includes regular follow-ups with a physician, physical therapist, and psychologist.

Typically, day treatment programs require a great deal of time and effort; patients may need to take time off from other therapies. The pain center psychologist will likely perform an evaluation and determine the relevant treatment targets for the rehabilitation. At this point, the primary care psychologist can provide input. Throughout the program, the primary care psychologist can be enlisted as a consultant for the patient. At discharge, the two psychologists should discuss the progress and further plans for the patient's care.

In outpatient care, the patient typically returns to the pain psychologist on a limited basis, generally for 6 to 10 sessions. The two psychologists need to discuss how the therapy issues, pain-specific and other psychological issues, should be targeted in each clinic.

At a pain center, the patient will likely undergo a comprehensive pain evaluation that includes a psychological assessment, mostly to understand the extent of psychosocial factors relevant to his or her pain, current mood and mental status, and coping skills. The communication between the pain psychologist and the primary care psychologist is critical at this point to create and coordinate treatment plans. Details of treatment plans are unique to each case and cannot be easily generalized. However, elements of the plan may include the acquisition of self-management skills for pain control (6–8 sessions).

Given the time-limited nature of the plan, long-standing psychosocial issues might not be a part of the treatment target. For those patients whose psychological health is significantly compromised, psychological intervention beyond what they receive at a pain center is needed. Concurrent psychopathology and pain rehabilitation often interact. The two psychologists should continue the collaborative relationship to prevent either of these factors from exacerbating the other to achieve optimal treatment outcomes.

Role of the Clinical Specialist

There are a number of clinical specialists who evaluate and treat back pain. In general, people visit their primary care physicians for an initial consultation when they first experience back pain. It seems intuitively reasonable for many patients to stay out of normal activities and remain sedentary until the pain subsides. However, a 2002 outcome review (Hagen, Hilde, Jamtvedt, & Winnem, 2002) indicated that prolonged bed rest for acute back pain may be detrimental, suggesting that a return to the normal life routine as soon as possible may be more beneficial.

For most patients, relatively simple treatments (nonsteroidal anti-inflammatory drugs, muscle relaxants) should be sufficient to heal their acute pain and associated disability. Some may elect to visit complementary clinical specialists such as chiropractors, acupuncturists, and massage therapists. Clinical efficacy of these modalities is not well studied; the existing evidence seems to suggest modest benefit at best.

For a minority of patients, back pain persists despite the appropriate course of therapy. These patients are generally referred to specialists, including neurologists, radiologists, surgeons, anesthesiologists, and other pain specialists for further diagnostic testing or specialized treatment. When pain remains intractable, some patients are referred to pain management programs.

Role of Opioid Analgesics in the Treatment of Chronic Low Back Pain

One of the most controversial issues in the treatment of chronic back pain is the use of opioid analgesics.[1] Historically, long-term use of opioids in the treatment of chronic noncancer pain was unanimously considered inappropriate. Many pain center treatment programs in the 1970s and the early 1980s attempted to eliminate opioid analgesics from a patient's regimen as a part of rehabilitation. However, several investigators began questioning this approach in the late 1980s (Melzack, 1990; Portenoy, 1989). These authors suggest that opioids could be used to better manage chronic pain, thereby improving quality of life and the chance of engaging in functional activities.

The efficacy of long-term opioid maintenance therapy for chronic pain has generated extensive controversy. One of the few truly long-term studies (Jamison, Raymond, Slawsby, Nedeljkovic, & Katz, 1998) reported that patients with back pain who received a titrated dose of sustained-release opioid showed decreased pain and emotional distress compared to those receiving only nonsteroidal anti-inflammatory drugs or a set dose of short-acting opioids. However, there were no improvements in activity levels or sleep, suggesting that opioid therapy alone is insufficient to rehabilitate patients with chronic low back pain and indicating that other therapy modalities in conjunction with opioid therapy are needed.

Another issue that deserves more attention is that of individual differences in treatment response. The response to medications varies greatly across patients, even among those with the same pain diagnosis taking the same class of opioid. Delineation of patient characteristics for positive treatment response to opioid therapy would clearly improve the clinical efficacy and cost effectiveness of chronic pain treatment.

A third problem is physicians' general lack of appropriate training in pain management and the persistence of misinformation and myths about opioid abuse, physical dependency, and addiction. Although these terms are often confused, they are not interchangeable. Patients using opioid analgesics *will* develop physical dependency and experience withdrawal on sudden termination of the medication. However, this does not mean that the physical dependency equals addiction. Addiction is defined as "behaviors that include one or more of the following: impaired control over drug use, compulsive use, continued use despite harm, and craving. Furthermore, addiction can only be understood as a pattern of behavior, rather than a single incident" (Savage, 1999, p. 911). The prevalence of addictive behaviors in this population ranges from 3% to 30%, depending on the definition of addiction and the nature of the patient sample (Chabal, Erjavec, Jacobson, Mariano, & Chaney, 1997; Cowan, Allan, & Griffiths, 2002; Fishbain, Rosomoff, & Rosomoff, 1992; Robinson et al., 2001).

Drug-Seeking Behaviors and Addiction Issues

Although the majority of patients with chronic pain are able to take opioid medications without adverse behavioral consequences, a minority of patients exhibit aberrant opioid-taking behaviors, such as excessive phone calls to the clinic to obtain early refills, noncompliant or compulsive misuse of opioid medications, obtaining opioid medications from multiple providers, diversion (i.e., selling opioids illegally to others), and prescription forgery. It is important for clinicians who treat patients with chronic pain to understand that there are multiple potential reasons underlying aberrant behaviors.

Many of these behaviors may be driven by "pseudoaddiction," in which the behaviors are the direct result of undertreated pain. In the case of pseudoaddiction, the aberrant behaviors disappear once the pain is adequately treated. Another possibility is that patients misuse opioid medications for managing their sleep and mood, particularly anxiety. The assumption that all drug-seeking behaviors represent addiction is certainly unwarranted.

The decision to continue or discontinue opioid use for these patients critically depends on how a clinician conceptualizes the drug-seeking behavior in question. Anecdotes suggest that clinicians are not very accurate in identifying patients who misuse or abuse their medications. Pharmacy records, now available in many states, and urine toxicology screening may be necessary to identify such patients more accurately. For example, the state of Utah has a mandated program that monitors all dispensed Schedule II–V drugs by all pharmacies in the state as well as mail order out-of-state pharmacies. The information includes the names of medications, dates prescribed, provider names, pharmacy names, dates filled, and dosages. Physicians may routinely send the request to receive the information from the state for every patient who receives an opioid prescription.

At our specialty pain management clinic, at which patients sign an agreement to receive opioids only from the clinic, evidence of obtaining opioids from multiple sources was significantly related to aberrant opioid-taking behaviors (Okifuji, Lassen, Ashburn, & Bradshaw, 2003).

A preliminary examination of problem behaviors associated with the use of opioid analgesics showed some interesting results (Rust, Okifuji, & Ashburn, 2003). In the study, 61% of the patients met at least one of the criteria listed in Table 19.3, and more than 23% met at least three criteria for aberrant opioid-taking behaviors. Those who met three or more criteria tended to (a) be younger and male, (b) have a past history of substance abuse, (c) have an injurious onset of pain, and (d) have a greater degree of mood disturbance. Interestingly, these patients were less likely to experience pain reduction over the course of the treatment.

SUMMARY

Low back pain is a prevalent, expensive, and debilitating problem in both primary care and spe-

Table 19.3 Criteria for the Aberrant Behaviors Associated With the Use of Opioid Analgesics

Requesting early refill of the prescription three times or more

Evidence suggestive of multiple providers prescribing opioids despite the signed agreement not to do so

Requesting another prescription, claiming their medicine was lost or stolen

Clinician's suspicion of abuse

Evidence of self-increasing dosage of opioids

Multiple calls regarding opioid issues

Evidence of obtaining medication illegally

cialty medical settings. It is clearly a biopsychosocial problem, and one for which psychological treatment can provide important relief. It is also clear that no isomorphic relationship exists between tissue damage and pain report. The dualistic concept of pain, only considering pain either as a somatic phenomenon or as a psychogenic problem, has been replaced with a more comprehensive, biopsychosocial model of pain as a perceptual process resulting from nociceptive input modulated on a number of different levels in the central nervous system. The current state of knowledge suggests that pain must be viewed as a complex phenomenon that incorporates physical, psychosocial, and behavioral factors. Failure to incorporate each of these factors will lead to an incomplete understanding of pain.

It is important that we understand the integrated nature of the psychosocial factors in chronic pain. Psychological distress may be a consequence of pain; however, psychological factors in turn contribute to the overall pain experience of patients.

The primary care psychologist should be prepared to intervene in three key target areas: pain beliefs, mood disturbance, and stress management. Low back pain can be relieved with activity, cognitive–behavioral therapy, and pain medication, preferably in combination. In complex or treatment-resistant cases, referral to a specialty pain clinic and close collaboration between the primary care psychologist and the pain psychologist will be necessary.

ACKNOWLEDGMENT   Support for the preparation of this chapter was provided in part by grants from the National Institute of Arthritis and Musculoskeletal and Skin Diseases (R01 AR43606).

Note

1. The term *narcotics* is sometimes interchangeably used to describe opioid analgesics. However, it should be noted that narcotics is a legal term, and it includes a range of nonopioid substances, such as cocaine. *Opioid* is a medical term describing a substance that binds to or otherwise affects the opiate receptors on the surface of the cell.

References

Adler, G., & Gattaz, W. F. (1993). Pain perception threshold in major depression. *Biological Psychiatry, 34*, 687–689.

Bandura, A., O'Leary, A., Taylor, C. B., Gauthier, J., & Gossard, D. (1987). Perceived self-efficacy and pain control: Opioid and nonopioid mechanisms. *Journal of Personality and Social Psychology, 53*, 563–571.

Bantick, S. J., Wise, R. G., Ploghaus, A., Clare, S., Smith, S. M., & Tracey, I. (2002). Imaging how attention modulates pain in humans using functional MRI. *Brain, 125(Pt. 2)*, 310–319.

Bigos, S., Bowyer, O., Braen, G., Brown, K., Deyo, R., Haldeman, S., et al. (1994). *Acute low back problems in adults* (AHCPR Publication No. 95-0642). Rockville, MD: Agency for Health Care Policy and Research, Public Health Service, U.S. Department of Health and Human Services.

Bruehl, S., Burns, J. W., Chung, O. Y., Ward, P., & Johnson, B. (2002). Anger and pain sensitivity in chronic low back pain patients and pain-free controls: The role of endogenous opioids. *Pain, 99*, 223–233.

Cassidy, J. D., Carroll, L. J., & Cote, P. (1998). The Saskatchewan health and back pain survey. The prevalence of low back pain and related disability in Saskatchewan adults. *Spine, 23*, 1860–1866, discussion 1867.

Chabal, C., Erjavec, M. K., Jacobson, L., Mariano, A., & Chaney, E. (1997). Prescription opiate abuse in chronic pain patients: Clinical criteria, incidence, and predictors. *Clinical Journal of Pain, 13*, 150–155.

Cowan, D. T., Allan, L., & Griffiths, P. (2002). A pilot study into the problematic use of opioid analgesics in chronic non-cancer pain patients. *International Journal of Nursing Studies, 39*, 59–69.

Craig, K., & Hill, M. (1999). Detecting deception and malingering. In A. Block, E. Kremer, & E. Fernandez (Eds.), *Handbook of pain syndromes* (pp. 41–58). Mahwah, NJ: Lawrence Erlbaum.

Crombez, G., Vlaeyen, J. W., Heuts, P. H., & Lysens, R. (1999). Pain-related fear is more disabling than pain itself: Evidence on the role of pain-related fear in chronic back pain disability. *Pain, 80*, 329–339.

DeGood, D., & Sjutty, M. (1992). Assessment of pain beliefs, coping and self-efficacy. In D. Turk & R. Melzack (Eds.), *Handbook of pain assessment* (pp. 214–234). New York: Guilford Press.

Feinmann, C., Ong, M., Harvey, W., & Harris, M. (1987). Psychological factors influencing postoperative pain and analgesic consumption. *British Journal of Oral and Maxillofacial Surgery, 25*, 285–292.

Fishbain, D. A., Rosomoff, H. L., & Rosomoff, R. S. (1992). Drug abuse, dependence, and addiction in chronic pain patients. *Clinical Journal of Pain, 8*, 77–85.

Flor, H., Birbaumer, N., Schugens, M. M., & Lutzenberger, W. (1992). Symptom-specific psychophysiological responses in chronic pain patients. *Psychophysiology, 29*, 452–460.

Flor, H., Fydrich, T., & Turk, D. C. (1992). Efficacy of multidisciplinary pain treatment centers: A meta-analytic review. *Pain, 49*, 221–230.

Fordyce, W. (1976). *Behavioral methods in chronic pain and illness*. St. Louis: C. V. Mosby.

Guzman, J., Esmail, R., Karjalainen, K., Malmivaara, A., Irvin, E., & Bombardier, C. (2002). *Multidisciplinary bio-psycho-social rehabilitation for chronic low back pain*. Cochrane Database Syst Rev. 1, CD 000963.

Hagen, K. B., Hilde, G., Jamtvedt, G., & Winnem, M. F. (2002). The Cochrane review of advice to stay active as a single treatment for low back pain and sciatica. *Spine, 27*, 1736–1741.

Hoffman, R. M., Wheeler, K. J., & Deyo, R. A. (1993). Surgery for herniated lumbar discs: A literature synthesis. *Journal of General Internal Medicine, 8*, 487–496.

International Association for the Study of Pain. (1986). Classification of chronic pain. Descriptions of chronic pain syndromes and definitions of pain terms. *Pain, 3*, S1–S226.

Jamison, R. N., Raymond, S. A., Slawsby, E. A., Nedeljkovic, S. S., & Katz, N. P. (1998). Opioid therapy for chronic noncancer back pain. A randomized prospective study. *Spine, 23,* 2591–2600.

Jamner, L., & Tursky, B. (1987). Discrimination between intensity and affective pain descriptors: A psychophysiological evaluation. *Pain, 30,* 271–283.

Jensen, M. C., Brant-Zawadzki, M. N., Obuchowski, N., Modic, M. T., Malkasian, D., & Ross, J. S. (1994). Magnetic resonance imaging of the lumbar spine in people without back pain. *New England Journal of Medicine, 331,* 69–73.

Jensen, M. P., Turner, J. A., Romano, J. M., & Karoly, P. (1991). Coping with chronic pain: A critical review of the literature. *Pain, 47,* 249–283.

Karadottir, H., Lenoir, L., Barbierato, B., Bogle, M., Riggs, M., Sigurdsson, T., Crigger, M., & Egelberg, J. (2002). Pain experienced by patients during periodontal maintenance treatment. *Journal of Periodontology, 73,* 536–542.

Karjalainen, K., Malmivaara, A., van Tulder, M., Roine, R., Jauhiainen, M., Hurri, H., & Koes, B. (2001). Multidisciplinary biopsychosocial rehabilitation for subacute low back pain in working-age adults: A systematic review within the framework of the Cochrane Collaboration Back Review Group. *Spine, 26,* 262–269.

Keefe, F. J., Brown, G. K., Wallston, K. A., & Caldwell, D. S. (1989). Coping with rheumatoid arthritis pain: Catastrophizing as a maladaptive strategy. *Pain, 37,* 51–56.

Kerns, R., Rosenberg, R., & Jacob, M. (1994). Anger expression and chronic pain. *Journal of Behavioral Medicine, 17,* 57–67.

Klenerman, L., Slade, P. D., Stanley, I. M., Pennie, B., Reilly, J. P., Atchison, L. E., Troup, J. D., & Rose, M. J. (1995). The prediction of chronicity in patients with an acute attack of low back pain in a general practice setting. *Spine, 20,* 478–484.

Loeser, J. (1992). *Desirable characteristics for pain treatment facilities.* Seattle, WA: IASP.

Longe, S. E., Wise, R., Bantick, S., Lloyd, D., Johansen-Berg, H., McGlone, F., & Tracey, I. (2001). Counter-stimulatory effects on pain perception and processing are significantly altered by attention: An fMRI study. *Neuroreport, 12,* 2021–2025.

Malter, A. D., Larson, E. B., Urban, N., & Deyo, R. A. (1996). Cost-effectiveness of lumbar discectomy for the treatment of herniated intervertebral disc. *Spine, 21,* 1048–1054, discussion 1055.

Manyande, A., Berg, S., Gettins, D., Stanford, S. C., Mazhero, S., Marks, D. F., & Salmon, P. (1995). Preoperative rehearsal of active coping imagery influences subjective and hormonal responses to abdominal surgery. *Psychosomatic Medicine, 57,* 177–182.

Marketdata-Enterprises. (2001). *Pain management programs: A market analysis.* Tampa, FL: Author.

Melzack, R. (1990). The tragedy of needless pain. *Science, 262,* 27–33.

Melzack, R., & Wall, P. (1965). Pain mechanisms: A new theory. *Science, 150,* 971–979.

Okifuji, A., Lassen, C. L., Ashburn, M. A., & Bradshaw, D. H. (2003). *Aberrant opioid taking behaviors in chronic non-cancer pain patients: Prevalence and predictors.* Manuscript submitted for publication.

Pilowsky, I., & Spence, N. (1976). Pain, anger, and illness behaviour. *Journal of Psychosomatic Research, 20,* 411–416.

Porro, C. A., Baraldi, P., Pagnoni, G., Serafini, M., Facchin, P., Maieron, M., & Nichelli, P. (2002). Does anticipation of pain affect cortical nociceptive systems? *Journal of Neuroscience, 22,* 3206–3214.

Portenoy, R. (1989). Opioid therapy in the management of chronic back pain. In C. Tollison (Ed.), *Interdisciplinary rehabilitation of low back pain* (pp. 137–157). Baltimore, MD: Williams and Wilkins.

Robinson, R. C., Gatchel, R. J., Polatin, P., Deschner, M., Noe, C., & Gajraj, N. (2001). Screening for problematic prescription opioid use. *Clinical Journal of Pain, 17,* 220–228.

Romano, J. M., & Turner, J. A. (1985). Chronic pain and depression: Does the evidence support a relationship? *Psychology Bulletin, 97,* 18–34.

Rudy, T. E., Kerns, R. D., & Turk, D. C. (1988). Chronic pain and depression: Toward a cognitive-behavioral mediation model. *Pain, 35,* 129–140.

Rust, H., Okifuji, A., & Ashburn, M. (2003). *Chronic opioid therapy and addiction in nonmalignant pain.* Unpublished manuscript.

Savage, S. R. (1999). Opioid therapy of chronic pain: Assessment of consequences. *Acta Anaesthesiology Scandania, 43,* 909–917.

Severeijns, R., Vlaeyen, J. W., van den Hout, M. A., & Weber, W. E. (2001). Pain catastrophizing predicts pain intensity, disability, and psychological distress independent of the level of physical impairment. *Clinical Journal of Pain, 17,* 165–172.

Taylor, V. M., Deyo, R. A., Cherkin, D. C., & Kreuter, W. (1994). Low back pain hospitalization. Recent United States trends and regional variations. *Spine, 19,* 1207–1212; discussion 1213.

Turk, D. (1996). Biopsychosocial perspective on chronic pain. In R. Gatchel & D. Turk (Eds.), *Psychological approaches to pain management: A practitioner's handbook* (pp. 3–32). New York: Guilford Press.

Turk, D. C., Okifuji, A., & Scharff, L. (1995). Chronic pain and depression: Role of perceived impact and perceived control in different age cohorts. *Pain, 61,* 93–101.

Turner, J. A., Ersek, M., Herron, L., & Deyo, R.

(1992). Surgery for lumbar spinal stenosis. Attempted meta-analysis of the literature. *Spine, 17,* 1–8.

Vlaeyen, J. W., Kole-Snijders, A. M., Boeren, R. G., & van Eek, H. (1995). Fear of movement/(re)injury in chronic low back pain and its relation to behavioral performance. *Pain, 62,* 363–372.

Waddell, G., Newton, M., Henderson, I., Somerville, D., & Main, C. J. (1993). A Fear-Avoidance Beliefs Questionnaire (FABQ) and the role of fear-avoidance beliefs in chronic low back pain and disability. *Pain, 52,* 157–168.

Wiesel, S. W., Tsourmas, N., Feffer, H. L., Citrin, C. M., & Patronas, N. (1984). A study of computer-assisted tomography. I. The incidence of positive CAT scans in an asymptomatic group of patients. *Spine, 9,* 549–551.

20

Cancer

Tiffany L. Tibbs
Kathleen L. Tarr

Few words evoke as much emotion as the word *cancer*, especially when it is uttered in reference to one's own or a loved one's health. These feelings are understandable as cancer occurs frequently and remains one of the leading causes of death for all age groups. In 2002, for example, it was estimated that there would be 1,284,900 new cases of cancer and 555,500 deaths in the United States alone (Jemal, Thomas, Murray, & Thun, 2002). Cancer most recently ranked as the second leading cause of death in both adults and children (Jemal et al., 2002).

Given the number of individuals who are diagnosed with cancer in the United States, it is quite likely that psychologists working in a primary care setting will encounter cancer patients and survivors in their practice. Primary care psychologists can play an important role in the care of these patients by addressing the range of issues that arise at diagnosis, during treatment, throughout survival, or when illness becomes terminal. This chapter highlights the key issues for psychologists who work with patients with cancer. First, we provide an overview of the medical aspects of cancer and treatment. We then review the psy-

chological issues that affect patients and family members over time and present a variety of psychotherapeutic interventions to help patients cope with cancer. Finally, we outline the benefits and challenges of working with cancer patients and the medical team.

MEDICAL TREATMENT OF CANCER: WHAT PSYCHOLOGISTS NEED TO KNOW

The term *cancer* is commonly used to denote a malignant growth. In contrast, *tumor* refers to a growth that may be malignant or benign. In many people's minds, however, the two are synonymous. Translated literally, the word *cancer* simply means "a crab." This is in reference to the first characteristic of cancer, the ability to invade surrounding tissues, much like the multiple legs of a crab. This invasiveness gives rise to the other two characteristics: the ability to recur at the same site and the ability to metastasize (to occur or recur at sites distant from the primary tumor, often in the lungs, liver, brain, or bone).

Cancer develops as a mutation in normal cellular structure or function. This abnormality may be minor enough to cause malignant growth, but still allow the cancer to be recognized as arising from and functioning like nearby normal tissue. At the other extreme may be a malignancy that has mutated to such an extent that it is no longer recognizable as any one tissue type. The extent of mutation is referred to as *tumor grade*. There are as many types of cancer as there are tissues, but there are some categories of cancer based on embryonic tissue origin. These are adenocarcinoma, squamous cell, or hematologic malignancies.

Staging and Prognosis

Treatment of cancer is dependent on accurate diagnosis of the type, extent of cellular abnormality, and extent of cancer involvement both locally (the site of the primary tumor) and as distant metastases. Although a diagnosis may be considered based on symptoms, findings from physical examination, or radiographically, a definitive diagnosis depends on examining a piece of the involved tissue under a microscope. This leads to a time period during which the patient is assumed, but not proven, to have cancer and will likely be undergoing extensive testing or invasive procedures for biopsy. This may include open surgical exploration.

Tumor staging has three components, referred to as the TNM stage.[1] In general, higher numbers for these components of staging indicate more advanced cancer and poorer prognosis. Thus, an individual with a T1N0M0 tumor has a small tumor with no involvement as either local lymphatic spread or distant metastatic spread. On the other extreme, an individual with a T4N2M1 staging has a large tumor, likely with local spread to adjacent tissues and evidence of distant spread to the lymph nodes and as metastases.

These multiple stages are often "condensed" into a four-stage classification (I–IV) as this has more prognostic value for each cancer type and helps to dictate treatment strategy. Stage I cancer has a very good prognosis and may be curable with removal of the primary tumor. In contrast, Stage IV cancer carries a poorer prognosis, and palliation may be the only treatment option.

Stages II and III are intermediate and will likely require progressively more aggressive treatment.

Prognosis in cancer refers to the likelihood that treatment will render a patient free of cancer or cured. Cure, however, usually refers to a 5-year time period, not necessarily indefinite or permanent absence of cancer. It should be noted that prognosis varies widely among different cancer types and even stages within the same cancer type. For example, testicular cancer is very curable, even at Stage IV, with 7,500 estimated new cases for 2002 and only 400 (5.3%) deaths expected (Jemal et al., 2002). On the opposite end of the spectrum, 169,000 new cases of lung cancer were expected in 2002, with 154,900 deaths (91.6%) (Jemal et al., 2002).

In general, however, newer forms of treatment have dramatically improved the prognosis of cancer patients. As mentioned, in 2002, it was estimated that there would be 1,284,900 new cases of cancer, and that 555,500 people would die in the United States (Jemal et al., 2002). This represents an increase in cases from previous years, yet mortality from cancer has continued to decline. For example, from 1974 to 1976, the 5-year survival rate for cancer from all sites in all ethnic groups was 50%. From 1992 to 1997, however, this survival rate increased to 62% (Jemal et al., 2002).

Cancer Treatment

Cancer treatment is highly individualized based on the type, grade, and extent of tumor. Other factors, such as the patient's medical history, also play a role. Treatment often involves multiple specialists, including the medical oncologist, the radiation oncologist, and the surgeon. There are three levels of cancer care, each with a different focus or goal of therapy: curative, palliative, and comfort care. Although palliative treatment and comfort care may at times be used interchangeably, palliative can also imply treatment aimed at minimizing symptoms and maintaining function. Comfort care always implies minimizing symptoms in preparation for death. A patient may progress from one to the next or may have only one type during the course of treatment. The first and most prominent type of cancer therapy is curative. As the name implies, the goal of treatment is for the patient to be and remain cancer free.

Surgery

Many treatment regimens start with resection, or surgical removal, of the primary tumor, although some regimens include presurgery chemotherapy or radiation therapy with the goal of reducing the tumor to a size that may be resected while sparing surrounding normal tissues. Postsurgery, the patient will experience pain of varying degrees at the surgical site. This is controlled by narcotic and nonnarcotic pain relievers. Additional effects may include difficulties with wound management, postoperative infections, and gastric effects such as nausea or constipation.

After adequate time for healing of the surgical site, most regimens continue with radiation therapy and/or chemotherapy. Even when the surgery is considered curative, the patient's best chance for remaining tumor free and having long-term survival may include postsurgical chemotherapy or radiation therapy. In this setting, the therapy is termed *adjuvant*. For example, a patient with colon cancer may have a complete tumor resection but still undergo chemotherapy to "mop up" any unapparent tumor cells.

Radiation

Radiation therapy is used in a number of different cancer types. Radiation therapy is the process of exposing the cancerous cells to irradiation. In the most typical form, the patient undergoes daily treatments for a period of several weeks. This has the advantage of delivering a higher dose to the tumor while minimizing side effects. However, the patient must have access to the therapy site, so daily travel or local arrangements for lodging may be necessary.

The side effects of radiation therapy depend on the site of treatment and effects on the surrounding tissues, but there are few effects at distant sites because the therapy is very focused. One of the most prominent side effects is burning of the skin at the therapy site, leading to discomfort or, at times, disfigurement. These effects usually fade after therapy is complete. There can also be side effects because of involvement of nearby structures. For example, radiation therapy of a neck tumor may lead to nausea because of involvement of the stomach or esophagus in the treatment field. Effects on adjacent structures can also be longer lasting. For example, if a lung tumor is irradiated, there may be scarring of surrounding lung tissue, leading to long-term decrease in pulmonary function. Newer radiation therapy techniques have become very efficient at localizing the tumor site and reducing or eliminating these side effects.

A second method of radiation therapy involves implanting radioactive beads or other carriers at the site of the tumor. This has the advantage of delivering prolonged irradiation to the tumor and minimizing side effects while also eliminating the need for daily treatments. Side effects from radioactive beads are often limited to local effects such as scarring of surrounding tissues; however, systemic effects such as bone marrow suppression or nausea may still be seen. Radioactive agents that are injected to concentrate in a target organ (such as thyroid or bone) may be especially likely to produce systemic effects.

Chemotherapy

Chemotherapy agents are delivered via a range of regimens. Most are intravenous medications and require placement of an infusion port or catheter that may remain in place for an extended time period. This gives the patient relief from multiple blood draws and intravenous infusions, but may lead to problems from infections or blood clots. Chemotherapy may be delivered daily or intermittently, ranging from weekly infusions to treatment for several days every 3 or 4 weeks. Duration may range from a few weeks to indefinite to maintain or prolong remission. Most chemotherapy is given in an outpatient setting, but a few agents require hospitalization for extended infusion times or close monitoring for side effects. The type, method of administration, and duration of chemotherapy are determined by a number of factors, including specific agent, cancer type, treatment protocol, and any other medical problems of the patient.

Chemotherapy agents generally affect the

whole body, and because cancerous cells may not be extremely different from normal cells, chemotherapy has many side effects. Cells that normally divide rapidly, such as blood cells and the lining of the gastrointestinal tract, are the most susceptible. Newer agents are able to exploit the specific genetic mutations of cancer cells and have fewer side effects. In addition, many medications are available to manage side effects, which may decrease the disruption of the patient's routine.

Side effects from chemotherapy may be immediate or long term. The long-term side effects include cardiac, pulmonary, and neurological problems. If an agent is known to produce one of the effects, the patient will be monitored so that the long-term consequences can be minimized. The most common immediate side effects are anemia and fatigue, infections from neutropenia (low white blood cell count), nausea and vomiting, mouth sores, diarrhea, and hair loss.

Growth factors such as erythropoietin and granulocyte-macrophage colony-stimulating factor may help increase red blood cells and white blood cells, respectively. These help decrease anemia, fatigue, and secondary infections or hospitalizations and improve quality of life. Many different medications are available to decrease the nausea associated with chemotherapy and help the patient maintain nutrition. Other medications can ease diarrhea and mouth sores. Hair lost will eventually regrow after chemotherapy is stopped. Interestingly, hair texture or color may be different at regrowth.

Hormonal Therapy

Hormonal therapy is a newer form of therapy directed at certain cancers that use naturally occurring hormones as "fuel." The prominent uses for this are for breast and prostate cancer. Hormonal therapies are most commonly administered as an oral medication, although injectable forms are also used. The most common side effects of these therapies are the result of blocking the specific hormone. For example, a woman undergoing hormonal therapy for breast cancer may experience the symptoms of menopause as her own estrogen and progesterone are "blocked." Patients with prostate cancer may undergo orchiectomy (surgical removal of the testes) or hormonal treatment.

Both of these suppress testosterone, which may result in both physical (impotence) and psychological (not feeling "like a man") side effects.

Bone Marrow Transplantation

Bone marrow transplantation is a form of treatment that deserves special mention. This is usually used for hematologic malignancies (leukemia and lymphoma), but has been investigated for other types of tumors. The treatment consists of high-dose chemotherapy with or without whole-body radiation as a conditioning regimen to totally destroy any traces of the cancer. These doses also destroy the patient's bone marrow, leaving the patient without the ability to produce blood cells and without the function provided by these blood cells, such as clotting or fighting infection. The bone marrow is reconstituted by an infusion of bone marrow or stem cells previously collected either from the patient or from a matched donor.

Bone marrow transplantation is often done when the patient is in remission and thus feels well. The treatment often results in a time period when the patient is fairly ill because of the side effects of the chemotherapy and is open to multiple infections. If a donor is used, the patient will likely be required to take lifelong immunosuppressive therapy to keep the donor white blood cells and immune system from attacking the patient's other tissues.

Although very useful for hematologic malignancies, the results have been mixed for other types of cancers. Bone marrow transplantation for other malignancies has been a focus of political activism, so discordant reports about treatment effectiveness can be confusing for the patient.

Follow-up

No matter which treatment the patient undergoes, monitoring response to treatment and lifelong monitoring for recurrence will be necessary. This may range from a blood test for a tumor marker (a substance secreted by a tumor, such as prostate-specific antigen for prostate cancer) to periodic computerized tomographic, magnetic resonance imaging, or positron emission tomographic scans, to periodic invasive procedures such as bone marrow biopsy. Thus, there are repeated periods of waiting until the patient finds out if he or she remains free of cancer.

Palliative and Comfort Care

Palliative Care

As noted, palliation is directed at controlling the symptoms of the cancer to allow the patient to continue to function as normally as possible. It may be the initial goal of therapy or may come after failure of curative therapy. Palliative care may consist of chemotherapy, hormonal therapy, or radiation therapy. For example, chemotherapy may be directed at limiting tumor growth and compression on nearby tissue. Some tumors metastasize to bone, so a course of radiation may decrease pain and possibility of fracture while not curing the patient of cancer at other locations. Palliative therapy also allows the patient to "buy time" as new treatments are evaluated and approved; curative therapy remains the ultimate goal.

Pain is an often-feared symptom of cancer and side effect of cancer treatment (management is reviewed in Cherny, 2000). There are many medication options to treat pain, and psychologists can offer adjuncts to symptom management (relaxation, imagery, or other cognitive–behavioral techniques discussed separately in this chapter). However, patients are often reluctant to seek adequate pain medication because of concerns about addiction.

Pain control is essential for maintaining good quality of life, and addiction is not commonly seen in this setting. In one study of 11,882 patients, only 4 cases of addiction were found (Porter & Jick, 1980). Addiction should also not be confused with tolerance. It is more common for patients to become "used to" the side effects and occasionally the main effects of pain medication. This is not the same as addiction (see the chapter 19 for more detail on the definition of addiction to pain medication; see Cherny, 2000, for a review of findings).

One of the more prominent side effects of pain medications is somnolence. This may initially make daily functioning difficult, especially for tasks such as driving. Although patients usually become tolerant to this effect, caution must still be exercised. Many states have laws prohibiting driving while taking a medication that could impair performance, even if the person is not clearly impaired at the time.

Other side effects include gastrointestinal effects such as nausea or constipation. These may be minimized by taking medications with food, increasing attention to nutritional elements such as fiber, changing medication, or using an additional medication directed at the side effect. Patients may be reluctant to discuss side effects, especially embarrassing ones, with their physician. Good communication is essential and can be encouraged.

Comfort Care

The goal of comfort care is to minimize the symptoms of cancer as the patient prepares for death. Curative treatment is neither a primary nor a secondary goal. Symptoms such as pain, anxiety, breathing difficulties, incontinence, and skin breakdown are all managed with the first and foremost goal of decreasing patient discomfort. Agencies such as Hospice are excellent resources for providing comfort care and offer services to support the family and other caregivers both before and after the patient's death. This is generally during the last 6 months of the patient's life. Hospice care usually occurs in the patient's home with the family as caregivers, but may also be available for patients in extended care facilities.

An important aspect of comfort care is clarity about end-of-life decisions. Although it is advisable for all patients to have written instructions for their end-of-life decisions and someone to carry out those wishes, for cancer patients this becomes essential. These documents are known by many names, such as advanced directive, health care power of attorney, care level, or end-of-life directive. These documents specify the level of care the patient wishes to undergo to avoid or postpone death. They can range in aggressiveness from comfort care only, to acceptance of certain medicines such as antibiotics, to accepting aggressive life-sustaining methods such as mechanical ventilation or defibrillation (shocking the heart). These decisions are very personal and having them carried out requires discussion with both the health care team and the patient's family and friends.

Clinical Trials

Because cancer treatment is such a rapidly changing area of medicine, many cancer patients may be involved in treatment via clinical trials or protocols. The type of treatment, and the goal of the treatment, may vary by type of trial and patient's prognosis. Phase 1 trials are the starting point for evaluating a potential new treatment. In these, a treatment (usually chemotherapeutic agent) that has shown promise in laboratory or animal studies is evaluated for safety and side effects in humans. At the same time, any possible anticancer activity is evaluated. The patients who agree to participate in these trials are often altruistic because the ability of these agents to cure or even palliate is unknown. Patients may express the hope that their participation will help someone else.

Phase 2 trials are the next step. Agents that have been shown to have some antitumor activity with acceptable toxicities are further evaluated. Usually, patients with specific types of cancer are evaluated, and optimal dosage is determined. Again, the agents are evaluated for clinical efficacy and acceptable toxicities. Cure or palliation is possible with these regimens, but they certainly are not guaranteed.

In Phase 3 trials, agents that have shown promise with specific cancers are evaluated directly against current standard treatment in a randomized clinical trial. Both the trial agent and the standard therapy are known to have the potential for cure or palliation. It is through these trials that new standards of care with better prognosis may be found. For these trials, the patients are randomly assigned to a treatment regimen, so both clinician and patient must believe that both arms are acceptable treatment options.

Complementary and Alternative Therapies

During the course of treatment, many patients may consider or adopt complementary or alternative therapies. Defined simply, complementary therapies enhance the standard medical treatments the patient is undergoing. Complementary therapies include such modalities as diet, exercise, relaxation, or vitamins. Relaxation is discussed in more detail separately in this chapter. In contrast, alternative therapies are adopted instead of conventional therapy. Although many patients are attracted by the claims of cure, these claims are largely based on anecdotal evidence.

Few of these therapies have been evaluated by rigorous, scientific means. In 1998, The National Cancer Institute established an Office of Cancer Complementary and Alternative Medicine to evaluate a wide range of these therapies. A variety of alternative and complementary therapies (nutrition, homeopathic approaches, acupuncture) are used by cancer patients to improve well-being, but a comprehensive review is not possible here (see Doan, 1998; Cassileth, 1998). It is important for patients to discuss these therapies with their health care team, especially because these treatments may counteract or interact with standard therapies. One patient's perspective is presented in the work of Harpham (2001).

Prevention and Screening

Screening for cancer is both well established and, in some cases, controversial. A wide variety of cancers, including breast, cervical, colon, skin, and testicular cancers, can be detected with screening tests. Methods range from observational (skin) to simple examination (testicular) to procedural (colon) or combinations of these (breast with self-exam, clinical breast exam, and mammography). Prevention of cancer is also an important area, particularly for smoking-related cancers. In addition, dietary factors and environmental factors play a role in cancer development and thus in prevention.

Genetic markers are an emerging area of focus in cancer development as more and more gene mutations that lead to cancer are identified. This has the advantage of allowing development of targeted therapies with greater efficacy and decreased side effects. However, this raises the issue of screening for genetic markers for cancer development in subsequent generations, with implications for possible interventive therapy and insurability issues. For example, a young female patient who is found to be positive for markers for breast cancer may face the decision to undergo double mastectomy or face a change in insurance coverage. Both individual and family genetic counseling can be an important aspect of these decisions.

PSYCHOLOGICAL ISSUES IN CANCER: WHAT PATIENTS AND FAMILIES ENCOUNTER THROUGHOUT THE PROCESS

At the Time of Diagnosis and During Treatment

At the time of diagnosis, patients and family members can experience a wide range of emotional responses, including shock, anger, denial, anxiety about treatment, sadness, despair, and fears about death. As patients learn about their disease and treatment, some relief may come with accurate information. Psychological distress has been shown to be prevalent at diagnosis and throughout the course of treatment, although it typically diminishes over time (Glanz & Lerman, 1992).

Several factors have been identified that affect patients' adjustment to cancer. Broadly, these factors include the intensity of medical and cancer-related problems, social support, economic resources, personality traits or premorbid psychological functioning, and length of time since treatment completion (Kornblith, 1998).

During treatment, a number of psychological issues can arise. Depression has been cited as one of the most common psychiatric complications of cancer, as has anxiety (Sellick & Crooks, 1999; Shapiro et al., 2001). Cancer survivors tend to show higher levels of depression, as compared to the normal population; however, their levels of depression, anxiety, and distress are significantly lower than those of psychiatric patients (Vantspijker, Trijsburg, & Duivenvoorden, 1997). Adjustment disorders are also commonly seen among cancer patients (Derogatis et al., 1983). Cancer has been conceptualized as a complex stressor, with a number of events that involve threat, pain, or loss, which can be traumatic (Baum & Posluszny, 2001). Some cancer treatments, particularly those that are more prolonged, extensive, or aver-

sive (e.g., bone marrow transplantation), may put patients at higher risk for distress (Cordova, Andrykowski, & Kenady, 1995).

Physical changes and side effects vary by type and intensity of treatment and can significantly impact quality of life during and after treatment. Depending on the location of the tumor, cancer surgery may result in physical changes, disfigurement, changes in functioning, and changes in body image (e.g., adjusting to a mastectomy, learning to manage a colostomy bag). Weight changes, hair loss, nausea, and vomiting associated with chemotherapy can certainly affect quality of life for patients. As mentioned, pain is a common experience and concern for cancer patients, and pain control is an important goal for the well-being of the patient. Fatigue is also a side effect of many cancer therapies, and survivors report fatigue is one of the most important issues following treatment (Harpham, 1999). Fatigue affects quality of life across domains by affecting the ability to engage in social, family, and employment activities.

After Treatment and During Survivorship

Cancer survivors move through three stages, from acute survival (from diagnosis through the first year), through extended survival (from the first year until 3 years later), and to permanent survival (after 3 years postdiagnosis) (Mullin, 1990). As more time passes, adjustment and quality of life typically improve (Gotay & Muraoka, 1998); for most patients, distress declines within a year following treatment (Glanz & Lerman, 1992). However, a significant minority of patients remains distressed after treatment, and "returning to normal" after cancer can be challenging.

After treatment, common concerns include fear of recurrence, fatigue, and readjustment to social roles and relationships (Bloom, 2002; Harpham, 1999). Although posttraumatic stress disorder among cancer patients is still under investigation, cancer patients report higher levels of posttraumatic stress symptoms, such as reexperiencing, avoidance, and hyperarousal, compared to normal controls (Alter et al., 1996).

In contrast to the negative effects of cancer, there is some evidence to suggest that cancer survivors have an equivalent, and in some cases enhanced, quality of life. Gotay and Muraoka (1998) reported that long-term survivors of adult-onset cancers are generally satisfied with their health and their lives. In fact, this review documented the positive coping strategies used by survivors and the benefits of having faced and survived a life-threatening disease. The experience of surviving cancer has been associated with positive changes in the quality of one's life (Cella, 1986). Many survivors acknowledge that cancer helped them to focus on important priorities, to have a greater appreciation for life, and to strengthen their religious faith or sense of purpose.

Facing Recurrence and Terminal Illness

Despite advances in screening and treatment, many patients face recurrence and terminal illness. This may be a recurrence of the original cancer, or it may be related to previous treatment. As cancer treatment has improved, an additional long-term effect has been noted with some treatments (especially older chemotherapy agents): a secondary cancer. Alternatively, this may be a second primary cancer because cancer survivors are at increased risk for other cancers.

Recurrence is associated with intense emotional reactions, the resurfacing of emotions from the initial diagnosis, guilt, and self-blame (Mahon, Cella, & Donovan, 1990). Patients' responses may vary from optimistic ("I beat it once, I will again") to extreme pessimism ("I can't do this again"). The patient's experience and reactions to the initial treatment may play a role in the response. Depression, common at diagnosis, is also commonly seen at recurrence and terminal stages of disease (Hotopf, Chidgey, Addington-Hall, & Ly, 2002). Existential and family concerns are increasingly important during these phases. Along with depression, anxiety and confusion are often important issues to address in palliative and comfort care (Barraclough, 1997).

Family Dynamics

To a large extent, cancer is a family issue. Family members may have fears about their own cancer risk if there is a genetic link. Regardless of the type of cancer, cancer has an impact on family stress, functioning, and decisions. As a result, there may be changes in family roles and relationships. Parents often report concern about their children's adjustment and may benefit from support or resources (Harpham, 1997).

In addition to the emotional stress of cancer in the family, there are often physical and financial demands on families as a result of the patient's needs. Increasingly, the family is called on to provide more care at home, and caregiver stress is receiving more attention (Chan & Chang, 1999). Spouses and family members may benefit from individual therapy, family therapy, or support groups for caregivers. Hospice services are also another good source of support for patients and family members at home.

COPING WITH CANCER:
HOW PSYCHOLOGISTS
CAN HELP PATIENTS

Psychotherapeutic interventions can help cancer patients reduce distress, improve mood, enhance quality of life, and develop coping skills. Research suggests that coping with cancer in an active, direct way leads to better adjustment (Holland & Rowland, 1990), and strategies based on avoidance are related to distress in cancer patients (Carver et al., 1993; Osowiecki & Compas, 1999). The following summary focuses on approaches in psychotherapy to help patients deal with the challenges of cancer. Psychotherapeutic techniques include supportive psychotherapy focused on existential issues, cognitive–behavioral techniques to manage symptoms, psychoeducational strategies to enhance communication and control, behavioral strategies to make health changes and solve problems, and a variety of group therapies, notably supportive-expressive and psychoeducational groups.

Address Existential Issues

Cancer can involve many losses: loss of health, loss of body, loss of fertility, loss of functioning, and, at times, loss of life. Psychologists are in a unique position to help patients grieve the losses they anticipate and experience. Facing the possibility and reality of death can be frightening. Patients may not feel comfortable discussing these issues with family, friends, physicians, or other professionals because of their own emphasis on or other people's investment in remaining positive and successfully curing cancer. Patients may also perceive other people's discomfort with discussions of death and dying and would rather not cause them distress. Often, patients appreciate having a safe place in psychotherapy to talk about these losses and fears.

Despite many losses, the experience of cancer can also provide an impetus to find purpose and meaning in life. Cancer patients often strive to find meaning in this experience, and cancer can provide the potential for positive psychological change (Andrykowski, Brady, & Hunt, 1993). Helping patients determine what is most important in their lives, exploring priorities, and addressing "unfinished business" are meaningful activities. Regardless of prognosis, cancer can provide the motivation to make changes in one's life.

Manage Symptoms

Clinicians who work with cancer patients are typically well versed in the general treatment of depression and anxiety. It is important to evaluate and treat comorbid depression, adjustment, and anxiety disorders to enhance a patient's quality of life as well as diminish the possible exacerbation of treatment difficulties (e.g., pain, fatigue, nonadherence). Given the stressful nature of cancer, patients are often taught a variety of stress management skills.

Psychologists also teach patients a variety of skills to manage the specific physical and psychological symptoms associated with cancer. Relaxation training (progressive muscle relaxation, deep breathing, self-hypnosis, visualization, guided imagery, meditation, etc.) can be extremely helpful to patients to reduce arousal during procedures, manage nausea, and enhance well-being. Systematic desensitization can be used to manage anticipatory nausea associated with chemotherapy as well as phobias or other problems with an anxiety component.

Psychologists can help patients with pain-related issues in a number of ways. Patients can be encouraged to communicate with physicians about pain levels and concerns. This communication can be used to clarify expectations, provide education about pain medication, and address concerns about the risk of addiction, thus preventing problems in the future. Teaching patients to accurately report the intensity, time course, and qualitative descriptors of pain may facilitate communication with the health care team. Patients also benefit from learning pain management strategies, such as relaxation, imagery/distraction, or other cognitive–behavioral techniques to enhance coping and control, as an adjunct to medication (Breitbart & Payne, 1998).

Fatigue is often a target for intervention. Psychologists can help patients learn energy conservation techniques, such as pacing activities and avoiding deconditioning.

Symptom management strategies should be conducted in collaboration with a patient's medical team, so that patients are encouraged to talk with physicians about treatable medical conditions (e.g., anemia-related fatigue), medications (antidepressants), and symptom levels (e.g., using a 10-point pain-rating scale to monitor the effectiveness of pain interventions).

Empower Patients

Cancer can make patients feel helpless, with little control over their own lives and health. Psychologists can empower patients to seek information in an effort to gain control, reduce uncertainty, and make the best treatment decisions possible. The amount of information gathered and the pacing of this process will depend on the patient. Encouraging patients to ask questions of their medical team, discuss options, and obtain second opinions can reassure them about the best course of treatment. Talking with other survivors can provide valuable advice about how to cope. Patients can also be encouraged to contact reputable organizations, such as the National Cancer Institute and American Cancer Society, for information. Patients may benefit from using other community resources such as "wellness communities," hospital information centers, and support groups.

Another way to gain control after a diagnosis of cancer is to change behaviors to improve health. Although some patients may not be ready to make behavioral changes at diagnosis, many patients decide to quit smoking, change their diet, or improve stress management, and there are psychological and physical benefits of doing so. Psychologists can help patients make a plan, garner support, monitor progress, prepare for pitfalls, and maintain lifestyle changes. Providing guidance to patients regarding these behavioral changes, in conjunction with referrals and support from other health care professionals, can help individuals gain control over important aspects of their health and well-being.

Helping patients prepare for medical visits and to communicate with the health care team is another potential area for intervention. Appointments are often anxiety provoking for patients, but they represent important opportunities to learn crucial information. Psychologists can normalize the emotional impact of appointments while helping patients maximize their use of appointments. For example, patients can be encouraged to bring written questions, take notes or tape-record discussions (with permission), or bring a family member or friend for support at appointments. Communication and assertiveness skills are important, especially when patients and health care providers have different ideas about the focus of treatment, prognosis, or quality of life.

One common example of this discrepancy is when a patient's expectation for a cure does not match the physician's estimate of a patient's prognosis. Another difficulty can arise when a physician recommends intensive treatment to give the best chance for control or cure, but the patient prefers to avoid anticipated side effects or does not want to undergo additional treatment. Helping patients clearly discuss their preferences or learn more information from their health care providers may be of benefit. Patients may appreciate the chance to explore their wishes, identify questions, or role-play discussions in therapy sessions.

Enhance Support

Research indicates a consistent relationship between emotional support and better quality of life for cancer patients (Helgeson & Cohen, 1996); thus, helping patients obtain and sustain support is an important focus of psychotherapeutic work. Often at the time of diagnosis, there is an outpouring of support from family and friends. This support can be extremely helpful, but it can also be challenging to manage, and sometimes well-intentioned efforts are not useful.

Psychologists can help patients assertively ask for support and accept help that matches their needs. For example, if a patient is overwhelmed by phone calls inquiring about the diagnosis, the patient could ask a family member to answer calls and provide information or encourage friends and family members to send cards in lieu of multiple phone calls. The timing of support is also important. For example, a patient may "take a rain check" on a friend's offer to help with meals or housework, to be "redeemed" once chemotherapy begins. Patients may expect and benefit from different types of support from different sources (Rose, 1990), and psychologists can help them choose the best sources for the task at hand. For example, patients may want to request practical support from a spouse or family member after surgery, but choose to discuss concerns about coping with chemotherapy with another cancer survivor.

Cancer patients often use support groups, and they are associated with psychological benefits such as reduced distress and pain (Spiegel, 2001). In addition, some group psychotherapy studies have demonstrated a positive effect on survival (Fawzy et al., 1993; Spiegel, Bloom, Kraemer, & Gottheil, 1989); the literature is still not consistent on this issue, and additional research is needed. Supportive-expressive group therapy was initially developed for patients with metastases and focuses on emotional expression and existential issues. Educational support groups generally provide information about one's disease and coping skills. Support groups can increase a sense of purpose and decrease isolation, but not all patients benefit from them. In at least one study, a short-term discussion group increased negative affect among participants (Helgeson, Cohen, Schulz, & Yasko, 2001). It is important for patients to consider which services meet their current support needs best.

EXPECTATIONS AND RELATIONSHIPS WITH MEDICAL TEAM AND CANCER PATIENTS: HOW PSYCHOLOGISTS CAN WORK EFFECTIVELY

Collaborative Care Arrangements

Many cancer centers have psycho-oncology services, which may include a variety of mental health and supportive services. Depending on the system, services may be initiated by a physician, through self-referral, through a standard screening process, or as a normal part of cancer care. Psychologists who work in cancer centers have unique opportunities to work with patients and staff in a flexible way. For example, psychological visits can be paired with medical appointments, or before or after surgery on an inpatient basis. For patients with anxiety disorders or anticipatory nausea, treatment can be conducted in vivo, with gradual exposure to the chemotherapy area, equipment, or other feared stimuli.

Psycho-oncologists often have opportunities to exchange information with medical professionals about a patient's psychological status and to learn about a patient's medications, side effects, or disease status. Collaborating with psychiatrists or the patient's medical practitioners regarding the potential need for psychotropic medications can facilitate better patient care.

Communication Strategies and Expectations of Medical Practitioners

Regardless of one's location in a cancer center, outpatient setting, or primary care office, it is important to inform referral sources about the range and parameters of psychological services and referrals. Before providing services, it is important to clarify the purpose of the referral. Does the physician want a psychological evaluation, and which specific questions are being asked (e.g., regarding cognitive status, psychological adjustment to cancer, suicidality)? Is the physician or is the patient requesting psychotherapy services?

Although federal legislation (Health Insurance Portability and Accountability Act, or HIPAA) established stronger safeguards of patient privacy,

reminding patients and referral sources about issues of confidentiality is still important. Depending on the nature of the problem and current level of care, it may be helpful to contact primary care physicians or oncologists (e.g., discussing patient's anticipatory nausea with the medical oncologist). Physicians may hope that, through psychological intervention, patients will agree to undergo recommended medical treatment.

Although this may occur (e.g., patient's depression remits, patient feels more able to handle another course of chemotherapy), in other cases it may not be the patient's goal to return to treatment (we discuss this in more detail below). In other cases, physicians may refer patients who are disruptive, use more resources, or have long-standing personality disorders. For example, physicians may refer a patient who is hypervigilant or, more extremely, has a somatization disorder in hopes that the patient will be "fixed" quickly. Psychological intervention can help, but this process takes time; in any case, it is not likely that a cancer patient will stop being watchful for symptoms. Physicians may benefit from information to help them adopt realistic expectations about such patients.

Avoiding Common Mistakes in Psychological Work With Cancer Patients

Psychotherapy with cancer patients can be rewarding, but a number of challenges accompany this work. As a therapist, it is important to examine and address one's own experiences with cancer personally, as well as feelings about death and dying, when working with patients who have cancer. Several other key issues, requiring balance and sensitivity, are illustrated here, with a description of possible challenges.

Remain Neutral and Objective Regarding Patient Choices

Physicians often refer patients who are having difficulty adhering to medications or are refusing a recommended course of treatment. Mental health professionals, in an effort to respond to the concerns of the referring physician, may make the mistake of "persuading" the patient to continue with or follow a course of treatment. It is important to avoid giving medical advice outside one's expertise and to remain neutral and objective when providing psychological evaluation and services. Rapport and honest reflection are more likely to occur in the absence of judgment, and the patient may be more open to returning for psychological services regardless of medical choices. By assessing the patient's psychological and mental status, understanding of treatment options, and reactions to possible consequences, the psychologist can then provide valuable information to aid both the patient and physician in the decision-making process.

Respect the Power of Hope

It is very important for patients to have hope about their lives, their treatment, and their goals. Finding a purpose and meaning in life within one's limits is very important, especially during later stages of disease (Scheier & Carver, 2001). However, in some patients, hopefulness borders on denial, and this may prevent them from making realistic plans for treatment or other activities in life. Common mistakes by therapists include encouraging false hope without the chance to examine realistic limits or, alternatively, forcing patients to focus on limits with no room for hope. Helping patients find a balance that allows hope with an acceptance of reality is a sensitive clinical issue.

Allow for a Range of Emotional Expression, Especially Regarding Mortality

Patients differ in their perceptions about what is most difficult about having cancer; in particular, patients vary with regard to their focus on their own mortality. It may be a mistake to avoid any discussion of death (and thus collude with patients). However, forcing patients to confront death or plan for it in a certain, prescribed way may increase their distress or damage the therapeutic relationship. There is a wide range of issues that may need to be addressed during therapy. For example, patients and their family members may have expectations for survival until a specific life event has occurred (e.g., graduation, anniversary, birthday). At times, these dreams are realized.

However, this expectation may not be realistic given the patient's clinical course and may cause distress for both the patient and the family if these expectations cannot be met. Providing a safe place for emotional expression to discuss all relevant issues, including those of death and dying, without forcing an agenda or time line is important.

Consider the Role of Positive Thinking

Many patients have read or heard about the ill effects of stress and the power of positive thinking, and patients often believe that positive thinking can have an impact on cancer progression. Although research in psychoneuroimmunology has identified some associations between stress and illness among healthy individuals, additional research is needed in cancer (Andersen, 2001). Tumor progression is a complex process, and it is unfair for patients to assume that their thoughts "caused" progression to occur. Stress management and positive thinking have an impact on quality of life and mood. In fact, psychologists often teach such positive cognitive strategies. However, it is important that patients understand the purpose of these interventions (to improve mood and quality of life) and do not blame themselves if their cancer worsens or recurs because they were not "positive" enough.

When to Refer to a Psycho-oncologist

Some of the mental health needs of cancer patients can be effectively addressed by a primary care psychologist who is comfortable treating patients with depression, anxiety, grief, and adjustment issues. However, there are specific situations for which one might consider a referral to a psycho-oncologist. This is recommended when the patient's concerns are directly linked to the hospital setting and would be best addressed there. For example, a patient with anticipatory nausea related to chemotherapy would be ideally be treated using systematic desensitization, working gradually with the patient in the actual medical setting. Other referrals may involve patients who have a specific phobia related to needles or procedures, which could interfere with successful treatment (e.g., initiating chemotherapy, preparation for radiation therapy, or undergoing additional biopsies). In these cases, it would be advantageous to work with a psycho-oncologist who is within the hospital setting, who has established collaborative relationships with other medical staff, and who is familiar with the medical procedures or equipment that are associated with the psychological problem. The professional's familiarity with the setting and expertise in treatment will make successful resolution more likely for the patient.

ADDITIONAL RESOURCES

Suggestions for further reading and professional development resources are available at this book's companion Web site: www.primarycarepsych.com.

Note

1. In TNM staging, *T* refers to the primary tumor size and ranges from 1 to 5 based on size and extension into surrounding normal tissues or organs, with higher numbers signifying larger, more extensive primary tumors. *N* refers to involvement of nearby or distant lymph nodes and ranges from 0 (no nodal involvement) to 3 (distant lymph nodes on the opposite side of the body from the primary tumor). *M* refers to the presence (M1) or absence (M0) of distant metastases involving other organs.

References

Anderson, B. (2001). A biobehavioral model for psychological interventions. In A. Baum & B. L. Anderson (Eds.), *Psychosocial interventions for cancer* (pp. 119–129). Washington, DC: American Psychological Association.

Andrykowski, M. A., Brady, M. J., & Hunt, J. W. (1993). Positive psychosocial adjustment in potential bone marrow transplant recipients: Cancer as a psychosocial transition. *Psycho-Oncology, 2*, 261–276.

Alter, C. L., Pelcovitz, D., Axelrod, A., Goldenberg, B., Harris, H., Meyers, B., Brobois, B., Mandel, F., Septimus, A., & Kaplan, S. (1996). Identification of PTSD in cancer survivors. *Psychosomatics, 37*, 137–143.

Barraclough, J. (1997). ABC of palliative care. Depression, anxiety, and confusion. *BMJ, 315*, 1365–1368.

Baum, A., & Posluszny, D. M. (2001). Traumatic stress as a target for intervention with cancer patients. In A. Baum & B. L. Anderson (Eds.), *Psychosocial interventions for cancer* (pp. 143–173). Washington, DC: American Psychological Association.

Bloom, J. R. (2002). Surviving and thriving? *Psycho-Oncology, 11*, 89–92.

Breitbart, W., & Payne, D. K. (1998). Pain. In J. Holland (Ed.), *Psycho-oncology* (pp. 450–467). New York: Oxford University Press.

Carver, C. S., Pozo, C., Harris, S. D., Noriega, V., Scheier, M. F., Robinson, D. S., Ketcham, A. S., Moffat, F. L., Jr., & Clark, K. C. (1993). How coping mediates the effect of optimism on distress: A study of women with early stage breast cancer. *Journal of Personality and Social Psychology, 65*, 375–390.

Cassileth, B. R. (Ed.). (1998). *The alternative medicine handbook: The complete reference guide to alternative and complementary therapies.* New York: Norton.

Cella, D. F. (1986). Psychological sequelae in the cured cancer patient. In D. J. Higby (Ed.), *Issues in supportive care of cancer patients* (pp. 149–171). Boston: Martinus-Nijhoff.

Chan, C. W., & Chang, A. M. (1999). Stress associated with tasks for family caregivers of patients with cancer in Hong Kong. *Cancer Nursing, 22*, 260–265.

Cherny, N. I. (2000). The management of cancer pain. *CA: A Cancer Journal for Clinicians, 50*, 70–116.

Cordova, M. J., Andrykowski, M. A., & Kenady, D. E. (1995). Frequency and correlates of posttraumatic stress disorder-like symptoms after treatment for breast cancer. *Journal of Consulting and Clinical Psychology, 63*, 981–986.

Derogatis, L., Morrow, G., Fetting, J., Penman, D., Piasetsky, S., Schmale, A., Heinrichs, M., & Carnicke, C. (1983). The prevalence of psychiatric disorders among cancer patients. *Journal of the American Medical Association, 249*, 751–757.

Doan, B. D. (1998). Alternative and complementary therapies. In J. Holland (Ed.), *Psycho-oncology* (pp. 817–827). New York: Oxford University Press.

Fawzy, F. I., Fawzy, N. W., Hyun, C. S., Gutherie, D., Gahey, J. L., & Morton, D. (1993). Malignant melanoma: Effects of an early structured psychiatric intervention, coping, and affective state on recurrence and survival six years later. *Archives of General Psychiatry, 50*, 681–689.

Glanz, K., & Lerman, C. (1992). Psychosocial impact of breast cancer: A critical review. *Annals of Behavioral Medicine, 14,* 204–212.

Gotay, C. C., & Muraoka, M. Y. (1998). Quality of life in long-term survivors of adult-onset cancers. *Journal of the National Cancer Institute, 90,* 656–667.

Harpham, W. S. (1997). *When a parent has cancer: A guide to caring for your children.* New York: HarperCollins.

Harpham, W. S. (1999). Resolving the frustration of fatigue. *CA: A Cancer Journal for Clinicians, 49,* 178–189.

Harpham, W. S. (2001). Alternative therapies for curing cancer: What do patients want? What do patients need? *CA: A Cancer Journal for Clinicians, 51,* 131–136.

Helgeson, V. S., & Cohen, S. (1996). Social support and adjustment to cancer: Reconciling the descriptive, correlational, and intervention research. *Health Psychology, 15,* 135–148.

Helgeson, V. S., Cohen, S., Schulz, R., & Yasko, J. (2001). Group support interventions for people with cancer: Benefits and hazards. In A. Baum & B. Andersen (Eds.), *Psychosocial interventions for cancer* (pp. 269–286). Washington, DC: American Psychological Association.

Holland, J., & Rowland, J. (Eds.). (1990). *Handbook of psychooncology: Psychologic care of the patient with cancer.* Newark, NJ: Oxford University Press.

Hotopf, M., Chidgey, J., Addington-Hall, J., & Ly, K. L. (2002). Depression in advanced disease: A systematic review. Part 1. Prevalence and case finding. *Palliative Medicine, 16,* 81–97.

Jemal, A., Thomas, A., Murray, T., & Thun, M. (2002). Cancer statistics, 2002. *CA: A Cancer Journal for Clinicians, 52,* 23–47.

Kornblith, A. B. (1998). Psychosocial adaptation of cancer survivors. In J. Holland (Ed.), *Psychooncology* (pp. 223–254). New York: Oxford University Press.

Mahon, S. M., Cella, D. F., & Donovan, M. I. (1990). Psychological adjustment to recurrent cancer. *Oncology Nursing Forum, 17,* 47–52.

Mullin, F. (1990). *Charting the journey: Almanac of practical resources for cancer survivors.* Mt. Vernon, NY: Consumers Union.

Osowiecki, D. M., & Compas, B. E. (1999). A prospective study of coping, perceived control, and psychological adaptation to breast cancer. *Cognitive Therapy and Research, 23,* 169–180.

Porter, J., & Jick, H. (1980). Addiction rare in patients treated with narcotics. *New England Journal of Medicine, 302,* 123.

Rose, J. H. (1990). Social support and cancer: Adult patients' desire for support from family, friends, and health professionals. *American Journal of Community Psychology, 18,* 439–464.

Scheier, M. F., & Carver, C. S. (2001). Adapting to cancer: The importance of hope and purpose. In A. Baum & B. L. Anderson (Eds.), *Psychosocial interventions for cancer* (pp. 15–36). Washington, DC: American Psychological Association.

Sellick, S. M., & Crooks, D. L. (1999). Depression and cancer: An appraisal of the literature for prevalence, detection, and practice guideline development for psychological interventions. *Psycho-oncology, 8,* 315–333.

Shapiro, S. L., Lopez, A. M., Schwartz, G. E., Bootzin, R., Figueredo, A. J., Bradnen, C. J., et al. (2001). Quality of life and breast cancer: Relationship to psychosocial variables. *Journal of Clinical Psychology, 57,* 501–519.

Spiegel, D. (2001). Mind matters—Group therapy and survival in breast cancer [editorial]. *New England Journal of Medicine, 345,* 1767–1768.

Spiegel, D., Bloom, J. R., Kraemer, H. C., & Gottheil, E. (1989). Effect of psychosocial treatment on survival of patients with metastatic breast cancer. *Lancet, 2,* 888–891.

Vantspijker, A., Trijsburg, R. W., & Duivenvoorden, H. J. (1997). Psychological sequelae of cancer diagnosis—A meta-analytical review of 58 studies after 1980. *Psychosomatic Medicine, 59,* 280–293.

21

Dementia and
Late-Life Depression

Christopher M. Callahan
Mary G. Austrom
Frederick W. Unverzagt

Caring for older adults, particularly those suffering from the common disorders of dementia and depression, presents a unique challenge to health care professionals for several reasons. First, older adults typically present with comorbid conditions. These comorbid conditions may include medical diseases such as heart disease, diabetes, or arthritis; nonspecific symptoms such as pain, fatigue, or insomnia; psychiatric conditions such as depression, anxiety, or substance abuse; or taking multiple medications with multiple side effects. Second, older adults are more likely to present with chronic rather than acute conditions. The chronic nature of these conditions renders them more complex and potentially less amenable to treatment. Third, the goals of care often are more appropriately focused on functional independence than longevity or cure. Diagnostic strategies, intervention, and treatments that might be appropriate for younger patients may be inappropriate for any given older adult if they lower current quality of life to obtain uncertain long-term benefits. Fourth, negotiating goals of care often involves not only the patient, but also family caregivers, other health care professionals involved

in the patient's treatments, and even third-party payers.

Although there is certainly increased chronic illness and disability in older adults, not all stresses among elders are because of medical illnesses or the side effects of treatment. Retirement, loss of role functioning, loss of loved ones, financial stressors, and awareness of unrealized or lost opportunities may all result in both physical and mental symptoms.

The challenges of caring for the older adult are best met first with a careful assessment of symptoms, careful history taking, and a longitudinal approach to care. Small therapeutic interventions and frequent reassessment for progress characterize care for older adults. A frequent geriatric aphorism suggests "Start low, go slow, but go!" Advice to move with caution in older adults should not be confused with a misperception not to proceed at all. The call for a longitudinal approach recognizes not only a chronic care model, but also the need to frequently adjust treatments, monitor for adverse events, and reconsider diagnoses if improvement does not match expectations. Finally, many of the treatments recommended by practitioners will require action, collaboration, and self-management on the part of the patient. Education, socioeconomics, culture, and self-efficacy all play a role in the success of self-management.

Cognitive changes are the most common sources of psychological complaints presented by older patients, and they are the focus of dementia and depression sections of the chapter. Although dementia and depression are the most prevalent psychological disorders among older adult primary care patients, delirium is the condition that often demands the most urgent attention.

DELIRIUM AS A MEDICAL EMERGENCY

The hallmark of delirium is an attention disorder. Older adults with cognitive impairment are particularly vulnerable to delirium. Delirium in older adults represents a medical emergency and is almost always caused by medical disorders outside the central nervous system (Francis, Martin, & Kapoor, 1990). Conditions such as acute infections outside the central nervous system, adverse drug events, dehydration, and low blood sugar more commonly cause delirium in older adults than head trauma, psychosis, or meningitis, for example. Also, the etiology of delirium is typically multifactorial, so that in many patients two or three causes combined can trigger symptoms.

One common instrument available to aid in the recognition of delirium is the confusion assessment method (CAM; Inouye, 1994). To diagnose delirium using the CAM, the clinician assesses the patient for (a) an acute change in mentation and a fluctuating course; (b) evidence of inattention; (c) evidence of disorganized thinking; and (d) an altered level of consciousness. The diagnosis of delirium requires presence of items a *and* b *and* either c or d. Patients diagnosed with delirium require an emergent evaluation by a physician. The following case report depicts the often-complicated presentation of an elderly patient with an acute change in condition.

Mrs. Jones is an 81-year-old white woman with a history of mild-to-moderate dementia, hypertension, and diabetes. The patient and her daughter have been receiving counseling from a psycholo-gist for caregiver stress. Mrs. Jones is still independent in her self-care and lives in an apartment next door to her daughter. The daughter must visit her mother daily to help prepare meals and assist with medications. Mrs. Jones frequently calls her daughter throughout the night for various concerns. At a recent primary care visit, the patient's blood pressure and blood sugar were elevated, and the primary care physician increased Mrs. Jones's diuretic and oral hypoglycemic agent.

Mrs. Jones and her daughter come to the psychologist's office for a scheduled visit 5 days after the primary care visit. The daughter is suggesting treatment for her mother's "depression." Over the last few days, the mother has become increasingly withdrawn and uncooperative. On exam, the psychologist notes that the patient is somewhat somnolent, and when she does engage in conversation, her speech is rambling and incoherent. This is a clear change in mentation since the prior examination. The daughter is instructed to take the patient to the emergency room immediately.

In the emergency room, the patient is noted to be dehydrated and hypotensive, and she has an elevated blood sugar and a urinary tract infection. On questioning the daughter, the physician finds that she recently began giving her mother an over-the-counter sleeping pill. Mrs. Jones's mentation returns to normal over the next week as each of these problems (infection, dehydration, medication side effects) is resolved.

In a patient without a baseline dementia, any one of the problems noted in this case would be less likely to precipitate delirium. However, in an older adult, these problems tend to cascade and interact and present as psychiatric symptoms rather than acute medical conditions.

CLINICAL EPIDEMIOLOGY OF DEMENTIA AND DEPRESSION

The psychologist practicing in or consulting with primary care clinics is very likely to encounter patients with dementia and other age-associated cognitive disorders. Population studies are consistent in showing that about 4% to 5% of community-dwelling persons older than 65 years suffer from dementia (Hendrie, Osuntokun, et al., 1995).

Prevalence rates increase dramatically with age, ranging from 1% to 2% for persons aged 65–74 years to 17% to 18% for persons aged 85 years and older. A meta-analysis indicated that the incidence of dementia also increases with increasing age, at less than 1% annually in those aged 65–74 years, but rising to 7% annually in those older than 84 years (Gao, Hendrie, Hall, & Hui, 1998). Among elders, mild cognitive impairment known as "cognitive impairment, no dementia" is more common than dementia, with studies reporting prevalence rates between 11% and 27% (Unverzagt, Gao, et al., 2001).

Although dementia and cognitive dysfunction are common in the primary care setting, they are frequently unrecognized by family members and care providers. A population-based study found that 21% of families failed to recognize memory loss in subjects subsequently diagnosed with dementia; of those recognizing a problem, only 47% sought medical assessment for the involved individual (Ross, Abbott, Petrovitch, et al., 1997). In another study, nearly 75% of subjects subsequently found to have moderate to severe cognitive dysfunction did not have a dementia diagnosis on the chart (Callahan, Hendrie, & Tierney, 1995).

These data suggest that the psychologist in primary care may be the first to recognize dementia or clinically important cognitive loss in a patient. As a result, skill in the differential diagnosis of memory loss in the aged as well as general clinical assessment acumen are critical. This environment places a premium on the psychologist's ability to address denial in family members, promote adaptive responding in the patient and caregiver, and negotiate complex and potentially charged family dynamics. In addition, these studies indicate that, at least for some of these patients, consultation skills will be required as the psychologist alerts the primary care team to a previously unrecognized, clinically important cognitive problem.

Dementia is a leading cause of death in older Americans and is associated with shortened life expectancy. Patients with dementia caused by Alzheimer's disease (AD) or cerebrovascular disease are 2 to 10 times more likely to die within 5 years than the general population (Ostbye & Steenhuis, 1999). In a longitudinal registry, median survival from onset of dementia was approximately 10 years (Heyman, Peterson, Fillenbaum, & Pieper, 1996), but community-based studies, owing to nonselectivity of the sample and presence of significant comorbidities, tend to show much shorter median survival times, ranging from 3 to 5 years (Perkins, Hui, Ogunniyi, et al., 2002). Male gender, older age, more severe cognitive impairment, presence of psychotic symptoms, and presence of extrapyramidal symptoms (i.e., symptoms similar to Parkinson's disease) have all been associated with shorter survival times (Heyman et al., 1996; Stern, Tang, Albert, et al., 2002). These data imply that psychologists working in this area may also need skills in the management of patients' and families' end-of-life concerns.

AD and dementia are both emotionally and economically costly. Persons older than 60 years, who often witness the untreatable and progressive loss of mental faculties, degradation of personality, and loss of independence and dignity associated with mid- and late-stage dementia, may be more fearful of AD than cancer. The emotional burden goes beyond fear of illness; family caregivers are at increased risk for depression and other psychiatric morbidity themselves. The economic cost of dementia is also extremely high. A 1991 study estimated the total cost associated with dementia, including direct costs of care and medications, unpaid caregiver costs, and disability and premature mortality, was $173,932 per patient for an annual national (U.S.) cost of $67 billion (Ernst & Hay, 1994). The high care costs of dementia, the fact that dementia prevalence and incidence reach their peak in old age, and the fact that persons over 85 years of age represent one of the fastest growing segments of the population all combine to make dementia one of the biggest public health problems this country will face in the coming years.

Depression is also a common problem among older adults. Because depression occurs in the context of multiple physical and psychosocial problems, it is often unrecognized by both the patient and the professional. Estimates of the percentage of older adults experiencing late-life depression vary depending on clinical setting. Prevalence of depressive disorders increases with the presence and severity of comorbid illness and disability, and may affect as many as 25% of older adults with disability. In nursing home settings, the prevalence of depressive disorders has been reported to be as high as 60% (American Association for Geriatric Psychiatry, 1996; Hirschfield, Keller, Panico, et al., 1997; Lebowitz, Pearson, Schneider, et al., 1997). Among the elderly seen in primary outpatient clinics, some form of depressive illness (major depressive disorder, dysthymia, or subsyndromal depression) has been reported in 17% to 37% of the patients (Callahan, Hendrie, & Tierney, 1996; Evans & Katonen, 1993).

Depression can be associated with an exacerbation of an existing physical illness and can lead to increased disabilities and pain intensity (Stewart, Greenfield, Hays, et al., 1989; Wells, Stewart, Hays, et al., 1989). Depression is also associated with increased mortality as a result of both suicide and its effect on comorbid medical illness. However, the explanation for the relationship between the increase in nonsuicidal mortality and depression remains unclear (Conwell, 1994). Annual health care costs are higher for patients with depression, but it is difficult to tease out which components of these costs are caused by depression and which are caused by comorbid conditions (Callahan, Hui, Nienaber, et al., 1994).

STRENGTHS AND WEAKNESSES OF THE PRIMARY CARE ENVIRONMENT

Quality improvement efforts have consistently demonstrated that late-life depression and dementia are underrecognized and undertreated by primary care physicians (Callahan, 2001). Although primary care settings are well designed for the care of acute conditions of mild to moderate severity, they are poorly designed for the longitudinal management of chronic conditions. Nonetheless, primary care physicians now spend the majority of their professional time in the care of patients with chronic conditions. Many primary care visits must therefore incorporate management of multiple conditions as well as preventive health measures. These "obvious" comorbid medical conditions may dominate the time-limited patient encounter, and this situation is exacerbated among older adults, who may also present with multiple disabilities.

In addition to physician and practice environment factors, other barriers to the diagnosis and treatment of dementia and depression include patient factors such as denial, poor adherence, or beliefs that treatments are ineffective or harmful. Further, providers complain of both real and imagined financial disincentives to treatment. The combination of these factors may contribute to a nihilistic perception that recognition and treatment are futile. However, there is a growing body of literature that demonstrates the effectiveness of treatment when barriers to care are addressed in a systematic manner (e.g., Unutzer, Katon, Callahan, et al., 2002). Psychologists who can bring additional health care resources and expertise to bear and contribute to a positive environment of treatment opportunity will find a receptive primary care audience of providers, patients, and families.

DIAGNOSIS AND TREATMENT OF DEMENTIA

Most definitions of dementia require a clinically significant decline in memory or new learning ability and a decline in another aspect of thinking (language, praxis, judgment, or reasoning). In combination, these cognitive impairments must result in a decline or loss of independence in activities of daily living. These problems cannot occur exclusively as part of a delirium or confusional state. A new emphasis in the fourth edition of the *Diagnostic and Statistical Manual of Mental Disorders* (*DSM-IV*) is the differentiation of dementias by etiology (American Psychiatric Association, 1994). Although the core set of symptoms listed above is common to all dementias, distinctive aspects of history or examination are incorporated into the diagnostic criteria for specific disorders. For example, the diagnosis of dementia of the Alzheimer type (AD) requires a gradually progressive course; the diagnosis of vascular dementia, on the other hand, requires specific focal neurological signs.

The syndromal criteria for dementia have been dominated by the phenomenology of AD, which is not surprising because AD is estimated to constitute, alone or in combination, two thirds to three quarters of all dementias (Barker, Luis,

Kashuba, et al., 2002; Hendrie, Osuntokun, et al., 1995). However, there is growing concern that vascular cognitive impairment fits poorly into a dementia mold based on AD. Specifically, the criteria for dementia overemphasize memory loss, treat vascular cognitive impairment as a single condition, and require marked cognitive losses, thus negating the possibility of intervention at an early or mild stage when treatment of vascular risk factors could avert further decline (Bowler, Munoz, Merskey, & Hachinski, 1998). These concerns have resulted in a profusion of diagnostic schemes for vascular dementia.

Much of medicine and most of psychology hinges on patient self-report of symptoms and status. Faith in this methodology is tenuous at best when it comes to evaluation of cognitive and memory problems. Of normal, community-dwelling elderly, 49% report memory decline, and one quarter to one third report losing things often (O'Connor, Pollitt, Roth, Brook, & Reiss, 1990). More than two thirds of depressed elderly will report memory loss; on the other hand, at least 40% of patients with dementia report their memory as normal (O'Connor et al., 1990). The clinician relying on self-report is left in the uncomfortable position of knowing that a fair proportion of normal and depressed elderly will report memory loss, but do not really have clinically significant problems in that area; an equally large proportion of demented patients will deny such a problem despite the fact that dementia's defining feature is memory loss.

With this kind of inaccuracy embedded in history taking, it is not surprising that clinicians look to more objective measures of function. There are single test screens and screening batteries from which to choose. By far the most well-studied instrument is the Mini-Mental State Examination (MMSE; Folstein, Folstein, & McHugh, 1975). It has much to recommend its use in the primary care environment: It is brief (completed in under 5 minutes in most cases), reliable (median test-retest reliability of .85 across several samples and follow-up times up to 2 months), and valid in detecting moderate to severe dysfunction (Tombaugh & McIntyre, 1992). The Community Screening Interview for Dementia (CSID; Hall, Ogunniyi, Hendrie, et al., 1996) and Cognitive Abilities Screening Instrument (CASI; Teng,

Hasegawa, Homma, et al., 1994) have been used in large cross-national epidemiological studies. The CSID is unique in including a brief informant interview of symptoms and functional status. The Modified Mini-Mental State (3MS; Teng & Chui, 1987) and Mattis Dementia Rating Scale (Mattis, 1973) have also been used in large registry studies. The Six-Item Screener (Callahan, Unverzagt, Hui, Perkins, & Hendrie, 2002) has the advantage of being extremely brief and can be completed over the telephone, as can the Telephone Interview for Cognitive Status (TICS; Welsh, Breitner, & Magruder-Habib, 1993). The Six-Item Screener questionnaire is shown in Table 21.1.

In the mid-1980s, British researchers published a structured interview and cognitive testing procedure for dementia called the CAMDEX (Roth, Tym, Mountjoy, et al., 1986). At about the same time, the Consortium to Establish a Registry for Alzheimer Disease (CERAD) neuropsychological battery was developed as part of a larger effort to standardize the clinical diagnostic assessment of subjects in Alzheimer disease research centers funded by the National Institutes of Health. In its basic form, it consists of five separate tests covering general cognition, verbal fluency, confrontation naming, constructional ability, and new learning. It has proven reliability and validity in a wide range of settings (Ganguli, Ratcliff, & Huff, 1991; Morris, Edland, Clark, et al., 1993; Morris, Heyman, Mohs, et al., 1989; Unverzagt, Hall, et al., 2001; Unverzagt, Hall, Torke, et al., 1996; Welsh, Butters, Mohs, et al., 1994; Welsh, Fillenbaum, Wilkinson, et al., 1995). The Repeatable Battery for the Assessment of Neuropsychological Status (RBANS) (Randolph, Tierney, Mohr, & Chase, 1998) represents a well-designed and well-constructed evolution of the CERAD approach with improved coverage of cognitive domains and better psychometric features of the component tests.

In the interest of efficiency, the following discussion of the strengths, weaknesses, and interpretative strategy of cognitive screening tests focuses on the MMSE alone, although much of this discussion applies to most, if not all, screening tests. A fallacy of cognitive screening is that a single cutoff score can have utility for all patients. Care must be taken in the interpretation of scores

Table 21.1 Six-Item Screener

I would like to ask you some questions that ask you to use your memory. I am going to name three objects. Please wait until I say all three words, then repeat them. Remember what they are because I am going to ask you to name them again in a few minutes. Please repeat these words for me: APPLE—TABLE—PENNY. *(Interviewer may repeat names 3 times if necessary but repetition not scored.)*

Did patient correctly repeat all three words?	*Yes*	*No*
	Incorrect	Correct
1. What year is this?	0	1
2. What month is this?	0	1
3. What is the day of the week?	0	1
What were the three objects I asked you to remember?		
4. *Apple* =	0	1
5. *Table* =	0	1
6. *Penny* =	0	1

Note. From "Six-item Screener to Identify Cognitive Impairment Among Potential Subjects for Clinical Research," by C. M. Callahan, F. W. Unverzagt, S. L. Hui, A. Perkins, and H. C. Hendrie, 2002, *Medical Care, 40,* p. 779. Copyright 2002 by Lippincott Williams & Wilkins, Inc. Reprinted with permission.

because factors other than brain disease, including age, gender, education, reading ability, and ethnicity can affect scores on the MMSE and similar instruments (Crum, Anthony, Basset, & Folstein, 1993; Murden, McRae, Kaner, & Bucknam, 1991; O'Connor, Pollitt, Treasure, Brook, & Reiss, 1989; Unverzagt et al., 1996; Weiss, Reed, Klingman, & Abyad, 1995). In fact, approximately 25% of normal elderly African Americans with low education score below the "standard" MMSE cutoff score of 24/30 (Unverzagt et al., 1996). It is critical that clinicians assure themselves of a good match between the patient under study and the normative values used to guide test score interpretation. Uncritical application of cut scores as well as unconsidered application of norms can result in gross errors of interpretation.

Clinicians need to be aware of another limitation in the use of the MMSE and similar cognitive screening tests. These measures all tend to be skewed negatively, which means performances are not well separated in the upper score range. Figure 21.1 displays cognitive scores from the CSID (Hall et al., 1996), which is very similar to the MMSE in design and psychometric properties. A community-based sample of 2,212 elderly African Americans was screened with the CSID,

and a subset of 351 was subsequently diagnosed as normal or demented based on a detailed clinical examination. Although very few normal subjects score in the lower range of scores on the CSID, there is significant overlap between normal and dementia groups in the upper range of CSID scores.

The figure graphically demonstrates how tests of this kind are prone to false negatives; that is, they tend to be insensitive to, or miss altogether, early and mild cases of dementia. In this situation, one reasonable strategy is to look for ominous patterns of errors within the MMSE irrespective of a high total score, for example, temporal disorientation or poor delayed recall of the three objects (Callahan et al., 2002). The clinician should also carefully review the history of the present illness as described by a reliable informant. If subtle warning signs are present in either scenario, a recommendation for comprehensive neuropsychological examination is indicated. In general, a diagnosis cannot be made from a screening test score. These simple tools indicate current level of cognitive dysfunction and indicate the need for further evaluation.

Patients with dementia may complain of memory loss, difficulty with concentration, or difficulty performing a cognitive task they have previously mastered. Patients may also present with more nonspecific symptoms, such as depression, poor appetite or sleep, behavioral disturbances, or decreased social interaction. Often, a family member has noted the decline from a prior level of cognitive function; the patient may or may not be aware of the difficulty, or when aware of the difficulty, the patient may minimize the level of disability. Alternatively, some older patients may present with a fear of cognitive impairment when none exists because of difficulty remembering the names of acquaintances or losing common objects such as eyeglasses or car keys. Thus, it is important to obtain specific examples of cognitive tasks that the patient finds difficult and to obtain specific examples from family members. As noted, it is also important to complete a standardized assessment of the patient's cognitive function so that the magnitude of the impairment may be quantified.

In addition to documenting specific problems with cognition, the clinician must also explore the potential effects of comorbid medical conditions (particularly those that may affect cognitive function either directly or indirectly) and obtain a complete listing of medications. Multiple prescription and nonprescription medication may have anticholinergic side effects or other detrimental effects on the central nervous system. When the presentation is clouded by comorbidity, depression, or medications, formal neuropsychological testing may be essential.

PSEUDODEMENTIA

Severe depression is not uncommon among elders. A large population study of persons older than 65 years found a point prevalence of major depression of 4.4% in women and 2.7% in men (Steffens, Skoog, Norton, et al., 2000). Depressed patients tend to score lower than control samples on neuropsychological tests of attention and memory (approximately 1 standard deviation lower), with 2% to 15% showing clinically significant cognitive impairment (Veiel, 1997). The causal basis of the cognitive deficit in depression is uncertain; however, some postulate that a central motivational deficit may affect effortful processing and

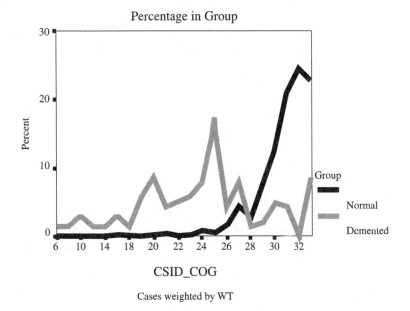

Cases weighted by WT

Figure 21.1   Cognitive scores from the Community Screening Interview for Dementia (CSID).

sustained attention, thus resulting in lowered cognitive performance.

Depressed elderly tend to report memory loss at high rates (O'Connor et al., 1990), thereby creating a challenge for differential diagnosis of depression versus dementia in this group. A careful history with the patient and an informant will usually reveal a clear psychosocial loss (e.g., divorce, death of a loved one, job loss, change in residence, interpersonal or vocational setback, loss of physical independence, illness) in the depressed patient that is temporally related to the onset of the subjective cognitive problems. The onset of problems tends to be abrupt or subacute, and there is often considerable variability in daily functioning. In these patients, it is rare to see a severe amnestic profile on neuropsychological testing. Psychotherapy and antidepressants (usually selective serotonin reuptake inhibitors [SSRIs] because of their limited anticholinergic side effects) are the treatments of choice; neuropsychological reevaluation should occur in 2 to 3 months.

Mild and severe depression can be present in patients with dementia and successfully treated with medications. In these cases, the depressed mood frequently occurs well after the memory loss has been noticed. In fact, in patients with mild depression, it is the frustration and worry associated with the loss of mental acuity and independence that precipitate depression. Unlike pseudodementia, the cognitive deficits of dementia persist even after euthymic mood is reestablished.

The neuropsychologist will act as a consultant to the primary care team in the evaluation of patients with suspected dementia. He or she will take a history from the patient and caregiver, perform a detailed psychometric assessment of several domains of function (cognitive, affective, and activities of daily living), interpret the scores based on best-available normative studies, and integrate the findings into a report that is sent to the referral source.

In a true consultant model, the primary care team integrates the findings of the consultant into their ongoing care of the patient. In other cases, the neuropsychologist will review the test findings with the patient and family and begin the process of caregiver education and support. Linking families with support organizations (e.g., Alzheimer's Association) and specialty providers (e.g., therapists experienced with caregiver adjustment) is a critical function of the neuropsychologist in this capacity.

The American Academy of Neurology published guidelines on the diagnosis and management of dementia (Doody, Stevens, Beck, et al., 2001; Knopman, Dekosky, Cummings, et al., 2001). In addition to making an explicit diagnosis, a search for reversible causes of cognitive impairment and important comorbid conditions is also recommended. This would include structural neuroimaging (head CT scan or MRI) and screening for depression, vitamin B_{12} deficiency, and hypothyroidism. Often, the diagnosis and evaluation for treatable conditions will have been completed prior to referral to the psychologist. However, practitioners must remain vigilant about the potentially deleterious effects of both prescription and nonprescription medications. Drugs with anticholinergic side effects (e.g., amitriptyline, loperamide, diphenhydramine) should be specifically avoided in older adults with dementia.

Over the past decade, a number of prescription and nonprescription pharmacological agents have been proposed in the prevention or treatment of dementia. Cholinesterase inhibitors or vitamin E have the strongest evidence base as pharmacological treatments (Doody, Stevens, Beck, et al., 2001). Other agents, such as selegiline, antioxidants, anti-inflammatories, ginkgo biloba, and estrogen, have not been clearly demonstrated to be beneficial. Many other agents are currently being investigated.

In addition to pharmacological treatment of dementia, patients and caregivers also benefit from treatment targeted to behavioral disturbances such as agitation, depression, psychosis, and repetitive behaviors. The newer atypical antipsychotic agents have been demonstrated to improve agitation and psychoses, but like any drugs used in older adults, the risk:benefit ratio of these medications in any given patient must be continually reevaluated. There is also evidence that currently available antidepressants are effective in the treatment of depression among patients with dementia. Tricyclic antidepressants with anticholinergic side effects should be avoided in favor of SSRIs in most older adults. Nonpharmacological management of behavioral disturbances is important both for the patient and the caregivers. These approaches are discussed in more detail next.

A psychologist can fill multiple roles in helping the dementia patient in the primary care setting. A crucial role is providing family support. The psychologist can educate the patient and the family regarding disease progression and prognosis, provide support, and monitor judgment and safety issues so that the patient can continue in an independent or community-dwelling role as long as possible (Guerriero Austrom & Hendrie, 2001; Richards & Hendrie, 1999). Particularly relevant is helping the family avoid feelings of isolation and hopelessness following a dementia diagnosis by the physician (Guerriero Austrom & Hendrie, 2001).

An important aspect of family support is caregiver education. Unlike other illnesses, caregiving for a person with dementia has the additional unique problem of dealing with memory loss. The educational process should include strategies for dealing with this symptom. It must be emphasized to the family caregiver that a patient with dementia who, for example, asks repetitive questions is not behaving this way intentionally. These behaviors are a manifestation of the disease, and caregivers must not take anything the patient says or does personally. This can help avoid conflicts, anger, and subsequent feelings of guilt. (Guerriero Austrom & Hendrie, 1992; Guerriero Austrom, Richards, & Hendrie, 1987; Hendrie, Unverzagt, & Guerriero Austrom, 1997).

In addition, there are a number of psychosocial interventions that may be helpful in the management of patients with dementia who develop symptoms of depression or agitation. For example, with depressed patients, emotion-oriented psychotherapy that validates their current feelings, and reminiscence therapy, which reviews important positive life events, have been reported beneficial in the mild to moderate stages of dementia (Small, Rabins, Barry, et al., 1997). Agitation often responds to an analysis of the antecedents of the behavior, followed by an appropriate intervention. For example, it is common for patients to become agitated at bath time. In this case, a review and modification of bath time procedures may be beneficial, including changing the time, personnel, or method of bathing. It is best

to prevent agitation or a catastrophic reaction if possible by avoiding the patient's exposure to the antecedent. Should the behavior get out of control, it is important to instruct the caregiver to remain calm and redirect the patient while protecting patient dignity (Guerriero Austrom & Hendrie, 2001; Hendrie et al., 1997).

One of the most effective interventions for family caregivers is a support group. Support groups can be extremely beneficial in alleviating family concerns by providing caregivers with a safe environment in which they can voice concerns and acquire additional information and help from caregivers in similar situations. Several studies of family caregivers have reported that the greatest decreases in the level of stress have followed group therapy sessions or participation in psychoeducational support groups. Many of the existing support groups are sponsored by the Alzheimer's Association. A referral to the local chapter is always advisable (Guerriero Austrom et al., 1987; Guerriero Austrom & Hendrie, 1992, 2001; Hendrie et al., 1997).

DIAGNOSIS AND TREATMENT OF LATE-LIFE DEPRESSION

DSM-IV criteria for major depressive disorder and dysthymia can be applied as well in the primary care clinic as in other settings (American Psychiatric Association, 1994). However, many patients present with symptoms that do not meet *DSM-IV* criteria for major depressive disorder or dysthymia. One of the problems in arriving at a diagnosis of depression is the fact that many primary care patients have associated medical illnesses with similar symptoms, for example, appetite loss, fatigue, and sleep disturbance. It is often unclear whether these symptoms should be attributed to the physical illness or to the depression. Because major depressive disorder is associated with significant disability (Hendrie, Callahan, et al., 1995), many practitioners propose that all symptoms should be counted to meet diagnostic criteria for depression regardless of their cause. This inclusive method will increase the chances that treatment is offered to the patient. The assumption that depressive symptoms are "understandable" contributes to the problem of undertreatment. In general, older adults meeting criteria for a major depressive disorder deserve treatment even if the symptom complex can be decomposed and serially attributed to organic causes.

When the diagnosis remains clouded, the neuropsychologist may be an invaluable consultant/liaison in conducting further diagnostic testing, considering a differential diagnosis, and intervening with patient and care team. The neuropsychologist may be in the best position to educate patient, family, and the primary care team on the effects of depression on cognition and daily function and to recommend effective forms of therapy (medications and psychotherapy).

Although there is some disagreement among experts whether the fundamental clinical presentation, symptom complex, and natural history of late-life depression differ from depression in younger age groups, practically speaking, late-life depression is harder to diagnose and manage. This is true for the same reasons that other chronic medical conditions are more difficult to diagnose and manage in older adults. Late-life depression rarely occurs in the absence of other chronic medical conditions in older adults. Therefore, the attribution of symptoms to psychiatric disease as opposed to medical disease becomes more difficult, it is more difficult to assess response to therapy and recognize relapse, and, even when recognized by physicians, older patients often prefer to ascribe psychiatric symptoms to medical illness. Furthermore, depression is a frequent concomitant of the many conditions common among older adults, including dementia, stroke, Parkinson's disease, myocardial infarction, hip fracture, chronic pain, and multiple losses, among others.

Side effects from medications are more common, patients are often on multiple medications, and physical and cognitive impairment can interfere with the older adult's participation in care. Older adults and their primary care physicians typically need additional resources to improve adherence to recommended guidelines for care, and this is an area in which psychologists can play an important role. In a multisite, randomized clinical trial, a collaborative care intervention resulted in significant improvements in treatment rates and outcome of care for depressed older adults (Unutzer et al., 2002).

Interpersonal Issues

Living with a depressed patient represents a tremendous burden for the spouse and family. This is a result of the still-widespread belief that depression does not represent a disease, and therefore the patient's behaviors, for example, of hopelessness and helplessness, are somehow volitional. It is also unfortunately true that mental illnesses, including depression, remain stigmatized particularly in the view of the elderly; therefore, many elderly people deny, avoid reporting the symptoms in themselves or loved ones, or refuse help.

Educational efforts should involve both the patient and the family. Psychologists can provide information about depression and what to expect from treatment. It is essential to explain to family members that the patient's behavioral manifestations are a result of the disease and not volitional. There is now considerable evidence that specific psychotherapies that can be administered by clinical psychologists are useful in patients with mild to moderate depression or in association with antidepressant medications. Often, these therapies are relatively short (average of 12 sessions) and quite goal oriented. Psychotherapies have included problem-solving, cognitive–behavioral, interpersonal, or brief focused psychodynamic therapy. Late-life depression can also be associated with grief and loss issues for many patients; therefore, grief therapy can also be beneficial. These issues are addressed in chapter 27.

Improving Communication Between the Psychologist and the Primary Care Practitioner

Managing patients with major neuropsychiatric disorders is a complex task. It is unlikely that a single health care professional will have the expertise available to provide comprehensive care to these patients and their families. Thus, the establishment of a multidisciplinary collaborative team that includes physicians, nurses, psychologists, and social workers is necessary. The collaborative team approach can provide the appropriate care management plan to address the medical, neuropsychological, and psychosocial needs of the patients and their families throughout the course of these chronic illnesses (Guerriero Austrom et al., 1987; Hendrie et al., 1997).

This team will be constituted differently for any given patient, but in addition to the primary care physician, the team might include a psychiatrist, psychologist, social worker, nurse, pharmacist, or a rehabilitation professional, among others. This team will rarely meet together face-to-face, and communications typically happen through written notes in a medical record. However, the psychologist is encouraged to facilitate a more interactive mode of communication with the primary care physician, especially for those cases that are particularly complex or when there seems to be a difference in opinion regarding care. A telephone call between the psychologist and the primary care physician or other health care professional may greatly improve care.

The psychologist's written communication with the primary care team will be a very important determinant of successful patient care and continued referrals. Many psychologists make the mistake of not keeping the primary care team apprised of the results of a consultation or the progress of psychotherapy. In addition to sharing written communication, all other common forms of communication in the medical arena may play a role. Individual primary care physicians will often have a preference for phone calls, face-to-face interactions, or E-mail in addition to traditional paper notes.

Consultation Notes

In general, when a request has been made for psychological or neuropsychological evaluation, the consultation note should take the form of a letter addressed to the referral source. The consult letter should be brief, 1 to 2 pages at most, and sent out within 2 weeks of the examination. Elements of an effective consultation note are listed in Table 21.2. Recognize that primary care physicians are accustomed to glancing over the first page of the assessment and moving directly to the diagno-

Table 21.2 Consultation Note Outline

Element	Contents/Length
History of the present illness[a]	One paragraph, two if information from an informant is included; description of the problem prompting the evaluation including onset and course; brief quotes from the patient describing the symptoms as appropriate; evaluations or treatments to date for presenting problem
Prior history	Review of pertinent, prior medical, psychiatric, family, and social history
Behavioral observations	Physical appearance, alertness, orientation, ability to provide history, language, affect, motor skills/movement, and cooperativeness; note threats to validity posed by poor effort or other factors
Examination and/or test results	Listing of the tests given and raw scores obtained
Diagnostic impression	Single line consisting of a *DSM* disorder (e.g., major depression) or neurobehavioral syndrome (e.g., frontal lobe syndrome)
Comment	Integrated biopsychosocial formulation of the patient, the basis of and rationale for the diagnosis, differential diagnoses considered, reasons they were ruled out or deemed unlikely, prognosis; diagnoses that may be unfamiliar to primary care providers (e.g., dissociative fugue) should be explained here
Treatment plan	Numbered or bulleted listing of further diagnostic studies that need to be done; medical/psychiatric treatments to be considered; psychological treatments to be considered, including form (e.g., group vs. individual), focus (e.g., assertiveness training vs. cognitive–behavioral treatment), and provider (name and contact number listed); suggestions for rehabilitation or compensatory strategies; psychosocial implications (e.g., guardianship, need for supervision, disability from occupation); and timing of any repeat assessment

[a]For dementia evaluations, a history of the present illness and a review of activities of daily living as provided by a reliable informant may be necessary.

sis and treatment sections. Within the treatment recommendations, serial listing of treatments or interventions that are not in the purview of the primary care physician is unwelcome. Specific action-oriented recommendations limited to 3 to 5 high-priority interventions will increase the likelihood of primary care physician adherence to recommendations.

Progress Notes

Psychotherapy progress notes should be sent to the primary care team at regular intervals, perhaps every 3 to 6 months for long-term patients. When psychotherapy terminates, a close-out note describing the history of treatment, response to same, and discharge status (e.g., fully improved, partially improved, unchanged, or worse) should be sent to the primary care team.

Verbal Exchanges

The primary care physician will highly value brevity with clarity in oral communications. Physicians' medical training contains a substantial formal and informal curriculum on quick, concise communication between physicians. A two- to three-sentence introduction to the patient and a similarly brief description of the problem will typically suffice. The primary care physician may ask a series of questions to fill in areas of ambiguity in the presentation and to hone in on areas of particular relevance to care of the patient. This is consistent with the typical physician–physician interaction. Oral communications will typically last 2 to 5 minutes, and this brevity should not be construed as disinterest on the physician's part. If there are professional disagreements on patient management, all clinicians involved should remember that, more often than not, disagreements are a result of miscommunication rather than true conflicts in how to care for the patient.

Primary care clinics are designed and primary care physicians are trained to allow a 10- to 20-minute face-to-face interaction between provider and patient on most occasions. Within these brief encounters, the primary care physician attempts to elicit history and symptoms, perform a directed physical examination, catalogue medication use, suggest or follow up diagnostic testing,

and complete education or counseling needs. Both patients and providers feel hurried, and both often report a sense of dissatisfaction with the encounter. To be an effective part of the team, the psychologists must be aware of this practice environment and its ramifications on patient care and practitioner time. Therapeutic maneuvers that may seem imperative to the psychologist may be a lower priority to the physician than treatment for medical illness or prevention health interventions. Quality care can still be achieved in this harried setting if the practitioner is supported by infrastructure that allows a team approach to care and a longitudinal approach to care. Negotiating the goals of care to optimize the patient's function is a hallmark of good geriatric care.

ACKNOWLEDGMENT Preparation of this chapter was supported in part by the National Institutes of Health (R01 AG 00956, P30 AG 10133, K07 AG 00868, and R01 HS10884).

References

American Association for Geriatric Psychiatry. (1996). Consensus update conference: Diagnosis and treatment of late-life depression. *American Journal of Geriatric Psychiatry, Supplement 1.*

American Psychiatric Association. (1994). *Diagnostic and statistical manual of mental disorders* (4th ed.). Washington, DC: Author.

Barker, W., Luis, C. A., Kashuba, A., et al. (2002). Relative frequencies of Alzheimer disease, Lewy body, vascular, and frontotemporal dementia, and hippocampal sclerosis in the Florida Brain Bank. *Alzheimer Disease and Associated Disorders, 16,* 203–212.

Bowler, J. V., Munoz, D. G., Merskey, H., & Hachinski, V. (1998). Fallacies in the pathological confirmation of the diagnosis of Alzheimer's disease. *Journal of Neurology, Neurosurgery, and Psychiatry, 64,* 18–24.

Callahan, C. M. (2001). Quality improvement research on late life depression in primary care. *Medical Care, 39,* 772–784.

Callahan, C. M., Hendrie, H. C., & Tierney, W. M. (1995). Documentation and evaluation of cognitive impairment in elderly primary care patients. *Annals of Internal Medicine, 122,* 422–429.

Callahan, C. M., Hendrie, H. C., & Tierney, W. M. (1996) The recognition and treatment of late life depression: A view from primary care. *International Journal of Psychiatry in Medicine, 26*, 155–171.

Callahan, C. M., Hui, S. L., Nienaber, N. A., et al. (1994). Longitudinal study of depression and health services use among elderly primary care patients. *Journal of American Geriatric Society, 42*, 833–838.

Callahan, C. M., Unverzagt, F. W., Hui, S. L., Perkins, A., & Hendrie, H. C. (2002). Six-item screener to identify cognitive impairment among potential subjects for clinical research. *Medical Care, 40*, 771–781.

Conwell, Y. (1994). Suicide in elderly patients. In L. S. Schneider, C. F. Reynolds, B. D. Lebowitz, et al. (Eds.), *Diagnosis and treatment of depression in late life* (pp. 397–418). Washington, DC: American Psychiatric Press.

Crum, R. M., Anthony, J. C., Basset, S. S., & Folstein, M. F. (1993). Population-based norms for the Mini-Mental State Examination by age and educational level. *Journal of the American Medical Association, 269*, 2386–2391.

Doody, R. S., Stevens, J. C., Beck, C., et al. (2001). Practice parameter: Management of dementia (an evidenced-based review). *Neurology, 56*, 1154–1166.

Ernst, R. L., & Hay, J. W. (1994). The US economic and social costs of Alzheimer's disease revisited. *American Journal of Public Health, 84*, 1261–1264.

Evans, S., & Katona, C. (1993). Epidemiology of depressive symptoms in elderly primary care attendees. *Dementia, 4*, 327–333.

Folstein, M. F., Folstein, S. E., & McHugh, P. R. (1975). Mini-Mental State: A practical method for grading the cognitive state of patients for the clinician. *Journal of Psychiatric Research, 12*, 189–198.

Francis, J., Martin, D., & Kapoor, W. N. (1990). A prospective study of delirium in hospitalized elderly. *Journal of the American Medical Association, 263*, 1097–1101.

Ganguli, M., Ratcliff, G., Huff, F. J., et al. (1991). Effects of age, gender, and education on cognitive tests in a rural elderly community sample: Norms from the Monongahela Valley Independent Elders Survey. *Neuroepidemiology, 10*, 42–52.

Gao, S., Hendrie, H. C., Hall, K. S., & Hui, S. (1998). The relationships between age, sex, and the incidence of dementia and Alzheimer disease: A meta-analysis. *Archives of General Psychiatry, 55*, 809–815.

Guerriero Austrom, M., & Hendrie, H. C. (1992). Quality of life: The family and Alzheimer's disease. *Journal of Palliative Care, 8*, 56–60.

Guerriero Austrom, M., & Hendrie, H. C. (2001). Family care for elders with dementia. In M. D. Mezey et al. (Eds.), *The encyclopedia of elder care* (pp. 254–256). New York: Springer.

Guerriero Austrom, M., Richards, B. S., & Hendrie, H. C. (1987). Alzheimer's disease: Providing care for the family. *Indiana Medicine, 80*, 648–651.

Hall, K. S., Ogunniyi, A. O., Hendrie, H. C., et al. (1996). A cross-cultural community based study of dementias: Methods and performance of the survey instrument Indianapolis, U.S.A., and Ibadan, Nigeria. *International Journal of Methods in Psychiatric Research, 6*, 129–142.

Hendrie, H. C., Callahan, C. M., Levitt, E. E., et al. (1995). Prevalence rates of major depressive disorders. The effects of varying the diagnostic criteria in an older primary care population. *American Journal of Geriatric Psychiatry, 3*, 119–131.

Hendrie, H. C., Osuntokun, B. O., Hall, K. S., et al. (1995). Prevalence of Alzheimer's disease and dementia in two communities: Nigerian Africans and African Americans. *American Journal of Psychiatry, 152*, 1485–1492.

Hendrie, H. C., Unverzagt, F.W., & Guerriero Austrom, M. (1997). The dementing disorders. *Psychiatric Quarterly, 68*, 261–279.

Heyman, A., Peterson, B., Fillenbaum, G., & Pieper, C. (1996). The Consortium to Establish a Registry for Alzheimer's Disease (CERAD). Part XIV: Demographic and clinical predictors of survival in patients with Alzheimer's disease. *Neurology, 46*, 656–660.

Hirschfeld, R. M., Keller, F. M. B., Panico, S., et al. (1997). The National Depressive and Manic-Depressive Association consensus statement on the undertreatment of depression. *Journal of the American Medical Association, 277*, 333–340.

Inouye, S. K. (1994). The dilemma of delirium. *American Journal of Medicine, 97*, 278–285.

Knopman, D. S., DeKosky, S. T., Cummings, J. L., et al. (2001). Practice parameter: Diagnosis of dementia (an evidence-based review). *Neurology, 56*, 1143–1153.

Lebowitz, B. D., Pearson, J. L., Schneider, L. S., et al. (1997). Diagnosis and treatment of depression in late life. *Journal of the American Medical Association, 278,* 1186–1190.

Mattis, S. (1973). *DRS: Dementia rating scale professional manual.* Odessa, FL: Psychological Assessment Resources.

Morris, J. C., Edland, S., Clark, C., et al. (1993). The Consortium to Establish a Registry for Alzheimer's Disease (CERAD). Part IV. Rates of cognitive change in the longitudinal assessment of probable Alzheimer's disease. *Neurology, 43,* 2457–2465.

Morris, J. C., Heyman, A., Mohs, R. C., et al. (1989). The Consortium to Establish a Registry for Alzheimer's Disease (CERAD). Part I. Clinical and neuropsychological assessment of Alzheimer's disease. *Neurology, 39,* 1159–1165.

Murden, R. A., McRae, T. D., Kaner, S., & Bucknam, M. E. (1991). Mini-Mental State Exam scores vary with education in blacks and whites. *Journal of American Geriatric Society, 39,* 149–155.

O'Connor, D. W., Pollitt, P. A., Roth, M., Brook, P. B., & Reiss, B. B. (1990). Memory complaints and impairment in normal, depressed, and demented elderly persons identified in a community survey. *Archives of General Psychiatry, 47,* 224–227.

O'Connor, D. W., Pollitt, P. A., Treasure, F. P., Brook, C. P. B., & Reiss, B. B. (1989). The influence of education, social class and sex on Mini-Mental State scores. *Psychological Medicine, 19,* 771–776.

Ostbye, T., Hill, G., & Steenhuis, R. (1999). Mortality in elderly Canadians with and without dementia: A 5-year follow-up. *Neurology, 53,* 521–526.

Perkins, A., Hui, S. L., Ogunniyi, A., et al. (2002). Risk of mortality for dementia in a developing country: The Yoruba in Nigeria. *International Journal Geriatric Psychiatry, 17,* 566–573.

Randolph, C., Tierney, M. C., Mohr, E., & Chase, T. N. (1998). The Repeatable Battery for the Assessment of Neuropsychological Status (RBANS): Preliminary clinical validity. *Journal of Clinical and Experimental Neuropsychology, 20,* 310–319.

Richards, S., & Hendrie, H. C. (1999). Diagnosis, management and treatment of Alzheimer's disease: A guide for the internist. *Archives of Internal Medicine, 159,* 789–798.

Ross, G. W., Abbott, R. D., Petrovitch, H., et al. (1997). Frequency and characteristics of silent dementia among elderly Japanese-American men: The Honolulu-Asia Aging Study. *Journal of the American Medical Association, 277,* 800–805.

Roth, M., Tym, E., Mountjoy, C. Q., et al. (1986). CAMDEX: A standardized instrument for the diagnosis of mental disorder in the elderly with special reference to the early detection of dementia. *British Journal of Psychiatry, 149,* 698–709.

Small, G. W., Rabins, P. V., Barry, P. P., et al. (1997). Diagnosis and treatment of Alzheimer disease and related disorders: Consensus statement of the American Association for Geriatric Psychiatry, the Alzheimer's Association, and the American Geriatrics Society. *Journal of the American Medical Association, 278,* 1363–1371.

Steffens, D. C., Skoog, I., Norton, M. C., et al. (2000). Prevalence of depression and its treatment in an elderly population—The Cache County study. *Archives of General Psychiatry, 57,* 601–607.

Stern, Y., Tang, M., Albert, M. S., et al. (2002). Predicting time to nursing home care and death in individuals with Alzheimer disease. *Journal of the American Medical Association, 277,* 806–812.

Stewart, A. L., Greenfield, S., Hays, R. D., et al. (1989). The functioning and well-being of patients with chronic conditions: Results from the Medical Outcomes Study. *Journal of the American Medical Association, 262,* 907–913.

Teng, E. L., & Chui, H. C. (1987). The Modified Mini-Mental State (3MS) Examination. *Journal of Clinical Psychiatry, 48,* 314–318.

Teng, E. L., Hasegawa, K., Homma, A., et al. (1994). The Cognitive Abilities Screening Instrument (CASI): A practical test for cross-cultural epidemiological studies. *International Psychogeriatrics, 6,* 45–58.

Tombaugh, T. N., & McIntyre, N. J. (1992). The Mini-Mental State Examination: A comprehensive review. *Journal of American Geriatric Society, 40,* 922–935.

Unutzer, J., Katon, W., Callahan, C. M., et al. (2002). Collaborative care management improves treatment and outcomes of late life depression: A multi-site randomized trial with 1,801 depressed older adults. *Journal of the American Medical Association, 288,* 2836–2845.

Unverzagt, F. W., Gao, S., Baiyewu, O., et al. (2001). Prevalence of cognitive impairment: Data from the Indianapolis Study of Health and Aging. *Neurology, 57,* 1655–1662.

Unverzagt, F. W., Hall, K. S., Ayou, P. O., et al.

(2001). Clinical utility of the CERAD Neuropsychological Battery in elderly Kenyans. *Journal International Neuropsychological Society, 7,* 192–193.

Unverzagt, F. W., Hall, K. S., Torke, A. M., et al. (1996). Effects of age, education, and gender on CERAD neuropsychological test performance in an African American sample. *Clinical Neuropsychologist, 10,* 180–190.

Veiel, H. O. (1997) A preliminary profile of neuropsychological deficits associated with major depression. *Journal of Clinical and Experimental Neuropsychology, 19,* 587–603.

Weiss, B. D., Reed, R., Klingman, E. W., & Abyad, A. (1995). Literacy and performance on the Mini-Mental State Examination. *Journal of American Geriatric Society, 43,* 807–810.

Wells, K. B., Stewart, A. L., Hays, R. D., et al. (1989). Functional status and well-being of depressed patients. *Journal of the American Medical Association, 262,* 914–919.

Welsh, K. A., Breitner, J. C. S., & Magruder-Habib, K. M. (1993). Detection of dementia in the elderly using the Telephone Screening of Cognitive Status. *Neuropsychiatry, Neuropsychology, and Behavioral Neurology, 6,* 103–110.

Welsh, K. A., Butters, N., Mohs, R. C., et al. (1994). The Consortium to Establish a Registry for Alzheimer's Disease (CERAD). Part V. A normative study of the neuropsychological battery. *Neurology, 44,* 609–614.

Welsh, K. A., Fillenbaum, G., Wilkinson, W., et al. (1995). Neuropsychological test performance in African-American and white patients with Alzheimer's disease. *Neurology, 45,* 2207–11.

22

Depression and Mood Disorders

Kenneth E. Freedland
Robert M. Carney
Judith A. Skala

Depression is one of the most common disorders seen in primary medical care clinics (Katon, 1987), and more patients are treated for depression by primary care providers than by mental health specialists (Regier et al., 1993). Depressive disorders cause substantial emotional distress, functional impairment, and disability (Wells & Sherbourne, 1999). They are associated with high utilization of primary care and other medical services (Carbone et al., 2000), and they are among the most expensive disorders in the United States in terms of health care expenditures and lost productivity (Simon et al., 2000).

Depression is associated with lifestyle risk factors for major chronic illnesses, including alcohol abuse, cigarette smoking, and physical inactivity (Hasin & Grant, 2002; Kritz-Silverstein, Barrett-Connor, & Corbeau, 2001). It is also an independent risk factor for the development of major medical illnesses such as coronary heart disease in initially healthy cohorts (Ferketich, Schwartzbaum, Frid, & Moeschberger, 2000) and for morbidity and mortality in medically ill patients (Carney,

Freedland, & Jaffe, 2001; de Groot, Anderson, Freedland, Clouse, & Lustman, 2001).

Patients seen by primary care providers tend to have less-severe forms of depression than do those treated by mental health specialists (Klinkman, Schwenk, & Coyne, 1997), but severely depressed patients also utilize primary health care services. Consequently, psychologists in primary care must be prepared to see mood disorders ranging from mild adjustment reactions to severe forms of depression, both in otherwise healthy and in medically ill patients.

The advent of the selective serotonin reuptake inhibitor antidepressants, clinical practice guidelines, and public awareness that depression is a treatable health problem has helped to make treatment of depression routine in many primary care practices. Nevertheless, underrecognition and undertreatment are still widespread (Young, Klap, Sherbourne, & Wells, 2001). Psychologists can contribute to the primary care of depressed patients by providing assessment, treatment, consultative, and educational services.

SCREENING FOR DEPRESSION

Whether routine screening for depression is a useful practice in primary care is controversial. The U.S. Preventive Services Task Force recommends it (Pignone, Gaynes, Lohr, Orleans, & Mulrow, 2001), but a review (Gilbody, House, & Sheldon, 2001) found that it often fails to improve referral or treatment practices. The utility of screening ultimately depends on how the information is used.

There are many screening instruments to choose from. According to a review by Schade, Jones, and Wittlin (1998), the most extensively studied questionnaires are the Geriatric Depression Scale (Yesavage et al., 1982), the Beck Depression Inventory (BDI; Beck, Ward, Mendelsohn, Mock, & Erbaugh, 1961), the General Health Questionnaire (Goldberg & Blackwell, 1970), the Zung Depression Scale (Zung, 1965), and the Center for Epidemiologic Studies Depression Scale (CES-D) (Radloff, 1977). On the other hand, a two-item instrument assessing only dysphoric mood and anhedonia has been shown to perform almost as well as lengthier questionnaires in detecting major depression (Brody et al., 1998). The new BDI-II is more compatible than the original BDI with the *Diagnostic and Statistical Manual of Mental Disorders*, fourth edition (*DSM-IV*; American Psychiatric Association [APA], 1994), and it performed well in a study of primary care patients (Arnau, Meagher, Norris, & Bramson, 2001). For patients who go on to be diagnosed with a depressive disorder, this versatile instrument can be used to measure the severity of depression before, during, and after treatment and to assess relapses and recurrences.

Many depressed patients have comorbid psychiatric conditions such as anxiety disorders or alcohol abuse. Screens for multiple disorders may be administered in addition to or in lieu of depression-specific instruments. The Patient Health Questionnaire (Spitzer, Kroenke, & Williams, 1999), a self-report form of the Primary Care Evaluation of Mental Disorders (PRIME-MD), is suitable for identifying common Axis I disorders in primary care patients. Brief screens for Axis II (personality) disorders are also available (Cloninger, 2000; Langbehn et al., 1999).

DIAGNOSTIC EVALUATION OF DEPRESSION

The evaluation of depressed patients should ascertain (a) the severity and duration of current symptoms; (b) the severity of functional impairment; (c) stressors and medical factors associated with the depressive episode; (d) past history of depressive episodes, treatments for depression, or family history of unipolar or bipolar mood disorders; and (e) comorbid psychiatric conditions. If suicidal features are identified, a detailed assessment of suicide risk should be conducted.

Clinical evaluations tend to be more thorough when structured interviews are used. Some standardized diagnostic interviews are specific to depression, and others cover a wider variety of psychiatric disorders. The Depression Interview and Structured Hamilton (Freedland et al., 2002) is a semistructured, depression-specific interview for medically ill patients. It is used to diagnose depressive disorders according to the *DSM-IV* criteria and to assess their severity on an embedded version of Williams's (1988) Structured Interview Guide for the Hamilton Depression scale. The Structured Clinical Interview for *DSM-IV* Axis I Disorders (SCID-I) (First, 1997) assesses all of the major Axis I disorders.

DEPRESSIVE DISORDERS

Major Depression

The symptoms of a major depressive episode include depressed mood; markedly diminished interest or pleasure in usual activities; significant changes in appetite or weight; insomnia or hypersomnia; psychomotor agitation or retardation; fatigue; thoughts of worthlessness or excessive or inappropriate guilt; diminished ability to think, concentrate, or make decisions; and recurrent thoughts of death or suicide. The *DSM-IV* criteria require that at least five of these symptoms have been present during the same 2-week period, that they represent a change from previous functioning, that either depressed mood or loss of interest or pleasure in usual activities is present, and that symptoms cause significant distress or functional impairment in social, occupational, or other domains. The Global Assessment of Functioning scale is used to assess the severity of functional impairment (APA, 2000a, pp. 32–34.)

In *DSM-IV*, the severity of a major depressive episode is classified as *mild* if five or six symptoms are present and they are causing only minor functional impairment, *severe* if eight or nine symptoms are present and they are causing marked functional impairment, or *moderate* if the severity is between mild and severe. Severe major depression is subclassified as psychotic if delusions or hallucinations are present and otherwise as nonpsychotic. Severe major depression is seen much less often in primary care than are mild or moderate episodes, and psychotic depression is rare.

In atypical major depression, there is usually hypersomnia rather than insomnia and increased appetite and weight gain rather than loss of appetite and weight. Other common features include leaden paralysis (i.e., behavioral inertia with a sensation of heaviness in the extremities) and interpersonal rejection sensitivity. In this instance, atypical is not synonymous with unusual; atypical features are present in between 1 of 5 and 1 of 4 of major depressive episodes (Posternak & Zimmerman, 2002). Atypical depression is about two or three times more common in women than in men, and it is more common in patients who are younger, anxious, socially phobic, and avoidant. It is also associated with adolescent onset of depression (Benazzi, 1999).

Major depressive disorder and dysthymia frequently follow a chronic or recurrent course, and subsyndromal symptoms are common between episodes (Judd et al., 1998). Comorbid depressive disorders are often chronic or recurrent in medically ill patients as well (Hance, Carney, Freedland, & Skala, 1996; Lustman, Griffith, Freedland, & Clouse, 1997). This is important to consider when depression occurs in the wake of a stressful medical crisis. Some patients who are depressed after such an event will remit spontaneously within a few weeks, with or without treatment. Many others, however, will not remit spontaneously and may continue to suffer from depression for months or even years. Thus, depression should never be dismissed as merely an understandable, passing reaction to a medical crisis or other stressful event.

Minor Depression

Minor depressive disorder was included in *DSM-IV* as a provisional diagnosis, in part because primary care physicians were seeing patients whose mild symptoms did not meet the *DSM-III-R* (APA, 1987) definition of major depression (Lyness, Caine, King, Cox, & Yoediono, 1999). The criteria for minor and major depression are identical, except that in a minor episode the patient has two to four symptoms. It is necessary to characterize the entire course of the episode from its onset to the present to differentiate between minor depression and major depression in partial remission. There is significant functional impairment in minor depression, although not quite as severe as in major depression (Rapaport & Judd, 1998).

Dysthymic Disorder

Dysthymia is a form of chronic depression that is usually less severe than chronic major depression. Depressed mood is the only cardinal symptom of dysthymia. Although anhedonia is a cardinal symptom of major and minor depression, it does not count at all as a symptom of dysthymia. In contrast, low self-esteem and hopelessness do count, despite not counting in major or minor depression. Poor appetite or overeating, insomnia or hypersomnia, fatigue, and poor concentration or indecision are symptoms both of dysthymia and of major and minor depression. In addition to depressed mood, at least two other symptoms must be present for at least two years.

If a major depressive episode occurs during the first 2 years of the mood disturbance, the correct diagnosis is either chronic major depression or major depression in partial remission rather than dysthymia. However, if a major depressive episode occurs during a dysthymic episode that has already lasted at least 2 years, the patient has major depression superimposed on dysthymia (i.e., "double depression"). It is difficult to differentiate between double depression and chronic major depression, but the distinction is important because the former is more difficult to treat. Treatment of double depression often yields a return to dysthymia rather than complete remission (McCullough et al., 2000).

Bipolar Disorders

Mood disorders are classified as either unipolar or bipolar, depending on whether the patient has ever had a manic or hypomanic episode. A manic episode is a period of abnormally elevated, expansive, or irritable mood, with other symptoms such as decreased need for sleep; flight of ideas; distractibility; increased activity; excessively risky activity; psychosis; severe impairments in social, occupational, and other areas of functioning; and need for hospitalization. In a mixed episode, the criteria for mania and a major depressive episode are met *concurrently*. Hypomanic and manic episodes are similar except that the former are less severe. The following table summarizes the principal *DSM-IV* criteria for bipolar disorders.

Disorder	Principal Criteria
Bipolar I	One or more manic or mixed episodes; may alternate with major depressive episodes
Bipolar II	One or more major depressive episodes, with one or more hypomanic and no manic episodes
Cyclothymia	Hypomanic and minor depressive episodes alternating over 2 or more years.

Bipolar I disorder is relatively rare in primary care patients, and other bipolar disorders are also less common than unipolar depression. Many patients with bipolar disorders delay or refuse to seek treatment for manic or hypomanic episodes (Lish, Dime-Meenan, Whybrow, Price, & Hirschfeld, 1994); treatment may have to be imposed on them.

When assessing a patient who is currently depressed, it is impossible to determine whether the patient has a unipolar or a bipolar disorder without determining whether there have been any previous manic, mixed, or hypomanic episodes. Furthermore, bipolar disorder cannot be ruled out in young, severely depressed patients who

have never had any manic or hypomanic episodes because they might start having them in the future (Goldberg, Harrow, & Whiteside, 2001). The risk is increased in patients who have ever been hospitalized for psychotic depression.

Bipolar disorders in first-degree relatives increase the patient's lifetime risk of bipolar disorder to between 5% and 10%, which is much higher than the risk in patients without any affected first-degree relatives (Karkowski & Kendler, 1997). Unipolar depression, particularly recurrent major depression, is also heritable, but less so than bipolar disorders (Kendler & Prescott, 1999). The lifetime risk of major depression is doubled or tripled in patients with a first-degree family history of major depression (Sullivan, Neale, & Kendler, 2000).

Patients who have a bipolar disorder need specialized psychiatric care, and manic episodes often require hospitalization, especially in the context of nonadherence to mood-stabilizing medications (Scott & Pope, 2002). However, the need for psychiatric services might not be immediately apparent if a depressed patient has an undiagnosed bipolar disorder. Antidepressants, particularly if taken without lithium or other mood-stabilizing medications, induce mania, hypomania, or rapid cycling in some patients with bipolar disorders (Altshuler et al., 1995). Consequently, on rare occasions, standard treatment of what appears to be typical major depression produces a psychiatric emergency instead of improvement (Preda, MacLean, Mazure, & Bowers, 2001).

A brief questionnaire to screen for bipolar spectrum disorders has been published (Hirschfeld et al., 2000). It may be especially useful when considering antidepressants for patients who have never been diagnosed as having a bipolar disorder, but who do have a family history of bipolar disorder.

Secondary Mood Disorders

The terms *primary* and *secondary* apply to relationships between one psychiatric disorder and another or between psychiatric disorders and medical illnesses. The most widely accepted definitions concern temporal, but not necessarily causal (etiological), relationships: A mood disorder is primary if its onset occurs in the absence of other psychiatric or major medical disorders and secondary if it occurs after the onset of another disorder (Guze, 1990). For example, an initial major depressive episode occurring after the onset of alcohol abuse may be called "depression secondary to alcohol abuse," but this does not necessarily mean that the alcohol abuse caused the depression.

Relatively few recent studies of relationships between mood disorders and medical conditions have described the depressive disorders as secondary. The lifetime onset of major depression often precedes the onset of any major medical illness by years or decades, and the onsets of major depressive episodes often precede rather than follow the onsets of acute medical conditions (Freedland, Carney, Lustman, Rich, & Jaffe, 1992). This is inevitable; whereas the modal lifetime onset of major depression is between adolescence and the mid-20s (Lavori et al., 1993), for most major medical illnesses it is in middle or old age. For example, 28% of patients hospitalized for acute myocardial infarction (MI) at an average age of 60 years had a major depressive episode at some point in their life before the myocardial infarction, 8% had one in the preceding year, 32% were depressed after the MI, and 42% of the depressed patients had a prior history of major depression, compared to only 22% of those who were not depressed after the MI (Lesperance, Frasure-Smith, & Talajic, 1996). Some patients in these studies have primary and some have secondary depression, but all can be (and often are) described as medically ill patients with *comorbid* major depression (Anderson, Freedland, Clouse, & Lustman, 2001).

It can be difficult to diagnose depression in medically ill patients because some symptoms (e.g., fatigue) are nonspecific. Several decision rules about whether to count such symptoms toward the diagnosis of depression have been proposed (Koenig, George, Peterson, & Pieper, 1997). In the inclusive approach, ambiguous symptoms such as fatigue are always counted; in the exclusive approach, they are never counted; in the substitutive approach, alternative symptoms such as crying are counted instead; and in the etiologic approach, they are counted only if they are judged to be caused by depression. A combina-

tion of the exclusive and etiologic approaches identifies the most severe and persistent cases of depression, but the inclusive rule is the most sensitive and reliable (Koenig et al., 1997).

The *DSM-IV* approach is inclusive, but with etiologic exceptions. It establishes a high threshold for attributing symptoms to medical illness, medication, or substance abuse; symptoms count toward the diagnosis of depression except if clearly and completely accounted for by the direct, physiological effects of a medical condition or medication. Symptoms rarely meet this stringent test, even if they *might* be, at least partially, caused by a medical condition or medication. Diagnostic uncertainty tends to increase along with the ratio of ambiguous symptoms to unambiguous symptoms, but *DSM-IV* resolves it by fiat. The key advantage of this approach is that it reduces the risks of underrecognition and undertreatment of depression in medically ill patients.

Some mood disorders are indeed caused by the direct, physiological effects of a medical condition. Thyroid disorders, for example, can cause depression. These conditions are classified in *DSM-IV* as mood disorders due to a general medical condition. Most conditions that are etiologically related to mood disorders are neurological, endocrine, or infectious diseases (Rundell & Wise, 1989).

Determination that a depressive episode is caused by medical illness requires consideration of its etiology. It is often impossible to determine that a patient's medical condition directly caused his or her mood disorder, especially if other there are other contributory factors, such as disability or interpersonal loss. Causality is a reasonable conclusion if the medical condition is a well-established cause of depression, the onset of the medical disorder preceded the mood disorder, and the severity of the mood disorder covaries with the severity of the medical condition. A corollary is that the mood disorder should improve along with successful treatment of the medical condition, even if no specific treatment is provided for the mood disorder (Hall, 1980). The level of thyroid-stimulating hormone should be obtained to screen for thyroid abnormalities, with the proviso that mildly abnormal TSH levels are often found in depressed patients without any identifiable thyroid disease (Placidi et al., 1998).

Some cases may be caused by pathophysiological conditions other than those usually associated with mood disorders due to a general medical condition. For example, late-onset depression (i.e., lifetime onset of depression after age 59 years) may in some cases be caused by subtle cerebrovascular disease (Krishnan, Hays, & Blazer, 1997). This has come to be called "vascular depression." However, the evidence is not yet strong enough to justify the conclusion that, when cerebrovascular disease and major depression occur together, the latter is caused by the former. Thus, these cases are generally classified as major depressive disorder on Axis I with cerebrovascular disease on Axis III.

The fact that a mood disorder is caused by a general medical condition does not imply that it should be left untreated. First, if the treatment for the medical condition is not very successful or if the condition is untreatable, it is likely to continue to cause depression. Second, some conditions are related to mood disorders in complex ways. For example, whether depression is a direct, physiological effect of a stroke rather than a reaction to stroke-related disability may depend on the location of the lesion (Morris et al., 1996). Third, depression due to a medical condition can be just as distressing and functionally disabling as depression due to other causes. Finally, medically ill patients are not immune to other causes of depression. For example, a stroke patient who loses his or her job, functional independence, and ability to communicate has many reasons to feel depressed, whether or not the stroke disrupted the brain's mood regulation system. For all of these reasons, depression caused by a general medical condition should be managed as a problem in its own right and not ignored as if it were an unimportant sequela of the medical illness.

It may or may not be advisable to withhold depression treatment until the medical illness has been brought under control; this is a case-by-case judgment. One factor to consider is whether there have been any relevant clinical trials. For example, nortriptyline has been shown efficacious for poststroke depression and superior to fluoxetine (Robinson et al., 2000). In contrast, there have not been any clinical trials for depression caused by thyroid disease, although a trial of

fluoxetine for major depression in patients with high or low thyroid indices found that significant thyroid function abnormalities were rare, and that subtle ones had no impact on treatment outcomes (Fava, Labbate, Abraham, & Rosenbaum, 1995).

Dysphoric mood is a side effect of a wide variety of medications, but few have been proven to cause major depression. For example, beta-blockers cause dysphoric mood, but not major depression (Carney et al., 1987). Antidepressants may be able to counteract the depressogenic effects of certain drugs. For example, paroxetine can prevent interferon-induced depression in malignant melanoma (Musselman et al., 2001).

SUBSYNDROMAL DEPRESSIVE SYMPTOMS

Subsyndromal depression refers to symptoms that do not meet the criteria for a defined depressive disorder. Some authors consider minor depressive disorder a form of subsyndromal depression, but others exclude it from their definition. There are several ways to have symptoms of depression without meeting the full criteria for a major or minor depressive episode or dysthymic disorder. One is to have an adjustment disorder with depressed mood, which is defined in DSM-IV as the development of subsyndromal depressive symptoms within 3 months of the onset of an identifiable stressor. Another is to have symptoms that might otherwise constitute a depressive disorder except that only some of the required features are present. For example, a patient might affirm a number of depressive symptoms, but deny the cardinal symptoms. A third way is to have a depressive disorder in partial remission.

Subsyndromal depressive symptoms are often prodromal to major depressive episodes, and patients who have persistent residual symptoms after a major depressive episode has gone into partial remission are at high risk for relapse (Judd, Akiskal, & Paulus, 1997). Subsyndromal depression is also associated with impairment in multiple domains of functioning and with poor health status (Williams, Kerber, Mulrow, Medina, & Aguilar, 1995). Thus, subsyndromal depressive symptoms should be regarded as clinically important even if they do not comprise an established Axis I mood disorder.

EPIDEMIOLOGY OF DEPRESSION

The landmark Epidemiologic Catchment Area study reported a lifetime prevalence of major depressive disorder of 5% and a 1-year prevalence of 3% in a large, community-based sample. The lifetime prevalence of dysthymia was 3%, but 42% of the dysthymic individuals also had a history of at least one major depressive episode (Weissman, Bruce, Leaf, Florio, & Holzer, 1991).

More recent estimates from the National Comorbidity Survey are considerably higher. This study reported lifetime and 1-year prevalence estimates of 17% and 10%, respectively, for major depressive episodes and 6% and 3%, respectively, for dysthymia. It also estimated a 10% lifetime prevalence for minor depression (Blazer, Kessler, McGonagle, & Swartz, 1994; Kessler, Zhao, Blazer, & Swartz, 1997). When a clinical significance requirement was added to the diagnostic criteria, the difference in prevalence estimates between the two studies narrowed (Narrow, Rae, Robins, & Regier, 2002). Uncertainty remains about the prevalence of these disorders, but depression clearly affects millions of individuals every year.

Among primary care patients, the prevalence of current major depression is about 10%, and the prevalence of dysthymia is about 2%, making depression the most common form of mental disorder encountered in primary care (Katon, 1987; Sartorius, Ustun, Lecrubier, & Wittchen, 1996). The prevalence of depression is higher in chronically medically ill patients than it is in medically healthy individuals. This has been found in a variety of different medical illnesses, such as diabetes (Anderson et al., 2001) and coronary heart disease (Carney et al., 2001).

Although much less prevalent than unipolar depression, bipolar spectrum disorders are more common than one might expect. The lifetime prevalence of bipolar I disorder is approximately 1% (Weissman et al., 1991). The lifetime prevalence for the entire spectrum of bipolar disorders (bipolar I, bipolar II, cyclothymia, and bipolar

disorder not otherwise specified) is between about 3% and 6% (Angst, 1998). Major depression is about twice as prevalent in women as men. In contrast, almost as many men as women have bipolar spectrum disorders (Weissman et al., 1991).

CHOICE OF TREATMENT

Barriers to Acceptance of Diagnosis or Treatment

Despite the suffering and other problems that depression can create, many patients deny their symptoms, and some who know they are depressed either do not seek or actively refuse treatment. Unfortunately, many other patients who do seek care for depression are unable to obtain effective treatment. Common barriers to revealing depression to primary care providers include lack of awareness that depression is a treatable disorder, shame, social stigma, and fear of consequences, such as loss of health insurance (Blumenthal & Endicott, 1996). Some of these obstacles may be reinforced by the patient's social environment or by religious teachings (Diala et al., 2001). Male and older patients tend to be more reluctant to be screened for depression than are female and younger patients (Nazemi, Larkin, Sullivan, & Katon, 2001).

Other barriers can interfere with treatment for patients who either complain of depression or accept a depression diagnosis. Some patients prefer antidepressants, others prefer psychotherapy, and still others reject treatment altogether (Lam, 2001). Many primary care patients are not offered an antidepressant despite a diagnosis of depression, and many of those who do receive a prescription are given an inadequate dose, for too little time, and without systematic follow-up to address problems such as side effects or treatment resistance (Harman & Reynolds, 2000). Some of the barriers are systemic (Pincus, 2003). For example, treatment is harder to obtain in some health maintenance organizations than in others (Grembowski et al., 2002).

Many patients ostensibly accept treatment but fail to adhere to it. Nonadherence and premature discontinuation of antidepressants increase the risk of relapses and recurrences of major depression (Melfi et al., 1998); rates of premature discontinuation of antidepressants have exceeded 50% in some studies (Bull et al., 2002). Some patients discontinue antidepressants because of side effects, but there are a number of other reasons as well (Thompson, Peveler, Stephenson, & McKendrick, 2000). Depression itself can interfere with treatment adherence (Carney, Freedland, Eisen, Rich, & Jaffe, 1995). It can be difficult to improve adherence, but fortunately it is not impossible. For example, adherence improves when physicians communicate clearly with patients about treatment for depression and when they follow up at least several times after prescribing antidepressants (Bull et al., 2002).

Some depressed primary care patients react negatively to being referred to a mental health specialist. The referral may be interpreted as a personal rejection or as a dismissal of the patient's complaints. Patients who believe this tend to greet the mental health specialist with skepticism and anger, if they do not decline the referral altogether, and this can set the stage for poor adherence to the psychiatric or psychological intervention. Primary care physicians can help to prevent these problems by assuring the patient that his or her medical problems and concerns are taken seriously; that depression is a common, treatable disorder that may take a long time to remit if left untreated; and that treatment is necessary because of the harmful emotional, psychosocial, interpersonal, and medical consequences of depression. The physician can also help by dispelling unwarranted fears and concerns about mental health care and by sharing accounts of similar patients who have benefited from treatment.

Effective Treatments

Antidepressants

Selective serotonin reuptake inhibitors are the first-line treatment for most cases of unipolar depression in a growing proportion of psychiatric and primary care practices (Petersen et al., 2002). There have been hundreds of clinical trials of antidepressants for depression. Most recent primary care treatment trials have tested selective serotonin reuptake inhibitors or newer antidepressants, including ones that affect both serotonin and norepinephrine receptors.

In general, newer agents are no more effective than long-established antidepressants, but they tend to have more benign side effect profiles (Williams, Mulrow, et al., 2000). The antidepressant response rate has been increasing in recent trials, but so has the placebo response rate, probably because of increased public awareness and acceptance of antidepressants (Walsh, Seidman, Sysko, & Gould, 2002). Consequently, treatment effect sizes have not increased very much, and the quest for more effective antidepressants continues. Nevertheless, many depressed patients benefit from currently available antidepressants, and current clinical practice guidelines revolve around providing antidepressant medications for patients with depressive disorders (American Psychiatric Association, 2000b; Schulberg, Katon, Simon, & Rush, 1998; Snow, Lascher, & Mottur-Pilson, 2000).

There are several important differences between the use of antidepressants in primary care and their use in psychiatric practice. Primary care patients tend to have milder cases of depression, less psychiatric comorbidity, and more medical comorbidity compared to depressed psychiatric patients (Cooper-Patrick, Crum, & Ford, 1994). Patients with comorbid medical illnesses are excluded from most antidepressant trials (Mulrow et al., 2000). Some antidepressants that are safe for medically well patients are contraindicated for patients with certain medical conditions. For example, tricyclic antidepressants are contraindicated for patients with cardiac conduction disorders. Patients with chronic medical illnesses often have to take multiple medications, which can decrease their willingness or financial ability to take any more medications as well as their adherence to treatment. Furthermore, there is a risk of adverse drug interactions between antidepressants and medications prescribed for other medical illnesses (Sheline, Freedland, & Carney, 1997). These factors make it especially important to monitor medically ill patients' responses to antidepressants. If intolerable side effects or drug interactions occur, options include adjusting the dosage of the initial antidepressant or switching to a different agent. Switching to a nonpharmacological treatment such as cognitive–behavioral therapy is also an option for some patients.

Decisions about the use of antidepressant medications for primary care patients should be informed by clinical trials conducted in primary care or other general medical settings (Williams, Mulrow, et al., 2000). The literature provides some support for the following conclusions:

1. About 50% to 60% of depressed primary care patients respond to antidepressants with a 50% or greater reduction in symptoms, which is comparable to the response rate in psychiatric patients.
2. Newer antidepressants are generally no more efficacious for primary care patients than are tricyclics, and they are more expensive. However, patients are less likely to discontinue selective serotonin reuptake inhibitors, and the overall cost of treatment is similar between newer and older antidepressants.
3. Frequent office visits during the first 2 months of pharmacotherapy may improve clinical outcomes (Schulberg et al., 1998).

Although major depression has been the target of most antidepressant studies, clinical trials have recently been conducted to evaluate the efficacy of antidepressants for minor depression and dysthymia (Barrett et al., 2001; Williams, Barrett, et al., 2000). The antidepressant response rates in these studies have been relatively high for minor depression, but so have the placebo response rates in the studies that have included placebo controls. Consequently, there is only equivocal evidence that antidepressants are efficacious for minor depression. Although the antidepressant response rate tends to be lower for dysthymia than for minor depression, the placebo response rate is also lower. Paroxetine has been significantly more efficacious than placebo in adults younger than 60 years with dysthymia (Barrett et al., 2001). In older adults, paroxetine was more efficacious for dysthymia than placebo only in the subgroups with high or intermediate baseline functioning (Williams, Barrett, et al., 2000). In short, there is much less evidence that antidepressants are efficacious for mild depressive disorders than there is for major depression.

Antidepressant therapy for medically ill primary care patients should also be informed by tri-als conducted in patients with the same medical illness as the patient in question. For example, the Sertraline Antidepressant Heart Attack Randomized Trial (SADHART) is the first, and so far the only, large, multicenter clinical trial of an antidepressant for major depression in patients who have recently had an acute myocardial infarction or unstable angina. The results showed that not only is sertraline relatively safe for these patients, but also its efficacy is questionable. In the total randomized sample, there was no difference in Hamilton depression scores between the sertraline and placebo arms and only a slight difference on the Clinical Global Impression scale. The results were more promising in the subgroup of patients with severe, recurrent major depressive disorder, but even in this subgroup, the difference in Hamilton change scores between the arms was less than 3 points (Glassman et al., 2002). This study should be taken into account in clinical decisions about how to treat depression in primary care patients with heart disease, especially because cardiac patients have been systematically excluded from most clinical trials of sertraline.

Unfortunately, there have not been any major, multicenter clinical trials for comorbid depression in most major chronic illnesses, and there have been very few methodologically adequate, single-site trials. Nevertheless, the available studies can impart important information about the treatment of comorbid depression in specific medical illnesses that cannot be gleaned from studies of otherwise medically well but depressed psychiatric patients. To date, for example, there have been two randomized, double-blind, placebo-controlled trials for antidepressants for depression in patients with diabetes. One showed that nortriptyline is efficacious for depression, but at the expense of worse glycemic control (Lustman, Griffith, Clouse, et al., 1997). The other found that fluoxetine is also efficacious for depression, and that it does not impair glycemic control. To the contrary, there was a trend toward *better* glycemic control in the patients who received fluoxetine (Lustman, Freedland, Griffith, & Clouse, 2000).

An evidence-based medicine review of 18 clinical trials of antidepressants for comorbid depression in specific medical illnesses (Gill & Hatcher, 2002) concluded that depressed patients with a wide range of physical diseases are more likely to improve when treated with antidepressants than with a placebo or with no treatment. These findings are helpful for primary care practitioners, but more studies of antidepressant safety and efficacy in medically ill patients are needed.

Psychotherapy

Dozens of different (or at least nominally different) psychotherapies have been used to treat depression (Corsini & Wedding, 2002), but very few have been tested in controlled clinical trials, and fewer still meet even lenient evidentiary standards for empirically supported therapies (Chambless & Hollon, 1998). More research has been conducted on cognitive–behavioral therapy (Beck, Rush, Shaw, & Emery, 1979) than any other psychotherapeutic treatment for depression, and more evidence supports its efficacy than any other form of psychotherapy. There is also growing evidence that interpersonal therapy (Klerman, Weissman, Rounsaville, & Chevron, 1984) and problem-solving therapy (Nezu, 1986) are efficacious treatments for depression (DeRubeis & Crits-Christoph, 1998).

Despite the relative strength of evidence supporting these therapies, many questions require further investigation, such as whether they produce consistently superior outcomes in comparison to nondirective, supportive counseling or other psychotherapies; whether they are efficacious not only in mild to moderate depression, but also in more severe cases; and how they fare in comparison to antidepressants. Nevertheless, cognitive–behavioral therapy and interpersonal therapy are now widely considered efficacious, both as alternatives and as adjuncts to pharmacotherapy for depression (Barkham & Hardy, 2001). Furthermore, there is growing evidence that they can decrease the risks of relapse and recurrence in major depressive disorder (Fava, Grandi, Zielezny, Rafanelli, & Canestrari, 1996).

There is considerable interest in whether combining antidepressant medications with cognitive or interpersonal therapy produces better depression outcomes than any of these treatments alone. Although there is still uncertainty, the weight of evidence suggests that combination therapy is probably superior to monotherapy (Thase et al., 1997). The evidence from one large multicenter clinical trial is striking. A sample of 681 adults with chronic major depression, many of whom had been depressed for quite a few years and had not benefited from previous treatments, were randomly assigned to 12 weeks of nefazodone, a cognitive–behavioral intervention, or both. In the intention-to-treat analysis, the overall response rates were 48% in both of the monotherapy groups and 73% in the combined group. Among the 519 patients who completed the study, the response rates were 55% for nefazodone, 52% for cognitive–behavioral therapy, and 85% for combination therapy (Keller et al., 2000). These are very encouraging findings for chronically depressed patients, especially for those who have tried other treatments without success.

In 1993, both the APA (1993) and the U.S. Department of Health and Human Services Agency for Health Care Policy and Research (AHCPR) (Depression Guideline Panel, 1993) issued clinical practice guidelines for the treatment of major depression. The APA guidelines were geared toward psychiatric treatment, and the AHCPR guidelines were developed for primary care. Both of them were criticized for underemphasizing empirically supported psychotherapies (Persons, Thase, & Crits-Christoph, 1996). A recent update of the primary care practice guidelines concluded that there is now more evidence to support the use of cognitive–behavioral, interpersonal, and problem-solving therapies in primary care (Schulberg et al., 1998).

Few studies have examined the efficacy of cognitive, interpersonal, or problem-solving therapies for depression in primary care. One study, for example, found that problem-solving therapy was significantly more efficacious than placebo for dysthymia, but somewhat less efficacious than paroxetine (Barrett et al., 2001). A review of 12 recent trials concluded that depressive-specific psychotherapies for major depression produced clinical outcomes better than usual care and comparable to those for antidepressants. It also concluded that there is only equivocal evidence that psychotherapy is efficacious for dysthymia or minor depression in primary care (Schulberg, Raue, & Rollman, 2002). However, research on psychotherapeutic interventions in primary care is still at a relatively early stage. Further studies of their feasibility, effectiveness, and cost effectiveness are needed.

As is true of antidepressant clinical trials, most studies of cognitive–behavioral and interpersonal psychotherapies for depression have been conducted in medically well populations. There have been relatively few randomized, controlled clinical trials of these interventions in patients with specific chronic medical illnesses. Furthermore, depression was neither an inclusion criterion nor the primary outcome in some of these studies. Nevertheless, there is growing evidence that cognitive–behavioral and interpersonal interventions can be effective treatments for depression in medically ill patients. For example, in a sample of patients with Type II diabetes, depression remitted in 85% of those randomly assigned to a combination of cognitive–behavioral therapy and supportive diabetes education compared to only 27% of those who received only the latter. Furthermore, the patients who received cognitive–behavioral therapy had better glycemic control at follow-up. Conversely, poor adherence to blood glucose monitoring predicted nonremission of depression (Lustman, Freedland, Griffith, & Clouse, 1998; Lustman, Griffith, Freedland, Kissel, & Clouse, 1998). This study illustrated that medical factors can affect the outcome of psychotherapeutic treatments for depression in medically ill patients.

Several small trials have tested psychotherapeutic treatments for depression and related problems in patients with HIV/AIDS, with promising results (Blanch et al., 2002). There have been similar trials in a number of other medical populations, such as patients with rheumatoid arthritis (Sharpe et al., 2001), cancer (Moorey, Greer, Bliss, & Law, 1998), chronic low back pain (Turner & Jensen, 1993), stroke (Lincoln, Flannaghan, Sutcliffe, & Rother, 1997); patients with cardiac arrhythmia with implanted defibrillators (Kohn, Petrucci, Baessler, Soto, & Movsowitz, 2000); and patients with stable coronary heart disease (Carney et al., 2000). As in the HIV/AIDS studies, these trials have produced promising results. Larger, well-designed trials are needed to determine which psychotherapeutic treatments are most effective in specific medical patient populations. In some populations, it will

also be important to determine whether interventions are more effective at particular stages of the medical illness. For example, it would be helpful to know if it is better to treat depression as soon as possible after coronary artery bypass graft surgery or to wait until the patient has had enough time to resume normal activities.

The National Heart, Lung, and Blood Institute has sponsored a large, multicenter clinical trial to determine if cognitive–behavioral therapy for depression or low perceived social support after an acute myocardial infarction reduces the risk of recurrent infarction and prolongs survival. The participants ($N = 2,481$) were randomly assigned either to usual care for these problems or to an intervention consisting of up to 6 months of individual cognitive–behavioral therapy, supplemented when feasible with cognitive–behavioral group therapy and when necessary with sertraline (ENRICHD Investigators, 2000). There was significantly greater improvement in depression and perceived social support in the intervention arm, but this did not translate into a significant difference in reinfarction-free survival (Berkman, Blumenthal, Burg, Carney, Catellier, Cowan, et al., 2003).

Enhancing Recovery in Coronary Heart Disease (ENRICHD) is the largest clinical trial ever conducted in the field of behavioral medicine. Although the primary hypothesis was not supported, the study has yielded many interesting findings. One of the most important implications of ENRICHD is that even though depression and social isolation are risk factors for mortality in patients who have had an acute myocardial infarction, and although cognitive–behavioral therapy can help to relieve these problems, we cannot promise patients that this will necessarily improve their medical prognosis. Discovering how to treat depression in ways that *do* improve prognosis is still a worthy goal, but the principal reason to treat it is to relieve emotional suffering and to improve functioning and quality of life. The same can also be said for the treatment of comorbid depression in other major medical illnesses such as cancer and HIV/AIDS.

Although there has been little research on this question, it is probably necessary to modify psychotherapeutic treatments that were developed for depressed but medically well individuals to the unique needs of depressed medical patients. For example, behavioral activation is a key ingredient in cognitive–behavioral therapy for depression, and it may even be the most important one (Jacobson et al., 1996), but it must be undertaken cautiously in medically ill patients to prevent serious adverse events. Patients recovering from an acute myocardial infarction, for instance, should be asked to consult with their physician before undertaking physical activities such as golf or gardening as part of a behavioral activation intervention.

The growing use of antidepressants in primary care, along with restrictions imposed by managed care on mental health services, has raised questions about whether psychotherapy is still a viable treatment option for depressed outpatients. Surveys have confirmed that, although more depressed patients are being treated, the proportion receiving antidepressants is growing, and the proportion receiving psychotherapy, at least as monotherapy, is shrinking. Furthermore, physicians are accounting for more of the "psychotherapy" that is being provided, and psychologists are accounting for less of it (Druss, Marcus, Olfson, Tanielian, & Pincus, 2003; Olfson, Marcus, Druss, Elinson, et al., 2002; Olfson, Marcus, Druss, & Pincus, 2002). Although some of these trends are clearly unfavorable, the surveys nevertheless showed that psychologists are still providing psychotherapeutic services for large numbers of depressed patients.

Other Nonpharmacological Interventions

Exercise is one of the most promising nonpharmacological interventions for depression. Antidepressants may have more rapid effects, but exercise can be an efficacious treatment for major depression if sustained for several months. Furthermore, patients who continue exercising on their own following a short-term exercise intervention for depression are less likely to relapse (Babyak et al., 2000). Interventions designed to improve social support also appear promising. Although there have been few trials of social support interventions per se, poor social support is a predictor of poor response to other treatments for depression (Dew et al., 1997). Thus, enhancing social support could be a useful adjunct to other therapies.

Ineffective Treatments

St. John's wort (hypericum extract) is a very controversial treatment for depression. Several trials have found this herbal remedy to be a safe and efficacious treatment for mild to moderate depression (Lecrubier, Clerc, Didi, & Kieser, 2002), but it fared no better than placebo in two trials for patients with major depression (Hypericum Depression Trial Study Group, 2002; Shelton et al., 2001). St. John's wort seems to be relatively safe for medically well individuals, although case reports suggest that it may have triggered manic or hypomanic episodes in some individuals (Nierenberg, Burt, Matthews, & Weiss, 1999). Furthermore, there are serious concerns about its safety in medical patients. It poses potentially serious risks, for example, for surgical patients, organ transplant recipients, and patients taking certain medications commonly prescribed for major medical illnesses (Ang-Lee, Moss, & Yuan, 2001). Patients who inquire about St. John's wort should be urged to talk with their physician about the potential risks of taking this or any other herbal remedy. Physicians should specifically inquire about whether their patients are taking any of these remedies for depression, insomnia, or premenstrual symptoms.

SUMMARY

Depression is one of the most common problems in primary care patients. Beyond emotional distress, depression often causes significant functional impairment and increased utilization of medical services, and it is a risk factor for suicidal behavior and for medical morbidity and mortality. Antidepressants, particularly selective serotonin reuptake inhibitors, are the first-line treatments for depression in primary care. There is also growing evidence that specific psychotherapeutic treatments, including cognitive–behavioral, interpersonal, and problem-solving therapies, are also efficacious treatments for depression. Unfortunately, currently available treatments fail in too many cases. Although efforts continue to develop more effective antidepressants and psychotherapeutic interventions for depression, innovative models of collaborative primary care are showing how to optimize the effectiveness of existing treatments.

References

Altshuler, L. L., Post, R. M., Leverich, G. S., Mikalauskas, K., Rosoff, A., & Ackerman, L. (1995). Antidepressant-induced mania and cycle acceleration: A controversy revisited. *American Journal of Psychiatry, 152,* 1130–1138.

American Psychiatric Association. (1987). *Diagnostic and statistical manual of mental disorders* (3rd ed., rev.). Washington, DC: Author.

American Psychiatric Association. (1993). Practice guideline for major depressive disorder in adults. *American Journal of Psychiatry, 150*(4 Suppl.), *Suppl*-26.

American Psychiatric Association. (1994). *Diagnostic and statistical manual of mental disorders* (4th ed.). Washington, DC: Author.

American Psychiatric Association. (2000a). *Diagnostic and statistical manual of mental disorders* (4th ed., text rev.). Washington, DC: Author.

American Psychiatric Association. (2000b). Practice guideline for the treatment of patients with major depressive disorder (revision). *American Journal of Psychiatry, 157*(4 Suppl.), 1–45.

Anderson, R. J., Freedland, K. E., Clouse, R. E., & Lustman, P. J. (2001). The prevalence of comorbid depression in adults with diabetes: A meta-analysis. *Diabetes Care, 24,* 1069–1078.

Ang-Lee, M. K., Moss, J., & Yuan, C. S. (2001). Herbal medicines and perioperative care. *Journal of the American Medical Association, 286,* 208–216.

Angst, J. (1998). The emerging epidemiology of hypomania and bipolar II disorder. *Journal of Affective Disorders, 50,* 143–151.

Arnau, R. C., Meagher, M. W., Norris, M. P., & Bramson, R. (2001). Psychometric evaluation of the Beck Depression Inventory-II with primary care medical patients. *Health Psychology, 20,* 112–119.

Babyak, M., Blumenthal, J. A., Herman, S., Khatri, P., Doraiswamy, M., Moore, K., Craighead, W. E., Baldewicz, T. T., & Krishnan, K. R. (2000). Exercise treatment for major depression: Maintenance of therapeutic benefit at 10 months. *Psychosomatic Medicine, 62,* 633–638.

Barkham, M., & Hardy, G. E. (2001). Counselling and interpersonal therapies for depression: Towards securing an evidence-base. *British Medical Bulletin, 57,* 115–132.

Barrett, J. E., Williams, J. W. J., Oxman, T. E., Frank, E., Katon, W., Sullivan, M., Hegel, M. T., Cornell, J. E., & Sengupta, A. S. (2001). Treatment of dysthymia and minor depression in primary care: A randomized trial in patients aged 18 to 59 years. *Journal of Family Practice, 50,* 405–412.

Beck, A. T., Rush, A. J., Shaw, B. F., & Emery, G. (1979). *Cognitive therapy of depression.* New York: Guilford Press.

Beck, A. T., Ward, C. H., Mendelsohn, M., Mock, J., & Erbaugh, J. (1961). An inventory for measuring depression. *Archives of General Psychiatry, 4,* 561–571.

Benazzi, F. (1999). Prevalence and clinical features of atypical depression in depressed outpatients: A 467-case study. *Psychiatry Research, 86,* 259–265.

Berkman, L. F., Blumenthal, J., Burg, M., Carney, R. M., Catellier, D., Cowan, M. J., et al. 2003. Effects of treating depression and low perceived social support on clinical events after myocardial infarction: The Enhancing Recovery in Coronary Heart Disease Patients (ENRICHD) randomized trial. *Journal of the American Medical Association, 289*(23) 3171–3173.

Blanch, J., Rousaud, A., Hautzinger, M., Martinez, E., Peri, J. M., Andres, S., Cirera, E., Gatell, J. M., & Gasto, C. (2002). Assessment of the efficacy of a cognitive-behavioural group psychotherapy programme for HIV-infected patients referred to a consultation-liaison psychiatry department. *Psychotherapy and Psychosomatics, 71,* 77–84.

Blazer, D. G., Kessler, R. C., McGonagle, K. A., & Swartz, M. S. (1994). The prevalence and distribution of major depression in a national community sample: The National Comorbidity Survey. *American Journal of Psychiatry, 151,* 979–986.

Blumenthal, R., & Endicott, J. (1996). Barriers to seeking treatment for major depression. *Depression and Anxiety, 4,* 273–278.

Brody, D. S., Hahn, S. R., Spitzer, R. L., Kroenke, K., Linzer, M., deGruy, F. V., III, & Williams, J. B. (1998). Identifying patients with depression in the primary care setting: A more efficient method. *Archives of Internal Medicine,* *158,* 2469–2475.

Bull, S. A., Hu, X. H., Hunkeler, E. M., Lee, J. Y., Ming, E. E., Markson, L. E., & Fireman, B. (2002). Discontinuation of use and switching of antidepressants: Influence of patient-physician communication. *Journal of the American Medical Association, 288,* 1403–1409.

Carbone, L. A., Barsky, A. J., Orav, E. J., Fife, A., Fricchione, G. L., Minden, S. L., & Borus, J. F. (2000). Psychiatric symptoms and medical utilization in primary care patients. *Psychosomatics, 41,* 512–518.

Carney, R. M., Freedland, K. E., Eisen, S. A., Rich, M. W., & Jaffe, A. S. (1995). Major depression and medication adherence in elderly patients with coronary artery disease. *Health Psychology, 14,* 88–90.

Carney, R. M., Freedland, K. E., & Jaffe, A. S. (2001). Depression as a risk factor for coronary heart disease mortality. *Archives of General Psychiatry, 58,* 229–230.

Carney, R. M., Freedland, K. E., Stein, P. H., Skala, J. A., Hoffman, P., & Jaffe, A. S. (2000). Change in heart rate and heart rate variability during treatment for depression in patients with coronary heart disease. *Psychosomatic Medicine, 62,* 639–647.

Carney, R. M., Rich, M. W., teVelde, A., Saini, J., Clark, K., & Freedland, K. E. (1987). Prevalence of major depressive disorder in patients receiving beta-blocker therapy versus other medications. *American Journal of Medicine, 83,* 223–226.

Chambless, D. L., & Hollon, S. D. (1998). Defining empirically supported therapies. *Journal of Consulting and Clinical Psychology, 66,* 7–18.

Cloninger, C. R. (2000). A practical way to diagnosis personality disorder: A proposal [Review]. *Journal of Personality Disorders, 14,* 99–108.

Cooper-Patrick, L., Crum, R. M., & Ford, D. E. (1994). Characteristics of patients with major depression who received care in general medical and specialty mental health settings. *Medical Care, 32,* 15–24.

Corsini, R. J., & Wedding, D. (2002). *Current psychotherapies* (6th ed.). Itasca, IL: F. E. Peacock.

de Groot, M., Anderson, R., Freedland, K. E., Clouse, R. E., & Lustman, P. J. (2001). Association of depression and diabetes complications: A meta-analysis. *Psychosomatic Medicine, 63,* 619–630.

Depression Guideline Panel. (1993). *Depression in*

primary care. Rockville, MD: U.S. Department of Health and Human Services, Public Health Service, Agency for Health Care Policy and Research.

DeRubeis, R. J., & Crits-Christoph, P. (1998). Empirically supported individual and group psychological treatments for adult mental disorders. *Journal of Consulting and Clinical Psychology, 66,* 37–52.

Dew, M. A., Reynolds, C. F., III, Houck, P. R., Hall, M., Buysse, D. J., Frank, E., & Kupfer, D. J. (1997). Temporal profiles of the course of depression during treatment. Predictors of pathways toward recovery in the elderly. *Archives of General Psychiatry, 54,* 1016–1024.

Diala, C. C., Muntaner, C., Walrath, C., Nickerson, K., LaVeist, T., & Leaf, P. (2001). Racial/ethnic differences in attitudes toward seeking professional mental health services. *American Journal of Public Health, 91,* 805–807.

Druss, B. G., Marcus, S. C., Olfson, M., Tanielian, T., & Pincus, H. A. (2003). Trends in care by nonphysician clinicians in the United States. *New England Journal of Medicine, 348,* 130–137.

ENRICHD Investigators. (2000). Enhancing Recovery in Coronary Heart Disease patients (ENRICHD): Study design and methods. *American Heart Journal, 139*(1, Pt. 1), 1–9.

Fava, G. A., Grandi, S., Zielezny, M., Rafanelli, C., & Canestrari, R. (1996). Four-year outcome for cognitive behavioral treatment of residual symptoms in major depression. *American Journal of Psychiatry, 153,* 945–947.

Fava, M., Labbate, L. A., Abraham, M. E., & Rosenbaum, J. F. (1995). Hypothyroidism and hyperthyroidism in major depression revisited. *Journal of Clinical Psychiatry, 56,* 186–192.

Ferketich, A. K., Schwartzbaum, J. A., Frid, D. J., & Moeschberger, M. L. (2000). Depression as an antecedent to heart disease among women and men in the NHANES I study. National Health and Nutrition Examination Survey. *Archives of Internal Medicine, 160,* 1261–1268.

First, M. B. (1997). *User's guide for the structured clinical interview for DSM-IV Axis I disorders (SCID-I)* (clinician version). Washington, DC: American Psychiatric Press.

Freedland, K. E., Carney, R. M., Lustman, P. J., Rich, M. W., & Jaffe, A. S. (1992). Major depression in coronary artery disease patients with vs. without a prior history of depression. *Psychosomatic Medicine, 54,* 416–421.

Freedland, K. E., Skala, J. A., Carney, R. M., Raczynski, J. M., Taylor, C. B., Mendes De Leon, C. F., Ironson, G., Youngblood, M. E., Rama Krishnan, K. R., & Veith, R. C. (2002). The Depression Interview and Structured Hamilton (DISH): Rationale, development, characteristics, and clinical validity. *Psychosomatic Medicine, 64,* 897–905.

Gilbody, S. M., House, A. O., & Sheldon, T. A. (2001). Routinely administered questionnaires for depression and anxiety: Systematic review. *British Medical Journal, 322,* 406–409.

Gill, D., & Hatcher, S. (2002). Antidepressants for depression in medical illness. Cochrane Database Syst Rev., CD001312.

Glassman, A. H., O'Connor, C. M., Califf, R. M., Swedberg, K., Schwartz, P., Bigger, J. T., Jr., et al. (2002). Sertraline treatment of major depression in patients with acute MI or unstable angina. *Journal of the American Medical Association, 288,* 701–709.

Goldberg, D. P., & Blackwell, B. (1970). Psychiatric illness in general practice. A detailed study using a new method of case identification. *British Medical Journal, 1,* 439–443.

Goldberg, J. F., Harrow, M., & Whiteside, J. E. (2001). Risk for bipolar illness in patients initially hospitalized for unipolar depression. *American Journal of Psychiatry, 158,* 1265–1270.

Grembowski, D. E., Martin, D., Patrick, D. L., Diehr, P., Katon, W., Williams, B., Engelberg, R., Novak, L., Dickstein, D., Deyo, R., & Goldberg, H. I. (2002). Managed care, access to mental health specialists, and outcomes among primary care patients with depressive symptoms. *Journal of General Internal Medicine, 17,* 258–269.

Guze, S. B. (1990). Secondary depression: Observations in alcoholism, Briquet's syndrome, anxiety disorder, schizophrenia, and antisocial personality. A form of comorbidity? *Psychiatric Clinics of North America, 13,* 651–659.

Hall, R. C. W. (1980). *Psychiatric presentations of medical illness: Somatopsychic disorders.* New York: SP Scientific and Medical Books.

Hance, M., Carney, R. M., Freedland, K. E., & Skala, J. (1996). Depression in patients with coronary heart disease. A 12-month follow-up. *General Hospital Psychiatry, 18,* 61–65.

Harman, J. S., & Reynolds, C. F., III. (2000). Removing the barriers to effective depression treatment in old age. *Journal of the American Geriatrics Society, 48,* 1012–1013.

Hasin, D. S., & Grant, B. F. (2002). Major depres-sion in 6050 former drinkers: Association with past alcohol dependence. *Archives of General Psychiatry, 59,* 794–800.

Hirschfeld, R. M., Williams, J. B., Spitzer, R. L., Calabrese, J. R., Flynn, L., Keck, P. E., Jr., et al. (2000). Development and validation of a screening instrument for bipolar spectrum disorder: The Mood Disorder Questionnaire. *American Journal of Psychiatry, 157(11)* 1873–1875.

Hypericum Depression Trial Study Group. (2002). Effect of *Hypericum perforatum* (St John's wort) in major depressive disorder: A randomized controlled trial. *Journal of the American Medical Association, 287,* 1807–1814.

Jacobson, N. S., Dobson, K. S., Truax, P. A., Addis, M. E., Koerner, K., Gollan, J. K., Gortner, E., & Prince, S. E. (1996). A component analysis of cognitive-behavioral treatment for depression. *Journal of Consulting and Clinical Psychology, 64,* 295–304.

Judd, L. L., Akiskal, H. S., Maser, J. D., Zeller, P. J., Endicott, J., Coryell, W., et al. (1998). A prospective 12-year study of subsyndromal and syndromal depressive symptoms in unipolar major depressive disorders. *Archives of General Psychiatry, 55,* 694–700.

Judd, L. L., Akiskal, H. S., & Paulus, M. P. (1997). The role and clinical significance of subsyndromal depressive symptoms (SSD) in unipolar major depressive disorder. *Journal of Affective Disorders, 45,* 5–17.

Karkowski, L. M., & Kendler, K. S. (1997). An examination of the genetic relationship between bipolar and unipolar illness in an epidemiological sample. *Psychiatric Genetics, 7,* 159–163.

Katon, W. (1987). The epidemiology of depression in medical care. *International Journal of Psychiatry in Medicine, 17,* 93–112.

Keller, M. B., McCullough, J. P., Klein, D. N., Arnow, B., Dunner, D. L., Gelenberg, A. J., et al. (2000). A comparison of nefazodone, the cognitive behavioral-analysis system of psychotherapy, and their combination for the treatment of chronic depression. *New England Journal of Medicine, 342,* 1462–1470.

Kendler, K. S., & Prescott, C. A. (1999). A population-based twin study of lifetime major depression in men and women. *Archives of General Psychiatry, 56,* 39–44.

Kessler, R. C., Zhao, S., Blazer, D. G., & Swartz, M. (1997). Prevalence, correlates, and course of minor depression and major depression in the National Comorbidity Survey. *Journal of Affective Disorders, 45,* 19–30.

Klerman, G. L., Weissman, M. M., Rounsaville, B. J., & Chevron, E. S. (1984). *Interpersonal psychotherapy of depression.* New York: Basic Books.

Klinkman, M. S., Schwenk, T. L., & Coyne, J. C. (1997). Depression in primary care—more like asthma than appendicitis: The Michigan Depression Project. *Canadian Journal of Psychiatry—Revue Canadienne de Psychiatrie, 42,* 966–973.

Koenig, H. G., George, L. K., Peterson, B. L., & Pieper, C. F. (1997). Depression in medically ill hospitalized older adults: Prevalence, characteristics, and course of symptoms according to six diagnostic schemes. *American Journal of Psychiatry, 154,* 1376–1383.

Kohn, C. S., Petrucci, R. J., Baessler, C., Soto, D. M., & Movsowitz, C. (2000). The effect of psychological intervention on patients' long-term adjustment to the ICD: A prospective study. *Pacing and Clinical Electrophysiology, 23*(4, Pt. 1), 450–456.

Krishnan, K. R., Hays, J. C., & Blazer, D. G. (1997). MRI-defined vascular depression. *American Journal of Psychiatry, 154,* 497–501.

Kritz-Silverstein, D., Barrett-Connor, E., & Corbeau, C. (2001). Cross-sectional and prospective study of exercise and depressed mood in the elderly: The Rancho Bernardo study. *American Journal of Epidemiology, 153,* 596–603.

Lam, R. W. (2001). Patients' preferences and counselling for depression in primary care. *Lancet, 357,* 575–576.

Langbehn, D. R., Pfohl, B. M., Reynolds, S., Clark, L. A., Battaglia, M., Bellodi, L., et al. (1999). The Iowa Personality Disorder Screen: Development and preliminary validation of a brief screening interview. *Journal of Personality Disorders, 13,* 75–89.

Lavori, P. W., Warshaw, M., Klerman, G., Mueller, T. I., Leon, A., Rice, J., & Akiskal, H. (1993). Secular trends in lifetime onset of MDD stratified by selected sociodemographic risk factors. *Journal of Psychiatric Research, 27,* 95–109.

Lecrubier, Y., Clerc, G., Didi, R., & Kieser, M. (2002). Efficacy of St. John's wort extract WS 5570 in major depression: A double-blind, placebo-controlled trial. *American Journal of Psychiatry, 159,* 1361–1366.

Lesperance, F., Frasure-Smith, N., & Talajic, M. (1996). Major depression before and after myocardial infarction: Its nature and consequences. *Psychosomatic Medicine, 58,* 99–110.

Lincoln, N. B., Flannaghan, T., Sutcliffe, L., & Rother, L. (1997). Evaluation of cognitive behavioural treatment for depression after stroke: A pilot study. *Clinical Rehabilitation, 11,* 114–122.

Lish, J. D., Dime-Meenan, S., Whybrow, P. C., Price, R. A., & Hirschfeld, R. M. (1994). The National Depressive and Manic-Depressive Association (DMDA) survey of bipolar members. *Journal of Affective Disorders, 31,* 281–294.

Lustman, P. J., Freedland, K. E., Griffith, L. S., & Clouse, R. E. (1998). Predicting response to cognitive behavior therapy of depression in type 2 diabetes. *General Hospital Psychiatry, 20,* 302–306.

Lustman, P. J., Freedland, K. E., Griffith, L. S., & Clouse, R. E. (2000). Fluoxetine for depression in diabetes: A randomized double-blind placebo-controlled trial. *Diabetes Care, 23,* 618–623.

Lustman, P. J., Griffith, L. S., Clouse, R. E., Freedland, K. E., Eisen, S. A., Rubin, E. H., Carney, R. M., & McGill, J. B. (1997). Effects of nortriptyline on depression and glycemic control in diabetes: Results of a double-blind, placebo-controlled trial. *Psychosomatic Medicine, 59,* 241–250.

Lustman, P. J., Griffith, L. S., Freedland, K. E., & Clouse, R. E. (1997). The course of major depression in diabetes. *General Hospital Psychiatry, 19,* 138–143.

Lustman, P. J., Griffith, L. S., Freedland, K. E., Kissel, S. S., & Clouse, R. E. (1998). Cognitive behavior therapy for depression in type 2 diabetes mellitus. A randomized, controlled trial. *Annals of Internal Medicine, 129,* 613–621.

Lyness, J. M., Caine, E. D., King, D. A., Cox, C., & Yoediono, Z. (1999). Psychiatric disorders in older primary care patients. *Journal of General Internal Medicine, 14,* 249–254.

McCullough, J. P., Jr., Klein, D. N., Keller, M. B., Holzer, C. E., III, Davis, S. M., Kornstein, S. G., et al. (2000). Comparison of *DSM-III-R* chronic major depression and major depression superimposed on dysthymia (double depression): Validity of the distinction. *Journal of Abnormal Psychology, 109,* 419–427.

Melfi, C. A., Chawla, A. J., Croghan, T. W., Hanna, M. P., Kennedy, S., & Sredl, K.

(1998). The effects of adherence to antidepressant treatment guidelines on relapse and recurrence of depression. *Archives of General Psychiatry, 55,* 1128–1132.

Moorey, S., Greer, S., Bliss, J., & Law, M. (1998). A comparison of adjuvant psychological therapy and supportive counselling in patients with cancer. *Psycho-Oncology, 7,* 218–228.

Morris, P. L., Robinson, R. G., de Carvalho, M. L., Albert, P., Wells, J. C., Samuels, J. F., et al. (1996). Lesion characteristics and depressed mood in the stroke data bank study. *Journal of Neuropsychiatry and Clinical Neurosciences, 8,* 153–159.

Mulrow, C. D., Williams, J. W., Jr., Chiquette, E., Aguilar, C., Hitchcock-Noel, P., Lee, S., et al. (2000). Efficacy of newer medications for treating depression in primary care patients. *American Journal of Medicine, 108,* 54–64.

Musselman, D. L., Lawson, D. H., Gumnick, J. F., Manatunga, A. K., Penna, S., Goodkin, R. S., et al. (2001). Paroxetine for the prevention of depression induced by high-dose interferon alfa. *New England Journal of Medicine, 344,* 961–966.

Narrow, W. E., Rae, D. S., Robins, L. N., & Regier, D. A. (2002). Revised prevalence estimates of mental disorders in the United States: Using a clinical significance criterion to reconcile 2 surveys' estimates [Comment]. *Archives of General Psychiatry, 59,* 115–123.

Nazemi, H., Larkin, A. A., Sullivan, M. D., & Katon, W. (2001). Methodological issues in the recruitment of primary care patients with depression. *International Journal of Psychiatry in Medicine, 31,* 277–288.

Nezu, A. M. (1986). Efficacy of a social problem-solving therapy approach for unipolar depression. *Journal of Consulting and Clinical Psychology, 54,* 196–202.

Nierenberg, A. A., Burt, T., Matthews, J., & Weiss, A. P. (1999). Mania associated with St. John's wort. *Biological Psychiatry, 46,* 1707–1708.

Olfson, M., Marcus, S. C., Druss, B., Elinson, L., Tanielian, T., & Pincus, H. A. (2002). National trends in the outpatient treatment of depression. *Journal of the American Medical Association, 287,* 203–209.

Olfson, M., Marcus, S. C., Druss, B., & Pincus, H. A. (2002). National trends in the use of outpatient psychotherapy. *American Journal of Psychiatry, 159,* 1914–1920.

Persons, J. B., Thase, M. E., & Crits-Christoph, P.

(1996). The role of psychotherapy in the treatment of depression: Review of two practice guidelines. *Archives of General Psychiatry, 53,* 283–290.

Petersen, T., Dording, C., Neault, N. B., Kornbluh, R., Alpert, J. E., Nierenberg, A. A., et al. (2002). A survey of prescribing practices in the treatment of depression. *Progress in Neuro-Psychopharmacology and Biological Psychiatry, 26,* 177–187.

Pignone, M., Gaynes, B. N., Lohr, K. N., Orleans, C. T., & Mulrow, C. (2001). Questionnaires for depression and anxiety. Systematic review is incomplete. *British Medical Journal, 323,* 167–168.

Pincus, H. A. (2003). The future of behavioral health and primary care: Drowning in the mainstream or left on the bank? *Psychosomatics, 44,* 1–11.

Placidi, G. P., Boldrini, M., Patronelli, A., Fiore, E., Chiovato, L., Perugi, G., & Marazziti, D. (1998). Prevalence of psychiatric disorders in thyroid diseased patients. *Neuropsychobiology, 38,* 222–225.

Posternak, M. A., & Zimmerman, M. (2002). The prevalence of atypical features across mood, anxiety, and personality disorders. *Comprehensive Psychiatry, 43,* 253–262.

Preda, A., MacLean, R. W., Mazure, C. M., & Bowers, M. B., Jr. (2001). Antidepressant-associated mania and psychosis resulting in psychiatric admissions. *Journal of Clinical Psychiatry, 62,* 30–33.

Radloff, L. S. (1977). The CES-D scale: A self-report depression scale for research in the general population. *Applied Psychological Measurement, 1,* 385–401.

Rapaport, M. H., & Judd, L. L. (1998). Minor depressive disorder and subsyndromal depressive symptoms: Functional impairment and response to treatment. *Journal of Affective Disorders, 48,* 227–232.

Regier, D. A., Narrow, W. E., Rae, D. S., Manderscheid, R. W., Locke, B. Z., & Goodwin, F. K. (1993). The de facto US mental and addictive disorders service system. Epidemiologic Catchment Area prospective 1-year prevalence rates of disorders and services. *Archives of General Psychiatry, 50,* 85–94.

Robinson, R. G., Schultz, S. K., Castillo, C., Kopel, T., Kosier, J. T., Newman, R. M., et al. (2000). Nortriptyline versus fluoxetine in the treatment of depression and in short-term recovery after stroke: A placebo-controlled, double-blind study. *American Journal of Psychiatry, 157,* 351–359.

Rundell, J. R., & Wise, M. G. (1989). Causes of organic mood disorder. *Journal of Neuropsychiatry and Clinical Neurosciences, 1,* 398–400.

Sartorius, N., Ustun, T. B., Lecrubier, Y., & Wittchen, H. U. (1996). Depression comorbid with anxiety: Results from the WHO study on psychological disorders in primary health care. *British Journal of Psychiatry—Supplementum,* (30), 38–43.

Schade, C. P., Jones, E. R. J., & Wittlin, B. J. (1998). A ten-year review of the validity and clinical utility of depression screening. *Psychiatric Services, 49,* 55–61.

Schulberg, H. C., Katon, W., Simon, G. E., & Rush, A. J. (1998). Treating major depression in primary care practice: An update of the Agency for Health Care Policy and Research Practice Guidelines. *Archives of General Psychiatry, 55,* 1121–1127.

Schulberg, H. C., Raue, P. J., & Rollman, B. L. (2002). The effectiveness of psychotherapy in treating depressive disorders in primary care practice: Clinical and cost perspectives. *General Hospital Psychiatry, 24,* 203–212.

Scott, J., & Pope, M. (2002). Self-reported adherence to treatment with mood stabilizers, plasma levels, and psychiatric hospitalization. *American Journal of Psychiatry, 159,* 1927–1929.

Sharpe, L., Sensky, T., Timberlake, N., Ryan, B., Brewin, C. R., & Allard, S. (2001). A blind, randomized, controlled trial of cognitive-behavioural intervention for patients with recent onset rheumatoid arthritis: Preventing psychological and physical morbidity. *Pain, 89,* 275–283.

Sheline, Y. I., Freedland, K. E., & Carney, R. M. (1997). How safe are serotonin reuptake inhibitors for depression in patients with coronary heart disease? *American Journal of Medicine, 102,* 54–59.

Shelton, R. C., Keller, M. B., Gelenberg, A., Dunner, D. L., Hirschfeld, R., Thase, M. E., et al. (2001). Effectiveness of St John's wort in major depression: A randomized controlled trial. *Journal of the American Medical Association, 285,* 1978–1986.

Simon, G. E., Revicki, D., Heiligenstein, J., Grothaus, L., VonKorff, M., Katon, W. J., & Hylan, T. R. (2000). Recovery from depression, work productivity, and health care costs among primary care patients. *General Hospital Psychiatry, 22,* 153–162.

Snow, V., Lascher, S., & Mottur-Pilson, C. (2000). Pharmacologic treatment of acute major depression and dysthymia. American College of Physicians-American Society of Internal Medicine. *Annals of Internal Medicine, 132,* 738–742.

Spitzer, R. L., Kroenke, K., & Williams, J. B. (1999). Validation and utility of a self-report version of PRIME-MD: The PHQ primary care study. Primary Care Evaluation of Mental Disorders. Patient Health Questionnaire. *Journal of the American Medical Association, 282,* 1737–1744.

Sullivan, P. F., Neale, M. C., & Kendler, K. S. (2000). Genetic epidemiology of major depression: Review and meta-analysis. *American Journal of Psychiatry, 157,* 1552–1562.

Thase, M. E., Greenhouse, J. B., Frank, E., Reynolds, C. F., III, Pilkonis, P. A., Hurley, K., et al. (1997). Treatment of major depression with psychotherapy or psychotherapy-pharmacotherapy combinations. *Archives of General Psychiatry, 54,* 1009–1015.

Thompson, C., Peveler, R. C., Stephenson, D., & McKendrick, J. (2000). Compliance with antidepressant medication in the treatment of major depressive disorder in primary care: A randomized comparison of fluoxetine and a tricyclic antidepressant. *American Journal of Psychiatry, 157,* 338–343.

Turner, J. A., & Jensen, M. P. (1993). Efficacy of cognitive therapy for chronic low back pain. *Pain, 52,* 169–177.

Walsh, B. T., Seidman, S. N., Sysko, R., & Gould, M. (2002). Placebo response in studies of major depression: Variable, substantial, and growing. *Journal of the American Medical Association, 287,* 1840–1847.

Weissman, M. M., Bruce, M. L., Leaf, P. J., Florio, L. P., & Holzer, C. E., III. (1991). Affective disorders. In L. N. Robins & D. A. Regier (Eds.), *Psychiatric disorders in America: The Epidemiologic Catchment Area study* (pp. 53–80). New York: Free Press.

Wells, K. B., & Sherbourne, C. D. (1999). Functioning and utility for current health of patients with depression or chronic medical conditions in managed, primary care practices. *Archives of General Psychiatry, 56,* 897–904.

Williams, J. B. (1988). A structured interview

guide for the Hamilton Depression Rating Scale. *Archives of General Psychiatry, 45*, 742–747.

Williams, J. W., Jr., Barrett, J., Oxman, T., Frank, E., Katon, W., Sullivan, M., et al. (2000). Treatment of dysthymia and minor depression in primary care: A randomized controlled trial in older adults. *Journal of the American Medical Association, 284*, 1519–1526.

Williams, J. W., Jr., Kerber, C. A., Mulrow, C. D., Medina, A., & Aguilar, C. (1995). Depressive disorders in primary care: Prevalence, functional disability, and identification. *Journal of General Internal Medicine, 10*, 7–12.

Williams, J. W., Jr., Mulrow, C. D., Chiquette, E., Noel, P. H., Aguilar, C., & Cornell, J. (2000). A systematic review of newer pharmacotherapies for depression in adults: Evidence report summary. *Annals of Internal Medicine, 132*, 743–756.

Yesavage, J. A., Brink, T. L., Rose, T. L., Lum, O., Huang, V., Adey, M., & Leirer, V. O. (1982). Development and validation of a geriatric depression screening scale: A preliminary report. *Journal of Psychiatric Research, 17*, 37–49.

Young, A. S., Klap, R., Sherbourne, C. D., & Wells, K. B. (2001). The quality of care for depressive and anxiety disorders in the United States. *Archives of General Psychiatry, 58*, 55–61.

Zung, W. W. (1965). A self-rating depression scale. *Archives of General Psychiatry, 12*, 63–70.

23

Diabetes

Russell E. Glasgow
Paul A. Nutting

The purpose of this chapter is to describe diabetes and the primary care–based management of diabetes, with emphasis on the role that psychologists can play. We summarize current evidence on behavioral interventions for this complex and challenging condition and make recommendations for practical strategies and ways to integrate behavioral and psychological interventions into primary care. These issues are important because diabetes is increasing markedly in prevalence and will continue to do so and because it is a prototypical chronic illness. Clinicians able to deal successfully with diabetes should also be well prepared to assist with other chronic illnesses.

Diabetes mellitus is a disorder of glucose metabolism that leads to an inability to use glucose in the peripheral tissues and results in elevated glucose levels in the blood. The onset of Type 1 diabetes mellitus occurs primarily in children and adolescents and was formerly known as insulin-dependent diabetes mellitus (IDDM) because affected individuals are committed to a lifetime regimen of regular injections of insulin. Type 2 diabetes mellitus (formerly known as non-insulin dependent diabetes mellitus or NIDDM) is more common, accounting for 90% of all cases of diabetes in the United States. Type 2 diabetes may be treated with diet and exercise, oral agents, or insulin.

There is encouraging recent evidence that the onset of Type 2 diabetes can be delayed or even prevented by addressing obesity and sedentary lifestyle (Pan et al., 1997). Approximately 40% of adults in the United States are obese, and 25% report limited physical activity. Individuals who are physically active on most days of the week may reduce their risk for onset of diabetes by as much as 40% (U.S. Preventive Services Task Force, 1996).

The care of diabetes is complicated and requires a team approach involving the patient, the primary care physician, and a variety of other health professionals. Psychologists can play a critical role in the overall care of this condition by working with both the patient and the primary care physician to increase the effectiveness of and support for the patient role in diabetes self-management. The profound effect of this condition on the daily life of affected individuals also leads to psychological, as well as medical, sequelae that should be addressed to optimize the individual's quality of life.

ETIOLOGY

The causes of Type 1 and Type 2 diabetes are very different. Type 1 diabetes is characterized by an absolute deficiency of insulin, believed to be caused by an autoimmune destruction of beta cells of the pancreas that produce insulin. Individuals with Type 1 diabetes are committed to lifelong administration of multiple daily injections of insulin or to the use of one of the newer continuous infusion devices ("insulin pumps").

Persons with Type 2 diabetes initially produce adequate insulin, but experience resistance to insulin activity at the cellular level. In an effort to drive glucose into the cells, the pancreas increases insulin production. Serum levels of glucose begin to rise when pancreatic production of insulin cannot keep pace with increasing cellular resistance. Eventually, the pancreas is unable to maintain the high level of insulin production, and supplemental insulin may be required.

EPIDEMIOLOGY

Diabetes is a leading cause of death, illness, and disability in the United States, affecting an estimated 16 million Americans (Centers for Disease Control and Prevention, 1997). Overall life expectancy for both Type 1 and Type 2 diabetes is shortened by as much as 7 years.

Microvascular and neuropathic complications cause substantial morbidity: Diabetic retinopathy is the leading cause of new cases of blindness among American adults. Diabetic nephropathy is the most common cause of end-stage renal disease. Diabetic neuropathy (and vascular disease) produce leg and foot ulcers that do not heal well, resulting in half of all lower extremity amputations in the United States (Reiber, Boyko, & Smith, 1995).

An even greater burden on the American public comes from the macrovascular complications of diabetes, which substantially increase risk of death and morbidity from coronary artery disease, stroke, and peripheral vascular disease. Individuals with diabetes are at greater risk for cardiovascular disease, and 70% of deaths in adults with diabetes are attributable to cardiovascular disease (National Diabetes Data Group, 1995). The atherogenic (cardiovascular) consequences of diabetes account for an enormous burden of suffering and rising health care expenditures. Recent estimates of annual direct and indirect costs of diabetes are $46 billion to $54 billion (American Diabetes Association [ADA], 1997).

TYPICAL COURSE OF THE ILLNESS

Onset of Type 1 diabetes generally occurs in childhood or adolescence, and Type 2 diabetes generally occurs in the middle adult years and increases in prevalence with advancing age. Type 2 diabetes is often associated with obesity and physical inactivity, and the epidemic of obesity in younger Americans is driving the average age of onset down to include more adolescents and young adults. The diagnosis may not be made for several years as the classic presentation of hyperglycemia and ketoacidosis, typical of Type 1 diabetes and often requiring hospitalization, is uncommon. Type 2 diabetes is more likely to present insidiously with frequent infections, often frequent vaginal candidiasis (yeast infection) in women, or frequent urinary tract infections in either gender. The classic triad of polyphagia (excessive hunger), polydipsia (excessive thirst), and polyuria (excessive urination) may signal onset of either Type 1 or Type 2 diabetes in some persons.

Both Type 1 and Type 2 diabetes are associated with serious complications resulting from microvascular (retina, kidney) and macrovascular (heart, brain, extremities) complications. Because the onset of Type 2 diabetes may be gradual and without marked symptoms, the initial diagnosis in some patients may result from clinical or laboratory examination consequent to checkups or hospitalization for other purposes that reveals early progression of complications affecting the kidney or retina.

WHO TREATS THIS CONDITION?

Primary care physicians provide approximately 80% of care for individuals with diabetes, although patients with Type 1 diabetes, children especially, may be more likely to receive a larger proportion of their care from endocrinologists or other specialists. There is general agreement that optimal care of diabetes requires a coordinated team approach with the patients themselves participating as active team members (Anderson & Funnell, 2000). Thus, there are important roles for behavioral scientists, dieticians, diabetes educators, nurse clinicians, exercise specialists, and others in the optimal management of diabetes (Anderson & Rubin, 2002).

Although the predominant form of primary care in the United States is based on an acute care model, there are strong arguments for the adoption of chronic care models in the management of diabetes (Glasgow et al., 1999; Wagner, Grothaus, et al., 2001). Such models include care management to coordinate care among different clinicians, information systems to support clinical decision making and sharing of critical information among team members, systems to track and reinforce needed elements of care, provision for enhancing the patient's self-management role, and provisions for redesigning the very structure of the diabetes office visit (Sadur et al., 1999).

TYPICAL TREATMENTS

The therapeutic objectives for diabetes include management of blood sugar levels, blood pressure, and lipid levels combined with diet management, weight control, and physical activity. When appropriate, cessation of smoking plays a central role in achieving optimal outcomes for diabetes as well. During the initial stage of development of Type 2 diabetes characterized by insulin resistance, treatment is focused on decreasing insulin resistance through weight loss and medications that reduce resistance. In the later stages of Type 2 diabetes, some individuals will also require insulin.

Control of Blood Sugar

Control of blood sugar for individuals with Type 1 diabetes is essential to maintain life and has been the principal objective of treatment since the isolation of insulin. There is now strong evidence that control of blood sugar reduces complications of both Type 1 (Diabetes Control and Complications Trial Research Group, 1993) and Type 2 diabetes (United Kingdom Prospective Diabetes Study [UKPDS] Group, 1998a). Although the concern of hypoglycemia associated with tight blood sugar control legitimately raises quality-of-life concerns, there is direct evidence that improved glycemic control is associated with improvements in patient-reported quality of life (Testa & Simonson, 1998). There are also well-validated blood glucose awareness training programs to help persons anticipate, recognize, and cope with hypo- and hyperglycemia (Cox et al., 1995, 1999). These programs are discussed in the section on psychological aspects.

Blood sugar levels are usually controlled by a combination of dietary management and use of medications. Type 1 diabetes requires use of insulin, and the oral agents play little or no role. In Type 2 diabetes, dietary management is usually augmented initially by oral agents, and insulin is added only when diet and oral agents do not achieve optimal control. Oral medications for diabetes generally fall into three classes, each with its own profile of actions, advantages, and disadvantages. Not uncommonly, more than one oral agent is used to take advantage of the combination of profiles achieved.

The first class of drugs stimulates the beta cells to release more insulin and consists of the sulfonylureas. These medications have been in use for nearly 50 years, and because they stimulate the release of insulin, they have hypoglycemia as a side effect in common. These drugs are generally taken one to two times a day, before meals. All sulfonylurea drugs have similar effects on blood sugar levels, but they differ in side effects, how often they are taken, and interactions with other drugs. Some sulfonylureas can interact with alcohol to cause vomiting and flushing or even relatively severe illness. The second class of diabetes drugs (metformin and the glitazones) sensitizes the liver, muscle, and fat cells to the insulin that is already present. The third class of oral agents (acarbose and meglitol) acts by slowing the breakdown of starches and certain sugars and reduces absorption from the diet. Their action slows the rise in blood sugar levels after a meal, and they are usually taken at the beginning of a meal.

Although used less commonly, insulin may be needed to supplement or even replace oral agents in individuals with more severe or long-standing diabetes. As a simplification, insulin can be considered long acting (NPH, lente, and ultralente) or short acting (regular and lispro). These may be used in combinations that best achieve the glycemic control needs of the individual patient. The practice of injecting a short-acting insulin immediately before a meal to control the postprandial glucose surge is becoming more common, particularly in Type 1 diabetes. All patients who use insulin require careful instruction in managing their insulin injections, monitoring their blood sugar, exercise, and management of hypoglycemic episodes.

Hypoglycemia is an unpleasant and potentially dangerous result of excessive lowering of blood sugar, most commonly resulting from insulin, but occasionally associated with oral agents (such as the sulfonyureas). As hypoglycemia initially develops, the patient notices excessive perspiration, hunger or nausea, tremors, tachycardia (rapid heart rate), and pallor. If hypoglycemia is prolonged or blood sugar levels fall further, patients suffer headache, lethargy, confusion, blurred vision, disorientation, bizarre behavior, and even coma.

Hypoglycemic episodes can be rapidly reversed by feeding rapidly absorbed foods, such as fruit juices, candy, or commercially available packets of "instant glucose," which can even be sufficiently absorbed if simply held in the mouth. More severe hypoglycemic episodes and those in patients unable to take sugar by mouth are treated with intravenous glucose. Many patients find a hypoglycemic episode extremely unpleasant and are hesitant to continue addressing their blood sugar as aggressively after experiencing a "hypo." Although validated instruments are available to assess fear of hypoglycemia (Cox, Irvine, Gonder-Frederick, Nowacek, & Butterfield, 1987), the clinician should at least ask patients to rate the intensity of their concern.

Blood sugar levels were traditionally monitored by repeated measures of the serum levels of glucose, and this remains an important strategy for patients with Type 1 diabetes to adjust their activities and medications to control better the peaks and valleys in blood sugar. The evidence for the value of blood glucose self-monitoring is not as strong for Type 2 diabetes. Because glucose levels fluctuate rapidly in response to dietary intake and exercise, it is difficult to obtain a clear picture of overall glucose control over time.

Over the past decade, the ability to estimate "average glucose levels" by measuring a chemical effect of blood glucose on the hemoglobin molecule (HgA1c) has largely replaced periodic monitoring of blood sugar by the primary care physician. The HgA1c provides an estimate of the "average" blood sugar level over the previous 2 to 3 months, and the ADA recommends checking levels every 3 months. There is good evidence for the relationship between HgA1c levels and delay of microvascular complications of diabetes; the relationships also exist for macrovascular complications, although the evidence is less strong. Generally, HgA1c levels below 7% are considered good glycemic control, and levels between 7% and 8% may be acceptable in some patients; levels above 9% are nearly always considered unacceptable. The exact HgA1c target for a given individual, however, remains a highly individualized determination that must take into account age, mental capacity, medical comorbidity, propensity to hypoglycemic episodes, and many other patient factors.

Management of Cardiovascular Risk Factors

Cardiovascular risk reduction in adults is as important as glycemic control (UKPDS Group, 1998b). About 60% of patients with newly diagnosed Type 2 diabetes have clinical or subclinical coronary heart disease, and over 70% of adults with diabetes die from cardiovascular or cerebrovascular causes. Because of this additional risk, special efforts are required to detect and manage other potentially concurrent cardiovascular risk factors, specifically smoking, hypertension, hyperlipidemia, obesity, diet, and physical activity.

All patients with diabetes should be carefully and routinely asked about smoking and other tobacco use. When discovered, the individual should be counseled about the risks and encouraged to join with the health care team and other community resources to develop a plan to quit that is tailored to their situation and preferences (Haire-Joshu, Glasgow, & Tibbs, 1999). (See also other chapters in this volume on smoking, obesity, and encouragement of behavior change.)

Blood pressure control for patients with Type 2 diabetes has a critical effect on overall mortality and on both micro- and macrovascular complications. Results from one prominent study suggested that effective control of blood pressure may be even more important than blood sugar control on microvascular complications (UKPDS Group, 1998a, 1998b). Primary care physicians will generally strive for blood pressure levels below 135/85 mmHg for patients with diabetes.

Management of lipids is also a strong component of preventing cardiovascular complications of diabetes. High-density lipoprotein (HDL) levels are protective, and low-density lipoproteins (LDLs) are associated with elevated risk of cardio- and cerebrovascular events. Most individuals with Type 2 diabetes have either a pattern of elevated LDL levels (above 130 mg/dl) or a pattern of depressed HDL levels (below 35 mg/dl) along with elevated triglycerides. The goal of lipid management is to reduce LDL levels to less than 100 mg/dl (or less than 100 mg/dl in patients who have current cardiovascular, cerebrovascular, or peripheral vascular disease) and elevate HDL levels above 45 mg/dl in men and above 55 mg/dl in women. Reduction in dietary fat, especially saturated fat, and use of the "statin" agents form the mainstay of lipid management. The ADA recommends monitoring of lipid levels every year or more often to achieve targets. Because current laboratory technology requires a fasting blood sample to estimate the LDL, total cholesterol, HDL, and their ratio are often measured because they can be obtained on a random blood sample; however, they do not provide an accurate estimate of LDL.

Patient Self-Management

To a greater extent than most other chronic illnesses, the management of diabetes requires a great deal of commitment and self-management activity by the affected individual. Patients and not the medical team ultimately determine the potentially critical contributions that will be made by dietary, exercise, weight management, blood sugar monitoring, and foot care activities. Patient attention and commitment to each component of self-management for diabetes has both short- and long-term implications for management of diabetes and quality of life.

For example, attention to foot care, including use of nonbinding and properly fitted shoes, along with frequent self-examination of the feet for redness and signs of early ulceration can prevent the intractable foot damage that often leads to amputation. Although physicians should examine the patient's feet on every visit, problems often develop quickly and can best be prevented and detected by the patient. This underscores the importance of a central role for the patient in tailoring and implementing a treatment plan to their preferences and life situation (Anderson & Funnell, 2000).

Demands of Regimens

The diabetes self-management regimen is one of the most challenging of any condition (Gerstein & Haynes, 2001; Glasgow & Eakin, 2000; Gonder-Frederick, Cox, & Ritterband, 2002). It involves an integrated sequence of consistent dietary and exercise behaviors, medication adherence, and regular blood glucose testing in appropriate temporal relationship to the various actions above, as well as series of preventive actions and regular laboratory checks. In addition to these daily activities, diabetes care also typically involves the management of comorbid illnesses or disease complications. Other important aspects of diabetes self-management include coping with social pressures inconsistent with regimen recommendations (e.g., holiday or birthday parties) and potential stigma or embarrassment. Because of the complexity of these issues, good communication between the patient and the health care team is especially important.

Not surprisingly, adherence to a diabetes regimen is typically far from optimal. A significant complexity is that the intensity of self-management effort required (the term preferred over patient adherence or compliance; Glasgow & Anderson, 1999) can vary considerably across different regimen components. For example, the efforts required for adequate blood glucose testing are often unrelated to the efforts required to achieve adequate physical activity. Recognizing these facts can help the clinician avoid the common trap of labeling a given patient "noncompliant." Ironically, noncompliance is one of the most typical reasons that patients are referred to psychologists by physicians. Instead of focusing on compliance or noncompliance as a global trait, the psychologist should focus on the specific behaviors of concern.

Similarly, the regimen expectations and aggressiveness of the medical interventions involved vary considerably across patients. Often, patients with Type 1 diabetes, more poorly controlled blood glucose levels, or at higher risk because of other comorbid conditions are placed on more aggressive medication regimens. These sometimes involve insulin self-adjustment, multiple shots of insulin per day, or an implantable insulin pump. Two landmark studies, the Diabetes Control and Complications Trial and the UKPDS, demonstrated that tighter metabolic control resulted in substantial reductions in microvascular and macrovascular complications and have led to the wider use of more aggressive treatment regimens.

PSYCHOLOGICAL ASPECTS OF DIABETES

When they are initially diagnosed with diabetes or when their regimen is "stepped up" (from no medication to oral medication or from oral medications to insulin), patients may have one of two quite different reactions. They may minimize the seriousness of their condition; for example, some patients will say that they do not have diabetes, but only "a little sugar." In contrast, especially if they have relatives who have experienced the complications of diabetes, they can become quite distressed about the incurable illness they have contracted. Understanding a patient's personal model of illness (Hampson, Glasgow, Toobert, & Strycker, 2000), which is how they understand their illness and its causes, consequences, and treatment expectations, is often an important initial step in working with diabetes patients.

Either initially or later during the course of their illness, patients with diabetes may become depressed. As we discuss below, depression may partially cause diabetes, be a result of diabetes, or complicate the presentation.

Family interactions have been best studied among adolescent patients with Type 1 diabetes, and it is clear that the management demands of the diabetes regimen are handled quite differently across families. Some families become overprotective or overcontrolling of diabetic family members, and research has indicated that diabetic children whose families have appropriate age-related expectations of them are usually in better metabolic control and are better adjusted (Anderson & Funnel, 2000). Recent research on adults with Type 2 diabetes has demonstrated several differences between ethnic and cultural groups in the impact of diabetes on the family (Fisher, Chesla, Mullan, Skaff, & Kanter, 2001).

One of the common concerns of patients with "brittle diabetes," who are subject to marked blood glucose excursions, is fear of hypoglycemia. More intensive insulin treatment is associated with a higher incidence of insulin reactions, whose consequences and experience can be serious and very distressing for both patients and family members. Because of this fear of hypoglycemia, many patients would rather live with high blood glucose levels, which can be relatively asymptomatic, rather than risk insulin reactions (Cox et al., 1987). Training programs for blood glucose awareness have been developed and found effective in improving blood glucose estimation, reducing hypoglycemic episodes, improving quality of life, and reducing motor vehicle accidents (Cox et al., 1999).

PSYCHOLOGICAL CONDITIONS COMORBID WITH DIABETES

There is growing evidence of an association between diabetes and depression (Anderson, Freedland, Clouse, & Lustman, 2001). Recent data suggest that the prevalence of depression in individuals with diabetes may be twice that observed in individuals without diabetes. The nature of the association is not clear. Especially among younger patients, there may also be a high incidence of eating disorders and self-image difficulties. The effect on diabetes of treating the comorbid depression is currently under study. Preliminary evidence suggests that treating depression via either pharmacological or cognitive–behavioral modalities may also improve diabetes (Lustman, Singh, & Clouse, 2002).

EFFECTIVE INTERVENTION APPROACHES

A variety of patient education and counseling approaches have been developed and evaluated for their effectiveness in helping patients cope with diabetes regimen tasks such as eating patterns, physical activity levels, medication taking and regimen "adherence," blood glucose testing, and combinations of these factors. Space does not permit detailed discussion of these studies, and reviews have been published elsewhere (Anderson & Rubin, 2002; Gonder-Frederick et al., 2002; Norris, Engelgau, & Narayan, 2001). In this section, we review key lessons learned from this research, with emphasis on studies that have been conducted under realistic clinical conditions or have been replicated and have potential to be adopted widely in primary care settings.

Most modern diabetes self-management education programs employ a patient-centered, collaborative, and empowerment-based approach (Anderson & Funnell, 2000). This approach recognizes patients as the primary decision makers concerning their diabetes and collaboratively negotiates goals and action plans using a problem-based adult learning approach (Anderson & Funnell, 1999). Thus, the clinician presents more questions than directives. In such a collaborative approach, the patient is recognized as the expert on his or her situation and on strategies that will be best personally. Although many clinicians state that they employ such an approach, in fact interactions are often provider directed and more didactic and advice giving than patient-centered and problem-solving. One hallmark of an empowerment approach is that goal setting is truly collaborative and not dominated by the clinician.

Diabetes interventions have their maximum impact when they are proactive, population based, and patient centered (Hiss, 1996). This is also a

change from the traditional role of the psychologist, who reactively meets with patients who have developed difficulties of some kind and are referred for help. This change to a population-based or "public-health psychology" (Glasgow et al., 1999) perspective is challenging for many health professionals and systems.

Several studies have found brief patient activation or counseling approaches conducted either immediately before or during medical office visits to be effective (Glasgow et al., 1997; Kaplan, Greenfield, & Ware, 1989). Key components of these interventions seem to be helping the patient identify issues and barriers to goal attainment, developing action plans using problem-solving methods, and having consistent follow-up after the office visit, often in the form of telephone calls. Although much more work remains, we are also starting to see promising interventions that are culturally appropriate and deliver effective interventions for minority patients and those of lower socioeconomic status. In particular, the community health centers supported by the Bureau of Primary Care have conducted a variety of innovative and low-cost programs tailored to particular low-socioeconomic and racial and ethnic minority populations and settings (http://bphc.hrsa.gov/programs/HDCProgramInfo.htm).

A useful heuristic for brief intervention approaches, known as the five A's, that has proven successful in other behavior change areas also seems appropriate for diabetes self-management support (Whitlock, Orleans, Pender, & Allan, 2002). As seen in Figure 23.1, this cycle of assess, advise, agree, assist, and arrange (follow-up) succinctly describes the component processes discussed above and illustrates that self-management should be viewed as an ongoing, iterative process, not a one-time "inoculation" that is done to the patient and that magically provides immunity to future problems.

These interventions and interactions do not occur in a vacuum, however, and need to be designed to be consistent with and to complement the patient's ongoing primary care (Glasgow, 1999). Self-management goals need to be shared and reinforced by all team members. Finally, just as interventions are generally more effective when tailored to patients' situations and preferences, so

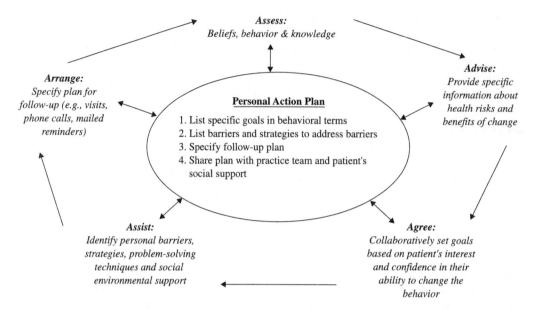

Figure 23.1   Self-management model with five A's. (From Glasgow, Funnell, et al., 2002; Whitlock et al., 2002.)

are self-management support plans (Glasgow, Davis, Funnell, & Beck, 2003).

NONPSYCHOTHERAPEUTIC APPROACHES

A variety of brief and distance intervention approaches have been tried, and there is evidence that a variety of intervention agents can effectively implement and deliver supportive diabetes self-care interventions if patients are appropriately trained and supervised (Brown & Harris, 1999; Glasgow, Toobert, Hampson, & Strycker, 2002). Lifestyle change interventions have most frequently evaluated the effects of different counselors or "health coaches." For example, Glasgow et al. (2003) found that nurse/certified diabetes educators, psychologists, dieticians, and a bachelor's level assistant all did equally well in implementing a CD-ROM-assisted dietary behavior change intervention; Brown and Harris (1999) as well as others have had success in training lay leaders (*promatoras*) to deliver components of their program. As demonstrated by Lorig et al. (1999), the key seems to be having a structured protocol so the coach is clear on what to do (and what not

to do), a good training program, and supervision. Developing such materials and training and supervision of paraprofessionals and other health personnel are important roles that psychologists can play in addition to direct delivery of services.

There is a great deal of current interest in Internet-based support groups, and a relatively large number of self-help books are available on coping with diabetes, including many published by the ADA. Although many individuals apparently find these resources valuable, there are few or no controlled studies of their reach (penetration) or effectiveness (Piette, 2002). Barrera, Glasgow, McKay, Boles, and Feil (2002) found that an Internet-only intervention did enhance perceptions of social support, and there is clearly a role for psychologists in designing Web site interventions and moderating online discussions.

INNOVATIVE COLLABORATIVE CARE ARRANGEMENTS

One of the largest changes in diabetes management over the past decade has been the switch from a "provider-centric" management model, with an almost exclusive focus on achieving the lowest possible blood glucose levels, to a patient-centered approach that involves the patient as an active decision maker and considers much broader outcomes, including especially patient quality-of-life issues (Anderson & Rubin, 2002).

Psychologists, dieticians, certified diabetes educators, exercise specialists, nurses, and others have demonstrated that they can function as key members of the patient's health care team, and most education programs recommend a team approach to diabetes care. The key challenges in such an approach are consistency in messages and goals addressed by the various team members and communication among team members and with the patient.

Some of the most exciting approaches have involved activating patients to help them interact with their providers and to ensure that they are receiving quality care. It is likely that the Internet explosion will further this trend over the next several years. Primary care group visits may be promising; in this model, a number of patients and their family members are seen conjointly, usually by a nurse coordinator and a physician. Although there are different variations of this basic approach (Sadur et al., 1999), most involve both a structured discussion and time for group members to raise questions or issues and for group discussion. The patients get to interact with their health care providers for a much longer time (often approximately 2 hours) and in a different role than usual. They also benefit from the comments and perspective of other patients with chronic illness. Psychologists could productively help physicians to plan, implement, and evaluate group visits in their practice.

One particular model that has recently achieved recognition is called the chronic care model; it proposes a series of evidence-based changes to make primary care more proactive, more planful, and more patient centered in how chronic illnesses like diabetes are treated (Wagner, 1998; Wagner, Glasgow, et al., 2001). Key components of the model most relevant to psychologists are patients' self-management support and linkages to community resources. These act in concert with other changes to create productive interactions between informed, activated patients and prepared, proactive clinicians. This framework enumerates a number of changes necessary to improve chronic illness care, and the framework suggests that all components (see Figure 23.2)

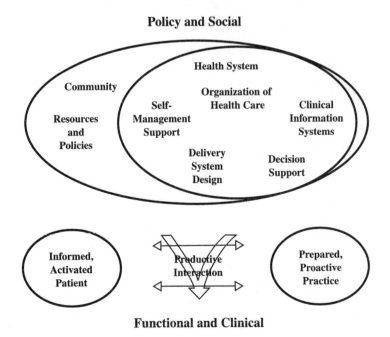

Figure 23.2 Elements of the chronic care model.

must be addressed to see meaningful improvement. For present purposes, it is important that self-management training be integrated and coordinated with other aspects of the patient's care.

EFFECTIVE COLLABORATION BETWEEN MEDICAL AND PSYCHOLOGICAL CLINICIANS

Physicians most commonly refer diabetes patients because of noncompliance, especially with lifestyle aspects of the regimen, including weight control, emotional problems such as depression, and family dysfunction. Unfortunately, it is also common that the psychologist or diabetes educator is consulted only after a patient has had a series of failure experiences. A related challenge to working with some physicians is their expectation that a single session of counseling or a short term of self-management training will somehow miraculously "cure" the patient.

Conversely, a service that is seldom requested but that can be enormously helpful is to have a behavioral specialist assist the team in designing a series of "rapid-cycle improvement" tests (Langley, Nolan, Nolan, Norman, & Provost, 1996) or evaluations of systems changes to help design more effective systems of diabetes and chronic illness care. Such consultation on designing "mini-experiments" of system changes (especially those related to ways of interacting with patients or self-management) should become an important area for psychologists in the future.

Several common mistakes made by psychologists who do not deal regularly with diabetes are noted in Table 23.1 along with more productive alternatives. Note that, of the five pitfalls listed, the last is the most serious and potentially the most damaging to effective teamwork.

From the primary care physician's perspective, diabetes can be a frustrating condition. For most components of the treatment, the locus of control rests with the patient, and the physician may feel powerless to affect patient outcomes and further frustrated at the patient's inability to follow various components of the management plan. In some cases, this is manifested by an unintentional tendency to "blame the patient." When this occurs, the behavioral scientist may be helpful to the primary care physician in clarifying the reasons for the patient's actions and in suggesting tools for improving communication and negotiation with the patient.

SUMMARY

Table 23.2 lists a number of lessons learned, both from research and from clinical experience with health care quality improvement programs for diabetes care. To summarize a number of the key points enumerated in this table, effective care needs to move from a provider-centered acute illness model that reactively addresses primarily urgent issues for patients who present for treatment—often after they have gotten into trouble. Instead, modern evidence-based care is popu-

Table 23.1 Common Pitfalls and Traps to Avoid and What to Do Instead

Avoid	Instead
Assuming the patient understands and agrees with regimen	Assess patient understanding and feelings about their regimen
Solving the problem for the patient	Assist patients to identify strategies that work for them
Focusing only on the patients who come in for help	Do outreach and follow-up
Trying to make too big a change or changing too many things at once	Focus on gradual change; use the continuity of primary care
Giving advice that conflicts with that from patient's primary care provider	Help the patient and physician to reach consensus

Table 23.2 Summary of Key Points

1. Patients, not providers, are responsible for their diabetes self-management (Anderson et al., 2000). The full implications of this change in perspective are seldom appreciated or acted on. *Psychologists can learn and teach motivational interviewing and empowerment skills* (Anderson & Funnell, 2000).

2. The diabetes regimen and its management are complex and multidimensional and are influenced by the interaction of a variety of personal, social, biological, and contextual factors, including one's family and the medical office interaction (Gonder-Frederick et al., 2002). *Psychologists should assess patients' personal models of diabetes and help patients identify barriers and supports in their social environment* (Hampson et al., 2000; Glasgow, Funnell, et al., 2002).

3. The five A's counseling model (Figure 23.1) reminds clinicians of core counseling principles and skills (Whitlock et al., 2002). These principles, like action plans for individual patients, need to be tailored to the specific office environment.

4. Self-management should not be considered a one-time "inoculation" handled via a referral process outside usual care, but rather as an iterative and ongoing process linked to other aspects of the patient's care (see Figure 23.2). *Psychologists should help primary care practices design ways to enhance follow-up and continuity of care.*

5. There is no magic bullet that will appeal to all patients or work in all situations. There are, however, general principles and replicated approaches that, when tailored to the patient population and clinical situation, will help to improve care when implemented consistently and include follow-up support (Norris et al., 2001).

6. Psychologists have many roles to play in diabetes care. Some of the most beneficial will involve transitioning from the traditional role of only being a referral resource for "problem patients" to being a more integrated partner in primary care. *This will include helping to design and evaluate practice innovations and training and supervising other staff.*

lation based, proactive, patient centered, and planned.

ACKNOWLEDGMENT Preparation of this chapter was supported by the National Institute of Digestive and Diabetes and Kidney Disease (NIDDK DK35524) and the Agency for Healthcare Research and Quality (AHRQ HS10123).

References

American Diabetes Association. (1997). Economic consequences of diabetes mellitus in the U.S. in 1997. *Diabetes Care, 21,* 296–309.

Anderson, B. J., & Rubin, R. R. E. (2002). *Practical psychology for diabetes clinicians: How to deal with the key behavioral issues faced by patients and health care teams* (2nd ed.). Alexandria, VA: American Diabetes Association.

Anderson, R. J., Freedland, K. E., Clouse, R. E., & Lustman, P. J. (2001). The prevalence of comorbid depression adults with diabetes: A meta-analysis. *Diabetes Care, 24,* 1069–1078.

Anderson, R. M., & Funnell, M. M. (1999). Putting Humpty Dumpty back together again. *Diabetes Spectrum, 12,* 19–23.

Anderson, R. M., & Funnell, M. M. (2000). *The art of empowerment: Stories and strategies for diabetes educators.* Alexandria, VA: American Diabetes Association.

Barrera, M., Jr., Glasgow, R. E., McKay, H. G., Boles, S. M., & Feil, E. G. (2002). Do Internet-based support interventions change perceptions of social support? An experimental trial of approaches for supporting diabetes self-management. *American Journal of Community Psychology, 30,* 637–654.

Brown, S. A., & Harris, C. L. (1999). Culturally competent diabetes education for Mexican Americans: The Starr County Study. *The Diabetes Educator, 25,* 226–236.

Centers for Disease Control and Prevention. (1997). *National diabetes fact sheet: National estimates and information on diabetes in the United States.* Atlanta, GA: U.S. Department of Health and Human Services, Centers for Disease Control and Prevention, Division of Diabetes Translation.

Cox, D., Gonder-Frederick, L., Polonsky, W., Schlundt, D., Julian, D., & Clarke, W. (1995). A multi-center evaluation of Blood Glucose Awareness Training-II. *Diabetes Care, 18,* 523–528.

Cox, D. J., Gonder-Frederick, L. A., Kovatchev, B. P., Young-Hyman, D. L., Donner, T. W., Julian, D. M., & Clarke, W. L. (1999). Biopsychobehavioral model of severe hypoglycemia II. Understanding the risk of severe hypoglycemia. *Diabetes Care, 22,* 2018–2025.

Cox, D. J., Irvine, A., Gonder-Frederick, L., Nowacek, G., & Butterfield, J. (1987). Fear of hypoglycemia: Quantification, validation, and utilization. *Diabetes Care, 10*, 617–621.

Diabetes Control and Complications Trial Research Group. (1993). The effect of intensive treatment of diabetes on the development and progression of long-term complications in insulin-dependent diabetes mellitus. *New England Journal of Medicine, 329*, 977–986.

Fisher, L., Chesla, C. A., Mullan, J. T., Skaff, M., & Kanter, R. A. (2001). Contributors to depression in Latino and European-American patients with Type 2 diabetes. *Diabetes Care, 24*, 1751–1757.

Gerstein, H., & Haynes, R. (2001). *Evidence-based diabetes care.* Hamilton, Ontario, Canada: B. C. Decker.

Glasgow, R. E. (1999). Outcomes of and for diabetes education research. *Diabetes Educator, 25*, 74–88.

Glasgow, R. E., & Anderson, R. M. (1999). In diabetes care, moving from compliance to adherence is not enough: Something entirely different is needed. *Diabetes Care, 22*, 2090–2092.

Glasgow, R. E., Davis, C. L., Funnell, M. M., & Beck, A. (2003). Implementing practical interventions to support chronic illness self-management in health care settings: Lessons learned and recommendations. *Joint Commission Journal on Quality and Safety, 29*, 563–574.

Glasgow, R. E., & Eakin, E. G. (2000). Medical office-based interventions. In F. J. Snoek & C. S. Skinner (Eds.), *Psychological aspects of diabetes care* (pp. 142–168). London: John Wiley and Sons.

Glasgow, R. E., Funnell, M. M., Bonomi, A. E., Davis, C., Beckham, V., & Wagner, E. H. (2002). Self-management aspects of the improving chronic illness care breakthrough series: Implementation with diabetes and heart failure teams. *Annals of Behavioral Medicine, 24*, 80–87.

Glasgow, R. E., La Chance, P., Toobert, D. J., Brown, J., Hampson, S. E., & Riddle, M. C. (1997). Long term effects and costs of brief behavioral dietary intervention for patients with diabetes delivered from the medical office. *Patient Education and Counseling, 32*, 175–184.

Glasgow R. E., Toobert, D. J., Hampson, S. E., & Strycker, L. A. (2002). Implementation, generalization, and long-term results of the "Choosing Well" diabetes self-management intervention. *Patient Education and Counseling, 48*, 115–122.

Glasgow, R. E., Wagner, E., Kaplan, R. M., Vinicor, F., Smith, L., & Norman, J. (1999). If diabetes is a public health problem, why not treat it as one? A population-based approach to chronic illness. *Annals of Behavioral Medicine, 21*, 159–170.

Gonder-Frederick, L. A., Cox, D. J., & Ritterband, L. M. (2002). Diabetes and behavioral medicine: The second decade. *Journal of Counseling and Clinical Psychology, 70*, 611–625.

Haire-Joshu, D., Glasgow, R. E., & Tibbs, T. L. (1999). Smoking and diabetes. *Diabetes Care, 22*, 1887–1898.

Hampson, S. E., Glasgow, R. E., Toobert, D. J., & Strycker, L. A. (2000). Beliefs versus feelings: A comparison of personal illness models and depression for predicting multiple outcomes in diabetes. *British Journal of Health Psychology, 5*, 27–40.

Hiss, R. G. (1996). Barriers to care in non-insulin-dependent diabetes mellitus, the Michigan experience. *Annals of Internal Medicine, 124*, 146–148.

Kaplan, S. H., Greenfield, S., & Ware, J. E., Jr. (1989). Assessing the effects of physician-patient interactions on the outcomes of chronic disease. *Medical Care, 27*, S110–S127.

Langley, G. J., Nolan, K. M., Nolan, T. W., Norman, C. L., & Provost, L. P. (1996). *The improvement guide: A practical approach to enhancing organizational performance.* San Francisco: Jossey-Bass.

Lorig, K. R., Sobel, D. S., Stewart, A. L., Brown, B. W., Bandura, A., Ritter, P., Gonzalez, V. M., Laurent, D. D., & Holman, H. R. (1999). Evidence suggesting that a chronic disease self-management program can improve health status while reducing hospitalization. *Medical Care, 37*, 5–14.

Lustman, P. J., Singh, P. K., & Clouse, R. E. (2002). Recognizing and managing depression in patients with diabetes. In B. J. Anderson & R. R. Rubin (Eds.), *Practical psychology for diabetes clinicians* (pp. 229–238). Alexandria, VA: American Diabetes Association.

National Diabetes Data Group. (1995). *Diabetes in America* (2nd ed.). Rockville, MD: National Institutes of Health.

Norris, S. L., Engelgau, M. M., & Narayan, K. M. (2001). Effectiveness of self-management training in Type 2 diabetes: Systematic review of randomized controlled trials. *Diabetes Care,* *24,* 561–587.

Pan, X. R., Li, G. W., Hu, Y. H., Wang, J. X., Yang, W. Y., An, Z. X., et al. (1997). Effects of diet and exercise in preventing NIDDM in people with impaired glucose tolerance: The Da Qing IGT and Diabetes Study. *Diabetes Care, 20,* 544.

Piette, J. (2002). Enhancing support via interactive technologies. *Current Diabetes Reports, 2,* 160–165.

Reiber, G. E., Boyko, E. J., & Smith, D. G. (1995). Lower extremity foot ulcers and amputations in diabetes. In M. I. Harris, C. C. Cowie, M. P. Stern, E. J. Boyko, G. E. Reiber, & P. H. Bennett (Eds.), *Diabetes in America* (2nd ed., pp. 409–428). Rockville, MD: National Institutes of Health.

Sadur, C. N., Moline, N., Costa, M., Michalik, D., Mendlowitz, D., Roller, S., et al. (1999). Diabetes management in a health maintenance organization: Efficacy of care management using cluster visits. *Diabetes Care, 22,* 2011–2017.

Testa, M. A., & Simonson, D. C. (1998). Health economic benefits and quality of life during improved glycemic control in patients with Type 2 diabetes mellitus. *Journal of the American Medical Association, 280,* 1490–1496.

United Kingdom Prospective Diabetes Study Group. (1998a). Effect of intensive blood-glucose control with metformin on complications in overweight patients with Type 2 diabetes. *Lancet, 352,* 854–865.

United Kingdom Prospective Diabetes Study Group. (1998b). Efficacy of atenolol and captopril in reducing risk of macrovascular and microvascular complications of Type 2 diabetes. *British Medical Journal, 317,* 713–720.

U.S. Preventive Services Task Force. (1996). *Guide to clinical preventive services* (2nd ed.). Baltimore, MD: U.S. Department of Health and Human Services.

Wagner, E. H. (1998). Chronic disease management: What will it take to improve care for chronic illness. *Effective Clinical Practice, 1,* 1–4.

Wagner, E. H., Glasgow, R. E., Davis, C., Bonomi, A. E., Provost, L., McCulloch, D., Carver, P., & Sixta, C. (2001). Quality improvement in chronic illness care: A collaborative approach. *Journal of Joint Commission on Health Care Quality, 27,* 63–80.

Wagner, E. H., Grothaus, L. C., Sandhu, N., Galvin, M. S., McGregor, M., Artz, K., et al. (2001). Chronic care clinics for diabetes in primary care: A system-wide randomized trial. *Diabetes Care, 24,* 695–700.

Whitlock, E. P., Orleans, C. T., Pender, N., & Allan, J. (2002). Evaluating primary care behavioral counseling interventions: An evidence-based approach. *American Journal of Preventive Medicine, 22,* 267–284.

24

Domestic Violence

L. Kevin Hamberger
Darshana Patel

DEFINING DOMESTIC VIOLENCE

Domestic violence is assaultive behavior that functions to dominate, control, and punish another in an intimate, supposedly peer relationship (Ganley, 1989). Domestic violence does not consist of a specific action or set of actions. Rather, domestic violence consists of a pattern of behaviors that occurs over time and has a specific function, namely, to dominate, control, or punish another. The function of the assaultive behavior is what actually defines it as battering or abusive.

Ganley (1989) identified four types of actions that generally constitute domestic violence: physical, sexual, property and pet destruction, and psychological terror tactics. Each type consists of a wide range of actions that could be distinguished by severity. However, it matters little whether the specific assaultive behavior consists of clubbing or stabbing, pushing or shoving, breaking things or punching walls, or making verbal or nonverbal threatening gestures. Because such actions evoke fear and terror, they have the ability to force a victim to do what she or he would not otherwise want to do, thus establishing control.

This understanding is especially important for medical health care providers because their training and practice often focus on injury severity and not on the functional aspects of domestic violence. By understanding and focusing on the common function of all abusive behavior, regardless of "severity," one appreciates how all forms of abusive behavior function to entrap victims and, over time, damage their health. Hence, all forms of domestic violence are to be taken seriously as requiring intervention.

Victims may also use violence against their oppressive partners. Sometimes, a superficial analysis of such actions leads to the conclusion that both partners are "mutually violent," and that "women are as violent as men." However, recent research, both with community-based clinical samples and medical system–based clinical samples, suggested that, overall, the primary problem in bidirectional violence is that of men battering women (Hamberger & Guse, 2002; Phelan, Hamberger, Hare, & Edwards, 2002; Vivian & Langhinrichsen-Rohling, 1994). Therefore, the focus of this chapter is women as victims of domestic violence in heterosexual relationships. We describe a collaborative approach to helping an abuse survivor within a family medicine practice setting. Using an extended case example, we illustrate and describe identification of the problem, initiation of the collaborative process, and maintenance of a collaborative care model to help the patient develop safety plans, cope with stress from the abuse, and access community resources for safety assistance.

PREVALENCE, COSTS, AND MORBIDITY OF DOMESTIC VIOLENCE

Partner violence victimization against women has been identified as a major health care problem. Battered women, as a group, are regular and frequent consumers of health care services across a variety of medical subspecialties, including emergency medicine, for which prevalence estimates range between 10% and 59% (Abbott, Johnson, Koziol-McClain, & Lowenstein, 1995; Waller, Hohenhaus, Shah, & Stern, 1996); maternal health care settings, for which prevalence rates range from about 2% to 29% before and during pregnancy (Hamberger & Ambuel, 2001); and family practice and internal medicine settings, with estimated rates of current domestic violence against women patients between 12% and 25% (Gin, Rucker, Frayne, Cygan, & Hubbell, 1991; Hamberger, Saunders, & Hovey, 1992; Johnson & Elliott, 1997).

The health consequences of partner violence against women are substantial. Compared to non-battered women, battered women had significantly more hospital admissions for both trauma- and nontrauma-related problems, such as medical admissions, miscarriage and elective abortion, maternal health problems, nontrauma-related surgeries, alcohol and drug problems, and psychiatric problems (Bergman & Brismar, 1991). Battered women seek help for genital injuries and sexually transmitted diseases, gastrointestinal symptoms, chronic pain syndromes (Coker, Smith, Bethea, King, & McKeown, 2000; Koss & Heslet, 1992), depression and depressive symptoms (Saunders,

Hamberger, & Hovey, 1993), posttraumatic stress disorder (Saunders, 1994), anxiety, sexual dysfunction, and obsessive-compulsive disorder (Gleason, 1993). These problems have a profound impact on the quality of life and health status of abuse victims and survivors. Such morbidity may be among the many factors that motivate abuse victims and survivors to visit their primary care physician for frequent, symptom-focused care.

Hence, primary care physicians can expect to see many women patients who are victims of partner violence; therefore, these physicians have an opportunity to help them through appropriate practice-based identification and intervention efforts. By extension, psychologists who work in primary care settings or who collaborate with primary care physicians are also positioned to provide treatment and other help to battered women patients. Such patients will likely be referred for a variety of mental health problems, as noted above, as well as problems related to health psychology, such as smoking cessation, pain management, chronic illness, or compliance with health regimens. Hence, psychologists working in primary care need to have the knowledge and skill necessary to help such patients effectively.

Ambuel, Hamberger, and Lahti (1997) as well as Hamberger and Ambuel (1998, 2001) described a model medical practice approach for identifying and helping abuse victims, emphasizing physician-initiated universal screening and case finding. Case finding involves actively including domestic abuse in the differential diagnosis when risk markers such as those reviewed above are noted.

Following identification of abuse, Ambuel et al. (1997) has recommended six steps for physicians to take in providing appropriate help to abuse victims and survivors: (a) provide emotional support to validate the patient's feelings and experience; (b) assess dangerousness and lethality; (c) begin safety planning; (d) provide the patient with community resource information; (e) document the domestic violence; and (f) offer frequent follow-up visits. Such a delineation of physician intervention parameters increases the physician's self-efficacy to identify and help partner violence victims (Hamberger et al., in press). In addition, Ambuel et al. (1997) has recommended that physicians collaborate with community experts and agencies to help abuse victims and survivors.

PRESENTATION OF ABUSE VICTIMS IN PRIMARY CARE

Although there is no single "profile" of battered women in primary care settings, the patient we describe throughout the remainder of the chapter, R. S., presented with many concerns and abuse dynamics frequently reported by other battered women. Hence, her story, together with the account of our intervention, illustrates key elements of collaborative practice to help partner violence victims in primary care.

Referral Question

With permission from R. S., the family physician contacted the psychologist, thus initiating collaboration. During the initial contact, the physician described R. S.'s symptom picture: tearfulness, difficulty sleeping, feeling "stressed out," and difficulty coping with everyday life. The family physician also described R. S. as irritable and in frequent conflict with family members, especially her husband. The physician indicated that she had assessed for domestic violence and noted that R. S. appeared to be the victim of fairly severe and frequent psychological and verbal abuse. Physical partner violence did not appear to be part of the picture.

The physician requested that the psychologist see the patient for assessment for individual therapy and possible couples therapy. Assessment for couples therapy was briefly considered. Because of the identification of psychological abuse, despite R. S.'s initial denial, concern was raised about the possibility of physical abuse, which could make conjoint counseling dangerous (Murphy & O'Leary, 1989). Both professionals agreed that a more thorough domestic violence assessment was indicated.

Patient Background Information

Family of Origin

The patient R. S. (not her actual initials) is a 33-year-old white woman, the youngest of three sisters and no brothers. Although not all partner abuse victims report trauma and abuse in their childhood experiences, R. S. described her biological father as controlling and abusive, and the family "walked on eggshells" around him. Her biological parents divorced when she was 10 years old. Her mother remarried when R. S. was 14 years old. The stepfather severely and frequently abused her mother. R. S. reported a history of emotional abuse as a child; she was told that she would never amount to anything, that she was stupid, and that she was to blame for her siblings' misbehaviors. These experiences are typical of children who grow up with and witness violence between parents (Edleson, 2000). R. S. reported physical abuse in the context of discipline that was extreme and severe. R. S. also reported sexual molestation by a stepbrother for a 2-year period during her teens that was not reported out of fear of reprisal and punishment. She also reported frequent and severe fighting with her siblings.

Other Violence History

Consistent with the findings of Edleson (2000) about the impact on children of growing up in an abusive family, R. S. described fights with neighborhood girls as a youth. In her first marriage, R. S. reported that her husband assaulted her two times in 11 years by throwing hot coffee on her and slapping her. R. S. also reported that another man she dated slapped her on one occasion.

Behavioral Health History

R. S. reported a familial history of depression and alcohol abuse and a history of prior individual therapy for depression, as well as psychotropic medication for depression and "cyclothymia." She had never been hospitalized for behavioral health problems. R. S. reported minimal benefits from her behavioral health interventions. R. S. denied any use of illicit street drugs. Alcohol use was described as infrequent heavy drinking episodes, in which she consumed 6 to 12 beers over the course of a 4- to 6-hour evening.

Marital History

R. S. divorced her first husband after 11 years of marriage, citing boredom and his infidelity. She had three children by her first marriage. R. S. met her current husband in a bar. She was attracted to his air of self-confidence and protectiveness of her. They married after a short courtship. He was the custodial parent of three children from his prior relationships. They had been married for 6 months at the time of her presentation.

Educational and Occupational History

R. S. completed high school. She reported being an average student. For the past 8 years, R. S. worked as a homemaker. In the past, she sold insurance. Recently, she purchased a computer and was working on developing a home-based clerical business.

Presenting Problem

R. S. presented for medical care for the first time since the delivery of her youngest child 3 years ago. Consistent with the findings of Saunders et al. (1993) that battered women are frequently diagnosed with depression and its various symptoms, her chief complaints were painful periods, difficulty sleeping, and feeling "stressed out" with daily challenges. R. S. reported taking paroxetine (Paxil) and quetiapine (Seroquel) in the past; although she had managed without medications for the past 2.5 years, she now felt she might need them again. R. S. had taken over-the-counter ibuprofen for relief of her menstrual symptoms, but over the past 2 years, the symptoms had increased in intensity, and she had gotten no relief from maximum-strength doses. She occasionally self-medicated with alcohol. R. S. reported a positive family history of depression. She denied suicidal ideation, but reported feeling stressed, irritable, sad, inadequate, and guilty much of the time. Her marriage of 6 months was "stressed out."

The physician also screened R. S. for partner abuse, using the case-finding approach described by Ambuel et al. (1997). That is, the physician integrated questions about abuse into broader inquiry about the stress that R. S. described in her life. The physician reasoned that R. S. was not likely to volunteer whether she was abused, but would acknowledge it if asked. When queried about abuse, R. S. admitted that her partner verbally abused her, and that they had severe arguments, but she denied physical violence. R. S. stated that her partner accused her of showing favor to her children over his, and that he retaliated by harshly disciplining her children. She reported feelings of futility that her marriage would stabilize. Her initial denial of physical abuse is neither uncommon nor surprising. Gerbert, Johnston, Caspers, Bleecker, and Rosenbaum (1996) have described a process that occurs over time through which battered women gradually test and develop trust in their clinicians to manage the disclosure of physical abuse without shaming or causing further harm.

PHYSICIAN–PSYCHOLOGIST COLLABORATION

Initial Referral Logistics

Specific preappointment issues were discussed with the family physician and subsequently with R. S. Initial psychologist–family physician discussion focused on expectations for coordination of care. The family physician would continue to follow R. S. regularly for monitoring of psychotropic medication and other, ongoing medical treatment. The psychologist and family physician agreed that, because many of R. S.'s current problems appeared related to depression, stress, and the psychological abuse to which she was subjected, they would have regular, monthly contacts related to medication changes, psychotherapy treatment plans, goals, and progress. The psychologist agreed to handle the informed consent procedures with R. S.

Methods of Assessment and Diagnosis

Medical Assessment Strategies

Initial medical assessment in this case was a clinical interview and physical exam. R. S.'s physical exam showed normal blood pressure but elevated pulse, which warranted further tests to rule out organic causes of tachycardia. R. S. denied chest pain and palpitations. Blood tests included those involving the thyroid and hemoglobin; these tests did show abnormalities. An electrocardiogram was conducted and was normal. The physician did a Pap smear and tested for sexually transmitted diseases to determine reasons for pain with menstruation. All of these tests were within normal limits, ruling out organic causes for her premenstrual symptoms. There were no bruises over her body. She reported no history of broken bones.

Because R. S. indicated she was depressed, the physician administered the Beck Depression Inventory (Beck, Wood, Mendelson, Mock, & Erbaugh, 1961) and the Hamilton Rating Scale for Depression (Hamilton, 1960), which confirmed that she was moderately depressed. R. S. denied suicidal ideation or plans. Because domestic violence screening was conducted verbally, the physician did not conduct further screening. However, a number of paper-and-pencil screening instruments are under development for use in primary care settings. These include the HITS (Sherin, Sinacore, Li, Zitter, & Shakil, 1998), a four-item instrument that asks respondents how often their partner physically *hurt*, *insulted*, *threatened with harm*, or *screamed* at them, and the WAST (Women Abuse Screening Tool; Brown, Lent, Sas, & Pederson, 1996), an eight-item screening instrument with a two-item short form. Both instruments have received some validation, and the WAST has also been acceptable to patients (the WAST items are shown in Table 24.1).

Psychological Interview Strategies

Because of concerns about abuse and the need to assess further for physical and sexual abuse, a strategic decision was made to limit psychological evaluation to interview assessment methods, without psychological tests, particularly because her family physician already had used psychometric instruments to confirm the depression. Most major psychological tests, such as the Minnesota Multiphasic Inventory or Millon Clinical Multiaxial Inventory tend to have pathology biases (Barnett & Hamberger, 1992). Many abused women do show signs of depression (Gleason, 1993) and posttraumatic stress disorder (Saunders, 1994). However, the very act of testing communicates to the abused woman that something is "wrong" with her. This communication is further reinforced by the test results, which typically are reported in terms of problems or deficits (Rosewater, 1987).

In contrast, interview assessment allows the

Table 24.1 Items From the Woman Abuse Screening Tool (WAST)

1. In general, how would you describe your relationship . . .
   a lot of tension   some tension   no tension

2. Do you and your partner work out arguments with . . .
   great difficulty   some difficulty   no difficulty

3. Do arguments ever result in you feeling put down or bad about yourself?
   often   sometimes   never

4. Do arguments ever result in hitting, kicking, or pushing?
   often   sometimes   never

5. Do you ever feel frightened by what your partner says or does?
   often   sometimes   never

6. Has your partner ever abused you physically?
   often   sometimes   never

7. Has your partner ever abused you emotionally?
   often   sometimes   never

8. Has your partner ever abused you sexually?
   often   sometimes   never

Note. Items 1 and 2 comprise the WAST-Short. "Often" is scored 1, and "never" is scored 3 for the long form. For the short form, a score of 1 is assigned to the most extreme positive response for each item (i.e., "a lot of tension" and "great difficulty"), and 0 is assigned to the other two response options. Adapted from Brown, Lent, Schmidt, and Sas (2000).

patient to tell her own story of abuse and survival. Interview methods are flexible and allow identification of specific strengths as well as deficits. Information gathering is collaborative and aims to determine both perceived needs and identified patient strengths and resourcefulness. A strengths-oriented approach is crucial in helping abuse victims and survivors heal (Walker, 1994). Although the patient has been physically and psychologically abused, she has also survived. A collaborative approach honors her ability to survive by making her a partner in the process.

What follows is a description of a thorough domestic violence assessment that examines not only forms of violence and abuse, but also the physical and emotional impact of the violence on the victim, knowledge of community resources, and safety plan information.

The interview with R. S. covered standard psychological history and intake topics, as noted above in the section Patient Background Information. In addition, the psychologist assessed R. S.'s abuse and violence experiences using a modified version of the Conflict Tactics Scales (CTS; Straus, 1979). The CTS is a 24-item checklist of behaviors listed in order of increasing severity, including psychological abuse and physical violence. Items range from doing or saying spiteful things to controlling social activities, yelling and screaming, or threatening violence. Physically violent behaviors range from grabbing and restraining to slapping, hitting with objects, beating up, or threatening with or using a knife or a gun. The CTS is widely used, and its psychometric properties have been well documented (Straus, 1990). There are other instruments that can be used to assess the spectrum of abuse that a patient is experiencing, such as the Index of Spouse Abuse (Hudson & McIntosh, 1981). These instruments can be accessed from the relevant literature citations.

Because the CTS measures only whether specific behaviors occurred, other interview questions assess current levels and changes in abuse frequency, duration, and severity. Other questions assess who began the pattern of abuse in the relationship and who initiates violence most often. Emotional and behavioral reactions are assessed to determine the impact of any bidirectional vio-

lence. Feelings of fear, anger, or indignation are queried, as are reactions such as retributive violence, increased efforts to control the partner, escape attempts, and acquiescing to avoid further violence (Hamberger & Guse, 2002).

Knowledge of safety resources is assessed, including informal resources such as friends and family members or resources for independent living. Assessment also covers knowledge of formal helping resources, such as local domestic violence advocacy centers and legal assistance resources. The patient is also asked about safety plans and whether she has constructed one, as well as strategies she has used in the past to avoid or escape abusive situations successfully.

R. S. attributed many of her symptoms to current marital stress. She described her partner as jealous and controlling. She also reported that the couple struggled with blended family issues such as mutual mistrust of stepchildren and stepparents, concerns about favoritism toward biological children, and uneven discipline of biological and stepchildren.

R. S. reported duration of physical violence of about 1 year. Average physical violence frequency was estimated at two to three times per month and increasing. Physical violence sustained from her partner ranged from pushing/shoving, to throwing objects such as keys or telephones at her, to beating her up. R. S. reported a full spectrum of psychological abuse, ranging from doing or saying spiteful things, to insulting and name calling, to verbal pressure for sex. R. S. also experienced threats from her partner to clear out the house, abandon her and her children, or have an affair. He also threatened violence, verbally or through use of nonverbal gestures. R. S. stated that she had assaulted her partner on one occasion when he was trying to forcibly remove her wedding ring from her finger.

R. S. reported that the physical violence sustained never resulted in an injury severe enough to require medical attention. However, she described the physical and psychological abuse as humiliating, threatening, and causing her to feel fearful for her safety and very angry. She also felt intimidated and controlled by her partner's demands. She reported having called the police on a number of occasions. However, her partner often knew the responding officers, and arrests were not made. R. S. denied homicidal, assaultive, or suicidal plans, impulses, or urges.

A Note About Batterers

In a section above, the need for batterers to control their partners was discussed primarily in the context of victims leaving the abusive relationship. A fair amount of research has described men who batter and abuse their partners. Most of the research on batterers suggests that there is no single profile of abusive men. Hamberger and associates (Hamberger & Hastings, 1986; Hamberger, Lohr, Bonge, & Tolin, 1996) and Holtzworth-Munroe and associates (Holtzworth-Munroe & Stuart, 1994; Holtzworth-Munroe, Stuart, Meehan, Herron, & Rehman, 2000) have identified three primary types of batterers. These include those who show little or no psychopathology and limit their violence primarily to their intimate partners; those who show strong antisocial tendencies and are generally violent with intimate partners and others; and those who show borderline personality organization and are primarily violent in intimate relationships, but also show generally violent tendencies. The last two types, antisocial and borderline organization, are relatively poor risks for domestic abuse abatement treatment and tend to show the highest rates of premature termination and recidivism.

Because R. S.'s partner did not participate in assessment, it is unknown which "type" he may have fit. Nevertheless, given the level of violence reported by R. S., the psychologist concluded that his violence was chronic and severe, making her living situation difficult and imminent escape from the relationship difficult, if not impossible and inadvisable, without considerable thought and support. It is against this backdrop that case conceptualization and treatment planning took place.

Case Conceptualizations

Physician's Conceptualization

Considering the initial presenting symptoms, the family physician concluded that the long-standing stressful family life and blended family issues, as well as a family history of depression, put R. S. at high risk of recurrent major depressive disorder. R. S. showed signs of depression and would benefit from medication as well as psychological intervention. Her futile efforts to "fix" her struggling marriage, the relentless blame experienced from her partner, and her subsequent guilt feelings had worn R. S. down. She appeared to feel isolated and trapped. Her mildly elevated pulse could be secondary to anxiety but needed further assessment. R. S.'s complaint of pain accompanying her menstrual periods combined with her normal pelvic exam and no other history of surgery or fracture also indicate a stress-related (rather than organic) etiology.

Psychologist's Conceptualization

Although R. S. experienced significant losses resulting from her recent divorce and new stressors related to remarriage and the challenges of integrating a blended family, the psychologist reasoned that lack of safety from living in an abusive relationship was the most clinically appropriate basis for conceptualizing R. S.'s clinical and treatment needs. Initially, psychological and verbal abuse were considered the primary types of abuse. During assessment, a history of physical abuse in the present relationship also emerged. Even if physical abuse had not been uncovered, addressing the problem of living in a highly emotionally and verbally abusive relationship would have been a top treatment priority.

Current research on psychological abuse suggests that its impact is multidimensional. Severe forms of threatening verbal abuse can induce fear of actual violence as well as sadness and anger (Follingstad, Rutledge, Berg, Hause, & Polek, 1990). Further, even subtle forms of verbal abuse, such as criticisms, put-downs, and ongoing negative comments can undermine the victim's confidence (Marshall, 1992). Psychological abuse in early marriage has been found to predict future physical abuse (Murphy & O'Leary, 1989). Generally, verbal and psychological abuse is ongoing, frequent, and relentless. Hence, its long-term impact can be to lower self-esteem and increase a sense of heightened alertness for problem interactions and a sense of futility at not being able to control such outbursts (Hamberger & Holtzworth-Munroe, 2000). In addition, the presence of physical abuse in R. S.'s clinical picture potentiates the impact of verbal and psychological abuse. Specifically, through the conditioning effects of combining psychological and physical abuse, psychological forms of abuse acquire the controlling functions of physical abuse (Ganley, 1989; Hamberger & Lohr, 1989).

Hence, for R. S. to live in a psychologically and verbally abusive relationship meant much more than having a few "spats" with her partner that could be worked out in couples counseling focusing on blended family issues. Rather, R. S. was an abuse victim. Her symptoms of depression and anxiety were viewed as responses to the crisis of living in an abusive, dangerous relationship (Hamberger & Holtzworth-Munroe, 2000). Therefore, the psychologist determined that the first treatment priority to propose would focus on helping R. S. develop safety plans and knowledge of community resources to help achieve safety from partner abuse and violence for herself and her children.

Assessment, Feedback, and Treatment Planning

Physician Diagnosis and Treatment Plan

The physician discussed with R. S. her initial assessment and formulated the following treatment plan with her:

1. Referral to a psychologist because the frequent abuse was a major stressor for her anxiety and depression.
2. Antidepressant medication with follow-up at 4 weeks. Note that the prescription was accompanied by an explanation of both the benefits and side effects of the medication and by an emphasis on the fact that taking antidepressants in no way indicated that the symptoms were "her fault."
3. Reduction of alcohol use.
4. Institution of other safety and health maintenance measures (e.g., not driving after drinking alcohol, locating a safe place to exercise).

Psychologist Diagnosis and Treatment Plan

The treatment plan was negotiated and developed collaboratively between the psychologist and R. S. The agreed-on goal was to decrease depression and anxiety by first addressing R. S.'s chronic lack of safety. To accomplish this goal, four objectives were developed:

1. Identify community-based resources for advocacy and safety. Hamberger, Ambuel, Marbella, and Donze (1998) found that battered women greatly valued their clinicians' willingness to provide information about community resources for safety. R. S. was not knowledgeable about such resources and their functions. The plan called for developing information about shelter and advocacy services, and legal advocacy programs, as well as identifying informal support networks such as friends and family who could be helpful in appropriate ways and times.
2. Develop safety plans. These included escape plans in case violence erupted unexpectedly or in the event of a rapidly escalating, explosive situation. The second type of safety plan consisted of identifying predictable types of partner behaviors or conflict situations that resulted in escalation and abusive behavior and specific steps to avoid violence. In addition, R. S. agreed to work on both short-term safety plans for managing safety issues on a day-to-day basis and long-term plans. Long-term safety plans included discussion and consideration of her relationship status and how to take emotional and physical care of herself while living in a relationship with an abusive partner (Hamberger & Potente, 1996).
3. Continue identification and discussion of abuse experiences to facilitate awareness of types of abuse and their impact on psychological and physical health. Such sensitization was designed to lead to development of "safe boundaries," including distinguishing limits of responsibility for self and others' feelings and actions and developing a self-image as an autonomous adult in an intimate relationship.
4. Identify personal strengths for coping and survival. Abuse victims and survivors frequently display great resourcefulness and courage in coping with abuse and its im-

pact. Yet, the intensity and relentlessness of the oppression they experience frequently leaves them with a sense of futility, fatigue, and resignation, that they are incapable of survival on their own. Therefore, it is important to help abuse victims appreciate their strengths and how they use them for healthy coping efforts (Walker, 1994).

Sharing the Treatment Plan With the Physician

With R. S.'s consent, the psychologist notified her family physician about the treatment plan. The physician was interested in R. S.'s overall health care, particularly safety, and willing to reinforce key concepts and issues addressed in psychotherapy.

Specific Psychological Treatment Approaches

Psychological treatment consisted of individual psychotherapy and focused on developing R. S.'s strengths and resources for achieving safety in her life. The treatment plan called for sessions spaced 1 to 2 weeks apart.

Developing Knowledge of Social Support Resources

Early in the intervention, R. S. learned about local emergency shelter and advocacy services. She had a working knowledge of law enforcement functions. However, she was uncertain about shelter services in her area and had no knowledge of legal advocacy services that could assist with legal proceedings or provide representation for restraining order petitions or other family law issues. Providing the patient with such knowledge can decrease her sense of isolation and provide her with options for taking action to seek safety from abuse. Such information also facilitates safety planning because the patient can identify concrete resources she can turn to for either emergency or long-term help.

Safety Planning

The second goal, safety planning, was accomplished by working through a detailed exercise developed by Hart and Stuehling (1992) and borrowing from the work of Hamberger and Potente (1996). For short-term planning for escaping explosive and violent situations, R. S. developed working mental maps of her residence. This included knowledge of multiple escape routes from different locations within the residence. Acute danger safety planning also included working with her children to develop signals to alert them to danger and the need to escape or call for emergency services. R. S. also prepared a package of necessary items to take in the event of a necessary quick escape. Of particular importance to R. S. was the development of a sufficiently large supply of cash to make an escrow account and first month's rent on a new apartment. She also identified her sister as a reliable emergency contact and safe house location.

R. S. also developed avoidance safety plans. She identified specific conflict-laden topics that typically resulted in abuse. She learned techniques for defusing and/or short-circuiting the escalation process. Examples included active listening, assertive verbal responding, and avoidance of accusatory language and name-calling (Hamberger & Potente, 1996). R. S. also practiced maintaining a safe distance during conflict situations and positioned herself near doorways or telephones.

Long-term safety planning involved making the decision to end the relationship if new violence recurred within a 6-month time frame. R. S. developed a personal savings plan to manage the first month's rent and escrow on an apartment. She also began reestablishing friendship networks while working on her relationship. She developed a sense of clarity and confidence that she could live independently, if necessary, although she preferred for her marital relationship to survive and grow.

Note that in the discussion about safety planning, emphasis is not placed on getting the patient to leave her partner as quickly as possible. There are two reasons for this. First, many battered women do not want to leave their partners or end the relationship. They only want the violence to end. Second, leaving a violent and abusive relationship can be very dangerous as it represents to the perpetrator the ultimate loss of control over his partner. Such a threat to control can precipitate stalking, increased violence, and even homicide. Therefore, a more patient-centered approach is to work with the patient to identify options for safety and allow her to decide how to maximize her safety, up to and including leaving the relationship with appropriate supports in place.

Work on Healing

As part of her therapy, R. S. also worked to identify and name her many abuse experiences. This exercise enabled R. S. to break the silence of her abuse and examine its impact on her emotional and physical well-being. Issues of insomnia, pain, moodiness, and loss of interest in sex were all considered part of the experience of chronic, relentless abuse. In addition, the psychologist encouraged R. S. to consult with her family physician about physical symptoms, particularly when they changed in intensity, to rule out any possible underlying medical condition. Similarly, R. S. frequently informed the psychologist about medication effects, including side effects and benefits, as well as any changes in medication her physician prescribed.

Through this process, R. S. began to view herself increasingly as an autonomous person who did not deserve to be abused or controlled. She identified boundaries and limits of responsibility for her own and her partner's feelings and actions. For example, R. S. came to understand her partner's obsessive jealousy as stemming from his own experience and not from any behavior on her part. She recognized her fear as a signal to implement her safety plan. She also came to understand that she did not have to live in an abusive relationship interminably, and that she could make decisions about the rest of her life.

Course of the Intervention

The psychologist and physician consulted on treatment with R. S. approximately once per month. The family physician informed the psychologist about medication changes and expected effects and side effects. The psychologist kept the physician abreast of current therapy issues. The physician in turn reinforced therapeutic insights and accomplishments and also supported R. S. when she struggled.

At times, the family physician learned about changes in the patient's life before the psychologist did. For example, on one occasion during safety planning, R. S. informed her physician that she had acquired a gun that she was keeping loaded in her nightstand. The physician advised her of the dangers of having a loaded gun in an abusive relationship and informed the psychologist of the discovery. The psychologist then reinforced the physician's concern with R. S. at the next visit. On another occasion, R. S. informed her physician prior to seeing the psychologist that she was planning on seeking a temporary restraining order, but did not know how to go about it. The physician notified the psychologist, who then gathered relevant information to provide R. S. during the next visit.

The final collaborative act between the psychologist and the physician occurred in the context of R. S.'s effort to obtain a temporary restraining order against her partner when the abuse again escalated. R. S. contacted both clinicians and asked them to testify in family court on their findings of abuse gathered in the course of their work with her. Both agreed to testify. Although neither was ultimately called to provide testimony, both cleared their schedules for the day and time of the scheduled restraining order hearing in the event that they would be called.

Intervention Outcome

R. S. was able to obtain a temporary restraining order, was able to maintain separation from her partner, and possessed legal leverage to enforce her safety. Following the hearing for a temporary restraining order, R. S. ended her involvement in psychotherapy as well as ongoing medical treatment with her family physician. There were two reasons for this decision. First, R. S. believed that she had, for the most part, accomplished her primary treatment goals. In addition, her insurance situation changed, requiring her to seek treatment (both medical and psychological) from other sources.

Results of Medical Treatment

After 4 weeks (and some initial mild side effects), R. S. responded well to antidepressant medication. She reported better control over her emotions and showed increased positive decision making and strategy development to respond to her husband's ongoing verbal and psychological abuse. R. S. also began to feel good enough to develop new friendships in her neighborhood and renew a relationship with her sister, whom she identified as helpful and emotionally supportive.

Results of Psychological Treatment

R. S. successfully developed and implemented safety plans. In particular, she successfully employed acute danger safety plans on three occasions, avoiding imminently explosive situations. She also successfully avoided or defused a number of less acute, but potentially dangerous, situations. However, she had occasional difficulty suppressing anger expressions and sarcasm, which frequently contributed to conflict escalation.

In terms of long-term safety plans, R. S. decided she could no longer tolerate her husband's abusive behavior and began to prepare to successfully leave. These efforts included reinforcing a supportive family and social network and saving enough money to enable her to live independently.

In terms of community resource utilization, she negotiated the family law and legal aid systems and was able to obtain a 2-year temporary restraining order. Prior to finally receiving the restraining order, R. S. also called police on one occasion following separation, when her partner attempted to enter her apartment uninvited.

Planning for Long-Term Treatment Strategies

Ideally, following treatment to facilitate knowledge of community resources and enhance safety, clinical attention would have turned to assessing R. S.'s need to address prior traumatic experiences that may also have had an impact on her depression and episodic alcohol abuse (Lechner, Vogel, Garcia-Shelton, Leichter, & Steibel, 1993). However, because treatment ended rather abruptly, its impact on R. S.'s depression and anxiety is less certain.

Further, extended treatment would also focus on her ability to live as an autonomous adult who could choose to live on her own without her abusive partner. This would be important because R. S. was committed to her marital relationship and desperately wanted it to succeed. Hence, separation could be expected to be stressful, particularly because she felt responsibility to her stepchildren. These issues were not addressed in the present intervention and are often related to depression and anxiety.

Finally, the impact of intervention on R. S.'s partner, although the target of intervention, is also uncertain. It is not known, for example, if he respected the terms of the restraining order. It is known that he called seeking information and referral for a local batterer intervention program.

Analysis of the Collaborative Process

Benefits to Practitioners

Battered women seek help from their primary care physicians (Hamberger et al., 1992; Johnson & Elliott, 1997); therefore, primary care physicians are in a prime position to identify and appropriately treat abuse victims and survivors (Ambuel et al., 1997). However, time pressure is a significant barrier to helping abuse victims (Sugg & Inui, 1992), and part of an appropriate intervention is to refer the patient to appropriate community resources (Hamberger et al., 1998). A psychologist appropriately trained in the area of domestic violence can devote the necessary time to assist the woman in safety planning and identifying necessary community resources. The physician plays an important role in reinforcing such planning and problem solving and provides relevant information to the psychologist. The psychologist can utilize the information provided by both patient and physician to implement effective treatment plans.

In the case of R. S., both the physician and the psychologist benefited from the unique perspectives with which each approached R. S.'s problems, and they were able to meld their individual perspectives together to develop a unified and complementary approach. In addition to the unique perspectives brought to the intervention by both the physician and psychologist, there was also considerable overlap between the two clinicians. Both shared a common interest in R. S.'s welfare and were primarily concerned with her safety and well-being. Hence, both framed their case conceptualization and subsequent treatment strategies within agreed-on parameters of patient safety. As such, medications were prescribed to enhance R. S.'s ability to focus on safety issues and problem solving. Psychological interventions also emphasized safety. Although it is generally viewed as inappropriate simply to medicate battered victims (Mandel & Marcotte, 1983), a combined approach emphasizing both psychosocial interventions and medical interventions is appropriate.

A further benefit of collaboration for both the physician and the psychologist is that information on the patient's status and situation was maximized. Sometimes, R. S. would share certain information with one clinician prior to seeing the other. Because the clinicians both worked in the same clinic, they could communicate regularly in the staffing office and leave each other memos or voice mail messages.

Collaboration Mitigates Transference and Countertransference Issues

Working in the area of domestic violence on any level, whether as a physician, psychologist, or other role, is very difficult. For many clinicians, delving into domestic violence with their patients brings feelings of loss of control, vulnerability, and a sense of opening Pandora's box (Sugg & Inui, 1992). Working with someone else's victimization can rekindle personal victimization experiences (Ambuel, Butler, Hamberger, Lawrence, & Guse, 2003).

In addition to the countertransference issues noted above, victims of partner violence sometimes also have coexisting characteristics that are viewed by clinicians as negative. These include intoxication and mental illness. Kurz (1990) observed that such patient characteristics among battered women are related to lower quality of care and punitive psychiatric labeling.

Further, Mandel and Marcotte (1990) found that some battered women received inappropriate medication interventions, and Ambuel et al. (1997) reported that clinicians sometimes respond to patients with such characteristics with victim blaming and refusal to make domestic vio-

lence part of their personal medical or psychological practice. In the present case, collaboration allowed both professionals to provide mutual support for coping with uncertainty and the inevitable frustrations.

Benefits to the Patient

The patient also benefited from collaboration. Because a major dynamic of domestic violence is isolation, R. S. benefited from multiple sources of support and feedback. The consistent messages she received from both her physician and psychologist provided a sense of validation so necessary for abuse victims to experience. She received consistent messages that the abuse was not her fault, that community resources existed to assist her, that safety was a primary concern, and that her physician and psychologist were going to try to help her achieve safety, not just treat her depressive and anxious symptoms.

Domestic abuse occasionally, and even frequently, is punctuated by crisis (Hamberger & Holtzworth-Munroe, 2000). The presence of multiple, coordinated helpers also meant that R. S. could turn to any one of them when necessary and receive appropriate, consistent support and help with problem solving. If her physician was not available, her psychologist generally was and vice versa. Hence, the collaborative working relationship forged by the physician and psychologist had the added benefit of providing a comprehensive safety net for R. S.

Difficulties Working With Domestic Violence in the Primary Care Setting

Domestic violence is a difficult and complex problem. Certainty is often elusive; there may be insufficient time to address all aspects of the problem fully in the usual encounter; domestic violence may evoke powerful emotions and clinician transference and countertransference reactions; and some states require clinicians to report domestic violence to law enforcement authorities. Sometimes, despite the best efforts of everyone involved, patient and helpers alike, violence recurs and, in the worst-case scenario, victims are killed.

Mandatory Reporting

Almost every state has laws requiring health care providers to report injuries stemming from criminal acts to authorities, and seven states have specific domestic violence mandatory reporting laws (Hyman, Schillinger, & Lo, 1995). However, the specifics differ across states. For example, some states require reporting on the basis of observed injuries. Other states require reporting on the basis of disclosure of domestic violence regardless of observed injuries. Further, some states require physicians, but not mental health professionals, to report disclosures of domestic violence. It will be necessary, therefore, for both physicians and psychologists to know the scope and parameters of their local reporting requirements. The effect of reporting on the treatment relationship also is a concern (Rodriguez, McLoughlin, Bauer, Paredes, & Grumbach, 1999).

Lack of Certainty and Clarity

There are few obvious answers and prescriptive solutions to any given patient's problem with domestic violence. Therefore, health care providers can become confused, frustrated, and disillusioned with efforts to screen and help domestic violence victims (Minsky, Pape, & Hamberger, 2000). The single best strategy to confront and resolve this problem is to become increasingly informed about the dynamics of domestic violence. Such knowledge will help clinicians understand behaviors that otherwise seem mystifying and confusing and can easily lead to victim blaming without a proper conceptual foundation. For example, when a battered patient returns to her partner, rather than castigate her as masochistic or having a borderline personality disorder, the behavior can be understood as part of the violence dynamic that includes financial and emotional dependency, and lack of options for independent living, as well as fear for safety when trying to end a violent relationship and understanding that ending the relationship will not guarantee an end to the violence.

SUMMARY

Domestic violence against women is a serious public and personal health problem. From a pub-lic health perspective, domestic violence exacts a tremendous cost to society, health care systems, families, and individual patients. From a personal health perspective, research is beginning to show that domestic violence lies behind considerable morbidity and health care utilization among its victims. In the worst scenarios, domestic violence results in premature death.

Because victims and survivors utilize health care resources so heavily, primary care physicians and psychologists who work with them are in a key position to identify and provide appropriate intervention to such patients. Battered patients can best be identified by screening all patients about safety and violence in the home and by asking patients with both obvious and subtle signs of distress, injury, and relationship problems about domestic violence.

When patients acknowledge domestic violence, primary care physicians and psychologists can collaborate to conduct thorough assessments and appropriate treatments. Such treatments involve the physician and psychologist adopting discipline-relevant interventions with common goals related to helping the patient find safety and make decisions about her life situation as an autonomous person. Domestic violence is a frequently confusing patient issue that can profoundly affect professional helpers, resulting in avoidance of the issue or less-optimal treatment of patients. Thorough knowledge of the dynamics of domestic violence and the ability to process personal feelings and experiences with partner violence are essential for providing appropriate help to abuse victims.

Because of the complexities of domestic violence, treatment outcome is not guaranteed. However, psychologists and physicians working together can provide care for battered patients even if a "cure" is not highly probable. Key elements of psychological treatment include development of acute and long-term safety strategies and dissemination of knowledge of community support resources such as shelter, legal advocacy, and financial assistance. In addition, informal resources such as family and friendship networks are identified and built into safety planning. A third key treatment component involves processing and healing from the trauma of living in a chronically oppressive, violent, and abusive relationship and helping the patient channel personal strengths into enhancing safety for herself and her children. Medical treatment can include psychotropic medication used judiciously and in the context of a supportive, informed therapeutic relationship. Key elements of collaborative psychologist–physician practice consist of regular communication, specification of clinician roles, and complementary support for the respective, discipline-specific interventions.

ADDITIONAL RESOURCES

Suggestions for further reading and professional development resources are available at this book's companion Web site: www.primarycarepsych.com.

References

Abbott, J., Johnson, R., Koziol-McLain, J., & Lowenstein, S. R. (1995). Domestic violence against women: Incidence and prevalence in an emergency department population. *Journal of the American Medical Association, 273,* 1763–1767.

Ambuel, B., Butler, D., Hamberger, L. K., Lawrence, S., & Guse, C. E. (2003). Female and male medical students' exposure to violence: Impact on well being and perceived capacity to help battered women. *Journal of Comparative Family Studies, 34,* 113–135.

Ambuel, B., Hamberger, L. K., & Lahti, J. (1997). The Family Peace Project: A model for training health care professionals to identify, treat and prevent partner violence. *Journal of Aggression, Maltreatment, and Trauma, 2,* 55–81.

Barnett, O. W., & Hamberger, L. K. (1992). The assessment of maritally violent men on the California Psychological Inventory. *Violence and Victims, 7,* 1–14.

Beck, A. T., Wood, E., Mendelson, M., Mock, J., & Erbaugh, J. (1961). Inventory for measuring depression. *Archives of General Psychiatry, 4,* 561–571.

Bergman, B., & Brismar, B. (1991). A 5-year follow-up study of 117 battered women. *American Journal of Public Health, 81,* 1486–1488.

Brown, J. B., Lent, B., Brett, P. J., Sas, G., & Pederson, L. L. (1996). Development of the Woman Abuse Screening Tool for use in family practice. *Family Medicine, 28,* 422–428.

Brown, J. B., Lent, B., Schmidt, G., & Sas, G. (2000). Application of the woman abuse screening tool (WAST) and WAST-Short in the family practice setting. *Journal of Family Practice, 49,* 896–903.

Coker, A. L., Smith, P. H., Bethea, L., King, M. R., & McKeown, R. E. (2000). Physical health consequences of physical and psychological intimate partner violence. *Archives of Family Medicine, 9,* 451–457.

Edleson, J. L. (2000). Children's witnessing of adult domestic violence. *Journal of Interpersonal Violence, 14,* 839–870.

Follingstad, D. R., Rutledge, L. L., Berg, B. J., Hause, E. S., & Polek, D. S. (1990). The role of emotional abuse in physically abusive relationships. *Journal of Family Violence, 5,* 107–120.

Ganley, A. L. (1989). Integrating feminist and social learning analyses of aggression: Creating multiple models for interventions with men who batter. In P. L. Caesar & L. K. Hamberger (Eds.), *Treating men who batter: Theory, practice and programs* (pp. 196–235). New York: Springer.

Gerbert, B., Johnston, K., Caspers, N., Bleecker, T., Woods, A., & Rosenbaum, A. (1996). Experiences of battered women in health care settings: A qualitative study. *Women and Health, 24,* 1–17.

Gin, N. E., Rucker, L., Frayne, S., Cygan, R., & Hubbell, A. (1991). Prevalence of domestic violence among patients in three ambulatory care internal medicine clinics. *Journal of General Internal Medicine, 6,* 317–322.

Gleason, W. J. (1993). Mental disorders in battered women: An empirical study. *Violence and Victims, 8,* 53–68.

Hamberger, L. K., & Ambuel, B. (1998). Dating violence. *Pediatric Clinics of North America, 45,* 381–390.

Hamberger, L. K., & Ambuel, B. (2001). Spousal abuse in pregnancy. *Clinics in Family Practice, 3,* 203–224.

Hamberger, L. K., Ambuel, B., Marbella, A., & Donze, J. (1998). Physician interaction with battered women: The women's perspective. *Archives of Family Medicine, 7,* 575–582.

Hamberger, L. K., & Guse, C. (2002). Men's and women's use of intimate partner violence in clinical samples. *Violence Against Women, 8,* 1301–1331.

Hamberger, L. K., Guse, C., Boerger, J., Pape, D., Minsky, D., & Folsom, C. (in press). Evaluation of a healthcare provider training program to identify and help partner violence victims. *Journal of Family Violence.*

Hamberger, L. K., & Hastings, L. (1986). Personality correlates of men who abuse their partners: A cross-validation study. *Journal of Family Violence, 1,* 323–346.

Hamberger, L. K., & Holtzworth-Munroe, A. (2000). Partner violence. In F. Dattilio and A. Freeman (Eds.), *Cognitive-behavioral strategies in crisis intervention* (2nd ed., pp. 339–361). New York: Guilford Press.

Hamberger, L. K., & Lohr, J. M. (1989). Proximal causes of spouse abuse: Cognitive and behavioral factors. In P. L. Caesar & L. K. Hamberger (Eds.), *Treating men who batter: Theory, practice and programs* (pp. 53–76). New York: Springer.

Hamberger, L. K., Lohr, J. M., Bonge, D., & Tolin, D. F. (1996). A large sample empirical typology of male spouse abusers and its relationship to dimensions of abuse. *Violence and Victims, 11,* 277–292.

Hamberger, L. K., & Potente, T. (1996). Counseling heterosexual women arrested for domestic violence: Implications for theory and practice. In L. K. Hamberger & C. Renzetti (Eds.), *Domestic partner abuse* (pp. 53–75). New York: Springer.

Hamberger, L. K., Saunders, D. G., & Hovey, M. (1992). Prevalence of domestic violence in community practice and rate of physician inquiry. *Family Medicine, 24,* 283–287.

Hamilton, M. (1960). A rating scale for depression. *Journal of Neurology and Neurosurgical Psychiatry, 23,* 56–62.

Hart, B., & Stuehling, J. (1992). *Personalized safety plan.* Reading, PA: Pennsylvania Coalition Against Domestic Violence.

Holtzworth-Munroe, A., & Stuart, G. (1994). Typologies of male batterers: Three subtypes and the differences among them. *Psychological Bulletin, 116,* 476–497.

Holtzworth-Munroe, A., Stuart, G. L., Meehan, J. C., Herron, K., & Rehman, U. (2000). Testing the Holtzworth-Munroe and Stuart (1994) batterer typology. *Journal of Consulting and Clinical Psychology, 68,* 1000–1019.

Hudson, W., & McIntosh, S. (1981). The Index of Spouse Abuse: Two quantifiable dimensions. *Journal of Marriage and Family, 43,* 873–888.

Hyman, A., Schillinger, D., & Lo, B. (1995). Laws mandating reporting of domestic violence. Do they promote patient well-being? *Journal of the American Medical Association, 273,* 1781–1787.

Johnson, M., & Elliott, B. A. (1997). Domestic violence among family practice patients in mid-sized and rural communities. *Journal of Family Practice, 44,* 391–399.

Koss, M. P., & Heslet, L. (1993). Somatic consequences of violence against women. *Archives of Family Violence, 1,* 53–59.

Kurz, D. (1990). Interventions with battered women in health care settings. *Violence and Victims, 5,* 243–256.

Lechner, M. E., Vogel, M. E., Garcia-Shelton, L. M., Leichter, J. L., & Steibel, K. R. (1993). Self-reported medical problems of adult female survivors of childhood sexual abuse. *Journal of Family Practice, 36,* 633–638.

Mandel, J. B., & Marcotte, D. B. (1983). Teaching family practice residents to identify and treat battered women. *Journal of Family Practice, 17,* 708–716.

Marshall, L. L. (1992). Development of the Severity of Violence Against Women Scales. *Journal of Family Violence, 7,* 103–121.

Minsky, D., Pape, D., & Hamberger, L. K. (2000, August). *Domestic violence: Qualitative analysis of barriers to identification and referral of victims in an urban healthcare setting.* Paper presented at the meeting of the American Psychological Association, Washington, DC.

Murphy, C. M., & O'Leary, K. D. (1989). Psychological aggression predicts physical aggression in early marriage. *Journal of Consulting and Clinical Psychology, 57,* 579–582.

Phelan, M. B., Hamberger, L. K., Hare, S., & Edwards, S. (2002, August). *Domestic violence among male and female emergency department patients.* Paper presented at the meeting of the American Psychological Association, Chicago, IL.

Rodriguez, M. A., McLoughlin, E., Bauer, H. M., Paredes, V., & Grumbach, K. (1999). Mandatory reporting of intimate partner violence to police: Views of physicians in California. *American Journal of Public Health, 89,* 575–578.

Rosewater, L. B. (1987). The clinical and courtroom application of battered women's personality assessments. In D. J. Sonkin (Ed.), *Domestic violence on trial: Psychological and legal dimensions of family violence* (pp. 86–94). New York: Springer.

Saunders, D. G. (1994). Posttraumatic stress symptom profiles of battered women: A comparison of survivors in two settings. *Violence and Victims, 9,* 31–44.

Saunders, D. G., Hamberger, L. K., & Hovey, M. (1993). Indicators of woman abuse based on a chart review at a family practice center. *Archives of Family Medicine, 2,* 537–543.

Sherin, K. M., Sinacore, J. M., Li, X., Zitter, R. E., & Shakil, A. (1998). HITS: A short domestic violence screening tool for use in a family practice setting. *Family Medicine, 30,* 508–512.

Straus, M. A. (1979). Measuring intrafamily conflict and violence: The Conflict Tactics (CT) Scales. *Journal of Marriage and the Family, 4,* 75–88.

Straus, M. A. (1990). The Conflict Tactics Scales and its critics: An evaluation and new data on validity and reliability. In M. A. Straus & R. J. Gelles (Eds.), *Physical violence in Ameri-*

can families (pp. 49–73). New Brunswick, NJ: Transaction Books.

Sugg, N. K., & Inui, T. (1992). Primary care physicians' response to domestic violence: Opening Pandora's box. *Journal of the American Medical Association, 267,* 3157–3160.

Vivian, D., & Langhinrichsen-Rohling, J. (1994). Are bi-directionally violent couples mutually victimized? A gender-sensitive comparison. *Violence and Victims, 9,* 107–124.

Walker, L. E. A. (1994). *Abused women and survivor therapy: A practical guide for the psychotherapist.* Washington, DC: American Psychological Association.

Waller, A. E., Hohenhaus, S. M., Shah, P., & Stern, E. A. (1996). Development and validation of an emergency department screening and referral protocol for victims of domestic violence. *Annals of Emergency Medicine, 27,* 754–760.

25

Eating Disorders

Barbara Cubic
Daniel Bluestein

At age 12 years, Tonya, a white female, presents with a 3-month history of severe, persistent headaches, significant fatigue, nausea, and a 20-pound weight loss. She has limited her activities considerably, but rarely misses school and continues to excel academically. Her physical exam, with the exception of her appearance, is unremarkable. Her only previous medical problem is asthma. As a mental health clinician, you have been asked to teach Tonya relaxation techniques to offset her headaches during the wait for an outpatient neurological consult. Would you consider the possibility that Tonya has an eating disorder? You should.

Why? The presentation is highly suggestive of anorexia nervosa, one of several eating disorders, which is rapidly increasing in prevalence. Tonya is female, white, prepubertal, possibly perfectionistic, and has had rapid weight loss without a known cause.

INTRODUCTION

Mixed messages abound in Western cultures regarding weight and exercise. Advertisements for fast-food restaurants with "supersized" meals are followed by promotions for weight loss products. Physicians underscore the importance of remaining health conscious, and at the same time images of "healthy" people portrayed by the media are often dangerously thin. Vulnerable adolescents who seek peer acceptance engage in destructive eating behaviors and develop aberrant ideas about their own bodies that only serve to further isolate them from others.

Consequently, over time Western cultures have developed two paradoxical problems with life-threatening complications: obesity and eating disorders. Anorexia nervosa has the highest mortality rate of any psychiatric condition. Simultaneously, recent estimates have suggested that each year obesity leads to more than 300,000 deaths and is becoming the nation's single most preventable cause of premature death and disability (for more about obesity, refer to chapter 32).

Changes in societal norms and national policies, comprehensive preventive strategies, and effective clinical treatments are all needed to address the increasing prevalence of eating disorders. Primary care settings offer a point of intervention in this regard, as an average family or pediatric practice with 5,000 patients should be expected to contain 25 to 60 patients with bulimia and approximately 25 patients with anorexia nervosa.

With dieting and body dissatisfaction becoming the norm, patients with eating disorders and the physicians who treat them are often unaware of the seriousness of the patients' behavior. This means it is infrequent that an eating disorder is a presenting problem for a visit to primary care, and mental health clinicians will often have to alert both the physician and the patient to the problem. Therefore, this chapter provides an overview of eating disorders, quick screening measures, and possible treatment options.

CLINICAL DESCRIPTIONS

Eating disorders represent the epitome of a biopsychosocial disorder because of the interplay between the mind and the body in these conditions. The central component of all eating disorders is a severe disturbance in eating behavior, often provoked by an exaggerated drive for thinness. This pathological eating pattern is often accompanied by a disturbance in body image and weight and maladaptive behaviors designed to offset weight gain. For some individuals, starvation and excessive exercise prevail, and for others binge eating and dangerous compensatory behaviors develop in an attempt to undo a binge.

Although most primary care patients will not meet full criteria for an eating disorder, many will exhibit significant disturbances in eating, exercise, and body-related beliefs. In fact, destructive eating behaviors and attitudes tend to be more prevalent than diagnosable conditions, especially among college-age females, with 27% to 66% reporting binging, 12% to 15% describing purging, 30% classifying themselves as restrained eaters (i.e., use extreme dieting methods periodically) (Rand & Kuldau, 1991), and 50% stating they are overweight even when underweight (Haberman & Luffey, 1998). Furthermore, the first year of college appears to be a high-risk time for the development of pathological eating in both genders even if no eating disorder develops. This may be related to the stress associated with this transi-

tional period and the limited supervision a young adult receives regarding eating and exercise behaviors.

Subclinical patterns of eating pathology are also often seen in younger patients before an eating disorder fully develops, in older patients who have achieved partial recovery from an eating disorder, and in weight-preoccupied individuals of all ages and gender. For example, female athletes and patients with diabetes may also have subclinical, but destructive, eating disturbances that can go unnoticed if the problems are attributed to the demands of the sport or the illness. These facts underscore the importance of awareness of eating-related problems and knowing how to differentiate the various forms of disordered eating.

Anorexia Nervosa

General Description

As the case of Tonya in the introduction suggests, anorexia nervosa affects females predominantly, although not exclusively; usually begins in adolescence or early adulthood; and is seen primarily in Western affluent societies. The cardinal characteristic is emaciation, achieved through rigorous exercise and drastic restriction of food (American Psychiatric Association [APA], 2000a), in other words, self-starvation.

Initially, anorexia nervosa is difficult to differentiate from typical dieting as both occur when concern about weight is provoked, often after being teased or at the onset of puberty's bodily changes. The hallmark difference is that in anorexia nervosa extreme measures of weight control are adapted and maintained. Purgative behaviors such as self-induced vomiting or abuse of laxatives, diuretics, and enemas commonly co-occur with the dietary restriction, especially if the individual was previously overweight. Body image concerns substantially exceed the typical preoccupation with body image seen in adolescents. As the eating disorder becomes all-consuming, creative steps are taken to disguise the disorder, such as taking over meal preparation to control food intake, cleaning up after meals to leave the table early, and wearing less-revealing clothes to hide weight loss. Approximately half of these individuals also develop bulimia nervosa symptoms, either during their illness or in alternation with anorexia (Cubic, 2001).

Anorexia nervosa frequently begins during a transitional period (e.g., puberty, entering college) or after a family stressor (e.g., parental divorce, older sibling leaving the home). Comorbid diagnoses of major depression, dysthymia, and obsessive-compulsive disorder are common (Walsh, Wheat, & Freund, 2000). Psychological theories often link the individual's sense of a lack of control over life circumstances and family relationships to the need for control over food intake and weight. Because the symptoms often begin near the onset of puberty, theories also emphasize a fear of maturing sexually and assuming adult responsibilities as fundamental to the disorder's development.

Epidemiology

The incidence of anorexia nervosa has steadily increased over the last few decades, with current lifetime prevalence rates ranging from 0.5% to 3.7%. The disorder occurs predominantly in white female adolescents and young adults, with a typical age of onset between 12 and 25 years (Cubic, 2001). Within male populations, homosexual men and men who pursue sports that emphasize thin body ideals or target weights are most at risk. Females who engage in activities that accentuate a lean physique (e.g., ballet, gymnastics) are particularly at high risk for anorexia nervosa, especially those reaching elite levels of competition (Smolak, Murnen, & Ruble, 2000).

Medical Complications

The mortality rates for anorexia nervosa are the highest of any psychiatric disorder (Ramsay, Ward, Treasure, & Russell, 1999), estimated at 5%. The primary causes of death include cardiac arrest caused by arrhythmias, inanition (exhaustion from lack of food), infection, hypothermia, and suicide. Death from anorexia nervosa is often very sudden and not always related to the severity of the disorder. The medical complications of severe anorexia nervosa are extensive and affect every system in the body. There are additional complications if the patient also binges or purges. Particular note should be paid to cardiovascular complications and electrolyte disturbances because these are implicated in mortality. Other complications are listed in Table 25.1.

Laboratory studies in anorexia nervosa may be normal, even in advanced disease. Amenorrhea is a cardinal manifestation of anorexia nervosa, and if it lasts longer than 6 months, it may lead to bone mineral loss (osteopenia and osteoporosis) and a higher rate of fractures of the lumbar spine and hip as a result. Infertility and atrophy of breast tissue are additional sequelae. Abnormal neuroimaging is found in more than half of individuals with the illness. Persistent deficits on neu-

Table 25.1 Medical Complications of Anorexia Nervosa

Systemic (heat-conserving adaptations)
  Hypotension, bradycardia (often <30 beats per minute), hypothermia

Skin
  Yellowish discoloration (hypercarotenemia)
  Dry skin (xerosis)
  Fine hairs on the face and arms (lanugo)
  Brittle nails
  Hair loss (alopecia)
  Blue tinge to hands and feet (acrocyanosis)

Cardiovascular
  Reduced heart muscle mass, mitral valve prolapse, QT interval prolongation

Hematologic (may be normal)
  Neutropenia, anemia, thrombocytopenia

Endocrine/metabolic (may normalize with treatment)
  Electrolyte abnormalities (see bulimia nervosa)
  Hypoglycemia
  Euthyroid sick syndrome (i.e., decreased triiodothyronine and thyroxine, normal or slightly decreased thyroid-stimulating hormone)
  Abnomal growth hormone secretion
  Excessive secretion of insulin
  Increased cortisol production
  Hypogonadotropic hypogonadism/hypoestrogenism/decreased levels of testosterone
  Infertility
  Growth arrest
  Osteopenia and osteoporosis
  Kidney stones

Gastrointestinal (see bulimia nervosa)

Neurological
  Reversible cortical atrophy, ventricular enlargement, peripheral neuropathy

ropsychological testing are also observed and are associated with poorer outcomes (APA, 2000b).

Prognosis

Full recovery from anorexia nervosa is rare, but achievable. The death rate is currently estimated at 5.6% per decade of life (Sullivan, 1995). However, patients receiving intensive treatment, often initially in inpatient facilities, have a more favorable prognosis. Following hospitalization, a good outcome is typically defined as weight restored to within 15% of target weight and a return of menstruation; close to half of patients achieve this goal. A poorer prognosis appears to be associated with an initial lower minimum weight, presence of vomiting, failure to respond to previous treatment, premorbidly disturbed family relationships, and being married. The relapse rate is high (4 of 10) during the first year of treatment (APA, 2000b).

Bulimia Nervosa

Melanie was a 16-year-old female who developed bulimia nervosa after an extensive diet. Prior to the onset of her eating disorder, at 5 feet, 4 inches tall, she weighed 138 pounds. Her self-imposed diet began when her father developed a serious life-threatening illness requiring 3 months of hospitalization. Melanie lost weight rapidly in the first 3 months of her diet, but soon began to lose control of her eating and began binging. She had heard about purging on a television show about eating disorders and decided it would offset her binges. Soon, she was binging and purging two to three times daily. The binges typically occurred on returning home from school when she had no supervision.

General Description

The principal characteristic of bulimia nervosa is the binge-purge cycle (APA, 2000a). Unlike anorexia nervosa, dieting is difficult to maintain over time; ultimately, control over eating is lost. Consumption of unplanned food or actual binges begins, and over time the frequency of binges increases. Because of embarrassment, the binge eating is a secretive behavior and often can go un-

discovered and unrevealed for years. During a binge, food is eaten quickly and in large quantities, often with the amount of food eaten ranging between 3 and 30 times the amount normally eaten in a day. The binge creates physical discomfort and extreme anxiety; subsequently, the individual engages in a compensatory behavior, often termed a *purge*, to offset weight gain. Typical compensatory behaviors are self-induced vomiting; abuse of laxatives, diuretics, or enemas; excessive exercise; and extreme dietary restriction. Following the binge-purge cycle, the individual with bulimia nervosa recommits to dieting, creating a state of hunger and increasing the likelihood of another binge. The body image disturbances seen in bulimia nervosa may be equivalent to those seen in anorexia nervosa (Williamson, Cubic, & Gleaves, 1993).

Binge and purge episodes are often precipitated by emotional stressors (e.g., boredom, loneliness, anger, depression). The most common form of purging is self-induced vomiting, although between 75% and 90% of bulimics use laxatives as a means of weight control, whether following a binge or between binges (Abraham & Llewellyn-Jones, 1997). In general, individuals who develop bulimia nervosa have low self-esteem and a propensity toward depression. On average, bulimics binge and purge 11 to 12 times a week, and a binge episode lasts for 1 hour. However, there is wide variation in binging and purging behavior, with 2 to 3 binge-purge cycles a week required to make the diagnosis, but many patients reported binging and purging 30 or more times a week. Binge foods typically are high in calories, easily prepared, and easily digested.

Individuals with bulimia nervosa show increased rates of anxiety disorders, chemical dependency, bipolar disorder, and personality disorders. Many individuals with the illness also show problems with impulse control, including sexual promiscuity, impulsive spending, and self-mutilation. Families members may have increased rates of substance abuse, affective disorders, and obesity (Walsh et al., 2000).

Epidemiology

Bulimia nervosa has a lifetime prevalence of 1.1% to 4.2% and an estimated prevalence rate of 8%

in female college populations (APA, 2000a). Although once believed to occur predominantly in middle- to upper-class white females, the disorder may be more prevalent in other groups than suspected. Approximately 10% of individuals with bulimia nervosa are male (Gordon, 2001b). A premorbid history of obesity and participation in sports requiring tight weight control (e.g., wrestling) appear to be risk factors for men. The age of onset for both bulimia nervosa and binge eating disorder (BED) varies considerably, but typically binging begins in late adolescence or early adulthood after a period of dieting. In bulimia nervosa, the onset of purging is usually within 6 months of the onset of binging.

Medical Complications

Although the medical problems in bulimia nervosa are dependent on the form of purging used, there are several similarities (see Table 25.2 for a detailed list). Although amenorrhea is not required to diagnose bulimia nervosa, irregular menses are common. Electrolyte, fluid, and acid-base disturbances are of significant concern for those who purge. The binge-purge cycle is thought to lower the basal metabolism rate, leading to insidious weight gain over time.

Throat problems and gastrointestinal complications are prominent. Abuse of ipecac to induce vomiting may cause cardiomyopathies (with sudden death). Individuals with bulimia nervosa who use self-induced vomiting will typically lose enamel on the back of the front teeth, suffer tooth decay, have calluses on the fingers from inserting them into the mouth, and show breakage of small facial blood vessels.

The mortality risks are unknown, but death from the disorder is believed to be rare (Mitchell, Pomeroy, & Adson, 1997). The endocrine problems seen in the disorder are similar to those in anorexia nervosa if the individual is at a substantially lowered body weight.

Prognosis

The outcome in bulimia nervosa is much better than in anorexia nervosa. Patients who complete treatment (either psychosocial or medication) show a 50% to 90% (mean 70%) reduction in

Table 25.2 Medical Complications of Bulimia Nervosa

Systemic
  Lower basal metabolism rate leading to insidious
    weight gain
Skin
  Calluses and cuts on fingers (Russell's sign)
  Breakage of small facial vessels
Gynecological
  Irregular menses
  Amenorrhea
Electrolyte, fluid, and acid–base disturbances
  Increased bicarbonate
  Hypochloremia
  Hypokalemia
  Hypomagnesemia
  Hyponatremia
  Hyper- and hypophosphatemia
Oropharyngeal
  Benign parotid gland enlargement
  Frequent sore throats
  Lacerations or contusions of the pharynx
  Dental discoloration
  Loss of enamel on the back of front teeth, tooth
    decay
Gastrointestinal
  Effects of self-induced vomiting
    Gastric dilation (leading to abdominal pain and
      bloating)
    Esophagitis
    Hematemesis (vomiting blood)
    Occult gastrointestinal bleeding
    Gastric rupture
    Aspiration pneumonia
  Effects of laxative abuse
    Diminished intestinal motility (leading to disten-
      sion and chronic severe constipation, hemor-
      rhoids, and rectal prolapse)

binge eating and purging (APA, 2000b). For example, Fichter and Quadflieg (1997) found about two thirds of those seeking treatment responded well; one fourth had an intermediate outcome, 10% had a poor outcome, and 1% died. Untreated patients have shown a 25% to 30% spontaneous recovery rate over 2 years (APA, 2000b).

Binge Eating Disorder

According to *DSM-IV*, BED is not considered a separate entity, and the diagnosis is subsumed under the category of eating disorder, not otherwise specified (APA, 2000a). However, the prevalence and impact of the condition warrants a brief discussion as many of these patients will present in the primary care setting with concerns about obesity and will seek weight loss advice, but will not seek direct psychological services.

BED is characterized by recurrent binges in the absence of purges. Although not limited to obese individuals, BED is most common in this group. BED is more equal in gender ratio than bulimia nervosa; in community samples, its prevalence is 2% to 5%. Clinical features include eating until uncomfortably full, eating when not physically hungry, eating alone, and feelings of depression or guilt. On average, 1,000 calories are consumed during a binge, but there is considerable diversity.

The average age of onset of the binges is 19 years, and weight gain gradually occurs because no compensatory behavior is utilized. Estimates are that 20% to 30% of patients who currently meet the diagnosis of BED may have previously had anorexia or bulimia nervosa, the latter being most common (APA, 2000a). Medical consequences are potentially severe, as repetitive binging, followed by unsuccessful, overly restrictive dieting can lead to escalating weight gain, morbid obesity, and attendant disorders such as diabetes, coronary disease, and sleep apnea. Common psychiatric comorbidities include depression and personality disorders.

Controversy exists over the most appropriate way to intervene with BED and whether treatment outcome is linked with successful elimination of binging, weight loss, or both. Studies have generally found that a high percentage of obese individuals can achieve significant weight loss through a variety of methods, but only 5% typically maintain this success after a 5-year follow-up period. These successful individuals are most likely to have achieved their weight loss through exercise (Brownell, 1995).

The prognosis for BED itself is less clear. Recent research suggested that successful psychological intervention that targets binging and its comorbid psychological issues leads to weight reduction in 25% of patients treated. Also, successful treatment of BED tends to improve later weight loss outcomes when these individual par-

ticipate in future weight loss programs (Peterson & Mitchell, 1999). Therefore, researchers are now seeking ways to incorporate both weight loss and psychological treatment components into BED treatment.

CULTURAL ISSUES

Cultural studies based in the United States have often measured disturbed eating behaviors and attitudes rather than frequency of diagnosable eating disorders; however, some general conclusions can be drawn. First, it appears that acculturation (i.e., the adoption of majority culture attitudes) places minorities at higher risk for developing eating disorders (Striegel-Moore et al., 2000). Second, there is evidence of differences in body size and dissatisfaction across groups. Hispanic and African American females generally have higher body mass indexes (BMIs) than whites and Asian Americans, but have less body image dissatisfaction. Whites appear to focus more on body size and shape, and Asian Americans tend to be less satisfied with racially distinct body features than weight (Mintz & Kashubeck, 1999). Third, the prevalence of eating disorders appears to vary across ethnicity. In contrast to whites, anorexia nervosa remains rare in all minority groups; Hispanics appear to be at equal risk for developing bulimia nervosa and BED; and African Americans have a lower prevalence of bulimia nervosa and equal or higher prevalence of BED. Native Americans may actually be at the highest risk for developing both bulimia nervosa and BED among all ethnic groups (Crago, Shisslak, & Estes, 1996).

DETECTION RATES IN PRIMARY CARE

Issues Regarding Detection

With dieting becoming the norm, it is often easy in a primary care setting to discount the possibility of eating disorders and to seek medical explanations when severe weight loss, signs of vomiting, or gastrointestinal distress are present. This is true despite the facts that patients with eating disorders, in contrast to their counterparts, see their doctors more frequently; report more concerns per visit, and have magnified social problems. Barriers to detection may include lack of training or awareness, inadequate continuity of care, and the high volume typical of many primary care settings.

Anorexia nervosa may be detected more frequently than bulimia nervosa because of the degree of weight loss present, but it is still seriously underdetected. Even when physicians are alerted to the possibility of anorexia nervosa, an average time lapse of 7.4 months occurs before referral to a mental health professional is made (Bryant-Waugh, Lask, Shafran, & Fosson, 1992). This delay increases medical complications and mortality and leads to a poorer prognosis. This tendency toward underdetection is even higher in younger children.

Because patients with bulimia nervosa may be of normal weight or slightly overweight and appear healthy, the disorder is often not considered in a differential diagnosis. However, in contrast to patients with anorexia nervosa, these patients often want assistance and may give subtle hints to their doctors in hope of diagnosis and treatment (Bursten, Gabel, Brose, & Monk, 1996). In fact, studies have shown that, when physicians do not respond to initial hints, more obvious ways of revealing the disorder will be attempted, including directly discussing overeating and purging or obtaining medical advice about the possible consequences of laxative, diuretic, or diet pill usage.

Also, anecdotal evidence suggested that once patients disclose binging or purging, they are less likely to lie about future eating problems. Ironically, instead of receiving treatment for bulimia nervosa or referral to a mental health professional, patients with bulimia nervosa often receive dieting advice or referral to a dietician, again, likely because of a low index of suspicion for eating disorders of any type.

Improving Detection Rates

Improving the detection of eating disorders could lead to earlier interventions, better prognoses, and reduction in medical expenses. Furthermore, despite the misconception that eating disorders are difficult to identify, research has shown that basic questions can alert clinicians to eating problems, especially in subclinical populations and patients with bulimia nervosa.

If there is suspicion of an eating disorder or if a patient is in a high-risk group, interviewing techniques such as transitioning and normalization will facilitate discussions. Open-ended, basic questions to encourage dialogue such as those shown in Table 25.3 may increase yield (Carlat, 1998; Freund, Graham, Lesky, & Moskowitz, 1993; Walsh et al., 2000). If the patient provides an affirmative response, then focused questions about the weight loss methods used should be asked in a matter-of-fact manner to decrease shame and embarrassment. For example, a history of binging or purging may be elicited by simple questions like "Do you go on eating binges in which you eat an unusually large amount of food within a 2-hour period?" or "Do you feel that you can't control your eating?" or "Do you ever make yourself vomit after you eat?"

When anorexia nervosa is suspected, confirmation of the diagnosis through clinical interview may be more difficult. Because anorexia nervosa is ego-syntonic, patients with the disorder are likely, when directly questioned, to deny any problems with eating. Even when patients are aware of the seriousness of the eating disorder, they may still conceal information secondary to embarrassment or fears of being forced to eat. Therefore, more rapport may be needed to obtain information about previous weights, patterns of weight loss, menstrual history, activities, sleep disturbances, and exercise habits.

Although most interviewing approaches have value, it matters less which specific question is asked and more that questions are asked at all. Simple awareness is key. The primary care psychologist has a vital role in fostering such awareness through education and support of primary care physician partners by suggesting the possibility that an eating disorder has been overlooked. Most primary care physicians appreciate constructive feedback and differing perspectives as they work so frequently with so many specialists.

TREATMENT OPTIONS

The main goals of treatment for all of the eating disorders are as follows:

Table 25.3 Basic Screening Questions

Introductory questions:
  Have you ever felt like you are overweight?
  Many young people have concerns about their weight or about food. Do you have any concerns in this area?
  Many young people have trouble with binge eating large amounts of food. Has this been a problem for you?
SCOFF questions (100% sensitivity and 87.5% specificity for detecting anorexia or bulimia nervosa):
  Do you make yourself sick because you feel uncomfortably full?
  Do you worry you have lost control over how much you eat?
  Have you recently lost more than one stone (14 pounds) in a 3-month period?
  Do you believe yourself to be fat when others say you are too thin?
  Would you say food dominates your life?

1. Enlistment of the patient's cooperation with treatment
2. Nutritional rehabilitation and normalization of weight (when needed)
3. Correction of medical and psychiatric sequelae of malnutrition
4. Facilitation of healthier behaviors and attitudes regarding eating and body image
5. Improved interpersonal and social functioning
6. Identification and treatment of comorbid psychopathology

Because eating disorders vary in severity and prognosis worsens with duration, early intervention is warranted. Treatment options range from management by a primary care physician, to well-coordinated multidisciplinary outpatient treatment approaches, to structured partial hospitalization, residential care, or inpatient treatment programs. A higher level of care should be considered if there is a rapid or persistent decline in oral intake or weight, previously unsuccessful treatment attempts, medical and psychological stressors, a return to a prior status warranting hospitalization previously, or comorbid psychiatric conditions (APA, 2000b).

Weight, cardiac functioning, metabolic status, and potential for suicide are the most critical physical parameters in determining the level of care needed. An intensive outpatient or inpatient treatment program should be considered if there is concern about medical instability or if the patient is 15% or more below the expected weight, typically around a BMI of 17. The target weight can be determined by calculating the patient's BMI: divide weight in kilograms by height in square meters. See Table 25.4 for BMI calculations.

Anorexia Nervosa

With anorexia nervosa, there must be awareness of the behavioral and physiological effects of starvation as well as the additional difficulties created by the volitional dietary restraint. As treatment begins, the patient will often feel the need to more rigidly restrict calories and pursue other symptomatic behavior.

Nutritional rehabilitation should focus on defining a healthy target weight range (e.g., BMI of 18.5–20) and reasonable rates of controlled weight gain (e.g., 2–3 lb/week for most inpatient and 0.5–1 lb/week for most outpatient programs) (Touyz & Beumont, 1997). Close communication regarding treatment and weight goals is required by an interdisciplinary team (e.g., a dietician, psychologist, and physician) so the patient

Table 25.4 BMI Calculations

BMI Score	Significance
>30	Obesity
25–29.9	Overweight
18.5–24.9	Normal range
18.5–20	Typical target BMI for patients with anorexia nervosa
<17	Consider intensive treatment or hospitalization
<12	Serious caution required during refeeding

does not receive mixed messages. From a clinical perspective, restoration and maintenance of 90% of ideal body weight would indicate success. Ideally, no more than 3,000 to 3,500 calories a day will be encouraged during the weight gain phase, and then the intake will be reduced to approximately 1,800 calories per day (Touyz & Beumont, 1997). Rapid or overfeeding is not recommended as refeeding syndrome, a potentially catastrophic complication, can occur. During early treatment, patients may experience abdominal pain and bloating, constipation, acne, and breast tenderness.

Psychotropic medications are not routinely prescribed to severely malnourished patients with anorexia nervosa because of increased risk of side effects. The cognitive effects of malnutrition, which may improve with weight restoration, also often interfere with systematic assessment of the need for medications. However, antidepressants, particularly selective serotonin reuptake inhibitors (SSRIs), can be used to treat comorbid depression or obsessive-compulsive problems, and antipsychotics may alter psychotic symptoms (APA, 2000b). The role of medications in relapse prevention is not clear; some studies suggested that antidepressants may be associated with less weight loss and fewer rehospitalizations. Regardless of medication choice, patients with anorexia nervosa should be seen by a psychiatrist experienced in anorexia management. Nonpsychotropic medications should include 1,000 to 1,500 mg per day of calcium and a multivitamin with 400 IU or more of vitamin D.

To date, no single type of psychosocial intervention has been superior in treating anorexia nervosa. However, there is mounting evidence that family therapy, which teaches parents how to regain control over their child's eating (especially younger children) (Lock, Le Grange, Agras, & Dare, 2001; Wood, Flower, & Black, 1998) is effective. The case of Sabrina illustrates this point.

At the time of her self-imposed diet, Sabrina was 12 years old, and her weight was at the 65th percentile for her age group. What began as a healthy diet soon turned into a restricted diet. Her parents were unaware that Sabrina was dieting. In time, Sabrina lost 32 pounds in less than 4 months and finally was hospitalized. During her hospital stay, family therapy began; this followed a structural model and was facilitated by the fact that the family was generally cohesive and the parents had good communication and cooperation skills. Therefore, the parents were successful in providing appropriate supervision and monitoring of their daughter's eating.

These approaches only focus partially on dismantling dysfunctional family dynamics. The main emphasis is on communication skills, psychoeducation, observation of family meals, and encouragement of non-food-related activities. The family therapy also challenges beliefs within the family contributing to the eating disorder (e.g., equation of thinness or perfection with self-worth, nonfostering of autonomy, inappropriate emotional expression), not just issues regarding eating.

Individual therapy approaches should utilize a combination of psychodynamic, supportive, and cognitive–behavioral techniques because of the complexity of anorexia nervosa. Throughout therapy, the detection of comorbid psychiatric disorders is important as treating these disorders increases the likelihood that the anorexia may be successfully treated. Early interventions should address patient education, help patients deal with weight gain and body image changes, provide support to patients and families, and utilize behavioral approaches. Once the patient's nutritional status is restored, long-term psychotherapy should address healthy ways to achieve a sense of control and self-worth and skill building (e.g., addressing lack of assertiveness, poor problem solving, limited communication). Emotional awareness training should also be considered because a high percentage of patients with anorexia nervosa are alexithymic (i.e., lack words for feelings) (Taylor, Parker, Bagby, & Bourke, 1996).

Bulimia Nervosa

Most patients with bulimia nervosa can be managed as outpatients unless medical instability develops. Controlled studies have established cognitive–behavioral therapy (CBT) as the most efficient and effective psychotherapy approach (Wilson, 1999). CBT-based self-help and guided self-help approaches have also produced significant reductions in binge eating (Peterson & Mitchell, 1999). Also, interpersonal therapy may be comparable to CBT by the end of treatment, but the gains achieved appear to occur at a slower rate (Peterson & Mitchell, 1999).

In CBT, the initial goal is to restore dietary control through goal setting, food monitoring, behavioral contracting for planned meals, stimulus control techniques, exposure with response prevention, and teaching alternative coping skills (e.g., relaxation, distraction, dealing with emotions directly). Longer term goals focus on food regulation, body and weight preoccupation, perfectionism, dichotomous thinking, and low self-esteem. Cognitive techniques, such as thought monitoring, are integrated throughout therapy; a sample of typical eating-disordered cognitions is listed in Table 25.5. It is important to note that, despite recurrent findings about the effectiveness of CBT in altering binging and purging, CBT is rarely used in the United States (Wilson, 1999). This finding has led advocates of CBT to argue for the dissemination of "therapist-friendly," manual-based CBT resources (e.g., Agras & Apple, 2001) for both bulimia nervosa and BED.

> Melanie's individual therapy focused on educating her about healthy strategies for weight control, encouraging her to record and discuss thoughts and feelings that preceded binges, and developing alternative strategies for dealing with high-risk situations (i.e., coming home from school). The family therapy focused on how both Melanie and her parents had distorted thoughts and dysfunctional lifestyles pertaining to eating and body image. The parents were encouraged to see how Melanie's bulimia nervosa was exacerbated by the dysfunctional thought and behavior patterns of the parents, and the parents were encouraged to make alterations. Melanie was able to decrease her binge-purge episodes to one to two times a month, but the family made very little progress.

Psychotropic medications may be indicated when patients show only partial improvement with therapy or if the severity of the disorder warrants rapid stabilization. Tricyclic and SSRI antidepressants have the strongest track record in decreasing binging and purging (APA, 2000b), and fluoxetine is now the only medication approved by the U.S. Food and Drug Administration for treatment of bulimia nervosa. The monoamine oxidase inhibitors also have empirical support, but their associated side effects and dietary restrictions mean they are not recommended as an initial treatment approach. Bupropion (Wellbutrin) can effectively diminish the frequency of binge eating, but is contraindicated in patients with bulimia nervosa because it places them at an increased risk for seizures.

Binge Eating Disorder

Treatments for BED have often been similar to those utilized for bulimia nervosa, and weight loss strategies are added if the patient is overweight. For example, Brownell's (1989) LEARN (Lifestyle, Exercise, Attitudes, Relationships, Nutrition) program might be utilized as a behavioral approach which stresses gradual rather than rapid weight loss.

Although BED has received limited empirical attention, research has shown that CBT is effective in reducing binge frequency, although it may not lead directly to weight loss (Wilson, 1999). As with bulimia nervosa, interpersonal therapy and antidepressant medications appear to be other promising treatment alternatives for BED, but also do not yield substantial weight loss unless combined with traditional weight loss programs (Wilfley & Cohen, 1997).

The primary treatment goals for BED include cessation of binge eating, improvement of physical health (possibly mediated in part by weight loss), reduction in psychological distress, and treatment of comorbid conditions. Initially, the treatment focuses on increased self-awareness of thoughts and behavior, psychoeducation, normalization of eating, and potential obstacles to progress. Patients are taught to eat at scheduled times to eliminate the role of dieting in binging and are educated about the negative impact of alternating between dieting and binging. Foods that typically would lead to a binge are identified, and problem solving and temptation exposure with response prevention approaches are used to assist patients in eating feared foods in moderation.

Table 25.5 Typical Cognitions in Eating-Disordered Patients

Control/perfection issues
  "Demonstrating control over food intake and weight shows self-discipline."
  "Giving in to sensations of hunger means that I am a failure."
  "Unless I can control my weight, my accomplishments in life mean nothing."
  "I must be perfect at everything I attempt."

Weight control beliefs
  "Gaining any amount of weight is terrifying."
  "I can be any weight I want to be if I simply try hard enough."
  "The only way to control my weight is to constantly check it."

Body image dissatisfaction
  "My body is disgusting."
  "If I gain any weight, I become completely unattractive and must avoid others."
  "If I feel negatively about something, it must be because my body is disgusting/fat."
  "Feeling fat and being fat are the same thing."

Minimization of the eating disorder
  "An eating disorder is not a serious problem."
  "I'll stop my eating-disordered behavior before I have any serious medical complications."
  "Having an eating disorder is part of who I am and therefore I cannot change it."

Feelings about obesity
  "People who are obese are lazy and overeat."
  "Being fat would be the end of the world."

Dealing with emotions
  "Being thin equals being happy."
  "I can't tolerate feeling negative emotions."
  "If I feel upset, then restricting my food intake will make me feel better."
  "If I eat, the anxiety will be intolerable, and I must purge, restrict, or compulsively exercise to avoid the
    anxiety."
  "My eating disorder helps me avoid dealing with things."

Eating habits
  "If I eat anything that was unplanned, I might as well have binged."
  "As long as I can 'undo eating' [i.e., purge], then there will be no negative consequences."
  "Chronic dieting is the only way to maintain long-term weight loss."

Acceptable foods
  "There are foods which are 'good' [i.e., acceptable] to eat and those which are 'bad' [i.e., forbidden]."
  "After eating fatty foods, I can literally see my body growing."
  "If I eat anything that is not on my diet, then I have 'blown it' for the day."

Once nutritional intake is normalized, the focus shifts to cognitive restructuring techniques, body image treatment approaches, and relapse prevention. Ultimately, the goal is for patients to identify precipitants to binges and modify dysfunctional thoughts and behaviors.

Pharmacological intervention may be useful in reducing binging in BED; however, the research is limited to date. SSRIs, used in high dosage, and tricyclic antidepressants have been shown to yield substantially greater reduction in binge eating than placebo, but the results may be short term; consistent sustained weight loss rarely occurs (Peterson & Mitchell, 1999). Gastric bypass surgery may also be considered for BED patients with morbid obesity and significant health-related problems and is fairly effective at decreasing binging and creating weight loss (Wilson, 1999). However, surgery candidates should undergo a thorough medical, nutritional, and psychological evaluation to rule out contraindications because of the risks associated with the surgery (i.e., death, gastrointestinal complications, weight regain if eating behavior does not change).

IMPROVING COMANAGEMENT

When eating disorders are viewed as self-inflicted or the medical risks are underestimated, empathy and understanding may be compromised. To complicate matters further, patient denial or ambivalence about treatment may lead to poor compliance, deceit, and hostility. Therefore, several initial steps are important to enhance the therapeutic alliance. Clinicians must convey empathy regarding the patient's struggle to normalize eating; be prepared to discuss issues related to their own body size, eating habits, and exercise routine (as their physique is clearly visible to the patient); and converse openly about the reality of societal pressures for thinness and achievement. Gender differences may also need to be discussed. Often, both male and female patients may feel as if male therapists cannot conceive of the pressures applied to females or a subset of males regarding thinness.

When treatment will be provided in the outpatient setting, primary care psychologist must be able to form a treatment team (via relationships with physicians, nutritionists, psychiatrists, and other mental health professionals) or should refer the patient to an eating disorders specialist. Collaborative psychoeducation should emphasize a target weight, nutritional goals, factors related to the development of eating disorders, the energy regulation model, set point theory, the impact of societal pressures for thinness, and the medical and physiological consequences of eating disorders. The impact of starvation on behavior and cognitive processes can be illustrated by discussing the findings of the Keys, Brozek, Henshel, Mickelsen, and Taylor (1950) study.

All treatment team members should encourage the patient to explore advantages and disadvantages of eating-disordered behaviors and beliefs (e.g., that thinner is better). Also, the treatment team should consistently encourage the patient to expand the notion of self as more than a body. Emphasis is on increasing the patient's recognition of strengths and weaknesses and how the composite of these characteristics leads to uniqueness.

Continued coordination of care is critical. Because the physician will be instrumental in determining the medical severity of the condition, he or she should be updated regularly on the course of therapy. Conversely, the primary care physician should keep the mental health clinician(s) appraised of any changes in physical status (in both positive or negative directions) and treat any complications caused by the eating disorder.

In outpatient treatment, the mental health clinician should assist the team in recognizing that the patient's diet and exercise should be monitored, but few immediate recommendations should be made. Reassurance should be given to the patient through simple statements such as "Our goal is not to make you fat," and clinicians should remember that quick recommendations convey a lack of understanding and often intensify fears of uncontrollable weight gain. Normalizing eating will be addressed over time when trust is established, and is best accomplished by integrating weight goals into a treatment contract that focuses on all of the issues associated with the eating disorder. The patient's current problems should be discussed as an understandable reaction to life experiences and messages learned during childhood and adolescence, and therapy will teach adaptive coping skills. Last, throughout treatment, the clinician must stay alert to trust and control issues because of possible abandonment issues, real or symbolic losses, or a history of abuse.

Mental health specialists also need to take a proactive role in providing education to primary care physicians and patients about the nature and treatment of eating disorders and preventive programming within the community. To do so, mental health specialists should offer to provide periodic professional presentations on the topic and serve as consultants to local primary care clinicians when cases arise. Because of the complexities involved in working with patients with eating disorders, clinicians may find it necessary to establish professional credibility in the area by obtaining continuing education in the field.

SPECIAL CONSIDERATIONS: PREGNANCY, DIABETES, ATHLETICISM

1. *Pregnancy.* Because of the prevalence of eating disorders in females of childbearing age, issues of

how to manage the disorders during pregnancy warrant attention. Obviously, it is ideal if the eating disorder is treated prior to pregnancy and if issues related to potential relapse are addressed in preconception counseling. Inadequate nutrition, binging, and purging and the use of teratogenic medications can result in fetal or maternal complications. Obstetric care should be transferred to an obstetrician who specializes in high-risk pregnancies. Nutritional and mental health counseling should continue throughout the course of the pregnancy and 3 to 6 months thereafter because, if symptoms abate spontaneously during pregnancy, the eating-disordered behaviors often return after delivery. Women with a history of anorexia nervosa, regardless of current status, are at greater risk for birth complications and delivery of a lower birth weight baby (Bulik et al., 1999). Body image issues are intensified dramatically during the pregnancy. Also, mothers with eating disorders have more difficulty breast-feeding (Stein, Woolley, Cooper, & Fairburn, 1994).

2. *Diabetes.* In adolescent females with diabetes, therapeutic focus on eating and weight gain with good glycemic control may increase susceptibility to abnormal eating. Subthreshold eating disorders and bulimia and anorexia nervosa are more common in this group of patients and may be associated with familial problems such as poor communication with both parents, mistrust of parental accessibility and responsiveness, family conflict, and poor social support (Hoffman, 2001). These issues may underlie dangerous behaviors such as insulin omission and resultant diabetic ketoacidosis. Thus, the possibility of an eating disorder should be considered with recurrent diabetic ketoacidosis or poor glycemic control that is resistant to attempts at improvement. Similarly, there are reports of male, Type 1 diabetic adolescent wrestlers omitting insulin doses to achieve weight goals, although disordered eating is less common with male gender. Multidisciplinary therapeutic strategies are needed and should include decreased dietary restraint, promotion of healthy eating, and psychological interventions.

3. *Athleticism.* The concurrence of eating disorders and athleticism is also commonly noted. Researchers have delineated a "female athlete triad" consisting of disordered eating, amenorrhea, and osteoporosis (Hobart & Smucker, 2000).

Many with the triad do not meet *DSM-IV* criteria for anorexia or bulimia nervosa yet manifest similar disordered eating behaviors. Eating disorders that are enmeshed in athleticism can often lead to severe bone demineralization, injury, and destruction of athletic careers. Risk factors include competitive drive and pressure from peers, family members, and coaches. The mental health clinician should remind primary care physicians that the preparticipation sports physical is an ideal screening opportunity for these types of problems.

PREVENTIVE STRATEGIES

In the United States, on any given day, 25% of males and 45% of females are dieting, and children as young as 6 years of age are now starting to diet (Gordon, 2001a). Non-Western cultures exposed to American media are now beginning to develop higher rates of eating disorders, underscoring the role of messages about thinness in the etiology of eating disorders and the need for prevention.

During routine encounters, clinicians should empathically discount societal messages that overestimate the importance of thinness, discuss body image concerns and healthy ways of maintaining weight, and prepare children and adolescents for the pubertal changes they will face. Physicians should be reminded to be cautious about suggesting dieting, especially in children and adolescents, unless serious weight concerns are present. Rather, encouragement of exercise and provision of sound nutritional advice is needed.

Primary care settings are also often ideal locations for eating-related support or therapy groups because the potential for stigmatization is less. Psychoeducation and prevention strategies can be readily incorporated into classes on nutrition and healthy lifestyle. Community-based preventive programming can focus on ways to build self-esteem, enhance body satisfaction, and provide healthy methods of weight control. Preventive programming should avoid discussions about techniques used by patients with eating disorders because impressionable females may often learn maladaptive weight control behaviors even when presentations on eating disorders are well intended.

SUMMARY

Eating disorders represent the epitome of a bio-psychosocial disorder because of the interplay between the mind and the body in these conditions. Anorexia nervosa, bulimia nervosa, and BED pose both medical and psychological threats to an individual and become increasingly difficult to treat with chronicity. Early detection and intervention improve prognosis, and prevention is ideal. Multidisciplinary coordination is needed, and empirically validated approaches (e.g., CBT or SSRIs for bulimia nervosa, family therapy for adolescents with anorexia nervosa) should be considered first-line approaches. Treatment should include close collaboration with the patient's physician, and more efforts should be made to educate primary care physicians on how to detect and treat these disorders.

ADDITIONAL RESOURCES

Suggestions for further reading and professional development resources are available at this book's companion Web site: www.primarycarepsych.com.

References

Abraham, S., & Llewellyn-Jones, D. (1997). *Eating disorders: The facts.* Oxford, U.K.: Oxford University Press.

Agras, W. S., & Apple, R. (2001). *Overcoming binge eating.* New York: The Guilford Press.

American Psychiatric Association. (1994). *Diagnostic and statistical manual of mental disorders* (4th ed.). Washington, DC: Author.

American Psychiatric Association. (2000a). *Diagnostic and statistical manual of mental disorders* (4th ed., text rev.). Washington, DC: Author.

American Psychiatric Association. (2000b). Practice guideline for the treatment of patients with eating disorders (revision). *American Journal of Psychiatry, 157*(Suppl.), 1–39.

Bender, R., Trautner, C., Spraul, M., & Berger, M. (1998). Assessment of excess mortality in obesity. *American Journal of Epidemiology, 147,* 42–48.

Brownell, K. D. (1989). *The LEARN program for weight control.* Philadelphia: University of Pennsylvania School of Medicine.

Brownell, K. D. (1995). Exercise and obesity treatment: Psychological aspects. *International Journal of Obesity, 19*(Suppl.), 122–125.

Bryant-Waugh, R. J., Lask, B. D., Shafran, R. L., & Fosson, A. R. (1992). Do doctors recognise eating disorders in children? *Archives of Disease in Childhood, 67,* 103–105.

Bulik, C., Sullivan, P., Fear, J., Pickering, A., Dawn, A., & McCullin, M. (1999). Fertility and reproduction in women with anorexia nervosa: A controlled study. *Journal of Clinical Psychiatry, 60,* 130–135.

Bursten, M. S., Gabel, L. L., Brose, J. A., & Monk, J. S. (1996). Detecting and treating bulimia nervosa: How involved are family physicians? *Journal of the American Board of Family Practice, 9,* 380–383.

Carlat, D. J. (1998). The psychiatric review of symptoms: A screening tool for family physicians. *American Family Physician, 58,* 1617–1624.

Crago, M., Shisslak, C. M., & Estes, L. S. (1996). Eating disturbances among American minority groups: A review. *International Journal of Eating Disorders, 19,* 239–248.

Cubic, B. A. (2001). Psychopathology. In D. Wedding (Ed.), *Behavior and medicine* (3rd ed., pp. 379–405). Kirkland, WA: Hogrefe and Huber.

Fichter, M. M., & Quadflieg, N. (1997). Six-year course of bulimia nervosa. *International Journal of Eating Disorders, 22,* 361–384.

Freund, K. M., Graham, S. M., Lesky, L. G., & Moskowitz, M. A. (1993). Detection of bulimia in a primary care setting. *Journal of General Internal Medicine, 18,* 236–242.

Gordon, A. (2001a). Eating disorders: 1. Anorexia nervosa. *Hospital Practice, 36,* 36–38.

Gordon, A. (2001b). Eating disorders: 2. Bulimia nervosa. *Hospital Practice, 37,* 71–72.

Haberman, S., & Luffey, D. (1998). Weighing in college students' diet and exercise behaviors. *Journal of American College Health, 46,* 189–191.

Hobart, J. A., & Smucker, D. R. (2000). The female athlete triad. *American Family Physician, 61,* 3357–3364.

Hoffman, R. P. (2001). Eating disorders in adolescents with type 1 diabetes. A closer look at a complicated condition. *Postgraduate Medicine, 109,* 67–74.

Keys, A., Brozek, J., Henshel, A., Mickelsen, O., & Taylor, H. L. (1950). *The biology of human starvation* (Vols. 1 and 2). Minneapolis: University of Minnesota Press.

Lock, J., Le Grange, D., Agras, W. S., & Dare, C. (2001). *Treatment manual for anorexia nervosa: A family-based approach.* New York: Guilford Press.

Mintz, L. B., & Kashubeck, S. (1999). Body image and disordered eating among Asian American and Caucasian college students. *Psychology of Women Quarterly, 23,* 781–796.

Mitchell, J. E., Pomeroy, C., & Adson, D. E. (1997). Managing medical complications. In D. M. Garner & P. E. Garfinkel (Eds.), *Handbook of treatment for eating disorders* (2nd ed., pp. 383–393). New York: Guilford Press.

Peterson, C. B., & Mitchell, J. E. (1999). Psychosocial and pharmacological treatment of eating disorders: A review of research findings. *Journal of Clinical Psychology, 55,* 685–697.

Ramsay, R., Ward, A., Treasure, J., & Russell, G. F. M. (1999). Compulsory treatment in anorexia nervosa. *British Journal of Psychiatry, 175,* 147–153.

Rand, C. S., & Kuldau, J. M. (1991). Restrained eating (weight concerns in the general population and among students). *International Journal of Eating Disorders, 10,* 699–708.

Smolak L., Murnen, S. K., & Ruble, A. E. (2000). Female athletes and eating problems: A meta-analysis. *International Journal of Eating Disorders, 27,* 371–380.

Stein, A., Woolley, H., Cooper, S. D., & Fairburn, C. G. (1994). An observational study of mothers with eating disorders and their infants. *Journal of Child Psychology and Psychiatry, 35,* 733–748.

Striegel-Moore, R. H., Schreiber, G. B., Lo, A., Crawford, P., Obarzanek, E., & Rodin, J. (2000). Eating disorder symptoms in a cohort of 11 to 16 year old back and white girls: The NHLBI growth and health study. *International Journal of Eating Disorders, 27,* 49–66.

Sullivan, P. K. (1995). Mortality in anorexia nervosa. *American Journal of Psychiatry, 152,* 1073–1074.

Taylor, G. J., Parker, J. D., Bagby, R. M., & Bourke, M. P. (1996). Relationships between alexithymia and psychological characteristics associated with eating disorders. *Journal of Psychosomatic Research, 41,* 561–568.

Touyz, S. W., & Beumont, P. J. V. (1997). Behavioral treatment to promote weight gain in anorexia nervosa. In D. M. Garner & P. E. Garfinkel (Eds.), *Handbook of treatment for eating disorders* (2nd ed., pp. 361–371). New York: Guilford Press.

Walsh, J. M., Wheat, M. E., & Freund, K. (2000). Detection, evaluation, and treatment of eating disorders: The role of the primary care physician. *Journal of General Internal Medicine, 15,* 577–590.

Wilfley, D. E., & Cohen, L. R. (1997). Psychological treatment of bulimia nervosa and binge eating disorder. *Psychopharmacology Bulletin, 33,* 437–454.

Williamson, D. A., Cubic, B. A., & Gleaves, D. H. (1993). Equivalence of body image disturbance in anorexia and bulimia nervosa. *Journal of Abnormal Psychology, 102,* 177–180.

Wilson, G. T. (1999). Cognitive behavior therapy for eating disorders: Progress and problems. *Behaviour Research and Therapy, 37*(Suppl. 1), S79–S95.

Wood, D., Flower, P., & Black, D. (1998). Should parents take charge of their child's eating disorder? Some preliminary findings and suggestions for future research. *International Journal of Psychiatry in Clinical Practice, 2,* 295–301.

26

Fibromyalgia and Chronic Fatigue Syndrome

Laurence A. Bradley
Graciela S. Alarcón
Leanne R. Cianfrini
Nancy L. McKendree-Smith

Fibromyalgia (FM) is characterized as a chronic, non–life-threatening, incurable but manageable condition that causes pain and widespread fatigue. Chronic fatigue syndrome (CFS) is described disorder that causes profound fatigue as well as joint and muscle pain. FM and CFS are characterized by similar symptoms and the absence of biological, diagnostic markers that might be used to distinguish them from one another and from other medical disorders (Demitrack, 1998). Both of these disorders primarily affect women.

The primary symptoms of FM are persistent, generalized, musculoskeletal pain and abnormal pain sensitivity (i.e., tenderness) at multiple anatomic sites; additional clinical manifestations include fatigue, sleep disturbance, stiffness of muscles and joints, subjective joint swelling, and joint laxity or hypermobility (Yunus, 1994). Individuals with FM also show abnormal pain sensitivity in response to pressure stimulation of deep muscle tissue (e.g., Wolfe et al., 1990) as well as to thermal and electrocutaneous stimulation of the skin (e.g., Gibson, Littlejohn, Gorman, Helme, & Granges, 1994). Finally, patients with FM fail to display diminished pain sensitivity in response to

counterstimulation procedures such as ischemic pressure (Lautenbacher & Rollman, 1997) and physical exercise (Vierck et al., 2001). However, modest responses to counterstimulation are also observed in samples of healthy women; thus, they are probably a sex-related phenomenon rather than a unique feature of FM (Staud, Robinson, Vierck, & Price, 2003).

CFS is characterized by persistent, debilitating fatigue as well as secondary symptoms such as myalgias, arthralgias, sleep disturbance, and postexertion malaise. It is not surprising, then, that clinic-based studies show that, among persons with CFS, between 35% and 70% meet criteria for FM (Aaron, Burke, & Buchwald, 2000; Bradley, McKendree-Smith, & Alarcón, 2001); one of these investigations also found that 64% of patients with FM also meet criteria for CFS (Aaron et al., 2000). As a consequence, some investigators have theorized that the FM and CFS labels represent different clinical expressions of the same disorder (e.g., Clauw & Chrousos, 1997). However, the severity of fatigue experienced by patients with CFS is far greater than that reported by patients with FM. In addition, individuals with

CFS do not display abnormal pain sensitivity unless they also fulfill the classification criteria for FM (Buchwald, 1996).

We first review the classification criteria for FM and CFS and then discuss current findings regarding the epidemiology and natural history of these two disorders. Next, we describe our current understanding of the pathophysiology of FM and CFS with particular emphasis on the physiological and psychosocial factors that contribute to musculoskeletal pain. Finally, we note that current treatment interventions for FM and CFS are very similar, and we review current literature regarding the outcomes of these interventions.

CLASSIFICATION CRITERIA, EPIDEMIOLOGY, AND NATURAL HISTORY

Classification Criteria

Fibromyalgia

The symptom complex associated with FM has been recognized for decades. However, it was not until 1990 that the American College of Rheumatology (ACR) developed reliable classification criteria for this disorder by comparing a large group of patients chosen to represent the FM syndrome from several samples of patients with other painful musculoskeletal disorders (chronic low back pain, rheumatoid arthritis [RA], and systemic lupus erythematosus [SLE]) (Wolfe et al., 1990). The classification criteria include the two variables that best differentiated the patients with FM from the comparison patient groups. These are (a) widespread pain, defined as pain above and below the waist, in the peripheral as well as in the axial skeleton, in the right and left sides of the body, and present for at least 3 months; and (b) low pain threshold levels in at least 11 of 18 defined anatomical sites (i.e., "tender points"), elicited by 4 kg pressure applied by the thumb (in the clinic) or a calibrated dolorimeter (in the laboratory) (see Table 26.1 and Figure 26.1). Many patients display low pain thresholds at more than 11 tender points as well as at other anatomical areas, including those that the ACR defined as nonpainful or "control" points.

Table 26.1 The 1990 American College of Rheumatology Classification Criteria for Fibromyalgia

I. History of widespread pain (≥3 months)
 • Left and right side of body
 • Above and below the waist
 • Axial skeletal pain
  • cervical spine, or
  • anterior chest, or
  • thoracic spine, or
  • low back

II. Tender point pain
 • Pain, on digital palpation, must be present in at least 11 of 18 specific tender point sites (9 points bilateral)

Occiput	Lateral epicondyle
Lower cervical	Gluteal
Trapezius	Greater trochanter
Supraspinatus	Knees
Second rib	

Note. Adapted from Wolfe et al. (1990).

The ACR classification criteria have produced relatively uniform characterization of patients with FM in clinical and research settings. However, two important issues regarding these criteria should be noted. First, the ACR did not distinguish between primary FM, which occurs independent of other rheumatic disorders, and secondary FM, which occurs in conjunction with or following the onset of other well-defined rheumatic disorders such as RA or SLE. Nevertheless, this distinction may be useful in the clinic setting (e.g., for treatment purposes) as well as in the research laboratory.

The second issue is that several factors may produce spurious effects on patients' pain threshold responses. For example, pain sensitivity within individuals may vary as a function of time of day (i.e., circadian rhythm), menstrual cycle phase, medication usage, or cognitive errors in labeling sensory events. Thus, it may be necessary to repeat tender point examinations on some patients before determining whether they fulfill the pain threshold criterion for FM. Okifuji, Turk, Sinclair, Starz, and Marcus (1997) published a manual and videotape that provide standardized instructions for identifying the ACR tender points and control points and for evaluating pain thresholds at these points.

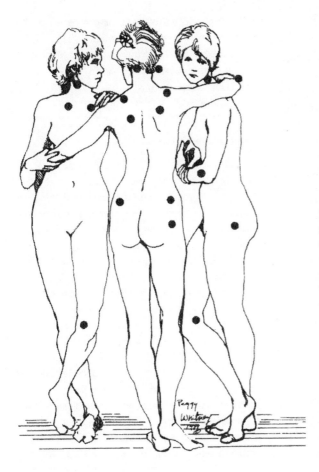

Figure 26.1 The 18 tender points used to evaluate persons for fibromyalgia. These consist of the left and right occiput, at the insertion of the suboccipital muscles; lower cervical, at the anterior aspect of the intertransverse spaces between C5 and C7; trapezius, at the midpoint of the upper border; supraspinatus, at the origin of the muscle, above the scapula spine near the medial border; second rib, at the second costochondral junction; gluteal, at the upper outer quadrant of buttocks; epicondyle (lateral), 2 cm distal to the epicondyle; greater trochanter, posterior to the trochanteric prominence; and knee, at the medial fat pad, proximal to the articular line. Adapted from Wolfe et al. (1990).

Chronic Fatigue Syndrome

The Centers for Disease Control and Prevention established the current classification criteria for CFS in 1994 (Table 26.2; Fukuda et al., 1994). These include two inclusion and two exclusion criteria. The first inclusion criterion consists of debilitating fatigue that persists or recurs over a period of at least 6 months. The second consists of the patient's report of at least four of eight additional symptoms present for at least 6 months. These symptoms include (a) impaired memory or concentration; (b) sore throat; (c) tender cervical or axillary lymph nodes; (d) myalgias; (e) arthralgias; (f) recurrent headaches that did not occur before the onset of debilitating fatigue; (g) unrefreshing sleep; and (h) postexertion malaise. The exclusion criteria are that (a) history, physical exam, and laboratory tests must rule out other medical conditions (including obesity) that could produce the debilitating fatigue; and (b) psychiatric evaluation must rule out major depressive disorder, bipolar disorder, psychotic disorders, dementia, anorexia, or bulimia.

Comorbid Conditions

Patients with FM and CFS frequently exhibit similar comorbid symptoms or conditions, such as stiffness in muscles and joints, abnormal functioning of the autonomic nervous system, irritable bowel syndrome, interstitial cystitis, chronic pelvic pain, temporal-mandibular joint disorders, cognitive impairment, and multiple chemical sensitivity syndrome (Aaron et al., 2000). Patients with FM also frequently report subjective joint swelling and joint laxity or hypermobility.

One of the most distressing symptoms associated with FM and CFS is sleep disturbance. A substantial number of patients report that they persistently find it difficult to fall asleep, wake up numerous times during the night, or fail to feel

Table 26.2 Centers for Disease Control and Prevention Classification Criteria for Chronic Fatigue Syndrome

I. Debilitating fatigue that persists or relapses >6 months

II. History, physical exam, laboratory tests do not indicate any other medical conditions that could account for persistent fatigue

III. Psychiatric evaluation excludes major depressive disorder, bipolar disorder, psychotic disorders, dementia, anorexia, or bulimia

IV. At least four symptom criteria present >6 months
- impaired memory or concentration
- sore throat
- tender cervical or axillary lymph nodes
- muscle pain or multijoint pain
- new headaches
- unrefreshing sleep
- postexertion malaise

Note. From Fukuda et al. (1994).

refreshed when they wake from sleep. These sleep disturbances tend to be associated with an abnormal pattern in the electroencephalographic (EEG) recordings of patients with FM and CFS during deep sleep (Moldofsky, Scarisbrick, England, & Smythe, 1975; Whelton, Salit, & Moldofsky, 1992). This abnormal pattern is characterized by a relatively fast-frequency alpha EEG wave superimposed on a slower frequency delta EEG during non-rapid eye movement (non-REM) sleep. Indeed, it has been shown that induction of this alpha-delta EEG abnormality by slow-wave sleep deprivation produces increased pain sensitivity among healthy men and women (Lentz, Landis, Rathermel, & Shaver, 1999; Moldofsky et al., 1975).

Some investigators have questioned whether the high frequency of sleep abnormalities among patients with FM and CFS might contribute to their frequent reports of impairment in memory, verbal fluency, and other cognitive functions (e.g., Park, Glass, Minear, & Crofford, 2001). The alpha-delta EEG abnormality is associated with slow speed of performance on complex cognitive tasks and fatigue in patients with FM (Cote & Moldofsky, 1997). It is not known whether sleep disturbance is associated with the deficits in memory

and complex cognitive tasks associated with CFS (Ross, Fantie, Straus, & Grafman, 2001).

Another sleep abnormality that frequently occurs in conjunction with FM and CFS is sleep apnea (Harding, 1998); chapter 37, Sleep Disorders, explores this problem in more depth.

Health Care Utilization

Patients with FM and CFS tend to be frequent users of health care services because of the primary symptoms of these disorders and the large number of comorbidities and secondary symptom manifestations involving almost every organ system. A good history should point the practitioner toward the correct diagnosis. Unfortunately, that is not always the case; in fact, these patients are very likely to undergo numerous noninvasive and even invasive diagnostic or therapeutic procedures that can produce negative personal and social consequences. For example, in extreme cases, patients with FM may be erroneously diagnosed with a more serious rheumatic disorder such as SLE and even treated with unnecessary and potentially toxic pharmacological agents. Table 26.3 summarizes clinical manifestations frequently reported by patients with FM and CFS, the providers from whom they are likely to seek care, and the tests or procedures usually ordered to define these symptoms (Alarcón, 1999).

It is important to note that, because of the many symptoms and high levels of health care system usage associated with FM and CFS, a sizable proportion of health care providers view patients with these disorders as (a) psychologically disturbed; (b) hypervigilant about common, unpleasant sensory experiences; or (c) somatizers who seek to "medicalize" their symptoms (e.g., Barsky & Borus, 1999). Perhaps the most important reason for this is that physicians generally are ill equipped to deal with patients who frequently exhibit significant psychopathology and report symptoms not associated with measurable biological markers. The negative attitudes exhibited by physicians are clearly perceived by the patients, who are likely to respond by seeking treatment from other, more sympathetic, health care professionals. This health care–seeking behavior generates additional medical costs, which may be justified if patients receive appropriate medical care

Table 26.3 Symptoms, Diagnostic Tests/Procedures, and Diagnoses in Patients With Fibromyalgia and Chronic Fatigue Syndrome Seeking Health Care

Type of Specialist	Symptoms Commonly Expressed	Potential Tests and Procedures	Possible Diagnoses[a]
Allergist	Allergies	Skin test, suppression tests	Allergies, multiple chemical sensitivities
Cardiologist	Palpitations, chest pain, syncope, hypotension	ECG, exercise tests, echocardiogram, conventional and magnetic resonance angiograms, cardiac catheterization, tilt table evaluations	Mitral valve prolapse, atypical angina, dysautonomia
Dentist	Dry mouth	Salivary gland biopsy	Sicca syndrome
Dermatologist	Pruritus, hives, skin rashes, photosensitivity	Skin biopsies	Dermatitis
Endocrinologist	Weakness, faintness	Fasting blood sugars, serum hormonal levels	Hypoglycemia
Gastroenterologist	Dysphagia, dyspepsia, abdominal pain, bloating, constipation, diarrhea	Endoscopies (upper and lower GI), radiographs, biopsies, abdominal CT scans and/or ultrasound, abdominal angiogram	Noncardiac chest pain Irritable bowel syndrome, gastroesophageal reflux
Gynecologist	Polyuria, dysuria, dyspareunia, "vaginitis," pelvic pain	Cystoscopies, colposcopies	UTI, cystitis, vaginitis, endometriosis
Internist	Malaise, fatigue, weakness	Various	Various
Neurologist	Dizziness, dysesthesias, vertigo, headache, syncope, seizures	CT scans and/or MRIs, MR angiogram, electrophysiological studies, lumbar puncture, biopsies	Headaches, restless legs syndrome, dysautonomia, anxiety
Neurosurgeon	Headache, neck, and/or back pain; dysesthesias	CT scans and/or MRIs, electrophysiological studies	Spinal stenosis, radiculopathy
Ophthalmologist	Dry eyes, blurred vision, double vision	Shirmer's test, fluorescein test	Sicca syndrome
Orthopedist	Neck and/or back pain	Radiographs, MRIs, and/or CT scans	"Arthritis"
Otorhinolaryngologist	Tinnitus, cough, headache, hoarseness, snoring, vertigo, dizziness	Audiograms, CT scans or MRIs, polysommography	Rhinitis, sinusitis, Meniere's disease, sleep apnea
Psychiatrist	Anxiety, depression, insomnia, decreased memory, sexual and/or physical abuse	MMPI, neurocognitive evaluation, other psychological tests	Anxiety, depression, abuse (sexual and/or physical)
Rheumatologist	Myalgias, arthralgias, Raynaud's phenomenon, weakness, neck and/or back pain	Serological tests, electrophysiological studies	"Latent" or "variant" lupus costochondritis, polymyalgia rheumatica, undifferentiated CTD

CT, computed tomography; CTD, connective disease; ECG, electrocardiogram; GI, gastrointestinal; MMPI, Minnesota Multiphasic Personality Inventory test; MRI, magetic resonance imagining; UTI, urinary tract infection. Modified from Alarcón (1999).
[a]Some of these diagnoses represent true associations. Others, unfortunately, are given to patients in an effort to explain their symptoms, but lack organic bases.

with which they are satisfied. However, the search for acceptance from a health care provider may lead some patients to a subgroup of health professionals who provide unproven or even questionable treatments to patients with FM and CFS. This may actually harm patients as well as increase the cost of their care.

Many patients with FM or CFS do not have a good understanding of current findings regarding the pathophysiology of their disorders. A productive initial patient encounter will include a discussion of these findings and their implications for treatment; it will use language that can be understood by persons without a medical background.

Epidemiology

A small number of population-based studies in North America have established the prevalence rates for FM and CFS; however, the incidence rates for these disorders are unknown. In addition, little is known concerning risk factors for these disorders except that individuals with hypermobile joints are predisposed to develop FM at a relatively early age (Goldman, 1991). Within adult populations, the prevalence of FM ranges between 2% and 3% (White, Speechly, Harth, & Ostliye, 1999; Wolfe, Ross, Anderson, Russell, & Hebert, 1995), whereas that for CFS varies between 0.2% and 0.4% (Jason et al., 1999). Both disorders primarily affect women; it has been found consistently that women comprise about 90% of persons with FM and 70% of those with CFS. The FM studies have not carefully examined ethnic group differences in the prevalence of this disorder, although one population-based study in Wichita, Kansas, revealed that "nonwhites" comprised 11% of persons identified as FM cases (Wolfe et al., 1995). A population-based study in Chicago, Illinois, revealed that 16% of the individuals identified as CFS cases were African American, and 28% were Latino (Jason et al., 1999).

There are no population-based studies of the prevalence of FM among children. However, clinic-based studies indicated that 25% to 40% of children with chronic musculoskeletal pain who are treated by pediatric rheumatologists meet the criteria proposed by Yunus for juvenile primary FM syndrome (Schanberg, Keefe, Lefebvre,

Kredich, & Gil, 1996; Yunus & Masi, 1985). Epidemiological studies of CFS among children are characterized by numerous methodological weaknesses. However, one of the better studies, performed in Australia, produced a prevalence estimate of 0.4% (Lloyd, Hickie, Boughton, Spencer, & Wakefield, 1990).

As noted, clinic-based investigations suggest a large amount of overlap in FM and CFS. However, there are no population-based studies of the prevalence of individuals who meet criteria for both disorders. Nevertheless, there appear to be three subgroups of persons with these disorders. These are persons with pain and fatigue who meet criteria only for CFS, those who meet criteria solely for FM, and those with both FM and CFS. Only persons with FM or FM and CFS display *allodynia*, abnormal pain responses to low levels of pressure stimulation at the tender points as well as at other anatomic sites. Individuals with CFS alone do not display allodynia in response to pressure stimulation (Buchwald, 1996). However, it is not known whether these individuals might show abnormal pain responses to stimuli other than pressure (see Figure 26.2).

Natural History

Longitudinal studies of adult patients with FM have yielded conflicting results. The initial studies of the natural history of FM found that most patients reported their symptoms persisted over periods ranging from 1 to 2 years (e.g., Waylonis & Perkins, 1994). Other studies revealed that up to 75% of patients with FM reported increased symptom severity over a 5-year period (e.g., Forseth, Forre, & Gran, 1999). However, there is a subgroup of individuals who report improvements in pain and other symptoms over time. For example, Poyhia, Da Costa, and Fitzcharles (2001) followed 59 women with FM over a 3-year period and found that one third of the cohort reported reductions in pain of at least 30% from baseline levels.

Studies of the natural history of CFS among adults have produced findings similar to those of the early FM investigations described above. The CFS studies indicated that spontaneous remissions occur in 8% or fewer of patients followed between 1 and 3 years (e.g., Bombardier & Buch-

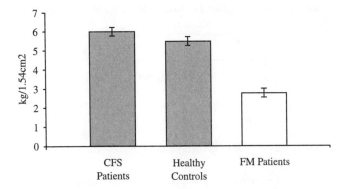

Figure 26.2 Mean (±*SEM*, standard error of measurement) pressure pain threshold levels of patients with chronic fatigue syndrome (CFS; *n* = 9), patients with fibromyalgia (FM; *n* = 22), and healthy controls (*n* = 25). Patients with CFS and healthy controls displayed significantly higher mean pain threshold levels than patients with Fm in response to dolorimeter stimulation applied to 10 of the 18 tender points used to classify individuals with FM according to the American College of Rheumatology classification criteria (Wolfe et al., 1990). There was no difference in mean pain threshold level between patients with CFS and healthy controls. There was no overlap of FM and CFS diagnoses in any of the patients.

wald, 1995). These studies have also suggested that illness duration is inversely related to persistence of fatigue (e.g., van der Werf, de Vree, Alberts, van der Meer, & Bleijenberg, 2002). Similarly, patients with persistent fatigue who do not fulfill the CDC for CFS are more likely to show spontaneous improvements in symptoms than individuals who fulfill the criteria for CFS (e.g., Valdini, Steinhardt, Valicenti, & Jaffe, 1988). Studies of the natural history of FM and CFS in children have used very small samples. Thus, it is not possible to produce reliable conclusions concerning natural history on the basis of these investigations.

PHYSIOLOGICAL AND PSYCHOSOCIAL FACTORS THAT INFLUENCE PAIN AND FATIGUE

Numerous investigators have performed case-controlled studies of physiological and psychosocial factors that differentiate patients with FM or CFS from healthy controls. Given the high degree of overlap between these disorders, it is not surprising that these studies have produced similar findings with regard to neuroendocrine and immune function as well as psychosocial factors. However, there also are important differences between patients with FM and CFS in levels of pain-related neuropeptides and measures of functional brain activity (see Table 26.4).

Physiological Factors

Genetic Factors

Male and female relatives of patients with FM are characterized by greater pain sensitivity and a higher frequency of FM than matched controls (e.g., Buskila & Neumann, 1997). This familial aggregation of pain sensitivity and FM suggests there may be a genetic predisposition to the development of FM, although it does not rule out the influence of learned illness behavior, particularly among the offspring of parents affected with FM (Pelligrino, Waylonis, & Sommer, 1989).

Well-designed studies of genetic factors that may contribute to these disorders have just begun to appear. Two independent laboratories have reported that patients with FM are significantly more likely than controls to show a functional

Table 26.4 Biological and Psychosocial Factors Associated with Pain in Fibromyalgia and Chronic Fatigue Syndrome

	Fibromyalgia	Chronic Fatigue Syndrome
Genetic factors	Higher frequency of a functional polymorphism in the promoter region of the 5-HTT gene	Chronic fatigue occurs more frequently in both members of monozygotic, compared to dizygotic, twin pairs
HPA axis abnormalities	Low 24-hour free urine cortisol Low CRH Low basal levels IGF-1 and growth hormone	Low 24-hour free urine cortisol Low CRH No consistent abnormalities in IGF-1 or growth hormone
Neuropeptide levels	Low serum serotonin and low CSF 5-HIAA levels High CSF levels of substance P, dynorphin A, nerve growth factor, and CGRP	High plasma 5-HIAA levels Normal CSF levels of substance P
Immune function	High blood plasma levels of proinflammatory cytokines (e.g., IL-1-α)	High blood serum levels of proinflammatory cytokines (e.g., IL-8, IL-1R antibody)
Brain structure	No cortical abnormalities	High number of cortical white matter lesions
Measures of functional brain activity	Hypoperfusion of the thalamus and caudate nucleus at rest Low levels of stimulation produce relatively high pain intensity ratings and increased perfusion in large number of brain regions	Inconsistent findings, although two studies reported brain stem hypoperfusion at rest No evidence at present
Psychiatric comorbidity	High frequency of depressive and anxiety disorders as well as lifetime psychiatric morbidity Psychiatric morbidity is greater among tertiary care patients than in community residents who do not seek treatment for FM symptoms	High frequency of depressive and anxiety disorders as well as lifetime psychiatric morbidity Psychiatric morbidity is greater in tertiary care patients than in primary care patients and community residents

CGRP, calcitonin gene-related peptide; CRH, corticotropin-releasing hormone; CSF, cerebrospinal fluid; 5-HTT, 5-hydroxytryptamine; 5-HIAA, 5-hydroxyindole acetic acid; IGF-1, insulin-like growth factor 1; IL, interleukin.

polymorphism in the promoter region of the serotonin transporter gene that has also been associated with affective disorders, anxiety-related traits, and migraine headaches (Cohen, Buskila, Neumann, & Ebstein, 2002; Offenbaecher et al., 1999). It is not yet known whether this functional polymorphism is associated with relatively low levels of serotonin and enhanced pain sensitivity in patients with FM or their female, first-degree relatives.

Buchwald and colleagues (2001) reported the preliminary results of a study of 146 female-female twin pairs, of whom at least 1 member reported fatigue that had persisted for at least 6 months. There was a significantly greater concordance rate for chronic fatigue among the monozygotic twins (55%) compared to the dizygotic twins (19%). This strongly suggested that there is a significant genetic contribution to the occurrence of chronic fatigue in family members. However, no candidate genes for CFS have been studied to date.

Neuroendocrine Function

Several neuroendocrine abnormalities have been described in patients with FM and CFS. The most consistent findings are those of the hypothalamic-pituitary-adrenal (HPA) axis; evidence for abnormalities in the HP-thyroid, the growth hormone (GH) axis, and the HP-gonadal (G) axis is just emerging. The HPA axis abnormalities include

(a) low 24-hour urinary free cortisol; (b) low hypothalamic levels of corticotropin-releasing hormone (CRH); and (c) exaggerated corticotropin response to the exogenous administration of CRH followed by a blunted cortisol response (Crofford et al., 1994; Demitrack & Crofford, 1998). Low levels of cortisol and CRH may disrupt the function of several biological systems involved in pain modulation, especially during exposure to stressors (Clauw & Chrousos, 1997).

Patients with FM also show low basal levels of GH and insulin-like growth factor 1 (IGF-1) (Bennett, Clark, Campbell, & Burckhardt, 1995). In contrast, studies of patients with CFS have not produced reliable evidence of abnormal GH axis function. Growth hormone has its peak secretion during Stage 4 of REM sleep, and it is involved in the maintenance of muscle homeostasis. Therefore, Bennett et al. (1992) proposed that sleep disturbances among patients with FM may lead to decreased GH secretion and subsequently to a vulnerability to muscle microtrauma and pain. Indeed, patients with FM display significant improvements in tender point scores and functional ability in response to GH injections compared to placebo (Bennett, Clark, & Walczyk, 1998).

Finally, both patients with FM and those with CFS exhibit impairments in autonomic nervous system functions such as increased sympathetic and decreased parasympathetic activity. These impairments contribute to several clinical phenomena, such as abnormal postural changes in blood pressure and heart rate (i.e., orthostatic intolerance), episodes of presyncope, difficulties with balance, cold intolerance, and other Raynaudlike symptoms (Gerrity et al., 2003). We have found it very useful to refer patients with these symptoms for evaluation of autonomic function and recommendations for treatment (such as prescriptions of the steroid fludrocortisone or exercise).

Abnormalities in Brain Structure

A large number of patients with CFS undergo magnetic resonance imaging (MRI) of the brain in an attempt to rule out the possibility that their persistent fatigue is caused by early multiple sclerosis. As a consequence, several investigators have compared MRI findings in patients with CFS and healthy controls. Three investigators found that patients with CFS, compared to controls, display a significantly greater number of cortical white matter lesions, primarily in the frontal area (e.g., Buchwald et al., 1992). It is not known, however, whether these white matter lesions actually contribute to the pathophysiology or symptoms of CFS.

A few physicians have suggested that Chiari Type 1 malformation may be responsible for the pain and orthostatic intolerance associated with FM and CFS. This malformation is a congenital hindbrain anomaly characterized by downward displacement of the cerebellar tonsils through the foramen magnum. It can lead to compression of cerebellar components, the lower brain stem, and the upper cervical spinal cord and produce a variety of neurological deficits. Unfortunately, most of the evidence regarding this potential association and the effects of spinal decompression surgery on patients with these disorders has appeared in newspaper articles, on national television programs, and on Internet Web sites (Garland & Robertson, 2001).

Although a subgroup of the patient community is highly interested in surgical intervention for their symptoms, the only prospective, blinded, study of the association between the Chiari 1 malformation and FM showed that the Chiari malformation was detected more frequently in healthy controls than in patients with FM (Clauw, Bennett, Petzke, & Rosner, 2000). In addition, a 2001 review found that the claimed association between orthostatic intolerance and Chiari malformation is almost entirely unsupported by peer-reviewed literature (Garland & Robertson, 2001). We suggest that patients with FM and CFS should be carefully evaluated for the presence of neurological deficits; those who display signs of such deficits should be referred for further evaluation. However, current data suggest that only a very small number of these patients will show structural abnormalities that require spinal decompression.

Abnormalities in Functional Brain Activity

Many investigators have used neuroimaging to determine whether the persistent musculoskeletal pain experienced by patients with FM and

CFS is associated with abnormalities in regional cerebral blood flow (rCBF) or other indices of functional brain activity. It has been shown consistently that patients with FM, compared to healthy controls, show significantly lower resting state levels of rCBF in the right and left thalamus or caudate nucleus (e.g., Mountz et al., 1995). Given that this abnormality is also observed in patients with persistent pain caused by neuropathy or metastatic cancer (e.g., Iadarola et al., 1995), it may be that inhibited thalamic or caudate rCBF represents a compensatory response to prolonged or augmented levels of excitatory neural input.

Indeed, Gracely, Petzke, Wolf, and Clauw (2002) measured the amount of mechanical pressure stimulation required by patients with FM and controls to produce moderate ratings of pain intensity (i.e., 11 on a 20-point scale). Patients with FM produced these ratings at about one half the intensity of stimulation required by the controls. Despite the group difference in stimulation intensity, both patients and controls showed significant increases in brain rCBF in the same seven brain structures (e.g., somatosensory cortex, cerebellum). This provides empirical evidence that relatively low levels of stimulation applied to mechanoreceptors produce augmented neural input in patients with FM.

Two studies have found that patients with CFS, compared to healthy controls, exhibit lower resting state levels of rCBF in the brain stem (Costa, Tannock, & Brostoff, 1995; Tirelli et al., 1998). Low brain stem rCBF levels may contribute to abnormal function of the locus ceruleus-norepinephrine/autonomic nervous system, which helps regulate descending antinociceptive pathways from the brain to the spinal dorsal horns (Clauw & Chrousos, 1997). Nevertheless, a study of 22 monozygotic twin pairs who were discordant for CFS found that the individuals with CFS did not differ from their healthy twins in resting state rCBF levels or in the number of visually detected perfusion abnormalities (Lewis et al., 2001).

Neuropeptide Abnormalities

Peripheral nociceptors that are activated by noxious stimuli (e.g., heat, pressure) generate signals transmitted along ascending neural pathways to the dorsal horns of the spinal cord, where they excite neurons through the release of several excitatory neurotransmitters. The main excitatory transmitter from the peripheral afferent fibers is glutamate, which acts on postsynaptic N-methyl-D-aspartate receptors of dorsal horn neurons. Other excitatory molecules include substance P and neurokinin A, both of which act on postsynaptic neurokinin receptors of the dorsal horn neurons (Pillemer et al., 1997). The signals generated by these neurons are then transmitted to the brain via their axons. However, the activity of several fibers that originate in brain stem sites and descend to the spinal dorsal horns may inhibit transmission of nociceptive input to the brain, primarily through the release of serotonin and norepinephrine.

Several investigators have compared patients with FM or CFS to healthy controls on blood serum or cerebrospinal fluid (CSF) levels of neurotransmitters involved in pain transmission and inhibition. With regard to pain transmission, it has been consistently found that patients with FM exhibit significantly greater levels of CSF substance P than healthy controls (Russell et al., 1994). Similar elevations are also shown in "nonpatients," community residents who meet the classification criteria for FM, but who do not seek medical care for their pain (Bradley, Sotolongo, Alberts, et al., 1999). This abnormality, however, is not found in patients with CFS who do not meet criteria for FM (Evengard et al., 1998).

Patients with FM also display elevated CSF levels of other excitatory neurotransmitters, such as dynorphin A, calcitonin gene-related peptide, and nerve growth factor (e.g., Giovengo, Russell, & Larson, 1999). Elevated levels of these neuropeptides and substance P are associated with a phenomenon that may occur following tissue and nerve injury, referred to as *central sensitization*. Central sensitization is characterized by hyperexcitability of both damaged nerves in the injured tissue and the spinal dorsal horn neurons; this produces enhanced responsiveness to a wide array of stimuli and abnormal pain sensitivity. Most FM investigators now posit that a phenomenon similar to central sensitization contributes to abnormal pain sensitivity in this disorder (e.g., Weigent, Bradley, Blalock, & Alarcón, 1998).

With regard to pain inhibitory neurotransmitters, several investigators have reported that patients with FM, compared to healthy persons, exhibit abnormal metabolism of serotonin and its precursor tryptophan, lower serum levels of serotonin, and lower CSF levels of 5-HIAA (5-hydroxyindole acetic acid) (e.g., Wolfe, Russell, Vipraio, Ross, & Anderson, 1997). Serotonin contributes to the activation of descending pain inhibitory pathways from the brain to the spinal dorsal horns and probably plays a role in stimulating the release of CRH from the hypothalamus (Holmes, Di Renzo, Beckford, Gillham, & Jones, 1982). In contrast, patients with CFS show increased plasma levels of 5-HIAA (Demitrack et al., 1992) and a prolactin response to buspirone indicative of enhanced serotonin neurotransmission (Bakheit, Behan, Dinan, Gray, & O'Keane, 1992).

Immune System Function

A large number of abnormalities in immune system function have been identified in persons with CFS. For example, it has been consistently found that patients with CFS exhibit elevated levels of proinflammatory cytokines, such as interleukin-1-alpha (IL-1 alpha), in blood plasma (Patarca-Montero, Antoni, Fletcher, & Klimas, 2001). These cytokines may interact with the nervous system in ways that have important implications for pain. For example, IL-1 normally interacts with CRH at the hypothalamus to promote activation of the HPA axis and inhibition of inflammatory processes. However, among persons with CFS, HPA axis dysregulation and low cortisol production may contribute to elevations in proinflammatory cytokines and to symptoms such as fatigue and muscle pain (Demitrack & Crofford, 1998).

This interaction between proinflammatory cytokines and the HPA axis may be enhanced by exposure to stressors. For example, even among healthy individuals, exposure to personally relevant stressors tends to produce increases in proinflammatory cytokines such as IL-6 and tumor necrosis factor-alpha (Goebel, Mills, Irwin, & Ziegler, 2000). The relationship between stressors and release of proinflammatory cytokines may be enhanced in patients with FM or CFS with im-

paired HPA axis function. In turn, this may contribute to the finding that persons with CFS report experiencing stressful life events, infections, and high fatigue levels during the 3 months prior to the onset of persistent fatigue (Theorell, Blomkvist, Lindh, & Evengard, 1999).

Relatively little effort has been devoted to the study of immune system function in patients with FM. However, several recent studies have shown that patients with FM, compared to controls, display significantly higher serum levels of proinflammatory cytokines such as IL-8 and IL-1R antibody (e.g., Gur et al., 2002). It remains to be determined whether stress-induced increases in these proinflammatory cytokines contribute to the relationships between exposure to stressors and increased pain intensity in patients with FM (Davis, Zautra, & Reich, 2001).

Psychosocial Factors

Psychological Distress and Psychiatric Morbidity

A large number of studies have documented that patients with FM or CFS who seek treatment in tertiary care centers, compared to healthy controls, are characterized by significantly higher scores on self-report measures of anxiety and depression as well as significantly higher levels of lifetime psychiatric morbidity (e.g., Buchwald, Pearlman, Kith, Katon, & Schmaling, 1997; Hudson, Goldenberg, Pope, Keck, & Schlesinger, 1992). For example, lifetime rates of affective disorders among patients with FM range from 20% to 86% (e.g., Aaron et al., 2000). Similarly, the lifetime rate of psychiatric disorders among patients with CFS is 82% (Buchwald et al., 1997).

The relationships between psychological distress and FM or CFS are quite complex. For example, we have found that there is no difference in number of lifetime psychiatric diagnoses between healthy individuals recruited from the community and community residents who meet criteria for FM but who have not consulted a physician for their painful symptoms during the preceding 10 years (i.e., FM nonpatients) (Aaron et al., 1996). This strongly suggests that high levels of psychological distress may contribute to the decision of individuals to seek health care for their FM symptoms, but are not necessary factors in the pathophysiology of the disorder.

Indeed, the results of our cross-sectional and longitudinal evaluations of these participants over a 30-month period are in accord with this interpretation. The cross-sectional study showed that, after controlling for demographic factors, time since onset of symptoms, and psychiatric morbidity, the four variables that best distinguished patients with FM from FM nonpatients were high levels of pain and negative affect, greater number of recent stressful experiences, and lower levels of self-efficacy for managing FM symptoms (Kersh et al., 2001). Longitudinal evaluation of 40 FM nonpatients showed that 10 individuals sought treatment from a physician during the 30-month follow-up (Aaron et al., 1997). Individuals who obtained medical care, relative to those who remained nonpatients, were more likely at baseline to report work-related stress, a psychiatric history of mood or substance abuse disorders, and use of prescription medication or medication for gastrointestinal disorders. However, the strongest predictor of seeking health care among these persons was the number of lifetime psychiatric diagnoses at baseline evaluation. These findings are consistent with the results of a population-based study in the United Kingdom that indicated, among women with widespread chronic pain, the risk of psychiatric illness among those who sought medical treatment was more than twice that of the women who did not seek medical care (MacFarlane et al., 1999).

It should be noted, however, that further analyses of the data derived from this population-based study have produced results that differ somewhat from those of our investigations. A 12-month follow-up assessment of the population (2,000–3,000 men and women), revealed that baseline reports of somatization symptoms (e.g., frequent vomiting, loss of voice, difficulty swallowing, frequent pain in the fingers and toes) were highly associated with the development of chronic widespread pain at follow-up (e.g., McBeth, Macfarlane, Benjamin, & Silman, 2001). One might suggest that this indicates FM is produced by somatic amplification. However, given that abnormal pain sensitivity was not evaluated in the subject population, we believe this finding simply shows that high numbers of medically unexplained symptoms at baseline predict the future development of chronic widespread pain. It does not indicate that medically unexplained symptoms accurately predict the development of both chronic widespread pain and the abnormal pain sensitivity that characterize FM.

Most studies of the association between CFS and psychological distress have examined associations between affective disorders and CFS. Similar to our findings regarding FM and psychiatric morbidity, it has been found that individuals with CFS in primary and tertiary care settings are characterized by higher frequencies of affective and anxiety disorders than persons with CFS in community settings. As expected, the frequencies of these disorders among patients with CFS in tertiary care settings are greater than those of patients with CFS in primary care settings (Katon & Walker, 1993). Two twin studies suggested that psychological distress rather than genetic factors or chronic pain in persons with CFS is associated with debilitating fatigue.

Roy-Byrne and colleagues (2002) found that, among monozygotic and dizygotic twin pairs who were discordant for chronic fatigue, the fatigued individuals reported higher levels of anxiety, somatic preoccupation, and social dysfunction than those without fatigue. However, the fatigued, monozygotic individuals did not differ from the fatigued, dizygotic individuals on these measures of distress. This suggests that genetic covariation does not strongly contribute to the association between chronic fatigue and psychological distress.

In a similar investigation, Aaron and colleagues (2002) evaluated both psychiatric morbidity and self-reports of psychological distress among monozygotic and dizygotic twin pairs who were discordant for chronic widespread or regional pain. The individuals with chronic pain were characterized by higher psychiatric morbidity and psychological distress than those without pain. However, these group differences were eliminated after controlling for the presence of CFS.

Emotional Trauma and Other Stressors

We noted in the section on neuroendocrine function that individuals with FM and CFS show similar abnormalities in HPA axis function at rest and in response to biological challenges associated with exposure to stressors. Indeed, there is evidence that women with FM, compared to women with osteoarthritis, report greater increases in pain after a 30-minute discussion of personally relevant stressful events (Davis et al., 2001). There currently are no reports of the effects of psychosocial stressors on pain or other symptoms associated with CFS. However, one study suggested a significant association between the onset of CFS and the experience of stressful life events, infection, and high fatigue levels (Theorell et al., 1999).

Patients with FM in tertiary care centers, compared to healthy controls, more frequently reported histories of sexual, physical, and emotional abuse (e.g., Alexander et al., 1998; Van Houdenhove et al., 2001). However, we found that nonpatients with FM did not differ from controls with regard to the frequency of sexual or physical abuse (Alexander et al., 1998). This suggests that, similar to our findings on psychiatric morbidity, high frequencies of abuse are associated with seeking treatment for FM at tertiary care centers, but are neither necessary nor sufficient for developing this disorder. Indeed, the results of a recent population-based study revealed that sexual or physical abuse is not a risk factor for the development of CFS (Taylor & Jason, 2001).

TREATMENT OF FIBROMYALGIA AND CHRONIC FATIGUE SYNDROME

Current interventions for the treatment or management FM and CFS are quite similar. Practice guidelines for CFS have been published (Royal Australasian College of Physicians, 2002); practice guidelines for FM are in preparation in the United States. These practice guidelines require the physician or medical director of the treatment team to develop an individualized management plan through active discussion with each patient.

Psychologists play an important role in formulating the management plan. First, psychologists may use structured interviews and brief, self-report questionnaires to achieve several important objectives: (a) obtain a history of events that may have precipitated the onset of the patient's

pain or fatigue as well as the course of these symptoms over time; (b) identify events that may precipitate increases in pain or fatigue and the events that follow (e.g., reinforce) these exacerbations; (c) evaluate the patient's daily activities to determine the extent to which the patient's behavior may exacerbate symptoms; (d) determine whether the patient has any friends or relatives who experience persistent pain or fatigue (i.e., evaluate possible modeling of illness behavior); and (e) evaluate the extent to which the patient experiences affective disturbance or psychiatric illness (Bradley & Mckendree-Smith, 2001). Psychologists can also usefully assess whether cognitive impairment may influence the patient's daily activities or ability to adhere to regimens. Finally, psychologists generally are asked to perform cognitive–behavioral interventions that will help patients develop improved skills for coping with persistent pain and fatigue.

Once the management plan is formulated, the physician/director of the treatment team should describe available pharmacological and behavioral (e.g., physical exercise, cognitive–behavioral therapy [CBT]) interventions as well as a schedule for provision of continuing medical care. It should be emphasized to the patient that treatment will probably not produce full remission of symptoms. However, an active collaboration between the treatment team and the patient is essential for the patient to achieve and maintain maximum functional capacity as well as reductions in pain and fatigue. Successful treatment may require endurance on the patient's part because satisfactory improvements may frequently take 6 to 9 months to occur.

The following review describes the current pharmacological and behavioral interventions frequently used for patients with FM or CFS. We limited our review to medications that currently are approved for use in the United States.

Pharmacological Interventions

Amitriptyline and Cyclobenzaprine

Initial pharmacological approaches for treating FM were influenced by the reports of low serotonin levels in patients with this disorder. Therefore, early studies focused on the efficacy of amitriptyline (Elavil), cyclobenzaprine (Flexeril), and other tricyclic antidepressants because they tend to increase the synaptic concentrations of serotonin throughout the central nervous system. The effects of the tricyclic antidepressants on symptoms of CFS have not been well studied because these medications tend to promote sedation or drowsiness. Amitriptyline is superior to placebo in decreasing patients' reports of pain intensity, sleep quality, and global symptom severity (e.g., Carette, McCain, Bell, & Fam, 1986). However, this medication rarely influences tender point counts or other measures of pain sensitivity. The outcomes produced by cyclobenzaprine are similar to those produced by amitriptyline (e.g., Bennett et al., 1988). However, cyclobenzaprine appears to induce more consistent improvements in patients' ratings of sleep than in pain intensity.

A meta-analysis of the influence of these medications on pain, sleep, fatigue, and other FM symptoms revealed a mean effect size of 0.43, indicating a moderate level of improvement (Arnold, Keck, & Welge, 2000). Nevertheless, there is strong evidence that the efficacy of these medications greatly diminishes over time (e.g., Carette et al., 1994).

Monoamine Oxidase Inhibitors

Monoamine oxidase inhibitors tend to increase concentrations of serotonin and catecholamine neurotransmitters throughout the central nervous system, and they do not have the sedating effects associated with the tricyclics described above. There are two studies of the effects of the monoamine oxidase inhibitors moclobemide and selegiline on patients with CFS. Both investigations revealed that these medications tend to improve subjective perceptions of vigor or energy (Hickie et al., 2000; Natelson et al., 1998). However, patients who take these medications should be carefully monitored for negative side effects such as agitation and insomnia.

Alprazolam, Selective Serotonin
Reuptake Inhibitors, and Other
Psychotropic Medications

Anxiety and depression tend to amplify pain perception. Therefore, alprazolam, the selective se-

rotonin reuptake inhibitors (SSRIs), and other psychotropics have been used to modify the pain associated with FM or CFS. Unfortunately, most of the outcome studies performed with these pharmacological agents are characterized by important methodologic weaknesses such as small sample sizes and low statistical power.

Nevertheless, two major findings have been produced to date in this literature. First, it has been shown that, among patients with FM, alprazolam and ibuprofen together produce significantly greater reductions than placebo in the tender point index and patients' ratings of disease severity (Russell, Fletcher, Michalek, McBroom, & Hester, 1991). The effects of these medications have not been assessed over prolonged follow-up periods, however.

Second, several trials suggested that fluoxetine, venlafaxine, and nefazodone produce significant improvements in symptoms of FM or CFS (e.g., Arnold et al., 2002; Dwight et al., 1998; Hickie, 2000). Two of these trials evaluated the effects of fluoxetine on patients with FM. A randomized, placebo-controlled trial (Arnold et al., 2002) revealed that fluoxetine, compared to placebo, produced significantly greater improvements in patients' reports of pain, fatigue, and depression on the Fibromyalgia Impact Questionnaire and the McGill Pain Questionnaire. In addition, Goldenberg and colleagues (Goldenberg, Mayskiy, Mossey, Ruthazer, & Schmid, 1996) reported that both fluoxetine and amitriptyline produced significant improvements in patients' reports of pain, sleep disturbance, and global well-being. However, a combination of these two medications produced greater improvements on these outcome measures than either of the drugs alone.

Venlafaxine and nefazodone are antidepressant medications that inhibit the reuptake of both serotonin and norepinephrine. Two open-label trials have produced preliminary evidence of the efficacy of these medications on patients with CFS. Dwight and colleagues (1998) found that venlafaxine produced clinically significant (>50%) reductions in FM symptoms in 6 of 11 patients who completed the open-label trial. Hickie (2000) reported similar effects in an open-label trial of nefazodone for patients with CFS. It was found that 8 of 10 patients reported moderate to marked improvements in sleep disturbance and mood, and 4 patients reported moderate to marked improvements in fatigue. Moreover, 5 patients returned either to work or to their previous levels of role function at the end of the trial. It is now necessary to determine whether similar improvements are produced by venlafaxine and nefazodone in randomized, placebo-controlled trials.

Behavioral Interventions

Aerobic Exercise

Exercise interventions produce positive effects on symptoms associated with both FM and CFS. However, there tends to be greater consistency in these positive effects in studies involving patients with CFS. McCain, Bell, Mai, and Halliday (1988) made a randomized, controlled study of the effects of aerobic exercise that has served as an excellent model for subsequent investigators. McCain and associates compared the outcomes produced by a 20-week cardiovascular fitness training program with those produced by training in flexibility exercises. It was found that cardiovascular fitness was superior to flexibility training in producing improvements in cardiovascular fitness indices, pain threshold, and subjective ratings of disease severity. Many investigators also reported that aerobic exercise programs are superior to flexibility training in improving cardiovascular fitness indices, attenuating clinical pain, and increasing physical function in patients with FM (e.g., Burckhardt, Mannerkorpi, Hendenberg, & Bjelle, 1994).

It should be noted, however, that some investigations have produced equivocal results regarding the benefits of aerobic exercise for FM (e.g., Ramsay et al., 2000). Moreover, a substantial number of studies indicated that the initial positive effects of exercise are not maintained at follow-up assessments as soon as 6 months (e.g., Gowans et al., 2001). Furthermore, there is no consensus regarding the type, intensity, and duration of exercise that should be delivered to patients with FM.

Contrary to the literature on exercise for FM, three randomized, controlled trials showed that graded exercise produces significant improvements on both physical and psychosocial outcome measures among patients with CFS. For example, Powell, Bentall, Nye, and Edwards (2001) compared the effects of three exercise interventions and standard medical care to the effects of standard care alone at posttreatment and at 1-year follow-up. The exercise interventions varied on the number of individualized training sessions delivered to participants (two to seven sessions) as well as the number of telephone "booster" calls made to participants during follow-up (0 to 7 weeks). It was found that, at the 1-year follow-up session, participants in all three exercise intervention groups, compared to those who only received standard medical care, reported significantly greater improvements on a standardized measure of physical function as well as on standardized measures of anxiety and depression. Moreover, there were no differences in outcomes among the three exercise treatment conditions.

Which factors might account for the differences in outcomes produced by aerobic exercise in patients with FM versus those with CFS? One factor may be that the abnormal pain sensitivity associated with FM may produce greater clinical pain experiences among the patients with FM during the early stages of exercise training. High levels of pain may represent barriers to the initiation or maintenance of a prescribed exercise program. Indeed, Mengshoel, Vollestad, and Forre (1995) reported that patients with FM, compared to sedentary healthy subjects, reported higher levels of exertion, fatigue, and exercise-induced extremity pain after aerobic exercise despite similar levels of cardiovascular fitness. Similar findings have been reported in recent laboratory studies of abnormal pain sensitivity in patients with FM (Vierck et al., 2001). As noted, this effect may be more highly related to female sex than to the pathophysiology of FM. Nevertheless, abnormal pain modulation may contribute to the inconsistent findings concerning exercise effects in persons with FM.

Cognitive–Behavioral Therapy

Comprehensive CBT interventions provide (a) education regarding current models of the pathophysiology of FM and CFS; (b) training in skills for managing pain, fatigue, and related symptoms; (c) opportunities to practice these self-management skills in the treatment setting as well as the home and work environments; (d) opportunities to alter the self-management skills as a function of the outcomes that are produced; and (e) practice of behaviors that may enhance maintenance of the self-management skills after termination of the CBT intervention (see Bradley, 1996, for a detailed description of these treatment components).

We should emphasize that it is very important to incorporate strategies for the prevention of relapse early in CBT treatment for FM and CFS. There are several relapse prevention strategies that may be incorporated in CBT protocols. The first is to teach patients to identify high-risk situations likely to trigger increases in pain or fatigue as well as provide opportunities to practice strategies for avoiding or coping with these situations. Second, it is important for patients to rehearse behavioral and cognitive strategies for coping with setbacks (e.g., reducing negative self-talk) and to practice using self-control skills to maintain frequent practice of coping skills in their home or work environments (e.g., self-monitoring and self-reinforcement). Third, a series of booster sessions following treatment termination should be incorporated that will reinforce patients for coping effectively with symptom flares and setbacks and provide an opportunity to develop alternative strategies for new coping problems that may emerge after termination. Finally, there is consistent evidence that including spouses or significant others in CBT protocols is associated with greater patient improvement. For example, training spouses in behavioral methods such as communication skills and social reinforcement for healthy behavior enhances the family's understanding of CBT treatment and may promote patients' practice and maintenance of learned coping skills (Keefe & Van Horn, 1993).

Many investigations without appropriate attention-placebo controls have shown that CBT interventions produce statistically or clinically significant reductions in patients' displays of pain sensitivity (e.g., tender point counts) and their ratings of pain, other clinical symptoms, and functional disability (e.g., Williams et al., 2002). Some of these investigations also reported that improvements in ratings of pain or functional ability were maintained for up to 30 months after

treatment termination (e.g., White & Nielson, 1995).

However, all of the CBT investigations with adequate attention-placebo controls produced negative findings regarding changes in self-reports of pain and measures of pain sensitivity, such as the tender point count (e.g., Vlaeyen et al., 1996). At present, then, CBT interventions cannot be considered superior to placebo for the treatment of FM. Nevertheless, we and our colleagues have successfully used CBT to help patients with FM better manage their pain.

What factors might account for the negative outcomes associated with the placebo-controlled trials? It is important to note that these trials have used treatment manuals based on those used successfully in trials of patients with diseases such as rheumatoid arthritis and osteoarthritis of the knee. Patients with these diseases, compared to patients with FM, are characterized by lower levels of psychological distress and generalized pain sensitivity. Therefore, future investigators may have to (a) modify patient inclusion/exclusion criteria to exclude patients with extremely high levels of psychological distress and (b) alter the content of CBT interventions that they may better help patients cope with abnormal, generalized pain sensitivity and its effects on their behavior and quality of life.

Early studies of the effects of CBT interventions for CFS produced negative findings (e.g., Lloyd et al., 1990). However, more recent studies have consistently found that CBT, compared to control conditions such as relaxation training and social support interventions (e.g., Deale, Chalder, Marks, & Wessely, 1997) produce significantly greater improvements on fatigue severity and functional impairment. Moreover, these investigations have reported that the outcomes for patients receiving CBT remain superior to those of the control condition patients at follow-up periods ranging from 14 months (Prins et al., 2001) to 5 years (Deale, Husain, Chalder, & Wessely, 2001). It should be noted, however, that, in contrast to the studies concerning CBT for patients with FM, the studies described above did not attempt to evaluate whether the CBT and control condition patients initially perceived their treatment interventions as equal in credibility or in their potential to reduce symptom severity. Thus, it is possible that the superior outcomes produced by the CBT interventions for CFS may be mediated in part by group differences in initial expectations for improvement. Nevertheless, it also may be that the superior outcomes produced by CBT for patients with CFS versus those with FM are caused in part by patient group differences in abnormal pain sensitivity.

SUMMARY

FM and CFS are frustrating, overlapping conditions frequently found in conjunction with psychological problems. These conditions are more common among women and are associated with higher levels of medical help-seeking. Primary care psychologists are likely to encounter patients with these conditions, although they should recognize that there are many individuals who are nonpatients who also would meet criteria for the conditions, but who do not present for treatment. Characteristics of those who do seek medical care for their FM and CFS are that they have significantly high levels of psychological distress and perhaps lower levels of social support. Although a number of promising avenues of research have suggested mechanisms that would produce the abnormal pain sensitivity characteristic of FM and the abnormal fatigue characteristic of CFS, etiological understanding is still developing. Treatment, both pharmacological and psychological, focuses mainly on management rather than "cure."

Primary care psychologists can help patients with FM and CFS, and can help primary care physicians manage these patients, by providing CBT, exercise-promoting interventions, and psychoeducation regarding the conditions. CBT, exercise, and medications can also help reduce fatigue and decrease pain; psychological treatment that does not overpromise relief from symptoms but offers the prospect of improved management as well as sensitive and empathic listening can help decrease patients' suffering.

ACKNOWLEDGMENTS Preparation of this chapter was supported by the National Institute of Arthritis, Musculoskeletal and Skin Disease (1 RO1 AR43136; P60 AR 48095) and the National Center for Research Resources (5M0100032).

References

Aaron, L. A., Arguelles, L. M., Ashton, S., Belcourt, M., Herrell, R., Goldberg, J., Smith, W. R., & Buchwald, D. (2002). Health and functional status of twins with chronic regional and widespread pain. *Journal of Rheumatology, 29,* 2426–2434.

Aaron, L. A., Bradley, L. A., Alarcon, G. S., Alexander, R. W., Triana-Alexander, M., Martin, M. Y., & Alberts, K. R. (1996). Psychiatric diagnoses are related to health care seeking behavior rather than illness in fibromyalgia. *Arthritis and Rheumatism, 39,* 436–445.

Aaron, L. A., Bradley, L. A., Alarcon, G. S., Triana-Alexander, M., Alexander, R. W., Martin, M. Y., et al. (1997). Work stress, psychiatric history, and medication usage predict initial use of medical treatment for fibromyalgia symptoms: A prospective analysis. In T. S. Jensen, J. A. Turner, & Z. Wiesenfeld-Hallin (Eds.), *Proceedings of the Seventh World Congress on Pain. Progress in pain research and management* (Vol. 8, pp. 683–691). Seattle, WA: IASP Press.

Aaron, L. A., Burke, M. M., & Buchwald, D. (2000). Overlapping conditions among patients with chronic fatigue syndrome, fibromyalgia, and temporomandibular disorder. *Archives of Internal Medicine, 160,* 221–227.

Alarcón, G. S. (1999). Fibromyalgia: Dispelling diagnostic and treatment myths. Is this common condition organic or affective? *Women's Health in Primary Care, 2,* 775–784.

Alexander, R. W., Bradley, L. A., Alarcón, G. S., Triana-Alexander, M., Aaron, L. A., Alberts, K. R., Martin, M. Y., & Stewart, K. E. (1998). Sexual and physical abuse in women with fibromyalgia: Association with outpatient health care utilization and pain medication usage. *Arthritis Care and Research, 11,* 102–115.

Arnold, L. M., Hess, E. V., Hudson, J. I., Welge, J. A., Berno, S. E., & Keck, P. E. (2002). A randomized, placebo-controlled, double-blind, flexible-dose study of fluoxetine in the treatment of women with fibromyalgia. *American Journal of Medicine, 112,* 191–197.

Arnold, L. M., Keck, P. E., & Welge, J. A. (2000). Antidepressant treatment of fibromyalgia: A meta-analysis and review. *Psychosomatics, 41,* 104–113.

Bakheit, A. M., Behan, P. O., Dinan, T. G., Gray, C. E., & O'Keane, V. (1992). Possible upregulation of hypothalamic 5-hydroxytryptamine receptors in patients with postviral fatigue syndrome. *British Medical Journal, 304,* 1010–1012.

Barsky, A. J., & Borus, J. F. (1999). Functional somatic syndromes. *Annals of Internal Medicine, 130,* 910–921.

Bennett, R. M., Clark, S. R., Campbell, S. M., & Burckhardt, C. S. (1992). Low levels of somatomedin C in patients with the fibromyalgia syndrome: A possible link between sleep and muscle pain. *Arthritis and Rheumatism, 35,* 1113–1116.

Bennett, R. M., Clark, S. C., & Walczyk, J. (1998). A randomized, double-blind, placebo-controlled study of growth hormone in the treatment of fibromyalgia. *American Journal of Medicine, 104*(3), 227–231.

Bennett, R. M., Gatter, R. A., Campbell, S. M., Andrews, R. P., Clark, S. R., & Scarola, J. A. (1988). A comparison of cyclobenzaprine and placebo in the management of fibrositis. A double-blind controlled study. *Arthritis and Rheumatism, 31,* 1535–1542.

Bombardier, C. H., & Buchwald, D. (1995). Outcome and prognosis of patients with chronic fatigue vs. chronic fatigue syndrome. *Archives of Internal Medicine, 155,* 2105–2110.

Bradley, L. A. (1996). Cognitive-behavioral therapy for chronic pain. In R. J. Gatchel & D. C. Turk (Eds.), *Psychological approaches to pain management: A practitioner's handbook* (pp. 131–147). New York: Guilford Press.

Bradley, L. A., & McKendree-Smith, N. L. (2001). Assessment of psychological status using interviews and self-report instruments. In D. C. Turk & R. Melzack (Eds.), *Handbook of pain assessment* (2nd ed., pp. 292–319). New York: Guilford Press.

Bradley, L. A., McKendree-Smith, N. L., & Alarcón, G. S. (2001). Pain complaints in patients with fibromyalgia versus chronic fatigue syndrome. *Current Review of Pain, 4,* 148–157.

Bradley, L. A., Sotolongo, A., Alarcón, G. S., Mountz, J. M., Alberts, K. R., et al. (1999). Dolorimeter stimulation elicits abnormal pain sensitivity and regional cerebral blood flow (rCBF) in the right cingulate cortex (CC) as well as passive coping strategies in nondepressed patients with fibromyalgia (FM). *Arthritis and Rheumatism, 42* (Suppl. 9), 342–347.

Bradley, L. A., Sotolongo, A., Alberts, K. R., Alarcón, G. S., Mountz, J. M., Liu, H. G., Kersh, B. C., Domino, M. L., DeWaal, D., Weigent, D. A., & Blalock, J. E. (1999). Abnormal regional cerebral blood flow in the caudate nucleus among fibromyalgia patients and nonpatients is associated with insidious symptom onset. *Journal of Musculoskeletal Pain, 7,* 285–292.

Buchwald, D. (1996). Fibromyalgia and chronic fatigue syndrome: Similarities and differences. *Rheumatic Disease Clinics of North America, 22,* 219–243.

Buchwald, D., Cheney, P. R., Peterson, D. L., Henry, B., Wormsley, S. B., Geiger, A., Ablashi, D. V., Salahuddin, S. Z., Saxinger, C., & Biddle, R. (1992). A chronic illness characterized by fatigue, neurologic and immunologic disorders, and active human herpesvirus type 6 infection. *Annals of Internal Medicine, 116,* 103–113.

Buchwald, D., Herrell, R., Ashton, S., Belcourt, M., Schmaling, K., Sullivan, P., Neale, M., & Goldberg, J. (2001). A twin study of chronic fatigue. *Psychosomatic Medicine, 63,* 936–943.

Buchwald, D., Pearlman, T., Kith, P., Katon, W., & Schmaling, K. (1997). Screening for psychiatric disorders in chronic fatigue and chronic fatigue syndrome. *Journal of Psychosomatic Research, 42,* 87–94.

Burckhardt, C. S., Mannerkorpi, K., Hendenberg, L., & Bjelle, A. (1994). A randomized, controlled clinical trial of education and physical training for women with fibromyalgia. *Journal of Rheumatology, 21,* 714–720.

Buskila, D., & Neumann, L. (1997). Fibromyalgia syndrome (FM) and nonarticular tenderness in relatives of patients with FM. *Journal of Rheumatology, 24,* 941–944.

Carette, S., Bell, M. J., Reynolds, W. J., Haráoui, B., McCain, G. A., Bykerk, V. P., Edworthy, S. M., Baron, M., Koehler, B. E., & Fam, A. G. (1994). Comparison of amitriptyline, cyclobenzaprine, and placebo in the treatment of fibromyalgia: A randomized, double-blind clinical trial. *Arthritis and Rheumatism, 37,* 32–40.

Carette, S., McCain, G. A., Bell, D. A., & Fam, A. G. (1986). Evaluation of amitriptyline in primary fibrositis: A double-blind, placebo-controlled study. *Arthritis and Rheumatism, 29,* 655–659.

Clauw, D. J., Bennett, R. M., Petzke, F., & Rosner, M. J. (2000). Prevalence of Chiari malformation and cervical stenosis in fibromyalgia. *Arthritis and Rheumatism, 43*(Suppl.), S173.

Clauw, D. J., & Chrousos, G. P. (1997). Chronic pain and fatigue syndromes: Overlapping clinical and neuroendocrine features and potential pathogenic mechanisms. *Neuroimmunomodulation, 4,* 134–153.

Cohen, H., Buskila, D., Neumann, L., & Ebstein, R. P. (2002). Confirmation of an association between fibromyalgia and serotonin transporter promoter region (5-HTTLPR) polymorphism, and relationship to anxiety-related personality traits. *Arthritis and Rheumatism, 46,* 845–847.

Costa, D. C., Tannock, C., & Brostoff, J. (1995). Brainstem perfusion is impaired in chronic fatigue syndrome. *Quarterly Journal of Medicine, 88,* 767–773.

Cote, K. A., & Moldofsky, H. (1997). Sleep, daytime symptoms, cognitive performance in patients with fibromyalgia. *Journal of Rheumatology, 24,* 2014–2023.

Crofford, L. J., Pillemer, S. R., Kalogeras, K. T., Cash, J. M., Michelson, D., Kling, M. A., Sternberg, E. M., Gold, P. W., Chrousos, G. P., & Wilder, R. L. (1994). Hypothalamic-pituitary-adrenal axis perturbations in patients with fibromyalgia. *Arthritis and Rheumatism, 37,* 1583–1592.

Davis, M. C., Zautra, A. J., & Reich, J. W. (2001). Vulnerability to stress among women in chronic pain from fibromyalgia and osteoarthritis. *Annals of Behavioral Medicine, 23,* 215–226.

Deale, A., Chalder, T., Marks, I., & Wessely, S. (1997). Cognitive behavior therapy for chronic fatigue syndrome: A randomized controlled trial. *American Journal of Psychiatry, 154,* 408–414.

Deale, A., Husain, K., Chalder, T., & Wessely, S. (2001). Long-term outcome of cognitive behavior therapy versus relaxation therapy for chronic fatigue syndrome: A 5-year follow-up study. *American Journal of Psychiatry, 158,* 2038–2042.

Demitrack, M. A. (1998). Chronic fatigue syndrome and fibromyalgia: Dilemmas in diagnosis and clinical management. *Psychiatric Clinics of North America, 21,* 671–697.

Demitrack, M. A., & Crofford, L. J. (1998). Evidence for and pathological implications of hypothalamic-pituitary-adrenal axis dysregulation in fibromyalgia and chronic fatigue syndrome. *Annals of the New York Academy of Sciences, 840,* 684–697.

Demitrack, M. A., Gold, P. W., Dale, J. K., Krahn, D. D., Kling, M. A., & Straus, S. E. (1992). Plasma and cerebrospinal fluid monoamine metabolism in patients with chronic fatigue syndrome: Preliminary findings. *Biological Psychiatry, 32,* 1065–1077.

Dwight, M. D., Arnold, L. M., O'Brien, H., Metzger, R., Morris-Park, E., & Keck, P. E. (1998). An open clinical trial of venlafaxine treatment of fibromyalgia. *Psychosomatics, 39,* 14–17.

Evengard, B., Nilsson, C. G., Lindh, G., Lindquist, L., Eneroth, P., Fredrickson, S., Tereniuo, L., & Henriksson, K. G. (1998). Chronic fatigue syndrome differs from fibromyalgia. No evidence for elevated substance P levels in cerebrospinal fluid of patients with chronic fatigue syndrome. *Pain, 78,* 153–155.

Forseth, D. O., Forre, O., & Gran, J. T. (1999). A 5.5 year prospective study of self-reported musculoskeletal pain and of fibromyalgia in a female population: Significance and natural history. *Clinical Rheumatology, 18,* 114–121.

Fukuda, K., Straus, S. E., Hickie, I., Sharpe, M. C., Dobbins, J. G., & Komaroff, A. (1994). The chronic fatigue syndrome: A comprehensive approach to its definition and study. *Annals of Internal Medicine, 121,* 953–959.

Garland, E. M., & Robertson, D. (2001). Chiari I malformation as a cause of orthostatic intolerance symptoms: A media myth? *American Journal of Medicine, 111,* 546–552.

Gerrity, T. R., Bates, J., Bell, D. S., Chrousos, G., Furst, G., Hedrick, T., Hurwitz, B., Kula, R. W., Levine, S. M., Moore, R. C., & Schondorf, R. (2003). Chronic fatigue syndrome: What role does the autonomic nervous system play in the pathophysiology of this complex illness? *Neuroimmunomodulation, 10,* 134–141.

Gibson, J. J., Littlejohn, G. O., Gorman, M. M., Helme, R. D., & Granges, G. (1994). Altered heat pain thresholds and cerebral event-related potentials following painful CO_2 laser stimulation in subjects with fibromyalgia syndrome. *Pain, 58,* 185–193.

Giovengo, S. L., Russell, I. J., & Larson, A. A. (1999). Increased concentrations of nerve growth factor in cerebrospinal fluid of patients with fibromyalgia. *Journal of Rheumatology, 26,* 1564–1569.

Goebel, M. U., Mills, P. J., Irwin, M. R., & Ziegler, M. G. (2000). Interleukin-6 and tumor necrosis factor-α production after acute psy-

chological stress, exercise, and infused isopro-
terenol: Differential effects and pathways.
Psychosomatic Medicine, 62, 591–598.

Goldenberg, D., Mayskiy, M., Mossey, C., Ruthazer, R., & Schmid, C. (1996). A randomized, double-blind corssover trial of fluoxetine
and amitriptyline in the treatment of fibromyalgia. *Arthritis & Rheumatism, 39*(11),
1852–1859.

Goldman, J. A. (1991). Hypermobility and deconditioning: Important links to fibromyalgia/
fibrositis. *Southern Medical Journal, 84,* 1192–
1196.

Gowans, S. E., deHueck, A., Voss, S., Silaj, A., Abbey, S. E., & Reynolds, W. J. (2001). Effect of
a randomized, controlled trial of exercise on
mood and physical function in individuals
with fibromyalgia. *Arthritis and Rheumatism,
45,* 519–529.

Gracely, R. H., Petzke, F., Wolf, J. M., & Clauw,
D. J. (2002). Functional magnetic resonance
imaging evidence of augmented pain processing in fibromyalgia. *Arthritis and Rheumatism,
46,* 1333–1343.

Gur, A., Karakoc, M., Nas, K., Remzi, Cevik, Den-
li, A., & Sarac, J. (2002). Cytokines and depression in cases with fibromyalgia. *Journal of
Rheumatology, 29,* 358–361.

Harding, S. M. (1998). Sleep in fibromyalgia patients: Subjective and objective findings. *American Journal of Medical Science, 315,* 367–376.

Hickie, I. (2000). Nefazodone for patients with
chronic fatigue syndrome. *Australian and New
Zealand Journal of Psychiatry, 33,* 278.

Hickie, I. B., Wilson, A. J., Wright, J. M., Bennett,
B. K., Wakefield, D., & Lloyd, A. R. (2000). A
randomized, double-blind, placebo-controlled
trial of moclobemide in patients with chronic
fatigue syndrome. *Journal of Clinical Psychiatry, 61,* 643–648.

Holmes, M. C., Di Renzo, G., Beckford, U.,
Gillham, B., & Jones, M. T. (1982). Role of
serotonin in the control of secretion of cortico-
trophin releasing factor. *Journal of Endocrinology, 93,* 151–160.

Hudson, J. I., Goldenberg, D. L., Pope, H. G.,
Keck, P. E., & Schlesinger, L. (1992). Comorbidity of fibromyalgia with medical and psychiatric disorders. *American Journal of Medicine, 92,* 363–367.

Iadarola, M. J., Max, M. B., Berman, K. F., Byas-
Smith, M. G., Coghill, R. C., Gracely, R. H.,
& Bennett, G. J. (1995). Unilateral decrease in
thalamic activity observed with positron emission tomography in patients with chronic neuropathic pain. *Pain, 63,* 55–64.

Jason, L. A., Richman, J. A., Rademaker, A. W.,
Jordon, K. M., Plioplys, A. V., Taylor, R. R.,
McCready, W., Huang, C. F., & Plioplys, S.
(1999). A community-based study of chronic
fatigue syndrome. *Archives of Internal Medicine, 159,* 2129–2137.

Katon, W. J., & Walker, E. A. (1993). The relationship of chronic fatigue to psychiatric illness in
community, primary care and tertiary care
samples. *Ciba Foundation Symposium, 173,*
193–204.

Keefe, F. J., & Van Horn, Y. (1993). Cognitive-behavioral treatment of rheumatoid arthritis
pain. *Arthritis Care and Research, 6,* 213–222.

Kersh, B. C., Bradley, L. A., Alarcon, G. S., Alberts, K. R., Sotolongo, A., Martin, M. Y.,
Aaron, L. A., Dewaal, D. F., Domino, M. L.,
Chaplin, W. F., Palardy, N. R., Cianfrini,
L. R., & Triana-Alexander, M. (2001). Psychosocial and health status variables independently predict health care seeking in fibromyalgia. *Arthritis and Rheumatism, 45,* 362–371.

Lautenbacher, S., & Rollman, G. B. (1997). Possible deficiencies of pain modulation in fibromyalgia. *Clinical Journal of Pain, 13,* 189–196.

Lentz, M. J., Landis, C. A., Rathermel, J., &
Shaver, J. L. F. (1999). Effects of selective
slow wave sleep disruption on musculoskeletal
pain and fatigue in middle aged women. *Journal of Rheumatology, 26,* 1586–1592.

Lewis, D. H., Mayberg, H. S., Fischer, M. E., Goldberg, J., Ashton, S., Graham, M. M., Buchwald D. (2001). Monozygotic twins discordant for chronic fatigue syndrome: Regional
cerebral blood flow SPECT. *Radiology, 219,*
766–773.

Lloyd, A. R., Hickie, I., Boughton, C. R., Spencer,
O., & Wakefield, D. (1990). Prevalence of
chronic fatigue syndrome in an Australian
population. *Medical Journal of Australia, 153,*
522–528.

MacFarlane, G. J., Morris, S., Hunt, I. M., Benjamin, S., McBeth, J., Papageorgiou, A. C., &
Silman, A. J. (1999). Chronic widespread pain
in the community: The influence of psychological symptoms and mental disorder on healthcare seeking behavior. *Journal of Rheumatology,
26,* 413–419.

McBeth, J., Macfarlane, G. J., Benjamin, S., & Silman, A. J. (2001). Features of somatization

predict the onset of chronic widespread pain: Results of a large population-based study. *Arthritis and Rheumatism, 44*, 940–946.

McCain, G. A., Bell, D. A., Mai, F. M., & Halliday, P. D. (1988). A controlled study of the effects of a supervised cardiovascular fitness training program on the manifestations of primary fibromyalgia. *Arthritis and Rheumatism, 31*, 1135–1141.

Mengshoel, A. M., Vollestad, N. K., & Forre, O. (1995). Pain and fatigue induced by exercise in fibromyalgia patients and sedentary healthy subjects. *Clinical and Experimental Rheumatology, 13*, 477–482.

Moldofsky, H., Scarisbrick, P., England, R., & Smythe, H. (1975). Musculoskeletal symptoms and non-REM sleep disturbances in patients with fibrositis syndrome and healthy subjects. *Psychosomatic Medicine, 37*, 341–351.

Mountz, J. M., Bradley, L. A., Modell, J. G., Alexander, R. W., Triana-Alexander, M., Aaron, L. A., Stewart, K. E., Alarcon, G. S., & Mountz, J. D. (1995). Fibromyalgia in women. Abnormalities of regional cerebral blood flow in the thalamus and the caudate nucleus are associated with low pain threshold levels. *Arthritis and Rheumatism, 38*, 926–938.

Natelson, B. H., Cheu, J., Hill, N., Bergen, M., Korn, L., Denny, T., & Dahl, K. (1998). Single-blind, placebo phase-in trial of two escalating doses of selegiline in the chronic fatigue syndrome. *Neuropsychobiology, 37*, 150–154.

Offenbaecher, M., Bondy, B., de Jonge, S., Glatzeder, K., Kruger, M., Schoeps, P., & Ackenheil, M. (1999). Possible association of fibromyalgia with a polymorphism in the serotonin transporter gene regulatory region. *Arthritis Rheumatology, 42*, 2482–2488.

Okifuji, A., Turk, D. C., Sinclair, J. D., Starz, T. W., & Marcus, D. A. (1997). A standardized manual tender point survey. I. Development of a threshold point for the identification of positive tender points in fibromyalgia syndrome. *Journal of Rheumatology, 24*, 377–383.

Park, D. C., Glass, J. M., Minear, M., & Crofford, L. J. (2001). Cognitive function in fibromyalgia patients. *Arthritis and Rheumatism, 44*, 2125–2133.

Patarca-Montero, R., Antoni, M., Fletcher, M. A., & Klimas, N. G. (2001). Cytokine and other immunologic markers in chronic fatigue syndrome and their relation to neuropsychological factors. *Applied Neuropsychology, 8*, 51–64.

Pellegrino, M. J., Waylonis, G. W., & Sommer, A. (1989). Familial occurrence of primary fibromyalgia. *Archives of Physical Medicine and Rehabilitation, 70*, 61–63.

Pillemer, S. R., Bradley, L. A., Crofford, L. J., Moldofsky, H., & Chrousos, G. (1997). The neuroscience and endocrinology of fibromyalgia. *Arthritis and Rheumatism, 40*, 1928–1937.

Poyhia, R., Da Costa, D., & Fitzcharles, M. A. (2001). Pain and pain relief in fibromyalgia patients followed for three years. *Arthritis and Rheumatism, 45*, 355–361.

Powell, P., Bentall, R. P., Nye, F. J., & Edwards, R. H. (2001). Randomised controlled trial of patient education to encourage graded exercise in chronic fatigue syndrome. *British Medical Journal, 322*, 387–390.

Prins, J. B., Bleijenberg, G., Bazelmans, E., Elving, L. D., de Boo, T. M., Severens, J. L., van der Wilt, G. J., Spinhoven, P., & van der Meer, J. W. (2001). Cognitive behaviour therapy for chronic fatigue syndrome: A multicentre randomised controlled trial. *Lancet, 357*, 841–847.

Ramsay, C., Moreland, J., Hol, M., Joyce, S., Walker, S., & Pullar, T. (2000). An observer-blinded comparison of supervised and unsupervised aerobic exercise regimens in fibromyalgia. *Rheumatology, 39*, 501–505.

Ross, S., Fantie, B., Straus, S. F., & Grafman, J. (2001). Divided attention deficits in patients with chronic fatigue syndrome. *Applied Neuropsychology, 8*, 4–11.

Royal Australasian College of Physicians. (2002). Clinical practice guidelines: Chronic fatigue syndrome. *Medical Journal of Australia, 178* (Suppl.), S17–S55.

Roy-Byrne, P., Afari, N., Ashton, S., Fischer, M., Goldberg, J., & Buchwald, D. (2002). Chronic fatigue and anxiety/depression: A twin study. *British Journal of Psychiatry, 180*, 29–34.

Russell, I. J., Fletcher, E. M., Michalek, J. E., McBroom, P. C., & Hester, G. G. (1991). Treatment of primary fibrositis/fibromyalgia syndrome with ibuprofen and alprazolam: A double-blind, placebo-controlled study. *Arthritis and Rheumatism, 34*, 552–560.

Russell, I. J., Orr, M. D., Littman, B., Vipraio, G. A., Alboukrek, D., Michalek, J. E., Lopez, Y., & MacKillip, F. (1994). Elevated cerebrospinal fluid levels of substance P in patients with the fibromyalgia syndrome. *Arthritis and Rheumatism, 37*, 1593–1601.

Schanberg, L. E., Keefe, F. J., Lefebvre, J. C., Kredich, D. W., & Gil, K. M. (1996). Pain coping strategies in children with juvenile primary fibromyalgia syndrome: Correlation with pain, physical function, and psychological distress. *Arthritis Care and Research, 9,* 89–96.

Staud, R., Robinson, M. E., Vierck, C. J., & Price, D. D. (2003). Diffuse noxious inhibitory controls (DNIC) attenuate temporal summation of second pain in normal males but not in normal females or fibromyalgia patients. *Pain, 101,* 167–174.

Taylor, R. R., & Jason, L. A. (2001). Sexual abuse, physical abuse, chronic fatigue, and chronic fatigue syndrome: A community-based study. *Journal of Nervous and Mental Disease, 189,* 709–715.

Theorell, T., Blomkvist, V., Lindh, G., & Evengard, B. (1999). Critical life events, infections, and symptoms during the year preceding chronic fatigue syndrome (CFS): An examination of CFS patients and subjects with a nonspecific life crisis. *Psychosomatic Medicine, 61,* 304–310.

Tirelli, U., Chierichetti, F., Tavio, M., Simonelli, C., Bianchin, G., Zanco, P., & Ferlin, G. (1998). Brain positron emission tomography (PET) in chronic fatigue syndrome: Preliminary data. *American Journal of Medicine, 105*(Suppl.), 54S–58S.

Valdini, A. F., Steinhardt, S., Valicenti, J., & Jaffe, A. (1988). A one-year follow-up of fatigued patients. *Family Practice Research Journal, 6,* 175–188.

Van der Werf, S. P., de Vree, B., Alberts, M., van der Meer, J. W. M., & Bleijenberg, G. (2001). Natural course and predicting self-reported improvement in patients with chronic fatigue syndrome with a relatively short illness duration. *Journal of Psychosomatic Research, 53,* 749–753.

Van Houdenhove, B., Neerinckx, E., Lysens, R., Vertommen, H., Van Houdenhove, L., Onghena, P., Westhovens, R., & D'Hooghe, M. B. (2001). Victimization in chronic fatigue syndrome and fibromyalgia in tertiary care: A controlled study on prevalence and characteristics. *Psychosomatics, 42,* 21–28.

Vierck, C. K., Staud, R., Price, D. D., Cannon, R. L., Mauderli, A. P., & Martin, D. A. (2001). The effect of maximal exercise on temporal summation of second pain (windup) in patients with fibromyalgia syndrome. *Journal of Pain, 2,* 334–344.

Vlaeyen, J. W., Teeken-Gruben, N. J., Goossens, M. E., Rutten-van Molken, M. P., Pelt, R. A., van Eek, H., & Heuts, P. H. (1996). Cognitive-educational treatment of fibromyalgia: A randomized clinical trail. I. Clinical effects. *Journal of Rheumatology, 23,* 1237–1245.

Waylonis, G. W., & Perkins, R. H. (1994). Posttraumatic fibromyalgia. A long-term follow-up. *American Journal of Physical Medicine and Rehabilitation, 73,* 403–412.

Weigent, D. A., Bradley, L. A., Blalock, J. E., & Alarcón, G. S. (1998). Current concepts in the pathophysiology of abnormal pain perception in fibromyalgia. *American Journal of Medical Science, 315,* 405–412.

Whelton, C. L., Salit, I., & Moldofsky, H. (1992). Sleep, Epstein-Barr virus infection, musculoskeletal pain, and depressive symptoms in chronic fatigue syndrome. *Journal of Rheumatology, 19,* 939–943.

White, K. C., Speechly, M., Harth, M., & Ostliye, T. (1999). The London fibromyalgia epidemiology study: The prevalence of fibromyalgia syndrome in London, Ontario. *Journal of Rheumatology, 26,* 1570–1576.

White, K. P., & Nielson, W. R. (1995). Cognitive-behavioral treatment of fibromyalgia syndrome: A follow-up assessment. *Journal of Rheumatology, 22,* 717–721.

Williams, D. A., Cary, M. A., Groner, K. H., Chaplin, W., Glazer, L. J., Rodriguez, A. M., & Clauw, D. J. (2002). Improving physical functional status in patients with fibromyalgia: A brief cognitive behavioral intervention. *Journal of Rheumatology, 29,* 1280–1286.

Wolfe, F., Ross, K., Anderson, J., Russell, I. J., & Hebert, L. (1995). The prevalence and characteristics of fibromyalgia in the general population. *Arthritis and Rheumatism, 38,* 19–28.

Wolfe, F., Russell, I. J., Vipraio, G., Ross, K., & Anderson, J. (1997). Serotonin levels, pain threshold, and fibromyalgia symptoms in the general population. *Journal of Rheumatology, 24,* 555–559.

Wolfe, F., Smythe, H. A., Yunus, M. B., Bennett, R. M., Bombardier, C., Goldenberg, D. L., Tugwell, P., Campbell, S. M., Abeles, M., Clark, P., et al. (1990). The American College of Rheumatology 1990 criteria for the classification of fibromyalgia. Report of the Multicenter Criteria Committee. *Arthritis and Rheumatism, 33,* 160–172.

Yunus, M. B. (1994). Fibromyalgia syndrome:

Clinical features and spectrum. In S. R. Pillemer (Ed.), *The fibromyalgia syndrome: Current research and future directions in epidemiology, pathogenesis, and treatment* (pp. 5–21). Binghamton, NY: Haworth Medical Press.

Yunus, M. B., & Masi, A. T. (1985). Juvenile primary fibromyalgia syndrome: A clinical study of thirty-three patients and matched healthy controls. *Arthritis and Rheumatism, 28,* 138–145.

27

Grief and End-of-Life Issues

Scott T. Michael
Julia Kasl-Godley
Steven Lovett
Antonette M. Zeiss

Despite the obvious prevalence of death and dying issues in primary care settings, they may be easily overlooked because of time pressures and beliefs that such issues are the domain of other settings (e.g., hospices, mental health care clinics, etc.). As a result, a large population of patients and their families may not receive needed and important care. Primary care psychologists are very likely to work with older patients and patients with life-limiting diseases in primary care settings. Furthermore, when patients die, their families may need clinical attention. The primary care psychologist is in a unique position to give care to this underserved population and to facilitate care from other clinicians in their setting who might otherwise be unaware of the needs of their patients.

Our aim in this chapter is to discuss some of the end-of-life and bereavement issues that primary care psychologists may face and to provide practical advice, based in the empirical literature, for addressing such issues.

END-OF-LIFE ISSUES IN PRIMARY CARE SETTINGS

Defining End-of-Life Care

Effective end-of-life care encompasses palliative and hospice care. Palliative care is the comprehensive management of the physical, psychological, social, spiritual, and existential needs of individuals with advanced disease that is life-limiting or refractory to disease-modifying treatment and the needs of their families (Task Force on Palliative Care, 1997). Conditions for which palliative care is appropriate include cancer, AIDS, congestive heart failure, chronic obstructive pulmonary disease, end-stage organ disease, dementia, and other progressive neurological diseases.

The goal of palliative care is to achieve the best possible quality of life for patients and their families. This goal is achieved through relief of suffering, pain and symptom management, psychosocial support, optimization of functional capacity, and respect for autonomy and the appropriate role of family and legal surrogates. Sensitivity to personal, cultural, and religious values, beliefs, and practices is emphasized (Task Force on Palliative Care, 1997).

Hospice is a form of palliative care provided to individuals with a known terminal illness who are expected to live 6 months or less and are no longer pursuing aggressive or curative treatments, although some interventions may be performed to maximize quality of life, such as blood transfusions to maintain energy level in leukemia patients. Goals include self-determined life closure, safe and comfortable dying, and effective grieving (National Hospice Organization Standards and Accreditation Committee, 1997).

Optimum palliative and hospice care require effective communication among health care professionals, patients, and families; integration, coordination, and continuity of care; an individualized, interdisciplinary plan of care that addresses the physical, psychological, and spiritual needs of the patient and family; assessment of clinical outcomes as well as patient and family satisfaction; and commitment to education and training of patients, family, and health care clinicians (cf. Field & Cassell, 1997; Task Force on Palliative Care, 1997). Psychologists and other mental health specialists in primary care settings are in a strong position to facilitate these components of good palliative care.

Providing End-of-Life Care Across the Disease Continuum

Needs of Patients

Psychologists in primary care can work with patients at different points on the disease continuum on a variety of end-of-life issues. The specific issues raised and the associated intervention approaches used will vary with the stage of illness, phase of treatment, and patient sociodemographic and personality characteristics (Baum, Thompson, Stollings, Garofalo, & Redinbaugh, 2001). In this section of the chapter, we review some of the most common issues and intervention strategies at different phases of the disease trajectory.

Psychologists who work with patients diagnosed recently with a life-threatening disease commonly need to address advance care planning, involving the patient, often with family members, and the treating physician or a member of the health care team. The purpose of advance care planning is to provide information about the illness (anticipated course and prognosis), clarify the patient's and family's values and goals, present a range of treatment options from aggressive life prolonging to supportive (Byock, 2001), and obtain an advanced directive, such as a living will or durable power of attorney, which provides legal directives regarding treatment preferences and surrogate authority.

Despite efforts to ensure that patients complete advanced directives, more than three quarters of patients do not do so (Emanuel, Barry, Stoeckle, & Emanuel, 1991); this can result in patients receiving interventions that they do not want. In addition, when advanced directives are completed, this tends to occur late in the progression of the disease or in the course of an institutional stay, suggesting the need for more timely end-of-life discussions and better integration of palliative care into mainstream hospital practice (Fins et al., 1999). Mental health specialists in primary care can assist recently diagnosed individuals with advance care planning by exploring their perception of the illness, their understanding of treatment options, and their decision-making process. Clinicians then can facilitate patients' communication of treatment preferences to physicians and family members.

Psychologists also can assist patients in managing the stress of their illness. Stress may have physiological, psychological, and behavioral consequences that can affect disease progression or health-related behaviors (Baum et al., 2001). Individuals' perceptions of their ability to cope with that stress and the meaning they ascribe to the disease are important mediating factors (Marteau, 1995). Additional factors that can influence adaptation to disease and may affect psychological reactions are the nature of the disease and prognosis, sociodemographic variables, cultural and religious beliefs, prior loss experiences, personality characteristics, and type of coping efforts. Individuals likely to experience greater distress are those for whom the disease is recurrent and protracted and results in limited mobility; those who are younger (under 40 years), female, and of higher socioeconomic status; those who have previous unresolved separation or loss experience; and those who react with resignation, withdrawal, and rumination, and lack active coping/problem-solving responses (Emanuel & Emanuel, 1998). In addition, denial may be problematic (and therefore is challenged) when it interferes with social relationships, physical and emotional well-being, decision planning, and treatment compliance; however, denial can be adaptive by reducing stress and allowing time to adjust to the situation (Burgess, 1994). It is likely that a moderate amount of avoidance may be helpful in the initial adjustment to a terminal diagnosis, but may lead to problems if it persists.

As the disease progresses, clinicians can help patients with the transition from more curative, life-prolonging interventions to more palliative approaches that focus on quality of life. For example, patients receiving chemotherapy and/or radiation for advanced cancer may be extremely debilitated by the treatment with little to no change in their disease. At some point, they may reevaluate the costs and benefits of treatment and consider discontinuing it. Psychologists can assist patients with this decision-making process. Within this context, psychologists can help patients consider what is most important to them at this point in their lives (e.g., what brings value, meaning, and sense of purpose) and how they want to live out the time they have left.

Interventions to facilitate effective coping over the course of curative and palliative treatment may include brief problem-focused or cognitive–behavioral approaches (e.g., cognitive restructuring, stress management, relaxation), psychoeducation, grief therapy, supportive therapy, and mobilization of social support and other services.

When working with individuals whose disease is terminal, mental health specialists in primary care often are helping patients maintain a meaningful quality of life and facilitating a "good death" (Emanuel & Emanuel, 1998). Factors that contribute to a good death have been identified through expert panels and interviews with clinicians, patients and family members. These groups show both convergence and disagreement on what they consider a good death (Steinhauser, Clipp, et al., 2000), underscoring the need to communicate openly with patients about their unique needs.

Terminally ill individuals describe certain factors as important to determining a good death, including the following:

1. Having a good relationship with health care professionals in which one feels comfortable talking about dying, death, and personal fears
2. Confronting and preparing for death (e.g., having affairs in order, knowing what to expect about physical condition, saying good-bye, resolving unfinished business)
3. Maintaining a sense of continuity with oneself and making meaning of one's life and death (e.g., remembering personal accomplishments, dealing with failures/regrets)
4. Having adequate pain and symptom management, including for psychological symptoms
5. Gaining affirmation as a whole person (e.g., maintaining dignity, being known as an individual and not just as a patient, being touched and listened to)
6. Achieving a sense of control, including involvement in treatment decisions and mental awareness
7. Maintaining and strengthening personal relationships
8. Not being burdensome to family or society
9. Having the ability to help others through sharing wisdom, modeling a meaningful path through the dying process, and teaching (e.g., Steinhauser, Christakis, et al., 2000)

Unfortunately, often people do not die the way they hope or desire. A majority of deaths occur in hospitals, where preferences concerning life-sustaining treatments frequently are not adequately discussed, documented, or adhered to and where discussions of existential or spiritual issues are rare (Fins et al., 1999; SUPPORT Principle Investigators, 1995). Dying patients often experience significant pain and other physical symptoms such as breathing difficulties, nausea, or constipation (Lynn et al., 1997); interpersonal strain, economic burden, and psychological distress (Bradley, Fried, Kasl, & Idler, 2000); and unmet concrete service needs such as for transportation and homemaking (Emanuel et al., 1991). Of all the unmet needs, psychosocial needs are the greatest (Rathbone, Horsley, & Goacher 1994), particularly among women and unmarried individuals. Referrals to hospice or home care, which could address many of these shortcomings, occur late or not at all. Only 20% to 25% of patients who die in the United States receive hospice care (National Hospice and Palliative Care Organization, 2001).

Most of these issues are amenable to psychological assessment and intervention. Psychosocial interventions address issues such as pain management; emotional problems (e.g., depression, anxiety); fears and adjustment to the dying process (e.g., changes in cognitive status, disability, diminished control, and changes in roles and status); grief reactions; existential and spiritual concerns; relationship problems; social isolation; and caregiver burden. The overarching goal is increasing psychological comfort and reducing suffering, building on the patients' strengths and adaptive behaviors. Psychological interventions can include patient and family education, supportive psychotherapy, cognitive–behavioral approaches (cognitive restructuring, guided imagery, relaxation, visualization, meditation, mindfulness), life review, and grief counseling.

Interventions may need to be modified, however (e.g., Kastenbaum, 2000). For example, psychologists working with terminally ill patients should be flexible about the length, frequency, and structure of the therapeutic encounter (e.g., briefer, more frequent, less formal) and the settings in which they see patients (e.g., in home, hospital). They may need to shift their expectations for what is possible in therapy, maintaining very simple and short-term goals.

The dying person sets the tone and pace of the sessions and may not address all of the issues that the psychologist thinks are necessary for achieving a good death. This outcome can lead to a sense of incompleteness and requires the clinician to develop increased tolerance of ambiguity and discomfort. It may be helpful to keep in mind that the way people approach dying is often how they approached living, and how they cope with dying will be similar to how they dealt with difficult stressors in the past. Additional differences in psychotherapy when working with terminally ill patients are: increased use of therapist self-disclosure, aimed at enhancing connection; reinforcing or validating the patient's experience; and therapist's greater awareness of personal emotional well-being and personal issues such as feelings about death and dying.

Psychological interventions should be considered in addition to pharmacological treatment and adjunctive therapies such as massage, music, and art. Unfortunately, few psychological interventions in the context of terminal illness have been rigorously evaluated. Partly for this reason, reviews of evidence-based interventions for patients with life-limiting illness that include practice guidelines for anxiety (Jackson & Lipman, 2000) and depression (Martin & Jackson, 2000) only briefly mention the potential value of psychotherapy. More research on the effectiveness of well-established psychological interventions with dying patients is needed.

Needs of Family Members

Family members of palliative care and hospice patients face many issues in the last phase of their loved ones' lives. They must provide emotional support and practical aid to their loved one, communicate with clinicians, take care of concrete matters (e.g., funeral arrangements), communicate last messages (e.g., thanks, forgiveness), accept the terminal illness and impending death, and grieve their loss. In addition, family members often experience anticipatory grief (Rando, 2000). Collectively, these physical and psychological tasks place significant demands and stress on family members (Haley, LaMonde, Han, Narramore, & Schonwetler, 2001. Existing studies report high levels of psychological distress among family caregivers (Haley et al., 2001) and disruption across several domains, including physical, financial, psychological, social, and spiritual (Cheng et al., 1994). Furthermore, patient and family coping are intertwined. For example, patients may sense family members' stress and want to protect them from further distress; thus, patients may not share fears or concerns, which inadvertently can place more stress on family members, who sense something is amiss but are not able to glean from the patient what it is.

Psychological interventions with family members can include psychoeducation, supportive psychotherapy, and cognitive–behavioral and problem-solving approaches. Targets may include increased or more effective communication, coping, and problem-solving skills; anticipatory grieving; and mobilization of support. Individual, group, or family approaches can be utilized.

Guidelines for Providing Effective Palliative Care

Several guidelines for intervention have been proposed that may improve the way palliative care is delivered (e.g., AGS Ethics Committee, 1995; Emanuel & Emanuel, 1998). The guidelines encompass communication, assessment, and intervention and can be useful to psychologists in primary care.

Communication guidelines emphasize open, honest communication between clinicians and the patient, family members, or designated decision makers regarding diagnosis and prognosis, range of treatment options, and goals for care. End-of-life discussions should include advanced care planning and an evaluation of factors that can influence decision making, such as depression, pain, fear of dependency, or fear of being a burden. Clinicians should elicit patients' concerns, fears, hopes, and expectations. It is important to focus on patients' perceptions as clinicians may underestimate the importance to patients of some issues (Goldberg, Guadagnoli, Silliman, & Glicksman, 1990). Furthermore, patients' concerns are associated with level of distress, with different types of concerns related to different psychological reactions (Heaven & Maguire, 1998). In addition, end-of-life conversations should be dynamic, evolving as the disease progresses, and respectful of patients' values and cultural norms as well as cohort- and gender-related attitudes. Psychologists should be aware of their own goals/values vis-à-vis those of the patient; it is important to be aware that what you as a clinician may think is important and meaningful in living and dying may be different from the views of the patient. Further details on thoughtful approaches to end-of-life discussions are available (e.g., Quill, 2000).

Guidelines for assessment and intervention include conducting a multidimensional assessment, preferably by an interdisciplinary team, which then develops a comprehensive care plan and intervenes accordingly. Multidimensional assessment explores legal, financial, social, spiritual, existential, psychological, and environmental issues that may affect the patient. Topics examined may include concrete issues such as the existence of advanced directives (e.g., living wills, durable power of attorney), the status of financial affairs, funeral or memorial service plans, or transportation needs. Psychological issues such as problematic family dynamics, existential concerns, and opportunities for growth may be concerns as well.

Psychological interventions for patients should focus on promoting a meaningful quality of life through maintaining realistic goals, ameliorating or preventing distressing symptoms, promoting interpersonal relationships, facilitating completion of "unfinished business," and providing continuity with self (e.g., identifying things of value to the patient, ways for the patient to continue to contribute and leave a legacy). Family member interventions are aimed at managing stress and caregiver burden, promoting connection with the patient, and identifying opportunities to help the family with grief and loss.

Although the primary care psychologist is integral to addressing end-of-life or palliative care needs of patients across the disease continuum, the complex needs of terminally ill patients easily can outstrip the resources of primary care clinics, particularly if an interdisciplinary team is not available. It may be necessary for the psychologist in primary care to target the most salient psychological needs of the patient and then refer to outside agencies or other services within the setting to provide the most appropriate level of care.

GRIEF ISSUES IN PRIMARY CARE SETTINGS

Normative Grieving

Models of "normative" adjustment to bereavement (e.g., Bowlby & Parkes, 1970) have long guided mental health specialists in working with grieving patients. These models utilize a concept referred to as the *grief work hypothesis* (Stroebe, 1992), which stipulates that purposely bringing thoughts of the deceased into awareness, processing the elements of the loss, and working toward detachment from the deceased is adaptive, and that suppression of this process is pathological.

Bowlby and Parkes (1970), for example, posited that bereaved individuals tend to move through phases of grief: (a) numbness, (b) yearning and searching for the deceased, (c) disorganization and despair, and (d) reorganization. Parkes (2001), however, emphasized that this model was never meant to be a static, linear one that delineated a precise course of grieving. He and Bowlby envisioned the model to be representative of the phases of grieving that many will pass through, but bereaved individuals are likely to oscillate between the phases, sometimes experiencing reactions characteristic of a "later" phase, then returning to an "earlier" phase. Parkes (2001) noted that misunderstanding of this point has led some therapists to attempt to "move" patients through each stage in a stepwise, orderly progression. Such efforts may alienate patients and cause them to feel unsupported and misunderstood. This is not to say that stage, or phase, models are incorrect or lack utility. Stage models offer clinicians, patients, and family members useful heuristics for understanding some of the commonly experienced aspects of the grieving process.

Myths About Grieving

Research has challenged other widely held beliefs about grief. Wortman and Silver (2001) culled the bereavement literature (including theories discussed above) in Euro-American culture and identified five primary assumptions that underlie most of the early writing; in their review of the empirical literature, however, they found these assumptions often were not supported, as reviewed below.

Myth 1: Intense distress inevitably follows a death.

A substantial minority of individuals (perhaps 20%–35%) neither display nor report intense distress.

Myth 2: Failure to experience distress is pathological and will lead to delayed grieving.

Research does not support the conception that failure to experience/display grief is pathological and the "delayed" grieving reaction has not been identified in empirical examinations.

Myth 3: Adaptive adjustment requires grief work.

Empirical research does not support consistently the value of "working through" a loss. Many individuals who engage in such grief work report higher levels of distress at follow-up than those who do not. For example, bereaved participants who engaged in an expressive writing paradigm did not report improved psychological adjustment or engage in fewer medical visits in comparison to a bereaved control writing group (Stroebe, Stroebe, Schut, Zech, & van den Bout, 2002).

Myth 4: Ongoing attachment to the deceased is problematic, and adaptation requires severing the attachment.

Maintaining an ongoing attachment to the deceased is not necessarily pathological. It is common for bereaved individuals to report sensing the presence of a lost loved one, talking to the deceased, and engaging in rituals and other activities (visiting cemeteries, lighting candles, etc.) meant to maintain a bond to the deceased.

Myth 5: In a suitable period of time (1–2 years), the bereaved individual will recover from the loss and resume previous levels of functioning.

There is often an expectation in Euro-American culture that there is a "just enough" level of grieving—not too little and not too much—and that those who fall outside these parameters are adapting poorly to their loss. Research, however, shows that the grief process can go on for longer periods without being pathological, and there is no specific time limit for how long grief should persist.

Taken together, these myths suggest that clinicians should be aware of their expectations for the grieving process and not try to impose a presumed model of "healthy" bereavement on a patient. When bereaved individuals quickly recover and move on with their lives, eliciting more grief is not indicated. Conversely, some may seem to grieve for a lengthy period of time, may seem to hold on to the deceased, or report intermittent periods of intense sadness and grief many years after the loss. Such patients may not be pathological, especially if they give signs of otherwise healthy functioning (e.g., good social and occupational functioning, being active and engaged). It is important to address clinically the stated needs of the patient rather than imposing a model of how the patient "should" feel.

Factors Associated With Adaptive Adjustment to Bereavement

Wortman and Silver (2001) also examined factors associated with adaptive and maladaptive adjustment to bereavement that were supported by the empirical evidence; these are discussed below.

1. *Social support* often is a very important factor in adjusting to bereavement. Lack of social support following a death is associated with poorer well-being (Nolen-Hoeksema & Larson, 1999). Helping patients mobilize their social support base following bereavement can be a brief, yet effective, intervention. Family members, friends, local bereavement support groups, and religious organizations with which the patient is affiliated can ameliorate distress (Nolen-Hoeksema & Larson, 1999).

2. *Hope and optimism* are associated with adaptive adjustment to bereavement and well-being following the loss of a loved one. Although hope (Michael & Snyder, 2002) and optimism (Nolen-Hoeksema & Larson, 1999) are considered different personality or coping constructs, they share a conceptual communality: positive expectancies for good things happening. Patients who express hopes for a positive future and can visualize better times ahead are more likely to adjust well to bereavement than those who express a pervasively negative view of the future. Nolen-Hoeksema and Larson (1999) followed over an 18-month period bereaved participants recruited from hospices and found that optimism 1 month after the loss was a unique predictor of lower levels of depression and distress at 12- and 18-month assessments after controlling for depression and distress at 1 month. For the psychologist in a primary care setting, who must make decisions about how to allocate time and resources, resiliency factors (hope, optimism, self-efficacy, hardiness) may indicate those who are likely to adjust adaptively to the loss of a loved one without a need for counseling or other clinician intervention. A more in-depth explanation and a copy of the Hope Scale are available in chapter 13.

3. *Finding meaning in the loss* is strongly associated with positive psychological outcomes (Davis, Nolen-Hoeksema, & Larson, 1998; Michael & Snyder, 2002) and physical health outcomes (Bower, Kemeny, Taylor, & Fahey, 1998). For example, Bower and colleagues (1998), in a study of HIV-positive men who experienced the death of a partner due to AIDS-related causes, found that a sense of meaning in the death predicted slower CD4 T-cell decline and lessened AIDS-related morbidity.

The type of meaning found also can be important. Davis et al. (1998) differentiated two aspects of meaning: making sense of the death and finding some benefit in the death. Making sense of the death appears to arise out of the need to reconstruct worldviews and shape meaningful life narratives that explain painful losses. In those for whom religion and spirituality are an important source of meaning in life, this likely will involve exploration of spiritual beliefs. Alternatively, finding benefits is a positive reframing coping strategy often found in those who respond adaptively to painful and traumatic life events (e.g., Affleck & Tennen, 1996). This strategy involves a sense of having grown and found some strength in the experience of an adverse life event. It also can include rethinking life goals and can lead to greater thoughtfulness and sensitivity toward others, finding previously unknown strengths, and very often, realizing the importance of relationships (Nolen-Hoeksema & Larson, 1999). Both types of meaning were associated with positive outcomes by Davis et al. (1998) and Michael and Snyder (2002).

Complicated Bereavement

For some individuals, the loss of a loved one results in a level of sustained distress and disruption in daily functioning that exceeds that of most other people; this response has been called *complicated grief* (Prigerson & Jacobs, 2001). In a primary care setting, rapid differentiation of those who are normatively grieving from those likely to experience a more complicated course would be helpful in allocating resources to those in need of greater attention. However, establishing clear criteria that distinguish complicated from uncomplicated grief has proved difficult. The *Diagnostic and Statistical Manual of Mental Disorders*, fourth edition (*DSM-IV*; American Psychiatric Association, 1994) does not contain a diagnostic category for complicated grief. It does provide guidance in differentiating uncomplicated bereavement from a major depressive disorder associated with bereavement. The diagnosis of a major depressive episode following the death of a loved one should not be made within the first 2 months following the loss unless at least one of the following is present: marked functional impairment, morbid preoccupation with worthlessness, suicidal ideation, psychotic symptoms, or psychomotor retardation.

Prigerson and colleagues (1999) proposed that complicated grieving is a distinct clinical disorder worthy of its own diagnostic category, with features that differentiate it from major depression. Two primary symptom clusters have been proposed (Prigerson & Jacobs, 2001). Cluster A encompasses separation distress symptoms (intrusive thoughts of the deceased, yearning, searching, excessive loneliness). Cluster B is made up of traumatic distress symptoms (purposelessness, numbness/detachment, difficulty acknowledging death, meaninglessness, subjective sense that part of self has died, shattered worldviews, assuming symptoms of the deceased, and excessive bitterness/anger about death). To meet a diagnosis of complicated grief, the bereaved patient must have at least three Cluster A and four Cluster B symptoms that last for 6 months or more and create significant impairment in functioning.

The review of the literature by Prigerson and Jacobs (2001) indicated that complicated grief predicts poorer health and psychological well-being beyond the variance accounted for by depressive symptoms. Given this finding and the statistically distinct factor structure of complicated grief from depression, the symptoms listed above can be a useful clinical tool for determining if a patient may be experiencing a complicated course of bereavement that necessitates further clinical attention. These symptoms are common in the acute stage of grief; thus, it is important to be aware of the 6-month time frame in evaluating the presence of a complicated grieving reaction.

Cultural Differences in Grieving

A full consideration of cultural differences in the grieving process is beyond the scope of this chapter. It is nonetheless important to note that such differences do exist and that we, who are each members of our own society/culture of upbringing, have internal, culturally based models of adaptive grieving. As clinicians, it is natural to apply the assumptions derived from our personal culture or society to our work with the bereaved.

We must be able, however, to suspend these assumptions when working with individuals from different cultures. For instance, within Euro-American culture, bereaved individuals, particularly the conjugally bereaved, are expected to grieve for a "sufficient" period of time, then move on with life and establish a new identity. But other cultures have very divergent ideas about maintaining ongoing bonds with the deceased (Stroebe, Gergen, Gergen, & Stroebe, 1992). Some cultures foster the belief that the widow or widower should maintain ongoing contact with the dead spouse (e.g., Japanese) or maintain a lifelong role as a widow (e.g., certain Latin-American and other cultures based on the Catholic religion). Other cultures (e.g., Hopi) hold that the dead should be forgotten as soon as possible and not discussed.

When working with bereaved patients from different cultures, we suggest asking patients about their cultural beliefs and using these as a basis for deciding together how best to be helpful. For example, the clinician may inquire, "For me to help you better, it would be useful if you could explain to me how issues like death and grief for a deceased loved one are thought of in your culture," or "There may be times in our work together when it would be useful to guide me in better understanding the beliefs of your culture so we can collaborate to find the best way to help you during this painful time." Furthermore, encouraging patients to seek out other members of their culture and clergy members, if relevant, may be beneficial. Chapter 11 provides additional material on cultural awareness and cultural competence.

A THERAPEUTIC APPROACH TO GRIEF

The conceptualization of grief offered by Bowlby and Parkes (1970) provides a framework for guiding psychological treatment of grief. They focused on symptoms of numbness, yearning and searching for the deceased (referred to as *pining*), disorganization and despair, and reorganization. Zeiss (2001) developed an intervention model that draws heavily on the perceived tasks and emotional experiences described in each phase of the model of Bowlby and Parkes. Her intervention model is divided into phases for ease of use, but it is important to restate that phases are useful heuristics and do not represent the process that each bereaved person necessarily will go through in a sequential fashion. For an alternate approach to grief therapy, see the work of Worden (2002). If the bereaved shows signs of posttraumatic stress in response to the death of a loved one such as automatic, intrusive, distressing imagery of the loved one that may have a gruesome aspect (e.g., morbid images of deceased in grave); intense fear response to such imagery; avoidance of any reminders of the deceased; withdrawing from others; and the like, the exposure-based approach to traumatic grief developed by Shear and colleagues (2001) may be particularly effective.

Addressing the Phases of Grieving: Overview of the Model

Before addressing interventions for the specific phases of grieving, it is important to present the overall philosophy behind the model and the nature of the therapeutic relationship it entails. This approach is based on a collaborative process in which the therapist shares the grief model with the patient to explain what a patient may expect during a grief experience. The therapist invites the patient to collaborate in determining how the patient's experience fits the model and what aspects of the grief process the patient finds especially difficult. Collaboration can render the process of thinking about one's personal grief experience controllable to patients. By identifying problems the patient is having, the therapist and patient can create joint solutions to facilitate the grieving process. While sharing the model, offering gentle support and showing a willingness to hear the person can be very powerful.

In Euro-American culture, it is common to avoid talking about death. Few people ask directly about the death and its impact for fear of causing more pain, and the bereaved avoids talking about it so that others do not feel uncomfortable. The psychologist can alter this process by educating the patient about the grief experience and asking how the person is doing, what he or she has been thinking about lately, and what kinds of problems have arisen. It is important to be respectful of each individual and not to push someone into processing grief, but this does not mean the topic of conversation should be avoided. Rather, we suggest gentle questions that invite the patient to talk, but are not intrusive or coercive. For instance, we might say to a patient whose spouse died a month ago and who now is actively pining, "You may want to tell me about your husband's death and how things have been for you since then. Perhaps you have some questions about what you have been experiencing or what may lie ahead for you."

If the grief is very recent, the therapist may decide to delay sharing the grief model in favor of encouraging instrumental support in the immediate aftermath of loss. Directly following the death of a loved one, a number of tasks must be addressed. Funeral arrangements must be made, the process of settling an estate needs to be initiated, and basic needs must be met (some patients may not have food and shelter). During this time, help patients to mobilize their social support network, if possible. Encourage them to ask family and friends for help. Perhaps they need someone to go to the funeral director's with them or to help them process a life insurance claim so that they may have money to pay for the funeral. As these initial needs are met, the patient's psychosocial needs are more apt to be addressed effectively, as described below.

When assessing grief for a bereaved patient, it is helpful for the clinician to remember that the patient may oscillate between numbness and feeling flooded by intense negative affect. We focus on numbness and despair (or pining) separately, but patients move back and forth between these experiences. For example, numbness may be the first reaction, which moves into a period of intense distress and sadness. As these feelings build, numbness may recur as the distress begins to feel overwhelming. Later, sadness and distress will return.

Numbness

Core thought: "This can't be true."

Many bereaved report that their initial reaction is one of disbelief. They may have a sense of unreality or depersonalization. This can have a dissociative aspect, but may be distinguished in terms of intensity and duration from dissociation that arises in a more complicated response to bereavement, such as traumatic grief. In normative grieving, patients may report feeling numb, that they are walking around in a haze, or that it seems like this could not really be happening. In traumatic grieving, the dissociation will have a more clinical aspect, characterized by intense derealization/depersonalization. For example, the person may feel outside of the body or report forgetting large blocks of time.

During a time of numbness, the clinician can normalize the response and offer support. For example, a patient may feel "cried out" by the time the funeral happens and not cry during the ceremony. Later, the patient may feel guilty for not crying. Normalizing such reactions can be very helpful. The clinician can explain that numbness is a body's way of taking care of the person when he or she is overwhelmed. We have sometimes used a circuit breaker metaphor: The breaker switches off as a way to protect the system from being burned out.

Pining

Core thought: "This is true, and I can't stand it."

Periods of serious despair and emotional pain that can feel overwhelming define the pining phase following a death. During this phase, it is common to feel both emotional pain (e.g., crying/sadness, emotional pain, and despair) and physiological pain (e.g., physical aching, difficulty breathing and rapid heart rate, restlessness). It may seem impossible to believe that life could go on after the loss. Being "present" with patients as they grieve, engaging them in conversations about and recollections of the loved one, and otherwise facilitating their focus on loss will be beneficial.

During this period of grieving, patients also may report having bizarre experiences, such as sensing the presence of the deceased, hearing the deceased's voice, or seeing the deceased when walking into a room where the deceased used to spend time. Although they can seem psychotic or hallucinatory, nonpsychotic patients commonly report such reactions, and the clinician can assuage the accompanying distress by normalizing these experiences. Some of the experiences and emotional states may be anomalous for bereaved patients, and they may fear there is something very wrong—even that they are "going crazy." Clinicians should not diagnose Axis I disorders if symptoms are better explained by bereavement.

This phase also has been referred to as *yearning and searching*. Searching behavior, such as thinking the deceased is seen briefly in a crowd, is a common, expectable reaction. Encourage patients to talk about any experiences that seem frightening or "crazy"; providing validation that these are normal and information about how they will change with time can be extremely helpful.

The clinician may collaborate with the patient to develop meaningful rituals that mark the grieving and loss. For example, some bereaved individuals may not subscribe to the spiritual practices of the deceased and will have participated in a funeral ceremony that does not reflect their views. Creating an alternative ritual based in the bereaved person's own beliefs may be helpful. Other rituals can help the bereaved to say goodbye, such as having the patient write the loved one a letter that contains special sentiments he or she would like to share.

The clinician should be sensitive to the tendency of the recently bereaved to make big decisions, especially during the pining phase. Bereaved individuals can sometimes be tempted to take radical action to deal with the immediate pain they are feeling, but these actions may make later phases of grieving more difficult. For example, some people choose to dispose of all of the deceased's belongings immediately, take down all pictures of the person, move, or quit a job. Some decisions must be made quickly (e.g., the person may need to move because of financial strains); however, the clinician can educate the patient about the tendency to want to make decisions too soon and collaborate with the patient to identify and reason through desired decisions as they arise. Again, it is important to be culturally sensitive during this time. For example, some cultural beliefs dictate that reminders of the deceased should be removed from the home environment.

Confrontation of Loss/Disorganization and Despair

Core thought: "I have to live with this every day; everything has changed."

In the immediate aftermath of a death, we are faced with the task of reconstructing a life that no longer includes that person. During this phase, patients report that they often feel as if they are "hitting a brick wall" as they try to plan for social activities, to make household decisions, to get through mealtimes—all the everyday experiences that used to be shared with the loved one and now must be done alone. Obviously, this is especially salient for a widowed spouse, but loss of a parent, sibling, special friend, or other loved one also interrupts all the roles of that person in one's life.

The bereaved patient will experience a multitude of emotions and thoughts during this time: sadness and depression; tearfulness; anhedonia with low motivation to do anything; anxiety about the future and the thought of being alone; and frustration and anger with themselves, treatment providers, and even the deceased. They may express anger at God or the world and later feel guilty for this anger or feel guilty about what they did and did not do for the deceased. If the loved one died following a long and draining illness, the patient may feel an initial sense of relief, but subsequently feel guilty for it. During this phase, one of the clinician's strongest tools will be "normalizing." Understanding that you are going through something that others have gone through and survived can be very comforting.

In coping with bereavement adjustment in this phase of disorganization, there are two primary coping orientations: loss orientation and restoration orientation (Stroebe & Schut, 1999). The bereaved person is likely to focus on a loss orientation—processing the loss and grief. But concurrently, the bereaved must focus on day-to-day tasks and how to cope with them effectively (restoration orientation). If the deceased was an integral part of the bereaved patient's own day-to-day life, certain tasks and roles will need to be filled. For example, the deceased may have paid all the bills, known where all the investments were, or driven the kids to school each morning. Furthermore, there may be subtle roles that the deceased fulfilled that are now empty, such as social coordinator. It is common for widowers to lose contact with their social circles because deceased wives maintained and nurtured the social contacts. As we have discussed, social support is crucial during adaptation to bereavement, and this protective factor may be lost if the bereaved patient feels inept or uncomfortable in contacting others. Usually, the clinician can help the bereaved patient face these demands with a problem-solving orientation and may act as an advocate in facilitating access to helpful services in the community.

In addition, during this phase of grief, it can be helpful to underscore the patient's own resourcefulness. As the bereaved patient manages each day, doing tasks that formerly would have been delegated to the lost loved one, the discovery of previously unused skills and knowledge can be a positive experience. At first, the bereaved patient will focus more on the feeling of being overwhelmed by the immensity of the task of recreating a new pattern of everyday life, but with increasing time, he or she likely will come to appreciate the capacity for effective action and will begin to notice an increased sense of self-efficacy. For example, one woman, after the death of her husband, began to realize that she could face her loss when she successfully changed the washer on a bathroom sink, something her husband had always done. Such moments can seem trivial in the face of the enormity of a loss, but for particular individuals, they represent the ability to face the tasks of everyday life and to re-create organization out of disorganization. This process leads to the last phase of grief, the period of reorganization.

Reorganization, Adaptation, and "Recovery"

Core thought: "Everything has changed, but I still have good experiences ahead."

We avoid the term *grief resolution* because it implies that grief is a problem that can be fixed and set aside in time. In reality, grief never goes away completely, and bereaved individuals will likely experience sadness and a sense of loss periodically throughout their lives. This phase of bereavement generally involves coming to terms with loss and rejoining the stream of life. There is a realization that life will go on, and that it can be meaningful and fulfilling without the presence of the deceased loved one, but that it is appropriate to continue to miss that person greatly. The grieving patient will start to recognize that, although grief will never go away, there is more to life than being defined as a "griever."

This is a time when most bereaved engage in meaning-finding activities. They are more likely to be able to tolerate distress and sadness that comes from thinking about the loved one and can contemplate what has happened and how life has changed. They also can remember good times shared with the deceased and share positive memories with other loved ones. The clinician can facilitate these remembrances and meaning-finding activities by being present with the patient and engaging in discussion. It is important not to force the point (e.g., "Can't you see a silver lining?") and is much better to follow the patient's lead (e.g., "You said you're starting to see how things can get better; can you tell me more about that?").

During the recovery phase, the bereaved patient typically will begin to resume old interests or may wish to initiate new ones. Instrumental support can be helpful. For example, perhaps the patient always wanted to take dance lessons, but felt that he or she could not because the deceased partner did not share this interest. Encouraging this interest and problem solving with the patient about getting involved in new activities can be helpful.

Practical Tips for Primary Care Settings

Primary care settings vary greatly in terms of modality of patient contact, time allotted for patient contact, and number of possible contacts. We offer several suggestions for concrete, supportive interventions that draw on our model and may be useful if the psychologist in a primary care setting is not able to implement the full model described in this chapter.

1. Approach bereaved patients in terms of their stated needs. Some patients may resolve their grief very quickly and report low levels of negative affect. Encouraging cognitive and emotional processing when patients are not currently involved in that process is not indicated. Ask patients what they feel they need and help facilitate this process. For example, if the patient wants only to get information about resources to handle practical matters, such as finding a "handyman" to take care of household repairs, helping the patient with that issue may be therapeutic.

2. Assess factors such as hope, social support, and finding meaning in the loss. Regardless of the issues they consider primary, patients demonstrating low levels of these factors may require more clinical attention or referrals to sources designed to increase levels of these factors. For example, the elderly widower who is not part of a religious congregation, reports feeling that he is too old to expect any good new things to come into his life, has no adult children living in the area, and whose wife made all social plans will need more help than someone with a supportive network, a likely source for finding meaning in the loss, and a more hopeful outlook.

3. Focus on enhancing family communication and support. The family is often the primary social support group and the most likely source of

ongoing support. Families, however, respond to the death of a loved one in many different ways, and family members may have very different ideas of how to grieve and address issues that arise out of the death (funeral arrangements, settling the estate, etc.). The clinician may choose to invite the family to meet for a session (or several) to facilitate communication among family members.

4. Encourage community involvement. Community-based groups, such as churches or support groups, are often beneficial. Churches and other spiritually based organizations can be excellent sources of social support and assistance at a time when the bereaved is trying to find meaning in the death. Many communities have bereavement-related support groups, or the primary care psychologist could help to organize one.

5. Encourage the patient to practice good self-care. Getting proper nutrition and sleep are crucial during this time. Many patients will not feel like eating, will ruminate at night, and will have difficulty sleeping. Let your patients know that it is okay to take care of themselves, and that this does not mean they are "bad" or not grieving properly. Taking some time out to exercise or seek the company of friends and family is very beneficial. However, families, although often an excellent source of support, can be stressful at times. The patient may need permission to take an occasional break from the family, see friends, or otherwise have some time alone.

6. Provide resources and referrals for use at a later time if necessary. The patient may not wish to talk about loss yet, or your setting may prohibit ongoing contact. There may come a time when resources will be helpful. It is worthwhile to compile a resource book that has handy information and referrals to bereavement-specific services in your community. Some resources that may be helpful are provided at this book's companion Web site (see "Additional Resources" below).

7. If you are concerned that a patient may be displaying complicated bereavement, assess more fully. The criteria of Prigerson et al. (1999) may be a useful guide for identifying individuals who may need additional services. Other factors associated with poorer outcomes in bereaved individuals that require assessment and possible

attention include current or prior psychiatric problems, excessive use of alcohol or other substances, lack of social support following the loss, minimal sense of hope or optimism about the future, and an inability to find meaning in the loss. In such cases, referral to more intensive mental health treatment resources can be important. In particular, the group at highest risk for suicide is older men whose spouses have died and who have physical health problems or substance abuse problems. Patients who fit these criteria should be encouraged to use psychosocial resources fully.

Acting as a Liaison Between Patients and Physicians and Other Clinicians

Mental health practitioners in primary care settings may be called on to act as a liaison between bereaved patients and physicians. Families may be looking for answers: What happened? What is next? In medical settings, physicians and other primary care clinicians often have very limited time and high patient caseloads, making lengthy discussions with families impractical. In addition, some physicians and other clinicians in primary care may be uncomfortable talking about death and avoid it, perhaps because of thoughts or feelings that they "failed" or will be blamed. Clinicians may feel that they have nothing to offer after their patient is deceased, and that their job is done. This attitude, however, can be off-putting and unsupportive to recently bereaved family members. Furthermore, in cases of slow health declines in terminal illnesses, clinicians may become a day-to-day feature of the family's life. The family relies on the support of clinicians in these cases, and when their family member finally dies, they often are faced with losing all contact with clinicians as well.

Psychologists can facilitate the process of having family members' pertinent questions answered and of "letting go" of the treatment team. The letting-go process will often involve work with both sides. Sometimes, this work will involve being supportive of the family and providing some form of contact as they adjust. A condolence letter from the treatment team can be helpful during these times. At other times, the focus may be on helping those who provided care to be supportive. This may involve assessing their prior experiences in responding to patient deaths and identifying what has worked effectively for them. It may also involve literally helping them find the words to say. Prigerson and Jacobs (2001) provided suggestions for clinicians to communicate with the bereaved. The clinician in a liaison role can help physicians learn what to say and, subsequently, to provide the support the family desires. Knowing what to say and feeling as if they are supported in their roles may make it easier for physicians to provide support to the family members.

SUMMARY

Psychologists in primary care settings have a unique opportunity to identify and assist patients and families with end-of-life and bereavement issues. Many of these individuals would never seek out such services through the mental health system on their own. Research has identified a variety of psychosocial issues that commonly arise in these situations that mental health practitioners are especially qualified to address.

Psychologists in primary care settings can help improve the quality of life for patients with a terminal illness and their families by providing the following:

- Emotional support
- Behavioral interventions to control pain and reduce stress
- Assistance in determining treatment preferences and advanced directives and communicating this to their physicians
- Help to patients to determine what a good death would be for them and what tasks must be accomplished for this to occur

Psychologists in primary care settings can assist individuals who have been bereaved by providing the following:

- Emotional support
- Normalization of the experience through education about the types of reactions that occur during the grieving process
- Assistance in ensuring that necessary daily activities are completed, social contacts are

maintained or increased, and major life decisions (e.g., selling the family house) are not made prematurely
- Identification of and assistance to individuals who may be experiencing a complicated grief reaction that is unusually intense, enduring, or disruptive to the person's life

This chapter describes specific approaches that psychologists in primary care settings can use to assist individuals with issues associated with the end of life and the grieving process. Many of the suggestions can be usefully employed even in settings that provide the opportunity for only minimal patient contact. It bears repeating that the best guide to determining which services to provide to patients is to ask them what they need. Facing death and grieving the loss of a loved one are intensely personal experiences that do not perfectly conform to any one model or theory. As psychologists in primary care settings, we have the unique opportunity both to share in and to facilitate individuals' struggles with these major life experiences.

ADDITIONAL RESOURCES

Suggestions for further reading and professional development resources are available at this book's companion Web site: www.primarycarepsych.com.

References

Affleck, G., & Tennen, H. (1996). Construing benefits from adversity: Adaptational significance and dispositional underpinnings. *Journal of Personality, 64,* 899–922.

AGS Ethics Committee. (1995). The care of dying patients: A position statement from the American Geriatrics Society. *Journal of the American Geriatrics Society, 43,* 577–578.

American Psychiatric Association. (1994). *Diagnostic and statistical manual of mental disorders* (4th ed.). Washington, DC: Author.

Baum, A., Thompson, D., Stollings, S., Garofalo, J. P., & Redinbaugh, E. (2001). Psychological and psychiatric practice in oncology populations. In J. Milgrom & G. D. Burrows (Eds.), *Psychology and psychiatry: Integrating medical practice* (pp. 155–181). New York: Wiley.

Bower, J. E., Kemeny, M. E., Taylor, S. E., & Fahey, J. L. (1998). Cognitive processing, discovery of meaning, CD4 decline, and AIDS-related mortality among bereaved HIV-seropositive men. *Journal of Consulting and Clinical Psychology, 66,* 979–986.

Bowlby, J., & Parkes, C. M. (1970). Separation and loss within the family. In E. J. Anthony (Ed.), *The child in his family* (pp. 197–216). New York: Wiley.

Bradley, E. H., Fried, T. R., Kasl, S. V., & Idler, E. (2000). Quality-of-life trajectories of elders in the end of life. *Annual Review of Gerontology and Geriatrics, 20,* 64–96.

Burgess, D. (1994). Denial and terminal illness. *American Journal of Hospice and Palliative Care, 11,* 46–48.

Byock, I. R. (2001). End-of-life care: A public health crisis and an opportunity for managed care. *American Journal of Managed Care, 7,* 1–10.

Cheng, W. C., Schuckers, P. L., Hauser, G., Burch, J., Emmett, J. G., Walker, B., Law, E., Wakefield, D., Boyle, D., Lee, M. & Thyer, B. A. (1994). Psychosocial needs of family caregivers of terminally ill patients. *Psychological Reports, 75,* 1243–1250.

Davis, C. G., Nolen-Hoeksema, S., & Larson, J. (1998). Making sense of loss and benefiting from the experience: Two construals of meaning. *Journal of Personality and Social Psychology, 75,* 561–574.

Emanuel, E. J., & Emanuel, L. L. (1998). The promise of a good death. *Lancet, 351*(Suppl. 2), 21–29.

Emanuel, L., Barry, M., Stoeckle, J., & Emanuel, E. (1991). Advance directives for medical care: A case for greater use. *New England Journal of Medicine, 324,* 889–895.

Field, M. J., & Cassel, C. K. (Eds.). (1997). *Approaching death: Improving care at the end-of-life.* Washington, DC: National Academy Press.

Fins, J. J., Miller, F. G., Acres, C. A., Bacchett, M. D., Huzzard, L. L., & Rapkin, B. D. (1999). End-of-life decision-making in the hospital: Current practice and future prospects. *Journal of Pain and Symptom Management, 17,* 6–15.

Goldberg, R., Guadagnoli, E., Silliman, R. A., & Glicksman, A. (1990). Cancer patients' concerns: Congruence between patients and primary care physicians. *Journal of Cancer Education, 5,* 193–199.

Haley, W. E., LaMonde, L. A., Han, B., Narra-
more, S., & Schonwetter, R. (2001). Family caregiving in hospice: Effects on psychological and health functioning among spousal caregivers of hospice patients with lung cancer and dementia. *Hospice Journal, 15,* 1–8.

Heaven, C. M., & Maguire, P. (1998). The relationship between patients' concerns and psychological distress in a hospice setting. *Psycho-Oncology, 7,* 502–507.

Jackson, K. C., & Lipman, A. G. (2000). Anxiety in palliative care patients. In A. G. Lipman, K. C. Jackson, & L. S. Tyler (Eds.), *Evidence based symptom control in palliative care* (pp. 23–35). Binghamton, NY: Pharmaceutical Products Press.

Kastenbaum, R. (2000). Counseling the elderly dying patient. In V. Molinari (Ed.), *Professional psychology in long term care* (pp. 201–226). New York: Hatherleigh Press.

Lynn, J., Teno, J. M., Phillips, R. S., Wu, A. W., Desbiens, N., Harrold, J., Claessens, M. T., Wenger, N., Kreling, B., & Connors, A. F. for SUPPORT investigators. (1997). Perceptions by family members of the dying experience of older and seriously ill patients. *Annals of Internal Medicine, 126,* 97–106.

Marteau, T. M. (1995). Health beliefs and attributions. In A. Broome & S. Llewelyn (Eds.), *Health psychology: Process and applications* (2nd ed., pp. 3–20). New York: Chapman and Hall.

Martin, A. C., & Jackson, K. C. (2000). Depression in palliative care patients. In A. G. Lipman, K. C. Jackson, & L. S. Tyler (Eds.), *Evidence based symptom control in palliative care* (pp. 71–89). Binghamton, NY: Pharmaceutical Products Press.

Michael, S. T., & Snyder, C. R. (2002). *Getting unstuck: The roles of hope, finding meaning, and rumination in the adjustment to the death of a loved one.* Manuscript in preparation.

National Hospice and Palliative Care Organization. (2001). *NHPCO facts and figures.* Alexandria, VA: Author.

National Hospice Organization, Standards and Accreditation Committee. (1997). *A pathway for patients and families facing terminal illness.* Alexandria, VA: Author.

Nolen-Hoeksema, S., & Larson, J. (1999). *Coping with loss.* Mahwah, NJ: Erlbaum.

Parkes, C. M. (2001). A historical overview of the scientific study of bereavement. In M. S. Stroebe, R. O. Hansson, W. Stroebe, & H. Schut (Eds.), *Handbook of bereavement research: Consequences, coping, and care* (pp. 25–

45). Washington, DC: American Psychological Association.

Prigerson, H. G., & Jacobs, S. C. (2001). Caring for bereaved patients: "All the doctors just suddenly go." *Journal of the American Medical Association, 286,* 1369–1376.

Prigerson, H. G., Shear, M. K., Jacobs, S. C., Reynolds, C. F., Maciejewski, P. K., Pilkonis, P. A., Wortman, C., Williams, J. B. W., Widiger, T. A., Rosenheck, R. A., Davidson, J., Frank, E., Kupfer, D. J., & Zisook, S. (1999). Consensus criteria for traumatic grief: A preliminary empirical test. *British Journal of Psychiatry, 174,* 67–73.

Quill, T. E. (2000). Initiating end-of-life discussions with seriously ill patients: Addressing the "elephant in the room." *Journal of the American Medical Association, 284,* 2502–2507.

Rando, T. A. (2000). Promoting healthy anticipatory mourning in intimates of the life-threatened or dying person. In T. A. Rando (Ed.), *Clinical dimensions of anticipatory mourning: Theory and practice in working with the dying, their loved ones, and their caregivers* (pp. 307–378). Champaign, IL: Research Press.

Rathbone, G. V., Horsley, S., & Goacher, J. (1994). A self-evaluated assessment suitable for seriously ill hospice patients. *Palliative Medicine, 1,* 29–34.

Shear, M. K., Frank, E., Foa, E., Cherry, C., Reynolds, C. F., Vander-Bilt, J., & Masters, S. (2001). Traumatic grief treatment: A pilot study. *American Journal of Psychiatry, 158,* 1506–1508.

Steinhauser, K. E., Christakis, N. A., Clipp, E. C., McNeilly, M., McIntyre, L., & Tulsky, J. A. (2000). Factors considered important at the end of life by patients, family, physicians, and other care providers. *Journal of the American Medical Association, 284,* 2476–2482.

Steinhauser, K. E., Clipp, E. C., McNeilly, M., Christakis, N. A., McIntyre, L. M., & Tulsky, J. (2000). In search of a good death: Observa-

tions of patients, families, and providers. *Annals of Internal Medicine, 132,* 825–832.

Stroebe, M. (1992). Coping with bereavement: A review of the grief work hypothesis. *Omega, 26,* 19–42.

Stroebe, M., Gergen, M. M., Gergen, K. J., & Stroebe, W. (1992). Broken hearts or broken bonds: Love and death in historical perspective. *American Psychologist, 47,* 1205–1212.

Stroebe, M., & Schut, H. (1999). The dual process model of coping with bereavement: Rationale and description. *Death Studies, 23,* 197–224.

Stroebe, M. S., Stroebe, W., Schut, H., Zech, E., & van den Bout, J. (2002). Does disclosure of emotion facilitate recovery from bereavement? Evidence from two prospective studies. *Journal of Consulting and Clinical Psychology, 70,* 169–178.

SUPPORT Principle Investigators. (1995). A controlled trial to improve care for seriously ill hospitalized patients: The study to understand prognoses and preferences for outcomes and risks of treatments (SUPPORT). *Journal of the American Medical Association, 274,* 1591–1598.

Task Force on Palliative Care. (1997). *Last acts, care and caring at the end of life. Precepts of palliative care.* Princeton, NJ: Robert Wood Johnson Foundation.

Worden, J. W. (2002). *Grief counseling and grief therapy: A handbook for the mental health practitioner* (3rd ed.). New York: Springer.

Wortman, C. B., & Silver, R. C. (2001). The myths of coping with loss revisited. In M. S. Stroebe, R. O. Hansson, W. Stroebe, & H. Schut (Eds.), *Handbook of bereavement research: Consequences, coping, and care* (pp. 405–429). Washington, DC: American Psychological Association.

Zeiss, A.(2001). *Grief and loss: A psychoeducational model of intervention.* (Unpublished training manual available from VA Palo Alto Health Care System (116B), 3801 Miranda Ave., Palo Alto, CA 94304.

28

Coronary Heart Disease and Essential Hypertension in Primary Care

Timothy W. Smith
Kelly M. Glazer

As in most industrialized nations, cardiovascular diseases comprise the leading cause of death in the United States. This has been the case for most of the last century and is likely to continue despite recent decreases in cardiovascular death rates. The majority of these deaths and the related burdens in health care expenditures, lost productivity, and human suffering involve coronary heart disease (CHD). This disease is the single leading cause of death among both men and women in America (American Heart Association [AHA], 2001). Despite recent declines in the incidence of this disease, over 12 million Americans are currently living with CHD. The AHA has estimated that 1 million individuals will have a first or recurrent heart attack this year.

Essential hypertension (EH) is a major contributor to CHD, increasing the likelihood of an individual developing and dying from CHD by a factor of two or more (AHA, 2001). EH also contributes to other major health problems, including cerebrovascular disease, congestive heart failure, renal disease, and peripheral vascular disease. Recent estimates have suggested that approximately 50 million Americans suffer from EH, but

only about two thirds of these individuals are aware of the condition, and only about half are receiving treatment for it. Even among those receiving treatment, only about a third have adequately controlled blood pressure (Joint National Committee, 2003). Hence, these two very prevalent cardiovascular conditions pose major public health burdens and clinical challenges.

Given their seriousness and prevalence, CHD and EH are common and important considerations in primary medical care. Further, several other medical conditions are related to these conditions (e.g., diabetes, obesity, congestive heart failure). Therefore, CHD and EH often influence the evaluation and management of other presenting problems in primary care. We review the psychosocial issues in medical care for these patients together not only because EH is a major risk factor for CHD and they often co-occur, but also because the behavioral issues in their management overlap to a considerable degree. For both conditions, we review pathophysiology and common medical care and then discuss psychosocial issues in the impact and management of the conditions, beginning with EH. We conclude with a general clinical outline for assessment and case conceptualization in EH and CHD that is intended to facilitate a comprehensive understanding of individual patients and to assist the primary care clinician in making decisions about prioritizing and implementing the many possible psychosocial interventions for these patients.

ESSENTIAL HYPERTENSION

Pathophysiology and Traditional Medical Care

Blood pressure reflects the force exerted against the arterial wall by circulating blood. Systolic blood pressure reflects the force associated with the contraction of the heart, whereas diastolic blood pressure reflects the force exerted between contractions. The physiological regulation of blood pressure is quite complex, but for the sake of simplicity can be seen as involving three factors.

First, blood pressure increases in proportion to cardiac output, which is the volume of blood ejected by the left ventricle of the heart with each contraction. More rapid and forceful contractions increase cardiac output and therefore raise blood pressure. Second, blood pressure rises in proportion to increases in peripheral resistance (the force blood flows against). Temporary changes in peripheral resistance typically reflect constriction and dilation of major vascular beds (e.g., muscles, digestive organs, etc.), whereas more permanent changes reflect conditions such as atherosclerosis (i.e., "hardening" of the arteries). Third, blood volume is positively related to blood pressure because the heart increases the force of contractions (i.e., increases in cardiac output) in direct proportion to the volume of blood returned to the heart by the venous circulation. Hence, with greater blood volume venous return increases and as a result so does cardiac output and ultimately blood pressure.

EH develops over time. It is generally characterized by a process in which increased cardiac output predominates in the earlier phases, whereas increased peripheral resistance and abnormalities in the regulation of blood volume through renal mechanisms (i.e., fluid retention) predominate in the later phases. These three simple de-

terminants of blood pressure are useful in understanding the mechanisms underlying drug treatments for EH, as well as the mechanisms underlying psychosocial influences on its development and behavioral interventions for its management.

Current definitions of various degrees of EH are listed in Table 28.1 (Joint National Committee, 2003). Because the risk of CHD, stroke, and other serious complications of EH increase across the full range of blood pressure, there are health benefits from reducing blood pressure at all levels above the current definitions of optimal. That is, although reductions from very high levels are a pressing medical priority, even reductions from "high-normal" levels can reduce risk of other serious conditions. The assessment of these various degrees of elevated blood pressure is not completely straightforward because blood pressure is highly variable across time and settings. Repeated measurements with approved devices and conducted by appropriately trained medical professionals are important.

Blood pressure measured in health care settings can be misleadingly high. It is presumed that anxiety and concerns about the evaluation by medical professionals can raise blood pressure temporarily, producing "white coat hypertension" that resolves after repeated testing. As a result, repeated assessments are often needed prior to reaching a sound diagnosis and certainly before initiating any intervention for EH. In some cases, ambulatory blood pressure (ABP) must be assessed. In this procedure, an occluding cuff is worn along with a small monitor containing a computerized memory. The resulting readings from these re-

Table 28.1 Joint National Committee (JNC7) Classification of Blood Pressure for Adults Aged 18 Years and Older

Category	Blood Pressure, mmHg		
	Systolic		Diastolic
Normal	<120	and	<80
Prehypertensive	120–139	or	80–89
Stage 1	140–159	or	90–99
Stage 2	160 and above	or	100 and above

Note. From Joint National Committee (2003).

peated measurements in the patient's natural environments are often better predictors of medical complications of EH (e.g., enlargement of the left ventricle of the heart [left ventricular hypertrophy]) and subsequent cardiovascular events (e.g., myocardial infarction [MI], cerebrovascular events, mortality) than are traditional clinic-based assessments. This is presumably because they provide a more accurate measure of "true" blood pressure and as a result a better indication of the total systemic burden of elevated blood pressure. Interestingly, nighttime blood pressure is also emerging as a valuable predictor of cardiovascular morbidity and mortality, and ABP monitoring is useful in obtaining this information as well (Blumenthal, Sherwood, Gullette, Georgiades, & Tweedy, 2002).

Following a reliable assessment of persistent elevations in blood pressure, standard medical evaluation turns to assessments of the presence and extent of any related end-organ damage (i.e., to the heart, kidneys, etc.) and the assessment of additional cardiovascular risk factors that inform treatment decisions. Further, some possible medical causes of hypertension may be assessed (e.g., some forms of kidney disease cause, rather than result from, hypertension), but these treatable problems account for fewer than 5% of cases with elevated blood pressure. The term *essential hypertension*, as opposed to secondary hypertension, refers to the elevation of blood pressure in the absence of such specific causes.

Once the diagnosis of EH is made and the level of related risk established, treatment typically involves a sequence of graded interventions, with the initial severity of hypertension and response to initial interventions guiding the selection and implementation of various treatment options. Mild and moderate hypertension are often treated initially with recommendations for lifestyle modification or behavioral changes. These include weight loss, increased physical activity, smoking cessation, and dietary changes (i.e., sodium and alcohol restrictions). As reviewed in this chapter, the efficacy of these behavioral interventions is supported by some well-controlled research, but such behavioral changes are difficult to maintain and often do not produce adequate blood pressure control.

Current medical guidelines (Joint National Committee, 2003) suggest that if after 6 months lifestyle changes do not produce sufficiently large and stable reductions in blood pressure (or in the case of more severe EH), medication should be initiated. Diuretics are a common first choice, and this class of medications lowers blood pressure by reducing blood volume. Beta-blockers are also common, either as a first-line or second-line medication class if diuretics do not provide adequate control. Beta-blockers reduce blood pressure through several mechanisms, including reductions in cardiac output. A large body of research indicated that, in mild and moderate EH, treatment with diuretics and/or beta-blockers is associated with reductions in blood pressure and reductions in the incidence of stroke, CHD, and cardiovascular death (Collins et al., 1990). Angiotensin-converting enzyme inhibitors and calcium channel blockers are also commonly used. These medications have also been found effective in reducing blood pressure, but their effectiveness in reducing subsequent cardiovascular morbidity and mortality is still under evaluation in large randomized controlled trials (for a review, see Blumenthal et al., 2002).

The basic approach to the pharmacological management of EH is to begin with low doses of one agent and increase the dosage until adequate treatment response is achieved. If this fails, then a second agent within a given class may be selected, or a different class may be initiated. In many cases, low doses of a drug from a second class are added (e.g., adding a beta-blocker to ongoing diuretic therapy) and are increased until control is achieved. Such combination treatments can produce adequate control with an additional benefit: The lower dosages may result in fewer side effects, which is important because unpleasant side effects are a common cause of nonadherence to antihypertensive medication regimens.

Often, when medication regimens with well-established efficacy produce poor results with a given patient, poor adherence is the cause. Simplifying the regimen (e.g., reducing doses), providing additional educational materials, increasing family support and family member education about the regimen, behavioral contracting, home blood pressure monitoring, the use of "pill packs" to provide cues for adherence, and telephone check-in calls have all been found to improve adherence, and improved adherence improves blood pressure control (for a review, see Blumenthal et al., 2002; chapter 14, this volume).

Behavioral and Psychosocial Risk Factors

A large body of observational epidemiological research has identified several important risk factors for the development of EH (for a review, see Blumenthal et al., 2002). EH is more common among older individuals, those with a positive family history of the condition, and among African Americans. At younger ages, EH is more prevalent among men than women. However, this sex difference decreases with age, eventually reversing at approximately 50 years of age. The more rapid age-related rise in blood pressure among women is presumably because of the occurrence of menopause. Of the modifiable behavioral risk factors for EH, obesity and physical inactivity are the most well established. Additional levels of risk are conferred by high levels of sodium and alcohol intake (Stamler, Stamler, & Neaton, 1993). Not surprisingly, these behaviors have been the focus of a large and still-growing body of intervention research examining the utility of related behavioral interventions in managing EH.

Several psychosocial risk factors for EH have been examined in observational epidemiological research, as well as in human and animal laboratory studies (Pickering, 1997). Many of these can be subsumed under the general rubric of psychological stress and negative emotions. Presumably, these factors contribute to the development of EH through autonomic nervous system and neuroendocrine influences on cardiac output, peripheral resistance, or blood volume regulation (Lovallo, 1997). For example, chronic job stress is associated with increased risk of EH and hypertensive end-organ damage such as left ventricular hypertrophy (for a review, see Smith & Hopkins, 2003). The tendency to experience high levels of anger and express it in maladaptive ways also confers increased risk of EH (Everson, Goldberg, Kaplan, Julkunen, & Salonen, 1998). As discussed next, these findings serve as the rationale for stress management approaches to the treatment of EH.

Psychosocial Treatment Approaches to Essential Hypertension

As noted, several "lifestyle" or behavioral interventions comprise the recommended initial treatment approach for EH and serve as adjunctive interventions for patients on pharmacological regimens. As an adjunct to medication, these behavior change approaches can produce additional reductions in blood pressure and sometimes can result in improved control to the extent that medication dosages can be reduced (Shapiro, Hui, Oakley, Pasic, & Jammer, 1997).

Controlled trials of exercise programs suggest some modest treatment benefits, with reductions in blood pressure of less than 5 mmHg when compared to appropriate control conditions. Weight loss interventions produce larger improvements (approximately 5–10 mmHg), but weight regain is a common problem. Restrictions of dietary sodium can produce small decreases in blood pressure for individuals with EH, but these improvements are generally limited to those individuals who are "salt sensitive" (i.e., larger increases in blood pressure in response to short-term increases in sodium intake). For many persons with EH, sodium restrictions are not necessary. Potassium supplementation, calcium supplementation, and reductions of alcohol intake among heavy drinkers to more moderate levels also produce modest but potentially beneficial improvements. In a comprehensive review of this literature, Blumenthal et al. (2002) concluded that weight loss for individuals who are above optimal weight is the most beneficial of these behavioral interventions. Unfortunately, weight loss of the magnitude that is likely to produce decreases in blood pressure (15–20 lb) is difficult to maintain (Wadden, Brownell, & Foster, 2002).

Historically, various stress management techniques have received considerable attention in the treatment of EH. After decades of research, many well-controlled trials are available to guide conclusions about the value of these approaches. Biofeedback and single-component stress management interventions (e.g., progressive muscle relaxation training) have been found to have small and often nonsignificant effects on blood pressure among persons with EH. In contrast, multicomponent approaches that combine arousal reduction techniques (e.g., relaxation training), cognitive restructuring of stress-engendering thoughts, behavioral skills training (e.g., problem solving, communication training), and other specific techniques produce larger reductions (Blumenthal et al., 2002; Linden & Chambers, 1994). These approaches reduced ABP as well (Linden, Lenz, & Con, 2001).

CORONARY HEART DISEASE

Pathophysiology and Typical Medical Management

CHD is a result of the formation of plaques or lesions in the coronary arteries (coronary artery disease; CAD). As early in life as middle childhood, these plaques begin as fatty streaks and increase in size with age. The size of the plaques increases as immune cells such as macrophages and foam cells are drawn to the sites of small injuries in the lining or endothelium of the arteries, and lipid molecules are deposited. Views of this process consider CAD as a process of chronic inflammation at these sites in the artery walls (Libby, Ridker, & Maseri, 2002). Eventually, the plaques may develop fibrous tissues or calcifications. CAD may progress for decades before noticeable symptoms emerge.

Plaques may increase in size to the point that they intrude into the opening within the artery (i.e., the lumen). When they functionally obstruct the blood flow capacity of the artery, they limit oxygen supply to the heart. Further, these lesions can disrupt the blood vessel's ability to dilate properly during times of high myocardial oxygen demand. Myocardial ischemia occurs when blood flow to the heart is not sufficient to meet its demand for oxygen during mental or physical stress. The ischemia can be "silent" or painless, or it can be accompanied by chest pains (i.e., angina pectoris) (for a review, see Smith & Ruiz, 2002a). In severe cases of angina, patients experience ischemia with little or no physical exertion. Lesions may be even further enlarged if they rupture and bleed because blood clots (thrombi) are likely to form at such sites. These changes can cause an abrupt and life-threatening increase in ischemia, as can portions of clots that break off, move "downstream," and occlude smaller vessels.

These acute thrombolytic blockages can cause nearly complete occlusions, restricting blood flow to a portion of the myocardium so severely that this portion of the heart muscle dies. This death of heart muscle is otherwise known as a *myocardial infarction* (MI) or *heart attack.* Ischemia may also affect the electrical stability of the heart, causing an arrhythmia. A severe arrhythmia, ventricular fibrillation, is characterized by profoundly disorganized beating. If the heart is not immediately treated to restore normal rhythm, ventricular fibrillation causes sudden cardiac death.

Medical care for CAD and CHD differs depending on the circumstances and specifics of clinical presentation. In routine assessment (i.e., nonemergency situations), patients undergo diagnostic procedures that assess presence of CAD and disease progression. Patients may undergo electrocardiogram (ECG) "stress testing" in which they are monitored by an electrocardiograph during exercise (e.g., on a treadmill or stationary bicycle) for ischemic changes (i.e., reversible ST segment depressions on the ECG tracing). Patients may also wear ambulatory ECG monitors (i.e., Holter monitors) to assess ischemia during daily activities.

Other diagnostic procedures include thallium scans, by which physicians monitor the uptake of thallium injected into the bloodstream into the myocardium before, during, and after exercise, and cardiac imaging techniques such as echocardiography, which assess abnormalities in ventricular wall motion caused by prior MI or transient ischemia (see Rozanski, 1998).

When the presence of CAD is detected, the location and severity of CAD is assessed through angiography with coronary arteriography. A catheter is inserted in the femoral or brachial artery and threaded into the coronary arteries. A radio-opaque dye is released, and high speed X-rays of the dye indicate the location and severity of CAD.

Some cases of CHD are managed through medication and lifestyle changes. Table 28.2 contains a list of common medications used to manage CHD. Although efficacy for these drugs has been demonstrated, their efficacy is often reduced by poor adherence. Patients with more severe CHD may also undergo surgical procedures. After diagnosis through angiography, physicians may choose to utilize percutaneous transluminal angi-

Table 28.2 Drug Classes Used in the Treatment of Coronary Heart Disease

Class	Example	Action
β-Blockers	Propranolol (Inderol)	Reduces heart rate and strength of contraction
Calcium blockers	Dilitiazem (Cardizem)	Vasodilators in peripheral and coronary arteries
Nitrates	Sublingual nitroglycerin	Coronary and peripheral vasodilation
Lipid-lowering agents	Lovastatin (Mevacor)	Improves lipid profiles
Angiotensin-converting enzyme inhibitors	Catopril (Capoten)	Antihypertensive, primary therapy in congestive heart failure
Inotropic agents	Digoxin (Lanoxin)	Increases cardiac contraction strength; stabilizes rhythm
Diuretics	Furosemide (Lasix)	Decreases blood volume
Anticoagulants	Warfarin (Coumadin), aspirin	Reduces blood clotting

oplasty (PCTA), in which a catheter is directed near the lesion, and a balloon tip is inflated to open the narrowed site, thus restoring blood flow. Physicians may insert small metal mesh tubes or stents into the artery to retard restenosis after PCTA. In other cases, physicians may opt to restore blood flow by mechanically rerouting blood from the aorta to the coronary circulation through a coronary artery bypass graft (CABG). In this surgery, a portion of a vein (usually the saphenous vein from the leg) is removed and attached to the aorta and to a site on the coronary artery past the blockage. The new route allows blood to flow freely to the myocardium. Typically, PCTA and CABG patients are treated with medication and lifestyle changes following discharge.

Regular exercise is a central component of treatment following MI, PCTA, or CABG, as well as for patients who are at risk for a coronary event. Although several studies reported null results, overall it appears that incorporating exercise into treatment for CHD reduces mortality and recurrent coronary events (O'Connor et al., 1989; Oldridge et al., 1988). Exercise programs may also be useful in increasing activity levels of CHD patients (Ades, Pashkow, & Nextor, 1997) and reducing depression (Blumenthal et al., 1999). Although exercise may lead to these beneficial outcomes, poor adherence to exercise regimens often prevents patients from achieving them.

A compelling example of the potential impact of behavioral interventions for the management of CHD is the impact of multicomponent interventions on the underlying disease process. Programs such as the Lifestyle Heart Trial (Ornish et al., 1990) involve a strict vegetarian diet, daily meditation and stress management, smoking cessation, and moderate activity. Patients who followed this program for 1 year demonstrated reductions in CHD severity and anginal episodes when compared with patients under standard medical care (Gould et al., 1992; Ornish et al., 1990). The extensiveness of this intervention raises concerns as to its usefulness in general practice (Billings, 2000), but the encouraging results highlight the possible benefits of behavioral modification.

Emotional Responses to Treatment

In the acute stages of a coronary event, patients are often quite distressed. However, this distress is often followed by a period of denial or minimization of the seriousness of the situation. Denial can be adaptive in the short term, possibly by reducing arousal (Levenson, Mishra, Hamer, & Hastillo, 1989). However, in the long term, denial can worsen prognosis by interfering with adaptive coping and needed lifestyle changes (Havik & Maeland, 1988; Levine et al., 1987). The acute stages of coronary events are also quite distressing for the spouses and family members of cardiac patients. Some report that the coronary event may be more distressing for the spouse than for the patient (Hilbert, 1996). Thus, it is important to recognize and address the symptoms of distress in the spouse and family members as well as in the patient during the acute stages of a coronary event (Delon, 1996).

Following a coronary crisis, most patients return to their prior levels of emotional functioning. However, employment often remains an ongoing concern. Some patients who were previously employed take longer to return to work or have a diminished capacity for work following MI or CABG. These patients often have more severe disease, are older, are less educated, have blue-collar jobs, and experience continuing emotional distress (Hlatky et al., 1986; Mark et al., 1992). Similarly, a minority of patients have lingering impairments in social functioning, marital and family adjustment, and sexual activity that influence quality of life (Swenson & Clinch, 2000).

Behavioral and Psychosocial Risk Factors

Several of the risk factors for the development of CHD are not modifiable; these include age, male sex, and family history of CHD. However, individuals with nonmodifiable risk factors can still influence their risk for CHD by reducing other modifiable biobehavioral factors. The three modifiable risk factors that have the strongest association with CHD are high cholesterol (low-density lipoprotein), hypertension, and smoking. Smoking is a particularly important risk factor to modify. Smoking cessation has been associated with a 50% reduction in mortality (Wilson, Gibson, Willan, & Cook, 2000). Other important risk factors include obesity, physical inactivity, and diabetes (Stamler et al., 1999; Wannamethee et al., 1998). These risk factors confer an interactive effect, presenting a greater risk than the simple sum of their independent effects when present together. See Table 28.3 for the recommended levels of each of these factors.

As noted, CHD is the leading cause of death for white and African American men and women in the United States, but risk disease and prognosis vary with gender and race. Although women may develop CHD later in life (i.e., postmenopause), they often have poorer prognosis and are less likely to be treated aggressively through CABG, PCTA, or medical therapy (Mosca et al., 1997).

Table 28.3 Risk Factor Goals

Low-density lipoprotein cholesterol	<100 mg/dl (ideal)
High-density lipoprotein cholesterol	>40 mg/dl
Triglycerides	<150
Blood pressure	<120/80 mmHg (ideal)
Nonsmoking status and no secondary exposure	
Body mass index	18.5–25 kg/m^2
Moderate intensity physical activity	>30 min/day
Vigorous exercise	>20 min three times per week
Fasting blood plasma glucose	<110 mg/dl

Note. Adapted from Pearson, Blair, Daniels, Eckels, Fair, Fortmann, et al. (2002).

Similar disparities are present between African American and white patients. African American patients are less likely to undergo cardiac catheterization and CABG than white patients (Laouri et al., 1997). Only recently has medical research begun to investigate these inequalities. Because many of the commonly used surgical and medical treatments for CHD were devised and tested on white male patients, research is needed into the most beneficial treatments for women and minorities.

Several psychosocial risk factors are associated with increased risk for CHD (for reviews, see Kop, 1999; Smith & Ruiz, 2002b). In both animal and human research, stress has been found to promote the development of CAD, predict the development of CHD in previously healthy persons, and precipitate the emergence of ischemic symptoms of CHD in individuals with established CHD. Specific types of stress found to confer risk of CHD and poor prognosis among patients with established CHD include job stress (Peter & Siegrist, 2000) and difficulties in close relationships (Matthews & Gump, 2002; Orth-Gomer et al., 2000).

Type A behavior pattern (TABP) is one of the most well-known risk factors for CHD. However, after several high-profile failures to replicate the association of TABP with CHD, researchers began to examine the specific components of this multifaceted constellation and quickly identified hostility as the critical component (Smith, 1992). Hostility has been linked to the occurrence and reoccurrence of CHD in prospective and retrospective studies (Miller, Smith, Turner, Guijarro, & Hallet, 1996). It is characterized by angry affect, cynical attitudes, and aggressive behavior (Smith, 1992). A second aspect of the TABP, social dominance (i.e., the tendency to exert influence or control over others), may also confer risk of CHD (Houston, Chesney, Black, Cates, & Hecker, 1992; Siegman et al., 2000).

A large number of well-controlled studies indicate that low levels of social support place individuals at greater risk for the initial development of CHD and for recurrent cardiac events and death among patients with established CHD (for a review, see Berkman, 1995). Social support has been defined differently from study to study, using the presence of a spouse or a confidant, the perception of being supported, and the availability of emotional support as indices of social environment.

Chronic negative affect, such as anxiety and depression, has been linked to the initial development and subsequent course of CHD (Kubzansky & Kawachi, 2000). Subclinical levels of depression as well as frank depressive disorders have been associated with increased incidence of CHD among previously healthy persons and poorer cardiovascular outcomes (i.e., recurrence, death) in CHD patients. These findings make it important for the psychologist working with cardiac patients to have highly developed skills in the assessment of depression. Challenges to accurate assessment of depression in the coronary patient include misinterpreting its presence as a "normal reaction" to a coronary event; difficulty distinguishing somatic symptoms such as fatigue common to both cardiac conditions and depression; depressed cardiac patients' reluctance to report depressive symptoms; and the presence of atypical depressive symptoms. In addition, cardiac patients may not be seeking psychological treatment. Therefore, psychologists working with cardiac patients must observe and interview skillfully and make use of less-well-established indices of negative affect such as exhaustion (e.g. Appels, Bar, Bruggerman, & De Baets, 2000), pessimism (Helgeson &

Fritz, 1999; Scheier et al., 1999), and hopelessness (Everson et al., 1996; Everson, Kaplan, Goldberg, Salonen, & Salonen, 1997).

Psychological Treatment Approaches to Coronary Heart Disease

Psychologists are well equipped to provide a range of interventions that can help patients' cardiac conditions improve and can help them resolve both the short-term and the long-term psychosocial consequences of the condition.

With regard to interventions that directly affect health outcomes, psychologists can help to improve the health and quality of life of cardiac patients by helping to improve adherence to recommended treatments. Simple adherence interventions have been demonstrated to be useful for smoking cessation (see chapter 38). For example, 30-minute counseling sessions along with follow-up phone calls produced reductions in smoking that were maintained for years (Rosal et al., 1998). Psychologists may also be involved in similar interventions to improve adherence to medication, dietary changes, and exercise (see chapter 14).

With regard to emotional responses to CHD, assessing and managing depressive symptoms are also ways psychologists can help improve quality of life in coronary patients. Patients may wonder what visiting with a psychologist has to do with their heart disease or be reluctant to discuss their emotional issues. To open discussion on depressive symptoms, Lespérance and Frasure-Smith (2000) recommended using simple questions: "How have you been coping with your heart disease lately? Have you been more tired or less active than usual? Have you felt more stressed than usual? Have you been less interested in interacting with others?"

Treatment of depressive symptoms is especially recommended in patients with more severe symptoms, greater impairment, past depressive episodes, comorbid stressors, and low levels of social support (Lespérance & Frasure-Smith, 2000). Pharmacotherapy and psychotherapy are treatment options for patients with significant depressive symptoms (see chapter 22).

Although pharmacological treatments for depression have been proven safe for cardiac patients, there has been little research on their efficacy. Importantly, several large controlled trials have suggested that psychosocial and psychopharmacological interventions for depression might improve medical prognoses in these patients (see Smith & Ruiz, 2002b, for a review). However, improved quality of life with successful treatment for depression is important even if positive effects on medical outcomes have not yet been convincingly demonstrated.

Stress management is becoming a common component of cardiac care and cardiac rehabilitation programs. A quantitative review of stress management interventions reported that these interventions reduced cardiac recurrences by over 40% (Dusseldorp, van Elderen, Maes, Meulman, & Kraaij, 1999). It appeared that treatments which improved emotional adjustment were most effective in reducing coronary events. Linden (2000) suggested that cost-effectiveness studies of stress management interventions will make them a standard element of coronary care.

There are a few promising interventions to reduce Type A behavior and hostility: Friedman and colleagues (1986) conducted a large controlled study in which patients with CHD were assigned to an intervention that included relaxation training, monitoring of Type A behavior, and other cognitive–behavioral techniques or provided with counseling about lifestyle changes. Patients in the intervention group reported reduced levels of Type A behavior as well as fewer cardiac events. The intervention also reduced mortality in patients with less-severe initial MI (Friedman et al., 1986; Powell & Thoresen, 1988). In another study, a hostility-reduction intervention reduced hostility levels as well as diastolic blood pressure (Gridon, Davidson, & Bata, 1999). Although this research suggested that reducing Type A behavior and hostility may have benefits, more research is needed to evaluate the effects of reducing hostility on longer term CHD outcomes.

BIOPSYCHOSOCIAL ASSESSMENT OF ESSENTIAL HYPERTENSION AND CORONARY HEART DISEASE

Effective clinical management of EH and CHD begins with a comprehensive, biopsychosocial understanding of each patient's presentation. Table 28.4 outlines an integrated approach to the assessment and management of patients with EH and CHD. For psychologists new to this topic, the background knowledge required for the application of this outline can be obtained through relevant volumes (e.g., Allan & Scheidt, 1996) and updated with the resources available through the American Heart Association (www.american heart.org).

The last source is also the single best resource for information written specifically for patients and their families. Through a variety of assessment and information sources, the psychologist must have information about each of these characteristics, even those that may be seen as falling outside traditional definitions of the psychologist's role (Smith & Nicassio, 1995). For example, to understand the demands the patients faces and the relative importance of various psychosocial issues, the psychologist must have an understanding of the illness and its treatment in the general case as well as the specific patient's presentation. In addition to understanding pathophysiology, illness severity, and the risk profile of the patient, health psychologists should understand diagnostic procedures and the course of treatment the patients will typically face.

Psychologists should assess current and past psychological conditions and coping skills as well as demographic information such as educational and vocational status. These factors will likely color the patient's adaptation to the illness and its treatment. Furthermore, psychologists should assess the patient's social and cultural resources, including marital/family functioning and his or her cultural views of disease. Finally, the psychologist should assess aspects of the health care and health insurance system because these factors influence the patient's ability to participate in treatment.

Ideally, a comprehensive psychosocial assessment such as this will be a part of usual patient care. Using this format to identify psychosocial issues, the treatment team can identify goals for each individual, creating a unified and prioritized approach to patient care. In the case of EH and CHD, rank-ordered priorities typically should include adherence to medication regimens, smoking cessation, weight loss (if appropriate) and reg-

Table 28.4 Outline for Psychosocial Assessment of Essential Hypertension and Coronary Heart Disease

The disease
  Degree of hypertension (see Table 28.1)
  Hypertensive end-organ damage
  Extent and location of coronary artery disease
  History and location of previous myocardial infarction
  Pumping effectiveness (left ventricular ejection fraction)
  Diagnosed arrhythmias
  Risk factors (see Table 28.3)
  Previous and planned diagnostic procedures
  Prior, current, and planned medical/surgical management
  Complexity and side effects of medication regimen

The patient
  DSM-IV Axis I conditions
  Personality characteristics and coping style
  Knowledge and conceptualization of illness and treatment, especially medication
  Educational and vocational status
  Impact of illness on subjective distress, social functioning, activity level, and self-care

The social and cultural context
  Level of job stress
  Quality of marital and family relationships
  Use and effectiveness of social support
  Family members' conceptualizations of medical condition
  Family members' understanding of medical regimen
  Risk factor status of family members
  Training in cardiopulmonary resuscitation and emergency care
  Patient–physician relationship and interactions
  Patient and family cultural background

The health care system
  Medical organization, setting, culture
  Insurance coverage for risk factor modification
  Geographical, social, psychological barriers to care
  Disability benefits and funding for vocational retraining

Note. DSM-IV, Diagnostic and Statistical Manual of Mental Disorders, fourth edition (American Psychiatric Association, 1994). Adapted from Smith and Nicassio (1995).

ular exercise training, sensible diet, stress management, and interventions for depression and anger. Importantly, limited resources and realistic limits on the demands for behavior change that can be placed on the patient will likely cause the psychologist to face difficult decisions about which of many psychosocial factors in a given case should be pursued and which should be postponed. A full understanding of the patient's unique situation will assist the psychologist in making recommendations to the treatment team and the patient.

SUMMARY

Cardiovascular diseases comprise the leading cause of death in most industrialized nations. CHD and EH are major components of this burden. For both these conditions, lifestyle factors (e.g., smoking, diet and body weight, exercise) are major contributors to risk. Further, psychosocial risk factors (e.g., stress and negative emotion, social isolation) and adherence to related medical regimens are additional important considerations in the psychological assessment and management of these conditions. Following comprehensive biopsycho-social evaluation of the patient, an integrated and prioritized set of psychological interventions can be a valuable addition to the routine medical/surgical management of these patients.

References

Ades, P. A., Pashkow, F. J., & Nestor, J. R. (1997). Cost-effectiveness of cardiac rehabilitation after myocardial infarction. *Journal of Cardiopulmonary Rehabilitation, 17,* 222–231.

Allan, R., & Scheidt, S. (Eds.). (1996). *Heart and mind: The practice of cardiac psychology.* Washington, DC: American Psychological Association.

American Heart Association. (2001). *2001 Heart and stroke statistical update.* Dallas, TX: Author.

American Psychiatric Association. (1994). *Diagnostic and statistical manual of mental disorders* (4th ed.). Washington, DC: Author.

Appels, A., Bar, F. W., Bruggerman, C., & De Baets, M. (2000). Inflammation depressive symptomatology, and coronary artery disease. *Psychosomatic Medicine, 62,* 601–605.

Berkman, L. F. (1995). The role of social relations in health promotion. *Psychosomatic Medicine, 57,* 245–254.

Billings, J. H. (2000). Maintenance of behavior changes in cardiorespiratory risk reduction: A clinical perspective from the Ornish Program for reversing coronary heart disease. *Health Psychology, 19*(Suppl. 1), 70–75.

Blumenthal, J. A., Babytak, M. A., Moor, K. A., Craighead, W. E., Herman, S., Khatri, P., et al. (1999). Effects of exercise training on older patients with major depression. *Archives of Internal Medicine, 159,* 2349–2356.

Blumenthal, J. A., Sherwood, A., Gullette, E. C. D., Georgiades, A., & Tweedy, D. (2002). Biobehavioral approaches to the treatment of essential hypertension. *Journal of Consulting and Clinical Psychology, 70,* 569–589.

Collins, R., Peto, R., MacMahon, S., Herbert, P., Fiebach, N., Eberlein, K., et al. (1990). Blood pressure, stroke and coronary heart disease: Part 2. Short-term reductions in blood pressure: Overview of randomized drug trials in their epidemiological context. *Lancet, 335,* 827–838.

Delon, M. (1996). The patient in the CCU waiting room: In-hospital treatment of the cardiac spouse. In R. Allan & S. Scheidt (Eds.), *Heart and mind: The practice of cardiac psychology* (pp. 421–432). Washington DC: American Psychological Association.

Dusseldorp, E., van Elderen, T., Maes, S., Meulman, J., & Kraaij, V. (1999). A meta-analysis of psychoeducational programs for coronary heart disease patients. *Health Psychology, 18,* 506–519.

Everson, S. A., Goldberg, D. E., Kaplan, G. A., Cohen, R. D., Pukkala, E., Tuomilehto, J., & Salonen, J. T. (1996). Hopelessness and risk of mortality and incidence of myocardial infarction and cancer. *Psychosomatic Medicine, 58,* 113–121.

Everson, S. A., Goldberg, D. E., Kaplan, G. A., Julkunen, J., & Salonen, J. T. (1998). Anger expression and incident hypertension. *Psychosomatic Medicine, 60*(6), 730–735.

Everson, S. A., Kaplan, G. A., Goldberg, D. E., Salonen, R., & Salonen, J. T. (1997). Hopelessness and 40-year progression of carotid atherosclerosis. *Arteriosclerosis, Thrombosis, and Vascular Biology, 17,* 1490–1495.

Friedman, M., Thoreson, C. E., Gill, J. J., Ulmer, D., Powell, L. H., Price, V. A., et al. (1986). Alteration of Type-A behavior and its effects on cardiac recurrences in post-myocardial infarction patients: Summary results of the Recurrent Coronary Prevention Project. *American Heart Journal, 112,* 653–665.

Gidron, Y., Davidson, K., & Bata, I. (1999). The short-term effects of a hostility-reduction intervention on male coronary heart disease patients. *Health Psychology, 18,* 416–420.

Gould, K. L., Ornish, D., Kirkeeide, R., Brown, S., Stuart, Y., Buchi, M., et al. (1992). Improved stenosis geometry by quantitative coronary arteriography after vigorous risk factor modification. *American Journal of Cardiology, 69*(9), 845–853.

Havik, O. E., & Maeland, J. G. (1988). Verbal denial and outcome in myocardial infarction patients. *Journal of Psychosomatic Research, 32,* 145–157.

Helgeson, V. S., & Fritz, H. L. (1999). Cognitive adaptation as a predictor of new coronary events after percutaneous transluminal coronary angioplasty. *Psychosomatic Medicine, 61,* 488–495.

Hilbert, G. A. (1996). Cardiac patients and spouses: Family functioning and emotions. *Clinical Nursing Research, 3*(3), 243–252.

Hlatky, M. A., Lam, L. C., Lee, K. L., Clap-Channing, N. E., Williams, R. B., Pryor, D. B., et al. (1995). Job strain and the prevalence and outcome of coronary artery disease. *Circulation, 92,* 327–333.

Houston, B. K., Chesney, M. A., Black, G. W., Cates, D. S., & Hecker, M. L. (1992). Behavioral clusters and coronary heart disease risk. *Psychosomatic Medicine, 54,* 447–461.

Joint National Committee on Detection, Evaluation, and Treatment of High Blood Pressure. (2003). *The sixth report of the Joint National Committee on Detection, Evaluation, and Treatment of High Blood Pressure (JNC VII).* Bethesda, MD: National Heart, Lung, and Blood Institute.

Kop, W. J. (1999). Chronic and acute psychological risk factors for clinical manifestations of coronary artery disease. *Psychosomatic Medicine, 61,* 426–487.

Kubzansky, L. D., & Kawachi, I. (2000). Going to the heart of the matter: Do negative emotions cause coronary heart disease? *Journal of Psychosomatic Research, 48,* 323–337.

Laouri, M., Kravitz, R. L., French, W. J., Yang, I., Milliken, J. D., Hilborne, L., Wachsner, R., & Brook, R. H. (1997). Underuse of coronary revascularization procedures: Application of a clinical method. *Journal of the American College of Cardiologists, 29*(5), 891–897.

Lespérance, F., & Frasure-Smith, N. (2000). Depression in patients with cardiac disease: The role of psychosomatic medicine. *Journal of Psychosomatic Research, 48,* 379–392.

Levenson, J. L., Mishra, A., Hamer, R. M., & Hastillo, A. (1989). Denial and medical outcome in unstable angina. *Psychosomatic Medicine, 51,* 27–35.

Levine, J., Warrenburg, S., Kerns, R., Schwartz, G., Delaney, R., Fontana, A., Gradman, A., Smith, S., Allen, S., & Cascione, R. (1987). The role of denial in recovery from coronary heart disease. *Psychosomatic Medicine, 49,* 109–117.

Libby, P., Ridker, P. M., & Maseri, A. (2002). Inflammation and atherosclerosis. *Circulation, 105,* 1135–1143.

Linden, W. (2000). Psychological treatments in cardiac rehabilitation: Review of rationales and outcomes. *Journal of Psychosomatic Research, 48,* 443–454.

Linden, W., & Chambers, L. (1994). Clinical effectiveness of non-drug treatment for hypertension: A meta-analysis. *Annals of Behavioral Medicine, 16,* 34–45.

Linden, W., Lenz, J. W., & Con, A. H. (2001). Individualized stress management for primary hypertension: A randomized trial. *Archives of Internal Medicine, 161,* 1071–1080.

Lovallo, W. (1997). *Stress and health.* Thousand Oaks, CA: Sage.

Mark, D. B., Lam, L. C., Lee, K. L., Clapp-Channing, N. E., Williams, R. B., Pryor, D. B., Califf, R. M., & Hlatky, M. A. (1992). Identification of patients with coronary disease at high risk for loss of employment. A prospective validation study. *Circulation, 86,* 1485–1494.

Matthews, K. A., & Gump, B. B. (2002). Work stress and marital dissolution increase risk of posttrial mortality in men from the Multiple Risk Factor Intervention Trial. *Archives of Internal Medicine, 162,* 309–315.

Miller, T. Q., Smith, T. W., Turner, C. W., Guijarro, M. L., & Hallet, J. J. (1996). A meta-analytic review of research on hostility and physical health. *Psychological Bulletin, 119,* 322–348.

Mosca, L., Manson, J. E., Sutherland, S. E., Langer, R. D., Manolio, T., & Barrett-Connor, E. (1997). Cardiovascular disease in women. *Circulation, 96,* 2468–2482.

O'Connor, G. T., Buring, J. E., Yusuf, S., Goldhaber, S. Z., Olmstead, E. M., Paffenbarger, R. S., Jr., & Hennekens, C. H. (1989). An overview of randomized trials of rehabilitation with exercise after myocardial infarction. *Circulation, 80,* 234–244.

Oldridge, N. B., Guyatt, G. H., Fisher, M. E., & Rimm, A. A. (1988). Cardiac rehabilitation after myocardial infarction. Combined experience of randomized clinical trials. *Journal of the American Medical Association, 260,* 945–950.

Ornish, D., Brown, S. E., Scherwitz, L. W., Billings, J. H., Armstrong, W. T., Ports, T. A., Melanahan, S. M., Kirkeeide, R. L., Brand, R. J., & Gould, K. L. (1990). Can lifestyle changes reverse coronary heart disease? *Lancet, 336,* 129–133.

Orth-Gomer, K., Wamala, S. P., Horsten, M., Schneck-Gustafsson, K., Schneiderman, N., & Mittleman, M. A. (2000). Marital stress worsens prognosis in women with coronary artery disease: The Stockholm Female Coronary Risk Study. *Journal of the American Medical Association, 284,* 3008–3014.

Pearson, T. A., Blair, S. N., Daniels, S. R., Eckels, R. H., Fair, J. M., Fortmann, S. P., et al. (2002). AHA guidelines for primary prevention of cardiovascular disease and stroke: 2002 update. *Circulation, 106,* 388–391.

Peter, R., & Siegrist, J. (2000). Psychosocial work environment and the risk of coronary heart disease. *International Archives of Occupational and Environmental Health, 73,* S41–S45.

Pickering, T. G. (1997). The effects of environmental and lifestyle factors on blood pressure and the intermediary role of the sympathetic nervous system. *Journal of Human Hypertension, 11*(Suppl.), S9–S18.

Powell, L. H., & Thoresen, C. E. (1988). Effects of Type-A behavioral counseling and severity of prior acute myocardial infarction on survival. *American Journal of Cardiology, 62,* 1159–1163.

Rosal, M. C., Ockene, J. K., Ma, Y., Herbert, J. R., Ockene, I. S., & Meriam, P. (1998). Coronary artery smoking intervention study (CASIS): 5-year follow-up. *Health Psychology, 17,* 476–478.

Rozanski, A. (1998). Laboratory techniques for assessing the presence and magnitude of mental stress-induced myocardial ischemia in patients with coronary artery disease. In D. S. Krantz & A. Boum (Eds.), *Technology and methods in behavioral medicine* (pp. 47–67). Mahwah, NJ: Erlbaum.

Scheier, M. F., Matthews, K. A., Owens, J. F., Schultz, R., Bridges, M. W., Magovern, G. J., & Carver, C. S. (1999). Optimism and rehospitalization after coronary artery bypass graft surgery. *Archives of Internal Medicine, 159,* 829–833.

Shapiro, D., Hui, K. K., Oakley, J. E., Pasic, J., & Jammer, L. D. (1997). Reduction in drug requirements for hypertension by means of a cognitive-behavioral intervention. *American Journal of Hypertension, 10,* 9–17.

Siegman, A. W., Kubzansky, L. D., Kawachi, I., Boyle, S., Vokonas, P. S., & Sparrow, D. (2000). A prospective study of dominance and coronary heart disease in the Normative Aging study. *American Journal of Cardiology, 86,* 145–149.

Smith, T. W. (1992). Hostility and health: Current status of a psychosomatic hypothesis. *Health Psychology, 11,* 139–150.

Smith, T. W., & Hopkins, P. N. (2003). Psychological considerations in essential hypertension, coronary heart disease, and end-stage renal disease. In L. A. Schein, H. S. Bernard, H. I. Spitz, & P. R. Muskin (Eds.), *Psychosocial treatments for medical conditions: Principles and techniques* (pp. 133–179). New York: Brunner-Routledge.

Smith, T. W., & Nicassio, P. C. (1995). Psychological practice in chronic medical illness: Clinical application of the biopsychosocial model. In P. C. Nicassio & T. W. Smith (Eds.), *Psychosocial management of chronic illness* (pp. 1–31). Washington, DC: Americal Psychological Association.

Smith, T. W., & Ruiz, J. M. (2002a). Coronary heart disease. In A. J. Christensen & M. Antoni (Eds.), *Chronic physical disorders: Behavioral medicine's perspective* (pp. 83–111). Oxford, U.K.: Blackwell.

Smith, T. W., & Ruiz, J. M. (2002b). Psychosocial influences on the development and course of coronary heart disease: Current status and implications for research and practice. *Journal of Counseling and Clinical Psychology, 70,* 548–568.

Stamler, J., Stamler, R., & Neaton, J. D. (1993). Blood pressure, systolic and diastolic, and cardiovascular risks. *Archives of Internal Medicine, 153,* 598–615.

Stamler, J., Stamler, R., Neaton, J. D., Wentworth, D., Daviglus, M. L., Garside, D., et al. (1999). Low risk-factor profile and long-term cardiovascular and noncardiovascular mortality and life expectancy: Findings for 5 large cohorts of young adult and middle-aged men and women. *Journal of the American Medical Association, 282,* 2012–2018.

Swenson, J. R., & Clinch, J. J. (2000). Assessment of quality of life in patients with cardiac disease: The role of psychosomatic medicine. *Journal of Psychosomatic Research, 48,* 405–415.

Wadden, T. A., Brownell, K. D., & Foster, G. D. (2002). Obesity: Responding to the global epidemic. *Journal of Consulting and Clinical Psychology, 70,* 510–525.

Wannamethee, S. G., Shaper, A. G., Walker, M., & Ebrahim, S. (1998). Lifestyle and 15-year survival free of heart attack, stroke and diabetes in middle-aged British men. *Archives in Internal Medicine, 158,* 2433–2440.

Wilson, K., Gibson, N., Willan, A., & Cook, D. (2000). Effect of smoking cessation on mortality after myocardial infarction. *Archives of Internal Medicine, 160,* 939–944.

29

Infertility

Margot Weinshel
Mimi Meyers
Constance N. Scharf

Infertility is defined as the inability to achieve a pregnancy after a year of regular sexual relations without the use of contraception or to carry a pregnancy to live birth (*Merck Manual*, 1992). For women who are 35 years or older, diagnostic testing may begin after as few as 6 months because this is a group whose fertility rates are steadily decreasing and for whom infertility treatments become less effective with age. If a couple has had three or more miscarriages, they are also considered to have infertility problems. Of those couples who have had at least one live birth, 10% will subsequently have difficulty conceiving; this condition is called *secondary infertility*.

Infertility has profound consequences for both members of a couple. By interrupting the couple's developmental life cycle and presenting the possibility of childlessness, infertility and its treatments are usually traumatic. It can challenge each person's deeply held beliefs, identity, sense of adequacy, and competence. Caught in the liminal "not-yet-pregnant" state (Greil, 1991) and burdened with the "social disability" of infertility (Menning, 1988), couples feel both alienated and

out of step with their peers. They yearn to be part of the mainstream, yet find themselves isolated and marginalized in a child-centered society that is acutely ignorant of the impact of infertility (Diamond, Kezur, Meyers, Scharf, & Weinshel, 1999; Meyers et al., 1995a; Sandelowski, 1993).

According to statistics compiled by the American Society for Reproductive Medicine (formerly known as the American Fertility Society, 2000–2002) infertility affects 6.1 million American women and their partners, or about 10% of the reproductive-age population. For 80% of this population, a medical diagnosis can be determined. The etiological factors are male and female related: sperm disorders (35% of couples), ovulatory dysfunction (20%), tubal dysfunction (30%), abnormal cervical mucus (5%), and unidentified factors (10%).

More than 95% of infertile people receiving medical interventions are treated with drug therapy or surgical procedures. About 80% of these couples will conceive within 4 to 5 years of diagnosis. Fewer than 5% of infertile couples will be treated with in vitro fertilization (IVF).

Although media coverage gives the impression that infertility is epidemic, affecting all women, age-related percentages are stable. The absolute number of infertile couples has increased, but this is related to the increased number of couples in the "baby boom" generation and the growing number who delay childbearing. As recently as 40 years ago, most women had completed their families by the time they were 35 (Hodder, 1997); currently, 20% of women delay having children until this age. The percentage of married couples experiencing infertility has remained at approximately 10% for the past 25 years (American Fertility Society, 2000–2002; Marrs, 1997).

Although perhaps not epidemic, infertility is prevalent enough that the primary care psychologist will certainly encounter patients who are struggling with it—or with its aftermath—and should be well prepared to assess its dimensions as well as provide help for its psychological consequences. This chapter addresses the medical, psychological, and couple issues related to infertility and suggests a variety of treatment approaches that can be helpful to the individual or family therapist working with individuals and couples in this population.

THE DIAGNOSIS AND MEDICAL TREATMENT OF INFERTILITY

The age of the woman is directly correlated to the chance of achieving pregnancy per menstrual cycle. At age 15 years, the pregnancy rate per menstrual cycle is 40% to 50%; at age 25 years, it drops to 30% to 35%; at age 35 years, it is reduced to 15% to 20%; and by age 45 years, there is only a 3% to 5% pregnancy rate per cycle (Marrs, 1997). The usual course of infertility recognition begins after several months of unprotected sex when one or both partners in the couple begin to worry that there may be an infertility problem.

Most often, it is the woman who becomes concerned first and consults with her primary care physician (often an obstetrician-gynecologist). Women may be advised to use ovulation kits and to have intercourse during the days in which they ovulate; couples are often advised to wait 1 year before beginning preliminary testing for infertility. If the woman is older than 30 years, this preliminary testing begins after six menstrual cycles. At some point during the course of infertility recognition, the couple may request referral to an infertility specialist.

Diagnosis and treatment of infertility differ for men and women. Many fewer procedures exist for men, and, with a few exceptions, treatments for women are more invasive and time consuming. Treatments are typically preceded by extensive diagnostic procedures: The woman's hormone levels, daily body temperature, sperm antibodies, and even postcoital secretions are analyzed. More invasive diagnostic examinations may include endometrial biopsy; hysterosalpingogram, in which a dye injection is followed by an X-ray of the uterus and fallopian tubes to reveal any uterine or tubal abnormalities; and laparoscopy, an outpatient surgical procedure that requires several incisions to view the peritoneal cavity, ovaries, fallopian tubes, and uterus. Current diagnostic procedures for men include hormonal-level assessments, sperm analysis (count and motility), and, in rare instances, testicular biopsy (which involves removing a piece of tissue from the testicle) or vasography (an X-ray following dye injection of the vas deferentia, seminal vesicles, and ejaculatory ducts) to determine whether there are obstructions or lesions. Treatments for male infertility include variocelectomy (an outpatient surgical procedure that divides and ties off the varicose veins in the testes), sperm washing to segregate viable sperm, donor sperm inseminations of his partner, and intracytoplasmic sperm injection (ICSI, explained further below).

If the workups show no physical problems in the woman and if the man's sperm is normal, intrauterine insemination can be performed by injecting the man's washed semen into the uterus via a catheter. The cost for this protocol is relatively low. Costs increase dramatically for more "aggressive" procedures, such as intrauterine insemination in conjunction with chomipene citrate (Serophene, Clomid), a medication taken orally for 5 days a month to increase the number of ovarian follicles, thus generating more eggs.

In addition to chomipene citrate, women are usually treated with a variety of fertility medications to hyperstimulate their ovaries. These drugs are costly as well as often difficult to tolerate; side effects can include depression, fatigue, anxiety, insomnia, headaches, and nausea. IVF is often used when a woman's fallopian tubes are blocked. Before IVF proper is begun, medications that stimulate egg production are administered so that the ovaries will produce multiple eggs; these eggs are surgically removed from the ovarian follicles and combined with the man's sperm in a culturing dish, which is then placed in an incubator. About 2 days later, three to five embryos are transferred to the woman's uterus.

If there are additional embryos, they are typically frozen, to be thawed for use in future IVF cycles should the woman fail to become pregnant in the first cycle or if the couple wants to try to have another child in the future. Couples who store their frozen embryos are charged monthly fees. Many wait until they are absolutely certain that another pregnancy is out of the question before they stop payment (thereby agreeing to have the embryos destroyed). This can be a difficult choice point for the couple and may trigger another wave of sadness for the loss of the potential child or children.

Current estimates of the success rate for IVF (defined as percentage of transfers resulting in live births) suggest that effectiveness declines with increasing age. For women younger than 35 years, the estimated success rate using IVF is 33%; for women aged 35 to 37 years, the rate is 27%; for women aged 38 to 40 years, the rate is 18%; and for women aged 41 to 42 years, the rate is 10% (Centers for Disease Control and Prevention [CDC], 2002).

When the man's sperm is compromised (e.g., low sperm count or sperm that cannot reach the egg successfully), IVF with donor sperm has been used. However, ICSI has essentially replaced this procedure. ICSI involves selecting a single sperm and delivering it directly through a catheter into the woman's retrieved egg. ICSI in combination with IVF represents a major breakthrough in assisted reproductive technology. This procedure is considered the leading method for treating male factor infertility because of its ability to achieve fertilization regardless of semen parameters or dysfunctional spermatozoa. Success rates for ICSI

in one study were 39% (Palermo, Colombero, Schattman, Davis, & Rosenwaks, 1996).

Egg donation has become possible in the last 20 years; the procedure entails synchronizing the donor's and recipient's reproductive cycles using hormones, extracting the donor's eggs and fertilizing them using the male partner's sperm, and transferring the embryo to the female partner's uterus. Because the donors are typically young healthy women with healthy eggs, the success rate for the use of donor eggs across all female recipients is relatively high, estimated at 43% (CDC, 2002). Couples may choose to use donated gametes (eggs or sperm) from a known donor—such as a sibling or friend—or from an anonymous donor. The number of children born from donated eggs jumped from 112 babies in 1989 to 2,922 in 2000 (CDC, 2002).

The use of donor eggs has expanded fertility treatments and radically changed the age at which women can become pregnant. Whereas previously a woman's "biological clock" was determined by her age, and consequently the age of her eggs, the advent of egg donation has extended a woman's childbearing years. There are at least two reports of women in their early 60s who have carried and delivered egg donor children (Dhillon, 2003; Kolata, 1997).

A study of egg donor recipients found that, for women in their 50s, pregnancy rates, multiple gestation rates, and spontaneous abortion rates were similar to those of younger women. Although there may be increases in other medical risks, the authors (Paulson et al., 2002, p. 2320) concluded that "there does not appear to be any definitive medical reason for excluding these women from attempting pregnancy on the basis of age alone." The American Society for Reproductive Medicine's ethics committee (1997), however, stated that using egg donation in postmenopausal women should be discouraged, and most fertility clinics have a cutoff age of between 47 and 55 years. Although some contend that it is unethical to impregnate women who might not live to see their children grow up, others believe that denying such women the chance to conceive would be "ageism" (Tarkan, 2002). The psychological issues raised in this increasing population, which includes parents, offspring, donors, and extended families, are complex and have yet to be researched.

Surrogacy procedures are those in which a surrogate female gives birth to the child. The pregnancy may result from fertilizing the surrogate's egg with the husband's sperm or from an embryo formed by the couple's egg and sperm that is transferred to the surrogate's uterus. Laws related to surrogacy are complex and very considerably from state to state.

Assisted reproductive technology, or ART, increases the chances for multiple births. Although most fertility clinics limit the number of implanted zygotes to four, multiple zygote transfers increase the chance of multiple births. ART pregnancies with fresh nondonor eggs result in multiple births 36% of the time, and with donor eggs, this figure is 43% of the time, versus 3% in the general population. With donor procedures, 36% are twins; 3.7% are triplets or more. With nondonor procedures, 28% are twins; 7.7% are triplets or more (CDC, 2002). Multiple births can pose medical problems. Babies are more likely to be born prematurely and have lower birth weight, which increases the risk of serious medical, developmental, and learning problems. This can add an additional component of distress for the infertile couple (Davis & Rosenwaks, 1996).

PSYCHOLOGY AND COUPLE DYNAMICS OF INFERTILITY

The impact of infertility on both individual psychology and couple interactions is profound. Comparisons between fertile and infertile women show that the latter have higher levels of anxiety, tension, guilt, anger, and depression (O'Moore, O'Moore, Harrison, & Carruthers, 1983). Respondents asked to rate their most stressful life experiences rated infertility as stressful as the death of a child or a spouse (Kedem, Mikulincer, Nathanson, & Bartov, 1990). Women struggling with infertility show levels of emotional distress similar to those of patients with cancer or heart disease (Tarkin, 2002).

Infertility inescapably involves mourning for a variety of losses (Menning, 1988; Myers, 1990). The obvious losses involve failure to conceive and miscarriage, but there are less-obvious losses as

well. These include the loss of normal expectations in the life cycle and reproductive privacy (Burns, 1990; Mahlstedt, 1985), as well as grief over the lost fantasized child (Boss & Greenberg, 1984).

The woman's monthly ovulation cycle and each infertility treatment protocol generate intense emotional oscillations: hope with each ovulation and/or new procedure and despair with the onset of each menstrual cycle, negative laboratory result, or miscarriage. Stillbirths following labor and delivery are especially painful (McDaniel, Hepworth, & Doherty, 1992). Unfortunately, these distressed and traumatized couples have neither the time nor the opportunity to grieve because they feel pressured by the "ticking clock" to initiate additional treatments.

Each partner may have a distinct set of psychological traumas related to the infertility, and each requires some time to resolve; thus, husband and wife are frequently "out of sync" with each other. For example, it is not unusual for one to be prepared to proceed with a medical intervention while the other is not. The pressure of time can further increase these tensions between partners; mutual support can be diminished, and decision making can become more difficult (Meyers et al., 1995b).

Because a wide range of crises for the couple may occur during diagnostic workups and treatments, preexisting couple problems not only are likely to surface, but also frequently worsen. The majority of couples report conflict, communication problems, disagreements over medical treatments, failure of empathy, and differential investments in the process (Burns, 1990). Distress appears to be greater for women; they report more dissatisfaction with themselves than with their marriages. In many cases, both partners tend to place the responsibility for the infertility on the woman; this can be so even when the male is infertile. When husbands are infertile, women often collude with their partners to keep the source of their infertility secret (Humphrey, 1986). Women typically take on the responsibilities of initiating medical treatment, making decisions, and following through with protocols.

The psychological distress and trauma resulting from infertility and its treatments may impair each partner's capacity to comfort and support the other (Meyers et al., 1995b). Partners may avoid discussing personal feelings related to infertility to protect each other from pain. Partners' different—and frequently clashing—coping and communication styles (Gottman, 1994) may further compound the problem. Conversations appear to be especially difficult if the male carries the infertility factor.

When spouses, usually wives, use family and friends as confidants rather than their partners, couple relationships usually suffer. Secrecy typically increases each partner's sense of isolation, guilt, and resentment. At times, it can even compromise the process of evaluating critical medical options. Couples may, for example, make hasty, ill-advised choices, defer timely decisions, or delegate one member to make decisions for which future consequences can be profound.

The longer the couple struggles with infertility, the greater their distance from their families and friends may become. On the one hand, they often avoid attending child-centered occasions, which for most families represent the bulk of time spent together. On the other hand, members of their families and other support systems may be uncertain about how to relate to the couple. In their misguided attempt to be helpful, friends and family may sidestep any discussions about infertility with the couple, or they may avoid the couple altogether.

At the same time that couples' connections to their standard networks shrink, their connections to and dependency on the medical system increase in frequency and intensity. It tends to be a one-down or submissive position because they are obliged to discuss their intimate sexual behavior with their physicians, nurses, and technicians and submit to a variety of physically intrusive, time-consuming, and personally embarrassing procedures. In this role, couples may try to conceal their distress; many fear that if they are not "good" patients, their physicians will withhold or give less than first-rate treatment (Diamond et al., 1999).

The necessary compliance to the rigid timetables dictated by medical protocols (Berg & Wilson, 1991), particularly the scheduling of sexual intercourse at times of greatest fertility, often turns enjoyable spontaneous lovemaking into a chore. Fertilization itself, ordinarily the outcome of partners in an intimate private union, may shift to an aseptic medical environment.

One source of tension between partners may arise out of differing attitudes toward the source of genetic material. Some feel that unless their children are conceived with their own gametes, there can be no continuity with the past and future. There are a number of issues central to the use of donor gametes that couples need to explore (Diamond et al., 1999). These issues are equally important whether the couple uses donor eggs or donor sperm. Many couples who have been through multiple infertility treatments and reach a point at which a donor gamete is the only option that allows for at least one partner's biological child may not pause to evaluate the ramifications of this choice.

The use of donor gametes raises many issues for the couple, for each partner, and for the child (Scharf & Weinshel, 2000). Aside from profound psychological, ethical, social, and legal questions, persons who use donor gametes must grapple with whether they should conceal or reveal the child's parentage, to whom they will make this information known, and whether gametes should be from known or anonymous donors. Although couples were once advised to keep donated gametes a secret (Walter, 1982), there is a growing movement to make this information open. Couples considering the use of a family member's—usually a sibling—gametes face unique dilemmas: The lines between generativity and sexuality can blur; role confusions and conflict can develop (Meyers et al., 1995b).

The Infertility Project of the Ackerman Institute (IPAI; Ackerman Institute for the Family, New York, NY), in researching and treating infertile couples, developed a phase-specific model that delineates five psychosocial stages and treatment recommendations for each phase. The phases are dawning, mobilization, immersion, resolution, and legacy (Diamond et al., 1999).

THE PHASES OF INFERTILITY

During the dawning phase, couples become increasingly aware that there seems to be a problem conceiving. Concern grows with each month's failure to conceive. By the end of the phase, this concern leads them to seek a medical consultation. Couple conflict may arise as it did with Mary, age 34 years, and John, age 38 years. Having tried to conceive a child for 10 months, Mary was distraught and wanted to go for infertility testing; John wanted to wait and could not understand Mary's distress.

Mobilization marks the decisive engagement with physicians as couples begin diagnostic testing. Although the couple may be concerned about the possibility of infertility, a definite diagnosis is likely to cause shock and disbelief, particularly in cases of secondary infertility. Problems may begin to emerge in the relationship as couples face the first loss of infertility: a "normal" problem-free conception. During this phase, couples are usually so focused on the medical arena that they are unlikely to present for psychological interventions.

Immersion is the most complex and demanding phase. As couples undergo more testing and medical treatments, they remain in a liminal, "not-yet-pregnant" state (Greil, 1991), a limbo from which they cannot move ahead into the next stage of the life cycle: becoming parents. Barbara, 35 years old, spoke of her experience this way: "My wish to have a child outweighs everything else that goes on for me physically and emotionally." Her 34-year-old husband Dan added: "We've gone so far, our savings are nearly depleted, yet it's impossible to imagine stopping at this point."

Tossed back and forth between the hope that they will have a child and despair that they may not, it is often the time of greatest turmoil in a couple's relationship. And for many it may seriously threaten the marriage: Becoming pregnant outweighs the risks of psychological and relational stress. One wife said, "If we ever have this baby, his or her parents may be divorced."

In the later stages of immersion, if they have been unable to conceive a child, couples may be offered the option of using donor gametes (sperm or eggs). Couples choose this option with varying degrees of understanding of possible future consequences. Some treat it as just one more rung on the treatment ladder; they lose sight of the fact that adding another person's gametes to the family equation is likely to mark a quantum leap in both social and psychological complexity. Among the complications associated with the option to use donor gametes is deciding who shall be told about the child's genetics. Some couples decide to be open, often comparing the donor procedure to adoption; other couples prefer to keep the matter private (Scharf & Weinshel, 2000).

The resolution phase involves ending medical treatment, acknowledging and mourning the loss of their ability to have a genetically related child. Couples begin to refocus on other family options such as adoption or life without children. This is the time when the couple must examine which is most important: their desire to parent (and adopt) or their desire to continue their genetic line (and eschew adoption). For those who choose not to adopt and for those who are unsuccessful in finding a child to adopt, many will strengthen their connection to other family members' children and/or develop mentoring relationships with children in their larger communities.

A not atypical couple, Ellen and George, experienced four failed IVF and three failed donor egg cycles. Although they had been advised by their physician to stop infertility treatments until they had dealt with their grief in couples counseling, they could not consider the possibility of adoption or a childless life. Toward the conclusion of therapy, they had adopted a baby girl.

The legacy phase encompasses the aftermath of the experience with infertility. Marital, sexual, and parenting problems may emerge as a consequence of the infertility, particularly when partners have not adequately handled the significant losses accompanying this experience. Alice and Barry, a professional couple in their late 50s, were thinking of divorce. Although a recent heart attack appeared to be the precipitant for the couple's distress, in taking the couple's history, the clinician queried them about the 8-year span between their marriage and the birth of their only son. They then described a 7-year struggle with infertility, and, as Barry put it, "That was the beginning of the end." Neither had fully understood the devastation that their struggle with infertility had wrought. Although there are some whose relationships have been so damaged by the infertility and its treatments that they divorce, couples who have been able to face this hardship together often find their marriages have been strengthened.

INFERTILITY AND PSYCHOTHERAPY

The modalities for the psychological treatment of infertility are similar to those for other acute and chronic illnesses. Many infertility patients find support groups (both group therapy and leaderless self-help groups) beneficial, although others find this modality too painful. The exposure to other couples' infertility experiences may even feel retraumatizing. Although individual therapy for women is useful, it tends to replicate medical procedures, which leave the male partner out of the loop. Because many of the issues raised by the infertility are interpersonal, therapies including the husband are recommended.

After the diagnosis of infertility, it is common for one or both partners to experience varying levels of anxiety or depression. Symptoms may increase and decrease throughout the various phases of the infertility experience. During the 1950s and 1960s, when medical diagnoses for infertility could be determined for only 30% to 40% of all infertile women (Eisner, 1963), reasons offered for nondiagnosed infertility were often related to the psychological problems of women. Hostility to women's mothers or partners and women's aggressive imitation of men were common explanations (Benedek, 1952). The focus of psychotherapy was on the woman and her ambivalence toward motherhood.

With the advent of sophisticated medical diagnostic procedures, physiological explanations can now be determined for 90% of infertile couples. As stated above, male and female factors for infertility are nearly equal. However, because a woman's body is the site of most treatments and because her identity may be more dependent on bearing and raising a child, she may experience more distress and be more receptive to psychotherapeutic intervention. But no matter who shows the most distress, the IPAI strongly recommends seeing the couple as the unit for psychotherapy. First, infertility is indeed a "couple issue." The distresses of infertility and its medical treatments are profound, and the effects reverberate: in each partner, in the couple dyad, in any future child, and in the couple's relationships with family, friends, and medical systems (Meyers et al., 1995b).

Second, there is a growing body of literature concerning the effects of social support on the re-siliency of those who experience physical and emotional stress (Perry, Difade, Musngi, Francis, & Jasobsberg, 1992). Although partners struggling with infertility will certainly benefit from the support of medical professionals and infertility communities such as RESOLVE, their ability to cope with the trauma is directly related to the strength of their close attachments (Johnson, 2002), namely, their partners. Lack of secure attachments not only makes them more vulnerable to traumatic distress, but also can affect medical compliance.

The following treatment recommendations were developed by the IPAI and are more fully delineated in the project's text, *Couple Therapy for Infertility* (Diamond et al., 1999). It is important for clinicians, especially those who are less experienced in working with infertility, to appreciate the extreme distress it generates. Clinicians should be careful not to attribute more dysfunction to the couple and more pathology to each partner than is warranted. The ordeal of infertility must be considered as the context in which the couple and individual issues emerge.

Telling the Story

One way to begin appreciating the ordeal of infertility—for the couple and the clinician—is to ask the partners to tell their joint and individual stories about the infertility. Not only is the gathering of information about experiences with infertility vital to a clinician's understanding, but also the telling itself is a necessary therapeutic step that appears to help couples step out of their current predicaments and take a look at the various ways in which infertility has engulfed their lives. It is also a time for each partner to hear about what the other partner has been experiencing as the ordeal evolved. And it is a time to explore the various coping styles and resources they have been able to utilize.

Normalizing the Infertility

Infertile couples often feel marginalized and isolated from their normal social networks. It is useful for clinicians to normalize the couple's experience by sharing similar experiences of other infertile couples. This is a standard protocol of the IPAI. Certainly identities were kept confidential and permission was obtained from couples, but the sharing of stories and coping strategies created a sense of community with others who were also struggling with infertility. Support groups have been found to be extremely helpful. The two major national self-help and information organizations offering such groups are RESOLVE: the National Infertility Association and the American Infertility Association.

Determine the Phase in Which
the Couple Finds Itself

Although it cannot be assumed that each couple's passage through the ordeal will be the same, the general progression through the various phases described here can serve as a useful map for the clinician. It not only suggests which issues are likely to be most salient for the couple but helps the clinician plan his or her clinical interventions. And although there are instances when couples can benefit from information regarding a specific phase, it is also important to recognize the uniqueness of each partner's and each couple's experience.

Nurturing the Couple's Relationship

Coping with infertility and its treatments can be so overwhelming that couples are likely to neglect their personal lives and their relationship. At first, couples make these sacrifices in response to the immediate crisis that infertility presents. As months or years of failed protocols accumulate, there is less time, energy, and incentive to have fun and enjoy each other's company. Couples need to invest a share of their time and energy in preserving their relationship; often the therapist must help them conjure up a future in which the infertility ordeal will have ended. Clinicians can suggest that couples create areas of their lives that can serve as infertility-free havens, such as designated evenings for enjoyment without the discussion of infertility.

Sexual Pleasure Versus the Chore
of Baby Making

Almost universally, infertility and its treatments have detrimental effects on the couple's sexual relationship. Over time, scheduled, nonspontaneous intercourse becomes a chore; some may even have aversive reactions to sex that persist into the legacy phase. The IPAI recommends that couples create a separation—both in their conceptualizations and in their behavior—between sexual intercourse for "baby making" and sexual intercourse for enjoyment. Specifically, it is suggested that they take the time, usually on days when there is little likelihood of becoming pregnant, to enjoy lovemaking.

Separate Sessions:
Speaking the Unspeakable

IPAI found that the "unspeakable" themes evoked by the infertility are likely to result in uncertainty and guardedness about what to share with one's partner. Because couples need a forum in which to express these thoughts, feelings, and fantasies—to "speak the unspeakable," the thoughts and fantasies that are generated by the infertility—separate sessions for each partner are scheduled within the first 4 weeks of a couple's sessions. The clinician explains that the goal of separate sessions is to help partners articulate what troubles them and to bring back to the conjoint sessions any significant issues that bear on the couple relationship. The number of separate sessions varies and is determined by the clinician and the couple. In these sessions, partners are often helped to realize that their concerns and feelings can be shared with the other partner without resulting in dire consequences, and that by speaking freely, they may strengthen the couple's bonds.

In her separate session, Laura told the therapist that after she learned of Jim's sterility, she was not only finding him sexually less attractive, but generally less manly, and she admitted treating him rather shabbily. In his session, Jim spoke of how much the sterility diagnosis had made him feel "less of a man"; for his part, he reported acting more dejected and "hangdog" around Laura. In each partner's separate session, the pros and cons of keeping these painful matters secret from the other were discussed. Each was encouraged and supported in their decision to talk about their feelings about the sterility together. The couple broached the topic on their own and reported back in the couple session. Once they could air their fears and feelings, a deeper intimacy and eventual sexual intimacy were fostered.

Facilitating Mourning

Loss is a leitmotif of the couple's encounter with infertility, and the kinds of losses are both tangible (e.g., failed medical protocols, miscarriages, stillbirths) and intangible (e.g., experiencing a trouble-free pregnancy, having a genetically related child, the anticipatory loss of not knowing whether they will ever have children). Related research concerning coping with the death of a child (Videka-Sherman, 1982; Videka-Sherman & Lieberman, 1985) found that women often became depressed, and their husbands withdrew from the relationship and engaged in tasks. The woman thereby suffered am additional loss. However, for the couples that stayed connected and grieved together, the grief was handled more effectively, and the relationship improved. There are none of the customary rituals, such as funeral services, wakes, or sitting shivah, for grieving the losses of infertility. Because these kinds of rituals facilitate the mourning process, IPAI encourages couples to create mourning rituals of their own.

Susan and Ben, a couple in their mid-30s, designed a mourning ritual for failed infertility procedures. After receiving the medical report that she had not conceived, Susan called Steve. Then each left work, and Steve met Susan at home with chocolates and a video. Cuddling in bed, watching the video, and eating the chocolate, they were able to comfort each other. They called this the "bed-and-chocolate ritual."

EXTRAPSYCHOTHERAPEUTIC APPROACHES

Domar and Kelly (2002) described the mind-body approach she developed for women diagnosed with infertility. The program is aimed at reducing stress and depression. It consists of a combination of group relaxation and meditation. Domar reported significant improvements in achieving pregnancies and live births.

RESOLVE and the American Infertility Association are national self-help groups with local chapters; both offer information and support and provide a needed sense of community for this marginalized population.

SUMMARY

The experience of infertility is one of the most difficult ordeals a couple can face. It typically elicits powerful feelings of loss, guilt, shame, and anger while challenging each partner's basic beliefs about themselves and the world around them. In so doing, it puts severe strains on the couple relationship. For this reason, the psychological and relational problems that are precipitated by infertility are handled most effectively when the couple faces the ordeal together.

Working together, couples may discover hidden resources, strengthen their communication skills, enhance their ability to function collaboratively, and—through empathic understanding of each other's experience—resolve conflicts and make decisions more effectively. More than one couple has called this phenomenon the "silver lining" of their ordeal. Working with the couple, the therapist can strengthen the couple's relationship as together they face the challenges of infertility. Primary care psychologists should be prepared to recognize when infertility may be part of a patient's or a couple's distress, effectively assess its impact, and provide empathic, nonpathologizing treatment.

References

American Fertility Society. (2000–2002). *Fact sheet: In vitro fertilization.* Birmingham, AL: Author.

American Society for Reproductive Medicine. (1997). Ethical considerations of assisted reproductive technologies. The Ethics Committee of the American Society for Reproductive Medicine. *Fertility and Sterility, 67* (5, Suppl. 1), i–iii, 1S–9S.

Benedek, T. (1952). Infertility a psychosomatic defense. *Fertility and Sterility, 3,* 527–541.

Berg, B. J., & Wilson, J. F. (1991). Psychological functioning across stages of treatment for infertility. *Journal of Behavioral Medicine, 14,* 11–26.

Boss, P., & Greenberg, J. (1984). Family boundary ambiguity: A new variable in family stress theory. *Family Process, 23,* 535–546.

Burns, L. H. (1990). An exploratory study of perceptions of parenting after infertility. *Family Systems Medicine, 8,* 177–189.

Burns, L. H. (1987). Infertility as boundary ambiguity: One theoretical perspective. *Family Process, 26,* 359–372.

Centers for Disease Control and Prevention. (2002). *Assisted reproductive technology success rates, national summary and fertility clinic reports.* Washington, DC: U.S. Department of Health and Human Services.

Davis, O. K., & Rosenwaks, Z. (1996). In vitro fertilization. In E. Adashi (Ed.), *Reproductive endocrinology, surgery and technology* (pp. 2320–2331). Philadelphia, PA: Lippincott-Raven.

Dhillon, A. (2003, April 12). At 65, is Indian the world's oldest mum? *South China Morning Post Publishers Limited, Hong Kong,* p. 3.

Diamond, R., Kezur, D., Meyers, M., Scharf, C. N., & Weinshel, M. (1999). *Couple therapy for infertility.* New York: Guilford Press.

Domar, A., & Kelly, A. (2002). *Conquering infertility: Dr. Alice Domar's mind/body guide to enhancing fertility and coping with infertility.* New York: Penguin Putnam.

Eisner, B. G. (1963). Some psychological differences between fertile and infertile women. *Journal of Clinical Psychology, 19,* 391–394.

Gottman, J. (1994). *What predicts divorce?* Mahwah, NJ: Erlbaum.

Greil, A. L. (1991). *Not yet pregnant.* New Brunswick, NJ: Rutgers University Press.

Hodder, H. F. (1997, November-December). The new fertility. *Harvard Magazine,* 66–98.

Humphrey, M. (1986). Infertility as a marital crisis. *Stress Medicine, 2,* 221–224.

Johnson, S. (2002). *Emotionally focused couple therapy with trauma survivors: Strengthening attachment bonds.* New York: Guilford Press.

Kedem, P., Mikulincer, M., Nathanson, Y. E., & Bartov, B. (1990). Psychological aspects of male infertility. *British Journal of Medical Psychology, 63,* 73–80.

Kolata, G. (1997, April 24). A record and big questions as woman gives birth at 63. *New York Times* (section 14, p. 3).

Mahlstedt, P. P. (1985). Psychological components of infertility. *Fertility and Sterility, 43,* 335–346.

Marrs, R. (with Bloch, L. F., & Silverman, K. K.).

(1997). *Dr. Richard Marrs' fertility book.* New York: Delacorte.

McDaniel, S. H., Hepworth, J., & Doherty, W. (1992). Medical family therapy with couples facing infertility. *American Journal of Family Therapy, 20,* 101–122.

Menning, B. E. (1988). *Infertility: A guide for the childless couple* (2nd ed.). New York: Prentice Hall.

Merck Manual (16th ed.). (1992). Philadelphia, PA: National.

Meyers, M. (1990). Male gender-related issues in reproduction and technology. In N. L. Stotland (Ed.), *Psychiatric aspects of reproductive technology* (pp. 25–34). Washington, DC: American Psychiatric Press.

Meyers, M., Weinshel, M., Scharf, C., Kezur, D., Diamond, R., & Rait, D. (1995a). An infertility primer for family therapists: I. Medical, social and psychological dimensions. *Family Process, 34,* 219–229.

Meyers, M., Weinshel, M., Scharf, C., Kezur, D., Diamond, R., & Rait, D. (1995b). An infertility primer for family therapists: II. Working with couples who struggle with infertility. *Family Process, 34,* 231–240.

O'Moore, A. M., O'Moore, R. R., Harrison, F. F., & Carruthers, M. (1983). Psychosomatic aspects in idiopathic infertility: Effects of treatment with autogenic training. *Journal of Psychosomatic Research, 27,* 145–151.

Palermo, G., Colombero, L., Schattman, G., Davis, O., & Rosenwaks, Z. (1996). Evolution of pregnancies and initial follow-up of newborns delivered after intracytoplasmic sperm injection. *Journal of the American Medical Association, 276,* 1893–1897.

Paulson, R., Boostanfar, R., Saadat, P., Mor, E., Tourgeman, D., & Slater, C. C. (2002). Pregnancy in the sixth decade of life: Obstetric outcomes in women of advanced reproductive age. *Journal of the American Medical Association, 288,* 2320–2323.

Perry, S., Difade, J., Musngi, G., Francis, A., & Jasobsberg, L. (1992). Predictors of posttraumatic stress disorder after burn injury. *American Journal of Psychiatry, 149,* 931–935.

Sandelowski, M. (1993). *With child in mind.* Philadelphia: University of Pennsylvania Press.

Scharf, C., & Weinshel, M. (2000). Infertility and late life pregnancies. In P. Papp (Ed.), *Couples on the fault line: New directions for therapists* (pp. 104–129). New York: Guilford Press.

Tarkan, L. (2002, October 8). Fertility clinics begin to address mental health. *New York Times*, p. F5.

Videka-Sherman, L. (1982). Coping with the death of a child: A study over time. *American Journal of Orthopsychiatry, 55,* 668–698.

Videka-Sherman, L., & Lieberman, M. (1985). The effects of self-help and psychotherapy intervention on child loss: The limits of recovery. *American Journal of Orthopsychiatry, 55,* 70–82.

Walter, H. (1982). Psychological and legal aspects of artificial insemination (AID): An overview. *American Journal of Psychotherapy, 36,* 91–102.

30

Irritable Bowel Syndrome and Other Functional Gastrointestinal Disorders

Charles K. Burnett
Douglas A. Drossman

This chapter reviews the pathophysiology, epidemiology, and treatment of functional gastrointestinal disorders (FGIDs). Although a number of FGIDs have been described, the majority of data on the course and treatment of these conditions have focused on irritable bowel syndrome (IBS). Throughout the chapter, we will focus on IBS as the prototypical FGID, unless specific reference is made to other conditions. Interest in FGIDs in children is growing, but far less information is available for pediatric populations and FGIDs. Consequently, this chapter focuses exclusively on adults.

OVERVIEW OF THE FUNCTIONAL GASTROINTESTINAL DISORDERS

The FGIDs are a set of conditions encompassing disturbances in the functioning of the digestive system that are not directly attributable to structural abnormalities or infection. Functional disorders affect the entire gastrointestinal system from throat to anus. A multinational, collaborative effort has been under way for several years to classify and develop diagnostic criteria for FGIDs. This diagnostic system, the Rome II criteria (Drossman, Corazziari, Talley, Thompson, & Whitehead, 2000), specifies positive diagnostic criteria for each disorder, similar to the *Diagnostic and Statistical Manual of Mental Disorders*, fourth edition (*DSM-IV*) criteria for psychiatric disorders (American Psychiatric Association, 1994).

Until relatively recently, functional disorders were diagnoses of exclusion; that is, they were diagnosed after no biological explanation for symptoms could be identified. The multinational committee developing the Rome II criteria assembled research documenting the pathophysiological and psychosocial evidence to support diagnoses of FGIDs as distinct disorders rather than as vague symptoms unexplainable by other means. In addition, the Rome II diagnostic manual provides the current status of epidemiology, pathophysiology, and treatment recommendations for each condition.

The currently recognized FGIDs are shown in Table 30.1, which indicates that the FGIDs are clustered by location in the gastrointestinal tract

Table 30.1 The Functional Gastrointestinal Disorders

Esophageal disorders
  Globus
  Rumination syndrome
  Functional chest pain of presumed esophageal origin
  Functional heartburn
  Functional dysphagia
  Unspecified functional esophageal disorder

Gastroduodenal disorders
  Functional dyspepsia
    Ulcerlike dyspepsia
    Dysmotilitylike dyspepsia
    Unspecified (nonspecific) dyspepsia
  Aerophagia
  Functional vomiting

Bowel disorders
  Irritable bowel syndrome
  Functional abdominal bloating
  Functional constipation
  Functional diarrhea
  Unspecified functional bowel disorder

Functional abdominal pain
  Functional abdominal pain syndrome
  Unspecified functional abdominal pain

Functional disorders of the biliary tract and the
    pancreas
  Gallbladder dysfunction
  Sphincter of Oddi dysfunction

Anorectal disorders
  Functional fecal incontinence
  Functional anorectal pain
    Levator ani syndrome
    Proctalgia fugax
  Pelvic floor dyssynergia

Functional pediatric disorders
  Vomiting
    Infant regurgitation
    Infant rumination syndrome
    Cyclic vomiting syndrome
  Abdominal pain
    Functional dyspepsia
      Ulcerlike dyspepsia
      Dysmotilitylike dyspepsia
      Unspecified (nonspecific) dyspepsia
    Irritable bowel syndrome
    Functional abdominal pain
    Abdominal migraine
    Aerophagia
  Functional diarrhea
  Disorders of defecation
    Infant dyschezia
    Functional constipation
    Functional fecal retention
    Functional nonretentive fecal soiling

and subcategorized according to predominant type of symptoms.

PATHOPHYSIOLOGY

Abnormal motor responses—motility disturbances—of the gastrointestinal tract are present in many gastrointestinal symptoms, such as vomiting and diarrhea. Furthermore, stressful experiences can evoke altered motility throughout the gastrointestinal system in healthy individuals as well as in patients with FGIDs. Individuals with FGIDs have been found to exhibit heightened motor responses to environmental and psychological stressors compared with normal controls (Kumar & Wingate, 1985). The degree of motor dysfunction does not correlate very highly with symptom reports, leading to the speculation that motor dysfunction may only partly contribute to the discomfort experienced by patients with these disorders.

Pain is a predominant symptom of most FGIDs. Notably, functional chest pain, functional abdominal pain syndrome, functional dyspepsia, functional anorectal pain syndromes, and IBS could be considered as primarily chronic or recurrent painful disorders. The concept of visceral hypersensitivity is useful in conceptualizing the pain component of FGIDs. Visceral hypersensitivity can be thought of as an amplification of visceral signals to the brain that can occur at various levels of the neural axis from the intestinal mucosal to the brain (Drossman, Camilleri, Mayer, & Whitehead, 2002). Thus, painful visceral signals may be experienced as more painful in persons with IBS (hyperalgesia), and even normal regulatory motor activity such as peristalsis may be perceived as painful (allodynia). The amplification of this visceral pain afferent system may be related to one or a combination of altered mucosal receptor sensitivity, spinal dorsal horn excitability, or dysregulation of the central pain modulation system (Drossman et al., 2002).

This understanding has raised interest that IBS be considered a disorder related to dysfunction of the brain-gut axis (Mayer & Raybould, 1990). This view emphasizes the role of reciprocal feedback circuits connecting visceral nociception, spinal sensory modulation, subcortical emotional sensitization, and cortical modulation of sensory information. Thus, external factors such as stressful events as well as internal emotional experiences can affect gastrointestinal sensations, motility, secretory activity, and inflammatory responses directly through cortical and subcortical effects on enteric nervous system functioning. Conversely, peripheral visceral sensory input can affect central pain levels, mood, cognitions, and behavior. Autonomic reactivity, especially as modulated by vagal afferents, is an important pathway in altering gastrointestinal function (Wood, Alpers, & Andrews, 1999).

Inflammatory factors may play a role in triggering or maintaining symptoms in FGIDs. Of a group of individuals with no prior history of bowel disorder who had an episode of acute gastroenteritis, 23% met criteria for IBS 3 months later. Although altered gastrointestinal motility was found in both symptomatic and asymptomatic individuals at follow-up, level of hypochondriasis and life stress predicted the persistence of IBS symptoms. Patients with IBS at 3 months also had increased levels of inflammatory cells in the colon (Gwee et al., 1999), and it has been proposed that psychological distress may serve to "upregulate" the peripheral sensory inflammatory signals that occur in postinfectious IBS (Drossman, 1999a). A 2002 study documented chronic inflammatory changes and evidence of neuropathy in jejunal biopsies of patients with IBS (Törnblom, Lindberg, Nyberg, & Veress, 2002) compared with controls. It appears, then, that a gastrointestinal trauma such as an acute inflammatory illness or even psychological trauma acting on the gut through efferent pathways can act as a sentinel event in establishing a brain-gut feedback loop perpetuating FGID symptoms.

FGIDs can essentially be considered chronic illnesses, with varying courses dependent on numerous biopsychosocial factors (Drossman, 1998; Engel, 1977). There is a growing appreciation for the central role that patient psychosocial factors play in the onset, maintenance, and exacerbation of the FGIDs (Drossman, 1998). Stress or psychophysiological arousal is well known to induce alterations in gastrointestinal functioning in healthy individuals and to worsen symptoms in FGID patients. Preexisting or comorbid Axis I and Axis II disorders are strongly associated with

symptom intensity, coping ability, and health care–seeking behavior (Drossman, Creed, et al., 2000; Drossman, Li, et al., 2000; Fullwood & Drossman, 1995). As is the case with most chronic illness, FGIDs have been shown to affect quality of life adversely (Whitehead, Burnett, Cook, & Taub, 1996).

Physical or sexual abuse have been implicated as factors that may amplify perception of visceral signals in FGIDs or the behavioral response to them (Drossman et al., 1990; Drossman, Li, Leserman, Toomey, & Hu, 1996), especially IBS. Despite the high prevalence of self-reported abuse of 30% to 56% of FGID patients seen in tertiary care centers (Drossman, Talley, Leserman, Olden, & Barreiro, 1995), an abuse history has not been shown to cause symptoms directly. Rather, abuse history is associated with the somatic or behavioral expression of psychological distress. Abuse may also contribute to upregulation of emotional and somatic hypervigilance, to heightened pain perception, and to maladaptive cognitions such as difficulty setting boundaries and feeling out of control. More severe abuse experiences, involving rape with penetration, threat of death, or repeated abusive experiences are associated with poorer health outcomes (Drossman et al., 1990, 1996). Studies using brain imaging are showing a possible mechanism for greater pain perception and reporting in patients with FGIDs and abuse history via dysfunction in the central nervous system's pain regulatory system located in the cingulate cortex (Drossman et al., 2003).

EPIDEMIOLOGY

Prevalence estimates for FGIDs vary by condition and across studies. However, data for a number of the FGIDs suggest point prevalence rates ranging from 2% to 3% for functional vomiting and functional abdominal pain to 25% for dyspepsia (Drossman, Creed, et al., 2000). IBS is the most well-researched functional disorder, and several studies have reported prevalence rates in the range of 10% to 20%. IBS is also more common among women than men. Individuals tend to consult physicians for IBS first between the ages of 30 and 50 years, prevalence decreases with advancing age, and African Americans and whites exhibit similar rates; Hispanics may report lower rates of IBS symptoms (Drossman et al., 2002).

TYPICAL COURSE
OF THE ILLNESS

As with most, if not all, medical conditions, FGIDs involve numerous aspects of physiological and psychological functioning. A critical feature of FGIDs is the general lack of evidence for structural abnormalities. Thus, even extensive medical evaluations typically fail to discover structural or biochemical abnormalities to be corrected. This leaves the physician with a finite set of medication options to use in attempting to treat symptoms or alter physiology to reduce symptom intensity. Surgical interventions such as cholecystectomy, hysterectomy, or exploratory laparotomy are common in patients with medication-resistant symptoms.

When even invasive procedures do not alleviate symptoms, the tendency is for physicians to retreat to a dualistic stance and attribute symptoms exclusively to psychopathology. The patient often feels his or her symptoms and experience of illness have been misunderstood, invalidated, and dismissed as "all in my head." This is frequently the point at which referrals are made to psychologists. Thus, one or more of the initial psychotherapy sessions is usually devoted to education about the mind-body or brain-gut connection in addition to more specific education about the particular FGIDs experienced by the patient.

TREATMENT

There is a progression of illness severity seen in FGID patients that is dependent on the type of referral source or practice setting. Patients with more refractory or severe symptoms tend ultimately to be referred to tertiary care settings, and those with more moderate symptoms often achieve satisfactory benefit from primary care or specialty (gastroenterology) interventions (Drossman, 1999b; Drossman et al., 2002). Patients seen in tertiary care settings also are more likely to exhibit severe psychological distress and Axis I

and II pathology than those seen in primary care settings. Data on health care seeking in patients with IBS indicated that the decision to consult a physician is strongly associated with neuroticism and Axis I and II diagnoses (Drossman et al., 1988; Drossman, Creed, et al., 2000; Whitehead, Bosmajian, Zonderman, Costa, & Schuster, 1988).

A major role of the psychologist in treating patients with FGIDs is an educational one. Busy medical clinics seldom allow for time for patient education, so FGID patients, especially those newly diagnosed, typically have a great need for information on their condition and treatment options. Just as with other chronic conditions, half of the battle often lies in joining with the patient in a shared view of the psychophysiological nature of the illness and its treatment. Several sessions may be required for some patients to learn to adopt a biopsychosocial viewpoint. Once this level of understanding has been achieved, more classically psychological treatment regimens can be used.

Typical Approaches

A graduated, multicomponent treatment approach to patients with IBS of varying severity levels was proposed by Drossman and Thompson (1992). This approach recognizes the increasing level of symptom severity and greater likelihood of comorbid psychological disorders seen in patients across primary, secondary, and tertiary care settings. Patients with mild symptoms (70% of patients) are typically initially seen in primary care settings and exhibit no noticeable psychopathology or significant disruption in their lives because of symptoms. They are best treated with education, reassurance, and possibly dietary modification or fiber supplementation. Patients with mild symptoms are less likely to require psychological treatment, but education regarding basic stress management could be of potential benefit.

Patients with moderate symptoms (25% of patients) are more likely to experience impairment in daily functioning and to have diagnosable psychological disorders. These individuals are likely to be referred to gastroenterologists for more extensive evaluation. Drossman and Thompson (1992) recommended pharmacological treatment and referral for psychological treatment for these patients.

Finally, patients with severe symptoms (5% of patients) have usually been refractory to treatment, have diagnosable psychopathology including Axis II psychopathology, and are usually referred to tertiary care settings. A multicomponent treatment strategy is most appropriate for patients with severe symptoms, including pharmacological treatment with antidepressants, psychological treatment, and physician behavioral management strategies such as limit setting and supportive counseling.

The next section presents a model, the biopsychosocial vicious cycle, for use in patient education and treatment planning. The vicious cycle concept is readily accepted by patients and has been helpful for educational and treatment planning purposes.

The Vicious Cycle

Ms. X., a middle-aged woman with a 5-year history of functional abdominal pain, is referred by her gastroenterologist for pain management and treatment for depression. She comes to the psychologist's office dysphoric and angry, exhibiting pain behaviors such as grimacing, abdominal holding, and rocking. She is periodically tearful. When asked for treatment goals, Ms. X. expresses puzzlement at being referred to a psychologist when all she wants is for someone to "cut it out" and rid her of her pain. Her previous medical history includes numerous tests and procedures, including endoscopies, radiological studies, cholycystectomy, hysterectomy, and exploratory surgeries with lysis of adhesions. She rates her pain at 6/10 on average, with multiple flares of up to 9/10 across an average week. Ms. X. has been tried on numerous antidepressant and pain medications with little impact on her pain.

Ms. X.'s bouncing knee, hand wringing, and urgent speech support her self-report of irritability and restlessness. When she can get to sleep, her sleep is interrupted by frequent awakenings with pain. She realizes that she is impatient with her children, harsh with her husband, short-tempered, and angry with the medical profession for failing to eliminate her pain.

Her predominant cognitions concern her growing sense of helplessness and feeling out of control. In addition to her anxiety, Ms. X. is also becoming increasingly dysphoric with catastrophizing automatic thoughts, such as "I can't take this anymore," "I can't live like this," and "I must have cancer or something terribly wrong with me that the physicians are missing."

Historically, Ms. X. married young, has effectively parented three children, and worked in a blue-collar job until going on disability because of her pain. Her husband is growing increasingly frustrated with her condition, and wants something done to fix her pain. Ms. X., along with two sisters, was shuffled among foster homes after her substance-abusing and physically and verbally abusive parents relinquished custody. One of her earliest memories is packing her few personal belongings to move to yet another foster home, separate from her sisters, and having no idea what might happen to her. Subsequently, one sister committed suicide, and the other lives a marginal lifestyle with multiple psychological and substance abuse problems.

Ms. X. reports that she is as distressed when her pain is better as she is when it is severe. She has observed that when she notices herself starting to feel slightly better, she is aware of "waiting for the other shoe to drop," and her pain inevitably increases. She has also recently noticed worsening back pain, headaches, and dyspepsia. Ms. X. wonders "what next" will go wrong with her body. She can no longer trust her body to function properly, and she is constantly aware of changing sensations throughout her body, especially visceral sensations.

Ms. X. is clearly caught in a vicious cycle in which her pain contributes to psychophysiological hyperarousal and negative, catastrophizing cognitions. Her state of hyperarousal energizes not only cognitive, but also attentional factors that draw her attention more and more to her pain and distress. Over time, as her attention becomes more focused on her pain, she perceives even subtle changes in symptom level as threatening and notices other novel sensations more readily. Her sense of being threatened by her body is enhanced by accumulating external stressors such as job loss and family pressures. Ms. X. has been sensitized to feeling out of control by her early abandonment experiences, so she feels helpless and increasingly desperate for help. She has had repeated surgical trauma to her abdomen in prior attempts to treat her pain, and these now are likely also contributing to the pain.

Ms. X. needs a way of understanding the vicious cycle in which she is caught in order to engage in psychological treatment. The therapist also could benefit from a model for conceptualizing the multiple factors affecting the etiology and maintenance of her symptoms and for planning effective treatment strategies. The biopsychosocial vicious cycle model has proven extremely useful as a clinical tool. The basic model is one of threat appraisal and reactivity (see Figure 30.1). In this model, the patient experiences an FGID symptom first, which immediately causes a physiological threat reaction, or state of autonomic arousal. As the individual perceives this reaction, various cognitions and emotions determine the psychological meaning of the threat-induced arousal in a process of appraisal, the third step. The individual then focuses on the original sensations giving rise to the threat response, as well as to even subtle changes in the symptom or other different sensations or symptoms that may arise. Fourth, the resulting selective attention increases the probability that further threat will be detected because of either subtle variations in the original symptom or novel and even unrelated sensations or symptoms. As arousal and selective attention build, more sources of threat or a more profound sense of threat increase arousal, cognitive and emotional investment, and selective attention.

The psychophysiological vicious cycle takes place within a social context, such that external sources of threat, arousal, thought and mood, or hypervigilance can energize the system. For example, marital distress can increase physiological arousal and affect mood to increase the likelihood that symptoms will be perceived. Early childhood experience of abuse can affect chronic physiological arousal, cognitions, mood, hypervigilance, and baseline level of perceived threat. In each of these instances, the biopsychosocial model posits worsening FGID symptoms with increases in physiological, psychological, or social threats over and above the threat value of the original sensations or symptom complex.

The biopsychosocial vicious cycle can be an important tool in patient education and treatment planning. Explaining symptoms in terms of this model helps to validate and normalize the individual's experiences with sometimes bewildering interactions among sensations, thoughts, moods, and illness-related experiences. Patients can often make the connection between thoughts, arousal, and symptoms within this context without hearing "it's all in your head." The vicious cycle concept also facilitates a paradigm shift from a strictly biomedical mode of thought to a more flexible and realistic biopsychosocial approach to symptom exacerbation and treatment options.

Each aspect of the vicious cycle model suggests a variety of treatment options. For example, medication is often the preferred treatment for specific sensations or symptoms. Reduction of physiological arousal may be facilitated by more behavioral techniques such as relaxation exercises, yoga, biofeedback, physical exercise, and the like. The thought and mood domain of the model provides a rationale for psychotherapy to improve affect and coping, for pain management, and to understand and modify maladaptive cognitions. Finally, attention management techniques such as distraction, hypnosis, and mindfulness meditation can be useful in reducing selective attention and hypervigilance to threatening sensations.

In the case of Ms. X., the majority of the second treatment session was used to explain and discuss the biopsychosocial vicious cycle model and how it relates to her experience of her symptoms. Although she was skeptical of the relationship between her thoughts and her symptoms, she readily acknowledged her hyperarousal. This provided an opening for introducing her to progressive muscle relaxation, breathing exercises, walking, and other arousal reduction techniques.

At a return visit 2 weeks later, Ms. X. reported that she had diligently practiced her arousal reduction homework and was amazed to find that her pain was a great deal better, now 2 to 3 on a scale of 10 with only one or two flares of 6/10 over the past week. Her skepticism had all but disappeared, and she was eager to press on with

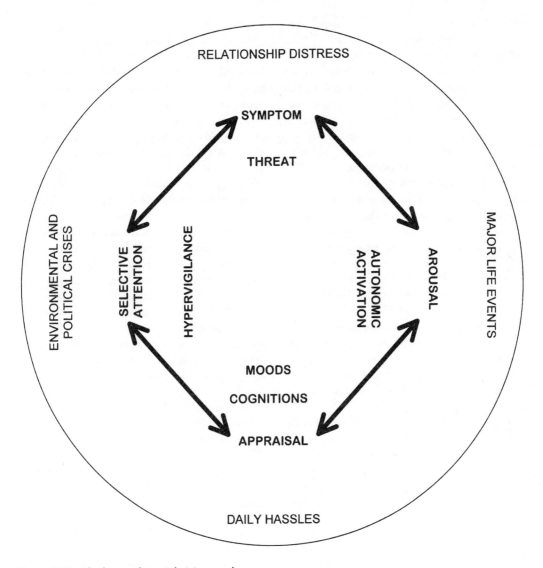

Figure 30.1   The biopsychosocial vicious cycle.

treatment. Over the ensuing eight sessions, Ms. X. enthusiastically explored the relationship among her thoughts, moods, developmental history, and symptoms. She worked on improving her communication with her husband and learned some basic strategies for managing her attention.

At the end of treatment, she was able to articulate the interrelationships among her symptoms, arousal, thoughts and moods, and hypervigilance as well as describe the various cognitive and behavioral techniques she had learned and applied to moderate each aspect of the vicious cycle. At a 6-month follow-up, Ms. X. was still practicing her techniques and was essentially symptom free.

Medical Treatment

A primary goal of medical evaluation of FGID patients is the exclusion of structural, neoplastic, or infectious causes for the reported symptoms. Despite the existence of positive diagnostic criteria for these disorders (Rome II; Drossman, Corazziari, et al., 2000), most physicians require some degree of medical evaluation prior to diagnosing a functional gastrointestinal disorder. Typically, routine blood work, fecal cultures for ova and parasites, and flexible sigmoidoscopy (or colonoscopy in a patient older than 50 years) are sufficient to rule out alternative etiologies for IBS symptoms (Drossman, 2001a). Upper gastrointestinal symptoms usually also merit an esophagoduodenoscopy to evaluate for acid reflux disease (gastroesophageal reflux disease, GERD), *Helicobacter pylori gastritis,* or ulcer disease.

Other more specific tests such as CT scans, MRIs, colonoscopies, tests for celiac sprue or lactose intolerance, specialized radiographic studies, or mucosal biopsies may be conducted if there is preliminary information from routine screening tests or the physical examination to suggest other diagnoses that could be detected by these imaging techniques. However, they should not be done based on the refractoriness of the patient's condition or patient requests to "do something." In these situations, performing unnecessary tests does not reassure the patient as some physicians believe; instead, it has the paradoxical effect of reinforcing the patient's belief that something is being missed.

The usual medical approach to treating FGIDs relies heavily on pharmacological management of symptoms. Extensive use of smooth muscle antispasmodics for lower gastrointestinal symptoms (e.g., dicyclomine [Bentyl], hyoscyamine [Levsin]), or acid-blocking agents for upper gastrointestinal symptoms (e.g., omeprazole [Prilosec], ranitidine [Zantac]), and antidepressants are common across the spectrum of FGIDs. Prokinetic medications (e.g., metoclopramide [Reglan]) are also used in treating gastric disorders. Tricyclic antidepressants have been effective in the treatment of FGIDs (Jackson et al., 2000), especially in diarrhea-predominant IBS, for which their anticholinergic side effects can be helpful in reducing abnormal motility and in improving stool form. Increased use of selective serotonin reuptake inhibitors has occurred over the past few years, especially in cases of constipation-predominant IBS with abdominal pain or in treating other FGID pain symptoms, although no treatment trials using SSRIs have been reported to date.

Medications targeting serotonin levels in the gastrointestinal system have been introduced. One such medication is alosetron (Lotronex), a 5HT-3 antagonist approved for treatment of diarrhea-predominant IBS. Unfortunately, dosing and prescribing practices led to its recall by the Food and Drug Administration in November 2000. It has been made available again for restricted use. Among newer medications available or under development, tegaserod (Zelnorm) has been available in the United States since summer 2002 for treatment of constipation-predominant IBS. Tegaserod appears to function to some degree as a prokinetic throughout the gastrointestinal system in addition to reducing constipation, bloating, and discomfort.

Many patients with FGID are on a number of other medications as well. Benzodiazepines may be prescribed for comorbid anxiety, nausea and vomiting, or spasm. However, there is little or no evidence that benzodiazepines are efficacious in treating FGIDs. The potential for interaction with other medications and dependency also argue against chronic use. Buspirone (Buspar) may have some specialized effects on muscle wall compliance in the gastrointestinal system, so it may be more appropriate for longer term use in patients with FGID.

Pain medications, both narcotic and nonnarcotic, are frequently prescribed for episodic or chronic use. A major drawback of heavy reliance on narcotic analgesics is "narcotic bowel" or the tendency for narcotics to disrupt normal gastrointestinal motility and afferent pain pathways, eventually exacerbating symptoms by producing intestinal distension, constipation, vomiting, and a paradoxical worsening of pain, leading to a vicious cycle of pain, narcotic, pain. Especially if short-acting narcotics are used (e.g., oxycodone [Percocet]), there is the risk of a "soar-crash" cycle in which symptoms recur hours after medication administration because of withdrawal effects, and thus the cycle continues (Rogers & Cerda, 1989). A wide variety of herbal and homeopathic substances may also be used by patients with FGID.

Psychological Treatment

Several psychological treatment approaches have been evaluated for FGIDs. As mentioned, however, most of the published treatment trials have been limited to patients with IBS. Three major psychological treatment strategies have been used in randomized clinical trials: hypnotherapy, cognitive–behavioral therapy (CBT), and brief psychodynamic psychotherapy.

Hypnotherapy

Several studies have demonstrated improvements in FGID symptoms following hypnotherapy. Most of the research has been conducted with IBS. Whorwell and colleagues (Houghton, Heyman, & Whorwell, 1996; Whorwell, Prior, & Colgan, 1987; Whorwell, Prior, & Faragher, 1984) reported on several studies using a series of hypnotherapy sessions focusing on relaxation and increasing control over bowel symptoms. Across studies, subjects with IBS experienced decreased pain, bloating, bowel pattern disturbance, and an enhanced sense of subjective well-being. Hypnotherapy was shown to be superior to wait list and placebo controls. Whorwell's findings have been replicated using group hypnotherapy (Harvey, Hinton, Gunary, & Barry, 1989) and by Galovski and Blanchard (1998), who also found decreased anxiety in subjects following hypnotherapy.

Interest in the use of hypnotherapy for FGIDs has continued with efforts to identify the mechanisms responsible for the observed reduction in symptoms. Palsson, Turner, Johnson, Burnett, and Whitehead (2002) again found reductions in IBS symptoms following a standardized series of seven hypnotherapy sessions. Reductions in subjects' general psychological distress and somatization were also found. Interestingly, almost no change in physiological parameters, such as rectal pain sensitivity and physiological reactivity, was observed. A slight decrease in skin conductance was observed, which may represent decreased autonomic reactivity following treatment.

Another study by Whorwell's group (Calvert, Houghton, Cooper, Morris, & Whorwell, 2002) extended the findings on the effectiveness of hypnotherapy in IBS in a study of hypnotherapy in patients with functional dyspepsia. Symptoms of fullness, early satiety, nausea, and vomiting were dramatically improved following a series of hypnotherapy sessions emphasizing imagery of improving gastric functioning. Hypnotherapy was superior to customary medical treatment and supportive therapy up to a year following treat-

ment. It appears, then, that hypnotherapy is beneficial in reducing symptoms and improving quality of life for patients with at least two of the more prevalent FGIDs.

Cognitive–Behavioral Therapy

A number of trials using cognitive and behavioral methodology for treatment of IBS have been reported. Interest in CBT as a treatment for FGIDs began with the work of Bennett and Wilkinson (1985), who found a multicomponent CBT program equal to medication in producing symptom reduction and superior in reducing anxiety. Lynch and Zamble (1989) found CBT was associated with symptom improvement and reduced anxiety compared with wait list controls. Multicomponent CBT in conjunction with standard medical therapy was also found to be superior to medical treatment alone in terms of symptom reduction and improved sense of well-being and quality of life in IBS patients (Heymann-Mönnikes et al., 2000).

Group CBT treatment has been reported to produce greater decreases in IBS symptoms than a wait list control (Van Dulmen, Fennis, & Bleijenberg, 1996) and to be superior to standard medical care, but equal in effectiveness to a psychoeducational control condition (Toner et al., 1998). A comparison of individual and group cognitive therapy found similar improvement in IBS symptoms regardless of treatment modality compared with standard medical care (Vollmer & Blanchard, 1998). Multicomponent group CBT has also been beneficial for treating functional chest pain (Potts, Lewin, Fox, & Johnstone, 1999).

A large series of studies using various combinations of cognitive therapy, patient education, and a variety of behavioral methods, such as progressive muscle relaxation and thermal biofeedback, has been conducted by Blanchard and colleagues (Blanchard, 2001; Blanchard & Scharff, 2002). This series of studies used standardized treatment protocols and the same outcome measures across trials assessing individual aspects of and combined multicomponent treatment for IBS. Active treatments have been compared to symptom-monitoring and attention-placebo groups. Overall, CBT treatments have been superior to attention-placebo and have demonstrated improvements in bowel symptoms up to 4 years following treatment. Of the various types of specific CBT treatments and treatment combinations evaluated, cognitive therapy alone has shown the most consistent and powerful effect on symptom reduction across studies (Blanchard & Scharff, 2002).

Data were released from a large multicenter study that involved over 400 patients with functional bowel disorders (e.g., IBS, functional constipation, functional abdominal pain) randomly assigned to CBT versus education or desipramine versus placebo groups (Drossman et al., in press). The data showed clear benefit for CBT over education and nonsignificant benefit for desipramine over placebo in the intention to treat analysis, but with significant benefit in the per protocol analysis. Outcome was assessed using a composite measure of patient-rated treatment efficacy, global well-being, pain ratings, and health-related quality of life. Thus, CBT was effective for treating functional bowel disorders, but desipramine may also be effective, providing the patient stays on the medication.

Psychodynamic Therapy

Brief psychodynamically oriented therapy has been used for treating IBS by two groups of investigators. Svedlund, Sjodin, Ottoson, and Dotevall (1983) compared groups receiving 7 to 10 sessions of psychodynamic psychotherapy with a group receiving conventional medical treatment. The psychotherapy groups exhibited improvements in pain and bowel function at 1-year follow-up. A similar study using an interpersonal model of dynamic psychotherapy was reported by Guthrie, Creed, Dawson, and Tomenson (1991). A 7-session individual treatment program was compared with customary medical care for patients with IBS. Patients in the treatment group reported significant improvement in bowel symptoms and had fewer return clinic visits over 3-month and 1-year follow-ups.

In general, data from treatment trials using a variety of psychological methodologies showed improvement in symptoms and enhanced quality of life or well-being compared to customary medical treatment or symptom monitoring. Studies

using an attention-placebo have found no difference in outcome between active treatment and controls. Although no trials have been reported directly comparing treatment strategies, some of the dismantling studies reported by Blanchard and Scharff (2002) pointed toward cognitive therapy as more efficacious than behavioral techniques. Excellent treatment manuals are available for CBT treatment of IBS (Blanchard, 2001; Toner et al., 2000). Additionally, hypnotherapy continues to generate interest and consistently good results in patients with IBS and, apparently, functional dyspepsia. After reviewing the data across all psychosocial treatment trials in patients with FGIDs, Drossman, Creed, and colleagues (2000) observed that, "Given the current state of knowledge, the psychotherapist should use the technique with which they [sic] are most experienced" (p. 215) when treating patients with FGID.

COMMON EMOTIONAL REACTIONS

Patients

Although patients with FGIDs can be conceptualized as generally reacting in a manner similar to patients with other chronic illnesses, several aspects of gastrointestinal disorders merit special consideration. Gastrointestinal disorders are generally "hidden" despite the potential to be quite disabling, making it more difficult to justify work absences, abrupt leave-taking in social and family situations, and other disruptions in roles and daily functioning.

From clinical experience, patients with FGID experience visceral pain as generally more mysterious, serious, and significant than nonvisceral somatic pain. Visceral symptoms, especially pain, seem to be accompanied by a heightened sense of severity and threat. This makes sense in that most of the bodily survival functions are housed within the viscera. In addition to increasing perceived threat, gastrointestinal dysfunction is a violation of a person's sense of "normalcy." Patients will often report that they formerly were not aware of gastrointestinal functions, but now can practically trace the path of food throughout the system. They usually long for a return to the time when digestion was automatic and occurred without conscious awareness. All of these perceptual features may be further enhanced among victims of abuse, who will generally be more vigilant to bodily signals.

Frequent yet generally unpredictable urges to defecate, eat, vomit, or pass gas can be extremely inconvenient and embarrassing. Efforts to avoid embarrassment often lead to dramatically restricted social, recreational, and job participation. Sometimes, obsessive preoccupations develop regarding scanning for and locating restrooms along customary travel routes and in every location a patient visits. Individuals also devise exit strategies for leaving social situations that become uncomfortable in case of a symptom flare. These patients may appear socially phobic, but may be exhibiting exaggerated defensive maneuvers in an attempt to reduce shame and embarrassment.

Patients with FGID often report feeling isolated from usual sources of social support such as friends and family members. Isolation often increases as symptoms worsen. Attempting to explain limitations imposed by FGIDs to others, even to intimates, often entails revealing unpleasant and highly personal information about bodily functions. Because most people are not accustomed to readily sharing such potentially embarrassing information with others, FGIDs are often accompanied by a substantial sense of shame. Individuals with prior history of abuse or other tendencies toward shame can be particularly vulnerable to psychological distress related to symptoms.

Another common reaction of patients with FGID is anger, both about being ill and about the medical profession. Anger directed at being ill often is based in loss. Patients with FGID commonly experience an intense sense of loss as social, recreational, and job opportunities and performance decline. Perceived loss of control over bodily functions can also increase anger. Medical professionals are frequently the targets of patient anger because of unexpressed or unresolved expectations for cure on the part of patients with FGID. The message that "there is nothing really wrong," conveyed with genuine relief by physicians following sometimes extensive medical evaluations, can be received as "it's all in my head" or "my situation is hopeless." Anger also accompanies violated assumptions of cause-effect

relationships between disease and illness, the widely held belief that there is a medical or surgical "fix" for pain and illness, and pervasive standards that pain and discomfort are wrong and mean that the physician has "missed something."

It is very important to assess and address these concerns early in therapy to facilitate patients' acceptance of a broader, more complex, and flexible biopsychosocial view of their particular disorder. A referral for psychological intervention is ideally perceived as enhancing the effects of medical treatment, but can also heighten patient concerns about abandonment by the physician and intensify catastrophizing cognitions, especially related to validity of the illness experience. This emphasizes not only the critical role of patient education about the nature of the FGIDs and the role and limitations of medical treatment, but also the importance of the therapeutic relationship in overcoming sometimes-repeated experiences of invalidation, especially in patients with abuse histories. Once these therapeutic tasks are accomplished, patients are in position to benefit maximally from more traditional psychotherapy.

Family

In contrast to the expectations of patients and family members regarding the course of many illnesses and injuries, FGIDs are almost by definition chronic or recurring. The normative illness model specifies an onset because of a specific cause, then a treatment that alleviates the condition. It appears more difficult generally for family members to accept FGIDs as chronic illnesses requiring management rather than expecting cure. Part of this difficulty stems from the hidden disability and unpredictability of symptoms, with patients exhibiting seemingly random periods of illness alternating with periods of apparently complete health. This variability can be puzzling and frustrating for family members, who quickly learn that there is little they can do to affect the patient's experience of illness. Existing family and couple dynamics affect the degree to which anger, withdrawal, and various control strategies are used to try to manage family members' affect and behaviors related to the illness. Thus, it is often beneficial to include partners and other family members in sessions devoted to educational and illness management strategies. Additional interpersonal or family therapy may be indicated when relationship distress appears to be affecting the FGID more directly through increased stress.

Clinicians

Physicians often find the treatment of patients FGID challenging and frustrating. Common issues faced by physicians include (a) discomfort with diagnostic uncertainty, (b) feeling pressured by patients to treat symptoms that are medically unexplained, (c) attempting to limit potentially risky diagnostic procedures and treatments that are unlikely to be effective or provide useful information, and (d) legitimizing patients' experience of illness without necessarily endorsing a specific disease etiology (Drossman, 2001b). Taken together, these physician-patient factors frequently contribute to a greater likelihood of dissatisfaction, fatigue, and lack of gratification when working with FGID patients versus patients with more "organic" disease.

Similar frustrations may be noted by psychologists working with patients with FGID. It is important for psychologists to avoid becoming caught between patients and physicians in struggles for further evaluation and treatment. Patients bring varying satisfaction with prior medical treatment to therapy and sometimes attempt to ally with the therapist against the physician, who is portrayed as invalidating or uncaring. This pattern is especially prevalent when Axis II disorders are present, but is not uncommon among patients with FGID in general. Physicians are often unable to devote the time for education, support, and counseling that patients with FGID really need. Psychologists are in a strategic position to serve these functions in true multidisciplinary fashion.

In an attempt to assist physicians and other health care workers in treating patients with FGID, Drossman (1994) provided 11 guidelines for promoting an environment of care that is responsive to patients and appropriate and satisfactory for clinicians:

1. Acknowledge the patient's distress and disability from the illness.
2. Educate.
3. Actively listen and respond to the patient's agenda(s).
4. Reframe the interaction to focus on what the patient is trying to say rather than the items of disagreement.
5. Do not look for cure.
6. Encourage the patient to be actively involved in care.
7. Offer tasks or responsibility in a graded fashion.
8. Address only psychological issues that the patient sees as relevant (at least initially).
9. Be clear and honest with your beliefs.
10. Be flexible.
11. Be available for ongoing care.

Although these are generally good suggestions for health care settings, they are especially important when treating patients with FGID who may have a history of multiple, unsatisfactory encounters with previous clinicians.

SUMMARY

Studies have contributed a great deal to understanding the prevalence, pathophysiology, and treatment of FGIDs. FGIDs remain among the most common disorders seen in primary and specialty medical practice. There has been a parallel growth in interest in FGIDs by both physicians and psychologists and in physician appreciation of the potential contribution of psychological treatments to patient care. Clinical trials have demonstrated efficacy for a range of therapeutic approaches for treating FGIDs, including hypnotherapy, interpersonal therapy, and CBT. Recent work has supported the efficacy of multicomponent treatment approaches including both medication and psychological treatment. Thus, the opportunity exists for rewarding multidisciplinary and multicomponent treatments involving both the medical and psychological specialties.

References

American Psychiatric Association. (1994). *Diagnostic and statistical manual of mental disorders* (4th ed.). Washington, DC: Author.
Bennett, P., & Wilkinson, S. (1985). Comparison of psychological and medical treatment of the

irritable bowel syndrome. *British Journal of Clinical Psychology, 24,* 215–216.

Blanchard, E. B. (2001). *Irritable bowel syndrome: Psychosocial assessment and treatment.* Washington, DC: American Psychological Association.

Blanchard, E. B., & Scharff, L. (2002). Psychosocial aspects of assessment and treatment of irritable bowel syndrome in adults and recurrent abdominal pain in children. *Journal of Consulting and Clinical Psychology, 70,* 725–738.

Calvert, E. L., Houghton, L. A., Cooper, P., Morris, J., & Whorwell, P. J. (2002). Long-term improvement in functional dyspepsia using hypnotherapy. *Gastroenterology, 123,* 1778–1785.

Drossman, D. A. (1994). Struggling with the controlling patient. *American Journal of Gastroenterology, 89,* 1441–1446.

Drossman, D. A. (1998). Presidential address: Gastrointestinal illness and the biopsychosocial model. *Psychosomatic Medicine, 60,* 258–267.

Drossman, D. A. (1999a). Mind over matter in the postinfective irritable bowel. *Gut, 44,* 306–307.

Drossman, D. A. (1999b). Review article: An integrated approach to the irritable bowel syndrome. *Alimentary Pharmacology and Therapeutics, 13*(Suppl. 2), 3–14.

Drossman, D. A. (2001a). Irritable bowel syndrome: How far do you go in the workup? *Gastroenterology, 121,* 1512–1515.

Drossman, D. A. (2001b). A biopsychosocial understanding of gastrointestinal illness and disease. In M. Feldman, B. Scharschmidt, & M. H. Sleisenger (Eds.), *Sleisenger and Fordtran's gastrointestinal disease* (pp. 2373–2385). Philadelphia, PA: Saunders.

Drossman, D. A., Camilleri, M., Mayer, E. A., & Whitehead, W. E. (2002). AGA technical review on irritable bowel syndrome. *Gastroenterology, 123,* 2108–2131.

Drossman, D. A., Corazziari, E., Talley, N. J., Thompson, W. G., & Whitehead, W. E. (2000). *Rome II: The functional gastrointestinal disorders.* McLean, VA: Degnon Associates.

Drossman, D. A., Creed, F. H., Olden, K. W., Svedlund, J., Toner, B., & Whitehead, W. E. (2000). Psychosocial aspects of the functional gastrointestinal disorders. In D. A. Drossman, E. Corazziari, N. J. Talley, W. G. Thompson, & W. E. Whitehead (Eds.), *Rome II: The functional gastrointestinal disorders* (pp. 158–245). McLean, VA: Degnon Associates.

Drossman, D. A., Leserman, J., Nachman, G., Li, Z., Gluck, H., Toomey, T. C., et al. (1990). Sexual and physical abuse in women with functional or organic gastrointestinal disorders. *Annals of Internal Medicine, 113,* 828–333.

Drossman, D. A., Li, Z., Leserman, J., Keefe, F. J., Hu, Y. J., & Toomey, T. C. (2000). Effects of coping on health outcome among female patients with gastrointestinal disorders. *Psychosomatic Medicine, 62,* 309–317.

Drossman, D. A., Li, Z., Leserman, J., Toomey, T. C., & Hu, Y. (1996). Health status by gastrointestinal diagnosis and abuse history. *Gastroenterology, 110,* 999–1007.

Drossman, D. A., McKee, D. C., Sandler, R. S., Mitchell, C. M., Cramer, E. M., Lowman, B. C., & Burger, A. L. (1988). Psychosocial factors in the irritable bowel syndrome. A multivariate study of patients and nonpatients with irritable bowel syndrome. *Gastroenterology, 95,* 701–708.

Drossman, D. A., Ringel, Y., Vogt, B., Leserman, J., Lin, W., Smith, J. K., et al. (2003). Alterations of brain activity associated with resolution of emotional distress and pain in a case of severe IBS. *Gastroenterology, 124,* 754–761.

Drossman, D. A., Talley, N. J., Leserman, J., Olden, K. W., & Barreiro, M. A. (1995). Sexual and physical abuse and gastrointestinal illness. Review and recommendations. *Annals of Internal Medicine, 123,* 782–794.

Drossman, D. A., & Thompson, W. G. (1992). The irritable bowel syndrome: Review and a graduated multicomponent treatment approach. *Annals of Internal Medicine, 116,* 1009–1016.

Drossman, D. A., Toner, B. B., Whitehead, W. E., Diamant, N. E., Dalton, C. B., Duncan, S., et al. (2003). A randomized trial of cognitive-behavioral treatment vs. education and desipramine vs. placebo in treatment of moderate to severe functional bowel disorder. *Gastroenterology, 125,* 19–31.

Engel, G. L. (1977). The need for a new medical model: A challenge for biomedicine. *Science, 196,* 129–136.

Fullwood, A., & Drossman, D. A. (1995). The relationship of psychiatric illness with gastrointestinal disease. *Annual Review of Medicine, 46,* 483–496.

Galovski, T. E., & Blanchard, E. B. (1998). The treatment of irritable bowel syndrome with hypnotherapy. *Applied Psychophysiology and Biofeedback, 23,* 219–232.

Guthrie, E., Creed, F., Dawson, D., & Tomenson, B. (1991). A controlled trial of psychological treatment for the irritable bowel syndrome. *Gastroenterology, 100*, 450–457.

Gwee, K. A., Leong, Y. L., Graham, C., McKendrick, M. W., Collins, S. M., Walters, S. J., et al. (1999). The role of psychological and biological factors in post-infective gut dysfunction. *Gut, 44*, 400–406.

Harvey, R. F., Hinton, R. A., Guinary, R. M., & Barry, R. E. (1989). Individual and group hypnotherapy in treatment of refractory irritable bowel syndrome. *Lancet, 1*, 424–425.

Heymann-Mönnikes, I., Arnold, R., Florin, I., Herda, C., Melfsen, S., & Mönnikes, H. (2000). The combination of medical treatment plus multicomponent behavioral therapy is superior to medical treatment alone in the therapy of irritable bowel syndrome. *American Journal of Gastroenterology, 95*, 981–994.

Houghton, L. A., Heyman, D. J., & Whorwell, P. J. (1996). Symptomatology, quality of life and economic features of irritable bowel syndrome: The effects of hypnotherapy. *Alimentary Pharmacology and Therapeutics, 10*, 91–95.

Jackson, J. L., O'Malley, P. G., Tomkins, G., Balden, E., Santoro, J., & Kroenke, K. (2000). Treatment of functional gastrointestinal disorders with antidepressant medications: A meta-analysis. *American Journal of Medicine, 108*, 65–72.

Kumar, D., & Wingate, D. L. (1985). The irritable bowel syndrome: A paroxysmal motor disorder. *Lancet, 2*, 973–977.

Lynch, P. N., & Zamble, E. (1989). A controlled behavioral treatment study of irritable bowel syndrome. *Behavior Therapy, 20*, 509–523.

Mayer, E. A., & Raybould, H. E. (1990). Role of visceral afferent mechanisms in functional bowel disorders. *Gastroenterology, 99*, 1688–1704.

Palsson, O. S., Turner, M. J., Johnson, D. A., Burnett, C. K., & Whitehead, W. E. (2002). Hypnosis treatment for severe irritable bowel syndrome: Investigation of mechanism and effects on symptoms. *Digestive Diseases and Sciences, 47*, 2605–2614.

Potts, S. G., Lewin, R., Fox, K. A., & Johnstone, E. C. (1999). Group psychological treatment for chest pain with normal coronary arteries. *Quarterly Journal of Medicine, 92*, 81–86.

Rogers, M., & Cerda, J. J. (1989). Editorial: The narcotic bowel syndrome. *Journal of Clinical Gastroenterology, 11*, 132–135.

Svedlund, J., Sjodin, I., Ottoson, J. O., & Dotevall, G. (1983). Controlled study of psychotherapy in irritable bowel syndrome. *Acta Psychiatrica Scandanvia, 67*(Suppl. 306), 1–86.

Toner, B. B., Segal, Z. V., Emmott, S. D., & Myran, D. (2000). *Cognitive–behavioral treatment of irritable bowel syndrome: The brain–gut connection.* London: Guilford Press.

Toner, B. B., Segal, Z. V., Emmott, S., Myran, D., Ali, A., DiGasbarro, I., & Stuckless, N. (1998). Cognitive-behavioral group therapy for patients with irritable bowel syndrome. *International Journal of Group Psychotherapy, 48*, 215–243.

Törnblom, H., Lindberg, G., Nyberg, B., & Veress, B. (2002). Full-thickness biopsy of the jejunum reveals inflammation and enteric neuropathy in irritable bowel syndrome. *Gastroenterology, 123*, 1972–1979.

Van Dulmen, A. M., Fennis, J. F. M., & Bleijenberg, G. (1996). Cognitive-behavioral group therapy for irritable bowel syndrome: Effects and long-term follow-up. *Psychosomatic Medicine, 58*, 508–514.

Vollmer, A., & Blanchard, E. B. (1998). Controlled comparison of individual versus group cognitive therapy for irritable bowel syndrome. *Behavior Therapy, 29*, 19–33.

Whitehead, W. E., Bosmajian, L., Zonderman, A. B., Costa, P. T., & Schuster, M. M. (1988). Symptoms of psychologic distress associated with irritable bowel syndrome. Comparison of community and medical clinic samples. *Gastroenterology, 95*, 709–714.

Whitehead, W. E., Burnett, C. K., Cook, E. W., & Taub, E. (1996). Impact of irritable bowel syndrome on quality of life. *Digestive Diseases and Sciences, 41*, 2248–2253.

Whorwell, P. J., Prior, A., & Colgan, S. M. (1987). Hypnotherapy in severe irritable-bowel-syndrome—further experience. *Gut, 28*, 423–425.

Whorwell, P. J., Prior, A., & Faragher, E. B. (1984). Controlled trial of hypnotherapy in the treatment of severe refractory irritable-bowel syndrome. *Lancet, 2*, 1232–1234.

Wood, J. D., Alpers, D. H., & Andrews, P. L. R. (1999). Fundamentals of neurogastroenterology. *Gut, 45*(Suppl. II), II6–II16.

31

Menopause

Laura A. Czajkowski
Kirtly Parker Jones

Menopause is an integral and natural part of a woman's life cycle. The progression from regular menstrual cycles and fertility to menopause is a complex experience that can be associated with psychological complaints, physiological symptoms, and the perceived loss of youth. It is estimated that one third of a woman's lifetime occurs during and after menopause. The decline of ovarian function also coincides with other important psychosocial changes in midlife. For both clinician and patient, it may be difficult to determine which midlife psychological symptoms are caused by the decline in normal ovarian function and which may just be concurrent.

The experience of menopause is unique to each individual and is modulated by health status, attributions regarding menopause, and the social and psychological meanings of midlife. The primary care psychologist may be in a unique position to identify and treat women who are at risk for a difficult transition. The decline in normal ovarian function is not necessarily synonymous with a decline in life quality; in fact, menopause may be viewed as an opportunity for physical, emotional, and spiritual transformation.

There is ample evidence that many of the complaints that occur during menopause can be treated. This chapter provides an overview of the biology of menopause and perimenopause. Common psychological, behavioral, and physiological complaints and their relation to menopause are reviewed. The efficacy of select treatment interventions is discussed.

PERIMENOPAUSE VERSUS MENOPAUSE

The onset of menopause is related to the lifetime supply of ova, and this number can vary between individuals. Only a few of the approximately 7 million ova present at 20 weeks gestation are actually destined to ovulate. By the first menstrual period, continuous loss of follicles has decreased the number of ova to about 300,000. This process continues throughout reproductive life whether or not women are ovulating (as during the use of oral contraceptives, pregnancy, or with anovulatory women).

By the time the woman reaches her early 40s,

the pool of ova remaining may be small enough that ovulation is less predictable. Most women will not notice any changes in their day-to-day symptoms, although some women may notice that their regular menstrual cycles become shorter.

The term *perimenopause* refers to the time prior to the last spontaneous menstrual cycle when menstruation becomes unpredictable. Longitudinal demographic studies suggested that this period of unpredictable cycles (cycles shorter or longer with "skipped" menstrual periods) averages about 4 years, but the range is quite variable. The hormonal pattern of the perimenopause is the absence of pattern. Estrogens may be higher than average one week (possible symptoms: headache and breast tenderness) and lower than average one week (possible symptoms: headache and hot flushes), and ovulation becomes unpredictable (possible symptoms: unpredictable vaginal bleeding and mood changes similar to premenstrual dysphoria). Research has indicated that women who struggle with psychological problems in midlife may actually have more symptoms in the perimenopause than after menopause.

Menopause is defined as the last spontaneous menstrual period when there has been no bleeding for 1 year. The average age of menopause in the United States is about 51. A woman who is a year past her last spontaneous menstrual cycle can be termed *postmenopausal*. With ovarian function unpredictable in the perimenopause, a woman can go a year without a period and then ovulate one more time.

Vasomotor flushes ("hot flushes") are the most common symptom of the menopause. Hot flushes can occur at any time of reproductive life; they are common in the perimenopause (when there are still adequate estrogen stores) and are even more common in the first years of the postmenopausal period. Up to 20% of women will continue to have hot flushes 5 years or more after the menopause.

The precise cause of hot flushes is not completely known; they are brief (3–5 minutes), centrally mediated events associated with peripheral dilatation, sweating, increased pulse rate, and slight decrease in core temperature. Norepinephrine may be one of the hypothalamic mediators of the flush (it is similar to the flush associated with anger or shame), and flushing is also seen with testosterone withdrawal, nicotine withdrawal, and narcotics withdrawal. Flushes are exacerbated by alcohol, caffeine, and anxiety.

Because hot flushes are more common in midlife and may be temporally associated with a number of psychological complaints, clinicians and patients often feel that the presence of flushes always indicates estrogen deficiency. Women who are still having menstrual periods are not estrogen deficient, although they may have hot flushes. Also, the presence of flushes may lead patients to believe that their other psychological symptoms are because of the perimenopause or menopause, and that hormonal management will deal with all of their symptoms. The only psychological symptoms that consistently improve with estrogen replacement are the sleep disturbances and night sweats associated with hot flushes.

COMMON COMPLAINTS

This section examines some of the health issues associated with both perimenopause and menopause; we discuss mood disturbances, sleep disturbances, sexual dysfunction, and memory complaints.

Mood

Several models have been developed to explain the interaction between depression and menopausal status. A biochemical model suggests that alterations in estrogen affect the synthesis and release of both serotonin and norepinephrine, neurotransmitters implicated in mood changes (Joffe & Cohen, 1998). It is suggested that the estrogen-serotonin interaction increases vulnerability to affective disorders. Women who develop depression may be biologically more sensitive to the effects of unstable estrogen levels and the impact on neurotransmitters. This explanation has been labeled the *estrogen withdrawal theory*.

An alternative explanation suggests that vasomotor events associated with estrogen decline (hot flushes, night sweats) contribute to depression and sleep disturbance. This premise is based on the observed improvement in psychological symptoms following administration of estrogen. The addition of estrogen reduces the vasomotor symptoms and contributes to mood stabilization.

Environmental models contend that negative mood and somatic symptoms are associated with social/lifestyle changes rather than natural menopausal transition. These factors include prior experience of negative mood, poor self-rated health, changes in roles and identity, negative feelings for partner, no partner, and daily stress (Dennerstein, Lehert, Burger, & Dudley, 1999).

Community-based surveys indicated that depression is approximately twice as common in women than in men (Kessler, 2000). There is an increased risk of a depressive episode during times of hormonal changes, as illustrated by premenstrual dysphoric disorders and postpartum depression. The relation between menopause and depression has been the subject of multiple investigations, yet the exact nature of this interaction remains elusive. The complexity of this literature is highlighted by the difficulties in defining terminology for both depressive disorders and menopause. Methodological limitations such as subject selection, variability of assessment instruments, and reliance on self-report data contribute to the lack of understanding.

The assumption of causality between menopause and depression is premature based on the evidence from large epidemiological investigations. These findings do not support an increased prevalence of depression with menopause (Avis, Kaufert, Lock, McKinlay, & Vass, 1994; Kaufert, Gilbert, & Tate, 1992; Weissman, 1979). The results of the Massachusetts Women's Health Study were not indicative of an increased prevalence of depression in menopause (Avis et al., 1994). The literature suggests that as women reach menopause, negative mood declines, and well-being significantly improves (Dennerstein, Lehert, & Guthrie, 2002).

The perimenopausal transition appears to be a time of increased vulnerability for depressive episodes, particularly among women with a history of depression (Ayubi-Moak & Parry, 2002; Maartens, Knottnerus, & Pop, 2002). Numerous studies have demonstrated an increase in psychological complaints during the perimenopausal period (Burt, Altshuler, & Rasgon, 1998; Schmidt, Roca, Bloch, & Rubinow, 1997).

There is evidence that a lifetime history of major depression is associated with an earlier decline in ovarian function and an earlier transition to perimenopause (Harlow, Wise, Otto, Soares, & Cohen, 2003). A history of depression may be predictive of increased vulnerability to psychological distress during perimenopause. Behavioral and psychosocial factors that may be predictive of depression during the perimenopause include stressful events, high trait anxiety, pessimism, present health status, and views regarding the midlife (Bromberger & Matthews, 1996; Kaufert, Gilbert, & Tate, 1992; Woods & Mitchell, 1997).

The evidence for estrogen replacement as a treatment for depression is variable and difficult to interpret in part because of methodological problems. For women without clinical depression, estrogen replacement has been found to improve mood and perceptions of quality of life (Dennerstein et al., 1993; Sherwin & Gelfand, 1985). However, estrogen replacement for women who meet criteria for clinical depression does not result in mood elevation (Thomson & Oswald, 1997). The efficacy of estrogen as a supplement to antidepressant medication in the treatment of major depressive disorder has been mixed (Rasgon et al., 2002). It appears that the impact of hormone replacement therapy (HRT) on quality-of-life measures is modified by the presence of vasomotor symptoms; women with flushes treated with estrogen reported improved quality of life (Hlatky, Boothroyd, Vittinghoff, Sharp, & Whooley, 2002).

Clearly, there are multiple issues to consider when treating women who are approaching menopause. A clear understanding of their expectations and beliefs regarding menopause, cultural beliefs, economic status, relationship, concurrent stressful events, and prior history of depression is necessary to formulate a treatment plan. Referral to the primary care provider is warranted for specific somatic symptoms of hot flushes, vaginal dryness, or loss of libido.

All mood disorders in perimenopausal or menopausal women should be treated, as at other times of life. A history of prior depression, postpartum depression, or premenstrual syndrome may be predictive of vulnerability to a recurrence of mood disorder associated with fluctuations of ovarian function. Certain women may be predisposed to psychological distress during the transition from perimenopause to menopause, because of biological sensitivity to hormonal fluctuations, lack of adequate psychological mechanisms for coping with change, or a combination of these factors.

Sleep

Sleep disruption increases with age and is equally distributed in men and women younger than 45 years. The transition to menopause may be associated with the disruption of sleep regulation: By midlife, women report approximately twice the insomnia rate of men older than 45 years (Jones & Czajkowski, 2000). There are longer latencies to sleep onset, increased middle-of-the-night awakenings, and an increased incidence of hypnotic usage (Aspland & Aberg, 1995). Women with hot flushes at night are more likely to report disturbed sleep, a greater number of intermittent awakenings, and a decreased sense of well-being (Shaver, Giblin, Lentz, & Lee, 1988).

As noted, women may experience episodes of hot flushes for several years. Kronenberg (1990) has reported that 50% to 85% of women have hot flushes over a period of 5 years. Hot flushes follow a circadian cycle, with a peak in both late evening and early morning. These sensations are usually more disturbing at night, when sleep is disrupted. Sleep disturbances caused by hot flushes may be improved with HRT (Polo-Kantola, Erkkola, & Helenius, 1998).

Insomnia is a common health complaint of perimenopausal women, including those who are not seeking treatment for menopausal symptoms (Moe, 1999). The incidence of insomnia in postmenopausal women ranges from 28% to 63% (Shaver & Zenk, 2000). Insomnia complaints in the menopausal transition may be coupled with other somatic concerns, including headache, dizziness, palpitations, depression, and weight gain. Hormone replacement decreases multiple nighttime awakenings associated with hot flushes, but does not promote sleep in menopausal patients without hot flushes.

A woman's likelihood of developing a breathing-related sleep disorder increases after menopause. Recent studies indicate that the risk of sleep-related breathing disorders is almost as high for postmenopausal women not taking HRT as it is for men (Cistulli, Barnes, Grunstein, & Sullivan, 1994). Sleep apnea is a disorder characterized by brief interruptions of breathing during sleep. Risk factors include snoring, obesity, decreased levels of physical activity, and high blood pressure. Excessive daytime sleepiness is one of the hallmarks of obstructive sleep apnea (see chapter 37, this volume, for additional information concerning sleep disorders).

Habits that promote sleep during the menopausal transition include limited caffeine intake; consistent exercise, including both aerobic and resistance training; cool bedroom environment; a bedtime ritual that induces comfort; a consistent sleep schedule (particularly wake-up time), and use of the bed only for sleep and intimacy. Misconceptions associated with sleep and menopause can be addressed through cognitive techniques. The therapeutic challenge is to reframe negative beliefs regarding both sleep and menopause. Chapter 37 on sleep disorders discusses these issues in greater depth.

Sexual Dysfunction

Sexuality is an important aspect of health and includes biological, psychological, social, emotional, cognitive, and cultural experiences. Menopause, with the concomitant decrease in estrogen and testosterone, can lead to decreased libido, dyspareunia secondary to vaginal dryness, reduced blood flow, and other sexual dysfunction (McCoy, 1998). Factors that affect sexual function include consistency of sexual activity prior to menopause and the quality of the relationship.

It is critical to assess all factors that affect sexual functioning, including, body image, general health status, relationship status, psychological issues, medication use, and beliefs about menopause and sexuality. Avis, Stellato, Crawford, Johannes, and Longcope (2000) found physical and mental health, marital status, and health behaviors to be better predictors of women's midlife sexual functioning than menopausal status. A healthy sexual relationship can be maintained through menopause with a realistic understanding of the changes that accompany aging (see chapter 36).

Memory

Changes in memory and executive functioning are probably the most disturbing psychological symptom experienced in midlife. Diminished cognitive efficiency can be exacerbated by chronic sleep disturbance, mood swings, and fluctuations in hormonal levels.

The research is inconclusive on the specific cognitive effects of menopause and HRT on cognition. Wise, Dubal, Wilson, Rau, and Bottner (2001), in a review of the neuroprotective aspects of estrogen, found that estrogen influences memory, cognition, and mood in healthy young and postmenopausal women. The findings suggest that estrogen may decrease the risk and delay the onset of neurodegenerative diseases such as Alzheimer's disease. Estrogen replacement early in menopause and continued for at least 5 years may decrease the incidence of Alzheimer's disease (Zandi et al., 2002). There was no consistent evidence that estrogen prevented memory loss or delayed cognitive decline (Mulnard et al., 2000). Continued study with large placebo-controlled trials will be necessary to determine the efficacy of estrogen in treating cognitive symptoms.

Published data from the Women's Health Initiative (Rapp et al., 2003) suggested that estrogen/progestin replacement therapy, when started late (average age 70 years) after menopause does not decrease the rate of dementia. Very long-term (longer than 15 years) prospective randomized trials starting at menopause may never be done, given the cost and complexity of these studies.

The primary care psychologist is ideally positioned to elicit women's personal beliefs and expectations regarding memory and aging. Providing information on normal changes associated with aging and challenging distorted attributions are essential components of treatment. In addition, incorporating habits that promote preservation of memory and recall is helpful. These habits may include decreasing consumption of alcohol and caffeine, increasing consumption of vegetables and fruits, exercising consistently, and incor-

porating mental activity into daily routines. Cognitive strategies designed for enhanced retrieval such as association, visualization, and rehearsal can also be implemented.

RISK FACTORS FOR DIFFICULT TRANSITION TO MENOPAUSE

Preexisting Beliefs

A woman's expectation of menopause affects her experience during the menopause. For some women, menopause is a relief, associated with diminished worry about an unwanted pregnancy. For others, it signals a loss of fertility and loss of youth and beauty. Menopause is also associated with culture and socialization. In a culture that emphasizes youth, middle-aged women may adopt a more negative view of self that can contribute to distress. Avis, Kaufert, Lock, McKinlay, and Vass (1993) found that women in Japan experienced a lower prevalence of hot flushes than women examined in the Manitoba Project or the Massachusetts Women's Health Study. Woods and Mitchell (1997) concluded that the attributional patterns of women regarding aging and menopause may contribute to negative events. Positive expectations regarding menopause and aging influence estimations of symptom severity and are associated with less-severe vasomotor symptoms.

There is limited research characterizing positive psychological concomitants of menopause. Dennerstein, Lehert, Dudley, and Guthrie (2001) conducted an investigation with a subset of the Melbourne Women's Midlife Health Project over a 9-year period. Predictors of positive mood during menopausal transition included a relationship, living with a partner, diminished interpersonal stress, positive attitudes toward aging, and a baseline level of positive mood.

Assessment

Examination of behavioral and psychosocial factors as well as menopausal status is essential to understand the complexities of affective changes. Components of the evaluation include questions regarding current menstrual history and present/ past history of psychological problems. The menstrual history includes the last menstrual period, the frequency and the durations of menses, and the relationship of affective complaints to menstrual cycles. Assessing the frequency and intensity of vasomotor flushes is helpful in determining whether sleep disturbances and memory changes are associated with frequent daily hot flushes (more than 8 per day). Women with daily frequent intense hot flushes benefit from estrogen replacement therapy with increased sleep quality and improved cognition. In the sexual history, questions related to vaginal dryness or painful intercourse may help define patients who may be helped by low-dose vaginal estrogens. A consultation with the patient's primary care provider (internist, family practitioner, or gynecologist) may be helpful in planning HRT. If a patient does not have a primary care provider, referrals with the specific questions will allow the patient's health care team to provide her with the best treatment options.

HORMONE REPLACEMENT THERAPY: RISKS AND BENEFITS

An exhaustive discussion of the risks and benefits of HRT (estrogen alone, or estrogen/progestin therapy) is beyond the scope of this chapter. It is important to remember that the recognized symptoms for which estrogen replacement therapy is indicated are hot flushes and vaginal atrophy. Estrogens have been proven to be effective for treatment of these symptoms by prospective randomized trials, and no other therapies are as effective. If the woman's uterus is intact, progestins are routinely added to estrogen replacement therapy to protect against the risk of endometrial cancer because there is an increased risk for women who have a uterus and take unopposed estrogens.

The data from the Women's Health Initiative Study comparing the risks and benefits of estrogen/progestin therapy versus placebo are difficult to apply to the symptomatic menopausal woman at 52 years of age. The risks of HRT that have been consistent over many studies are the small increased risk of thromboembolic events ("clots")

and the small increase in the detection of breast cancer. This increase leads to one extra thrombosis per 1,000 women per year in women taking estrogen/progestin therapy compared to women taking placebo. The increased risk of detecting breast cancer is approximately one extra breast cancer per 1,000 women per year who are taking estrogen/progestin therapy compared to women taking placebo.

The Women's Health Initiative recruited older (average age 63 years), asymptomatic women for their prospective randomized trial of estrogen/ progestin versus placebo. This study also looked at adverse outcomes such as cardiovascular disease and stroke. There was a very small increase in heart attack and stroke in estrogen/progestin users compared to placebo users of about one extra event per 1,000 women per year in women taking estrogen/progestin compared to placebo. There was a small decrease in the rate of osteoporotic fractures and colon cancer in the estrogen/ progestin users compared to placebo users. The recommendations from the Women's Health Initiative Study were that hormone replacement should be used for women with symptoms, although it should not be continued indefinitely.

ALTERNATIVE TREATMENTS

There has been ambivalence about the use of HRT by women and concerns regarding long-term safety. Fewer than 40% of women who started HRT continue using the medication after 1 year (Taylor, 2001). Potential side effects such as vaginal bleeding, perceived weight gain, mood changes, cramping, bloating, headache, and fear of cancer contribute to the avoidance of HRT. Alternative treatments include plant estrogens, natural hormones, and botanicals. These options may be attractive to women because they provide a sense of control and choice.

Alternative treatments generally address vasomotor symptoms, decreased libido, mood changes, and fatigue. Taylor (2001) stated that most of the botanicals used to treat midlife and menstrual disorders are relatively safe. However, efficacy studies for botanicals such as black cohosh, *dong quai*, Chinese herbs, ginseng, and isoflavones (plant phytoestrogens) have shown limited improvement in symptoms compared to placebo. It is important to note that the placebo effect for hot flushes and menopausal symptoms and libido is quite large, with many studies showing a 30% to 40% improvement in symptoms with placebo alone.

Although conventional HRT has become less appealing to women, alternative practices demand the same scrutiny in terms of safety and efficacy. Practitioners need to be knowledgeable about alternatives to assist women in designing a plan to match a desired lifestyle.

Midlife health concerns include heart disease, elevated blood pressure, weight gain, hypercholesterolemia, osteoporosis, diminished muscle mass, and joint disease. Many women desire lifestyle changes that both address menopausal symptoms and promote wellness. Accurate assessment of present practices is critical in developing an effective intervention program in collaboration with the woman's physician. Elements of assessment include questions on nutrition, vitamin usage, exercise, tobacco/substance usage, and family or work demands.

Women may consider behavioral or psychological interventions to manage menopausal symptoms. Interventions include stress management, physical activity, decreased alcohol and caffeine consumption, smoking cessation, low-fat and low-cholesterol diets, and education. Exercise in particular has been associated with reduction in menopausal symptoms. For example, Hammar, Berg, and Lindgren (1990) suggested that exercise reduced depressive symptoms and prevented hot flushes. In this study with 1,200 women aged 52 to 54 years, the presence of hot flushes and sweats was 50% less in physically active postmenopausal women. Perception of mood was more positive in physically active women regardless of menopausal state (Slavin & Lee, 1997).

SUMMARY

Menopause marks a change of the reproductive system as well as changes in the social and psychological environment. There is no evidence of a normative menopausal syndrome. Although the underlying mechanisms are complex, the symptoms reliably associated with menopause include vasomotor symptoms (hot flushes, night sweats) and vaginal atrophy. The existing studies on menopause have several methodological and conceptual limitations. These include sampling and generalizability of findings, distinction between natural and surgical menopause, the limited number of population-based prospective studies, the need for randomized controlled trials, control of preexisting group differences, and limited measures of outcome.

Most women do not have significant complaints during the transition into menopause and perhaps focus on the benefits of this transition. Diminished well-being, depressive symptoms, and major clinical depression in the perimenopause and postmenopause can be explained by both declining levels of estrogen and multiple psychosocial factors. It is imperative that clinicians consider all aspects of a woman's life in their assessment, as the association between menopause and quality of life remains multifactorial. Clinicians need to adopt a holistic model to promote women's health across the lifespan.

ADDITIONAL RESOURCES

Suggestions for further reading and professional development resources are available at this book's companion Web site: www.primarycarepsych.com.

References

Asplund, R., & Aberg, H. (1995). Body mass index and sleep in women aged 40 to 64 years. *Maturitas, 22,* 1–8.

Avis, N. E., Brambilla, D., McKinlay, S. M., & Vass, K. (1994). A longitudinal analysis of the association between menopause and depression. Results from the Massachusetts Women's Health Study. *Annals of Epidemiology, 4,* 214–220.

Avis, N., Kaufert, P., Lock, M., McKinlay, S., & Vass, K. (1993). The evolution of menopausal symptoms. *Balliere's Clinical Endocrinology and Metabolism, 7,* 17–31.

Avis, N. E., Stellato, R., Crawford, S., Johannes, C., & Longcope, C. (2000). Is there an association between menopause status and sexual functioning? *Menopause: The Journal of the North American Menopause Society, 7,* 297–309.

Ayubi-Moal, I., & Parry, B. (2002). Psychiatric aspects of menopause depression. In S. Kornstein & A. Clayton (Eds.). *Women' s mental health: A comprehensive textbook* (pp. 132–143). New York: Guilford Press.

Bromberger, J., & Matthews, K. (1996). A longitudinal study of the effects of pessimism, trait anxiety, and life stress on depressive symptoms in middle-aged women. *Psychology and Aging, 11,* 207–213.

Burt, Y. K., Altshuler, L., & Rasgon, N. (1998). Depressive symptoms in the perimenopause; prevalence, assessment and guidelines for treatment. *Harvard Review of Psychiatry, 6,* 121–132.

Dennerstein, L., Lehert, P., Burger, H., & Dudley, E. (1999). Mood and menopausal transition. *Journal of Nervous and Mental Disease, 187,* 685–691.

Dennerstein, L., Lehert, P., Dudley, E., & Guthrie, J. (2001). Factors contributing to positive mood during the menopausal transition. *Journal of Nervous and Mental Disease, 189,* 84–89.

Dennerstein, L., Lehert, P., & Guthrie, J. (2002). The effect of the menopausal transition and biopsychosocial factors on well being. *Archives in Women's Mental Health, 5,* 15–22.

Dennerstein, L., Smith, A., Morse, C., Burger, H., Green, A., Hopper J., & Ryan, M. (1993). Menopausal symptoms in Australian women. *Medical Journal of Australia, 159,* 232–236.

Hammar, M., Berg, C., & Lindgren, R. (1990). Does physical exercise influence the frequency of postmenopausal hot flushes? *Acta Obstetrics Gynecology Scandinavia, 69,* 409–412.

Harlow, B., Wise, L., Otto, M., Soares, C., & Cohen, L. (2003). Depression and its influence on reproductive, endocrine, and menstrual cycle markers associated with perimenopause. *Archives of General Psychiatry, 60,* 29–36.

Hlatky, M., Boothroyd, D., Vittinghoff, E., Sharp, P., & Whooley, M. (2002). Quality of life and depressive symptoms in postmenopausal women after receiving hormone therapy: Results from the Heart and Estrogen/Progestin Replacement Study (HERS) trial. *Journal of the American Medical Association , 287,* 591–597.

Joffe, H., & Cohen, L. S. (1998). Estrogen, serotonin, and mood disturbance: Where is the therapeutic bridge. *Biological Psychiatry, 44,* 798–811.

Jones, C., & Czajkowski, L. (2000) Evaluation and management of insomnia in menopause. *Clinical Obstetrics and Gynecology, 43,* 184–197.

Kaufert, P. A., Gilbert, P., & Tate, R. (1992). The Manitoba Project. A re-examination of the link between menopause and depression. *Maturitas, 14,* 143–155.

Kessler, R. C. (2000). Gender differences in major depression: Epidemiological findings. In E. Frank (Ed.), *Gender and its effects on psychopathology* (pp. 61–84). Washington, DC: American Psychiatric Press.

Kessler, R. C., McGonagle, K., Swartz, M., Blazer, D., & Nelson, C. (1993). Sex and depression in the National Comorbidity Survey 1: Lifetime prevalence, chronicity, and recurrence. *Journal of Affective Disorders, 29,* 85–96.

Kronenberg, F. (1990). Hot flashes: Epidemiology and physiology. *Annals of the New York Academy of Science, 592,* 52–86.

Maartens, L., Knottnerus, J., & Pop, V. (2002). Menopausal transition and increased depressive symptomatology: A community based prospective study. *Maturitas, 42,* 195–200.

McCoy, N. (1998). Methodological problems in the study of sexuality and the menopause. *Maturitas, 29,* 51–60.

McKinlay, J. B., McKinlay, S. M., & Brambilla, D. J. (1987) Health status and utilization behavior associated with menopause. *American Journal of Epidemiology, 125,* 110–121.

Mulnard, R. A., Cotman, C. W., Kawas, C., van Dyck, C. H., Sano, M., Doody, R., et al. (2000). Estrogen replacement therapy for treatment of mild to moderate Alzheimer's disease: A randomized controlled trial. Alzheimer's Disease Cooperative Study. *Journal of the American Medical Association, 283,* 1007–1015.

Polo-Kantola, P., Erkkola, R., Helenius, H., Irjala, K., & Polo, O. (1998). When does estrogen replacement therapy improve sleep quality? *American Journal of Obstetrics and Gynecology, 187,* 1002–1009.

Rapp, S., Espeland, M., Shumaker, S., Handerson, V., Brunner, R., Manson, J., et al. (2003). Effect of estrogen plus progestin on global cognitive function in postmenopausal women: The Women's Health Initiative Memory Study— A randomized controlled trial. *Journal of the American Medical Association, 289,* 2663–2672.

Rasgon, N., Altshuler, L., Fairbanks, L., Dunkin, J., Davtyan, C., Elman, S., & Apkin, A. (2002).

Estrogen replacement therapy in the treatment of major depressive disorder in perimenopausal women. *Journal of Clinical Psychiatry*, 63(Suppl. 7), 45–48.

Schmidt, P. J., Roca, C., Bloch, M., & Rubinow, D. R. (1997). The perimenopause and affective disorders. *Seminars in Reproductive Endocrinology*, 15, 91–100.

Shaver, J. E., Giblin, E., Lentz, M., & Lee, K. (1988). Sleep patterns and stability in perimenopausal women. *Sleep*, 11, 556–561.

Shaver, J., & Zenk, S. (2000). Sleep disturbance in menopause. *Journal of Women's Health Gender Based Medicine*, 9, 109–118.

Sherwin, B., & Gelfand, M. (1985). Sex steroid and affect in the surgical menopause: A double blind, cross-over study. *Psychoneuroendocrinology*, 10, 325–335.

Slavin, L., & Lee, C. (1997). Mood and symptoms reporting among middle-aged women: The relationship between menopausal status, hormone replacement therapy and exercise participation. *Health Psychology*, 16, 203–208.

Taylor, M. (2001). Botanicals: Medicines and menopause. *Clinical Obstetrics and Gynecology*, 44, 853–863.

Thomson, J., & Oswald, I. (1997). Effects of oestrogen on the sleep, mood, anxiety of menopausal women. *British Medical Journal*, 2, 1317–1319.

Weissman, M. M. (1979). The myth of involutional melancholia. *Journal of the American Medical Association*, 242, 742–744.

Wilbur, J., Miller, A., & Montgomery, A. (1995). The influence of demographic characteristics, menopausal status, and symptoms on women's attitudes toward menopause. *Women and Health*, 23, 19–39.

Wise, P., Dubal, D., Wilson, M., Rau, S., & Bottner, M. (2001). Minireview: Neuroprotective effects of estrogen—new insights into mechanisms of action. *Endocrinology*, 142, 969–973.

Woods, N., & Mitchell, E. (1997). Pathways to depressed mood for midlife women: Observations from the Seattle Midlife Women's Health Study. *Research in Nursing and Health*, 20, 119–129.

Zandi, P., Carlson, M., Plassman, B., Welsh-Bowman, K., Mayer, L., Steffens, D., & Breitner, J. (2002). Hormone replacement therapy and incidence of Alzheimer's disease in older women. The Cache County Study. *Journal of the American Medical Association*, 288, 2123–2129.

32

Obesity: Assessment and Treatment

David B. Sarwer
Kelly C. Allison
Robert I. Berkowitz

Although excess body weight is often considered an aesthetic issue, obesity represents a significant health problem in the United States. Obesity is strongly associated with morbidity (NHLBI, 1998). Obese individuals are at increased risk for, and frequently suffer from, a variety of significant health problems, including cardiovascular disease (heart disease and hypertension), Type II diabetes, osteoarthritis, sleep apnea, and certain cancers. Obesity-related health problems were estimated to have cost the country approximately $100 billion in 1995 (Wolf & Colditz, 1998); the amount today is likely much higher. Obese individuals also are at increased risk for mortality. Obese individuals have a 30% greater risk of premature death compared to normal-weight individuals. For those with severe obesity, the risk of death is approximately 100% greater (Manson et al., 1995).

Obesity is associated with psychosocial difficulties as well. Obese individuals are frequently stigmatized, if not discriminated against, in a variety of settings (Puhl & Brownell, 2001). Obese children and adolescents often are teased and socially rejected by their peers in school, which likely has a profound effect on the child's self-esteem and body image (Sarwer & Thompson, 2002). Overweight college applicants often are not accepted; if admitted, they frequently receive poorer grades (Solovay, 2000). Obese adults often encounter difficulty in employment settings. As compared to average weight individuals, obese persons are frequently not hired for jobs, particularly those that involve interactions with customers. When hired, obese individuals often receive lower salaries than their average-weight colleagues (e.g., Roehling, 1999). Intentionally or not, obese individuals are stigmatized in public settings, such as when flying on airplanes or attending movies or sporting events.

Even as experts attempt to educate the public on the multifactorial nature of obesity, many individuals see obesity as a result of an inability to control personal impulses or a moral failing, further adding to its stigmatization. Most unfortunately, some medical professionals who work with obese individuals also hold these beliefs (e.g., Harris, Hamaday, & Mochan, 1999), which may compromise their ability to treat these persons. In addition, it likely deters some obese individuals from seeking treatment (Rand & MacGregor, 1990).

This chapter discusses the assessment and treatment of obesity by mental health professionals who work in a primary care setting. The chapter begins with a brief overview of the etiology of obesity. We then highlight some general considerations when working with obese individuals, touching on issues of psychopathology, race, and age. The assessment of an obese patient is detailed. Treatment guidelines and the behavioral management of obesity, either alone or in combination with pharmacological or surgical treatment, are reviewed.

THE ETIOLOGY OF OBESITY

Obesity describes an excess of body fat and is best categorized by the body mass index (BMI). BMI is the ratio of weight to height and can be calculated by dividing an individual's weight in kilograms by height in meters squared (Figure 32.1). Both the National Institutes of Health (NHLBI, 1998) and the World Health Organization (WHO, 1998) have defined being overweight as having a BMI of 25.0 to 29.9 kg/m^2. Obesity is defined as a BMI of 30.0 kg/m^2 or above. The most recent statistics suggested that 64.5% of Americans are overweight, and 30.5% are obese (Flegal, Carroll, Ogden, & Johnson, 2002). Most experts believe that obesity results from the interaction of genetic and environmental factors.

Genetic Factors

Although heredity is thought to play a significant role in the development of obesity, the specific genes that contribute to human obesity have yet to be identified (Price, 2002). It appears that a combination of genes, perhaps as many as 250 or more, influence body weight. Genes are thought to explain up to 40% of the variance in BMI in humans (Price, 2002). Furthermore, they are thought to account for individual differences in metabolic rate, weight gain, and body fat distribution (Bouchard, 1994).

Environmental Factors

There is little, if any, evidence to suggest that changes in genetic makeup have occurred in the last several decades. Thus, most experts believe that environmental changes best account for the dramatic increase in the rate of obesity in the United States and other westernized countries. As related to obesity, the current environment has been categorized as a "toxic environment" (Horgen & Brownell, 1998, 2002). The almost unlimited availability of, and frequent reliance on, high-fat and high-calorie foods from countless fast-food and take-out restaurants, convenience stores, and other retail locations has likely contributed to the obesity epidemic. It is not, however, just the nature of the food, but also the amount. As a society, we are fascinated by large portion sizes almost to the point at which we feel cheated if we are served a recommended portion size.

Furthermore, many of the major household inventions of the past century, from washing machines and televisions to cordless/cellular phones, computers, and video games have made many Americans more sedentary. In some respects, television completes the vicious cycle. Endless advertisements for calorically dense foods and the restaurants that serve them likely contribute to our overconsumption of these products. As simple as it sounds, eating too much and exercising too little have likely been the primary catalyst of the increasing rate of obesity.

CONSIDERATIONS IN WORKING WITH OBESE INDIVIDUALS

Given the current prevalence of obesity, mental health professionals working in a primary care setting will likely be presented with numerous opportunities to work with obese patients. Physicians frequently do not have the time, interest, or training to provide weight loss treatment. Thus, internal and family medicine physicians, as well as obstetrician-gynecologists, pediatricians, cardiologists, and other specialists may refer their obese patients to primary care psychologists for assessment and/or modification of eating and exercise habits.

Behaviorally based treatment is rather straightforward and can be easily learned by the psychologist with a background in cognitive–behavioral theory and technique. As a result, weight loss

Body Weight (in pounds) According to Height (in inches) and Body Mass Index

Height (inches)	Body Mass Index																
	19	20	21	22	23	24	25	26	27	28	29	30	31	32	33	34	35
	Body Weight (pounds)																
58	91	96	100	105	110	115	119	124	129	134	138	143	148	153	158	162	167
59	94	99	104	109	114	119	124	128	133	138	143	148	153	158	163	168	173
60	97	102	107	112	118	123	128	133	138	143	148	153	158	163	168	174	179
61	100	106	111	116	122	127	132	137	143	148	153	158	164	169	174	180	185
62	104	109	115	120	126	131	136	142	147	153	158	164	169	175	180	186	191
63	107	113	118	124	130	135	141	146	152	158	163	169	175	180	186	191	197
64	110	116	122	128	134	140	145	151	157	163	169	174	180	186	192	197	204
65	114	120	126	132	138	144	150	156	162	168	174	180	186	192	198	204	210
66	118	124	130	136	142	148	155	161	167	173	179	186	192	198	204	210	216
67	121	127	134	140	146	153	159	166	172	178	185	191	198	204	211	217	223
68	125	131	138	144	151	158	164	171	177	184	190	197	203	210	216	223	230
69	128	135	142	149	155	162	169	176	182	189	196	203	209	216	223	230	236
70	132	139	146	153	160	167	174	181	188	195	202	209	216	222	229	236	243
71	136	143	150	157	165	172	179	186	193	200	208	215	222	229	236	243	250
72	140	147	154	162	169	177	184	191	199	206	213	221	228	235	242	250	258
73	144	151	159	166	174	182	189	197	204	212	219	227	235	242	250	257	265
74	148	155	163	171	179	186	194	202	210	218	225	233	241	249	256	264	272
75	152	160	168	176	184	192	200	208	216	224	232	240	248	256	264	272	279
76	156	164	172	180	189	197	205	213	221	230	238	246	254	263	271	279	287

Height (inches)	Body Mass Index																
	36	37	38	39	40	41	42	43	44	45	46	47	48	49	50	51	52
	Body Weight (pounds)																
58	172	177	181	186	191	196	201	205	210	215	220	224	229	234	239	244	248
59	178	183	188	193	198	203	208	212	217	222	227	232	237	242	247	252	257
60	184	189	194	199	204	209	215	220	225	230	235	240	245	250	255	261	266
61	190	195	201	206	211	217	222	227	232	238	243	248	254	259	264	269	275
62	196	202	207	213	218	224	229	235	240	246	251	256	262	267	273	278	284
63	203	208	214	220	225	231	237	242	248	254	259	265	270	278	282	287	293
64	209	215	221	227	232	238	244	250	256	262	267	273	279	285	291	296	302
65	216	222	228	234	240	246	252	258	264	270	276	282	288	294	300	306	312
66	223	229	235	241	247	253	260	266	272	278	284	291	297	303	309	315	322
67	230	236	242	249	255	261	268	274	280	287	293	299	306	312	319	325	331
68	236	243	249	256	262	269	276	282	289	295	302	308	315	322	328	335	341
69	243	250	257	263	270	277	284	291	297	304	311	318	324	331	338	345	351
70	250	257	264	271	278	285	292	299	306	313	320	327	334	341	348	355	362
71	257	265	272	279	286	293	301	308	315	322	329	338	343	351	358	365	372
72	265	272	279	287	294	302	309	316	324	331	338	346	353	361	368	375	383
73	272	280	288	295	302	310	318	325	333	340	348	355	363	371	378	386	393
74	280	287	295	303	311	319	326	334	342	350	358	365	373	381	389	396	404
75	287	295	303	311	319	327	335	343	351	359	367	375	383	391	399	407	415
76	295	304	312	320	328	336	344	353	361	369	377	385	394	402	410	418	426

Figure 32.1   BMI chart.

treatment can become another intervention in the toolbox of the mental health professionals working in behavioral medicine settings. Psychologists not interested in working with obese patients or those who do not have the time to provide ongoing treatment can frequently identify appropriate clinicians through eating disorder programs. The primary care psychologist, however, can still play an important role in assessment. Before working with obese persons, the mental health professional should consider obesity in specific populations, and certain additional considerations.

Obesity and Psychopathology

Few differences in general psychopathology between obese and average-weight individuals have been found (e.g., Friedman & Brownell, 1995; Wadden & Stunkard, 1985). Nonetheless, many medical professionals and laypersons believe that obesity is related to depressed mood. Two large studies of national samples have identified a relationship between BMI and depression (Carpenter, Hasin, Allison, & Faith, 2000; Istvan, Zavela, & Weidner, 1992). Obese individuals who present for weight loss treatment often report greater symptoms of depression than persons of average weight (Wadden & Stunkard, 1985). However, depressive and other psychological symptoms may be as much a result of obesity as a cause of it.

Obesity in Specific Populations

Minority populations, particularly minority women, are disproportionately affected by obesity. Based on the National Health and Nutrition Examination Survey, 49.7% of African American and 39.7% of Hispanic American women were classified as obese (Flegal et al., 2002). These percentages are approximately 10% to 20% greater than those for white women (30.1%). For men, 28% of African Americans and 28.9% of Hispanic Americans are overweight or obese, comparable to 27.3% of white men (Flegal et al., 2002). Higher prevalence of overweight and obesity compared to whites has been found in samples of other minority groups, including Puerto Rican, Cuban American, American Indian, Alaskan Na-

tive, and Western Samoan (Kumanyika, 1994). Minorities and men of all racial and ethnic groups typically are underrepresented among those who seek weight loss treatment.

The problem of child and adolescent obesity has received increased attention in the past several years. In 1999, 13% of children and 14% of adolescents were considered obese (Flegal, Caroll, Kuczmarski, & Johnson, 1998). These percentages have increased 4% and 5%, respectively, since 1965. Family-based behavioral treatment programs (similar to adult programs, discussed in detail in the "Behavioral Treatment" section) appear to be most effective in producing weight loss compared to other treatment approaches (Jelalian & Saelens, 1999). Effective treatment, however, is often at odds with barriers from the environment, family, peers, and the child (Faith, Saelens, Wilfley, & Allison, 2001). At present, little is known about the effectiveness of pharmacological and surgical treatment of childhood obesity. (A detailed discussion of the treatment of pediatric obesity is provided in Goldfield, Raynor, & Epstein, 2002.)

Additional Considerations

As noted in the introduction, medical professionals (and psychologists) are not immune to holding derogatory attitudes about the obese. Unless changed, these beliefs may negatively color interactions with the patient.

It is also important to consider some practical issues. The mental health professional's environment must be able to accommodate not only overweight, but also severely obese persons. Chairs in both the reception area and the clinician's office should be without arms so patients can sit comfortably. If working in a medical office, the mental health professional should ensure that examination gowns and blood pressure cuffs are large enough for obese persons. Finally, the scale should be placed in a private location and be able to accommodate severely obese individuals, ideally up to at least 800 lb. Nothing may be more demoralizing for obese individuals than to present for weight loss treatment and not be able to be weighed because the scale cannot accommodate them.

ASSESSMENT OF
THE OBESE PATIENT

The mental health professional's assessment of obese patients will often occur after a physician has performed a comprehensive physical exam and recommended weight loss treatment. The assessment has at least three goals (Wadden & Phelan, 2002). First, the assessment helps the clinician and patient better understand the biological and behavioral factors that may contribute to the patient's obesity. Second, it allows for an assessment of the psychosocial consequences of obesity. Finally, it provides a forum for discussing the patient's weight loss goals.

The mental health professional's assessment should include four factors categorized by the phrase BEST treatment (Sarwer & Wadden, 1999; Wadden & Phelan, 2002; Wadden & Sarwer, 1999). BEST represents the (a) biological, (b) environmental, (c) social/psychological, and (d) temporal factors associated with a weight loss effort. This interview can be augmented with paper-and-pencil assessment tools, such as the Weight and Lifestyle Inventory (Wadden & Foster, 2001) and the Beck Depression Inventory–II (Beck, Steer, & Brown, 1996).

Biological Factors

The medical evaluation may reveal the presence of a number of obesity-related disorders, including hypertension, hyperlipidemia, diabetes mellitus, heart disease, and osteoarthritis. Other syndromes such as Prader-Willi syndrome, hypothalamic or pituitary tumors, hypothyroidism, and polycystic ovarian syndrome may also be present with obesity. These disorders can be treated simultaneously with weight reduction. In addition, several medications may be associated with weight gain. Examples include systemic steroids for asthma or arthritis, Depakote (valproate) for seizure disorders, and sulfonylurea drugs for non-insulin-dependent diabetes mellitus. Many of the antipsychotics (e.g., clozapine and risperidone), antidepressants (e.g., tricyclics and monoamine oxidase inhibitors), mood stabilizers (e.g., lithium and valproic acid), and some anxiolytics are associated with unwanted weight gain (Ackerman & Nolan, 1998). Behavioral weight loss treatment can help minimize the weight gain associated with these medications.

Assessing the age of onset and family history of obesity can offer important information about genetic susceptibility to obesity. Prepubescent onset of obesity is generally associated with increased fat cell number and greater adult body weight (Krotiewski et al., 1980). Severe obesity, in particular, often occurs across generations.

Environmental Factors

A key environmental factor associated with obesity is the patient's eating habits. Ideally, patients will have completed records of food and beverage intake over several days prior to the assessment (see Figure 32.2). These records will reveal the general composition of the diet, the approximate daily calorie intake, and specific eating patterns and habits. In the absence of food records, it is useful to ask patients to describe food and beverage intake over the past 24 hours, as well as consumption on a typical weekday and weekend day. Obese persons often consume large amounts of high-caloric beverages, including regular soda, sweetened iced tea, and fruit juice. Unfortunately, many individuals are unaware that these calories can make a significant contribution to their weight. Thus, the professional should specifically ask about beverage intake. The presence of binge eating should be assessed. *Binge eating* is defined as consumption of a large amount of food (i.e., an amount that would be considered large by others) in a brief period of time, accompanied by a feeling of loss of control (Spitzer et al., 1992). Binge eating disorder occurs in only about 2% of the population, but is found in approximately 15% to 20% of obese persons treated in specialty clinics (Yanovski, 1993). Obese binge eaters may require psychotherapeutic treatment either before or in addition to weight reduction, as discussed in a separate section.

In addition, physical activity should be assessed. The mental health professional should ask about participation in traditional forms of scheduled exercise, such as jogging or aerobics. Furthermore, patients should be asked about daily lifestyle activity, such as stair use and walking.

Day 1		Date:_____	
Food & Amount	Place	Time	Calories
BREAKFAST			

_____
_____
_____

Total calories from this meal _____
LUNCH

_____
_____
_____

Total calories from this meal _____
DINNER

_____
_____
_____

Total calories from this meal _____
SNACKS

_____
_____
_____

Total calories from this meal _____

Total calories for the day: _____

ACTIVITY/EXERCISE   MINUTES

_____
_____

Day 2		Date:_____	
Food & Amount	Place	Time	Calories
BREAKFAST			

_____
_____
_____

Total calories from this meal _____
LUNCH

_____
_____
_____

Total calories from this meal _____
DINNER

_____
_____
_____

Total calories from this meal _____
SNACKS

_____
_____
_____

Total calories from this meal _____

Total calories for the day: _____

ACTIVITY/EXERCISE   MINUTES

_____
_____

Figure 32.2   A food record.

Many obese individuals are often quite sedentary, frequently because of the physical discomfort associated with activity.

Social/Psychological Factors

The assessment of the social and psychological factors associated with obesity incorporates many elements of any general psychological assessment. The interviewer should inquire about the psychiatric history. The presence of current psychopathology, particularly depression, should be assessed. Mild forms of depression, or those related to patients' current weight, often can be treated simultaneously with weight reduction. The occurrence of a major depressive episode, however, likely contraindicates behavioral treatment of obesity (Sarwer, Womble, & Berkowitz, 2001).

Among obese patients treated in university- and hospital-based clinics, approximately 25% to 35% of individuals present with comorbid psychopathology (Fitzgibbon, Stolley, & Kirschenbaum, 1993). Many of these conditions can negatively affect behavioral weight control treatment. Bulimia nervosa (binge eating with loss of control, which is accompanied by compensatory behaviors including vomiting, laxative abuse, or excessive exercise) warrants treatment independent of weight reduction. Persons actively abusing substances and those who are actively psychotic are inappropriate for weight loss treatment.

As in other psychological assessments, the mental health professional should inquire about other dimensions of patients' lives that may be related to or influenced by obesity. These areas include social and romantic relationships, job satisfaction, and current life goals. It is important to understand how these areas may be influenced by weight loss.

Timing Factors

The mental health professional also should determine the current interest and motivation for weight loss. In a primary care setting, patients may be motivated to lose weight for health reasons and because of the recommendation of their physicians. Distressing events such as an increase in clothing size or viewing an unflattering picture, also may prompt patients to lose weight. The level of life stress at the present time should be determined. Weight maintenance rather than weight loss should be encouraged during periods of high stress. An understanding of a patient's motivations and stress level will help both patient and practitioner determine the readiness to change maladaptive behaviors. (See chapter 14 for a more detailed discussion of motivation and behavior change.)

Establishing Realistic Treatment Goals

The assessment should conclude with a discussion of the goals for treatment. Guidelines from the National Heart, Lung, and Blood Institute (NHLBI) emphasize two goals (NHLBI, 1998). The first is to attain a 10% loss from the initial body weight over a period of 6 months. The second goal of treatment is the prevention of weight regain.

Unfortunately, these treatment goals are frequently at odds with patients' weight loss goals. Patients often begin a weight loss effort hoping to reach a specific weight, often one that is 20% to 35% less than their current weight (Foster, Wadden, & Vogt, 1997b; Jeffery, Wing, & Randall, 1998; O'Neil, Smith, Foster, & Anderson, 2000). Thus, one of the greatest challenges for professionals working with obese patients is helping them adopt more realistic weight loss goals, typically 5% to 15% of initial weight. Several scientific panels have concluded that weight losses of this magnitude can frequently improve obesity-related comorbidities and improve psychosocial status (Agricultural Research Service, 1995; Insti-

tute of Medicine, 1995; NHLBI, 1998; WHO, 1998). Thus, the traditional goal of weight reduction—helping patients reach their ideal body weight (which was unattainable for the vast majority of patients)—has been replaced by this more attainable goal (Foster & Kendall, 1994; Wadden, Sarwer, & Berkowitz, 1999).

The health benefits of these more realistic losses should be emphasized. Patients also should be educated about improvements in mobility, appearance, body image, and self-esteem that are associated with a weight loss as low as 10% (Sarwer et al., 2001). Such discussion may be particularly important for patients with a biological predisposition for obesity. These patients may be able to achieve these weight losses; however, it may be unlikely that these individuals will attain an average body weight (BMI 25 kg/m^2 or less) and maintain that weight for an extended period of time.

TREATMENT OF OBESITY IN A PRIMARY CARE SETTING

The 1998 NHLBI guidelines provided specific recommendations for the treatment of obesity. They were made based on the patient's BMI and the presence of significant comorbid medical conditions or risk factors. Wadden, Brownell, and Foster (2002) also have proposed a conceptual scheme of a three-stage process for selecting a weight loss treatment approach (see Figure 32.3). Similar to the NHLBI guidelines, this approach provides recommendations based on BMI. It also provides suggestions for treatment options of different intensity.

Behavior modification strategies, either as part of a self-directed or self-help program or as practiced by a mental health professional working in a primary care setting, can be utilized regardless of a patient's BMI or comorbid conditions. For patients with a BMI less than 30 kg/m^2 who have failed self-directed or self-help programs, behavior modification with a psychologist is an appropriate treatment option. For patients with a BMI from 30 to 40 kg/m^2, behavior modification can be used in combination with low-calorie diets or pharmacotherapy. Behavior modification is also

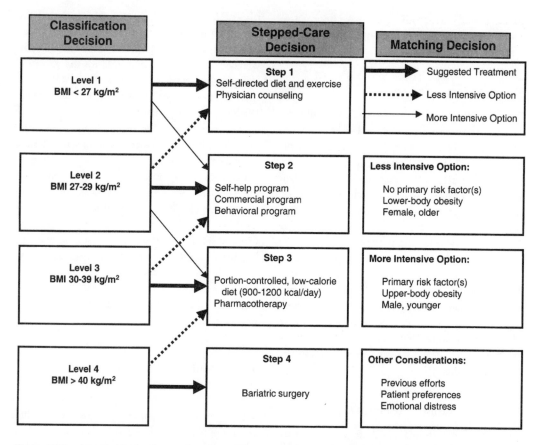

Figure 32.3 A conceptual scheme showing a three-stage process for selecting a treatment approach. The first step, the classification decision, divides people into four levels based on body mass index (BMI). This level dictates which of four steps would be appropriate in the second stage, the stepped-care decision. This indicates that the least intensive, costly, and risky approach will be used from among the treatment alternatives. The solid arrow between the two boxes identifies the treatment most likely to be appropriate. The third stage, the matching decision, is used to make a final treatment selection, based on the assessment of the patient's need for weight reduction as judged by the actual presence of comorbid conditions or other risk factors. The dashed arrow between boxes indicates a reduced need for weight reduction because of the absence of risk factors. The thin arrow shows the more intensive treatment option, appropriate for persons with a significant comorbid condition. For example, many patients with a BMI of 27–29 kg/m^2 do not have health complications. The appropriate treatment for such individuals would include a commercial program or a behavioral or self-help approach. By contrast, the practitioner may wish to consider pharmacotherapy with an individual with a BMI of 29 kg/m^2 who also has Type II diabetes. Patients with significant psychiatric problems or who want more support in changing diet and exercise habits can be referred for adjunct care. Reprinted with permission of Thomas A. Wadden and Kelly Brownell.

an important treatment component for persons with a BMI above 40 kg/m^2 who undergo bariatric surgery. The discussion here outlines behavior modification strategies for patients in all three groups.

Behavioral Treatment

Behavioral treatment of obesity relies on a functional analysis of behavior to help obese individuals identify and modify inappropriate eating, exercise, and thinking habits that contribute to their obesity. As in many behavioral psychotherapeutic approaches, patients are taught to identify antecedents, behaviors, and consequences. The approach also involves cognitive treatment strategies; patients are taught to identify negative cognitions associated with eating and exercise.

Behavioral treatment acknowledges the role of genetic, metabolic, and hormonal influences on body weight. Nevertheless, the focus of treatment is on providing patients with a set of skills with which to control their obesity, regardless of its etiology. The basic skills include self-monitoring, problem solving, stimulus control, and nutrition education. The approach often includes the use of treatment manuals, such as the *LEARN Program for Weight Control* (Brownell, 1991), which provide additional structure in a step-by-step format. There are many elements of behavioral treatment (Wadden & Phelan, 2002; Wing, 1998); the discussion here focuses on three key components: self-monitoring, nutrition education, and exercise. Treatment can be provided either individually or in a group setting.

Self-Monitoring

Self-monitoring is the cornerstone of behavioral treatment of obesity (Sarwer & Wadden, 1999; Wadden & Sarwer, 1999). It provides a detailed record of food and beverage intake (see Figure 32.2). Patients frequently report that self-monitoring makes them more aware of what they consume, which often leads to decreased intake. In addition to recording what and how much they eat and drink each day, patients indicate the time, place, activity, and emotions experienced while eating. This more detailed monitoring helps patients identify maladaptive eating patterns that

can be targeted for change. Problem-solving and stimulus control techniques can be taught to disrupt these patterns. Stimulus control can modify the precursors of eating and therefore create a more restricted set of environmental events related to eating.

For example, monitoring forms may reveal that an individual eats snack foods while watching certain television programs. A corresponding intervention may involve avoiding food intake while watching television or limiting consumption to a carefully selected, healthy snack. Eating triggered by strong emotional experiences often requires cognitive interventions that involve identifying negative, irrational thoughts (e.g., "I am a failure when it comes to losing weight") and then restructuring those thoughts with appropriate counterstatements.

Completion of self-monitoring forms is thought to be critical to long-term behavior change. Nevertheless, it has some limitations. Patients may underestimate their caloric intake by as much as 50% (Lichtman et al., 1992). Some patients are resistant to completing food records. Some indicate little interest in recording their intake, and others report being too busy to keep records. These situations also warrant cognitive interventions.

Nutrition Education

Most behavioral modification weight reduction programs include nutrition education. This can be provided in a consultation with a dietician or by a psychologist with a good working knowledge of nutrition. Many behavioral programs provide general nutrition education rather than prescribe a rigid diet. The recommended diet is composed of no more than 30% calories from fat, 12% from protein, and the remainder from carbohydrate (Agricultural Research Service, 1995). The Food Guide Pyramid (National Livestock and Meat Board, 1993) encourages individuals to consume 6 to 11 servings of bread, cereal, rice, and pasta; 3 to 5 servings of vegetables; 2 to 4 servings of fruit; 2 to 3 servings of milk, yogurt, and cheese; and 2 to 3 servings of meat, poultry, fish, and eggs each day. Using these serving guidelines, women and men trying to lose weight usually limit their calories to 1,200 and 1,500 kcal, respectively (nondieting women and men typically consume 1,800 and 2,500 kcal/day, respectively). To meet the caloric intake range, patients often need to eat at the low end of the recommended number of bread servings (i.e., 6 to 8 servings).

Patients are instructed to consume foods that they enjoy without avoiding "forbidden foods," typically high-fat, high-sugar foods such as chocolate, cookies, and ice cream. Patients are encouraged to develop plans to learn how to eat reduced portion sizes of these foods in moderation. For example, they may be asked to eat ice cream out of a smaller bowl or to order the small serving size of French fries in restaurants. As a result, patients typically do not feel deprived, and they may be less likely to overindulge when they eventually eat a forbidden food.

Low-calorie (1,000 kcal/day) or very low-calorie (800 kcal/day) diets can also be used as part of a behavioral weight loss program. These diets frequently use liquid meal replacement products (e.g., Slimfast or Optifast) to help patients reduce their calories to these amounts in a nutritious, safe manner. Patients typically use these products for 12 to 16 weeks and then are returned to a 1,500 kcal/day diet. This approach is often appealing to patients as it can produce a rapid initial weight loss. Unfortunately, weight regain typically occurs more quickly than in diets with less dramatic calorie reductions. These approaches should only be used in combination with comprehensive medical and nutritional monitoring.

Exercise

The physical and mental health benefits of regular exercise are undeniable (NHLBI, 1998). Somewhat surprising to both medical professionals and laypersons alike, however, is that exercise appears to make only a modest contribution to weight loss. The addition of regular exercise to a 1,200 kcal/day diet used in most behavioral programs of 16 to 18 weeks increases weight loss by only 2 to 3 kg (Perri, McAdoo, McAllister, Laurer, & Yancey, 1986; Wadden, Vogt, et al., 1997). Thus, the practitioner should avoid overstating the weight-reducing effects of exercise. Nevertheless, regular exercise appears to be an important part of long-term weight maintenance. Numerous studies

show that those patients who lose weight and keep it off exercise regularly (Ballor & Poehlman, 1994; Klem, Wing, McGuire, Seagle, & Hill, 1997; Saris, 1998).

Many experts talk about two broad categories of exercise: programmed activity and lifestyle activity. Programmed activity involves regularly planned periods (i.e., 20–40 minutes) of physical exertion at a high-intensity level (i.e., 60%–80% maximum heart rate). Examples of programmed activity include running, swimming, cycling, and aerobic workouts. Lifestyle activity involves engaging in behaviors of daily living that increase activity levels. Examples include taking the stairs instead of the elevators or escalators and parking farther away from building entrances. The main goal of this form of activity is to increase energy expenditure without worrying about the level of intensity.

For obese patients hesitant to engage in programmed activity because of physical or psychological discomfort, lifestyle activity is a more amenable option. At least one study has suggested that a program of diet and increased lifestyle activity (30 minutes/day) may be just as beneficial to health as a program consisting of diet plus vigorous activity (three step-aerobic classes per week) (Andersen et al., 1999). Current recommendations suggest that adults should engage in at least 30 minutes a day of moderate-intensity activity (Pate et al., 1995).

Behavioral programs typically encourage patients to increase both forms of activity (Fox, 1992). Walking, which falls into both categories, may be an ideal form of exercise for obese individuals (Andersen et al., 1999). Use of a pedometer that monitors the number of steps taken can help patients increase their daily walking. In addition, patients should be encouraged to schedule walks. A schedule of programmed activity begins with walking two or three times a week for about 10 to 20 minutes at a time. Over time, patients should target a goal of at least 150 minutes of activity per week (4–5 days per week for 40–45 minutes each day). This amount of exercise has been shown to improve weight loss over an 18-month period (Jakicic, Winters, Lang, & Wing, 1999). Patients unable to reach these goals, however, should also be reminded that any amount of exercise is better than none at all.

THE EFFECTIVENESS OF BEHAVIOR THERAPY FOR OBESITY

Most of the research on the behavioral treatment of obesity has taken place in clinical trials conducted in university-based hospital settings. The results from both short-term and long-term studies can provide some information on the effectiveness of treatment offered in other settings.

Short-Term Behavioral Treatment

A review of the behavioral treatment studies suggests that behavioral approaches produce weight losses consistent with the current weight loss recommendations. In several studies, women lost 9% of their starting body weight, on average, in a 20-week treatment period (for a review, see Sarwer & Wadden, 1999; Wadden, Sarwer, et al., 1999; Wing, 2002). These weight losses also are consistent with the weight losses achieved by the majority of the antiobesity drugs available over the past decade (e.g., Davidson et al., 1999; Sjostrom et al., 1998). The similarity of weight losses for both behavioral and pharmacological treatments for obesity is often surprising to patients and practitioners alike because weight loss medications are often mischaracterized, particularly by the popular press, as the "magic bullet" of weight control (Sarwer et al., 2001).

Patients typically regain about 30% to 35% of their weight in the year following treatment (Wadden, Sternberg, Letizia, Stunkard, & Foster, 1990). Even with weight regain, most patients still meet the criteria of success—a 5% weight loss maintained for at least 1 year—proposed by the Institute of Medicine (1995). Unfortunately, weight gain generally increases over time, and patients frequently regain 100% of their weight loss within 5 years (Wadden et al., 1990). Although discouraging, this finding is not surprising if obesity is thought of as a chronic disorder similar to hypertension or diabetes. Continuous, long-term care is needed for those disorders and is increasingly thought to be necessary for obesity (Wadden et al., 2002). Thus, practitioners are strongly advised to encourage patients to think of weight loss behaviors as long-term changes in lifestyle rather than short-term changes in behavior.

Long-Term Behavioral Treatment

Several studies have demonstrated benefits of long-term behavioral treatment (Perri et al., 1988; Viegener et al., 1990; Wing et al., 1994). In one investigation, patients who attended group maintenance sessions every other week for 1 year following weight reduction maintained 13.0 kg of their 13.2 kg end-of-treatment weight loss. Those who did not attend these sessions maintained less than half that amount (Perri et al., 1988). Maintenance sessions appear to provide patients the support and motivation needed to continue to practice weight control skills, such as keeping food records, exercising regularly, and weighing themselves at least weekly (Wadden, Sarwer, et al., 1999).

Although there appear to be some benefits to long-term treatment, three limitations exist (Wadden, Sarwer, et al., 1999). First, increasing treatment duration is not associated with substantially larger weight losses. Second, follow-up visits need to occur at least every other week to sustain a 10% weight loss. Infrequent contact is not likely to be sufficient to sustain patients' attention to and motivation for behavior change. Finally, long-term behavioral treatment appears to delay, rather than prevent, weight regain. When maintenance sessions are discontinued, patients regain weight. These results suggest the need for chronic care, which may be difficult to provide in a primary care setting (Wadden, Sarwer, et al., 1999). The use of a weight loss medication in combination with behavioral weight control therapy, however, may assist with the long-term maintenance of weight loss.

BEHAVIORAL AND PHARMACOLOGICAL TREATMENT OF OBESITY

Two medications are currently approved by the Food and Drug Administration for the long-term treatment of obesity. (For a detailed discussion of the pharmacological treatment of obesity, interested readers are referred to Bray, 2002.) Sibutramine (Meridia) is a serotonin and norepinephrine reuptake inhibitor that increases feelings of satiety or fullness, ultimately resulting in a decrease in appetite (Lean, 1997). Orlistat (Xenical) is a gastrointestinal lipase inhibitor that prevents the absorption of fat in the digestive system (Sjostrom et al., 1998). Despite the very different mechanisms of action for these medications, studies have found that both produce weight losses of approximately 7% to 10% (i.e., Bray et al., 1996, 1999; Hill et al., 1999; James et al., 2000; Sjostrom et al., 1998), similar to those typically found from behavioral treatments. However, achieving sustained weight loss behaviorally seems to take much more time and effort for both the patient and the practitioner.

Pharmacological agents induce weight loss by modifying *internal* signals associated with eating. In contrast, behavioral modification induces weight loss by helping patients modify their *external* environment. As the two treatments differ in their mechanisms of action, they may serve to augment each other and produce increased weight losses. Studies of both previously available medications (Craighead, Stunkard, & O'Brien, 1981; Wadden et al., 1997), as well as those of sibutramine (Wadden, Berkowitz, Sarwer, Prus-Wisniewski, & Steinberg, 2001), suggested that a combined approach to treatment may maximize patients' weight losses.

BEHAVIORAL AND SURGICAL TREATMENT OF OBESITY

Bariatric surgery ("stomach stapling") for obesity is becoming an increasingly popular option for individuals with severe obesity. Patients must have a BMI of 40 kg/m^2 or higher, or more than 35 kg/m^2 with the presence of one or more obesity-related comorbidities. Patients typically receive one of two basic surgical procedures. The vertical banded gastroplasty (VBG) involves the creation of a small stomach pouch at the base of the esophagus (approximately 50 ml in size), which severely limits food intake. The gastric bypass procedure also involves the creation of a small stomach pouch. However, the remaining area of the stomach and part of the intestine (duodenum) are bypassed by attaching the small pouch to the jejunum. The bypass works both by limiting food intake and by creating malabsorption of calories. The typical weight losses associated with

both procedures are between 25% and 35% of the patient's preoperative body weight (Albrecht & Pories, 1999; Kral, 1998). (A more detailed discussion of bariatric surgery is provided in Latifi, Kellum, DeMaria, and Sugerman, 2002, or Wadden et al., 2001.) Cosmetic procedures such as liposuction are not a treatment for obesity; liposuction typically results in very modest weight losses.

Psychologists may encounter bariatric surgery patients preoperatively because many surgeons require a psychological evaluation prior to surgery. These evaluations are quite similar to the basic behavioral assessment described in this chapter. As part of the evaluative process, several additional questions must be addressed:

- Does the patient's BMI and comorbidity profile warrant the procedure?
- Has the patient exhausted more conservative treatment options, including self-directed diets, commercial programs, behavioral programs, nutritional counseling, and weight loss medications?
- Is the patient free of psychopathology (most typically major depression) that may affect his or her ability to learn and adhere to the rigorous demands of the postoperative diet?
- Does the patient have an appreciation of the significant behavioral changes required to achieve a successful postoperative result?

If the answer to any of these questions is no, the psychologist should recommend delaying surgery until additional psychoeducation or psychiatric treatment has occurred.

Psychologists also may encounter bariatric surgery patients postoperatively. Some patients have a difficult time adjusting to the postoperative diet or reducing their portion sizes. Others may experience difficulties with depression or other psychopathology that was not addressed preoperatively. For others, changes in physical appearance and body image may warrant psychotherapeutic care.

ADDITIONAL CLINICAL ISSUES

Psychologists working in a primary care setting also may encounter obese patients who are struggling with other issues related to their obesity. These issues include binge eating, night eating, and body image dissatisfaction. (See chapter 25 for a more detailed discussion of eating disorders.)

Binge Eating Disorder

Obese persons may suffer from binge eating disorder (BED), which is currently a provisional diagnosis under additional research in the *Diagnostic and Statistical Manual of Mental Disorders*, fourth edition (*DSM-IV*; American Psychiatric Association, 1994). It is defined as eating a very large amount of food in a discrete period of time (2 hours) while feeling out of control. The binges are accompanied by at least three of the following: eating much more rapidly than usual; eating until feeling uncomfortably full; eating large amounts of food when not physically hungry; eating alone because of embarrassment; and feeling disgusted with oneself, depressed, or very guilty after eating. These episodes are not accompanied by purging behaviors (i.e., vomiting, laxative abuse, or excessive exercise) seen in bulimia nervosa. The diagnosis requires an average of two binges per week for a period of 6 months. BED afflicts both white and minority women to similar extents; men of all racial groups are diagnosed less frequently (Smith, Marcus, Lewis, Fitzgibbon, & Schreiner, 1998).

Diagnosis of BED can be challenging because of the difficulty in determining what constitutes an amount of food "definitely larger than what most people would eat during a similar period of time or under similar circumstances" (APA, 1994, p. 787). The Eating Disorders Examination–Questionnaire (Fairburn & Cooper, 1993) or the Questionnaire on Weight and Eating Patterns (Yanovski, 1993) can be used to assess possible episodes. A general guideline for a binge would be ingestion of at least two large platefuls of food or three main course servings. Ultimately, reports of a loss of control during the eating episode may help distinguish a binge episode from a large meal.

Psychiatric comorbidity is common in persons with BED. Depression is consistently reported, and Axis II disorders may be present. If severe enough, these conditions should take priority in treatment, especially because the number of binge episodes decreases in response to treatment of other existing disorders (Stunkard & Allison, 2003).

Cognitive–behavioral therapy for BED, administered in individual, group, and self-help formats, is effective in decreasing binge episodes (e.g., Agras, Telch, Arnow, Eldredge, & Marnell, 1997; Marcus, Wing, & Fairburn, 1995; Wilfley et al., 1993). Interpersonal treatment approaches also show significant reductions in binging (Wilfley et al., 1993; Wilfley & Cohen, 1997). None of these interventions, however, typically produces significant weight loss. Pharmacotherapy, usually with antidepressants, may be effective in the short term, but once it is discontinued, the bingeing predictably returns (Alger, Schwalberg, Bigaoutte, Michaelek, & Howard, 1991; Hudson et al., 1998).

Night Eating Syndrome

There has been increased interest in night eating syndrome (NES) over the past few years. NES consists of four core symptoms: morning anorexia, evening hyperphagia, nocturnal awakenings, and eating during waking episodes. NES is often accompanied by a depressed mood, especially later in the day. Although NES occurs in both normal weight and overweight individuals, NES is thought to promote obesity. It is present in approximately 1.5% of the general population (Rand et al., 1997), but occurs more often in obese persons seeking weight loss treatment (15%; Stunkard et al., 1996) and bariatric surgery (42%; Hsu, Betancourt, & Sullivan, 1996). The disorder appears to occur frequently in both men and minority populations.

Many persons with NES are embarrassed by their behaviors and have been advised by physicians to "just stop eating at night." However, NES sufferers feel compelled to eat when they awaken and believe that they cannot fall back to sleep without eating. Some patients may repeat this pattern two to four times each night. Most persons with NES are awake, to varying degrees, and determined to eat. They sometimes go to extremes to stop themselves, such as locking their refrigerators or locking themselves in their bedrooms. The nighttime ingestions characteristic of

NES are not "binges"; rather, they are snacks, such as peanut butter, cakes, chips, or readily available leftover foods. Most night eaters typically return to bed shortly after they have eaten and fall asleep readily once their cravings have been satisfied. In the morning, NES sufferers have no appetite and often do not eat until the afternoon.

Three quarters of night eaters report a stress-related onset of their symptoms. Cortisol, a stress-related hormone, is characteristically elevated over a 24-hour period (Birketvedt et al., 1999). Accordingly, NES may worsen in periods of heavy stress. Other hormonal findings indicate that melatonin and leptin, which should rise at night to help maintain sleep and suppress appetite, respectively, do not increase as expected (Birketvedt et al., 1999). Although melatonin is available over the counter, reports do not support its effectiveness as a potential treatment. Hypnotics and over-the-counter sleeping pills also do not seem effective.

Initial reports suggested that sertraline (Zoloft) may be effective in reducing NES when used at doses similar to those used for treating bulimia (O'Reardon, Stunkard, & Allison, 2004). Promotion of good sleep hygiene and enforcing a regular daytime eating pattern also may be helpful. These strategies do not appear sufficient, however. Exploration of patients' beliefs about their need to eat during the night may be fruitful, as well as reenforcement of coping strategies for dealing with daytime stressors.

Body Image Dissatisfaction

Body image dissatisfaction is pervasive, with greater than 50% of women and more than two fifths of men reporting dissatisfaction with their appearance (Garner, 1997). For most individuals, the focus of this dissatisfaction is on features commonly associated with excess body weight—abdomen, hips, and thighs—but often it occurs independently of actual body weight (Foster et al., 1997a; Sarwer, Wadden, & Foster, 1998). Overweight and obese women frequently report heightened body image dissatisfaction, which often has a detrimental impact on their behavior (Rosen, Orosan, & Reiter, 1995; Sarwer et al., 1998). Studies also have suggested that, among overweight and obese women, body image dissatisfaction is related to decreased self-esteem and increased depressive symptoms (Foster et al., 1997b; Sarwer et al., 1998).

Body image dissatisfaction appears to play a significant role in motivating weight loss efforts (Sarwer & Thompson, 2002). Several studies have found that weight loss results in improvement in body image (e.g., Cash, 1994; Foster et al., 1997a). Other studies have suggested that obese women can experience improvement in body image without weight loss in programs that focus on improving self-esteem and body image with cognitive–behavioral interventions (Polivy & Herman, 1992; Rosen et al., 1995). Ramirez and Rosen (2001) combined a behavioral weight control program with a cognitive–behavioral body image program and reported a 10% reduction in weight coupled with improvements in body image, self-esteem, and eating concerns. Such combined approaches hold promise in helping obese patients deal with the physical and psychological effects of obesity (Sarwer & Thompson, 2002).

SUMMARY

As an increasing proportion of the Western population continues to suffer from obesity and its related medical illnesses, psychologists working in the primary care setting will be called on to assess and treat this epidemic. Thorough assessment of weight and dieting history as well as identification of detrimental lifestyle choices are essential in selecting appropriate treatment options. Patients must be adequately motivated to change their lifestyles through decreased caloric intake and increased lifestyle activity, and practitioners should help patients accept a modest weight loss goal of 5% to 15%. Psychologists working in a primary care setting can use behavioral modification strategies, including self-monitoring of food and beverage consumption, nutrition education, and physical activity, to help obese individuals meet these weight loss goals.

Special populations may need additional consideration. Severely obese patients who undergo bariatric surgery require special assessment preoperatively and continued follow-up postoperatively. Obese patients with disorders such as depression, BED, or NES often require additional treatment.

In the final analysis, maintenance of weight loss for any overweight or obese individual requires lifelong changes that should be viewed in the same context and with the same importance as those made in response to any other chronic medical illness. The psychologist working in the primary care setting can play a significant role in helping obese individuals both make and sustain these behavioral changes.

ADDITIONAL RESOURCES

Suggestions for further reading and professional development resources are available at this book's companion Web site: www.primarycarepsych.com.

ACKNOWLEDGMENTS This chapter was supported, in part, by funding from the National Institute of Diabetes and Digestive and Kidney Diseases (NIDDK), grant K23 DK60023-01 to Dr. Sarwer and grant R01 DK054713-01 to Dr. Berkowitz. Dr. Allison's work was supported by NIDDK grant R01 DK56735-03.

References

Ackerman, S., & Nolan, L. J. (1998). Body weight gain induced by psychotropic drugs: Incidence, mechanisms and management. *CNS Drugs, 9*, 135–151.

Agras, W. S., Telch, C. F., Arnow, B., Eldredge, K., & Marnell, M. (1997). One-year follow-up of cognitive-behavioral therapy for obese individuals with binge eating disorder. *Journal of Consulting and Clinical Psychology, 65*, 343–347.

Agricultural Research Service. (1995). *Report of the Dietary Guidelines Advisory Committee on the Dietary Guidelines for Americans*. Washington, DC: USDA.

Albrecht, R. J., & Pories, W. J. (1999). Surgical intervention for the severely obese. *Balliere's Clinical Endocrinology and Metabolism, 13*, 149–172.

Alger, S. A., Schwalberg, M. D., Bigaoutte, J. M., Michalek, A. V., & Howard, I. J. (1991). Effect of a tricyclic antidepressant and opiate antagonist on binge-eating behavior: A double-blind, placebo-controlled study. *American Journal of Clinical Nutrition, 53*, 365–371.

American Psychiatric Association. (1994). *Diagnostic and statistical manual of mental disorders* (4th ed.). Washington, DC: Author.

Andersen, R. E., Wadden, T. A., Bartlett, S. J., Zemel, B. S., Verde, T. J., & Franckowiak, S. C. (1999). Effects of lifestyle activity vs. structured aerobic exercise in obese women: A randomized trial. *Journal of the American Medical Association, 281*, 335–340.

Ballor, D. L., & Poehlman, E. T. (1994). Exercise training enhances fat-free mass preservation during diet-induced weight loss: A meta-analytical finding. *International Journal of Eating Disorders, 18*, 35–40.

Beck, A. T., Steer, R. A, & Brown, G. K. (1996). *Beck Depression Inventory–II (BDI-II) manual*. San Antonio, TX: Harcourt Brace.

Birketvedt, G., Florholmen, J., Sundsfjord, J., Osterud, B., Dinges, D., Bilker, W., & Stunkard, A. J. (1999). Behavioral and neuroendocrine characteristics of the night-eating syndrome. *Journal of the American Medical Association, 282*, 657–663.

Bouchard, C. B. (1994). Genetics of obesity: Overview and research direction. In C. B. Bouchard (Ed.), *The genetics of obesity* (pp. 223–233). Boca Raton, FL: CRC Press.

Bray, G. A. (2002). Drug treatment of obesity. In T. A. Wadden & A. J. Stunkard (Eds.), *Handbook of obesity treatment* (pp. 317–338). New York: Guilford Press.

Bray, G. A., Blackburn, G. L., Ferguson, J. M., Greenway, F. L., Jain, A. K., Mendel, C. M., Mendles, J., Ryan, D., Schwartz, S. L., Scheinbaum, M. L., & Seaton, T. B. (1999). Sibutramine produces dose-related weight loss. *Obesity Research, 7*, 189–198.

Bray, G. A., Ryan, D. H., Gordon, D., Heidingsfeldrer, H., Cerise, F., & Wilson, K. (1996). A double-blind randomized placebo-controlled trial of sibutramine. *Obesity Research, 4*, 263–270.

Brownell, K. D. (1991). *The LEARN program for weight control*. Dallas, TX: American Health.

Brownell, K. D., & Wadden, T. A. (1991). The heterogeneity of obesity: Fitting treatments to individuals. *Behavioral Therapy, 22*, 153–177.

Carpenter, K. M., Hasin, D., Allison, D. B., & Faith, M. S. (2000). Relationships between obesity and *DSM-IV* major depressive disorder, suicide ideation, and suicide attempts: Results from a general population study. *American Journal of Public Health, 90*, 251–257.

Cash, T. F. (1994). Body image and weight changes

in a multisite comprehensive very-low-calorie diet program. *Behavior Therapy, 25*, 239–254.

Craighead, L. W., Stunkard, A. J., & O'Brien, R. M. (1981). Behavior therapy and pharmacotherapy for obesity. *Archives of General Psychiatry, 38*, 763–768.

Davidson, M. H., Hauptman, J., DiGirolamo, M., Foreyt, J. P., Halsted, C. H., Heber, D., et al. (1999). Weight control and risk factor reduction in obese subjects treated for 2 years with orlistat: A randomized controlled Trial. *Journal of the American Medical Association, 281*, 235–242.

Fairburn, C. G., & Cooper, Z. (1993). The eating disorders examination. In C. G. Fairburn & G. T. Wilson (Eds.), *Binge eating: Nature, assessment, and treatment* (pp. 317–360). New York: Guilford Press.

Faith, M. S., Saelens, B. E., Wilfley, D. E., & Allison, D. B. (2001). Behavioral treatment of childhood and adolescent obesity: Current status, challenges, and future directions. In J. K. Thompson & L. Smolak (Eds.), *Body image, eating disorders, and obesity in youth: Assessment, prevention and treatment* (pp. 313–340). Washington, DC: American Psychological Association.

Fitzgibbon, M. L., Stolley, M. R., & Kirschenbaum, D. S. (1993). Obese people who seek treatment have different characteristics than those who do not seek treatment. *Health Psychology, 12*, 342–345.

Flegal, K. M., Caroll, M. D., Kuczmarski, R. J., & Johnson, C. L. (1998). Overweight and obesity in the United States: Prevalence and trends, 1960–1994. *International Journal of Obesity, 22*, 39–47.

Flegal, K. M., Carroll, M. D., Odgen, C. L., & Johnson, C. L. (2002). Prevalence and trends in obesity among US adults. *Journal of the American Medical Association, 288*, 1723–1727.

Foster, G. D., & Kendall, P. C. (1994). The realistic treatment of obesity: Changing the scales of success. *Clinical Psychology Review, 14*, 701–736.

Foster, G. D., Wadden, T. A., & Vogt, R. A. (1997a). Body image before, during and after weight loss treatment. *Health Psychology, 16*, 226–229.

Foster, G. D., Wadden, T. A., & Vogt, R. A. (1997b). What is a reasonable weight loss? Patients' expectations and evaluations of obesity treatment outcomes. *Journal of Consulting and Clinical Psychology, 65*, 79–85.

Fox, K. R. (1992). A clinical approach to exercise in the markedly obese. In T. A. Wadden & T. B. VanItallie (Eds.), *Treatment of the seriously obese patient* (pp. 354–382). New York: Guilford Press.

Friedman, M. A., & Brownell, K. D. (1995). Psychological correlates of obesity: Moving to the next research generation. *Psychological Bulletin, 117*, 3–20.

Garner, D. M. (1997). The 1997 body image survey results. *Psychology Today, 30*, 30–41.

Goldfield, G. S., Raynor, H. A., & Epstein, L. H. (2002). Treatment of pediatric obesity. In T. A. Wadden & A. J. Stunkard (Eds.), *Handbook of obesity treatment* (pp. 532–555). New York: Guilford Press.

Harris, J. E., Hamaday, V., & Mochan, E. (1999). Osteopathic family physicians' attitudes, knowledge, and self-reported practices regarding obesity. *Journal of the American Osteopathic Association, 99*, 358–365.

Hill, J. O., Hauptman, J., Anderson, J. W., Fujioka, K., O'Neil, P. M., Smith, D. K., Zavoral, J. H., & Aronne, L. J. (1999). Orlistat, a lipase inhibitor, for weight maintenance after conventional dieting: A 1-year study. *American Journal of Clinical Nutrition, 69*, 1108–1116.

Horgen, K. B., & Brownell, K. D. (1998). Policy changes as a means for reducing the prevalence and impact of alcoholism, smoking, and obesity. In W. R. Miller & N. Heather (Eds.), *Treating addictive behaviors* (2nd ed., pp. 105–118). New York: Plenum Press.

Horgen, K. B., & Brownell, K. D. (2002). Confronting the toxic environment. In T. A. Wadden & A. J. Stunkard (Eds.), *Handbook of obesity treatment* (pp. 95–106). New York: Guilford Press.

Hsu, L. K. G., Betancourt, S., & Sullivan, S. P. (1996). Eating disturbances before and after vertical banded gastroplasty: A pilot study. *International Journal of Eating Disorders, 19*, 23–34.

Hudson, J. I., McElroy, S. L., Raymond, N. C., Crow, S., Keck, P. E., Carter, W. P., Mitchell, J. E., Strakowski, S. M., Pope, H. G., Coleman, B. S., & Jeffrey, J. M. (1998). Fluvoxamine in the treatment of binge eating disorder: A multicenter placebo-controlled, double-blind trial. *American Journal of Psychiatry, 155*, 1756–1762.

Institute of Medicine. (1995). *Weighing the options: Criteria for evaluating weight management programs.* Washington, DC: U.S. Government Printing Office.

Istvan, J., Zavela, K., & Weidener, G. (1992). Body weight and psychological distress in NHANES I. *International Journal of Obesity, 16,* 999–1003.

Jakicic, J. M., Winters, C., Lang, W., & Wing, R. R. (1999). Effects of intermittent exercise and use of home exercise equipment on adherence, weight loss, and fitness in overweight women: A randomized trial. *Journal of the American Medical Association, 282,* 1554–1560.

James, W. P. T., Astrup, A., Finer, N., Hilsted, J., Kopelman, P., Rossner, S., Saris, W. H. M., & Van Gaal, L. F., for the STORM Study Group. (2000). Effect of sibutramine on weight maintenance after weight loss: A randomised trial. *Lancet, 356,* 2119–2126.

Jeffery, R. W., Wing, R. R., & Randall, R. M. (1998). Are smaller weight losses or more achievable weight loss goals better in the long term for obese patients? *Journal of Consulting and Clinical Psychology, 66,* 641–645.

Jelalian, E., & Saelens, B. E. (1999). Intervention for pediatric obesity: Treatments that work. *Journal of Pediatric Psychology, 24,* 223–248.

Klem, M. L., Wing, R. R., McGuire, M. T., Seagle, H. M., & Hill, J. O. (1997). A descriptive study of individuals successful at long-term maintenance of substantial weight loss. *American Journal of Clinical Nutrition, 66,* 239–246.

Kral, J. G. (1998). Surgical treatment of obesity. In G. A. Bray, C. Bouchard, & W. P. T. James (Eds.), *Handbook of obesity* (pp. 977–993). New York: Marcel Dekker.

Krotiewski, M., Garellick, G., Sjostrom, L., Persson, G., Bjuro, T., & Sullivan, L. (1980). Fat cell number, resting metabolic rate, mean heart rate, and insulin elevation while seeing and smelling food as predictors of slimming. *Metabolism, 29,* 1003–1012.

Kumanyika, S. K. (1994). Obesity in minority populations: An epidemiological assessment. *Obesity Research, 2,* 166–182.

Latifi, R., Kellum, J. M., DeMaria, E. J., & Sugerman, H. J. (2002). Surgical treatment of obesity. In T. A. Wadden & A. J. Stunkard (Eds.), *Handbook of obesity treatment* (pp. 339–356). New York: Guilford Press.

Lean, M. E. J. (1997). Sibutramine—a review of clinical efficacy. *International Journal of Obesity, 21,* 30S–36S.

Lichtman, S. W., Pisarka, K., Berman, E. R., Pestone, M., Dowling, H., Offenbacher, E., Weisel, H., Heshka, S., Matthews, D. E., & Heymsfield, S. B. (1992). Discrepancy between self-reported and actual caloric intake and exercise in obese subjects. *New England Journal of Medicine, 327,* 1893–1898.

Manson, J. E., Willett, W. C., Stampfer, M. J., Colditz, G. A., Hunter, D. J., Hankinson, S. E., Henekens, C. H., & Speizer, F. E. (1995). Body weight and mortality among women. *New England Journal of Medicine, 333,* 677–685.

Marcus, M. D., Wing, R. R., & Fairburn, C. G. (1995). Cognitive behavioral treatment of binge eating vs. behavioral weight control on the treatment of binge eating disorder. *Annals of Behavioral Medicine, 17,* S090.

National Livestock and Meat Board. (1993). *Food guide pyramid.* Chicago: Author.

NHLBI Obesity Education Initiative Expert Panel. (1998). Clinical guidelines on the identification, evaluation, and treatment of overweight and obesity in adults: The evidence report. *Obesity Research, 6,* 51S–209S.

O'Neil, P. M., Smith, C. F., Foster, G. D., & Andersen, D. A. (2000). The perceived relative worth of reaching goal weight. *International Journal of Obesity, 24,* 1069–1076.

O'Reardon, J. P., Stunkard, A. J., & Allison, K. C. (2004). Clinical trail of sertraline in the treatment of night eating syndrome. *International Journal of Eating Disorders, 35*(1) 16–26.

Pate, R. R., Pratt, M., Blair, S. N., Haskell, W. L., Macera, C. A., Bouchard, C., Buchner, D., Ettinger, W., Heath, G. W., King, A. C., Kriska, A., Leon, A. S., Marcus, B. H., Morris, J., Paffenbarger, R. S., Jr., Patrick, K., Pollock, M. L., Rippe, J. M., Sallis, J., & Wilmore, J. H. (1995). Physical activity and public health: A recommendation from the Centers for Disease Control and Prevention and the American College of Sports Medicine. *Journal of the American Medical Association, 273,* 402–407.

Perri, M. G., McAdoo, W. G., McAllister, D. A., Laurer, J. B., & Yancey, D. Z. (1986). Enhancing the efficacy of behavior therapy for obesity: Effects of aerobic exercise and a multi component maintenance program. *Journal of Consulting and Clinical Psychology, 54,* 670–675.

Perri, M. G., McAllister, D. A., Gange, J. J., Jordan, R. C., McAdoo, W. G., & Nezu, A. M. (1988). Effects of four maintenance programs on the long-term management of obesity. *Journal of Consulting and Clinical Psychology*, 56, 529–534.

Polivy, J., & Herman, C. P. (1992). Undieting: A program to help people stop dieting. *International Journal of Eating Disorders*, 11, 261–268.

Price, R. A. (2002). Genetics and common obesities: Background, current status, strategies, and future prospects. In T. A. Wadden & A. J. Stunkard (Eds.), *Handbook of obesity treatment* (pp. 73–94). New York: Guilford Press.

Puhl, R., & Brownell, K. D. (2001). Bias, discrimination, and obesity. *Obesity Research*, 9, 788–805.

Ramirez, E. M., & Rosen, J. C. (2001). A comparison of weight control and body image therapy for obese men and women. *Journal of Consulting and Clinical Psychology*, 69, 440–446.

Rand, C. S. W., & MacGregor, A. M. C. (1990). Morbidly obese patients' perceptions of social discrimination before and after surgery for obesity. *Southern Medical Journal*, 83, 1390–1395.

Rand, C. S. W., MacGregor, M. D., & Stunkard, A. (1997). The night eating syndrome in the general population and among the post-operative obesity surgery patients. *International Journal of Eating Disorders*, 22, 65–69.

Roehling, M. V. (1999). Weight-based discrimination in employment: Psychological and legal aspects. *Personnel Psychology*, 52, 969–1016.

Rosen, J. C., Orosan, P., & Reiter, J. (1995). Cognitive behavior therapy for negative body image in obese women. *Behavior Therapy*, 26, 25–42.

Saris, W. H. M. (1998). Fit, fat, and fat-free: The metabolic aspects of weight control. *International Journal of Obesity*, 22, S15–S21.

Sarwer, D. B., & Thompson, J. K. (2002). Obesity and body image disturbance. In T. A. Wadden & A. J. Stunkard (Eds.), *Handbook of obesity treatment* (pp. 447–464). New York: Guilford Press.

Sarwer, D. B., & Wadden, T. A. (1999). The treatment of obesity: What's new, what's recommended. *Journal of Women's Health and Gender Based Medicine*, 8, 483–492.

Sarwer, D. B., Wadden, T. A., & Foster, G. D. (1998). Assessment of body image dissatisfaction in obese women: Specificity, severity, and clinical significance. *Journal of Consulting and Clinical Psychology*, 66, 651–654.

Sarwer, D. B., Womble, L. G., & Berkowitz, R. I. (2001). Behavioral treatment of obesity in the primary care setting. In B. Gumbiner (Ed.), *Obesity* (pp. 202–221). Philadelphia: American College of Physicians Press.

Sjostrom, L., Rissanen, A., Andersen, T., Boldrin, M., Golay, A., Koppeschaar, H. P. F., et al. (1998). Randomized placebo-controlled trial of orlistat for weight loss and prevention of weight regain in obese patients. *Lancet*, 352, 167–172.

Smith, D. E., Marcus, M. D., Lewis, C. E., Fitzgibbon, M., & Schreiner, P. (1998). Prevalence of binge eating disorder, obesity, and depression in a biracial cohort of young adults. *Annals of Behavioral Medicine*, 20(3), 227–232.

Solovay, S. (2000). *Tipping the scales in injustice: Fighting weight-based discrimination*. Amherst, NY: Prometheus Books.

Spitzer, R. L., Devlin, M., Walsh, T. B., Hasin, D., Marcus, M. D., Stunkard, A. J., et al. (1992). Binge eating disorder: A multisite field trial of the diagnostic criteria. *International Journal of Eating Disorders*, 11, 191–203.

Stunkard, A. J., & Allison, K. C. (2003). Two forms of disordered eating in obesity: Binge eating and night eating. *International Journal of Obesity & Related MetabolicDisorders*, 27(1), 1–12.

Stunkard, A. J., Berkowitz, R., Wadden, T., Tanrikut, C., Reiss, E., & Young, L. (1996). Binge eating disorder and the night eating syndrome. *International Journal of Obesity*, 20, 1–6.

Viegener, B. J., Perri, M. G., Nezu, A. M., Renjilian, D. A., McKelvey, W. F., & Schein, R. L. (1990). Effect of an intermittent, low-fat, low-calorie diet in the behavioral treatment of obesity. *Behavior Therapy*, 21, 499–509.

Wadden, T. A., Berkowitz, R. I., Sarwer, D. B., Prus-Wisniewski, R., & Steinberg, C. M. (2001). Benefits of lifestyle modification in the pharmacologic treatment of obesity: A randomized trial. *Archives of Internal Medicine*, 161, 218–227.

Wadden, T. A., Berkowitz, R. I., Vogt, R. A., Steen, S. N., Stunkard, A. J., & Foster, G. D. (1997). Lifestyle modification in the pharmacologic treatment of obesity: A pilot investigation of a potential primary care approach. *Obesity Research*, 6, 278–284.

Wadden, T. A., Brownell, K. D., & Foster, G. D. (2002). Obesity: Responding to the global epidemic. *Journal of Consulting and Clinical Psychology, 70,* 510–525.

Wadden, T. A., & Foster, G. D. (2001). *Weight and lifestyle inventory.* Philadelphia: University of Pennsylvania Press.

Wadden, T. A., & Phelan, S. (2002). Behavioral assessment of the obese patient. In T. A. Wadden & A. J. Stunkard (Eds.), *Handbook of obesity treatment* (pp. 186–228). New York: Guilford Press.

Wadden, T. A., & Sarwer, D. B. (1999). Behavioral treatment of obesity: New approaches to an old disorder. In D. Goldstein (Ed.), *The management of eating disorders* (pp. 232–246). Totowa, NJ: Humana Press.

Wadden, T. A., Sarwer, D. B., & Berkowitz, R. I. (1999). Behavioral treatment of the overweight patient. *Balliere's Clinical Endocrinology and Metabolism, 13,* 93–107.

Wadden, T. A., Sarwer, D. B., Womble, L. G., Foster, G. D., McGuckin, B. G., & Schimmel, A. (2001). Psychosocial aspects of obesity and obesity surgery. *Surgical Clinics of North America, 81,* 1001–1024.

Wadden, T. A., Sternberg, J. A., Letizia, K. A., Stunkard, A. J., & Foster, G. D. (1990). Treatment of obesity by very-low-calorie diet, behavior therapy and their combination: A five-year perspective. *International Journal of Obesity, 51,* 167–172.

Wadden, T. A., & Stunkard, A. J. (1985). Social and psychological consequences of obesity. *Annals of Internal Medicine, 103,* 1062–1067.

Wadden, T. A., Vogt, R. A., Anderson, R. E., Bartlett, S. J., Foster, G. D., Kuehnel, R. H., et al. (1997). Exercise in the treatment of obesity: Effects of four interventions on body composition, resting energy expenditure, appetite, and

mood. *Journal of Consulting and Clinical Psychology, 65,* 269–277.

Wilfley, D. E., Agras, W. S., Telch, C. F., Rossiter, E. M., Schneider, J. A., Cole, A. G., Sifford, L., & Raeburn, S. D. (1993). Group cognitive-behavioral therapy and group interpersonal psychotherapy for the nonpurging bulimic individual: A controlled comparison. *Journal of Consulting and Clinical Psychology, 61,* 296–305.

Wilfley, D. E., & Cohen, L. R. (1997). Psychological treatment of bulimia nervosa and binge eating disorder. *Psychopharmacology Bulletin, 33,* 437–454.

Wing, R. R. (1998). Behavioral approaches to the treatment of obesity. In G. A. Bray, C. Bouchard, & W. P. T. James (Eds.), *Handbook of obesity* (pp. 855–873). New York: Marcel Dekker.

Wing, R. R. (2002). Behavioral weight control. In T. A. Wadden & A. J. Stunkard (Eds.), *Handbook of obesity treatment* (pp. 301–316). New York: Guilford Press.

Wing, R. R., Blair, E. H., Marcus, M. D., Epstein, L. H., & Harvey, J. (1994). Year-long weight loss treatment for obese patients with Type 2 diabetes: Does including an intermittent very-low-calorie diet improve outcome? *American Journal of Medicine, 97,* 354–362.

Wolf, A. M., & Colditz, G. A. (1998). Current estimates of the economic costs of obesity in the United States. *Obesity Research, 6,* 97–106.

World Health Organization. (1998). *Obesity: Preventing and managing the global epidemic.* Geneva: World Health Organization.

Yanovski, S. Z. (1993). Binge eating disorder: Current knowledge. *Obesity Research, 1,* 306–324.

33

Personality Disorders:
Old Dilemmas and New Tools
for the Primary Care Psychologist

Leonard J. Haas
Michael K. Magill
David Duncan

The well-trained psychologist has considerable experience in the assessment and treatment of personality-disordered (Axis II) patients. Indeed, it would not be surprising if the majority of long-term patients in the average psychologist's practice were suffering from some degree of personality disorder because psychotherapy has long been considered the treatment of choice for Axis II conditions. Nonetheless, this chapter will be useful to the primary care psychologist because the evidence base for assessing and treating personality disorders has been rapidly expanding and is changing dramatically (although some old problems have not yet been resolved); because personality disorders are prevalent in primary care; and because an appreciation of personality disorders is necessary for effectively treating the complex comorbid cases that emerge in primary care.

Primary care psychologists can help in several important ways to manage personality-disordered patients in primary care. Despite the common assumption that personality disorders cannot be effectively treated in the time-limited environment of primary care, some personality-disordered patients in primary care are amenable to long-term psychotherapy. For these patients, the primary care psychologist can effectively coordinate patient management with the primary care physician, to the great benefit of both the patient and the primary care practice.

However, many personality-disordered patients will refuse or otherwise be inappropriate for long-term psychotherapy. The primary care psychologist can still help these patients and the primary care physician a great deal with repeated courses of short-term psychotherapy in times of crisis; with psychological evaluation plus collaboration with the patient's primary care physician; or simply with a collegial consulting relationship with the physician and office staff to provide support as they provide ongoing care to these difficult patients.

In this chapter, we provide a brief overview of the personality disorders; highlight current controversies and new developments, particularly in the areas of focused psychopharmacology and focused psychotherapy; and identify ways that the primary care psychologist can help the personality-disordered primary care patient and the primary care physician.

OVERVIEW OF PERSONALITY DISORDERS

Personality disorders are defined as "recurrent patterns of interpersonal difficulty" (American Psychiatric Association [APA], 1994) that cause the patient—and those with whom the patient interacts—undue distress and impairment. Such patients may experience a range of negative emotional states (e.g., anger, fear, loneliness), but do not attribute these uncomfortable feelings to their own actions. Instead, the patient blames others (parents, family, employers, the environment) for the difficulties (Magill & Haas, 2002).

The *Diagnostic and Statistical Manual of Mental Disorders*, fourth edition (*DSM-IV*; APA, 1994) describes 10 specific Axis II diagnoses categorized into three clusters, plus personality disorder not otherwise specified (NOS), not part of any cluster. In addition, passive-aggressive and depressive personality disorders are included in Appendix B, "Criteria Sets and Axes Provided for Further Study" (APA, 1994). Table 33.1 provides a summary of the 10 *DSM-IV* personality disorders. The three clusters and their defining characteristics are as follows: Cluster A, the *odd-eccentric* disorders, comprises the paranoid, schizoid, and schizotypal personality disorders; Cluster B, the *dramatic-emotional* disorders, comprises the antisocial, borderline, histrionic, and narcissistic personality disorders; and Cluster C, the *anxious-fearful* disorders, comprises the avoidant, dependent, and obsessive-compulsive personality disorders.

Epidemiology

Because of problems with the reliability of diagnosis, it is somewhat difficult to determine the prevalence of personality disorders. Nonetheless, recent reviews that attempt to account for measurement variability seem to converge on similar figures; for example, in a review of pre-*DSM-IV* epidemiological studies of personality disorders that attempted to take measurement limitations into account, Weissman (1993) concluded that prevalence rates are in the range of 6% to 14%. Current prevalence estimates range from 6% to 10% of the U.S. population (Maffei et al., 1997). As noted in Table 33.1, prevalence of the different disorders varies considerably.

Etiology

Causal theories of personality disorder are numerous, and a full consideration of them is beyond the scope of this chapter (see Millon & Davis, 1996, for a review). Genetics, neurobiology, early environment, psychological conflict, and medical conditions have all been implicated in the development of personality disorders. In addition to single-factor models of causation, in-

Table 33.1 Prominent Features and Prevalence of Personality Disorders

Disorder	Prominent Traits, Behaviors, Affects	Prevalence Estimate
Paranoid	Suspicious, humorless, wary	0.5%–0.25%
Schizoid	Social withdrawal, eccentric; cold, aloof, distant	7.5%
Schizotypal	Peculiar, oddly superstitious; tense	3%
Antisocial	Superficially charming, exploitive, manipulative, conscienceless	Males 3%, females 1%
Borderline	Demanding, rejection sensitive, abandonment fears, unstable labile affect (often depressed/angry)	2% (males < females)
Histrionic	Dramatic, extroverted, attention seeking	2%–3% (males < females)
Narcissistic	Entitled, demanding	>1%
Avoidant	Social inhibition, "inferiority complex," anxious	0.5%–1.0%
Dependent	Clinging, indecisive, submissive; tolerant of abuse	Unknown
Obsessive-compulsive	Perfectionistic, inflexible, emotionally constricted	1%

teractional or diathesis-stress models have been postulated (e.g., Linehan, 1993; Millon, 1990) that incorporate biological vulnerability plus a "toxic" interpersonal environment. Research is limited on most causal theories, in part because of the difficulty of conducting the necessary developmental and longitudinal studies, but findings with stronger empirical support are emerging.

Regarding genetics, it is estimated that the heritability of normal personality traits is in the range of 50% to 60%, and similar rates have been shown for the majority of personality disorder dimensions. However, this varies by trait. For example, Livesley, Schroeder, Jackson, and Jang (1994) showed nonsignificant genetic effects for insecure attachment, intimacy problems, and submissiveness. At the level of specific disorders, there is modest evidence for familial transmission of borderline and schizotypal personality disorders and limited genetic evidence (twin studies) for schizotypal personality disorder (Crits-Christoph & Barber, 2002; Torgersen, 1994).

Multiple neurotransmitter abnormalities have been identified in patients diagnosed with personality disorders (Gurvits, Koenigsberg, & Siever, 2000), although the direction of causality has not been established.

Although medical conditions can cause personality changes, their role in the causation of personality disorders is less clear. Personality disturbances, particularly those of sudden onset, may be a result of tumors, head trauma, cerebrovascular disease, Huntington's disease, epilepsy, central nervous system infections, endocrine conditions, autoimmune conditions, and lead poisoning (Magill & Haas, 2002). A much more common cause of personality disorder (although it may also be a consequence) is substance abuse.

The diathesis-stress approach is supported indirectly by interesting evidence for situational stress as a cause of personality disorder. It is noteworthy that although *DSM-IV* does not consider a stress-induced personality disorder, this is an option in the current version of the *International Classification of Diseases*, 10th revision (*ICD-10*; World Health Organization, 1990). Reich (1999) found that Axis I disorders could activate a long-term disorder of personality ("trait personality disorder"), a temporary disorder ("state personality disorder"), or no disorder. He presented

suggestive data that family history of personality disorders, history of suicide attempts, strong reaction to criticism, and strong need for approval was more common in "trait personality disorder" patients.

CONTINUING CONTROVERSIES

In this section, we discuss six continuing controversies with implications for diagnosis, patient education, indirect intervention through the primary care physician, and treatment.

Is Axis II Really Different From Axis I?

Recent research concerning personality disorders highlights the artificial statistical distinction between Axis I and Axis II disorders and focuses on the continuity of symptoms. It is noteworthy in this regard that high rates of Axis I comorbidities characterize patients with many personality disorders. For example, there are particularly high rates of comorbidity between substance use disorders and antisocial personality disorder; obsessive-compulsive disorder and obsessive-compulsive personality disorder; and social phobia and avoidant personality disorder (Reich et al., 1994). In addition, differentiating between dysthymia and depressive personality disorder is quite difficult (Ryder, Bagby, & Dion, 2001), and borderline personality disorder is well known to be associated with a variety of Axis I conditions (Crits-Christoph & Barber, 2002).

Are the Clusters Reliably Distinct?

Endler and Kocovski (2002) noted that cluster categories are not theoretically or empirically derived. Although Cluster C disorders appear to share significant variance, Cluster B disorders are quite heterogeneous, and Cluster A disorders have one classification (schizotypal personality disorder) that fits better into Axis I as a schizophrenia spectrum disorder; indeed, it is so categorized in *ICD-10* (World Health Organization, 1992).

Are the Specific Personality Disorders Reliably Distinct?

The 10 specific personality disorders have limited reliability (Endler & Kocovski, 2002) and are

CLINICAL CONDITIONS

highly comorbid with each other. If a patient meets criteria for one personality disorder, there is an 80% probability that he or she will meet criteria for a second (Livesley, 1998). The vast body of literature on narcissistic and borderline personality types reviewed by Aronson (1989) shows a lack of consensus on the definition of these disorders. The validity of most of the diagnoses has not been established (Endler & Kocovski, 2002). Parker and colleagues (2002), among others, argued that there are underlying dimensions of personality-disordered functioning that would provide more accurate targets for intervention and cut across a number of diagnoses.

Are Personality Disorders Continuous or Discontinuous From "Normal" Personality Types?

The question of whether the diagnostic category "personality disorder" is one end of a continuum (with the other end being "normalcy") has been the subject of considerable debate and conflicting research findings. Impairment, as measured in the Global Assessment of Functioning scale (APA, 1994), has been shown to be continuous when attributed to personality disorders. In other words, the presence of certain personality disorder traits even at a "subclinical" level is associated with impairment (Nakao, Gunderson, Philips, & Tanaka, 1992). The current system emphasizes discontinuity of the conditions and focuses on personality traits. However, it is unclear whether the personality traits are inherently maladaptive, maladaptive only in certain contexts, or maladaptive only above a certain level of intensity. One way to interpret the findings is that continuity is better demonstrated for some traits than others (Endler & Kocovski, 2002). For example, there is strong evidence of discontinuity for the traits of schizotypal personality disorder, in contrast with the weaker evidence for the discontinuity of the defining traits of antisocial personality disorder and borderline personality disorder.

An important practical implication of one's position on this debate is the choice of assessment tool because certain measures are dimension based and others are categorical. For example, the Schedule for Nonadaptive and Adaptive Person-

ality (SNAP; Clark, McEwen, Collard, & Hickok, 1993) is a dimensional tool, whereas the Millon Clinical Multiaxial Inventory (MCMI-III; Millon, Millon, & Davis, 1994) is categorical.

Which Personality Dimensions or Traits Are Most Significant?

Among clinicians and theorists who espouse the dimensional approach to understanding personality disorders, different researchers argue for different numbers of personality traits. Coker, Samuel, and Widiger (2002) advocated using the five-factor model of personality. Crits-Christoph and Barber (2002) argued for a four-dimensional model involving difficulties with perception, cognition, affect, or behavior.

In an interesting synthesis of current thinking on this issue, Parker and colleagues (2002) argued for 17 underlying dimensions of functioning, as summarized in Table 33.2. They noted that descriptors of personality disorders can emphasize personality style, disordered personality function-

Table 33.2 Constructs of Disordered Personality Functioning

1. Disagreeableness
2. Inability to care for others
3. Lack of cooperation
4. Causes discomfort to others
5. Ineffectiveness
6. Lack of empathy
7. Failure to form and maintain interpersonal relationships
8. Failure to learn from experience
9. Impulsivity
10. Inflexibility
11. Maladaptability
12. Immorality
13. Extremes of optimism
14. Self-defeating
15. Lack of self-directedness
16. Lack of humor
17. Tenuous stability under stress

Note. Adapted from Parker et al. (2002).

ing, or both. For example, impulsivity is an aspect of most personality disorders (e.g., "overly impulsive" is characteristic of borderline, antisocial, and paranoid personality disorders). Other dimensions of functioning may be bipolar in that both extremes of the dimension are problematic. This approach makes it easy to link the functioning of personality disorders to broader constructs such as emotional intelligence and the negotiation of important life tasks. Impulsivity, inflexibility, and difficulty learning from experience, as well as self-defeating coping strategies, appear to be particularly important higher-order constructs. These dimensions of functioning may be useful in quantifying the severity of a categorical personality disorder.

Are Axis II Diagnoses Clinically Useful?

Clinical experience certainly suggests that many patients object strenuously to being diagnosed as "personality disordered," and it is not uncommon for people in their family and social network to use these diagnoses as accusations. Critics of the utility of these diagnoses suggest that, in the absence of clear-cut evidence for distinct Axis II conditions, the target areas of dysfunction should be considered Axis I problems. The personality style should then be assessed, not to diagnose the patient on Axis II, but rather to understand the context of the difficulties (Livesley & Jang, 2000). Advocates of the utility of the Axis II diagnostic categories suggest that awareness of the Axis II conditions is clinically important because "standard brief treatments for Axis I conditions often fail when Axis II pathology is also present" (Crits-Christoph & Barber, 2002, p. 619), and failure to diagnose personality disorder can obscure the reasons for difficulty treating Axis I symptoms. As Crits-Christoph and Barber (2002) also noted, "Personality pathology complicates and interferes with the treatment of almost every Axis I problem" (p. 623). It certainly complicates medical treatment as well. This would argue that the primary care psychologist should help the primary care physician understand the personality disorder of the patient so that inappropriate blame is not leveled at the patient, and that appropriate treatment is offered (Haas, Sanyer, & White, 2001).

RECENT POSITIVE DEVELOPMENTS

Despite the controversies, there is no question that a class of patients exists who are resistant to current psychiatric and psychological treatments, who are in repeated difficulty, and who have trouble exercising good judgment and taking responsibility for their actions. Several developments, many aimed specifically at the patient with borderline personality disorder, are promising tools for the primary care psychologist. These include focused psychotherapy and targeted pharmacotherapy. In addition, the treatment guidelines for borderline personality disorder (APA, 2001) contain several useful suggestions. Several of these that may be particularly useful in the primary care setting are highlighted in Table 33.3.

Psychotherapy

Psychological treatment developments have included more attention to cognitive therapies

Table 33.3 Selected Suggestions From the Borderline Personality Disorder Guidelines

1. Develop a therapeutic alliance.
2. Make sure that the patient agrees with and accepts the treatment plan.
3. Ensure that the patient feels understood and accepted.
4. Collaborate with the patient in solving practical problems.
5. Provide education about the disorder and its treatment.
6. Consider psychoeducation for families or others who live with patients.
7. Be aware of and manage potential splitting and boundary problems.
8. Elicit patient preferences about treatment.
9. Help the patient take appropriate responsibility for his or her actions.
10. Minimize self-blame for past abuse, but encourage responsibility for avoiding current self-destructive patterns.
11. Promote reflection rather than impulsive action.
12. Encourage thinking through the consequences of actions.

Note. Adapted from American Psychiatric Association (2002).

(Beck & Freeman, 1990; Linehan, 1993). There have also been guidelines endorsing psychotherapy issued by the APA (2001), although these have been heavily criticized for their poor empirical support and heavy emphasis on psychodynamic treatment. Overall, mounting evidence shows that active psychotherapy of a variety of types can be effective for personality disorders (Benjamin & Karpaik, 2001; Perry, Banon, & Ianni, 1999).

Perry and colleagues (1999) reviewed 15 studies reporting empirical data on the outcome of personality disorders after either short- or long-term psychotherapy. They concluded that all studies of active psychotherapies of personality disorders reported positive outcomes at termination and at follow-up. When "recovery" (e.g., no longer meeting criteria for a personality disorder diagnosis) was used as a criterion, mean recovery rate was 51.8% after a mean of 78 sessions over a mean of 67 weeks (1.3 years). In general, their review suggested that recovery is more likely with higher initial level of functioning and the ability to maintain a good therapeutic alliance and to tolerate distressing affect.

In general, improvement rates are highest for the three Cluster C disorders, intermediate for borderline personality disorder, and lowest for schizotypal personality disorder (Karterud et al., 1992). For the most part, these were long-term treatment courses, lasting a median of 28 weeks with a median of 40 sessions. The range of treatment lengths was 2 weeks to 2 years, and there was a significant relationship between duration of treatment and effect size. Perry et al. (1999) concluded that psychotherapy speeds recovery by a factor of seven over the natural history of borderline personality disorders, the best studied of the disorders.

The best-designed psychotherapy trials reviewed by Crits-Christoph and Barber (2002) are of dialectical behavior therapy (DBT) for borderline personality disorder. DBT consists of weekly group and individual sessions. The group is psychoeducational, teaching interpersonal skills, distress tolerance, reality acceptance, and emotion regulation skills, and the individual therapy sessions involve direct problem-solving techniques as well as empathy and acceptance. Specific treatment goals include decreasing suicidal behavior,

decreasing "therapy-interfering behaviors," decreasing behaviors that interfere with quality of life, increasing behavioral skills, decreasing behaviors related to posttraumatic stress, and increasing respect for self.

Although these data are encouraging, there are significant obstacles to providing long-term or group-plus-individual treatment for primary care patients with personality disorders. Brief intermittent treatment or consultation with the primary care physician may be all that is feasible. Clinical experience suggests that brief focused treatment may help in managing crises and may allow more substantial personality change to continue afterward. In addition, because the relationship between the primary care physician and the personality-disordered patient is often long term, providing helpful consultation may be a method of fostering a therapeutic relationship between patient and physician (Haas, Sanyer, & White, 2001).

Pharmacotherapy

Advances in understanding of the neurochemistry of personality disorders and positive results of therapeutic trials suggest that medications targeted to specific symptom complexes may be useful for many patients with personality disorders. Current clinical research focuses on four dimensions of dysfunction: cognitive or perceptual organization, behavioral control (particularly impulsivity/aggression), affective stability, and anxiety suppression (Koenigsberg, Woo-Ming, & Siever, 2002). Appropriate targets of pharmacotherapy include the acute presentations of aggression, suspiciousness, and psychoticlike thinking in the Cluster A patient; the rejection-sensitivity, affective instability, inappropriate intense anger, depressive mood "crashes," and temper outbursts of the Cluster B patient; the impulsivity, self-destructive behavior, and rash judgments characteristic of the Cluster B patient; and the anxiety and somatic preoccupation characteristic of the Cluster C patient.

In addition, the Axis I–Axis II overlap is another reason to focus pharmacotherapy on target symptoms. It is quite likely that unidentified Axis I pathology will affect internal distress. In patients with both major depression and a personality disorder who were treated for their depression, for example (Fava et al., 1994), a significant proportion no longer met criteria for a personality disorder when their depressive symptoms were treated.

Difficulties with pharmacotherapy include medication abuse in the form of overdose or noncompliance (Koenigsberg et al., 2002) and increased clinician liability with concomitant need for careful attention to and documentation of informed consent because no medication is approved by the FDA for any personality disorder.

Even highly effective medication regimens must be accompanied by active management. Patients often need encouragement and careful monitoring of their medication regimen because of several sources of resistance: unwillingness to "be on drugs" because this indicates that they are "crazy"; expense; and unwanted side effects such as weight gain or sexual problems.

Psychotherapy remains critical for the treatment of many personality disorders even with medication. Clearly, the psychologist must help address the potentially unrealistic expectations of the patient for cure. Helping patients identify symptoms that cause serious internal or social impairment will clarify treatment goals and contractual roles. In addition, reactions to medication and difficulties in compliance with prescriptions may themselves become psychotherapy foci because they often demonstrate the patient's characteristic defense mechanisms.

Specific medication recommendations by cluster are presented next; they were drawn from reviews by Kapfhammer and Hippius (1998) and Koenigsberg et al. (2002).

Cluster A (Odd-Eccentric) Disorders

Specific dimensions for target symptom relief in Cluster A odd-eccentric disorders may include cognitive distortion, suspiciousness, and interpersonal sensitivity leading to relational distress. The disturbances in the cognitive and perceptual domains of schizotypal personality disorder have been most thoroughly studied; these may appear as psychoticlike symptoms, deficitlike symptoms, and cognitive disorganization. Patients with schizotypal personality disorder show processing deficits similar to those characteristic of schizophrenia.

Cognitive perceptual distortions may be related to dysfunction within the dopaminergic system (Kirrane & Siever, 2000). For patients with relatively "pure" schizotypal personality disorder, risperidone treatment is associated with improvement, and cognitive dysfunction, sustained attention, working memory, and learning may benefit from enhanced dopaminergic activity or other catecholaminergic agents (Koenigsberg et al., 2003).

Fluoxetine has been helpful in decreasing obsessive symptoms, rejection sensitivity, depressive symptoms, anxiety, and psychoticism. However, because of the significant overlap of schizoid personality disorder with borderline personality disorder, major depressive disorder, and pronounced somatic sensitivity leading to medication intolerance, results are somewhat difficult to interpret. Despite, or indeed because of, this comorbidity, the selective serotonin reuptake inhibitors (SSRIs) are likely to benefit the majority of patients with schizotypal personality disorder; for those with limited comorbidity, low-dose atypical antipsychotics will be well tolerated and beneficial.

Cluster B Disorders

In Cluster B, the major dimensions of difficulty are impulsivity/aggression, psychosis proneness, and affective lability. Diminished serotonin has been implicated in impulsive/aggressive behavior directed toward the self, as in suicide attempts, as well as that directed toward others. Impulsivity plays a role in both borderline personality disorder symptoms and suicidality. Impulsivity-moderating drugs are among the more beneficial pharmacological treatments for borderline personality disorder (Hirschfeld, 1997; Soloff, Lynch, & Moss, 2000). The mood stabilizers have a definite role in managing the affective instability and impulsivity, even though the exact mechanism of action is not known. Improvements in behavior may occur even without subjective benefit. Lithium is the most scientifically studied and may have a particular role in decreasing suicide risk, although it is limited by its narrow therapeutic window. Valproic acid may improve impulsive aggression in patients unresponsive to SSRIs. Carbamazepine also may be particularly beneficial in patients with affective instability and aggression associated with rage outbursts and electroencephalogram changes. Anecdotal reports suggested that lamotrigine maybe useful for episodic aggression and other types of impulsive behavior (Kapfhammer & Hippius, 1998).

Serotonergic disruption seems to occur across all diagnostic categories; at least one functional imaging study (Siever et al., 1999) reported blunted serotonergic activity in relevant brain regions in impulsive/aggressive patients. Affective instability may also share blunted serotonergic neurotransmission associated with impulsivity.

Borderline personality disorder is associated with serotonin dysregulation; neuroimaging studies have shown abnormalities in brain function and structure among individuals with borderline personality disorders, especially individuals with a history of abuse. Several medication algorithms are included in the APA guideline (2001). First-line treatment for both disinhibited anger and affective dysregulation is an SSRI (12-week trial). Serotonergic agents seem to decrease impulsivity among borderline patients as well as improve other symptoms, such as anger, suicidality, and irritability. Fluoxetine had a clinically and statistically significant effect in reducing anger and depression in a sample of patients with borderline personality disorder that was mild to moderately severe (Salzman et al., 1995). SSRIs are the best studied and now are considered first-line agents for impulsive aggressive symptoms and affective dysregulation (APA, 2001). Monoamine oxidase inhibitors (MAOIs) have moderate scientific support for efficacy, especially for atypical depressive features, although the risk of life-threatening interactions limits their utility.

Antipsychotic medication for borderline personality disorder has shown global, but modest, effect on symptoms. Newer atypical antipsychotics have not been well studied, although olanzapine and risperidone have been shown in case reports and open label trials to be effective with patients with borderline personality disorder, especially those who self-mutilate.

There is limited evidence that dopaminergic dysfunction accounts for the pseudopsychotic symptoms that led to the early conceptualization of the "borderline psychotic," similar to individuals with schizophrenia. A single challenge study did demonstrate that patients with borderline personality disorder exposed to amphetamine are prone to psychoticlike symptoms. Lack of a genetic relationship between borderline personality disorder and the psychotic disorders further distinguishes these disorders.

The limited number of studies, small number of subjects, extensive comorbidities, and methodological designs limit conclusive recommendations. For patients with psychoticlike phenomena presenting for acute treatment, atypical antipsychotics may increase the likelihood of tangible gain. However, these benefits must be weighed against lack of evidence for maintenance or continuation therapy, risk of metabolic effects, extrapyramidal symptoms, and even long-term effect on mood.

Although benzodiazepines have been helpful in the control of anxiety in Cluster B patients, there is no scientific evidence for the efficacy of benzodiazepines in the management of anxiety in borderline personality disorder. In addition, there is a disconcertingly high rate of disinhibition, particularly anger and aggression, and there is the risk of drug abuse. Longer acting benzodiazepines are preferred.

Several studies have suggested that noradrenergic agents such as the tricyclics improve mood, but may worsen irritability and impulsivity, particularly suicidality, among patients with borderline personality disorder.

In addition, alterations in the endogenous opioid system may account for the abnormal physiological response to pain shown in self-mutilating behavior. The opioid antagonists have been studied to a limited extent; this is because of the "addictive" quality some patients ascribe to their self-injurious behavior. Open-label studies suggested that these agents may help decrease self-injury and dissociative phenomena.

Antisocial personality disorders seems associated (less clearly) with subtle frontal dysfunction and reduced autonomic arousal and reactivity to distressing stimuli. Pharmacological treatments have shown little benefit, except for treatment of aggressive behaviors.

Cluster C Disorders

The anxiety and inhibition common to the Cluster C personality disorders have been associated with autonomic nervous system disturbances mediated by the serotonergic and noradrenergic systems. The high rates of association between avoidant personality disorder and social phobia suggest that anxiety, regardless of whether it is considered Axis I or Axis II, could be effectively treated similarly. As an example, a study of patients with avoidant personality disorder found 89% of them diagnosed with generalized social phobia (Tyrer, Casey, & Ferguson, 1991). Two controlled trials suggested that the MAOI phenelzine decreases avoidant personality features and anxiety. The "reversible MAOI" moclobemide has shown similar effects. Benzodiazepines have also been helpful. SSRIs have demonstrated efficacy in treatment of social phobia. It is likely that they would also be useful treatments for avoidant personality disorder, although thus far no studies of this have been done.

PERSONALITY DISORDERS IN PRIMARY CARE

Although "unreasonable behavior is not unexpected in primary care" (Sugarman, 2000, p. 400), not all of this acting out is a result of personality disorder. Personality disorders are quite prevalent among primary care patients, particularly in patients with Axis I disorders, and certain disorders are more likely than others to be represented and referred to the primary care psychologist. Patients with personality disorders are often labeled "difficult" by primary care clinicians (Hahn et al., 1996; Haas et al., 2002). These disorders affect the doctor–patient relationship, make it difficult to manage a medical condition, or result in confusing requests for medical services (Searight, 1992). Nonetheless, personality disorders are often unrecognized and untreated in primary care settings. A 1994 epidemiological study (Samuels, Nestadt, Romanoski, Folstein, & McHugh, 1994) found that only 20% of community-dwelling individuals with Axis II diagnoses were receiving treatment. In this section, we explore each of the clusters in relation to the primary care setting and provide impressions drawn from clinical experience and clinical literature (e.g., Groves, 1978; Oldham, 1994).

Cluster A Disorders

As noted, Cluster A disorders are often marked by mistrust or interpersonal aversion. Individuals with Cluster A personality disorders do not typically seek medical treatment and often resist psychiatric referral (Reich, Boerstler, Yates, & Nduaguba, 1989). They are less likely to be seen in primary care because of their dislike of physical examinations and difficulty enduring close contact with clinicians. Patients with paranoid personality disorder tend to avoid care because of their underlying expectation of harm or trickery by the clinician. Patients with schizoid personality disorder may delay coming for medical visits until their problems are severe; they may give limited information in response to questions and appear eager for medical visits to end. Patients with schizotypal personality disorder have difficulty with physical examinations and with direct communication with the physician.

Cluster B Disorders

Patients with Cluster B disorders (particularly, but not only, antisocial personality disorders) can be manipulative and drug seeking or disability claim seeking, but as noted, disorders in this cluster are extremely diverse. Borderline personality disorders are the most common Cluster B disorders in the general population and the most commonly encountered in primary care, perhaps because these patients experience the greatest distress and impairment. Borderline personality disorder complicates the diagnosis and treatment of depression and anxiety, and most patients seeking help for these problems go to primary care physicians. Patients with borderline personality disorder often have fragile, stormy, or inappropriate relationships with their primary care physicians (Nowlis, 1990). They can be exquisitely sensitive to loss or change in the health care team, and referrals can elicit fear of abandonment and rejection. Dividing the staff and polarizing them into good and bad is also characteristic of borderline personality disorder. Borderline personality disorder underlies many cases of Munchausen syndrome and false accusations of providers' sexual improprieties. Gross et al. (2002) noted that patients with borderline personality disorder are often described as difficult, demanding, manipulative, noncompliant, or disruptive. They found that approximately half of patients with borderline disorder in their study practice were recognized by the primary care physician, and only half of these patients had received mental health treatment in the previous year. Narcissistic personality disorder prevalence may be lower in a primary care population because admitting medical problems is incompatible with the patient's inflated sense of self and grandiose feelings of uniqueness. Antisocial personality disorder prevalence may be higher in a primary care population because of its contribution to inappropriate disability-compensation–seeking and drug-seeking.

Cluster C Disorders

Cluster C disorders are heavily comorbid with Axis I depression and anxiety disorders. Medical help is more frequently sought by these patients because of the prominence of worry. Avoidant personality disorder prevalence may be lower in a primary care population because these patients may be afraid to ask questions and delay seeking medical attention. Dependent and obsessive-compulsive personality disorders are most common (Zimmerman, 1994). Patients with dependent personality disorder are often very difficult for primary care physicians as they often attempt to get the physician to make decisions for them, have endless questions that prolong their visits (perhaps so that they feel cared for), and are "noncompliant" (i.e., have difficulty with self-care responsibilities). Obsessive-compulsive personality disorder prevalence may be higher in a primary care population; these patients may seek multiple opinions about the diagnosis and may meticulously document their symptoms.

HELPING THE PATIENT MAINTAIN A PARTNERSHIP WITH THE PRIMARY CARE PHYSICIAN

Awareness of the Condition

As noted, physicians often complain about "difficult patients," many if not all of whom are likely to have a personality disorder (Schafer & Nowlis,

1998). Livesley's (2000) recommendation (specific to borderline personality disorder, but generally applicable) was that "the most appropriate stance . . . is to be empathetic, supportive, and validating" (p. 2). Paré and colleagues (Paré, Banon, & Ianni, 1999) suggested a number of strategies for managing patients with personality disorders, including

1. Learning to take the patient's perspective
2. Using medication judiciously to manage target symptoms
3. Developing an explicit treatment contract
4. Appreciating the patient's original need to develop these extreme coping strategies

Oldham (1994) suggested that several distinct personality traits that cause difficulty in the medical setting are related to increased likelihood of particular personality disorders, and that particular physician responses may be helpful (these are summarized in Table 33.4).

Patient Education

Data about the underlying genetic and neurobiological abnormalities of personality disorders provide a physiological explanation that can be useful to patients: "Patients may be strangely reassured when told that their lapses, misperceptions, and judgments errors may be caused by a neuropsychological deficit. . . . It may be much easier to see oneself as flawed (but able to develop coping tools) rather than to see oneself as (1) dumb, bad, or manipulative or (2) the victim of developmental failures" (O'Leary, 2000, p. 56).

Treatment discontinuation is a particular problem and should be addressed preventively with the patient. The NIMH (National Institute of Mental Health) treatment of depression collaborative research program (Shea et al., 1990) found a 31% dropout rate for personality disorders across all treatments: Cluster B 40%, Cluster A 30%, and Cluster C 28%. Dropout rates for group therapy are particularly high (e.g., Budman, Demby, Soldz, & Merry, 1996); however, adding individual sessions seems to improve acceptability to patients.

Table 33.4 Personality Disorders (PDs) in the Medical Setting: Traits, Likely Diagnoses, Meaning of Illness, and Helpful Physician Responses

Personality Trait	Likely Axis II Disorder	Meaning of Illness to Patient	Helpful Physician Response Style
Dependent, over-demanding	Dependent PD, borderline PD	Abandonment and rejection	Balanced approach combining empathic recognition of patient's need for reassurance and anxiety about being alone with limit setting, clarity, consistency, and structure
Orderly and compulsive	Obsessive-compulsive PD	Loss of control	Respect for patient's need to be as much in control as possible; provide complete information, including test results, as quickly as possible; engage patient's participation in treatment planning, scheduling
Dramatizing	Histrionic PD	Threat to physical intactness and attractiveness	Respectful and professional manner without abbreviating time spent with the patient
Self-sacrificing (self-defeating style)	Dependent PD, passive-aggressive PD, depressive PD	Combination of prospect of pain and of kindness from others	Spend adequate time to hear detailed symptomatology, anticipate ambivalence/lack of enthusiasm on improvement
Self-important	Narcissistic PD	Threat of having to rely on others; prospect of being cared for by inferiors (threat of being dismissed, demeaned)	Nondefensive acceptance of "less-experienced" status; readiness to call in the experts
Detached	Schizoid PD, schizotypal PD, avoidant PD	Too-intense close contact with others; threat to privacy	Respect patient's need for privacy and distance; insist on adequate time for necessary medical care
Suspicious	Paranoid PD	Vulnerability; threat of being harmed by strangers	Inform patient about hospital procedures; provide exact details of medical procedures (especially risks and benefits), acknowledge validity of tension, guardedness
Manipulative	Antisocial PD	Chance to work hidden agenda (e.g., escaping criminal justice system, maintaining drug dependence)	Provide only clearly medically indicated treatments; request psychiatric consult if malingering likely

Note. Adapted from Oldham (1994).

PRACTICAL TREATMENT PLANNING

Mindful of the constraints of the primary care environment, we present here a suggested algorithm for deciding on the focus of primary care psychological treatment for the personality-disordered patient:

1. *Identify the major dimensions of the patient's difficulty.* Although this may be difficult, if the primary care psychologist and the patient can agree on a set of key issues or themes that run through the various crises the patient will inevitably present, therapy can proceed despite the conceptual difficulties of diagnosis, comorbidities, and subsyndromal presentations.

2. *Activate the patient's sense of personal responsibility for change in this area of conflict.* This may be the foundation of most successful interpersonal approaches to psychotherapy for these conditions. Parker et al. (2002) underscored *lack of self-directedness*, which includes the tendency to blame others and ignore choices one could make to solve personal problems as a crucial dimension of personality functioning to be addressed. In the analysis of defensive style, this has been called *projection* or *immature defenses*; Table 33.5 lists

Table 33.5 Defense Levels and Their Respective Individual Defenses

7 High adaptive level: anticipation, affiliation, altruism, humor, self-assertion, self-observation, sublimation, suppression

6 Mental inhibitors (compromise, formation) level: (a) obsessional defenses: isolation of affect, intellectualization, undoing; (b) hysterical defenses: repression, dissociation; other neurotic defenses: reaction formation, displacement

5 Minor image-distorting level: devaluation, idealization, omnipotence

4 Disavowal level: denial, rationalization, projection

3 Major image-distorting level: splitting of self and others' images, projective identification, autistic fantasy

2 Action level: acting out, help-rejecting complaining (hypochondriasis), passive-aggression, apathetic withdrawal

1 Level of defensive dysregulation, psychotic denial, psychotic distortion, delusional projection

Note. Adapted from Paré and Rosenbluth (1999).

other aspects of defensive functioning. Identifying areas of functioning that are more mature or more successful can also be a useful avenue to therapeutic change.

3. *Determine whether the identified areas of difficulty should be addressed with psychotherapy, psychopharmacology, or both.* As noted, certain core aspects of difficulty can be targeted with proper medications. However, it is also clear that adherence to a medication regimen is difficult for many patients with personality disorders. The same holds true for psychotherapy; it can be effective if treatment is maintained. Brief intermittent therapy may be helpful for primary care patients with a personality disorder, although brief treatments appear to shows higher relapse rates (Parker et al., 2002). If each episode of care can help the patient to learn strategies for avoiding the vicious circles and self-defeating behavior in which he or she is prone to engage, brief repeated episodes of treatment should still should be helpful.

Treatment planning should ideally include the patient as an active participant in the choice; the costs and benefits of each possibility should be addressed. Given the data on length of recovery time for untreated personality disorder noted by Perry et al. (1999), the risk of remaining untreated should be addressed as well.

4. *Determine whether social skills training would be useful.* Recent work, particularly that based on Linehan's (1993) DBT model, suggested that social skills training or psychoeducational approaches in groups can be effective, particularly with borderline personality disorders. However, this requires a support structure that includes ongoing training and consultation for the group leaders and combines individual therapy with the group sessions. Limited availability of trained therapists may reduce the feasibility of this option.

SUMMARY

Personality disorders are common in primary care patient populations, and their symptoms are frequently overlooked or untreated. A sophisticated understanding of the issues involved in successful treatment of the various personality disorders may allow the primary care psychologist to provide considerable help to these patients. In addition, the primary care psychologist can be helpful to the primary care physician by offering a flexible range of approaches at different levels of involvement with the personality-disordered patient.

Long-term psychotherapy, although best supported in research settings, is less likely to be feasible or effective in primary care settings. In contrast, brief intermittent psychotherapy, time-limited social skills training, and providing consultation to the primary care team regarding management may be both feasible and effective ways to help the primary care patient with a personality disorder.

Regardless of the patient's interpersonal unpleasantness, the primary care physician will in most cases maintain a long-term relationship. For some patients, this may be the most sustained relationship with a helping professional that they will ever manage. Even when a patient's behavior poses difficult interpersonal challenges, the physician may be able to care effectively for medical problems. The psychologist may be of great help to personality-disordered patients and their physicians by offering repeated courses of brief, supportive psychotherapy in times of crisis and at the same time support the continuation of the patient's relationship with the primary care physician.

In addition, via close collaboration with primary care physicians, psychologists can offer help of several other types to personality-disordered patients and the primary care physicians caring for them. For example, a close working relationship between the primary care psychologist and the primary care physician may improve the acceptability of psychotherapy to the patient and reduce the chances that a referral is experienced as an abandonment. Anecdotally, we have found that barriers to accepting treatment are greatly reduced if the physician is able to invite the psychologist into the examination room to meet the patient during a regular "medical" office visit. It also facilitates the physician's ability to make it clear that he or she is adding helpful professionals to the treatment team rather than substituting one clinician for another. Often, this process is facilitated if the physician indicates that a "partner who specializes in medical behavioral issues" can see the patient and offer advice to both the patient and physician about ongoing care.

Even if the psychologist never directly sees the personality-disordered patient, care for the patient can be greatly improved if the physician and office staff can turn to the psychologist for informal consultation, advice, and support. Often, this will help them develop effective strategies to manage the patient's medical problems in the context of challenging behavior. As a last resort, the psychologist can help the physician work through the ethical and behavioral issues surrounding potential or actual termination of the doctor-patient relationship.

An appreciation of and congenial approach to the patient's physical complaints is essential in working with the personality-disordered patient, as it is in other aspects of primary care psychology. Somatic symptoms are likely to be the common currency of the primary care patient in distress whether Axis I or Axis II is the focus of the disturbance. Pain and physical symptoms are common complaints among personality-disordered patients because this is the way in which they will get attention in a medical setting. The recognition that physical complaints in the personality-disordered patient can serve as a defense mechanism against fears of abandonment and unmet dependency needs is a significant advantage for both the psychotherapist and the primary care physician. This awareness also illuminates the extreme resistance to psychological referrals shown by some of these patients.

References

American Psychiatric Association. (1994). *Diagnostic and statistical manual of mental disorders* (4th ed.). Washington, DC: Author.

American Psychiatric Association. (2001). Practice guideline for the treatment of patients with borderline personality disorder. *American Journal of Psychiatry, 158*, 1–52.

American Psychiatric Association. (2002). Work Group on Borderline Personality Disorder. *Practice Guideline for the Treatment of Patients With Borderline Personality Disorder*. Arlington, VA: Author.

Aronson, T. (1989). A critical review of psychotherapeutic treatments of the borderline personality, historical trends and future directions. *Journal of Nervous and Mental Disease,* *177,* 511–527.

Beck, A., & Freeman, A. A. (1990). *Cognitive therapy of personality disorders.* New York: Guilford Press.

Benjamin, L., & Karpaik, C. (2001). Personality disorders. *Psychotherapy: Theory, Research, Practice, Training, 38,* 487–491.

Budman, S. H., Demby, A., Soldz, S., & Merry, J. (1996). Time-limited group psychotherapy for patients with personality disorders: Outcomes and dropouts. *International Journal of Group Psychotherapy, 46*(3), 357–377.

Clark, L., McEwen, J., Collard, L., & Hickok, L. (1993). Symptoms and traits of personality disorder: Two new methods for their assessment. *Psychological Assessment, 5,* 81–91.

Coker, L. A., Samuel, D. B., & Widiger, T. A. (2002). Maladaptive personality functioning within the big five and the five-factor model. *Journal of Personality Disorders, 16,* 385–401.

Crits-Christoph, C., & Barber, N. (2002). Psychosocial treatments for personality disorders. In P. Nathan & J. Gorman (Eds.), *A guide to treatments that work* (pp. 611–624). New York: Oxford University Press.

Endler, N. S., & Kocovski, N. L. (2002). Personality disorders at the crossroads. *Journal of Personality Disorders, 16,* 487–502.

Fava, M., Bouffides, E., Pava, J. A., McCarthy, M. K., Steingard, R. J., & Rosenbaum, J. F. (1994). Personality disorder comorbidity with major depression and response to fluoxetine treatment. *Psychotherapy and psychosomatics, 62,* 160–167.

Gross, R., Olfson, M., Gameroff, M., Shea, S., Feder, A., Fuentes, M., et al. (2002). Borderline personality disorder in primary care. *Archives of Internal Medicine, 162,* 53–60.

Groves, J. E. (1978). Taking care of the hateful patient. *New England Journal of Medicine, 298,* 883–887.

Gurvits, I. G., Koenigsberg, H. W., & Siever, L. J. (2000). Neurotransmitter dysfunction in patients with borderline personality disorder. *Psychiatric Clinics of North America, 23,* 27–40, vi.

Haas, L. J., Sanyer, O. N., & White, G. (2001). Caring for the frustrating patient. *Clinician Reviews, 11,* 75–87.

Hahn, S., Kroenke, K., Spitzer, R. L., Brody, D., Williams, J. B., Linzer, M., et al. (1996). The difficult patient: Prevalence, psychopathology, and functional impairment. *Journal of General Internal Medicine, 11,* 1–8.

Hirschfeld, R. M. (1997). Pharmacotherapy of borderline personality disorder. *Journal of Clinical Psychiatry, 58*(Suppl. 14), 48–52; discussion 53.

Kapfhammer, H. P., & Hippius, H. (1998). Special feature: Pharmacotherapy in personality disorders. *Journal of Personality Disorders, 12,* 277–288.

Karterud, S., Vaglum, S., Friis, S., Irion, T., Johns, S., & Vaglum, P. (1992). Day hospital therapeutic community treatment for patients with personality disorders: An empirical evaluation of the containment function. *Journal of Nervous and Mental Disease, 180,* 238–243.

Kirrane, R. M., & Siever, L. J. (2000). New perspectives on schizotypal personality disorder. *Current Psychiatry Reports, 2,* 62–66.

Koenigsberg, H., Woo-Ming, A., & Siever, L. S. (2002). Pharmacological treatments for personality disorders. In P. Nathan & J. Gorman (Eds.), *A guide to treatments that work* (2nd ed., pp. 625–641). New York: Oxford University Press.

Koenigsberg, H. W., Reynolds, D., Goodman, M., New, A. S., Mitropoulou, V., Trestman, R. L., et al. (2003). Risperidone in the treatment of schizotypal personality disorder. *Journal of Clinical Psychiatry, 64,* 628–634.

Linehan, M. (1993). *Cognitive-behavioral treatment of borderline personality disorders.* New York: Guilford Press.

Livesley, W. (1998). Suggestions for a framework for an empirically based classification of personality disorder. *Canadian Journal of Psychiatry, 43,* 137–147.

Livesley, W. (2000). Introduction. *Journal of Personality Disorders, 14,* 1–2.

Livesley, W. J., & Jang, K. L. (2000). Toward an empirically based classification of personality disorder. *Journal of Personality Disorders, 14,* 137–151.

Livesley, W. J., Schroeder, M. L., Jackson, D. N., & Jang, K. L. (1994). Categorical distinctions in the study of personality disorder: Implications for classification. *Journal of Abnormal Psychology, 103,* 6–17.

Maffei, C., Fossati, A., Agostoni, I., Barraco, A., Bagnato, M., Deborah, D., et al. (1997). Interrater reliability and internal consistency of the Structured Clinical Interview for *DSM-IV* Axis II personality disorders (SCID-II), version 2.0. *Journal of Personality Disorders, 11,* 279–284.

Magill, M. M., & Haas, L. J. (2002). Selected psychiatric and behavioral problems in primary care. In R. Taylor (Ed.), *Family medicine: Principles and practice* (6th ed., pp. 301–317). New York: Springer.

Millon, T. (1990). *Toward a new personology: An evolutionary model.* New York: Wiley.

Millon, T., & Davis R. (1996). *Disorders of personality: DSM-IV and beyond.* New York: Wiley.

Millon, T., Millon, C., & Davis, R. (1994). *MCMI-III Manual.* Minneapolis, MN: NCS Assessments.

Nakao, K., Gundersen, J., Philips, K., & Tanaka, N. (1992). Functional impairment in personality disorders. *Journal of Personality Disorders, 6,* 24–33.

Nowlis, D. P. (1990). Borderline personality disorder in primary care. *Journal of Family Practice, 30,* 329–335.

Oldham, J. M. (1994). Personality disorders: Current perspectives. *Journal of the American Medical Association, 272,* 1770–1776.

O'Leary, K. M. (2000). Borderline personality disorder: Neuropsychological testing results. *Psychiatric Clinics of North America, 23*(1), 41–60.

Paré, M. F., & Rosenbluth, M. (1999). Personality disorders in primary care. *Primary Care, 26,* 243–278.

Parker, G., Both, L., Olley, A., Hadzi-Pavlovic, D., Irvine, D., & Jacobs, D. (2002). Defining disordered personality functioning. *Journal of Personality Disorders, 16,* 503–522.

Perry, J. C., Banon, E., & Ianni, F. (1999). Effectiveness of psychotherapy for personality disorders. *American Journal of Psychiatry, 156,* 1312–1321.

Reich, J. (1999). Empirical evidence for stress induced personality disorders. *Psychiatric Annals, 29,* 701–706.

Reich, J., Boerstler, H., Yates, W., & Nduaguba, M. (1989). Utilization of medical resources in persons with *DSM-III* personality disorders in a community sample. *International Journal of Psychiatry in Medicine, 19,* 1–9.

Reich, J., Perry, J. C., Shera, D., Dyck, I., Vasile, R., Goisman, R. M., et al. (1994). Comparison of personality disorders in different anxiety disorder diagnoses: Panic, agoraphobia, generalized anxiety, and social phobia. *Annals of Clinical Psychiatry, 6,* 125–134.

Ryder, A., Bagby, R., & Dion, K. L. (2001). Chronic, low grade depression in a nonclinical sample: Depressive personality or dysthymia? *Journal of Personality Disorders, 15,* 84–93.

Salzman, C., Wolfson, A. N., Schatzberg, A., Looper, J., Henke, R., Albanese, M., et al. (1995). Effect of fluoxetine on anger in symptomatic volunteers with borderline personality disorder. *Journal of Clinical Psychopharmacology, 15,* 23–29.

Samuels, J. F., Nestadt, G., Romanoski, A. J., Folstein, M. F., & McHugh, P. R. (1994). *DSM-III* personality disorders in the community. *American Journal of Psychiatry, 151,* 1055–1062.

Schafer, S., & Nowlis, D. P. (1998). Personality disorders among difficult patients. *Archives of Family Medicine, 7,* 126–129.

Searight, H. R. (1992). Borderline personality disorder: Diagnosis and management in primary care. *Journal of Family Practice, 34,* 605–612.

Shea, M. T., Pilkonis, P. A., Beckham, E., Collins, J. F., Elkin, I., Sotsky, S. M., et al. (1990). Personality disorders and treatment outcome in the NIMH Treatment of Depression Collaborative Research Program. *American Journal of Psychiatry, 147,* 711–718.

Siever, L. J., Buchsbaum, M. S., New, A. S., Spiegel-Cohen, J., Wei, T., Hazlett, E. A., et al. (1999). d,l-Fenfluramine response in impulsive personality disorder assessed with [18F]-fluorodeoxyglucose positron emission tomography. *Neuropsychopharmacology, 20,* 413–423.

Soloff, P. H., Lynch, K. G., & Moss, H. B. (2000). Serotonin, impulsivity, and alcohol use disorders in the older adolescent: A psychobiological study. *Alcoholism, Clinical and Experimental Research, 24,* 1609–1619.

Sugarman, P. (2000). Personality disorder in primary care. *The Practitioner, 244,* 400–407.

Torgersen, S. (1994). Genetics in borderline conditions. *Acta Psychiatrica Scandinavica Supplementum, 379,* 19–25.

Tyrer, P., Case, P., & Ferguson, B. (1991). Personality disorder in perspective. *British Journal of Psychiatry, 159,* 463–471.

Weissman, M. (1993). The epidemiology of personality disorders. *Journal of Personality Disorders, 7,* 44–62.

World Health Organization. (1992). *International classification of diseases and related health problems* (10th rev.). Geneva: Author.

Zimmerman, M. (1994). Diagnosing personality disorders: A review of issues and research models. *Archives of General Psychiatry, 51,* 225–245.

34

Rape, Sexual Assault, and PTSD: Strategies for the Primary Care Psychologist

Gretchen A. Clum

Kelly R. Chrestman

Patricia A. Resick

Psychologists in primary care settings are in a unique position to address the potentially pervasive effects of sexual assault and abuse in a large segment of the victimized population. There are two factors that make the primary care setting an important venue for identification and treatment of sexual assault victims: First, the sexual assault victim is more likely to seek care in medical settings than in mental health settings; second, victims report poorer health and greater physical symptoms than nonvictims. Both of these factors suggest that identification of the sexual assault or abuse victim in primary care settings can lead not only to appropriate psychological interventions, but also set the stage for an integration of psychological and medical care services that can address a fuller spectrum of problems.

In this chapter, we provide an overview of the prevalence of sexual assault and abuse in the general population and in primary health care settings. We also discuss acute and chronic reactions to sexual assault and provide information on the physical health sequelae associated with sexual assault and abuse. Suggestions and strategies for

screening in both medical and mental health care settings and for expanded assessments within the mental health care setting are reviewed. We discuss treatment strategies for the most common psychological disorder associated with sexual assault and abuse, namely, posttraumatic stress disorder (PTSD). Finally, we discuss opportunities for integrating mental and physical health care to address more effectively the breadth of outcomes associated with sexual assault and abuse and recommend new directions for intervention in primary care settings.

PREVALENCE OF SEXUAL ASSAULT

Sexual assault has been identified as a public health problem in part because of the large number of individuals affected by sexual assault in childhood and adulthood. In a recent national sample of women, lifetime prevalence rates of completed rape were estimated at 17.6% (Kilpatrick, Edmunds, & Seymour, 1992; Tjaden & Theonnes, 1998). In primary care settings, rates of rape and sexual assault are even higher, with estimates placed at over 30% (Koss, Koss, & Woodruff, 1991; Walker, Torkelson, Katon, & Koss, 1993). Rates of male rape, although lower, still constitute a considerable number of victims, ranging from 1% to 3% (Tjaden & Theonnes, 1998). Retrospective rates of childhood sexual abuse reported by adult men and women indicate sexual abuse in 27% of children (Finkelhor, Hotaling, Lewis, & Smith, 1990).

SEXUAL ASSAULT IN PRIMARY CARE

Generally, individuals with mental health diagnoses are more likely to seek treatment from physicians than mental health professionals (Norquist & Regier, 1996). This pattern also applies to sexual assault victims, who tend to utilize medical rather than psychological services after assault (Kimerling & Calhoun, 1994). Further, individuals diagnosed with PTSD are unlikely to seek mental health care at all (Kessler, Sonnega, Bromet, Hughes, & Nelson, 1995; Kessler et al., 1995). Childhood sexual abuse is also associated with increased use of primary care services, more emergency department visits, and increased cost of services in adult women when compared to nonvictims (Walker et al., 1999). The higher prevalence of sexual assault and abuse victims in primary care settings and the research on use of medical services point to the fact that many undiagnosed sexual assault and abuse victims will be utilizing primary care services and underutilizing mental health services. This underscores the importance of ensuring that the primary care setting includes appropriate resources to help these patients.

PSYCHOLOGICAL CONSEQUENCES OF SEXUAL ASSAULT AND ABUSE

There are both immediate and long-term psychological effects of rape and related traumas. We touch on each of these issues in turn in the following sections.

Immediate Postassault Psychological Reactions

The immediate negative psychological effects of rape and sexual assault include generalized anxiety and fear, flashbacks, nightmares, emotional numbing or dissociation, and phobic avoidance of assault-related situations (Rothbaum, Foa, Riggs, Murdock, & Walsh, 1992). Acute stress disorder (ASD), introduced in the *Diagnostic and Statistical Manual of Mental Disorders*, fourth edition (*DSM-IV*; American Psychiatric Association, 1994), is a reaction to trauma that includes dissociative symptoms, intrusive symptoms, avoidance, and hyperarousal (see Table 34.1). The symptoms of ASD must cause significant distress or impairment, last between 2 days and 4 weeks, and occur within a 4-week period after the trauma. ASD has been suggested as a set of reactions that constitutes risk for PTSD.

Table 34.1 Acute Stress Disorder

Diagnostic Criteria for Acute Stress Disorder

A. Exposure (as victim or witness) to a traumatic event that
   1. involved actual or threatened death or serious injury (to self or others), and that
   2. evoked fear, helplessness, or horror

B. Three or more dissociative symptoms during or after the experience:
   1. subjective sense of numbing, detachment, or emotional unresponsiveness
   2. reduced awareness of surroundings
   3. derealization
   4. depersonalization
   5. dissociative amnesia

C. Persistent reexperiencing of the event (one or more): recurrent images, thoughts, dreams, illusions, flashbacks, or distress when reminded of the event.

D. Symptoms of cognitive or behavioral avoidance of trauma reminders.

E. Symptoms of anxiety or increased arousal.

F. Symptoms last 2 days to 4 weeks and occur within 4 weeks of the trauma.

G. Significant distress or functional impairment.

Note. Adapted from American Psychiatric Association (2000).

Long-Term Mental Health Effects

PTSD is the most frequent mental health diagnosis after a sexual assault or rape. A diagnosis of PTSD requires exposure to a Criterion A stressor, which means that the person has been exposed to an event that involved actual or threatened death or injury or a threat to the physical integrity of self or others. In addition, subjective reactions to the event must include intense fear, helplessness, or horror.

The symptoms of PTSD are currently divided into three symptom clusters (reexperiencing, avoidance, and hyperarousal symptoms), and these symptoms are anchored to the Criterion A event (Table 34.2). One reexperiencing symptom, three avoidance/numbing symptoms, and two hyperarousal symptoms are required for a diagnosis. Symptoms must be present for 1 month or longer, and PTSD cannot be diagnosed until 1 month postassault. Symptoms must cause significant distress or impairment. Acute PTSD is defined as lasting from 1 to 3 months, with chronic PTSD diagnosed when symptoms persist for 3 months or longer.

Retrospective studies revealed the lifetime PTSD prevalence rate among sexually assaulted women ranged from 49% to 60% (Breslau, Davis, Andreski, Federman, & Anthony, 1998; Rothbaum et al., 1992), with current prevalence rates at 12% to 13% (Resnick, Kilpatrick, Dansky, Saunders, & Best, 1993). PTSD symptoms do tend to improve over the course of time; however, a substantial percentage of women continue to meet diagnostic criteria long after the rape or assault. Rates of PTSD are higher at 3 months for rape victims than for victims of nonsexual crimes (Foa, Hearst-Ikeda, & Perry, 1995; Foa, Rothbaum, Riggs, & Murdock, 1991).

Current data on PTSD in primary care settings make clear that the condition is far from rare, but do not indicate what percentage of primary care PTSD cases result from rape or sexual assault. A screening study conducted within a primary care setting found that 11.8% of the sample met criteria for current full or partial PTSD (Stein, McQuaid, Pedrelli, Lenox, & McCahill, 2000). In a large study of PTSD in a primary care setting, PTSD was diagnosed in 34% of the sample screened

after medical evidence or screens indicated the likelihood of undetected anxiety or depressive disorders. PTSD was second only to major depression in terms of functional impairment associated with the disorder (Schonfeld et al., 1997). It has been proposed that PTSD may be the most common undetected anxiety disorder in primary care (Fifer et al., 1994); in a large health maintenance organization study that examined diagnoses associated with mental health referrals, PTSD

Table 34.2 Posttraumatic Stress Disorder

Diagnostic Criteria for Posttraumatic Stress Disorder

A. Exposure (as victim or witness) to a traumatic event that
   a. involved actual or threatened death or serious injury (to self or others), and that;
   b. evoked fear, helplessness, or horror

B. Persistent reexperiencing of the event as evidenced by:
   1. Distressing thoughts of the traumatic event, or
   2. Distressing dreams of the event, or
   3. Reliving the experience (e.g., flashbacks), or
   4. Psychological distress when reminded of the event (internally or externally), or
   5. Physiological reactivity to reminders of the event

C. Avoidance and/or general numbing of responsiveness, as evidenced by three or more of the following:
   1. Efforts to avoid thoughts or feelings related to the event
   2. Efforts to avoid activities or situations related to the event
   3. Psychogenic amnesia
   4. Diminished interest in usual activities
   5. Social detachment
   6. Restricted range of affect
   7. Sense of a "foreshortened future"

D. Persistent symptoms of increased physiological arousal (two or more):
   1. Sleep disturbances, or
   2. Irritability or outburst of anger, or
   3. Difficulty concentrating, or
   4. Hypervigilance, or
   5. Exaggerated startle response

E. Greater than 1 month's duration of symptoms

F. Significant distress or functional impairment

Note. Adapted from American Psychiatric Association (2000).

was diagnosed in almost 40% of the referred sample (Samson, Benson, Beck, Price, & Nimmer, 1999).

Emergence of Mental Health Problems Coexistent With Posttraumatic Stress Disorder

PTSD often co-occurs with other disorders; the most frequent are major depression, other anxiety disorders, and substance use disorders (Kessler, Sonnega, Bromet, Hughes, & Nelson, 1995, Resnick et al., 1993). In the primary care study mentioned in the preceding section, 85% of the identified PTSD cases had comorbid disorders (Schonfeld et al., 1997). In some cases, the relationship among sexual assault, PTSD, and other disorders is complex and cyclical.

For example, Kilpatrick and colleagues (Kilpatrick, Acierno, Resnick, Saunders, & Best, 1997) found that assault victims were more likely to abuse drugs and alcohol. Drug use in turn was associated with increased risk for additional assaults and hence possible perpetuation of symptoms. Evidence suggested, in fact, that when comorbidity is present, PTSD symptoms frequently precede the onset of substance abuse and depressive symptoms (Kessler et al., 1995, 1997). It is important to consider comorbidity when assessing for PTSD; likewise, routine assessment of PTSD in individuals with these common comorbid conditions should be considered.

Other Outcomes Associated With Sexual Assault

Other problems associated with abuse and sexual assault include negative health behaviors such as increased substance use, cigarette smoking, disordered eating (for review see Laws and Golding, 1996; Resnick, Acierno, & Kilpatrick, 1997); high-risk sexual behavior; and avoidance of reproductive health care (Farley, Golding, & Minkoff, 2002). These negative health behaviors have been conceptualized as possible attempts to reduce trauma-related symptoms such as sleep problems (Nishith, Resick, & Mueser, 2001) or intrusion and hyperarousal (Stewart, 1996) or as trauma-related avoidance of activities (e.g., gynecological exams) that trigger traumatic memories.

A broader conceptualization of posttrauma reactions after childhood abuse or repeated victimization is found in the cluster of symptoms termed *complex PTSD*. This conceptualization encompasses symptoms such as emotion dysregulation, dissociative symptoms, somatization, and self-harming behaviors. Borderline personality disorder and dissociative symptoms and disorders are also found (e.g., Briere & Elliot, 1994; Dancu, Riggs, Hearst-Ikeda, Shoyer, & Foa, 1995).

HEALTH CONSEQUENCES OF RAPE AND ABUSE

Trauma of any kind is strongly related to poorer health in men and women. Excellent reviews of the empirical literature on trauma, PTSD, and health are available (see Resnick et al., 1997; Schnurr & Jankowski, 1999), and an extensive review of medical comorbidity and trauma with a focus on gender issues is also available (Kimerling, Clum, McQuery, & Schnurr, 2002); thus, this topic is not covered in detail. A brief summary of this literature suggests that exposure to trauma and trauma severity are associated with increased reports of physical symptoms across bodily systems, morbidity (such as heart disease), and mortality. Trauma victims report more physical symptoms and poorer overall health.

The traumas of rape, sexual assault, and abuse have also demonstrated associations with medical problems. Female victims of violence are more likely to have gastrointestinal symptoms and disorders (Walker, Gelfand, Gelfand, Koss, & Katon, 1995), premenstrual and menstrual symptoms (Golding, 1996; Moellner, Bachmann, & Moellner, 1993), chronic pelvic pain and other chronic pain syndromes (Jamieson & Steege, 1997), reproductive or urinary tract symptoms (Cunningham, Pearce, & Pearce, 2003; Waigandt, Wallace, Phelps, & Miller, 1990), sexual dysfunctions (Becker & Skinner, 1983; Becker, Skinner, Abel, & Cichon, 1986; Letourneau, Resnick, Kilpatrick, Saunders, & Best, 1996), and gynecological problems (Waigandt et al., 1990). The apparent association between sexual assault and reproductive health issues should be tempered with the caveat that these medical outcomes are likely not specific to the trauma of sexual assault; however, their presence may be helpful in guiding screening efforts. Mounting evidence suggests that the effects of trauma on health outcomes may be at least partially accounted for by mental health diagnoses such as PTSD and depression and biological and behavioral changes associated with these diagnoses (Miranda, Meyerson, Marx, & Tucker, 2002; Wolfe, Schnurr, Brown, & Furey, 1994). This research suggests that screening efforts in the medical setting may be better aimed at assessment of mental health symptoms rather than trauma history.

SCREENING, INTERVENTION, AND REFERRAL

Mental Health Screening in the Acute Postassault Period

In the acute postassault period, victims may seek care in emergency room settings. An ideal standard of care would involve psychosocial intervention in addition to a standardized rape exam and prophylactic care (for sexually transmitted infections and pregnancy). If the opportunity exists for intervention in the acute postassault period, a review by Resnick and colleagues that covers issues of screening, assessment, and intervention with recent assault victims in emergency department settings will be useful (Resnick, Acierno, Holmes, Dammeyer, & Kilpatrick, 2000).

There are mixed results in terms of the utility of early psychological interventions aimed at reducing PTSD. One early intervention study in a small sample of sexual assault victims resulted in reductions in PTSD at the close of the study that were, however, not sustained at later follow-up (Foa, Hearst-Ikeda, & Perry, 1995). However, when Bryant, Harvey, Dang, Sackville, and Basten (1998) focused only on individuals with a diagnosis of ASD, early intervention was effective in preventing more chronic problems in motor vehicle accident survivors. Resnick and colleagues reported preliminary data on a brief emergency room intervention using video education in the acute assault period that may be helpful in preventing PTSD by reducing acute assault-related anxiety (Resnick, Acierno, Holmes, Kilpatrick, & Jager, 1999). Thus, although in the formative stages, early intervention strategies to reduce postassault psychopathology appear promising.

Screening for Chronic Postassault Consequences in Medical Settings

The initial challenge in primary care settings is identifying the sexual assault and abuse victims who may benefit from additional medical or mental health intervention. Screening for traumatic events and associated symptoms is a necessary step in identifying those victims in primary care settings. However, screening is not always routinely conducted. Barriers to screening in primary care settings that have been identified include time constraints, physician's attitudes and discomfort with querying about traumatic events, and concerns of both physicians and patients about reporting assault or abuse.

Psychologists can play a role in educating physicians about the prevalence and outcomes of traumatic events such as sexual assault and informing them about patient attitudes and concerns (see Table 34.3). In spite of some physicians' concerns about patient discomfort with screening, patients tend to be in favor of routine assessment of violence and believe that physicians can help with violence issues (Friedman, Samet, Roberts, Hudlin, & Hands, 1992). As is evident from Table 34.3, patients are concerned about privacy and confidentiality issues and about health outcomes associated with sexual assault (data from Kilpatrick et al., 1992). Physicians should be prepared to ask about patient concerns and provide accurate information and appropriate treatment.

General principles for effective screening of sexual assault and trauma symptoms, whether in medical or other settings, include that it be done routinely and with everyone, with follow-up conducted in a private setting (Resnick et al., 2000). An ideal screen would include a history of both traumatic events and associated symptoms. However, because time constraints may be a barrier to screening, brief, symptom-focused screens could be conducted during the medical history before the physician appointment. The Primary Care PTSD Screen (Prins, Kimerling, Cameron, Ouimette, & Shaw, 1999), presented in Table 34.4, is a brief, symptom-focused screen that could be

Table 34.3 Concerns of Rape Victims

Concerns of Rape Victims	Percentage of All Victims Concerned	Percentage of Victims Raped in Last 5 Years Concerned
Victim's relatives knowing about assault	71	66
Victim blaming	69	66
People outside family knowing about assault	68	61
Victim's identity revealed in the news media	50	60
Becoming pregnant	34	61
Contracting a sexually transmitted disease	19	43
Contracting HIV/AIDS	10	40

Note. Data from Kilpatrick, Edmunds, and Seymour (1992).

administered. Suggested guidelines for indication of a positive diagnosis and recommendation for referral include answering yes to any two items or yes to the hyperarousal item (Item 3). The PTSD Checklist–Civilian Version (Weathers, Huska, & Keane, 1991) is also a brief PTSD screen that has good sensitivity and specificity with female veterans in a primary care setting (Lang, Laffaye, Satz, Dresselhaus, & Stein, 2003). The authors recommend a cutoff of 28 to 30 in screening for PTSD. A brief discussion of trauma reactions and symptoms is appropriate, and a brief assessment of the current impact of symptoms on the patient's daily functioning is recommended.

Physician reactions to patient disclosure are important. This may be the first feedback sexual assault or abuse victims have received; thus, a brief statement of empathy ("I'm sorry this happened to you") and a brief statement normalizing any symptoms are appropriate. ("The thoughts and feelings you are describing are very common after an experience like you have told me about. Many people who have had this experience report similar reactions.") Supportive and empathic responses are always helpful, as are indications that the clinician wants to help, particularly if prior disclosures have been met with negative reactions. However, it is important to note that this does not require detailed discussion of the traumatic events. In fact, unless physicians have more than average training in mental health issues, extensive assessment should not be conducted (Prins et al., 1999).

To address barriers focused on physician and patient concerns about reporting sexual assault or abuse, psychologists can assist with the development of protocols to help physicians determine if there are current threats or safety issues for the

Table 34.4 Primary Care Posttraumatic Stress Disorder (PC-PTSD) Screen

In your life, have you ever had any experience that was so frightening, horrible, or upsetting that, in the past month, you . . .

1. Have had nightmares about it or thought about it when you did not want to?
   Yes   No

2. Tried hard not to think about it or went out of your way to avoid situations that reminded you of it?
   Yes   No

3. Were constantly on guard, watchful, or easily startled?
   Yes   No

4. Felt numb or detached from others, activities, or your surroundings?
   Yes   No

Note. Adapted from Prins et al. (1999).

patient and how to respond to them. The limits of confidentiality and guidelines for reporting sexual assault or abuse in each state should be understood so that appropriate reporting, safety plans, and referrals to mental health professionals or community agencies can be provided to patients (Prins et al., 1999; Resnick et al., 2000).

Screening for Chronic Postassault Consequences in Specialty Mental Health/ Substance Abuse Settings

Many of the above issues apply to screening for sexual assault, abuse, and other trauma in mental health or substance abuse settings. Rates of trauma and PTSD are greater in both mental health and substance abuse settings, indicating an important need for screening and assessment in these patients. Because of the high rates of comorbidity associated with PTSD, it is possible that individuals who present with substance abuse, depression, and other anxiety disorders may have PTSD as well. Thus, if possible, screening for trauma and associated symptoms should also be done routinely and in a more comprehensive manner in substance abuse or mental health settings.

Note, however, that screening in the absence of available resources for treatment may do more harm than good (Greene & Kimerling, 2004). Thus, psychologists should be prepared to identify protocols and procedures that will maximize screening efforts in both medical and specialty settings by placing an emphasis on how the screen will be used and forging partnerships with physicians or other health care practitioners involved in the screening process.

MORE COMPREHENSIVE ASSESSMENT OF THE PSYCHOLOGICAL CONSEQUENCES OF RAPE AND SEXUAL ASSAULT

If screening in medical, mental health, or substance abuse settings indicates that trauma-related symptoms might be an issue, a more comprehensive assessment should be conducted. This will set the stage for case conceptualization and treatment planning, but it is also an opportunity to provide education and feedback about trauma symptoms. A fuller assessment should focus on the trauma history, the presence of PTSD symptoms, the existence of concurrent psychological problems (particularly substance abuse), and interpersonal or quality-of-life issues. We touch on each of these in turn next.

Trauma History

A comprehensive trauma assessment not only will assess the occurrence of a sexual assault, but also will query about prior history of assaults, both physical and sexual, and other potentially traumatic events, such as exposure to violence, community violence, natural disaster, and the like. Trauma assessments should also use behavioral definitions of events rather than terminology that may prevent a person from endorsing its occurrence. For example, queries using terms like "rape" or "sexual abuse" may not result in endorsement; queries using a specific behavioral definition such as "forced to have vaginal intercourse when I did not want to" may be clearer to the individual and less difficult to endorse.

An assessment of traumatic events should assess age of occurrence and severity of the event utilizing current Criterion A definitions to gauge severity. For example, if a patient endorses a physical assault, she or he should be queried about life threat and reactions such as fear, helplessness, or horror. Multiple assessments are available for both children and adults that assess a wide variety of possible traumatic events; some assessments were developed specifically for use with women (e.g., the Life Stressor Checklist Revised [Wolfe & Kimerling, 1997]). Whether or not self-report instruments are used, the clinical interview maybe the best tool to identify a specific Criterion A event that will serve as the focus for the PTSD assessment.

Posttraumatic Stress Disorder Assessment

Once the traumas have been specified, a fuller assessment of PTSD can be conducted. The Criterion A event that will be the focus of the PTSD assessment may be the one identified as the most severe, the initial event, or the most recent. If the patient has difficulty identifying a single event, further inquiry about the content of intrusive thoughts may help identify which event is most salient, or a combination of traumatic events can be used to anchor the PTSD assessment. A comprehensive list of PTSD assessments for adults and children is available on the National Center for PTSD Web site (www.ncptsd.org/publications/assessment).

The Clinician Administered PTSD Scale is an empirically supported clinical interview that provides frequency and severity information, descriptive cues to assist with making distinctions in frequency and severity, and cutoffs for meeting symptom criteria for each PTSD symptom cluster and overall diagnosis (Blake et al., 1995; Weathers, Keane, & Davidson, 2001).

A thorough PTSD assessment should also assess whether substance abuse is present and whether substance use functions as a coping strategy to deal with trauma-related symptoms (Stewart, 1996). This is a particular concern in women and female adolescents because evidence suggests that PTSD is likely to precede substance use disorders in these groups (Deykin & Buka, 1997; Stewart, Ouimette, & Brown, 2002). Understanding how PTSD influences substance use and substance use influences PTSD is important for psychoeducation, the development and use of alternate coping strategies, the identification of triggers for substance use, and strategies for relapse prevention.

Finally, a comprehensive assessment will include obtaining information on quality of life, functional impairment, health problems and behaviors, and self-harming behaviors or suicidal ideation as well as an understanding of how the sexual assault or abuse has affected relationships, both intimate and casual.

TREATMENT FOR PTSD

Adults

A comprehensive guide for medication and psychotherapy for the treatment of PTSD has been compiled as part of the Expert Consensus Guideline Series (1999). This document is highly recommended as a resource for primary care psychol-ogists, psychiatrists, and health care providers. It provides guidelines for medication selection and dosage, psychotherapy selection, and assistance with decision making for tailoring treatments to patient needs and situational issues such as treatment setting. Although a full summary of the guide is not possible here, we review several empirically validated, short-term cognitive–behavioral therapies (CBTs) for PTSD in greater depth. Several treatments for PTSD have demonstrated efficacy in symptom reduction, with exposure-based and cognitive interventions demonstrating the strongest effect sizes (Cason, Grubaugh, & Resick, 2002). There is some evidence that, although PTSD is more prevalent in women than in men, men are also more likely to benefit from treatment (Cason et al., 2002).

Exposure-based therapies, such as prolonged exposure (Foa et al., 1991), are based on emotional processing models of PTSD. Specifically, prolonged exposure combines imaginal exposure to the traumatic memory and in vivo exposure to trauma-related situations, places, and activities that are avoided by the individual, not because they are dangerous, but because they evoke traumatic memories or feelings. By confronting rather than avoiding the traumatic memory and the triggers associated with it, the patient is able to process information about the trauma more accurately. As the traumatic memory is confronted and processed, symptoms are reduced, and unhelpful, trauma-related cognitions are revised. Prolonged exposure is provided in 90-minute sessions for 8 to 10 sessions and has been shown to be efficacious in the treatment of rape- and assault-related PTSD.

Cognitive processing therapy (CPT; Resick & Schnicke, 1992) combines exposure with cognitive therapy focused on trauma-related cognitions such as safety, trust, esteem, and intimacy. CPT targets attempts to maintain old beliefs about self or the world or "assimilated cognitions" (e.g., "I must have caused the rape somehow") as well as extreme change in beliefs as a result of the rape or "accommodated cognitions" (e.g., "No man can be trusted"). CPT is conducted in 12 sessions and has demonstrated efficacy in the treatment of PTSD symptoms, depression, and guilt (Resick, Nishith, Weaver, Astin, & Feuer, 2002).

Other cognitive–behavioral interventions, such as stress inoculation training (SIT; Kilpatrick, Veronen, & Resick, 1982), include skills training, such as relaxation and progressive muscle relaxation, as well as coping strategies, to prepare patients to deal with trauma-related cognitions, physical reactions, and emotions. With SIT, a stress inoculation model is used in which exposure to feared situations is done in a hierarchical manner and coupled with coping skills. Efficacy in treating PTSD has also been demonstrated with SIT.

Children and Adolescents

To date, randomized controlled trials of interventions focused on treating abuse sequelae in children and adolescents have focused largely on sexual abuse and have been grounded in cognitive–behavioral theory (Pine & Cohen, 2002). The interventions have focused on PTSD symptoms and other outcomes, such as anxiety and behavioral problems, associated with the experience of abuse. Pine and Cohen (2002) reviewed the evidence for efficacy of cognitive–behavioral interventions and concluded that treatment effects were significant, compared to both attention-control and other active treatments.

Much like the CBTs for PTSD in adults, interventions with children and adolescents typically incorporate some aspect of exposure, in many instances utilizing gradual exposure. Pine and Cohen (2002), in their review of the cognitive–behavioral treatment literature regarding children and adolescents, summarized components that have been incorporated into successful interventions: cognitive processing, exposure, and stress inoculation strategies. They noted also that simultaneous intervention with parents using cognitive–behavioral strategies and parent training strategies is frequently incorporated (Pine & Cohen, 2002) and may be a predictor of successful treatment outcome (Cohen & Mannarino, 2000).

The treatment outcome research on children and adolescents does not currently provide specific information about adolescents. However, reactions and trauma-related symptoms in adolescents appear to parallel more closely those found in adult samples than the reactions and symptoms

of young children. Thus, modifications of treatment strategies used with adults or children to developmentally appropriate levels may be useful when treating adolescents.

Adults With Child Abuse Histories

In an attempt to address some of the adulthood problems associated with child sexual abuse not addressed by standard PTSD treatments, Cloitre, Koenen, Cohen, and Han (2002) developed a short-term intervention focused on the development of skills to promote affect regulation and interpersonal skills such as conflict management and negotiation. The treatment requires 16 sessions over a 12-week period in two distinct phases. The first phase (8 sessions, 1 hour a week) is focused on skill development in the affect and interpersonal arenas, and the second phase is modified exposure therapy (8 sessions, 90 minutes per session, twice a week). This intervention resulted in significant improvements in affect regulation problems, interpersonal skills deficits, and PTSD symptoms when compared with a wait list control.

Primary Care Interventions

Although interventions for PTSD treatment tailored to the primary care setting have not been tested, some brief treatment models have received preliminary support. Foa and colleagues (Foa, Hearst-Ikeda, et al., 1995) have tested a four-session adaptation of prolonged exposure therapy with good results. Researchers from this group are also testing the feasibility of clinician-directed self-help and bibliotherapy interventions for reducing symptoms of anxiety in primary care patients. Innovations such as these hold promise for the large group of patients who may prefer to receive treatment in the primary care clinic.

Treatment of Comorbid Conditions in Adults

Several treatment manuals address comorbid conditions, but the efficacy of these treatments is not firmly established. The most common conditions comorbid with PTSD, as noted in the discussion of coexisting conditions, are anxiety, depression, and substance abuse. Because several of the controlled studies of PTSD discussed here excluded individuals with active substance abuse or dependence, their generalizability to treatment of comorbid conditions such as substance use disorders is unknown. However, given the high rates of comorbidity identified between PTSD and other disorders, particularly substance abuse, treatment of comorbid conditions should be a consideration in assessment and intervention planning. It is also noteworthy that clinically significant decreases in depression were observed in studies that addressed PTSD diagnoses (e.g., Resick et al., 2002). Examples of multifocus approaches are reviewed next.

1. Multiple channel exposure therapy (Falsetti & Resnick, 2000), has demonstrated preliminary efficacy in reducing symptoms of PTSD and panic symptoms in sexual assault victims (Falsetti, Resnick, Davis, & Gallagher, 2001).

2. An integrated treatment that focuses on both PTSD and substance abuse is Seeking Safety (Najavits, Weiss, Shaw, & Muenz, 1998), a 24-session CBT therapy that emphasizes becoming and staying safe, discontinuation of substance use, and enhancing coping skills, self-worth, and self-care. There are 24 modules that can be used in any order and in multiple formats (individual, group). Seeking Safety does not include direct exposure techniques focused on the traumatic event. An open trial of the therapy demonstrated reductions of PTSD and substance use symptoms, as well as acceptability to the patient sample. A controlled study comparing Seeking Safety, relapse prevention treatment, and a treatment-as-usual control group found that Seeking Safety and relapse prevention therapy were both efficacious in reducing PTSD and substance use symptoms, as well as general psychiatric distress, at close of therapy (Hien, Cohen, Litt, Miele, & Capstick, in press).

3. Concurrent treatment of PTSD and cocaine dependence (Brady, Dansky, Back, Foa, & Carroll, 2001) addresses comorbid PTSD and cocaine abuse. The therapy combines CBT for cocaine with exposure-based techniques for PTSD in a sequential manner. Data from an open trial study suggested that the therapy resulted in reduced symptoms of PTSD and cocaine use at therapy close and at 6-month follow-up, with an effect size similar to exposure-based therapies for PTSD without substance use disorder. However, a high percentage of participants did not complete the study (Brady et al., 2001).

In conclusion, the treatments addressing comorbid PTSD and substance use disorders require more controlled studies with longer term follow-up to demonstrate efficacy. Depending on the severity of the substance use and PTSD, treatment effects for comorbid PTSD and substance use disorder may be difficult to sustain in the long term without ongoing maintenance (Ouimette, Moos, & Finney, 2000); thus, relapse prevention, follow-up strategies, and booster sessions should be incorporated into termination planning. When queried, patients suggested a preference for receiving treatment that focuses on both their substance use and PTSD symptoms concurrently rather than treating each disorder independently (Brown, Stout, & Gannon-Rowley, 1998). It is important to note that there is no evidence to support the concern that treatment of both PTSD and substance abuse leads to increased substance abuse.

INTEGRATING HEALTH-RELATED ISSUES INTO POSTTRAUMATIC STRESS DISORDER TREATMENT

Negative health behaviors such as smoking and substance use, coupled with lack of positive health care practices such as exercise, gynecological exams, and proper nutrition, are important targets for intervention. Victims of sexual assault and abuse should be educated about the interrelationships of mental and physical health variables and helped to understand how these negative health behaviors relate to trauma symptoms. Simple monitoring of trauma-related symptoms and urges to smoke, for example, could be a useful intervention to help patients understand triggers and reduce smoking urges. Clinicians are encouraged to assess the relationship between trauma symptoms and health behaviors in treatment planning.

PTSD-positive patients who carry diagnoses of health conditions or disease should also be educated about the role that PTSD and negative health behaviors can play in the exacerbation of illness. For example, a patient with heart disease and PTSD may engage in negative health behaviors, such as smoking, that can amplify disease. There is evidence to suggest that treating PTSD symptoms may improve some physical symptoms or disease states. For example, a case study of a woman with comorbid PTSD and irritable bowel syndrome revealed that successful treatment of PTSD alleviated the primary IBS symptoms (Weaver, Nishith, & Resick, 1999).

The majority of individuals do not receive rape-related medical exams (Resnick et al., 2000); thus, if the psychologist's patient has not received a thorough medical exam or does not have a primary care physician, he or she should be encouraged to obtain these. However, the psychologist should make clear to the primary care physician the patient's rape history or abuse history and provide consultation if necessary to facilitate the sensitive care of these patients. Psychologists can also assist with this process by preparing patients for medical procedures to be conducted, addressing any anxiety concerning medical procedures, and assisting patients with the formulation of medical questions and concerns. Psychologists should follow up with patients after the medical exam to address any ongoing issues and to "debrief" if necessary.

SUMMARY

The majority of patients with problems related to sexual assault and abuse are currently not served and may not wish to be served by specialty mental health clinicians. These patients seek care from primary care physicians for a variety of health problems directly and indirectly affected by the presence of PTSD and other mental health diagnoses. If patients are not amenable to referrals to mental health clinicians, these patients may be best served by offering them practical, timely interventions designed to address both their immediate concerns and the root causes of their problems in the primary care setting.

Although there are a few brief interventions for rape and sexual assault symptoms that may be suited to primary care settings (e.g., Foa, Hearst-Ikeda, et al., 1995; Resnick et al., 1999), there is a need for new, innovative approaches to treating trauma and PTSD that suit the context of service delivery in a primary care setting. For example, psychologists could educate and provide ongoing consultation to a primary care team that provides core behavioral health interventions to manage symptoms or increase coping skills, with the interventions adapted to fit within the primary care timetable. Psychologists should work to develop new strategies for identification and intervention in the primary care setting and strive to play an important role in the health and mental health care of these patients.

The most basic opportunity for intervention may also be the most important: simply asking about abuse and assault history. With this information, psychologists can work with the patient and other clinicians to develop a plan of action to address patient needs. Intervention can result in improved quality of life and better mental and physical health. Intervention may also prevent revictimization and the increasing risk for negative outcomes that revictimization brings.

References

American Psychiatric Association. (1994). *Diagnostic and statistical manual of mental disorders* (4th ed.). Washington, DC: Author.

Becker, J. V., Skinner, L. J., Abel, G. G., & Cichon, J. (1986). Level of postassault sexual functioning in rape and incest victims. *Archives of Sexual Behavior, 15*, 37–49.

Blake, D. D., Weathers, F. W., Nagy, L. M., Kaloupek, D. G., Gusman, F. D., Charney, D. S., et al. (1995). The development of a clinician-administered PTSD scale. *Journal of Traumatic Stress, 8*, 75–90.

Brady, K. T., Dansky, B. S., Back, S. E., Foa, E. B., & Carroll, K. M. (2001). Exposure therapy in the treatment of PTSD among cocaine-dependent individuals: Preliminary findings. *Journal of Substance Abuse Treatment, 21*, 47–54.

Breslau, N., Davis, G. C., Andreski, P., Federman, B., & Anthony, J. C. (1998). Epidemiological findings on posttraumatic stress disorder and co-morbid disorders in the general population. In B. Dohrenwend (Ed.), *Adversity, stress, and psychopathology* (pp. 319–330). London: Oxford University Press.

Briere, J. N., & Elliott, D. M. (1994). Immediate and long-term impacts of child sexual abuse. *The Future of Children, 4*, 54–69.

Brown, P. J., Stout, R. L., & Gannon-Rowley, J. (1998). Substance use disorder-PTSD comorbidity: Patients' perceptions of symptom interplay and treatment issues. *Journal of Substance Abuse Treatment, 14,* 1–4.

Bryant, R. A., Harvey, A. G., Dang, S. T., Sackville, T., & Basten, C. (1998). Treatment of acute stress disorder: A comparison of cognitive behavior therapy and supportive counseling. *Journal of Consulting and Clinical Psychology, 66,* 862–866.

Cason, D., Grubaugh, A., & Resick, P. (2002). Gender and PTSD treatment: Efficacy and effectiveness. In R. Kimerling, P. Ouimette, & J. Wolfe (Eds.), *Gender and PTSD* (pp. 305–334). New York: Guilford Press.

Cloitre, M., Koenen, K. C., Cohen, L. R., & Han, H. (2002). Skills training in affective and interpersonal regulation followed by exposure: A phase-based treatment for PTSD related to childhood abuse. *Journal of Consulting and Clinical Psychology, 70,* 1067–1074.

Cohen, J. A., & Mannarino, A. P. (2000). Predictors of treatment outcome in sexually abused children. *Child Abuse and Neglect, 24,* 983–994.

Cunningham, J., Pearce, T., & Pearce, P. (2003). Childhood sexual abuse and medical complaints in adult women. *Journal of Interpersonal Violence, 3,* 131–144.

Dancu, C. V., Riggs, D. S., Hearst-Ikeda, D., Shoyer, B. G., & Foa, E. B. (1996). Dissociative experiences and posttraumatic stress disorder among female victims of criminal assault and rape. *Journal of Traumatic Stress, 9,* 253–267.

Deykin, E. Y. & Buka, S. L. (1997). Prevalence and risk factors for posttraumatic stress disorder among chemically dependent adolescents. *American Journal of Psychiatry, 154,* 752–757.

Expert consensus guideline series. Treatment of posttraumatic stress disorder. (1999). *Journal of Clinical Psychiatry, 60*(Suppl. 16), 3–76.

Falsetti, S. A., & Resnick, H. (2000). Cognitive behavioral treatment for PTSD with comorbid panic attacks. *Journal of Contemporary Psychotherapy, 30,* 163–179.

Falsetti, S. A., Resnick, H., Davis J., & Gallagher, N. G. (2001). Treatment of posttraumatic stress disorder with comorbid panic attacks: Combining cognitive processing therapy with panic control treatment techniques. *Group Dynamics, 5,* 252–260.

Farley, M., Golding, J. M., & Minkoff, J. R. (2002). Is a history of trauma associated with a reduced likelihood of cervical cancer screening? *Journal of Family Practice, 51,* 827–831.

Fifer, S. K., Mathias, S. D., Patrick, D. L., Mazonson, P. D., Lubeck, D. P., & Buesching, D. P. (1994). Untreated anxiety among adult primary care patients in a health maintenance organization. *Archives of General Psychiatry, 51,* 740–750.

Finkelhor, D., Hotaling, G., Lewis, I. A., & Smith, C. (1990). Sexual abuse in a national survey of adult men and women: Prevalence, characteristics, and risk factors. *Child Abuse and Neglect, 14,* 19–28.

Foa, E. B., Hearst-Ikeda, D., & Perry, K. J. (1995). Evaluation of a brief cognitive-behavioral program for the prevention of chronic PTSD in recent assault victims. *Journal of Consulting Clinical Psychology, 63,* 948–955.

Foa, E. B., Riggs, D. S., & Gershuny, B. S. (1995). Arousal, numbing, and intrusion: Symptom structure of PTSD following assault. *American Journal of Psychiatry, 152,* 116–120.

Foa, E. B., Rothbaum, B. O., Riggs, D. S., & Murdock, T. B. (1991). Treatment of posttraumatic stress disorder in rape victims: A comparison between cognitive-behavioral procedures and counseling. *Journal of Consulting Clinical Psychology, 59,* 715–723.

Friedman, L. S., Samet, J. H., Roberts, M. S., Hudlin, M., & Hans, P. (1992). Inquiry about victimization experiences. A survey of patient preferences and physician practices. *Archives of Internal Medicine, 152,* 1186–1190.

Golding, J. M. (1996). Sexual assault history and women's reproductive and sexual health. *Psychology of Women Quarterly, 20,* 101–121.

Green, B., & Kimerling, R. (2004). Trauma, PTSD, and health. In P. Schnurr & B. Green (Eds.), *Trauma and health: Physical health consequences of exposure to extreme stress.* Washington, DC: American Psychological Association.

Hien, D. A., Cohen, L. R., Litt, L. C., Miele, G. M., & Capstick, C. (in press). Promising empirically supported treatment for women with comorbid PTSD and substance use disorders. *American Journal of Psychiatry.*

Jamieson, D. J., & Steege, J. F. (1997). The association of sexual abuse with pelvic pain complaints in a primary care population. *American Journal of Obstetrics and Gynecology, 177,* 1408–1412.

Kessler, R. C., Crum, R. M., Warner, L. A., Nelson, C. B., Schulenberg, J., & Anthony, J. C. (1997). Lifetime co-occurrence of *DSM-III-R* alcohol abuse and dependence with other psychiatric disorders in the National Comorbidity

Survey. *Archives of General Psychiatry, 54,* 313–321.

Kessler, R. C., McGonagle, K. A., Zhao, S., Nelson, C. B., Hughes, M., Eshleman, S., et al. (1994). Lifetime and 12-month prevalence of *DSM-III-R* psychiatric disorders in the United States. Results from the National Comorbidity Survey. *Archives of General Psychiatry, 51,* 8–19.

Kessler, R. C., Sonnega, A., Bromet, E., Hughes, M., & Nelson, C. B. (1995). Posttraumatic stress disorder in the National Comorbidity Survey. *Archives of General Psychiatry, 52,* 1048–1060.

Kilpatrick, D. G., Edmunds, C. N., & Seymour, A. K. (1992). *Rape in America: A report to the nation.* Arlington, VA: National Victim Center & Medical University of South Carolina.

Kilpatrick, D., Veronen, L. J., & Resick, P. (1982). Psychological sequelae to rape: Assessment and treatment strategies. In D. M. Dolays, R. L. Meredith, & A. R. Ciminero (Eds.), *Behavioral medicine: Assessment and treatment strategies* (pp. 473–497). New York: Plenum Press.

Kilpatrick, D. G., Acierno, R., Resnick, H. S., Saunders, B. E., & Best, C. L. (1997). A 2-year longitudinal analysis of the relationships between violent assault and substance use in women. *Journal of Consulting Clinical Psychology, 65,* 834–847.

Kimerling, R., & Calhoun, K. S. (1994). Somatic symptoms, social support, and treatment seeking among sexual assault victims. *Journal of Consulting Clinical Psychology, 62,* 333–340.

Kimerling, R., Clum, G. A., McQuery, J. S., & Schnurr, P. P. (2002). PTSD and medical comorbidity. In R. Kimerling, P. Ouimette, & J. Wolfe (Eds.), *Gender and PTSD* (pp. 271–302). New York: Guilford Press.

Koss, M. P., Koss, P. G., & Woodruff, W. J. (1991). Deleterious effects of criminal victimization on women's health and medical utilization. *Archives of Internal Medicine, 151,* 342–347.

Lang, A. J., Laffaye, C., Satz, L. E., Dresselhaus, T. R., & Stein, M. B. (2003). Sensitivity and specificity of the PTSD Checklist in detecting PTSD in female veterans in primary care. *Journal of Traumatic Stress, 16,* 257–268.

Laws, A., & Golding, J. M. (1996). Sexual assault history and eating disorder symptoms among white, Hispanic, and African-American women and men. *American Journal of Public Health, 86,* 579–582.

Letourneau, E. J., Resnick, H. S., Kilpatrick, D. G.,

Saunders, B. E., & Best, C. L. (1996). Comorbidity of sexual problems and posttraumatic stress disorder in female crime victims. *Behavior Therapy, 27,* 321–336.

Miranda, R., Jr., Meyerson, L. A., Marx, B. P., & Tucker, P. M. (2002). Civilian-based posttraumatic stress disorder and physical complaints: evaluation of depression as a mediator. *Journal of Traumatic Stress, 15,* 297–301.

Najavits, L. M., Weiss, R. D., Shaw, S. R., & Muenz, L. R. (1998). Seeking safety: Outcome of a new cognitive-behavioral psychotherapy for women with posttraumatic stress disorder and substance dependence. *Journal of Traumatic Stress, 11,* 437–456.

Nishith, P., Resick, P. A., & Mueser, K. T. (2001). Sleep difficulties and alcohol use motives in female rape victims with posttraumatic stress disorder. *Journal of Traumatic Stress, 14,* 469–479.

Norquist, G. S., & Regier, D. A. (1996). The epidemiology of psychiatric disorders and the de facto mental health care system. *Annual Review of Medicine, 47,* 473–479.

Ouimette, P. C., Moos, R. H., & Finney, J. W. (2000). Two-year mental health service use and course of remission in patients with substance use and posttraumatic stress disorders. *Journal of Studies on Alcohol, 61,* 247–253.

Pine, D. S., & Cohen, J. A. (2002). Trauma in children and adolescents: Risk and treatment of psychiatric sequelae. *Biological Psychiatry, 51,* 519–531.

Prins, A., Kimerling, R., Cameron, R., Ouimette, P., Shaw, J., Trailkill, A., Sheikh, J., & Gusman, F. (1999, November). *The Primary Care PTSD Screen (PC-PTSD).* Paper presented at the 15th annual meeting of the International Society for Traumatic Stress Studies, Miami, FL.

Resick, P. A., Nishith, P., Weaver, T. L., Astin, M. C., & Feuer, C. A. (2002). A comparison of cognitive-processing therapy with prolonged exposure and a waiting condition for the treatment of chronic posttraumatic stress disorder in female rape victims. *Journal of Consulting Clinical Psychology, 70,* 867–879.

Resick, P. A., & Schnicke, M. K. (1992). Cognitive processing therapy for sexual assault victims. *Journal of Consulting Clinical Psychology, 60,* 748–756.

Resnick, H., Acierno, R., Holmes, M., Dammeyer, M., & Kilpatrick, D. (2000). Emergency evaluation and intervention with female victims of rape and other violence. *Journal of Clinical Psychology, 56,* 1317–1333.

Resnick, H., Acierno, R., Holmes, M., Kilpatrick, D. G., & Jager, N. (1999). Prevention of post-rape psychopathology: Preliminary findings of a controlled acute rape treatment study. *Journal of Anxiety Disorders, 13,* 359–370.

Resnick, H. S., Acierno, R., & Kilpatrick, D. G. (1997). Health impact of interpersonal violence. 2: Medical and mental health outcomes. *Behavioral Medicine, 23,* 65–78.

Resnick, H. S., Kilpatrick, D. G., Dansky, B. S., Saunders, B. E., & Best, C. L. (1993). Prevalence of civilian trauma and posttraumatic stress disorder in a representative national sample of women. *Journal of Consulting Clinical Psychology, 61,* 984–991.

Rothbaum, B. O., Foa, E. B., Riggs, D. S., Murdock, T. B., & Walsh, W. (1992). A prospective examination of post-traumatic stress disorder in rape victims. *Journal of Traumatic Stress, 5,* 455–475.

Samson, A. Y., Bensen, S., Beck A., Price, D., & Nimmer, C. (1999). Posttraumatic stress disorder in primary care. *Journal of Family Practice, 48,* 222–227.

Schnurr, P. P., & Jankowski, M. K. (1999). Physical health and post-traumatic stress disorder: Review and synthesis. *Seminars in Clinical Neuropsychiatry, 4,* 295–304.

Schonfeld, W. H., Verboncoeur, C. J., Fifer, S. K., Lipschutz, R. C., Lubeck, D. P., & Buesching, D. P. (1997). The functioning and well-being of patients with unrecognized anxiety disorders and major depressive disorder. *Journal of Affective Disorders, 43,* 105–119.

Stein, M. B., McQuaid, J. R., Pedrelli, P., Lenox, R., & McCahill, M. E. (2000). Posttraumatic stress disorder in the primary care medical setting. *General Hospital Psychiatry, 22,* 261–269.

Stewart, S. H. (1996). Alcohol abuse in individuals exposed to trauma: A critical review. *Psychology Bulletin, 120,* 83–112.

Stewart, S. H., Ouimette, P., & Brown, P. J. (2002). Gender and the comorbidity of PTSD with substance use disorders. In R. Kimerling, P. Ouimette, & J. Wolfe (Eds.), *Gender and PTSD* (pp. 232–270). New York: Guilford Press.

Tjaden, P., & Thoennes, N. (1998). *Prevalence, incidence, and consequences of violence against women: Findings from the National Violence Against Women Survey.* Washington, DC: U.S. Department of Justice, Bureau of Justice Statistics.

Waigant, A., Wallance, D. C., Phelps, C., Miller, D. A. (1990). The impact of sexual assault on physical health status. *Journal of Traumatic Stress, 3*(1), 93–102.

Walker, E. A., Gelfand, A. N., Gelfand, M. D., Koss, M. P., & Katon, W. J. (1995). Medical and psychiatric symptoms in female gastroenterology clinic patients with histories of sexual victimization. *General Hospital Psychiatry, 17,* 85–92.

Walker, E. A., Torkelson, N., Katon, W. J., & Koss, M. P. (1993). The prevalence rate of sexual trauma in a primary care clinic. *Journal of American Board Family Practice, 6,* 465–471.

Walker, E. A., Unutzer, J., Rutter, C., Gelfand, A., Saunders, K., VonKorff, M., et al. (1999). Costs of health care use by women HMO members with a history of childhood abuse and neglect. *Archives of General Psychiatry, 56,* 609–613.

Weathers, F., Huska, J., & Keane, T. (1991). The PTSD Checklist–Civilian Version (PCL-C). Boston, Mass: National Center for PTSD.

Weathers, F. W., Keane, T. M., & Davidson, J. R. (2001). Clinician-administered PTSD scale: A review of the first ten years of research. *Depression and Anxiety, 13,* 132–156.

Weaver, T. L., Nishith, P., & Resick, P. (1999). Prolonged exposure therapy and irritable bowel syndrome: A case study examining the impact of a trauma-focused treatment on a physical condition. *Cognitive and Behavioral Practice, 6,* 68.

Wolfe, J., & Kimerling, R. (1997). Gender isues in the assessment of posttraumatic stress disorder. In J. Wilson & T. M. Keane (Eds.), *Assessing psychological trauma and PTSD* (pp. 192–238). New York: Guilford Press.

Wolfe, J., Schnurr, P. P., Brown, P. J., & Furey, J. (1994). Posttraumatic stress disorder and warzone exposure as correlates of perceived health in female Vietnam War veterans. *Journal of Consulting Clinical Psychology, 62,* 1235–1240.

35

Sexual Disorders Affecting Men

Joseph LoPiccolo

The male sexual dysfunctions include low sexual desire, premature ejaculation, male orgasmic disorder, and erectile dysfunction. Although some men may seek treatment of these problems from a "sex therapist" or a mental health practitioner, it is more common for a man with a sexual concern to go to his general practitioner or to a urologist. Men generally do not like to think of the cause of their sexual problem as "in their head," but rather seek a physical cause and a quick, medical solution to the problem (Pridal, 2001).

When these men are then referred to the psychologist who works in the primary care setting, a number of differences from the standard "sex therapy" situation require the clinician to make some modifications to standard treatment procedures. Even more important, the psychologist's approach to the patient needs to be different from that in other settings regarding male sexual dysfunction cases. This chapter covers the issues involved in working with men with sexual problems who are seen in a primary health care setting. The issue of how medical conditions—and medications—may cause sexual problems is covered. Although this chapter is phrased in terms of heterosexual men, most of the information is applicable to homosexual men as well. As an example of the type of cases seen by psychologists who work in medical settings, consider the following case:

> A man was referred for erectile failure and low sex drive after Viagra failed to help his problem. He is an insulin-dependent diabetic with juvenile onset. What does the psychologist need to assess, and which treatment might be offered to this man?

This case is discussed at the end of this chapter.

THE INITIAL APPROACH

In sex therapy settings, typically a couple seeks treatment, and they often expect to enter psychotherapy. In primary care, typically a man comes in alone and expects medical treatment for what he considers a physically based problem. Therefore, the clinician should start by asking the patient about *his* understanding of why he has been referred to a psychologist and how he feels about this referral. Sometimes, the patient will state that he is totally puzzled by this referral: "Dr. Smith said I should see you—I don't know why!"

Other patients, as mentioned in the introduction, will be bothered by the idea that the problem is mental and may require extensive therapy. Single patients worry that psychological therapy requires a partner. Married patients or those with partners may be reluctant to include the partner or may believe that the partner will refuse to attend therapy.

In these types of cases, the therapist suggests that, before trying to resolve any such issues, patient and therapist explore the problem. It may be suggested that, rather than being deep seated "in the head," many sexual problems are based on issues such as lack of information or simple misinformation about normal changes in sexual functioning with aging. Rather than needing extensive therapy, many problems are handled through education, suggestions for things for the person/couple to try, suggestions to the doctor about medications or devices plus sexual techniques, and so forth.

Early in this discussion, the psychologist should acknowledge for the patient how difficult it is for a man to talk about having a sexual problem and how much trouble this causes in relationships (if the patient has one). The patient should be given feedback on how he has managed this challenging situation well, and that therapy will respect his rights; that is, this sort of therapy does not involve his giving up control or asking him to do things contrary to his values or beliefs. Patients may have concerns regarding issues such as whether therapy will involve sexual activities they object to, such as masturbation, genital caressing, oral sex, or the use of sexual aids such as vibrators. I always tell patients that there are standard elements to treatment programs, but they can always be modified to better fit individual needs and preferences.

If the patient has a wife or sexual partner, the clinician then does need to raise the issue of her possible participation. If the patient has not discussed possible treatment with her, this is the obvious first step for him. As a general rule, women tend to be a bit more willing to enter therapy. I

suggest to the man that I will be willing to meet with his partner alone, for one session, if she wishes because he had one such session, and she might feel more comfortable "having a chance to tell her view of things." Wives rarely take this option, but I have enough positive feedback from them about the offer that I continue to make it. Obviously, it is virtually essential to have involvement of the sexual partner of a man participating in therapy, and if his talking with her does not go well, the psychologist may suggest a session just to discuss the possibility of starting therapy, or even just a telephone conversation about this. Again, these procedures are not necessary in other practice settings.

Another difference that arises in primary care settings is that more single men—men without a sexual partner, that is—are seen. These men can be helped, as discussed in the sections on each of the dysfunctions.

TREATMENT PROCEDURES

Erectile Dysfunction

Men who are having problems with erection are perhaps the patients most commonly referred to the psychologist in primary care settings. Although it has been known for some time that both psychological and physiological factors are involved in the etiology of most men's erectile problems (LoPiccolo, 1999), one type of patient referred is still the "psychogenic" erectile failure case. That is, this man's examination by the referring physician has revealed no abnormalities in terms of penile blood flow/pressure, pelvic reflexes, hormones, and so forth. Another category of referral, in recent years, is for "Viagra failure." Sildenafil (Viagra) does work for about 70% of cases, and when it does not and there are no abnormal physical findings, a referral to the psychologist is made. Although these men may initially be distressed by referral for psychotherapy, they often respond well to brief, directive cognitive–behavioral therapy.

Many of the cases in which no physiological basis for the erectile failure was found are men in their 50s or 60s experiencing the normal aging changes in sexual response. That is, a young man does not require direct tactile stimulation of the penis to produce erection; kissing and caressing his wife or even thinking about sex or looking at sexy pictures can produce an erection. But as a man ages, direct physical stimulation of the penis becomes necessary to produce erection.

Many men never become aware of this change because their lovemaking has always included penile touching. However, some couples have not done penile touching, perhaps because the man would ejaculate rapidly if they did or the woman may have been a bit inhibited. As a younger man, the male partner did not need this touching to become erect, but as he aged, he developed erectile failure.

When the older man is not receiving direct penile stimulation, explaining this normal aging change and exploring whether his partner will be willing and able to provide such stimulation can lead to a dramatic therapeutic effect. If she has a strong negative reaction to this idea, further assessment is needed. Some women are simply a product of the culture or family in which they were raised and feel that such genital caressing is abnormal or unusual. Although these cases usually respond well to simple information and reassurance, other women may require much more. Some women have an aversion to touching male genitalia based on a history of childhood sexual abuse or adult rape, for example. This type of case is best treated by referral to a specialist in the complex issues involved in treatment of survivors of sexual victimization.

Similarly, the single most common cause of Viagra failure is exactly this same issue: lack of sexual stimulation, again in an older man. Although the Viagra package literature states that sexual stimulation plus Viagra is what produces erection, cases are seen in which the man has taken his pill and received very little, if any, direct penile caressing and did not obtain an erection. The man reports that he is very aroused and stimulated and wonders why the Viagra is not working. So, neither the prescribing physician nor the product literature has been clear about exactly what is meant by "stimulation"—caressing of the penis.

Of course, erection of the penis is not determined by anything as simple as caressing, especially once problems have begun to occur. The issue stressed by sex therapy is "performance anxiety and the spectator role" (Masters & Johnson, 1970). Standard sex therapy reduces performance anxiety by eliminating attempts at intercourse and having the woman stimulate the penis, but stopping if the man begins to get an erection. This makes it impossible for the man to fail, thus eliminating performance anxiety and allowing arousal to occur. Next, the couple learns to insert his flaccid penis in the vagina, so that again failure is impossible, and anxiety is reduced.

All of these procedures are useful in primary care settings and apply to the issue of Viagra failures. Many of these cases respond well to simple instructions involving Viagra plus penile caressing and not attempting intercourse, just enjoying the sensations, and exploration of the male caressing the female's genitals. That is, some performance anxiety is reduced if the man can provide pleasure—and perhaps even orgasm—for his partner without using his penis (LoPiccolo, 1999).

Medical Factors in Erectile Failure

The other category of men with erectile failure is those whose problem is caused by a medical condition or is a side effect of medication. A listing of medications that have been noted to interfere with erections is shown in Table 35.1. The data in Table 35.1 are drawn primarily from review articles by Broderick and Foreman (1999) and by Ashton, Young, and LoPiccolo (2001). It might be noted, however, that there are no really good data on just how commonly such side effects occur; widely different rates of occurrence appear in different research studies. Such differences suggest that there may be differences in individual susceptibility to such side effects. Although some such differences may relate to psychological/behavioral factors, it is also the case that simply switching the patient to another medication may result in improved functioning without any psychological intervention.

The medical conditions that influence erection are those that damage the innervation of the penis, the blood flow to the penis, or the hormonal system. Diabetes, which has effects on the small arteries and produces neurological demyeliniza-

Table 35.1 Sexual Effects of Medications

Medication	Erection	Orgasm	Desire	Medication	Erection	Orgasm	Desire
	May Cause Problems In				*May Cause Problems In*		
Antianxiety				Cardiovascular–antihypertensives and diuretics			
Alprazolam		x		Acetazolamide	x		
Chlordiazepoxide		x		Alphamethyldopa	x	x	x
Diazepam		x		Atenolol	x		
Lorazepam		x		Amiloride	x		x
Antidepressants				Bendroflumethiazide	x		
Amitriptyline	x	x	x	Chlorthalidone	x		x
Amoxapine	x	x	x	Clonidine	x		x
Citalopram	x	x	x	Dichlorphenamide	x		x
Clomipramine	x	x	x	Guanadrel	x	x	
Doxepin		x		Guanethidine	x	x	x
Fluoxetine	x	x		Methazolamide	x		x
Imipramine	x	x	x	Metoprolol	x		x
Iproniazid	x	x		Oxyprenolol	x		x
Isocarboxazid	x	x		Phenoxybenzamine	x	x	
Lithium	x		x	Phentolamine			x
Maprotiline	x	x	x	Pindolol	x	x	x
Mebanazine		x		Propranolol	x	x	x
Nortriptyline	x	x	x	Reserpine	x	x	x
Pargyline	x	x		Spironolactone	x		x
Paroxetine	x	x	x	Miscellaneous			
Phenelzine	x	x		Amphetamine	x	x	
Protriptyline	x	x	x	Anisotropine	x		
Sertraline	x	x	x	Baclofen	x	x	
Trimipramine	x	x	x	Babiturates	x		
Venlafaxine		x		Cimetidine	x		x
Antipsychotics				Clofibrate	x		x
Benperidol	x		x	Dicyclomine		x	
Butaperazine	x	x	x	Fenfluramine	x		x
Chlorpromazine	x	x	x	Hexocyclium	x		
Chlorprothixene	x	x	x	Homatropine	x		
Fluphenazine	x	x	x	Hydralazine	x		
Haloperidol	x		x	Mepenzolate	x		
Mesoridazine	x		x	Methantheline	x		
Perphenazine	x		x	Metoclopramide	x		x
Pimozide	x	x	x	Naproxen		x	
Sulperide	x		x	Oxybutinin	x		
Thiothixine	x		x	Phenytoin	x		x
Thioridiazine	x	x	x	Primadone	x		x
Trifluoperazine	x		x	Propantheline	x		
				Tridihexethyl	x		

Note. Medications are listed by generic name only; for trade names of psychotropic medications, see Table A.1.

tion, has been found to produce erectile dysfunction in up to 50% of patients (Lewis & Mills, 1999). Despite this high incidence, some physicians will not directly ask their diabetic patients about their sexual functioning; some physicians were even taught not to ask about sexual functioning for fear of offending the patient or of causing anxiety by questions suggesting to the patient that diabetes can result in sexual dysfunction. These attempts to protect the patient may lead to the patient being too embarrassed to report his erectile failure to the physician; the physician's silence on the subject of sexuality is misinterpreted as indicating that sex is *not* something to be discussed with the doctor. So, if erectile failure does occur, these patients may be referred to the psychologist for some other complaints, such as depression with unknown causation.

Similarly, the various forms of cardiovascular disease, including hypertension, ischemic heart disease, peripheral vascular disease, and hyperlipidemia, may damage the arteries and chambers of the penis, leading to insufficient flow to the penis, inability to trap blood in the penis, or excessive venous drainage. Patients with chronic renal failure are also at risk, with high rates of erectile dysfunction seen in dialysis patients.

Another category of erectile dysfunction is the male with surgical (or accidental) trauma. The most common of these cases, of course, involve men who have had the prostate removed. Some of these individuals with severe surgical damage will not be referred to the psychologist, but rather will have a penile prosthesis implanted, and they may be told of this possibility prior to surgery. These patients are told that "nerve-sparing" surgery may be not possible given the state of their cancer and their prostate. Sometimes, however, this is not known in advance, and the patient and his wife may discover during recovery that sexual functioning no longer occurs.

Some urologists have their patients (and their wives) participate in a presurgical education program that prepares them for the somewhat unpredictable outcome of prostatectomy, and this is an area in which the primary care psychologist can really be useful. In such a program, the issues of maximizing penile stimulation, reducing performance anxiety, and giving pleasure to the woman in ways that do not require the male to have an erection are all very helpful to the patient with surgical or traumatic impairment of erectile capability. Of course, consultation with the attending physician regarding options such as medication, vasoactive injections, or even prosthetic implants may also need to be explored in such cases.

The role of the sex hormones in erection problems has become much less clear as research on the subject has advanced (Randeva, Davison, & Bouloux, 1999). Moderately low levels of testosterone, within the normal range, do not result in erectile problems. True testicular failure, resulting from pituitary or hypothalamic disorders, will cause erectile failure, but these cases are typically treated by endocrinologists, and referral to psychologists is rare.

Premature Ejaculation

Premature ejaculation is a relatively common concern; some studies have found as many as 25% of couples troubled by the rapidity with which the man reaches ejaculation. The *Diagnostic and Statistical Manual of Mental Disorders*, fourth edition (*DSM-IV*; American Psychiatric Association, 1994) defined premature ejaculation as occurring with minimal sexual stimulation before, on, or shortly after penetration and before the person wishes it. The *DSM* notes that factors such as age, novelty of the situation or partner, and recent frequency of sexual activity must be taken into account before making the diagnosis.

This definition does not adequately guide the clinician in making a diagnosis of premature ejaculation. Most of the men who seek treatment for this problem are genuine cases of rapid ejaculation. That is, they cannot tolerate much preintromission stimulation of the penis and ejaculate very rapidly after penile entry. However, some patients who seek treatment are not really rapid ejaculators and are better served by information and reassurance than by therapy. For example, if a man and his partner engage in 30 minutes of foreplay during which they caress each other's genitals, both manually and orally, and then have "only a minute or two" of vigorous, unrestrained intercourse, should this be considered premature ejaculation? Probably not, although the issue of how the partner is going to reach orgasm may need to be addressed.

At the other extreme, men may be seen who are able to have a very long duration of intercourse, but only with such actions as wearing three condoms, biting his tongue so the pain interferes with his arousal, having intercourse in a position that puts stress on an old injury, or visualizing having sex with his mother-in-law (these are all real cases). In other cases, nothing so dramatic is done to prolong intercourse; it is more what is *not* done. In these cases, the couple engages in a very limited range of foreplay activities; the woman cannot do anything to the man; and he may have to avoid focusing his attention on her while he "gets her ready" so that intercourse can last for some time. Thus, the issue is not just how long intercourse lasts, but what the couple's sexual interaction is like and what their emotional experience is during foreplay and during intercourse.

In contrast to that of erectile failure, the etiology of premature ejaculation is much less complex: There are no known medical conditions or medications involved in the etiology of premature ejaculation (Ashton et al., 2001).

In specialty sex therapy clinics or mental health settings, couples seeking treatment for premature ejaculation are taught to use a technique of stimulation of the penis, briefly squeezing where the glans joins the shaft, pausing, and repeating this several times before the man is brought to orgasm. This procedure, developed by Masters and Johnson (1970), works extremely well. Over the course of a few sessions, the couple progresses to vaginal insertion, then to thrusting; in each of these steps, the number of squeeze/pauses is reduced to zero before moving on to the next step.

In primary care settings, certain issues may need to be addressed that may or may not occur in mental health settings. First, in primary care settings, more men will be seen who do not have a sexual partner. Although it might seem that having the man do the treatment on his own through manual masturbation would not generalize to the much more arousing situation involving a partner, this has not proven to be the case. In treating many such cases, it has been found that

rather good results do occur, as in the following case:

A man, prior to treatment, reached orgasm in 2 or 3 minutes of masturbation and in less than 30 seconds (at most) of intercourse. After solo treatment, he was able to masturbate for around 10 minutes on average, with no pauses, using good erotic stimuli (books and videos). When he began having sexual activity with a woman, intercourse did not last 10 minutes, but it did last "a couple of minutes" the first time and was soon lasting 4 to 5 minutes regularly thereafter.

It might be noted that there is considerable interest by medical practitioners in the treatment of premature ejaculation with pharmacological agents, most commonly the antidepressants in the selective serotonin reuptake inhibitor class (Ashton et al., 2001). This use came about because a side effect of these drugs makes orgasm delayed or even impossible for patients taking them. The primary care psychologist might take an active role in pointing out (to both the medical staff and patients) that behavioral retraining of the ejaculation response is easy, very effective, and, with the aid of video and written training materials, can be done with small amounts of professional time. In addition, there are some serious negative issues with the use of pharmacological treatment: The patient must take an expensive medication regularly; dosage is variable; there are other side effects; and a dose high enough to produce ejaculatory delay may reduce orgasmic intensity or sex drive and even prevent orgasm entirely (Nitenson & Cole, 1993; Segraves, 1993).

Another issue in some primary care cases concerns low frequency of sexual activity. For all men, time to reach climax is related to frequency; low frequency leads to rapidity. Many men seen for concern about premature ejaculation will disagree, saying something like, "No, I tried masturbating the day before, and it didn't help!" The issue is that it is frequency, not just recently having had an orgasm, that matters. This is relevant because men are seen who are having sex at a low frequency for various reasons, once per week or less, for example. For these men, the training program is very effective, but the reasons for the low frequency should also be explored.

Orgasmic Dysfunction

Male orgasmic dysfunction (previously called *inhibited orgasmic disorder*) is defined as persistent or recurring delay of or absence of orgasm despite normal sexual stimulation and excitement. The sexual activity must be of sufficient focus, intensity, quality, and duration that orgasm would be expected considering the patient's age.

In contrast to premature ejaculation, orgasmic dysfunction is virtually never lifelong; these men previously were able to reach orgasm without difficulty. Also, in contrast to premature ejaculation, medical conditions and medication side effects are extremely common as the causes of male orgasmic dysfunction (Segraves & Segraves, 1993).

Any neurological disorder that interferes with sensation or inhibits sympathetic arousal or injury to the spinal cord itself (in the area from the ninth thoracic to the fourth sacral spinal cord segments) has the potential to interfere with orgasm. The orgasm reflex is more easily impaired than is erection, so some men with neurological pathology will be able to attain erection, but will not be able to reach orgasm and will be very frustrated by this condition.

Medications that cause orgasmic dysfunction are shown in Table 35.1. Medications that inhibit sympathetic arousal, particularly the SSRIs, some antianxiety agents, and some antihypertensives are the most commonly seen pharmacological causes of orgasmic disorder. As noted, actual rates of occurrence of interference with sexual function (in this case, orgasm) cannot be definitively stated for any medication, but it is clear that the indicated medications do have this effect on some patients.

As is the case with erectile failure, performance anxiety and efforts to achieve orgasm can lead to even less arousal and less chance of orgasm happening. Thus, a psychological component is added to the physiological or pharmacological etiology of orgasmic dysfunction.

Treatment of orgasmic dysfunction involves teaching the patient to increase sexual stimulation while initially forbidding orgasm, thus eliminating performance anxiety. Next, procedures that may serve to trigger orgasm are taught, with an explanation to the patient that these trigger the orgasm reflex, but that his is not to focus on trying to attain orgasm. These triggers include caressing of the scrotum, testes, and perineal area. For men with neuropathy, an effective treatment is stimulation of the anal area; this can be with the finger or with a vibrator. Patients accept this technique very well if it is explained that this is not some exotic, "kinky," or "homosexual" sexual practice, but that there is simply a reflex involved. That is, just as tapping the knee causes the foot to move, anal stimulation causes an orgasm.

Hypoactive Sexual Desire

Men who are referred for loss of sexual interest or drive present an especially challenging problem for psychologists who work in primary care settings. Having a high level of sexual interest is a major element in the "normal male" gender role for men in our culture. Men who have low interest in sex have been found to be resistant to seeking psychotherapy for this problem and usually do so only when under pressure from their partner (Pridal & LoPiccolo, 2000). When these men are told that their problem does not have a medical cause and are referred to a psychologist, their reaction is often quite negative.

As noted in the section on medical factors, low testosterone does have a negative effect on sexual drive level. However, this condition is rather uncommon in men who suffer from low drive, as are any other medical factors. Table 35.1 does indicate the drive suppressing effects of some medications, but the low drive of patients referred to the psychologist usually has no organic or pharmacological basis.

A major issue that arises in working with these men concerns careful assessment to be sure that there actually is a "low desire" problem. That is, loss of sexual drive is to be expected in men with other sexual dysfunction problems. Men with erectile failure often develop low sexual desire because the failure and humiliation of sexual encounters with no erection is quite sufficient to suppress sexual interest. How can one feel an urge to have another frustrating and disappointing experience? These cases are best treated as erectile failure cases, but careful differential diagnosis is needed. That is, the reason some men have erectile failure is that they do not have any desire to actually have sex with their partners; they attempt sex under pressure to placate the partner and their lack of any sexual interest results in no arousal (erection) during the sexual encounter.

Arriving at an understanding of the cause-effect relationship between low drive and sexual dysfunction requires the clinician to assess carefully for a number of very sensitive issues. Does the patient's low drive reflect relationship difficulties, or is it even the case that the man does have a sex drive, but not for the partner who has brought him into therapy? Questions about sexual interests of any sort, masturbation fantasy material, and even interest in "deviant" or paraphiliac sex need to be raised.

Some men will admit to such things, which places the clinician in a somewhat difficult position. If the man wishes to change the underlying cause of his apparent low sexual drive, couple therapy is indicated. However, some men do not wish to do so. One man with low drive who came to treatment under pressure from his wife admitted that he actually *did* have a good level of sexual drive, but for the woman with whom he was having an affair, not his wife. When asked why he had sought treatment, the patient replied, "I've always wanted sex. I was afraid that if I didn't seem concerned about my not wanting to make love, my wife might get suspicious and figure out what was going on."

In cases with some "secret" that causes low drive for sexual activity with the partner, the therapist should present the patient with the reality that sexual interest in the complaining partner is not likely to be obtained until the underlying issues are addressed. This may involve subsequent referral to a marital specialist.

For most cases of low drive, another major issue is simply making it possible for the man to enter therapy. For men with low drive, helping them to see that they have suffered a loss and have something to gain from therapy is crucial. As long as the man sees coming to treatment as just for the benefit of his sexually frustrated partner, therapy is not likely to succeed.

Treatment of low sexual drive is complex and is discussed fully in works such as those of Pridal and LoPiccolo (2000) or Zilbergeld (1999). The basic approach involves trying to find what is blocking the man's awareness of his sexual drive and then using a combination of cognitive, couple systemic, and behavioral interventions to make it possible for the man to experience sexual desire.

SUMMARY

The psychologist who works in a primary medical care setting faces a challenging situation in terms of patient resistance to taking a "psychological" approach to sexuality problems. However, this work can be very rewarding. It is true that the training of many physicians did not include much focus on sexual issues; this, coupled with the time demands of the physician's clinical practice, may lead to cases when the psychologist can be very helpful to the patient.

The case presented at the beginning of this chapter can now be examined:

A man was referred for erectile failure and low sex drive after Viagra failed to help his problem. History revealed that he is an insulin-dependent diabetic, with juvenile onset. His erection problems had been occurring for about 2 years and were very upsetting to him and his wife, who accompanied him on referral.

On assessment, the man stated that he had only tried Viagra three times, and that he was still "losing my erection." Questioning revealed that he was able to get an erection during foreplay, and that intercourse lasted "some time" before he lost the erection. When asked how long he was sustaining erection and intercourse, the wife replied, "I don't know for the first time, but I looked at the clock the other two times, and it was about 3 hours. That's part of why we are here; the darn Viagra didn't help him, and now a I have a vaginal infection!"

They had actually been referred by her gynecologist after he learned what had caused her vaginal irritations that had become infected. When I asked the man how long he had been able to keep his erection and sustain intercourse before beginning Viagra, both he and his wife agreed that the duration of intercourse had become about 30 to 45 minutes in the last few years. I then asked if he was actually reaching an orgasm and learned that he was not.

Although he was thinking of his problem as one of erectile failure, he actually was suffering from orgasmic dysfunction. He told me that his prescribing physician had not asked about whether he reached orgasm or even suggested that it was normal to lose one's erection after many minutes of intercourse if orgasm does not occur. He also had not been informed that orgasmic dysfunction was often seen in diabetic men.

This couple, in consultation with the physician, did not resume using Viagra and began the treatment program for orgasmic dysfunction. With scrotal and perianal stimulation, he was able to reach orgasm, and follow-up indicated that they were both now quite pleased with their sexual relationship.

This case illustrates that careful assessment is the starting point for all successful treatment. Although interviewing is best, a simple questionnaire that asks about desire, arousal, and orgasm can be quite useful. One such instrument is a 29-question (multiple-choice format) form that can be filled out quickly by patients (Nowinski & LoPiccolo, 1979).

The failure of the prescribing physician to obtain an adequate assessment of the patient's problem also points to the need for health and mental health professionals to obtain specialty training in sexuality. Workshops at the annual conventions of such organizations as the Society for Sex Therapy and Research (Washington, DC) present good continuing education opportunities. A good single volume on current treatment of sexual problems is the book edited by Leiblum and Rosen (2000).

Even with some reading and continuing education, the general practice psychologist may wish to refer some patients to a specialist. Candidates for referral include men with complicated relationship problems that are part of the etiology

of their problems. Other cases that may need specialist treatment include those involving a history of child sexual abuse, current paraphiliac arousal, or other more complicated sexual issues. The Society for Sex Therapy and Research has a category of "clinical member," which requires specialty training and experience; this provides a source of professionals to whom referrals can be made with an expectation of competence on the part of the practitioner.

References

American Psychiatric Association. (1994). *Diagnostic and statistical manual of mental disorders* (4th ed.). Washington, DC: Author.

Ashton, A. K., Young, C. M., & LoPiccolo, J. (2001). Premature ejaculation and male orgasmic disorder. In G. O. Gabbard (Ed.), *Treatments of psychiatric disorders* (Vol. 2, pp. 1911–1934). Washington, DC: American Psychiatric Publishing.

Broderick, G. A., & Foreman, M. M. (1999). Iatrogenic erectile dysfunction: Pharmacologic and surgical therapies that alter male sexual behavior and erectile performance. In C. Carson, R. Kirby, & Goldstein, I. (Eds.), *Textbook of erectile dysfunction* (pp. 149–170). Oxford, U.K.: Isis Medical Media.

Leiblum, S. R., & Rosen, R. C. (Eds.). (2000). *Principles and practice of sex therapy* (3rd ed.) New York: Guilford Press.

Lewis, R. W., & Mills, T. M. (1999). Risk factors for impotence. In C. Carson, R. Kirby, & I. Goldstein (Eds.), *Textbook of erectile dysfunction* (pp. 141–148). Oxford, U.K.: Isis Medical Media.

LoPiccolo, J. (1999). Psychological assessment of erectile dysfunction. In C. Carson, R. Kirby, & I. Goldstein (Eds.), *Textbook of erectile dysfunction* (pp. 183–194). Oxford, U.K.: Isis Medical Media.

Masters, W., & Johnson, V. (1970). *Human sexual inadequacy.* Boston: Little, Brown.

Nitenson, N. C., & Cole, J. O. (1993). Psychotropic induced sexual dysfunction. In D. L. Dunner (Ed.), *Current psychiatric therapy* (pp. 353–359). Philadelphia: Saunders.

Nowinski, J., & LoPiccolo, J. (1979). Assessing sexual behavior in couples. *Journal of Sex and Marital Therapy, 5,* 225–243.

Pridal, C. G. (2001). Male gender role issues in the treatment of sexual dysfunction. In G. R.

Brooks & G. E. Good (Eds.), *The new handbook of psychotherapy and counseling with men* (pp. 309–334). San Francisco: Jossey-Bass.

Pridal, C. G., & LoPiccolo, J. (2000). Multi-element treatment of desire disorders: Integration of cognitive, behavioral, and systemic therapy. In S. R. Leiblum & R. C. Rosen (Eds.), *Principles and practice of sex therapy* (pp. 57–84). New York: Guilford Press.

Randeva, H. S., Davison, R. M., & Bouloux, M. G. (1999). Endocrinology. In C. Carson, R. Kirby, & I. Goldstein (Eds.), *Textbook of erectile dysfunction*. Oxford, U.K.: Isis Medical Media.

Segraves, R. T. (1993). Affective disorders, antidepressants and sexual dysfunction. *Sexual and Marital Therapy, 8,* 213–215.

Segraves, R. T., & Segraves, K. B. (1993). Medical aspects of orgasm disorders. In W. O'Donohue & J. Geer (Eds.), *Handbook of sexual dysfunctions* (pp. 225–252). Boston: Allyn and Bacon.

Zilbergeld, B. (1999). *The new male sexuality* (rev. ed.). New York: Bantam Books.

36

Sexual Disorders Affecting Women

Amy Heard-Davison

Julia R. Heiman

Brittany Briggs

Although estimates vary regarding the prevalence of sexual dysfunction among women (Simons & Carey, 2001), sexual problems are certainly not rare and often are associated with decreased well-being and relationship satisfaction (Laumann, Paik, & Rosen, 1999). A variety of interventions that relieve sexual symptoms and improve relationship functioning are available (e.g., Heiman, 2002; Rosen & Leiblum, 1995), although specialty training in treating sexual dysfunction is not available in many clinical psychology programs.

Sexual disorders in women typically are the result of multiple factors, which can make accurate assessment and effective treatment difficult. Our goal in this chapter is to provide psychologists and other clinicians in primary care settings with the basic skills and resources for assessment and treatment of sexual problems in women. To this end, we briefly describe the four main categories of female sexual dysfunction (FSD; i.e., desire disorders, arousal disorders, orgasm disorders, and sexual pain disorders) and their potential etiological factors, outline guidelines for assessment and methods of treatment for each dysfunction, and highlight issues specific to primary care settings.

Because female sexual functioning is multifactorial, attempts to identify a medication that would be as effective for women as sildenafil (Viagra) has been for men have met with limited success (e.g., Basson, McInnes, Smith, Hodgson, & Koppiker, 2002; Caruso, Intelisano, Lupo, & Angello, 2001; Modelska & Cummings, 2003). To date, no medication has been approved by the Food and Drug Administration (FDA) for the treatment of any of the FSDs, although we expect this to change within the next 5 years.

The search for effective medications has stimulated increased interest in basic research on the biological mechanisms involved in female sexual function. However, there is concern that assessment and treatment of female sexual response will become "medicalized," and that a quest for medications to "cure" female sexual problems will miss important variables (e.g., Bancroft, Loftus, & Long, 2003; Moynihan, 2003; Tiefer, 2002). Current conceptualizations indicate that a more inclusive model of female sexuality that encompasses organic, interpersonal, and psychological factors is more likely to provide accurate information that will guide successful treatments (e.g., Bancroft, 2002; Heiman, 2000; Rosen & Leiblum, 1995).

THE FEMALE SEXUAL DYSFUNCTIONS: DEFINITION

The FSDs are divided into four major categories: desire, arousal, orgasm, and pain. Three of these correspond with the sexual response cycle originally proposed by Masters and Johnson (1966) and revised by Kaplan (1974) to a triphasic model. The fourth category, pain, is not related to normal sexual functioning. Disturbances in any of these areas may constitute a dysfunction and often are caused by some physiological and/or psychological factors or a combination of both according the text revision of the *Diagnostic and Statistical Manual of Mental Disorders*, fourth edition (*DSM-IV-TR*; American Psychiatric Association [APA], 2000).

According to the *DSM-IV-TR*, any sexual problem must be persistent or recurrent in nature and cause marked distress or interpersonal difficulty to be considered diagnostically significant. In addition, the *DSM-IV-TR* outlines specifiers for the sexual dysfunctions that provide additional information relevant to etiology and treatment. These specifiers indicate (a) onset, (b) context, and (c) etiology. *Onset* may be *lifelong* (present since the beginning of sexual activity) or *acquired* (noted after a period of undisturbed sexual functioning). *Context* indicates whether the problem is *generalized* (occurs in every situation regardless of the type of stimulation or partner) or *situational* (happens only with certain partners, activities, or settings).

Etiology is specified (if possible) as caused by psychological factors, as caused by a general medical condition, or as substance induced. Axis I disorders must be ruled out as the primary cause for the dysfunction (e.g., major depressive disorder can present as low sexual desire, anxiety disorder symptoms can interfere with adequate sexual arousal). Another classification system, the International Consensus Panel (ICP) definitions (Basson et al., 2000), allows ICP-identified disorders

to be classified as "mixed," or related to both psychological and biological factors.

Given the current state of the somewhat-limited conceptualization and database of female sexual functioning, it is no surprise that there is some disagreement as to how exactly sexual disorders in women should be defined. The *DSM-IV-TR* (APA, 2000) and *International Classification of Diseases*, 10th revision (*ICD-10*; World Health Organization, 1992) contain standards used for diagnosis of the FSDs. In 2000, an International Consensus Development Conference on Female Sexual Dysfunction was convened to slightly expand definitions and classifications for the sexual dysfunctions to include more recent scientific findings (Basson et al., 2000), and further discussions were under way in 2003. This chapter presents the diagnostic criteria used in the *DSM-IV-TR* along with the expanded definitions found in the ICP definitions.

Sexual Desire Disorders

Hypoactive Sexual Desire Disorder

Hypoactive sexual desire disorder (HSDD) is characterized by a decrease in or absence of sexual thoughts and fantasies and a decreased desire to engage in sexual activity, taking into account factors that may affect sexual functioning, such as age (APA, 2000). The ICP expands the definition to include a lack of receptivity to sexual advances by a partner as indicating low desire (Basson et al., 2000). Prevalence data indicate that this is the most common sexual problem reported by women, both in community and medical settings, with estimates ranging from 5% to 46%, depending on the population sampled (the highest rates were found in postmenopausal women; Simons & Carey, 2001).

Sexual Aversion Disorder

Aversion to and avoidance of genital contact with a sexual partner is characterized as *phobic aversion* and is the key symptom of this rather uncommon problem (APA, 2000; Basson et al., 2000).

Female Sexual Arousal Disorder

Physiological sexual arousal in women is characterized by vaginal lubrication, swelling of the genitals, and increased vasocongestion in the pelvis. Difficulties achieving or maintaining these responses until the completion of sexual activity are characteristic symptoms of female sexual arousal disorder (FSAD) (APA, 2000). In addition to genital responses, the ICP includes lack of subjective excitement or "other somatic responses" in its criteria (Basson et al., 2000). Limited data are available for estimates of FSAD prevalence, in part because these symptoms rarely present in isolation, but a large community sample found 21% of women reported trouble with lubrication (Laumann et al., 1999).

Female Orgasmic Disorder

Both *DSM-IV-TR* and ICP definitions list two criteria for orgasmic disorder in women: (a) delayed or absent orgasm following a normal excitement phase and (b) difficulty despite sufficient sexual stimulation (APA, 2000; Basson et al., 2000). Diagnosing this disorder requires that the clinician assess the patient's sexual history, her knowledge of her own sexual functioning, her level of comfort in transferring this knowledge to her partner, and her partner's responsiveness to her sexual wishes. Prevalence data for problems with orgasm vary widely, although it is estimated that they are more common in primary care settings (5% lifetime to 42% current) than in the general population (Simons & Carey, 2001).

Sexual Pain Disorders

Dyspareunia

In the *DSM-IV-TR*, dyspareunia includes genital pain before, during, or after intercourse (APA, 2000). The ICP definition extends the *DSM-IV-TR* definition to include another category, noncoital sexual pain disorder, which covers noncoital genital pain (Basson et al., 2000). Again, prevalence estimates vary by study depending on the criteria used and range from 3% to 46% in medical settings. The higher estimates include pain resulting from lack of lubrication and vaginismus (Simons & Carey, 2001).

Vaginismus

Vaginismus is characterized by involuntary spasms of the outer third of the vagina that interfere with coitus. The ICP definition includes spasm produced by "vaginal penetration" by any object, such as a speculum or finger. Most of the prevalence data for vaginismus come from medical patients, with one study finding that it was the most common dysfunction reported by women (N = 104) in a primary care setting (Read, King, & Watson, 1997).

ETIOLOGY

As noted in the introduction, the etiology of sexual dysfunction in women is multifactorial and poorly defined. Table 36.1 lists some of the factors associated with sexual problems in women. These variables are based primarily on knowledge of physiology, research findings in men, or correlational studies.

EPIDEMIOLOGY

The epidemiological measurement of sexual functioning is dependent on the wording of questions, the definition of dysfunction, and the population of interest. Prevalence rates of sexual problems in community samples range from 25% to 63% (Heiman, 2002). In the National Health and Social Life Survey, which used a random sample of 1,749 women in the United States aged 18 to 59 years, 43% of women with partners reported some sort of sexual problems in the past year (Laumann et al., 1999; Laumann, Gagnon, Michael, & Michaels, 1994). Of these, 32% reported lack of interest, 26% inability to achieve orgasm, 16% dyspareunia, 23% sex was not pleasurable, 12% anxiety about performance, and 21% trouble lubricating.

Data from several studies have indicated that desire problems are the most prevalent disorder in women (e.g., Ernst, Foldenyi, & Angst, 1993; Lindal & Stefansson, 1993; Ventegodt, 1998). However, it is important to note that the presence of sexual symptoms in 43% of women does not necessarily indicate that all of these women met criteria for clinical diagnosis (Laumann et al., 1999). Interestingly, a community-based study of heterosexual women found that problems in the areas of desire, arousal, and orgasm were not pre-

Table 36.1 Factors That May Contribute to Sexual Dysfunction

	Biological Factors	Psychosocial Factors	Medications
HSDD	Menopause (low androgens)[a,b] Endocrine disorders[e] Lactation (high prolactin)[b,e] Hysterectomy[b,d] Radiation[i] General health[d] Depression[d,h] Fatigue[i]	Increasing age[c,d] Decreased well-being[c,g] Relationship problems[e,h] Partners dysfunction[g] History of sexual force[c] Gender identity issues[d] Sexual identity issues[d] Negative body image[d]	Antidepressants (+SSRIs)[b,e,f] Neuroleptics[e] Atypical antipsychotics[d,e] Chemotherapy[i] Sedative-hypnotics[i] Narcotics[i] Beta blockers[i] Calcium blockers[i] Anti-hypertensives[i] Oral contraceptives[b]
FSAD	Menopause[a,e,h] Diabetes[e,j] Multiple sclerosis[k] Hypertension[e] Obesity[e] Hysterectomy[d] Depression[e,i]	Increasing age[d] Alcohol and drug abuse[e] Smoking[e] Relationship problems[e,h] Anxiety[h,l] Childhood sexual abuse[c] History of sexual force[c]	SSRIs[e,f] Anticholinergics[e] Alcohol[e] Heroin[b] Methadone[b]
FOD	Diabetes[e] Neuropathy[e] Multiple sclerosis[k] Depression[e,h]	Younger age[c] Relationship problems[e,h]	SSRIs[e,f] β-Blockers[e] Cocaine (chronic use)[b] Amphetamines[b]
Sexual pain	Poor health[c] Menopause[g] Vulvar vestibulitis[m] Vulvar or vaginal atrophy[m] Fibroids[m] Ovarian cyst[m] Depressive symptoms[m]	Negative sexual attitudes[m] Relationship problems[m] Anxiety[m]	No medications have been identified as directly related to genital pain

Note. The current state of knowledge and the frequent overlap of factors do not allow accurate estimates of the prevalence for individual causes.
[a]Sarrel (2000). [b]Meston and Frolich (2000). [c]Laumann, Paik, and Rosen (1999). [d]Heiman and Meston (1997). [e]Stahl (2001b). [f]Rosen, Lane, and Menza (1999). [g]Dennerstein, Lehert, Burger, and Dudley (1999). [h]Dunn, Croft, and Hackett (1999). [i]Maurice (1999). [j]Spector, Leiblum, Carey, and Rosen (1993). [k]Mattson, Petrie, Srivastava, and McDermott (1995). [l]Barlow (1986). [m]Meana, Binik, Khalife, and Cohen (1997a).

dictive of self-reported distress in the sexual relationship or in regard to their own sexuality (Bancroft et al., 2003).

The rates of sexual dysfunction in primary care settings are higher than those found in community samples (Simons & Carey, 2001). In a primary care setting in Britain, 87% of women ($N = 98$) reported they were usually or always satisfied with their sexual relationship, but 68% reported general sexual difficulties, and 42% reported a specific sexual dysfunction (Read et al., 1997). In the Read et al. sample, vaginismus and anorgasmia were the most common difficulties noted (30% and 23%, respectively). In another study of women presenting to a gynecology clinic, difficulty with occasional vaginal tightness (28%), orgasm (58%), genital pain (37%), and sexual anxiety/inhibition (49%) were reported (Rosen, Taylor, Leiblum, & Bachmann, 1993). Comorbidity rates among the FSDs also were consistent with previous findings, with 67% of women seen in primary care reporting disturbances in more than one area. In a study of 475 women with HSDD who participated in a pharmaceutical trial, Segraves and Segraves (1991) found that 41% had at least one other sexual disorder, and 18% had disorders in all three categories (i.e., desire, arousal, and orgasm).

Studies attempting to identify medical and psychiatric conditions associated with sexual dysfunctions have found a high degree of comorbidity with anxiety, depressive symptoms, marital problems, and other sexual disorders (e.g., Donahey & Carroll, 1993; Dunn, Croft, & Hackett, 1999; Meana, Binik, Khalife, & Cohen, 1997a). Both the high rate of sexual dysfunctions associated with the selective serotonin reuptake inhibitors (Rosen, Lane, & Menza, 1999) and symptoms of untreated major depression are associated with desire, arousal, and orgasm problems (Kennedy, Dickens, Eisfeld, & Bagby, 1999). Emotional problems and fair-to-poor physical health are also both associated with a significant increase in the risk for these problems (Laumann et al., 1999).

COURSE OF FEMALE SEXUAL DYSFUNCTIONS

Because of the diversity of sexual disorders and the multiple and interacting etiological factors, there is no typical course for the FSDs. Because these disorders often begin long before (sometimes years before) medical and/or psychological treatment is sought, sexual symptoms frequently follow a "relapsing-and-remitting" course in which women exhibit periods of low functioning alternating with relatively normal, satisfactory functioning. Three factors affect the course of sexual dysfunctions: (a) history of the disorder (e.g., primary [lifelong] disorders are typically more treatment refractory); (b) consequences in the relationship (e.g., relationships that have experienced a significant decline in their level of emotional intimacy will likely have greater difficulty improving the level of sexual intimacy); and (c) strategies for coping (e.g., couples with a broader range of adaptive coping skills have an advantage).

ASSESSMENT: TAKING A SEXUAL HISTORY

Guidelines for Brief Assessment of Sexual Functioning

To determine the sexually relevant variables, their relationship to one another, and their influ-ence on the sexual dysfunction, it is important that the clinician obtain a thorough and specific sexual history (cf. Heiman & Meston, 1997; Williams, 1995). Assessment in the primary care setting may be more focused than a traditional sexual history because patients and physicians may expect treatment or referral recommendations after a single evaluation session. Fully defining the problem expediently is of special importance. To this end, it is helpful to have access to information about the patient's medical health and the reason for the referral.

The following steps outline a brief but thorough assessment that takes between 30 and 60 minutes. Assessment should begin with a description of past and current sexual symptoms. This should indicate to the clinician which area(s) of sexual functioning should be most fully explored and be augmented by a brief description of functioning in the other areas. Next, any medical issues that could be related to the problem should be reviewed, including use of medications, alcohol, or other substances. Finally, the impact on the patient's emotional and relationship health and strategies for coping should be determined. Because physical and sexual abuse are associated with problems in sexual, emotional, and physical health, all evaluations should determine the presence and extent of any abuse. Questions regarding the key elements in a sexual history are presented in Table 36.2.

Special Issues in Sexual History Taking

Because of the sensitivity of sexual feelings and behavior, it is especially important that patients and clinicians feel comfortable discussing this information (Wincze & Carey, 2001). In a primary care setting, clinicians may increase their level of comfort by reminding themselves that the information they are discussing is relevant, and that they possess the interest and skills to assess sexual functioning accurately and provide appropriate treatment or referrals. Assessing the patient's level of comfort with discussing her sexuality and (if necessary) briefly explaining the reason for the assessment, including how the information will be used and who will have access to it, may be helpful. Sensitivity to cultural differences in discussing sexuality is also important. It may begin

Table 36.2 Categories and Areas of Interest for Inclusion in a Sexual History

Category	Questions/Areas of Interest
Screening for sexual problems	Are you currently sexually active? When was the last time you had sex? When was the last time you masturbated? Are you satisfied with your response/frequency? Have you noticed any changes or problems in your sexual response? Is there any aspect of your sexuality that you would like to change (and receive treatment for)?
Perception of the problem	Why are you coming in for treatment? Duration (lifelong/acquired) and specificity (global/situational) of problem. How has this affected your relationship? What has your partner said about the problem? (Ask if partner is not present to assess their perception of the problem)
Developmental events	Menstruation and relationship to sexual response. Health of pregnancies, deliveries, breastfeeding, and impact on sexuality. Menopause and its affect on sexual functioning.
Prior sexual experiences	Any important childhood events related to sexuality. How was sex handled/discussed in your family? First sexual experience and reactions to it. Number of sexual partners. Satisfaction with sexual functioning. Masturbation frequency? When did you start?
Unwanted sexual experiences (Research indicates that although some women experience these as traumatic and show long-term consequences, others report neutral feelings and no subsequent effects on functioning.)	History of unwanted or coercive sexual experiences? (How many and with whom?) Age of patient and age of partner at the time. Have you ever spoken with anyone about those experiences? Do you believe that it/they is/are affecting your current relationships or sexual functioning? Does your partner know about that experience?
General sexual health	Are your partners men, women, or both? Are you in a monogamous sexual relationship, or do you have multiple partners? Are you using birth control? What type? Do you currently have or have you had any STDs? Are you using condoms to prevent disease?
Sexual symptoms	When did your sexual problems begin? What was going on in your life at that time? Are you distressed by the sexual problem? What have you done to try to manage this problem? (Prior treatment, change in activity/stimulation, reading/education) How has this affected your relationship? If problems in more than one category: Which symptom did you notice first? Which problem is most troublesome to you?
Desire	Do you have sexual thoughts? How much interest do you have in sex (with self/partner/others)? Who typically initiates sexual activity? How do you respond when your partner initiates?

Table 36.2 Continued

Category	Questions/Areas of Interest
Arousal	Have you noticed a change in your level of arousal? Do you have problems with lubrication or genital swelling? Does the problem occur all the time? Is there any situation in which it is better?
Orgasm	Are you orgasmic? Are you having any difficulties having an orgasm? What percentage of the time did you previously/do you now achieve orgasm?
Pain	Where is your pain located? When does it occur (during or after intercourse, with other types of touch/stimulation)? How would you describe the pain (burning, stabbing, aching)? What percentage of the time do you have sex without pain?
Relationship functioning	Describe your current relationship. How important is sex for you in your relationship? Strategies for managing conflict/problems. How are you coping with your sexual problem? How is your partner's sexual functioning?

Note. STD, sexually transmitted disease.

by asking patients about their level of comfort with answering questions alone versus in the presence of their partner.

The clinician may use a subset of the questions listed in Table 36.2 to ask about specific symptoms and how the patient has been affected. In addition, several self-report measures designed to assess FSD are available (cf. Leiblum & Rosen, 2000; Wincze & Carey, 2001). Because recognizing all of the contributing variables may be difficult if the woman alone is interviewed, including the partner can be very useful (factual as well as interactional information can be obtained).

Screening for Sexual Problems

Not all women with sexual dysfunction will present with sexual complaints. Thus, questions that can be used as an initial screen to determine the presence of sexual symptoms may be necessary and are presented at the beginning of Table 36.2. All individuals who express dissatisfaction or distress in their couple relationship should be asked about their sexual relationship and screened for dysfunction.

TREATMENT: CONDUCTING SEX THERAPY

Although it might be expected that sexual disorders are treated using multimodal interventions (e.g., a combination of medical and/or psychological treatments), there are few outcome studies for FSD. Using the criteria established by the 1995 American Psychological Association Task Force on the Promotion and Dissemination of Psychological Procedures, Heiman (2002) concluded that only one treatment (directed masturbation for primary orgasmic disorder) has been demonstrated to have well-established efficacy, and that one treatment (directed masturbation for secondary orgasmic disorder) is probably efficacious. Although treatment for primary anorgasmia has an 80% to 90% success rate for reaching orgasm during masturbation, it is less successful for achieving orgasm via intercourse or partner stimulation

(Rosen & Leiblum, 1995). Despite promising findings from studies of treatments for genital pain, there remains a need for controlled comparison studies to establish empirically validated medical and psychological treatments for FSD (Heiman, 2002; Rosen & Leiblum, 1995).

Who Treats Female Sexual Dysfunction?

Women with sexual dysfunction may first consult their primary care physician or gynecologist, who may provide reassurance, education, or medical intervention, depending on the nature and severity of the problem and/or their physician's own comfort and knowledge level. However, many patients report that their physicians do not appear to be comfortable discussing this topic and elicit limited information regarding their problems (Maurice, 1999). Psychologists working with women or couples may provide basic interventions and information in accordance with their training and experience. Women also may go to clinicians who specialize in sexual and relationship problems.

Problems that may be managed successfully by medical and/or mental health professionals with limited training in sex therapy include short-term loss of desire precipitated by a specific event, primary anorgasmia in otherwise healthy women, arousal problems because of insufficient stimulation or lack of lubrication, primary vaginismus, or conditions secondary to a medical problem. These sexual dysfunctions often respond to education, bibliotherapy, support, or medication. It may be best to consult with or refer to a sex therapist when the symptoms include long-term loss of sexual desire; unexplained problems with sexual pain, arousal, or orgasm; treatment-resistant problems; or severe relationship problems with impaired sexual functioning.

At what point should the woman be referred to a sex therapist or specialist? The first is when the problem exceeds the competence of the primary care psychologist; the second is when the clinician is uncomfortable or uninterested in discussing and potentially prescribing a range of sexual behaviors. It is also important to note that women who have a primary (lifelong) disorder, a history of physical or sexual abuse, or problems in multiple areas of sexual functioning are likely to benefit from more specialized assessment and treatment. Should nonsexual psychiatric problems be treated first? For patients with sexual problems that coexist with anxiety, depression, or substance abuse, acute psychiatric symptoms should be treated adequately before sexual problems can be addressed (Wincze & Carey, 2001).

General Guidelines

Treatments for FSD offered by mental health professionals in a primary care setting are typically brief and problem focused because of system resources and patient expectations. Wincze and Carey (2001) outlined a three-stage model for conducting intensive but brief sex therapy that is focused and flexible enough to address the variety of issues that may present in medical environments. The components are (a) information gathering and collaborative goal setting (between the patient and both mental and medical health providers), (b) working toward goals using specific treatment strategies (sex therapy techniques and/or individual or couple psychotherapy), and (c) reviewing treatment gains to facilitate generalization and promote relapse prevention.

One potential advantage for clinicians working in the primary care setting is the ease of collaborating with the patient's physician. This can decrease the time required to obtain a full assessment by having quick access to laboratory data and to medical findings, which may in turn facilitate medication treatment, if indicated. In the case of a sexual dysfunction caused by a medical condition, it also may provide an opportunity for the psychologist to educate the physician about ways to talk with patients and address their concerns.

When providing sex therapy, as in taking the sexual history, psychologists should take extra steps to put patients at ease and not respond in ways that may make them feel uncomfortable or "abnormal." One common mistake is prescribing an exercise (e.g., masturbation training or use of erotica) before assessing patient attitudes toward the activity. Prior to any intervention, it is important to explore the patients' beliefs, emotional states, and any past or current resistance to interventions. Noncompliance with exercises should be discussed to clarify if it is related to negative feelings or a lack of motivation. Another clinician mistake is setting up unrealistic performance expectations or goals for the patient or the partner, such as unattainable frequency of sexual activities. Because many sexual problems have performance anxiety as a maintaining factor, patients should be asked to review their perception of the goals for each exercise to be careful about re-creating this pattern.

For HSDD, couple treatment may be superior to individual treatment (Trudel et al., 2001). However, for the other dysfunctions, we do not have clear empirical guidelines for when to treat the individual versus the couple. Often, the decision is made in part based on the willingness of the woman and her partner to participate in therapy. Primary anorgasmia is typically treated individually, at least initially. With sexual pain, individual treatment can be augmented by intermittent sessions with the partner to discuss the impact on their relationship and encourage the return to sexual activity after the pain has been addressed and relaxation strategies have been mastered.

When working with couples, it is important to avoid blaming one partner or siding with either partner. Clinicians should help partners understand that they are not the sole source of relationship problems and to address their feelings of guilt, anger, and resentment. In addition, stressing that both are the source of the solution can be a useful shift in perspective. Wincze and Carey (2001) also suggested regularly reviewing the issues that each partner needs to work on individually. This can help distinguish individual issues from relationship issues and to emphasize that both partners are equally involved in the change process and treatment outcome.

Interventions

A series of specific techniques have been developed for use in treating sexual problems. Based on the predisposing, precipitating, and maintaining factors identified during assessment, these techniques consist of psychological and sexual therapies that can be combined with hormonal supplementation if indicated. Following is a partial list and brief description of some that are used commonly. More in-depth information about these techniques and their implementation can be found in the work of Leiblum and Rosen (2000) and Wincze and Carey (2001).

Education

Most interventions involve at least some form of sexual education. Topics aim to normalize sexual behavior and may include the following: providing information about basic sexual anatomy; exploring sexual myths, attitudes, and beliefs; providing normative data; and suggesting helpful resources.

Sensate Focus Exercises

These couple exercises were originally developed by Masters and Johnson (1970) and still form the basis for treatment of many sexual difficulties. The primary goals of sensate focus are to reduce performance demands, increase focus on sensual and/or sexual sensations, and facilitate nonverbal sexual communication. Because worrying about sexual performance can interfere with sexual response, clinicians should take special precautions to stress the importance of the non-goal-oriented sensual encounter by being "in the moment," fully attending to either giving or receiving stimulation, and not striving to reach orgasm. The exercises themselves should be tailored to the problem addressed; generally, they consist of explicit instructions to patients describing the four basic steps: nongenital pleasuring, genital pleasuring, containment without thrusting when vaginal intercourse is an issue, and thrusting/intercourse. Throughout all steps, sexual arousal and orgasm are not the goals, and intercourse is usually prohibited to ensure that couples remain focused on the sensual experience.

Cognitive Restructuring

Addressing faulty assumptions and beliefs may improve sexual functioning. In addition, negative emotions such as anxiety during the sexual encounter have been associated with sexual dysfunction (e.g., Barlow, 1986) and appear to be mediated by perceptual and attentional processes (Rosen & Leiblum, 1995). Intrusive thoughts or images that occur during sexual activity should be identified, along with ways to reduce these thoughts and increase the focus on erotic sensations or images. When working with the couple, it is important to address both partners' negative emotions and cognitive interference.

Masturbation Training

Masturbation training is outlined in a book written for women with anorgasmia (Heiman & Lo-Piccolo, 1988). Women are taken through a series of exercises designed to increase their awareness of their physical and/or psychological responses and determine what they find pleasurable. The use of vibrators is explained and often recommended.

Sexual Fantasy Training/Use of Erotica

Sexual fantasy training/use of erotica exercises are designed to increase women's awareness about their potential for sexual fantasies, integrate them into their sexual lives to increase arousal, and as a result, broaden their exposure to sexual stimuli and what they find erotic.

Communication Training

Couples are taught basic strategies for communicating to resolve conflict, acquire constructive disclosure and listening skills, foster sexual communication, and facilitate sexual interactions with the goal of building sexual and emotional intimacy.

Medications

As noted in the introduction, there are currently no FDA-approved medications for treating FSD. However, the current understanding of the hormonal and physiological processes involved in female sexual functioning has led to the investigation of hormonal, pharmaceutical, and herbal agents believed to be effective in treating various aspects of the female sexual response (cf. Bartlik & Goldberg, 2000; Heiman, 2002). Current guidelines for hormonal therapy to treat sexual dysfunction rely more on clinical response than a prescribed regimen. When making referrals for hormone replacement therapy as a treatment for FSD, it is important to discuss with each physician his or her level of comfort and experience in this area.

Estrogen

Estrogen is a primary female hormone involved in genital vasocongestion, lubrication, and sexual sensitivity (e.g., Meston & Frolich, 2000; Stahl, 2001a). Although few data from randomized trials are available, estrogen replacement is often clinically used to treat dyspareunia and vaginal dryness in postmenopausal women (Meston & Frolich, 2000; Rosen & Leiblum, 1995). However, patients and practitioners should carefully weigh the risks and benefits of long-term use in light of data from a recent clinical trial that showed negative health consequences associated with extended use of hormone replacement therapy (Writing Group, 2002).

Testosterone

The hormone testosterone is responsible for sexual desire and interest in both men and women (Davis, 1998a; Meston & Frolich, 2000). There is mounting evidence that testosterone therapy for women with low levels of bioavailable or "free" testosterone has a positive effect on sexual libido, activity, satisfaction, pleasure, and orgasm (Davis, 1998b, 1999; Shifren et al., 2000). Although testosterone is not currently approved by the FDA for treatment of FSD, there are protocols in the literature for its use in clinical practice to treat HSDD (e.g., Bartlik, Legere, & Andersson, 1999; Davis, 1998a, 1999).

Other Hormones

Other hormones that have been identified as contributors to sexual functioning include prolactin, oxytocin, and cortisol (Meston & Frolich, 2000). Assessing the role of oral contraceptives in FSD is important because progesterone, a hormone found in these preparations, is associated with decreased sexual desire.

Sildenafil Citrate

The use of sildenafil citrate (Viagra) to treat erectile dysfunction in men has received much positive attention. However, trials of this medication in women have had less positive results, with most studies finding no change in subjective ratings of sexual arousal (Basson et al., 2002; Laan, van Lunsen, Everaerd, Heiman, & Hackbert, 2000; Laan et al., 2002). Caruso and colleagues (2001) did demonstrate improvement in sexual functioning among young women with FSAD administered 25 or 50 mg of sildenafil. In light of these findings, Heiman (2002) concluded that "given the lack of genital focus of women, it is possible that genitally targeted pharmacological agents would be best compared to and combined with psychological treatments" (p. 75).

Treatments for Specific Disorders

Hypoactive Sexual Desire Disorder

Low desire is a problem that is highly case specific and very heterogeneous and is treated by a wide array of medical and psychological methods (Rosen & Leiblum, 1995). Two primary intervention approaches, cognitive–behavioral and systemic, use couple therapy to treat HSDD. The cognitive–behavioral intervention approach emphasizes the identification of attitudinal and environmental factors involved in low desire and offer specific, problem-focused interventions (Wincze & Carey, 2001). These treatments focus on maladaptive patterns such as mind reading and negative automatic thoughts about or during sex that are managed using specific strategies through the use of thought records, communication training, and conflict resolution (Beck, 1978). Group couple therapy using these methods has resulted in positive changes in areas of sexual desire and couple intimacy (Trudel et al., 2001). Systemic interventions for HSDD target sexual interactions between partners on multiple levels or subsystems. Treatment focuses on problems in any of the subsystems that create sexual polarization and emotional distancing between partners, thus impacting sexual functioning (cf. Heiman, 2001; Schnarch, 1991; Verhulst & Heiman, 1988).

In practice, many therapists combine these approaches into a multimodal strategy and apply them in either an individual or group therapy format. Specific techniques that may be used to treat HSDD include sexual education, conflict resolution, cognitive restructuring, masturbation training, sexual fantasy training, and sensate focus. Testosterone therapy has also been used to augment sex therapy, with some clinical reports of success (Bartlik et al., 1999).

Female Sexual Arousal Disorder

Although FSAD is distinguished for the purpose of clinical diagnosis and research, it is rare that women only present with FSAD symptoms (Segraves & Segraves, 1991). Instead, FSAD symptoms typically occur in combination with problems with orgasm, desire, or genital pain. Commonly used techniques for treating FSAD that may be applied in individual or couple therapy include cognitive restructuring, sexual education, sensate focus, masturbation training, sexual fantasy training, sexual skills training, and communication training. Estrogen therapy may be used to treat FSAD symptoms in postmenopausal women. As noted, sildenafil or other vasocongestive agents may be of some use.

Female Orgasmic Disorder

As noted in the section on conducting sex therapy, directed masturbation with or without concomitant individual or couple therapy has demonstrated efficacy for primary orgasmic disorder. Sexual education, sensate focus, sexual skills training, sexual fantasy training, cognitive restructuring, and relaxation exercises are often used in conjunction with masturbation training to address physiological and psychological barriers to sexual response. There are some clinical reports indicating that adjunctive therapy with sildenafil or buspirone may assist in reducing SSRI-related anorgasmia (Gelenberg, Delgado, & Nurnberg, 2000; Nurnberg, Lauriello, Hensley, Parker, & Keith, 1999). It is noteworthy that SSRIs may produce anorgasmia in as many as 57% of women (Kennedy, Eisfeld, Dickens, Bacchiochi, & Bagby, 2000; Rosen et al., 1999).

Genital Pain Disorders

Traditionally, the sexual pain disorders have been divided into two separate categories: dyspareunia and vaginismus. However, these two categories are not mutually exclusive, and it is difficult to differentiate patients empirically by diagnosis on the basis of symptom presentation (Van Lankveld, Brewaeys, Ter Kuile, & Weijenborg, 1995). Instead, viewing them along a continuum and conceptualizing them as a pain disorder, rather than a sexual dysfunction, may be more helpful for identifying etiology and for facilitating treatment (Binik, Bergeron, & Khalife, 2000; Meana, Binik, Khalife, & Cohen, 1997b). For instance, many individuals with medical conditions such as chronic vaginal infections and vulvar vestibulitis develop chronic perineal and abdominal muscle tension accompanied by contractions on intromission.

Further support for this model comes from a clinical outcome study comparing surgery, biofeedback, and cognitive–behavioral group therapy for vulvar vestibulitis. Results showed significant pain reductions in all three groups at posttreatment and at 6-month follow-up (Bergeron et al., 1997). Collaborative care arrangements with physicians and physical therapists to manage medical issues, address muscle tension, and improve psychosocial functioning can be beneficial for these patients. Relaxation training, biofeedback, and dilators in conjunction with individual or couple therapy that may include sensate focus, sexual education, cognitive restructuring, and communication training are often effective.

Illustrative Case Example

This case is an amalgam of several we have seen in an academic medical center outpatient setting. We present it for the purpose of demonstrating the complexity of potential etiological factors that are commonly seen in women with sexual disorders at a primary care clinic.

A 28-year-old, married, African American female who worked as a chemical engineer and had a 2-year-old son was referred by her physician after coming in for her annual exam and stating, "I'm just not interested in sex." She reported that she never had any sexual fantasies, but denied past difficulty with lubrication or orgasm. She stated that since her pregnancy, she often was "not into sex" and only had an orgasm 50% of the time (compared with 90% before giving birth). She de-

nied past or present sexual pain. She reported that she had two partners before her marriage, and that sex had been "OK." She waited until 1 year after her son's birth to marry his father because she was concerned about how they handled conflicts over money and sex. She was still breastfeeding and worked 50 hours per week. She had been on oral contraceptives for 18 months and was on no other medication. She drank alcohol occasionally and complained of "stress" and fatigue. Although her husband had always initiated sex and was fine with that, he became very frustrated by their lack of sexual activity (past frequency twice per week; current frequency twice per month) and had been working longer hours to avoid being at home.

Diagnosis: Hypoactive sexual desire disorder (secondary, global, worsening). Also meets criteria for female sexual arousal disorder and female orgasmic disorder.

Possible etiological factors: Hormonal changes (oral contraceptives and breastfeeding); couple conflict aggravated by desire discrepancy; limited time and energy; lifelong history of low sexual desire; physiological changes postpregnancy and delivery affecting her arousal and orgasm.

Treatment recommendations: Couple therapy to increase emotional intimacy and sexual fantasy training; education regarding stress and time management with individual therapy if anxiety or depressive symptoms are present; medical referral for fatigue and hormone profile; gynecological examination.

SUMMARY

Sexual disorders in women constitute a wide range of difficulties and are associated with decreased quality of life and relationship dissatisfaction. Because the FSDs are more prevalent in medical populations, clinicians working in the primary care setting are likely to encounter women with sexual problems. There is still much to discover and understand about the interactions of causal factors and how best to combine treatments to maximize response. Use of the tools provided in this chapter will help guide treatment planning through careful assessment of sexual functioning, knowledge of causal factors, and implementation of commonly used techniques for conducting sex therapy.

ADDITIONAL RESOURCES

Suggestions for further reading and professional development resources are available at this book's companion Web site: www.primarycarepsych.com.

References

American Psychiatric Association. (2000). *Diagnostic and statistical manual of mental disorders* (4th ed., text revision). Washington, DC: Author.

Bancroft, J. (2002). The medicalization of female sexual dysfunction: The need for caution. *Archives of Sexual Behavior, 31,* 451–455.

Bancroft, J., Loftus, J., & Long, J. S. (2003). Distress about sex: A national survey of women in heterosexual relationships. *Archives of Sexual Behavior, 32,* 193–208.

Barlow, D. H. (1986). Causes of sexual dysfunction: The role of anxiety and cognitive interference. *Journal of Consulting and Clinical Psychology, 54,* 140–148.

Bartlik, B., & Goldberg, J. (2000). Female sexual arousal disorder. In S. R. Leiblum & R. C. Rosen (Eds.), *Principles and practice of sex therapy* (pp. 85–117). New York: Guilford Press.

Bartlik, B., Legere, R., & Andersson, L. (1999). The combined use of sex therapy and testosterone replacement therapy for women. *Psychiatric Annals, 29,* 27–33.

Basson, R., Berman, J., Burnett, A., Derogatis, L., Ferguson, D., Fourcroy, J., Goldstein, I., Graziottin, A., Heiman, J., Laan, E., Leiblum, S., Padma-Nathan, H., Rosn, R., Segraves, K., Seagraves, R. T., Shalosigh, R., Sipski, M., Wagner, G. & Whipple, B. (2000). Report of the International Consensus Development Conference on Female Sexual Dysfunction: Definitions and classifications. *Journal of Urology, 163,* 888–893.

Basson, R., McInnes, R., Smith, M. D., Hodgson, G., & Koppiker, N. (2002). Efficacy and safety of sildenafil citrate in women with sexual dysfunction associated with female sexual arousal disorder. *Journal of Women's Health and Gender-Based Medicine, 11,* 367–377.

Beck, A. T. (1978). *Love is never enough.* New York: Harper and Row.

Bergeron, S., Binik, Y., Khalife, S., Meana, M., Berkley, K. J., & Pagidas, K. (1997). The treatment of vulvar vestibulitis syndrome: Towards a multimodal approach. *Sexual and Marital Therapy, 12,* 305–311.

Binik, Y. M., Bergeron, S., & Khalife, S. (2000). Dyspareunia. In S. R. Leiblum & R. C. Rosen (Eds.), *Principles and practice of sex therapy* (pp. 155–180). New York: Guilford Press.

Caruso, S., Intelisano, G., Lupo, L., & Agnello, C. (2001). Premenopausal women affected by sexual arousal disorder treated by sildenafil: A double-blind, cross-over, placebo-controlled study. *British Journal of Obstetrics and Gynecology, 108,* 623–628.

Davis, S. R. (1998a). The clinical use of androgens in female sexual disorders. *Journal of Sex and Marital Therapy, 24,* 153–163.

Davis, S. R. (1998b). The role of androgens and the menopause in the female sexual response. *International Journal of Impotence Research, 10,* S82–S83.

Davis, S. R. (1999). The therapeutic use of androgens in women. *Journal of Steroids, Biochemical and Molecular Biology, 69,* 177–184.

Dennerstein, L., Lehert, P., Burger, H., & Dudley, E. (1999). Factors affecting sexual functioning in women in the mid-life years. *Climacteric, 2,* 254–262.

Donahey, K. M., & Carroll, R. A. (1993). Gender differences in factors associated with hypoactive sexual desire. *Journal of Sex and Marital Therapy, 19,* 25–40.

Dunn, K. M., Croft, P. R., & Hackett, G. I. (1999). Association of sexual problems with social, psychological, and physical problems in men and women: A cross sectional population survey. *Journal of Epidemiology and Community Health, 53,* 144–148.

Ernst, C., Foldenyi, M., & Angst, J. (1993). The Zurich study: XXI. Sexual dysfunctions and disturbances in young adults. *European Archives of Psychiatry and Clinical Neuroscience, 243,* 179–188.

Gelenberg, A. J., Delgado, P., & Nurnberg, H. G. (2000). Sexual side effects of antidepressant drugs. *Current Psychiatry Reports, 2,* 223–227.

Heiman, J. R. (2000). Orgasmic disorders in women. In S. R. Leiblum & R. C. Rosen (Eds.), *Principles and practice of sex therapy* (pp. 118–153). New York: Guilford Press.

Heiman, J. R. (2001). Sexual desire in human relationships. In W. Evaraerd, E. Laan, & S. Both (Eds.), *Sexual appetite, desire and motivation: Energetics of the sexual system* (pp. 117–134). Amsterdam: The Royal Netherlands Academy of Arts and Sciences.

Heiman, J. R. (2002). Sexual dysfunction: Overview of prevalence, etiological factors, and treatments. *Journal of Sex Research, 39,* 73–78.

Heiman, J. R., & LoPiccolo, J. (1988). *Becoming orgasmic. A sexual growth program for women* (rev. expanded ed.). New York: Prentice Hall.

Heiman, J. R., & Meston, C. M. (1997). Evaluating sexual dysfunction in women. *Clinical Obstetrics and Gynecology, 40,* 616–629.

Kaplan, H. S. (1974). *The new sex therapy.* New York: Brunner/Mazel.

Kennedy, S. H., Dickens, S. E., Eisfeld, B. S., & Bagby, R. M. (1999). Sexual dysfunction before antidepressant therapy in major depression. *Journal of Affective Disorders, 56,* 201–208.

Kennedy, S. H., Eisfeld, B. S., Dickens, S. E., Bacchiochi, J. R., & Bagby, R. M. (2000). Antidepressant-induced sexual dysfunction during treatment with moclobemide, paroxetine, sertraline, and venlafaxine. *Journal of Clinical Psychiatry, 61,* 276–281.

Laan, E., van Lunsen, R. H., Everaerd, W., Heiman, J. R., & Hackbert, L. (2000, June). *The effect of sildenafil on women's genital and subjective sexual response.* Paper presented at the 26th annual meeting of the International Academy of Sex Research, Paris, France.

Laan, E., van Lunsen, R. H., Everaerd, W., Riley, A., Scott, E., & Boolell, M. (2002). The enhancement of vaginal vasocongestion by sildenafil in healthy premenopausal women. *Journal of Women's Health and Gender-Based Medicine, 11,* 357–365.

Laumann, E. O., Gagnon, J. H., Michael, R. T., & Michaels, S. (1994). *The social organization of sexuality.* Chicago: University of Chicago Press.

Laumann, E. O., Paik, A., & Rosen, R. C. (1999). Sexual dysfunction in the United States: Prevalence and predictors. *Journal of the American Medical Association, 281,* 537–544.

Leiblum, S. R., & Rosen, R. C. (2000). *Principles and practice of sex therapy* (3rd ed.). New York: Guilford Press.

Lindal, E., & Stefansson, J. G. (1993). The lifetime prevalence of psychosexual dysfunction among 55 to 57 year-olds in Iceland. *Social Psychiatry and Psychiatric Epidemiology, 28,* 91–95.

Masters, W., & Johnson, V. (1966). *Human sexual response.* Boston: Little, Brown.

Masters, W., & Johnson, V. (1970). *Human sexual inadequacy.* Boston: Little, Brown.

Mattson, D., Petrie, M., Srivastava, D. K., & McDermott, M. (1995). Multiple sclerosis: Sexual dysfunction and its response to medications. *Archives of Neurology, 52,* 862–868.

Maurice, W. L. (1999). *Sexual medicine in primary care.* St. Louis, MO: Mosby.

McCarthy, B. W., & McCarthy, E. (1984). *Sexual awareness: Enhancing sexual pleasure.* New York: Carol and Graf.

Meana, M., Binik, Y. M., Khalife, S., & Cohen, D. (1997a). Biopsychosocial profile of women with dyspareunia. *Obstetrics and Gynecology, 90,* 583–589.

Meana, M., Binik, Y. M., Khalife, S., & Cohen, D. (1997b). Dyspareunia: Sexual dysfunction or pain syndrome? *Journal of Nervous and Mental Disease, 185,* 561–569.

Meston, C. M., & Frohlich, P. F. (2000). The neurobiology of sexual function. *Archives of General Psychiatry, 57,* 1012–1030.

Modelska, K., & Cummings, S. (2003). Female sexual dysfunction in postmenopausal women: Systematic review of placebo-controlled studies. *American Journal of Obstetrics and Gynecology, 188,* 286–293.

Moynihan, R. (2003). The making of a disease: Female sexual dysfunction. *British Medical Journal, 326,* 45–47.

Nurnberg, H. G., Lauriello, J., Hensley, P. L., Parker, L. M., & Keith, S. J. (1999). Sildenafil for sexual dysfunction in women taking antidepressants. *American Journal of Psychiatry, 156,* 1664.

Read, S., King, M., & Watson, J. (1997). Sexual dysfunction in primary medical care: Prevalence, characteristics and detection by the general practitioner. *Journal of Public Health Medicine, 19,* 387–391.

Rosen, R. C., Lane, R. M., & Menza, M. (1999). Effects of SSRIs on sexual function: A critical review. *Journal of Clinical Psychopharmacology, 19,* 67–85.

Rosen, R. C., & Leiblum, S. R. (1995). Treatment of sexual disorders in the 1990s: An integrated approach. *Journal of Consulting and Clinical Psychology, 63,* 877–890.

Rosen, R. C., Taylor, J. F., Leiblum, S. R., & Bachmann, G. A. (1993). Prevalence of sexual dysfunction in women: Results of a survey study of women in an outpatient gynecological clinic. *Journal of Sex and Marital Therapy, 19,* 171–188.

Sarrel, P. M. (2000). Effects of hormone replacement therapy on sexual psychophysiology and behavior in postmenopause. *Journal of Women's Health and Gender-Based Medicine, 9,* S25–S32.

Schnarch, D. (1991). *Constructing the sexual crucible.* New York: Norton.

Segraves, K. B., & Segraves, R. T. (1991). Hypoactive sexual desire disorder: Prevalence and comorbidity in 906 subjects. *Journal of Sex and Marital Therapy, 17,* 55–58.

Shifren, J. L., Braunstein, G. D., Simon, J. A., Casson, P. R., Buster, J. E., Redmond, G. P., Burki, R. E., Ginsburg, E. S., Rosen, R. C., Leiblum, S. R., Caramelli, K. E., & Mazer, N. A. (2000). Transdermal testosterone treatment in women with impaired sexual function after oopharectomy. *New England Journal of Medicine, 343,* 682–688.

Simons, J. S., & Carey, M. P. (2001). Prevalence of sexual dysfunctions: Results from a decade of research. *Archives of Sexual Behavior, 30,* 177–219.

Spector, I. P., Leiblum, S. R., Carey, M. P., & Rosen, R. C. (1993). Diabetes and female sexual function: A critical review. *Annals of Behavioral Medicine, 15,* 257–264.

Stahl, S. M. (2001a). The psychopharmacology of sex, part 1: Neurotransmitters and the 3 phases of the human sexual response. *Journal of Clinical Psychiatry, 62,* 80–81.

Stahl, S. M. (2001b). The psychopharmacology of sex, part 2: Effects of drugs and disease on the 3 phases of human sexual response. *Journal of Clinical Psychiatry, 62,* 147–148.

Tiefer, L. (2002). Sexual behaviour and its medicalisation. Many (especially economic) forces promote medicalisation. *British Medical Journal, 325,* 45.

Trudel, G., Marchand, A., Ravart, M., Aubin, S., Turgeon, L., & Fortier, P. (2001). The effect of a cognitive-behavioral group treatment program on hypoactive sexual desire in women. *Sexual and Relationship Therapy, 16,* 145–164.

Van Lankveld, J. J. D. M., Brewaeys, A. M. A., Ter Kuile, M. M., & Weijenborg, P. T. M. (1995). Difficulties in the differential diagnosis of vaginismus, dyspareunia and mixed sexual pain disorder. *Journal of Psychosomatic Obstetrics and Gynecology, 16,* 201–209.

Ventegodt, S. (1998). Sex and the quality of life in Denmark. *Archives of Sexual Behavior, 27,* 295–307.

Verhulst, J., & Heiman, J. R. (1988). A systems perspective on sexual desire. In S. R. Leiblum & R. C. Rosen (Eds.), *Sexual desire disorders* (pp. 243–270). New York: Guilford Press.

Williams, S. (1995). The sexual history. In M. Lipkin Jr., S. M. Putnam, & A. Lazare (Eds.), *The medical interview: Clinical care, education and research* (pp. 235–250). New York: Springer-Verlag.

Wincze, J. P., & Carey, M. P. (2001). *Sexual dysfunction: A guide for assessment and treatment.* New York: Guilford Press.

World Health Organization. (1992). *International Statistical Classification of Diseases and Related Health Problems* (1989 revision). Geneva: Author.

Writing Group for the Women's Health Initiative Investigators. (2002). Risks and benefits of estrogen plus progestin in healthy postmenopausal women: Principal results from the women's health initiative randomized controlled trial. *Journal of the American Medical Association, 288,* 321–333.

37

Sleep Disorders

Laura A. Czajkowski
Kenneth R. Casey
Christopher R. Jones

Sleep disorders are prevalent, treatable, and frequently undiagnosed. Approximately one third of the adult population complains of occasional insomnia. Some 70 million Americans have clinically significant sleep problems. Daytime sleepiness resulting from sleep deprivation is very common. The average total sleep time has decreased by an estimated 25% over the last century in the U.S. Sleep disorders such as obstructive sleep apnea (OSA), restless legs syndrome/periodic limb movement syndrome (RLS/PLMS), and narcolepsy frequently result in sleepiness. Excessive daytime sleepiness produces impaired quality of life, diminished attention/concentration and cognitive performance, impaired productivity, and increased risk of vehicle and occupational accidents. The National Sleep Foundation (2002) reported that 51% of the American workforce experiences symptoms of sleepiness that interfere with productivity.

Primary care physicians seldom investigate sleep complaints in depth. Detailed assessment of sleep quality is also frequently lacking in psychological evaluations. The primary care psychologist is ideally positioned to recognize sleep pathology associated with psychiatric disorders or chronic medical illness. There is ample evidence that many sleep complaints can be treated successfully. However, the application of an effective intervention, which may have broad patient benefit, is contingent on recognition of the problem. This chapter provides an overview of sleep, descriptions of common sleep disorders, and a review of evaluation and treatment strategies.

OVERVIEW OF SLEEP

Sleep behavior is characterized by diminished mobility, closed eyes, and decreased responsiveness. It is distinguished from coma by a return to consciousness spontaneously or following stimuli. In the past, sleep was defined as simply the absence of wakefulness (Chokroverty, 1999). It is now recognized that sleep is actively modulated by the brain and is characterized by an orderly progression of different sleep stages, each associated with particular electrophysiological patterns.

Sleep can be divided into two distinctive states: non-rapid eye movement (NREM) sleep and rapid eye movement (REM) sleep. Sleep stages are described by changes in brain waves, eye movements, and motor tension. There are four stages of successively "deeper" NREM sleep. Stage I sleep is normally a brief transitional state. Stage II sleep accounts for 45% to 50% of the total sleep time. Stages III and IV slow wave sleep (SWS) are associated with minimal responsiveness to external stimulation. NREM sleep accounts for 75% to 80% of sleep time in adults.

REM sleep comprises 20% to 25% of total sleep time and consists of a tonic and a phasic stage. Distinguishing features of REM sleep include muscle atonia, rapid eye movements, and dream generation. Dream mentation is associated with sensory and motor excitation; however, movement is not executed because of inhibition of motor neurons during REM sleep. REM sleep is characterized by an irregular respiratory rhythm, acceleration of heart rate, and blood pressure variation.

A sleep cycle consists of a period of NREM sleep followed by a period of REM sleep. This cycle typically lasts 90 to 110 minutes. There are four to six sleep cycles in the course of a night. SWS is dominant in the beginning of the night, whereas REM sleep increases in prominence throughout the night. Overall, with each sleep cycle, the time spent in REM tends to increase, and the time spent in SWS decreases.

The average total sleep time in adults is 7 to 8 hours, although the amount of sleep necessary to support daytime functionality varies. Both circadian and homeostatic processes regulate sleep. Circadian rhythms (circa, approximately; dian, day), which influence the timing of sleep, are generated by the suprachiasmatic nucleus of the brain and are entrained to the light-dark cycle. Sleep is also influenced by homeostatic drive, a physiological process that gradually increases sleepiness as the period of being awake lengthens. The homeostatic sleep drive and the circadian rhythm influence sleep and wakefulness in about equal proportion.

Purpose of Sleep

The specific function of sleep is not clearly understood, but several theories have been proposed (Chokroverty, 1999). Two theories of particular interest to mental health practitioners are the restoration theory and memory reinforcement/consolidation theory. The restorative theory suggests that sleep provides restoration to body tissue in NREM and brain tissue in REM sleep. This hypothesis is based on the increase in secretion of anabolic hormones and decreased levels of catabolic hormones during sleep and the subjective perception of feeling refreshed after NREM sleep.

REM sleep is associated with growth and maintenance of the nervous system in young organisms. There is evidence that REM sleep is associated with learning and memory consolidation. REM sleep brain wave activity is similar to wakefulness. Positron emission tomography scans of the brain have demonstrated higher metabolic activity during REM than during NREM or wakefulness (Marquet et al., 1990). Data suggested improvement in memory retention after REM compared to NREM. In addition, REM deprivation interferes with memory acquisition and consolidation (Dujardin, Guerrien, & Leconte, 1990).

Developmental Course of Sleep

Sleep requirements, sleep architecture, and sleep quality change across the life span. Total sleep time decreases with age, and the percentage of time spent in REM and SWS also decreases with age. The average sleep duration for a 1-month-old infant is 16 hours; an 80-year-old may spend 6 hours a day asleep.

Infancy

Organization of brain function into the states of wakefulness, NREM, and REM with a 24-hour rhythm is a developmental priority during infancy. An infant's sleep cycle is shorter than that of an adult (50 minutes vs. 90 minutes). The onset of infant sleep often begins with REM. An infant's sleep is 50% REM. The proportion of REM decreases during childhood to the adult value of 20%.

Childhood

Total sleep time gradually decreases in childhood, with 10 hours the average for a 6-year-old. Transition to school, birth of siblings, parental stability, and developmental fears may affect children's sleep. Children who experience more uncontrollable negative events may experience middle-of-the-night awakenings and difficulty with morning awakening. Among children, 20% to 30% have complaints of sleep disturbance regarded as significant problems by the family. The most common sleep problems in childhood are sleepwalking, sleep talking, sleep terrors, nightmares, and enuresis.

Adolescence: Sleep Phase Delay

Sleep wake patterns change dramatically in association with the multiple physical, emotional, psychological, and social transitions of adolescence. An excellent review of this area is that of Carskadon and Acebo (2002). Research findings indicated that the need for sleep does not decrease during adolescence. In fact, an average of just over 9 hours is required for optimal alertness. However, there is an increase in the level of daytime sleep tendency. The delay in bedtime observed in adolescence is in part caused by biological regulatory processes (homeostatic drive and the circadian influences). Carskadon and Acebo (2002) speculated that changes within the circadian timing system reflect a reorganization of the biological system that favors a delayed sleep pattern.

Behavioral characteristics of adolescent delayed sleep phase include inability to fall asleep at night; later bedtimes and rising times, especially on the weekend; decreased total sleep time during the week; makeup sleep on the weekends; and marked discrepancy between school night and weekend night sleep patterns. The consequences of a delayed sleep pattern are often compounded by early school start times. These adolescents are often sleep deprived and may experience impaired school performance and depression (Carskadon, Wolfson, Acebo, Tzischinsky, & Seifer, 1998).

Psychologists who are referred adolescents for behavioral problems—common ones are school truancy, increased agitation, mood changes, or failing grades—must assess their sleep habits. These problems may be misinterpreted as a lack of motivation and interest or as rebelliousness. Frequently, antidepressants are prescribed with-

out significant changes in the sleep pattern. Recognition of the biological tendency to delay sleep, in conjunction with an assessment of behavioral predisposing factors, is critical for successful treatment. Interventions include regular exercise, consistent sleep and rise times, and no naps. In severe cases, a referral to an accredited sleep center is warranted to implement bright light chronotherapy.

Aging

Aging is associated with additional changes in sleep architecture and disrupted sleep patterns. In a large epidemiological study, Foley, Monjan, and Brown (1995) reported that 50% of older Americans have chronic sleep disturbance characterized by difficulty with sleep initiation, decreased total sleep time despite increased time in bed, multiple nighttime awakenings, early morning awakening, and daytime napping. Data from sleep studies demonstrated reduction or absence of SWS and a decrease in REM sleep. There are more frequent shifts in sleep stage, and more of the night is spent in lighter sleep. The elderly may experience significant daytime sleepiness. Czeisler and colleagues (2000) suggested that sleep fragmentation is associated with age-related changes in the promotion of sleep by the circadian pacemaker as well as a reduced homeostatic drive for sleep.

Sleep complaints among the elderly may result from physiological sleep changes of normal aging, medical illness, physical pain and discomfort, psychiatric disorders, neurological deficits, or medication usage. Appropriate assessment includes a comprehensive sleep history, sleep diaries, reports from the bed partner or caregiver, medical history, medication history, and psychiatric history. Specific sleep disorders prevalent in this population include insomnia, sleep-disordered breathing, periodic limb movements and REM sleep-behavior disorder.

Nonpharmacological approaches to insomnia in the elderly should be considered. Exercise, consistent bedtime and rising time; reduction or avoidance of napping; exposure to bright outdoor sunlight, particularly in the late afternoon or early evening; and avoidance of caffeine, alcohol, and stimulant medication near bedtime may be helpful. Morin and colleagues (Morin, Colecchi, Stone,

& Sood, 1999) examined the efficacy of behavioral approaches with the elderly. The findings indicated that cognitive–behavioral therapy was as effective as medication in the initial phase and had better long-term outcomes.

Elderly individuals, with and without dementia, residing in extended care facilities have fragmented sleep, excessive sleepiness during the day, and nocturnal wandering. They are susceptible to circadian rhythm disorders secondary to daytime napping, chronic bed rest, lack of activity, and lack of exposure to bright light. There is also a high prevalence of sleep-disordered breathing in this population. Sleep continuity may be enhanced by entrainment cues to strengthen circadian rhythm such as exposure to bright light, consistent physical activity, and regular social interaction.

Sleep disturbance in the elderly is a growing concern because of aging of the population. Currently available assessment and treatment approaches are inadequate. Further study is warranted to identify more effective interventions to improve the quality of life in this population.

ASSESSMENT OF
SLEEP DISORDERS

A comprehensive sleep history focusing on the duration, precipitants, and severity of the sleep complaint is indispensable to determine etiology and establish a treatment plan. Other important elements of the clinical assessment include attributions associated with the complaint, daytime functioning, past treatment approaches, sleep environment, work/school schedule, medical history, medication history, substance usage, and psychiatric history. The elements of a sleep assessment are listed in Table 37.1. There are sleep-specific questionnaires, including the Pittsburgh Sleep Quality Index (Buysse, Reynolds, Monk, Berman, & Kupfer, 1989), Epworth Sleepiness Scale (Johns, 1992), and the CCNY Semistructured Interview for Insomnia (Spielman & Anderson, 1999).

Identification of the sleep complaint should incorporate questions designed to detect the presence of difficulties with sleep onset, maintenance, early awakenings, or nonrefreshing sleep. It is im-

Table 37.1 Elements of a Sleep Assessment

Sleep complaint	Time to sleep onset
	Number of awakenings
	Duration of awakenings
	Total sleep time
Sleep pattern	Quality of sleep
	Frequency and duration
Daytime consequences	Fatigue
	Sleepiness
	Cognitions regarding sleep
Causative elements	Precipitating
	Changed patterns since onset
	Irregular work schedule
	School schedule
	Factors that increase sleep complaint
	Factors that decrease sleep complaint
Past treatment	Changes in sleep schedule
	Prescription medication
	Over-the-counter medication
Present sleep schedule	Weekday
	Weekends
	Naps
History of sleep complaints	Childhood
	Adolescence
	Adulthood
Differential	Breathing-related sleep disorder
	Restless legs syndrome/periodic limb movements in sleep
	Idiopathic insomnia
	Parasomnia
	Narcolepsy
Medical history	Illness
	Chronic problems
	Medication
	Substance usage
	Exercise
Psychopathology	Affective disorders
	Anxiety
	Posttraumatic stress disorder
	Attention-deficit/hyperactivity disorder
	Treatment

portant to determine the specifics of the sleep-wake schedule. The response "I sleep well" could be mistakenly construed as intact sleep. However, on further questioning, it may indicate sleeping throughout a 24-hour period, indicating excessive sleepiness.

Queries associated with the sleep-wake schedule include time in bed, lights out, estimated time to sleep onset, awakening after sleep onset, secondary sleep latencies, final awakening, estimated total sleep time, and circadian tendencies. Recording the sleep schedule on the weekend or vacation days may be important. Daytime functioning can be illuminated by asking about the duration and frequency of naps and complaints of sleepiness, such as dozing or inattention. Changes in work performance, social activities, and mood are documented. The behavior and attributions associated with delays to sleep onset and with awakenings contribute to understanding possible etiology.

Information from the bed partner is helpful for confirmation and evaluation of problems not evident to the patient. Questions regarding breathing pattern, choking, breath holding, snoring, twitching, or leg jerks are incorporated. Symptoms associated with nightmares, night terrors, nocturnal panic, sleepwalking, or motor behaviors in sleep should be recorded.

In addition to the medical history and family history, a complete sleep evaluation should assess medication use, including all over-the-counter medication. Also important are details regarding alcohol, nicotine, and caffeine consumption. Identification of a mood disorder or anxiety is important, but complicated because many of the daytime consequences of sleep disruption (discouragement, fatigue, distractibility, social/interpersonal relationship problems) may also be mood or anxiety symptoms. Systematic analysis regarding the course of symptoms and the relationship between mood and sleep is critical to diagnosis. Sleep disturbance is often associated with other mental health issues. Therefore, a sleep evaluation includes assessment of psychiatric disorders, including substance abuse, eating disorders, schizophrenia, posttraumatic stress disorder, and somatoform disorders.

Sleep questionnaires and diaries are used for both assessment and treatment. Sleep diaries provide information on the subjective experience of sleep. Sleep logs generally include bedtime, rising time, sleep latency, number and duration of awakenings, naps, and the use of sleep aids. Completion of sleep logs may contribute to the patient's more realistic appraisal of sleep quality. Actigraphy, which employs a device worn on the wrist that records motion, may be used to evaluate sleep-wake patterns in combination with other assessment procedures.

Much of the current understanding of sleep and its disorders is based on polysomnography (PSG; overnight sleep study). PSG is an intensively monitored record of electrophysiological parameters and respiratory and cardiac function gathered in a specialized facility designed to provide a "homelike" sleeping environment. PSG is the standard assessment for many sleep-related problems, such as OSA.

Excessive daytime sleepiness is a challenge to evaluate because it is a highly subjective state of perception. If chronic sleepiness develops gradually, the subject may perceive it as normal. Sleepiness will vary according to circumstances, activity level, affective state, and social context. For example, sleepiness is less likely to be recognized during physical labor than during sedentary repose. Subjects may use different terms, such as "tiredness" or "fatigue," in place of "sleepiness." Several imperfect tests have been developed to attempt quantitative measurement of sleepiness. The most widely used of these tests are based on self-administered questionnaires as described above. However, such questionnaires leave much open to the subject's interpretation.

More extensive testing of sleepiness, such as "nap testing," can be performed at sleep centers. These tests include the multiple sleep latency test, a test to measure how long it takes the subject to fall asleep, and the maintenance of wakefulness test, which measures how long the patient can remain awake. These studies are particularly important in the clinical diagnosis of narcolepsy.

COMMON SLEEP DISORDERS

Sleep complaints are produced by a wide range of sleep disorders, including insomnia, excessive sleepiness, parasomnias, circadian rhythm disorders, and breathing-related sleep disorders. This section is a review of the most prevalent sleep problems.

Insomnia

A typical insomniac might state, "I am exhausted and cannot function during the day. Lack of sleep is ruining my life . . . my ability to work, my marriage, and how I act with my family. I am so tired all day . . . and am desperate for sleep. I dread the night because I know I will be awake."

It is estimated that 30% to 35% of the adult population experience occasional insomnia. The National Sleep Foundation (2002) report indicated that 10% to 20% of American adults have chronic insomnia of many years' duration. Chronic insomnia increases with age and is more common in women. Shocat (1999) estimated the occurrence of insomnia in a primary care population as 69%, with 19% of patients complaining of chronic symptoms. Factors associated with insomnia include psychiatric illness, the specific sleep disorders described in this chapter, medical problems, and psychological arousal (Chesson et al., 2000).

Insomnia is a complaint of poor sleep that can incorporate difficult sleep initiation, multiple nighttime or early morning awakenings, short total sleep time, or diminished sleep quality. It is associated with changes in daytime functioning with complaints of low energy, fatigue, malaise, diminished cognitive abilities, and alteration in behavior or emotional state. The subjective experience of insomnia and its daytime consequences may exceed objective demonstration. Emotional arousal and appraisal are significant mediating factors that contribute to the development and maintenance of insomnia (Sateia, Doghramji, Hauri, & Morin, 2000).

Insomnia sustained for weeks or months induces heightened anxiety, negative expectations, and desperately frustrating efforts to sleep, which result in more time in bed awake. A circular pattern emerges with mounting concern over sleep throughout the day and increased anxiety at night. The learned association between bedtime and the failure to sleep maintains the arousal. The consequences of poor sleep are magnified, and sleep becomes the perceived cause of all errors, inefficiency, mood changes, and interpersonal conflict.

Clarification of predisposing, precipitating, and perpetuating factors as well as assessment of maladaptive cognitive and behavioral responses to the insomnia are crucial for effective treatment. Certain personality traits predispose individuals to develop insomnia. Ongoing patterns of ruminative thought, worry/anticipation of failure, and hypervigilance increase the susceptibility to insomnia and perpetuate the problem. Precipitating events associated with the onset of insomnia are important to identify, particularly when the onset of sleep disturbance is recent. Examples include changes in relationships, family, finances, health, schedule, or occupation. In persistent insomnia, the triggering event may not be linked with the sleep disturbance at the time of evaluation. Poor sleep habits contribute to maintenance of insomnia; these include excessive time in bed, inconsistent bedtimes, variable arising times, napping, incompatible in-bed behavior (e.g., studying, television watching, computer use), increased caffeine consumption, alcohol usage, reliance on sleep medication, excessive cognitive arousal, and preoccupation with sleep.

Elucidating and understanding the factors associated with insomnia are important in designing an intervention. Treatment is targeted at the behaviors that disrupt the sleep-wake cycle and increase both cognitive and physiological arousal. The efficacy of nonpharmacological treatment of insomnia is well established and results in consistent and stable sleep enhancement (Morin, Hauri, et al., 1999). Cognitive–behavioral therapy for insomnia consists of several components, such as education, implementing healthy sleep habits, stimulus control, sleep restriction, and relaxation strategies. Circadian rhythm disorders are addressed by correcting the timing of the sleep-wake cycle and implementing light therapy.

Sleep education, including an overview of sleep physiology, is intended to promote an understanding of the factors contributing to sleep disruption by addressing the dysfunctional beliefs and misperceptions that maintain insomnia. Cognitive therapy for insomnia targets these maladaptive thoughts by interrupting the chain of negative thought and identifying realistic expectations for sleep.

Healthy sleep habits incorporate lifestyle and environmental factors that have an impact on sleep. Sleep-promoting practices should encompass consistent routines and bedtime rituals; reduced intake of caffeine, tobacco, and stimulants; avoidance of alcohol at bedtime; regular exercise; and a safe, dark, quiet sleep environment.

Stimulus control instructions are designed to reestablish the bed as a cue for rapid sleep onset by decreasing behaviors incompatible with sleep. Instructions include going to bed only when sleepy, limiting the use of the bed to sleep and sexual activity, leaving the bedroom when unable to sleep, returning to bed only when sleepy, maintaining a consistent wake-up time regardless of sleep duration, and avoiding daytime napping. Successful implementation of these practices requires close monitoring with daily sleep logs and providing explanations for the intervention.

Sleep restriction is utilized to increase sleep efficiency by consolidating sleep. It increases the drive for sleep by limiting the amount of time spent in bed each night and decreases the association between bed and being awake. Once sleep is consolidated, a slow and gradual increase of the time in bed is begun. Adherence to this protocol requires close supervision with considerable reassurance.

Insomniacs exhibit physiological and cognitive arousal during the day and night (Bonnet & Arand, 1995). Relaxation therapies are used to reduce arousal in conjunction with cognitive–behavioral therapy for insomnia. It is important to clarify that the relaxation goal is decreasing arousal rather than inducing sleep. Progressive muscle relaxation, guided imagery, biofeedback, and diaphragmatic breathing all have been used successfully for insomnia management.

Many clinicians are unduly pessimistic regarding management of insomnia. Insomnia, indeed, is a complex complaint with multifactorial etiologies, but with individualized treatment approaches it is highly treatable. Symptoms of insomnia can be alleviated by specific cognitive–behavioral therapy sleep practices. Chronic and resistant insomniacs should be referred to an accredited sleep center with experience in the evaluation and treatment of these problems.

Obstructive Sleep Apnea

The wife of a 48-year-old man complains that his snoring has become unbearable. She also notes that he seems to be struggling to breathe in his sleep. Over the past 5 years, he has gained 40 pounds. He is a transit bus driver who claims that he is not sleepy during the day. Two years ago, he saw an otolaryngologist, who performed "some kind of throat surgery" that seemed to help his snoring, but only for a period of 6 months. He has hypertension and diabetes mellitus. He insists that he is not going to use "that face mask thing" he has heard about.

OSA and similar breathing-related sleep disorders are the most common conditions evaluated by overnight polysomnography. Epidemiological data from Young and colleagues (1993) indicated that 9% of women and 24% of men aged 30 to 60 years demonstrate sleep-disordered breathing. Perhaps 5% of all adults in Western countries have undiagnosed sleep apnea (Young, Evans, Finn, & Palte, 1997). Even relatively mild abnormalities may be associated with an increased risk of hypertension, manifestations of coronary artery disease, and stroke. Patients with OSA are more likely than controls to utilize health care resources prior to diagnosis. OSA is also correlated with diminished quality of life and decreased work or school performance (Redline et al., 1997).

The development of OSA is related to upper-airway anatomy and physiology (Kuna & Remmers, 2000). It must be emphasized that OSA does not occur exclusively in obese, middle-aged men. Obstruction most often occurs when upper airway muscle tone is decreased compared to wakefulness. With inspiratory respiratory effort, the airway collapses, and airflow is dramatically reduced or ceases completely. Breathing is restored as the patient awakens, but at the expense of continuity of sleep. Tremendous "physiological stress" results from the pattern of repetitive strangulation, with stimulation of the sympathetic nervous system and dramatic changes in cardiopulmonary hemodynamics.

The presenting signs and symptoms of OSA are becoming familiar through media reports. Snoring is most often loud and disruptive, but may not be reported by the patient, particularly if sleep is not witnessed. Similarly, observed apnea episodes may not be reported. The typical patient complains of unrefreshing sleep, nocturnal choking, excessive daytime sleepiness, difficulty concentrating during mundane tasks, irritability, morning headaches, or just a general lack of "energy." Less-obvious associated problems may include nocturia and enuresis, nocturnal heartburn, depression, and worsening dementia.

At present, effective diagnosis of sleep-disordered breathing requires PSG (Chesson et al., 1997). The accuracy of prediction of the presence and severity of OSA, even by the most astute clinician, is notoriously poor (Hoffstein & Szalai, 1993). Very little additional information is contributed by so-called screening tests, such as limited montage monitoring or overnight oxygen saturation monitoring. Furthermore, selection of therapeutic interventions is facilitated by overnight PSG testing.

Treatment of sleep apnea is often unsatisfactory. Over-the-counter remedies, including nasal dilator strips and throat sprays, are largely ineffective and probably best avoided. Surgical correction of upper airway anatomy may be helpful if major abnormalities are present (e.g., a large overbite or massively enlarged tonsils). For most patients, however, the benefit of surgery is only transient. Occasionally, patients with prominent snoring but mild OSA respond to a variety of dental devices that position the jaw and tongue forward. By far the best treatment available today is continuous positive airway pressure (CPAP), consisting of a nasal interface (occasionally also covering the mouth) connected to a blower that provides a column of air pressure, thereby pneumatically splinting the airway open (Grunstein & Sullivan, 2000). Although CPAP may seem unwieldy and inconvenient, its ability to correct OSA and improve sleep quality can be dramatic and perhaps lifesaving. Unfortunately, if the patient is unable to recognize a meaningful improvement in alertness and quality of life, the "compliance" rate of using CPAP is frustratingly poor (Barbe et al., 2001).

Narcolepsy

A 35-year-old man is sent for psychological evaluation after an unrevealing medical workup for a 10-year history of "chronic fatigue." Evaluation uncovers home and marital stress mostly related to the financial impact of being fired for sleeping on a job that became more sedentary. He has also taken on more child care duties at night because of his wife's employment, which has cut his habitual nightly sleep time down from 8 to 7 hours. He appears neither fatigued nor sleepy in your office but assures you he could fall asleep "any time of day if I'm not up and around doing something." Frightening vivid visual hallucinations as he is drifting off to sleep at night are infrequent, and he denies any convincing description of narcoleptic cataplexy. According to his wife, he has only mild intermittent snoring.

Narcolepsy is a neurogenetic syndrome of excessive daytime sleepiness despite adequate nighttime sleep time and sleep quality. Defective hypocretinergic neurotransmission has recently been identified as an important etiological factor (Mignot, 2000). The prevalence of approximately 0.05% (Guilleminault & Anagnos, 2000) is higher than previously thought. The risk of a narcoleptic parent having a narcoleptic child is approximately 1% to 2%. The neurological exam and intelligence are normal. Onset is typically in the teens or 20s, but can be in the 50s or later.

Narcoleptic sleepiness is most evident in sedentary, monotonous, and predictable nonthreatening situations. It is therefore not necessarily obvious when the patient is being interrogated by a health care professional. Narcoleptic sleepiness is behaviorally quite similar to that seen in any normal but sleep-deprived person. Contrary to popular belief, falling asleep while walking or with no warning at all is very unusual in narcoleptics. Sudden, brief, bilateral muscle weakness of varying distribution without loss of consciousness and precipitated by sudden emotion (cataplexy) is pathognomonic for narcolepsy, but is not reported in all cases. Auxiliary features of transient paralysis and frightening vivid visual hallucinations at sleep onset or awakening, periodic leg movements during sleep, and unexplained awakenings from sleep are also not found in all cases.

As in any chronic condition with symptoms the patient cannot control, chronic psychological distress may evolve, which in turn can exacerbate the symptoms. Suspected cases should be referred to a sleep disorders center because diagnosis relies heavily on a combination of the subtleties of the history plus overnight PSG and daytime nap studies. So-called genetic tests for narcolepsy are of little clinical use, and most patients will not benefit from spinal fluid hypocretin level testing.

At this time, there is no cure for narcolepsy. Management efforts are directed at patient education regarding driving and other safety considerations, vocational counseling, sleep hygiene, scheduling adequate nighttime sleep and short daytime naps, stimulant medications, and if appropriate, anticataplectic drugs.

Restless Legs Syndrome/Periodic Limb Movement Syndrome

A seemingly healthy 45-year-old female complains of gradually worsening difficulty initiating sleep over a 10-year period. Similar, but transient, episodes of insomnia accompanied her two pregnancies. There is no evidence for depressive or anxious traits, and her family practitioner finds no evidence of general medical or neurological abnormalities. Her blood count, liver, kidney, blood sugar, and thyroid tests are all normal. She attributes her sleep problem to disagreeable leg sensations when she lies down at night, but does not have these paresthesias during a daytime clinic visit and has difficulty describing exactly what they feel like or precisely where they are located. The family doctor is beginning to wonder whether her condition is psychological.

Restless legs syndrome (RLS) is a neurological cause of sleep-onset insomnia (Montplaisir, Nicolas, Godbout, & Walters, 2000) that may, in moderate or severe cases, also cause multiple awakenings. The prevalence is unknown, with estimates ranging from 0.5% to 15%, depending on ascertainment method and symptom severity. Severity usually increases with age. Most cases are familial and consistent with an autosomal dominant mode of inheritance. Onset is usually before the age of 50 years, sometimes during childhood and sometimes with exacerbation during pregnancy. There is often a family history of similar symptoms. RLS may also occur in association with chronic renal failure and iron deficiency. The International Restless Legs Study Group criteria for RLS are listed in Table 37.2.

It is the urge to move that seems to keep patients awake. In most cases, sufferers deny leg

Table 37.2 International Restless Legs Study Group Criteria for the Diagnosis of Restless Legs Syndrome

1. Desire to move the limbs, usually associated with paresthesias or dysesthesias.[a]
2. Motor restlessness.
3. Symptoms are worse or exclusively present at rest, with at least partial and temporary relief by activity.
4. Symptoms must be worse in the evening or during the night.

[a]Dysesthesia: An unpleasant *abnormal sensation*, whether spontaneous or evoked.

pain, itching, or cramping and describe the sensation as deep in the skin and difficult to localize precisely, but not in the joints. PSG is neither necessary nor sufficient and is not even confirmatory. Although common in RLS, not all patients will manifest periodic limb movements in sleep to bed partner observation or PSG demonstration. Furthermore, periodic leg movements are very common in the elderly, sleep apneics, narcoleptics, and even normal individuals. Syndromes that closely mimic RLS include the motor restlessness of akathesia, Parkinsonism, and painful peripheral neuropathy.

Evaluation should include screening for renal failure and for insufficient iron storage. Serum ferritin, rather than a simple hematocrit, is required to screen for low iron storage (Sun, Chen, Ho, Earley, & Allen, 1998). Sleep center referral may be indicated when (a) the diagnosis is in doubt; (b) bed partner observations suggest periodic leg movements in the setting of a sleep complaint, but the patient denies RLS symptomatology; or (c) treatment is ineffective.

Treatment is often difficult as there is no cure, and patients may eventually develop tolerance, even to dopamine agonists. Therefore, a search for exacerbating factors is important. Such factors include insufficient sleep time, caffeine after noon, diphenhydramine, alcohol at bedtime, antidepressant medication, and any cause of sleep fragmentation, such as obstructive sleep apnea. The dopamine agonists are the most efficacious drugs for symptomatic relief. Generally, benzodiazepines and related sedative hypnotics are of limited benefit in mild cases. Opiates can be very effective, but are not generally used as drugs of first choice. In children, clonidine is often used.

Circadian Rhythm Disorders: Delayed and Advanced Sleep Phase Syndromes, Jet Lag, and Shift Work Problems

A 20-year-old college sophomore with an otherwise excellent academic record complains of poor grades in her morning classes. She excels on her soccer team, which practices in the afternoons. Her most productive study time is 9 p.m. to 1 a.m. On the weekends, she "parties" until 2:30 a.m. and sleeps soundly until noon. An extensive medical workup for chronic fatigue was uninformative and eventually abandoned because it became apparent that her "fatigue" was limited to the hours before noon. Her father and her brother are "night owls."

The 24-hour sleep-wake cycle, along with myriad other bodily rhythms, is significantly influenced by a hypothalamic circadian pacemaker. When the hypothalamic circadian system is stressed (e.g., jet lag or shift work) or genetically programmed for an unwanted sleep-wake schedule, complaints may ensue.

Delayed sleep phase syndrome (DSPS) is the most common of the circadian disorders and appears to be a lifelong trait in many people. It is usually most prominent in those aged 15 to 25 years (Baker & Zee, 2000). Such "night people" easily delay their bedtime and often are incapable of initiating sleep before midnight. Long sleep times with difficulty awakening before 9 a.m. to noon are typical. Manifestations of adolescent DSPS are discussed in a separate section above.

Simply advising the patient to go to bed earlier and wake up to the alarm clock ignores the patient's neurological reality and is rarely effective. Management is difficult and should be referred to psychologists or sleep centers with interest in this disorder. Sleep hygiene, sleep logs, and individualized timing of bright early morning light and dim early evening light may be successful, but require considerable patient insight and motivation. The use of melatonin is still under investigation.

Treatment may also require psychiatric consultation to manage comorbid depression, social work consultation if a chaotic home situation precludes consistent limit setting, and educator consultation if academic failure that reinforces school avoidance is suspected. In adulthood, people with DSPS often end up working late shifts. If they attempt a conventional work schedule without treatment, they will appear to be sleep-deprived and exhausted sleep-onset insomniacs; their biological clocks keep them up late, and their social responsibilities wake them up early.

Advanced sleep phase syndrome (ASPS) is much less common in the young adult years than DSPS, but becomes prominent after middle age. Thus, as in DSPS, there are thought to be both genetic and developmental susceptibilities. Young adults with genetic (occasionally autosomal dominant) ASPS tend to fall asleep early and awaken early (Jones et al., 1999). They may also present with fatigue and early morning awakening insomnia if domestic responsibilities keep them up late and their biological "clock" wakes them up early. Symptomatic ASPS before the age of 40 years is sufficiently unusual and difficult to manage that referral to a sleep center with particular expertise in treating circadian disorders is indicated.

Early morning awakening is common in the elderly; approximately 30% of the geriatric population suffer from this even in the absence of depression. Current hypotheses of sleep maintenance insomnia in the elderly emphasize a combination of factors: (a) decreased capacity of the brain to generate deep sleep, (b) increased bodily stimuli that disrupt sleep, and (c) an advance in the circadian morning wake-up time to an earlier hour. Although of uncertain efficacy, current management recommendations for the circadian component emphasize bright light in the evening hours, increased daytime activity, and in some cases, curtailing the afternoon nap.

The syndrome of jet lag is thought to be a combination of sleep deprivation directly related to the travel plus loss of synchrony between the various internal sleep and body rhythms, as well as difficulty catching up on sleep at the destination (Arendt, Stone, & Skene, 2000). It may take the circadian system days to weeks to adjust to local time, depending on the individual and the number and direction of time zones crossed. Typical symptoms of such temporal stress include fatigue, apathy, irritability, difficulty staying awake in the day, difficulty getting to sleep at night, and gastrointestinal complaints.

Management of jet lag begins with adjusting the sleep and light exposure level closer to that of the destination days before departure. Factors that exacerbate sleep loss such as alcohol, caffeine, and stress should be minimized. For very short trips, it is probably better to try to stay on one's home schedule. For longer stays, guidelines have been devised to estimate the optimal timing of bright light and dark exposure on arrival. However, there are significant interindividual differences in biological rhythms, and bright light exposure at the wrong biological time can delay adaptation.

Sedatives have been reported to cause "travelers amnesia" (Morris, 1987). In our experience, other hypnotics (e.g., zolpidem) increase the risk of sleepwalking. Melatonin has some theoretical advantages, but the timing of the dose is critical and complicated to estimate. Until more effective strategies are devised, safety considerations such as avoiding prolonged driving or other critical tasks in a sleep-deprived state are paramount.

Shift work is conceptually related to jet lag in the sense that the imposed rest-activity cycle changes faster than the week or two required by the brain's circadian system. Chronic sleep deprivation is the result. Symptoms are also similar, including impaired vigilance while driving and increased irritability at home. Similar advice as noted above regarding the deleterious effects of caffeine, alcohol, and nicotine on sleep should be given. Sleep-disordered breathing syndromes or any other source of sleep disruption should be considered and treated aggressively if found. Most important, the patient should negotiate with family and friends whether (a) shift work can be tolerated any longer, (b) a second job is feasible, (c) the timing of domestic responsibilities in effect constitutes a second job, (d) a light- and noiseproof sleeping place where the patient is not interrupted during the day can be maintained.

Parasomnias: Sleepwalking, Sleep Talking, and Rapid Eye Movement Behavior Disorder

A 70-year-old female is found to have facial bruises; she is reluctant to explain how she was injured. Her husband is a mild-mannered man with no history of impulsive or violent behavior, and the patient states he has always been gentle with her. His behavior has not changed in that regard, but he has become much more forgetful and has much less of any substance to talk about. Eventually, she admits that her husband punched her while she was asleep. The husband claims he dreamed there was an intruder intent on harming his wife, and he woke up from his wife's shouting thinking he had punched the intruder.

Parasomnias are unwanted behaviors developing from sleep. In their most common form, they consist of talking, walking, or screaming episodes that arise out of deep NREM sleep in young children. The prevalence in children is thought to be in the 1%–15% range, but most cases never come to medical attention (American Sleep Disorders Association, 1997). Occasionally, the sleepwalking begins in adolescence or continues into adulthood. A positive family history of sleep walking/talking or enuresis is often present.

If injuries have occurred or are thought to be imminent, referral to a sleep disorders center is reasonable for diagnostic confirmation. It is also important to determine whether there are exacerbating factors such as sleep apnea. Particularly in children, nonpharmacological treatments are sought. Relaxation and hypnosis at bedtime (Broughton, 2000) and scheduled awakenings 15 to 30 minutes before the behaviors typically occur (D'Cruz & Vaughn, 2001) have demonstrated efficacy.

In elderly males, a history of violent sleep behavior with dream reports that are congruent with this behavior should raise the possibility of REM behavior disorder (RBD), particularly if there is a background of dementia (Mahowald & Schenck, 2000). In this condition, the normal REM sleep inhibition of skeletal muscle activity is significantly diminished, and patients may literally "act out" violent dreams. RBD may be a harbinger of Parkinson's or Alzheimer's disease or other degenerative brain disorders. Antidepressants, particularly chronic use of venlafaxine or fluoxetine, and alcohol withdrawal are also implicated. Whether cholinergic treatments for Alzheimer's disease exacerbate RBD is controversial. The prevalence is unknown, but RBD is probably not rare in the elderly. In contrast to the non-REM parasomnias, psychological counseling and treatment do not decrease the frequency or severity of RBD episodes.

It is impossible to distinguish between REM and NREM parasomnias by history alone. Sleep center referral is strongly recommended for consultation and PSG confirmation of the diagnosis because the most effective treatment (clonazepam) has potentially serious side effects on fall risk, cognition and memory, and sleep-disordered breathing.

SLEEP AND PSYCHIATRIC DISORDERS

Mood Disorders

Depressive disorders are associated with changes in sleep continuity, increased initial sleep latency, increased middle-of-the-night awakenings, early morning awakenings, decreased SWS, decreased latency to REM sleep, and increased REM density. It is difficult to determine whether the sleep changes are a result of depression or a precursor to the depressive episode. Depression is also associated with complaints of distressing dreams and daytime fatigue. Insomnia and depression frequently coexist. An estimated 60% of depressed subjects report sleep disturbance. Hypersomnia is reported with bipolar disorder and seasonal affective disorder. Insomnia may be a precursor of manic episodes in bipolar patients.

Anxiety

Generalized anxiety, panic disorder, posttraumatic stress disorder, and obsessive-compulsive disorder are associated with sleep disturbance. Common complaints include difficulty with sleep initiation and/or maintenance and unrefreshing sleep. Sleep disturbance and diminished sleep time contribute to exacerbation of the anxiety. Patients diagnosed with panic episodes may experience nocturnal panic attacks during the transition from stage 2 to SWS. Recurrent nocturnal panic attacks contribute to fear of sleep and perpetuate insomnia.

Schizophrenia

Significant sleep disruption may occur with schizophrenia, particularly with exacerbation of the disorder. Sleep patterns are characterized by reduced REM latency and decreased SWS. Complaints include increased nighttime awakenings, daytime fatigue, frightening dreams, and napping. The sedating effect of antipsychotic medication generally improves sleep onset and continuity. The adverse effects of antipsychotics include daytime sedation.

PSYCHOTROPIC MEDICATIONS AND SLEEP

The impact of psychotropic medications on sleep quality and sleep architecture is complex. It is difficult to isolate effectively the various effects on sleep of underlying pathology, coexisting conditions, effects of other medications, and individual variations in response. Nonetheless, a few generalizations and cautions are appropriate.

Tricyclic Antidepressants, Selective Serotonin Reuptake Inhibitors, and Monoamine Oxidase Inhibitor Antidepressants

The tricyclic antidepressants (amitriptyline, doxepin, imipramine, trimipramine, clomipramine, desipramine, nortriptyline) have been the type of antidepressant most studied with PSG. Overall, these drugs contribute to sedation, increased sleep continuity with decreased arousals, and REM suppression. The effects on REM suppression may be dose related. These medications are also associated with RLS/periodic leg movements that can disrupt overall sleep quality. Although there are possible detrimental effects, low-dose tricyclic antidepressants are commonly prescribed in the treatment of insomnia.

The selective serotonin reuptake inhibitors are associated with higher rates of sleep disorders, including RLS, PLMS, and insomnia (Dorsey, Lukas, & Cunningham, 1996). These medications are stimulating and contribute to generalized alerting effects (Sharpley & Cowen, 1995). PSG findings indicate delay to sleep onset, increased REM latency, decreased REM, and decreased sleep efficiency with sleep fragmentation (Gursky & Krahn, 2000).

Monoamine oxidase inhibitors have been found to suppress REM sleep. There may be a significant increase in REM following withdrawal of the medication. Objective findings include an overall decrease in sleep continuity with increased arousals, decreased total sleep time, and increased latency to REM (Gursky & Krahn, 2000).

Other Antidepressants

Trazadone is frequently prescribed for the treatment of insomnia and has been extensively studied regarding its effects on sleep. There is improvement in sleep initiation, sleep efficiency, depth of sleep, increased REM latency, and REM suppression. Nierenberg, Adler, Peselow, Zornberg, and Rosenthal (1994), in a double-blind, placebo-controlled study, found trazadone was effective for sleep promotion and improved sleep quality when used to counter the sleep-fragmenting effects of selective serotonin reuptake inhibitor antidepressants.

Nefazodone has been associated with improved sleep quality and increased REM time in both normal controls and depressed subjects. A multicenter, double-blind, placebo-controlled investigation by Rush and colleagues (1998) with depressed outpatients demonstrated improved sleep quality. Subjects taking nefazadone had decreased sleep fragmentation, improved sleep efficiency, and increased total REM sleep time.

Anxiolytics

Benzodiazepines have long been used for the treatment of insomnia and have been shown to reduce time to sleep onset, increase sleep efficiency, increase REM latency, and suppress REM. Benzodiazepines dramatically increase sleep spindle density in PSG recordings. Potential side effects of this class of drugs include potential addiction, withdrawal effects, rebound insomnia, amnesic effects, and residual sedation. These effects are affected by both dose and duration of action.

The continued use of sedative/hypnotic medications in the treatment of insomnia is problematic. Although it is easier to take medication than to initiate a behavioral program, the unfortunate result of reliance on medication is often escalating doses, tolerance, and diminished efficacy in the insomniac's ability to sleep. Eventually, the patient comes to believe that sleep is only possible with medication. The available evidence clearly supports greater efficacy of behavioral approaches over pharmacological interventions in the treatment of chronic insomnia (Morin, Hauri, et al., 1999). In addition, worsening of apnea and impairment of recovery through arousal occurs with all sedating medications, including benzodiazepines and opiates. If medication dependence has developed, treatment of the sleep disorder requires education, institution of healthy sleep habits, cognitive restructuring, and gradual tapering off of the medication dose.

CAFFEINE, ALCOHOL, AND SLEEP

Caffeine

Although there are individual sensitivities to caffeine consumption, ingestion of 500 mg of caffeine produces effects similar to 5 mg of amphetamine (Gillin & Drummond, 2000). Symptoms of insomnia, delirium, dyspnea, and cardiac irregularities are associated with caffeine consumption above 1 g. Caffeine is present in many beverages, chocolate, ice cream, yogurt, and over-the-counter analgesics and cold remedies. Although caffeine may be listed as an added ingredient, the amount of caffeine may not be disclosed. Levels of caffeine vary across products, serving size, and preparation. Brewed coffee contains about 100 to 150 mg of caffeine, soft drinks 40 to 75 mg in a 12-ounce serving, and cold preparations 15 to 60 mg per tablet.

The stimulant properties of caffeine can interfere with both sleep onset and sleep maintenance, thereby reducing total sleep time. The half-life of caffeine in young individuals is 3 to 7 hours. Consequently, the effects of caffeine can last as long as 8 to 14 hours. There is also a reduction in the capacity to metabolize and eliminate caffeine with increased age. Subsequently, caffeine consumption in the afternoon may have an impact on the quality of sleep in middle age. Recognition of the impact of caffeine is critical for an accurate assessment and treatment of sleep complaints in children, pregnant women, adults, and in the elderly because many patients are unaware of their actual caffeine intake.

Alcohol

Alcohol is one of the most commonly used sleep aids in the general population. It is estimated that 13% of the population between the ages of 18 and 45 years use alcohol to help sleep. Initially, alcohol promotes sleep onset; however, it disrupts the second half of the sleep period. Alcohol is metabolized quickly; subsequently, the second half of the night may be characterized by shallow disrupted sleep, increased REM sleep, nightmares, or sympathetic arousal such as tachycardia and sweating. It may also increase the risk of injury or falls during the night.

Sleep-disordered breathing is dramatically worsened by alcohol. Alcohol enhances upper airway collapse at the same time it increases the drive to breathe. When apneas subsequently develop, they are more prolonged and dangerous because alcohol tends to limit the ability to awaken and resume respiration.

Sleep patterns in alcoholics are generally disturbed, with complaints of insomnia, parasomnias, and circadian rhythm disorders. Sleep onset is rapid, but sleep duration is relatively short. Disrupted sleep patterns characterized by prolonged sleep latency, sleep fragmentation, and diminished total sleep time may persist for up to 2 years of abstinence. The treatment of sleep problems in the recovering alcoholic is challenging and may require the expertise of a sleep specialist in conjunction with an interdisciplinary team.

CONCLUSION

This chapter highlighted a few of the more common sleep disorders. We outlined the devastating impact of disrupted sleep on health and well-being. By paying attention to the sleep habits and sleep problems of patients, mental health practitioners are in a uniquely advantageous position to help resolve sleep disorders. There are few interventions that can so dramatically improve patients' lives at so little cost.

Sleep medicine is one of the fastest growing areas of medical science. The foundations of this science were established quite recently. The 2003 annual meeting of the Association of Professional Sleep Societies celebrated the 50th anniversary of the discovery of REM sleep. Obstructive sleep apnea, which has been described in the literature for centuries, was defined scientifically only about 30 years ago. There is still much to be learned as more attention is paid to the measurement, analysis, and subsequent understanding of sleep and its disorders.

In the near future, sleep medicine will be recognized as a separate specialty area for training and practice. It will remain an essentially multi-disciplinary discipline, both in the laboratory and the clinic. Mental health practitioners, as well as geneticists, physiologists, neurologists, pulmonologists, pediatricians, primary care physicians, and surgeons all have important roles in the recognition and management of sleep disorders.

ADDITIONAL RESOURCES

Suggestions for further reading and professional development resources are available at this book's companion Web site: www.primarycarepsych.com.

References

American Sleep Disorders Association. (1997). *ICSD—International classification of sleep disorders, revised: Diagnostic and coding manual* (pp. 142–147, 177–180). Rochester, MN: Author.

Arendt, J., Stone, B., & Skene, D. (2000). Jet lag and sleep disruption. In M. H. Kryger, T. Roth, & C. Dement (Eds.), *Principles and practice of sleep medicine* (3rd ed., pp. 591–599). Philadelphia, PA: Saunders.

Baker, S. K., & Zee, P. C. (2000). Circadian disorders of the sleep-wake cycle. In M. H. Kryger, T. Roth, & C. Dement (Eds.), *Principles and practice of sleep medicine* (3rd ed., pp. 606–614). Philadelphia: Saunders.

Barbe, F., Mayoralas, L. R., Duran, J., Masa, J. F., Maimo, A., Montserrat, J. M., et al. (2001). Treatment with continuous positive airway pressure is not effective in patients with sleep apnea but no daytime sleepiness. A randomized, controlled trial. *Annals of Internal Medicine, 134*, 1015–1023.

Bonnet, M. H., & Arand, D. L. (1995). 24-Hour metabolic rate in insomniacs and matched normal sleepers. *Sleep, 18*, 581–588.

Broughton, R. J. (2000). NREM arousal parasomnias. In M. H. Kryger, T. Roth, & C. Dement (Eds.), *Principles and practice of sleep medicine* (3rd ed., 693–706). Philadelphia: Saunders.

Buysse, D. J., Reynolds, C. F., Monk, T. H., Berman, S. R., & Kupfer, D. (1989). The Pittsburgh Sleep Quality Index: A new instrument for psychiatric practice and research. *Psychiatry Research, 28*, 193–213.

Carskadon, M., & Acebo, C. (2002). Regulation of sleepiness in adolescents: Update, insights, and speculation. *Sleep, 25*, 606–616.

Carskadon, M., Wolfson, A., Acebo, C., Tzischinsky, O., & Seifer, R. (1998). Adolescent sleep patterns, circadian timing and sleepiness at a transition to early school days. *Sleep, 21*, 871–881.

Chesson, A. L., Jr., Ferber, R. A., Fry, J. M., Grigg-Damberger, M., Hartse, K. M., Hurwitz, T. D., et al. (1997). The indications for polysomnography and related procedures. *Sleep 20*, 423–487.

Chesson, A., Hartse, K., Anderson, W., Davilia, D., Johnson, S., Littner, M., Wise, M. & Rafecas, J. (2000). Practice parameters for the evaluation of insomnia. *Sleep, 23*, 237–241.

Chokroverty, S. (1999). An overview of sleep. In S. Chokroverty (Ed.) *Sleep disorders medicine: Basic science, technical considerations, and clinical aspects* (pp. 7–20). Boston: Butterworth Heinemann.

Czeisler, C. A., Dijk, D. J., Kronauer, R. E., Brown, E. N., Duffy, J. F., Allan, J. S., Shanahan, T. L., Rimmer, D. W., Ronda, J. M., Mitchell, J. F., Silva, E. J., & Emens, J. S. (2000, May 19). Is there an intrinsic period of the circadian clock? *Science, 290*, 1174–1175.

D'Cruz, O. F., & Vaughn, B. V. (2001). Parasomnias—an update. *Seminars in Pediatric Neurology, 8*, 251–257.

Dorsey, C. M., Lukas, S. E., & Cunningham, S. L. (1996). Fluoxetine-induced sleep disturbance in depressed patients. *Neuropsychopharmacology, 14*, 437–442.

Dujardin, K., Guerrien, A., & Leconte, P. (1990). Sleep, brain activation, and cognition. *Physiology and Behavior, 47*, 1271–1278.

Foley, D. J., Monjan, A., & Brown, S. L. (1995). Sleep complaints among elderly persons: An epidemiological study of three communities. *Sleep, 18*, 425–432.

Gillin, J. C., & Drummond, S. (2000) Medication and substance abuse. In M. Kryger, T. Roth, & W. Dement (Eds.), *Principles and practice of sleep medicine* (3rd ed., pp. 1176–1195). Philadelphia: Saunders.

Grunstein, R., & Sullivan, C. (2000). Continuous positive airway pressure for sleep breathing disorders. In M. H. Kryger, T. Roth, & C. Dement (Eds.), *Principles and practice of sleep medicine* (3rd ed., pp. 894–912). Philadelphia: Saunders.

Guilleminault, C., & Anagnos, A. (2000). Narcolepsy. In M. H. Kryger, T. Roth, & C. Dement (Eds.), *Principles and practice of sleep medicine* (3rd ed., pp. 676–686). Philadelphia: Saunders.

Gursky, J., & Krahn, L. (2000). The effects of antidepressants on sleep: A review. *Harvard Review Psychiatry, 8*, 298–306.

Hoffstein, V., & Szalai, J. P. (1993). Predictive value of clinical features in diagnosing obstructive sleep apnea. *Sleep, 16*, 118–122.

Johns, M. W. (1992). Reliability and factor analysis of the Epworth Sleepiness Scale. *Sleep, 15*, 376–381.

Jones, C. R., Campbell, S. S., Zone, S. E., Cooper, F., DeSano, A., Murphy, J., Jones, B., Czajkowski, L., & Ptacek, L. J. (1999). Familial advanced sleep-phase syndrome: A short period circadian variant in humans. *Nature Medicine, 5*, 1062–1065.

Kuna, S., & Remmers, J. E. (2000). Anatomy and physiology of upper airway obstruction. In M. H. Kryger, T. Roth, & C. Dement (Eds.), *Principles and practice of sleep medicine* (3rd ed., pp. 840–858). Philadelphia: Saunders.

Mahowald, M. W., & Schenck, C. H. (2000). REM sleep parasomnias. In M. H. Kryger, T. Roth, & C. Dement (Eds.), *Principles and practice of sleep medicine* (3rd ed., pp. 724–741). Philadelphia: Saunders.

Marquet, P., Dive, D., Salmon, E., Sadzot, B., Franco, G., Poirrier, R., et al. (1990). Cerebral glucose utilization during sleep-wake cycle in man determined by positron emission tomagraphy and 2-fluoro-2-deoxy-d-glucose method. *Brain Research, 513*, 136–143.

Mignot, E. (2000). Pathophysiology of narcolepsy. In M. H. Kryger, T. Roth, & C. Dement (Eds.), *Principles and practice of sleep medicine* (3rd ed., pp. 663–675). Philadelphia: Saunders.

Montplaisir, J., Nicolas, A., Godbout, R., & Walters, A. (2000). Restless legs syndrome and periodic limb movement disorders. In M. H. Kryger, T. Roth., & C. Dement (Eds.), *Principles and practice of sleep medicine* (3rd ed., pp. 742–752). Philadelphia: Saunders.

Morin, C., Colecchi, C., Stone, J., & Sood, R. (1999). Behavioral and pharmacological therapies for late life insomnia. *Journal of the American Medical Association, 281*, 991–999.

Morin, C., Hauri, P., Espie, C., Spielman, A., Buysse, D., & Bootzin, R. (1999). Nonpharmacologic treatment of chronic insomnia. *Sleep, 22*, 1134–1156.

Morris, H. H. (1987). Traveler's amnesia: Transient global amnesia secondary to triazolam. *Journal of the American Medical Association, 258*, 945–946.

National Sleep Foundation. (2002). *Sleep in America poll.* Washington, DC: Author.

Nierenberg, A., Adler, L., Peselow, E., Zornberg, G., & Rosenthal, M. (1994). Trazadone for antidepressant associated insomnia. *American Journal of Psychiatry, 151*, 1069–1072.

Redline, S., Strauss, M., Adams, N., Winters, M., Roebuck, T., Spry, K., Rosenberg, C., & Adams, K. (1997). Neuropsychological function in mild sleep-disordered breathing. *Sleep, 20*, 160–167.

Rush, A. J., Armitage, R., Gillin, J. C., Yonkers, K. A., Winokur, A., Moldofsky, H., Vogel, G. W., Kaplita, S. B., Fleming, J. B., Montplaisir, J., Erman, M. K., Albala, B. J., & McQuade, R. D. (1998). Comparative effects of nefazodone and fluoxetine on sleep in outpatients with major depressive disorder. *Biological Psychiatry, 44*, 3–14.

Sateia, M., Doghramji, K., Hauri, P., & Morin, C. (2000). Evaluation of chronic insomnia. An American Academy of Sleep Medicine review. *Sleep, 23*, 243–308.

Sharpley, A., & Cowen, P. J. (1995). Effect of pharmacologic treatments on the sleep of depressed patients. *Biological Psychiatry, 37*, 85–98.

Shocat, T. (1999). Insomnia in primary care. *Sleep, 22*, s359–s365.

Spielman, A., & Anderson, M. (1999). The clinical interview and treatment planning as a guide to understanding the nature of insomnia: The CCNY insomnia interview. In S. Shokroverty (Ed.), *Sleep disorders medicine basic science, technical considerations, and clinical aspects* (pp. 385–426). Boston: Butterworth-Heinemann.

Sun, E. R., Chen, C. A., Ho, G., Earley, C. J., & Allen, R. P. (1998). Iron and the restless legs syndrome. *Sleep, 21*, 371–377.

Young, T., Evans, L., Finn, L., & Palte, M. (1997). Estimation of the clinically diagnosed proportion of sleep apnea syndrome in middle aged men and women. *Sleep, 20*, 705–706.

Young, T., Palta, M., Dempsey J., Skatrud, J., Weber, S., & Badr, S. (1993). The occurrence of sleep-disordered breathing among middle aged adults. *New England Journal of Medicine, 328*, 1230–1235.

38

Smoking Cessation Treatment

Lori Pbert
Roger Luckmann
Judith K. Ockene

Smoking is the leading preventable cause of morbidity and mortality in the United States, causing more than 430,000 deaths each year (Centers for Disease Control and Prevention, 1999). The health benefits of quitting smoking are substantial, decreasing the risk of heart attack, stroke, lung and other cancers, and chronic lung disease (U.S. Department of Health and Human Services, 1990). Despite the enormous health consequences of smoking and benefits of stopping, 23% of American adults continue to smoke (U.S. Department of Health and Human Services, n.d.).

Approximately 70% of smokers are seen by a primary care physician each year and average between three and four visits (National Center for Health Statistics, 1996), making the primary care setting an excellent venue for routinely identifying smokers and providing treatment. Unfortunately, only about half of smokers seen by a physician report receiving advice or counseling to quit (e.g., Thorndike, Rigotti, Stafford, & Singer, 1998), and even fewer (2%–15%) are offered any form of assistance, including provision of specific counseling steps, referral to treatment programs, or prescription for smoking cessation medications

(e.g., Goldstein et al., 1997). Psychologists and other mental health professionals working in the primary care setting have tremendous opportunities to address nicotine dependence, both within the context of their own clinical practice and in consultation to other primary care clinicians.

Psychologists currently deliver smoking treatment at an unknown rate. Because the constraints they face are similar to those faced by primary care physicians—time pressure, competing demands, difficulty obtaining reimbursement, and perception that such interventions are not part of their professional responsibility—it is likely that few psychologists routinely provide such services in primary care. However, psychologists are well trained to provide the types of behavioral interventions demonstrated as most effective in treating nicotine dependence. Psychologists could readily become key members of comprehensive primary care smoking treatment programs as well.

In this chapter, we describe nicotine dependence and present the clinical practice guideline for delivering the evidence-based treatment strategies currently recommended for smoking cessation treatment. Concrete strategies for assisting the smoker are provided, including both cognitive–behavioral and pharmacotherapy approaches. Because the primary care psychologist will likely encounter patients with medical conditions, alcoholism, and other psychiatric disorders as well as pregnant women and adolescent patients, we also focus on approaches that can be tailored to such patients. Finally, we present strategies for working effectively with medical colleagues as well as mistakes to avoid.

NICOTINE DEPENDENCE AND RELATED FACTORS

Nicotine dependence is classified as a substance use disorder in the *Diagnostic and Statistical Manual of Mental Disorders*, fourth edition (*DSM-IV*; American Psychiatric Association [APA], 1994). A prominent feature of dependence is nicotine withdrawal, which can include the following signs or symptoms experienced within 24 hours after abrupt cessation of nicotine use or a reduction in the amount of nicotine used: (a) dysphoric or depressed mood; (b) insomnia; (c) irritability, frustration, or anger; (d) anxiety; (e) difficulty concentrating; (f) restlessness; (g) decreased heart rate; and (h) increased appetite or weight gain (APA, 1994). Symptoms begin within a few hours of abstinence or significant reduction of tobacco use, increase over 3 to 4 days, and then gradually decrease over 1 to 3 weeks (Gritz, Berman, & Bastani, 1992). Change in appetite and problems with concentration appear to persist longer than do feelings of restlessness and irritability. Persons who take in more nicotine typically have stronger withdrawal symptoms and a more difficult time stopping smoking, but considerable variability occurs (Hughes, Higgins, & Hatsukami, 1990).

Physiological Factors in Nicotine Dependence

Nicotine exerts a number of neurochemical effects on the brain that are believed to contribute to the maintenance of cigarette smoking. The first are noradrenergic effects in the locus ceruleus thought to involve the neurotransmitter norepinephrine and to mediate symptoms of with-

drawal such as craving and irritability. Nicotine also exerts dopaminergic effects in the nucleus accumbens, which involves the release of dopamine and results in pleasurable feelings (Leshner, 1996). The smoker therefore takes in nicotine to avoid withdrawal and to obtain the pleasurable, immediate peripheral and central effects of nicotine (Pomerleau & Pomerleau, 1984).

Investigators have long noted that a smoker's primary use of cigarettes is to regulate emotional states (Tomkins, 1966). Early laboratory studies concluded that smoking significantly reduces fluctuations or changes in mood or affect during stress (Pomerleau & Pomerleau, 1987; Schachter, 1978). However, more recent evidence suggested that smokers experience higher stress levels than nonsmokers and recent quitters, and that the perceived reduction in tension and stress may be a function of the physiological dependence on nicotine (Parrott, 1999). Although desire to end the symptoms of withdrawal largely interferes with initial efforts to quit smoking, the active benefits of nicotine (e.g., improved concentration and the anorexic, stimulant, and perceived anxiolytic effects) clearly maintain the desirability of smoking and contribute to relapse for many persons.

Psychological Factors in Nicotine Dependence

The pleasurable physiological effects of nicotine become paired with the many activities and emotions associated with smoking (e.g., talking on the phone, driving, being in the work setting, feeling stressed or bored). These situations and emotions become "triggers" for the urge to smoke, and for many people smoking becomes a habitual behavior with little conscious forethought. Evaluating the functional uses of smoking for the person, such as a way to take a break from work or family chores or to handle daily stressors, can help identify areas in which the person will need to develop strategies other than smoking to help him or her function without cigarettes. In addition to identifying triggers, it is important to help the patient increase his or her self-efficacy or confidence in handling such situations and emotions without cigarettes. Considerable evidence shows that high self-efficacy predicts success in stopping smoking, whether the person is dealing with specific problem situations or with withdrawal symptoms (Ward, Klesges, & Halpern, 1997).

Social Factors in Nicotine Dependence

The social and cultural environments of smokers affect their ability to stop smoking. Individuals who experience more social support for cessation and have fewer smokers in their environment are more successful at stopping smoking (Gulliver, Hughes, Solomon, & Dey, 1995). Women whose husbands smoke have a more difficult time quitting than women whose husbands do not smoke (Royce, Corbett, Sorensen, & Ockene, 1997).

As the percentage of smokers decreases among more highly educated groups, the "hard core" smoker may continue to smoke despite social pressures against doing so (Kristeller, 1994) or may be a member of a social group in which there are social pressures to continue to smoke. The individual who is a member of the latter group and is one of the first in his or her group to stop smoking may have stronger personal reasons to quit than the other group members. Helping such individuals to address the social pressures to continue to smoke or including spouses or significant others in treatment may be particularly useful.

ASSESSMENT AND TREATMENT: AN OVERVIEW

The clinical practice guideline developed by the Agency for Healthcare Research and Quality (AHRQ), *Treating Tobacco Use and Dependence*, provides an assessment and intervention model for the treatment of nicotine dependence, as well as evidence-based treatment strategies that incorporate the National Cancer Institute's 5A strategy: ask, advise, assess, assist, and arrange follow-up (Fiore, Bailey, Cohen, et al., 2000). We recommend that the primary care clinician routinely assess and document smoking status at every clinical contact (ask). All current smokers should be provided clear, strong, and personalized advice to stop smoking (advise) and assessed for their willingness to quit at each contact (assess). For those smokers who are willing to quit, further assessment should occur, taking into account the physiological, psychological, and social

factors maintaining their smoking behavior, and brief intervention with follow-up should be provided (assist and arrange). When appropriate, referral to a psychologist or other mental health specialist may be made for more intensive treatment. Smokers who are not willing to quit may benefit from a brief motivational intervention to help facilitate motivation and future quitting efforts, and those who have recently quit should be offered interventions to help prevent relapse.

The psychologist or other mental health professional has the following potential roles in instituting the 5A strategy in a primary care setting:

1. Institute the 5As and incorporate all components of the model into your own clinical practice.
2. Assist primary care clinics in establishing a system for routinely screening patients for tobacco use, documenting use in the medical record (e.g., by adding smoking status to vital signs, noting tobacco dependence in the problem list, including in computerized assessments, asking on patient questionnaires), and prompting clinicians to deliver brief intervention and to refer patients to more intensive treatment as appropriate.
3. Provide training to primary care colleagues, both physicians and other clinicians, in how to deliver effective advice, assess willingness to quit, and provide counseling or motivational intervention.
4. Provide consultation and treatment for more intensive treatment and follow-up, including the development of specialized treatment programs to which primary care clinicians can refer their patients.

ASSESSMENT OF MOTIVATION AND READINESS TO QUIT

Because nicotine dependence is a chronic, relapsing disorder, often requiring five to seven attempts before maintained abstinence is achieved (U.S. Department of Health and Human Services, 1990), stopping smoking is a long-term process of change that takes place in stages over time. The psychologist or other mental health clinician is likely to receive referrals for patients who vary tremendously in their level of motivation or readiness to stop smoking, from not thinking about quitting, to taking steps to quit, to having quit and returned to smoking.

It is therefore important that the psychologist understand the full range of motivation and how best to intervene at each stage. It also is important to articulate to primary care clinicians that, as a behavior change specialist, you can assist the smoker at any level of motivation and encourage referrals of patients at all stages. It also is useful to help the physician understand that, by listening to the patient and using what he or she says, you can help move the patient along the continuum of change.

A description of the stages of change relevant for current smokers—precontemplation, contemplation, and preparation—with percentage of smokers falling into each of these categories and recommended clinician intervention is presented in Table 38.1. Many patients with psychiatric disorders fall into the precontemplation stage of change (e.g., Hall et al., 1995). Individuals in the action and maintenance stages of change are no longer smoking. They are at particular risk for relapse during the action stage, and the best approach is to work on relapse prevention (refer to the section "Preventing Relapse and Maintaining Change").

ASSISTING THE SMOKER WHO IS READY TO QUIT

For the smoker who is ready to make a quit attempt, the clinician's role is to assist in developing a quit plan and to support the individual through the quitting process. In developing a treatment plan, the clinician should consider the physiological, psychological, and social aspects of the patient's dependence and the strategies in the AHRQ clinical practice guideline (Fiore et al., 2000) summarized in Table 38.2.

Addressing Physiological Dependence: Nicotine Fading and Pharmacotherapy

Nicotine replacement therapy (NRT) and bupropion are proven effective treatments for nicotine dependence and, unless contraindicated, should be offered to all smokers of 10 or more cigarettes per day interested in quitting (Fiore et

al., 2000). Evaluation of physiological dependence is not required to justify pharmacotherapy, but it can be useful in preparing a quit plan. The Fagerstrom Test for Nicotine Dependence (Heatherton, Kozlowski, Frecker, & Fagestrom, 1991) (Table 38.3) is an excellent tool for assessing level of dependence. Table 38.4 summarizes behavioral strategies aimed at dealing with withdrawal symptoms.

Nicotine Fading: Brand Switching and Gradual Reduction

Nicotine fading (Foxx & Brown, 1979) has two components: brand switching to a cigarette with a lower nicotine level and gradual reduction of number of cigarettes smoked. Brand switching one or more times over several weeks in combination with reducing the number of cigarettes smoked by about one half per week can reduce withdrawal symptoms in heavy smokers. However, brand switching alone is likely not effective because smokers compensate for the lower nicotine level by vent blocking, puffing more frequently, or inhaling more deeply (Massachusetts Department of Public Health, 1997). Cessation rates are approximately equal for those who quit "cold turkey" and those who gradually reduce the number of cigarettes smoked (Fiore et al., 2000); patient preference should determine the approach selected. If nicotine fading is used, it should be combined with behavioral management strategies such that "lower need" cigarettes are eliminated first, and awareness of the function of each cigarette is increased.

Pharmacotherapy for Nicotine Dependence

Although most primary care physicians have a basic knowledge of pharmacotherapy for smoking cessation, many may not have the detailed understanding required to make the optimum recommendation for many smokers. Psychologists providing smoking cessation treatment should be able to offer informed recommendations on pharmacotherapy in consultation with their patients' primary care physicians.

Smokers who try to quit without the aid of pharmacotherapy typically have less than a 10% chance of succeeding even when highly moti-

Table 38.1 Stages of Change of Current Smokers and Recommended Clinician Intervention

Stages of Change[a]	Description	% of Smokers[b]	Clinician's Goal	Recommended Intervention[c]
Precontemplation	Not thinking about stopping smoking May be unaware of the risks of smoking, unwilling to consider making a change, or discouraged regarding ability to quit	40	Raise doubt about their intention to continue smoking by stimulating ambivalence; encourage patient to generate risks and problems associated with smoking and potential benefits of quitting	Motivational intervention, the 5Rs: 1. Relevance—encourage patient to consider why quitting is personally important 2. Risk—ask patient to identify potential negative consequences of tobacco use (e.g., personal and family health risks, financial cost, role model for children) 3. Rewards—ask patient to identify potential benefits of stopping tobacco use, highlighting the most relevant for patient 4. Roadblocks—ask patient to identify barriers to quitting; note elements of treatment that could address barriers; review past quit attempts to identify problems and successful coping skills 5. Repetition—repeat motivational intervention at each visit
Contemplation	Expresses ambivalence regarding stopping smoking Thinking about quitting and seeking information about smoking and stopping Not ready to commit to quit; uncertain about desire or ability to stop	40	Help patient resolve ambivalence by tipping the balance in favor of quitting	
Preparation	Ready to stop smoking in the next month May have made serious quit attempt in past year or have taken steps toward stopping (e.g., cutting down on number of cigarettes smoked, telling others of intent to quit)	20	Help patient determine best course of action to take Develop strategies and skills needed to make a successful quit attempt	See the section "Assisting the Smoker Who Is Ready to Quit"

[a]From DiClemente et al. (1991).
[b]From Velicer et al. (1995).
[c]From Fiore et al. (2000).

Table 38.2 Strategies for Assisting Smokers Who Are Ready to Quit

Action	Strategies for Implementation
1. Help the patient develop a quit plan	*Set a quit date*, preferably within the next week. *Tell* family, friends and coworkers of intent to quit and request understanding and support. *Anticipate challenges* to planned quit attempt, particularly during the critical first few weeks, including nicotine withdrawal symptoms, and prepare to address them. *Remove* cigarettes from environment.
2. Provide practical counseling (problem solving/skills training)	*Abstinence*—Total abstinence is essential. "Not even a single puff after the quit date." *Past quit experience*—Review to identify high-risk situations and what helped and hurt. *Anticipate triggers or challenges*—Discuss challenges/triggers and how patient will successfully address them. *Alcohol*—Consider limiting or abstaining from alcohol during the quitting process as alcohol is highly associated with relapse. *Other smokers in the household*—Encourage patient to quit with housemates or ask that they not smoke in their presence.
3. Provide intratreatment social support	Provide a *supportive clinical environment* while encouraging the patient in his or her quit attempt, clearly stating the clinic staff's availability to assist the patient.
4. Help patient obtain extra-treatment social support	Encourage the patient to *ask their spouse/partner, friends, and coworkers to support* his or her quit attempt.
5. Recommend the use of pharmacotherapy unless contraindicated	Recommend the use of *nicotine replacement therapy or nonnicotine pill, bupropion* (see section on pharmacotherapy).
6. Provide supplementary materials	Provide patient with *self-help materials* appropriate to his or her age, culture, race, and educational level.
7. Schedule follow-up contact, either in person or via telephone	*Follow-up* should occur within the first week after the quit date. *If abstinent at follow-up*, congratulate success, address problems encountered and challenges anticipated, and monitor pharmacological aids used. *If smoking occurred*, review circumstances leading to smoking, elicit recommitment to total abstinence, address problems encountered and challenges anticipated, review pharmacological aid use and problems, and consider referral to more intensive, specialized treatment.

Note. Adapted from Fiore et al. (2000). Used with permission.

vated to quit (Fiore, Smith, Jorenby, & Baker, 1994). Pharmacotherapies for smoking cessation include five first-line drugs (four types of NRT and sustained-release bupropion [bupropion SR]), two second-line drugs (nortriptyline and clonidine), and some combinations of two NRTs (see Table 38.5). Although published studies suggested that all five first-line medications have produced similar results in clinical trials (Fiore et al., 2000), the nicotine patch and bupropion SR are the best studied, best tolerated, and most widely used.

Use of any one of the five first-line medications approximately doubles a smoker's chance of quitting successfully (Fiore et al., 2000). The NRT combinations may increase long-term quit rates even more (Blondal, Gudmundsson, Olafsdottir, Gustavsson, & Westin, 1999; Fagerstrom, Schneider, & Lunell, 1993). As noted in the section "Addressing Physiological Dependence," all adult smokers of 10 or more cigarettes per day should be encouraged to use some form of pharmacotherapy each time they make a quit attempt. Light smokers (<10 cigarettes per day) have not been included in clinical trials of medications for smoking cessation, so it is not possible to make an evidence-based recommendation for them, but guidelines support the use of appropriately tailored NRT and bupropion SR in selected light smokers (Fiore et al., 2000). There are relatively few studies on the safety and efficacy of pharmacotherapy for smoking cessation among adolescents, but some experts suggested that cautious use of medications in appropriately adjusted doses may be justified (Fiore et al., 2000).

Nicotine replacement therapy

NRT is currently available in five delivery systems (transdermal patch, chewing gum, nasal spray, inhaler, and lozenge) that are about equally effective, although few studies have been done to compare them directly (Fiore et al., 2000). All forms of NRT deliver about half of the amount of nicotine provided by smoking a pack of cigarettes

under typical conditions of use, but the timing and rates of delivery differ (for example, transdermal patches deliver nicotine continuously over a 16- or 24-hour period; nicotine nasal spray raises blood nicotine levels more quickly than the gum or the inhaler and may be more effective in rapidly reducing acute nicotine craving in the highly dependent smoker) (Henningfield, 1995).

The disadvantages of the gum, the inhaler, and the spray include difficulty complying with multiple dose regimens as well as common adverse effects associated with the irritant properties and the disagreeable taste of nicotine. Some studies suggested that regular counseling that includes careful instruction in the delivery technique is required to maximize the effect of the nicotine gum (Cepeda-Benito, 1993).

Table 38.4 shows the commonly recommended duration of therapy for all forms of NRT currently available. Treatment for more than 8 weeks does not appear to increase the long-term quit

Table 38.3 Fagerstrom Test for Nicotine Dependence

	0 Points	1 Point	2 Points	3 Points	Score
1. How soon after you wake up do you smoke your first cigarette?	After 60 minutes	31–60 minutes	6–30 minutes	Within 5 minutes	
2. Do you find it difficult to refrain from smoking in places where it is forbidden, e.g., in church, at the library, cinema, etc.?	No	Yes			
3. Which cigarette would you hate most to give up?	All others	The first one in the morning			
4. How many cigarettes/day do you smoke?	10 or fewer	11–20	21–30	31 or more	
5. Do you smoke more frequently during the first hours of waking than during the rest of the day?	No	Yes			
6. Do you smoke if you are so ill that you are in bed most of the day?	No	Yes			
Total					

Classification of Dependence

0–2	Very low
3–4	Low
5	Moderate
6–7	High
8–10	Very High

Note. From Heatherton et al. (1991). Used with permission.

Table 38.4 Coping With Nicotine Withdrawal

Symptom	Cause	Duration	What to Do
Cough	Body is getting rid of mucus that has blocked airways	A few days	Drink plenty of fluids, use cough drops, hard candies, cough syrup at night to sleep
Lightheadedness	Body is getting extra oxygen	1 or 2 days	Take extra caution, get up and change positions slowly, drink water
Headache	More oxygen in the system and less carbon monoxide	1–2 weeks	Pain relievers, drink plenty of water, relaxation exercises, warm bath
Constipation, gas, stomach pain	Intestinal movement decreases for a brief period	1–2 weeks	Drink plenty of fluids, add fiber to diet (fruit, vegetables, whole grains), exercise
Irritability	Body's craving for nicotine	2–4 weeks	Walk, cut down on caffeine, deep breathing, hot baths, know it will pass
Insomnia	Nicotine affects brain wave function	2–4 weeks	Cut down on caffeine and avoid after 6 p.m., relaxation exercises, hot shower
Fatigue	Nicotine is a stimulant	2–4 weeks	Exercise, take naps, get plenty of rest, do not push yourself
Difficulty concentrating	Body needs time to adjust to lack of stimulation from nicotine	A few weeks	Plan workload, avoid additional stress, allow extra time, make "to do" lists, relaxation exercises
Hunger, increased appetite	Craving for cigarettes may be confused with hunger pangs	A few weeks	Drink water or low-calorie drinks, have low-calorie snacks on hand
Dysphoric or depressed mood, emotionality	Adjustment to life without nicotine and tobacco	A few weeks	Talk to a friend, take time out, get support
Craving for a cigarette	Withdrawal from nicotine, an addictive drug	A few weeks	Wait out the urge and remind yourself they last only a few minutes, deep breathe, distract yourself, drink water, take a walk

rate (Fiore et al., 2000). Tapering the dose of NRT before stopping therapy does not show a significant advantage over abrupt discontinuation. Flexible tailoring of dose and duration of NRT therapy according to the user's preferences and responses is a reasonable approach supported by clinical trials.

There are few contraindications to the use of NRT. Smoking any cigarettes while using the patch is strongly discouraged in all patients, but available evidence suggests that patch users who do smoke some cigarettes are not at high risk of any serious adverse events (Joseph et al., 1996).

Using two transdermal patches at a time has been recommended by some experts as a means of providing more complete nicotine replacement for heavy smokers, but so far clinical trials of high-dose patching have not shown a significantly higher quit rate for this approach compared to use of a single patch (Dale et al., 1995).

Combining the nicotine patch with another form of NRT (gum, spray, inhaler) offers the theoretical advantage of providing nicotine supplementation for acute cravings while also providing a continuous dose of nicotine to prevent withdrawal symptoms and cravings. Combinations of the nicotine patch with nicotine gum and nicotine nasal spray have been studied (Blondal et al., 1999; Fagerstrom et al., 1993) and reported to be safe and possibly to double the quit rate compared to the patch alone. Combining the patch with another NRT can become the treatment of choice even for first-time quitters. It may be reasonable to suggest an NRT combination therapy to more addicted smokers so they may supplement the patch with ad lib gum or an inhaler when needed.

Bupropion

Bupropion SR is an antidepressant demonstrated effective in several clinical trials in helping smokers manage cravings and withdrawal during quit attempts. Its most important contraindication is a history of a seizure or being at risk for seizures. Similar to NRT, bupropion typically has doubled long-term quit rates in clinical trials (Fiore et al., 2000). There is limited evidence to suggest that combining bupropion with the nicotine patch may have a small advantage over monotherapy. Bupropion's potential for reducing relapse rates and weight gain when used long term makes it an attractive agent for smokers with a history of multiple failed quit attempts and for overweight smokers. (Hays et al., 2001). One study showed that prolonged use (for 12 months) of bupropion SR following smoking cessation can modestly reduce expected weight gain as long as the medication is continued and may even result in an overall modest reduction in weight gain following discontinuance of the medication (Hays et al., 2001).

Second-line drugs (nortriptyline and clonidine) are also effective (Fiore et al., 2000), but the high frequency of adverse reactions (e.g., sedation and dry mouth) limit their use to smokers who are unable to receive or tolerate first-line medications. Ineffective medications include some antidepressants in the selective serotonin reuptake inhibitor class, naltrexone, and benzodiazepines (Hughes, Stead, & Lancaster, 2002a, 2002b; Wong, Wolter, Croghan, Offord, & Hurt, 1999).

Selecting the optimum pharmacotherapy

Selecting the optimum pharmacotherapy for an individual smoker requires a combination of art and science. After contraindications, ease of access to a medication and cost of medication may be the next most important considerations. If a smoker found that a medication was effective in promoting short-term abstinence in the past, it may be wise to recommend it again and then to attend to factors related to the smoker's relapse. When a medication was not effective in the past, a careful history of a quit attempt may elucidate reasons for its failure (e.g., compliance issues, inadequate dose, breakthrough craving), which can guide a decision on repeat use of the agent.

Depressive symptoms may emerge during smoking cessation among susceptible individuals, especially those with a history of depression (Borrelli et al., 1996); depression may also increase the risk of relapse (Burgess et al., 2002). Antidepressants such as bupropion SR or nortriptyline might prevent the development of depression during smoking cessation and thus increase the likelihood of success (Hayford et al., 1999), and they could be recommended to such patients. One small study also offered some initial support for the safety and efficacy of prescribing bupropion SR to smokers taking a selective serotonin reuptake inhibitor and in remission from depression (Chengappa et al., 2001).

Addressing Psychological Dependence: Cognitive and Behavioral Interventions

Cognitive and behavioral interventions for smoking have been developed from those used to treat a wide range of behavioral and addictive disorders (Bandura, 1969). Compared with no treatment, these interventions have been found typically to double quit rates (Fiore et al., 2000). The cognitive–behavioral approach encompasses assessment and intervention.

First, past quit attempts are reviewed to identify the reasons why the quit attempts were made, what methods the smokers used (e.g., cold turkey, tapering, pharmacological aids), problems experienced (including withdrawal symptoms), strategies that helped, and what led to relapse. The key is to assist the patient in reframing past

Table 38.5 First Line Medications for Treating Nicotine Dependence

Product	Nicotine Patches[a]	Nicotine Gum[a]	Nicotine Inhaler	Nicotine Spray	Bupropion SR
Brand names	Nicotrol CQ, Nicoderm, generic (various store brands)	Nicorette, generic (various store brands)	Nicotrol inhaler	Nicotrol NS	Zyban, Wellbutrin[b]
Product strengths	7 mg, 14 mg, 21 mg per patch (for typical systems that deliver 17, 32, 52 mg per day of nicotine)	2 mg (for average smokers, ≤24 cigarettes/day); 4 mg (for heavy smokers, >24 cigarettes/day)	10 mg/cartridge	10 mg/ml	150 mg
Amount of nicotine delivered[c]	16-hour patch: 15 mg/day; 24-hour patches: 7 mg/day, 14 mg/day, 21 mg/day	Up to 0.8 mg per 2-mg piece; up to 1.5 mg per 4-mg piece	Up to 2 mg per cartridge	0.5 mg in 2 sprays	N/A
Special directions for use	Apply to nonhairy part of body	Alternately chew and park for 20 minutes; nicotine absorbed through oral mucosa when gum is parked; avoid acidic beverages	Take frequent puffs over 20 minutes; nicotine absorbed through oral mucosa; avoid acidic beverages	Two sprays in each nostril	None
Dosing intervals and maximum doses	16-hour patch: 16 hours on, 8 hours off; 24-hour patch: replace every 24 hours (option to remove at bedtime)	1 piece every 1 to 2 hours and as needed for craving; maximum 24 pieces per day	Multiple puffs on a cartridge every 1–2 hours or as needed; 6–16 cartridges per day; maximum 16 cartridges per day	1–2 doses/hour (1 dose = 2 sprays or 1 per nostril)	150 mg/day (Days 1–3), 150/twice per day (after Day 3)
Time to peak plasma level	5–10 hours	20–30 minutes	15 minutes	5–7 minutes	3 hours
Manufacturer's recommended treatment duration[d]	16-mg patch: 6 weeks; 24-hour patches: initial, 21 mg for 4 weeks; taper, 14 mg and 7 mg for 2 weeks each	Initial: 6 weeks; taper: 6 weeks	Initial: up to 12 weeks; taper: 12 weeks	Initial: up to 8 weeks; taper: 4–6 weeks	7–12 weeks; maintenance: up to 6 months

Adverse reactions (treatment of reaction)	50% experience mild irritant skin reactions (rotate and use steroid cream), rare allergic skin reaction; vivid dreams, sleep disturbances while on the patch 24 hours (remove at bedtime)	Mouth soreness, hiccups, dyspepsia, and jaw ache (usually mild and transient; correct technique)	40% experience mouth and throat irritation (may resolve with regular use); dyspepsia	Local transient irritation in the nose and throat, watery eyes, sneezing and cough	Dry mouth; insomnia (avoid bedtime dose); shakiness
Absolute contraindications	_Previous hypersensitivity reaction to any of the products (i.e., serious allergic reaction); heart attack within 6 weeks or unstable angina_				
	Heart attack within 6 weeks; unstable angina; serious heart arrhythmia; uncontrolled hypertension; active peptic ulcer disease for all NRT	Allergy to menthol		Active rhinitis; active sinusitis	History of seizure; current or prior diagnosis of bulimia or anorexia nervosa; concurrent or recent use of monoamine oxidase inhibitors
	Severe eczema or other skin diseases that may be exacerbated by the patch	Severe temporomandibular joint disease or other jaw problems; dentures			
Relative contraindications/precautions	_Moderate or severe hepatic or renal impairment for all products_				
	Active hyperthyroidism; peripheral vascular disease for all NRT				
	Hot work environment (reduced patch adhesion); mild-moderate skin disease	Any jaw problem that affects gum chewing; dental appliances affected by gum	Oral or pharyngeal inflammation	Asthma; nasal polyps	Agitation; anxiety; insomnia; history of head trauma or other risk factor for seizure
Pregnancy category[e]	D	C	D	D	B

[a] Available without prescription.

[b] Zyban is brand name for bupropion SR marketed for smoking cessation with support materials; Wellbutrin is brand name for bupropion SR marketed for depression.

[c] Typical cigarette delivers 1–3 mg of nicotine.

[d] Manufacturer recommendations based on duration of treatment in initial clinical trials. Many independent trials of NRT suggest treatment for 8 weeks is as effective as longer treatments for most, but shorter and longer intervals are reasonable depending on individual smoker.

[e] Pregnancy categories: B, No evidence of risk in humans; adequate, well-controlled studies in pregnant women have not shown increased risk of fetal abnormalities despite adverse findings in animals, or in the absence of adequate human studies, animal studies show no fetal risk; the chance of fetal harm is remote, but remains a possibility. C, Risk cannot be ruled out; adequate, well-controlled human studies are lacking, and animal studies have shown a risk to the fetus or are lacking as well; there is a chance of fetal harm if the drug is administered during pregnancy, but the potential benefits may outweigh the potential risks. D, Positive evidence of risk. Studies in humans, or investigational or postmarketing data, have demonstrated fetal risk; nevertheless, potential benefits from the use of the drug may outweigh the potential risk. For example, the drug may be acceptable if needed in a life-threatening situation or serious disease for which safer drugs cannot be used or are ineffective.

efforts to stop smoking as learning experiences and to apply what was learned to the current quit attempt.

Second, current smoking patterns are assessed. In which situations and in response to what feelings or emotions does the patient most feel like smoking? These are triggers to smoking. Asking the smoker to rate the level of need for each cigarette on a scale of 1 (low need) to 5 (high need) is often helpful. Behavioral self-monitoring, which involves the patient recording the time, place, situation, mood, thoughts, and need level associated with each cigarette smoked, can be very informative for both the patient and clinician at this stage to identify specific areas needing attention.

You can then help the patient develop specific cognitive–behavioral coping strategies to address anticipated problems and triggers, such as the following:

1. Anticipate and avoid high-risk situations and cues that bring on an urge to smoke (e.g., negative mood, being around other smokers, drinking alcohol).
2. Remove oneself from the trigger situation.
3. Substitute other behaviors incompatible with smoking cigarettes when urges arise (e.g., taking a walk, going to a smoke-free environment, deep breathing or other relaxation exercise).
4. Learn cognitive strategies to reduce negative moods.
5. Develop and use assertiveness, refusal skills, and other skills to manage the triggers.
6. Use cognitive restructuring to reshape positive beliefs about smoking or to counteract irrational thinking, replacing maladaptive thoughts with more constructive thoughts.

Such practical counseling assists the smoker in developing the problem-solving skills necessary to address the psychological dependence on smoking.

Addressing Social Influences

The psychologist or other mental health professional can address social influences in two ways. First, the psychologist can establish a supportive clinical environment including (a) encouraging the patient in his or her quit attempt by noting the availability of effective treatments and that half of all individuals who have ever smoked have now quit and communicating belief in the patient's ability to quit; (b) communicating caring, concern, and willingness to help by asking how the patient feels about quitting and being open to discussing the patient's fears about quitting, ambivalence, and difficulties experienced; and (c) encouraging the patient to talk about the quitting process by asking about the patient's reasons for wanting to quit, concerns or worries about quitting, and successes achieved and difficulties encountered while quitting (Fiore et al., 2000). The psychologist also can share these approaches with the referring primary care clinician so that the clinician may similarly develop a supportive environment for the patient when seen in the primary care clinic.

Second, the psychologist can help patients increase social support from friends, family, and coworkers for their efforts to quit. The psychologist can model through videotapes or demonstration how to request support from others and have the patient practice these skills. The psychologist can inform patients of community resources such as "quit lines" and Web sites and invite support persons to treatment sessions or assign patients to serve as support "buddies" for one another (Fiore et al., 2000). Role playing to resist social pressures to smoke is another important component of treatment.

Addressing Smoking Cessation and Weight Gain

The average weight gain for sustained quitters is 5 to 6 kg (Froom, Melamed, & Benbasal, 1998). Although such weight gain does not present a medical risk at all comparable to that of smoking a pack of cigarettes a day, it is a common reason for many people to start use of tobacco, continue use, and return to it. Several factors have been implicated in weight gain, including an increase in metabolism from nicotine intake (Perkins, 1992), which may result in weight gain during the quitting process even without increased caloric intake (Fiore et al., 2000) and a heightened preference for sweets while smoking (Grunberg, 1982).

These biological factors, along with the use of food as a behavioral substitute, make weight gain an important issue to address when helping smokers quit (Klesges, Meyers, & Klesges, 1989). However, there is no published empirically tested treatment that successfully addresses weight gain while quitting. Dieting while attempting to quit increases the rate of relapse (Ockene et al., 2000). The AHRQ guideline (Fiore et al., 2000) suggests discussing issues of weight gain with patients before they quit and preparing them for the high probability of gaining weight when they quit.

In addition, remind the patient that quitting smoking is the current priority, and that support is available if the patient would like to work on weight loss after successful cessation. A focus on weight loss should be delayed until the patient is no longer experiencing withdrawal symptoms and feels secure in his or her ability to remain smoke free. Encouraging patients to engage in sensible lifestyle changes such as increasing physical activity, eating plenty of fruits and vegetables, and avoiding alcohol use is also suggested. There is evidence that increasing physical activity can help decrease weight gain and support maintenance (Froom et al., 1998). As noted, both nicotine gum and bupropion SR may delay or reduce weight gain.

PREVENTING RELAPSE AND MAINTAINING CHANGE

As many as 70% of those individuals who stop smoking resume smoking, or relapse, within a year. The strongest predictor of relapse is a "slip" within a relatively brief period of time (average 18–60 days) after cessation (Ockene et al., 2000). The psychologist will therefore want to implement a system to deliver minimal relapse prevention interventions routinely to all individuals who have recently stopped smoking.

The AHRQ guideline recommends that the individual be congratulated on any success, provided strong encouragement to remain abstinent, and encouraged to discuss (a) benefits the patient may derive from stopping smoking; (b) any success experienced, such as reduced withdrawal symptoms and duration of abstinence; and (c) any problems encountered or anticipated in maintaining abstinence, such as weight gain, depression, alcohol, or other smokers in the household (Fiore

et al., 2000). More intensive prescriptive relapse prevention interventions should be delivered when an individual experiences problems in maintaining abstinence and should be tailored to the specific problems encountered. These interventions are presented in Table 38.6.

For those individuals who have a physical health problem related to their smoking, as of January 1, 2002, the psychologist and other health care clinicians now may use six new reimbursement codes under the *Current Procedural Terminology (CPT)* coding system for the initial assessment and ongoing treatment of nicotine dependence. These codes are for health and behavior assessment and treatment services for behavioral, social, and psychophysiological procedures for the prevention, treatment, and management of physical health problems (American Psychological Association, n.d.). They do not require psychiatric diagnoses, which eliminates a major obstacle to affording treatment for many patients.

SMOKING CESSATION TREATMENT IN SPECIAL POPULATIONS

The typical primary care physician cares for many patients with serious cardiopulmonary conditions and major psychiatric disorders and is likely to be the main provider of smoking cessation treatment for these patients even though many may also receive some care from psychiatrists, cardiologists, pulmonologists, and other specialists. Pediatricians and family physicians are key providers of advice on smoking for adolescents; many family physicians and obstetrician-gynecologists provide prenatal care for pregnant women. Each of these patient populations poses some special challenges but also offers some unique opportunities to reduce medical risks dramatically.

Smoking Cessation and Cardiopulmonary Disease

Cigarette smoking is a potent, major risk factor for both the development of coronary heart disease (CHD) (angina and myocardial infarction) and its progression (Schoenberger, 2002). Smoking approximately doubles the lifetime risk of CHD; among individuals who have had a myo-

Table 38.6 Prescriptive Relapse Prevention

Problems	Responses
Lack of support for cessation	Schedule follow-up visits or telephone calls with the patient.
	Help the patient identify sources of support in his or her environment.
	Refer the patient to an appropriate organization that offers cessation counseling or support.
Negative mood or depression	If significant, provide counseling, prescribe appropriate medications, or refer the patient to a specialist.
Strong or prolonged withdrawal symptoms	If the patient reports prolonged craving or other withdrawal symptoms, consider extending the use of an approved pharmacotherapy or adding/combining pharmacological medications to reduce strong withdrawal symptoms.
Weight gain	Recommend starting or increasing physical activity; discourage strict dieting.
	Reassure the patient that some weight gain after quitting is common and appears to be self-limiting.
	Emphasize the importance of a healthy diet.
	Maintain the patient on pharmacotherapy known to delay weight gain (e.g., bupropion SR; NRTs, particularly nicotine gum).
	Refer the patient to a specialist or program.
Flagging motivation/ feeling deprived	Reassure the patient that these feelings are common.
	Recommend rewarding activities.
	Probe to ensure that the patient is not engaged in periodic tobacco use.
	Emphasize that beginning to smoke (even a puff) will increase urges and make quitting more difficult.

Note. Reprinted from Fiore et al. (2000). Used with permission.

cardial infarction, continued smoking increases the risk of death or repeated infarction by 22% to 47% (Schoenberger, 2002). Cigarette smoking is the most important cause of chronic obstructive pulmonary disease (COPD) (chronic bronchitis and emphysema).

For individuals with a diagnosis of CHD or COPD, smoking cessation can dramatically improve their prognosis (Schoenberger, 2002). Smokers who quit after having a heart attack have been reported to reduce their risk of death or reinfarction by up to 50% (Schoenberger, 2002). Smokers with early COPD have shown objective improvement in baseline lung function, a return to normal age-related rates of decline in lung function, and a reduction in COPD symptoms (Kanner, Connett, Williams, & Buist, 1999). The benefits in reduced risks and reduced symptoms from smoking cessation may appear within months of cessation for patients with CHD and COPD (Schoenberger, 2002).

The well-documented substantial short-term and long-term benefits from cessation and the life-threatening nature of the risks of continued smoking provide potentially powerful motivation to quit for smokers with CHD and COPD. Studies of smoking cessation after myocardial infarction and coronary artery bypass surgery have shown that even subjects in the control groups quit smoking at relatively high rates, ranging from 30% to 45% (Hajek, Taylor, & Mills, 2002; Tonstad, 2002). The behavioral interventions evaluated nearly double the already high quit rates of the control group. Quit rates among subjects with COPD in control groups in clinical trials are not as high as the rates among CHD patients (Tashkin et al., 2001; Tonstad, 2002). A variety of interventions, including counseling and pharmacotherapy, increase long-term quit rates among patients with COPD (Pederson, Wanklin, & Lefcoe, 1991; Tashkin et al., 2001; Tonstad, 2002). Psychologists may be especially well equipped to take maximum advantage of the motivators for quitting in primary care patients with CHD and COPD. Except for patients within 6 weeks of a heart attack or experiencing unstable angina or serious heart rhythm disturbances, all forms of NRT can be offered to these patients. Bupropion is also an option, even in the early postinfarction period.

Smoking Cessation and Alcohol

The primary care psychologist will likely see patients with both tobacco use and alcohol abuse as these two conditions have been found to be moderately to strongly related (e.g., Kozlowski et al., 1993). Among identified alcoholic persons, the incidence of smoking has been between 80% and 90% in all studies; alcoholic persons also are more likely to smoke heavily (Bien & Burge, 1990). Consequently, most patients seen in primary care who have been identified as suffering from alcoholism will smoke, many of them at a level that is acutely health endangering.

Although individuals in substance abuse treatment report that it is difficult to quit smoking while undergoing substance abuse treatment, working on smoking cessation does not increase relapse to alcohol use (Kalman, 1998; Hughes et al., 1996). In fact, in some instances smoking cessation has been found to be associated with *decreased* relapse back to alcohol use (Kalman, 1998). There is evidence that alcohol may interact with nicotine, increasing tolerance to the more immediate effects of alcohol, thus setting the stage for high-risk drinking (Kalman, 1998).

However, smoking may be used as a coping strategy to avoid alcohol use in response to urges to use alcohol during early sobriety (Kalman, 1998). Kalman noted that alcoholic individuals with greater nicotine dependence (a) more often report that they cope with drinking urges by smoking; (b) are more likely to have stronger urges to smoke when abstaining from alcohol; and (c) are more likely to be concerned about maintaining sobriety while quitting smoking, particularly during the early phases of sobriety.

The American Psychiatric Association practice guideline for tobacco treatment in individuals with alcoholism therefore recommends that the timing of smoking cessation in relationship to alcohol abuse treatment should be determined by the patient (Hughes et al., 1996). The AHRQ clinical practice guideline also supports the provision of smoking cessation treatments for individu-als receiving treatment for chemical dependency, recommending both counseling and pharmacotherapy (Fiore et al., 2000).

Smoking Cessation and Psychiatric Disorders

Smoking is more prevalent and cessation is less common in individuals with a current or past history of significant mental health disorders, including depression and schizophrenia (American Psychiatric Association, 1996; Breslau, 1995; Covey, Glassman, & Stetner, 1998; Glassman, 1993; Ziedonis, Kosten, Glazer, & Frances, 1994). The evidence is less clear regarding the increased prevalence of smoking among individuals with anxiety disorders (Glassman, 1993; Parrott, 1999).

Increasing attention is being paid to the role of smoking in psychiatric disorders in regard both to the role of the central nervous system effects of nicotine and to the apparent special value of smoking to psychiatric patients (Glassman, 1993). Some psychiatric patients may be actively self-medicating through their use of cigarettes (Hall, 1980). Also, there is evidence that smoking interacts with psychoactive medications, and that abstinence from smoking affects medications commonly used to treat psychiatric disorders (Hughes et al., 1996) (see Table 38.7).

Patients who are depressed or who have a history of depression not only have difficulty with cessation, but also are at increased risk of experiencing dysphoric mood states and relapse of major depressive disorder after cessation (Covey et al., 1998) and may experience more extreme symptoms of withdrawal (Glassman, 1993). Although the detrimental effect of depression on smoking cessation has been found in both men and women, it may be particularly important in the treatment of women because of the increased incidence of depression and dysphoric mood states in women (Borrelli, Bock, King, Pinto, & Marcus, 1996).

The period of time during which major depressive symptoms return after stopping smoking varies with each individual and may be as short as a few weeks or as long as a few months after quitting. Therefore, individuals who have a history of depression or who reported having experienced depression in association with previous

Table 38.7 Effect of Smoking Cessation on Psychoactive Medications

Increases Blood Levels	Does Not Increase Blood Levels	May or May Not Affect Blood Levels
Clomipramine	Amitriptyline	Alprazolam
Clozapine	Chlordiazepoxide	Chlorpromazine
Desipramine	Ethanol	Diazepam
Dexmethyldiazepam	Lorazepam	
Doxepin	Midazolam	
Fluphenazine	Triazolam	
Haloperidol		
Imipramine		
Oxazepam		
Nortriptyline		
Propranolol		

Note. Medications are listed by generic name only; for trade names of psychotropic medications, see Table A.1.

quit attempts should be advised to consider psychotherapy or pharmacological treatment of depression if they begin to experience dysphoria (Hughes et al., 1996).

A high rate of smoking and difficulty with cessation are also observed in patients with schizophrenia (Ziedonis et al., 1994). Nicotine may reduce drug-induced side effects experienced by these patients, and nicotine withdrawal symptoms can mimic drug-induced side effects (i.e., increased restlessness) as well. In persons with schizophrenia, quitting smoking also may temporarily worsen drug-related movement disorders, and continued smoking may bring about a need for an increase in the required dosage of antipsychotics (Goff, Henderson, & Amico, 1992; Hughes et al., 1996; Menza, Grossman, Van Horn, Cody, & Forman, 1991).

Little empirical evidence is available regarding the treatment of nicotine dependence in psychiatric patients (see Hughes et al., 1996, for a discussion of intervention issues). In the psychiatric patient for whom smoking cessation is critical for medical reasons, a comprehensive intervention plan—one that includes the treatment components outlined in this chapter—is indicated. In particular, behavior therapy focused on the development of coping and social skills is important. Adjustment of medication may be needed as well. As more inpatient services limit access to

smoking or become smoke free, use of the nicotine patch, particularly for persons who smoke heavily, is recommended. In addition, a clear staff policy regarding smoking that does not undermine the smoke-free policy of the treatment unit is imperative.

Smoking Cessation and Pregnancy

Smoking by pregnant women is associated with an increased risk of prenatal death, low birth weight, and preterm delivery (Rodriguez-Thompson, 2002). About 25% of women of reproductive age are current smokers; only 20% to 30% of pregnant smokers abstain completely from smoking throughout their pregnancy (Rodriguez-Thompson, 2002). Because any pharmacotherapy can pose a risk to a fetus, the implementation of effective, intensive behavioral interventions is especially important for pregnant women.

A variety of behavioral interventions have been shown in clinical trails to be modestly effective in promoting smoking cessation (Dolan-Mullen, Ramirez, & Groff, 1994). NRT and bupropion may be used to treat pregnant women, but should be considered only after behavioral therapy has been tried and has failed (Rodriguez-Thompson, 2002). Although nicotine itself has several known adverse effects on the developing fetus, the use of NRT may be less risky than continued smoking because NRT typically cuts nicotine levels to half compared to smoking and eliminates exposure to carbon monoxide and multiple other toxins in tobacco smoke. Bupropion is classified as a Pregnancy Class B medication, indicating that animal studies have shown no serious adverse effects on fetuses, and that so far limited information about its use in humans does not suggest adverse effects on pregnancy outcomes.

Smoking Cessation and Adolescents

Adolescent smoking is the most powerful predictor of adult smoking (Chassin, Presson, Rose, & Sherman, 1996). Nearly 90% of adult smokers smoked their first cigarette and 71% were daily smokers before 18 years of age (U.S. Department of Health and Human Services, 1994). The most recent National Youth Tobacco Survey found 28% of high school students reported current smoking, defined as smoking in the past 30 days (Centers for Disease Control and Prevention, 2001).

Although the most serious health outcomes associated with smoking typically emerge later in life, adolescent smokers show evidence of airway obstruction, slowed growth in lung function, and higher rates of cough and other respiratory symptoms compared to nonsmokers (Gold et al., 1996; Prokhorov, Emmons, Pallonen, & Tsoh, 1996). In addition, the earlier that individuals begin to smoke, the higher their risk for cancer, heart disease, stroke, and chronic obstructive lung disease (Davis, Shelton, Watanabe, & Arnold, 1989), nicotine addiction (Taioli & Wynder, 1991), and possibly their risk of developing anxiety disorders and depression (Goodman & Capitman, 2000; Johnson et al., 2000). If current tobacco use patterns continue, an estimated 5 million youths between the ages of 0 and 17 years in 1995 (approximately one in three adolescent smokers) will die of a smoking-related disease.

Although cessation is less common among adolescents than adults, interest in quitting is strong: Nearly three fourths of adolescent smokers have seriously thought about quitting, 64% reported having made a quit attempt, and 40% of daily smokers reported having tried to quit at least once and failed (U.S. Department of Health and Human Services, 1994). Cessation and suc-

cessful abstinence are more common in smokers who began smoking at or after 17 years of age (American Academy of Pediatrics, 1988). Among 17-year-old smokers, 40% reported that they would be interested in cessation treatment (U.S. Department of Health and Human Services, 1994).

Primary care settings provide key opportunities for delivering smoking cessation treatment to young smokers because between 63% and 85% of adolescents are seen by pediatricians, family practitioners, and other clinicians for preventive care visits each year (Hedberg, Byrd, Klein, Auinger, & Weitzman, 1996; Igra & Millstein, 1993; Klein, Wilson, McNulty, Kapphahn, & Collins, 1999). Existing guidelines recommend that clinicians routinely screen for smoking and deliver strong messages regarding abstaining from smoking and stopping smoking to children and adolescents (e.g., American Academy of Pediatrics, 1988; Fiore et al., 2000).

The AHQR clinical practice guideline recommends that counseling and behavioral interventions shown to be effective with adults (i.e., those presented in this chapter) should be considered for use with adolescents, with the content of these interventions modified to be developmentally appropriate (Fiore et al., 2000). Regarding the use of pharmacotherapy in treating adolescent smokers, the guideline suggests clinicians may consider prescriptions for bupropion SR or NRT when there is evidence of nicotine dependence and the desire to stop smoking.

WAYS TO WORK EFFECTIVELY WITH YOUR MEDICAL COLLEAGUES

As a trained behavior change specialist, the psychologist is an exceptional resource for medical colleagues in the primary care setting. Based on our extensive experience with such collaborations, we make the following recommendations:

1. Educate medical colleagues about establishing comprehensive systems to screen and treat smokers and offer training or inservices to assist them in building the skills and confidence necessary to deliver brief, effective treatment in the course of routine care.

2. Ensure that medical colleagues are aware that you are available to treat their patients who smoke.

3. Reinforce that you can help with smokers at all stages of readiness to quit, and that they can encourage smokers to consider quitting and to work with you.

4. Inform physicians who refer patients to you of your assessment, your recommendations, and your treatment plan and provide updates on the progress of treatment.

5. If possible, make arrangements to go on rounds with medical colleagues or be involved in case management meetings to discuss patients who smoke and take the opportunity to provide informal coaching regarding medical advice giving and brief motivational interventions.

6. Explore colleagues' past experience in treating patients for nicotine dependence, eliciting their frustrations and possible negative attitudes toward smokers in an accepting, nonjudgmental manner, assisting them to accept those reactions, and educating them regarding the nature of nicotine addiction, the stages of change for smokers, the chronic nature of the condition, and the availability of effective treatments to assist smokers.

7. Work with your medical colleagues and health care setting to institute the nonpsychiatric reimbursement codes under the *Current Procedural Terminology* coding system for the initial assessment and ongoing treatment of nicotine dependence. These codes are for health and behavior assessment and treatment services for behavioral, social, and psychophysiological procedures for the prevention, treatment, and management of physical health problems (American Psychological Association, n.d.).

COMMON MISTAKES TO AVOID IN WORKING WITH SMOKERS

Based on our clinical experience, the following are errors commonly made by both psychologists and medical clinicians when working with smokers and strategies to address these concerns:

1. Lecturing the individual regarding the risks of the smoking behavior and what he or she needs to do to quit. The use of a patient-centered approach is more appropriate and effective; it explores the patient's concerns regarding continued smoking and past quit experiences and, through the use of open-ended questions, helps the patient consider the best strategies for quitting.

2. Failing to consider pharmacotherapy options if the patient had not had success with them in the past because of inappropriate use. Assess prior use and determine the best approach based on the patient's needs, including education and guidance on proper medication use.

3. Considering (and verbalizing) a quit attempt ending in relapse to be a failure. It takes multiple quit attempts to maintain abstinence, and every attempt is an opportunity to learn what worked well and what problem spots need addressing to improve the likelihood of maintained abstinence with the next quit attempt.

4. Failing to address smoking and smoking cessation in patients who express little or no interest in quitting. Individuals move through stages of change and each stage benefits from interventions tailored to that level of readiness to quit: For the individual not wanting to quit, a patient-centered approach to exploring the patient's perception of his or her personal risks of smoking and potential benefits of quitting along with barriers of concern and strategies and treatments available to address these barriers is recommended.

SUMMARY

Cigarette smoking is the leading preventable cause of morbidity and mortality in the United States (Centers for Disease Control and Prevention, 1999). Psychologists and other mental health professionals working in the primary care setting have many opportunities to address nicotine dependence within the context of their own clinical practice and in consultation to other primary health care clinicians. There are now evidence-based treatment guidelines on which to base interventions (Fiore et al., 2000). These guidelines help the clinician in assessing the unique needs of each smoker and assisting the smoker by addressing physiological, psychological, and social dependence through pharmacotherapy and cognitive–behavioral interventions. From a behavioral perspective, the clinician can assist the smoker in developing or enhancing skills to manage stress, emotions, and situational triggers without the use of cigarettes, with an emphasis on the patient attributing changes in smoking behavior to their personal abilities and skills rather than to willpower or to the external aspects of treatment (Bandura, 1977a, 1977b). From a pharmacological perspective, all smokers, and particularly those who demonstrate a high level of physiological dependency on nicotine, would benefit from NRT or bupropion to allow them to work on the behavioral aspects of quitting while receiving some relief from the physiological withdrawal symptoms. The psychologist can begin to discuss NRT or bupropion and recommend that the patient speak with his or her primary care clinician to make a final decision on the most appropriate pharmacotherapy. Also, the patient may benefit from relapse prevention intervention as well as more intensive help when problems in maintaining abstinence are experienced. Special clinical populations, such as patients with medical conditions, pregnant women, and adolescents, require special considerations when treating them for nicotine dependence. Finally, there are specific strategies mental health clinicians can use to maximize their effectiveness in working with medical colleagues in the primary care setting and resources that they and their patients can turn to in their efforts to help smokers become smoke free.

ADDITIONAL RESOURCES

Suggestions for further reading and professional development resources are available at this book's companion Web site: www.primarycarepsych.com.

References

American Academy of Pediatrics, Committee on Psychosocial Aspects of Child and Family Health. (1988). *Guidelines for health supervision II*. Elk Grove, IL: Author.

American Psychiatric Association. (1994). *Diagnostic and statistical manual of mental disorders* (4th ed.). Washington, DC: Author, 1994.

American Psychiatric Association. (1996). Practice guideline for the treatment of patients with nicotine dependence. *American Journal of Psychiatry, 153*, 1–31.

American Psychological Association. (n.d.). *Practice directorate announces new health and behavior CPT codes*. Retrieved October 17, 2002, from http://www.apa.org/practice/cpt_2002.html

Bandura, A. (1969). *Principles of behavior modification*. New York: Holt, Rinehart, and Winston.

Bandura, A. (1977a). Self-efficacy: Toward a unifying theory of behavioral change. *Psychology Review, 84*, 191–215.

Bandura, A. (1977b). *Social learning theory*. Englewood Cliffs, NJ: Prentice Hall.

Bien, T., & Burge, R. (1990). Smoking and drinking: A review of the literature. *International Journal of Addiction, 25*, 1429–1454.

Blondal, T., Gudmundsson, L. J., Olafsdottir, I., Gustavsson, G., & Westin, A. (1999). Nicotine nasal spray with nicotine patch for smoking cessation: Randomised trial with six year follow up. *British Medical Journal, 318*, 285–288.

Borrelli, B., Bock, B., King, T., Pinto, B., & Marcus, B. H. (1996). The impact of depression on smoking cessation in women. *American Journal of Preventive Medicine, 12*, 378–387.

Borrelli, B., Niaura, R., Keuthen, N., Goldstein, M. G., DePue, J. D., Murphy, C., et al. (1996). Development of major depressive disorder during smoking-cessation treatment. *Journal of Clinical Psychiatry, 57*, 534–538.

Breslau, N. (1995). Psychiatric co-morbidity of smoking and nicotine dependence. *Behavior Genetics, 25*, 95–101.

Burgess, E. S., Brown, R. A., Kahler, C. W., Niaura, R., Abrams, D. B., Goldstein, M. G., et al. (2002). Patterns of change in depressive symptoms during smoking cessation: Who's at risk for relapse? *Journal of Consulting and Clinical Psychology, 70*, 356–361.

Centers for Disease Control and Prevention. (1999). Cigarette smoking among adults—United States 1997. *Morbidity and Mortality Weekly Report, 48*, 993–996.

Centers for Disease Control and Prevention. (2001). Youth tobacco surveillance—United States. *Morbidity and Mortality Weekly Report, 50*, 1–86.

Cepeda-Benito, A. (1993). Meta-analytical review

of the efficacy of nicotine chewing gum in smoking treatment programs. *Journal of Consulting and Clinical Psychology, 61,* 822–830.

Chassin, L., Presson, C. C., Rose, J. S., & Sherman, S. J. (1996). The natural history of cigarette smoking from adolescence to adulthood: Demographic predictors of continuity and change. *Health Psychology, 15,* 478–484.

Chengappa, K. N., Kambhampati, R. K., Perkins, K., Nigam, R., Anderson, T., Brar, J. S., et al. (2001). Bupropion sustained release as a smoking cessation treatment in remitted depressed patients maintained on treatment with selective serotonin reuptake inhibitor antidepressants. *Journal of Clinical Psychiatry, 62,* 503–508.

Covey, L. S., Glassman, A. H., & Stetner, F. (1998). Cigarette smoking and major depression. In M. S. Gold & B. Stimmel (Eds.), *Smoking and illicit drug use* (pp. 35–46). Binghamton, NY: Haworth Medical Press.

Dale, L. C., Hurt, R. D., Offord, K. P., Lawson, G. M., Croghan, I. T., & Schroeder, D. R. (1995). High-dose nicotine patch therapy. Percentage of replacement and smoking cessation. *Journal of the American Medical Association, 274,* 1353–1358.

Davis, J. W., Shelton, L., Watanabe, I. S., & Arnold, J. (1989). Passive smoking affects endothelium and platelets. *Archives of Internal Medicine, 149,* 386–389.

DiClemente, C. C., Prochaska, J. O., Fairhurst, S. K., Velicer, W. F., Velasquez, M. M., & Rossi, J. S. (1991). The process of smoking cessation: An analysis of pre-contemplation, contemplations, and preparation stages of change. *Journal of Consulting and Clinical Psychology, 59,* 295–304.

Dolan-Mullen, P., Ramirez, G., & Groff, J. (1994). A meta-analysis of randomized trials of prenatal smoking cessation interventions. *American Journal of Obstetrics and Gynecology, 171,* 1328–1334.

Fagerstrom, K., Schneider, N., & Lunell, E. (1993). Effectiveness of nicotine patch and nicotine gum as individual versus combined treatments for tobacco withdrawal symptoms. *Psychopharmacology, 111,* 271–277.

Fiore, M. C., Bailey, W. C., Cohen, S. J., Dorfman, S. F., Goldstein, M. G., Gritz, E. R., et al. (2000). *Treating tobacco use and dependence: Clinical practice guideline.* Rockville, MD: U.S. Department of Public Health and Human Services, Public Health Service Agency for Healthcare Research and Quality.

Fiore, M. C., Smith, S. S., Jorenby, D. E., & Baker, T. B. (1994). The effectiveness of the nicotine patch for smoking cessation. A meta-analysis. *Journal of the American Medical Association, 271,* 1940–1947.

Foxx, R., & Brown, R. (1979). Nicotine fading and self-monitoring for cigarette abstinence or controlled smoking. *Journal of Applied Behavior Analysis, 12,* 111–125.

Froom, P., Melamed, S., & Benbasal, J. (1998). Smoking cessation and weight gain. *Journal of Family Practice, 46,* 460–464.

Glassman, A. H. (1993). Cigarette smoking: Implications for psychiatric illness. *American Journal of Psychiatry, 150,* 546–553.

Goff, D. C., Henderson, D. C., & Amico, E. (1992). Cigarette smoking in schizophrenia: Relationship to psychopathology and medication side effects. *American Journal of Psychiatry, 149,* 1189–1194.

Gold, D. R., Wang, X., Wypij, D., Speizer, F. E., Ware, J. H., & Dockery, D. W. (1996). Effects of cigarette smoking on lung function in adolescent boys and girls. *New England Journal of Medicine, 335,* 931–937.

Goldstein, M. G., Niaura, R., Willey-Lessne, C., De Pue, J., Eaton, C., Rakowski, W., et al. (1997). Physicians counseling smokers. A population-based survey of patients' perceptions of health care provider-delivered smoking cessation interventions. *Archives of Internal Medicine, 157,* 1313–1319.

Goodman, E., & Capitman, J. (2000). Depressive symptoms and cigarette smoking among teens. *Pediatrics, 106,* 748–755.

Gritz, E. R., Berman, B., & Bastani, R. (1992). A randomized trial of a self-help smoking cessation intervention in a nonvolunteer female population: Testing the limits of the public health model. *Health Psychology, 11,* 280–289.

Grunberg, N. (1982). The effects of nicotine and cigarette smoking on food consumption and taste preferences. *Addictive Behavior, 7,* 317–331.

Gulliver, S. B., Hughes, J. R., Solomon, L. J., & Dey, A. N. (1995). An investigation of self-efficacy, partner support, and daily stresses as predictors of relapse to smoking in self quitters. *Addiction, 90,* 767–772.

Hajek, P., Taylor, T., & Mills, P. (2002). Brief intervention during hospital admission to help patients to give up smoking after myocardial infarction and bypass surgery: Randomised controlled trial. *British Medical Journal, 324,* 87–89.

Hall, G. H. (1980). Pharmacology of tobacco smoking in relation to schizophrenia. In G. Hemmings (Ed.), *Biochemistry of schizophrenia and addiction: In search of a common factor* (pp. 199–207). Baltimore, MD: University Park Press.

Hall, R. G., Duhamel, M., McClanahan, R., Miles, G., Nason, C., Rosen, S., et al. (1995). Level of functioning, severity of illness, and smoking status among chronic psychiatric patients. *Journal of Nervous and Mental Disorders, 183,* 468–471.

Hayford, K. E., Patten, C. A., Rummans, T. A., Schroeder, D. R., Offord, K. P., Croghan, I. T., et al. (1995). Efficacy of bupropion for smoking cessation in smokers with a former history of major depression or alcoholism. *British Journal of Psychiatry, 174,* 73–178.

Hays, J. T., Hurt, R. D., Rigotti, N. A., Niaura, R., Gonzales, D., Durcan, M. J., et al. (2001). Sustained-release bupropion for pharmacologic relapse prevention after smoking cessation. A randomized, controlled trial. *Annals of Internal Medicine, 135,* 423–433.

Heatherton, T., Kozlowski, L., Frecker, R., & Fagestrom, K. O. (1991). The Fagerstrom Test for Nicotine Dependence: A revision of the Fagerstrom Tolerance Questionnaire. *British Journal of Addiction, 86,* 1119–1127.

Hedberg, V. A., Byrd, R. S., Klein, J. D., Auinger, P., & Weitzman, M. (1996). The role of community health centers in providing preventive care to adolescents. *Archives of Pediatrics and Adolescent Medicine, 150,* 603–608.

Henningfield, J. (1995). Nicotine medications for smoking cessation. *New England Journal of Medicine, 333,* 1196–1203.

Hughes, J. R., Fiester, S., Goldstein, M. G., Resnick, M. P., Rock, N., & Ziedonis, D. (1996). Practice guideline for the treatment of patients with nicotine dependence. American Psychiatric Association. *American Journal of Psychiatry, 153*(10 Suppl.), 1–31.

Hughes, J. R., Higgins, S. T., & Hatsukami, D. (1990). Effects of abstinence from tobacco: A critical review. In L. T. Kozlowski, H. M. Annis, H. D. Cappell, F. B. Glaser, M. S. Goodstadt, Y. Israel, et al. (Eds.), *Research advances in alcohol and drug problems* (Vol. 10, pp. 317–398). New York: Plenum.

Hughes, J. R., Stead, L., & Lancaster, T. (2002a). Antidepressants for smoking cessation. Cochrane Database of Systematic Reviews, CD00031.

Hughes, J. R., Stead, L., & Lancaster, T. (2002b). Anxiolytics for smoking cessation. Cochrane Database of Systematic Reviews, CD002849.

Igra, V., & Millstein, S. G. (1993). Current status and approaches to improving preventive services for adolescents. *Journal of the American Medical Association, 269,* 1408–1412.

Johnson, J. G., Cohen, P., Pine, D. S., Klein, D. F., Kasen, S., & Brook, J. S. (2000). Association between cigarette smoking and anxiety disorders during adolescence and early adulthood. *Journal of the American Medical Association, 284,* 2348–2351.

Joseph, M., Norman, M., Ferry, H., Prochaska, A. V., Westman, B. C., Steele, B. G., et al. (1996). The safety of transdermal nicotine as an aid to smoking cessation in patients with cardiac disease. *New England Journal of Medicine, 335,* 1792–1798.

Kalman, D. (1998). Smoking cessation treatment for substance misusers in early recovery: A review of the literature and recommendations for practice. *Substance Use and Misuse, 33,* 2021–2047.

Kanner, R. E., Connett, J. E., Williams, D. E., & Buist, A. S. (1999). Effects of randomized assignment to a smoking cessation intervention and changes in smoking habits on respiratory symptoms in smokers with early chronic obstructive pulmonary disease: The Lung Health Study. *American Journal of Medicine, 106,* 410–416.

Klein, J. D., Wilson, K. M., McNulty, M., Kapphahn, C., & Collins, K. S. (1999). Access to medical care for adolescents: Results from the 1997 Commonwealth Fund Survey of the Health of Adolescent Girls. *Journal of Adolescent Health, 25,* 120–130.

Klesges, R., Meyers, A., & Klesges, L. (1989). Smoking, body weight and their effects on smoking behavior: A comprehensive review of the literature. *Psychology Bulletin, 106,* 204–230.

Kozlowski, L. T., Henningfield, J. E., Keenan, R. M., Lei, H., Leigh, G., Jelinek, L., et al. (1993). Patterns of alcohol, cigarette, and caffeine and other drug use in two drug abusing populations. *Journal of Substance Abuse and Treatment, 10,* 171–179.

Kristeller, J. (1994). The hard-core smoker: Finding

a definition to guide intervention. *Health Values, 18*, 25–32.

Leshner, A. I. (1996). Understanding drug addiction: Implications for treatment. *Hospital Practice (Office of Education), 31*, 47–54, 57–59.

Massachusetts Department of Public Health. (1997). *Cigarette nicotine disclosure report as required by Massachusetts general laws.* Chapter 307B, CMR 660.000.

Menza, M. A., Grossman, N., Van Horn, M., Cody, R., & Forman, N. (1991). Smoking and movement disorders in psychiatric patients. *Biological Psychiatry, 30*, 109–115.

National Center for Health Statistics. (1996). *Health: United States (1995)* (Publication No. 96–1232). Hyattsville, MD: Public Health Service.

Ockene, J. K., Emmons, K. M., Mermelstein, R. J., Perkins, K. A., Bonollo, D. S., Voorhees, C. C., et al. (2000). Relapse and maintenance issues for smoking cessation. *Health Psychology, 19*(1, Suppl.), 17–31.

Parrott, A. C. (1999). Does cigarette smoking cause stress? *American Psychologist, 54*, 817–820.

Pederson, L., Wanklin, J., & Lefcoe, N. (1991). The effects of counseling on smoking cessation among patients hospitalized with chronic obstructive pulmonary disease: A randomized clinical trial. *International Journal of Addiction, 26*, 107–119.

Perkins, K. (1992). Metabolic effects of cigarette smoking. *Journal of Applied Physiology, 72*, 401–409.

Pomerleau, C., & Pomerleau, O. (1987). The effects of a psychosocial stressor on cigarette smoking and subsequent behavioral and physiological responses. *Psychophysiology, 24*, 278–285.

Pomerleau, O., & Pomerleau, C. (1984). Neuroregulators and the reinforcement of smoking: Towards a biobehavioral explanation. *Neuroscience Biobehavioral Review, 8*, 503–513.

Prokhorov, A. V., Emmons, K. M., Pallonen, U. E., & Tsoh, J. Y. (1996). Respiratory response to cigarette smoking among adolescent smokers: A pilot study. *Preventive Medicine, 25*, 633–640.

Rodriguez-Thompson, D. (2002). Smoking and pregnancy. In B. D. Rose (Ed.), *UptoDate.* Wellesley, MA. Retrieved May 2, 2003, from http://www.uptodate.com

Royce, J. M., Corbett, K., Sorensen, G., & Ockene, J. (1997). Gender, social pressure, and smoking cessations: The Community Intervention Trial for Smoking Cessation (COMMIT) at baseline. *Social Science & Medicine, 44*, 359–370.

Schachter, S. (1978). Pharmacological and psychological determinants of smoking. *Annals of Internal Medicine, 88*, 104–114.

Schoenberger, J. A. (2002). *Preventive cardiology: Cardiovascular risk of smoking and benefits of smoking cessation.* In B. D. Rose (Ed.), *UptoDate.* Wellesley, MA. Retrieved May 2, 2003, from http://www.uptodate.com

Taioli, E., & Wynder, E. L. (1991). Effect of the age at which smoking begins on frequency of smoking in adulthood. *New England Journal of Medicine, 325*, 968–969.

Tashkin, D., Kanner, R., Bailey, W., Buist, S., Anderson, P., Nides, M., et al. (2001). Smoking cessation in patients with chronic obstructive pulmonary disease: A double-blind, placebo-controlled, randomised trial. *Lancet, 357*, 1571–1575.

Thorndike, A. N., Rigotti, N. A., Stafford, R. S., & Singer, D. E. (1998). National patterns in the treatment of smokers by physicians. *Journal of the American Medical Association, 279*, 604–608.

Tomkins, S. (1966). Psychological model for smoking behavior. *American Journal of Public Health, 56*, 17–20.

Tonstad, S. (2002). Use of sustained-release bupropion in specific patient populations for smoking cessation. *Drugs, 62*(Suppl. 2), 37–43.

U.S. Department of Health and Human Services. (1990). *The health benefits of smoking cessation* [DHHS Publication No. (CDC) 90–8416, pp. 580–616]. Washington, DC.: U.S. Department of Health and Human Services, Public Health Service, Centers for Disease Control, Center for Chronic Disease Prevention and Health Promotion, Office on Smoking and Health.

U.S. Department of Health and Human Services. (1994). *Preventing tobacco use among young people: A report of the surgeon general.* Atlanta, GA: Centers for Disease Control and Prevention, National Center for Chronic Disease Prevention and Health Promotion, Office on Smoking and Health.

U.S. Department of Health and Human Services. (n.d.). *1997–2001 National health interview surveys.* Centers for Disease Control and Prevention, National Center for Health Statistics. Retrieved July 18, 2002, from http://www.cdc.gov/nchs

Velicer, W. R., Fava, J. L., Prochaska, J. O., Abrams, D. B., Emmons, K. M., & Pierce, J. P. (1995). Distribution of smokers by stage in three representative samples. *Preventive Medicine, 24,* 401–411.

Ward, K. D., Klesges, R. C., & Halpern, M. T. (1997). Predictors of smoking cessation and state-of-the-art smoking interventions. *Journal of Social Issues, 53,* 129–145.

Wong, G. Y., Wolter, T. D., Croghan, G. A., Croghan, I. T., Offord, K. P., & Hurt, R. D. (1999). A randomized trial of naltrexone for smoking cessation. *Addiction, 94,* 1227–1237.

Ziedonis, D. M., Kosten, T. R., Glazer, W. M., & Frances, R. J. (1994). Nicotine dependence and schizophrenia. *Hospital & Community Psychiatry, 45,* 204–206.

39

Somatoform Disorders

David Servan-Schreiber
Gary Tabas
Randall E. Kolb
Leonard J. Haas

Although somatoform disorders are among the most common psychiatric conditions in primary care patient populations (Spitzer et al., 1994), they are not disorders that psychologists commonly treat. This is largely because patients with these disorders resist considering their conditions as psychological; they are fixated on finding biological causes for their suffering. When patients with somatoform disorders present themselves for mental health treatment, it is essential that the psychologist collaborate with the primary care clinician. This chapter explores the processes underlying somatoform disorders, reviews the effective treatment of these disorders, and suggests ways in which the primary care psychologist can effectively collaborate with both the patient and the other clinicians involved in the patient's care.

Somatization is the process in which emotional distress or difficult life situations are experienced as physical symptoms. Patients who somatize present with persistent physical complaints for which physicians cannot find a physiological explanation. The condition is common; for example, 25% to 50% of primary care visits do not identify a serious medical problem as the cause of the chief complaint (Katon, 1984; Kroenke, Arrington, & Mangelsdorff, 1990).

Somatizing patients use inordinate amounts of health care resources. Smith, Miller, and Monson (1986) estimated that patients with somatization disorder generated costs nine times greater than the average medical patient. Despite such large amounts of medical attention, somatizing patients report high levels of disability and suffering, in one study greater than that experienced by depressed patients (Escobar et al., 1987). Finally, physicians report that somatizing patients are among the most frustrating to treat (Lin et al., 1991). Doctors are robbed of a sense of effectiveness as the multiple complaints do not fit into usual diagnostic categories, and the patients do not fit well into a typical office schedule.

Failure to recognize this disorder and manage it appropriately leads to frustrating, costly, and potentially dangerous interventions that do not reduce suffering or identify occult disease. Medical treatment outcome studies have begun to point toward management strategies and psychological interventions that reduce comorbidity and cost of treatment and significantly improve the doctor–patient relationship.

DIAGNOSIS

Somatization is frequently a diagnosis of exclusion. That is, the diagnosis is made only after a long process of excluding all possible physiological causes for the complaints. To avoid the frustration, errors, and cost of this approach, the clinician can instead seek to make an earlier, positive diagnosis of somatization. Servan-Schreiber (1998) described the key features necessary for the diagnosis: (a) several nonspecific symptoms in different organ systems, (b) a chronic course, and (c) symptoms that are in excess of objective findings.

Somatization is a not a specific disease, but rather a process with a spectrum of expression (Katon et al., 1991; Kroenke et al., 1994, 1997). Mild somatoform disorder is exemplified by stress-related exacerbation of common symptoms (e.g., headache, lightheadedness, or low back pain in the context of a divorce, new family member, or new job). The condition can also be expressed in severe unrelenting symptoms that leave a patient completely disabled and withdrawn from most aspects of personal and occupational functioning.

Although the *Diagnostic and Statistical Manual of Mental Disorders*, fourth edition (*DSM-IV*; American Psychiatric Association, 1994) has defined several different somatoform disorders and investigators have suggested additional criteria for syndromes seen commonly in office settings, making fine distinctions does not help the primary care physician manage these patients. The majority of somatoform disorders seen in medical practice are diagnosable as undifferentiated somatoform disorder (Simon, 2001). Once the process of somatization is identified, the management principles are similar for the different somatoform disorders.

Table 39.1 lists many of the symptoms and syndromes affecting patients who somatize. Most of these symptoms are similar to those reported by patients with organic pathology. If isolated, they would require a full medical workup. However, in the somatizing patient, there are too many symptoms in too many organ systems, and they last too long. The intensity of the symptoms often strikes the physician as out of proportion to the healthy appearance of the patient. Similarly, although the syndromes listed can be reflections of organic pathology, in the somatizing patient they are often nonspecific.

The diagnosis of somatization is complicated by the fact that there is a significant overlap between psychiatric/psychological disorders and somatization disorders. Finding evidence of a psychiatric condition does not rule out somatization; rather, it can be a clue to the diagnosis.

Nonspecific somatic symptoms such as fatigue, aches and pains, palpitations, sweating, or nausea are common complaints of patients with depression and anxiety (Bridges & Goldberg, 1985; Koenig, Cohen, Blazer, Krishnan, & Sibert, 1993; Kroenke et al., 1994; Mulsant, Ganguli, & Seaberg, 1997; Waxman, McCreary, Weinrit, & Carner, 1985). In addition to comorbidity of somatization with depression, which has been estimated to be as high as 60%, significant comorbidity has been found between somatization and anxiety disorders such as panic or obsessive-compulsive disorder (up to 50%), personality disorders (up to 60%) (Kroenke et al., 1994; Rost, Akins, Brown, & Smith, 1992), and substance abuse disorders (e.g., Walker et al., 1988). Goldberg, Novack, and Gask (1992) reported that the risk for a psychiatric disorder in a primary care patient increased linearly with the number of somatic complaints. Finally, somatization is strongly associated with a history of childhood sexual and physical abuse (Morrison, 1989; Walker et al., 1988). Morse, Suchman, and Frankel (1997) have provided a review and qualitative analysis.

Perhaps the greatest challenge to primary care physicians in making the diagnosis is that the existence of a somatization disorder does not exclude the presence of an organic medical condition. The careful primary care clinician will follow the recommendations of Servan-Schreiber, Kolb, and Tabas (2000) in ruling out organic medical conditions and evaluating for psychiatric conditions when pursuing the positive diagnosis of somatization. Ideally, a careful physical examination is performed, and reasonable laboratory tests are ordered. It is also critical to obtain and

Table 39.1 Common Symptoms and Syndromes Reported by Somatizing Patients

Gastrointestinal symptoms	Reproductive organ symptoms
Vomiting	Burning sensations in sexual organs
Abdominal pain	Dyspareunia
Nausea	Painful menstruation
Bloating and excessive gas	Irregular menstrual cycles
Diarrhea	Excessive menstrual bleeding
Food intolerances	Vomiting throughout pregnancy
Pain symptoms	**Syndromes**
Diffuse pain (e.g., "I hurt all over")	Food allergies
Pain in extremities	Atypical chest pain
Back pain	Temporomandibular joint syndrome
Joint pain	Tinnitus
Pain during urination	Hypoglycemia
Cardiopulmonary symptoms	Irritable bowel syndrome
Shortness of breath at rest	Chronic fatigue syndrome
Palpitations	Fibromyalgia
Chest pain	Vitamin deficiency
Dizziness	Seizures (pseudoseizures)
	Premenstrual syndrome
Pseudoneurological symptoms	Multiple chemical sensitivity
Amnesia	Low back pain
Difficulty swallowing	
Headaches	
Loss of voice	
Deafness	
Double or blurred vision	
Blindness	
Fainting	
Difficulty walking	
Muscle weakness	
Difficulty urinating	

Note. Syndromes derived from the list proposed by Blackwell and De Morgan (1996).

review previous records. The patient's history must be evaluated judiciously because patients with somatization disorders are unable to assess the severity of their condition accurately. This forces the clinician to skillfully interpret past diagnoses and test results. The clinician also will have evaluated for signs and symptoms of depression, anxiety disorders, and substance abuse, which can all present with nonspecific somatic complaints. The physician may need to elicit non-somatic psychiatric symptoms tactfully because the patient may prefer to remain focused on the physical symptoms for fear of seeing his or her condition labeled as "psychiatric" rather than "medical."

Patients will be open to discussing their emotional problems only after a careful medical history has been taken; this is true as well for histories of sexual or physical abuse. Only after the patient feels that the physician is inquiring out of genuine concern rather than with the purpose of blaming the symptoms on a history of childhood trauma will such a history be disclosed. Using a genogram that includes medical history as well psychosocial information such as substance abuse provides a helpful way of eliciting information.

PATHOPHYSIOLOGY

No one fully understands the pathophysiology of somatization. However, three psychological mechanisms are often cited: amplification of bodily sensations, adoption of the sick role, and dissociation.

Amplification of Bodily Sensations

Worries about physical disease can focus the patient's attention on common variations in bodily sensations to the point that they become disturbing and unpleasant. At the very least, these sensations provide confirmatory evidence for the suspected presence of pathology. The perception of such altered sensations then feeds into the patient's concerns, increases anxiety, and thereby amplifies the sensations further. This mechanism is well established in the pathophysiology of panic attacks and has been documented in somatization as well (Barsky, 1992; Pennebaker, 1982).

Adoption of the Sick Role

In somatizing patients, complaints wax and wane in response to stressful life situations (Mechanic, 1978). In fact, somatization has often been conceived of as the expression of psychic pain in the form of bodily complaints in people who do not have the vocabulary for, or societal option of, presenting their distress in any other way (Barsky & Klerman, 1983). When the patient's own expectations cannot be met, instead of acknowledging the stress and dealing with it cognitively, the patient may deny its existence and become physically ill.

There may be significant individual, familial, or cultural pressures to express distress primarily through physical symptoms and the sick role. At the individual psychological level, the "sick role" may afford relief from stressful or impossible interpersonal expectations (primary gain) and, in most societies, may provide attention, caring, and even sometimes monetary rewards (secondary gain). This is not malingering (consciously faking the symptoms) because the patient is not aware of the process through which the symptoms arise, cannot will them away, and does genuinely suffer from the reported ills. The individual may have deeply encoded the lessons of early family life that, although emotional expressions of distress are ignored, physical complaints get attention.

The family system itself may have stabilized around a particular member's sick role. When a family system is stressed, identifying one person as a patient may provide a focus that stabilizes the system and alleviates feelings of anxiety within the family system. Members "know" how to interact with each other. The behavioral patterns can become recurrent and form family "rules" about how each member is to act. The patterns may become dysfunctional in that one member (usually a female) may take on the role of being weak and defective. The physician may reinforce this troublesome dynamic by focusing medical attention on the somatizing patient's disability and illness. The family system often has a powerful tendency to resist change, even change that seems desirable, such as the improved health or function of the identified patient.

These processes are all supported by cultural beliefs in a fundamental difference between "physical" (e.g., real, nonvolitional, medically treatable) complaints and "mental" (e.g., ephemeral, volitional, not medically treatable) conditions. For the patient who comes from a culture in which failure is not acceptable but illness is, concerns may not be expressed in any other way than by becoming physically sick.

Dissociation

Patients with somatization report dissociative symptoms much more commonly than patients with other psychiatric conditions (van der Kolk et al., 1996). Examples of such symptoms include flashbacks, out-of-body experiences, and depersonalization. It is therefore likely that some somatized symptoms also result from dissociation (i.e., activation in the central nervous system) of somatic representations of pain or other physical sensations in the absence of physical stimulation. The phenomenon may be analogous to that of phantom limb pain: Although there is no observable tissue damage in the area of the reported pain, the central nervous system behaves "as if" tissue damage were present (Servan-Schreiber, 1998).

PRINCIPLES OF TREATMENT

The following 10 recommendations, although addressed primarily to mental health clinicians, are applicable to both medical and mental health aspects of the treatment of the somatizing patient.

First, strive to understand the patient's suffering and to develop a concerned attitude. From the standpoint of the physician, the patient's symptoms seem exaggerated and his or her worries irrational; however, the patient's suffering is always real. Even in the clearest cases of organic pathology, suffering is poorly correlated with the extent of tissue damage (Melzack & Wall, 1982). Failure to acknowledge this suffering and disability is experienced as trivializing and impairs the doctor–patient alliance (Servan-Schreiber, Tabas, & Kolb, 2000). An empathic stance that acknowledges the suffering can avoid this debate. It is important to accept the patient's belief in the reality of the symptoms.

Second, agree on an explanation of the symptoms that is mutually acceptable to at least the primary care clinician and the patient (preferably to family members and all members of the clinical team as well). "For the person in distress the perceived location of suffering is in the body: telling a patient that his bodily distress is because of emotions that he does not feel is experienced as a devaluing of his experience of illness" (Epstein, 1996, p. 4). Patients and many clinicians may falsely dichotomize somatic stress into real and psychological. This creates major barriers to effective treatment (Simon, 2001). From the psychologist's perspective, this can become a subtle (or overt) clash of health beliefs, such that patients attempt to "prove" to the psychologist that it is fruitless to "explain away" their suffering with reference to their emotional or interpersonal conflicts.

Note that patients are often reassured when a specific name is given to the condition; even if they do not meet full criteria, they might be told, for example, "you have a variation of fibromyalgia" if the main complaints are related to pain and fatigue (Servan-Schreiber, Tabas, & Kolb, 2000). It is also important that the explanation of the patient's condition emphasize what it is *not* (e.g., life threatening). A suggested explanation is offered by Servan-Schreiber, Tabas, and Kolb (2000, p. 1076): "The results of my examination and of the tests we conducted show that you do not have any life-threatening illness. However, you do have a serious and disabling medical condition, which I see often but is not completely understood. Though no treatment is available that can cure it completely, there are a number of interventions that can help you deal with the symptoms better than you have so far."

Third, establish reasonable treatment goals. It is particularly important to identify the patient's primary concerns. Some patients may be seeking pain relief, others may be preoccupied with fear of a serious illness, still others may recognize that these symptoms are stress related and would like to work on lowering their stress (Simon, 2001). Some patients may have quite unrealistic goals (such as "complete cure"), and it is important to address and modify these. Realistic goals might include improved functioning; experiencing increased well-being despite some pain; or tolerance of reasonable uncertainty regarding health status.

Fourth, agree on appropriate use of medical care, especially arranging care that does not require new symptoms to gain access. Recommended primary care arrangements largely focus on scheduling brief but regular office visits (e.g., 15 minutes every 4 weeks) that do not require the patient to develop new symptoms to receive medical attention (Servan-Schreiber, Tabas, & Kolb, 2000; Simon, 2001). This is justified to the patient by stressing the importance of following them closely to help them deal with their current symptoms and to make sure that no new life-threatening condition is developing.

Such regular visits (monthly or more frequently) have been shown to reduce significantly the cost of caring for patients with somatization disorder without affecting their satisfaction with the care they receive (Smith et al., 1986). Regular visits have also been shown to reduce the number and duration of hospitalizations. During these brief visits, the physician listens for any new symptoms, conducts a brief physical exam that helps rule out any new or worrisome condition, and provides the patient with the important benefits of the "laying on of hands." The physician also begins to shift the focus from physical symptoms to the psychosocial context that may be affecting their expression. A time-honored opening that is comfortable for both doctor and patient is: "How have your symptoms interfered with your everyday life?" Somatizing patients are always ready to discuss how symptoms are affecting their life. This question gets around the threatening suggestion that stress or other psychological factors may be *causing* the symptoms. Yet, it will lead to important information about a link between life circumstances and symptoms, especially when it is followed by gentle prompts such as: "Tell me more about your [boss, husband, children, girlfriend, etc.]."

Primary care physicians can also efficiently use the BATHE technique (addressing the *b*ackground of the issue, the *a*ffect associated with it, what *t*roubles the patient most about it, how the patient is *h*andling it, and providing *e*mpathy) (Lieberman, 1997; Stuart & Lieberman, 1993), which is a simple and effective questioning sequence that focuses the conversation on psychosocial factors and often provides emotional relief. Other useful interventions during these regular visits include recommendations for antidepressant medications, stress management programs, lifestyle changes, and benign medical treatments.

Fifth, emphasize a collaborative relationship (Table 39.2) between the physician and psychologist. The primary care psychologist should ensure that a sensible diagnostic and treatment process is under way before assuming that psychotherapy or any other aspect of psychological treatment can commence. Not uncommonly, the patient will have been referred by the primary care physician because the physician has said, "There's nothing I can do for you," or more destructively, "It's all in your head." Patients who have been subjected to this medical approach may appear in the psychologist's office ostensibly seeking treatment, but covertly attempting to demonstrate that it will fail to help their clearly misdiagnosed medical problems. Particularly in such cases, careful collaboration (Simon, 2001) is the key to avoiding ineffective treatment or, worse, triangulation between the patient and the physician. Collaboration works better than referral, and it reinforces the idea that somatic symptoms are being taken seriously; thus, the psychologist who has referred a patient should try hard to insist on a collaborative arrangement. The psychologist should recognize that mental health treatment may be episodic, whereas medical treatment may be lifelong for patients with more severe forms of the disorder. A productive role for the primary care psychologist is as consultant to the patient and the physician. A useful description of psychological treatment is "stress management for patients with chronic illness." As noted, it is important at the outset of treatment to deal directly with any resentment the patient may have at being "turfed" to a psychologist.

Sixth, focus treatment on functional goals. The focus should be on symptom management, not on diagnosis and cure. The patient is likely to believe that pain or discomfort signals the presence of a diagnosable disease; that health is the absence of discomfort; that medicine is an exact science; and that persistence of the symptoms should prompt more vigorous diagnostic efforts (Simon, 2001). In contrast, the psychologist, in conjunction with the primary care physician, should emphasize that physical symptoms are common and often have no specific medical cause; that health is the ability to function and enjoy life despite discomfort; and that persistence of symptoms is annoying and unfortunate, but does not imply an incorrect diagnosis.

Excessive probing for the underlying conflict will likely be less productive than helping the patient manage stresses and symptoms. Cognitive–behavioral therapy addressed to symptom sensitivity and exaggerated fear of disease should be applied. Although the psychotherapeutic treat-

Table 39.2 Principles of Collaborative Treatment of Somatization

Do

    Help the patient maintain a productive relationship with one designated physician.

    Help the patient arrange for and keep frequent, brief, regular visits not contingent on new complaints.

    Allow patients to keep the "sick role," but improve their functioning rather than removing their symptoms.

    Encourage patients to explore psychosocial issues.

    Encourage benign treatments and enjoyment time.

Don't

    Allow patients to get the message, "It's all in your head."

    Enable patient's pursuit of invasive diagnostic tests, medications, and surgical interventions.

    Enable referrals to specialists.

    Enable the patient's focus on symptoms.

ment of somatoform disorders is very much like that used for working with anxiety and affective disorders, there is the constant risk that treatment will be diverted into a discussion of whether the clinician believes the symptoms are "real."

Effective cognitive–behavioral therapy for somatizing patients starts from the mutual agreement that whatever the patient has been thinking and doing about the condition has not helped very much so far. It then proceeds to challenge ineffective beliefs and maladaptive behaviors in a gentle and caring manner (Deale, Chalder, Marks, & Wessely, 1997; Hellman, Budd, Borysenko, McClelland, & Benson, 1990; Martin, Nathan, Milech, & van Keppel, 1989; Speckens et al., 1995; van Dulmen, Fennis, & Bleijenberg, 1996; Warwick, Clark, Cobb, & Salkovskis, 1996).

The "stress biopsy" procedure (Blackwell & De Morgan, 1996) has been found helpful as well; in this procedure, the patient is asked to imagine a typical stressful situation and to take note of emotions and bodily sensations. This may help demonstrate the link between stress and somatic symptoms, which can then be pursued by keeping a diary of symptoms together with related life situations. Other important aspects of psychological treatment involve predicting relapses and modeling hopeful tolerance of uncertainty (McDaniel, Campbell, & Seaburn, 1990).

Seventh, include significant others in the treatment. For the psychologist, this may mean joint sessions with the primary care physician and patient or sessions that include the patient's family. McDaniel et al. (1990) recommend family therapy in most cases.

Eighth, consider ancillary support, such as self-help groups or "stress management" groups. Group sessions, particularly those focused on stress management and functional improvement, can be very helpful and can also prevent the patient's social network from shrinking. Be somewhat cautious about self-help groups, however, because some groups strongly reinforce the patient role and encourage a search for "understanding" physicians who recognize the serious physiological problems and offer miracle cures. Some centers have developed brief group therapy programs for somatizing patients; these programs have been shown effective in improving function and reducing distress (Kashner, Rost, Cohen, Anderson, & Smith, 1995). The sessions combine general advice, such as stress management, problem solving, and social skills training, with specific interventions targeted at the mechanisms of amplification and the need to be sick that underlie somatization.

Ninth, encourage nonspecific treatments or quality-of-life improvements. Interventions directed at reducing specific sources of stress are most helpful, but nonspecific improvements such as encouraging improved sleep hygiene, greater amounts of physical activity, and relaxation techniques are useful as well. Physical exercise is particularly important, even in patients who believe themselves physically impaired.

The clinician should emphasize the importance of pleasurable private time. Beyond exercise, this may include not only yoga classes or meditation, but also bowling or nature walks, which under the general title of "stress management," can be presented as necessary medical treatments. In addition, complementary medicine approaches such as acupuncture, chiropraxy, massage therapy, or homeopathy may have very positive effects. They do not challenge the patient's view of the self as ill, but provide a framework within which the patient learns to take responsibility for his or her health. At the same time, these modalities are also much safer than the diagnostic and surgical procedures that are often offered with very little rationale by conventional medicine.

Tenth, help to arrange appropriate pharmacotherapy. Although pharmacotherapy (primarily with selective serotonin reuptake inhibitors) is often very beneficial, it does not address the two essential mechanisms of symptom amplification: the need to be sick and dissociation discussed previously. For this reason, pharmacotherapy can only be thought of as an adjunct to the regular visits with the primary care physician, which remains the core of the treatment plan for the more persistently somatizing patients. The side effects of some medications, particularly antidepressants, may affect somatoform patients badly. Conversely, the side effects of some antidepressants can be used to help reduce symptoms that distress patients. For example, more sedating antidepressants can be prescribed for patients who have anxiety or insomnia.

OBSTACLES TO EFFECTIVE TREATMENT

Unrealistic Goals

Perhaps the most common issue in both medical and psychological management is the problem of setting inappropriate goals. It is important to recognize that in severe cases—such as those of patients with full-blown somatization disorder— symptoms are unlikely to improve and suffering will persist. If the unspoken goal of the treatment plan is to relieve the patient from illness, the physician and patient soon become frustrated and tempted to engage in a new flurry of diagnostic tests and invasive procedures.

As noted, a much more appropriate goal is that of helping the patient cope with his or her symptoms. The focus should be on functioning rather than on illness. The physician can help the patient tolerate uncertainty by demonstrating the ability to continue caring for the patient without a clear etiology for the symptoms. Treatment is successful if it keeps the patient out of the hospital and the emergency room and if it reduces exposure to iatrogenic complications. In addition, clinicians can take comfort in recognizing how much frustration they are sparing colleagues and inpatient or emergency department staff.

Care That Parallels or Replicates the Patient's Dysfunctional History

Patients who have a history of abuse tend to mistrust physicians and other authority figures. Abused women have repeatedly been subjected to negation and ridiculing of their feelings by figures of authority. In their experience, rejection and abandonment usually follow this abuse. Such patients react strongly to anything that evokes this past treatment. Yet this is precisely what they encounter when their complaints are dismissed as being "all in your head" or they are accused of being "in denial" about their emotional conflicts. Ironically, the physician who accedes to the patient's demand for more tests and studies may subject the patient to procedures that are painful or invasive. If this invasive approach is followed by actual dismissal when it does not produce the expected relief of symptoms, the angry and rebellious response of the patient is not surprising.

A history of negative interactions with physicians is a common characteristic of patients with somatization. Patients may similarly engage in power struggles with psychologists who insist that they use emotional language to express emotional distress. Clinicians who are out of touch with their negative emotional reactions to somatizing patients seem more likely to dismiss them, creating a feeling of rejection in the patient that exacerbates the somatization disorder.

Patient Insistence on Further Tests

The primary care psychologist can help maintain a productive physician-patient relationship. For example, patients may insistently request more tests, telling the psychologist that they still worry that a life-threatening condition is present. For example, they may say, "How does my doctor know that I don't have a brain tumor? A CT scan hasn't been done." There are two effective approaches to this situation. The first one is to reassure the patient that frequent and regular medical visits will catch worrisome symptoms early on, and that as long as they are being followed in this way, they do not need to worry about missed diagnoses. When the patient insists nevertheless, the second option is to ask the patient if he or she believes that a negative test result would reassure him or her for at least a year about not being gravely ill. If the patient says yes, he or she should be asked to rate his or her level of anxiety (e.g., on a scale of 0 to 10). After the test has been completed, the patient should be asked to rate this anxiety again. In this way, the physician/psychologist team (or the physician alone) will be in a strong position to demonstrate to the patient the futility of pursuing such diagnostic procedures when the next request will arise, even if it is for a different symptom.

Patient Focus on Obtaining Pain Medications

Repeated complaints of pain can be as distressing to the physician as they are to the patient. In general, it is best to stick to the benign treatments mentioned here. They provide evidence of caring and some degree of relief without risks of complications. Acetaminophen and low-dose nonsteroidal anti-inflammatory drugs can be prescribed as long as they are not contraindicated. Complaints of pain are often a good opportunity to introduce or reintroduce the suggestion of antidepressants. Patients who have resisted taking such medications even when clearly indicated for their depressive or anxiety symptoms may be very willing to try a course of treatment when the goal is the relief of pain rather than focused on psychiatric symptoms. Opioid medications are generally contraindicated, and the physician's approach can be reinforced by the psychologist by explaining that narcotic analgesics are associated with significant side effects—especially constipation, sedation, and impaired cognition—as well as the progressive development of tolerance. Yet, they are unlikely to provide much benefit (as Barsky noted, "There is no pill that can cure, and no surgery that can excise, the need to be sick" [1997, p. 677]). When the physician feels that a narcotic analgesic may be indicated for long-term use, preparations with slow onset of action and long half-lives should always be preferred because they are not used to induce a "high" and have lower street value.

Emergence of a Comorbid Medical Condition

Somatizing patients are not immune to common medical conditions. Especially as they grow older, they are as likely as any other patient group to develop common diseases such as osteoarthritis, coronary artery disease, or cancer. The psychologist can help the patient clarify whether they have developed another condition and (if the primary care physician is skeptical) help the patient negotiate productively for treatment.

Additional Obstacles to Treatment

Additional issues may need to be addressed by the primary care psychologist if the patient sees the psychologist as a sympathetic advocate who can press for more access to medical care or when the patient needs help in understanding the impact of his or her behavior on the now-less-sympathetic physician. Careful feedback about and intervention in these conflicts can help the patient obtain productive care.

Frequent Telephone Calls

Physicians often feel helpless and angry when faced with frequent phone calls from somatizing patients. Phone calls can become a burden that threatens the balance of the doctor–patient relationship. The physician should draw the patient's attention to the problem in a respectful way that reaffirms the intention to provide care.

A time-honored approach consists of emphasizing the physician's feelings and needs (which cannot be challenged) rather than emphasizing the patient's duties and obligations (which are perceived as arbitrary rules). A typical statement may be: "It is hard for me to give you the care and attention that you deserve when I feel frustrated by spending so much time on the phone with so few positive results for you." It may then be appropriate to propose more frequent regular visits or to set an explicit limit to the number and length of calls, such as: "I understand that there may be times when you feel you cannot wait for your next office visit." This could be followed by either "Maybe this means that we should increase the frequency of the visits" or "I am comfortable with us having one or two 10-minute phone calls between visits, but I feel frustrated when it gets beyond that. Can we agree on that limit?"

Frequent Emergency Department Visits

Visits to the emergency department create chaos. They often result in inconsistent care and mixed messages from physicians who are seeing the patient for the first time and can be alarmed by the patient's presentation. Such visits may lead to exposure to new iatrogenic complications from unnecessary procedures and inappropriate admissions to the hospital. This chaos only reinforces the patient's impression that he or she is suffering from a life-threatening medical condition, and it can seriously impair the primary care physician's treatment plan.

The problems triggered by repeated emergency department visits should be discussed directly with the patient, who should be reminded that the regular ambulatory clinic visits are meant to take care of all of his or her medical needs. A shorter interval between visits can be negotiated, but with a reminder that they are expected to help the patient avoid emergency department visits. In the majority of cases, this takes care of the problem.

At the same time, it may be necessary to agree on a protocol for that particular patient with the staff of the emergency department. Specifically, it can be agreed that repeating tests and inpatient admissions will be avoided unless the patient presents new objective findings on the physical exam or routine laboratory tests.

Threat of Lawsuit

The fear of legal action often interferes with the care of somatizing patients. Physicians feel justified in ordering unnecessary diagnostic tests to protect themselves against remotely possible organic causes for the patient's most recent complaint. However, this institutional dysfunction is clearly damaging to somatizing patients as it reinforces and worsens their belief in the possibility of a life-threatening medical condition ("because the doctor ordered am MRI of my head, she must be afraid that I may really have a brain tumor") and their maladaptive behavior ("because an MRI was needed last time, it may be needed again because the headache is even worse now"). The fear of lawsuits may be most acute in the emergency department setting when the patient is hunched over in pain and insisting on immediate admission to the hospital.

Physicians should recognize that a caring attitude toward the patient and the patient's family and a well-documented reasoning process is the best defense against lawsuits (Levinson, Roter, Mullooly, Dull, & Frankel, 1997). The more typical pattern, which combines a cynical attitude ("It's all in your head") with simultaneously ordering "cover my back" diagnostic tests or prescriptions is just as likely to lead to lawsuits and has the additional disadvantage of running counter to the ongoing treatment plan.

CONCLUSION

The treatment of somatizing patients relies heavily on a solid and respectful relationship with a single primary care physician. When the patient becomes more aware of the importance of stress in his or her life, the treatment plan can be augmented by cognitive therapy—either individual or in group format. This should be labeled as "techniques for living with chronic illness" and be conducted by a therapist skilled in dealing with somatizing patients. The combination of these two approaches has been shown to reduce suffering and improve function. In the most severely afflicted patients, the physician and psychologist should accept the fact that somatization can be a chronic and seriously disabling illness for which limited goals are appropriate.

With experience and skill, the frustration usually associated with the care of such patients can be transformed into the gratifying experience of knowing that one is avoiding chaos and providing a suffering patient with the best treatment available.

References

American Psychiatric Association. (1994). *Diagnostic and statistical manual of mental disorders* (4th ed.). Washington, DC: Author.

Barsky, A. J. (1992). Amplification, somatization, and the somatoform disorders. *Psychosomatics, 33,* 28–34.

Barsky, A. J. (1997). A 37-year-old man with multiple somatic complaints. *Journal of the American Medical Association, 278,* 673–679.

Barsky, A. J., & Klerman, G. L. (1983). Overview: hypochondriasis, bodily complaints, and somatic styles. *American Journal of Psychiatry, 140,* 273–283.

Blackwell, B., & De Morgan, N. P. (1996). The primary care of patients who have bodily concerns. *Archives of Family Medicine, 5*(8), 457–463.

Bridges, K., & Goldberg, D. (1985). Somatic presentation of *DSM-III* psychiatric disorders in primary care. *Journal of Psychosomatic Research, 29,* 563–569.

Deale, A., Chalder, T., Marks, I., & Wessely, S. (1997). Cognitive behavior therapy for chronic fatigue syndrome: A randomized controlled trial. *American Journal of Psychiatry, 154,* 408–414.

Epstein, R. (1996, October). *Unexplained somatic symptoms: Embodied suffering in the era of managed care.* Paper presented at the Association for the Behavioral Sciences and Medical Education, Orcas Island, WA.

Escobar, J. I., Golding, J. M., Hough, R. L., Karno, M., Burnam, M. A., & Wells, K. B. (1987). Somatization in the community: Relationship to disability and use of services. *American Journal of Public Health, 77,* 837–840.

Goldberg, R. J., Novack, D. H., & Gask, L. (1992). The recognition and management of somatization. What is needed in primary care training. *Psychosomatics, 33,* 55–61.

Hellman, C. J., Budd, M., Borysenko, J., McClelland, D. C., & Benson, H. (1990). A study of the effectiveness of two group behavioral medicine interventions for patients with psychosomatic complaints. *Behavioral Medicine, 16,* 165–173.

Kashner, T. M., Rost, K., Cohen, B., Anderson, M., & Smith, G. R., Jr. (1995). Enhancing the health of somatization disorder patients. Effectiveness of short-term group therapy. *Psychosomatics, 36,* 462–470.

Katon, W. (1984). Panic disorder and somatization. Review of 55 cases. *American Journal of Medicine, 77,* 101–106.

Katon, W., Lin, E., Von Korff, M., Russo, J., Lipscomb, P., & Bush, T. (1991). Somatization: A spectrum of severity. *American Journal of Psychiatry, 148,* 34–40.

Koenig, H. G., Cohen, H. J., Blazer, D. G., Krishnan, K. R., & Sibert, T. E. (1993). Profile of depressive symptoms in younger and older medical inpatients with major depression. *Journal of American Geriatric Society, 41,* 1169–1176.

Kroenke, K., Arrington, M. E., & Mangelsdorff, A. D. (1990). The prevalence of symptoms in medical outpatients and the adequacy of therapy. *Archives of Internal Medicine, 150,* 1685–1689.

Kroenke, K., Spitzer, R. L., deGruy, F. V., 3rd, Hahn, S. R., Linzer, M., Williams, J. B., Brody, D., & Davies, M. (1997). Multisomatoform disorder. An alternative to undifferentiated somatoform disorder for the somatizing patient in primary care. *Archives of General Psychiatry, 54,* 352–358.

Kroenke, K., Spitzer, R. L., Williams, J. B., Linzer, M., Hahn, S. R., deGruy, F. V., 3rd, & Brody, D. (1994). Physical symptoms in primary care. Predictors of psychiatric disorders and functional impairment. *Archives of Family Medicine, 3,* 774–779.

Levinson, W., Roter, D. L., Mulooly, J. P., Dull,

V. T., & Frankel, R. M. (1997). Physician-patient communication: The relationship with malpractice claims among primary care physicians and surgeons. *Journal of the American Medical Association, 277,* 553–559.

Lieberman, J. A. R. (1997). BATHE: An approach to the interview process in the primary care setting. *Journal of Clinical Psychiatry, 58,* 3–6.

Lin, E. H., Katon, W., Von Korff, M., Bush, T., Lipscomb, P., Russo, J., & Wagner, E. (1991). Frustrating patients: Physician and patient perspectives among distressed high users of medical services. *Journal of General Internal Medicine, 6,* 241–246.

Martin, P. R., Nathan, P. R., Milech, D., & van Keppel, M. (1989). Cognitive therapy vs. self-management training in the treatment of chronic headaches. *British Journal of Clinical Psychology, 28*(Pt. 4), 347–361.

McDaniel, S. H., Campbell, T., & Seaburn, D. (1990). *Family oriented primary care: A manual for medical providers.* New York: Springer-Verlag.

Mechanic, D. (1978). Effects of psychological distress on perceptions of physical health and use of medical and psychiatric facilities. *Journal of Human Stress, 4,* 26–32.

Melzack, R., & Wall, P. (1982). *The challenge of pain.* New York: Penguin.

Morrison, J. (1989). Childhood sexual histories of women with somatization disorder. *American Journal of Psychiatry, 146,* 239–241.

Morse, D. S., Suchman, A. L., & Frankel, R. M. (1997). The meaning of symptoms in 10 women with somatization disorder and a history of childhood abuse. *Archives Family Medicine, 6,* 468–476.

Mulsant, B. H., Ganguli, M., & Seaberg, E. C. (1997). The relationship between self-rated health and depressive symptoms in an epidemiological sample of community-dwelling older adults. *Journal American Geriatric Society, 45,* 954–958.

Pennebaker, J. (1982). *The psychology of physical symptoms.* New York: Springer-Verlag.

Rost, K. M., Akins, R. N., Brown, F. W., & Smith, G. R. (1992). The comorbidity of *DSM-III-R* personality disorders in somatization disorder. *General Hospital Psychiatry, 14,* 322–326.

Servan-Schreiber, D. (1998). Coping effectively with patients who somatize. *Women's Health in Primary Care, 1,* 435–447.

Servan-Schreiber, D., Kolb, N. R., & Tabas, G. (2000). Somatizing patients: Part I. Practical diagnosis. *American Family Physician, 61*, 1073–1078.

Servan-Schreiber, D., Tabas, G., & Kolb, R. (2000). Somatizing patients: Part II. Practical management. *American Family Physician, 61*, 1073–1078.

Simon, G. (2001). Management of somatoform and factitious disorders. In P. Nathan & J. Gorman (Eds.), *A guide to treatments that work* (2nd ed., pp. 447–461). New York: Oxford University Press.

Smith, G. R., Jr., Miller, L. M., & Monson, R. A. (1986). Consultation-liaison intervention in somatization disorder. *Hospital Community Psychiatry, 37*, 1207–1210.

Speckens, A. E., van Hemert, A. M., Spinhoven, P., Hawton, K. E., Bolk, J. H., & Rooijmans, H. G. (1995). Cognitive behavioural therapy for medically unexplained physical symptoms: A randomised controlled trial. *British Medical Journal, 311*, 1328–1332.

Spitzer, R. L., Williams, J. B., Kroenke, K., Linzer, M., deGruy, F. V., 3rd, Hahn, S. R., Brody, D., & Johnson, J. G. (1994). Utility of a new procedure for diagnosing mental disorders in primary care. The PRIME-MD 1000 study. *Journal of the American Medical Association, 272*, 1749–1756.

Stuart, M., & Lieberman, J. (1993). *The fifteen minute hour: Applied psychotherapy for the primary care physician.* Westport, CT: Praeger.

van der Kolk, B. A., Pelcovitz, D., Roth, S., Mandel, F. S., McFarlane, A., & Herman, J. L. (1996). Dissociation, somatization, and affect dysregulation: The complexity of adaptation of trauma. *American Journal of Psychiatry, 153*(7, Suppl.), 83–93.

van Dulmen, A. M., Fennis, J. F., & Bleijenberg, G. (1996). Cognitive-behavioral group therapy for irritable bowel syndrome: Effects and long-term follow-up. *Psychosomatic Medicine, 58*, 508–514.

Walker, E., Katon, W., Harrop Griffiths, J., Holm, L., Russo, J., & Hickok, L. R. (1988). Relationship of chronic pelvic pain to psychiatric diagnoses and childhood sexual abuse. *American Journal of Psychiatry, 145*, 75–80.

Warwick, H. M., Clark, D. M., Cobb, A. M., & Salkovskis, P. M. (1996). A controlled trial of cognitive-behavioural treatment of hypochondriasis. *British Journal of Psychiatry, 169*, 189–195.

Waxman, H. M., McCreary, G., Weinrit, R. M., & Carner, E. A. (1985). A comparison of somatic complaints among depressed and nondepressed older persons. *Gerontologist, 25*, 501–507.

40

Stress

Bruce N. Carpenter
Patrick R. Steffen

STRESS IN THE PRIMARY CARE SETTING

Stress is a process so widespread and fundamental to our conceptions of functioning that it is difficult to imagine practicing primary care psychology without frequently encountering it. Nearly everyone reports experiencing stress from time to time, even though it is often so embedded in daily activities that one may not recognize symptoms or conceptualize experiences from a stress perspective. Although commonplace, stress is hardly benign, with significant numbers of primary care patients experiencing major problems arising primarily from stress and many others having medical and psychological difficulties exacerbated by stress.

Epidemiology

Moderate levels of stress are so common as to be considered normal, but some data are available on more extreme forms and consequences. For example, estimates suggest as many as one in five persons experiences high levels of work-related stress (see chapter 41, this volume). Psychological symptoms experienced in sufficient intensity to warrant diagnosis of a mental disorder also occur at substantial rates. According to the *Diagnostic and Statistical Manual of Mental Disorders*, text revision (*DSM-IV-TR*; American Psychiatric Association, 2000), upward of one third of individuals exposed to severe trauma (e.g., being in an automobile accident) qualify for having acute stress disorder; the lifetime prevalence for posttraumatic stress disorder is about 8%, and adjustment disorder affects up to 8% of the young and the elderly, 12% of general hospital inpatients referred for mental health consultation, and 50% of those experiencing a significant stressor (including medical stressors). In addition to rates in psychological contexts, the medical conditions in which stress appears to play an important causal role are among the most common.

Major Consequences

The consequences of the stress process are often significant. The psychological, behavioral, and physiological processes activated in the stress process are quite varied, often including depression, anxiety, and withdrawal. The cognitive, behavioral, and physiological processes may also include alarm, worry, tension, lowered concentration, negative emotions, shifts in self-image, and general autonomic arousal. Performance declines, emotional dysregulation ensues, and relationships may be damaged. Further, the drive to reduce stress can be so intense as to strongly promote behaviors, such as drug, alcohol, and tobacco use, that have negative long-term consequences that outweigh the short-term benefits.

Of particular interest in the primary care setting, a picture is emerging of stress playing a major causal role in important health problems such as heart disease. Patients with significant stress are more likely to complain of poor health and are less likely to be active, effective participants in their own care. They are also more likely to develop serious, chronic medical conditions.

Common Misconceptions

Given the attention in both popular and professional outlets, we might hope for a high level of accurate knowledge and widespread use of appropriate interventions. Unfortunately, this is not the case. Misconceptions abound, such as "stress is the same for everybody," "widely used stress management techniques are the best," "if there are no symptoms then there is no stress," and "only major stress symptoms require attention" (Miller & Smith, 1993).

Often, misconceptions arise from overly simplistic notions of stress. For example, two common misconceptions are that "stress is caused by external events and people" and that "stress is all in your head." In fact, both internal and external processes are important.

Two other competing misconceptions are that "stress is inevitable—there is little we can do to avoid or eliminate it," and that "stress is of your own making." Certain elements of the environment may be out of our control, but internal processes are also important and can be largely controlled.

A third set of competing misconceptions is "if one doesn't feel/create stress, one can't achieve as much" versus "stress is always bad for you." This is partly semantics regarding what is meant by

stress, but also arises from recognition that looking for challenge and meaning can expose us to stressful difficulties, but that stress itself is not the goal and can often be reduced or eliminated without giving up real goals.

The Stress Process as a True Interface of Biology and Psychology

Discussion of stress often arises within a psychological context, so some assume that stress is a psychological process or that stress itself is a "mental disorder." Whereas psychiatric conditions for which stress is a major causal factor are included among the mental disorders, stress should not be equated with a subset of its consequences. There are indeed important psychological aspects to the stress process, but it is better thought of as a true blend of mind and body. Biological features are critical to the process, including initiation of the process by biological stressors (e.g., deprivation of all sorts), activation of bodily mechanisms (e.g., neural and hormonal pathways), and bodily consequences, which can be short term (e.g., muscle tension, elevated blood pressure, gastric secretion, headache) or long term (e.g., increased risk for heart disease or ulcers). Further, the process is mediated through psychological and biological mechanisms. These are important reasons why stress is so often a part of difficulties encountered in primary care.

A GENERAL MODEL FOR STRESS

Because of conflicting and ambiguous lay conceptions of stress, we follow the lead of others (e.g., Folkman & Lazarus, 1985) in considering stress a process linking several elements. The elements most commonly proposed and their primary linkages are illustrated in Figure 40.1. The stress process is precipitated by an actual or perceived demand, or stressor, that exceeds readily available resources. When efforts to meet demands are either unsuccessful or rapidly deplete resources, cognitive and physiological processes (e.g., alarm, worry, tension, hyperarousal) are triggered. People attempt to deal with these through additional action mechanisms, called *coping*. Although there is a constant interplay among evaluation, coping,

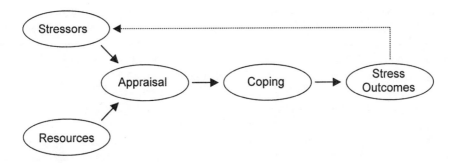

Figure 40.1 A general model of the stress process.

and outcome, the model orders them according to their primary causal contribution. Finally, negative stress outcomes, by virtue of taxing our adaptive adequacy, become stressors themselves.

Placing the General Model in Context

Stress in General Models of Disease

Stress is increasingly included in broader models of illness. Perhaps the most fundamental model of disorder is the diathesis-stressor model (cf. Dersh, Polatin, & Gatchel, 2002). The diathesis refers to a predisposition, usually distal (distant in time and similarity to presenting symptoms) and often thought of as a vulnerability; the stressor refers to the more proximal events that overwhelm the person, preying particularly on the vulnerability, and manifesting symptomatology that focuses on diathesis (weaknesses). Thus, a person with a powerful diathesis may succumb to illness merely under the stresses of normal living, whereas someone with mild diathesis may not experience symptoms unless subjected to powerful stressors. This general model has generated several variants such as the cognitive vulnerability–transactional stress model (Hankin & Abramson, 2001) and the vulnerability–stress-coping model (Gaebel et al., 2000).

Transactional and Ecological Elements

The general model of stress becomes more powerful when viewed from transactional and ecological perspectives. The transactional perspective specifies that there is interplay between patient behavior and the stress response—each triggers the other and adds to a growing feedback cycle. People contribute to the process of stress, at times even unknowingly seeking out stressors or responding in ways that accentuate and perpetuate the process.

Consider the transactional model's utility in understanding heart disease. Heart disease is overwhelmingly a disease of lifestyle behaviors and stress, with genetics and family history estimated to account for only about 10% of the variance in morbidity and mortality (see chapter 28). The transactional model encourages a focus on what leads up to and maintains unhealthy lifestyles and unhealthy ways of coping with stress. For example, in the case of hostility and heart disease, a strong focus is on how hostile people may unintentionally maintain their stress levels by eliciting stressful reactions from others, which in turn leads them to feel justified in their hostile treatment of others, and the process goes on.

The ecological perspective encourages recognition that processes and interventions occur within a context, with maximizing and limiting aspects (e.g., Quick, Nelson, Quick, & Orman, 2001). Environmental and internal "press" varies across persons and situations; therefore, effective coping always depends on context and will vary widely across persons, situations, and time.

Stressors

Stressors—conditions or events that place demands on us—can be significant in and of themselves, as in *major life events* (e.g., Johnson & Miller, 1997), such as divorce, surgery, an automobile accident, or death of a loved one. Negative events are more strongly related to psychological and physiological difficulties than positive events such as getting married (Sarason, Johnson, & Siegel, 1978), perhaps because negative events threaten our sense of well-being or lack the stress-buffering meaning of positive events.

Severe traumas such as war and natural disasters have been shown to have profound effects on mental and physical health, with posttraumatic stress disorder and sudden death from heart attack among the more prominent afflictions (Krantz & McCeney, 2002). Even short-lived natural disasters have been shown to have long-term aftereffects. The impact of the Northridge earthquake on the people in Southern California persisted for months, even though the actual stressor was quite brief. Those reporting higher levels of distress and worry also displayed immune system dysregulation over time (Segerstrom, Solomon, Kemeny, & Fahey, 1998; Solomon, Segerstrom, Grohr, Kemeny, & Fahey, 1997).

In contrast, small, everyday demands, sometimes called *daily hassles* (e.g., Kanner, Coyne, Schaefer, & Lazarus, 1981), achieve significance by their cumulative effect across hassles and across time. Indeed, stressors in general appear to have a cumulative effect (e.g., Singer, 1980); experience with extreme stressors in particular appears to make us more vulnerable, even for years.

Which features of demands, then, maximize stressful potential? Obviously, stressors are more stressful when they are undesirable, significant, chronic, or more salient (Pynoos et al., 1987). An example is work stress. Working in a stressful atmosphere for a short period usually does not result in significant stress. In contrast, being exposed to work stress over a period of months and years has been shown to have negative effects on health (Schnall, Schwartz, Landsbergis, Warren, & Pickering, 1998). For example, Baum and Fleming (1993), in a study of the stress of living in the vicinity of the Three Mile Island nuclear disaster, showed that uncertainty about negative effects was related to increased psychological stress and heightened physiological arousal over a period of years following the disaster.

In addition, demands are more stressful if they are unpredictable, uncontrollable, novel (Leventhal, Patrick-Muller, & Leventhal, 1998; Sattler, Kaiser, & Hittner, 2000), or ambiguous and accompany a history of failure with the stressor, or they require change (Maddi, Bartone, & Puccetti, 1987). Chronic noise is an example; people who perceive they have control over the amount of noise experienced, even if they do not exercise that control, report lower levels of stress (Weinstein, Quigley, & Mordkoff, 2002).

People who feel in control show decreased blood pressure and stress hormone responses to stressors compared to those who perceive they cannot control the situation (Singer, Lundberg, & Frankenhauser, 1978; Weinstein et al., 2002). Similarly, ambiguous situations can lead to increased stress through doubts about exactly what will happen and what is needed to cope effectively, increasing the likelihood of chronic arousal (Folkman, Shaefer, & Lazarus, 1979). If a person can prepare for an excessive demand, can influence it when it comes (or just believe it can be influenced), or view it as part of something desired (such as the stress of getting married), the feeling is generally less overwhelming than otherwise.

Resources

Resources are the tools available to meet demands. Resources can be classified in a variety of ways: (a) they can be tangible (e.g., money, help from a friend) or intangible (e.g., attitudes about self); (b) they can be personal (e.g., intelligence, personality, coping skills, knowledge of a problem) or environmental (e.g., social network, access to information); or (c) they can be actual or merely perceived. Indeed, psychological reactions, which in turn trigger physical reactions, seem to arise primarily from the belief that there is a stressor-resource mismatch; thus, perception of resources is often more powerful than actual resources in driving the stress process. Having "generic" resources available may be inadequate for avoiding stress because resources work best when they fit the demand at hand (Quick et al., 2001).

Three important personal resources are self-esteem, self-efficacy, and hardiness. When people have positive self-esteem, they are less likely to interpret or respond to an event as emotionally loaded or stressful (Whisman & Kwon, 1993). They cope better when stress occurs, yielding positive feedback that further increases self-esteem. People with low self-esteem, however, perceive themselves as having inadequate coping skills, are less likely to cope actively, and appear to hold more fatalistic beliefs.

Self-efficacy refers to the belief that one can succeed at something (Bandura, 1977). Belief in personal abilities to deal with stressful life events is more likely to lead to coping success (Bandura, Reese, & Adams, 1982) and to manageable or benign appraisals.

Finally, hardiness involves a combination of feeling in control, commitment, and viewing demands as challenges rather than threats (Kobasa, 1979). Hardy individuals report having developed fewer illnesses during extended stressful periods than less-hardy individuals (Kobasa, Maddi, Puccetti, & Zola, 1985).

A major resource for moderating stress is social support. The existence of strong, meaningful relationships acts as a coping mechanism that moderates the effects of stress by increasing the perceived available resources. People with social support believe they are loved and cared for, esteemed and valued, and part of a social network, such as a family or community organization, and that they can receive needed support and mutual aid in times of need.

Finally, an important resource is socioeconomic status (SES). This has been called the social gradient because there is a direct relationship between SES and health (Adler & Ostrove, 1999). For example, it has been estimated that those in the lower levels of SES are nearly three times more likely to die of heart disease than those in the highest level of SES (Krantz & McCeney, 2002). In addition to reduced access to health care, lower SES status typically translates into more "hassles" in daily life and more difficulty securing basic living necessities.

Appraisal

It is against the perception of resources that the stressfulness of demands is judged, introducing another reason why there is wide variability in response to stressors. Lazarus and Folkman (1984) articulated two main forms of appraisal: (a) primary appraisal, in which the extremeness of the challenge and its threat are evaluated; and (b) secondary appraisal, in which the avenues open

to deal with the challenge are evaluated, and in light of those avenues, what is likely to happen is evaluated. Appraisal is primarily a cognitive activity that may often be rather automatic and take place outside awareness.

A variety of conditions predispose people to appraise in particular ways. First, past experience with similar situations affects appraisal. For example, if the current situation involves public speaking, the amount of current stress partly depends on the degree of success or failure in similar, past situations (Bandura, 1977). If people felt competent previously, then stress levels will be reduced; if they felt inadequate, then current stress levels will be higher. Second, cultural differences can affect how a situation is perceived; that is, the meaning of an event can vary among people of differing backgrounds. Third, and so obvious that it is often overlooked, reality affects appraisal. Whereas an appraisal at a single point in time might allow denial of the true difficulty of a situation, over the long run, reality in the form of performance feedback typically informs people of their capacities. An interesting irony is that it is relatively easy to undervalue personal capacities and then experience failure not from incompetence, but as a reaction to the greater stress experienced by overappraising; in contrast, overvaluing capacities is more readily corrected by the harsh realities of consequent failure.

Coping

We prefer limiting the term *coping* to the context of the stress process; thus, day-to-day adaptive behaviors are excluded. From this approach, coping includes behaviors that arise in response to the stress process, that is, when stressors are judged as significantly taxing resources. For a variety of reasons, it helps to expect coping to encompass behaviors engaged in intentionally or with an expectation (although perhaps unconscious) that the behavior will help (e.g., Carpenter, 1992). In contrast, we do not require that coping be effective (one might cope in ways that do not help, that have positive and negative features, or that make things worse).

Coping can be extremely varied, as reflected in the variety of interventions proposed in this chapter. One popular coping classification system is that of Lazarus and Folkman (1984), in which they distinguish problem-focused coping from emotion-focused coping. The former includes activities intended to lessen the stressor, whereas the latter includes behaviors that lessen stress responses (primarily negative arousal).

Stress Outcomes

The psychological, behavioral, and physiological processes of stress are in part adaptive—as we seek to meet unusual demands, we must rise to the challenge. However, they come at some expense to psychological and physical functioning. This is especially true when the stress, including the stress response, is extraordinary, as in trauma, or when it is chronic, as is increasingly true in our complex, competitive society.

Balance and Adaptation

It is useful to understand how the human body operates under normal conditions as well as under stress. Balance and adaptation are two key concepts in physiological regulation. In the 19th century, Claude Bernard put forth the concept of the *milieu interieur*, the idea that the body needs to maintain internal balance or a steady state for healthy functioning (Chrousos & Gold, 1992). Later, Walter Cannon (1932) expanded on this by creating the terms *homeostasis* and *fight-or-flight reaction* to facilitate the idea that the body can adapt internally to stressful situations by shifting physiological functioning to cope with the external environment.

Sterling and Eyer (1988) proposed the concept of *allostasis* to emphasize that most physiological systems do not have one fixed set point and to account for the fact that the body's physiological systems interact and affect each other. In this view, the internal milieu is flexible and varies according to perceived and anticipated demand, and the interaction of the multiple systems is governed and organized by the brain. An example is blood pressure. The set point for blood pressure varies depending on posture (lying down, sitting, or standing), activity (e.g., walking or running), and emotional state (e.g., calm or angry). Blood pressure is affected by multiple body systems, in-

cluding the sympathetic nervous system and the adrenal medulla, the hypothalamic-pituitary-adrenal axis, and the renin-angiotensin system, as well as by feeding behavior (water and salt intake).

Allostasis, then, is stability through change (Sterling & Eyer, 1988). When things are going well, the body maintains internal balance while coping with the external environment. Under severe or chronic stressors, the internal balance is disrupted, leading to susceptibility to disease. McEwen and Stellar (1993) coined the term *allostatic load* to address the impact of stress on the body over time. Allostatic load is a process by which chronic levels of stress negatively affect health through prolonged exposure to elevated stress hormones and dysregulation of physiological systems. Three factors that determine whether a situation contributes to stress are physiological proneness, the demands of the situation, and the resources available.

Physiological Vulnerability

A key individual difference that affects reaction to potential stressors, often considered apart from other resources, is physiological proneness. Two factors that contribute to physiological proneness are temperament and traumatic events experienced during childhood. Research has shown that infants can have quite different temperaments, with some overly sensitive to stimuli and more prone to negative moods (e.g., Strelau, 2001). For these infants, the world is a more stressful place from the beginning of the life cycle. Childhood traumatic stressors can also predispose an otherwise healthy child to become more sensitized to stressful situations. For example, several studies documented that sexually abused children display a sensitized stress response, releasing abnormal levels of stress hormones in response to laboratory stressors (De Bellis, Chrousos, et al., 1994; De Bellis, Lefter, Trickett, & Putnam, 1994). This sensitized stress response has been shown to continue into the adult years. Heim et al. (2000) found that women who were sexually abused during childhood had a significantly more reactive stress hormone response to laboratory stressors compared to nonabused women.

EFFECTS OF STRESS

Stress consequences often play a diagnostic role by alerting us that excessive stress is present. Further, stress can result in biomedical, psychological, and psychophysiological problems, any of which may be important targets of stress intervention. To aid the practitioner, we review here some of the major stress effects.

Adaptation

When demands exceed resources, a series of predictable physiological responses occurs. The body's first response to a stressful situation has been called the fight-or-flight response (Chrousos & Gold, 1992). This is because the body prepares for action by the increased release of norepinephrine and epinephrine, which raises heart rate and blood pressure and prepares the muscles for immediate use. Levels of cortisol, a metabolic hormone that plays a central role in the stress response, also rise, which increases energy metabolism in the body. These physiological changes are adaptive in the short run, with mobilization of resources placing the body at an optimal level of alertness and readiness to act.

Stress can result in significant elevations in blood pressure, immune suppression, muscle tension and tension headaches, and fatigue (Herbert & Cohen, 1993b). For example, a longitudinal study of work stress found that changes in stress levels predict blood pressure changes over time (Schnall et al., 1998). When stress levels increased, blood pressure levels also increased, and when stress decreased, blood pressure levels also decreased. Similarly, in a study of susceptibility to infection, Cohen, Tyrrell, and Smith (1991) demonstrated that increased psychological stress increased the likelihood of being infected by a cold virus.

Major Medical Consequences

Studies suggested that long-term stress plays a role in development of important medical conditions such as heart disease, chronic immune problems, and ulcers (Black & Garbutt, 2002; Krantz & McCeney, 2002) and thereby has an impact on general disease morbidity and mortality. Stress contributes to an increase in myocardial ischemia, and these stress-induced ischemic events are significantly related to higher rates of fatal and nonfatal cardiac events (Jiang et al., 1996). Chronic stress has also been found to play a prominent role in blood vessel damage and the development of atherosclerosis (Black & Garbutt, 2002).

Chronic stressors also negatively affect immune function, which is of serious concern for people coping with diseases such as cancer and HIV/AIDS. In a study of women with breast cancer, women with abnormal cortisol rhythms had a shorter life expectancy than those with normal cortisol levels (Septhon, Sapolsky, Kraemer, & Spiegel, 2000). It was hypothesized that the immunosuppression caused by the elevated cortisol levels led to more rapid progression of the cancer. In studies of HIV-positive men, increased stress was related to decreased immune functioning (Antoni, LaPerriere, Schneiderman, & Fletcher, 1991; Leserman et al., 1997). A follow-up study found that cognitive–behavioral stress management intervention reduced stress levels and bolstered immune functioning (Antoni et al., 2000).

Major Psychological Consequences

In addition to the physiological impact of stress, there are significant emotional and behavioral effects. Feelings of anxiety frequently accompany stressful situations, and the symptoms associated with both significantly overlap. For example, both anxiety and stress symptoms include difficulties with concentration, sleep disturbances, muscle tension, and irritability (see *DSM-IV* [American Psychiatric Association, 1994] diagnostic criteria for the anxiety disorders). The same is true with depression and mood disorders, which share many of the above symptoms with anxiety and stress. Other emotional changes that frequently occur with stress include lability and hyperreactivity of mood states, particularly when a stressor is uncontrollable or unpredictable.

Prolonged stress can result in chronic depression and anxiety. This is particularly true when it appears that the stress is a constant part of life and is not likely to end in the near future. Long-term chronic stress can also lead to feelings of hopelessness and helplessness if there is a large disparity between the demands of the stress and the availability of coping resources. When repeated attempts to cope with the situation are unsuccessful, the individual can be left emotionally exhausted and fragile and will likely develop a negative sense of self. Continued failure to cope successfully can result in emotional withdrawal and apathy.

Interaction of Psychological and Medical Consequences

Both immediate and prolonged emotional changes play a key role in the relationship between stress and physical health. Measures of personality (Friedman & Booth-Kewley, 1990), depression (Herbert & Cohen, 1993a; Musselman & Nemeroff, 2000), and hostility (Miller, Smith, Turner, Guijarro, & Hallet, 1995) have all been found to mediate the relationship between stress and physical health outcomes. Common behavioral symptoms associated with stress include increased withdrawal, avoidance, and negative health behaviors. People usually avoid unpleasant situations and will attempt to distance themselves from stress. A specific example of avoidance in health settings is poor adherence to treatment. High levels of stress have been found to reduce adherence to treatment regimens. For example, in a study of diabetic patients, higher perceived stress was related to poorer glycemic control and more avoidant coping (Frenzel, McCaul, Glasgow, & Shafer, 1988). In a study of stress and exercise adherence, it was found that both increased frequency of stress and higher levels of perceived stress resulted in decreased levels of exercise and lower self-efficacy (Stetson, Rahn, Dubbert, Wilner, & Mercury, 1997).

Increased stress is also related to increases in unhealthy behavior. Stressed individuals are more likely to use cigarettes and alcohol, consume more fat and unhealthy foods, and engage in less physical activity (Conway, Vickers, Ward, & Rahe, 1981; Wiebe & McCallum, 1986). These behaviors are significant factors in the development and progression of heart disease and represent another pathway through which stress affects health. Highly stressed individuals are also more likely to suffer accidental injuries at home,

during sports activities, on the job, and while driving than are less-stressed individuals (Johnson, 1986).

INTERVENTIONS

Stress management/reduction interventions are well suited to the primary care setting. It is often easier for patients to accept the idea that they must lower their stress levels than it is to convince them that they suffer from a somatoform or other anxiety disorder. In fact, *stressed* is frequently the term primary care patients use to describe a wide range of psychological symptoms. The primary care psychologist can address stress with an equally wide range of therapeutic tools.

Analysis

As in all interventions, adequate evaluation and analysis should occur prior to actual intervention so that the therapist and, ideally, the patient understand how the stress process is occurring and how the intended intervention is likely to affect the process. Because patients often fail to see connections between stress and its varied outcomes, therapists must ask about demands, anxiety, a sense of being overwhelmed, and the like. For many patients, simply asking will bring out the necessary information. We recommend routine assessment of stress processes when patients present with (a) stress complaints; (b) conditions for which stress may play a major, but often hidden, causal role (e.g., depression, anxiety, hypertension, heart disease, ulcers); or (c) a pattern of vulnerability to stress (e.g., low SES, past coping failures, history of abuse or difficult childhood, hostility, emotional reactive and threat-sensitive temperaments, social isolation).

Inventories and structured interviews are available to provide more detailed and norm-referenced assessment (see chapter 41 on work stress and health). Some useful ones include the Life Stressors and Social Resources Inventory (Moos & Moos, 1997), the Occupational Stress Inventory (Osipow, 1998), the Perceived Stress Scale (Cohen, Kamarck, & Mermelstein, 1983), and the Stress Profile (Nowack, 1999). Some measures are specifically designed for non–mental health medical personnel, such as the Parenting Stress Index (Abidin, 1995).

Collaboration

In primary care settings, effective collaboration rather than mere referral is often required; medical components typical of stress reactions frequently require medical interventions, and collaboration heightens therapeutic efficacy through greater unity in the intervention process. We emphasize four points of collaboration already familiar to those in primary care.

First, educating and equipping medical personal can help them to assess adequately, incorporate stress interventions when appropriate, and increase accurate referrals to therapists. Collaboration is increased when physicians see that "psychosomatic" concerns do not mean replacing traditional medicine with "all-in-your-head" beliefs, but rather mean that psychological processes are relevant and can be effectively treated.

Second, case consultation can help physicians, with therapists framing patient concerns within the stress model and proposing appropriate psychosocial interventions that support the medical care. Indeed, many such interventions can be implemented without psychotherapy referral (e.g., money management, education).

Third, therapists can assist with patient education and access to community resources. Stress intervention can often be managed by patients themselves: numerous workshops on stress, time, and money management; on goal and priority setting; on education and career enhancement; and on overcoming negative behaviors are available through adult education, community programs, employee assistance programs, or health organizations. Finally, a subset of patients may need more intense involvement by therapists, such as through psychotherapy or ongoing case management.

Points of Intervention

Traditional Versus Model-Driven Approaches

Stress intervention is often conceptualized as "stress management." We see two concerns with

this. First is an assumption that stress is a given and can merely be managed. We agree this is sometimes true, but the approach magnifies a fatalist view that appears unnecessary. Indeed, more fundamental change is preferred and often needed in which general resilience to stress is enhanced, usually through lifestyle changes. Second, the approach promotes the use of a grab bag of management tools such as time management, priority management, diversion, exercise, meditation, social support activation, and relaxation training. We agree that these tools can be effective and propose using all of them, but they are most effective when used in a systematic, model-driven approach.

Our general model of the stress process (Figure 40.1) provides a context for discussing potential points of intervention. Indeed, conceptualizing patients' difficulties within such a model provides both a broader perspective on potential points of intervention and better matching of interventions to patients as required by the ecological perspective. We now focus in turn on interventions for each of the five components of the stress process.

Stressors

A key element in the stress response is the presence of significant demands. Intervention can therefore take the form of managing demands. This can range from eliminating some demands (e.g., turning down a request) to reducing them (e.g., accepting a more modest request instead) to merely gatekeeping some stressors (attending to demands in turn; e.g., informing others of when new requests will be attended to), with the common goal of lowering the overall stressor load. Stressors can often be significantly reduced through greater patient involvement in "selecting" stressors. Simply helping a patient sort through perceived stressors and clarify priorities may result in effective shifting of demands. Clarifying the actual demands posed by potential stressors can also be equally effective. Frequently, patients exaggerate demands or are so avoidant that they have no clear notion of what stressors actually demand of them; thus, clarifying may result in significant reappraisal. For those who take on too many demands, clarifying the relationship between excessive demands and stress outcomes may increase their vigilance and effort at setting priorities and limits.

Interventions that generalize beyond the immediate situation of stress often involve giving patients tools for managing demands or helping them overcome tendencies to invite or retain demands. These can take many forms, such as (a) assertiveness training to resist unnecessary demands by others; (b) examination of illogical beliefs, schemas, or dynamic pressures regarding worth deriving from meeting others' demands; (c) training in time management; (d) referral for debt counseling; or (e) overcoming anxieties, compulsive tendencies, or other barriers that keep them from reducing unnecessary demands.

A particularly effective way to remove demands is to solve or fulfill them. This is closest to what Lazarus and Folkman (1984) called "problem-focused coping." The goal is to work the problem so it is removed, reduced, or perceived as dealt with and hence manageable. This is an active, nonavoidant form of coping that requires effort and attention. Consequently, it often heightens stress initially, although the payoff comes when stress is removed. Examples include (a) consolidating debt; (b) tackling a looming assignment head-on; (c) seeking marriage counseling; (d) changing jobs; or (e) ending a problematic relationship. Obviously, bigger stress reduction occurs by solving major life problems, but major stressors may seem overwhelming or demand more than patients can give at the time. Daily hassle reduction can be as effective, but usually requires attacking multiple stressors for significant impact; thus, therapists must take care not to dilute focus, but still provide meaningful results.

The ecological model posits that active attempts to eliminate stressors will be ineffective when stressors are unlikely to be reduced. That is, one expends effort, with increasing stress, without benefit. Therapy, then, might focus on helping patients stop such ineffective coping. One poignant example is parents with children suffering from serious, irreparable disability who insist on seeking ineffective treatments. It is not surprising that models of adjustment to such situations see this active coping as an ineffective, energy-draining stage of refusal, with later, more adaptive stages focusing on acceptance and accommodation.

Resources

Activating and enhancing resources is an important component of stress management. Ecological concerns are particularly important. Patients may employ resources out of habit rather than through considerations of which are most relevant or available. A dependent patient may ask for help reflexively when social resources are irrelevant, or an independent person may refuse help when it is readily available. Therapy focusing on resource management typically evaluates potential resources, helps the patient match resources to demands based on likely effectiveness, and then devises and supports strategies for accessing the resources.

Often, patients are deficient in key resources. Some of these deficits may not be amenable to change, such as low intelligence or low income. Frequently, however, relevant resources can be enhanced. Information seeking can prepare patients for action, as well as increase their sense of control. Self-esteem and self-efficacy are powerful personal resources, and interventions abound for strengthening them. Skills training of various types (e.g., study skills, time management, and social skills) prepares patients to meet demands. The importance of relationships in general functioning cannot be overstated; thus, even when patients present with nonrelational concerns, improving the quality and quantity of relationships leads to a host of benefits that have an impact on the stress process (Carpenter & Scott, 1992).

Social support is a particularly effective and well-researched resource (e.g., Cohen, Gottlieb, & Underwood, 2001); thus, we make only two points. First, benefit arises from both the perception of social support (a belief that people would help you if you asked) and actual social support (including its host of functions, e.g., emotional support, esteem building, information, sounding board, and manpower). Second, both major models of social support are supported by research: stress buffering (when stressed, the impact of social support is especially helpful) and main effects (social support enhances functioning regardless of stress status).

An understanding of resources can also help the therapist appreciate patient vulnerabilities and perhaps devise compensatory or intervention strategies or steer therapy away from a focus on stressors for which ecologically adequate resources simply are not available. A therapist should be less likely to suggest complex interventions to a patient with limited cognitive abilities or to suggest costly interventions to poor patients without external supports. Similarly, a patient's personality or life circumstances might be a risk factor for certain stressors (e.g., hostility in heart disease, for which an intervention might focus on resolving conflict; cf. Vollrath, 2001).

Reappraisal

Whereas appraisal is regarded as the ongoing process of evaluating demands, resources, and likely outcomes, we refer to the more intentional, effortful reevaluation that occurs within psychotherapy as *reappraisal*. Because of the critical role of appraisal in triggering the stress response, it is a prime focus for intervention. Although belief systems and schemas are fairly automatic and somewhat resistant to change, the primary care therapist has numerous tools for examining, making salient, and challenging dysfunctional evaluations.

Frequently, we find that patient perceptions of inadequacy to meet demands and of likely outcomes are significantly exaggerated. That is why working with patients to perceive demands and resources more accurately (see Stressors and Resources sections) is so helpful. However, merely clarifying demands can heighten anxiety, and merely listing resources can seem too abstract. Beyond heightened accuracy, the patient needs a clear realization that demands can indeed be managed and outcomes, even if unpleasant, are tolerable. The goal is to help the patient, through accurate perception of the situation, obtain a sense of self-efficacy and a belief in successful stress management.

Thus, we view reappraisal as a conscious decision that either a demand can adequately be met or that negative consequences are acceptably small. The more clearly the patient accepts either of those conclusions, the greater the reduction in the stress response. As mentioned, those who ex- aggerate their ability to cope usually experience pressure from reality to correct their misperceptions. Therefore, reappraisal in therapy usually has the goal of changing overly pessimistic evaluations to more reasonable, rather than overly optimistic, levels.

Note also that reappraisal is not merely a verbal gimmick; rather, as reappraisal occurs, patient reactivity is lowered, and adaptation is more functional; that is, stress is reduced. Further, because appraisal is sensitive to data, the resulting reduction in arousal and negative thinking can be powerful feedback—if the patient's attention is directed to it—that the new, more benign appraisal is "on the mark."

Coping

Because we define coping as intentional responses activated by stress arousal, essentially everything we discuss in this section on interventions can be considered coping. However, we use this section to draw attention to a few additional key points.

To apply ecological principles of coping properly, it is helpful to consider prominent distinctions. We have alluded to several above, particularly the avoidant-nonavoidant distinction (e.g., Suls & Fletcher, 1985). Avoidant strategies, such as distraction and avoidance, work best on short-term stressors, for which nonavoidant strategies may be too costly in terms of effort and arousal because the stressor will end soon anyway. In contrast, avoidance of potentially long-term stressors eventually yields more negative consequences than do nonavoidant strategies because, with the former, problems are neither solved nor reduced. Nonavoidant strategies are usually inferior when people have little control over the stressor; in this case avoidant strategies seem superior regardless of temporal factors. When stressors are powerful, it is hard to use avoidant coping, even if quite temporary. Research suggests that a more detached form of focus is more effective than either avoidance or a focus on emotion (how bad it is); that is, attention to benign aspects of the unpleasant situation is in keeping with the demand to attend, but prevents turning it into a catastrophe.

It is important to avoid concluding that demands arising from the environment overwhelm the role of personality and other individual differences, sometimes called *coping styles*. The ecological model reminds us that matching coping to stressors is valuable. Nevertheless, individual difference variables can be valuable in predicting stress responses. For example, Miller (1992) considered "monitoring" and "blunting" to be attributes that function much like personality traits. Monitors attend closely to demands and reactions, and are thereby quite stress prone, and blunters distract themselves or avoid threatening information. Other research suggests that coping responses tend to be relatively stable and consistent, in part because of their link to personality traits (Ferguson, 2001; McCrae, 1992).

Finally, except with rather transient stressors, building *resilience* is often more effective than managing *vulnerability*. Resilience arises not from few stressors, but from a healthy lifestyle, a healthy self-image, a history of successful coping, and a wealth of resources. Interventions might include weight reduction, exercise programs, and job skills training, as well as targeted coping for specific stressors.

Stress Outcomes

When intervention focuses on stress outcomes, the emphasis is typically on counteracting the arousal associated with the stress response. A primary form of intervention here is medication, and its effectiveness should not be understated, although recidivism rates are higher than with psychological interventions, suggesting either maintenance medication or combining approaches. Psychological coping activities that target symptoms are sometimes called *defense oriented* because they act primarily to protect the self from hurt or disorganization rather than to respond to the demand. Although at times referred to as primitive, with an assumption that they are neurotic, they can be quite effective. Thus, crying, repetitive talking, and mourning can serve a reparative function (as highlighted in models of the bereavement process), although they are usually an early stage response rather than the solution to the stress. Other mechanisms can include denial and repression, which can be functional when they reduce anxiety and protect the sense of self from devaluation. Thus, it may be important for

therapists to postpone effort to overcome denial and the like until other coping mechanisms are in place.

A more direct approach to counteract the stress response is to actively seek change in the emotional component leading to arousal. This is essentially what Lazarus and Folkman (1984) meant by emotion-focused coping. Examples include relaxation training, distraction, exercise, yoga, meditation, and the introduction of activities that elicit positive emotions.

SUMMARY

Primary care therapists routinely see patients for whom stress is a major component of their complaints. Fortunately, stress is now one of the more extensively researched areas of mental health practice, and conceptualizing patient difficulties from a stress perspective allows a new level of understanding and opens an array of useful intervention techniques. Indeed, many of the techniques are already known by therapists and require little new training; however, they can be more accurately applied when treatments are planned from the stress perspective.

We propose a model of stress with five major components. Demands (or *stressors*) are weighed against *resources*, determining the degree of overload on a patient. Psychological reactions are mediated through patient *appraisal* of balance between demands and resources, thereby calling on *coping* behaviors and ultimately yielding short- and long-term stress *outcomes*.

With this framework, the specific stress process of the patient becomes clearer, and the best points for intervention can be determined. In fact, interventions can occur at any or all of these points. Generally, interventions help stress-laden patients reduce demands, increase resources and their utilization, appraise more accurately (and often more benignly), employ the most effective coping behaviors, and counteract negative outcomes when possible. A typical treatment attacks the problems at several of these points and may include multiple interventions at each. Further, taking into account the personal and environmental limitations and resources of the patient (the ecological perspective) can guide the therapist's choice of interventions for each point in the model for maximum benefit.

ADDITIONAL RESOURCES

Suggestions for further reading and professional development resources are available at this book's companion Web site: www.primarycarepsych.com.

References

Abidin, R. R. (1995). *The parenting stress index professional manual.* Odessa, FL: Psychological Assessment Resources.

Adler, N. E., & Ostrove, J. M. (1999). SES & health: What we know and what we don't. *Annals of the New York Academy of Sciences, 896,* 3–15.

American Psychiatric Association. (1994). *Diagnostic and statistical manual of mental disorders* (4th ed.). Washington, DC: Author.

American Psychiatric Association. (2000). *Diagnostic and statistical manual of mental disorders* (4th ed., text rev.). Washington, DC: Author.

Antoni, M. H., Cruess, D. G., Cruess, S., Lutgendorf, S., Kumar, M., Ironson, G., et al. (2000). Cognitive-behavioral stress management intervention effects on anxiety, 24-hr urinary norepinephrine output, and T-cytotoxic/suppressor cells over time among symptomatic HIV-infected gay men. *Journal of Consulting and Clinical Psychology, 68,* 31–45.

Antoni, M. H., LaPerriere, A., Schneiderman, N., & Fletcher, M. A. (1991). Stress and immunity in individuals at risk for AIDS. *Stress Medicine, 7,* 35–44.

Bandura, A. (1977). Self-efficacy: Toward a unifying theory of behavioral change. *Psychological Review, 84,* 191–215.

Bandura, A., Reese, L., & Adams, N. E. (1982). Microanalysis of action and fear arousal as a function of differential levels of perceived self-efficacy. *Journal of Personality and Social Psychology, 43,* 5–21.

Baum, A., & Fleming, I. (1993). Implications of psychological research on stress and technological accidents. *American Psychologist, 48,* 665–672.

Black, P. H., & Garbutt, L. D. (2002). Stress, inflammation, and cardiovascular disease. *Journal of Psychosomatic Research, 52,* 1–23.

Cannon, W. B. (1932). *The wisdom of the body.* New York: Norton.

Carpenter, B. N. (1992). Issues and advances in coping research. In B. N. Carpenter (Ed.), *Personal coping: Theory, research, and application* (pp. 1–13). New York: Praeger.

Carpenter, B. N., & Scott, S. M. (1992). Interpersonal aspects of coping. In B. N. Carpenter (Ed.), *Personal coping: Theory, research, and application* (pp. 93–110). New York: Praeger.

Chrousos, G. P., & Gold, P. W. (1992). The concepts of stress and stress system disorders. *Journal of the American Medical Association, 267,* 1244–1252.

Cohen, S., Gottlieb, B. H., & Underwood, L. G. (2001). Social relationships and health: Challenges for measurement and intervention. *Advances in Mind Body Medicine, 17,* 129–141.

Cohen, S., Kamarck, T., & Mermelstein, R. (1983). A global measure of perceived stress. *Journal of Health and Social Behavior, 24,* 385–396.

Cohen, S., Tyrrell, D. A., & Smith, A. P. (1991). Psychological stress and susceptibility to the common cold. *New England Journal of Medicine, 325,* 606–612.

Conway, T. L., Vickers, R. R., Ward, H. W., & Rahe, R. H. (1981). Occupational stress and variation in cigarette, coffee, and alcohol consumption. *Journal of Health and Social Behavior, 22,* 155–165.

De Bellis, M. D., Chrousos, G. P., Dorn, L. D., Burke, L., Helmers, K., Kling, M. A., et al. (1994). Hypothalamic-pituitary-adrenal axis dysregulation in sexually abused girls. *Journal of Clinical Endocrinology and Metabolism, 78,* 249–255.

De Bellis, M. D., Lefter, L., Trickett, P. K., & Putnam, F. W. (1994). Urinary catecholamine excretion in sexually abused girls. *Journal of the American Academy of Child and Adolescent Psychiatry, 33,* 320–327.

Dersh, J., Polatin, P. B., & Gatchel, R. J. (2002). Chronic pain and psychopathology: Research findings and theoretical considerations. *Psychosomatic Medicine, 64,* 773–786.

Ferguson, E. (2001). Personality and coping traits: A joint factor analysis. *British Journal of Health Psychology, 6,* 311–325.

Folkman, S., & Lazarus, R. S. (1985). If it changes it must be a process: A study of emotion and coping during three stages of a college examination. *Journal of Personality and Social Psychology, 48,* 150–170.

Folkman, S., Shaefer, C., & Lazarus, R. S. (1979).

Cognitive processes as mediators of stress and coping. In V. Hamilton & D. M. Warburton (Eds.), *Human stress and cognition: An information processing approach* (pp. 265–298). New York: Wiley.

Frenzel, M. P., McCaul, K. D., Glasgow, R. E., & Schafer, L. C. (1988). The relationship of stress and coping to regimen adherence and glycemic control of diabetes. *Journal of Social and Clinical Psychology, 6,* 77–87.

Friedman, H. S., & Booth-Kewley, S. (1990). The disease prone personality: A meta-analytic view of the concept. *American Psychologist, 42,* 539–555.

Gaebel, W., Jaenner, M., Frommann, N., Pietzcker, A., Koepcke, W., Linden, M., et al. (2000). Prodromal states in schizophrenia. *Comprehensive Psychiatry, 41,* 76–85.

Hankin, B. L., & Abramson, L. Y. (2001). Development of gender differences in depression: An elaborated cognitive vulnerability-transactional stress theory. *Psychological Bulletin, 127,* 773–796.

Heim, C., Newport, D. J., Heit, S., Graham, Y. P., Wilcox, M., Bonsall, R., et al. (2000). Pituitary-adrenal and autonomic responses to stress in women after sexual and physical abuse in childhood. *Journal of the American Medical Association, 284,* 592–597.

Herbert, T. B., & Cohen, S. (1993a). Depression and immunity: A meta-analytic review. *Psychological Bulletin, 113,* 472–486.

Herbert, T. B., & Cohen, S. (1993b). Stress and immunity in humans: A meta-analytic review. *Psychosomatic Medicine, 55,* 364–379.

Jiang, W., Krantz, D. S., Waugh, R. A., Coleman, R. E., Hanson, M. M., Frid, D. J., et al. (1996). Mental stress-induced myocardial ischemia and cardiac events. *Journal of the American Medical Association, 275,* 1651–1656.

Johnson, J. H. (1986). *Life events as stressors in childhood and adolescence.* Newbury Park, CA: Sage.

Johnson, S. L., & Miller, I. (1997). Negative life events and time to recovery from episodes of bipolar disorder. *Journal of Abnormal Psychology, 106,* 449–457.

Kanner, A. D., Coyne, J. C., Schaefer, C., & Lazarus, R. S. (1981). Comparison of two modes of stress measurement: Daily hassles and uplifts versus major life events. *Journal of Behavioral Medicine, 4,* 1–39.

Kobasa, S. C. (1979). Stressful life events, person-

ality, and health: An inquiry into hardiness. *Journal of Personality and Social Psychology, 37,* 1–11.

Kobasa, S. C., Maddi, S. R., Puccetti, M. C., & Zola, M. A. (1985). Effectiveness of hardiness, exercise and social support as resources against illness. *Journal of Psychosomatic Research, 29,* 525–533.

Krantz, D. S., & McCeney, M. K. (2002). Effects of psychological and social factors in organic disease: A critical assessment of research on coronary heart disease. *Annual Review of Psychology, 53,* 341–369.

Lazarus, R., & Folkman, S. (1984). *Stress, appraisal, and coping.* New York: Springer.

Leserman, J., Petitto, J. M., Perkins, D. O., Folds, J. D., Golden, R. N., & Evans, D. L. (1997). Severe stress, depressive symptoms, and changes in lymphocyte subsets in human immunodeficiency virus-infected men: A 2-year follow-up study. *Archives of General Psychiatry, 54,* 279–285.

Leventhal, H., Patrick-Muller, L., & Leventhal, E. A. (1998). It's long-term stressors that take a toll: Comment on Cohen et al. (1988). *Health Psychology, 17,* 211–213.

Maddi, S. R., Bartone, P. T., & Puccetti, M. C. (1987). Stressful events are indeed a factor in physical illness: Reply to Schroeder and Costa. *Journal of Personality and Social Psychology, 52,* 833–843.

McCrae, R. R. (1992). Situational determinants of coping. In B. N. Carpenter (Ed.), *Personal coping: Theory, research, and application* (pp. 65–76). New York: Praeger.

McEwen, B. S., & Stellar, E. (1993). Stress and the individual: Mechanisms leading to disease. *Archives of Internal Medicine, 153,* 2093–2101.

Miller, L. S., & Smith, A. D. (1993). *The stress solution.* New York: Simon and Schuster.

Miller, S. M. (1992). Monitoring and blunting in the face of threat: Implications for adaptation and health. In L. Montada, S. Filipp, & M. J. Lerner (Eds.), *Life crises and experiences of loss in adulthood* (pp. 255–273). Hillsdale, NJ: Lawrence Erlbaum.

Miller, T. Q., Smith, T. W., Turner, C. W., Guijarro, M. L., & Hallet, A. J. (1995). A meta-analytic review of hostility and physical health. *Psychological Bulletin, 119,* 322–348.

Moos, R. H., & Moos, B. S. (1997). Life Stressors and Social Resources Inventory: A measure of adults' and youths' life contexts. In C. P. Zalaquett & R. J. Wood (Eds.), *Evaluating stress: A* book of resources (pp. 177–190). Lanham, MD: Scarecrow.

Musselman, D. L., & Nemeroff, C. B. (2000). Depression really does hurt your heart: Stress, depression, and cardiovascular disease. *Progress in Brain Research, 122,* 43–59.

Nowack, K. (1999). *The stress profile.* Los Angeles: Western Psychological Services.

Osipow, S. H. (1998). *The occupational stress inventory–revised.* Odessa, FL: Psychological Assessment Resources.

Pynoos, R. S., Frederick, C., Nader, K., Arroyo, W., Steinberg, A., Eth, S., et al. (1987). Life threat and posttraumatic stress in school-age children. *Archives of General Psychiatry, 44,* 1057–1063.

Quick, J. C., Nelson, D. L., Quick, J. D., & Orman, D. K. (2001). An isomorphic theory of stress: The dynamics of person-environment fit. *Stress and Health: Journal of the International Society for the Investigation of Stress, 17,* 147–157.

Sarason, I. G., Johnson, J. H., & Siegel, J. M. (1978). Assessing the impact of life changes: Development of the Life Experiences Survey. *Journal of Consulting and Clinical Psychology, 46,* 932–946.

Sattler, D. N., Kaiser, C. F., & Hittner, J. B. (2000). Disaster preparedness: Relationships among prior experience, personal characteristics, and distress. *Journal of Applied Social Psychology, 30,* 1396–1402.

Schnall, P. L., Schwartz, J. E., Landsbergis, P. A., Warren, K., & Pickering, T. G. (1998). A longitudinal study of job strain and ambulatory blood pressure: Results from a three-year follow-up. *Psychosomatic Medicine, 60,* 697–706.

Segerstrom, S. C., Solomon, G. F., Kemeny, M. E., & Fahey, J. L. (1998). Relationship of worry to immune sequelae of the Northridge earthquake. *Journal of Behavioral Medicine, 21,* 433–450.

Septhon, S. E., Sapolsky, R. M., Kraemer, H. C., & Spiegel, D. (2000). Diurnal cortisol rhythm as a predictor of breast cancer survival. *Journal of the National Cancer Institute, 92,* 994–1000.

Singer, J. E. (1980). Traditions of stress research: Integrative comments. In I. G. Sarason & C. D. Spielberger (Eds.), *Stress and anxiety* (Vol. 7, pp. 3–10). Washington, DC: Hemisphere.

Singer, J. E., Lundberg, U., & Frankenhaeuser, M. (1978). Stress on the train: A study of urban commuting. In A. Baum, J. E. Singer, & S. Valins (Eds.), *Advances in environmental psychology* (Vol. 1, pp. 41–56). Hillsdale, NJ: Lawrence Erlbaum.

Solomon, G. F., Segerstrom, S. C., Grohr, P., Kemeny, M., & Fahey, J. (1997). Shaking up immunity: Psychological and immunological changes after a natural disaster. *Psychosomatic Medicine, 59,* 114–127.

Sterling, P., & Eyer, J. (1988). Allostasis: A new paradigm to explain arousal pathology. In S. Fisher & J. Reason (Eds.), *Handbook of life stress, cognition, and health* (pp. 629–649). New York: Wiley.

Stetson, B. A., Rahn, J. M., Dubbert, P. M., Wilner, B. I., & Mercury, M. G. (1997). Prospective evaluation of the effects of stress on exercise adherence in community residing women. *Health Psychology, 16,* 515–520.

Strelau, J. (2001). The role of temperament as a moderator of stress. In T. D. Wachs & G. A. Kohnstamm (Eds.), *Temperament in context* (pp. 153–172). Mahwah, NJ: Lawrence Erlbaum.

Suls, J., & Fletcher, B. (1985). The relative efficacy of avoidant and nonavoidant coping strategies: A meta-analysis. *Health Psychology, 4,* 249–288.

Vollrath, M. (2001). Personality and stress. *Scandinavian Journal of Psychology, 42,* 335–347.

Weinstein, S. E., Quigley, K. S., & Mordkoff, J. T. (2002). Influence of control and physical effort on cardiovascular reactivity to a video game task. *Psychophysiology, 39,* 591–598.

Whisman, M. A., & Kwon, P. (1993). Life stress and dysphoria: The role of self-esteem and hopelessness. *Journal of Personality and Social Psychology, 65,* 1054–1060.

Wiebe, D. J., & McCallum, D. M. (1986). Health practices and hardiness as mediators in the stress-illness relationship. *Health Psychology, 5,* 425–438.

41

Work Stress and Health

Paul J. Hartung
Mark A. Penn

Live neither in the past nor in the future, but let each day's work absorb your entire energies, and satisfy your widest ambition.—Sir William Osler, M.D., to his students

In the name of God, stop a moment, cease your work, look around you.— Leo Tolstoy, *Anna Karenina*

People strained by work stress often experience a variety of health problems. Such problems range from the behavioral to the psychological to the physical. Behavioral problems include lowered job performance, absenteeism, and violence. Psychological manifestations of work stress include depression, anxiety, and relationship conflicts. Physical problems linked to work stress include heart disease, immune system disorders, and neurological impairments. Work-related stress may in fact play a causative, contributory, or exacerbating role in any one of the psychological disorders and medical conditions described in this handbook.

Estimates indicate that stress-related problems account for 70% of visits to primary care physicians (Boone & Christensen, 1997). Disability claims associated with work stress rank as the most rapidly growing form of work-related illness for which individuals seek workers' compensation (King, 1995). Upward of 11 million workers report levels of work stress that threaten their health (Sauter, Murphy, & Hurrell, 1990). The annual incidence of occupational disease and work-generated illness approximates 400,000 cases (Savickas, 2001).

Clinicians practicing in primary care medical settings must understand work stress and the way it manifests itself in behavioral, psychological, and physical problems. Doing so can aid in identifying, treating, and preventing problems that arise from work stress and thereby promote worker health. Although patients are not typically referred specifically for work-related problems, the stress, depression, anxiety, and other emotional conditions with which they present often relate to their work.

This chapter provides clinicians with an understanding of work and the effects of work stress on individual health and well-being. The chapter seeks to help clinicians develop and implement treatment plans that will benefit their patients who experience work stress. The first part of the chapter (a) considers the nature and meaning of work in the context of the developing person; (b) articulates work stress in terms of stress, strain, and coping; and (c) identifies common clinical problems linked to work stress. The second part of the chapter then addresses issues related to diagnosis, prevention, treatment, and management of clinical problems arising from work stress and strain that clinicians typically encounter in primary care practice.

WORK AND HUMAN DEVELOPMENT

Work constitutes a primary context of human development and a core component of the human life structure. As a context of development, work provides at minimum a pathway to sustenance and potentially an avenue for cultivating a sense of identity, direction, and meaning in life through making a social contribution (Erikson, 1968). Developing industry, competence, and the capacity to work remain integral to human growth and development (Erikson, 1950). For centuries and in the writings of preeminent scholars such as Sigmund Freud and Alfred Adler, successful participation in work has been extolled as a cardinal virtue of life and a hallmark of the effectively functioning person.

As a prime dimension of the life structure, work entails a universal human activity and a location for enacting a social role. The work role, along with roles in other life domains such as family and community, provides a primary source of personal identity and shapes the life structure. Work as paid employment may typically occupy about one third of a worker's waking hours. It also often spills over to other, nonwork spheres as workers stressed by the vicissitudes and demands of work life bring their jobs and career concerns to their home, leisure, and community lives (Conrad, 1988). Estimates indicate that the average American work week comprises 52 hours, with workers logging 46 hours per week on the job and an additional 6 hours at home (cf. Robinson, 1998).

Within the life structure of the developing person, work can indeed absorb energies or exhaust them, yielding fulfillment or disdain. Working either too much or too little can debilitate or discourage. Work can increase creativity or diminish it. Allowing participation in work to contract or expand beyond appropriate boundaries can be detrimental to health. Just as work represents a cultural imperative, our culture and society also expect individuals to balance work with involvement in love, play, worship, and community. Striking a balance between work and nonwork so that each complements rather than conflicts with the other is essential to health and well-being. Contention and competition between and among life roles such as parent, worker, citizen, student, spouse, and friend make achieving such balance a difficult task. The centrality of work in the lives of women and men in contemporary developed societies compels the primary care clinician to inquire routinely about the stress patients experience at work, how they cope with it, and to what extent they are able to negotiate and integrate work and multiple role demands.

Work as a vital life context and core element of the life structure certainly has the potential to promote human development by cultivating identity, promoting success, nurturing relationship, and advancing community. However, many individuals clearly experience the physical, emotional, mental, social, interpersonal, and organizational aspects of work and the workplace as stressful and feel unfulfilled, if not undone, by the promise of work (Hepburn, Loughlin, & Barling, 1997). The centrality of work as a cultural mandate, social institution, and personal endeavor makes it a prime source of satisfaction as well as stress and strain. When workers appraise their work environments as meeting their needs and expectations, job satisfaction results. Stress on the job can compromise and lessen levels of job satisfaction and create strain.

WORK STRESS, STRAIN, AND COPING

To understand and manage the range of behavioral, psychological, physical, and other problems that can arise from or be exacerbated by work stress, such as those outlined in this handbook, the clinician must comprehend the dynamic interplay among stress, strain, and coping (see chapter 40). Beginning with the work of physiologist Walter Cannon and Hans Selye, the concept of stress in health and illness has been variously defined. Selye (1971) described stress as rate of wear and tear resulting from any demand on the body. Generally, stress has been regarded in one of three ways: (a) as a stimulus or activating event, quantified in Holmes and Rahe's Social Readjustment Rating Scale (1967), which ranks major life events by severity; (b) as a response to environmental stimuli engendering a biopsychosocial state; and (c) as the interaction of person and environment. From this last perspective, *stress* denotes a subjective experience resulting from an individual's interpretation of an event or situation as tension or pressure inducing and prompting a coping response.

Selye (1956) emphasized that stress per se is not necessarily bad. Rather, particular responses to stress may be undesirable and unhealthy. Selye defined *eustress* as healthy or positive stress (e.g., physical exercise or mental challenge) and *distress* as unhealthy or negative stress (e.g., excessive physical or mental demands). *Work stress* means a perceived tension or pressure in reaction to the specific stimulus demands of work and the workplace.

When stressed, individuals attempt to resolve the conditions prompting the stress by making *coping* responses aimed at altering aspects of themselves or the environment to alleviate the experience of stress. If coping responses and strategies prove ineffective such that stress overwhelms and injures the individual, strain ensues. *Strain* signifies the debilitating outcome of stress coupled with ineffective or insufficient coping resources to manage stress and manifested in any of the full range of behavioral, psychological, and physical problems. When stress levels exceed coping resources, strain results.

In sum, stress is a perception, coping is a behavior to deal with stress, and strain is a damaging condition that results when mechanisms, strategies, and resources for coping with stress fail. Work environments create stress, which workers attempt to cope with and resolve. Coping effectiveness and level of stress intensity interact to de-

termine the level of strain experienced. Higher levels of stress and lower coping resources yield higher levels of strain.

WORK STRESSORS

Six categories of work *stressors* (i.e., any condition or event that causes stress) have been identified in the occupational stress literature (cf. Cooper, 1983; Osipow & Spokane, 1987; Sauter et al., 1990; Spokane & Ferrara, 2001). These stressors arise from the conditions of the work environment and interact with the unique characteristics of the individual worker to induce stress or strain. The six categories of job stressors are as follows:

1. *Intrinsic job factors*: work overload or underload, shift work, long hours, travel, risk and danger, new technology, physical environment
2. *Role stressors*: role ambiguity, role overload, role insufficiency (e.g., inadequate amount of work), responsibility for others
3. *Career development*: job insecurity, uncertain career path in an organization
4. *Work relationships*: interpersonal conflicts, lack of support
5. *Organizational structure*: lack of autonomy, low decision-making latitude, lack of control
6. *Work–nonwork interface*: conflict between work and other domains such as family and leisure, "spillover" stress from interactions between multiple roles

Familiarity with common work stressors aids the clinician in assessing, diagnosing, treating, and preventing problems arising from them. It is also important for the clinician to distinguish between acute and chronic stress. Acute stress has a recognizable and sometimes predictable onset, with a short-term, limited course of usually less than 6 months. Nearly one third of the working population experience *chronic work stressors*, defined as stressors of variable duration, that are enduring, and are of non-specific onset. A suggested guideline for determining whether a stressor is acute or chronic is to consider its duration, onset, and likelihood of recurrence (Hepburn et al., 1997). Work stressors of long duration (>6 months), unspecified onset, and likely recurrence may be characterized as chronic.

An early study suggested that, at any given time, 33% of the workforce experience chronic work stressors (Kahn, Wolfe, Quinn, Snoek, & Rosenthal, 1964). Later reports have indicated that 25% to 53% of workers rate work as the single greatest stressor in their lives, and that work-related problems prompt more health complaints than any other life stressor, including financial or family problems (National Institute for Occupational Safety and Health, 1999; Spielberger & Reheiser, 1995). It is estimated that, at least once per week, 90% of family physicians encounter in their practices illness or injury linked to work stressors (Savickas, 2001). The pervasiveness of the problem demands that the clinician routinely assess levels of work stress and address its role in the concerns of individuals who present for treatment.

MEASURING WORK STRESS

Stress assessment has traditionally focused on measuring strain using both physiological and self-report methods. Physiological measures of strain include electroencephalography, electromyography, electrodermal responses or galvanic skin responses, electrocardiography, blood pressure, and blood volume. Self-report measures of strain include the Minnesota Multiphasic Personality Inventory (Hathaway & McKinley, 1952) and the State-Trait Anxiety Inventory (Spielberger, Gorsuch, & Lushene, 1970).

In the consulting room, the Occupational Stress Inventory–Revised (OSI-R; Osipow, 1998) offers clinicians a valuable tool for specifically appraising the interaction of work stress, strain, and coping in adults aged 18 years and older. The OSI-R contains 140 items and three questionnaires that measure three domains of occupational adjustment: occupational stress, psychological strain, and coping resources. The Occupational Roles Questionnaire of the OSI-R measures work stress in terms of role ambiguity, role overload, role insufficiency, role boundary, responsibility, and physical environment stressors. The Personal Strain Questionnaire assesses perceived levels of vocational, psychological, interpersonal, and physical strain. The Personal Resources Questionnaire mea-

sures recreation, self-care, social support, and rational/cognitive coping. Completing the OSI-R requires 30 minutes, and it can be machine or hand scored.

The Job Stress Survey (JSS; Spielberger & Vagg, 1999) provides a second tool for measuring work stress of adults aged 18 years and older. The JSS contains 30 items describing common workplace stressors that individuals rate in terms of perceived severity and frequency of occurrence, and requires 10 to 15 minutes to complete. Subscale scores for levels of job pressure and lack of organizational support provide an index of job stress related to the job itself and to lack of support from supervisors, coworkers, or the policies and procedures of the organization.

> I am doomed to an eternity of compulsive work. No set goal achieved satisfies. Success only breeds a new goal. The golden apple devoured has seeds. It is endless.—Bette Davis, *The Lonely Life*, 1962

WORK-RELATED SYNDROMES

Work stress and strain can be associated with a variety of biopsychosocial problems. There also exist identifiable syndromes clinicians encounter that have direct links to work. Type A behavior pattern (TABP) comprises a constellation of personality and psychological characteristics that, in interaction with the occupational environment, place an individual at risk for behavioral, psychological, and physical problems (Friedman, 1969). TABP comprises a combination of predispositions, behaviors, and emotional responses used to deal with environmental conditions and changes.

Research has consistently indicated that individuals with TABP are more alert, aggressive, competitive, time conscious, impatient, self-confident, orderly, self-controlled, well organized, deeply involved with work, and less able to relax when away from work. TABP manifests in individuals possessing these behavioral dispositions and, when combined with an aggravating occupational situation, has been implicated in such outcomes as emotional exhaustion, personality disintegration, and interpersonal conflicts. A review of the occupational stress and cardiovascular disease literature indicated a definite causal link between TABP and risk or incidence of coronary heart disease (Byrne, 2000). Type A behavior has been considered as an explanatory root of workaholism.

Workaholism or *work addiction* represents a second work-related syndrome characterized by an obsession with work and compulsive work involvement to the point of unwillingness or inability to disengage from work activity regardless of external demands. Workaholism involves avoiding responsibility to family and friends while earning praise from employers and work colleagues, displaying work habits that invariably exceed normal coworker expectations, high work drive, and perfectionism (McMillan, O'Driscoll, Marsh, & Brady, 2001). Rather than retreat appropriately from work, individuals with workaholism engage in or think about work anytime and anywhere, prompting significant life imbalance. Research has suggested links between workaholism and Type A behavior, obsessive-compulsive disorder, and hypomania (McMillan et al., 2001).

A third commonly recognized syndrome intimately related to work stress is *job burnout*. Emotional exhaustion, depersonalization, and a low sense of work efficacy constitute the triad of the burnout syndrome, which develops gradually over time (Maslach & Jackson, 1986). Typically, emotional exhaustion from interpersonal contact occurs first, prompting callous depersonalization toward others, especially those one serves, and eventually a lowered sense of accomplishment.

Taking a developmental process view of burnout helps to identify and track the organizational conditions and individual worker characteristics that often combine to produce burnout (Burke & Richardsen, 1996). Organizational conditions include strained interpersonal work relationships, high job demands, lack of autonomy, and low social support. Individual variables include high levels of personal empathy, sensitivity, dedication, and idealism, as well as obsessiveness, overenthusiasm, and overidentification with others. Occupations with high levels of people contact (e.g., human service professions) have been associated with higher prevalence of burnout. A wide range of presenting symptoms may accompany burnout, including withdrawal, overt anger and blaming, and abuse of food, alcohol, or other substances.

MANAGING WORK STRESS AND STRAIN

Mrs. P., a 45-year-old African American woman, works as the principal of a local private elementary school. She presents to her primary care doctor with vague upper abdominal pains. Married for 21 years, Mrs. P. is the mother of four children, ages 11, 14, 17, and 20 years. Significant history reveals that her 17-year-old son has been rebellious and has run away from home on several occasions over the past year. Mrs. P. questions her abilities to serve as principal of the school.

Primary care clinicians play an instrumental role in helping patients like Mrs. P. deal with work stress and strain. At times, the link between a presenting symptom and a particular stressor may be obvious to the patient, who may then openly discuss it with the clinician. At other times, the cause of a presenting symptom remains unclear and difficult to discern. On occasion, a physical symptom may not surface, and the clinician uncovers a problem through careful questioning. In any event, establishing and maintaining an effective therapeutic relationship with the patient is a prerequisite to the assessment, diagnosis, and management of work stress and strain.

Assessment and Diagnosis

Patients often present to the clinician's office with a variety of complaints that implicate work stress as part of the problem. Conducting a pertinent and thorough history to assess these complaints and make a proper diagnosis initiates the encounter. The clinical interview provides the richest source of data about the patient's stressors, perception, coping, and arousal reduction strategies (Boone & Christensen, 1997). Using objective measures such as the OSI and JSS in tandem with the interview adds incremental validity to comprehending the patient's stress, strain, and coping.

Assessment begins by identifying stress symptoms and precipitating stressors. Symptoms may relate to an alarm reaction, defined as an immediate response to a perceived challenge, and comprise palpitations, shallow rapid breathing, muscle tension, dryness of the throat, nausea, anxiety, dizziness, and sweating. As stress on the body increases, physical problems typically surface in the form of tension and migraine headaches, irritable bowel syndrome, impaired resistance to colds and other viral illnesses, dermatitis, asthma, backache, gastritis, and high blood pressure. Emotional issues arise as depression, suicidal ideation, and anxiety. Mental dysfunction emerges as accidents or near accidents, loss of clarity of thought, reduced performance, difficulty concentrating, constant tardiness, absenteeism, more frequent mistakes and excuses, increased misunderstandings with coworkers and family, and sudden loss of short-term memory (Onciul, 1997).

An effective assessment requires the clinician to clarify the nature of the patient's concerns and examine the origins of the symptoms and the contexts in which they occur. Ascertaining details about the patient's family and other life circumstances in addition to work proves necessary and helpful in this regard. In so doing, associated issues of family, marital, or parenting problems may emerge. Inquiries should also be made about health risk factors such as smoking and alcohol and other substance abuse, as well as about domestic violence issues and suicidal ideation. Often, the patient will minimize or deny the importance of major life stressors, which demands that the clinician remain sensitive to the temporal relationship between symptom onset and occurrence of major stressful life events (Ancha & Tucker, 2001).

A thorough assessment proceeds to inquiries into the patient's beliefs, expectations, self-perceptions, and needs that influence how the patient perceives and copes with stressors. To further assess patients in the context of their work, the clinician conducts a work-focused interview that examines key questions such as the following:

- How important is work in your life overall?
- How well do you believe your job fits with who you are?
- What is your level of satisfaction with your job?
- Do you work excessive hours or perform more than one job?
- Are organizational goals and expectations clearly defined and understood?

- How much input do you have in decision making?
- What are your relationships like with management and coworkers?
- What are the physical conditions at your place of employment?
- How would you describe your personality style?
- How do you cope with problems that you encounter at work?
- Who do you turn to when you need someone to talk to? Are they easily accessible? Are you satisfied with that relationship? Are they supportive? What other support systems do you have?

Case Assessment. *Mrs. P. experienced stress resulting from role overload and perceived role inadequacy. She perceived herself as unqualified for the role of principal because she lacked formal training for the position. This perception was despite the fact the school system in which she worked did not require such training. She possessed an educational degree and earned the appointment as principal based on her several years of diligent work on the school board and her demonstrated remarkable leadership and organizational skills.*

Too much work, too little assistance, and too few employees, prompted by the school's budget constraints, created a situation in which Mrs. P. experienced tremendous job stress. Propelled by a strong sense of commitment and duty, however, she felt obliged to work long hours, receive low pay, and deal with complex issues to help the school succeed. Mrs. P. defined her preferred role as "helper" rather than leader. She felt unable to get away from her job because of the immense workload to which she felt compelled to attend.

In addition to these problems, Mrs. P. experienced added pressure and family strain brought on by her child's rebellious behavior. Her husband, a manager at a local corporation who also worked long hours, provided Mrs. P. with support, yet she felt ineffective in dealing with her rebellious child. Mrs. P. reported no substance abuse or domestic violence history. She presented no other symptoms or physical problems. Physical exam and workup for the abdominal problems revealed no identifiable physical cause for her stated abdominal pains.

Management

A well-designed treatment and management plan follows appropriate assessment and diagnosis. A patient facing complex and multifaceted issues requires a management plan equally comprehensive and multidimensional. Such a plan, particularly when the issues confronted extend beyond the expertise of the primary care clinician, often requires appropriate consultation and a multidisciplinary approach. Contributing or underlying psychosocial issues must be addressed. The clinician uses the management plan to help define a patient's work capacity, identify needed job changes, and act as the patient's advocate with the employer (Frumkin, 2000).

During treatment, the clinician may act as a consultant or coach to fully inform the patient about his or her choices and encourage the patient to implement changes. In this regard, the clinician gives feedback about stress patterns revealed by the diagnostic workup, offers strategies for health promotion, and identifies potential consequences to the patient for adherence and nonadherence to the management plan (Boone & Christensen, 1997). Patients' confidence in their ability to recover increases when the clinician helps them to break the seemingly overwhelming problems into segments as well as providing an overview of the longer term goals (Ancha & Tucker, 2001).

Within the treatment decision-making process, the clinician shares responsibility with the patient rather than assuming full responsibility for decision making. Any and all recommendations made by the clinician involve enlisting the cooperation and active participation of the patient. As summarized in Table 41.1, the management plan for work stress and strain can be multifaceted, entailing two types of strategies: person based, dealing with changing the individual, and organization based, dealing with changing the workplace. Each of these strategies merits discussion in turn.

Person-Based Strategies

Reassurance/behavior management

Appropriate reassurance means conveying optimism about the patient's ability to influence his

Table 41.1 A Summary of Person-Based and Organization-Based Strategies for Managing Work Stress

Person-based strategies
  Reassurance/behavior management
  Psychotherapy
  Medication
  Social support
  Spirituality
  Complementary and alternative medicine
  Education

Organization-based strategies
  Organizational change
  Prevention
  Employee assistance programs

or her health. This involves explaining to the patient that a variety of strategies and options for examining and changing habits of thought and action exist, and that the clinician will work collaboratively with the patient to do so. Encouraging the patient also involves framing beneficial lifestyle changes as the patient's choice and empowering the patient with a sense of control. Specific techniques of relaxation training, guided imagery, and meditation offer useful ways to buffer work stress (Boone & Christensen, 1997).

Behavior management also takes the form of stress management programs that teach workers about the nature and sources of stress, the effects of stress on health, and personal skills to reduce stress. Integral components of stress management include identifying and addressing stressors, appropriately reframing concerns presented, and effectively challenging and disputing negative thoughts. Although some studies provide evidence to support formal stress management programs, they do potentially pose two major disadvantages: (a) the beneficial effects of these programs on stress symptoms often are short lived, and (b) such programs typically ignore important root causes of stress because they attend only to the worker and not to changing conditions in the work environment (National Institute for Occupational Safety and Health, 1999).

Other behavioral modification methods include addressing diet and exercise in consultation with the primary care physician. Ensuring that the patient maintains proper eating habits and a nutritional regimen adequate to handle job demands proves essential. A review of a patient's dietary habits, often in consultation with a dietitian, assists the clinician to determine if any adjustments may be appropriate. Evidence indicates that exercise improves health and well-being. Therefore, the clinician can encourage the sedentary patient to exercise regularly (30 minutes, three to four times per week) as a good beginning. Any patient with risk factors for problems prompted by exercise should be evaluated by the primary care physician to determine the patient's capacity to follow such a plan.

Psychotherapy

Psychotherapy, particularly cognitive–behavioral approaches, may prove highly effective for altering dysfunctional beliefs and unproductive coping habits that amplify strain (Ancha & Tucker, 2001). Psychotherapy becomes critical for patients who need more assistance in developing insight into their interpretations of and responses to stress and identifying more effective coping mechanisms through personality restructuring. Teaching cognitive restructuring and simple coping techniques, as well as encouraging the patient to set appropriate and realistic goals, understand personality issues, and recognize strengths all form useful components of psychotherapeutic interventions.

Medication

Problems interfering with performance of job or daily activities warrant more serious consideration of medication usage. Selective serotonin reuptake inhibitors (SSRIs) have replaced the chronic use of benzodiazepines in the treatment of anxiety. The SSRIs rank as the most commonly prescribed class of antidepressants for the treatment of depression. Doses for anxiety disorders are usually lower than those for depression to minimize some of the undesirable side effects. It is imperative that the clinician consult with the primary care physician to understand any medication prescribed as well as its side effects. Patients need to be cautioned about potential effects that might interfere with their work or everyday life activities.

Social support

Social support constitutes a key person-based management strategy. Support from family, friends, clergy, community, and others often mitigates strain. Social supports identified in the assessment form a critical part of the management plan; individuals who lack social supports should be encouraged to develop a support network. This extends to striking a balance between work and nonwork arenas, which may involve actively scheduling and taking time for family, friends, leisure, and other pursuits. Another strategy in this regard involves prompting patients to identify and interview, or at least observe, peers who cope successfully with excessive demands to discover some potential alternative coping strategies.

Spirituality

Exploring the role of spirituality in patients' lives offers another important person-based strategy for managing work stress. Patients often wish that their clinician would inquire about their personal spirituality, religious faith, and beliefs and incorporate them in treatment (Pulchalski & Romer, 2000). Recognizing this fact, Pulchalski and Romer described a spiritual assessment tool, using the acronym FICA, to inquire about the patient's faith, influence of spiritual beliefs on behavior, community connection, and how the patient would like the clinician to address spirituality. Personal beliefs should not be imposed on patients, but the importance of patients' own spiritual beliefs in helping them heal should be understood. Accessing their spiritual support system often helps patients to deal better with stressful life events.

Complementary and alternative medicine

Some patients may consider and pursue use of alternative treatments, such as herbs and vitamins. It is important to ask the patient about this, as well as about the use of over-the-counter medications in addition to medications prescribed by other clinicians. Supplements and herbs can be harmful, or there may be harmful cumulative or interactive effects with other medications. It is also helpful to inquire about other alternative medicine techniques. The clinician may need to help patients sort out the various methods and help them identify which methods are most beneficial and which methods may be not useful or may be harmful in their management plan.

Education

Patient education forms a vital person-based management plan strategy. Patients must understand that sometimes they cannot solve the problem right away, yet they can do some things to gain a sense of control, including challenging and easing unrealistic expectations about time required to reach problem resolution. The clinician can encourage and help the patient to identify realistic alternatives in this regard. The clinician should also think epidemiologically; could the problem be far reaching and shared by others in the community (Frumkin, 2000)? Helping patients to understand that the problem is not unique to them can be beneficial.

Organization-Based Strategies

Organizational change

Person-based strategies for addressing work stress and strain focus on individual change and therefore typically prove easier and less costly to implement. In contrast, organization-based strategies, involving system and environmental change, often prove expensive and disruptive (Hurrell & Murphy, 1998). The clinician may not be able to affect directly how the organization conducts its business, but may need to become an advocate for the patient in effecting change. Working alone or in collaboration with the patient's physician, the clinician could prepare, with the patient's involvement and permission, information for the company regarding the issues and difficulties the patient faces, along with some suggestions, if appropriate, on how to improve the situation. In most cases, the clinician will work with the patient to assist him or her in understanding the company's perspective and how the patient can better respond to the situation. Specific organization-based changes that can prevent job stress include the following (cf. Sauter et al., 1990):

1. Establishing fair employment policies, a suitable work environment, and sharing the rewards of the organization

2. Designing jobs to provide meaning, stimulation, and opportunities for skill utilization and career development
3. Clearly defining worker roles, responsibilities, and goals and ensuring that workload meets worker capabilities and resources
4. Giving workers opportunities to participate in decision making and actions affecting their jobs
5. Improving communications: reduce uncertainty about career development and future employment prospects
6. Providing opportunities for social interaction, support, and cohesive team building
7. Establishing work schedules compatible with nonwork demands and responsibilities

Case Plan. *The clinician encouraged Mrs. P. to discuss with the school board her issue of feeling inadequate and lacking assistance in getting the job done. The clinician discussed with and urged Mrs. P. to pursue the possibility of communicating her perspective to the board that some things might not get done within the current organizational structure, and that she needed help with prioritizing. Mrs. P. and the clinician also considered that she take time away from the job given her over 75-hour work week at the school. Mrs. P. worked with the clinician to learn time management as well as assertiveness skills to assist her in her confronting the board and delegating responsibilities to staff. Tapping her interest in art, the clinician recommended that Mrs. P. take time each week for art-related leisure activities.*

Prevention

Primary prevention strategies offer a vehicle for culture change and involve altering organizational climate and practices to prevent stress onset. Secondary prevention concerns prompt detection and management of stress by increasing awareness and improving the stress management skills of the individual through training and educational activities. The role of secondary prevention essentially involves damage limitation, often addressing the consequences rather than the sources of stress, which may be inherent in the organizational structure or culture, requiring the individual to develop and strengthen personal resistance to stress.

Tertiary prevention concerns the treatment-rehabilitation-recovery process of individuals who suffer from serious ill health as a result of strain. Interventions at the tertiary level typically involve counseling services for employee problems in the work or other domain and typically are provided by in-house counselors or outside agencies in the form of employee assistance programs. An organizational problem or crisis, such as escalating rates of employee sickness, absence, or turnover typically prompt action to reduce work stress. Organizations benefit from implementing stress prevention not only in terms of cost reduction or containment, but also as a means of maintaining and improving organizational health and increasing worker productivity (Cooper & Cartwright, 1997).

Employee assistance programs

Employee assistance plans (EAPs) provide valuable counseling services delivered by in-house or external clinicians for employees with personal or work-related problems. Evidence supports the efficacy of counseling as a means of improving employee well-being and the cost benefits of the organization (Cooper & Cartwright, 1997). The clinician can recommend access to EAP services when available at the patient's workplace, remaining open to consulting with the counselor, if desired by the patient, to collaboratively assist the patient in problem resolution.

Follow-up. *Six months later (following three visits), Mrs. P. reported significant progress. Her abdominal symptoms had subsided, and she communicated her issues to the school board. Because the board so valued her as an employee, they encouraged her to pursue additional training, which the school would help finance, and she would commence with the upcoming summer break. Although budget constraints precluded hiring additional help for Mrs. P. at present, the board worked with her to establish priorities and set reasonable expectations. In addition, Mrs. P. convinced her son and husband to participate in family therapy, which eased these strained relationships and contributed to her feeling less stressed and more satisfied in her work and family life.*

SUMMARY

Work comprises a primary context of human development and a fundamental element of identity. It also represents a prime source of stress that, when experienced as strain, may lead to a variety of health problems across behavioral psychological and physical domains. The centrality of work in people's lives demands that the primary care clinician routinely inquire about the stress patients experience at work, how they cope with it, and to what extent they are able to negotiate and integrate work and multiple role demands. Often, work stress underlies depression, anxiety, and other emotional problems that patients present in the consulting room. Equipped with an understanding of work stress and work-related syndromes such as TABP, workaholism, and job burnout, clinicians practicing in primary care medical settings can act to identify, treat, and prevent problems arising from work stress and promote worker health.

References

Ancha, L., & Tucker, P. (2001). A comprehensive approach to stress in primary care. *Journal of the Oklahoma State Medical Association, 94,* 451–454.

Boone, J. L., & Christensen, J. F. (1997). Stress and disease. In M. D. Feldman & J. F. Christensen (Eds.), *Behavioral medicine in primary care: A practical guide* (pp. 265–276). Stamford, CT: Appleton and Lange.

Burke, R. J., & Richardson, A. M. (1996). Stress, burnout, and health. In C. L. Cooper (Ed.), *Handbook of stress, medicine, and health* (pp. 101–117). New York: CRC Press.

Byrne, D. G. (2000). The frustration of success: Type A behavior, occupational stress, and cardiovascular disease. In D. T. Kenny, J. G. Carlson, F. J. McGuigan, & J. L. Sheppard (Eds.), *Stress and health: Research and clinical applications* (pp. 411–436). Amsterdam: Harwood.

Conrad, P. (1988). Health and fitness at work: A participant's perspective. *Social Science and Medicine, 26,* 545–550.

Cooper, C. L. (1983). Identifying stressors at work: Recent research developments. *Journal of Psychosomatic Research, 27,* 369–376.

Cooper, C. L., & Cartwright, C. (1997). An intervention strategy for workplace stress. *Journal of Psychosomatic Research, 43*, 7–16.

Erikson, E. H. (1950). *Childhood and society.* New York: Norton.

Erikson, E. H. (1968). *Identity: Youth and crisis.* New York: Norton.

Friedman, M. (1969). *Pathogenesis of coronary artery disease.* New York: McGraw-Hill.

Frumkin, H. (2000). Occupational and environmental medicine and primary care. *Occupational and Environmental Medicine, 27*, 813–829.

Hathaway, S., & McKinley, J. C. (1952). *Minnesota Multiphasic Personality Inventory.* Minneapolis: University of Minnesota Press.

Hepburn, C. G., Loughlin, C. A., & Barling, J. (1997). Coping with chronic work stress. In B. H. Gottlieb (Ed.), *Coping with chronic stress* (pp. 343–366). New York: Plenum Press.

Holmes, T. H., & Rahe, R. H. (1967). The Social Readjustment Rating Scale: A cross-cultural study of Western Europeans and Americans. *Journal of Psychosomatic Research, 14*, 391–400.

Hurrell, J. J., Jr., & Murphy, L. R. (1998). *Psychological job stress.* Philadelphia: Lippincott-Raven.

Kahn, R. L., Wolfe, D. M., Quinn, R. P., Snoek, J. D., & Rosenthal, R. A. (1964). *Role stress: Studies in role conflict and ambiguity.* New York: Wiley.

King, P. M. (1995). The psychosocial work environment: Implications for workplace safety and health. *Professional Safety, 40*, 36–39.

Maslach, C., & Jackson, S. E. (1986). *Maslach burnout inventory manual* (2nd ed.). Palo Alto, CA: Consulting Psychologists Press.

McMillan, L. H. W., O'Driscoll, M. P., Marsh, N. V., & Brady, E. C. (2001). Understanding workaholism: Data synthesis, theoretical critique, and future design strategies. *International Journal of Stress Management, 8*, 69–91.

National Institute for Occupational Safety and Health. (1999). *Stress at work* (U.S. Department of Health and Human Services Publication No. 99–101). Cincinnati, OH: National Institute for Occupational Safety and Health.

Onciul, J. V. (1997). ABC of work related disorder. Stress at work. *British Medical Journal (Clinical Research Edition), 313*, 745–748.

Osipow, S. H. (1998). *Occupational stress inventory–revised edition.* Odessa, FL: Psychological Assessment Resources.

Osipow, S. H., & Spokane, A. R. (1987). *Manual for the occupational stress inventory: Research version.* Odessa, FL: Psychological Assessment Resources.

Pulchalski, C. M., & Romer, A. L. (2000). Taking a spiritual history allows clinicians to understand patients more fully. *Journal of Palliative Medicine, 3*, 129–137.

Robinson, B. E. (1998). *Chained to the desk: A guidebook for workaholics, their partners and children and the clinicians who treat them.* New York: New York University Press.

Sauter, S. L., Murphy, L. R., & Hurrell, J. J., Jr. (1990). Prevention of work-related psychological disorders: A national strategy proposed by the National Institute for Occupational Safety and Health (NIOSH). *American Psychologist, 45*, 1146–1158.

Savickas, M. L. (2001). Work and health. In D. Wedding (Ed.), *Behavior and medicine* (3rd ed., pp. 209–218). Seattle, WA: Hogrefe and Huber.

Selye, H. (1956). *The stress of life.* New York: McGraw-Hill.

Selye, H. (1971). The evolution of the stress concept: Stress and cardiovascular disease. In L. Levi (Ed.), *Society, stress, and disease* (Vol. 1, pp. 299–311). London: Oxford University Press.

Speilberger, C. D., Gorsuch, R. L., & Lushene, R. E. (1970). *Manual for the State-Trait Anxiety Inventory.* Palo Alto, CA: Consulting Psychologists Press.

Speilberger, C. D., & Reheiser, E. C. (1995). Measuring occupational stress: The job stress survey. In R. Crandall & P. L. Perrewe (Eds.), *Occupational stress: A handbook* (pp. 51–69). Philadelphia: Taylor and Francis.

Speilberger, C. D., & Vagg, P. R. (1999). *Job stress survey.* Odessa, FL: Psychological Assessment Resources.

Spokane, A. R., & Ferrara, D. (2001). Samuel H. Osipow's contributions to occupational mental health and the assessment of stress: The Occupational Stress Inventory. In F. T. L. Leong & A. Barak (Eds.), *Contemporary models in vocational psychology: A volume in honor of Samuel H. Osipow* (pp. 79–96). Mahwah, NJ: Erlbaum.

Appendix A

Psychotropic Medications in Primary Care

Denise Small

HOW TO USE THIS APPENDIX

This appendix provides information on dosing, "clinical pearls," side effects, and certain precautions for most FDA-approved psychotropic medications likely to be encountered in the primary care setting (Tables A.1–A.13). Psychiatric medications not commonly encountered in primary care settings are excluded; thus, the appendix does not cover the following: "typical" antipsychotics (Haldol, Thorazine, etc.); addiction medications (ReVia, methadone); and antiepileptic medications not used for psychiatric purposes (Dilantin, phenobarbital). The dosing guideline tables are separated according to therapeutic uses and listed alphabetically as follows: attention-deficit/hyperactivity disorder (ADHD) medications, antidepressants, antipsychotics, anxiolytics, hypnotics-sedatives, and mood stabilizers (the exception to this is Table A.11, which combines side effects and precaution information for the anxiolytics and hypnotics). Within each table, the medications are listed alphabetically by generic name, with the trade name in parentheses. Because medications have both a brand and generic name, Table A.1 provides an alphabetical listing of both trade and generic names with their corresponding trade or generic name. The table also lists the primary therapeutic use for the medication to make identifying the drug information easier.

The dosing guideline tables provide information regarding the following:

- Commonly prescribed indications: The indications listed are both labeled (FDA approved) and off-labeled (commonly used for this purpose in clinical practice despite lack of specific FDA approval for the specific disorder) uses for the medications.
- Average daily dose for the specific indication: The dosages listed are for adults with the exception of those listed for ADHD medications. For the ADHD medications, reference to adult dosing may be found in the clinical pearls table for selected medications.
- Clinical pearls: The clinical pearls provide information not readily available from tertiary references. The clinical pearls section provides an alphabetical list by medication

class unless there is no medication class for the particular agent; in this case, the generic name is listed.

- Duration of action is listed for the stimulants.
- Onset of effect is given for the hypnotic-sedative agents

The following tables are included in this appendix:

References

Biederman, J. (2002). Practical considerations in stimulant drug selection for the attention-deficit/hyperactivity disorder patient—efficacy, potency and titration. *Today's Therapeutic Trends, 20,* 311–328.

Brown, C. S. (2001). Depression and anxiety disorders. *Obstetrics and Gynecology Clinics of North America, 28,* 241–268.

Cada, D. J., Covington, T. R., & Generali, J. A. (Eds.). *Drug facts and comparisons.* St. Louis, MO: Wolters Kluwer.

Carli, V., Sarchiapone, M., & DeRisio, S. (2002).

Mirtazapine in the treatment of panic disorder. *Archives of General Psychiatry, 59,* 661–662.

Carta, M. G., Hardoy, M. C., Grunze, H., & Carpiniello, B. (2002). The use of tiagabine in affective disorders. *Pharmacopsychiatry, 35,* 33–34.

Citrome, L., & Volavka, J. (2002). Optimal dosing of atypical antipsychotics in adults: A review of the current evidence. *Harvard Review of Psychiatry, 10,* 280–291.

DeBattista, C., & Schatzberg, A. F. (2001). Universal psychotropic dosing and monitoring guidelines. *Pharmacy Practice, 3,* 60–70.

Edwards, I. R. (2003). Withdrawing drugs: Nefazodone, the start of the latest saga. *Lancet, 361,* 1240.

Gelenberg, A. J., & Chesen, C. L. (2000). How fast are the antidepressants. *Journal of Clinical Psychiatry, 61,* 712–721.

Gill, M. A., Wincor, M. Z., & Park, E. H. (1999). The pharmacist's role in sleep disorders. *Pharmacy Times, 65,* 103–115.

Grimsley, S. R. (1995). Anxiety disorders. In L. Y. Young & M. N. Koda-Kimble (Eds.), *Applied therapeutics: Clinical use of drugs* (6th ed., pp. 73-1–73-31). Vancouver, WA: Applied Therapeutics.

Grunze, H., Erfurth, A., & Marcuse, A., Amann, B., Normann, C., & Walden, J. (1999). Tiagabine appears not to be efficacious in the treatment of acute mania. *Journal of Clinical Psychiatry, 60,* 759–762.

Hulisz, D., & Strayer, B. E. (2001). Power over panic disorder. *Pharmacy Times, 67,* 67–74.

Hurley, S. C. (2002). Lamotrigine update and its use in mood disorders. *Annals of Pharmacotherapy, 36,* 860–873.

Kupfer, D. J., & Reynolds, C. F. (1997). Management of insomnia. *New England Journal of Medicine, 336,* 341–346.

Lacy, C. F., Armstrong, L. L., Goldman, M. P., & Lance, L. L. (Eds.). (2002–2003). *Drug information handbook* (10th ed.). Hudson, OH: Lexi-Comp.

Meijer, W. E., Heerdink, E. R., van Eijk, J. T., & Leufkens, H. G. (2002). Adverse events in users of sertraline: Results from an observational study in psychiatric practice in The Netherlands. *Pharmacoepidemiology Drug Safety, 11,* 655–662.

Montejo-Gonzalez, A. L., Llorca, G., & Izquierdo, J. A. (1997). SSRI-induced sexual dysfunction: Fluoxetine, paroxetine, sertraline, and fluvoxamine in a prospective, multicenter, and descriptive clinical study of 344 patients. *Journal of Sex and Marital Therapy, 23,* 176–194.

Novak, V., Kanard, R., Kissel, J. T., & Mendell, J. R. (2001). Treatment of painful sensory neuropathy with tiagabine: A pilot study. *Clinical Autonomic Research, 11,* 357–361.

Parker, G., & Malhi, G. (2001). Are atypical antipsychotic drugs also atypical antidepressants. *Australian New Zealand Journal of Psychiatry, 35,* 631–638.

Pliszka, S. R., Greenhill, L. L., Crimson, M. L., Sedillo, A., Carlson, C., Conners, K., et al. (2000). The Texas Children's Medication Algorithm Project: Report of the Texas Consensus Conference Panel on Medication Treatment of Childhood Attention Deficit/Hyperactivity Disorder. Part II: Tactics. *Journal of American Academy of Child and Adolescent Psychiatry, 39,* 920–927.

Puzantian, T., & Stimmel, G. L. (2002, October). Review of psychotropic drugs. *Pharmacy Practice News,* (Suppl.), 21–26.

Schaffer, L. C., Schaffer, C. B., & Howe, J. (2002). An open case series on the utility of tiagabine as an augmentation in refractory bipolar outpatients. *Journal of Affective Disorders, 71,* 259–263.

Schweitzer, J. B., Cummins, T. K., & Kant, C. A. (2001). Attention-deficit/hyperactivity disorder. *Medical Clinics of North America, 85,* 757–777.

Sheehan, D. V., & Harnett-Sheehan, K. (1996). The role of SSRIs in panic disorder. *Journal of Clinical Psychiatry, 57*(Suppl. 10), 51–58.

Smith, D., Dempster, C., Glanville, J., Freemantle, N., & Anderson, I. (2002). Efficacy and tolerability of venlafaxine compared with selective serotonin reuptake inhibitors and other antidepressants: A meta-analysis. *British Journal of Psychiatry, 180,* 394–404.

Strattera [package insert]. (2002). Indianapolis, IN: Eli Lilly.

Suppes, T., Chisholm, K. A., Dhavale, D., Frye, M. A., Altshuler, L. L., McElroy, S. L., et al. (2002). Tiagabine in treatment refractory bipolar disorder: A clinical case series. *Bipolar Disorders, 4,* 283–289.

Taketomo, C. K., Hodding, J. H., & Kraus, D. M. (Eds.). (2002–2003). *Pediatric dosage handbook* (9th ed.). Hudson, OH: Lexi-Comp.

Tandon, R. (2002). Safety and tolerability: How do the newer generation atypical antipsychotics compare? *Psychiatric Quarterly, 73,* 297–311.

Weinstein, R. S. (1995). Panic disorder. *American Family Physician, 52,* 2055–2063.

Wilens, T. E., Spencer, T. J., Biederman, J., Girard, K., Doyle, R., Prince, J., et al. (2001). A controlled clinical trial of bupropion for attention deficit hyperactivity disorder in adults. *American Journal of Psychiatry, 158,* 282–288.

Williams, R., & Phil, M. (2001). Optimal dosing with risperidone: Updated recommendations. *Journal of Clinical Psychiatry, 62,* 282–289.

Worrel, J. A., Marken, P. A., Beckman, S. E., & Ruthter, V. L. (2000). Atypical antipsychotics agents: A critical review. *American Journal of Health Systems Pharmacy, 57,* 238–258.

Table A.1 Alphabetical Listing of Drug Names and Their Corresponding Names and Therapeutic Use

Drug Name	Corresponding Name	Therapeutic Class/Use[a]
Abilify	aripiprazole	Dopamine system stabilizer: partial agonist (listed in Table A.7)
Adderall	amphetamine/ dextroamphetamine	ADHD
alprazolam	Xanax	Anxiolytic
Ambien	zolpidem	Hypnotic
amitriptyline	Elavil	Antidepressant
amoxapine	Asendin	Antidepressant
amphetamine/ dextroamphetamine	Adderall	ADHD
Anafranil	clomipramine	Antidepressant
aripiprazole	Abilify	Dopamine system stabilizer: partial agonist (listed in Tables A.7 and A.8)
Asendin	amoxapine	Antidepressant
Atarax	hydroxyzine	Anxiolytic and hypnotic
Ativan	lorazepam	Anxiolytic and hypnotic
atomoxetine	Strattera	ADHD
Aventyl	nortriptyline	Antidepressant and ADHD
Benadryl	diphenhydramine	Hypnotic
bupropion	Wellbutrin, Zyban	Antidepressant and ADHD
Buspar	buspirone	Anxiolytic
buspirone	Buspar	Anxiolytic
carbamazepine	Carbatrol, Tegretol	Mood stabilizer
Carbatrol	carbamazepine	Mood stabilizer
Catapres	clonidine	ADHD
Celexa	citalopram	Antidepressant
chloral hydrate	Somnote	Hypnotic
chlordiazepoxide	Librium	Anxiolytic
citalopram	Celexa	Antidepressant
clomipramine	Anafranil	Antidepressant
clonazepam	Klonopin	Anxiolytic and hypnotic
clonidine	Catapres	ADHD
clorazepate	Tranxene	Anxiolytic and hypnotic
clozapine	Clozaril	Atypical antipsychotic
Clozaril	clozapine	Atypical antipsychotic
Concerta	methylphenidate	ADHD
Cylert	pemoline	ADHD
Dalmane	flurazepam	Hypnotic
Desyrel	trazodone	Antidepressant and hypnotic
Dexedrine	dextroamphetamine	ADHD
dexmethylphenidate	Focalin	ADHD
dextroamphetamine	Dexedrine	ADHD
diazepam	Valium	Anxiolytic
diphenhydramine	Benadryl	Hypnotic
doxepin	Sinequan	Antidepressant
Effexor	venlafaxine	Antidepressant and ADHD

Table A.1 Continued

Drug Name	Corresponding Name	Therapeutic Class/Use[a]
Elavil	amitriptyline	Antidepressant
escitalopram	Lexapro	Antidepressant
Eskalith	lithium	Mood stabilizer
estazolam	ProSom	Hypnotic
fluoxetine	Prozac, Sarafem	Antidepressant
flurazepam	Dalmane	Hypnotic
fluvoxamine	Luvox	Antidepressant
Focalin	dexmethylphenidate	ADHD
gabapentin	Neurontin	Mood stabilizer
Gabitril	tiagabine	Mood stabilizer
Geodon	ziprasidone	Atypical antipsychotic
guanfacine	Tenex	ADHD
Halcion	triazolam	Hypnotic
hydroxyzine	Atarax, Vistaril	Anxiolytic and hypnotic
imipramine	Tofranil	Antidepressant, ADHD
isocarboxazide	Marplan	Antidepressant
Keppra	levetiracetam	Mood stabilizer
Klonopin	clonazepam	Anxiolytic and hypnotic
Lamictal	lamotrigine	Mood stabilizer
lamotrigine	Lamictal	Mood stabilizer
Lexapro	escitalopram	Antidepressant
Librium	chlordiazepoxide	Anxiolytic
lithium	Lithobid, Eskalith	Mood stabilizer
Lithobid	lithium	Mood stabilizer
lorazepam	Ativan	Anxiolytic and hypnotic
Ludiomil	maprotiline	Antidepressant
Luvox	fluvoxamine	Antidepressant
maprotiline	Ludiomil	Antidepressant
Marplan	isocarboxazide	Antidepressant
Metadate	methylphenidate	ADHD
Methylin	methylphenidate	ADHD
methylphenidate	Methylin, Metadate, Ritalin, Concerta	ADHD
mirtazapine	Remeron	Antidepressant
Nardil	phenelzine	Antidepressant
nefazodone	Serzone	Antidepressant
Neurontin	gabapentin	Mood stabilizer
nortriptyline	Pamelor, Aventyl	Antidepressant and ADHD
olanzapine	Zyprexa	Atypical antipsychotic
oxazepam	Serax	Anxiolytic and hypnotic
oxcarbazepine	Trileptal	Mood stabilizer
Pamelor	nortriptyline	Antidepressant and ADHD
Parnate	tranylcypromine	Antidepressant
paroxetine	Paxil	Antidepressant
Paxil	paroxetine	Antidepressant
PemAdd	pemoline	ADHD

(continued)

Table A.1 Continued

Drug Name	Corresponding Name	Therapeutic Class/Use[a]
pemoline	PemAdd, Cylert	ADHD
phenelzine	Nardil	Antidepressant
ProSom	estazolam	Hypnotic
protriptyline	Vivactil	Antidepressant
Prozac	fluoxetine	Antidepressant
quetiapine	Seroquel	Atypical antipsychotic
Remeron	mirtazapine	Antidepressant
Restoril	temazepam	Hypnotic
Risperidal	risperidone	Atypical antipsychotic
risperidone	Risperidal	Atypical antipsychotic
Ritalin	methylphenidate	ADHD
Sarafem	fluoxetine	Antidepressant
Serax	oxazepam	Anxiolytic and hypnotic
Seroquel	quetiapine	Atypical antipsychotic
sertraline	Zoloft	Antidepressant
Serzone	nefazodone	Antidepressant
Sinequan	doxepin	Antidepressant
Somnote	chloral hydrate	Hypnotic
Sonata	zaleplon	Hypnotic
Strattera	atomoxetine	ADHD
Surmontil	trimipramine	Antidepressant
Tegretol	carbamazepine	Mood stabilizer
temazepam	Restoril	Hypnotic
Tenex	guanfacine	ADHD
Tofranil	imipramine	Antidepressant and ADHD
Topamax	topiramate	Mood stabilizer
topiramate	Topamax	Mood stabilizer
Tranxene	clorazepate	Anxiolytic and hypnotic
tranylcypromine	Parnate	Antidepressant
trazodone	Desyrel	Antidepressant and hypnotic
triazolam	Halcion	Hypnotic
Trileptal	oxcarbazepine	Mood stabilizer
trimipramine	Surmontil	Antidepressant
Valium	diazepam	Anxiolytic
venlafaxine	Effexor	Antidepressant and ADHD
Vistaril	hydroxyzine	Anxiolytic and hypnotic
Vivactil	protriptyline	Antidepressant
Wellbutrin	bupropion	Antidepressant and ADHD
Xanax	alprazolam	Anxiolytic
zaleplon	Sonata	Hypnotic
ziprasidone	Geodon	Atypical antipsychotic
Zoloft	sertraline	Antidepressant
zolpidem	Ambien	Hypnotic
Zonegran	zonisamide	Mood stabilizer
Zyban	bupropion	Antidepressant and ADHD
Zyprexa	olanzapine	Atypical antipsychotic

Note. Trade names are capitalized; generic names are lower cased. ADHD, attention-deficit/hyperactivity disorder.
[a]Refers to use described in this appendix; the medications may have other uses or class names described elsewhere.

Table A.2 ADHD Medications: Dosing Guidelines in Children and Adolescents and Clinical Pearls

Medication[a]	Average Daily Dose Range (mg/day)	Duration of Action (hours)	Clinical Pearls
Amphetamine/dextroamphetamine (Adderall and Adderall XR)	Immediate release, up to 40; XR, up to 30	Immediate release, 4–6; XR, 10–12	Also used to treat ADHD in adults; may cause or worsen tics; some clinicians feel that stimulants are underdosed in adolescents and adults
Atomoxetine (Strattera)	Children/adolescents ≤70 kg: 1.2 mg/kg/day; children/adolescents >70 kg: 80–100		Dosing in adults is same as in children/adolescents >70 kg
Bupropion (Wellbutrin and Wellbutrin SR)	3–6 mg/kg/day, not to exceed 300		Dosing in adults is the same as for depression in adults
Clonidine (Catapres)	Children <45 kg: up to 0.2; children >45 kg: up to 0.4		Not as effective for ADHD compared to stimulants, but can help treat tics; commonly used as an adjunct to stimulants
Dexmethylphenidate (Focalin)	Up to 20		
Dextroamphetamine (Dexedrine and Dexedrine Spansules)	Up to 40	Immediate release, 4–6; spansules 6–8	May cause or worsen tics; some clinicians feel that stimulants are underdosed in adolescents and adults
Guanfacine (Tenex)	Children <45 kg: up to 2; children >45 kg: up to 4		Less sedating compared to clonidine
Imipramine (Tofranil)	2–4 mg/kg/day		Also useful for enuresis
Methylphenidate (Ritalin, Methylin, Metadate ER, Methylin ER, Concerta, Ritalin SR, Metadate CD, and Ritalin LA)	Children ≥6 years old: immediate release tablets, 10–60; Concerta, 18–54; Metadate CD, 20–60; Ritalin LA, 20–60	Immediate release, 3–6; Concerta, 12; Metadate CD, 6–8; Ritalin LA, 6–8; SR and ER, 5–8	ER and SR may be given in place of regular tablets once daily dose is titrated using regular-release tablets, and the titrated dose corresponds to sustained-release tablet size; some clinicians feel that stimulants are underdosed in adolescents and adults; dosing in adults is the same as in children; may cause or worsen tics
Nortriptyline (Pamelor, Aventyl)	2 mg/kg/day		
Pemoline (Cylert and PemADD)	56.25–75		Need to monitor liver function tests at baseline and every 2 weeks thereafter; may cause or worsen tics
Venlafaxine (Effexor)	Children <40 kg: up to 50; children ≥40 kg: up to 75		Studies used immediate-release tablets

[a]Trade names are in parentheses.

Table A.3 ADHD Medications: Side Effects and Certain Precautions[a]

Medication	Common Side Effects and Certain Precautions
Amphetamine	Elevation in blood pressure, overstimulation, "zombie state," restlessness, insomnia, tremor, unmasking or exacerbation of tics, anorexia, suppression of growth in children with long-term use; if dose is high, may taper to discontinue rather than abruptly stopping
Atomoxetine	Insomnia, dry mouth, decreased appetite, upset stomach, nausea or vomiting, dizziness, problems urinating, and decreased libido; may be discontinued without tapering
Bupropion	See Table A.5
Clonidine/guanfacine	Dizziness, drowsiness, dry mouth, sedation, depression, constipation; withdrawal hypertension on abrupt discontinuation, taper to discontinue
Dextroamphetamine	Elevation in blood pressure, overstimulation, "zombie state," restlessness, insomnia, tremor, exacerbation of tics, anorexia, suppression of growth in children with long-term use; if dose is high, may taper to discontinue rather than abruptly stopping
Methylphenidate	Headache, anorexia, nervousness, insomnia, tachycardia, unmasking or exacerbation of tics, suppression of growth in children with long-term use; if dose is high, may taper to discontinue rather than abruptly stopping
Pemoline	Insomnia, unmasking or exacerbation of tics, anorexia, irritability, headache, rash; hepatic dysfunction (must monitor at baseline and every 2 weeks thereafter)

[a]Does not include all side effects of each medication; check manufacturer's package insert for complete list.

Table A.4 Antidepressants: Dosing Guidelines in Adults and Clinical Pearls

Medication[a]	Class	Indication	Adult Dosage Ranges (mg/day)	Clinical Pearls
Amitriptyline (Elavil)	Tricyclic anti-depressant	Depression Pain	50–150 25–100	
Amoxapine (Asendin)	Tricyclic anti-depressant	Depression	200–300	
Bupropion (Wellbutrin, Wellbutrin SR) (Zyban)		Depression ADHD Smoking cessation	300 300 300	Bupropion: Bupropion extended-release tablets may be split; tablets should be used soon after splitting because of rapid degradation on exposure to moisture; the tablets cannot be crushed or chewed. Bupropion has been added to an SSRI to reverse SSRI-induced sexual dysfunction or to boost inade-quate efficacy.
Citalopram (Celexa)	Selective serotonin reuptake inhibitor	Depression Panic disorder	20–40 20–60 (doses vary per study)	
Clomipramine (Anafranil)	Tricyclic anti-depressant	OCD Panic disorder	100–250 50–200	
Desipramine (Norpramin)	Tricyclic anti-depressant	Depression Panic disorder	100–200 100–300	
Doxepin (Sinequan)	Tricyclic anti-depressant	Depression or depres-sion/anxiety	30–150	
Escitalopram (Lexapro)	Selective serotonin reuptake inhibitor	Depression	10–20	
Fluoxetine (Prozac, Prozac Weekly)	Selective serotonin reuptake inhibitor	Anxiety Bulimia Depression	10–40 60 20–80 (90 mg weekly cap may be initiated 7 days after last 20 mg daily dose)	

(*continued*)

Table A.4 Continued

Medication[a]	Class	Indication	Adult Dosage Ranges (mg/day)	Clinical Pearls
		OCD	20–60	
		PTSD	10–80	
		Panic disorder	20–40	
		Social phobia	10–60	
(Sarafem)		Premenstrual dysphoric disorder	20 given continuously or intermittently	
Fluvoxamine (Luvox)	Selective serotonin reuptake inhibitor	Anxiety	50–200	
		OCD	100–300	
		Depression	100–300	
		Panic disorder	75–150	
Imipramine (Tofranil)	Tricyclic antidepressant	Depression	50–150	
		Panic disorder	100–300	
Isocarboxazid (Marplan)	Monoamine oxidase inhibitor	Depression	40	
Maprotiline (Ludiomil)	Tetracyclic antidepressant	Depression/anxiety	75–150	
Mirtazapine (Remeron)	Tetracyclic antidepressant	Depression	15–45	Mirtazapine: Increased appetite and weight gain are inversely related to dose.
		GAD	15–45	
Nefazodone (Serzone)		Depression	300–600	
		PTSD	100–600	
		GAD	200–600	
		Panic disorder	200–600	
Nortriptyline (Pamelor, Aventyl)	Tricyclic antidepressant	Depression	75–150	

Drug (trade name)	Class	Indication	Dose (mg/day)[a]	Paxil CR:
Paroxetine (Paxil and Paxil CR)	Selective serotonin reuptake inhibitor	Depression	Paxil: 20–50	25–62.5
		Anxiety	20–50	
		OCD	Target 40 (20–60)	
		Panic disorder	Target 40 (10–60)	12.5–75
		PTSD	20–50	
		Social anxiety	20–60	
Phenelzine (Nardil)	Monoamine oxidase inhibitor	Depression	60–90 and reduce dose for maintenance	
Protriptyline (Vivactil)	Tricyclic anti-depressant	Depression	15–40	
Sertraline (Zoloft)	Selective serotonin reuptake inhibitor	Anxiety	25–150	
		Depression	50–200	
		OCD	50–200	
		Panic	50–200	
		PTSD	50–200	
Tranylcypromine (Parnate)	Monoamine oxidase inhibitor	Depression	30	
Trazodone (Desyrel)		Depression	150–400	
		GAD	150–400	
		Insomnia	See Table A.10	
Trimipramine (Surmontil)	Tricyclic anti-depressant	Depression	50–150	
Venlafaxine (Effexor, Effexor XR)		Depression	Immediate release and XR: 75–225	
		GAD	75–225	
		OCD	150–375	

Note. ADHD, attention-deficit/hyperactivity disorder; GAD, generalized anxiety disorder; OCD, obsessive-compulsive disorder; PTSD, posttraumatic stress disorder; SSRI, selective serotonin reuptake inhibitor.

[a]Trade names are in parentheses.

Table A.5 Antidepressants: Comparative Side Effects[a,b]

Medication	Anticholinergic Effects[c]	Sedation	Orthostatic Hypotension	Sexual Dysfunction	Type of Antidepressant
Amitriptyline	++++	++++	++++	+++	Tricyclic
Amoxapine	++	++	+	+++	Tricyclic
Bupropion	0	0	0	0	Other
Citalopram	0	0–+	0	++++	Selective serotonin reuptake inhibitor
Clomipramine	++++	++++	++	++++	Tricyclic
Desipramine	+	++	++	+++	Tricyclic
Doxepin	+++	++++	++	+++	Tricyclic
Escitalopram	0	0–+	0	++++	Selective serotonin reuptake inhibitor
Fluoxetine	0	0	0	++++	Selective serotonin reuptake inhibitor
Fluvoxamine	0	Varies based on reference	0	++++	Selective serotonin reuptake inhibitor
Imipramine	+++	+++	++++	+++	Tricyclic
Maprotiline	++	++	++	++	Tetracyclic
Mirtazapine	+	+++ (inversely related to dose)	+	0	Tetracyclic
Nefazodone	0	++	+	0	Other
Nortriptyline	++	++	+	++++	Tricyclic
Paroxetine	+	+	0	++++	Selective serotonin reuptake inhibitor
Protriptyline	+++	+	++	+++	Tricyclic
Sertraline	0	0/+	0	++++	Selective serotonin reuptake inhibitor
Trazodone	+	++++	+++	0	Other
Trimipramine	+++	+++	+++	+++	Tricyclic
Venlafaxine	0	+	0/+	+++	Serotonin-norepinephrine reuptake inhibitor

[a]0 = none; + = mild; ++ = moderate; +++ = high; ++++ = very high.
[b]Does not include all side effects of each medication; check manufacturer's package insert for complete list.
[c]Anticholinergic effects: dry mouth, blurred vision, urinary retention, constipation.

Table A.6 Antidepressants: Additional Side Effects and Certain Precautions[a,b]

Medication	Additional Side Effects and Certain Precautions
Bupropion	Agitation, insomnia, confusion, headache, dizziness, tremor, tachycardia, dry mouth, blurred vision, constipation, nausea and vomiting; lowers seizure threshold—use extreme caution in patients with a history of seizure, cranial trauma, and in patients using concomitant medication that lowers seizure threshold; contraindicated for patients with current or prior diagnosis of bulimia or anorexia because of greater incidence of seizures; may cycle BPAD patients into mania/hypomania (some data show it is less likely than the SSRIs to cycle patients into mania)
Maprotiline	Photosensitization, restlessness, diarrhea, nausea; contraindicated for patients with known or suspected seizure disorder or during acute phase of a myocardial infarction; withdrawal with abrupt discontinuation, taper to discontinue; use with caution in patients with cardiovascular problems
Mirtazapine	Increased appetite and weight gain (inversely related to dose), tremor, edema; may cycle patients into mania/hypomania; withdrawal with abrupt discontinuation possible, taper to discontinue
Monoamine oxidase inhibitors (MAOIs)	Orthostatic hypotension, tachycardia, dizziness, headache, tremors, memory impairment, constipation, nausea, diarrhea, increased anxiety, agitation, dry mouth, edema, sexual dysfunction, anorexia, hypersomnia and insomnia, weight gain; withdrawal with abrupt discontinuation, taper to discontinue
Nefazodone	Nausea, confusion, dry mouth, insomnia (somnolence is more common; see Table A.5), agitation, edema, constipation; concerns with liver toxicity; removed from the market in Sweden by company (see clinical pearls for more information); may cycle patients into mania/hypomania; withdrawal with abrupt discontinuation possible, taper to discontinue
Selective serotonin reuptake inhibitors (SSRIs)	Nausea, diarrhea, insomnia and somnolence, dry mouth, hyponatremia, headache, nervousness, dyspepsia
	SSRIs normally cause weight loss; however, there are reports of weight gain, and paroxetine has the greatest incidence of weight gain compared to other SSRIs
	May cycle patients into mania/hypomania; drug interactions caused by effects on liver metabolism; withdrawal with abrupt discontinuation is greatest with paroxetine and lowest with fluoxetine, taper to discontinue
Trazodone	Priapism, nervousness, headache, edema, weight gain/loss; contraindicated in acute recovery phase following a myocardial infarction; withdrawal with abrupt discontinuation, taper to discontinue; may cycle patients into mania/hypomania
Tricyclic antidepressants	Photosensitivity reaction, cardiac arrhythmias, weight gain, tremor; lower seizure threshold, caution in patients with preexisting seizure disorder; may cycle patients into mania/hypomania; contraindicated in acute recovery phase following a myocardial infarction; withdrawal with abrupt discontinuation, taper to discontinue
Venlafaxine	Headache, nervousness, constipation and diarrhea, nausea, dry mouth, dizziness, sweating; induces or worsens hypertension (dose related) so use caution in patients with hypertension; may cycle patients into mania/hypomania; withdrawal with abrupt discontinuation, taper to discontinue

Note. BPAD, bipolar affective disorder.
[a]See Table A.5 for comparative side effects of anticholinergic, sedation, orthostatic hypotension, and sexual dysfunction.
[b]Does not include all side effects of each medication; check manufacturer's package insert for complete list.

Table A.7 Atypical Antipsychotics: Dosing Guidelines in Adults and Clinical Pearls

Medication[a]	Indication	Average Daily Dose Range (mg/day)	Clinical Pearls
Clozapine (Clozaril)	Schizophrenia	300–450 Dosing in mood disorders is not established	Reserved for refractory patients because of problematic side effects and strict monitoring parameters
Olanzapine (Zyprexa)	Bipolar mania	10–15 (but range used is 5–20)	Doses up to 50 mg have been used in schizophrenia studies; the higher doses did continue to demonstrate efficacy and were well tolerated
	Schizophrenia	10–30 (maximum dose stated by company is 20) Dosing in mood disorders is not established	Total body clearance is greater in smokers compared to nonsmokers An intramuscular form is currently under study
Quetiapine (Seroquel)	Schizophrenia	300–800 (many clinicians will target 400–600) Dosing in mood disorders is not established	Doses up to 1,200 mg and greater have been used in studies; the higher doses did continue to demonstrate efficacy and were well tolerated
Risperidone (Risperidal)	Schizophrenia	3–6 Dosing in mood disorders is not established	Risk of EPS is dose related; doses above 6 mg are associated with a greater incidence of EPS Intramuscular risperidone will be available soon; this is a long-acting injection and has the same indication as the oral agents
Ziprasidone (Geodon)	Schizophrenia	40–200 (target 120–160) Dosing in mood disorders is not established	Must take with food Available in intramuscular form for treatment of acute agitation in schizophrenic patients (not for long-term treatment of schizophrenia)
Dopamine system stabilizer (partial agonist) Abilify (Aripiprazole)	Schizophrenia	10–15	Approved up to 30 mg

Note. EPS, extrapyramidal side effects.
[a]Trade names are in parentheses.

Table A.8 Atypical Antipsychotics: Comparative Side Effects[a]

Medication	Anticholinergic Effects[b]	EPS[c]	Orthostatic Hypotension	Prolactin Elevation	Sedation	Weight Gain	Comments
Clozapine	+++	+/–	+++	0	+++	+++	Withdrawal
Olanzapine	+–++	+	+	+/–	++	+++	with abrupt
Quetiapine	+/–	+/–	++	+/–	++	+–++	discontinu-
Risperidone	+/–	+–++ (dose related)	++	+++	+	+–++	ation, taper to discon-
Ziprasidone	+/–	+	+	+/–	+–++	+/–	tinue
Aripiprazole	No comparative data at this time; based on current data, aripiprazole should cause little to no prolactin elevation; weight gain has been reported, but the difference between aripiprazole and placebo is slight; it can cause orthostatic hypotension and sedation; incidence of EPS is similar to placebo except for akathisia, which occurred slightly more often with aripiprazole						

[a]0 = none; +/– = minimal to very low; + = mild; ++ = moderate; +++ = high; + does not include all side effects of each medication; check manufacturer's package insert for complete list.
[b]Anticholinergic effects: dry mouth, blurred vision, urinary retention, constipation.
[c]EPS, extrapyramidal side effects: akathisia, pseudoparkinsonism, dystonic reactions.

Table A.9 Anxiolytics: Dosing Guidelines in Adults and Clinical Pearls

Medication[a]	Indication	Average Daily Dose Range (mg/day)	Rate of Onset and Clinical Pearls
Benzodiazepines			
Alprazolam (Xanax and Xanax XR)	Anxiety Panic	Xanax: 0.75–4 2–6 (doses up to 10 mg have been used) Xanax XR: 3–6 (some may require doses above 6 mg)	Intermediate rate of onset
Chlordiazepoxide (Librium)	Anxiety	15–100	Intermediate rate of onset
Clonazepam (Klonopin)	Anxiety Panic disorder Insomnia	1–3 up to 6 in some cases 1–3, most do not exceed 4 See Table A.10	Fast rate of onset
Clorazepate (Tranxene)	Anxiety Panic disorder Insomnia	7.5–60 7.5–60 See Table A.10	Fast rate of onset
Diazepam (Valium)	Anxiety Panic disorder	Varies: 4–40 Varies: 2–40	Very fast rate of onset
Lorazepam (Ativan)	Anxiety Panic disorder Insomnia	2–6 (up to 10 have been used) 3–4 up (up to 10 mg have been used) See Table A.10	Intermediate rate of onset; does not have active metabolites
Oxazepam (Serax)	Anxiety Panic disorder	30–120 40–120	Slow rate of onset; does not have active metabolites
Miscellaneous anxiolytics			
Buspirone (Buspar)	Anxiety	Target dose of 30 (maximum dose of 60)	May take several weeks to see full effect; not appropriate to use "as needed" (prn)
Hydroxyzine (Atarax and Vistaril)	Anxiety Insomnia	200–400 with a maximum dose of 600 See Table A.10	

[a]Trade names are in parentheses.

Table A.10 Hypnotics: Dosing Guidelines in Adults and Clinical Pearls

Medication[a]	Average Dosage Range (mg)	Onset of Effect (min)	Clinical Pearls
Chloral hydrate (Somnote)	500–1,000 (up to 2,000)	30–60	Rapid tolerance develops over a 5- to 14-day period of continued use
Clonazepam (Klonopin)	0.5–2	20–60	
Clorazepate (Tranxene)	3.75–15	30–60	
Diphenhydramine (Benadryl)	12.5–50		Disadvantages: daytime hangover, anticholinergic effects and tolerance may develop after 1–2 weeks of continued use
Doxylamine (Unisom)	25		Disadvantages: daytime hangover, anticholinergic effects and tolerance may develop after 1–2 weeks of continued use
Estazolam (ProSom)	1–2	60–120, some reports of 15–30	
Flurazepam (Dalmane)	15–30	30–60	Prone to excessive hangover
Hydroxyzine (Atarax and Vistaril)	25–50		Anticholinergic effects are less than with diphenhydramine; if used for a long period of time and with multiple daily doses, may wish to taper to discontinue to avoid cholinergic rebound
Lorazepam (Ativan)	1–4	30–60	
Oxazepam (Serax)	15–30	30–60	
Temazepam (Restoril)	7.5–30	60–120	Need to take 1–2 hours prior to bedtime
Trazodone (Desyrel)	25–150	30–60	
Triazolam (Halcion)	0.125–0.25	30, some reports of up to 120	Not recommended for patients with comorbid psychiatric illness
Zaleplon (Sonata)	10, range 5–20	30	May be administered in the middle of the night to reestablish sleep with no next-day hangover; no clear tolerance or withdrawal syndrome
Zolpidem (Ambien)	10	30	No next-day hangover; no clear tolerance or withdrawal syndrome when dosed correctly

[a]Trade names are in parentheses.

Table A.11 Anxiolytics and Hypnotics: Side Effects and Certain Precautions[a]

Medications	Side Effects and Certain Precautions
Antihistamines (diphenhydramine, doxylamine, hydroxyzine)	Anticholinergic effects, drowsiness, orthostatic hypotension, dizziness, nausea, headache, photosensitivity reactions; if used for a long period of time and by multiple daily dosing, may wish to taper to discontinue to avoid cholinergic rebound
Benzodiazepines (alprazolam, chlordiazepoxide, clonazepam, clorazepate, diazepam, estazolam, flurazepam, lorazepam, oxazepam, temazepam, triazolam)	Drowsiness, ataxia, confusion, dizziness, depression, disinhibition (paradoxical reaction), dry mouth, diplopia, dependence, memory disturbance; withdrawal with abrupt discontinuation, taper to discontinue
Buspirone	Nausea, headaches, dizziness, drowsiness and insomnia, nervousness
Chloral hydrate	Disorientation, incoherence, paranoid behavior, gastric irritation, nausea and vomiting, ataxia, dependence; do not abruptly discontinue, taper to discontinue
Trazodone	See antidepressants
Zaleplon	Drowsiness, dizziness/lightheadedness, nausea, myalgia; no clear tolerance or withdrawal syndrome
Zolpidem	Drowsiness, dizziness, diarrhea and constipation, lightheadedness, nausea; no clear tolerance or withdrawal syndrome when dosed correctly

[a]Does not include all side effects of each medication; check manufacturer's package insert for complete list.

Table A.12 Mood Stabilizers: Dosing Guidelines in Adults and Clinical Pearls

Medication[a]	Indication	Average Daily Dose Range (mg/day)	Clinical Pearls
Carbamazepine (Carbatrol, Tegretol, Tegretol XR)	Trigeminal neuralgia Bipolar disorder	400–800 Based on serum concentrations (see clinical pearls) and therapeutic response, but general range is 800–1200 mg	Plasma concentrations of 6–12 μg/ml are not established for efficacy in mood disorders, but rather are used to monitor for toxicity; numerous drug interactions
Gabapentin (Neurontin)	Epilepsy Postherpetic neuralgia Neuropathic pain	900–1,800 1,800–3,600 Dosing in mood disorders is not established (see clinical pearls)	Data in mood disorders is poor, yet case reports do show efficacy; not a first-line choice, but data suggest it may be helpful as adjunctive therapy in patients with refractory bipolar disorder Efficacy in social phobia
Lamotrigine (Lamictal)	Epilepsy	If on valproic acid: 100–200 If on an enzyme inducing agent: 300–500 If not on agents listed above: not established but reasonable to assume dosing would fall between the two regimens Dosing in mood disorders is not established Typical range is 50–500, with average dose range between 100 and 300	May be more beneficial for the management of the depressed phase of bipolar rather than mania; patients in all phases of bipolar have responded; however, there is conflicting information
Levetiracetam (Keppra)	Epilepsy	1,000–3,000 Dosing not established for mood disorders	Renally excreted and dosage adjustment necessary in renal impairment; limited data in mood disorders, with one case reporting demonstrated efficacy in treatment of acute mania
Lithium (Eskalith, Eskalith CR, Lithobid)	Bipolar disorder	900–2,400 Target a concentration between 0.6 and 1.2 mEq/L for prophylaxis and up to 1–1.5 mEq/L for acute mania	Not as effective for mixed mania or rapid cycling
Oxcarbazepine (Trileptal)	Epilepsy	Up to 1,200 Dosing not established for mood disorders	One study showed greater incidence of hyponatremia compared to carbamazepine
Tiagabine (Gabitril)	Epilepsy	Up to 56 Dosing not established for mood disorders	Mixed results in treating bipolar as an add-on agent; many studies showed limited to no efficacy, with a few open-label studies and case reports showing efficacy in some patients; small studies for neuropathic pain demonstrated some benefit; data emerging for treatment of anxiety disorders

(*continued*)

Table A.12 Continued

Medication[a]	Indication	Average Daily Dose Range (mg/day)	Clinical Pearls
Topiramate (Topamax)	Epilepsy	Up to 400 Dosing in mood disorders is not established	Blunts appetite and induces weight loss; often used to help counteract weight gain from other psychotropic medications; currently recommended as an adjunctive medication to other mood stabilizers
Valproic acid (Depakote, Depakene)	Bipolar	Target a serum concentration of 50–125 µg/ml	Especially useful for rapid cycling and mixed episodes; also used to prevent migraine headache attacks
Zonisamide (Zonegran)	Epilepsy	Up to 400	Has been dosed up to 600 mg and above, but side effects are more frequent at doses of 300 mg and above; has been used adjunctively and as monotherapy for mood disorders

[a]Trade names are in parentheses.

Table A.13 Mood Stabilizers: Side Effects and Certain Precautions[a]

Medication	Common Side Effects and Certain Precautions
Carbamazepine	Dizziness, drowsiness, unsteadiness, nausea/vomiting, rash; tapering to discontinue is recommended
Gabapentin	Somnolence/fatigue, dizziness, ataxia, nausea/vomiting, weight gain, edema, diplopia; tapering to discontinue is recommended
Lamotrigine	Dizziness, ataxia, nausea, diplopia, headache, somnolence, rash; tapering to discontinue is recommended
Levetiracetam	Somnolence, asthenia, dizziness, nervousness, vertigo
Lithium	Polydipsia, polyuria, fine hand tremor, nausea, fatigue, weight gain, rash, hair loss, dizziness, diarrhea; tapering to discontinue is recommended
Oxcarbazepine	Headache, dizziness, drowsiness, nausea/vomiting, diplopia; tapering to discontinue is recommended
Tiagabine	Dizziness, asthenia, somnolence, nausea, nervousness, ataxia, depression, diarrhea
Topiramate	Somnolence, dizziness, ataxia, psychomotor slowing, speech disorders, nervousness, nystagmus, difficulty with memory, nausea, diplopia, anorexia, difficulty with concentration/attention, confusion, tremor; tapering to discontinue is recommended
Valproic acid	Nausea/vomiting, tremor, somnolence, dizziness, ataxia, diarrhea, diplopia, weight gain, hair loss, can increase ammonia; tapering to discontinue is recommended
Zonisamide	Somnolence, dizziness, anorexia, headache; do not give if patient is allergic to sulfonamides; tapering to discontinue is recommended

[a]Does not include all side effects of each medication; check manufacturer's package insert for complete list.

Appendix B

Could the Symptoms Be Caused by the Patient's Medication? A Guide to Assessment

Karen Gunning

Many commonly used medications have been implicated over the past 50 years as causing or worsening symptoms of depression and other psychiatric disorders. The careful clinician should of course consider whether the use (or misuse) of prescription or over-the-counter (OTC) medications might be the cause of the patient's symptoms; this appendix provides some assistance with that process. The appendix also highlights the significant difficulties that emerge when the clinician attempts to make this determination.

Medications may cause symptoms (also known as *adverse reactions* or *side effects*), and at times these symptoms may be psychological, behavioral, or emotional. In addition to directly causing psychological symptoms, medications may produce symptoms in several other ways: by suggestion (the *nocebo effect*), by unmasking an underlying disorder, by interacting with other medications, when overdosed, or when discontinued. In addition, a patient may be intolerant of a variety of medications, a condition known as *multiple-drug intolerance* (Davies, 2003). It is therefore essential that a careful medication history be elicited, and

Table B.1 provides guidelines for the elements of such a history.

Having ascertained which medications the patient is taking or has taken, the clinician can then review the material in this appendix to determine if there may be a link between the medication and the patient's symptoms.

To obtain evidence about medication-induced psychological symptoms, Medline records from 1965 to 2003 were searched using the Medline Medical Subject Heading, or MESH, term "mental disorders (chemically induced)" along with the MESH terms for individual medications. In addition, reports or research findings concerning medications associated with adverse psychiatric effects were gleaned from review articles, textbooks, and computerized drug information databases.

Medications for which published evidence was found are listed in Tables B.2 and B.3. Table B.2 details the evidence for psychiatric side effects of classes of medications, and Table B.3 details the evidence for specific medications. Table B.3 lists medications alphabetically by generic name, followed by the trademarked name.

Table B.1 Elements of the Comprehensive Medication and Drug History

1. Allergies and symptoms experienced
2. Drug sensitivities and reaction experienced
3. Current prescription medications and date started
4. Current over-the-counter medications and date started
5. Medications taken in the past; when and why discontinued
6. Current and previous drug interactions experienced (patient could be asked if he or she had ever experienced a problem caused by "mixing" two or more medications)
7. Family history of benefits or problems with certain medications (prescription or over-the-counter)
8. History of problems with dependence on prescription drugs or drugs of abuse
9. Nicotine use/history
10. Alcohol and caffeine use/history
11. History of specific side effects from medications that resulted in medication discontinuation

Table B.4 provides a guide to the levels of evidence available for each conclusion. As can be readily seen, there are few conclusions for which the quality of the published evidence is at Level I or II. Considerable caution must be used in drawing causal conclusions because studies can fail to rule out alternative explanations for the emergence of symptoms, including concomitant medical diagnosis; base rate of symptom(s) in patients with the medical disorder; concomitant use of illicit drugs; and previous diagnosis of a psychiatric condition. Because it is unfortunately rather common for studies to have such methodological problems, the Naranjo criteria detailed in Table B.5 can be helpful in evaluating the conclusions from case reports and poorly controlled studies.

ADDITIONAL INFORMATION

Overdose and Withdrawal

Medication classes such as amphetamines, anabolic steroids, anticholinergic agents, and salicylates, when taken in doses several times higher than prescribed or when taken for extremely long periods of time, may cause delirium, mania, hallucinations, and paranoia; these symptoms are not associated with usual therapeutic doses of these medications.

Selective serotonin reuptake inhibitors (SSRIs), when abruptly discontinued, may cause agitation, insomnia, anorexia, dizziness, ataxia, diarrhea, fatigue, auditory hallucinations, nightmares, confusion, and relapse of previous depressive symptoms (Zajecka, Tracy, & Mitchell, 1997). Symptoms of serotonin withdrawal typically begin within 1 to 5 days of abrupt discontinuation (depending on the half-life of the specific SSRI) and may last days to weeks if not treated by temporarily restarting the SSRI and proceeding with a more gradual tapering of the dose.

Drug/Disease Interactions

As an example of the potential confusion caused by attributing the patient's symptoms to the medication, the often repeated "fact" that benzodiazepines can cause depression is better understood as the medication providing symptomatic relief for an underlying depression, with the discontinuation of the benzodiazepine unmasking the underlying depression (Patten & Love, 1997).

Multiple-Drug Intolerance

As noted, the medication history may reveal that the patient changes medications repeatedly because of nonspecific symptoms, including weakness, fatigue, or vague feelings of poor health. These effects are often experienced with several different drug classes, with varying pharmacological effects. This has been termed multiple-drug intolerance and may predict adverse reactions to other agents in the future (Davies, Jackson, Ram-

Table B.2 Drug Classes Reported to Cause Adverse Psychiatric Effects

Class	Example	Reported Effects	Comments	Level of Evidence	References
Amphetamines	Methylphenidate	Hallucinations, delusions, paranoia, depression with withdrawal	Primarily in abuse and overdose	Level IV abuse and over-dose Level V animal data in withdrawal	Harris, 2000 Kokkinidis, 1986
Anabolic steroids	Testosterone	Mania, aggression, depression with withdrawal, irritability	Primarily in men in situations of abuse and supraphysiological dosing	Level II (small RCT)	Pope, 2000 Pope, 1994 Uzych, 1992
Angiotensin converting enzyme inhibitor (ACEI)	Lisinopril	Changes in well-being (positive and negative) and acute mania (rare)	Difficult to differentiate drug versus disease in negative effects or drugs versus previous therapy in positive effects	Level IV	Jern, 1988 Zubenko, 1984
Anticholinergic agents	Atropine	Visual hallucinations, amnesia, delirium, agitation; "mad as a hatter"	Effects primarily reported in overdose, rarely with therapeutic doses; effects also reported with transdermal scopolamine (for motion sickness) and ophthalmic agents; children and elderly more susceptible	Level I	Moreau, 1986 Tune, 2001 Barker, 1990
Tricyclic antidepressants	Amitriptyline	Mania; also anticholinergic effects (see above)	Primarily seen in overdose; also in elderly and very young patients	Level I	Livingston, 1983 Oxman, 1996
Anticonvulsants	Phenytoin	Two groups of effects: (1) fatigue, cognitive slowing, antianxiety, antimanic (barbiturates, benzodiazepines, valproate, gabapentin, tiagabine, and vigabatrin); (2) activating, anxiogenic, antidepressant (lamotrigine, felbamate)	Difficult to separate psychiatric effects from those that may be caused by underlying disease state; much debate about the significance of drug effects	Levels III/IV	Schmitz, 1999 Ketter, 1999
Barbiturates	Phenobarbital	Hyperactivity, depression, psychosis	Especially in children and in withdrawal (migraine headaches/barbiturate addiction)	Level III	Domizio, 1993

(continued)

Table B.2 Continued

Class	Example	Reported Effects	Comments	Level of Evidence	References
Benzodiazepines	Diazepam	Withdrawal frequently causes delirium; may also cause mania; depression; amnesia; anxiety; anger or violence; impulsive, suicidal, or self-harming behavior; schizophrenialike symptoms	Use may obscure underlying depression and delay treatment; cognitive effects in elderly reported; effects potentiated by alcohol	Level III	Zalsman, 1998 Sumner, 1998 Cole, 1993
Beta-blockers	Atenolol	Depression, psychosis, delirium, anxiety, hallucinations, nightmares	Perhaps the best-studied drug-induced psychiatric effect (or lack thereof); early studies with poor design suggested an association; more recent studies, with appropriate definitions and diagnostic criteria, do not support an association	Level I to support a lack of effect of beta-blockers on psychiatric disorders	Ried, 1998 Ko, 2002 Gerstman, 1996 Beers, 1990
Calcium channel blockers	Nifedipine	Cognitive decline (elderly), depression, delirium, confusion	Most case reports with flunarizine (not available in the United States)	Level IV	Hullett, 1988 Maxwell, 1999
Cephalosporin antibiotics	Cephalexin	Psychosis, confusion, encephalopathy	Associated with high intravenous doses and decreased renal function	Level IV	Herd, 1989
Corticosteroids	Prednisone	Mania, "steroid psychosis," depression	Substantial evidence, credible pathophysiological and pharmacological explanations	Level II	Wada, 2000 Brown, Kahn, 1999 Brown, Rush, 1999
Dopamine receptor agonists	Pergolide	Hallucinations, "sleep attacks," delirium, psychosis	Substantial evidence, credible pathophysiological and pharmacological explanation (excessive dopaminergic activity)	Level I	Etminan, 2001 Young, 1997

Drug class	Drug	Effects	Comments	Level	Reference
Estrogens	Estradiol	Depression, panic attacks; also improvement in mood and well-being	Improvement in quality of life, positive mood changes often investigated as an end point in studies of estrogen replacement therapy; diagnosis often confounded, but consistent positive effect seen; three case reports of estrogen-associated panic attacks	Level IV for depression and panic; Level II for mood improvement	Dembert, 1994 Soares, 2003
Fluoroquinolones	Ciprofloxacin	Delirium, acute psychosis, mania ("antibiomania"); one case report of sleepwalking	Difficult to differentiate between the effects of drug versus infection and hypoxia; most reports with ciprofloxacin and ofloxacin	Level IV	Abouesh, 2002
H₁ blockers (antihistamines)	Diphenhydramine	Delirium; see anticholinergic agents; depression reported in abuse	Delirium especially in elderly	Level I	Agostini, 2001
H₂ blockers	Ranitidine	Confusion, delirium, mania	Especially in elderly; most reports with cimetidine, may be dose related and thus drug–drug interactions and renal/hepatic dysfunction may increase risk	Level III	Rodgers, 2001 Cantu, 1991
HMG CoA reductase inhibitors (statins)	Atorvastatin	Depression, sleep disturbances	Very limited case reports, most from European countries	Level V	Lechleitner, 1992
Monoamine oxidase inhibitors (MAOIs)	Tranylcypromine	Delirium, psychosis	Seen primarily in overdose/abuse and withdrawal; also increased risk if L-tryptophan is used with MAOI	Level IV	Goff, 1985
Nonsteroidal anti-inflammatory agents (NSAIDS)	Ibuprofen	Delirium, sedation, confusion; some retrospective trials have demonstrated a decreased incidence of Alzheimer's disease in chronic NSAID users	Seen primarily in elderly (delirium, confusion)	Level IV (delirium and confusion) Level III (Alzheimer's disease)	Karplus, 1998 Clark, 1992

(continued)

Table B.2 Continued

Class	Example	Reported Effects	Comments	Level of Evidence	References
Opioid analgesics	Morphine	Delirium, mania, agitation, anxiety, hallucinations	Very difficult to separate drug effect from effects of condition being treated, especially in patients at the end of life; with meperidine, associated with decreased renal function; most cases reported with meperidine; dose related	Level IV	Morita, 2002
Salicylates	Aspirin	Delirium	Usually with chronic overdose, especially in elderly	Level V	Steele, 1986
Selective serotonin reuptake inhibitors (SSRIs)	Fluoxetine	Anxiety, panic attacks, mania	Mania exacerbation in bipolar patients decreased in those also treated with lithium; risk increased with abrupt drug withdrawal; initiation with high dose associated with increased risk of initial anxiety	Level II	Henry, 2001 Preda, 2001
Sulfonamides	Sulfamethoxazole/trimethoprim	Delirium, panic	Some association with intravenous use	Level V	Abouesh, 2002 Zealberg, 1991

Table B.3 Specific Medications Reported to Cause Adverse Psychiatric Effects

Drug[a]	Use	Reported Effects	Comments	Level of Evidence	References
Acetazolamide (Diamox)	Glaucoma, altitude sickness	Depression, delirium, confusion	Increased risk with renal failure	Level V	Rowe, 1977 Schwenk, 1995
Acyclovir (Zovirax)	Antiviral	Delirium, mania	Only reports are in patients with renal failure, primarily with intravenous use	Level IV	Revankar, 1995
Amantadine (Symmatrel)	Antiviral, antiparkinsonian	Mania, delirium, "night terrors," mood changes (elevation/depression)	Most reports in elderly patients with Parkinson's disease; may be associated with medication withdrawal	Level IV	Flaherty, 1981 Factor, 1998
Baclofen (Lioresal)	Antispasmodic	Mania, psychosis, hallucinations	Seen more frequently after sudden withdrawal or in patients with underlying mental disorders; also associated with high doses or decreased elimination	Level IV	Yassa, 1988
Bupropion (Wellbutrin)	Antidepressant	Mania, nightmares, hallucinations	Associated with high doses	Level V	Goren, 2000
Buspirone (Buspar)	Antianxiety agent	Mania, serotonin syndrome	Associated with concurrent use of other serotonergic drugs	Level IV	McDaniel, 1990
Chloroquine (Aralen)	Antimalarial	Mania, depression, sleep disturbances, nightmares, agitation, anxiety	Increased in patients with preexisting mental disorders, more common with mefloquine than chloroquine	Level II	Barrett, 1996
Clarithromycin (Biaxin)	Antibiotic	Mania, delirium	Reported in patients also taking with SSRIs and corticosteroids, possibly because of cytochrome P450 drug interactions	Level IV	Pollack, 1995
Clonidine (Catapres)	Antihypertensive	Depression, sedation, delirium	Most reports from 1970s; very few case reports	Level V	Paykel, 1992
Clozapine (Clozaril)	Antipsychotic	Obsessive-compulsive disorder, delirium, psychosis	Delirium and psychosis more frequent with rapid withdrawal; emergence of obsessive-compulsive symptoms is probably unmasking of existing condition	Level II for obsessive-compulsive behaviors Level IV for delirium/psychosis	DeHaan, 1999
Cyclobenzaprine (Flexeril)	Muscle relaxant	Delirium, mania, psychosis	Only reported in elderly patients	Level IV	Douglass, 2000

(continued)

Table B.3 Continued

Drug[a]	Use	Reported Effects	Comments	Level of Evidence	References
Cycloserine (Seromycin)	Antituberculosis, antibiotic	Psychosis, paranoia, confusion	Associated with high doses, first 2 weeks of therapy, and more common in those with preexisting psychiatric disorders; some effects may be prevented with pyridoxine	Level V (no case reports, probably because of infrequent use of agent)	Eli Lilly, 1996
Dapsone	Leprosy	Manic depression, depression, psychosis	May be dose related, seen mostly in overdose	Level IV	Sheela, 1993
Dextromethorphan (Robitussin DM, Delsym)	Cough suppressant	Mania, psychosis, hallucinations	High doses when abused	Level IV	Price, 2000
Digoxin (Lanoxin)	Heart failure, arrhythmias	Delirium, pseudodepression, hallucinations	Toxicity (even at therapeutic levels) often misdiagnosed as depression because of vague symptoms (anorexia, weakness, dizziness, delirium), especially in elderly	Level IV	Eisendrath, 1987
Disulfiram (Antabuse)	Alcohol abuse deterrent	Psychosis, delusions, delirium	Hard to distinguish drug effects from condition treated; one small, well-designed prospective randomized trial demonstrated a very low rate of psychiatric effects	Level III (for lack of association with psychiatric adverse effects)	Branchey, 1987
Efavirenz (Sustiva)	HIV antiviral	Severe depression, suicidal thoughts	Up to 2% in patients with previous psychiatric history	Level I (from randomized placebo controlled trials)	Puzantian, 2002
Ephedrine	Stimulant	Agitation, anxiety, psychosis	Dose related, seen particularly when used in combination with caffeine in herbal products	Level I	Shekelle, 2003
Ganciclovir (Cytovene)	Intravenous antiviral used for cytomegalovirus	Hallucinations, agitation	Two case reports, one in patient with decreased renal function	Level IV	Chen, 1992
Ifosfamide (Ifex)	Chemotherapy	Hallucinations, confusion, agitation	Primarily in elderly, patients with decreased renal function	Level IV	Heim, 1981

Drug	Indication	Psychiatric symptoms	Level	Comments	Reference
Interleukin 2 (Proleukin)	Immunomodulator used for cancer treatment	Behavioral changes, agitation, delusions, hallucinations	Level I	Dose related; occur at end of dosing interval, reversible after drug discontinuation	Denicoff, 1987
Interferon alfa (2 A = Roferon, 2 B = Intron)	Hepatitis C treatment, malignant melanoma, hairy cell leukemia, Kaposi's sarcoma, lymphoma	Irritability, depression, delirium, anxiety	Level I	Increased incidence with prolonged treatment, higher dose, and weight loss during treatment; no increase with history of psychiatric disorder; dose reduction or SSRI may reduce effects; withdrawal occasionally reported to cause depression	Renault, 1987
Isoniazid	Tuberculosis	Mania, psychosis, obsessive-compulsive neuroses	Level IV	Risk factors include increased age, increased dose, decreased hepatic function, alcohol abuse, and history of psychiatric disorders; may be a result of pyridoxine (vitamin B_6) deficiency	Alao, 1998
Isotretinoin (Accutane)	Acne	Depression, suicidal ideation, psychosis	Level II	Informed consent required (since 2001) before dispensing; ranked number 5 in FDA adverse event database for drug-associated depression; the only nonpsychiatric drug in the top 10 for suicide attempts; findings confounded by association between acne and depression	Wysowski, 2001 Jick, 2000 Ng, 2003
Levodopa (Sinemet, with carbidopa)	Parkinson's disease	Psychosis, delirium, delusions, mania	Level I	Most significant in elderly patients, may be exacerbated by use of anticholinergic agents; mood swings may be associated with "on/off" motor symptoms; confounded by psychiatric symptoms that occur as a result of disease progression	Sweet, 1976 Young, 1997
Levonorgestrel (Norplant)	Contraceptive implant	Depression, anxiety, obsessive-compulsive disorder	Level IV	Case reports in patients without previous psychiatric history; resolution occurred within month of implant removal	Wagner, 1996

(continued)

Table B.3 Continued

Drug[a]	Use	Reported Effects	Comments	Level of Evidence	References
Mefloquine (Larium)	Antimalarial	Mania, depression, insomnia, nightmares, agitation, anxiety, hallucinations, psychotic behavior	28% with mild/moderate neuropsychiatric adverse effects in prospective trial; may be caused by inhibition of acetylcholinesterase; 80% seen in first 3 weeks of treatment; warnings added to package insert in 2002; avoid use in patients with active or recent history of major psychiatric disorders; prolonged effects after discontinuation have been reported; over 40 case reports	Level II	Ronn, 1998 Van Riemsdijk, 1997, 2002 Roche Laboratories, 2002
Methyldopa (Aldomet)	Antihypertensive	Depression, anxiety	Sedation common (may be misdiagnosed as depression); does not appear to cause more depression than other antihypertensive drugs	Level IV	DeMuth, 1983
Methylphenidate (Ritalin)	Stimulant	Mania, obsessive-compulsive disorder, anxiety	Often confounded by underlying and undiagnosed psychiatric issues that present as ADHD is treated	Level IV	Kouris, 1998
Metoclopramide (Reglan)	Antinausea	Mania, depression	Extrapyramidal (movement-related) effects may be confused with psychiatric effects	Level V	Anfinson, 2002
Metronidazole (Flagyl)	Antibiotic	Panic attacks, mania ("antibiomania"), confusion	Possible association with high doses	Level IV	Schentag, 1982 Abouesh, 2002
Nevirapine (Viramune)	HIV antiviral	Delirium, psychosis	Similar structure to efavirenz (similar adverse psychiatric effects reported)	Level IV (three case reports)	Wise, 2002
Quinidine (Quinadex)	Antiarrhythmic	Delirium, psychosis, confusion, depression	Primarily in elderly, may appear long after start of therapy	Level IV	Johnson, 1990

Drug	Indication	Adverse effect	Comments	Level	Reference
Reserpine	Antihypertensive	Depression	Related to dose and duration of treatment; less common with doses of less than 0.5 mg/day; effects may last long after drug discontinuation	Level I	Prisant, 1991
Selegiline (Eldepryl)	Parkinson's disease	Psychosis	Unclear if drug related or disease related	Level IV	Boyson, 1991; Young, 1997
Sumatriptan (Imitrex)	Migraine headaches	Panic	Known adverse effects of feelings of heaviness, tightening and tingling, particularly in head or chest may be misdiagnosed as anxiety or panic	Level V	Loi, 1996
Thyroid hormone (Synthroid)	Thyroid replacement	Anxiety, agitation, psychosis (hyperthyroidism); depression, fatigue, anxiety (hypothyroidism)	Not true adverse effects, but rather a result of either over- or undertreatment of underlying thyroid condition	Level II	Denicoff, 1990
Trazodone (Desyrel)	Sleep aid, antidepressant	Delirium, mania	Bulimia may be risk factor for delirium, several case reports in bulimic patients; mania reported with use and with sudden trazodone withdrawal	Level IV	Damlouji, 1984
Venlafaxine (Effexor)	Antidepressant	Mania, hypomania	May exacerbate underlying bipolar disease; all case reports have occurred in patients with bipolar depression	Level IV	Wilson, 1997
Zolpidem (Ambien)	Sleep aid	Visual hallucinations, delirium	Risk factors for delirium with zolpidem include advanced age, female, low albumin (all associated with higher serum levels); most reports of visual hallucinations have occurred in patients also on antidepressant therapy	Level IV	Brodeur, 2001

[a]Trade names are in parentheses.

Table B.4 Levels of Evidence

Level I: Strong evidence based on a systematic review of prospective cohort studies, or on well-designed randomized controlled trial(s)

Level II: Retrospective cohort studies

Level III: Very small cohort studies

Level IV: Case series or multiple case reports

Level V: Effects inferred from expert opinion, physiology, pharmacology, or single case reports

Note. From the Oxford Center for Evidence Based Medicine Levels of Evidence at www.cebm.net/levels_of_evidence.asp.

say, & Ghahramani, 2003). These vague symptoms are also similar to the somatic symptoms of depression and may serve to confuse the diagnosis of a primary psychiatric illness versus one secondary to medications. Patients may misidentify symptoms of their psychiatric illness as being caused by their medications. Davies et al. found, in hypertensive patients, significant associations between nonspecific medication adverse effects and diagnosed panic attacks and depression, as well as a significant association between the percentage of patients with a psychiatric diagnosis and the number of episodes of nonspecific drug intolerance.

Table B.5 The Naranjo Criteria for Judging the Likelihood That a Medication Is Causing a Symptom

Adverse effects under these criteria are classified as definite, probable, possible, or doubtful.

Definite association
  Reasonable temporal sequence with drug administration
  Improvement on removal of the drug
  Reappearance of the effect on reexposure

Probable association
  Reasonable temporal sequence with drug administration
  Improvement on removal of the drug

Possible association
  Symptoms may be explained by the characteristics of the disease

Doubtful association
  Other patient factors likely to cause symptoms

Note. From Naranjo, Busto, Sellers, et al. (1991).

There was no association between psychiatric illness and *specific* drug intolerance (side effects with pharmacological explanations). Of clinical importance, patients with multiple-drug intolerance more frequently had inadequate blood pressure control and thus the potential for increased cardiac morbidity and mortality.

Nocebo Responses

A *nocebo* (Latin for "I will harm" vs. placebo, "I will please") refers to symptoms and physiological changes that follow the administration of an inert substance that the patient believes to be active (Barsky, Saintfort, Rogers, & Borus, 2002). Barsky and colleagues reported that nocebo effects are more likely to occur in patients starting a new medication who expect to have side effects, those who have been told they will have side effects, and those who have experienced side effects with other medications in the past.

In addition, nocebo effects are more likely in patients with specific psychological characteristics (anxiety, depression, somatization), in women, among patients taking heavily advertised agents, and among patients who take medication of a specific color. Identification of patients at risk for nonspecific adverse effects may allow both patients and providers greater insight on management when these effects appear. Management strategies may include starting at a very low dose of medication and titrating slowly, discussing the nocebo phenomenon directly, evaluating with the patient the possibility of misattribution of symptoms, determining if the patient is dissatisfied with his or her medical care, and listening to patient concerns regarding medication.

References

Abouesh, A., Stone, C., & Hobbs, W. R. (2002). Antimicrobial-induced mania (antibiomania): A review of spontaneous reports. *Journal of Clinical Psychopharmacology, 22,* 71–81.

Agostini, J. V., Leo-Summers, L. S., & Inouye, S. K. (2001). Cognitive and other adverse effects of diphenhydramine use in hospitalized older patients. *Archives of Internal Medicine, 161,* 2091–2097.

Alao, A. O., & Yolles, J. C. (1988). Isoniazid induced psychosis. *Annals of Pharmacotherapy*, *32*, 889–891.

Anfinson, T. J. (2002). Akathisia, panic, agoraphobia and major depression following brief exposure to metoclopramide. *Psychopharmacology Bulletin*, *36*, 82–93.

Barker, D. B., & Solomon, D. A. (1990). The potential for mental status changes associated with systemic absorption of anticholinergic ophthalmic medications: Concerns in the elderly. *DICP: The Annals of Pharmacotherapy*, *24*, 847–850.

Barrett, P. J., Emmine, P. D., Clarke, P. D., & Bradley, D. J. (1996). Comparison of adverse events associated with use of mefloquine and combination of chloroquine and proguanil as antimalarial prophylaxis: Postal and telephone survey of travelers. *British Medical Journal*, *313*, 525–528.

Barsky, A. J., Saintfort, R., Rogers, M. P., & Borus, J. F. (2002). Nonspecific medication side effects and the nocebo phenomenon. *Journal of the American Medical Association*, *287*, 622–627.

Beers, M. H., & Passman, L. J. (1990). Antihypertensive medications and depression. *Drugs*, *40*, 792–799.

Boyson, S. L. (1991). Psychiatric effects of selegiline. *Archives of Neurology*, *48*, 902.

Branchey, L., Davis, W., Lee, K. K., & Fuller, R. K. (1987). Psychiatric complications of disulfiram treatment. *American Journal of Psychiatry*, *144*, 1310–1312.

Brodeur, M. R., & Stirling, A. L. (2001). Delirium associated with zolpidem. *Annals of Pharmacotherapy*, *35*, 1562–1564.

Brown, E. S., Khan, D. A., & Nejtek, V. A. (1999). The psychiatric side effects of corticosteroids. *Annals of Allergy Asthma Immunology*, *83*(6, Pt. 1), 495–503.

Brown, E. S., Rush, A. J., & McEwen, B. S. (1999). Hippocampal remodeling and damage by corticosteroids: Implications for mood disorders. *Neuropsychopharmacology*, *21*, 474–484.

Cantu, T. G., & Korek, J. S. (1991). Central nervous system reactions to histamine-2 receptor blockers. *Annals of Internal Medicine*, *114*, 1027–1034.

Chen, J. L., Brocavich, J. M., & Lin, A. Y. (1992). Psychiatric disturbances associated with ganciclovir therapy. *Annals of Pharmacotherapy*, *26*, 193–195.

Clark, D. W., & Ghose, K. (1992). Neuropsychiatric reactions to non-steroidal anti-inflammatory drugs (NSAIDs). The New Zealand experience. *Drug Safety*, *7*, 460–465.

Cole, J. O., & Kando, J. C. (1993). Adverse behavioral events reported in patients taking alprazolam and other benzodiazepines. *Journal of Clinical Psychiatry*, *54*(Suppl.), 49–61.

Damlouji, N. F., & Ferguson, J. M. (1984). Trazodone induced delirium in bulimic patients. *American Journal of Psychiatry*, *141*, 434–435.

Davies, S. J., Jackson, P. R., Ramsay, L. E., & Ghahramani, P. (2003). Drug intolerance due to nonspecific adverse effects related to psychiatric morbidity in hypertensive patients. *Archives of Internal Medicine*, *163*, 592–600.

De Haan, L., Linszen, D. H., & Gorisira, R. (1999). Clozapine and obsessions in patients with recent-onset schizophrenia and other psychotic disorders. *Journal of Clinical Psychiatry*, *60*, 364–365.

Dembert, M. L., Dinneen, M. P., & Opsahl, M. S. (1994). Estrogen-induced panic disorder. *American Journal of Psychiatry*, *151*, 1246.

Demuth, G. W., & Ackerman, S. H. (1983). Alpha-methyldopa and depression: A clinical study and review of the literature. *American Journal of Psychiatry*, *140*, 534–538.

Denicoff, K. D., Joffe, R. T., Lakshmanan, M. C., et al. (1990). Neuropsychiatric manifestations of altered thyroid state. *American Journal of Psychiatry*, *147*, 94–99.

Denicoff, K. D., Rubinow, D. R., Papa, M. Z., et al. (1987). The neuropsychiatric effects of treatment with interleukin 2 and lymphokine activated killer cells. *Annals of Internal Medicine*, *107*, 293–300.

Domizio, S., Verrotti, A., Ramenghi, L. A., et al. (1993). Anti-epileptic therapy and behavior disturbances in children. *Childs Nervous System*, *9*, 272–274.

Douglass, M. A., & Levine, D. P. (2000). Hallucinations in an elderly patient taking recommended doses of cyclobenzaprine. *Archives of Internal Medicine*, *160*, 1373.

Eisendrath, S. J., & Sweeney, M. A. (1987). Toxic neuropsychiatric effects of digoxin at therapeutic serum concentrations. *American Journal of Psychiatry*, *144*, 506–507.

Eli Lilly and Company. (1996). *Product information: Seromycin®, cycloserine.* Indianapolis, IN: Author.

Etminan, M., Samii, A., Takkouche, B., et al. (2001). Increased risk of somnolence with the new dopamine agonists in patients with Parkinson's disease: A meta-analysis of randomized controlled trials. *Drug Safety*, *24*, 863–868.

Factor, S. A., Molho, E. S., & Brown, D. L. (1998). Acute delirium after withdrawal of amantadine in Parkinson's disease. *Neurology, 50*, 1456–1458.

Flaherty, J. A., & Bellur, S. N. (1981). Mental side effects of amantadine therapy: Its spectrum and characteristics in a normal population. *Journal of Clinical Psychiatry, 42*, 344–345.

Gerstman, B., Jolson, H., Bauer, M., et al. (1996). The incidence of depression in new users of beta-blockers and selected antihypertensives. *Journal of Clinical Epidemiology, 49*, 809–815.

Goff, D. C. (1985). Two cases of hypomania following the addition of L-tryptophan to a monoamine oxidase inhibitor. *American Journal of Psychiatry, 142*, 1487–1488.

Goren, J. L., & Levin, G. M. (2000). Mania with bupropion: A dose-related phenomenon? *Annals of Pharmacotherapy, 34*, 619–621.

Harris, D., & Batki, S. L. (2000). Stimulant psychosis: Symptom profile and acute clinical course. *American Journal of Addiction, 9*, 28–37.

Heim, M. E., Fiene, R., Schick, E., et al. (1981). Central nervous system side effects following ifosfamide monotherapy of advanced renal carcinoma. *Journal of Cancer Research and Clinical Oncology, 100*, 113–116.

Henry, C., Sorbara, F., Lacoste, J., et al. (2001). Antidepressant-induced mania in bipolar patients: Identification of risk factors. *Journal of Clinical Psychiatry, 62*, 249–255.

Herd, A. M., Ross, C. A., & Bhattacharya, S. K. (1989). Acute confusional state with postoperative intravenous cefazolin. *British Medical Journal, 5*, 393–394.

Hullett, F. J., Potkin, S. G., Levy, A. B., & Ciasca, R. (1988). Depression associated with nifedipine-induced calcium channel blockade. *American Journal of Psychiatry, 145*, 1277–1279.

Jern, S. (1988). Evaluation of mood and the effect of angiotensin-converting enzyme inhibitors. *Drugs, 35*(Suppl. 5), 86–88.

Jick, S. S., Kremers, H. M., & Vasilakis-Scaramozza, C. (2000). Isotretinoin use and risk of depression, psychotic symptoms, suicide and attempted suicide. *Archives of Dermatology, 136*, 1231–1236.

Johnson, A. G., Day, R. O., & Seldon, W. A. (1990). A functional psychosis precipitated by quinidine. *Medical Journal of Australia, 153*, 47–49.

Karplus, T. M., & Saag, K. G. (1998). Nonsteroidal anti-inflammatory drugs and cognitive function: Do they have a beneficial or deleterious effect? *Drug Safety, 19*, 427–433.

Ketter, T. A., Post, R. M., & Theodore, W. H. (1999). Positive and negative psychiatric effects of antiepileptic drugs in patients with seizure disorders. *Neurology, 53*(5, Suppl. 2), S53–S67.

Ko, D. T., Hebert, P. R., Coffey, C. S., et al. (2002). Beta blocker therapy and symptoms of depression, fatigue, and sexual dysfunction. *Journal of the American Medical Association, 288*, 351–357.

Kokkinidis, L., Zacharko, R. M., & Anisman, H. (1986). Amphetamine withdrawal: A behavioral evaluation. *Journal of Life Sciences, 38*, 1617–1623.

Kouris, S. (1998). Methylphenidate induced obsessive compulsiveness. *Journal of American Academy of Child Adolescent Psychiatry, 37*, 135.

Lechleitner, M., Hoppichler, F., Konwalinka, G., et al. (1992). Depressive symptoms in hypercholesterolemic patients treated with pravastatin. *Lancet, 340*, 910.

Livingston, R. L., Zucker, D. K., Isenberg, K., & Wetzel, R. D. (1983). Tricyclic antidepressants and delirium. *Journal of Clinical Psychiatry, 44*, 173–176.

Loi, V., Lai, M., Pisano, M. R., et al. (1996). Sumatriptan and panic-like symptoms. *American Journal of Psychiatry, 153*, 1505.

Maxwell, C. J., Hogan, D. B., & Ebly, E. M. (1999). Calcium-channel blockers and cognitive function in elderly people: Results from the Canadian Study of Health and Aging. *CMAJ: Canadian Medical Association Journal, 161*, 501–506.

McDaniel, J. S., Ninan, P. T., & Magnuson, J. V. (1990). Possible induction of mania by buspirone. *American Journal of Psychiatry, 147*, 125–126.

Moreau, A., Jones, B. D., & Bann, V. (1986). Chronic central anticholinergic toxicity in manic depressive illness mimicking dementia. *Canadian Journal of Psychiatry, 31*, 339–341.

Morita, T., Tie, Y., Tsunoda, J., et al. (2002). Increased plasma morphine metabolites in terminally ill cancer patients with delirium: An intra-individual comparison. *Journal of Pain and Symptom Management, 23*, 107–113.

Naranjo, C. A., Busto, U., Sellers, E. M., et al. (1981). A method for estimating the probability of adverse drug reactions. *Clinical Pharmacology Therapy, 30*, 239–245.

Ng, C. H., & Schweitzer, I. (2003). The association

between depression and isotretinoin use in acne. *Australian New Zealand Journal of Psychiatry, 37,* 78–84.

Oxman, T. E. (1996). Antidepressants and cognitive impairment in the elderly. *Journal of Clinical Psychiatry, 57*(Suppl. 5), 38–44.

Patten, S. B., & Love, E. J. (1997). Drug Induced Depression. *Psychotherapy and Psychosomatics, 66,* 63–73.

Paykel, E. S., Fleminger, R., & Watson, J. P. (1982). Psychiatric side effects of antihypertensive drugs other than reserpine. *Journal of Clinical Psychopharmacology, 2,* 14–39.

Pollack, P. T., Sketris, I. S., MacKenzie, S. L., & Hewlett, T. J. (1995). Delirium probably induced by clarithromycin in a patient receiving fluoxetine. *Annals of Pharmacotherapy, 29,* 486–488.

Pope, H. G., & Katz, D. L. (1994). Psychiatric and medical effects of anabolic-androgenic steroid use. A controlled study of 160 athletes. *Archives of General Psychiatry, 51,* 375–382.

Pope, H. G., Kouri, E. M., & Hudson, J. L. (2000). Effects of supraphysiologic doses of testosterone on mood and aggression in normal men: A randomized controlled trial. *Archives of General Psychiatry, 579,* 133–140.

Preda, A., MacLean, R. W., Mazure, C. M., & Bowers, M. B., Jr. (2001). Antidepressant-associated mania and psychosis resulting in psychiatric admissions. *Journal of Clinical Psychiatry, 62,* 30–33.

Price, L. H., & Lebel, J. (2000). Dextromethorphan-induced psychosis. *American Journal of Psychiatry, 157,* 304.

Prisant, L. M., Spruill, W. J., Fincham, J. E., et al. (1991). Depression associated with antihypertensive drugs. *Journal of Family Practice, 33,* 481–485.

Puzantian, T. (2002). Central nervous system adverse effects with efavirenz: Case report and review. *Pharmacotherapy, 22,* 930–933.

Reid, L. D., McFarland, B. H., Johnson, R. E., et al. (1998). Beta blockers and depression: The more the murkier? *Annals of Pharmacotherapy, 32,* 699–708.

Renault, P. F., Hoofnagle, J. H., Park, Y., et al. (1987). Psychiatric complications of long term interferon alfa therapy. *Archives of Internal Medicine, 147,* 1577–1580.

Revankar, S. G., Applegate, A. L., & Markovitz, D. M. (1995). Delirium associated with acyclovir treatment in a patient with renal failure. *Clinical Infectious Diseases, 21,* 435–436.

Roche Laboratories. (2002). *Product information: Lariam®, mefloquine.* Nutley, NJ: Author.

Rodgers, P. T., & Brengel, G. R. (1998). Famotidine-associated mental status changes. *Pharmacotherapy, 18,* 404–407.

Ronn, A. M., Ronne-Rasmussen, J., Gotzsche, P. C., & Bygbjerg, I. C. (1998). Neuropsychiatric manifestations after mefloquine therapy for *Plasmodium falciparum* malaria: Comparing a retrospective and a prospective study. *Tropical Medicine and International Health, 3,* 83–88.

Rowe, T. O. (1977). Acetazolamide delirium. *American Journal of Psychiatry, 134,* 587–588.

Schentag, J. J., Ziemniak, J. A., Greco, J. M., et al. (1982). Mental confusion in a patient treated with metronidazole—a concentration-related effect? *Pharmacotherapy, 6,* 384–387.

Schmitz, B. (1999). Psychiatric syndromes related to antiepileptic drugs. *Epilepsia, 40*(Suppl. 10), S65–S70.

Schwenk, M. H., St. Peter, W. L., Meese, M. G., et al. (1995). Acetazolamide toxicity and pharmacokinetics in patients receiving hemodialysis. *Pharmacotherapy, 15,* 522–527.

Sheela, A., Thachil, R. T., & Sridhar, C. B. (1993). Dapsone poisoning. *Journal of Tropical Medicine and Hygiene, 96,* 274–276.

Shekelle, P. G., Hardy, M. L., Morton, S. C., et al. (2003). Efficacy and safety of ephedra and ephedrine for weight loss and athletic performance: A meta-analysis. *Journal of the American Medical Association, 289,* 1537–1545.

Soares, C. N., Poitras, J. R., & Prouty, J. (2003). Effect of reproductive hormones and selective estrogen receptor modulators on mood during menopause. *Drugs Aging, 20,* 85–100.

Steele, T. E., & Morton, W. A. (1986). Salicylate induced delirium. *Psychosomatics, 27,* 455–456.

Sumner, D. D. (1998). Benzodiazepine-induced persisting amnestic disorder: Are older adults at risk? *Archives of Psychiatric Nursing, 12,* 119–125.

Sweet, R. D., McDowell, F. H., Feigenson, J. S., Loranger, A. W., & Goodell, H. (1976). Mental symptoms in Parkinson's disease during chronic treatment with levodopa. *Neurology, 26,* 305–310.

Tune, L. E. (2001). Anticholinergic effects of medication in elderly patients. *Journal of Clinical Psychiatry, 62*(Suppl. 21), 11–14.

Uzych, L. (1992). Anabolic–androgenic steroids and psychiatric-related effects: A review. *Canadian Journal of Psychiatry, 37,* 23–28.

Van Riemsdijk, M. M., Ditters, J. M., Sturkenboom, M. C., Tulen, J. H., & Ligthelm, R. J. (2002). Neuropsychiatric events during prophylactic use of mefloquine before travelling. *European Journal of Clinical Pharmacology, 58,* 441–445.

Van Riemsdijk, M. M., Van Der Klauw, M. M., Van Heest, J. A. C., Reedeker, F. R., & Ligthelm, R. J. (1997). Neuropsychiatric effects of antimalarials. *European Journal of Clinical Pharmacology, 52,* 1–6.

Wada, K., Yamada, N., Suzuki, H., Lee, Y., & Kuroda, S. (2000). Recurrent cases of corticosteroid-induced mood disorder: Clinical characteristics and treatment. *Journal of Clinical Psychiatry, 61,* 261–267.

Wagner, K. D. (1996). Major depression and anxiety disorders associated with Norplant. *Journal of Clinical Psychiatry, 57,* 152–157.

Wilson, R., & Jenkins, P. (1997). Suspected complication of treatment with venlafaxine [letter]. *Journal of Clinical Psychopharmacology, 17,* 323.

Wise, M. E., Mistry, K., & Reid, S. (2002). Drug points: Neuropsychiatric complications of nevirapine treatment. *British Medical Journal, 324,* 879.

Wysowski, D. K., Pitts, M., & Beitz, J. (2001). An analysis of reports of depression and suicide in patients treated with isotretinoin. *Journal of American Academy of Dermatology, 45,* 515–519.

Yassa, R. Y., & Iskandar, H. L. (1988). Baclofen-induced psychosis: Two cases and a review. *Journal of Clinical Psychiatry, 49,* 318–320.

Young, B. K., Camicioli, R., & Ganzini, L. (1997). Neuropsychiatric adverse effects of anti-parkinsonian drugs. Characteristics, evaluation and treatment. *Drugs Aging, 10,* 367–383.

Zajecka, J., Tracy, K. A., & Mitchell, S. (1997). Discontinuation symptoms after treatment with serotonin reuptake inhibitors: A literature review. *Journal of Clinical Psychiatry, 58,* 291–297.

Zalsman, G., Hermesh, H., & Munitz, H. (1998). Alprazolam withdrawal delirium: A case report. *Clinical Neuropharmacology, 21,* 201–202.

Zealberg, J. J., Lydiard, R. B., & Christie, S. (1991). Exacerbation of panic disorder in a woman treated with trimethoprim-sulfamethoxazole. *Journal of Clinical Psychopharmacology, 11,* 144–145.

Zubenko, G. S., & Nixon, R. A. (1984). Mood-elevating effect of captopril in depressed patients. *American Journal of Psychiatry, 141,* 110–111.

Index